e2.50

Sou... ...Asia

■ Let's Go researchers have to make it on their own.

■ No other guidebook is as comprehensive.

■ Let's Go is completely revised each year.

Let's Go Publications

Let's Go: Alaska & The Pacific Northwest
Let's Go: Britain & Ireland
Let's Go: California
Let's Go: Central America
Let's Go: Eastern Europe
Let's Go: Ecuador & The Galápagos Islands
Let's Go: Europe
Let's Go: France
Let's Go: Germany
Let's Go: Greece & Turkey
Let's Go: India & Nepal
Let's Go: Ireland
Let's Go: Israel & Egypt
Let's Go: Italy
Let's Go: London
Let's Go: Mexico
Let's Go: New York City
Let's Go: Paris
Let's Go: Rome
Let's Go: Southeast Asia
Let's Go: Spain & Portugal
Let's Go: Switzerland & Austria
Let's Go: USA
Let's Go: Washington, D.C.

Let's Go **Map Guide:** Boston
Let's Go **Map Guide:** London
Let's Go **Map Guide:** New York City
Let's Go **Map Guide:** Paris
Let's Go **Map Guide:** San Francisco
Let's Go **Map Guide:** Washington, D.C.

LET'S GO

The Budget Guide to
Southeast Asia

1997

Pai C. Yang
Editor

Melanie Quintana Kansil
Associate Editor

Valérie E. Valtz
Associate Editor

Macmillan

HELPING LET'S GO

If you want to share your discoveries, suggestions, or corrections, please drop us a line. We read every piece of correspondence, whether a postcard, a 10-page e-mail, or a coconut. All suggestions are passed along to our researcher-writers. Please note that mail received after May 1997 may be too late for the 1998 book, but will be retained for the following edition. **Address mail to:**

> **Let's Go: Souteast Asia**
> **67 Mt. Auburn Street**
> **Cambridge, MA 02138**
> **USA**

Visit Let's Go at **http://www.letsgo.com,** or send e-mail to:

> **Fanmail@letsgo.com**
> **Subject: "Let's Go: Southeast Asia"**

In addition to the invaluable travel advice our readers share with us, many are kind enough to offer their services as researchers or editors. Unfortunately, the charter of Let's Go, Inc. enables us to employ only currently enrolled Harvard-Radcliffe students.

Published in Great Britain 1997 by Macmillan, an imprint of Macmillan General Books, 25 Eccleston Place, London SW1W 9NF and Basingstoke.

Maps by David Lindroth copyright © 1997, 1996, 1995, 1994, 1993, 1992, 1991, 1990, 1989, 1988 by St. Martin's Press, Inc.

Map revisions pp. 2-3, 263, 367, 378-379, 401-407, 499, 513, 514-515, 541, 563, 583, 605, 611, 629, 633, 669, 673, 678-679 by Let's Go, Inc.

Published in the United States of America by St. Martin's Press, Inc.

ISBN: 0 333 68669 1

First edition
10 9 8 7 6 5 4 3 2 1

Let's Go: Southeast Asia is written by Let's Go Publications, 67 Mt. Auburn Street, Cambridge, MA 02138, USA.

About Let's Go

Back in 1960, a few students at Harvard University banded together to produce a 20-page pamphlet offering a collection of tips on budget travel in Europe. This modest, mimeographed packet, offered as an extra to passengers on student charter flights to Europe, met with instant popularity. The following year, students traveling to Europe researched the first, full-fledged edition of *Let's Go: Europe*, a pocket-sized book featuring honest, irreverent writing and a decidedly youthful outlook on the world. Throughout the 60s, our guides reflected the times; the 1969 guide to America led off by inviting travelers to "dig the scene" at San Francisco's Haight-Ashbury. During the 70s and 80s, we gradually added regional guides and expanded coverage into the Middle East and Central America. With the addition of our in-depth city guides, handy map guides, and extensive coverage of Asia, the 90s are also proving to be a time of explosive growth for Let's Go, and there's certainly no end in sight. The first editions of *Let's Go: India & Nepal* and *Let's Go: Ecuador & The Galápagos Islands* hit the shelves this year, and research for next year's series has already begun.

We've seen a lot in 37 years. *Let's Go: Europe* is now the world's bestselling international guide, translated into seven languages. And our new guides bring Let's Go's total number of titles, with their spirit of adventure and their reputation for honesty, accuracy, and editorial integrity, to 30. But some things never change: our guides are still researched, written, and produced entirely by students who know first-hand how to see the world on the cheap.

HOW WE DO IT

Each guide is completely revised and thoroughly updated every year by a well-traveled set of 200 students. Every winter, we recruit over 120 researchers and 60 editors to write the books anew. After several months of training, Researcher-Writers hit the road for seven weeks of exploration, from Anchorage to Ankara, Estonia to El Salvador, Iceland to Indonesia. Hired for their rare combination of budget travel sense, writing ability, stamina, and courage, these adventurous travelers know that train strikes, stolen luggage, food poisoning, and marriage proposals are all part of a day's work. Back at our offices, editors work from spring to fall, massaging copy written on Himalayan bus rides into witty yet informative prose. A student staff of typesetters, cartographers, publicists, and managers keeps our lively team together. In September, the collected efforts of the summer are delivered to our printer, who turns them into books in record time, so that you have the most up-to-date information available for *your* vacation. And even as you read this, work on next year's editions is well underway.

WHY WE DO IT

At Let's Go, our goal is to give you a great vacation. We don't think of budget travel as the last recourse of the destitute; we believe that it's the only way to travel. Living cheaply and simply brings you closer to the people and places you've been saving up to visit. Our books will ease your anxieties and answer your questions about the basics—so you can get off the beaten track and explore. Once you learn the ropes, we encourage you to put Let's Go away now and then to strike out on your own. As any seasoned traveler will tell you, the best discoveries are often those you make yourself. When you find something worth sharing, drop us a line. We're Let's Go Publications, 67 Mt. Auburn St., Cambridge, MA 02138, USA (e-mail: fanmail@letsgo.com).

HAPPY TRAVELS!

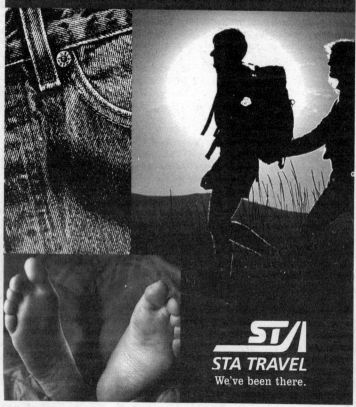

Contents

Maps

Acknowledgements

Top thanks to our stellar RWs—this is your book. Alejandro, Philbert, and Jeremiah for keeping our days inspired and our nights intense. Michelle for the SEAS support. Liz for returning from NY. Mike C. for being a happy, lovely, and musical person. Sales for keeping us sane. Katie Ü. for the dancin'. Pear for amusing us. Jeremy for the hair. Derek for Frodo and Rama. Amanda for fighting for us. Jonathan and Mark for the revisions. Dan O. & Dave F. for computers and the website. SoRelle for being our mother. Alex for fulfilling our proofing needs. GI Jake & Allison for eds. Joe L., Mike S., Chuck T., Laura S., and Nancy L. for their nimble fingers. Yori for working overtime. Ted G. for worshipping our perfection. Jesse G. for his insight. Josh F. & Lara Bennett for the helping hand. You know who for being beautiful. And, of course, Priscilla for sending us west to paradise. It's been bohemian. **—Club SEAS**

Mel and Val, the D&D bad-asses: thanks for your dedication, laughter, and decorating talent. Love: Chia, Munnie, Hanna, Nicky, Kong, and the Cupcakes. Victoria and Delou, here's to the future. Thanks: Christina for kicking me; Cindy for Oxford and beyond; Krzys for all the coffee talks; Gene for the chats; Cathy and Nora for being mentors & friends; Mom & Dad for your sacrifices. Kisses to all my siblings. **—PCY**

Pai: good luck in the world beyond from the center of you-know-what. Val: Yo! What's the cheeze!?! Cheers to Bali, HK, Tokyo, and the dynasty. Love and aloha to Mom, Papi, Jing-Jing, and Zane for the happy travels and everything else. Mahalos to: Biff (our protector), Mike C. for the fun, and of course, John (S.), Brian (Cake), Ronimal, Lizabee, Emily, Dan, and Matt. Club SEAS is in da' house! Wheeeee!! **—MQK**

Pai: here's to delinquency, Euro-trash, and us. Mel: for being my fellow and favorite bad-ass. But did we ever laugh? For once, words fail me. Thanks. Vundus: eeezarat? Way-hey! Eeezasausage!!! Maman et Papa: love from the caboose. Bisoux. Thanks to: Beau for froofiness; Mike C. for smiling; Biff "Big Boy" Rourke (wink, wink); Matt for the fun; Shan for not complaining; Sjoukje and Claire, I miss you. Thbbbbb!! **—VEV**

Editor	Pai C. Yang
Associate Editor	Melanie Quintana Kansil
Associate Editor	Valérie E. Valtz
Managing Editor	Elisabeth Mayer
Publishing Director	Michelle C. Sullivan
Production Manager	Daniel O. Williams
Associate Production Manager	Michael S. Campbell
Cartography Manager	Amanda K. Bean
Editorial Manager	John R. Brooks
Editorial Manager	Allison Crapo
Financial Manager	Stephen P. Janiak
Personnel Manager	Alexander H. Travelli
Publicity Manager	SoRelle B. Braun
Associate Publicity Manager	David Fagundes
Associate Publicity Manager	Elisabeth Mayer
Assistant Cartographer	Jonathan D. Kibera
Assistant Cartographer	Mark C. Staloff
Office Coordinator	Jennifer L. Schuberth
Director of Advertising and Sales	Amit Tiwari
Senior Sales Executives	Andrew T. Rourke
	Nicholas A. Valtz, Charles E. Varner
General Manager	Richard Olken
Assistant General Manager	Anne E. Chisholm

Researcher-Writers

Eric Dean Bennett *Lombok, Sumbawa, Flores, Sulawesi*
Equipped with resolute pragmatism, a hearty sense of irony, and a metaphorical outlook on life, Eric forged his way across Indonesia. A "certified woodsman," Eric proved to be unstoppable as he sailed through unchartered waters for *Let's Go*. With only paper and pen, Eric transmogrified his experiences into well-written prose with a touch of cynicism, which left his editors speechless. He has an uncanny ability to use the alphabet mercilessly in his town descriptions, and his artistry was unmatched. Through it all, he remained calm and sensible, offering lucid observations on the traveler's life.

Evan Erlanson *Peninsular Malaysia, Singapore, Pulau Bintan*
Evan was on a one-man mission through Malaysia, making his way down the west coast and then up the east coast, with a stopover in Singapore in between. As an avid student of Chinese history and economic development in Asia, Evan overwhelmed his editors with keen insight into the new Malaysia. A perfectionist in every respect, Evan took time to make all his prose and maps just right, while supplying details on the cultures he encountered. Not only was Evan's copy utterly brilliant and scintillating, but it was absolutely deeeelicious. Let there be no doubt that Evan was the team's culinary correspondent.

Bentsion Harder *Northeast Thailand, Laos, North Vietnam*
Though his pre-*Let's Go* stint may be the *high* point of his trip, Ben quickly fell in love with the *farang*-deprived stretches of Isaan. Transfixed by the beauty of the Mekong region, he filled kilo-sized copy with anthropological observations, tales of fruitless romances, and allusions to the Chevalier de Krak. A full dose of Laotian hospitality from the yuppies of Savannakhet prepared Ben for a hellish, buttock-bruising bus ride to Vietnam. In Hanoi, Ben joined up with fellow researcher Ben W. and together they prank called their editors at midnight after a night on the town. Back in Cambridge, we asked if he would do anything differently? "Next time, I'll stay away from that Larium stuff!" That's right, Ben: drugs are bad.

Robert Hopper *Hong Kong, Sarawak, Sabah*
From Hong Kong's steamy fetish shops to Borneo's jungled interiors, the dashing and debonair Robert warded off amorous advances left and right, resisted the decadent temptation to wear shorts, and kept us enthralled with his marginalia, trashy tabloids, and installments of *Every Woman's Dream*. A two-time *Let's Go* researcher, Robert was ready for anything. He didn't panic when the rare Kinabalu rat fell on his face. He didn't run away when the carnivorous pitcher plant attacked him. He just stared in amazement when his foot swelled up to the size of a melon. And he merely laughed when the orangutans stripped him butt-naked. Alas, what else could we expect from our valiant and spunky Robert?

Holly Leitzes *West Java and South Sumatra*
Always upbeat and on the ball, Holly attacked her itinerary enthusiastically. A world traveler and adventurer, Holly proved to be a steady and stellar researcher of indomitable spirits, conquering mighty Krakatau, Gede, and Jakarta without batting an eyelash. Undaunting in her goal, Holly pushed herself to the limits, finishing her itinerary well ahead of schedule, and returned back to Cambridge in no time at all to surprise her unsuspecting editors. A wonderful, fun-loving person, Holly never once allowed the travails of her job get to her. She endured long bus rides, pesky mosquitoes, and weariness with her usual grace and grit.

Joseph Lind *Central and Northern Thailand*
A connoisseur of Thai culture, Joe eagerly returned to his old haunt. Ever-changing Thailand, though, was not quite the same as he remembered. This time around, Joe found the dogs, monkeys, and chickens a little more rambunctious. Even the Thai police took Joe under their wing and allowed him to partake in their clandestine midnight activities. With a sound knowledge of the Thai language under his belt, Joe gained a unique perspective on the country, evident in his meticulous, detailed copy. Ever faithful to his editors back in Cambridge, Joe sent back beautiful embroidery and batiks, for which he deserves huge thanks.

Jojo Liu *Central Java, East Java, Bali*
Efficient, matter-of-fact, and tough, Jojo left a trail of dust and broken hearts through Java and Bali. Not one to be so easily distracted from the task at hand, she became every rapacious Indonesian man's worst nightmare, quelling all would-be admirers with a scathing look. Instead, she focused on sending back organized and humorous prose that reflected her shrewdness and sensitivity. Impervious to everything—except a slight cold—Jojo kept ahead on her itinerary, climbing every mountain in her way in search of the hidden treasures of Java and Bali, as well as the island's many cultures. Jojo is truly a woman of self-sufficient means.

Mark Roth *Northern and West Coast Sumatra*
Despite bone-jarring bus rides, lava-spewing volcanoes, and torrential rainfall, our fearless Mark plumbed the depths of the Sumatran wilderness, *never* once contemplating the dangers involved. With command of Bahasa Indonesia, he tackled unruly Medan and conservative Aceh, even managing to charm the most unfriendly of Bataks. With his fetching Finnish looks, Mark soon gathered a string of adamant admirers across Northern Sumatra eager and willing to lend him a helping hand. Whenever he could find a phone, Mark regaled his editors for hours at a time with his crazy adventures. A perfect R-W in every respect, Mark sent us lengthy, sagacious copy that was always complete, always thorough, and always amusing.

Phuc Truong *Central and Southern Thailand, North East Coast Malaysia*
Claiming that Bangkok was just too tame for him, Phuc scurried off to the glamourous beaches and tropical surf of the south. Summoning all his might, Phuc was on such a rampage through Thailand that word of his researching prowess reached as far away as Cambridge. But Full Moon Fever hit him real hard on Ko Phangan and all that hedonism brought out Phuc's wild side. Despite it all, Phuc went to great lengths—hiking to distant beaches, wading through water to get to boats, and nearly wiping himself out on a motorbike—to send us back what we needed. Not at all put out, Phuc bounced right back and continued on his merry way.

Benjamin Wilkinson *South Vietnam, East Coast Thailand, Cambodia*
Copious and exhaustive in all of his research and writing, this *Let's Go* veteran battled vicious dogs on the beaches of Thailand, then traversed the hinterlands of Cambodia. Flaunting flawless Vietnamese, Ben wheedled staunch embassy officials in Phnom Penh for a visa to enter Vietnam, where he quickly became Saigon's most popular and eligible bachelor. From unexpected rendezvous on the bus to prank calling his editor at midnight and from drinking draft beer with the proletariat to gorging himself with the yummiest food he ever had, Ben found bliss in Nam—so much so that he never returned! If you should encounter the young, sailor-tongued Ben in your travels, take a picture with him and send him our regards.

How to Use This Book

It's been a good first year, but we think it will be even better with this book, the second edition of *Let's Go: Southeast Asia*. This year we've revisited all of our favorite destinations, as well as adding brand-new coverage, including Sabah, Sarawak, Sulawesi, Lombok, Sumbawa, and Flores—regions sure to challenge even the most adventurous travelers.

The book begins with a general **Essentials** section, which discusses preparations you should make before a journey to Southeast Asia, as well as general information that will be useful once you're there. A short **Customs and Culture** section follows, offering a brief overview of the etiquette, food, and religious traditions of the region. Countries are arranged alphabetically, and each has **Essentials** and **Life and Times** sections, which provide practical, historical, and cultural background specific to the nation. Country chapters begin with the capital city, and continue in a logical path as much as local geography permits. Within city listings, **Orientation** and **Practical Information** sections lay out the town and compile crucial data. **Accommodations, Food,** and **Entertainment** sections follow, ranked with each sections listings according to what we believe to be the best values. **Sights** sections are arranged in an orderly geographical pattern whenever possible.

Travel in Southeast Asia requires a great deal of stamina and patience, and it's not always safe. By all means let your adventurous spirit guide you, but pay attention to our **boldfaced warnings** and **white-boxed warnings** which alert you to situations you should be aware of or special precautions you should take in specific regions. On a lighter note, *Let's Go* also has **gray boxes,** which feature interesting tangents we think are worthy of inclusion. Subjects run the gamut from local legends to historical anecdotes to hot political issues. This book also devotes sections to the issues of **responsible tourism** (see page 52) and **human rights** (see specific country introductions) that are unique within the series to this *Let's Go* guide.

As editors of a guide to Southeast Asia, we've made a conscious effort not only to bring you to the greatest experiences of the region, but also to include the perspectives of the people we write about and to present a picture of everyday life in Southeast Asia. Our goal has been to tap into a point of view that may run counter to commonly held perceptions of the "exotic Far East." With that said, we hope you find this book to be useful, informative, and entertaining; have a blast, and be sure to send us lots of mail!

SOUTHEAST ASIA

Stretching from the hypothermic highlands of Laos and Vietnam to the equatorial islands of Indonesia, the vast and diverse region of Southeast Asia incorporates a patchwork of complex influences. It is the continuing project of thousands of years of sea trade, religious dissemination, colonial influence, expanding empires, political strategies, and ethnic identifications. For every country and people these factors have played differing roles in forming unique identities. The origins of the various ethnicities are the subjects of legend and speculation: the Tai-Kadai people who came from southern China and formed the Thai and Lao kingdoms, the Malays from Indonesia who intermarried with Indian traders and princes to become the Khmer people, and a few dashes of Chinese migration thrown in for good measure. Indian influence is perhaps the one factor that provides a semblance of unity to Southeast Asia, where Hinduism, Buddhism, the *Ramayana,* and Indic philosophies continue to comingle with local custom and subtly define the region. The great kingdoms of Siam and Angkor to the north, and of Srivijaya and Majapahit to the south, all borrowed from the Indian subcontinent to build their own empires. From these shared beginnings, however, the countries of Southeast Asia have taken on their own identities. Islam swept through the island trade routes of Southeast Asia from the 7th to 13th centuries, Vietnam came under increasing Chinese influence, while Thailand remained impervious to foreign penetration. Kingdoms have mixed, matched, and migrated; European powers have divided, conquered, and colonized; and in the wake of colonialism, nation-states have formed, collapsed, and rebuilt themselves. As one visits the region, it becomes clear that although nationalism is alive and well in Southeast Asia, the modern boundaries are but the current face of a captivating jigsaw puzzle that has been worked for millennia.

Essentials

Any number of factors could draw a traveler to Southeast Asia. The decadent hedonist might go to soak up sun on the islands, sample the mouth-watering cuisines, and escape the pressures of the western world. The avid anthropologist could be attracted by the diversity of people, cultures, and societies found in this tropical zone. Encompassing a plethora of traditions, religions, and races, there is no single Southeast Asian culture and, consequently, no one set of rules; what might be appropriate in one country might not be in another. There are, nonetheless, certain facts which all travelers to this region should be equipped with; these are covered in the following section. Reading this information carefully might enable you to avoid certain problems you could encounter.

PLANNING YOUR TRIP

■ When to Go

The weather in Southeast Asia is hot and humid, with temperatures fluctuating around 27°C (80°F) year round, anywhere south of highland Vietnam. Most countries have a rainy season, which ranges from May to September in the north, and runs later

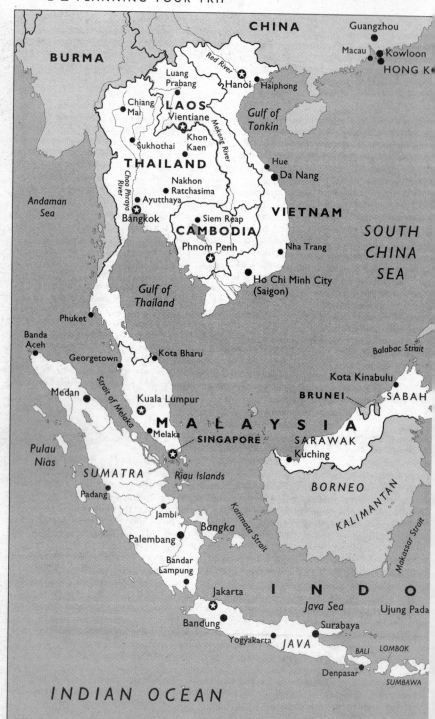

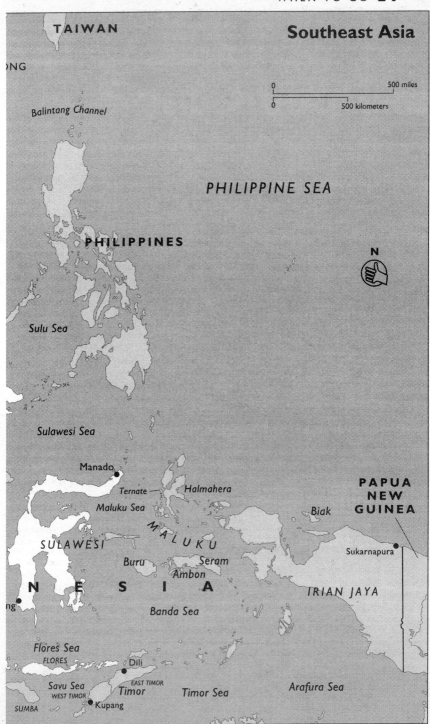

in the year the farther south you travel; by the time you get to Bali the rainy season lasts from November to May. The closer to the equator, the more consistently hot the weather is, and the less difference seasonal changes make. Please see the **Appendix** for a Climate Chart which gives more detail.

Another consideration for the traveler are tourist seasons; most countries have both high and low periods for tourism. These may depend upon anything from the rainy season to school vacations. What low season means for you is reduced services and reduced traffic at reduced prices; certain beaches and islands may close down all together. High seasons will bring floods of people to every popular beach and resort, as well as inflated prices. On the up side, however, more services will be available for the traveler. In such a diverse region there is no definitive answer on when to go. Something is always available for the budget traveler with a sense of adventure and a flexible itinerary.

■ Useful Information

GOVERNMENT INFORMATION OFFICES

Hong Kong Tourist Association (http://www.hkta.org): Australia: Level 5, 55 Harrington St., The Rocks, Sydney, NSW 2000 (tel. (02) 251 28 55; fax 247 88 12). **Canada:** 9 Temperance St., 3rd Fl., Toronto, Ont. M5H 1Y6 (tel. (416) 366-2389; fax 366-1098). **Europe, Africa, and the Middle East:** 4th/5th Fl., 125 Pall Mall, London SW1Y 5EA, England (tel. (0171) 930 47 75; fax 930 47 77). **New Zealand:** P.O. Box 2120, Auckland (tel. (09) 575 27 07; fax 575 26 20). **South Africa:** c/o Development Promotions Ltd. 7th Fl., Everite House, 20 De Korte St., Braamfontein 2001 (tel. (011) 339 48 65; fax 339 24 74). **US: East:** 5th Fl., 590 5th Ave., New York, NY 10036-4706 (tel. (212) 869-5008; fax 730-2605). **Central:** Suite 200, 610 Enterprise Dr., Oak Brook, IL 60521 (tel. (630) 575-2828; fax 575-2829). **West:** Suite 1220, 10940 Wilshire Blvd., Los Angeles, CA 90024-3915 (tel. (310) 208-4583; fax 208-1869).

Indonesia Tourist Promotion Office: Australia and the South Pacific: Level 10, 5 Elizabeth St., Sydney, NSW 2000 (tel. (02) 233 36 30; fax 233 36 29). **Europe:** Wießenhuttenstraße 17, D.6000 Frankfurt/Main 1 Germany (tel. (069) 233 677; fax 230 840). **North America:** 3457 Wilshire Blvd., Los Angeles, CA 90010-2203 (tel. (213) 387-2078; fax 380-4876). **UK and Scandanavia:** 3-4 Hanover St., London W1R 9HH (tel. (0171) 493 00 30; fax 493 17 47).

Tourism Malaysia: Australia: 65 York St., Sydney, NSW 2000 (tel. (02) 299 44 41; fax 262 20 26); 56 William St., Perth, WA 6000 (tel. (09) 481 04 00; fax 321 14 21). **Canada:** 830 Burrard St., Vancouver, BC V6Z 2K4 (tel. (604) 689-8899; fax 689-8804). **UK:** 57 Trafalgar Sq., London WC2N 5DU (tel. (0171) 930 79 32; fax 930 90 15). **US: East:** 595 Madison Ave., Suite 1800, New York, NY 10022 (tel. (212) 754-1113; fax 754-1116). **West:** 818 W. 7th St., Los Angeles, CA 90017 (tel. (213) 689-9702; fax 689-1530).

Singapore Tourist Promotion Board (http://www.travel.com.sg/sog): Australia: 8th Fl., St. Georges Ct., 16 St. Georges Terr., Perth, WA 6000 (tel. (09) 325 85 78; fax 221 38 64); Level 11, AWA Building, 47 York St., Sydney NSW 2000 (tel. (02) 290 28 88; fax 290 25 55). **Canada:** The Standard Life Centre, 121 King St. W., Suite 1000, Toronto, Ont. M5H 3T9 (tel. (416) 363-8898; fax 363-5752). **New Zealand:** 3rd Fl., 43 High St., P.O. Box 857, Auckland (tel. (09) 358 11 91; fax 358 11 96). **UK:** 1st Fl., Carrington House, 126-130 Regent St., London W1R 5FE (tel. (0171) 437 00 33; fax 734 21 91). **US: East:** 590 5th Ave., 12th Fl., New York, NY 10036 (tel. (212) 302-4861; fax 302-4801). **Central:** 180 N. Stetson Ave., 2 Prudential Plaza, Suite 1450, Chicago, IL 60601 (tel. (312) 938-1888; fax 938-0086). **West:** 8484 Wilshire Blvd., Suite 510, Beverly Hills, CA 90211 (tel. (213) 852-1901; fax 852-0129). **South Africa:** 52 3rd Ave., Parktown North 2193, P.O. Box 81432, Parkhurst 2120 (tel. (011) 788 07 01; fax 442 75 99).

Tourism Authority of Thailand (TAT): Australia: Level 2, National Australia Bank House, 255 George St., Sydney NSW 2000 (tel. (02) 247 75 49; fax 251 24 65). **Canada: East:** 250 St. Clair Ave. W, Suite 306, Toronto, Ont. M4V 1R6 (tel. (416)

925–9329; fax 925-2868). **West:** 10551 Shellbridge Way, Suite 157, Richmond, BC V6X 2W9 (tel. (604) 231-9030; fax 231-9031). **UK:** 49 Albemarle St., London WIX 3FE (tel. (0171) 499 76 79; fax 629 55 19). **US: East:** 5 World Trade Ctr., Suite 3443, New York, NY 10048 (tel. (212) 432-0433; fax 912-0920). **Central:** 303 E. Wacker Dr., Suite 400, Chicago, IL 60601 (tel. (312) 819-3990; fax 565-0359). **West:** 3440 Wilshire Blvd., Suite 1100, Los Angeles, CA 90010 (tel. (213) 382-2353; fax 389-7544).

No official overseas tourist offices for **Cambodia, Laos,** or **Vietnam.**

TRAVEL ORGANIZATIONS

American Automobile Association (AAA) Travel Related Services, 1000 AAA Dr. (mail stop 100), Heathrow, FL 32746-5080 (tel. (407) 444-8411). Offers travel services and auto insurance (free for members, small fee if not). To become a member, call 800-926-4222 in the US for the nearest office.

Council on International Educational Exchange (Council), 205 East 42nd St., New York, NY 10017-5706 (tel. (888) COUNCIL (268-6245); fax (212) 822-2699; e-mail info@ciee.org; http://www.ciee.org). A private, nonprofit organization, Council administers work, volunteer, and academic programs around the world. They also offer identity cards, including the ISIC and the GO25, and a range of publications, including the magazine *Student Travels* (free). Call or write for more information.

Federation of International Youth Travel Organizations (FIYTO), Bredgade 25H, DK-1260 Copenhagen K, Denmark (tel. (45) 33 33 96 00; fax 33 93 96 76; e-mail mailbox@fiyto.org), is an international organization promoting educational, cultural and social travel for young people. Member organizations include language schools, educational travel companies, national tourist boards, accommodation centers and other suppliers of travel services to youth and students. FIYTO sponsors the GO25 Card.

International Student Travel Confederation, Herengracht 479, 1017 BS Amsterdam, The Netherlands (tel. (31) 20 421 28 00; fax 20 421 28 10; e-mail istcinfo@istc.org; http://www.istc.org). The ISTC is a nonprofit confederation of student travel organizations whose focus is to develop, promote, and facilitate travel among young people and students. Member organizations include International Student Rail Association (ISRA), Student Air Travel Association (SATA), ISIS Travel Insurance, and the International Association for Educational and Work Exchange Programs (IAEWEP).

USEFUL PUBLICATIONS

Although *Let's Go* tries to cover all aspects of budget travel, we can't put *everything* in our guides. The travel publishers listed below offer some more detailed information on everything from restaurants to music festivals to geography. Most of the books listed can be ordered directly from the publisher.

Graphic Arts Center Publishing Company, P.O. Box 10306, Portland, OR 97210 (tel. (503) 226-2402 or (800) 452-3032; fax 223-1410; e-mail sales@gacpc.com). Pick up etiquette and plumb the national psyches of Hong Kong, Indonesia, Malaysia, Singapore, Thailand, or Vietnam with their *Culture Shock!* series.

Hippocrene Books, Inc., 171 Madison Ave., New York, NY 10016 (tel. (212) 685-4371; orders (718) 454-2366; fax (718) 454-1391). Free catalogue. Publishes travel reference books, travel guides, foreign language dictionaries, and language learning guides for over 100 languages.

Specialty Travel Index, 305 San Anselmo Ave., Suite 313, San Anselmo, CA 94960 (tel. (415) 459-4900; fax 459-4974; e-mail spectrav@ix.netcom.com; http://www.spectrav.com). Published twice yearly, this is an extensive listing of "off the beaten track" and specialty travel opportunities. One copy US$6, one-year subscription (2 copies) US$10.

Superintendent of Documents, U.S. Government Printing Office, P.O. Box 371954, Pittsburg, PA 15250-7954 (tel. (202) 512-1800; fax 512-2250). Open Mon.-Fri. 7:30am-4:30pm. Publishes *Your Trip Abroad* (US$1.25), *Health Information*

The Ramayana

The most obvious Indian influence on Southeast Asia that travelers encounter are the representations of characters, stories, and morals from the *Ramayana,* a Hindu epic that has inspired thousands of dances, paintings, and shadow puppet performances across the region. It is believed that the *Ramayana* was written about 500 BC by the sage Valmiki, and is probably based on actual events which took place between 1000 and 700 BC. Here is a brief synopsis:

Lord Rama was crown prince of the kingdom of Kosala, living in the capital city, Ayodhya. Beloved by all his subjects, Rama won the hand of beautiful Sita, the princess of a neighboring kingdom, by snapping in two an unbendable bow that Shiva had presented to Sita's father. Rama was all set to inherit the throne from his father, Dasaratha, when one of Dasaratha's wives tricked him into promising to make her son Bharatha king instead. Rama, Sita, and Rama's brother Lakshmana were exiled to the forest for 14 years.

While Rama and Lakshmana hunted wild beasts and protected ascetics, Ravana, the ten-headed king of the demons, began to eye Sita. One morning a servant of Ravana's appeared before Sita in the form of a golden stag. Sita urged Rama to go capture the creature, and while Rama was gone, Ravana abducted Sita to his island kingdom of Lanka. Rama was at a loss while Ravana kept Sita in his palace and lavished gifts on her, hoping to win her over. However, Rama and Lakshmana soon met the clever monkey Hanuman and won the favor of the monkey king, Sugriva. Huge armies of men and monkeys went to attack Lanka. Hanuman, whose father was the wind god, led the charge across the strait, throwing down rocks for the others to use as stepping stones. After a terrifying celestial battle Ravana was slain by one of Rama's arrows.

By this time, the 14 years of exile had elapsed and it was time for Rama to reclaim his throne, which Bharatha gladly handed over to him. The whole capital erupted in celebration as Rama learned that he was in fact an *avatara* (incarnation) of Vishnu. But there was one matter left to settle—Sita had been living in Ravana's household for months, and her chastity was questioned. Rama made Sita submit to a fire-ordeal, yet she emerged untouched by the flames. Still, rumors persisted, and when Sita became pregnant with twins, Rama was persuaded to banish her to the forest. There Sita met Valmiki, to whom she told the story of the *Ramayana.* And after her sons were born, Sita asked the earth to swallow her up. Meanwhile, in Ayodhya, Rama's kingdom decayed.

for International Travel (US$14), and "Background Notes" on all countries (US$1 each). Postage is included in the prices.

Transitions Abroad, 18 Hulst Rd., P.O. Box 1300, Amherst, MA 01004-1300 (tel. (413) 256-3414; fax 256-0375; e-mail trabroad@aol.com). Invaluable magazine lists publications and resources for overseas study, work, and volunteering. Also publishes *The Alternative Travel Directory,* a comprehensive guide to living, learning, and working overseas (US$20; postage US$4).

Travel Books & Language Center, Inc., 4931 Cordell Ave., Bethesda, MD 20814 (tel. (800) 220-2665; fax (301) 951-8546; e-mail travelbks@aol.com). Sells over 75,000 items, including books, cassettes, atlases, dictionaries, and a wide range of specialty travel maps. Free comprehensive catalogue upon request.

Wide World Books and Maps, 1911 N. 45th St., Seattle, WA 98103 (tel. (206) 634-3453; fax 634-0558; e-mail travelbk@mail.nwlink.com; http://nwlink.com/travelbk). A good selection of travel guides, travel accessories, and maps.

INTERNET RESOURCES

Along with everything else in the 90s, budget travel is moving rapidly into the information age. And with the growing user-friendliness of personal computers and internet technology, much of this information can be yours with the click of a mouse.

There are a number of ways to access the **Internet.** Most popular are commercial internet providers, such as **America Online** (U.S. tel. (800) 827-6394) and **Com-**

puserve (U.S. tel. (800) 433-0389). Many employers and schools also offer gateways to the Internet, often at no cost—unlike the corporate sort listed above. The Internet itself can be used in many different forms, but the World Wide Web and Usenet newsgroups are the most useful to 'net-surfing budget travelers.

The World Wide Web

Increasingly the Internet forum of choice, the **World Wide Web** provides its users with graphics and sound, as well as textual information. These benefits, and the huge proliferation of "web pages" (individual sites within the World Wide Web) have made the Web the most active and exciting of the destinations on the Internet. The introduction of **search engines** (services that search for web pages under specific subjects) has aided the search process. **Lycos** (http://a2z.lycos.com) and **Infoseek** (http://guide.infoseek.com) are two of the most popular. **Yahoo!** is a slightly more organized search engine; check out its travel links at http://www.yahoo.com/Recreation/Travel. It is often better to go to a well known site, and start "surfing" from there, through links from one web page to another. The following sites are good for surfing for budget travel information.

Dr. Memory's Favorite Travel Pages (http://www.access.digex.net/~drmemory/ cyber_travel.htm). Dr. Memory has links to hundreds of different web pages of interest to travelers of all kinds.

Rent-A-Wreck's Travel Links (http://www.rent-a-wreck.com/raw/travlist.htm) are very good and very complete.

Big World Magazine (http://boss.cpcnet.com/personal/bigworld/bigworld.htm), a budget travel 'zine, has a web page and a collection of links to travel pages.

City.Net (http://www.city.net) is a very impressive collection of regional- or city-specific web pages. You just select a geographic area, and it provides you with links to web pages related to it.

The CIA World Factbook (http://www.odci.gov/cia/publications/95fact) has tons of vital statistics on the country you want to visit. Check it out for an overview of a country's economy or an explanation of their system of government.

The Student and Budget Travel Guide (http://asa.ugl.lib.umich.edu/chdocs/ travel/travel-guide.html) is just what it sounds like.

Foreign Language for Travelers (http://www.travelang.com) can help you brush up on your Thai and other languages.

Newsgroups

One primary means of transmission and discussion of information across the Internet are forums known collectively as Usenet, and individually as **newsgroups,** which can be your best source for up-to-the-minute information. New groups are always sprouting up. Unfortunately, not all groups are available from all systems. Your system administrator can usually add new groups on request. A caveat: **most newsgroups are unmoderated,** so the quality of conversation and reliability of information is not always certain.

There are several types of newsgroups. The "soc" groups primarily address social issues and socializing; try **soc.culture.thai, soc.culture.malaysia, soc.culture.vietnamese,** or that of the country of your choice. Another good choice is **soc.culture.asean,** which discusses the member nations of ASEAN. The "alt" groups are a less formalized collection of newsgroups; good examples are **alt.culture.indonesia** and **alt.current-events.singapore.** "Rec" groups, such as **rec.travel.air** are oriented toward the arts, hobbies, or recreation. Some systems also provide access to the "ClariNet" newsgroups, read-only (copyrighted) groups that compile the latest wire service news; **clari.news.asia** is an example of such a group.

▓ Documents and Formalities

When traveling to Southeast Asia, be sure to file all applications several weeks or months in advance of your planned departure date. Remember, you are relying on government agencies that are sometimes notoriously inefficient at completing these transactions. If you don't plan ahead, a backlog in processing can spoil your plans.

When you travel **always carry on your person two or more forms of identification,** including at least one photo ID. Many establishments, especially banks, require several IDs before cashing traveler's checks. A passport combined with a driver's license or birth certificate usually serves as adequate proof of your identity and citizenship. **Never carry all your forms of ID and your valuable travel documents together,** however, in case of theft or loss. Be sure to **photocopy all important documents and credit cards** before you leave home; leave these with someone you trust and can contact easily in case of an emergency. Also, carry half a dozen extra passport-size photos for the sundry visa, ID, and other applications you may need to fill out. If you plan an extended stay, register your passport with the nearest embassy or consulate. Students should carry proof of their status (see **Youth and Student Identification** below) in order to take advantage of the various student discounts that are available on the road.

For many countries in Southeast Asia, a visa is required to enter. A visa is an endorsement that a foreign government stamps into a passport, allowing the bearer to stay in that country for a specified purpose and period of time. Most visas cost US$10-70 and let you spend about a month in a country, within six months to a year from the date of issue. Please see **Entrance Requirements and Visas** below for country-specific information.

For more information, U.S. travelers can send for *Foreign Entry Requirements* (US$0.50) from the **Consumer Information Center,** Pueblo, CO 81009 (tel. (719) 948-3334). The **Center for International Business and Travel (CIBT),** 25 W. 43rd St. #1420, New York, NY 10036 (tel. (800) 925-2428 or (212) 575-2811 from NYC), secures visas for travel to and from all countries. The service charge varies.

EMBASSIES AND CONSULATES

Cambodia

Royal Kingdom of Cambodia Embassy: US: 4500 16th St. NW, Washington, D.C. 20011 (tel. (202) 726-7742; fax 726-8381).

Hong Kong

Served by the **British embassies and consulates. US: Embassy:** 3100 Massachusetts Ave. NW, Washington, D.C. 20008 (tel. (202) 462-1340). **Consulates: East:** 845 Third Ave., New York, NY 10022 (tel. (212) 745-0200). **Central:** Suite 1300, The Wrigley Bldg., 400 N. Michigan Ave., Chicago, IL 60611 (tel. (312) 346-1810). **South:** First Interstate Bank Plaza, Suite 1990, 1000 Louisiana, Houston, TX 77002 (tel. (713) 659-6270). **West:** 11766 Wilshire Blvd., Suite 400, Los Angeles, CA 90025-6538 (tel. (310) 477-3322). Call the embassy for additional addresses. **British High Commission: Australia:** Commonwealth Ave., Yarralumla, Canberra, ACT 2600 (tel. (616) 270 66 66). **Canada:** 80 Elgin St., Ottawa, Ont. KIP 5K7 (tel. (613) 237-1530). **New Zealand,** 44 Hill St., Wellington 1 (tel. (644) 472 60 49).

Indonesia

Indonesian Consulate General: Australia: South: Beulah Park, 44 Gawler Place S.A. 5067, Adelaide (tel. (08) 430 87 42). **Southeast:** 236-238 Maroubra Rd., Maroubra, Sydney, NSW 2035 (tel. (02) 344 99 33; fax 349 68 54). **Canada:** 129 Jarvis St., Toronto, Ont. M5C 2H6 (tel. (416) 360 4020; fax 360 4295). **US: East:** 5 E. 68th St., New York, NY 10021 (tel. (212) 879-0600; fax 570-6206). **Central:** 2 Illinois Center, Suite 1422, 233 N. Michigan Ave., Chicago, IL 60601 (tel. (312) 938-0101; fax 938-3148). **West:** 3457 Wilshire Blvd., Los Angeles, CA 90010 (tel. (213) 383-5126; fax 487-3971).

Consulate of the Republic of Indonesia: Australia: North: 20 Harry Chan Ave., Darwin Northern Territory (tel. (089) 41 00 48; fax 41 27 09). **West:** 134 Adelaide Terr., P.O. Box 6683, East Perth, WA 6004 (tel. (09) 221 58 58; fax 221 56 88). **Southeast:** 72 Queen Rd., Melbourne, VIC 3004 (tel. (03) 525 27 55; fax 525 15 88). **Canada:** 15124-42 Ave., Edmonton, AB TGH 5LG (tel. (403) 430-8742; fax

988-9768). **US: Central:** 10900 Richmond Ave., Houston, TX 77042 (tel. (713) 785-1691; fax 780-9644). **West:** 1111 Columbus Ave., San Francisco, CA 94133 (tel. (415) 474-9571; fax 441-4320); 98-1032 Alania St., Aiea, HI 96701 (tel. (808) 488-0138).

Embassy of the Republic of Indonesia: Australia: 8 Darwin Ave., Yarralumla, Canberra, ACT 2600; P.O. Box 616, Kingston 2604 (tel. (06) 250 86 00; fax 250 86 66). **Canada:** 287 MacLaren St., Ottawa, Ont. K2P OL9 (tel. (613) 236 7403; fax 563 2858). **New Zealand:** 70 Glen Rd., P.O. Box 3543, Kelburn Wellington (tel. (04) 475 86 97; fax 475 93 74). **UK:** 38 Grosvenor Square, London WIX 9AD (tel. (0171) 499 76 61; fax 491 49 93). **US:** United Nations, 325 E. 38th St., New York, NY 10016 (tel. (212) 972-8333; fax 972-9780); 2020 Massachusetts Ave. NW, Washington, DC 20036 (tel. (202) 775-5200; fax 775-5365).

Laos

Embassy of the Lao PDR: Australia: 1 Dalman Crescent, O'Malley, Canberra, ACT 2606 (tel. (06) 286 45 95; fax 290 19 10); **US:** 2222 S St. NW, Washington, D.C. 20008 (tel. (202) 332-6416; fax 332-4923).

Permanent Mission of the Lao PDR to the UN: 317 E. 51st St., New York, NY 10022 (tel. (212) 832-2734; fax 750-0039).

Malaysia

Embassy of Malaysia: South Africa: Carlton Hotel, Main St., Johannesburg 2000 (tel. 330 19 11; fax 880 48 94). **US:** 2401 Massachusetts Ave. NW, Washington, D.C. 20008 (tel. (202) 328-2700; fax 483-7661); 550 S. Hope St., Ste. 400, Los Angeles, CA 90071 (tel. (213) 892-1238; fax 892-9031). **Consulate General of Malaysia: US:** 313 E. 43rd St., New York, NY 10017 (tel. (212) 682-0232; fax 983-1987).

High Commission of Malaysia: Australia: 7 Perth Ave., Yarralumla, Canberra, ACT 2600 (tel. (06) 273 15 43). **Canada:** 60 Boteler St., Ottawa, Ont. KIN 8Y7 (tel. (613) 237-5183; fax 237-4852). **New Zealand:** 10 Washington Ave., Brooklyn, Wellington (tel. (03) 85 24 93; fax 85 69 73). **UK:** 45 Belgrave Sq., London SWIX 8QT (tel. (0171) 235 80 33; fax 235 51 61).

Singapore

Embassy of the Republic of Singapore: US: 3501 International Pl. NW, Washington, D.C. 20008 (tel. (202) 537-3100).

Consulate General of the Republic of Singapore: Canada: Suite 1305, 999 W. Hastings St., Vancouver, BC V6C 2W2 (tel. (604) 669-5115). **US: West:** 2424 SE Bristol #320, Newport Beach, CA 92707 (tel. (714) 476-2330). **Central:** c/o Personnel Decisions Inc., 2000 Plaza VII, 45 S. 7th St., Minneapolis, MN 55402 (tel. (612) 337-3643).

Singapore High Commission: Australia: 17 Forster Crescent, Yarralumla, Canberra, ACT 2600 (tel. (06) 273 39 44). **New Zealand:** 17 Kabul St., P.O. Box 13-140, Khandallah, Wellington (tel. (04) 479 20 76). **South Africa:** 173 Beckett St., Arcadia, Pretoria 0083 (tel. (12) 343 43 71). **UK:** 9 Wilton Crescent, London SW1X 8SA (tel. (0171) 235 83 15).

Thailand

Royal Thai Consulate General: Australia: 75-77 Pitt St., 2nd Fl., Sydney, NSW 2000 (tel. (02) 241 25 42/3). **Canada: East:** 1155 René-Lévesque Ouest, Suite 2500, Montréal, QU H3B 2K4 (tel. (514) 871-9941; fax 875-8967). **Central:** 44th Fl., Scotia Plaza, 40 King St. W., 4th Fl., Toronto, Ont., M5H 3Y4 (tel. (416) 367-6750); 8625 112 St., Edmonton, AB T6G 1K8 (tel. (403) 439-3576; fax 432-1387). **West:** 736 Granville St., Suite 106, Vancouver, BC V6Z 1G3 (tel. (604) 687-1143; fax 687-4434). **UK: England:** 35 Lord St., Liverpool 2 (tel. (051) 225 05 04); **Scotland:** Pacific House, 70 Wellington St., Glasgow G2 6SB (tel. (041) 248 66 77). **US: East:** 351 E. 52nd St., New York, NY 10022 (tel. (212) 754-1770; fax 754-1907). **Central:** 35 E. Wacker Dr., Suite 1834, Chicago, IL 60601 (tel. (312) 236-2447). **West:** 801 N. La Brea Ave., Los Angeles, CA 90038 (tel. (213) 937-1894).

Royal Thai Embassy: Australia, 111 Empire Circuit, Yarralumla, Canberra, ACT 2600 (tel. (06) 273 11 49). **Canada,** 180 Island Park Dr., Ottawa K1Y OA2 (tel. (613) 722-4444). **UK,** 29-30 Queen's Gate, London SW7 5JB (tel. (0171) 589 01

73). **New Zealand,** 2 Cook St., P.O. Box 17-226, Karori, Wellington (tel. (04) 76 86 18). **US,** 1024 Wisconsin Ave., Washington, DC 20007 (tel. (202) 994-3608).

Vietnam

Embassy of Vietnam: Australia, 6 Tim Berra Crescent, Canberra, ACT 2600 (tel. (06) 286 60 58; fax 286 45 34). **UK,** Victoria 12-14, W. 8, London (tel. (0171) 937 19 12; fax 937 61 08). **US,** 1233 20th St., NW, Suite 501, Washington, D.C. 20036 (tel. (202) 861-0737; fax 861-0917).

PASSPORTS

Travelers in Southeast Asia must have a valid passport. Before you leave, **photocopy the page of your passport that contains your photograph, identifying information, and passport number.** Carry this photocopy in a safe place apart from your passport, and leave another copy at home. To help prove your citizenship, and further facilitate the issuance of a new passport, consulates recommend you carry an expired passport or an official copy of your birth certificate in a part of your baggage separate from other documents.

If you do lose your passport, it may take weeks to process a replacement, and the new one may be valid only for limited time. In addition, any visas stamped in the old passport will be irretrievable. If this event occurs, immediately notify the local police and the nearest embassy or consulate of your home country. To expedite its replacement, you need to know all information previously recorded and show identification and proof of citizenship. Most consulates can issue new passports within two days if given proof of citizenship. In an emergency, ask for immediate temporary traveling papers that will permit you to re-enter your home country. Your passport is a public document belonging to your nation's government. You may have to surrender it to a foreign government official; if you don't get it back in a reasonable amount of time, inform the nearest diplomatic mission of your home country.

United States

Citizens may apply for a passport, valid for 10 years (five years if under 18) at any federal or state courthouse or post office authorized to accept passport applications, or at a **U.S. Passport Agency,** located in Boston, Chicago, Honolulu, Houston, Los Angeles, Miami, New Orleans, New York, Philadelphia, San Francisco, Seattle, Stamford, or Washington, D.C. Parents must apply in person for children under age 13. You must apply in person if this is your first passport, if you are under age 18, or if your current passport is more than 12 years old or was issued before your 18th birthday. You must submit the following: 1) proof of citizenship (a certified birth certificate, certification of naturalization or of citizenship, or a previous passport); 2) identification bearing your signature and either your photograph or physical description (e.g. an unexpired driver's license or passport, student ID card, or government ID card); and 3) two identical, passport-size (2in. x 2in.) photographs with a white background taken within the last six months. It will cost US$65 (under 18 US$40); passports can be renewed by mail or in person for US$55. Processing takes two to four weeks. Passport agencies offer **rush service** for a surcharge of US$30 if you have proof that you're departing within ten working days (e.g., an airplane ticket or itinerary). If your passport is lost or stolen in the U.S., report it in writing to Passport Services, U.S. Department of State, 111 19th St., NW, Washington D.C. 20522-1705 or to the nearest passport agency. For more info, contact the U.S. Passport Information's **24-hour recorded message** (tel. (202) 647-0518).

Canada

Application forms in English and French are available at all passport offices, post offices, and most travel agencies. Citizens may apply in person at any one of 28 regional Passport Offices. Travel agents can direct the applicant to the nearest location. Canadian citizens residing abroad should contact the nearest Canadian embassy or consulate. Along with the application form, a citizen must provide: 1) citizenship documentation (an original birth certificate, or a certificate of citizenship); 2) two identical passport photos taken within the last year; 3) any previous Canadian passport; and 4) a CDN$60 fee (paid in cash, money order, or certified check) to Passport Office, Ottawa, Ont. K1A OG3. The application and one of the photographs must be signed by an eligible guarantor (someone who has known the applicant for two years and whose profession falls into one of the categories listed on the application). Processing takes approximately five business days for in-person applications and three weeks for mailed ones. Children under 16 may be included on a parent's passport, although some countries require children to carry their own passports. A passport is valid for five years and is not renewable. For additional info, call (800) 567-6868 (24 hr.; from Canada only) or call the Passport Office in Québec at (819) 994-3500, in Metro Toronto (416) 973-3251, and in Montréal (514) 283-2152. Refer to the booklet *Bon Voyage, But...* for further help and a list of Canadian embassies and consulates abroad. It's available free of charge from passport offices.

Britain

British citizens, British Dependent Territories citizens, British Nationals (overseas), and British Overseas citizens may apply for a **full passport.** Children under 16 may be included on a parent's passport, however, some countries require children to have their own passports. Processing by mail usually takes four to six weeks. The London office offers same-day, walk-in rush service; arrive early.

Ireland

Citizens can apply for a passport by mail to either the Department of Foreign Affairs, Passport Office, Setanta Centre, Molesworth St., Dublin 2 (tel. (01) 671 16 33), or the Passport Office, 1A South Mall, Cork (tel. (021) 627 25 25). Obtain an application at a local Garda station or request one from a passport office. The new Passport Express Service offers a two week turn-around and is available through post offices for an extra IR£3. Passports cost IR£45 and are valid for 10 years. Citizens under 18 or over 65 can request a three-year passport that costs IR£10.

Australia

Citizens must apply for a passport in person at a post office, a passport office, or an Australian diplomatic mission overseas. An appointment may be necessary. Passport offices are located in Adelaide, Brisbane, Canberra City, Darwin, Hobart, Melbourne, Newcastle, Perth, and Sydney. A parent may file an application for a child who is under 18 and unmarried. Application fees are adjusted frequently. For more info, call toll-free (in Australia) 13 12 32.

New Zealand

Application forms for passports are available in New Zealand from travel agents and Department of Internal Affairs Link Centres, and overseas from New Zealand embassies, high commissions, and consulates. Completed applications may be lodged at Link Centres and at overseas posts, or forwarded to the Passport Office, P.O. Box 10-526, Wellington. Processing takes 10 working days from receipt of a correctly completed application. An urgent passport service is also available. The application fee for an adult passport is NZ$80 in New Zealand, and NZ$130 overseas for applications lodged under the standard service.

South Africa

Citizens can apply for a passport at any Home Affairs Office. Two photos, either a birth certificate or an identity book, and a SAR80 fee must accompany a completed application. South African passports remain valid for 10 years. For further information, contact the nearest Department of Home Affairs Office.

ENTRANCE REQUIREMENTS AND VISAS

Cambodia

The easiest way to obtain a visa is upon arrival at Pochentong Airport in Phnom Penh. One-month visas are issued immediately for US$20. Those traveling overland from Vietnam can apply for visas in Ho Chi Minh City for US$20, which takes two days to process. Bangkok offers quick service: many travel agencies will grant visas in one day for an average US$25. **Visa extensions** can be made by the Immigration Office in Phnom Penh for up to six months.

Hong Kong

Without a visa, British citizens may stay in Hong Kong for up to 12 months, Australian, Canadian, and New Zealand citizens may stay three months, and South African and U.S. citizens may stay one month (with proof of onward passage).

Indonesia

Visitors from any country must carry a passport valid for at least six months from their date of entry and proof of onward passage. Residents of South Africa need a visa to enter the country. No visas are necessary for residents of Australia, Canada, Ireland, New Zealand, the U.K., and the U.S. if entering through one of the gateway cities (please see the **Getting Around** section of Indonesia on page 109). Travelers entering through another city must obtain a visa (valid for one month, but extendable). Visitors without a special visa may not stay longer 60 days.

Laos

Visa regulations change constantly, and no one seems able to give a definitive answer. Officially, every tourist enters the country on a 15-day tourist visa and is assigned to one of Vientiane's 20-odd travel agencies. It's best to apply for a visa from an embassy in Bangkok, Hanoi, or Phnom Penh first. Citizens of countries that have an embassy in Vientiane can get valid visas which must be stamped in Bangkok. For all others, it's possible to obtain quasi-legal visas in Nong Khai, Thailand, but problems can often arise once in Laos. **Visa extensions** can be made through the travel agency listed on your visa for US$3-5. Apply at least five days before the expiration date, otherwise you will be fined US$5 for every day you overstay your visa upon exiting the country.

Malaysia

Travelers to Malaysia from Australia, New Zealand, the U.K., and the U.S. can travel in Malaysia for up to three months without a visa. South African citizens can travel without a visa for up to one month. For longer stays contact the Malaysian Embassy or consulate. Travelers who wish to travel around Malaysia and return must apply for a **re-entry permit** (US$5).

Singapore

Travelers holding passports from Australia, New Zealand, the U.K., the U.S., and numerous other countries can enter and remain in Singapore for less than 14 days without a visa. Those planning to stay longer should apply for an **extension** at the Immigration Office at least two days before the grace period ends.

Thailand

Citizens from most western countries need not obtain visas if they plan to be in Thailand for less than one month (with proof of departure). Thailand issues two main types of visas: **tourist visas** (up to 60 days, US$15) and **non-immigrant visas** for business or employment (up to 90 days, US$20). These visas may be obtained at a Thai consulate in your home nation. Thirty-day transit visas may not be extended. For those who wish to take sojourns to nearby countries, a **re-entry permit** is required to return. Applications should be made at the main Immigration Office well before departure. When exiting Thailand, make sure to get an **exit stamp** on your passport.

If not, you will have exited the country *illegally*, and the next time you come to Thailand, you will face deportation.

Vietnam

The Vietnamese government grants 30-day single-entry tourist visa at any consulate. You must have a passport valid for at least nine months after your stay in Vietnam, two completed and signed visa application forms, and two recent passport size photos. A single-entry visa costs US$25, while a double-entry visa will set you back US$40. It's often easier to obtain a visa for Vietnam at travel agencies in Bangkok, which offer visas within four days for US$60. Express visas are also available, but are not as reliable and cost significantly more. For this you should have at least two passport-sized photos handy although you may need up to six in some places. Visas specify where travelers can enter and leave the country. For any changes of entry/exit points, go to the Foreign Ministry in Hanoi or Ho Chi Minh City. It's not unheard of for tourists to have a 30-day visa, only to have officials validate it for a week. Check immediately to see how many days you've been granted. If the validation stamp does not match your visa, you may be able to get it changed at the border checkpoint; if not, apply for an extension with the Ministry of Foreign Affairs. Overstaying your visa, no matter how short, is a serious violation. **Visa extensions** are no longer granted to tourists.

CUSTOMS: ENTERING

Cambodia

Standard international customs laws apply in Cambodia: 200 cigarettes, 1L of alcohol, and unlimited amounts of currency are allowed in the country. Weapons and drugs are banned from the country. The government takes drug trafficking very seriously. As one embassy official said, **those who are caught with drugs "will not come out of Cambodia alive,"** and drug abusers, including users of marijuana, opium, and cocaine "will be shot." Keep that in mind.

Hong Kong

Travelers can import up to 200 cigarettes, 50 cigars, or 250g of tobacco, and 1L of wine or spirits. Arms may be taken into custody, and must be declared. You must obtain a permit to bring ivory into or out of Hong Kong.

Indonesia

Visitors to Indonesia can carry a maximum of 2L of alcoholic beverages, 50 cigars or 200 cigarettes or 100g of tobacco, and perfume for personal use only. No radios, TV sets, narcotics, arms or ammunition, Chinese medicine, or text in Chinese characters may be imported. Upon entry, visitors must declare any cars, photographic equipment, typewriters, and tape recorders, and these must be re-exported. Although any amount of foreign currency may be taken in or out of the country, the import or export of more than Rp50,000 is prohibited. Quarantine permits are required for fruit, plants, and animals, and advance approval is required for transceivers. Movies or videos must be cleared by the Film Censor Board.

Laos

Travelers to Laos may bring in up to 200 cigarettes, 1L of alcohol, and perfume (for personal use only), as well as any foreign currency. Lao laws prohibit weapons, drugs, and pornography.

Malaysia

Travelers can bring in 1L of alcohol, 200 cigarettes, food preparations not exceeding RM75 in value, and gifts not exceeding RM200 in value. There is no restriction on the import or export of currency. Prohibited from import are pornography, prejudicial publications, knives, most broadcast receivers, and all goods originating from Israel. **The punishment for importing or exporting illegal drugs is the death penalty,** including opium, marijuana, heroin, morphine, etc. A permit is necessary to import

ESSENTIALS

precious stones (apart from reasonable amounts of jewelry), gold (except coins issued by the Central Bank of Malaysia and personal jewelry), toy or real arms, CBs, animals, plants, and soil.

Singapore

Travelers can bring in, duty free, 1L of spirits, wine, or beer, but no tobacco products, and up to S$400 in gifts, food preparations, etc. Prohibited from importation are chewing gum, chewing tobacco or imitation tobacco, cigarette lighters, obscenity, "seditious and treasonable material," and toy currency. **"Death for drug traffickers under Singapore law."** Possession equals trafficking under their laws. There are no currency restrictions.

Thailand

Travelers can bring in 250g tobacco, 200 cigarettes, 50 cigars, and 1L of liquor duty-free, as well as one still camera with five rolls of film, or one movie camera with three rolls of film. Narcotics, including opium, heroin, cocaine, marijuana, and morphine, are prohibited. The penalty for possession can range from a imprisonment to death, depending on the drug and whether or not the prosecutor can prove that you were trying to sell it. Fruits and vegetables should be left at home. Also, nix the firearms and pornography. Tourists entering the country must bring in a minimum of US$400 per person or US$800 per family.

Vietnam

Customs declaration forms ask visitors to declare quantities and makes of cameras, video and camcorders, tape recorders, and all other electric equipment being taken into the country. Foreign currency in excess of US$10,000 must be declared. Drug trafficking, weapons, and explosives are banned in Vietnam. The government is not hesitant about doling out harsh penalties, including capital punishment. In addition, objects deemed subversive and impure to Vietnamese society, such as pornography, will be confiscated.

CUSTOMS: GOING HOME

Having passed the test to get into the country of your choice, you have not yet completed the customs challenge. Certain Southeast Asian countries have regulations for exiting the country as well. In addition, upon returning home, you must declare all articles you acquired abroad and pay a duty on the value of those articles that exceed the allowance established by your country's customs service. Goods and gifts purchased at duty-free shops abroad are not exempt from duty or sales tax at your point of return; you must declare these items as well. "Duty-free" merely means that you need not pay a tax in the country of purchase. The Southeast Asian countries not listed have no exiting customs regulations.

Leaving Southeast Asia

Cambodia: Upon leaving Cambodia, there is an US$8 airport tax. Duty free allowances include 200 cigarettes, 1L of alcohol, and perfume (for personal use only).

Laos: There's a US$5 airport tax for all international flights. Duty-free allowances include two bottles of liquor and 500 cigarettes. In addition, no antiques or **Buddha images** can leave the country without the authorization of the government.

Thailand: The Thai government is adamant about enforcing the few exit laws they do have. **No Buddha images, Bodhisattva images, or fragments thereof** may be taken out of the country unless you're a worshiping Buddhist or you are using them for cultural exchanges or academic purposes. A license must be obtained from the Fine Arts Department if you want to take any Buddha images or objects of art out of Thailand. To apply for a license, send your enquiries to: The National Museums Division, Bangkok; The Chiang Mai National Museum, Chiang Mai; or the Songkhla National Museum, Songkhla, or call the National Museum in Bangkok (tel. (02) 261 661). **These rules do not apply to souvenirs** or other objects bought in department stores. For any art purchased in the country, keep receipts handy for presentation to customs officials.

Vietnam: Duty free allowances include 200 cigarettes, 1L of alcohol, perfume (for personal use), foreign currency, and unlimited jewelry. Antiques will not be allowed out of the country without approval from the Ministry of Culture and Information. No dong allowed out of the country. Upon leaving from Ho Chi Minh City, there is an airport tax of US$8; from Hanoi US$6. You need to show both your customs form and immigration card when leaving the country, otherwise you could be fined for losing them.

Entering Home Countries

United States: Citizens returning home may bring US$400 worth of accompanying goods duty-free and must pay a 10% tax on the next US$1000. All purchases must be declared, so have sales slips ready. Goods are considered duty-free if they are for personal or household use (including gifts) and cannot include more than 100 cigars, 200 cigarettes (1 carton), and 1L of wine or liquor. You must be over 21 to bring liquor into the U.S. If you mail home personal goods of U.S. origin, you can avoid duty charges by marking the package "American goods returned." For more information, consult the brochure *Know Before You Go,* available from the U.S. Customs Service, Box 7407, Washington, D.C. 20044 (tel. (202) 927-5580).

Canada: Citizens who remain abroad for at least one week may bring back up to CDN$500 worth of goods duty-free once per calendar year. Canadian citizens or residents who travel for a period between 48 hours and six days can bring back up to CDN$200 with the exception of tobacco and alcohol. Goods except tobacco and alcohol may be shipped home under this exemption, as long as you declare them when you arrive. Citizens of legal age may import up to 200 cigarettes, 50 cigars, 400g loose tobacco, 400 tobacco sticks, 1.14L wine or alcohol, and 24 355mL cans/bottles of beer; the value of these products is included in the CDN$500. For more information, write to Canadian Customs, 2265 St. Laurent Blvd., Ottawa, Ont. K1G 4K3 (tel. (613) 993-0534).

Britain: Citizens or visitors arriving in the UK from outside the EC must declare any goods in excess of the following allowances: 200 cigarettes, 100 cigarillos, 50 cigars, or 250g tobacco; still table wine (2L); strong liquors over 22% volume (1L); or fortified or sparkling wine, other liquors (2L); perfume (60 cc/mL); toilet water (250 cc/mL); and UK£145 worth of all other goods including gifts and souvenirs. You must be over 17 to import liquor or tobacco. Goods obtained duty and tax paid for personal use within the EC do not require any further customs duty. For more info about UK customs, contact Her Majesty's Customs and Excise, Custom House, Nettleton Road, Heathrow Airport, Hounslow, Middlesex TW6 2LA (tel. (0181) 910 37 44; fax 910 37 65).

Ireland: Citizens must declare everything in excess of IR£34 (IR£17 per traveler under 15 years of age) obtained outside the EC or duty- and tax-free in the EC above the following allowances: 200 cigarettes; 100 cigarillos; 50 cigars; or 250g tobacco; 1L liquor or 2L wine; 2L still wine; 50g perfume; and 250mL toilet water. You must be over 17 to bring in tobacco or alcohol. For more information, contact The Revenue Commissioners, Dublin Castle (tel. (01) 679 27 77; fax 671 20 21; e-mail taxes§ior.ie; http:ttwww.revenue.ie) or The Collector of Customs and Excise, The Custom House, Dublin 1.

Australia: Citizens may import AUS$400 (under 18 AUS$200) of goods duty-free, as well as 1.125L alcohol and 250 cigarettes or 250g tobacco. You must be over 18 to import either of these. There's no limit to the amount of Australian and/or foreign cash that may be brought into or taken out of the country. However, amounts of AUS$5000 or more, or the equivalent in foreign currency, must be reported. All foodstuffs and animal products must be declared on arrival. For information, contact the Regional Director, Australian Customs Service, GPO Box 8, Sydney NSW 2001 (tel. (02) 213 20 00; fax 213 40 00).

New Zealand: Citizens may bring home up to NZ$700 worth of goods duty-free if they are intended for personal use or are unsolicited gifts. The concession is 200 cigarettes (1 carton) or 250g tobacco or 50 cigars or a combination of all three not to exceed 250g. You may also bring in 4.5L of beer or wine and 1.125L of liquor.

The World At a Discount

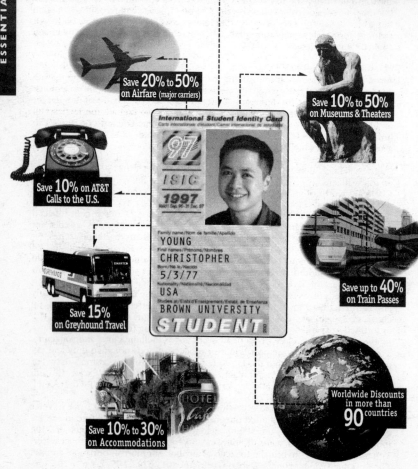

Save 20% to 50% on Airfare (major carriers)

Save 10% to 50% on Museums & Theaters

Save 10% on AT&T Calls to the U.S.

Save 15% on Greyhound Travel

Save up to 40% on Train Passes

International Student Identity Card
Carte internationale d'étudiant/Carnet internacional de estudiante

97
ISIC
1997
Valid 1 Sep. 96–31 Dec. 97

Family name/Nom de famille/Apellido
YOUNG
First names/Prénoms/Nombres
CHRISTOPHER
Born/Né le/Nacido
5/3/77
Nationality/Nationalité/Nacionalidad
USA
Studies at/Établid'Enseignement/Establ. de Enseñanza
BROWN UNIVERSITY
STUDENT

Save 10% to 30% on Accommodations

Worldwide Discounts in more than 90 countries

The International Student Identity Card
Your Passport to Discounts & Benefits

With the ISIC, you'll receive discounts on airfare, hotels, transportation, computer services, foreign currency exchange, phone calls, major attractions, and more. You'll also receive basic accident and sickness insurance coverage when traveling outside the U.S. and access to a 24-hour, toll-free Help Line. Call now to locate the issuing office nearest you (over 555 across the U.S.) at:

Free 40-page handbook with each card!

1-888-COUNCIL (toll-free)

For an application and complete discount list, you can also visit us at **http://www.ciee.org/**

Council
CIEE: Council on International Educational Exchange

Only travelers over 17 may bring tobacco or alcohol into the country. For more information, consult the *New Zealand Customs Guide for Travelers,* available from customs offices, or contact New Zealand Customs, 50 Anzac Ave., Box 29, Auckland (tel. (09) 377 35 20; fax 309 29 78).

South Africa: Citizens may import duty-free: 400 cigarettes; 50 cigars; 250g tobacco; 2L wine; 1L of spirits; 250mL toilet water; and 50mL perfume; and other items up to a value of SAR500. Amounts exceeding this limit but not SAR10,000 are dutiable at 20%. Certain items such as golf clubs and firearms require a duty higher than the standard. Goods acquired abroad and sent to the country as unaccompanied baggage do not qualify for any allowances. You may not export or import South African bank notes in excess of SAR500. Persons who require specific information or advice concerning customs and excise duties can address their inquiries to the Commissioner for Customs and Excise, Private Bag X47, Pretoria 0001, which distributes the pamphlet *South African Customs Information,* for visitors and residents. South Africans residing in the U.S. should contact the Embassy of South Africa, 3051 Massachusetts Ave., NW, Washington, D.C. 20008 (tel. (202) 232-4400; fax 244-9417) or the South African Home Annex, 3201 New Mexico Ave. #380 NW, Washington, D.C. 20016 (tel. (202) 966-1650).

YOUTH, STUDENT, & TEACHER IDENTIFICATION

The **International Student Identity Card (ISIC)** is the most widely accepted form of student identification. Although invaluable in well-traveled areas like Western Europe, its usefulness is unfortunately limited in Southeast Asia. Flashing this card may get you some discounts, but usually on bigger ticket items (such as domestic plane tickets). It may be worth getting however, simply to get a discount fare on your plane ticket there—some budget travel agencies require that you have an ISIC to get student fares. Another nice benefit is that the card provides accident insurance of up to US$3000 with no daily limit. Cardholders also have access to a toll-free Traveler's Assistance hotline whose multilingual staff can provide help in medical, legal, and financial emergencies overseas.

Many student travel offices issue ISICs, including Council Travel, Let's Go Travel, and STA Travel in the U.S.; Travel CUTS in Canada; and any of the organizations under the auspices of the International Student Travel Confederation (ISTC) around the world. When you apply for the card, request a copy of the *International Student Identity Card Handbook,* which lists by country some of the available discounts. You can also write to Council for a copy. The card is valid from September to December of the following year. The fee is US$18. Applicants must be at least 12 years old and degree-seeking students of a secondary or post-secondary school. Because of the proliferation of phony ISICs, many airlines and some other services require other proof of student identity: a signed letter from the registrar attesting to your student status and stamped with the school seal and/or your school ID card. The US$19 **International Teacher Identity Card (ITIC)** offers similar but limited discounts, as well as medical insurance coverage. For more info on these handy cards consult the organization's new web site (http:\\www.istc.org).

Federation of International Youth Travel Organizations (FIYTO) issues a discount card to travelers who are under 26 but not students. Known as the **GO25 Card,** this one-year card offers many of the same benefits as the ISIC, and most organizations that sell the ISIC also sell the GO25 Card. A brochure that lists discounts is free when you purchase the card. To apply, you will need a passport, a valid driver's license or copy of a birth certificate, and a passport-sized photo with your name printed on the back. The fee is US$16, CDN$15, or UK£5. For information contact Council in the U.S. or FIYTO in Denmark (see **Useful Organizations,** above).

INTERNATIONAL DRIVER'S PERMIT

Travelers planning to rent automobiles in Southeast Asia should obtain an **International Driving Permit (IDP),** which is required in certain countries. A valid driver's license from your home country must always accompany the IDP. Call an automobile association such as AAA to find out if your destination country requires the IDP. Although most car rental agencies don't require the permit, it may be a good idea to get one anyway, in case you're in a position (such as an accident or stranded in a smaller town) where the police may not read or speak English. IDPs must be issued in countries before departure.

■ Money Matters

Living on a tight budget in Southeast Asia is fairly easy. Some travelers, however, become obsessed with spending as little as possible, each day making it a goal to spend less money than the day before, living off tasteless gruel, sleeping on bug-infested mattresses, and doing laundry as seldom as possible. Not only is this usually unnecessary, but it can also deprive the visitor of experiencing some of the delights the region has to offer. Unless you have extravagant tastes, you should be able to travel comfortably in most places (excluding Hong Kong and Singapore) with less than US$15-20 each day. Prices tend to increase in remote areas where competition is lacking, but even in these places your wallet should not suffer too much.

CURRENCY AND EXCHANGE

Some easy, practical information can help you save your money from the start. For one, avoid exchanging money at luxury hotels and restaurants, which will likely gouge you on both exchange and commission rates; the best deal is usually found at major banks. In main cities, currency exchange booths controlled by major banks are everywhere. Although commission rates at the booths may be slightly higher, they are convenient and keep longer hours than the banks. In rural areas, look for branches of banks you recognize from larger cities. See **Money Matters** for each country for more information.

One alternative to changing money at banks is to do so through the black market. There is a high demand for U.S. dollars in most Southeast Asian countries, and independent individuals are often willing to offer a more advantageous rates for your hard currency. Keep in mind that since this process is not legal, there are risks involved. One way to determine whether it's wise to use the black market in a particular city or town is to talk with other travelers and see what they recommend.

You may find it difficult to exchange home currency abroad; bank tellers might not even recognize such common currencies as the Australian or New Zealand dollar in some Southeast Asian countries. As a result, it's a good idea to take U.S. dollars with you. If you're using traveler's checks or bills, be sure to carry some in small denominations (US$50 or less), especially for times when you are forced to change at unsatisfactory rates.

Remember that unless a commission rate is charged, service charges will eat up a chunk of your money each time you convert. To minimize losses, tourists exchange large sums of money at once, but never more than they can safely carry. It helps to plan ahead; travelers caught without local currency in a rural or out of the way area with no currency exchange center may be forced into particularly disadvantageous deals. Avoid converting more money than you can spend, as it may be near impossible to change your foreign currency back to that of your home country.

TRAVELER'S CHECKS

Carrying large amounts of cash, even in a money belt, is unwise. Traveler's checks, which can almost always be replaced if lost or stolen, are far safer. Although not all establishments, especially small, rural, or family-run shops, accept traveler's checks, your peace of mind will far outweigh any occasional inconvenience. Companies don't supply traveler's checks in regional currencies, so buy checks in your home currency. Large notes will spare you long waits at the bank; small ones will minimize your losses if you just need a little cash to tide you through the train ride from one big city to the next. Banks usually sell traveler's checks for a 1-2% commission.

Expect red tape and delay in the event of theft or loss of traveler's checks. To expedite the refund process, keep check receipts separate from the checks and store them in a safe place or with a traveling companion; leave a list of check numbers with someone at home and the numbers of those you cash, and ask for a list of refund centers when you buy your checks. American Express and Bank of America have over 40,000 centers worldwide. Keep a separate supply of cash or traveler's checks for emergencies. Never countersign checks until you're prepared to cash them. And always bring your passport and another form of identification with you when you plan to use the checks.

American Express: Call (800) 221-7282 in the US and Canada; in the UK (0800) 52 13 13; in New Zealand (0800) 44 10 68; in Australia (008) 25 19 02). Elsewhere, call US collect (801) 964-6665. Traveler's checks are now available in 11 major currencies, purchasable for a small fee at American Express Travel Service Offices, banks, American Automobile Association offices (AAA members can buy the checks commission-free), and even over America Online. They're the most widely recognized worldwide and the easiest to replace if lost or stolen. Cardmembers can also purchase checks at American Express Dispensers at Travel Service Offices at airports and by ordering them via phone (US tel. (800) ORDER-TC (673-3782)). American Express offices cash their checks commission-free (except where prohibited by national governments), although they often offer slightly worse exchange rates than banks. You can also buy checks which can be signed by either of two people traveling together.

Citicorp: Call (800) 645-6556 in the US and Canada; in the UK (44) 181 297 4781; from elsewhere call US collect (813) 623-1709. Sells both Citicorp and Citicorp Visa traveler's checks in major currencies for a commission of 1-2%. Checkholders are enrolled for 45 days in the Travel Assist Program (24-hr. hotline tel. (800) 250-4377 or collect (202) 296-8728) which provides travelers with English-speaking doctor, lawyer, and interpreter referrals, as well as check refund assistance and general travel information. Citicorp's World Courier Service guarantees hand-delivery of traveler's checks when a refund location is not convenient.

Thomas Cook MasterCard: Call (800) 223-9920 in the US and Canada; elsewhere call US collect (609) 987-7300; from the UK call (0800) 622 101 free or (1733) 50 29 95 collect or 31 89 50 collect. Offers checks in major currencies. Commission 1-2% for purchases. Lower commissions at Thomas Cook offices. No commission if cashed at a Thomas Cook office.

Visa: Call (800) 227-6811 in the US; in the UK (0800) 895 492; from anywhere else in the world call (017 333 189 49) collect. If you call any of the above numbers and give them your zip code, they will tell you where the closest office to you to purchase their traveler's checks is. Any kind of Visa traveler's checks can be reported lost at the Visa number.

CREDIT CARDS

While the past few years have brought an increasing acceptance of credit cards in Southeast Asia, they remain of limited use to the penniless pilgrim. There is, nonetheless, a great deal of variation in credit card acceptance. Generally, plastic is accepted at major hotels, department stores, expensive boutiques, and fine restaurants. Credit cards are not as well received at guest houses, shops frequented by locals, sidewalk merchants, food vendors, and bus and train ticket vendors. In some circumstances, however, a card can prove invaluable. You can charge expenses incurred at most hospitals, and many foreign banks allow you to withdraw money from ATM machines with a credit card. Perhaps the greatest advantage of these cards, however, is that they can enable you to purchase an airplane ticket should you need to leave a country in an emergency. The most commonly accepted cards are **Visa** and **MasterCard,** followed by **American Express** and **Diner's Club.**

MasterCard (U.S. tel. (800) 999-0454) and **Visa** (U.S. tel. (800) 336-8472) credit cards are sold by individual banks. Benefits depend on the type of card. If obtaining a MasterCard or Visa for travel purposes, ask bankers about specific travel services.

American Express (tel. (800) CASH-NOW (528-4800) in the U.S.) has a hefty annual fee (US$55) but offers a number of services. AmEx cardholders can cash personal checks at AmEx offices abroad. U.S. Assist, a 24-hour hotline offering medical and legal assistance in emergencies, is also available (tel. (800) 554-2639 in U.S. and Canada; from abroad call U.S. collect (301) 214-8228). Cardholders can also take advantage of the American Express Travel Service; benefits include assistance in changing airline, hotel, and car rental reservations, sending mailgrams and international cables, and holding mail at most AmEx offices around the world. Credit cards require extra vigilance. Report lost or stolen cards immediately, or you may be held responsible for forged charges. Write down the card-cancellation phone numbers for your bank and keep them separate from your cards.

CASH CARDS

Automatic Teller Machines (ATMs) offer 24-hour access to funds from home. ATMs are not as prevalent in Southeast Asia as in North America, but some banks in larger cities are connected to an international money network, often PLUS (U.S. tel. (800) 843-7587) or CIRRUS (U.S. tel. (800) 4-CIRRUS (424-7787)). All major banks in Thailand now offer this service for customers. Similarly, Singapore and Hong Kong provide ATMs at almost every turn. Use of these handy devices is increasing in Vietnam as well, although still largely limited to upscale establishment. In contrast, Indonesia just began CIRRUS service in 1994 and Jakarta lags far behind, as do the major cities in Malaysia; service in Laos and Cambodia is virtually non-existent. Many ATMs outside major cities accept only cards from banks within the country, so don't count on a town's ATM to save your neck. CIRRUS service is often associated with a specific bank. Look for the following: Hong Kong, Citicard; Indonesia, Bank Bali or Citibank; Malaysia, Southern Bank Berhad; Thailand, Siam Commercial Bank.

MONEY FROM HOME

Sending money abroad is complicated, expensive, and extremely frustrating. Avoid wiring money by carrying a credit card, personal checks, or a separate stash of emergency traveler's checks. Other than ATMs, an **American Express card** offers the easiest way to obtain money from home; AmEx allows any of its cardholders to draw cash from their checking accounts at any of its offices—up to US$1000 every 21 days. For more information, call **American Express** (tel. (800) 543-4080; in Canada (800) 933-3278). AmEx also offers Express Cash, with over 100,000 ATMs located in airports, hotels, banks, and shopping areas around the world. Express Cash withdrawals are automatically debited from the cardmember's specified bank account or line of credit. AmEx members may withdraw up to US$1000 in a seven-day period. There is a 2% transaction fee for each cash withdrawal with a US$2.50 minimum. To enroll in Express Cash, cardmembers in the U.S. may call 1-800-CASH NOW, outside the U.S. call collect (904) 565-7875. Unless using the AmEx service, avoid cashing checks in foreign currencies, since they usually take weeks and a US$30 fee to clear.

If you must have money, and are prepared to pay for it, **Western Union** (U.S. tel. (800) 325 6000) money wiring service is available throughout most of Southeast Asia outside of Cambodia and Laos. Credit card transfers do not work overseas; you must send cash. Thai post offices also offer an **International Money Order Service,** with reciprocal service between Thailand and 27 countries, including the U.S., the U.K., and Australia. It takes one day for the money to be received in the city post office, up to three days for the money to reach up-country.

In emergencies, U.S. citizens can have money sent via the **Overseas Citizens Service** at American Citizens Services, Consular Affairs, Public Affairs Staff, Room 4831, U.S. Department of State, Washington, D.C. 20520 (tel. (202) 647-5225; at night and on Sun. and holidays 647-4000; fax 647-3000; http://travel.state.gov). For a fee of US$15, the State Department forwards money within hours to the nearest consular office, which then disburses it according to instructions. The office serves only Americans in the direst of straits abroad. The quickest way to have the money sent is to cable the State Department through Western Union.

TIPPING AND BARGAINING

Tipping is still uncommon in Southeast Asia. A few upscale hotels or restaurants might expect you to tip approximately 10% of the bill, but aside from these, few people count on receiving a tip. That being said, almost no one will refuse the extra kip, riel, dong, or baht if they are offered; on the contrary, this money should be quite welcome. By most standards in the region, you're practically rolling in money, since the average yearly income for some is as low as US$150. If you feel you have received excellent service and would like to show your appreciation, don't hesitate to dip your hand in your pocket and pull out a few coins.

Where bargaining is concerned, the rule is simple: if no price is indicated, do it. In general, department stores, hotels, and guest houses are the only places where prices are seldom subject to negotiation. Such places usually indicate their status with a prominent "fixed price" sign to ward off the wiles of deal-hunters. Markets are good places to practice bargaining techniques as well. A good rule of thumb is to initially offer half of the asked price and settle for paying a little more than this. Knowing a few words of the local language guarantees better luck in bringing down prices, since the merchant will assume you've been in the country long enough to know roughly what things should cost. You might be surprised to find yourself arguing fiercely over the equivalent of US$0.13 and swearing under your breath at the merchant who won't lower his or her price any more. Keep a cool head. Bargaining should be treated like a game and executed with a smile. A friendly and polite attitude will also get you far, as locals regard displays of ill temper as a sign of bad breeding. For more information, consult the **Essentials** section of each country.

BRIBERY

Common throughout the region, with the notable exceptions of Singapore and Hong Kong, is **bribery.** For such incursions as traffic tickets, or minor customs violations, an offer of money or foreign- (especially American-) made goods may suddenly shed new light on the situation. Some chocolates, a shirt, or cold hard cash can work equally well depending on the scenario. Travelers may have to go through the same shenanigans they do when bargaining before reaching a satisfactory conclusion. While bribery is common, and sometimes expected, there are risks involved, as with anything illegal. *Let's Go* urges travelers to use their own discretion.

■ Safety and Security

SAFETY

Tourists are particularly vulnerable to crime for two reasons: they often carry large amounts of cash and are not as street-savvy as locals. To avoid such unwanted attention, try to **blend in** as much as possible. Respecting local customs (in many cases, this means dressing more conservatively) can often placate would-be hecklers. The gawking camera-toter is a more obvious target than the low-profile local look-alike. Walking directly into a café or shop to check your map beats checking it on a street corner. Look over your map before leaving the hotel room so that you can act as if you know where you're going. Muggings are more often impromptu than planned. Walking with nervous, over-the-shoulder glances can be a tip that you have something valuable to protect.

Especially if you are traveling alone, be sure that someone at home knows your itinerary. Never say that you're traveling alone. Women in particular may wish to refer to an imaginary husband, father, or uncle to defuse potentially sticky situations. Refer to **Women Travelers** on page 39 and **Traveling Alone** on page 43 for more information. Both men and women may want to carry a small **whistle** to scare off attackers or attract attention, and it's not a bad idea to jot down the number of the police if you'll be in town for a couple days.

When walking at night, you should turn day time precautions into mandates. Stick to busy well-lit streets and avoid dark alleyways. Do not attempt to cross through parks, parking lots or any other large, deserted areas. A blissfully isolated beach in daytime can become a treacherous nightmare as soon as night falls. When exploring a new city, extra vigilance is wise, but no city should force you to turn precautions into panic. When you get to a place where you'll be spending some time, find out about unsafe areas from the tourist office, from the manager of your hotel or hostel, or from a local whom you trust. Whenever possible, *Let's Go* warns of unsafe neighborhoods and areas, but only your eyes can tell you for sure if you've wandered into one. Buildings in disrepair, vacant lots, and general desertedness are all bad signs. Pay attention to your surroundings—a district can change character drastically in the course of a single block. Simply being aware of the flow of people can tell you a great deal about the relative safety of the area. Many notoriously dangerous districts have safe sections; look for children playing, women walking in the open, and other signs of an active community. If you feel uncomfortable, leave as quickly and directly as you can. Although caution is always in order when traveling, don't allow your fear of the new to close off whole worlds to you. Careful, persistent exploration can build confidence and make your stay in an area that much more rewarding.

There's no sure-fire set of precautions that will protect you from all of the situations you might encounter when traveling. A good self-defense course can give travelers more concrete ways to react to different types of aggression and probably increase confidence. In the U.S., **Model Mugging** is a national organization with offices in several major cities. They teach a very effective, comprehensive course on self-defense. Contact Lynn S. Auerbach on the East Coast (tel. (617) 232-7900); Alice Tibits in the Midwest (tel. (612) 645-6189); and Cori Couture on the West Coast (tel. (415) 592-7300). Course prices vary from US$400-500. Community colleges also frequently offer self-defense courses at more affordable prices. U.S. residents may also wish to write the U.S. Department of State for helpful publications, including a pamphlet entitled *A Safe Trip Abroad*.

SECURITY

Among the more colorful aspects of large cities are the **con artists** and hustlers often work in groups; children, unfortunately, are among the most effective at the game. Be aware of certain classics: sob stories that require money, "free" visits to gem factories, and "good price for you, my friend" assertions. Often at major tourist attractions, hordes of small children accost foreigners, ostensibly friendly and curious, while their nimble fingers search through pockets and bags. You don't need to be rude or avoid all eye contact with children, but be aware that a smiling face may be trying to distract you from a wandering hand. Contact the police if a hustler is particularly insistent or aggressive. It is also important to be wary of touts. While in many cases these offers of free transportation or special tours are well meant and perfectly safe, it's always wise to exercise caution.

Don't put money in a wallet in your back pocket. Never count money in public and carry as little cash as possible. If you carry a purse, buy a sturdy one with a secure clasp, and carry it crosswise on the side, away from the street with the clasp against you. For packs, buy a small combination padlock to slip through the two zippers and secure the pack shut. Even these precautions do not always suffice, since purse-snatching moped riders sometimes tote knives to cut the straps.

A **money belt** is the best way to carry cash and other valuables; you can buy one at most camping supply stores. The best combination of convenience and invulnerability is the nylon, zippered pouch with belt that should sit inside the waist of your pants or skirt. A **neck pouch** is equally safe, although far less accessible. Refrain from pulling out your neck pouch in public; if you must, be very discreet. Avoid using the ever-popular fanny-pack for holding anything precious (even if it's worn on your stomach), as valuables will be highly visible and easy to steal.

Be particularly watchful of your belongings on **buses** (for example, carry your backpack in front of you where you can see it), don't check baggage on trains especially if you're switching lines, and don't trust anyone to "watch your bag for a second." **Trains** are notoriously easy spots for thieving. Professionals wait for tourists to fall asleep and then carry off everything they can. When traveling in pairs, sleep in alternating shifts; when alone, use good judgement in selecting a train compartment, and never stay in an empty one.

Lockers are useful if you plan on sleeping outdoors or don't want to lug everything with you, but don't store valuables in them. Never leave your belongings unattended; even the most demure-looking hostel (convents included) may be a den of thievery. If you feel unsafe, look for places with either a curfew or a night attendant. When possible, leave expensive jewelry, valuables, and anything you couldn't bear to part with at home. Always keep valuables on your person if staying in low-budget hotels where someone else may have a passkey or dormitory-style surroundings.

Travel Assistance International by Worldwide Assistance Services, Inc. in the U.S. provides its members with a 24-hour hotline for emergencies. Their year-long traveler package (US$226) includes medical and travel insurance, financial assistance, and help in replacing lost documents. Call (800) 821-2828 or 828-5896, or write them at 1133 15th St. NW, Suite 400, Washington, D.C. 20005-2710.

DRUGS AND ALCOHOL

It's no secret that drugs are widely available in Southeast Asia and while most people do not visit the region solely for this distraction, some travelers will undoubtedly find themselves partaking at one point or another. While we can't do anything to prevent you from using **illegal drugs,** we can highlight the possible consequences of drug use particular to Southeast Asia. This part of the world takes drug use and abuse very seriously. Laws vary from country to country, but buying or selling *any* type of drug may lead to anything from a prison sentence to the death penalty. Some countries do not differentiate between "hard" drugs and more mainstream ones such as marijuana. A meek "I didn't know it was illegal" will not suffice. You are subject to the laws of the country in which you are traveling, and it's your responsibility to familiarize yourself with these laws before leaving. Remember that **your home country cannot help you if you get into trouble** with the law in another country, particularly in Southeast Asia.

If you carry **prescription drugs** while you travel, it's vital to have a copy of the prescriptions themselves readily accessible at country borders so there'll be no potentially inconvenient misunderstandings.

The attitude toward **alcohol** varies considerably throughout the region. In some parts, beer and spirits are key elements for many social functions; in others you might be looked down upon for even requesting an alcoholic beverage. Generally speaking, the predominantly Muslim countries (Indonesia and Malaysia) are strict where alcohol is concerned while Buddhist countries are more accepting. In all countries, however, drinking among women is frowned upon and you will rarely, if ever, see a local woman imbibing anything alcoholic. Foreign women might receive odd looks from locals if drinking in public outside of urban or heavily touristed areas. Wild drunken revelry is disapproved of by everyone, to say the least; public displays of drunkenness are offensive and will not always be tolerated by the locals.

Another thing to keep in mind is that liquor is not under the same kind of standardized regulation that it might be in your home country. As a result, you may never know exactly how much you are imbibing until you find yourself getting very familiar with the toilet in your guest house.

■ Health

BEFORE YOU GO

A hectic trip can take its toll on your health, especially in an equatorial climate. Keeping your body strong will help ward off serious maladies: eat properly, drink lots of fluids, get plenty of sleep, and don't overexert yourself. To minimize the effects of jet lag, adjust to the region's schedule as soon as possible. During the hot season, take precautions against heatstroke and sunburn: drink lots of liquids, wear a hat and sunscreen, and stay inside midday.

Although shots have not been a prerequisite for visiting most of Southeast Asia for over a decade, bring an updated copy of your immunization records. You are only required to get shots if you are coming from contaminated areas of the world. On the safe side, shots for typhoid, hepatitis A and B, Japanese encephalitis, rabies, and cholera are available. Undergoing an elaborate inoculation regimen before your trip is necessary only if you will be doing extensive trekking in rural or heavily forested areas. Consult your doctor well before leaving to determine if you will need any such routine, as many inoculation series can take weeks or months to complete.

For up-to-date information about which vaccinations are recommended for your destination, and region-specific health data, the **United States Centers for Disease Control and Prevention (CDC)** is an excellent source of information for travelers around the world and maintains an international travelers' hotline (tel. (404) 332-4559; fax 332-4565; http://www.cdc.gov). You can also write directly to the Centers for Disease Control and Prevention, Travelers' Health, 1600 Clifton Rd. NE, Atlanta, GA 30333. The CDC publishes the booklet *Health Information for International Travelers* (US$14), an annual global rundown of disease, immunization, and general health advice, including risks in particular countries.

You may wish to assemble a **first-aid kit,** including: antiseptic soap, aspirin, decongestant, antihistamine, acetaminophen (Tylenol) to lower fever, diarrhea medicine such as Immodium AD, motion sickness medicine, Pepto-Bismol, anti-bacterial ointment, a thermometer, bandages, insect repellent, a syringe (to be on the safe side), and a Swiss Army knife with tweezers and scissors.

Travelers with **corrective lenses** should bring an extra pair, a copy of the prescription, and a pair of glasses in case your eyes are tired or you lose a lens. Furthermore, roads in this part of the world tend to be quite dusty, so contacts may get irritating. Traveling does not always provide the most sanitary conditions for inserting and removing contact lenses—think ahead to avoid doing so on a lurching, crowded *bemo*. Bring extra solution, enzyme tablets, and eyedrops, as prices can be sky-high. Those who use heat disinfection may want to consider switching to chemical cleansers for the duration of the trip.

Bring an up-to-date, detailed copy of any **medical prescriptions** you require (in legible form, stating the medication's trade name, manufacturer, chemical name, and dosage), and carry an ample supply of all medication—matching your prescription with a foreign equivalent is not always economical, easy, or safe. Distribute medication between carry-on and checked baggage in case one goes astray. Travelers with a chronic medical condition requiring regular treatment should consult their doctors before leaving. People with diabetes, for example, may need advice on adapting insulin levels for flights across multiple time zones. Bring a statement describing any pre-existing medical conditions, especially if you will be bringing insulin, syringes, or any narcotics.

Those with medical conditions (e.g. diabetes, allergies to antibiotics, epilepsy, heart conditions) may want to obtain a stainless steel **Medic Alert** identification tag (US$35 the first year, and US$15 annually thereafter), which identifies the disease and gives a 24-hour collect-call information number. Contact Medic Alert at (800) 825-3785, or write to Medic Alert Foundation, 2323 Colorado Avenue, Turlock, CA 95382. Diabetics can contact the **American Diabetes Association**, 1660 Duke St., Alexandria, VA 22314 (tel. (800) 232-3472) to receive copies of the article "Travel and Diabetes" and a diabetic ID card, which carries messages in 18 languages explaining the carrier's diabetic status.

The U.S. Department of State compiles Consular Information Sheets on health, entry requirements, and other issues for all countries. For quick information on travel warnings, call the Overseas Citizens' Services (tel. (202) 647-5225). To receive the same Consular Information sheets by fax, dial (202) 647-3000 directly from a fax machine and follow the recorded instructions. The State Department's regional passport agencies in the U.S., field offices of the U.S. Chamber of Commerce, and U.S. embassies and consulates abroad provide the same data, or send a self-addressed, stamped envelope to the Overseas Citizens' Services, Bureau of Consular Affairs, #4811, U.S. Department of State, Washington, D.C. 20520. If you are HIV positive, call (202) 647-1488 for country-specific entry requirements or write to the Bureau of Consular Affairs, CA/P/PA, U.S. Department of State, Washington, D.C. 20520. For more general health information, contact the **American Red Cross,** which publishes *First-Aid and Safety Handbook* (US$15) available for purchase by calling or writing to the American Red Cross, 285 Columbus Ave., Boston, MA 02116-5114 (tel. (800) 564-1234). In the U.S., the American Red Cross also offers many first-aid and CPR courses, which are well-taught and relatively inexpensive.

If you are concerned about being able to access medical support while traveling, contact one of these two services: **Global Emergency Medical Services (GEMS)** provides 24-hour international medical assistance and support coordinated through registered nurses who have on-line access to your medical information, your primary physician, and a worldwide network of screened, credentialed English-speaking doctors and hospitals. Subscribers also receive a pocket-sized, personal medical record that contains vital information in case of emergencies. For more information call (800) 860-1111, fax (770) 475-0058, or write 2001 Westside Drive, Suite 120, Alpharetta, GA 30201. The **International Association for Medical Assistance to Travelers (IAMAT)** offers a membership ID card, a directory of English-speaking doctors around the world who treat members for a set fee schedule (US$55 for office visits, more for house calls and night/weekend aid), and detailed charts on immunization requirements, various tropical diseases, climate, and sanitation. Membership is free, though donations are appreciated and used for further research. Contact chapters in the **U.S.,** 417 Center St., Lewiston, NY 14092 (tel. (716) 754-4883; fax 836-3412; e-mail iamat@sentex.net; http://www.sentex.net/iamat), **Canada,** 40 Regal Road, Guelph, Ont., N1K 1B5 (tel. (519) 836-0102) or 1287 St. Clair Avenue West, Toronto, Ont., M6E 1B8 (tel. (416) 652-0137; fax (519) 836-3412), or **New Zealand,** P.O. Box 5049, Christchurch 5.

ON-THE-ROAD AILMENTS

Pay attention to the warning signals that your body may send you. You may feel fatigue and discomfort, not because of any specific illness, but simply because your body is adapting to a new climate, food, water quality, or pace when you arrive. Once you get going, however, some of the milder symptoms that you may safely ignore at home may be signs of something more serious; your increased exertion may wear you out and make you more susceptible to illness. The following paragraphs list some health problems you may encounter and their symptoms.

Water and Food

Purify any suspicious water by boiling it or treating it with iodine. **The tap water in Southeast Asia is not safe** for teeth-brushing, even in the finest resort hotels. Don't rinse your toothbrush under the faucet and keep your mouth closed in the shower (you'll quickly get the hang of it). Except in Singapore, make it a rule not to drink the water. Bottled purified water is available virtually throughout the region but make sure that the top is still tightly sealed when you buy it. In restaurants, be sure that your bottled beverage has been opened in front of you. Also, ask the waiter if the ice has been made from purified water. If you're not sure, insist on having your drink without ice. If there is no purified water, order a soft drink. Presumably, coffee and tea are all right to drink because the water has been boiled, but travelers should always ask first.

With minor exceptions, food is safe to eat. Peel your own fruit and never eat raw food, especially shellfish or other seafood. Stay away from salads, since uncooked vegetables are full of untreated water. Make sure that the cooked food you eat is still hot and always wash your hands before eating (moist towelettes work well here, too). Food sold in markets might look tempting, but isn't necessarily hygienic. Steer clear of items which may have been washed in dirty water or fried in rancid cooking oil. Other than that, the only thing to worry about is getting acquainted with the nature of local food. Slowly adjusting yourself to the region's cooking will help ease the transition for your stomach. Have quick-energy, non-sugary foods with you to keep your strength up; you'll need plenty of protein and carbohydrates.

The Heat

Overwhelming heat can stop even the most ambitious adventurers dead in their tracks, ergo it's very important to avoid heat exhaustion and heat stroke. The symptoms of **heat exhaustion** include fatigue, dizziness, headaches, and a feeling of lightness. The cause of heat exhaustion is, not surprisingly, dehydration. If you think you are suffering from heat exhaustion, get out of the sun and sit down in a cool area. Drink cool non-alcoholic fluids and avoid physical exertion.

Heat stroke, very serious and sometimes fatal, takes heat exhaustion to a more dangerous level. Symptoms include high body temperature, cessation of sweating, flushed skin, unbearable headaches, delirium, convulsions, and unconsciousness. It is vital to get the victim of heat stroke to a hospital, but in the meantime, make sure to place wet towels on the victim and place him or her in a cool area. If that is absolutely impossible, at least be sure to continually fan the victim.

To prevent yourself from getting heat exhaustion or heat stroke, drink plenty of fluids; drinking the recommended eight glasses of water per day (minimum) should become second nature. Stay away from diuretics such as alcohol, caffeinic sodas, coffee, and tea.

Other Maladies

Less debilitating than heatstroke, but still dangerous, is **sunburn.** Many travelers are shocked to find themselves toasted to a crisp despite a cover of thick clouds overhead. If you're prone to burning, carry sunscreen with you, and apply it liberally and often. Be wary of sunscreens with SPF higher than 15 or 20; higher ratings won't be of extra help, but do cost more. Wear a hat and sunglasses and a lightweight long-sleeved shirt to avoid burns and the risk of skin cancer. If you do get burned, drink more fluid than usual to cool you down and help the skin recover faster.

For some travelers, their visit to Southeast Asia will mean an introduction to **prickly heat,** a rash that develops when sweat is trapped under the skin. The groin area is very susceptible to this rash, especially in men. To alleviate itchiness, bathe often in cool water and sprinkle talcum powder over the affected area.

Southeast Asia's moist, hot weather can irritate the skin in other ways as well. Various **fungal infections** (athlete's foot, jock itch, etc.) should be prevented by washing often and drying thoroughly. Wear loose-fitting clothes made of natural, absorbent fibers like cotton.

The most common problem for travelers is **diarrhea.** It has many causes, including food poisoning, bacteria, viruses, and simply adjusting to new food. To prevent it from happening to you, wash your hands before eating, protect food from swarming flies, and stay away from scummy-looking restaurants. For regular diarrhea without other symptoms, fluid loss and dehydration are the biggest concerns; lots of non-diuretic liquids are needed to combat the effects. Try a rehydration drink: a glass of safe water, ½ teaspoon of sugar or honey, and a pinch of salt. Down several of these mixtures daily, rest, and wait for the illness to run its course. Alternatively, you can purchase a ready-made rehydration mixture at many pharmacies in the region, which might be easier than making your own. Also good are soft drinks and salted crackers.

Give yourself time, but if you develop a fever or your symptoms don't go away after four or five days, you may have picked up a food- or water-borne disease. For severe cases, consult a doctor to see if antibiotics are necessary. A remedy like Immodium AD can help to relieve symptoms, but prevent your body from washing out the undesirable agent. This can complicate serious infections; avoid anti-diarrheals if you suspect you have been exposed to contaminated food or water, which puts you at risk for cholera, typhoid fever, and other diseases.

Learn of regional hazards and always be aware of snakes and other dangerous animals in the wild, even if you're on a well traveled route. Avoid animals with open wounds and beware of touching any animal at all in Southeast Asia. A more common problem is insects. **Insect bites,** particularly from mosquitoes, will plague your visit to Southeast Asia. Many are most active from dusk until dawn, and carry dangerous diseases (malaria, Lyme, and others—see below). Be sure to wear repellent, long sleeves, long pants, and socks. Tropical-weight cottons can keep you comfortable in the heat without being thick or heavy. In especially mosquito-dense areas, tuck long pants into socks. The most you can do for prevention is use an insect repellent containing **DEET** which can be bought in spray or liquid form. The CDC recommends using flying-insect-killing spray in sleeping quarters at night, and, for greater protection, spraying clothing and bedding with **permethrin,** an insect repellent licensed for use on clothing. Natural repellents can also be useful; taking vitamin B-12 pills regularly can eventually make you smelly to insects, as can garlic pills. Apply calamine lotion to insect bites to alleviate the itching or, if you can find a tub, soak in a bath with baking soda (just dump a half–cup or so into a lukewarm bath) or oatmeal (Aveeno packages several oatmeal mixtures which you can buy at home). **Tiger balm,** a cold-heat ointment, is a favorite Chinese method, and is readily available in pharmacies or from street vendors.

Parasites (tapeworms, etc.) are fairly uncommon but irksome afflictions. They can enter your body through your feet, so don't walk around barefoot outside. They can also find their way into your stomach through undercooked meat or dirty vegetables. **Giardia** is a serious parasitic disease contracted by ingesting untreated water from lakes or streams. A stool test from a doctor will uncover these critters, which can be flushed away with the help of medicine. Symptoms of general parasitic infections include swollen glands or lymph nodes, fever, rashes, itchiness, digestive complications, eye problems, and anemia. Don't let these nasty creatures shrivel you from the inside out—wear shoes, drink purified water, and avoid uncooked food.

Schistosomiasis is another parasitic disease, this one caused when the larvae, found in fresh water, of the flatworm penetrate the unbroken skin. Swimming in fresh water, especially in rural areas, should be avoided. If your skin is exposed to untreated water, the CDC recommends immediate and vigorous rubbing with a towel and/or the application of rubbing alcohol to reduce the risk of infection. If infected, you may notice an itchy localized rash; later symptoms include fever, fatigue, painful urination, diarrhea, loss of appetite, night sweats, and a hive-like rash on the body. Known foci for Schistosomiasis are east of Kuala Lumpur in Malaysia, east Cambodia and the border with Laos, the Mekong River, the Thai border with Laos, and a few villages in Nakhon Si Thammarat Province in Thailand. Schistosomiasis can be treated with drugs.

Travelers to **higher altitudes** in north Laos or Vietnam must allow their bodies a couple of days to adjust to lower oxygen levels in the air before exerting themselves. If you're planning long alpine hikes, give yourself an adjustment period of a day or two before you start out. Also be careful about alcohol; at high altitudes where there's less oxygen, it will hit you harder than you might expect.

Serious Infectious Diseases

Malaria is the most serious disease that travelers to Southeast Asia (except Singapore and Hong Kong) are likely to contract. It is caused by a parasite carried by the female *Anopheles* mosquito, who usually bites at night. Because the incubation period for the disease varies, it could take up to weeks or months for an infected person to show any symptoms. When the disease does hit, the first symptoms include headaches, chills, general achiness, and fatigue. Since early stages resemble the flu, you should see a doctor for any flu-like sickness that occurs after travel in risk areas. Next comes a very high fever and sweating. In some cases, vomiting and diarrhea also show up. If you think you may have malaria, go to the nearest hospital immediately and have a blood test. While traveling and for up to a year later, seek medical attention to treat any flu-like symptoms. Malaria can be fatal: anemia, kidney failure, coma, and finally death can result if left untreated.

Malaria is generally found in heavily forested areas which seldom see visitors from abroad. It's virtually, but not entirely, impossible to get malaria in urban cities, towns, and most villages. The least danger exists in Thailand, Java, and Bali, except near the dense forests around border areas. The best way to combat malaria is to listen to your physician, carry lots of insect repellent, and stay away from uninhabited jungle areas. The CDC says that preventive medication against malaria is not necessary if you only visit relatively urban areas; however, as mentioned above, precautions should be taken to avoid being bitten by mosquitoes. If you do decide to visit rural or jungle areas, there are various forms of medication (no shots are available) that you can take to prevent you from catching malaria. Some doctors may prescribe mefloquine (sold under the name Lariam), or, for travelers in Thailand, the CDC recommends the drug doxycycline. Both of these drugs, and other malaria treatments, however, can have very serious side effects. There are many other people for whom such medications may be a great risk; be sure to consult your physician before requesting such prescriptions or starting any sort of malaria-preventive regimens. In particular, neither drug should be taken by pregnant women or small children.

Aedes mosquitoes also carry a virus that causes **dengue fever,** an "urban viral infection," which exhibits flu-like symptoms similar to malaria, but certain characteristics differentiate it from its more famous cousin. Dengue fever has two stages and is characterized by their sudden onset. Stage one lasts from two to four days, and its symptoms include chills, high fever, severe headaches, swollen lymph nodes, muscle aches, and in some instances, a pink rash on the face. Then the fever quickly disappears, and profuse sweating follows. For 24 hours there is no fever, but a rash unexpectedly appears all over the body. If you think you have contracted dengue fever, see a doctor, drink plenty of liquids, and remain in bed. It's also very important that you reduce the fever by taking acetaminophen (Tylenol). **Do not take aspirin for dengue fever.** Unfortunately, the only prevention for the disease is to avoid dengue mosquitoes, which bite during the day.

Japanese encephalitis rounds out the list of communicable diseases carried by mosquitoes. It has just been recently introduced into Southeast Asia. The Culex mosquito carries the virus for Japanese encephalitis, which is most prevalent during the rainy season in rural areas near rice fields and livestock pens. Symptoms are flu-like—chills, headache, fever, vomiting, muscle fatigue—and delirium. Its symptoms are similar to those of malaria but the fatality rate of Japanese encephalitis is much higher, so it's vital to admit yourself into a hospital as soon as any symptoms arise. A vaccine, JE-VAX, is available and is effective for a year; you can be vaccinated against this disease with a three-shot series given a week apart or on a longer, safer schedule. Serious side-effects have been associated with the vaccine, so travelers should consider whether it's necessary. The CDC claims that there's little chance that a traveler will be infected if proper precautions are taken, such as using mosquito repellents containing DEET and sleeping under bednets.

Every year, a **cholera** epidemic makes its way east from India and Bangladesh, landing around the end of the cool season, just in time for summer. Except for Hong Kong and Singapore, most of Southeast Asia is vulnerable to outbreaks. Cholera is an intestinal disease caused by bacteria found in contaminated food, characterized by explosive and interminable diarrhea, unstoppable vomiting, dehydration, muscle cramps, and lethargy, all of which come suddenly; unless quickly treated, the symptoms could prove fatal in a short time. It's crucial for the cholera-infected to find a hospital immediately. In the meantime, the patient should guzzle liquids to battle dehydration. Cholera is passed from person to person through contaminated food or water, human waste, and unsanitary cooking methods. The CDC recommends that travelers near infected areas peel their own fruit and eat only thoroughly cooked food. Consider getting a 50% effective vaccine if you have stomach problems (e.g. ulcers), are using an anti-acid therapy, will be in unsanitary conditions in epidemic areas, or camping a good deal.

Typhoid fever, caused by a bacteria, is spread through contaminated food, water, human waste, and contact with an infected person. It's common in villages and rural areas. Symptoms of the disease gradually creep up on the victim. For the first week or so, a fever slowly rises, sometimes accompanied by vomiting and diarrhea. Next, a rash may appear, and delirium and dehydration seize the victim. Headaches, fatigue, loss of appetite, and constipation are also associated symptoms. If left untreated, the patient may develop life-threatening pneumonia. It's imperative to find medical care as soon as possible. Typhoid fever is treatable with antibiotics, and a vaccine is available, although it is only 70-90% effective. The CDC recommends vaccination for those going to small cities or towns off the beaten track, or those staying longer than six weeks. Drink only bottled or boiled water and eat only thoroughly cooked food to lower the risk of infection.

Hepatitis A and **hepatitis B** are prevalent in areas with poor sanitation; both are caused by viruses attacking the liver. Hepatitis A, like typhoid fever, is spread through contaminated water and food with viruses present in human feces. It's therefore important to be wary of uncooked foods that may have been tainted during handling, such as fresh fruits, vegetables, and shellfish. It can also be transmitted from direct person-to-person contact. Fatigue, vomiting, nausea, fever, loss of appetite, dark urine, jaundice, light stools, and aches and pains are among the symptoms. At particular risk are travelers, especially those visiting rural areas, coming into close contact with local people, or eating in settings with poor sanitation. Hepatitis B, in contrast, is spread through the transfer of bodily fluids, such as blood, semen, and saliva, from one person to another. Its incubation period varies and can be much longer than the 30-day incubation period of hepatitis A. Thus, a person may not begin having symptoms until many years after infection.

While they have no known cure, vaccinations are available to protect travelers from both types of hepatitis. Protection from hepatitis A requires a shot of immune globulin, which is given about a week before departure and after all other immunizations have been completed. There is a new vaccine on the market, Havrix, which you should ask your doctor about. For protection against hepatitis B, a three-shot series given in six months is required. The CDC recommends the hepatitis B vaccination for health-care workers, sexually active travelers, long-term visitors who will have extensive contact with the local population, and anyone planning on seeking any medical treatment while in Southeast Asia.

Visitors should keep in mind that **rabies** is a common but little-publicized disease in Southeast Asia. Transmitted through the saliva of infected animals, it's fatal if not treated. Avoid close contact with other animals, especially strays. If you are bitten by an animal, wash the wound thoroughly with soap and water to help reduce the chance of infection, and seek medical care immediately. Once you begin having symptoms of rabies (thirst and muscle spasms), the disease is in its terminal stage. If possible, try to locate the dog which bit you to determine whether it does indeed have rabies. If you plan on traveling to an area which has a heavy concentration of rabid animals (such as bats or wild dogs), there are three shots you should get; it takes one year to receive them in series.

Women's Health

Women traveling in unsanitary conditions are vulnerable to **urinary tract** and **bladder infections** (cystitis), common and severely uncomfortable bacterial diseases that cause a burning sensation and painful (sometimes frequent) urination. A strong antibiotic usually gets rid of the symptoms within a couple of days. Other recommendations are to drink enormous amounts of vitamin C-rich juice (any citrus sort), plenty of water, and to urinate frequently. Untreated bladder infections can become very serious, leading to kidney infections or pelvic inflammatory disease. Treat an infection the best you can while on the road; if it persists, see a doctor and definitely check with one when you get home. If you are prone to vaginal **yeast infections** or thrush, take an over-the-counter medication along with you, as treatments may not be readily available elsewhere.

Sanitary napkins and tampons are sometimes hard to find overseas; your preferred brands may not be available, so it's advisable to bring your own. O.B. brand tampons have minimal packaging and occupy less space in baggage. Refer to *The Handbook for Women Travellers* by Maggie and Gemma Moss, published by Piatkus Books, or see the women's health guide *Our Bodies, Ourselves,* published by the Boston Women's Health Collective, for more info specific to women's health on the road.

AIDS, HIV, AND STDS

While most travelers venture to Southeast Asia to see the sights, some go to the region seeking pleasure of a different sort. These travelers may never get to see the temples of Luang Prabang or the steps of Borobudur. Instead, they see the crusty streets of Patpong and the bowels of quasi-legal bars, massage parlors, and discotheques. Above and beyond the fact that prostitution is exploitative and illegal, individuals emerging from their night have very likely contracted one of the venereal diseases which infect the prostitutes they visit. Every year, VD clinics make a killing on visitors who need medical help during their stay.

Hepatitis B is discussed above. **Syphilis** is a common STD spread through the exchange of infected bodily fluids during sexual intercourse, but is curable with penicillin. If left untreated, however, syphilis travels through three stages. In the first stage, which generally appears around three weeks after infection, soft cankers appear on the genitals, accompanied by enlarged lymph nodes. Three weeks later, the second stage appears, bringing fever, rashes, painful joints, and more cankers and enlarged lymph nodes. If the victim still does not seek medical help, the disease enters its third stage, which lasts indefinitely—a very long period of apparent remission. Many years later, a sudden onset of inflammation in the heart and central nervous system occurs and normally leads to death.

Gonorrhea is another widespread and pestilent STD. It is transmitted from person to person like syphilis, but its incubation period is shorter, lasting anywhere from three to seven days. Symptoms include discharge of pus and infection of the urethra. If left untreated, gonorrhea causes considerable discomfort. The disease can be treated with penicillin. Another STD, **chlamydia,** has symptoms identical to those of gonorrhea, but is resistant to penicillin treatment. Chlamydia can cause sterility, and often has no detectable symptoms whatsoever.

Herpes, caused by a virus, is a terribly uncomfortable STD for which there is no known cure. At the end of the 2-10 day incubation period, lesions begin to form at the site of the infection, whether it be the genital area, the mouth, or the hand. Protected sex does not necessarily keep contact with infected areas from occurring. The only way to be sure is to check for sores before touching the other individual and to pick sexual partners carefully. Lesions can eventually go away, but often recur throughout one's lifetime.

For more information in the U.S., call the **CDC's STDs Hotline,** (800) 227-8922. Council's brochure, *Travel Safe: AIDS and International Travel,* is available at all Council Travel offices.

AIDS is a growing problem in Southeast Asia. Some estimates put the proportion of HIV-positive prostitutes still working the bars and massage parlors of Bangkok at 50%. Tragically, most infected prostitutes and their customers are not aware that they carry the HIV virus. Most information on AIDS in Southeast Asia is on Thailand for two reasons: Thailand's prostitution problem is internationally realized, and the Thai government acknowledges and is making efforts to combat the disease. In other areas, the relevant information about the population is minimal or non-existent. AIDS is found throughout Southeast Asia, and the CDC claims that heterosexual contact is the primary mode of transmission there. The World Health Organization (WHO) estimates that in Southeast Asia there are 2.5 million HIV-infected persons and 250,000 AIDS cases; only 13,000 of those are in Thailand.

While not everyone who is HIV positive has AIDS, any person who is HIV positive can transmit this virus, which impairs the immune system and ultimately leads to death. The WHO estimates that 4.5 million people worldwide are living with AIDS, and about 13 million people are infected with HIV. Over 90% of adults newly infected with HIV acquired it through heterosexual sex. While relatively few women were HIV positive 10 years ago, they now represent 50% of all new HIV infections. By the year 2000, the WHO estimates that the number of AIDS cases worldwide will increase to 20 million, with between 30 and 40 million people infected with HIV, which spreads through sexual contact, needle-sharing, and blood transfusions. The most common mode of transmission is unprotected anal or vaginal intercourse. If infected blood, semen, vaginal secretions, or breast milk come into contact with the blood of a non-infected person, transmission often occurs.

The best advice is to follow all the precautions you should follow at home (always use a condom with spermicide, avoid sex with strangers or with people who engage in high-risk behavior such as IV drug use or promiscuous or unprotected sex), and stay away from prostitutes. Many prostitutes do not know that they are infected, and even if they did, there's no guarantee they would tell their customers. Often an infected person exhibits no symptoms for up to 10 years. It's not until the final stage of the disease that the patient has lost a considerable amount of the immunity to diseases normally found in healthy human beings. The final stage of AIDS is terminal, and there's no cure in sight.

Condoms help prevent the transmission of the virus, but only abstinence is 100% effective. Unprotected (without a condom) anal intercourse is believed to be the most risky form of sexual contact; vaginal intercourse follows, and then oral sex. Safe sex means using a latex condom and water-based lubricant every time you have intercourse. Condoms made of natural materials, like lambskin, *do not protect against transmission of HIV* because they are more porous than latex. Even if semen can't get through these pores, HIV can. Oil-based lubricants (like Vaseline) destroy the integrity of latex, opening the pores wider and rendering them useless in the prevention of HIV or even causing them to tear. It may not always be easy to buy condoms, and when it is, they may not be of very high-quality. For this reason, it's a good idea to take a supply of high-quality western-made condoms with you. Condoms treated with spermicide are thought to provide extra protection. They should be stored in a cool, dark place. Heat deteriorates condoms; never carry them in a wallet or pants pocket. A new condom should be used for each and every act of sexual intercourse in which semen, vaginal fluids or blood may be transmitted.

Never share needles; this is an easy way to transmit the virus through infected blood. Needles should be thoroughly flushed three times with soapy water, three times with bleach, and three more times with soapy water. If bleach is unavailable, washing needles with soapy water alone is the next best thing. Ideally, you should not use a needle already employed by another.

If you think you could have been exposed to HIV, you might want to get an HIV Antibody Test. This test detects only the presence of HIV antibodies, not the virus itself. Once infection has occurred, there is a window period of three to six months during which the body reacts to the virus and begins to make the antibodies that the test detects. For this reason, it makes no sense to get tested until at least three to six months after the suspect incident.

For more info on AIDS, call the **CDC's 24-hour Hotline** at (800) 342-2437. (TTY (800) 243-7889, Mon-Fri 10am-10pm; Spanish (800) 344-7332, daily 8am-2am.) The **World Health Organization** (tel. (202) 861-3200), provides statistics on AIDS internationally. In Europe call (011) 42 22 791 21 11 (Switzerland) or write directly to the World Health Organization, attn: Global Program on AIDS, 20 Avenue Appia, 1211 Geneva 27, Switzerland. Another resource is the U.S. Department of State (tel. (202)

647-1488; fax 647-3000). You can also try the **Bureau of Consular Affairs,** #6831, Department of State, Washington, D.C. 20520.

GETTING HELP

Tourist centers are full of pharmacies selling everything from cough drops to condoms, and some pharmacists are competent enough in English to understand what you need. The majority of pharmacies can fill a prescription with a note from a doctor. Few pharmacies are open 24 hours. In an emergency, head to the nearest major hospital, which is almost certainly open all night and has an in-house pharmacy.

Outside the major tourist centers, the going is a bit rougher, although every provincial capital should have at least one small drugstore. Serious problems most typically arise for those who are deep in the jungle or at small village outposts, as the pharmacy is likely to be replaced by an herbal medicine store.

In remote towns and other un-touristed areas, try to get someone who speaks the local language to call for you if you need help, since the language barrier may otherwise be insurmountable. Direct phone lines are often unavailable in guest houses. High-end hotels often have English-speaking staff, direct phone lines, and transportation. Those seeking referrals should contact their embassy; these diplomatic missions often have lists of English-speaking doctors for the major tourist areas.

■ Insurance

Beware of buying unnecessary travel coverage—your regular policies may well extend to many travel-related accidents. **Medical insurance** (especially university policies) often covers costs incurred abroad. **Medicare's** foreign travel coverage is not valid in Southeast Asia. Canadians are protected by their home province's health insurance plan for up to 90 days after leaving the country; check with the provincial Ministry of Health or Health Plan Headquarters for details. Australia has Reciprocal Health Care Agreements (RHCAs) with several countries; when traveling in these nations Australians are entitled to many of the services that they would receive at home. The Commonwealth Department of Human Services and Health can provide more information. Your **homeowners' insurance** (or your family's coverage) often covers theft during travel. Homeowners are generally covered against loss of travel documents (passport, plane ticket, etc.) up to US$500. Don't count on being automatically insured, however, or you may find yourself a few thousand dollars lighter needlessly. Contact your insurance provider to find out the extent of your coverage.

ISIC and **ITIC** provide US$3000 worth of accident and illness insurance and US$100 per day up to 60 days of hospitalization. They also offer up to US$1000 for accidental death or dismemberment, up to US$25,000 if injured due to an airline, and up to US$25,000 for emergency evacuation due to an illness. The cards also give access to a toll-free **Traveler's Assistance Hotline** (in the U.S. and Canada tel.(800) 626-2427; elsewhere call collect to the U.S. (713) 267-2525) whose multilingual staff can provide help in emergencies overseas.To supplement ISIC's insurance, **Council Travel** offers the inexpensive Trip-Safe plan with options covering medical treatment and hospitalization, accidents, baggage loss, and charter flights missed due to illness; Council and **STA** also offer more comprehensive and expensive policies. **American Express** cardholders receive automatic car rental (except for collision) insurance and travel accident insurance on flight purchases made with the card. Call Customer Service for inquiries (U.S. tel. (800) 528-4800).

Remember that insurance companies usually require a copy of the police report for thefts, or evidence of having paid medical expenses (doctor's statements, receipts) before they will honor a claim and may have time limits on filing for reimbursement. Always carry policy numbers and proof of insurance. Check with each insurance carrier for specific restrictions and policies. Most of the carriers listed below have 24-hour hotlines.

Access America, 6600 West Broad St., P.O. Box 11188, Richmond, VA 23230 (tel. (800) 284-8300; fax (804) 673-1491). Covers trip cancellation/interruption, on-the-spot hospital admittance costs, emergency medical evacuation, sickness, and baggage loss. 24-hr. hotline.

The Berkley Group/Carefree Travel Insurance, 100 Garden City Plaza, P.O. Box 9366, Garden City, NY 11530-9366 (tel. (800) 323-3149 or (516) 294-0220; fax 294-1096). Offers two comprehensive packages including coverage for trip cancellation/interruption/delay, accident and sickness, medical, baggage loss, bag delay, accidental death and dismemberment, and travel supplier insolvency. Trip cancellation/interruption may be purchased separately at a rate of US$5.50 per US$100 of coverage. 24-hr. worldwide emergency assistance hotline.

Globalcare Travel Insurance, 220 Broadway, Lynnfield, MA 01940 (tel. (800) 821-2488; fax (617) 592-7720; e-mail global@nebc.mv.com; http://nebc.mv.com/globalcare). Complete medical, legal, emergency, and travel-related services. On-the-spot payments and special student programs, including benefits for trip cancellation and interruption GTI waives pre-existing medical conditions with their Globalcare Economy Plan for cruise and travel, and provides coverage for the bankruptcy or default of cruiselines, airlines, or tour operators.

Travel Assistance International, by Worldwide Assistance Services, Inc., 1133 15th St. NW, Suite 400, Washington, DC 20005-2710 (tel. (800) 821-2828 or (202) 828-5894; fax 828-5896); e-mail wassist@aol.com). TAI provides members with a 24-hr. hotline for travel emergencies and referrals. Their Per-Trip (starting at US$52) and Frequent Traveler (starting at US$226) plans include medical, travel, and financial insurance, translation, and lost document/item assistance.

Travel Guard International, 1145 Clark St., Stevens Point, WI 54481 (tel. (800) 826-1300 or (715) 345-0505; fax 345-0525). Comprehensive insurance programs starting at US$44. Programs cover trip cancellation and interruption, bankruptcy and financial default, lost luggage, medical coverage abroad, emergency assistance, accidental death. 24-hr. hotline.

Travel Insured International, Inc., 52-S Oakland Ave., P.O. Box 280568, East Hartford, CT 06128-0568 (tel. (800) 243-3174; fax (203) 528-8005). Insurance against accident, baggage loss, sickness, trip cancellation and interruption, travel delay, and default. Covers emergency medical evacuation and automatic flight insurance.

Wallach and Company, Inc., 107 West Federal St., P.O. Box 480, Middleburg, VA 20118-0480 (tel. (800) 237-6615; fax (540) 687–3172; e-mail wallach.r@mediasoft.net). Comprehensive medical insurance including evacuation and repatriation of remains and direct payment of claims to providers of services. Other optional coverages available. 24-hr. toll-free international assistance.

■ Alternatives to Tourism

While some travelers desire simply to roam across Southeast Asia devoid of heavy baggage and obligations, others might prefer to focus on finding temporary employment or volunteer work. Many go to Southeast Asia intending to stay only a week or two, but become so enchanted with the region they decide to remain for a while. Fortunately for these people, Southeast Asia offers numerous work, volunteer, and study possibilities, especially for native English speakers. Researching your options will most likely require time, diligence, and persistence, but your efforts should always be rewarded.

STUDY

Foreign study programs vary tremendously in expense, academic quality, living conditions, degree of contact with local students, and exposure to the local culture and language. Local libraries and bookstores are helpful sources for current information on study abroad. While there are not as many programs available in Southeast Asia as in other regions, they are around, it just takes a bit more effort to find them. Check out the organizations below for a start.

American Field Service (AFS), 220 E. 42nd St., 3rd Fl., New York, NY 10017 (tel. (800) 237-4636 or AFS-INF0, 876-2376; fax (212) 949-9379; http//www.afs.org/usa). AFS offers summer, semester, and year-long homestay international exchange programs for high school students and graduating high school seniors and short-term service projects for adults. Financial aid available. Exchanges in Hong Kong, Indonesia, and Thailand.

College Semester Abroad, School for International Training, Admissions, Kipling Rd., P.O. Box 676, Brattleboro, VT 05302 (tel. (800) 336-1616; fax 258-3500). Runs semester and year-long programs featuring cultural orientation, intensive language study, homestay, and field and independent study. Programs cost US$8200-10,300, all expenses included. Financial aid available and US financial aid is transferrable. Most US colleges will transfer credit for semester work done abroad. Programs available in Indonesia, Thailand, and Vietnam.

Council sponsors over 40 study abroad programs throughout the world. Contact them for more information (see **Travel Organizations** on page 5).

International Association for the Exchange of Students for Technical Experience (IAESTE), 10400 Little Patuxent Pkwy. #250, Columbia, MD 21044-3510 (tel. (410) 997-3068; http://www.softaid.net/aipt/aipt/html). Operates 8- to 12-week programs in over 50 countries, including Thailand, for college students who have completed two years of study in a technical field. Non-refundable US$50 application fee; apply by Dec. 10 for summer placement.

International Schools Services, Educational Staffing Program, 15 Roszel Rd., P.O. Box 5910, Princeton, NJ 08543 (tel. (609) 452-0990; fax 452-2690; e-mail edustaffing%ISS@mcimail.com). Recruits teachers and administrators for schools in many countries including Laos, Vietnam, and Malaysia. All instruction in English. Applicants must have a bachelor's degree and two years of relevant experience. Nonrefundable US$75 application processing fee.

Peterson's Guides, P.O. Box 2123, Princeton, NJ 08543-2123 (tel. (800) 338-3282; fax (609) 243-9150; http://www.petersons.com). Their comprehensive *Study Abroad* annual guide lists programs in countries all over the world and provides essential information on the study abroad experience in general. Purchase a copy at your local bookstore (US$27) or call their toll-free number in the US

World Learning, Inc., Summer Abroad, P.O. Box 676, Brattleboro, VT 05302 (tel. (800) 345-2929 or (802) 257-7751; http://www.worldlearning.org). Founded in 1932 as the Experiment in International Living, it offers high school programs in Thailand as well as language-training programs with elective homestays. Programs are 3-5weeks long. Positions as group leaders are available world-wide if you are over 24, have previous in-country experience, are fluent in the language, and have experience with high school students.

WORK AND VOLUNTEER

There's no better way to submerge yourself in a foreign culture than to become part of its economy. The good news is that it's very easy to find a temporary job abroad; the bad news is that unless you have connections, it will rarely be glamorous and may not even pay for your plane ticket over.

Officially, you need a special visa that will allow you to be employed in the country of your choice. Please inquire at the embassy or consulate of the country you wish to work in for more specific information on obtaining such a visa. To avoid such complications, teaching English abroad is a common and practical choice. There are many books which list work-abroad opportunities. Note especially the excellent guides put out by **Vacation Work.**

Volunteering can also be an extremely valuable and rewarding experience on both the giving and receiving ends. There are quite a few organizations that can set you up with programs throughout Southeast Asia. If you're a full-time student at a U.S. university, one easy way to get a job abroad is through work permit programs run by the **Council on International Educational Exchange (Council)** and its member organizations (see **Travel Organizations** on page 5). In order to avoid scams from fraudulent employment agencies that demand large fees and provide no results, educate yourself

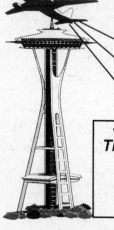

using publications from the following sources. Use these resources as a start to your search for gainful employment, or volunteer work.

Addison-Wesley, One Jacob Way, Reading, MA 01867 (tel. (800) 822-6339). Publishes *International Jobs: Where They Are, How to Get Them* (US$16).

The Archaeological Institute of America, 656 Beacon St., Boston, MA 02215-2010 (tel. (617) 353-9361; fax 353-6550), puts out the *Archaeological Fieldwork Opportunities Bulletin* (US$11 non-members) which lists over 250 field sites throughout the world. This can be purchased from Kendall/Hunt Publishing, 4050 Westmark Dr., Dubuque, Iowa 52002 (tel. (800) 228-0810).

Council (see **Travel Organizations** on page 5) offers 2- to 4-week environmental or community service projects in over 30 countries around the globe through its Voluntary Services Department (US$250-750 placement fee). Participants must be at least 18 years old.

Office of Overseas Schools, A/OS Room 245, SA-29, Dept. of State, Washington, D.C. 20522-2902 (tel. (703) 875-7800). Teaching jobs abroad.

Peace Corps, 1990 K St. NW, Washington, D.C. 20526 (tel. (800) 424-8580; fax (202) 606-4469; http://www.peacecorps.gov). Write for their "blue" brochure, which details applicant requirements. Opportunities in a variety of fields in developing nations around the world. Volunteers must be U.S. citizens willing to make a 2-year commitment.

Transitions Abroad Publishing, Inc., 18 Hulst Rd., P.O. Box 1300, Amherst, MA 01004-1300 (tel. (800) 293-0373; fax (413) 256-0373; e-mail trabroad@aol.com). Publishes a bi-monthly magazine listing all kinds of opportunities and printed resources for those seeking to study, work, or travel abroad. The possibilities are almost endless. They also publish *The Alternative Travel Directory,* a truly exhaustive listing of information for the "active international traveler." For subscriptions (U.S. US$20 for 6 issues, Canada US$26, other countries US$38), contact them at *Transitions Abroad,* Dept. TRA, Box 3000, Denville, NJ 07834.

Vacation Work Publications, 9 Park End St., Oxford OX1 1HJ, UK (tel. (01865) 24 19 78; fax 79 08 85). Publishes a wide variety of guides and directories with job listings and info for the working traveler. Opportunities for summer or full-time work in numerous countries. Write for a catalogue of their publications.

Volunteers for Peace, 43 Tiffany Rd., Belmont, VT 05730 (tel. (802) 259-2759; fax 259-2922; e-mail vfp@vermontel.com; http://www.vfp.org). A non-profit organization that arranges for speedy placement in over 800 workcamps in more than 60 countries, including Thailand and Vietnam. Many camps last for 2 to 3 weeks and are comprised of 10 to 15 people. Most complete and up-to-date listings provided in the annual *International Workcamp Directory* (US$12). Registration fee US$175. Some work camps are open to 16 and 17 year olds for US$200.

Volunteers in Asia, Inc., Box 4543, Stanford, CA 94309 (tel. (415) 723-3228; fax 725-1805). Coordinates volunteers in Indonesia, Thailand, Laos, and Vietnam to teach English. Also offers undergraduate opportunities.

World Teach, Harvard Institute for International Development, 1 Eliot St., Cambridge, MA 02138-5705 (tel. (617) 495-5527; fax 495-1599; e-mail worldteach@hiid.harvard.edu; http://www.hiid.harvard.edu). Volunteers teach English, math, science, and environmental education to students of all ages in developing areas of Thailand and Vietnam. Bachelor's degree required. Room and board are provided during their period of service. Rolling admission.

LONGER STAYS

Many travelers to Southeast Asia choose to linger instead of making whirlwind trips. The culture is so rich, and a comfortable lifestyle so affordable, that the lure of staying on is hard to resist. While there you may want to seek gainful employment; please refer to the above section to get more information on starting this search.

Once you've got yourself a source of funds, housing will probably be the most pressing concern. In this we can only suggest looking around the town of your choice for some real estate agencies who may be able to arrange rentals or leases for you. In many countries in the region foreigners cannot own property. Be sure to

check out your area of choice for such laws, as well as certain visa, residency, and taxation regulations which could easily thwart your best laid plans. Renting a room or bungalow in a guest house is also a very common housing solution for the ex-pat, ask the owner of one that appeals to you for a reduced rate.

Food shopping and the other details of living should not be difficult to arrange. Markets are everywhere, as we are sure you will discover, and we at *Let's Go* attempt to list the most significant markets and supermarkets in the towns we visit to give you a good start. If you so wish, you can also easily arrange to live in further luxury with some hired help. Ask around, and you can generally find someone who would love to help you out for a salary you might consider obscenely low.

■ Specific Concerns

WOMEN TRAVELERS

Women exploring on their own inevitably face additional safety concerns. Always trust your instincts; if you'd feel better somewhere else, move on. Always carry extra money for a phone call, bus, or taxi. *Let's Go* lists emergency numbers in the Practical Information listings of most cities. Consider staying in hostels which offer single rooms that lock from the inside, or in religious organizations that offer rooms for women only. Stick to centrally-located accommodations and avoid late-night treks. In Muslim countries the law prohibits Muslim women from walking alone at night. Although this law does not technically apply to westerners, expect strange looks and even comments or severe harassment should you find yourself outside alone after daylight hours. Hitching is never safe for lone women, or even for two women traveling together. Choose train compartments occupied by other women or couples; ask the conductor to put together a women-only compartment if he doesn't offer to do so first.

When in Southeast Asia, the less you look like a tourist, the better off you'll be. Look as if you know where you're going (even when you don't) and consider approaching women or couples for directions if you're lost or feel uncomfortable. Dress conservatively, particularly in rural areas. Although you may dress more liberally in Bangkok and other major cities, stay away from revealing tank tops and short shorts once out of town. In Muslim countries, you should dress fairly modestly even in the city, although locals do not expect to see westerners completely covered; shawls or veils would probably be overdoing it.

You may be harassed, nonetheless, regardless of your attire. Your best answer to verbal harassment is no answer at all (a reaction is what the harasser wants). Wearing a conspicuous wedding band may help prevent such incidents, as well as pretending you are on your way to meeting a father, uncle, husband, or brother. In crowds, you may be pinched or squeezed by oversexed slimeballs. The look on the face is the key to avoiding unwanted attention. Feigned deafness, sitting motionless, and staring at the ground will be more effective deterrents to the aggressor than a brash, incoherent stream of verbal abuse. If need be, turn to an older woman for help in an uncomfortable situation; her stern rebukes will usually be enough to embarrass the most persistent jerks.

Don't hesitate to seek out a police officer or a passerby if you are being harassed. Be aware that it has been reported that small-town police are sometimes not terribly enlightened about women. They, as well as some other men, may assume that a women traveling alone is looking for sex. Don't hesitate to call the police in an emergency, but don't place all your trust in them, particularly in un-touristed areas. Use your own discretion, and be prepared to deal with hassles.

Carry a whistle or an airhorn on your keychain, and don't hesitate to use it in an emergency. A **Model Mugging** course will not only prepare you for a potential mugging, but will also raise your level of awareness of your surroundings as well as your confidence (see **Safety and Security** on page 21). All of these warnings and suggestions should not discourage women from traveling alone. Don't take unnecessary risks, but don't lose your spirit of adventure either.

For general information in the U.S., contact the **National Organization for Women (NOW),** which boasts branches across the country that can refer women travelers to rape crisis centers and counseling services, and provide lists of feminist events. Main offices include 22 W. 21st St., 7th Fl., **New York,** NY 10010 (tel. (212) 260-4422); 1000 16th St. NW, 7th Fl., **Washington, D.C.** 20004 (tel. (202) 331-0066); and 3543 18th St., **San Francisco,** CA 94110 (tel. (415) 861-8960). Some other helpful resources are listed below.

Handbook for Women Travelers, by Maggie and Gemma Moss (UK£9). Encyclopedic and well-written. From Piaktus Books, 5 Windmill St., London W1P 1HF (tel. (0171) 631 07 10).

Directory of Women's Media, available from the National Council for Research on Women, 530 Broadway, 10th Fl., New York, NY 10012 (tel. (212) 274-0730; fax 274-0821). The publication lists women's publishers, bookstores, theaters, and news organizations (mail orders, US$30).

A Journey of One's Own, by Thalia Zepatos (Eighth Mountain Press US$17). The latest thing on the market, interesting and full of good advice, plus a specific and manageable bibliography of books and resources.

Women Travel: Adventures, Advice & Experience by Miranda Davies and Natania Jansz (Penguin, US$13). Info on specific foreign countries plus a decent bibliography and resource index. The sequel *More Women Travel* is US$15.

Women Going Places, a women's travel and resource guide emphasizing women-owned enterprises. Geared towards lesbians, but offers advice appropriate for all women. US$14 from Inland Book Company, 1436 W. Randolph St. Chicago, IL 60607 (tel. (800) 243-0138) or order from a local bookstore.

OLDER TRAVELERS

Travel in Southeast Asia has the potential to be particularly taxing for the senior citizen. There may, however, be some extra benefits to age, including greater respect from the people you encounter. For more information on senior traveling, investigate some of the books and organizations listed below.

AARP (American Association of Retired Persons), 601 E St. NW, Washington, D.C. 20049 (tel. (202) 434-2277). Members 50 and over receive benefits and services including the AARP Motoring Plan from AMOCO (800) 334-3300), and discounts on lodging, car rental, and sight-seeing. Annual fee US$8 per couple; lifetime membership US$75.

National Council of Senior Citizens, 1331 F St. NW, Washington, D.C. 20004 (tel. (202) 347-8800). Memberships are US$12 a year, US$30 for three years, or US$150 for a lifetime. Individual or couple can receive hotel and auto rental discounts, a senior citizen newspaper, use of a discount travel agency, supplemental Medicare insurance (if you're over 65), and a mail-order prescription drug service.

Pilot Books, 103 Cooper St., Babylon, NY 11702 (tel. (516) 422-2225). Publishes a large number of helpful guides including *The International Health Guide for Senior Citizens* (US$5, postage US$2). Call or write for a complete list of titles.

Unbelievably Good Deals and Great Adventures That You Absolutely Can't Get Unless You're Over 50, by Joan Rattner Heilman. After you finish reading the title page, check inside for some great tips on senior discounts and the like. Contemporary Books, US$10.

BISEXUAL, GAY, AND LESBIAN TRAVELERS

Attitudes regarding sexual orientation vary substantially across Southeast Asia. See the **Essentials** sections of each country for more detailed descriptions. Information for Vietnam, Laos, and Cambodia is practically non-existent. Travelers to these three countries should keep in mind that the people here are conservative and religious, and often disapprove public displays of affection, heterosexuals included. Listed below are contact organizations and publishers which offer materials addressing concerns for bisexual, gay, and lesbian travelers.

Damron Travel Guides, P.O. Box 422458, San Francisco, CA 94142 (tel. (415) 255-0404). Publishes *Damron's Accommodations,* listing gay and lesbian hotels around the world (US$19). Mail order available; add US$5 shipping.

Ferrari Guides, P.O. Box 37887, Phoenix, AZ 85069 (tel. (602) 863-2408; fax 439-3952; e-mail ferrari@q-net.com). *Ferrari Guides' Gay Travel A to Z* (US$16), *Ferrari Guides' Men's Travel in Your Pocket* (US$14), *Ferrari Guides' Women's Travel in Your Pocket* (US$14). Available in bookstores or by mail order.

Gay's the Word, 66 Marchmont St., London WC1N 1AB, UK (tel. (0171) 278 7654). The largest gay and lesbian bookshop in the UK. Mail order service available. No catalogue of listings, but they will provide a list of titles on a given subject. Open Mon.-Sat. 10am-6pm, Thurs. 10am-7pm, Sun. 2-6pm.

Giovanni's Room, 345 S. 12th St., Philadelphia, PA 19107 (tel. (215) 923-2960; fax 923-0813; e-mail gilphilp@netaxs.com). International feminist, lesbian, and gay bookstore with mail-order service. Carries many of the publications listed here.

International Gay Travel Association, Box 4974, Key West, FL 33041 (tel. (800) 448-8550; fax (305) 296-6633; e-mail IGTA@aol.com; http://www.rainbowmall.com/igta. An organization of over 1100 companies serving gay and lesbian travelers worldwide. Call for lists of travel agents, accommodations, and events.

International Lesbian and Gay Association (ILGA), 81 rue Marché-au-Charbon, B-1000 Brussels, Belgium (tel./fax (32) 25 02 24 71; e-mail ilga@ilga.org). Provides political information, such as homosexuality laws of individual countries.

Spartacus International Gay Guides, published by Bruno Gmunder, Postfach 110729, D-10837 Berlin, Germany (tel. (30) 615 00 30; fax 615 91 34). Lists bars, restaurants, hotels, and bookstores around the world catering to gays. Also lists hotlines for gays in various countries and homosexuality laws for each country. Available (US$32.95) in bookstores and in the US by mail from Giovanni's Room.

DISABLED TRAVELERS

Call ahead to make arrangements with airlines and make sure adequate facilities are available. Southeast Asia, excluding Hong Kong and Singapore, is ill-equipped to deal with disabled travelers. Hospitals cannot be relied upon to replace broken braces or prostheses successfully; their orthopedic materials, even in Bangkok and Jakarta, are faulty at best. Facilities for disabled travelers are generally poor. Public transportation (trains, buses, *songthaew, tuk-tuk,* etc.) is completely inaccessible. While the classier hotels often have elevators (which may not be wheelchair accessible), most budget accommodations don't. Rural areas have no sidewalks, let alone ramps, and larger cities are packed with curbs and steps.

Attitudes toward people with disabilities vary across the region. In Laos and Cambodia, where an uncommonly high percentage of the population are amputees (from old land-mines and cluster-bombs), disabilities are not uncommon. Thai people with disabilities, however, rarely come out in public; in Thai culture, a person with a disability is a poor reflection on his or her family. Despite this, travelers who aren't shy will find many people eager to aid them.

Call or write to the **World Institute on Disability** at 510 16th St., Suite 100, Oakland, CA 94612 (tel. (510) 763-4100; fax 763 4109) for information on disability rights advocates around the world. For information on access in Hong Kong and Singapore, write to their tourist promotion offices (see **Useful Information** on page 4). In Thailand, Mr. Narong Patibatsarakich is the **Chairperson of the Council of Disabled People of Thailand** (tel. (02) 583 30 31; fax 583 6518), and can help provide info on Thailand's resources for the disabled. The following organizations provide information or publications that might be of assistance.

American Foundation for the Blind, 11 Penn Plaza, New York, NY 10011 (tel. (212) 502-7600), open Mon.-Fri. 8:30am-4:30pm. Provides information and services for the visually impaired. For a catalogue of products, contact Lighthouse Y, 10011 (tel. (800) 829-0500).

Mobility International, USA (MIUSA), P.O. Box 10767, Eugene, OR 97440 (tel. (514) 343-1284 voice and TDD; fax 343-6812). International headquarters in Brussels, rue de Manchester, 25, B-1070 Brussels, Belgium (tel. (322) 410 62 97; fax 410 68 74). Contacts in 30 countries. Information on travel programs, international work camps, accommodations, access guides, and organized tours for those with physical disabilities. Membership US$25 per year, newsletter US$15. Sells the periodically updated and expanded *A World of Options: A Guide to International Educational Exchange, Community Service, and Travel for Persons with Disabilities* (US$14, non-members US$16). Also offers a series of courses that teach strategies helpful for travelers with disabilities. Call for details.

Society for the Advancement of Travel for the Handicapped (SATH), 347 Fifth Ave., #610, New York, NY 10016 (tel. (212) 447-7284; fax 725-8253). Publishes quarterly travel newsletter *SATH News* and information booklets (free for members, US$13 each for nonmembers) with advice on trip planning for people with disabilities. Annual membership US$45, students and seniors US$25.

Twin Peaks Press, P.O. Box 129, Vancouver, WA 98666-0129 (tel. (360) 694-2462, orders only MC and Visa (800) 637-2256; fax 696-3210). Publishers of *Travel for the Disabled,* which provides travel tips, lists of accessible tourist attractions, and advice on other resources for disabled travelers (US$20). Also publishes *Directory for Travel Agencies of the Disabled* (US$20), *Wheelchair Vagabond* ($15), and *Directory of Accessible Van Rentals* (US$10). Postage US$3 for first book, US$1.50 for each additional book.

VEGETARIAN AND KOSHER TRAVELERS

Although much Southeast Asian food contains meat or uses meat bases, *Let's Go* lists many **vegetarian** eating options. Vegetarian dishes abound throughout the region, making Southeast Asia a vegi-friendly destination. While **kosher** meals are next to nonexistent, the Muslim presence in Southeast Asia makes **halal** food a large part of the cuisine (especially in the Malay-speaking world). If you are strict in your observance, consider preparing your own food on the road.

North American Vegetarian Society, P.O. Box 72, Dolgeville, NY 13329 (tel. (518) 568-7970), a good resource for information in the US. They can obtain for you other travel-related publications, such as *Transformative Adventures,* a guide to vacations and retreats (US$15), and *Vegetarian Asia* (US$10). Membership to the Society is US$20; family membership is US$26 and members receive a 10% discount on all publications.

The Jewish Travel Guide (US$12, postage US$1.75) lists synagogues, kosher restaurants, and Jewish institutions in over 80 countries. Available from Ballantine-Mitchell Publishers, Newbury House 890-900, Eastern Ave., Newbury Park, Ilford, Essex, UK IG2 7HH (tel. (0181) 599 88 66; fax 599 09 84). Available in the US from Sepher-Hermon Press, 1265 46th St., Brooklyn, NY 11219 (tel. (718) 972-9010; US$14 plus US$2.50 shipping).

TRAVELERS WITH CHILDREN

Traveling in Southeast Asia with young children is not the best way to assure yourself a hassle-free trip. Hygienic environments are scarce and proper medical facilities cannot be found on every street corner. The combination of the deadly heat, swarming mosquitoes, and dirty water might prove to be too much for a young child. All this said, it's possible to bring children along, so long as you take extra precautions and remain especially alert to potential dangers. When deciding where to stay, remember the special needs of young children. If you rent a car, make sure the rental company provides a car seat for younger children. These may be difficult to get from even international rental companies, and near impossible from local rental agencies, so prepare to trek around looking for one It's important that each child carries some sort of identification in case of an emergency or if he or she gets lost. Some of the following publications offer tips for adults traveling with children or distractions for the kids themselves. You can also contact the publishers to see if they have other related publications that you might find useful.

Backpacking with Babies and Small Children (US$10). Published by Wilderness Press, 2440 Bancroft Way, Berkeley, CA 94704 (tel. (800) 443-7227 or (510) 843-8080; fax 548-1355).

Travel with Children, by Maureen Wheeler (US$11.95, postage US$1.50). Published by Lonely Planet Publications, Embarcadero West, 155 Filbert St., #251, Oakland, CA 94607 (tel. (800) 275-8555 or (510) 893-8555, fax 893-8563; e-mail info@lonelyplanet.com; http://www.lonelyplanet.com). Also P.O. Box 617, Hawthorn, Victoria 3122, Australia.

TRAVELING ALONE

Lone travelers have greater opportunities to meet and interact with locals. On the other hand, they may also be a more visible target for robbery and harassment. With some common sense and extra precautions, however, these dangers can be greatly reduced. People traveling alone should take public transportation, if possible, and never hitch rides. Lone travelers should also inspect all hotel rooms, moving elsewhere if the locks of a particular hotel seem suspect. Be very careful about joining up with strangers and pay special attention to the information in the **Safety** section above. If questioned, never admit that you are traveling alone. And try to maintain regular contact with someone at home who knows your itinerary.

The lone traveler should not travel to any highly rural areas without the assistance of a guide. Every year, news stories emerge of the solo foreign traveler found robbed and killed in some remote jungle area or simply having disappeared. If you wish to trek, make sure that you sign up for a tour with a reputable trekking agency. An amusing, yet informative book to read is Jay Ben-Lesser's **A Foxy Old Woman's Guide to Traveling Alone** (Crossing Press, US$11), which offers anecdotes and tips for anyone interested in solitary adventure.

■ Packing

Pack light. This means you. Your backpack or suitcase may be feather-light when you buy it or drag it out of storage and as buoyant as your enthusiasm all the way to the airport, but as soon as the plane lands it will become a ponderous, hot, uncomfortable nuisance. Before you leave, pack your bag and take it for a walk. Try to convince yourself that you're in Southeast Asia already, sweltering in the high heat and humidity. You're hiking up mountains which peak above the clouds and through flora denser than the porridge you had for breakfast. You're diving to catch an elderly monk about to fall off the bus. You're sprinting down hostel hallways, trying desperately to escape roving bands of curious cockroaches, leaping lizards and rambunctious rats. As a general rule, pack only what you absolutely need, then take half the clothes and twice the money. A *New York Times* correspondent recommends that you take "no more than you can carry for half a mile at a dead run." This may be extreme, but you get the idea.

Electricity

Electricity throughout most of Southeast Asia is 220V AC, enough to fry any 110V North American appliance. In rural areas, however, especially in Indonesia, Vietnam, and Laos, 110V may be common. In Cambodia, most areas outside of Phnom Penh are 110V. Be sure to check before using your appliances. Visit hardware stores for a converter (which changes the voltage) and an adapter (which changes the shape of the plug). To order a converter by mail (about US$20) or to receive their free and enlightening pamphlet, *Foreign Electricity is No Deep Dark Secret*, write to Franzus

Company, Murtha Industrial Park, P.O. Box 142, Beacon Falls, CT 06403 (tel. (203) 723-6664; fax 723-6666). Or simply leave the hair dryer and electric razor at home.

LUGGAGE

There are many different ways in which you can tote your belongings during your journey. Which option you choose should depend on what you are planning on doing during your trip, where you are going, and most importantly, how quickly and with what method you will be getting around.

Backpack: If you plan to cover most of your itinerary by foot or intend to ride a great deal on buses, the unbeatable luggage is a sturdy backpack with several external compartments. Some convert into a more normal-looking suitcase. This applies particularly to travelers who wish to trek to remote villages or hike through national parks. In general, **internal-frame** packs are easier to carry and more efficient for general traveling purposes. If you'll be doing extensive camping or hiking, you may want to consider an **external-frame** pack, which offers added support, distributes weight better, and allows for a sleeping bag to be strapped on. External-frame packs have been known to get caught and mangled in baggage conveyors; tie down loose parts to minimize risk. In any case, get a pack with a strong, padded hip belt to transfer weight from your shoulders to your legs. Whichever style you choose, avoid excessively low-end prices. Quality packs cost anywhere from US$150 to US$420. Packs with several compartments are best, but beware of ones with many outside zippers or flaps that could make a pickpocket's dream come true. An empty **lightweight duffel bag** packed inside your luggage will be useful; once abroad you can fill your luggage with purchases and keep your dirty clothes in the duffel.

Suitcase/trunk/other large or heavy luggage: While you won't see an abundance of these among travelers in this region, they're fine if you plan to live in one or two cities and explore from there. Hard-sided luggage is more durable and doesn't

wrinkle your clothes, but it's also heavier. Soft-sided luggage should have a PVC frame, a strong lining to resist bad weather and rough handling, and its seams should be triple-stitched for durability.

Daypack or courier bag: A smaller bag, in addition to your pack, is indispensable for plane flights, sight-seeing, picnics, and keeping some of your valuables on you. Make sure it's big enough to hold lunch, a camera, a water bottle, and *Let's Go*. Get one with secure zippers and closures.

Money belt or neck pouch: Guard your money, passport, railpass, and other important articles in either one of these, and keep it with you *at all times*. The best combination of convenience and security is the nylon, zippered pouch with belt that should sit *inside* the waist of your pants or skirt (though not too inconveniently). Neck pouches should be worn under at least one layer of clothing. Money belts and neck pouches are available at any good camping store.

CLOTHING AND FOOTWEAR

To get a good sense of the weather in Southeast Asia, imagine being in a steaming sauna for three weeks. Take only clothes that are practical in high average temperatures and near 100% humidity. Dark colors hide wear, tear, and stains, but lighter fabrics and colors will be cooler. Generally, natural fibers or cotton blends are most comfortable. The clothing you bring should be loose fitting, or you'll have to deal with the uncomfortable task of peeling an absolutely drenched shirt off your body. Also bear in mind that you can find plenty of cheap cotton clothing all over Southeast Asia, and while it might not be of high quality, it will serve most purposes.

In picking out your travel clothes, consider the time of year you are going and the destination (please consult the Climate Chart in the **Appendix** on page 737). Although most of the region is uniformly hot and humid, some places are cooler, especially in the mountains, and you might need a light sweater or jacket.

Casual clothing is generally recommended and, in most cases, appropriate. Light cotton shirts, t-shirts, trousers, jeans, shorts (not too tight or short, especially for women), skirts, and blouses should form the nucleus of your wardrobe. Modest clothing is required for entrance to mosques, temples, certain museums, and palaces, and highly recommended for travel in Malaysia and Indonesia. For men, this means a dress shirt and slacks; for women, a summer dress that covers the knees and shoulders, or a blouse and skirt/pants that do the same.

Comfortable **walking shoes** are essential. This is not the place to cut corners since blisters, corns, and sharp, shooting pains in your feet will provide obvious obstacles to your enjoyment of the trip. For those seeking the ultimate in comfort, **sandals** are recommended. If you take a quick survey of footwear among those living in Southeast Asia, you will learn that almost everyone wears sandals all the time. They're especially useful because your shoes will be coming off every time you enter homes, many guest houses, or beach-side rooms. If you aren't in the mood to shell out US$50 for expensive designer brands, don't despair. Cheap sandals are sold everywhere in the region, although larger sizes are often unavailable. For heavy-duty trekking, a pair of sturdy lace-up **hiking boots** will help out. A double pair of socks—light, absorbent cotton inside and thick wool outside—will cushion feet and keep them dry. Break in your shoes before you go, however; bring some moleskin (sold at camping/sporting goods stores) along to protect the tender areas and blisters on your feet. If you only want one pair of shoes, that evolutionary cross-breed the "sneaker-hiking boot" can serve as well as a hardcore boot for most treks, and may be more comfortable for the rest of your trip's activities. In addition, a pair of flip-flops can protect you against the foliage and fungi that lurk in some hostel showers.

Rain gear is essential. A waterproof jacket and a backpack cover can take care of you and your stuff at a moment's notice, which is often all you'll get. A little more cumbersome, a lightweight poncho can cover you and your and pack well and serve as a ground cloth. Gore-Tex, that waterproof and breathable miracle fabric, is mandatory if you plan on hiking.

PACKING LIST

The following is a suggested packing list; though not exhaustive, you might find some these miscellaneous items valuable: rain gear (umbrella, ponchos, garbage bags), medical kit (bandages, moleskin, tweezers, sunscreen, rubbing alcohol), insect repellent, safety pins, pocketknife (Swiss army knife), small notebook, pen, pocket phrasebook, maps, compass, petite alarm clock, sewing kit, sunglasses, sun hat, plastic water bottle, flashlight (torch), towel, whistle, Ziploc bags (for damp clothes, soap, food, etc.), waterproof matches, string (makeshift clothesline and lashing material), padlock, rubber bands, earplugs, electrical tape (for patching tears), bandanas, clothespins, and a personal stereo (walkman) with headphones. Some items that are not always available in Southeast Asia include deodorant, cold-water soap, condoms, tampons/pads, contact-lens solution, and razors. You may want to consider bringing plenty of these to be on the safe side.

Most toiletries are available in cities, so don't panic if you happen to forget your toothbrush. Keep in mind that fragrant deodorants, shampoos, and soaps attract insects and other (unwelcome) forest creatures with reckless abandon. Finding a non-scented items is your best bet. For cold-water soap, all-natural **Dr. Bronner's Castile Soap,** sold at camping and health food stores, is usable for anything from washing clothes, bathing, and shampooing to brushing your teeth (although the taste is heinous). If you are straight and sexually active, you will need to worry about contraception. Women on the Pill should bring enough to allow for possible loss or extended stays, and should bring a prescription, since forms of the Pill vary a good deal. Though condoms are available, bring your favorite brand before you go; availability and quality vary (usually between poor and non-existent). It might be wise to carry a towel, soap, and toilet paper for those out-of-the-way places or very cheap hotels. To be on the safe side, buy anything you forgot to bring as soon as you arrive, so you don't find yourself in a small village at a loss. There's more information in the **Alternative Accommodations** section on page 58.

TRAVEL IN SOUTHEAST ASIA

■ Getting There

BUDGET TRAVEL AGENCIES

Students and people under 26 ("youth") with proper identification qualify for reduced airfares. These are rarely available from airlines or travel agents, but instead from student travel agencies like **Let's Go Travel, STA, Travel CUTS, USTN** and **Council Travel.** These agencies negotiate special reduced-rate bulk purchases with the airlines, then resell them to the youth market. Return-date change fees also tend to be low (around US$25 per segment through Council or Let's Go Travel). Most flights are on major airlines. In peak season, however, some agencies may sell seats on less reliable chartered aircraft. Student travel agencies can also help non-students and people over 26, but probably won't be able to get the same low fares.

Council Travel (http://www.ciee.org/cts/ctshome.htm), the travel division of Council, is a full-service travel agency specializing in youth and budget travel. They offer railpasses, discount airfares, hosteling cards, guide books, budget tours, travel gear, and student (ISIC), youth (GO25), and teacher (ITIC) cards. US offices include: Emory Village, 1561 N. Decatur Rd., **Atlanta,** GA 30307 (tel. (404) 377-9997); 2000 Guadalupe, **Austin,** TX 78705 (tel. (512) 472-4931); 273 Newbury St., **Boston,** MA 02116 (tel. (617) 266-1926); 1138 13th St., **Boulder,** CO 80302 (tel. (303) 447-8101); 1153 N. Dearborn St., **Chicago,** IL 60610 (tel. (312) 951-0585); 10904 Lindbrook Dr., **Los Angeles,** CA 90024 (tel. (310) 208-3551); 1501 University Ave. SE, **Minneapolis,** MN 55414 (tel. (612) 379-2323); 205 E. 42nd St., **New**

York, NY 10017 (tel. (212) 822-2700); 953 Garnet Ave., **San Diego,** CA 92109 (tel. (619) 270-6401); 530 Bush St., **San Francisco,** CA 94108 (tel. (415) 421-3473); 4311½ University Way, **Seattle,** WA 98105 (tel. (206) 632-2448); 3300 M St. NW, **Washington, D.C.** 20007 (tel. (202) 337-6464). **For US cities not listed,** call 800-2-COUNCIL (226-8624). Also 28A Poland St. (Oxford Circus), **London** W1V 3DB (tel. (0171) 437 7767).

STA Travel, 6560 Scottsdale Rd. #F100, Scottsdale, AZ 85253 (tel. (800) 777-0112 nationwide; fax (602) 922-0793). A student and youth travel organization with over 100 offices worldwide offering discount airfares for young travelers, railpasses, accommodations, tours, insurance, and ISICs. 16 offices in the **US:** 297 Newbury St., **Boston,** MA 02115 (tel. (617) 266-6014); 429 S. Dearborn St., Chicago, IL 60605 (tel. (312) 786-9050); 7202 Melrose Ave., Los Angeles, CA 90046 (tel. (213) 934-8722); 10 Downing St., Ste. G, **New York,** NY 10003 (tel. (212) 627-3111); 4341 University Way NE, Seattle, WA 98105 (tel. (206) 633-5000); 2401 Pennsylvania Ave., **Washington, D.C.** 20037 (tel. (202) 887-0912); 51 Grant Ave., **San Francisco,** CA 94108 (tel. (415) 391-8407); **Miami,** FL 33133 (tel. (305) 461-3444). **UK:** 6 Wrights Ln., **London** W8 6TA (tel. (0171) 938 47 11 for North American travel). **New Zealand:** 10 High St., **Auckland** (tel. (09) 309 97 23). **Australia:** 222 Faraday St., **Melbourne** VIC 3050 (tel. (03) 349 69 11).

Let's Go Travel, Harvard Student Agencies, 67 Mt. Auburn St., Cambridge, MA 02138 (800-5-LETS GO (553-8746) or (617) 495-9649). Railpasses, HI-AYH memberships, ISICs, ITICs, FIYTO cards, guide books (including every *Let's Go*), maps, bargain flights, and a complete line of travel gear. All items available by mail; call or write for a catalogue (or see the catalogue in center of this publication).

Campus Travel, 52 Grosvenor Gardens, London SW1W 0AG (http://www.campustravel.co.uk). 41 branches in the UK. Student and youth fares on plane, train, boat, and bus travel. Flexible airline tickets. Discount and ID cards for youths, travel insurance for students and those under 35, and maps and guides. Puts out travel suggestion booklets. Telephone booking service: in Europe (0171) 730 34 02; in

North America (0171) 730 21 01; worldwide (0171) 730 81 11; in Manchester (0161) 273 17 21; in Scotland (0131) 668 33 03.

Journeys, 4011 Jackson Rd., Ann Arbor, MI 48103 (tel. (800) 255-8735; fax (313) 665-2945; e-mail journeysni@aol.com; http://www.journeys-intl.com). Offers small-group, guided explorations of 32 different countries in Asia, Africa, the Americas, and the Pacific. Free newsletter for prospective travelers.

Students Flights Inc., has over 100 offices worldwide: 5010 East Shea Blvd., #A104, **Scottsdale,** AZ 85254 (tel. (602) 951-1177; fax (602) 951-1216); **Los Angeles,** CA (tel. (310) 338-8616); 1450 City Councillors St., #1450, **Montréal,** QU H3A 2E6 (tel. (800) 361-7799 or (514) 845-9137; fax 845-9137); **Toronto,** Ont. (tel. (416) 415-1060).

Travel CUTS (Canadian Universities Travel Services Limited): 187 College St., **Toronto,** Ont. M5T 1P7 (tel. (416) 979-2406; fax 979-8167; e-mail mail@travel-cuts). Canada's national student travel bureau and equivalent of Council, with 40 offices across Canada. Also in the UK, 295-A Regent St., **London** W1R 7YA (tel. (0171) 637 31 61). Discounted domestic and international airfares open to all; special student fares to all destinations with valid ISIC. Issues ISIC, FIYTO, GO25, and HI hostel cards, as well as railpasses. Offers free *Student Traveller* magazine and information on the Student Work Abroad Program (SWAP).

Travel Management International (TMI), 3617 Dupont Ave. South, Minneapolis, MN 55409 (tel. (612) 661-8187 or (800) 245-3672). Diligent, prompt, and very helpful travel service offering student fares and discounts.

Unitravel, 117 North Warson Rd., St. Louis, MO 63132 (tel. (800) 325-2222; fax (314) 569-2503). Offers discounted airfares on major scheduled airlines from the US to Europe, Africa, and Asia.

Usit Youth and Student Travel, 19-21 Aston Quay, O'Connell Bridge, Dublin 2 (tel. (01) 677 81 17; fax 679 88 33). In the US: New York Student Center, 895 Amsterdam Ave., New York, NY, 10025 (tel. (212) 663-5435). Additional offices in Cork, Galway, Limerick, Waterford, Maynooth, Coleraine, Derry, Athlone, Jordanstown, Belfast, and Greece. Offers low cost tickets and flexible travel arrangements all over the world. Supplies ISIC and FIYTO-GO 25 cards.

Wasteels, 7041 Grand National Dr. #207, Orlando, FL 32819 (tel. (407) 351-2537; in **London** (0171) 834 70 66). European chain, with over 200 locations. Information in English can be requested from the London office (tel. (4471) 834 70 66; fax 630 76 28). Sells Wasteels BIJ tickets, which are discounted (30-45% off regular fare) 2nd class international point-to-point train tickets with unlimited stopovers (must be under 26 on the first day of travel); sold *only* in Europe.

WST Charters, 65 Wigmore St., London W1H 0JU (tel. (0171) 224 05 04; fax 224 61 42). Offers student and youth fares to destinations worldwide. Sells ISIC.

AIR TRAVEL

Finding a cheap airfare in the deliberately mysterious and confusing airline industry can be easier if you understand its system better than most people do. Call every toll-free number and don't be afraid to ask about discounts. Have several knowledgeable **travel agents** guide you. Travel agents may not want to spend time finding the cheapest fares (for which they receive the lowest commissions), but if you travel often, you should definitely find an agent who will cater to you and your needs, and track down deals in exchange for your frequent business. **TravelHUB** (http://www.travel-hub.com) can help you search for travel agencies on the web.

Students and people under 26 should never need to pay full price for a ticket. Seniors can also get great deals; many airlines offer senior traveler clubs or airline passes and discounts for their companions as well. Sunday newspapers often have travel sections that advertise bargain fares from the local airport. Outsmart airline reps with the phone-book-sized *Official Airline Guide* (check your local library; at US$397, the tome costs as much as some flights), a monthly guide listing nearly every scheduled flight in the world (with prices) and toll-free phone numbers for all the airlines. *The Airline Passenger's Guerrilla Handbook* (US$15; last published in 1990) is a more renegade resource. On the web, try the **Air Traveler's Handbook** (http://

www.cis.ohio-state.edu/hypertext/faq/usenet/travel/air/handbook/top.html),
which offers thorough information on air travel.

Most airfares peak between mid-June and early September. Midweek (Mon.-Thurs.
morning) roundtrip flights run about US$40-50 cheaper than on weekends. If you
embark and disembark at large cities rather than at small towns, you'll most likely
obtain a more competitive fare. Return-date flexibility is usually not an option for the
budget traveler; traveling with an "open return" ticket can be pricier than fixing a
return date and paying to change it. Whenever flying internationally, pick up your
ticket well in advance of the departure date, have the flight confirmed within 72
hours of departure, and arrive at the airport at least two hours before your flight.

Commercial Airlines

The commercial airlines' lowest regular offer is the **APEX** (Advance Purchase Excursion Fare); specials advertised in newspapers may be cheaper, but have more restrictions and fewer available seats. APEX fares provide you with confirmed reservations
and allow "open-jaw" tickets (landing in and returning from different cities). Generally, reservations must be made seven to 21 days in advance, with seven- to 14-day
minimum and up to 90-day maximum stay limits, and hefty cancellation and change
penalties (fees rise in summer). Book APEX fares early during peak season, as by May
you'll have a hard time getting the departure date you want.

Even if you pay an airline's lowest published fare, you may waste hundreds of dollars. For the adventurous or the bargain-hungry, there are other, perhaps more inconvenient or time-consuming options, but before shopping around it's a good idea to
find out the average commercial price in order to measure just how great a "bargain"
you are being offered.

Ticket Consolidators

Ticket consolidators resell unsold tickets on commercial and charter airlines at
unpublished fares. The consolidator market is by and large international. Consolidator flights are the best deals if you are traveling on short notice (you bypass advance
purchase requirements, since you aren't tangled in airline bureaucracy), on a high-
priced trip, to an offbeat destination, or in the peak season, when published fares are
jacked way up. There's rarely a maximum age or stay limit, but unlike tickets bought
through an airline, you won't be able to use your tickets on another flight if you miss
yours, and you'll have to go back to the consolidator to get a refund, rather than the
airline. Keep in mind that these tickets are often for coach seats on connecting (not
direct) flights on foreign airlines, and that frequent-flyer miles may not be credited.
Decide what you can and can't live with(out) before shopping.

Consolidators come in three varieties: wholesale, who sell only to travel agencies;
specialty agencies (both wholesale and retail); and **"bucket shops"** or discount retail
agencies. Private consumers can deal directly only with the latter, but you have
access to a larger market if you use a travel agent, who can also get tickets from
wholesale consolidators. Look for bucket shops' tiny ads in weekend papers (in the
U.S., the *Sunday New York Times* is best). In London, the **Air Travel Advisory
Bureau** (tel. (0171) 636 50 00) provides a list of consolidators.

Among the many reputable and trustworthy companies are, unfortunately, some
shady wheeler-dealers. In the U.S. contact the local **Better Business Bureau (BBB)** to
learn about a company's track record. Although not necessary, it's preferable to deal
with consolidators close to home so you can visit them in person if necessary. Ask to
receive your tickets as quickly as possible so you have time to fix any problems. Get
the company's policy in writing: insist on a receipt that gives full details about the
tickets, refunds, and restrictions, and a record of who you talked to and when. It may
be worth paying with a credit card (2-5% fee) so you can stop payment if you never
receive your tickets. Beware of the "bait and switch" gag; shyster firms will advertise
a super-low fare and then tell a caller that it has been sold. Although this is a viable
excuse, if they can't offer you a price near the advertised fare on *any* date, it's a scam

to lure in customers—report them to BBB. Ask also about accommodations and car rental discounts; some consolidators have fingers in many pies.

For destinations worldwide, try: **Airfare Busters,** with offices in Washington, DC (tel. (800) 776-0481), Boca Raton, FL (tel. (800) 881-3273), and Houston, TX (tel. 232-8783); **Pennsylvania Travel,** Paoli, PA (tel. (800) 331-0947); **Cheap Tickets,** offices in Los Angeles, CA, San Francisco, CA, Honolulu, HI, Overland Park, KS, and New York, NY, (tel. (800) 377-1000); and **Moment's Notice,** New York, NY (tel. (718) 234-6295; fax 234-6450), a discount club which books air tickets, tours, and hotels for individuals for an annual fee of US$25. For a processing fee, depending on the number of travelers and the itinerary, **Travel Avenue,** in Chicago, IL (tel. (800) 333-3335) will search for the lowest international airfare available and even give you a rebate on fares over US$300.

Kelly Monaghan's *Consolidators: Air Travel's Bargain Basement* (US$7, plus US$2 shipping) from the Intrepid Traveler, P.O. Box 438, New York, NY 10034 (e-mail intreptrav@aol.com), is an invaluable source for more information and lists of consolidators by location and destination. Cyber-resources include **World Wide** (http://www.tmn.com/wwwanderer) and Edward Hasbrouck's incredibly informative **Airline ticket consolidators and bucket shops** (http://www.gnn.com/gnn/wic/wics/trav.97.html).

Charter Flights

The theory behind a **charter** is that a tour operator contracts with an airline (usually one specializing in charters) to fly extra loads of passengers to peak-season destinations. Charter flights fly less frequently than major airlines and have more restrictions, particularly on refunds. They're also almost always fully booked, and schedules and itineraries may change or be cancelled at the last moment (as late as 48 hours before the trip, and without a full refund); you'll be much better off purchasing a ticket on a regularly scheduled airline. As always, pay with a credit card if you can; consider traveler's insurance against trip interruption.

Try **Interworld** (tel. (305) 443-4929), **Travac** (tel. (800) 872-8800), or **Rebel** in Valencia, CA (tel. (800) 227-3235) or Orlando, FL (tel. (800) 732-3588). Don't be afraid to call every number and hunt for the best deal.

Courier Companies and Freighters

Those who travel light might want to consider flying as a **courier.** The company hiring you will use your checked luggage space for freight; you can only bring carry-ons. Couriers are responsible for the safe delivery of the baggage claim slips to a representative at the desired destination—don't screw up or you'll be blacklisted. Couriers usually never see the parcels they are transporting—the company handles it all—and airport officials know this and do not hold couriers responsible for the cargo. Companies require that couriers be over 18, have a valid passport, and procure their own visa (if necessary). Most flights are roundtrip only with short fixed-length stays (usually one week). Only single tickets are issued (but a companion may be able to get a next-day flight), and most flights leave from New York. **NOW Voyager,** 74 Varick St. #307, New York, NY 10013 (tel. (212) 431-1616), acts as an agent for many courier flights worldwide primarily from New York. Other agents to try are **Halbart Express,** 147-05 176th St., Jamaica, NY 11434 (tel. (718) 656-5000), **Courier Travel Service,** 530 Central Ave., Cedarhurst, NY 11516 (tel. (516) 763-6898), and **Discount Travel International** (tel. (212) 362-3636).

You can also go directly through courier companies in New York, or check a bookstore or library for handbooks such as *Air Courier Bargains* (US$15 plus US$3.50 shipping from the Intrepid Traveler, P.O. Box 438, New York, NY 10034). *The Courier Air Travel Handbook* (US$10, plus US$3.50 shipping) explains how to travel as an air courier and contains names, phone numbers, and contact points of courier companies; order it from Bookmasters, Inc., P.O. Box 2039, Mansfield, OH 44905 (tel. (800) 507-2665). **Travel Unlimited,** P.O. Box 1058, Allston, MA 02134-1058, publishes a comprehensive, monthly newsletter detailing all possible options for courier travel, often 50% off discount commercial fares (one-year subscription US$25, outside the U.S., US$35).

A final caveat for the budget conscious: don't get caught up in the seemingly great deals. Always read the fine print and check for restrictions and hidden fees. There are amazingly cheap fares waiting to be unearthed, but you can't get something for nothing. **Ford's Travel Guides,** 19448 Londelius St., Northridge, CA 91324 (tel. (818) 701-7414; fax 701-7415) lists **freighter companies** that take passengers worldwide. Ask for their *Freighter Travel Guide and Waterways of the World* (US$16, plus US$2.50 postage if mailed outside the U.S.).

■ Border Crossings

Due to the occasional instability in the region, certain borders are either dangerous or illegal to cross. Please refer to the towns of specific border crossings for more information. In general, the borders with **Malaysia, Indonesia,** and **Singapore** are not problematic. Crossing into **Burma** overland is difficult; the Lao-Burmese border is closed as of now and the crossing from Thailand is very dangerous. Travel overland into **Cambodia** from Thailand or Laos is illegal, but the border with Vietnam is open. Entering **Vietnam** overland is possible from Laos and Cambodia, as long as the point of entry is specified on your visa. Crossings into **China** are possible from Laos and Vietnam but also usually necessitate specific permits or visas. In all cases be sure to check the current situation before crossing any border.

ONCE THERE

■ Responsible Tourism

Responsible tourism has been interpreted in a number of ways by authors, travelers, and organizations. There's no set list of activities which do or do not make you a responsible tourist, and no objective criteria exists that can be used to judge your fellow traveler's guilt or innocence. Being responsible does not mean never going on a trek or never getting a glass of water from a resort development. Rather, responsible tourism means understanding the short- and long-term effects of your actions, seriously considering these effects, and realizing you are responsible for them. Only looking at part of the picture does not lead to a responsible decision. This is especially true with spending your money. When purchasing a good or service, the baht, ringgit, or riel does much more than simply provide for you—it influences the growth of industries and the lives of those who work in them. Responsible tourism means being aware of these factors and weighing them in order to make a responsible decision.

As a traveler, there are certain measures you can take to minimize your impact on the countries you visit. It would be wise to turn off the lights and the air conditioning when you leave a room, and make sure that the doors and windows are shut when the air conditioning is on. When in Thailand, you may not want to eat tiger shrimp (the gigantic striped ones) as they are bred in toxic tanks carved out of mowed down mangrove forest. Products made of sea turtle shells may seem like ideal souvenirs, but they are at the expense of the globally endangered species. Try to avoid accepting excess packaging, particularly styrofoam boxes as they are not biodegradable. Woman may want to consider buying feminine hygiene products with minimal packaging; O.B. brand tampons, which have no applicator and come in small, discreet boxes, are increasingly available throughout Southeast Asia. Choose glass soda bottles over marginally recyclable plastic equivalents, and try to reuse plastic bags.

After some time in this part of the world, travelers undoubtedly realize that the bucket showers and squat toilets are significantly more water-efficient than their western counterparts. To be even more water-friendly, carry a refillable water bottle or canteen. While the water in Southeast Asia does present a credible health hazard, tourists can bring purifying tablets or iodine drops from home to treat it. This method saves you from buying countless plastic water bottles which will probably end up floating down the Mekong or decomposing next to railroad tracks.

The Peace Corps has recycling stations at several locations around Southeast Asia. The recycling effort of the Peace Corps depends on help from volunteers, and your assistance at any one of these place will be more than welcome. For more information, contact the Peace Corps (see **Alternatives to Tourism** on page 35 for contact numbers). There remains little information regarding responsible tourism in Southeast Asia. Should you happen to uncover a great "ecotourism" operator or have further ideas on how to be a low-impact tourist, we at *Let's Go* would love to hear of them. Please do not hesitate to call or write to us.

■ Getting Around

While there are numerous transportation options in Southeast Asia, departure times are subject to change on a monthly, weekly, or even daily basis. As a result, the schedules listed are as of summer 1996 and may not be applicable to your date of travel. Rely more on the frequency of a bus, train, or boat than on the exact times listed. We suggest that travelers check with the stations the day before their intended travel and double check times the morning of departure.

Budget travelers usually have to resort to traveling on land, as airfares can be steep to some destinations. Given the various stages of development and infrastructure among Southeast Asian countries, **road safety** can range anywhere from smooth highways (Hong Kong, Singapore, Peninsular Malaysia, and Thailand) to pot-holed, dirt affairs (Laos, Cambodia, Vietnam, East Malaysia, and Indonesia). Major roads in all the countries are paved, but only in the former are they well-lit and flanked with traffic signs and signals. The latter countries and regions lack traffic regulations and speed limits altogether. More remote areas of each country rely on dirt roads which become rivers of mud during the rainy season, making land travel near impossible. Regardless of the road conditions, however, drivers are usually the primary threat to the safety of roads. Where road regulations are well-enforced, drivers are more likely to obey speed limits and traffic rules. In the less developed countries, however, where there is no central authority to enforce traffic rules, drivers are reckless and aggressive, and licensing regulations seem to be a mystery. In addition, road travel at night tends to be treacherous, as buses and trucks swerve at high speeds as if they ruled the roads, forcing smaller vehicles to slow down. More importantly, visibility is limited, and this becomes especially dangerous along coastal and narrow, winding roads. On buses, foreigners may want to sit in the front seats, where there's more leg room, and from where it will be easier to get out should an accident occur.

BY PLANE

Often the most expensive option, planes are nonetheless important for travel within the region, such as to Cambodia, where the only overland border crossing is a bus from Ho Chi Minh City. See specific country listings for advice on the best way to get around the country you are planning on visiting. For greater flexibility and cheaper prices, purchase plane tickets for trips across the region once you are in Southeast Asia. Check specific countries and their cities for the major carriers and budget travel offices.

BY TRAIN

Trains are often the best way to travel long distances in Southeast Asia, especially for overnight rides, when you may need a sleeper car. Train service is, however, really only a viable option on Java and in Thailand, Malaysia, and Singapore. Rail systems are not extensive in much of the rest of Indonesia, expensive and uncomfortable in Vietnam, unsafe in Cambodia, and simply nonexistent in Laos. Beware of travel agencies which claim to sell train tickets; while some are licensed to do so, many also sell fake train tickets and run away with a good deal of money. The safest thing to do is to buy a ticket directly from a train station.

BY BUS

Next to traveling by train, bus travel is the most popular way for budget travelers to get around Southeast Asia (except in Cambodia). Bus travel is cheap and can be more convenient than trains, since buses can go where tracks cannot. Riding in a regular bus is often a suffocating, mind-numbing experience; taking an air-conditioned bus is only mind-numbing. Despite the awful traffic in and around large cities, most people expect their bus drivers to get from point A to point B as fast as possible—and the driver usually tries to accommodate. Expect to hear much grinding of gears and blaring of horns. Also, those with air-conditioning (when it works) provide a degree of climate control not found on most trains. Many long-legged western travelers find front seats to be the most comfortable.

Buses are often crowded, so buy **tickets** early at the bus terminal. As with train tickets, it's generally unwise to buy bus tickets from random travel agencies; often they are selling nothing more than useless slips of paper.

Many **private companies** offer their own bus services. Compared to government buses, private ones tend to have faster, more reckless drivers and charge a tiny bit more. Some private bus companies offer excellent service, while others should not hold an operating license; there are so many private operators in the country that it is difficult to know the quality of an operation until you're already on a bus and screaming down the highway.

BY BOAT

Travel by boat—be it by luxury inter-island ferry or motorized dugout canoe—is an exciting alternative to those oh-so-comfortable Southeast Asian buses and trains. Indeed, travelers intending to explore more remote regions of the north (specifically Laos and Cambodia), where planes, trains and even automobiles are scarce, may find boats the only option. In Cambodia, travel along the country's river system is often the safest way to reach the major cities north and northeast of Phnom Penh. As with other modes of transportation, the degree of comfort and safety varies widely. PELNI, Indonesia's national ferry line, operates cruise ship quality service linking major cities within the archipelago, while in Laos travelers must make their own arrangements with individual boat captains and may find themselves sharing their seat with a pig, chicken, or other barnyard friend (provided there is a "seat" at all of course). Be aware that the extent of travel possible along rivers can vary according to the season and water levels.

BY MINIVAN OR PICK-UP TRUCK (UTILITY)

Large minivans/pick-ups/utes are the consistent favorite for local transportation, and virtually every town has an organized (or not so organized) system. They often run like buses, with fixed routes within a town or between towns, and fares fixed according to distance. In Thailand the vehicles are called *songthaew,* literally "two rows." The name describes the way *songthaew* passengers sit: along two rows of seats in the covered bed of a small pick-up. In Indonesia and Malaysia, *bemo,* colts, Daihatsus, *angkutan kota (angkot),* or *sudako,* as they are randomly called, are more like small buses or vans, but the same principles apply. They typically seat 10 to 40 people, depending on the size of the vehicle and its passengers. Often, those who can't be bothered to wait for a seat simply hang on the back.

Some *songthaew* or *angkot* have a button on the roof that passengers press to signal the driver where they want to get off. If the one you're on doesn't have a button, it's customary to tap on a metal railing a few times with a coin until the driver figures out that you want off. In many towns, these vehicles can be chartered as private transport, with fares hammered out by driver and passenger.

BY MOTO-TRISHAW

To some, the "roving buzzsaw" is a convenient boon and a symbol of the Southeast Asian experience; to others it's merely a diesel fume-belching beast. Fans of the *tuk-tuk* (in Thailand) and *bajaj* (in Indonesia) argue that these small covered three-wheeled motorcycles are cheap compared to taxis, more convenient than buses and *songthaew/angkot,* small enough to dart through heavy traffic, and a tad safer than motorcycle taxis. Much of this, of course, depends upon the driver. Detractors criticize the spunky *tuk-tuk* for the damage it does to the environment and human ears. A *bajaj* can seat one to three, depending upon the size of the passengers. Low ceilings, minimal leg room, and narrow seats (not to mention a vibrating action that threatens to dismantle the vehicle's slipshod frame) could make a six-foot person forgo an auto-trishaw ride forever.

BY TRISHAW

Trishaws, not to be confused with *tuk-tuk* or *bajaj,* are tricycle rickshaws powered by the legs of drivers, many of whom have been driving them for years, ignoring the allure of their more glamorous motorized cousins. Found all across Southeast Asia, they are known as *samlor* in Thailand and *becak* (BAY-cha) in Malaysia and Indonesia, and cyclos in Cambodia and Vietnam. The benefit of riding in a trishaw comes from having the vehicle all to yourself; negatives include the longer traveling time, the potential of inhaling vicious amounts of air pollution, and the sorrow of seeing an old man labor away.

BY CAR

Driving a car in Southeast Asia is not for the faint of heart. Besides swerving to avoid cars and motorcycles, travelers have to remember to drive on the left in most places and learn to dodge people, dogs, and water buffalo. In addition, there's a general disrespect for the lines on the road, as vehicles race to pass one another. A car is usually unnecessary in large cities where efficient transportation abounds. Also, some rental companies do not offer insurance, and a serious accident often means spending some time in jail or the hospital, as well as shelling out a large sum of money to cover damages. If you absolutely must have a car, keep your international driver's permit and a substantial amount of money handy. The cost of renting a compact four-door sedan is typically ten times the cost of a night's stay at a guest house.

BY MOTORCYCLE, MOPED, AND SCOOTER

Motorcycles, mopeds, and scooters are probably more useful than cars for travelers. If you don't want to drive your own, they can also be hired as taxis, especially in Cambodia, Vietnam, and Thailand. Generally, motorized two-wheelers can weave in and out of congested traffic, and come in handy when touring island or jungle roads. Unfortunately, riding these puppies is worthy of a Surgeon General's warning (almost all our researchers have consistent track records of moped misfortune). The greatest number of traffic fatalities fall under the "motorcyclist" heading. In many areas, and all of Thailand, a helmet is required by law, but you will not always be provided with one. Unless you have a death wish however, you shouldn't get on a motorcycle or motorbike without one; traffic fatalities in the region tend to be frighteningly high, especially for these types of vehicle. As with a car, you'll find yourself dodging new and exciting obstacles. Remember that the larger vehicle has the right of way. Motorcycle rental shops are abundant near major tourist stops.

BY BICYCLE

If driving a car or riding a motorcycle is that hairy, and the largest vehicle can crush all smaller ones in its path, is it any surprise that few travelers ride bicycles in big cities? Rural towns with countryside or archaeological sights within biking distance are the places where bicycles really become worth the small change they're rented for.

BY THUMB

> *Let's Go* urges you to use common sense and consider all the risks involved before hitchhiking. We do not recommend hitchhiking to anyone.

Hitchhiking is uncommon in Southeast Asia, since transportation tends to be inexpensive. It's also dangerous, especially along highways; most cars and trucks do not travel at speeds that make it possible to stop and pick up hitchers. Even if a ride can be flagged down, the language barrier can easily create problems for the hitcher, who might find him/herself traveling to the wrong destination (and perhaps being asked for an unexpected fee upon arrival). As always, women should take extra precautions, and in general probably should not hitchhike at all.

■ Accommodations

Southeast Asia has a variety of inexpensive alternatives to hotels and motels. Before you set out, try to locate guest houses and hostels along your route and make reservations, especially if you plan to travel during peak tourist seasons. Many places still don't take reservations, but it's worth a try, especially in the larger cities and major tourist destinations. Even if you find yourself in dire straits, don't spend the night under the stars; it's often uncomfortable and unsafe, and sometimes illegal, even in national parks and forest areas.

HOTELS

In general, hotels offer the most comfort, but a price must be paid for this luxury. The cheapest hotels are akin to cheap motels. The typical inexpensive hotel provides basic amenities (soap, towel, toilet paper) in a sizable room that's sometimes carpeted. A private bathroom, hot water, and a bathtub are common. You also will not have to worry about bringing bedding, as this is usually provided. Rooms often have air-conditioning and some basic furnishings, even a television and refrigerator in more upscale locations. Most hotels require that visitors be registered on the hotel's log book. Be as careful with your valuables as you would elsewhere.

HOSTELS

As a rule, hostels are dorm-style accommodations where the sexes sleep apart, often in large rooms with bunk beds. Some hostels allow families and couples to have private rooms. You must bring or rent your own sleep sack (two sheets sewn together); sleeping bags may not be allowed. Hostels frequently have kitchens and utensils for guests' use, and some have storage areas and laundry facilities. Many also require communal chore, usually lasting no more than 15 minutes, from guests.

Hostels are not as prevalent in Southeast Asia as they are in other parts of the world. A few **Hostelling International (HI)** affiliates can nonetheless be found. To stay in HI hostels, membership is usually required. Hostelling International is the largest such organization, although others such as Backpackers Resorts International, Budget Backpackers Hostels, or Federation of International Youth Hostels may be worth considering. If you have Internet access, check out the **Internet Guide to Hostelling** (http://hostels.com). Reservations for HI hostels may be made via the International Booking Network (IBN), a computerized system which allows you to book to and from HI hostels (more than 300 centers worldwide) months in advance for a nominal fee. Credit card bookings may be made over the phone–contact your local hosteling organization for more details. For membership, contact the HI affiliate in your home country. Getting membership before you go is a much better idea than waiting until you're on the road if you plan to stay in HI establishments.

Hostelling Membership

Hostelling International-American Youth Hostels (HI-AYH), 733 15th St. NW, Suite 840, Washington, D.C. 20005 (tel. (202) 783-6161; fax 783-6171; http://www.taponline.com/tap/travel/hostels/pages/hosthp.html). HI-AYH maintains 34 offices and over 150 hostels in the US. 12-month HI memberships: adults US$25, under 18 US$10, over 54 US$15, and US$35 for family cards. Membership package includes *Hostelling USA: The Official Guide to Hostels in the United States* (filled with info on travel discounts, maps, and activities). All this can be purchased at many travel agencies, local council offices, and the national office.

Hostelling International-Canada (HI-C), 400-205 Catherine St., Ottawa, Ont. K2P 1C3 (tel. (613) 237-7884; fax 237-7868). Canada-wide membership/customer service line (800) 663-5777. IBN Booking centers in Edmonton, Montréal, Ottawa, and Vancouver. Membership fees: 1-yr., under 18 CDN$12; 1-yr., over 18 CDN$25; 2-yr., over 18 CDN$35; lifetime CDN$175.

Youth Hostels Association of England and Wales (YHA), Trevelyan House, 8 St. Stephen's Hill, St. Albans, Hertfordshire AL1 2DY, England (tel. (01727) 85 52 15; fax 84 41 26). Enrollment fees are: UK£9.30; under 18 UK£3.20; UK£18.60 for both parents with children under 18 enrolled free; UK£9.30 for one parent with children under 18 enrolled free; UK£125.00 for lifetime membership.

An Óige (Irish Youth Hostel Association), 61 Mountjoy St., Dublin 7 (tel. (01) 830 45 55; fax 830 58 08; http://www.touchtel.ie). One-year membership is IR£7.50, under 18 IR£4, family IR£7.50 for each adult with children under 16 free.

Youth Hostels Association of Northern Ireland (YHANI), 22 Donegall Rd., Belfast BT12 5JN, Northern Ireland (tel. (01232) 31 54 35; fax 43 96 99). Annual memberships UK£7, under 18 UK£3, family UK£14 for up to 6 children.

Scottish Youth Hostels Association (SYHA), 7 Glebe Crescent, Stirling FK8 2JA (tel. (01786) 45 11 81; fax 45 01 98). Membership UK£6, under 18 UK£2.50.

Australian Youth Hostels Association (AYHA), Level 3, 10 Mallett St., Camperdown, NSW 2050 (tel. (02) 565 16 99; fax 565 13 25; e-mail YHA@zeta.org.au). AUS$42, renewal AUS$26; under 18 AUS$12.

Youth Hostels Association of New Zealand (YHANZ), P.O. Box 436, 173 Gloucester St., Christchurch 1 (tel. (643) 379 99 70; fax 365 44 76; e-mail hostel.operations@yha.org.nz; http://yha.org.nz/yha). Annual membership fee NZ$24.

Hostel Association of South Africa, P.O. Box 4402, Cape Town 8000 (tel. (21) 419 18 53; fax 21 69 37). Membership SAR45; Students SAR30; Group SAR120; Family SAR90; Lifetime SAR225.

GUEST HOUSES

The guest house is the single-handed savior of the budget traveler's wallet. Surprisingly enough, the large availability of guest houses is a relatively new phenomenon and is gaining momentum in some countries faster than others. Guest houses, while providing minimal to no amenities, are generally very adequate and comfortable. The typical single is a small room (roughly 3m x 3m or smaller), and travelers must usually provide their own soap, towels, and toilet paper. Expect shared baths with showers and a squat toilet that you flush by manually pouring water through its drain. Many guest houses also operate a small restaurant catering to their guests. Make sure that you see the room you are about to rent and accept its condition. Feel free to check the lock, lights, fan, and bathroom.

Keep in mind that you are ultimately responsible for all personal belongings; guest houses can be dens of thievery—don't think your fellow travelers are immune. While most guest houses run honest operations, it only takes one exception to ruin a fine trip. Keep valuables and important documents on your person. Many guest houses offer luggage storage and safe deposit boxes; you must determine whether or not these are actually safe. Be aware of a guest house's specific policies and obey them; meet payments as requested, observe rules regarding eating, drinking, or smoking in a room. In addition, many guest houses do not allow outside guests (read: prostitutes, but this applies to fellow travelers). This measure is implemented to protect the guest house, which may be accused of robbery when a guest's "friend" runs off with the guest's valuables.

ALTERNATIVE ACCOMMODATIONS

While not as easy to find in Southeast Asia as in other places, alternatives to renting a room are around. Most of these options are more appropriate for the traveler who is planning on staying an extended period of time in the region. Please see **Longer Stays** on page 37 for more information on this.

One option is lodging in exchange for work. You should investigate **Willing Workers on Organic Farms** below, and let us know if you find any other resources for Southeast Asia. Another option is renting or exchanging homes, which you can begin investigating with the organizations below.

Barclay International Group, 150 West 52nd St., New York, NY 10022 (tel. (800) 845-6636 or (212) 832-3777; fax 753-1139), arranges hotel alternative accommodations (apartment, condo, cottage, or villa rentals) in Thailand. Most are equipped with kitchens, telephones, TV, concierge, and maid service. Rentals are pricey, starting around $500 per week low season. Useful for families with children, business travelers, or kosher/vegetarian travelers, as the apartments tend to be cheaper than comparably-serviced hotels.

The Invented City: International Home Exchange, 41 Sutter St., Suite 1090, San Francisco, CA 94104 (tel. (800) 788-CITY (US only) or (415) 252-1141 from abroad; fax 252-1171; e-mail invented@aol.com). Listing of 1700 homes worldwide. For US$50, you get your offer listed in 1 and receive 3 catalogues. It works via a simple swap, with details being worked out between members.

Willing Workers on Organic Farms, Postfach 615, CH-9001 St. Gallen, Switzerland (e-mail fairtours@gu.apc.org.), compiles a list of organic farms worldwide which provide beds and meals in exchange for labor. Send 2 international reply coupons for more info.

CAMPING

National parks are the most common places to camp. Some offer tents, established camp sites, bungalows, and a cafeteria. Prospective campers need to invest in good camping equipment. For more information on backpacks, see **Packing** on page 43. Most of the better **sleeping bags,** down (lightweight and warm), or synthetic (cheaper, heavier, more durable, and warmer when wet), have ratings for specific minimum temperatures. The lower the mercury, the higher the price. Expect to pay at least US$65 for a synthetic bag and up to US$270 for real feathers. **Sleeping bag pads** range US$13-25, while air mattresses go for about US$25-50. The best **tents** are free-standing with frames and suspension systems, set up quickly, and require no staking. Good two-person tents start at about US$135, for four US$200. Other camping basics include a battery-operated **lantern** (never gas), a plastic **groundcloth,** and collapsible **water sacks. Campstoves** come in all sizes, weights, and fuel types, but none is truly cheap (US$30-120) or light. In general, **cooking equipment** can prove more of an albatross than a convenience—consider your eating requirements and preferences carefully. A **canteen, Swiss army knife, waterproof matches,** and **insect repellent** are essential items to throw in with your gear.

■ Keeping in Touch

MAIL

Mail can be sent internationally through **Poste Restante** (the international phrase for General Delivery) to most cities or towns; it's well worth using and much more reliable than you might think. Mark the envelope "HOLD" and address it legibly in English to: Vundy <u>VALTZ</u> (or legal name of addressee), *Poste Restante,* City, City Code, Country. The last name should be capitalized and underlined. The mail will go to a special desk in the central post office, unless you specify a branch post office. As a rule, it's best to use the largest post office in the area; sometimes, mail will be sent there regardless of what you write on the envelope.

When picking up your mail, bring a passport or another ID. If the clerks insist that there's nothing for you, have them check under your first name as well. In a few countries you may have to pay a minimal fee per item received. *Let's Go* lists post offices in the Practical Information section for each city and most towns.

Aerogrammes, printed sheets that fold into envelopes and travel via airmail, are available at post offices. Be sure to mark all airmail *par avion*, which is universally understood. Most post offices charge exorbitant fees or simply refuse to send Aerogrammes with enclosures. Allow *at least* two weeks for mail to or from Southeast Asia. Much depends on the national postal system.

If regular airmail is too slow, there are a few faster, more expensive, options. Both **Federal Express** (U.S. tel. (800) 463-3339) and **DHL** (U.S. tel. (800) CALL DHL) operate throughout Southeast Asia. Federal Express costs (all prices for pick-up, under 8 oz. of 8½x11 in. paper): US$32.50 to Jakarta, Kuala Lumpur, Bangkok, and Ho Chi Minh City; US$28.50 to Hong Kong and Singapore; and US$44.00 to Phnom Penh. Delivery takes three to four business days (no service to Laos). **DHL** are (prices for under 30 pages and 8 oz. of documents): US$35 to Singapore and Hong Kong (three business days); US$35 to Jakarta, Bangkok, and Kuala Lumpur; and US$71 to Vientiane, Phnom Penh, and Ho Chi Minh City. Shipping anything but documents is more expensive. For documents to Ho Chi Minh City, use the official name—do not label it as Saigon.

Surface mail is the cheapest and slowest way to send mail, and is really only appropriate for sending large quantities of items you won't need to see for a while. Distinguish your airmail from surface mail by explicitly labeling "airmail" in the appropriate language. When ordering books and materials from abroad, always include one or two **International Reply Coupons (IRCs)**—a way of providing the postage to cover delivery. IRCs are available from local post offices (US$1.05).

American Express offices throughout the world act as a mail service for cardholders if you contact them in advance. Under this free service, they hold mail for 30 days, forward upon request, and accept telegrams. Address such letters as you would for *Poste Restante,* but indicate that it is "Client Mail." Some offices offer these services to non-cardholders (especially those who have purchased AmEx Travelers' Cheques), but you must call ahead to make sure. Check the **Practical Information** section of the countries you plan to visit; *Let's Go* lists AmEx office locations for most large cities. A complete list is available free from AmEx (US tel. (800) 528-4800) in the booklet *Traveler's Companion.*

TELEPHONES

International Subscriber Dialing (ISD) and **International Home Country Direct (HCD)** provide international telephone service. ISD calls can be made with or without the help of an operator. Without operator assistance, an ISD call may be made from any phone with international service by dialing **001+country code+area code+phone number.** Prices are lowest for calls within Asia, North America, and Europe, and higher for calls to the rest of the world. For **operator assistance,** dial 100. An operator can assist you with either a personal call, station-to-station call, collect call, or calling card call. ISD telephones are often available at post offices.

In **HCD** calls, special phones are pre-connected to operators within the country whose name appears on the phone. These calls are charged to the called party like collect calls. Access codes are listed in the specific countries.

You can make direct international calls from certain **pay phones.** In some countries, pay phones are card-operated; some even accept major credit cards. For specific information on international calls, check the **Keeping in Touch** sections of specific countries and the **Practical Information** section of the town you are in.

English-speaking operators are often available for both local and international assistance. Operators in most countries can place **collect calls** for you. It's cheaper to find a pay phone and deposit just enough money to be able to say "Call me" and give your number (though some pay phones can't receive calls).

A **calling card** is another cheap alternative; your local long-distance phone company will have a number for you to dial while traveling (either toll-free or charged as a local call) to connect instantly to an operator in your home country. The calls (plus a small surcharge) are then billed either collect or to a calling card. For more information, call **AT&T Direct** (tel. (800) 331-1140, from abroad (412) 553-7458), **Sprint** (tel. (800) 877-4646), or **MCI WorldPhone** and **World Reach** (tel. (800) 996-7535). MCI's WorldPhone also provides access to MCI's **Traveler's Assist,** which gives legal and medical advice, exchange rate information, and translation services. For similar services for countries outside the U.S., contact your local phone company. In Canada, contact Bell Canada **Canada Direct** (tel. (800) 565-4708); in the U.K., British Telecom **BT Direct** (tel. (800) 34 51 44); in Ireland, Telecom Éireann **Ireland Direct** (tel. (800) 25 02 50); in Australia, Telstra **Australia Direct** (tel. 13 22 00); in New Zealand, **Telecom New Zealand** (tel. 123); and in South Africa, **Telkom South Africa** (tel. 09 03).

Phone rates tend to be highest in the morning, lower in the evening, and lowest on Sunday and late at night. Also, remember **time differences** when you call. Southeast Asian countries ignore daylight savings time. See the **Keeping in Touch** section in each country for specific time differences.

OTHER COMMUNICATION

Domestic and international **telegrams** offer an option slower than telephones but faster than post. Fill out a form at any post or telephone office; cables to North America arrive in one or two days. To send a telegram overseas from the U.S., **Western Union** (tel. (800) 325-6000) charges US$14.32, plus US$9 outside the U.S., plus about 76¢ per word, including name and address (no service to Laos or Cambodia).

Telegrams can be expensive, so you may wish to consider **faxes,** for more immediate, personal, and cheaper communication. Most towns across Southeast Asia have telephone offices where you can send and receive faxes.

International editions of *Time* and *Newsweek* are usually available, as is the daily English language newspaper the *International Herald Tribune* which is affiliated with *The New York Times* and *Washington Post.* Some major cities also offer a local daily English language newspaper.

CUSTOMS AND CULTURE

■ Food and Drink

Much of Southeast Asian cuisine is influenced by or imported from other countries, most notably China and India, resulting in unique and eclectic flavors. The staple food of the region is **rice,** eaten at every meal including breakfast. Glutinous rice (sweet or sticky rice) is also eaten, usually with cold salads or pickles. Rice can also be eaten sweet (particularly popular in Laos) or fried, such as Indonesian *nasi goreng.* Rice noodles are a similar staple food often added to salads and soups. Accompanying the rice are typically dishes of meat, fish, vegetables, curry, pickles, or soups. These dishes are shared between everyone at the table. Fermented fish is popular in Cambodia, while the Laotians consume more pork, chicken, and duck, and Indonesians prepare a large variety of vegetable dishes.

Wherever you go in Southeast Asia, the cuisine is notoriously spicy, using **chili peppers** liberally. Tourist restaurants typically cater to the more tender tongue of western travelers and go lightly on the chilis, but local eateries serve up spicy food unless specifically told otherwise. Other condiments include lemon grass, fish sauce, tamarind, mint, ginger, garlic, shrimp paste, peanut sauce, and coconut. In Indonesia and Malaysia, coconut (or coconut milk) is used in almost every dish, such as *nasi lemak* (rice cooked in coconut milk with cucumbers, peanuts, and boiled egg) and *soto* *ayam* (coconut cream soup with chicken). In Thailand the emphasis is chili, whereas in Vietnam, fish sauce is the flavor of choice.

Salads are popular throughout Southeast Asia, but they bear little resemblance to those in the west. They are, rather, delicious blends of fruits and vegetables, served either hot or cold. *Som tam* (or *tum som* in Laos) is a popular dish in Thailand and Laos, consisting of unripe papaya mixed in a mortar with lemon, shrimp paste, chilis, garlic, tamarind, tomatoes, and even meat. The meal-sized Vietnamese *bun* is a cold salad of lettuce, cucumbers, shredded carrots, thin rice noodles, grilled meat or egg rolls topped with peanuts.

Few meals are complete without dessert, usually assuming the form of fresh fruit, glazed bananas, ice cream, or a sweet drink. The tropical climate lends itself to a year-long season of **fruit**, including varieties never seen in the west. These are sold for unbelievably low prices at street vendors and markets. **Drinks** vary throughout the region, but share a common element: incredible sweetness. A Vietnamese speciality, called *mia da,* consists of pressed sugarcane with ice, while a popular Thai drink is the sweet yogurt-based *lassi. Teh tarik,* Indian vanilla tea poured from cup to cup to cool, is served at the end of meals in Malaysia, while *es kelapa muda,* young coconut shaved into sweetened coconut milk and served with ice, can be bought on the street and in most restaurants in Indonesia.

Although tourists can always find restaurants, especially in well-touristed areas, it can be more fun and interesting to try food from street stalls. Caution should be exercised, however, as hygiene is not always a priority among vendors. With common sense and a good eye, tourists can often tell whether a certain vendor is relatively safe to eat at, so never eat anything that seems at all questionable.

Attitudes toward liquor vary within the region. In the strongly Muslim countries of Malaysia and Indonesia, alcohol is often not served in restaurants that do not cater to westerners. In other countries, however, it's usually easily procurable. This may obscure the fact of different perceptions of drunkenness and liquor. Public drunkenness is generally frowned upon, particularly for women.

■ Getting Along

There's little that characterizes Southeast Asian society more than its high regard for manners and courtesy. To achieve this and to avoid confrontation, indirectness is often employed, which many westerners misinterpret as timidity or meekness. Southeast Asian cultures frown upon public displays of emotion, as it is considered impolite to raise one's voice or gesture frantically. Arguing or a loss of temper are regarded as poor breeding. Similarly, public displays of affection are also discouraged. Members of the opposite sex rarely even hold hands in public, and tourists who wish to gain the esteem of locals would do well to follow suit.

The people of this region tend to be modest and unassuming, both in social interactions and physical appearance. Men and women alike dress conservatively. While short skirts and tank tops are commonplace in the west, it's usually inappropriate attire in this region, especially in more conservative and religious locals, as well as places less frequented by tourists.

Other common practices in the west can be considered rude or even offensive in this region. The head is believed to be where a person's spirit abides, and as such, is considered the most sacred part of the body. It's rude to touch another person on the head, even a small child; doing so might well attract shocked stares from locals. Likewise, the feet are considered to be the lowest and most impure part of the body, so pointing one's feet at someone or something (especially if it's sacred) should be avoided. Stepping over people, food, or books will also cause offense.

When greeting someone, especially an elder, typical western gestures of handshakes or a casual slap on the back are inappropriate. Instead, locals press their hands together in front of the chest, and bowing the head slightly. In Thailand, this is called the *wai* and in Laos the *phanom.* Casual physical contact is not the status quo, so even simple gestures such as tapping a waitress on the shoulder may be met with reproval. Similarly, typical western gestures to call someone's attention, such as the beckoning wave, are used only for animals, and can easily cause offense.

■ Religion

BUDDHISM

Buddhism is the predominant religion for most of mainland Southeast Asia, both in its Theravada and Mahayana forms. Buddhism's basis consists of the concepts of *dharma* (Buddha's guide to right actions and belief), *karma* (the belief that one is fully responsible for one's own actions in past, present, and future lives), and *sangha* (the ascetic community within which man can improve his *karma*). Its stress is on the "Middle Way," achievable through adherence to the Four Noble Truths and the Noble Eightfold Path. In most regions it blends with other indigenous religious traditions to create a belief unique to that locale.

Theravada Buddhism, which originated in Sri Lanka, first spread to Cambodia from the Thai kingdom of Sukhothai. Today, it is the predominant religion of Laos, Cambodia, and Thailand. Although of the same basis, **Mahayana Buddhism** differs from Theravada in its less monastic emphasis, and has a greater foothold in Central Asia, China, Japan, and Vietnam. As such, it's the principal religion among the Buddhists of Vietnam, Chinese-Malaysians, and Chinese-Indonesians.

It's important for travelers to respect the practices of this philosophy. Thailand is particularly serious regarding religious respect. Defacing or harming religious objects (including climbing onto a giant Buddha) is punishable by imprisonment, and exportation of Buddha images is prohibited. Buddhist monks cannot come into physical contact with women, so female travelers should take care not to sit next to, touch, or hand anything directly to a monk. Respect toward Buddhist objects, monks, and **appropriate dress and behavior in wats** (temples) will ensure that the traveler does not run into unforeseen problems. Temple visitors should dress appropriately (no shorts or tank tops) and hats must not be worn upon entering the grounds. Seek permission to see the main sanctuary *(wiharn)* and take off shoes before entering. Once inside, tourists should take heed not to sit cross-legged in front of the Buddha—that would be pointing your toe at the Holy One. Instead, sit down and bend your legs to the side, keeping toes and soles away from the Buddha. In addition, avoid pointing fingers at sacred images and keep your head lowered when talking to a monk. A small offering or donation would be a welcome gesture.

ISLAM

Islam is a monotheistic religion based on five pillars: belief in Allah as the one god and Muhammed as his prophet, prayer five times per day, the *haj* (pilgrimage to Mecca), giving alms to the poor, and Ramadan. Although the religion originated in the Middle East, the largest Muslim country is Indonesia, whose population is over 90% Muslim. West Sumatra and Aceh Province are most devout. Malaysia is overwhelmingly Muslim as well, being the most conservative in Kota Bharu and the Kelantan state. In this country, however, religion is inextricably tied with the law and government. As such, Muslims are answerable to the state for infractions of religious nature. Beyond Indonesia and Malaysia, there are some significant Muslim minorities in the other countries of the region. Southern Thailand's Islamic community has frequently expressed discontent in the Buddhist country and a desire to join the Federation of Malaysia. Throughout Islamic areas travelers should take care to respect the religion. The most visible way to demonstrate this is usually through dress. Modest dress, particularly for women, is in order: covered shoulders and long pants or a long skirt. Entrance to mosques often requires further measures.

Temple Etiquette in Bali

When visiting Balinese temples, dress modestly (no shorts or bare shoulders) and wear a sash. If possible, wear a sarong and have a Balinese person help you tie it properly. Never walk in front of a person who is praying or take flash photos at a ceremony. Balinese Hindus in mourning are not allowed to enter temples for several days; the loss of a loved one is seen as a distraction that hinders the ability to be open and empty—a state necessary to be receptive to god. People bleeding or menstruating are also seen as distracted and requested to not enter.

When you enter the *pura* (temple), kneel or sit cross-legged before the covered tables. A *pemanku* (lay priest) brings incense to visitors and a *canang sari* (offering), a palm leaf box filled with flowers. Close your eyes and raise pressed palms to your forehead twice. Repeat this three more times, but with flower petals between the fingertips. Then hold out your open palms as the *pemanku* sprinkles you with *tirtha* (holy water). Next, cup your hands (right over left) and slurp three times from the *tirtha* that he or she pours in. The fourth time the *pemanku* pours *tirtha* in your hands, splash it on your head; the fifth time on your face. The *pemanku* gives you wet rice grains to press onto your forehead and throat, or may press do that for you. Finally, he or she will hand you a flower. Break it in two and place each half behind an ear by crossing your arms before you; the flower in your right hand goes behind the left ear, and vice-versa.

OTHER FAITHS

Once the religion of Indonesia and the kingdom of Angkor in Cambodia, **Hinduism** was slowly displaced by the expansion of Buddhism and Islam. Today, only the Balinese practice the religion. Hindu temples still dot the landscape of Southeast Asia, however, and its myths, particularly the *Ramayana*, still influence the artistic traditions here. **Christianity,** although not widely practiced, is present, as well, especially in the northern areas of Indonesia. Some islands like Timor and Flores, as well as the Malaysian state of Sabah are predominantly Christian. **Confucianism** and **Taoism** are often worshipped hand in hand among the Chinese and Vietnamese. More indigenous to the hundreds of ethnic groups in this region are **phi,** the cult of spirit worship, **animism,** and **ancestor worship,** all of which are still practiced by locals, often co-existing and practiced with other major religions.

Let's Go Picks

After traipsing through mountains and jungles, we've come up with the following as some of our favorite destinations. Of course, they're entirely subjective and you need not live by it. In Southeast Asia, there are plenty of secluded locales still awaiting discovery. Feel free to send us a postcard of your own greatest hits.

Most Stupendous Natural Wonders: 4000 Islands Region (L), you guessed it, thousands of small islets dotting the Mekong River. **Cameron Highlands (M),** cool hill resort overlooking vast tea plantations. **Erawan Falls (T),** seven levels of cascades, the centerpiece of a Garden-of-Eden park. **Gunung Kerinci (I),** soars up from West Sumatran highlands, blushed pink from cinnamon trees. **Gunung Krakatau (I),** the remains of an active volcano, but still smoking and spitting lava. **Mulu Caves (M),** world's longest system of caves with some surreal subterranean splendors.

Best Beaches: Gapang Beach (I), peaceful stretch of sand squished between mountains and an ocean rich with coral. **Golden Beach (M),** glittering silken silica and austere coastal cliffs. **Kampung Juara (M),** isolated and removed from tourism development. **Pantai Kuta (I),** still the preeminent spot, despite the Eurobathers. **Long Beach (M),** shallow, but ultra-fine white sand does intimate things to your feet. **Parangtritis (I),** desert-like with miles and miles of black sand. **Phra Nang Beach (T),** sand as soft as chalk and few visitors.

Best Watersports: Ayung River (I), just above Ubud, good rafting through Bali's rice-terraced interior. **Coral Island (M),** no mystery in the name; enough marine life to keep snorkelers happy. **Krabi (T),** paddle your own boat around hidden coves. **Lagundi Bay (I),** surf-central, with 3m-high waves and friendly sea turtles; coral reefs repose offshore. **Nusa Lembongan (I),** protected land, great for snorkeling, diving, and surfing. **Pai River (T),** 180km of rafting through the heart of Northern Thailand. **Sipidan Island (M),** vivid flora and fauna, excellent for diving and snorkeling.

Best Monuments/Ruins/Temples: Angkor (C), ancient temples with smiling faces taken over by banyan trees. **Mesjid Raya Baiturrahman (I),** with black domes and minarets, straight out of an Arabian tale. **Borobudur (I),** many terraced steps lead to serene Buddhas. **Doi Suthep (T),** sacred pilgrimage sight on top of an imposing mountain. **Melaka (M),** the whole city is a sight, with some splendid mosques and Chinese temples. **Phu Thawk (T),** mountain temple standing alone on a rocky outcrop with views of the valley below.

Best Nightlife: Bali (I), those who want cheap beer and wet t-shirt contests, go to Kuta; those who want a Euro-disco feel and diverse clientele, go to Legian. **Kuching's esplanade (M),** not exactly romping, but nightlife indeed with lots of people to just hang out with. **Petticoat Lane (HK),** opulent decor and Dr. Seuss furniture make for great socializing. **Kuala Lumpur's Saturday night market (M),** on Jl. Tunku Abdul Rahman, has the best food, folks, and fun.

Best Places With No Significant Sights Whatsoever: Cibodas (I), in the heart of the Puncak. **Mamasa Valley (I),** tranquil beauty, rolling hills, great treks. **Rach Gia (V),** village with friendly locals, a massive market, and delicious seafood. **Sangkhom (T),** drowsy mountain hamlet, surrounded by waterfalls and cliffs. **Taiping (M),** truly the town of everlasting peace; you can just sit in the lake gardens and smile serenely. **Tetebatu (I),** nestled in the foothills of Mt. Rinjani overlooking fields of rice. **Vang Vieng (L),** quiet town in a quiet country—what more do you want?

CAMBODIA

Like the majestic temple towers of Angkor breaking through the dense jungles that vie to smother the ancient city, Cambodia transcends its crippling history. Once the brilliant gem and artistic leader of Southeast Asia, Cambodia is now trying to resurrect its cultural traditions in an effort to heal the pain of the country's recent tragedy. During the Khmer Rouge's brief but interminable four-year reign, more than one million Cambodians were murdered.

The Cambodian people have endured far more than their share of sorrow, and their legacy has wrought an inescapable, if not indelible, stain on the urban fabric. Crippled soldiers loll on the sidewalks, and far too many children have grown up parentless as a result of the Khmer Rouge genocide. Unlike most other people in Southeast Asia, Cambodians are wary of foreigners. This, coupled with the continuing struggle between the new government and the insurgent Khmer Rouge, make traveling through Cambodia difficult, although not impossible. The diligent traveler who can breach the barriers into Cambodia will find a country in the process of rebirth, with the exuberant laughter of children and the beaming smiles of people proudly displaying an ancient heritage nearly eradicated less than 20 years ago.

ESSENTIALS

■ Geography

Cambodia sits near the southern tip of the Indochinese Peninsula, covering 181,035sq.km, roughly the size of England and Wales. The country is enclosed by mountains, and its lowland interior is one of savannas, dense forests, and rich, fertile alluvial plains. In the northeast, the Eastern Highlands rise to form a natural border with Laos. The Dangkrek Mountains run the length of the northern border with Thailand, while the Cardamom and Elephant Mountains can be found in the west and southwest of the country. The Mekong River flows 500km through the east and curves by Phnom Penh, where it divides into the Lower Mekong and Bassac Rivers. Also running by the capital is the Tonle Sap River, which flows 100km downriver from the Tonle Sap (Great Lake), the largest fresh-water pond in Southeast Asia at 3000sq.km. During the rainy season, between June and October, the Mekong usually floods, overflowing into the Tonle Sap River which then reverses its course and deposits the excess water into the Tonle Sap, doubling the lake's size.

■ When to Go

To avoid the rain and scorching heat, the best time to visit Cambodia is between November to March, the cool and dry season. Temperatures during these months range 17-27°C (63-8°F). During the rainy season (Apr.-Oct.), temperatures range from 27-35°C (81-95°F), with humidity up to 90%. Phnom Penh receives an average rainfall of 1.4m annually. The hottest month is April, when temperatures can be as high as 38°C (100°F). Information on the temperature during the month(s) you will be visiting can be found in the Climate Chart in the **Appendix** on page 737.

■ Money

US$1=2380.00riel	1000riel=US$0.42
CDN$=1740.21riel	1000riel=CDN$0.575
UK£1=3675.88riel	1000riel=UK£0.272
IR£1=3625.454riel	1000riel=IR£0.027
AUS$1=1763.818riel	1000riel=AUS$0.567
NZ$1=1442.994riel	1000riel=NZ$0.693
SARand=667.590riel	1000riel=SARand0.149

The Cambodian monetary unit is the **riel (r).** There are 50, 100, 200, and 500 riel notes and the exchange rate fluctuates frequently. In Cambodia, the US$ acts as a second currency and is widely accepted at many hotels, guest houses, and restaurants; in fact, some places will only take US$. *Let's Go* lists prices in both riel and US$. It would be wise to keep small US$ bills handy. **Tipping** is not necessary, but much appreciated—the average Cambodian makes about US$5 per month.

■ Getting Around

Most tourists choose to travel in Cambodia **by plane.** Buses and trains, while they exist, are not recommended as long as the Khmer Rouge continue to menace the people. **They have been known to kill tourists. Stay away from any land travel, especially at night.** Inexpensive daily flights connect cities within the country. There is a US$4 airport tax on all domestic flights.The other safe alternative to flying is to take a boat. If you do choose to risk land travel, there is the option to move around **by car;** renting a car or hiring a taxi are two popular options. Most roads are unpaved and have fallen into bad condition, making them virtually impassable at some points. **Because of roving Khmer Rouge rebels, bandits, and even government soldiers, avoid road travel at night.**

■ Keeping in Touch

The **postal service** in Cambodia is somewhat unreliable. Mail can take as long as two weeks to and from Cambodia. *Poste Restante* service is available in Phnom Penh. **Postal codes** are not used in Cambodia. **Telephones** in Phnom Penh are still scarce but gradually making their presence known. Many locations use cellular phones, and these numbers begin with 015, 017, 018, or 023, and are followed by 6 digits. **Long-distance calls** placed from Cambodia can be costly. **Collect call** rates sometimes go as high as US$8 per minute to North America and Europe. Some places do accept incoming calls for a small charge, whenever possible, *Let's Go* has listed these places. IDD calls can be placed from Telstra phone booths found around Phnom Penh. **HCD numbers:** Telecom Australia, 1 800-881-061; AT&T, 1 800-881-001. Cambodia is seven hours ahead of Greenwich Mean Time (GMT).

■ Staying Safe

> When traveling through the countryside or exploring ancient ruins, stay on well-trodden paths. Tourists have been killed by land mines.

Cambodians have seen a lifetime's worth of crime and violence in a few short years; it is without surprise then that crime rates here are at a minimum. What little crime exists is often found on the poorly-lit streets at night and in raucous bars frequented by locals. **Petty thievery** is a serious problem in Phnom Penh. Keep your valuables close to you. Of course, crime is not the biggest threat to your safety in this country; the 8 to 10 million **anti-personnel mines** littering the land and roving **bandits and Khmer Rouge rebels** should be your biggest concern. It's wrong to assume that all crimes are coordinated and executed by the Khmer Rouge; bandits and government soldiers are not without blame for attacks on westerners. Check with your embassy or find out from expatriates about travel conditions outside of Phnom Penh before venturing out yourself. The situation changes frequently; what we have reported is the situation as of summer 1996.

■ Hours and Holidays

Most government offices open at 7:30am and close at 11:30am for a mid-day break; they re-open from 2:00pm until 5:00pm. Businesses tend to keep roughly the same hours, although they generally open a half hour later. Festivals and holidays in Cambodia commemorate, among other things, the king, the land, the water, and the religion. Many businesses close during official holidays but not necessarily during long, lengthy festivals. Keep these dates in mind when planning your trip:

January 7: National Day celebrates the defeat of the Khmer Rouge in 1979.
February 7&8: Vietnamese and Chinese New Year.
April-May: The Royal Ploughing ceremony (Bonn Chroat Preah Nongkal) is the first of many agrarian festivals taking place throughout these two months.
April: New Year's (Bonn Chaul Chnam), a 3-day affair at the end of the harvest.
May 1: Labor Day.
May 9: Genocide Day, remembering Khmer Rouge atrocities.
September: Spirits Commemoration Festival.
October: Bonn Kathen, all month.
October 31: King Norodom Sihanouk's Birthday.
November 9: Independence Day.
November: Bonn Om Tuk, a 3-day Water Festival (varies with lunar year).

LIFE AND TIMES

■ The People of Cambodia

In 1971, estimations placed the Cambodian population at eight million, but after the Khmer Rouge holocaust, that number decreased to five million. High birth rates, however, and the repatriation of refugees from Thailand have brought the population back to 8.8 million again. Nearly half are under the age of 15. It is estimated that two million refugees have emigrated.

KHMER

It is believed that the Khmers, who make up 85% of Cambodia's population today, have inhabited the country since 2000 BC. Theories claim that the Khmer followed the Mekong River south into Cambodia from either southwest China or the Khasi Hills of northeast India. Still others contend that the Khmers come from Indonesia. Regardless of where they originated, the Khmers intermarried with other ethnic groups of Thai, Indian, Chinese and Vietnamese who later migrated into the region, but continue to remain predominant.

KHMER LOEU

The **Khmer Loeu,** or Upland Khmer, lived in forested mountains of northeastern Cambodia until the Vietnam War pushed them down to the lowlands. Like most hill tribes in Southeast Asia, the Khmer Loeu are animists and practice slash-and-burn agriculture. There are four subdivisions of this group. The **Brao** still live in the northeast along the Lao border, the **Kuy** in the northwest, the **Pear** in the Cardamon Mountains to the west, and the **Saoch** in the Elephant Mountains to the southwest. The Khmer Loeu are slowly assimilating into mainstream Cambodian culture.

CHINESE

Today, the **Chinese** constitute only 3% of the population, but prior to Pol Pot's time, their numbers were far greater and they dominated Cambodian politics and commerce. Large groups of Chinese began to migrate to Cambodia in the 18th and 19th centuries, settling down, intermarrying, and trading. They were able to integrate in Cambodian society without repercussions, and did not sacrifice their distinctiveness even after intermarriage with Khmers. When civil war erupted, many Chinese fled. Of those who remained, few survived the Khmer Rouge holocaust.

VIETNAMESE

Unlike the Chinese, the **Vietnamese** (or the pejorative *yuon*, as the Khmers call them) have struggled to assimilate into Cambodian society. Driven by centuries of animosity toward Vietnamese invaders, the Khmers have in the past and continue to persecute this ethnic minority. Pogroms as recently as 1970 sanctioned the murder of Vietnamese victims and soon after, the rise of the Khmer Rouge saw a mass exodus of the Vietnamese who feared for their lives. Following the Vietnamese invasion in 1979, however, many of these people returned to Cambodia, feeling safer with the presence of the military. Today, the Vietnamese comprise only a scant 5% of the population, but the Khmer Rouge continue to rouse animosity for the them.

CHAM AND MALAY

Most **Chams** are descendents of the former Champa kingdom in southern Vietnam who were forced out of their homeland by the Vietnamese between the 15th and 18th centuries. The **Malays,** on the other hand, were invited to settle in Cambodia by

King Chan who converted to Islam in the mid-17th century. Nowadays, most Chams and Malays, making up 3% of the population, live along the Mekong River north of Phnom Penh. The Khmer Rouge ruthlessly persecuted this minority group, wiping out half the Cham-Malay population and destroying the majority of their mosques, only today are they recovering from this devastation.

■ History

The fertile plains of Cambodia were once the foundation of powerful empires, including civilizations as early as 3000 years ago. The country itself, lying on the trade routes between China and India, is a patchwork of traditions absorbed by the people and blended into a distinct Khmer culture that, at its height, influenced the entire region of Southeast Asia.

EARLY KINGDOMS AND INDIANIZATION

The first recorded civilization arose in the 1st century AD. Called **Funan** by the Chinese, this kingdom dominated Southeast Asia for the next five centuries. Situated on the lower reaches of the Tonle Sap and the Mekong Rivers, Funan developed into a prosperous fishing, rice cultivation and trade center. Indeed, Roman, Greek, Persian, and Indian artifacts have been found in the area near Oc Eo, Vietnam, which is believed to have been Funan's main port. With increasing prosperity, Funan was able to subjugate its neighbors, extending its boundaries south to the Malay peninsula and east across most of present-day Vietnam.

Contact with foreigners through merchants, diplomats, and Brahmins fostered the spread of **Hindu** culture to Southeast Asia, changing the history, art, culture, and politics of the region. The arrival of Indian immigrants in the 4th and 5th centuries hastened this process of Indianization, so that by the end of the 5th century, Indian culture was thoroughly integrated into Funan life. The people adopted the use of a Sanskrit-based script, the worship of Hindu gods, and art styles influenced by the Gupta period in India.

In the 6th century, internal conflicts plagued the empire, rendering it vulnerable to aggression from hostile neighbors. Eventually, Funan was slowly displaced by the rising powers of **Chenla,** an Indianized dynasty originally centered in the Lao southern province of Champassak. By the end of the 7th century, Funan had become a mere vassal state to Chenla, but marriages between the two royal families managed to retain the political, social, and religious culture of the former empire.

Chenla's rulers sought to expand their kingdom by annexing present-day Laos and Thailand. In the 8th century, however, dynastic upheaval split the empire into two rival kingdoms. **Land Chenla,** centered north of the Tonle Sap, had an agrarian-based economy and was able to maintain a relatively stable existence, while **Water Chenla,**

Sun, Moon, Star

According to Khmer legends, the people of Cambodia were born from the union of the heavens. An Indian Brahman priest, Kaundinya, followed a most exciting dream which came to him, and eventually came to the edge of a vast great lake. There he married the beautiful Soma, daughter of the Naga king. From their union sprang forth the lunar dynasty (Funan). The Naga drank the waters of the lake, uncovering a fertile delta for the people to cultivate. Some time later, in a land not too far away from Funan, an ascetic named Kambu married the beautiful and celestial Mera. They gave birth to a powerful kingdom, the solar dynasty (Chenla), and their descendants were known as Kambuja, the "sons of Kambu." It didn't take long for both houses to realize that a match made in heaven would unite the two kingdoms. The moon prince married the sun princess; but he betrayed his own people and aligned himself with Chenla, which subsumed Funan without difficulty.

situated on the lower Mekong, was vanquished by the Javanese empire of **Sailendra** after a period of constant internal conflict.

THE GOLDEN AGE OF ANGKOR

As the final step to the complete subjugation of the kingdom, Chenla's royal family was taken to the Javanese court. It was not until 800 AD, when **Jayavarman II** (802-50) returned to his family's Khmer state, that the former Chenla was freed from the suzerainty of Java. In 802 he founded the empire of **Kambuja** (from which Cambodia, or Kampuchea, took its name), beginning the history of a unified Cambodia. This empire, however, is better known as **Angkor,** named for the temple complex built near Jayavarman II's capital city as a lasting tribute to his descendents. Jayavarman II revived the Hindu cult of **devaraja,** or god-king, granting him divine status, through which he was able to rule unchallenged as the absolute monarch. Kambuja marked the beginning of Cambodia's golden age, bringing the kingdom unprecedented power and brilliant achievements in art and architecture.

From the 9th to the 14th century, Angkor thrived under the rule of strong and capable monarchs. **Indravarman I** (877-89) began construction of an elaborate system of canals and reservoirs that are believed to be the cornerstone of Kambuja's prosperity, freeing the kingdom from dependence on the monsoons and providing large surpluses of rice. Under **Suryavarman II** (1113-50), Kambuja stretched to the Irrawady River in Burma to the west, Vietnam to the east, China to the north, and the Malay peninsula to the south. Despite such strong military victories, Suryavarman II's greatest achievement lies in the construction of **Angkor Wat,** the largest religious edifice in the world. Unfortunately, his reign was followed by 30 years of insurrection and incursion by the neighboring **Champa** kingdom in southern Vietnam which eventually captured and sacked Angkor in 1177.

The rise of **Jayavarman VII** (1181-1218), the last great king of Angkor, to the throne ended Champa's hold on the struggling empire. This king, whose reign marked the pinnacle of Kambuja's power, drove out and conquered the Chams, bringing them under Khmer rule. Unlike his predecessors, Jayavarman VII was an avid believer of **Mahayana Buddhism,** rather than the cult of *devaraja*. He sponsored the construction of numerous temples, including the building of Angkor Thom and the Bayon temple complexes, as well as rest houses, hospitals, and roads throughout the kingdom. Although a distinguished king, Jayavarman VII's religion undermined his legitimacy, while his extravagant projects drained income from Kambuja's irrigation system. The wars and the public works, however long-lasting they may be, severely sapped the financial and human capital of the empire.

After Jayavarman VII's death, Kambuja entered a long period of decline from which it never emerged. Furthermore, the spread of **Theravada Buddhism,** challenged the royal Hindu and Mahayana Buddhist cults. The humanitarian and egalitarian teachings of this religion were in direct opposition to the lavish life-style of the royal court which kept the peasants at the mercy of the throne. At this time, increased southward migration of the Tai-Kadai peoples from Mongol China began to displace the Khmers. The rising Lao kingdom of Lane Xang seized Kambuja's northern territories while the Thais waged perpetual war on the weakened kingdom. The capture of Angkor Thom by the Thai kingdom of Ayutthaya (Sukhothai's successor) hailed the final defeat of the Angkor Empire in 1431.

COLONIAL RULE AND INDEPENDENCE

For the next five centuries, known as Cambodia's "dark ages", the remnants of Angkor struggled to maintain its existence, marked by economic, political, and cultural stagnation. By the mid-19th century, Cambodia had become hopelessly trapped in the territorial struggle between Thailand and Vietnam until France intervened by claiming the kingdom for itself.

France was already heavily involved with Vietnam, and sought to expand its influence in the region to ultimately gain control of the Mekong against the threat of the

British in Burma and the Thais next door. In 1863, the French annexed Cambodia as a protectorate to thwart its rivals. For the next two decades, the French colonialists exploited Cambodia's people and natural resources, turning the country into a vast rubber plantation and rice market. When King Norodom blatantly refused to accept anymore mistreatment from their oppressors in 1884, he was forced at gun point to surrender Cambodia completely to France as a colony. In order to gain royal support and a biddable ally, the French interfered with the succession, passing over the crown prince in favor of Norodom's brother Sisowath, for whom they provided an extravagant life style. The new king's collaboration with French rule essentially halted any nationalist movements similar to those of its neighbors.

When the Japanese seized Indochina during World War II, they allowed the French to remain in nominal control, while the Axis power continued on its military rampage through Southeast Asia. In 1941, the French crowned 18-year-old **Prince Norodom Sihanouk,** the grandson of Norodom, king of Cambodia. In their efforts to install a puppet government, the French underestimated Sihanouk. Japan's calls for "Asia for the Asiatics" kindled anti-European feelings and galvanized nationalist struggles throughout Indochina. In Cambodia, the **Khmer Issarak** (Freedom Front) arose as the foremost nationalist movement. With persuasion from Japan, Sihanouk declared independence for his country and dissolved all treaties with the French. Nevertheless, the new Democrat-controlled government represented the interests of a pro-French elite, intent on retaining its privileges.

When the French returned in late 1945, they were compelled to keep promises made by the Free French during the war. Consequently, Cambodia's colonial status was nullified and the absolute monarchy abolished. Sihanouk, however, remained a figurative head of state, trying to negotiate with the French for full independence while attempting to placate supporters of the pro-communist Khmer Issarak and the Viet Minh who were suspicious of his relations with France.

As the war between the French and the Viet Minh intensified during the late 1940s, the turmoil spilled into Cambodia. Even though the Viet Minh had stirred anti-French sentiment, the French successfully managed to divide the Cambodians. Two factions of the Issarak emerged: the dominant was strongly pro-Viet Minh while the other was largely anti-communist and wary of the Vietnamese. Under the auspices of the Viet Minh, the pro-communist Issarak formed Cambodia's first communist party, the **Khmer People's Revolutionary Party (KPRP).** Meanwhile, in Paris, Cambodian students such as **Saloth Sar (Pol Pot), Khieu Samphan,** and **Ieng Sary**—known as the "Paris Circle"—were introduced to Marxism and eventually joined the French Communist Party, the most militant and Stalinist in Western Europe. This group would come to play an important role in the development of communism in Cambodia, profoundly altering the course of its modern history.

With increased anti-French activities in Vietnam and Laos, as well as the insurgent guerilla war waged by the Khmer Issarak, France eventually granted complete independence to Cambodia on **November 9, 1953,** less than two weeks before their defeat at Dien Bien Phu. The **Geneva Accords** of 1954 recognized Sihanouk's Royal government as the sole legitimate authority in Cambodia. The Paris Circle remained, however, to shape the destiny of the communist movement in Cambodia.

CIVIL WAR

For the people of Cambodia, independence meant freedom from an absolute monarchy. Sihanouk was pressured to abdicate in 1955, although he remained a popular leader. Using his influence, Sihanouk played a neutrality card that kept his country out of the war raging in Vietnam and Laos in the 1960s. When civil war broke out in South Vietnam, Sihanouk gave his support to the north Vietnamese rebels. In an effort to thwart American involvement in Cambodia, Sihanouk broke all diplomatic relations with the U.S. in 1965. Much to the indignation of the U.S., Sihanouk also allowed the Viet Cong to run the **Ho Chi Minh Trail** through Cambodia. His ambiguity and constant shifting between right and left incurred much resentment from the political elite in Cambodia. This and his refusal to cooperate with the U.S. prompted the American-backed coup of 1970 by army Commander-in-Chief **Lon Nol,** who immediately abolished the monarchy and declared the **Khmer Republic.**

Sihanouk fled into exile and his revolutionary troops joined forces with the communist **Khmer Rouge** (a term Sihanouk used for all leftist groups, but later signified Pol Pot and his supporters, who gained control of the KPRP in 1960) to incite revolts throughout the country while the North Vietnamese burrowed further into Cambodia in its clandestine activities. In April 1970, B-52 and fighter bombers dropped hundreds of tons of bombs on eastern Cambodia as a prelude to invasion by American and South Vietnamese troops. Sihanouk set up a government-in-exile, which was immediately recognized by the communist regimes of Beijing and Hanoi and attracted the support of Khmer Rouge leaders. Civil war broke out between the two governments soon after.

During the next two years, revolutionary forces were successful in their guerilla attacks, isolating Phnom Penh from the rest of the country. At times, it was believed that they held 80% of Cambodia's territory. By 1973, they would be ready to launch an immediate, and probably successful coup on the capital. However, the US increased bombings that year, pushing revolutionary forces back and killing most of Sihanouk's supporters. As a result, the Khmer Rouge emerged as the dominant faction of the rebel insurgents.

REIGN OF TERROR

In 1975, the Khmer Rouge increased their offensive to gain control of Cambodia, finally seizing Phnom Penh on April 17, and renamed the country **Democratic Kampuchea.** Thus began one of the world's most brutal reigns of terror. The leaders of the Khmer Rouge, the so-called Paris Circle, were perhaps the most intellectually elite of Asia's communist leaders and took drastic actions toward state-building as a result of strong communist convictions. Many of these men blamed western oppression for impeding development in their country and contended that modernization could be achieved without industrialization.

As a means to creating an agrarian society, Pol Pot and his Khmer Rouge forces exterminated their opposition and forced the Cambodian people to the countryside, where they were pressed into slave labor. Cities were destroyed, modern facilities were sabotaged, and currency use was terminated. For the Khmer Rouge, it was no longer 1975, but Year Zero. People who wore glasses or spoke foreign languages were executed without remorse. During their reign, the Khmer Rouge massacred an estimated 1.4 million people (other estimates reach as high as 2.3 million) in a horrific holocaust unknown since Adolf Hitler's gas chambers. There was no room in the new society for personal expression of any sort. People were forced to work diligently, accept poor living conditions and food rations, refrain from lavish displays of wealth, swallow their grief over the loss of loved ones, and reject their religion. Violation of these rules meant imminent execution. To avoid such a fate, about two million people fled their homeland; many died along the way.

THE VIETNAMESE INTERVENTION

For nearly four years, the world sat back and watched the death of the Cambodian people. Finally, on December 25, 1978, Vietnamese forces invaded the country, successfully driving out the Khmer Rouge within two weeks. Nevertheless, the United Nations condemned Vietnam's occupation of Kampuchea; nobody else, however, was willing to intervene. A new government was set up for the **People's Republic of Kampuchea (PRK)** under **President Heng Samrin** and **Prime Minister Hun Sen.** Many different factions resisted Vietnamese rule, including Thailand, China, and Democratic Kampuchea, represented by Sihanouk (even though he had previously distanced himself from the Khmer Rouge) before the UN Security Council. In an unbelievable move in September 1979, the UN General Assembly passed over the PRK, instead, recognizing the Khmer Rouge as the representative government of the

Cambodian people in the United Nations. By the next year, 25 countries (mostly communist regimes) had recognized the PRK as the new legitimate government, but more than 80 countries continued to regard the Khmer Rouge as the sole authority. The Heng Samrin government, despite its unpopularity among the Cambodian people and the rest of the world, tried to restore the social and economic order of Kampuchea in the face of daunting odds.

THE NEW KINGDOM OF CAMBODIA

After more than 10 years of keeping the Khmer Rouge at bay, Vietnam withdrew its forces from Cambodia in September 1989 under harsh criticism and embargo. The Paris peace agreement in October 1991 allowed the UN to deploy the **United Nations Transit Authority in Cambodia (UNTAC),** by far their largest peacekeeping force to date, to monitor the ongoing civil war and resettle refugees back into the country. They oversaw the elections for a coalition government in May 1993, ensuring for the first time that all Cambodians had a chance to vote. In September, Sihanouk returned to his country and was crowned king of Cambodia again. That same year, the PRK was renamed Cambodia in an attempt to erase the horror and pain of the Khmer Rouge era from the memories of the people.

■ Cambodia Today

The annihilation and flight of the educated elite has posed a challenge to rebuilding the internal structures of the country. Left without a skilled workforce, Cambodia is struggling to keep up with a changing global market. Since the 1993 elections, the new government, led by co-prime ministers **Prince Ranariddh** and Hun Sen, has had to face both the challenge of development and the continued threat presented by the Khmer Rouge, who attempted a coup as recently as 1994. In an effort to remove reminders of the Khmer Rouge's reign of terror from the country, the government has been debating whether to destroy some of Phnom Penh's most important monuments which were constructed during this brutal era.

Emerging from decades of war and turmoil, the Cambodian government is eager to open trade with the rest of the world. When U.S. Secretary of State Warren Christopher visited the country in August 1995, the first visit of an American government official in 40 years, the prime ministers asked him to help Cambodia obtain most-favored-nation trading status from U.S. Congress. America is willing to help Cambodia on the path to development but, in return, expects certain policies to be changed, including the legality of marijuana and the on-going human rights violations. Cambodia is expected to join the Association of Southeast Asian Nations (ASEAN) in 1997 which will significantly help its economy, as will the expected development of the Mekong River region.

With a war still raging in the countryside and a new government which, albeit freely elected, tends to be authoritarian, Cambodia remains far from attaining the peace, stability, and national cohesion which foster economic and political development. Whether Cambodia can overcome the economic and social upheavals it is experiencing and eventually become a full-fledged exporter remains to be seen.

HUMAN RIGHTS

Under the UNTAC mandate, Cambodia adhered to most major international human rights instruments and people enjoyed the basic rights they had been deprived of during the previous decades of civil war and repressive government. A free press was permitted for the first time and non-governmental organizations concerned with economic development were formed.

All that changed at the end of 1993, however, when the mandate terminated, and a new constitution was drawn up. Although some of the rights and freedoms encompassed in international human rights standards were retained, these were not entirely adhered to and recent years have seen a steady augmentation of human rights violations. While progress has been made in some areas, notably in the training in human rights standards for police and military personnel, the rights to freedom of association, assembly, and expression have of late been threatened by the Royal Government. Eager to avoid negative press, the current government has imprisoned several newspaper editors who expressed anti-government sentiments, as well as prominent critics of the government.

■ The Arts

ARCHITECTURE

The Cambodian people have inherited one of the most remarkable artistic legacies the world has ever known—the **Angkor temples.** Although Khmer art in all its forms was inspired by Indian culture, it was the genius of the native peoples that gave expression and content to their greatest achievement.

Jayavarman II, greatly inspired by the artistic traditions of Sailendra, dreamt of establishing a powerful empire that would be supported by a strong religious cult expressed through the medium of art. Sailendra monarchs claimed the title of "Mountain Kings," and Jayavarman II also wanted to enshrine himself and his descendants in a heavenly mountain. Khmer temples were consequently modeled after **Mount Meru,** the sacred mountain dwelling of the gods, which houses the king's divinity and source of power—his **linga.** The first few structures were based on the old Chenla style—brick pyramids that are sometimes tiered—until Jayavarman II brought in architects from Java and Champa to help design temples at Kulen and the Roluos.

It was not until the 10th century, however, when Kambuja finally consolidated its power that Cambodian art flourished. Built of pinkish sandstone and laterite, early temples were simple representations of Mount Meru, consisting of a tiered pyramid topped with a sanctuary. Later temples built in the 12th century, most notably Angkor Wat, evolved into ornate and grandiose affairs which represented the Hindu world in microcosm. Angkor Wat, with its walls, moat, and gates, served as a temple consecrated to Vishnu, as well as a heavenly palace for the *devaraja*. The walls enclosing temple complexes signify the earth, while the moats, canals, and *baray* (reservoirs) symbolize the oceans. Khmer buildings are usually oriented east to west, with the main gates to the east. The galleries and walls of the temples are covered with exquisite bas-relief carvings depicting scenes from Hindu epics and Khmer history. Typical Angkorian architecture also includes ornate lintels, false windows and doors, and pathways to the main entrance flanked by serpentine *naga*.

The advent of Buddhism into Khmer society did little to change the art of the kingdom; this new religion in fact thrived side by side with the Hindu cult. The only difference was that god-kings were no longer incarnations of the Hindu gods, but of Buddha himself. The reign of Jayavarman VII, marked a period of colossal Buddhist architecture, many of which are Cambodia's most famous. For more information see **Angkor,** page 95.

DRAMA AND DANCE

Aside from its famous temples, Angkor civilization also saw the birth of **classical dance,** a highly stylized dance form that has influenced both Thailand and Laos. In ancient times, the dance was a religious tradition, performed in honor of the temple gods to bring divine blessing to the king and his people. Today, classical dance is being revived in a broad artistic movement sweeping through the country.

Based on the sacred dances of the *apsaras,* the mythological celestial nymphs of ancient Cambodia, classical dance retells the great Indian epics, particularly the *Ramayana*. When Ayutthaya plundered Angkor, they took the Khmer dancers back with them and the art of classical dance in Cambodia died out. In their efforts to assert themselves over the Khmer people, however, the Thais reintroduced classical dance to the Cambodian people. The dance remained Khmer in style, with the exception of the use of elaborate masks and ornate costumes adopted by the Thais.

The national dance of Cambodia is the **lamthon,** a dance with slow graceful gestures of the hands and arms. *Lamthon* dancers are women who perform barefoot in order to execute their movements with ease and elegance. In the country, folk plays and **shadow plays** are highly loved by the people. Shadow plays, brought to Cambodia from Java by the first *devaraja*, are based on stories from the *Ramayana* and are often interwoven with Khmer legends.

OTHER ART FORMS

Cambodia's artistic tradition of **hand-weaving** has persisted for centuries. The production of the lovely material used for **sarong** and **krama** scarves remains a vibrant art form. Using crude hand-looms, village girls turn out beautiful silk and cotton in simple linear and plaid patterns, as well as more complicated designs using tie-dyed thread. Vegetable dyes are specially mixed for each **sampot** (traditional women's sarong), so that no two lengths of material are exactly the same. Cambodian craftsmen once excelled in gold and silver work and produced exquisite **jewelry** and silver boxes. Despite its popularity and demand under the French, the craft has languished in the present century.

SOUTHERN CAMBODIA

■ Phnom Penh

In Cambodia, all roads lead to Phnom Penh. Founded as a religious shrine in 1433, the capital remains the center of Cambodian Buddhism; and distances along the national highways are measured from the tall, crumbling spire of Wat Phnom's stupa. It is here that the Tonle Sap, Bassac, and Mekong Rivers converge, rivers which brought prosperity and preeminence to the Angkor court in the 12th century and, eventually, figures of a far less glorious variety in 1863: the first French explorers. Bewitched by her tranquil backwater charm, they promptly incorporated Cambodia into their *Union Indochinoise*. In the 1920s they boasted of "their" city as the "Paris of the East." Today the *colons* are long gone, but French influence has left an indelible stamp on Phnom Penh's physical and culinary landscape: yellow colonial mansions stud the broad palm-lined boulevards of the city's northern sector, while vendors still peddle warm *baguettes* each morning.

Nearly destroyed by Pol Pot's marauders, the graceful, upturned arches of Phnom Penh's many wats still dominate the skyline of a capital city that has yet to see a skyscraper. Temples which traditionally provided shelter for the destitute and disabled now also play host to some of the countless English schools opening up Phnom Penh. "Hello, how are you?" competes with the *sutra* as the most popular mantra.

Perhaps it is the recent memory of genocide that explains why Phnom Penh has yet to wholeheartedly throw itself into the capitalist rat race, as Saigon and Bangkok have already with orgiastic abandon. Unlike in her sister capitals, a 15-minute drive down Phnom Penh's Preah Monivong Boulevard will leave you standing amongst rice paddies, where the only pedestrians are grinning, half-naked children. For the moment, Phnom Penh remains in limbo—full of the influences of a rich and varied past, but as yet uncertain as to where tomorrow's road may lead.

In Cambodia, the U.S. dollar acts as a second currency and is widely accepted at many hotels, guest houses, and restaurants; in fact, some places will only take U.S. dollars. *Let's Go* lists prices in both dollars and riel. It would be wise to keep small U.S. dollar bills handy.

GETTING THERE AND AWAY

By Plane

Flights into Phnom Penh arrive at **Pochentong International Airport,** 3km west of the city. Customs, immigration, and baggage claim cost $20. Taxis downtown should cost about $7, while motorcycle taxis cost $3.

   Silk Air, 219B M.V. Preah Monivong (tel. 364 545), on the first floor of the Pailin Hotel, has daily flights to **Singapore** for $230 (open Mon.-Fri. 8am-noon, Sat. 8am-1pm). **Thai Airways,** 19 P. 106 (tel 722 335), just northwest of the Old Market, offers daily flights to **Bangkok** for $138 (open Mon.-Fri. 8am-noon and 2-4pm, Sat. 8am-noon). **Vietnam Airlines,** 35 R.V. Samdech Preah Sihanouk (tel./fax 364 460), flies daily to **Ho Chi Minh City** for $70 (open Mon.-Sat. 8-11:30am and 2-5pm). **Lao Aviation,** 58B R.V. Samdech Preah Sihanouk (tel./fax 426 563), offers two flights per week to **Vientiane** for $150 (open Mon.-Sat. 8-11:30am and 2-5pm). **Malaysia Airlines,** 172-184 M.V. Preah Monivong (tel. 426 688), on the first floor of the Diamond Hotel, has four flights per week to **Kuala Lumpur** for $190 (open Mon.-Fri. 8am-5pm, Sat. 8am-noon).

By Bus

Buses to **Ho Chi Minh City** (Saigon) are clearly marked in English and leave daily at 5am, arriving there at 3pm. Tickets should be purchased a day in advance ($6). The station is located on P. 182. To get there from the Central Market, head down M.V. Charles de Gaulle and take a right at the first traffic rotary with a crocodile and an *apsaras* in the middle. The bus station is past P. 211 on the left and the ticket office is across the street (open daily 5-10am and 2-5pm).

By Taxi

Taxis to **Vietnam** can be hired across Monivong Bridge at the taxi stand opposite the Chbam Pao Market. The three-hour ride costs $25 for the vehicle (fit as many bodies as possible into the tiny Toyota). Most travelers find they are expected to slip a Cambodian policeman a five-spot or so as a "gift." **Note:** Visas must indicate arrival by car and specify point of entry or entry will be denied.

ORIENTATION

Despite the city's small size, many tourists in Phnom Penh are overwhelmed by the complex web of poorly marked and unpaved side streets. The capital's naming system only adds to the confusion. Each of the three governments that have held power since 1975 renamed the major streets at least once, and many addresses on buildings and business cards have yet to catch up. Picturing the city as roughly triangular in shape makes navigation easier. The three main north-south boulevards start off quite close together—the point of the pyramid. Beginning at the **Tonle Sap River, Preah Sisowath Quay** traces the river bank to form the eastern leg of the triangle. **Moha Vithei Preah Norodom** (*moha vithei,* abbreviated M.V., means "boulevard") begins at **Wat Phnom** in the north and runs past the **Victory Monument. M.V. Preah Monivong,** a commercial, financial, and residential street rolled into one, runs in a roughly straight line between two traffic rotaries—one near the **Friendship Bridge** in the north and the other just before **Monivong Bridge** in the south. Most of the sights, accommodations, and restaurants are located between M.V. Preah Monivong and the Tonle Sap River. **M.V. Charles de Gaulle** runs diagonally southwest from the Central Market, forming the western leg of the triangle. Running east-west, **Rukhak Vithei Samdech Preah Sihanouk** (*rukhak vithei,* abbreviated R.V., means "avenue") and **M.V. Mao Tse Toung** link the north-south thoroughfares. South of R.V. Samdech Preah Sihanouk, the triangle widens out into the **Khmer district,** while M.V. Mao Tse Toung forms the base of the triangle. The numbered *phlauv* (small streets, abbr. P) and *vithei* (larger streets, abbr. V) tend to run east-west if they are even-numbered, and north-south if they are odd.

CAMBODIA

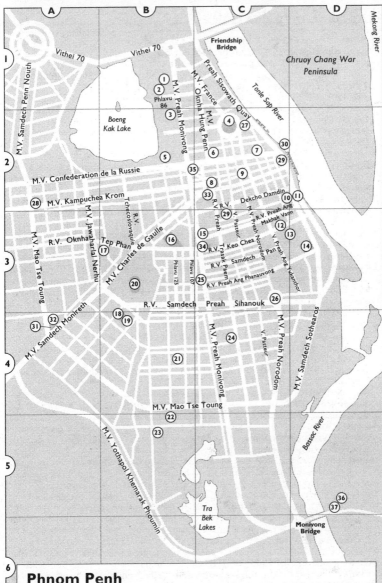

Phnom Penh

Access Medical
Services, 24
Bangkok Bank, 9
Boengkak Amusement
Park, 2
Bus Station, 32
Bus Station, 37
Bus to Ho Chi Minh
City, 17
Calmette Hospital, 1
Cambodian
Commercial Bank, 35

Central Market, 8
Chba Ampao Market, 36
Inter-City Bus Station, 18
Local Bus Station, 33
Ministry of Culture, 34
Ministry of Information, 3
Ministry of Tourism, 25
Municipal Theater, 31
National Museum of
Art, 12
Old Market, 7

Olympic Market, 19
Olympic Stadium, 20
O Russei Market, 16
Phnom Penh
Tourism, 11
Police, 29
Post Office, 27
Railway Station, 5
Royal Palace, 13
Silver Pagoda, 14
Small Boat Rental, 30

S.O.S. International
Medical Center, 28
Thai Farmers Bank, 6
Tuol Sleng Genocide
Museum, 21
Tuol Tum Pong
Market, 23
Wat Koh, 15
Wat Ounalom, 10
Wat Phnom, 4
Wat Tuol Tum Pong, 22
Victory Monument, 26

PRACTICAL INFORMATION

Tourist Offices: Phnom Penh Tourism, 313 Preah Sisowath Quay (tel. 723 949), at the convergence of Sisowath and M.V. Samdech Sothearos, in a large white colonial building. Look here for up-to-date safety information concerning travel outside the city, but no maps. Open Mon.-Fri. 7am-11:30am and 2-5:30pm. **Ministry of Tourism,** 3 M.V. Preah Monivong (tel. 426 107), on the corner of Monivong and P. 232. Provides lists of travel agencies and accommodations, as well as a few brochures. Some employees speak good English and can give tips on travel outside the capital. Open Mon.-Fri. 7:30-11am and 2-5pm. **Note:** Any information given here regarding safety outside Phnom Penh should be double-checked at western consulates or embassies.

Tourist Police: Office of Foreign Affairs (*Bureau des Etrangers*), on P. 154 off Pasteur St. Office oversees the many NGOs operating in Phnom Penh. Some English spoken. Open Mon.-Sat. 7:30-11:30am and 2-3:30pm. Any emergency should be reported to the relevant embassy immediately.

Tours and Travel: Hanuman Tourism, 188 P. 13 (tel. 428 457), just north of the National Museum. Very friendly staff speaks fluent English and can handle the most complex international flights. Open Mon.-Sat. 8am-6pm. **Diethelm Travel,** 8 P. 3 (tel. 426 648), between the Royal Palace and Wat Ounalom. Foreign staff speaks excellent English. Licensed representative for Swiss Air and local carriers. Open Mon.-Fri. 7:30-11:30am and 1:30-5:30pm, Sat. 7:30-11:30am.

Embassies and Consulates: Australia, Villa 11, P. 254 (tel. 426 000). Consular services 8am-noon and 1-4:30pm. Also handles concerns of **Canadian citizens. Lao PDR,** 15-17 M.V. Mao Tse Toung (tel. 426 441). Visa office open Mon.-Fri. 8am-noon and 2-5pm. 15-day transit and tourist visas cost $35 for citizens of the US, UK, Australia, and New Zealand. Canadian citizens $42. 3-day processing; you must leave passport with embassy. **Thailand,** 75 M.V. Preah Monivong (tel. 261 82). Visa applications available Mon.-Fri. 8:30am-noon. Visa pick up 2-5pm. 2-mo. tourist visa (1 entry $15, 2 entries $30). 3 days to process. Emergency same-day processing available. **UK,** 27-29 P. 75 (tel. 427 124). Consular services Mon.-Tues., Thurs.-Fri. 8am-noon and 1:30-5pm, Wed. 8am-1pm. Also handles concerns of **New Zealand citizens. US,** 16-18 P. 228 (tel. 426 436). Consular services Mon.-Fri. 1:00-4:30pm. Up-to-date safety info for travelers. Requests that Americans planning to leave Phnom Penh, particularly for western provinces, check with the embassy first. **Vietnam,** 436 M.V. Preah Monivong (tel. 362 531). Visa applications available Mon.-Fri. 7:30am-11am and 2:30-4pm, Sat. 7:30-noon. Single entry, 1-mo. visa $50. Visa must be stamped according to the means of entry into Vietnam to avoid being turned away at the border.

Immigration Offices: on P. 200, off M.V. Preah Norodom. Sign reads *Direction des Etrangers.* 1-week visa extensions $20, 1-mo. $30, 3-mo. $60, 6-mo. $100. 3-4 days processing. Open Mon.-Fri. 7:30-10:00am and 2-4pm, Sat. 7:30am-noon.

Currency Exchange: Cambodian Commercial Bank, 26 M.V. Preah Monivong (tel. 426 208). Head toward the train station past Monorom Hotel; it's on the right. No commission for US$. Visa and MC cash advances, minimum $100, maximum $2000 (no commission). Open Mon.-Fri. 8am-3:30pm. **Thai Farmers Bank,** 114 R.V. Kramuen Sar (tel. 724 035), north of the Central Market at the corner of P. 53. Does not exchange U.S. dollars for riel. 2% surcharge. Visa cash advances ($10 flat commission, limit of $800 per day). Open Mon.-Fri. 8am-3:30pm. The scads of **money changers** lining the sidewalks around the Central Market offer rates of about 100r higher than the banks.

American Express: Located at **Diethelm Travel,** 8 P. 3 (tel. 426 648). No surcharge on AmEx purchases and can issue traveler's checks. Also accepts Visa and MC. Open Mon.-Fri. 7:30-11:30am and 1:30-5:30pm, Sat. 7:30-11:30am.

Air Travel: Royal Air Cambodge, 206A M.V. Preah Norodom (tel. 428 055). To: **Siem Reap** (daily, $55); **Rattanakiri** (4 per week, $55); and **Sihanoukville** (3 per week, $40). Open Mon.-Fri. 8am-noon and 1-5:30pm, Sat. 8am-noon.

Trains: Station (tel. 724 115), in a large, yellow art deco building set back from M.V. Preah Monivong past Monorom Hotel. Two railway lines, one running northwest to Battambang and the other southwest to Sihanoukville. Trains for **Battam-**

bang leave every other day, stopping at **Romeas, Pursat,** and **Moung.** Trains for **Sihanoukville** also leave every other day, stopping at **Takeo** and **Kampot.** All tickets 2700r. Train service is frequently disrupted by fighting, particularly along the northwest line. **Note:** For westerners, train travel is considered highly dangerous and should be avoided as long as the current unrest persists.

Buses: Three private bus companies have recently opened in Phnom Penh. **D.H. Cambodia** (tel. 720 076), at the southeast corner of the terminal at the intersection of P. 63 and P. 154. Service to: **Sihanoukville** (7am and 2:30pm, 3hr., 12,000r); **Kampong Chnang** (6:40am, 10:30am and 2:30pm, 2hr., 5000r); **Kampong Cham** (2pm, 2hr., 5000r); and **Kampot** (7am and 12pm, 2hr., 10,000r). **G.S.T. Ltd.** has daily buses to **Sihanoukville** (7am and 1pm, 2hr., 12,0000r). Both bus companies leave from Psar Thmei. **Wing Ly Express Co.,** 26 P.199 (tel. 933 531), 3 blocks south of the Olympic Market, has daily buses to **Sihanoukville** (12,000r) and **Kampong Cham** (7:30am and 1:30pm, 2hr., 6000r). Public buses to **Pursat, Battambang,** and **Sisophan** also leave from the Central Market. Most buses leave at 5:30am. **Note:** Travel on public bus to the far-western provinces is considered highly dangerous.

Taxis: With the opening of a bus service to **Sihanoukville,** taxis are no longer the most popular way to reach the coast, but prices have dropped considerably. To **Kampot** (4hr., $4) and **Sihanoukville** ($6). Taxis congregate at the Central Market. Newer and cleaner taxis also leave from the Hotel Sofitel Cambodiana but charge higher prices. **Note:** When traveling beyond Phnom Penh by car, always leave early in the day so as to be off the roads well before nightfall.

Boats: Boat travel is a fast, fun, and safe way to reach cities along major rivers. **The Golden Sea Shipping Co.** (tel. 015 917 832), 2km beyond the Friendship Bridge along Rte. 5, offers service to **Siem Reap** (6hr., $25), **Kampong Cham** (2hr., $6), and **Kratie** (4hr., $15). Many boats overload with passengers, but Golden Sea is not known to do this and tends to be the most safety-conscious. All boats leave at 7am. Most guest houses also arrange express boat service to Siem Reap.

Local transportation: Cyclos (three-wheeled trishaws) and **motorcycle** drivers go anywhere in the city and its environs for low fares. "Moto" drivers also take passengers to sites out of town such as Choeng Ek, Tonle Bati, and Odong. For intracity rides 500-1000r is average, but expect to pay a bit more after dark. For trips to the "Killing Fields," drivers outside the Capitol Guest House tend to be best as they speak the most English.

Rentals: Lucky Lucky Motorcycles, 413 M.V. Preah Monivong (tel. 722 788), just north of the Hong Kong Hotel near Wat Koh. Rents by the day: small bikes $4, big bikes $7. Passport deposit. Open daily 7am-5:30pm.

English Language Bookstore: Bert's Books and Guest House, 79 Preah Sisowath Quay (tel. 360 806), 1 block east of the post office. Sells an eclectic range of paperbacks starting from 2300r. Carries guides to Angkor and Khmer-English dictionaries. Up-to-date safety information. Open Mon.-Fri. 7:30am-9pm.

Pharmacies: Many drug stores sporting signs with green crosses dot the streets of Phnom Penh, but travelers should be aware that a high percentage of drugs sold in these shops are either out of date or flat-out fake. Bring plenty of whatever prescription drugs you need. **Pharmacie de la Gare,** 124 M.V. Preah Monivong (tel. 426 288), just before the train station, is cleaner than most pharmacies. French and some English spoken. Open daily 6:30-11:30am and 1:30-7pm.

Hospitals: Health care and hygiene standards in Cambodia are well below those in the west. For serious medical emergencies, fly immediately to Bangkok. **Hospital Calmette,** 3 M.V. Preah Monivong (tel. 426 948), arranges ambulance service. French and some English spoken. **S.O.S. International Medical Center,** 83 M.V. Mao Tse Toung (tel. 015 912 765). Specializes in emergency care, and evacuation to Bangkok. French doctor on call 24hr. English and French spoken. Open Mon.-Fri. 8:30am-8:30pm, Sat. 8:30am-noon.

Emergency: (tel. 117). Free at phone booths.

Police: Nationale Commissariat Central (tel. 722 353). Reports of corruption within Phnom Penh's finest are widespread; even members of the government candidly advise that dealing with the police might bring more trouble than good.

Post Offices: GPO (tel. 723 500), on P. 13 past the Old Market in a large, yellow colonial building. A tall, easily visible radio tower is next door. *Poste Restante.* Overseas calls, fax, and telegram service available. Phone cards for local phone booths sold here. Open Mon-Fri. 7am-6pm, Sat.-Sun. 7am-5pm. No postal code.

Telephones: IDD calls can be made from all Telstra phone booths located at the GPO, the Ministry of Tourism, and outside many of the hotels on M.V. Preah Monivong. Pay phones do not use coins, but paper phone cards which are sold at the GPO and many hotels. **Telephone code:** 23.

ACCOMMODATIONS

Narin Guest House No. 50, 50 P.125. Take a left after the Ministry of Tourism and Narin's on the left of the fourth street after the Polo Club. More than the good food ($1-3), clean rooms, and charming neighborhood, it's the management that makes it one of Phnom Penh's best. Narin and his siblings bend over backwards for their guests. Perks include free reign of the fridge, drinking water, and stereo. Two shared bathrooms with flush toilets. Dorms $1.50. Singles $3. Doubles $5. Narin arranges transport via boat to Siem Reap.

Bert's Books and Guest House, 79 Preah Sisowath Quay (tel. 360 806), on the river 1 block west of the GPO. A friendly, laid-back place run by Bert, a great source of up-to-the-minute info on Cambodia. Guests talk for hours on the 3rd floor garden terrace overlooking the river. Clean, spacious rooms with private bathroom. Singles $5. Doubles $7. Bert's guests get discounts at several nearby restaurants. Fax and e-mail service available.

Cloud-9, 9 P. 93 (tel. 368 289), near the intersection with M.V. Preah Monivong. Guests stay for days, lolling on hammocks under the thatched roof porch built on stilts over Boeng Kak Lake, though a new reggae bar with a pool table next door may disturb the tranquility a bit. Pleasant, social atmosphere. Restaurant serves cheap food. "Business center" arranges visas to Laos and Vietnam, as well as boat tickets to Siem Reap. Dorms $2. Singles $3, with bathroom $4. Doubles $4.

City Lotus Restaurant and Guest House, 76 P. 172 (tel. 362 409), behind Monivong Hospital between P. 63 and 51. Cool and quiet, City Lotus offers hotel-quality rooms at guest house prices. All rooms have attached bathroom. Mr. Peter, the Malaysian owner, studied in the UK and speaks fluent English. The small restaurant on the ground floor serves cheap delicious food (about $3). Singles and doubles with fan $7, with A/C $10. Will add beds to singles upon request.

The Last Home, 47 P. 108 (tel. 724 917), 2 blocks west of the Old Market, diagonally across the park from the Thai Airways office. One of the finest locations in the city; the first floor beer garden overlooks a park. Bosse, the German owner, offers quality rooms with remote control fans at rock-bottom prices. Dorms $2. Singles $4. Doubles $5. Guests get free transport to and from the airport.

Amara Hotel, 176 P. 63 (362 824), on the corner of P. 282. Coming down R.V. Samdech Preah Sihanouk from the Victory Monument, P. 63 is just before Lucky Supermarket. This small colonial-style hotel has spacious, tiled, open-air hallways and rooms that are large enough to be squash courts. All rooms have bathroom, A/C, and fridge. Singles/doubles $10. Some of the rooms have fabulous views of Wat Lang Ka. "Business center" in the lobby has fax and IDD telephone service.

Capitol Guest House and Restaurant, 14 P. 182 (tel. 641 04), 1 block off Monivong just before O Russei Market. Very well-known, it's one of the older budget guest houses in Phnom Penh. Upstairs rooms are clean, if a bit shabby. Neighborhood can be loud. The owner, a veritable guest house tycoon, speaks good English. Trips to Tonle Bati, Chœng Ek, and Siem Reap can be arranged here, as can visas to Vietnam. Restaurant downstairs. Singles $3, with bathroom $4. Doubles and triples with bathroom $6 and $7 respectively.

Mid-Range Accommodations

Renakse Hotel, 44 M.V. Samdech Sothearos (tel. 722 457), opposite the grounds of the Royal Palace. This rambling, yellow stucco building is nestled back from the road amid a lush tropical garden. Relax in a creaking wicker chair in the open-air lobby and play out your *Indochine* fantasies. Rooms with dark wood paneling, bathrooms, and A/C. Current renovations may increase prices. Singles $22, doubles $27.50. Staff can arrange excursions to Siem Reap.

La Paillote, 234 P. 53 (tel./fax 426 513), across the street from the Central Market. Many come to La Paillote for the excellent French restaurant on the ground floor. For those travelers itching for a chance to dust off the credit card or use a pile of riel, La Paillote offers recently renovated rooms at $20 for a single and $30 for a double. Some of the rooms have nice views and the location is unparalleled. Includes satellite TV, fully-stocked fridge (goodies are extra, of course), A/C, and IDD phones. Reservations are advised. Visa and MC.

FOOD

For the cheapest eats in town, make tracks for one of the city's many **markets.** At 5:30pm, **food stalls** begin to materialize near Wat Koh and the Victory Monument. A number of cheap Khmer and Chinese restaurants are concentrated along M.V. Preah Monivong south of the intersection with R.V. Preah Samdech Sihanouk. More expensive local and foreign restaurants can be found along Sisowath Quay, near the Royal Palace. A popular Khmer dish is *loc lac*, a meat dish eaten with rice and particularly tasty when made with venison, and *amox* (fish cooked in banana leaves).

Phnom Khieu, 138 R.V. Samdech Preah Sihanouk, on the corner with P. 63. The proprietors owned a restaurant in France for years before returning to Cambodia. The small, intimate interior with A/C and patio shaded by a willow tree might be found on any quiet *rue* in Paris. The excellent food, however, is strictly Cambodian. Generous portions at inexpensive prices ($2.50-5). Open daily 6am-11pm.

Kim Ly Restaurant, 336 M.V. Preah Monivong, on the corner with P. 282. Hidden beneath a broad awning and tinted glass doors, Kim Ly serves fabulous food in an unassuming locale. Offers 14 soups, 8 vegetable dishes, 10 desserts, 36 western entrees, and a whopping 65 Chinese and Khmer dishes to drool over—all priced $1.50-14. Specialties include Szechuan soup ($3), king prawns with garlic ($14), and stuffed mushrooms ($3). Open daily 11am-10pm.

Apsara, 361 Preah Sisowath Quay (tel. 427 081), beneath the Foreign Correspondents' Club of Cambodia. Wicker chairs on the sidewalk invite gazing at the river. Apsara is a wonderful introduction to Cambodian cuisine. Malee, the friendly proprietor, can recommend dishes. The house speciality is *amox*. Chicken salad $2, venison *loc lac* $5. Most dishes $2-5. Open daily 11am-2:30pm and 3:30-10pm.

Raksmey Boeng Kak Restaurant (tel. 681 04), off P. 86 on the shores of Boeng Kak Lake. Take P. 86 just past the Ministry of Information; at the mosque take a right and it's about 250m down the dirt access road. Combines delicious seafood with a great location. Popular with well-heeled locals and therefore feeds few tourists. Menu has Khmer, Chinese, and French sections. The English-speaking *maître d'* can recommend local dishes, such as sauteed shrimp with lemon grass (7000r). Most dishes 7000-12,000r. Open daily 10am-10pm.

Ponlok, 319-323 Preah Sisowath Quay (tel. 426 051). This large 3-story eatery is one of the most popular in town, with balconies overlooking the river. At night the restaurant is ablaze with lights and expatriates. The Chinese and Khmer fare is excellent, especially the shrimp and noodle dishes. Traditional goodies like fried sparrow also available. Menus in French and English; has pictures if words fail. Most dishes 7000-20,000r. Open daily 11am-10pm.

Kirirom Restaurant, on the corner of P. 106 and Preah Sisowath Quay, opposite the Old Market. Kirirom is the first of several seafood joints off Sisowath along the Tonle Sap River. Come here for traditional Khmer food and a spectacular heat lightning show visible from the porch. French and English menu offers French dishes and the usual Khmer specialties in various incarnations. Try the classic smoked fish with mango (7000r). Most dishes 7000r for a regular portion and 24,000r for big boys and girls. Vegetarian dishes 3000r. Noodle soup served for breakfast. Boats can be chartered here for $10 an hour. Open daily 6am-10pm.

CAMBODIA

MARKETS

Phnom Penh supports more than seven markets, all of which serve food. The market scene is an excellent way to mingle with the Khmer people, many of whom cannot afford to eat at restaurants but readily take their day-time victuals here. Most vendors set up shop at about 6:30am, and don't leave until 5pm. For shopping, markets are best visited during the early morning hours.

The **Central Market** is the hub of Phnom Penh. Most of the major streets originate here or pass near it. A large Art Deco structure built in the 1930s, the market now barely houses half of the countless merchants who peddle their goods here. This is the place to purchase up-to-date maps of the city, regional maps, Angkor guides, and Khmer-English phrasebooks. Northeast of the Central Market along P. 108 and P. 15 is the **Old Market** (Psar Char). If you want silk by the yard, this is the place. A large number of silk dealers ply their beautiful bolts of cloth, beginning at $7 per skirt length. The atmosphere here is less touristy and the vendors less pushy.

The **O Russei Market** sprawls along the corner of M.V. Charles de Gaulle and P. 182 near the Olympic Stadium (this should not be confused with the Olympic Market located south of the stadium). The food market is one of the largest and most pungent, since a large number of the city's garlic vendors congregate here. Beyond the food, the byzantine corridors of this market proffer the usual range of goods.

Between the O Russei and Tuol Tom Pong Markets, along P. 199 south of the Olympic Stadium lies the mammoth **Olympic Market.** Just recently constructed, this cement phenomenon is cool, clean, and orderly—in short, not much fun. While there are a few silk vendors and Chinese merchants hawking fake gold jewelry, it is the Wal-Mart of Phnom Penh's market scene, and of little interest to most travelers.

Tuol Tom Pong Market (more commonly known as the Russian Market) sprawls out along P. 155 past the wat of the same name. In addition to boasting a large number of fruit vendors and food stalls, the market wins high marks for its beautiful silk and cotton print sarongs and *krama* (the combination scarf, headdress, and bathing suit). Tuol Tom Pong Market is located in the heart of the Khmer district and affords a glimpse of Phnom Penh that is largely absent in the more heavily touristed quarters north off R.V. Samdech Preah Sihanouk.

SIGHTS

Despite its colonial reputation as "Paris of the East," gung-ho sightseers and museum-goers will find a dearth of options in Phnom Penh. Indeed, all of the "sights" can easily be covered in a single day, with plenty of time for a mid-day siesta. Most guest houses can arrange a motorcycle driver to take visitors around, or one can simply be flagged down on the street. This should cost around $5, perhaps a dollar or two more for a trip out to the Choeng Ek "Killing Fields." While many government-operated tourist attractions claim to be closed on Mondays, do not despair; money talks in Phnom Penh and, as it turns out, can also open the doors of the National Museum.

Wat Phnom, the most sacred sight in Phnom Penh, is located on M.V. Preah Norodom north of the Old Market. According to legend, one Madame Penh founded a monastery atop an artificial hill here to house several statues of the Buddha that she discovered hidden inside a log. The current *wiharn,* or sanctuary, houses a number of Buddha relics, and is quite beautiful: frescoes in rich crimson and gold decorate the walls and ceiling. The small park at the base of Wat Phnom is popular with families and school children; vendors come here to peddle coconuts, soda, and mouth-watering glasses of sugarcane juice. Festivals and ceremonies are frequently conducted at the large pavilion just south of the hill.

Along M.V. Sothearos south of Wat Ounalom lies the **Royal Palace** and **Silver Pagoda** complex. The tall, yellow walls that enclose this mammoth compound prevents prying eyes from getting a good look at the magnificent architecture behind them. Unfortunately for would-be visitors, now that King Norodom Sihanouk has returned to the country, the grandeur of the palace is no longer accessible to the public. Thankfully, the Silver Pagoda still is. The entrance to the pagoda's compound is across the street from the Ministry of Justice. (Open Tues.-Sun. 7:30-11:30am and 2:30-5pm; admission $2, camera fee $2, and video camera fee $5; ticket booth tel. 255 69.) English or French guides can be hired for about $3; there is no set rate. During the brief walk from the main gate to the entrance of the pagoda, a glimpse of the Royal Palace can be had. Starting at the entrance and walking clockwise (toward the river), a series of fading frescoes portraying scenes from the *Ramayana* decorate the entire length of the wall. A large stupa holds the ashes of King Ang Duong (1845-59). The pavilion beyond it shelters a statue of King Norodom. The statue, which originally depicted Napoleon III of France, was decapitated and the head replaced with a likeness of the Cambodian king. A pavilion along the south wall contains a large golden footprint of the Buddha.

Occupying the center of the compound is the Silver Pagoda, which derives its name from the 5000 silver blocks covering the floor (most of which are now safely protected by rugs). An exquisite **emerald Buddha** dating from the 1600s surveys the room, hence the pagoda is sometimes referred to as the Temple of the Emerald Buddha or Wat Phra Kaew. Other treasures include a Buddha statue made in the likeness of King Norodom inlaid with thousands of sparkling diamonds, as well as a Burmese Buddha made from marble.

North of the Royal Palace along P. 13 is the **National Museum of Arts** (open Tues.-Sun. 8-11am and 2-5:30pm; admission $2). Although designed by a French architect, the museum is a beautiful example of Khmer-style architecture. The somewhat meager collection inside contains small statues dating mostly from the pre-Angkor period, an oddly gruesome assortment of statuary appendages, and wooden and stone figures from Angkor Wat. A central garden, framed by four symmetrical pools, contains the statue of the Leper King taken from the Terrace of the Leper King in Angkor Thom. Unfortunately, little here is labeled in English.

For a powerful glimpse into the horror of the Khmer Rouge reign, go to **Tuol Sleng Genocide Museum** on P. 103. Look for the large "Museum of Genocidal Crimes" sign on P. 350 (open daily 8-11am and 2-5pm; admission $1; photography permitted). At this former high school-turned-detention center, some 20,000 people were imprisoned and tortured; only seven are known to have survived. The rest—men, women, and children, including priests, doctors, teachers, farmers, and several foreigners—met their deaths at the "Killing Fields" of Choeng Ek. Tuol Sleng has been left largely as it was in 1979. Visitors are free to wander through the buildings, parts of which contain gruesome torture chambers complete with gory black and white photos of the victims. Most moving is the series of rooms containing nothing but pictures of the prisoners, evidence of the cold-blooded efficiency of Pol Pot's butchers. Not for the squeamish, since some of the photos were taken after death. The museum culminates with a map of Cambodia made entirely of skulls.

Revisit the legacy of Pol Pot's atrocities at the **Choeng Ek "Killing Fields,"** some 17km south of the city (open daily 8-11am and 2-5pm; admission $2). This was the end of the line for more than 40,000 victims of "Brother Number One's" brutal reign of terror. Prisoners from Tuol Sleng Detention Center were taken here for "liquidation." A stupa was erected in 1988; encased in glass are the skulls of some of the exhumed bodies, arranged by sex and age. Peace has returned to the surrounding villages, and behind the stupa, cows now graze amongst the mass grave, while bits of bone and clothing still litter the ground. (See **Reign of Terror** on page 72.)

Phnom Penh also has a number of wats, many of which were partly or wholly destroyed by the Khmer Rouge in the late 1970s. Unlike the originals, new, restored wats reflect communist architecture's penchant for concrete. They remain, however, important fixtures in the urban community, serving as schools and shelters for the poor and disabled. **Wat Ounalom,** located on the corner of P. 154 and Preah Sisowath Quay, is the headquarters of Cambodian Buddhism. Its library, destroyed by the Khmer Rouge, once housed the complete works of the Cambodian Buddhist Institute. The first temple was built in 1443 to hold one of the Buddha's hairs. **Wat Tuol**

Tum Pong, on the corner of M.V. Mao Tse Toung and P. 155 just before the market named for it, is worth a visit for those passing in the are. Students recite their lessons at the school located on the temple grounds, and budding linguists greet visitors with enthusiastic hellos. South of the Central Market on M.V. Preah Monivong lies **Wat Koh,** which is home to some of the many English schools cropping up all over the city. Native English speakers are welcomed; visitors can expect to be squired around by enthusiastic teachers and asked to give some cameo appearances in class. The rust-colored **Victory Monument** at the juncture of R.V. Samdech Preah Sihanouk and M.V. Preah Norodom is a tall Angkor-inspired structure signifying independence from the colonial yoke. It was built in 1954 following the end of French colonial rule. (See **Colonial Rule and Independence** on page 70.)

ENTERTAINMENT

For some culture beyond the usual museums and pagodas, there is little in the way of regularly scheduled entertainment. Those looking for a little relaxation rather than hard-core entertainment may want to seek out **Seeing Hands Massage** at Wat Saravan on P. 178, one block east of M.V. Preah Norodom. Founded to provide employment for blind Cambodians who face discrimination in Khmer culture, Seeing Hands created a sensation in the expat community upon opening. Try a one hour *shiatsu* massage conducted in an airy pavilion to the accompaniment of flute music for the low price of $2. Appointments may need to be made in advance. (Open Mon.-Sat. 9am-7pm.)

The other popular form of entertainment consists of dance, drama, and music. Unfortunately, finding traditional Khmer dancing here can be as difficult as finding traditional Khmer dancing in say, Varengeville-sur-mer. For budget travelers, the best bet is to inquire at the Ministry of Tourism and the Phnom Penh tourist office. The Ministry occasionally sponsors traditional music and dance performances at the **Chaktomuk Conference Hall** on Preah Sisowath Quay just north of the Cambodiana Hotel. As a last resort, the kitschy **Mekong Island Park,** intended as an "authentic showcase" of traditional Cambodian culture and sponsored in part by Tiger Beer, performs Khmer music and theater. The boat leaves from the Cambodiana Hotel daily at 9:45am and returns at 4pm. Tickets, including lunch and the shows, cost $28. For information, call the Cambodiana at 262 88.

Another option can be found at the **Magic Circus Café and Theater,** 111P. 360, which lies between the Sydney International Hotel and the Tuol Sleng Genocide Museum. When Delphine, a theater buff, first arrived in Phnom Penh four years ago, she noticed there was a shortage of venues for Cambodia's artists. Her solution was the Magic Circus—dinner theater Phnom Penh-style, with a different act each weekend (performances Fri., Sat., and Sun. at 8:30pm; admission Fri.-Sat. $2, Sun. $1). Musicians, dancers, and shadow puppeteers, to name a few, perform at the small outdoor stage. The artists are all professional, and the Circus is the only place in town with Khmer performing arts every week. Magic Circus has an artsy decor, achieved with the use of trick candles. The menu is simple and limited—couscous, chili con carne, and cheese fondue ($5).

The cheapest way to observe traditional Khmer music and dance is to visit the **Université Royale des Beaux-Arts** on P. 70 north of the French Embassy. Here, the faculty is struggling to preserve traditional Khmer art forms, which were virtually wiped out by Pol Pot and are now threatened by the increasing popularity of television and imported films and music. Students come to the dilapidated campus to learn the *apsaras* dance, Khmer flute music, and scenes from the *Ramayana.* Quiet, unobtrusive foreigners are welcome. Classes are taught Mon.-Sat. 7-11am. To get there, head north on Monivong and take a left at the rotary—slightly beyond the Thai Embassy. The university is on the right about 20m past the intersection.

Another way to observe Cambodian culture is to take an evening stroll along the **Tonle Sap River.** Every evening at around 6pm many families gather to relax and picnic. Food stalls sell snacks near the pavilion opposite the Royal Palace. Devotees flock to two small shrines flanking the pagoda, and street musicians often entertain the orderly crowds with traditional Khmer music. This area, roughly from the pavilion to Kirirom Restaurant, is well-lit by Phnom Penh standards (meaning there are functioning street lamps), and children cavort on the lawn until 8 or 9pm. Inquire at your guest house for the latest line on safety in the city after dark.

NIGHTLIFE

Beyond a preponderance of seedy fly-by-night "discos" catering to sins of the flesh, Phnom Penh's night scene is fairly meager. There are several very mellow, rather expensive bars and a few late-running restaurants. Most of the bars are quite clearly either Cambodian or foreign. Residents report that Khmer bars can get quite rowdy.

CAMBODIA

Dis, 46 P. 78, 2 blocks west of the National Museum, opposite Wat Saravan. Recently opened, Dis is owned by Alex and Ali, 2 transplanted Connecticut Yankees. Their aim was to capture the feel of a Lower East Side Manhattan bar. Free pool and some of the hippest tunes in town are the chief incentives to go. Drinks $1.60-3. Angkor on tap $1.20. No cover. Popular with young expats and travelers alike. Doesn't really start happening until 10 or 11pm. Open daily 9pm-3am.

Heart of Darkness Café, 26 P. 51, near the corner of P. 51 and 173. The name says it all. This rather run-down bar features a wonderfully hokey demonic decor, complete with black "hearts of darkness" covering the lamps, and a stone head of Jayavarman VII bathed in red light. The stereo blasts sweet American and British rock music, and a bald pool table stands in the back room. Beer $1.50, mixed drinks $1.50-3. No cover or minimum. Laid-back management. The preeminent backpacker/English teacher hangout. Open daily 7pm-2am.

Foreign Correspondent's Club of Cambodia (FCC), 363 Preah Sisowath Quay (tel. 427 757), north of the Royal Palace on the river. It's the preeminent expat/journalist/NGO haunt. Boisterous and cool, FCC has more booze than a Kennedy family reunion. Mixed drinks $3.20-3.80. Serves Tiger, Guinness, Heineken, and Angkor beer. Serves trendy yuppie-nosh like hummus, baba ghanoush, and sundried tomato focaccia ($3-7). English-language films shown every Sunday 5:30 and 8pm ($2). Bar with pool, air hockey, and football downstairs. IDD and fax services available. Open daily 7am-until the last customers straggle home.

Rock Café, 315 Preah Sisowath Quay (tel. 223 88), on the river north of the Royal Palace near Ponlok. Much more mellow than Heart of Darkness, Rock Café is a great place to quaff a beer or two with friends. Bona fide satellite-TV equipped bar inside. Pool table and good music. During happy hour (6-7pm) all drinks $1, after that $1.50. Margarita pitcher $8. The western food is cheaper than at most places ($1.50-3). Open daily 9:30am-2am.

Cactus, 94 R.V. Samdech Preah Sihanouk, west of the Victory Monument near Lucky Supermarket. Look for the illuminated green cactus out front. Owned by Luc, a Frenchman from Tahiti, Cactus is one of the primary Francophone bars in this former French possession, and very popular on the weekends. The decor is quaint *faux* Taco Bell. Cocktails $3-5, *apéritifs* from $2.50. The beer list includes Guinness, Kronenberg, and Miller ($2.50). Full-service restaurant with an all-you-can-eat couscous fest every Tuesday night ($9). The salad bar ($2) is also stuff-your-face. Open daily 9:30am-2am.

SHOPPING

While perhaps not yet a shopper's paradise, Phnom Penh is by no means purgatory either. Exploring the city's chaotic, pungent markets is often far more fun and rewarding than the purchase itself. Of course, there are other venues for the serious shopper in search of higher quality products.

Wat Than Handicrafts, on M.V. Preah Norodom just before the Royal Air Cambodge office. Part of an effort to aid some of the more than 35,000 men and women disabled by land mines in Cambodia. Participants are trained in a certain skill, such as tailoring, weaving, or carpentry, and their products are sold at the Wat Than showroom. Items include silk pillows, clothing, and pocketbooks (prices start at around $3). Tailor-made outfits are also available upon special order. For those with large backpacks, fine furniture can also be ordered. Open Mon.-Sat. 7:30am-5:30pm.

Sambath Neary Khmer (tel. 018 813 583), on the corner of P. 136 and 63, facing the south side of the Central Market. For shoppers seeking some serious silk, this small outfit sells raw Cambodian and Thai silk in a plethora of patterns. Material is sold in skirt lengths, beginning at $20. One piece is enough for two skirts. The helpful proprietors can recommend tailors to have the silk made into stunning outfits. Open daily 7am-5pm.

■ Near Phnom Penh

Many travelers often slight the ruins outside of Phnom Penh in favor of the much more impressive temple complex of Angkor. Nonetheless, there are several worthwhile sights, each of which can be easily visited in half a day. The easiest way to reach them is by motorcycle; most drivers take tourists for about $10-15 depending on the distance. It is possible to rent personal transportation, but this is not advised, as the ruins tend to be located a bit off the beaten track, and can be difficult to find. Expeditions are best mounted early so as to minimize the number of hours spent on the back of an uncomfortable bike along dusty roads in searing heat.

Ta Phrom and **Yeah Peau Temple** are located 32km south of Phnom Penh along Rte. 2. The turn-off is on the right; look for a gate with three large Angkor-inspired towers. The first Phrom temple was constructed in the 7th century. The current one is believed to have been erected during the rule of Jayavarman VII (1191-1218). Built of laterite and sandstone in the Bayon style, the workmanship, which is at times shoddy, contrasts markedly with both Phnom Chissor temple and Angkor Wat. Originally constructed as a Brahmanic temple, it was later reconsecrated as a Buddhist one. The lintel above the north gate depicts the mythical stirring of the sea. The false windows with half-drawn curtains carved in the main, cross-shaped sanctuary are unique in Khmer architecture.

The nearby lake of **Tonle Bati** is a popular weekend retreat for urbanites. For a few thousand riel, small, elevated thatched-roof shacks can be rented along the water's edge. Vendors offer beer, fried chicken, and sundry other tasty treats.

Twenty-two km down the road, **Phnom Chissor** temple rises high above the pancake-flat plains of Takeo Province. The turn-off is on the left just beyond a district high school. From there, a dusty dirt track winds 6km through a small village and past lush rice fields to the foot of the *phnom*. The kings had elephants, but now visitors must walk up the 500-plus steps. The view more than compensates for the schlep, though, as Takeo Province spreads out beneath it. Built in 1150 of laterite and sandstone, the temple was a regular stop on the god-king pilgrimage circuit. The central sanctuary houses the original reclining Buddha statue. In order to protect it from thieves, however, the monks have hidden it behind a cluster of new images. The original can only be viewed by clambering back into the tiny sanctuary with a candle, which is cheerfully provided for a 500r tip.

Facing east forming a direct line with Phnom Chissor stand two laterite gates, **Sen Thomol** and **Sen Ravang.** On their way to Phnom Chissor, the Brahman priests would bathe in Tonle Oun, the sacred lake in front of the first gate. The original steps are still visible leading down to the gates. Tragically, this lovely temple was nearly destroyed in 1973 when U.S. aircraft from South Vietnam bombed the surrounding region in search of the Viet Cong. The modern pagoda next to the ruins houses a very valuable statue of the Buddha. The resourceful monks, to guard against art thieves, spray painted the stone statue silver. It is the fat one in the center surrounded by other more modern images.

The Foxy Madame

According to legend, an Angkor king, passing through the hamlet of Tonle Bati, spied the foxy young Madame Peau. As it was his prerogative as god-king, he lay down with her and then continued on his royal way. The resulting child, a boy named Phrom, went to live at the Angkor court. When he returned years later, he too spotted the lovely Peau, who had not aged. Blissfully ignorant of her true identity, he proposed. Peau, horrified, suggested that the men and women of the village have a race to see who could build a temple fastest. Phrom readily agreed, but his team of young studs was bested by the cunning maidens. Phrom's temple has better withstood the test of time, however, for Peau's temple is now nothing but a pile of rubble.

ODONG

Be aware that bands of soldiers frequently supplement their $12 per month salary by setting up impromptu road blocks on the way to Odong. Often they choose not to harass foreigners, but if they do, travelers should just fork over 1000r and let the driver do the talking.

Forty km north of Phnom Penh along Rte. 5 is the historic capital of **Odong.** Here Cambodia's monarchs ruled between 1618 and 1866. A small Buddhist community of six monks lives at the back of **Phnom Preah Reach Throap** (the tall ridge running roughly north-south) and tends the ruins. The main attraction is the ruins of **Phnom Chet Ath Roeus,** a large *wiharn* built in 1911 during the reign of King Sisowath. Originally, the brick and stone structure housed a large statue of the Buddha, which was demolished along with the sanctuary by the Khmer Rouge in 1977. Today it is a popular weekend getaway and families from the city picnic in the stand of trees at the base of the hill, visiting the temple to take in the spectacular view and carve their initials into the rubble.

Farther down the ridge are three tall stupas, the first of which houses the ashes of King Monivong (1927-41). Several smaller, crumbling stupas are visible below the main ridge at its northernmost extremity. Locals believe that a large, vicious tiger and probably several deadly cobras inhabit these structures. At the base of the ridge is a pavilion housing the bones of some Khmer Rouge victims. Odong was the site of pitched fighting between Khmer Rouge and Vietnamese forces in the late 70s. Although authorities report the area has been completely de-mined, care should be taken to stay on well-trodden paths. The dirt access road to Odong is opposite a Cambodian People's Party office on the left.

The road to Odong passes several small mosques, a testament to the large Cham minority that remains in Cambodia despite ruthless Khmer Rouge persecution. Most of them merit little more than a glance, but **Nur Ul-Ihsam Mosque,** located about 38km from Phnom Penh near Odong, should be explored, if only briefly. Built more than 50 years ago, the mosque was trashed by Pol Pot's marauders. Since restored, it now holds prayer five times per day. The local population is quite open, and visitors are welcome to observe the noontime prayers.

■ Sihanoukville (Kompong Som)

No part of Cambodia, outside Phnom Penh, has seen more rapid change since the 1992 peace accords than Sihanoukville. During the Pol Pot years, the city was virtually destroyed; it was rebuilt with Soviet assistance during the 80s (which explains some of the classic neo-Stalinist architecture). Now, as the country's only deep-water port, this city of 30,000 inhabitants may well be the key to the kingdom's economic survival, particularly as long as the border with Thailand remains closed to legal commerce. Tourism development has also followed apace; in 1992 there were four hotels on the peninsula, now there are more than 30. The real reasons for this building boom are the miles of white sand and turquoise water which surround the town on three sides. Tourism officials in Phnom Penh speak wistfully of the day when Sihanoukville will become an international resort *à la* Phuket, Thailand. Until then, however, Sihanoukville's beaches remain largely deserted and the visitor's only dilemma will be deciding where on the vast strip of silica to lay out a blanket. Sihanoukville is an ideal spot to hang with the rucksack and spend a few days lolling in the sun and feasting on cheap seafood. Keep in mind that the rainy season means business here, and sunny days can be in short supply between May and October.

GETTING THERE AND AWAY

Now that the U.S. Agency for International Development has completed rebuilding Rte. 4, reaching Sihanoukville has never been easier. Deluxe **air conditioned buses** complete with free water and karaoke now can be found on the road from Phnom Penh several times a day (3hr., $5). See **Practical Information** below for details. **Shared-taxis,** previously the only way to get there by road, can still be hired for about $6 one way from the Central Market. Although the route is now considered safe, always make sure to be off the road well before sunset. Royal Air Cambodge flies to Sihanoukville three times per week ($40 one way). Sihanoukville is also accessible by train from Phnom Penh, but this is not considered wise for foreigners.

ORIENTATION

Travelers may find it tough to get their bearings in Sihanoukville, primarily because the town is so spread out, encompassing a large, hilly spit of land jutting out into the Gulf of Thailand. The bus companies usually disgorge their passengers along a narrow street bordering a park. One block south of the park is **Vithei Ekareach** (Independence Rd.), Sihanoukville's main drag. It runs roughly east-west through the center of town, intersecting **Vithei Sophakmongkol** at the Sorya Hotel. After about 2km (heading east), Ekareach takes a large bend, passing the **hospital** and several hotels before ending at a large **rotary** topped by gaudy golden lions. Taking a left at the rotary brings you to **Hoachateol Beach;** turning right leads to **Sokkha Beach.** The two most popular guest houses and the **international post** are located about 2km west of town. Maps are available at Sam's Guest House.

PRACTICAL INFORMATION

Tourist Offices: At the opposite end of the park from the Cambodian Farmer's Bank, look for the large blue sign. Even less helpful than its big brother in Phnom Penh. The well-meaning staff speaks some English but has no maps (this will change soon) and almost no information. Open Mon.-Fri. 7-11:30am and 2-5pm. **Sam's Restaurant and Guest House** runs an informal information service and can give you the latest on the safety situation.

Currency Exchange: Cambodian Farmer's Bank, (tel. 724 705), on V. Sophakmongkol on the hill on the way into town. Changes traveler's checks to riel at no commission. Open Mon.-Fri. 8am-3:30pm. **Cambodian Commercial Bank** (tel. 5593 12), on V. Ekareach about 300m before the Sorya Hotel. MC, Visa cash advance (no commission) and traveler's checks. Open Mon.-Fri. 8am-3pm.

Buses: Three bus companies offer daily bus service to Phnom Penh, all are located near the park 1 block north of the Sophakmongkol-Ekareach intersection. **DH Cambodia Group,** opposite the Cambodia Farmer's Bank (4 per day, 6:45am-2pm, 3hr., 12,000r). **Wing Ly** (tel. 933 531), on the park near the tourist office (3 per day, 7am-noon, 3hr., 12,000r).

Air Travel: The airfield is 30km north of the city on the road to Phnom Penh.

Trains: Station, northwest of town near the port. Trains to **Phnom Penh** every other day. **Warning:** Train travel is considered highly unsafe for westerners.

Ferries: Daily ferries to **Koh Khong** leave from the pier at Tumnoprolork village (12:30pm, 2hr., 500r).

Rentals: Motorbikes can be rented from **Mealy Chenda Guest House** ($6 per day) or the **Violet English School** on V. Sophakmongkol next to the Cambodian Farmer's Bank ($6 per day). Violet English school also rents **cars** ($20 per day, with driver $25 per day).

Local Transportation: Short of renting your own wheels, motorcycle taxi is the most efficient way to get around. From the bus companies to Mealy or Sam's should cost 1000r. If you're staying at one of the more far-flung establishments and need to get into town early, it might be wise to arrange in advance for a moto to pick you up, as they can be hard to find outside town.

Markets: Sihanoukville's **Central Market** (Psar Loer) is more a spot for local-color fanatics than shop-aholics unless, of course, you're in the market for fake wrist watches, fake gems, or fake designer clothes. The mammoth **food section,** however, is very real, and sprawls at the back of the market as do a number of noodle shop stalls. Open daily 5am-6pm. A raucous **night market (**open 6-11pm) sets up just north of the Central Market near the Okinawa Thmey Hotel.

Medical Services: The **public hospital** is located on the left, on the eastern end of V. Ekareach, 2km from the center of town. Some English spoken.

Police: (tel 348 574) on V. Ekareach. On the hill about 1km west of the center of town. No English spoken.

Post Offices: At the western end of town near Victory Beach. From Sam's Guest House walk toward the port. Take a right at the large white building with the green roof; the post office is on an alley behind it. Telephone services to Phnom Penh—sometimes. Open Mon.-Fri. 7-11am and 2:30-5pm.

Telephones: Overseas calls can be placed from the **business center** on the first floor of the Thmorda Hotel next to the Sorya Hotel on V. Ekareach (tel. 343 287). **Telephone code:** 015.

ACCOMMODATIONS

Despite the glut of hotels in Sihanoukville, there are few decent budget accommodations. During the week, when most of the larger hotels stand empty, good deals can be had on air-conditioned rooms.

Sam's Restaurant and Guest House, 2km from town on the road to the port, above Independence Beach. A bit far from town, but Vic, the British owner, may pay your moto fare from the bus stop. The restaurant serves up some of the best guest house food around, including plenty of vegetarian dishes (most plates $2.50). During the high season, Vic runs popular snorkeling trips to the islands off Sihanoukville, topped off with a seafood barbecue on the beach. Dorms $2. Wooden rooms with double bed and attached bath $6 (low season $4).

Mealy Chenda Guest House, on the bluff above Independence Beach, 2km from the center of town. Mealy Chenda's new rooftop restaurant has a magnificent view of the numerous emerald islets and the international port spread out below. If their hilltop rooms are full, they have overflow rooms in another building near the post office. Singles with shared bathroom $3. Doubles $5.

Angkor Inn (tel. 034 320 027), on a dirt side street 1 block west of the Sorya Hotel, opposite the Angkor Arms pub. Near the top of the guest house hierarchy, the Angkor Inn offers new, squeaky clean rooms with hotel quality amenities. The locals come for the pool in the lobby. Rooms with one double bed, flush toilet, and shower $6, with A/C and hot water $8.

Kompong Som Hotel (tel. 034 933 551), on V. Ekareach diagonally opposite the Hawaii Hotel near the center of town. A recent addition to Sihanoukville's growing horde of cookie-cutter-style Chinese hotels. The comfy leather armchairs in the lobby are as homey as it gets. Spacious, nearly-sterile rooms with A/C and flush toilet/shower for $10, with two single beds $13. Triples $15.

Okinawa Thmey Hotel (tel. 015 917 721). From the Central Market head north on the market road; at the intersection turn right and the hotel is across the street, right in the middle of the noisy night market. The bright red carpeting in the halls seems a bit presumptuous given Okinawa's decidedly un-grand appearance. Nonetheless, for those who can't find a room at other guest houses, this is the next best deal. Clean but shabby rooms with bathroom and fan $5. Larger rooms with TV, fridge, and A/C $10. Even larger rooms with same features $15.

FOOD

Both of the guest houses on Victory Beach boast wide selections of cheap Khmer and western food, thus many backpackers elect to take their meals here. The more adventurous should head for Sihanoukville's **night market,** one block north of the Central Market, where noodle dishes and fruit shakes abound (open daily 6-11pm). Additional **food stalls** crop up along V. Ekareach near the center of town (6-11pm).

Claude's, at the far eastern end of Hoachateol Beach, next to the Seaside Hotel. Since opening four years ago, Claude's has become a Sihanoukville legend, serving excellent French cuisine. Seafood is the speciality; grilled shrimp $6 and Dieppe-style fish (cooked in a clay pot with white wine sauce) $6.50. Pleasant bar area attracts a francophone crowd. Claude also runs snorkeling and diving expeditions; ask at the restaurant. Open daily 7:30am-when everyone goes home.

Koh Pos Restaurant, at the southwestern-most tip of the peninsula between the Independence Hotel and Victory Beach. Where Prime Minister Hun Sen goes to eat when he's in town, and it's no wonder: situated on a secluded beach just inches from the water, people come more for the scenery and the view than the food. Mostly seafood (2-8000r). Stuffed crab 3000r, grilled fish with lemon 8000r. If you're going by motor taxi, arrange for your driver to meet you afterwards, otherwise it'll be tough finding transportation. Open daily 9am-9:30pm.

Angkor Arms (tel. 015 342 695), on the corner of V. Ekareach 1 block south of the Sorya Hotel and diagonally opposite the Hawaii Hotel. Center of the expat scene, it's one of the few places in town where you can drink a beer free from pushy taxi girls and karaoke. Excellent pizza ($7), sandwiches ($2.50), and pasta ($4). A slew of beers and liquors you won't find elsewhere in this neck of the woods (Baileys, Kahlua, etc.) $2-5 per shot. Open daily 4pm-midnight.

SIGHTS

As far as tourism is concerned, Sihanoukville's *raison d'etre* are the miles of sugary sand that ring the town on three sides. There is little for hard-core sight-seers or culture-vultures to sink their teeth into. There is no excuse, however, for not making a pilgrimage to **Wat Ckottanien,** which sits atop the high ridge between the town and the port; the views from the balcony of the monks quarters are spectacular. To get there, head north on the road to Phnom Penh, take a right at the Cambrew brewery, and follow the dirt road up the ridge. The wat is about 1km from the brewery. Several hundred meters beyond the temple, past a cellular phone antennae, and the oddly situated water treatment facility, the panoramic view of the city, the bay, and the port is even more breathtaking.

BEACHES

Despite the hotel-building boom that has rocked Sihanoukville since the peace agreement, the town's gorgeous beaches have been mercifully spared the kind of development which blights so many beaches in Southeast Asia. Beyond the odd seafood joint or refreshment vendors, they have been left largely as nature intended them (jet skis, thankfully, have been banned, at least for the time being). During the week travelers can expect to have the sand and the waves virtually to themselves.

There are three principle beaches that ring the town's southern half. All are about the same in terms of quality (sand, cleanliness, etc.). All of them are several km from town, and most accommodations are easily reached by motorbike. At the southeastern-most end of the peninsula is **Hoachateol Beach.** Not frequented much by locals but popular with guests of the medium-sized Seaside Hotel across the road, it is virtually empty during the low season. Further west is **Sokkha Beach,** by far and away the most popular. Some locals claim it has the softest sand. The concentration of food stalls can get pretty thick, but they remain unobtrusively out of sight beneath the palm trees. At the far end of Sokkha Beach sits the **Sokkha Restaurant** with nearly 30 different kinds of seafood to feast on (5000-12,000r). Windsurfers and inner tubes can be rented from a little stack under the pine trees just beyond the restaurant (windsurfers $3 per hour). Just down the road and around a rocky neck is **Independence Beach,** which is not as nice as Hoachateol or Sokkha, but has overgrown gardens and crumbling sculptures. Still, the water is clean and clear and there aren't as many vendors as on Sokkha. The old **Independence Hotel** sits atop the small bluff at the end of Independence Beach. Built in the early 60s, it has since been abandoned, although the tropical gardens that line the driveway are still beautiful. Now the place exudes a slightly spooky feel, as if it could be the site of a Stephen King novel. **Victory Beach** has little to recommend itself; just down shore from the post, its sand is frequently littered with trash and debris.

NORTHERN CAMBODIA

■ Siem Reap

Siem Reap is to Angkor what Kathmandu is to the Himalayas, a gateway city to one of the world's greatest attractions. The city marks an important victory for the Khmers over their neighboring enemies in a long, constant war during the 14th century; the name Siem Reap means "Siamese Defeated." During the 1950s the khaki-clad set braved the heat and mosquitoes for a glimpse of the magnificent ruins (before scurrying back to the Grand Hotel for a few icy mint juleps, of course). Cambodia's searing 20-year tragedy, during which Siem Reap was nearly destroyed, proved just a nightmarish interlude; the ink was scarcely dry on the 1991 peace accords before hotels and guest houses began to sprout up at a rate even the god-king's builders would have admired. Being a one-hit wonder doesn't bother Siem Reap, not when its single hit happens to be a stupendous world attraction. For travelers who struggle through Phnom Penh's chaotic, dusty streets, suffer eight-hour "express" boat trips, and vertebrae-crunching truck rides, reaching Siem Reap can be a little like arriving at the Emerald City.

Despite its position as the gateway to Angkor, Siem Reap remains to a large extent a small provincial seat: only a few of the streets have names; fewer still are paved. Perhaps most refreshing about the town is the warmth of its people. Despite years of oppression and hardship, locals have retained a real pride in their town and its magnificent heritage. They know that the sweaty flat-footed foreigners are here only to experience and share in that treasure, not to take advantage of their children. A compliment, no matter how rudimentary or simple, never fails to evoke a smile of pride and understanding in return.

GETTING THERE AND AWAY

Presently there are only two routes to Siem Reap: by **boat** up the Tonle Sap River and across the lake, or by **plane.** Upon arrival at the dock, touts will likely descend on tourists. The standard fare into town is $2, but most moto or taxi drivers wave the fee in an effort to woo travelers to a particular guest house; wherever you stay, however, they still get a commission. Visitors are under no obligation to stay at a particular establishment. Taxis ($3 per person) and motorcycles ($1) can take tourists into town. Because plane tickets are relatively cheap, many travelers choose to take the boat up to Siem Reap and then fly out, which gives them more time to explore Angkor's glories. There's a $5 arrival and departure airport tax.

ORIENTATION

Fresh from the maze-like side streets of Phnom Penh, travelers to Siem Reap should have about as much trouble finding their way around town as Christopher Columbus would have sailing to the other side of his jacuzzi. The only tricky thing is that almost none of the streets are named or numbered. Heading north from Tonle Sap, the road forks at the **old bus station** into **Vithei Sivutha** on the left, and the **west bank river road** on the right. Most guest houses listed stretch out along the southern section of V. Sivutha. About 2km later, Sivutha intersects **Route 6,** which runs west to the **airport** and east to the **Central Market.** The very peaceful west bank river road passes the **post office** before also intersecting with Rte. 6. This road runs past the traffic circle, the Grand Hotel, and on to Angkor Wat 7km down. Another road follows the east bank of the **Siem Reap River.** The dirt road one block east of the river road is **Vithei Wat Bo,** an important road for backpackers to know, as several of the most popular guest houses are located here. V. Wat Bo intersects Rte. 6 just east of the east bank river road intersection.

PRACTICAL INFORMATION

Tourist Offices: (tel. 579 96), opposite the Grand Hotel on the road to Angkor Wat. Short on printed information and maps, but many of the employees here speak good English. Tickets to the temples can be purchased here (1-day $20, 2-days $40, 1-week $60). Motorcycle with driver $7-10 per day. Car and driver $25 per day also available. Guides licensed with the Guide Association of Khmer Angkor (English, French, and Chinese) can be hired for $20 per day. Open Mon.-Fri. 7:30-11:30am and 2-5pm, Sat. 7:30-11:30am.

Currency Exchange: National Bank of Cambodia (tel. 015 914 009), just off V. Sivutha beyond Bakheng Hotel. Exchanges traveler's checks at 2% commission. No commission on dollars to riel exchange. Open Mon.-Fri. 7:30am-4pm. **Cambodian Commercial Bank** (tel. 015 914 442), south of Hotel de la Paix along V. Sivutha. Visa and MC cash advances; 2% commission on traveler's checks exchange; no commission for dollars to riel. Open Mon.-Fri. 8am-3pm.

Tours and Travel: Diethelm Travel, 4 Rte. 6 (tel. 963 5244), about 2km west of the river on the left opposite Angkor Tourism. Tickets to **Bangkok** should be purchased 1 week in advance. Organizes pricey package tours. Open Mon.-Sat. 7-11am and 2-5:30pm. **Royal Air Cambodge,** 362 Rte. 6 (tel. 963 422), 0.5km west of the intersection with V. Sivutha on the left just before Diethelm Travel. Tickets to **Phnom Penh** (daily, 8am and 2:30pm, $55 one way) can be purchased up to 1 day in advance. Open Mon.-Fri. 8am-noon and 2-4pm, Sat. 8am-noon.

Pharmacies: There are several small pharmacies along Rte. 6 east of the bridge on the way to the market.

Medical Services: Siem Reap Provincial Hospital, along a side street off V. Sivutha. Heading north, take a right at Cambodian Commercial Bank; it's opposite the Apsara Tours branch office. Cambodian doctors are on call Mon.-Fri. 7-11am and 2-5pm, Sat. 6am-noon. Some French, but little English spoken. Travelers requiring serious medical treatment should return to Phnom Penh immediately.

Police: On the corner of Rte. 6 and V. Sivutha. Little English spoken.

Post Offices: GPO (tel. 063 963 441), along the west bank of the Siem Reap River just north of the Cambodian People's Party office. *Poste Restante* is a shot in the dark. Open daily 7am-5pm.

Telephones: International calls can be made from the **post office,** which has the cheapest rates in town ($5 per minute). Siem Reap's new Telstra phone booths also make international calls with a phone card ($4.80 per minute). The **Angkor International Communications** center (tel. 963 444) on V. Sivutha just before the intersection with Rte. 6 offers fax and phone service ($8 per minute). Calls can be received without charge.

ACCOMMODATIONS

Just four years ago, Siem Reap boasted only four guest houses. Today there are over 30, with more on the way. Guest houses run the gamut from sumptuous mahogany and teak affairs to dirty, unkempt Attica-style boarding houses. Countless accommodations line V. Sivutha north of the Hotel de la Paix. Three new guest houses with higher rates ($10-20 per night) congregate on V. Sivutha near Monorom Restaurant. They have nicer rooms than many of the low-end hotels.

The Mahogany Guest House, 0593 V. Wat Bo (tel. 630 086), about 30m south of the intersection with Rte. 6. The setting, in a large mahogany house with the finest veranda in town, is its biggest advantage. Two buffalo heads with blinking red eyes add a touch of the bizarre. Small rooms, but neat as a pin, and the rich wood walls more than make up for size. Shared bathrooms. Beer, water, and soda in the fridge. Singles on ground floor $4, upstairs $5. Doubles $5 and $6, respectively.

Sun Rise Guest House No. 592, 592 V. Wat Bo (tel. 015 635 883), between Mom's Guest House and Mahogany Guest House. Newly wed managers Keo and Sophanney speak good English and keep the atmosphere cheery and cozy. The 10 rooms are picture-perfect: high ceilings, funky red-and-green floor paper, and a few pictures of favorite Khmer pop divas. Shared bathrooms and baths with mounted shower heads. Drinking water available. Singles $4. Doubles $5.

Apsaras Angkor Guest House No. 279, 279 Rte. 6 (tel. 015 914 494), about 50m west of the bridge past the Grand Hotel, opposite an old wat near Chenla Guest House, set back from the main road. Apsaras' plentiful rooms and excellent services have made it a favorite. Two buildings: rooms in the original house are small and dark but homey, while rooms in the new building are larger, lighter, and airier but more institutional. Clean and sweet-smelling bathrooms. All 18 rooms have monster ceiling fan and portable closet. Singles $5. Doubles $7. Triples $6. A small restaurant serves good, cheap food (800-4000r).

Chenla Guest House No. 260, 260 Rte. 6, about 50m west of the bridge past the Grand Hotel on the left opposite an aging wat. Owned by the sister of Narin (of Guest House No. 50 fame in Phnom Penh), Chenla continues the family tradition of cheap, clean rooms in an intimate, friendly environment. Those in the front building are slightly cramped. Rooms in the back building are larger, lighter, and painted a smurfy robin's egg blue. Shared bathrooms, with flush toilets and showers, are spotless. All rooms have fans. Singles $2. Doubles $4. Recently completed third building boasts gorgeous rooms with A/C and private bath $15.

Mom's Guest House, 0099 V. Wat Bo, adjacent to Sun Rise Guest House. "Mom" may have a large family, but there's room in her heart for you, too. The owner keeps the mahogany floor spotless. Beds sport garish Barbie-skirt pink covers with matching mosquito nets. Large ceiling fans are loud but keep the small rooms cool. Shared bathrooms. Two doubles with bath are located in Mom's sister's house. While more pricey, they are brand new, with tiled floors and double windows. Drinking water is on Mom. Singles $5. Doubles $6.

Garden House, 0129 V. Wat Bo, opposite Bayon Restaurant just south of the intersection with Rte. 6. Set back from the road amid a tropical garden, this small guest house has a Swiss Family Robinson-type atmosphere in a traditional Khmer-style house. Intimate and friendly. Ideal for travelers who shun the beer-drinking socializing of larger establishments. Owners speak fluent French. All rooms have windows, doubles have ceiling fans. Shared bathrooms. Singles $5. Doubles $6.

Green Garden Home, 051 V. Sivutha, about 200m south of the intersection with Rte. 6; look for the blue sign. Owned by a friendly, francophile couple, who maintain 4 airy double rooms with private bathrooms, full-length mirrors, and towels. The fruit tree and flower garden, however, is the real jewel. All rooms are doubles ($6, with A/C $12). Rooms in the newly constructed guest house with a lovely garden terrace $8, with A/C $12. Free drinking water.

Vimean Thmei Hotel, 012 V. Sivutha (tel. 963 494), at the southern end of V. Sivutha. The least expensive of the three mini-hotels in the area. Clean, spacious, no-frills rooms. All rooms with flush toilet and shower. Rooms with 2 beds and fan $10, with A/C $15. Larger rooms with A/C $20.

FOOD

Don't expect too much variety from Siem Reap's many inexpensive restaurants, but count on filling, satisfying Khmer, Chinese, and Thai dishes for under $3. Many establishments cater primarily to visitors; those who wish to mix with the locals can head to the small **night market** on V. Sivutha opposite the old bus station. Here, delicious Khmer meals of noodles can be had for 4000r. A small **fruit market** is next to the market. **Food vendors** also line the east bank of the river south of Rte. 6.

Arun Restaurant, along the east bank of the river about 50m north of the intersection with Rte. 6 on the right. An exemplary open-air restaurant, Arun has gained a large following among the backpacker crowd for its good Cambodian and Chinese food at rock-bottom prices (average $2) and Bayon-size portions. Try the fried chicken in coconut cream—a Khmer Khlassic. Open daily 10am-10pm.

Chhouk Rath Restaurant, on the corner of V. Sivutha and Rte. 6. The owners and their children run the show, and the kids will be happy to arrange a duel between their pet Siamese fighting fish. But the main event is the excellent Khmer, Thai, and western food at knock-out prices (less than $2). Mouth-watering Thai-style fried noodles, steamed vegetables, *loc lac,* and fruit shakes compete favorably with food stall prices. Breakfast also served. Open daily 6am-10pm.

The Green House Restaurant (tel. 630 467), located on Rte. 6 about 20m west of the intersection with V. Sivutha. Perhaps the nicest setting in Siem Reap. The entrance leads through a scruffy tropical garden, and guests are seated under a high-ceilinged open-sided wooden pavilion. The emphasis here is on Thai-Cambodian dishes. *Tom yam* with veggies, or meat and fried shrimp with curry are excellent. Other "international" foods include Chinese, Italian, and Indian. Order ahead for the large shrimp pizza ($6). Most dishes $1-3. Open daily 10am-10pm.

Monorom Restaurant, on V. Sivutha opposite Hotel Vimean Thmei, about 100m north of the old bus station. This Chinese dive serves some of the best food in town. While the large interior opening onto the street may be pretty mundane, the food is anything but. Most dishes $1.50-8 depending on the size of the serving. Don't miss the roast duck ($3) or the mixed fried vegetables ($1.20). Open daily 6:30-9am and 11am-2pm and 4-9pm.

Bayon Restaurant, on V. Wat Bo, 30m south of the intersection with Rte. 6. Proximity to popular guest houses, reasonably priced food, and pleasant setting have made Bayon the pre-eminent traveler hangout. The menu ($2-4) is a blend of Thai, Khmer, and western cooking. Splurge on sautéed chicken in basil leaves ($2) or on the prawn curry served in a coconut ($3). Proving once more that it ain't easy bein' green in Cambodia, fried frog is available in garlic, ginger, or chili paste varieties ($2). Excellent breakfast deals for less than $2. Open daily 5am-9:30pm.

SIGHTS

With one of the world's most stunning sights just 7km up the road, most travelers don't spend much time exploring Siem Reap itself. Apart from the market and souvenir shops, the few interesting places to visit can be seen in a few hours. The **Siem Reap Crocodile Farm** is on V. Sivutha south of the old bus station on the way to the Tonle Sap. These massive reptiles have remained largely unchanged since the dinosaur days (that was about the last time their cages were cleaned out, too). Visitors can watch little boys herd the brutes with shovels and marvel at why they don't become Khmer tartar. (Open daily 6am-6pm; admission 1000r.)

A **memorial** to Khmer Rouge atrocities is located on the road to Angkor. Take the dirt road turn-off located at the "Welcome" sign 0.5km past the Grand Hotel. Follow the road to a small wat. A ramshackle wooden pavilion filled waist deep with human skulls and bones is a stark, grisly reminder of the Khmer Rouge massacres.

For those who can't get enough of Angkor architecture, **Wat Leah,** located along the east bank of the river north of Arun Restaurant, has two well-preserved Angkor-period brick sanctuaries behind the modern pagoda. One of the lintels, in fine condition, depicts the *Churning of the Sea of Milk* (see **Angkor Wat** on page 98).

SHOPPING

They say 1500 *apsaras* now grace the inner walls of Angkor Wat—the rest have left and opened up souvenir stalls in Siem Reap. A number of shops line Rte. 6 just east of the river near the V. Wat Bo intersection. They are a riel a dozen and do not merit individual description—most sell soapstone Bayons, wooden carvings, Angkor Wat relief paintings, and, of course, *apsaras* in every size and medium.

The **Central Market,** located about 1km down Rte. 6, east of the river, is open daily from sunrise to sunset (6:30am-5:30pm), a beehive of activity and well worth the 15-minute walk. Maps of the Angkor complex (but not, unfortunately, of Siem Reap) can be purchased here for around $2. The produce section is located in the back. The **Old Market,** located along the southern end of the west bank river road near Ta Phrom Hotel, has just recently been rebuilt. The aisles are broad, the ceilings high, and the air sweet-smelling—telltale signs that the designers have foreign tourists in mind. A number of pushy souvenir vendors set up shop here between 7am and 6pm. As usual, there is a small food section.

Half of Siem Reap will try to sell you Angkor t-shirts, most of which are of poor quality. For higher quality shirts try the **Mine Field Studio,** located on the road to Angkor Wat past the Grand Hotel on the right, where the New Zealander owner of the infamous Mine Field Bar has abandoned pubs in favor of t-shirts, wall hangings, and masks. Beautiful silk-screened and hand-painted shirts ($10-15) depict the temples and scenes from the bas-reliefs that decorate them. The ever-popular "Danger! Mines!" shirt is also sold here. Worth a trip to hear colorful stories from the owner, an experienced sage on Southeast Asia. (Open daily 7am-7pm.)

■ Angkor

GETTING THERE AND AWAY

The most common way for travelers not affiliated with pricey package tours to see the temples is simply to hire a motorcycle and driver which together cost about $6 per day. Drivers can be arranged through guest houses in Siem Reap, at the tourism office, or on the street. Likewise, cars with drivers can also be hired for $20 per day.

It is also possible for travelers to rent their own motorbikes (or bicycles, if you're a world class cyclist or masochist) at guest houses for $6 or $7 per day. While this is considered legal by the tourist office, they and the many guards frown upon it, especially after a recent accident involving a local and a tourist in which the former was killed. Travelers planning to explore the temples on their own should limit their excursions to the main sights of Angkor Wat and Angkor Thom. Beyond the well-established access roads, navigation can be tricky.

The current admission prices for a ticket into Angkor is $20 for a one-day pass, $40 for a three-day pass, and $60 for a one-week pass. Tickets can be purchased directly from the tourist office or on-site from roving ticket salesmen.

PRACTICAL INFORMATION

General Concerns

The government claims all of the area around Angkor has been de-mined, but take this with a large grain of salt and **stay on well-trodden paths.** While looking out for land mines, keep in mind that the jungles are home to **poisonous snakes.** Potentially most dangerous are the small bright green **kraits** which, while innocuous-looking, can be deadly. King **cobras** with enough venom to bring down a bull elephant are rare, but not unheard of. Travelers should be wary of isolated, pitch-dark chambers. A flashlight will be immensely useful in your explorations. A final **warning:** do not remove any stone fragments from the temples, no matter how small. The Cambodian government takes theft of their national heritage very seriously, and all bags are searched at the airport upon departure.

Touring Tips

Angkor's magnificent ruins hold enough secrets for several lifetimes worth of exploration. Most of us, unfortunately, have slightly less than that amount of time to spend here. Many visitors try to cover as much ground as possible on the first day, including the major sites, and then spend the remaining time either returning to those monuments that were particularly intriguing or venturing farther afield. However one chooses to tour the temples, try to get an early start. By 11am temperatures will rise to over 39°C (100°F), and the genius of the Khmer architects is difficult to appreciate with sweat stinging your eyes. Motorcycle drivers can take tourists early to see the sunrise. Daytrippers to the ruins should bring a map of the temple complex, a flashlight, drinking water, a guidebook to the monuments, and extra film.

Keep in mind that the safety situation is always changing. As of this writing some of the more isolated sights north of Angkor Thom were still closed to foreigners due to the threat of bandits who attacked and killed an American tourist on the road to Bantaey Srei in February 1995. As a result, temples in this area are off-limits. Inquire at guest houses or the tourist office for the latest line and be careful.

Food at Angkor

Several small restaurants located beneath the trees opposite Angkor Wat offer reasonably priced food and a place to escape the merciless sun. Another eating option is to pick up a *baguette* and munch it in the cool shadows of the world's most spectacular outdoor restaurant.

COSMOLOGY AND THE ROLE OF RELIGION

The frequently asked question, just what religion were the Angkor Khmer, elicits a complicated answer. The Angkor kings practiced a faith that became an amalgamation of Hinduism and Buddhism, in which the relative influence of one over the other varied depending upon the beliefs of a particular ruler. All were manipulated to fit the cult of *devaraja*. Thus, Jayavarman II and his immediate successors in the first period of the Angkor era, during which Hinduism predominated, were seen as the earthly incarnation of Shiva the destroyer. Three hundred years later, following the adoption of Mahayana Buddhism under Jayavarman VII, the god-kings were no longer seen as Hindu deities like Shiva or Vishnu but as the earth-bound incarnations of the Buddha, and life went on. The line between Hinduism and Buddhism in Angkorian Cambodia was always a fuzzy one. Buddhism, for instance, atheistic in most practices, recognized Hindu deities. The Bayon, Jayavarman VII's many-faced masterpiece, was consecrated to Buddhism, yet some of the bas-reliefs which adorn its walls depict scenes from the Hindu epics.

Throughout the Angkor period, Hindu cosmology dictated the layout of the temple complexes. Each temple complex was intended to symbolize the Hindu-Buddhist universe in microcosm. Angkor Wat, the mother of all Angkor temples, is an excellent example of this cosmology due to its high state of preservation. Picture yourself standing on the third level of the central sanctuary, facing west. The grounds of the complex spread out before you. Beginning at the western extreme is the moat, representing the oceans. Similarly, the thick laterite walls which enclose the temple symbolize the earth. At the center of the monument, the five towers, the arrangement of which is known as a quincux, represent Mount Meru, the Hindu deities' Himalayan retreat and center of creation. Many early Khmer temples were built on mountaintops for this reason. Later on, the Angkor builders simulated mountains by erecting their temples atop mounds of dirt—multi-tiered, laterite structures stacked like a wedding-cake. Classic examples of these "temple mountains" can be seen at Prey Rup and Bakong.

CAMBODIA

Angkor

TO SISOPHON

TO PHNOM PENH

ANGKOR

Wat Phnom Bok

Banteay Samre

Roluos River

Prei Prasat

Prasat To

East Baray

Prasat Pou Teng

Lolei

Preah Ko

Bakong

Prasat Trapeang Phong

ROLUOS GROUP

Prasat O Kaek

Prasat Prei Monti

Svay Pream

Prasat Totoeng O Thngai

Prasat Komnap

Ta Som

Krol Ko

Neak Pean

Leak Neang

East Mebon

Prey Rup

Kuk Taleh

Banteay Prei

Preah Khan

Ta Nei Thommanom

Takeo

Sra Srang

Top

Bat Chum

Prasat Kravan

Kuk Bangro

Tram Neak

Prasat Daunso

Prasat Kok Thlok

Prasat He Phka

Krol Romeas

Chau Say Tevoda

Ta Prohm

Banteay Kdei

ANGKOR THOM

Angkor Wat

Wat Preah Einkosei

Town Market

Prasat Rsei

Prasat Kuk O Chrung

Baksei Chamkrong

Phnom Bakheng

Killing Field Memorial

Siem Reap River

Post Office

Police Station

Banteay Thom

Airport

Prasat Ta Noreay

Prasat Prei

Prasat Patri

SIEM REAP

Wat Athvea

Prasat Kok Po

Prasat Phnom Rung

West Baray

West Mebon

Prasat Kas Ho

Wat Chedei

TO PHNOM KROM

Ak Yom

Inside Angkor Thom

Baphuon, 3
Bayon, 2
Beng Thom, 1
East Gate, 12
North Gate, 15
North Khleang, 8
Phimeanakas, 4
Preah Palilay, 5
Preah Pithu, 9
South Gate, 13
South Khleang, 10
Terrace of the Elephants, 6
Terrace of the Leper King, 7
Victory Gate, 11
West Gate, 14

Angkor: A Cast of Characters

A number of deities and mythical creatures adorn the Angkor monuments:

apsaras: These celestial waifs, which sprang forth during the *Churning of the Sea of Milk* (see Angkor Wat on page 98) have become virtually synonymous with Khmer architecture. Typically they are depicted facing outward with only their faces in profile. Angkor Wat *apsaras*, widely regarded as the most beautiful nymphs of the temples, appear individually. The Bayon creatures, by contrast, appear in groups of three.

Ganesha: The Hindu god of wisdom, Ganesha is the son of Shiva and Parvati. He was created by Parvati to guard her bath. When Shiva came to Parvati, Ganesha refused to let the powerful god see his wife. Unable to defeat the little boy, Shiva called upon Vishnu for help and together, they decapitated him. In her wrath, Parvati wrought destruction on the world. Finally, to appease his wife, Shiva placed the head of an elephant on Ganesha's body and brought him back to life.

Garuda: A late addition to Angkor's characters, this half-man, half-bird enemy of the *naga* can often be found with its chum, Vishnu.

Makara: This demonic brute of a sea monster possesses a fantastic, horrible mug, vaguely reminiscent of a Chinese dragon-dance costume, and is often represented on lintels. Lolei, one of the Roluos temples near Angkor, contains a particularly fine representation. This beast is often portrayed with ugly, hideous creatures coming out of his mouth, such as *naga*.

Naga: These mythical, multi-headed serpents, so named after the Sanskrit word for snake, are legion at Angkor and guard the causeway leading to Angkor Wat. Possibly the most typical motif in Southeast Asia, *naga* play an important role in Khmer legends, in particular the birth of Funan (see **Sun, Moon, and Star** on page 69). According to Hindu myths, the *naga* swallowed the waters of life and was either ruptured by Indra or squeezed by Vishnu's entourage to set these waters free.

Vishnu: An important Hindu deity, Vishnu was widely worshipped during the height of the Angkor period. Married to Laksmi, he is frequently portrayed with four arms, although he has the ability to assume an *avatara* (earthly incarnation) when necessary. He can be seen in the bas-reliefs of Angkor Wat both in his human form and as a tortoise during the *Churning of the Sea of Milk*. He is often depicted with a *garuda*, his sidekick.

Although the name Angkor Wat implies a place of worship as in modern Buddhist wats, many of the tower sanctuaries you will see were used solely to house religious objects. They were rarely visited except by the king himself and high-ranking clergymen. This explains the preponderance of fake windows and doors in the architecture of the period—adequate light simply was not necessary.

For a more in depth look at the complex and the engrossing world of Angkor monuments, pick up a copy of Dawn Rooney's *A Guide to Angkor*, published by Asia Books, at a bookstore. Pirated copies are available at the markets in Phnom Penh and Siem Reap.

■ The Grand Circuit

The following summaries are arranged in the order many travelers choose to see the monuments. Beginning at Angkor Wat this "Grand Circuit" proceeds clockwise on a roughly rectangular track. During the high season (Oct.-May), it may be wise to do the Grand Circuit in reverse, since almost everyone goes the same way and starts at about the same time. All of the sights can be seen in a single day if one goes early and does not dawdle.

ANGKOR WAT

Located approximately 6km north of Siem Reap just south of Angkor Thom, this magnificent laterite and sandstone complex was constructed during the reign of Suryavarman II (1113-50). Thirty years in the making, the massive temple was consecrated to Vishnu and is believed to be a funereal temple, which would explain why it faces west, the direction associated with death in Hindu cosmology. With its distinctive five tower quincux symbolizing the peaks of Mount Meru, it is a classic example of the "temple mountains" designed to represent the Hindu universe.

Flawless in every respect and widely regarded as the crowning achievement in classical Khmer art and architecture, Angkor Wat is also the best preserved of the major sights. Visitors could easily spend an entire day marveling at its beauty and grandeur. Don't miss an inch, but be sure to pay particular attention to the bas-reliefs which line the walls of the first-level gallery. The reliefs, the longest in the world, progress counter-clockwise beginning on the western side. The first panel depicts the battle of Kuruksetra, from the Hindu epic *Mahabharata*. A very disheartening vision of the 32 hells in Hindu mythology lines the second half of the south wall. Large demons make *piñatas* out of the heads of the damned. Perhaps the most famous relief in all of Angkor, the *Churning of the Sea of Milk,* adorns the eastern face of the gallery. In this scene the gods and the demons have put aside their differences in order to attain *amrita*, the nectar of immortality. Vasuki, the serpent, has offered to act as the egg-beater, and Vishnu kindly assumes the shape of a turtle to support the effort. Hanu-man, a monkey, stands on his shell, directing the operation. From this divine example of conflict resolution, the enchanting *apsaras,* or celestial waifs with dimensions that would shame Kate Moss, were created. The north wall depicts Vishnu's defeat of Bana the Demon King, a curious-looking hellion mounted on a rhino. Also portrayed on the second half of the gallery is an epic battle between the gods and the demons. All of the heavyweights, including Vishnu, Shiva, and Brahma, are represented. Completing the circuit, the northern panel of the west gallery depicts the battle of Lanka from the Hindu epic the *Ramayana,* which pitted the mild-mannered hero Rama against the demon Ravana, easily recognizable with his 10 heads and 20 arms.

Mounting the steps to the second level, the Gallery of 1000 Buddhas (of which only a few fragments remain) is on the right, and the Hall of Echoes is on the left. Temple explorers can stand in one corner of the Hall of Echoes, pound their chest like Tarzan, and feel the room reverberate (this trick can be repeated at numerous temples). The third level of the temple commands a stunning view of the perfectly symmetrical complex. Angkor Wat has by no means lost its spiritual value in favor of backpacking pilgrims; monks from the adjacent pagodas frequently conduct ceremonies here (indeed, the monks are credited with the temple's excellent state of preservation, as they have lived nearby for centuries and tended the site). Angkor Wat is best seen at sunrise or sunset.

PHNOM BAKHENG

Just north of Angkor Wat and slightly to the west, Phnom Bakheng was built by Yaso-varman I (889-900) in the late 9th century. Many travelers struggle up the very steep, rocky slope of this bona fide temple mountain at the end of a hard day's thrash through Angkor to enjoy a spectacular sunset and stunning view of Angkor Wat just below Phnom Bakheng to the southeast. The temple itself is built on five laterite tiers. Originally, 109 towers graced the *phnom,* corresponding to the animal zodiac cycle. The central tower is open on all four sides; come first and foremost for the view (5pm is ideal). The five towers of Angkor Wat present a perennial Kodak moment. To the south Phnom Krom, the mountain on the other side of Siem Reap, can be seen, as well as the West Baray sparkling amid a field of green to the west.

ANGKOR THOM

Lying roughly 1.5km north of Angkor Wat is the large temple complex of Angkor Thom, constructed by Jayavarman VII (1181-1219) on the site of earlier structures. The last and greatest of the Angkor Empire's capitals, it shares a cosmological layout similar to Angkor Wat's: a moat symbolizes the oceans, walls the land, and towers the peaks of Mount Meru. Within this vast former city (laid out in a 3km by 3km square)

CAMBODIA

are some of the most impressive ruins, including the Bayon, Baphuon, Phimeanakas, the Terrace of Elephants, and the Terrace of the Leper King. When entering the Angkor Thom (literally "great city") from the south, you cross a causeway lined with 54 statues of gods and demons. The Angkor Conservancy has removed many of the remaining original heads to prevent their theft and replaced them with replicas. The entry tower is topped by a *bayon* whose enigmatic grin has captivated artists, archaeologists, and travelers alike for 150 years.

The Bayon

Sprawling in the exact center of Angkor Thom, this temple was erected by Jayavarman VII and dedicated to Buddhism. Built about 100 years after Angkor Wat, the Bayon is unique in several respects: first, it has no surrounding laterite wall, and second, its outstanding reliefs depict, in addition to the usual epic stories, scenes of everyday life in Angkorian Cambodia that provide archaeologists with one of their only windows into this mysterious world. Tourists should try to visit the Bayon early. Surrounded by trees which also shade a modern pagoda, the experience of watching a new day begin is sublime. Before the motorcycles and vendors appear in force, the only sounds are of the jungle and perhaps a few aging nuns silently padding through the temple's labyrinthine passageways, lighting fresh sticks of incense.

The faces are believed to represent the Bodhisattva Avalokitesvara, the king's divine benefactor. The Bayon contains two sets of bas-reliefs that are viewed clockwise, unlike Angkor Wat. The lower gallery adorns the outer wall and depicts everyday life in the capital. The southern gallery is widely regarded to be the finest of Bayon's bas-reliefs. The panels begin with a depiction of a battle between the Khmers and the Chams; Khmer soldiers can be identified by their lack of headgear. The lower tier of reliefs presents a more peaceful view of Angkor life. Citizens observe cockfights, play board games, and pick lice from each other's hair. The northern gallery, only some of which was completed, contains a depiction of an Angkor circus complete with acrobats, jugglers, and Gunther Gable-Williams. The upper gallery of bas-reliefs contains stories from the Hindu epics.

Baphuon

A few hundred meters northwest of the Bayon stands the Hindu temple of Baphuon, built during the second half of the 11th century by Udayadityavarman II (1050-66). Intended to symbolize Mount Meru, the central sanctuary is located on top of a massive sandstone base. A reclining Buddha, built from the rubble of a collapsed gallery, can be seen lying along the length of the western wall. Access to the temple is gained by crossing a long elevated sandstone causeway, beginning near the Terrace of the Elephants. Presently, a team of French and Cambodian archaeologists is in the process of restoring Baphuon.

Phimeanakas

Situated just north of Baphuon, this Hindu monument was erected by three successive kings, Rajendravarman (944-68), Jayavarman V (968-1001), and Udayadityavarman I (1001-02). It is worth a visit primarily for the view from the top of the central sanctuary. The scramble up a very steep set of laterite "stairs" can be challenging and is best attempted early in the day.

Terrace of the Elephants

First laid out by Suryavarman I (1002-50), the Terrace of the Elephants (also called the Royal Terrace) stretches for 300m from the Baphuon to the beginning of the Terrace of the Leper King, past Phimeanakas. While gazing east from the Terrace, imagine a bustling city sprawled out before your eyes in what used to be the Grand Plaza, Angkor Thom's main square. The bas-relief elephants plodding in profile along the wall are remarkable for their realism. Along the wall near the Terrace of the Leper King is a carving of a five-headed horse, perhaps the mythical Balaha.

CAMBODIA

Terrace of the Leper King

Also another legacy of Jayavarman VII, this monument, north of the Terrace of the Elephants, was dedicated to Buddhism. Two galleries of bas-reliefs line this terrace. Mythological creatures and stunning half-naked *apsaras* decorate the outer wall. The well-preserved inner wall was discovered only recently by archaeologists.

The statue of the Leper King himself is a copy; the National Museum in Phnom Penh now houses the original. The mystery of the rotund little man remains an enigma. Historians suspect that Jayavarman VII may have suffered from leprosy. Others believe the statue portrays either Yama, the god of death, or Kubera, the god of wealth. A third theory holds that the figure represents David Leper-man, god-king of late night television.

PREAH KHAN

Located northwest of the Bayon outside of Angkor Thom, Preah Khan was built by Jayavarman VII in the late 12th century as a Buddhist temple in memory of his father. An official World Heritage Site, it features a small pavilion just beyond the gate on the left, which contains an interesting series of diagrams and photographs explaining the restoration process. Grab your fedora; this largely unrestored temple hidden away in lush emerald jungle is straight out of an Indiana Jones flick. The light that filters through the leafy canopy of towering banyan trees plays off the gray sandstone such that you'd swear that the *apsaras* in the corner of your eye just moved. Literally, Preah Khan means "sacred sword," and some archaeologists believe that the small two-story building located in the northeast corner of the compound, a rarity in Khmer architecture, might once have housed this Asian Excalibur. Visitors enter the temple from the west, but the original entry point, as usual in Hindu and Buddhist architecture, faces east. For an excellent view of the cross-shaped layout of the main sanctuary, it is possible to scramble up the rubble onto the top of the gallery just east of the sanctuary. Continuing along the west-east axis will eventually bring you to the east gate. The roots of several large *ponro* trees now envelop the laterite wall like the tentacles of a giant squid. **Warning:** This site is mined between 6pm and 6am in order to prevent further ransacking of the temple.

NEAK PEAN

Neak Pean, a Buddhist temple situated east of Preah Khan along the Grand Circuit access road was built by The Man (yes, Jayavarman VII) during the last decades of the 12th century. This small yet engrossing temple is made up of five ponds. A temple stands in the exact center of the large, central pond. Neak Pean is said to represent Lake Anauatapa, a sacred body of water in the Himalaya. The four symmetrical ponds, one at each cardinal point, represent the earth's four main rivers. A stone horse, believed to be the sacred steed, Balaha, drags several marooned sailors toward the island sanctuary in the middle of Neak Pean.

TA SOM

Lying east along the access road from Neak Pean, Ta Som, built by Jayavarman VII, is a contemporary of Neak Pean and was dedicated to Buddhism. A small temple with one sanctuary, it is unrestored and largely in ruins. A four-faced *bayon* casts its inscrutable smile over you as you enter from the west. In typical Khmer style, the false windows of the main sanctuary have half-drawn "curtains." Continue through to the east gate, whose *bayon* is now almost entirely in the clutches of fig tree roots. Damage caused by creeping vegetation such as this has been a principle threat to the preservation of the Angkor monuments.

EAST MEBON

Built by Rajendravarman II in the 10th century as a Hindu monument in memory of his parents, East Mebon stands in the middle of the East Baray southwest of Ta Som.

As your motorcycle speeds south to Mebon across pancake-flat rice paddies, picture the setting as it was during the Angkor period, when the East Baray was filled with water which may or may not have been used to irrigate the fields necessary to feed the great capital city. At that time, Mebon was accessible only by boat. The five main towers, a new architectural innovation, here and at Prey Rup are precursors to Angkor Wat's towers. This classic temple mountain representing Mount Meru sits atop a three-tiered artificial hill constructed of laterite blocks. Entry is through the east gate—notice the *singha* (lions) which guard the steps to the second level. Eight brick tiers, each supported by eight-sided sandstone columns, face the four cardinal points. Note also the elephants at the corners of the first two levels.

PREY RUP

Due south 0.5km of Mebon lies Prey Rup, a Hindu temple built by Rajendravarman II in the second half of the 10th century. A contemporary of East Mebon, but much more impressive, this multi-tiered structure affords a panoramic view of the East Baray to the north. (Mebon should be visible through the trees from the main sanctuary.) The two halls (or what is left of them) running parallel to the laterite wall as you enter from the east are believed to have housed pilgrims who had made the long journey to worship Shiva, the Hindu deity to which Rup was consecrated. The stone sarcophagus-like structure just past the rest halls may have been a crematorium. The five central towers atop a sandstone tier are typical of Khmer architecture during this period: all have false doors and open to the east.

On the short jaunt between Mebon and Prey Rup, lies the road leading to the enchanting Banteay Srei temple some 30km to the north. Alas, as of this writing Banteay Srei remained off-limits following the death of an American woman there. Check with the tourist office to see if this unfortunate situation has changed.

BANTEAY KDEI

Banteay Kdei is a Buddhist temple built by Jayavarman VII, southeast of Prey Rup near the Sra Sang reservoir. A *bayon* oversees the entrance to this unrestored temple. Take care while exploring Banteay Kdei, as many of the enclosed buildings are off-limits. Nothing would spoil a visit to Angkor quicker than a five-ton sandstone block on the noggin. The statue of the Buddha in the central sanctuary was vandalized by the Khmer Rouge, who cut off its original head (probably sitting in a private collection in Paris or New York now). Look carefully to see the very faint images of the Buddha etched in the walls of the sanctuary. Before heading on to the Ta Prohm, be sure to walk over to the Sra Sang reservoir. A stone platform lined with *naga* leads down to the water, and Sra Sang village is visible to the north.

TA PROHM

Located west of the Prey Rup, bordering Banteay Kdei, Ta Prohm was built at the end of the 12th century by Jayavarman VII as a Buddhist temple in memory of his mother. Set deep in the jungle, the noises of which provide an eerie soundtrack to your exploration, this vast crumbling temple competes with the Bayon and Angkor Wat as the most impressive of Angkor's treasures. Standing alone in a ruined sanctuary, creepers and fig trees all around you, it is not difficult to imagine how Henri Mouhot, who "rediscovered" Angkor in 1860, must have felt, for the site has changed little since then, save for young capitalists selling refreshments. Inscriptions found by archaeologists reveal that 79,365 people were employed in the upkeep of Ta Prohm during its hey-day. It is certainly huge, and a map is helpful to ensure you don't miss anything. Ten-year-old "guides" may lead you around whether you request it or not. Be careful while squirming through tiny "doors" the kids can wriggle through with ease. Massive banyan trees now hold a death-grip on many of the ruined galleries. A number of carvings and inscriptions decorate the walls of the galleries surrounding the central sanctuary. Many visitors make special early morning trips to Ta Prohm because of its stunning beauty in the morning light.

■ Near Angkor

WEST BARAY

West of Angkor Thom, a superb view of the half-filled lake can be had from the top of Phnom Bakheng. Believed to date from the 11th century, the West Baray was perhaps built during the reign of Udayadityavarman II. Though the debate over its function rages on, the *baray*, of which approximately half is still full of water, makes an interesting side trip for those with the time. Teenagers from Siem Reap often come here to swim and King Sihanouk, who maintained a royal residence in Siem Reap, used to take his guests water-skiing here. A small, largely destroyed temple, **West Mebon,** stands in the center of the *baray;* it is reachable by boat.

ROLUOS GROUP

About 10km southeast of Siem Reap, this collection of three temples represents the very earliest Angkor period. It is believed that Jayavarman II made his capital of Hariharalaya here in the middle of the 9th century. All three temples were originally consecrated to Hinduism. Two of the three monuments, Lolei (north of the other two off Rte. 6) and Preah Ko (south off Rte. 6 and north of Bakong) are quite small. They can be seen easily in an hour. **Lolei,** the site of a modern Buddhist wat, boasts a few beautiful lintels on the four brick towers of the main sanctuary. The door frames were each hewn from a single sandstone block, a characteristic of early Angkor architecture. **Preah Ko,** or "Sacred Ox," consists of a central sanctuary with six brick towers. It has ornate sandstone false doors and eight-sided sandstone columns. **Bakong,** the largest and most impressive of the Roluos Group, was once the ancient capital of Hariharalaya. It is a classic temple mountain, and its single central tower sits atop a five-tiered laterite base. The temple is entered from the east by crossing a causeway lined with *naga* over a now dry moat. A large modern pagoda is situated at the base of the temple. Stone elephants stand at every corner of the tiers, growing smaller at each level. The four central towers afford an excellent view of the surrounding countryside and of the remarkable symmetry of the Bakong temple.

■ Rattanakiri (Ban Lung)

Historically, Rattanakiri was not an integral part of the Khmer kingdom. Situated in the mountainous northeast along the border with Laos and Vietnam, its population of fiercely independent minorities resisted lowland hegemony for centuries. In the late 19th century, the province was ceded rather arbitrarily to Cambodia by the French. Even the Khmer Rouge left the ethnic minorities largely to their own devices, and consequently, Rattanakiri remains perhaps Cambodia's safest region.

Today the population remains a vibrant mix of Jorai, Krung, and Kravet people who continue to dwell in small, insular communities and practice swidden agriculture. Since 1986, when Ban Lung was made the provincial capital, increasing numbers of Khmer, Vietnamese, and Chinese have entered Rattanakiri. Sadly, economics threaten to accomplish what had previously been impossible; the Phnom Penh government is presently considering schemes to resettle large numbers of ethnic minorities to the lowlands in order to better exploit the region's rich timber reserves.

ORIENTATION AND PRACTICAL INFORMATION

With only one main road, finding one's way around **Ban Lung** is no difficult undertaking. The dirt strip **airfield** is located about 500m south of town. Heading north on the airport road brings you to the intersection with **Route 19,** Ban Lung's incongruously wide artery, running east-west through town and on to the Vietnamese border only

70km away. Taking a right at the *naga* pillars in the center of town leads to the **Royal Air Cambodge Office** (open daily 8am-noon), which offers four flights per week to Phnom Penh ($55 one way). All flights must be reconfirmed. Past the airline office is a **police station** followed by Ban Lung's very utilitarian **market** boasting a large assortment of high-quality Vietnamese-made consumer goods and several dirty food stalls. A few stands at the front of the market sell a fairly meager assortment of hill-tribe handicraft (wicker backpacks 5000r). **Rattanakiri Provincial Hospital** is about 2km north of the airport road-Rte. 19 intersection; it's not for the faint of heart. The **post office** (open daily 7:30-11am and 2-4:30pm) is 1km east of the *naga* pillar, next to the **telecommunications office** (tel. 974 006). There is no international service. (Open daily 7:30-11am and 2-4:30pm.) The **telephone code** is 075.

ACCOMMODATIONS AND FOOD

The **Mountain Guest House** (tel. 974 047), Ban Lung's optimal accommodation, is on Rte. 19 about 50m east of the intersection with the airport road. Large, clean rooms with double beds, fan, and shared bathroom go for $5. The congenial Chinese owners speak several languages including some English. A free breakfast of bread, rolls, and tea is served early every morning. The **Ban Lung Guest House,** on a side street to the left just before the market, offers simple, spotless rooms with shared bath for $4. Those who crave A/C can try the *other* **Ban Lung Guest House** (tel. 974 066), which is 100m from the airport on the way into town. Rooms with private flush toilet and shower are $5, with A/C $10. The **Restaurant Rattanakiri** is just west of the airport road-Rte. 19 intersection. Bound to be a highlight of any visit to Ban Lung, this place has a pleasant location and an English menu. Venison *loc lac* costs 3500r, scrumptious fried fish 3000r. Eat here twice and you're a regular. (Open daily 7am-10pm.)

SIGHTS

There is little to see in Ban Lung proper; one of the most entertaining activities is simply to take a stroll around town in the evening. Expect to be the center of attention, particularly among the four-to-ten-year-old set who will smile, wave, and greet you with a friendly "bye bye." Two km west of the airport road intersection on Rte. 19 is **Wat Phnom Suay.** At the top of Phnom Suay, about 1km beyond the temple along the dirt path that runs through the temple grounds, is a large statue of the **sleeping Buddha.** The Enlightened One has seen better days, but the view from the top, with the jagged peaks of the Central Highlands rising in the distance, is magnificent, especially at sunset. Three km east on Rte. 19 is **Yak Lom Lake,** a small crater lake. According to legend, when the winds whistle over the lip of the crater in the right direction, a vortex forms in the middle. This whirlpool allegedly swallowed a rowboat full of picnickers during the Vietnam War era. The water is quite clear and the swimming excellent. To get there, head east on Rte. 19 past several rubber plantations. After 2km, there's a round-about topped with Soviet-esque statues of hill tribesmen. Take a right here, and the lake is 1.5km farther, past a hill-tribe village.

■ Near Ban Lung

The principle attractions around Ban Lung are human. The region is a patchwork of highland minorities, many of whom continue to live as they have for a millennia in small, isolated communities. Indeed, during the rainy season (May-Nov.), many villages may be largely, if not completely, deserted. At this time families head off into the forest to clear and cultivate mountain (dry) rice, their staple crop.

Since the roads are unmarked and the villages are frequently hidden away from the main roads, the best way to see the countryside is to hire a motorcycle in Ban Lung ($12 per day; inquire at the Mountain Guest House).

There are several **Krung villages** west of town. A typical settlement consists of a meeting house where men and women gather to conduct ceremonies, a "groom house," often elevated far above other structures, where young men of marrying age sleep, and a number of individual family dwellings. There are also two fairly unimpressive **waterfalls** located 4 and 16km from the main road.

Forty km northwest of Ban Lung is **Virochey District.** The two-hour motorbike ride passes through several picturesque villages before reaching the district town, which is nothing more than a few buildings on the banks of the Tonle Sap River. The population is an equal mix of Lao, Khmer, and Chinese. Across the river is a small Chinese settlement, which has been around for more than 300 years. A Kravet village stands at the confluence of the Tonle Sap and Oraly rivers, about a 40-minute walk from the Chinese village, but it is deserted during the rainy season.

East on the road to Vietnam is **Bokeo District,** home to several Lao and hill-tribe villages, a waterfall, and several **sapphire mines.** Uncut stones are about $2. Sixty km south of Ban Lung stands the small town of **Lumphat,** famed for its **gold mines.** Lumphat can be visited in a day from Ban Lung (road conditions permitting), but plan on spending the night if you wish to visit the mines. **Note:** the American Embassy advises foreigners to exercise caution while visiting mines, although Rattanakiri is generally considered to be one of the safest provinces in Cambodia.

CAMBODIA

HONG KONG

For many tourists, hyper-kinetic Hong Kong stirs up well-worn stereotypes of the Far East: gliding junks, incense-clouded temples, kittenish *cheongsam*-clad Suzie Wongs, and Fu Manchu tycoons presiding over *hong* cartels. The junks and temples are still here, albeit somewhat obscured by McDonald's dazzling golden arches, shelves upon shelves of Gap khakis, and pitched battles waged in the streets between Janet Jackson and Chinese opera divas for audio supremacy. Change has come to Hong Kong and here are the signs o' the times. Suzie has been promoted to bar hostess, while other working girls claw their way to the top as corporate-level lady bosses. The *taipan* of Hong Kong's mythical past have stepped off the pages of James Clavell's novels and into Armani suits as eager business moguls carrying cellular phones. This capitalist ant colony proudly claims the world's highest per capita use of fax machines and other high-tech gadgets. And indeed, Mr. Rolex, Mrs. Rolls-Royce, and little Rémy Martin lead a peaceful, cheek-by-jowl co-existence with rhinoceros-horn aphrodisiacs, rickshaws, and roast duck banquets.

As 1997 approaches, however, the pace seems to have taken on a decidedly more introspective flavor, as residents who have not left (yet) attempt to divine what Hong Kong's next incarnation will be. Work continues 24 hours a day on the new multi-million dollar cuttlefish-shaped convention center where the hand-over ceremonies are scheduled to proceed, while construction of Hong Kong's state of the art airport is actually ahead of schedule. Yet even with the addition of such decidedly optimistic baubles to Hong Kong's capitalistic skyline, there remains an undercurrent of stale dissatisfaction over more intangible issues like freedom of speech. How will Beijing officials react to advocacy of Taiwan's independence, or other issues perceived as undermining China's sovereignty? Drop by after the stroke of midnight on June 30, 1997, and find out for yourself.

ESSENTIALS

■ Getting There and Away

Hong Kong International Airport (flight info tel. 2769 7531) is in Kowloon, the peninsula north of Hong Kong Island. There is a HK$100 airport tax per person. The extensive and inexpensive **airbus system** (tel. 2745 4466) is the easiest way to dart from the airport in A/C luxury to major districts in Hong Kong. To get from the airport to **Tsim Sha Tsui,** take the A1 bus (HK$12.30). A2 runs to **Central** and **Wan Chai,** A3 to **Causeway Bay,** and A5 to **Taikoo** and **North Point,** each costs HK$19; children under 12 ride half-price. Carry exact fare. Buses run daily 7am-midnight, except A5 and A7, which run 7am-11:30pm. A map of routes is available at the airport station; buses depart every 10-15 minutes. **Taxi cabs** wait outside the airport terminal. A ride from the airport to Tsim Sha Tsui runs about HK$50; from the airport to Causeway Bay, HK$100. There's a HK$20 surcharge for crossing the harbor, plus HK$5 for each piece of luggage. Cab jockeys will often understand English street names, but it's helpful to have addresses written in Chinese characters.

■ Orientation

At the tip of the **Kowloon** peninsula, sandwiched between the airport and Hong Kong Island, is **Tsim Sha Tsui,** the city's tourist center, glistening with upscale boutiques, bars, and restaurants. **Hong Kong Island** lies across Victoria Harbor, accessible by the Mass Transit Railway's island line and the Star Ferry. To the west, **Sheung Wan** is a honeycomb of cluttered streets and alleys. Eastward, **Central** and **Admiralty** sprout vertigo-inducing skyscrapers. Infamous **Wan Chai** is one stop east of Admiralty on the MTR. **Causeway Bay,** with its 13-story colossus of malls, is the next stop on the MTR. The southern part of Hong Kong Island is predominantly rural and slowly dissolves into talcum beaches at **Repulse Bay.** Farther west is **Aberdeen,** moored to the grandiose floating Christmas tree of an eatery, the Jumbo Floating Restaurant, widely touted on posters of Hong Kong.

■ Money

US$1=HK$7.730	HK$1=US$0.129
CDN$1=HK$5.652	HK$1=CDN$0.177
UK£1=HK$11.939	HK$1=UK£0.084
IR£1=HK$11,775	HK$1=IR£0.085
AUS$1=HK$5.729	HK$1=AUS$0.175
NZ$1=HK$4.687	HK$1=NZ$0.213
SARand1=HK$2.168	HK$1=SARand0.461

Legal tender is the **Hong Kong dollar** (HK$) which has 100 **cents.** Government-issued coins are bronze-colored for 10¢, 20¢, and 50¢; silver-colored for $1, $2, $5, and $10. Private banks issue notes in denominations of $10, $20, $50, $500, and $1000 for those wild mornings of *dim sum* bacchanalia. Currency can be exchanged at banks, hotels, or money changers, although banks usually have the best rates. There are also some 24-hour automatic currency exchange machines called EA$YEXCHANGE located at a few Wing Lung banks.

All major credit cards are accepted throughout Hong Kong. ATMs hooked up to international money networks can be found around the city, as well as in Kowloon and the New Territories. **Tipping** is fairly customary for taxi drivers, bellboys, and other attendants. In restaurants, a 10% service charge is usually added automatically, and they expect to keep the change. In places where no service charge is included, a 10% tip is sufficient. **Bargaining** is inappropriate in some places such as large boutiques and department stores where prices are indicated. In many smaller shops and boutiques, however, it's acceptable and even expected. Don't hesitate to ask the shop owner if he or she will give you a "special price."

■ Getting Around

MASS TRANSIT RAILWAY (MTR)

There's no subway station near the airport, but everywhere else Hong Kong's super-efficient MTR is the most stress-free means of transport (HK$4-12.50). Vending machines spit out tickets which are scanned at the entry gate and must be returned at the exit gate. Since cashiers are often not at the station, exact change is necessary. Each ticket is good for 90 minutes after it's scanned the first time. Three MTR lines link major areas in southern Kowloon and northern Hong Kong Island. Each station has multiple exits. To get out at the point nearest your destination, look for the red signs to guide you to well-known sights and landmarks. Rush hour is from 7:30-9:30am and 5:30-7:30pm. The system runs 6am-12:30am. The **Mass Transit Railway Information** can be reached at 2750 0170.

BUSES AND TAXIS

Hong Kong's star-quality **bus system** generally costs around HK$1.50-32, payable in exact change as you board. Snag a schedule with listed fares from any tourist office. On Hong Kong Island, **China Motor Bus** runs cream-and-blue buses (tel. 2565 8556) and **Citybus** operates orange buses (tel. 2873 0818). On Kowloon, cream-and-red caravans are run by **Kowloon Motor Bus** (tel. 2745 4466). **Taxis** are abundant and rea-

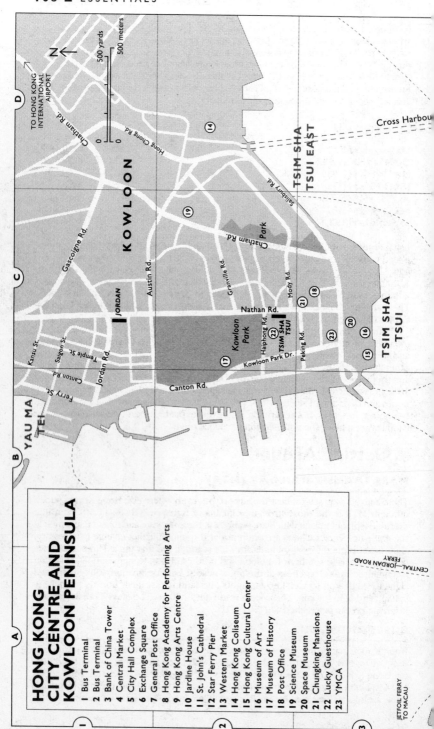

HONG KONG CITY CENTRE AND KOWLOON PENINSULA

1 Bus Terminal
2 Bus Terminal
3 Bank of China Tower
4 Central Market
5 City Hall Complex
6 Exchange Square
7 General Post Office
8 Hong Kong Academy for Performing Arts
9 Hong Kong Arts Centre
10 Jardine House
11 St. John's Cathedral
12 Star Ferry Pier
13 Western Market
14 Hong Kong Coliseum
15 Hong Kong Cultural Center
16 Museum of Art
17 Museum of History
18 Post Office
19 Science Museum
20 Space Museum
21 Chungking Mansions
22 Lucky Guesthouse
23 YMCA

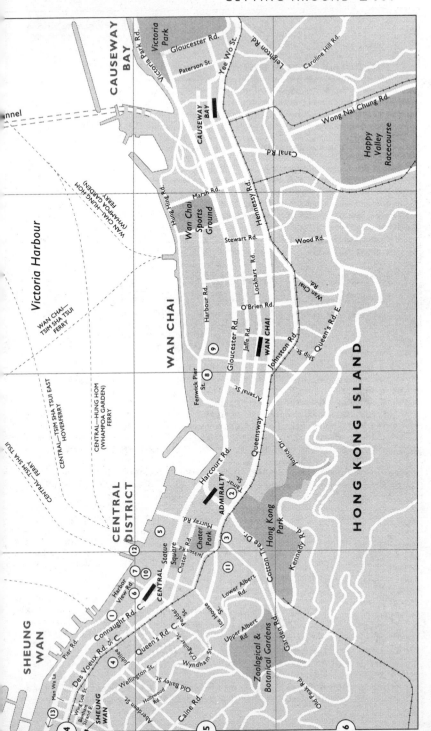

sonably priced. Many major thoroughfares have taxi stands. Meters start at HK$14, then it's HK$1.20 per 200m. If you are crossing the harbor, you must pay HK$20 for the cab's roundtrip tunnel toll.

KOWLOON-CANTON RAILWAY(KCR) AND TRAM

The **KCR** (tel. 2602 7799) runs from Kowloon Station to the Chinese border (HK$29, children and seniors pay half). Stored value tickets are accepted, except for trips to the Chinese border at Lo Wy. The **tram system** links points along north Hong Kong Island. Any destination costs HK$1.20 (half price for children), 6am-1am. Board at the rear and pay as you exit. The tram's last stop is written on the front of the vehicle in English. Contact **Hong Kong Tramways** (tel. 2559 8918).

BOATS

Boats offer a scenic way to scamper across the harbor. **Star Ferry** (tel. 2366 2576) links Tsim Sha Tsui and Central (6:30am-11:30pm, lower deck HK$1.70, upper deck HK$2). Ferries also connect Hong Kong Island with Macau and other outlying islands from piers west of the Star Ferry concourse. The tourist office has schedules. For inquiries call **Hong Kong Ferry Co.** (tel. 2542 3082). **Boats** also run between Central and Hung Hom (7am-7:20pm, lower deck HK$2, upper deck HK$2.50).

■ Practical Information

Tourist Offices: Multilingual Telephone Information Service (tel. 2807 6177). Open Mon.-Fri. 8am-6pm, Sat.-Sun. and public holidays 9am-5pm. **Hong Kong Tourist Association (HKTA): HK International Airport,** accessible only to arriving passengers. Indispensable bus and ferry schedules and maps. *Official Hong Kong Guide's* "Month in Focus" gives a rundown of current sports, festivals, and performing arts. Do-it-yourself walking tour guides available for HK$30, as well as free brochures about shopping, restaurants, and cultural sites. Free info packets in baggage-claim area. English spoken. Open daily 8am-10:30pm. **Central Hong Kong,** Jardine House, 1 Connaught Place, Shop 8, Basement. Leave the Central MTR station (Jardine House exit), and turn right onto the pedestrian overpass. Follow the signs. English spoken. Open Mon.-Fri. 9am-6pm, Sat. 9am-1pm. Closed public holidays. **Star Ferry Concourse (Kowloon),** left of the lower deck entrance. Open Mon.-Fri. 8am-6pm, Sat.-Sun. and holidays 9am-5pm. **Macau Tourist Information Bureau,** Room 3705 Shun Tak Centre, 168-200 Connaught Rd., Central (tel. 2540 8180).
Tours and Travel: Hong Kong Youth Hostels Association, Shek Kip Mei Estate, Block 19, Room 225, Shamshuipo, Kowloon (tel. 2788 1638). Open Mon., Wed., and Fri. 9:30am-5:30pm, Tues. and Thurs. 9:30am-7pm, Sat. 9:30am-1pm. **Sincerity Travel,** 921A Star House (tel. 2730 3269), next to the Star Ferry pier, Tsim Sha Tsui. English spoken. Open Mon.-Fri. 9:30am-7:30pm, Sat. 9:30am-6:30pm, Sun. 11am-6pm. Major credit cards accepted (2.25% surcharge).
Embassies and Consulates: Australia, Harbour Centre, 24th Fl., 25 Harbour Rd., Wan Chai (tel. 2827 8881). Open Mon.-Fri. 9am-noon and 2-4pm. **Canada,** Exchange Square Tower 1, 12th Fl., Central (tel. 2810 4321). Open Mon.-Tues. and Thurs.-Fri. 8:30am-4pm, Wed. 8:30am-noon. **Malaysia,** Malaysia Bldg., 23rd Fl., 50 Gloucester Rd., Wan Chai (tel. 2527 0921). Open Mon.-Fri. 9am-1pm and 3-5pm. **New Zealand,** 2705 Jardine House, 1 Connaught Rd., Central (tel. 2877 4488). Open Mon. and Wed.-Fri. 9am-12:30pm and 2-4pm, Tues. 10am-12:30pm and 2-4pm. **Singapore,** 901 Admiralty Centre, Tower 1, 9th Fl., Admiralty (tel. 2527 2212). Open Mon.-Fri. 10am-12:30pm and 2:30-5:30pm. **Thailand,** Fairmont House, 8th Fl., 8 Cotton Tree Dr., Central (tel. 2521 6481). Open Mon.-Fri. 9am-noon and 2-5pm. **UK,** Bank of America Tower, 9th Fl., 12 Harcourt Rd., Admiralty (tel. 2523 0176). Open Mon.-Fri. 8:30am-5:15pm. **US,** 26 Garden Rd., Central (tel. 2523 9011). Open Mon.-Fri. 8:30am-5:30pm.
Immigration Offices: Hong Kong Immigration Department, Immigration Tower, 7 Gloucester Rd., Wan Chai (tel. 2829 3000). Open Mon.-Fri. 8:45am-

4:30pm, Sat. 9am-11:30am. For visa extensions bring your passport, airplane ticket, and HK$115 to the 6th floor where you will have to fill out form ID91. **Immigration Hotline** (tel. 2824 6111).

Currency Exchange: Hang Seng Bank, at every subway station. Offers basic services. Open Mon.-Fri. 9am-5pm., Sat. 9am-1pm. Major banks cluster in one area. From the Star Ferry Pier, **Hong Kong and Shanghai Banking Corporation** is in front. **Bank of China** is to the left. Most are open Mon.-Fri. 9am-4:30pm, Sat. 9am-12:30pm. **American Express** cardholders can use Jetco **ATMs. MC** and **Visa** holders can use Hong Kong Bank's 'Electronic Money' ATMs.

American Express: Central, New World Tower, 16-18 Queen's Rd., Central, (tel. 2885 9366). MTR: Central MTR (China Bldg. exit). Exit opposite the Landmark Bldg. Turn right, take a left onto Queen's Road Central after the China Bldg. branch of the Hong Kong Bank. AmEx office is about half-block down, in the New World Tower. Mail held for 30 days free for members and those with AmEx traveler's checks. No charge for changing traveler's checks. Banking services available Mon.-Fri. 9:30am-4pm, Sat. 9:30am-noon. Other services available Mon.-Fri. 9am-5pm, Sat. 9am-12:30pm. **Tsim Sha Tsui,** Cheung Lee Communications Bldg., 25 Kimberly Rd. Turn onto Kimberly Rd. from Nathan Rd. It's just past the Carnarvon Rd. intersection on the left. No charge for cashing traveler's checks, but no client mail. Banking services open Mon.-Fri. 9:30am-4pm, Sat. 9:30am-noon. Other services Mon.-Fri. 9am-5pm, Sat. 9am-12:30pm.

Luggage Storage: Hong Kong International Airport (tel. 769 78 95), in the departure and arrival halls. HK$40 per piece for the first day, HK$60 per piece for the second day. Prices go up from there. Open daily 6:30am-1am.

English Bookstores: Bookazine Ltd., Shop No. 102-103, Chater Rd., Alexandra House, 1st Fl., Central (tel. 2521 1649). MTR: Central (Alexandra House exit). Wide selection of magazines, travel guides, and fiction. English spoken. Open Mon.-Sat. 9am-7pm, Sun. and holidays 10am-6pm.

Pharmacies: Yau Ma Tei Jockey Club Clinic, 145 Battery St., Yau Ma Tei. Open Mon.-Fri. 8:45am-12:30pm and 1:45-4:30pm, Sat. 8:45am-12:30pm.

Medical Services: Queen Mary Hospital, Pok Fu Lam Rd., Hong Kong Island (tel. 2855 3838, non-office hr. 2855 3111). **Queen Elizabeth Hospital,** 30 Gascoigne Rd., Kowloon (tel. 2958 8888).

Emergency: tel. 999.

Post Offices: GPO, 2 Connaught Place, Central (tel. 2921 2333). Immediately to the right of Star Ferry. From MTR Jardine House exit, take a right and get onto the pedestrian overpass. Follow signs for Jardine House; it's in front of the post office. *Poste Restante* held for 2 months. Open Mon.-Fri. 8am-6pm, Sat. 8am-2pm. **Tsim Sha Tsui,** Hermes House, Ground Fl., 10 Middle Rd. (tel. 2366 4111). MTR: Tsim Sha Tsui MTR (Nathan Rd. exit). Pass Chungking Mansions and turn left onto Middle Rd. Hermes House is at the end of the street on the left. *Poste Restante* held for 2 months. Open Mon.-Fri. 8am-6pm, Sat. 8am-2pm.

Telephones: Change, credit card, and phonecard phones. Pick up phonecards at Hong Kong Telecom Service centers, HKTA offices, or 7-Eleven and Circle K stores. Local calls cost HK$1 regardless of the call's length. For home country operators, call the **HCD number** for your country: British Telecom, 800-0044; Canada Direct, 800-1100; New Zealand Telecom, 800-0064; Telecom Australia, 800-0161; Telecom Eireann, 800-0353; Telekom South Africa, 800-0027; AT&T, 800-1111; MCI, 800-1121; Sprint, 800-1877.

▒ Hours and Holidays

Business hours are 9am to 5pm on weekdays (many offices take a lunch break from 1 to 2pm) and 9am to noon on Saturday. Most shops open every day at 10am, except during Lunar New Year, when almost everything shuts down for a few days. Public holidays and festivals for 1997 are as follows.

January 1: New Year's Day.
February 7 & 8: Lunar New Year, a 15-day festival. Most businesses close for at least three days.

April 4: Ching Ming Festival. Families visit graves and make offerings to ancestors.
March 30: Easter.
May 10: Tin Hau Festival, celebrated at temples to Tin Hau, Goddess of the Sea.
June 17: Queen Elizabeth's birthday (the following Monday is also a holiday).
June 20: Dragon Boat (Tuen Ng) Festival. "Dragon boats" race to drums.
August 26: Liberation Day (the previous Saturday is also a holiday).
August-September: Festival of the Hungry Ghosts. Offerings are burned in the
    streets, and various locations stage Chinese opera.
September 28: Mid-Autumn Festival. Paper lanterns are lit in public places.
October 21: Chung Yeung Festival. People visit ancestral graves to make offerings.
December 25: Christmas Day.
December 26: Boxing Day.

LIFE AND TIMES

■ The People of Hong Kong

Chinese constitute about 98% of Hong Kong's population, the majority of whom are
of Cantonese descent and colony born and bred. The entire population is just under
six million people, however, so there's plenty of room within that 2% for Filipinos,
Indians, Americans, Britons, and others. The fishing population of long-time islanders,
the **Tanka,** make up a small percentage as well.

■ History

Hong Kong, from *Heung Gong,* meaning "fragrant harbor," was largely ignored by
the Chinese before the mid-1800s, although it has been inhabited for thousands of
years. The original inhabitants were probably the **Yueh,** a tribe of boat-people and
fishermen whose descendents, the Tanka, still live in the area. At the beginning of the
first century AD, the region of what is now Hong Kong came under Chinese control.
Little was written about it until 1000 years later, when it served as a garrison town
and the center of pearl harvesting for Tanka divers. Around this time, discord within
China brought the Five Great Clans south. These northern Cantonese families settled
on the southern tip, and established the province of **Canton.**
    In the 17th century the **Qing** dynasty evacuated the area to control piracy. This
experiment was short-lived, and the sparsely populated region became a haven for
northern farmers, known as **Hakka** (guests). With this new economic base, the Cantonese families began to consolidate control over the market. British merchants
began trading in Canton in the late 17th century, along with other Europeans who
were vying for trade, and began converting this handful of small fishing villages into a
thriving commercial base, exchanging **opium** for Chinese silks, spices, and silver. As
the Chinese government saw capital leaving the country in exchange for a population of addicts, they restricted British trade. The drug smugglers persevered, and at
the beginning of the 19th century the opium trade had more than doubled. In 1821
the British established themselves in Hong Kong, gaining a strategic economic position. When threatened with a full-scale, enforced ban on drug trafficking, the British
attempted negotiations, and then struck with their naval hardware, claiming Hong
Kong Island as a British territory in 1841 and then invading the mainland. Beginning
with the **Treaty of Nanking,** the British and their western allies forced China to cede
the area collectively known as "Hong Kong." Hong Kong Island and its surrounding
waters were taken in the First Opium War (1842), Kowloon in the second (1860),
and the New Territories were acquired in a 99-year lease in 1898.
    The Japanese invasion of China, the establishment of the People's Republic of
China, and the Korean War drove millions of Cantonese and others to Hong Kong,
bringing many professionals to the tiny island. During the late 60s, China's Cultural

Revolution kept Hong Kong on edge, as its citizens realized that it would take little effort for China to subsume the tiny island. Instead, China became Hong Kong's largest trade partner. The British and Chinese eventually questioned how useful a split colony would be to either power, once the New Territories and much of Kowloon reverted to China. To simplify things Britain signed the **Sino-British Joint Declaration** in 1984 so that all of Hong Kong will return to China at **the stroke of midnight on June 30, 1997.**

▓ Hong Kong Today

Despite China's guarantee to maintain the current economy and life-style of Hong Kong until at least 2047, the impending turnover broadcasts financial and philosophical shock waves through the community, and has sent scores scurrying to the U.S., Canada, and Australia, and then scurrying right back again, with promises of permanent resident status if they return before the turnover. Pro-democracy movements are apprehensive as well, under the steady realization that the colonial administration will soon be replaced by equivalent figures from Beijing, leaving Hong Kong perpetually subservient. With many of the details of the takeover yet to be ironed out, the island's inhabitants hold their breath for what the future has in store.

Those living on borrowed time seem to take it in stride: Mandarin language schools are making big bucks, and the growing number of Cantonese who speak the northern dialect casually remark that they are rehearsing for 1997. Western-owned businesses covertly look for methods to increase Chinese visibility of their company. Meanwhile, the furious pace of life rumbles recklessly on for its inhabitants. Yuppies cruise the Lan Kwai Fong district, shuttling among transplanted pubs and trendy clubs with names like "Post-1997." Wizened sooth-sayers predict destinies, fruit-vendors hack up watermelons with Zen-like calm, and old men still lounge around temples, hunched over backgammon. More subtle manifestations are already afoot, as Queen Elizabeth's picture has been removed from the Territory's stamps and coins and replaced with Hong Kong's state flower, and the word Royal has been taken down from many public buildings. Yet nobody can determine how far off kilter the city will be thrown when Beijing comes to collect the rent. Many feel the future is up for grabs, but that there are more ways things can go wrong than right. Beyond it all, Taiwan looks on as well, believing that China's handling of Hong Kong will be an omen, good or bad, regarding the likelihood of the two countries ever reuniting. For now, however, the Fragrant Harbor is reassuringly redolent with the intoxicating smell of free-enterprise.

HUMAN RIGHTS

Human rights issues are becoming real and pressing concerns as the British colony mobilizes for the change-over to China, a country with a less-than-sparkling record on this front. With this date rapidly approaching, the island's residents and protectors are concerned that the freedom of expression and lack of oppression which they enjoy today will no longer be safeguarded. Even if a human rights guardian were to be implemented, China has suggested that it would be disbanded come mid-1997. China has already warned the island that the press will have to answer when the time comes; self-censorship has become the rule of thumb for Hong Kong's newspapers today as they hedge their bets against future eventualities.

▓ Arts and Recreation

Hong Kong's roots in Sino-British traditions have created a city where there are at least two ways of doing everything. **Chinese opera,** or *wayung,* can be found in the intricate but campy Cantonese style, with its extraordinary and sometimes incomprehensible costumes and movements, as well as in the older and more classical Beijing style. Hong Kong has two popular modern orchestras, one which specializes in western fare and one which plays Chinese classics.

Less cosmopolitan, but no less fun, **puppet plays** abound. Telling the stories of China's dynasties through shadow plays is a popular form of puppetry. The lion dances, with their martial arts-like movements, are important in festivals. For some bubble-gum music fun, Hong Kong's **Canto-Pop** has a light rock sound, but northwestern folk music is influencing the creation of a new, indigenous rock.

For a peaceful recreational pursuit, **mahjong,** the classic Chinese game of memory and strategy, is popular, as the traveler can discern by the characteristic clicking that often lasts all night long in Chinese hangouts. Martial arts are the exercise of choice in the frantic city. **Shadow boxing** and its hyper cousin **kung fu** are excellent ways to calm the system and maintain your abs of steel.

ON THE MAINLAND

■ Kowloon

The nine legendary dragons *(kow lung)* comprising this 11sq.km peninsula seem to have released Kowloon to the powers of Tsim Sha Tsui ("Sharp Sandy Point"), Hong Kong's retail mecca for disoriented shoppers hoping to return home with a bargain-priced bauble or too-cheap-to-be-true electronic gizmo. Thousands of foreigners mill around Nathan Rd., eyeballing the maze of streets filled with restaurants, bars, boutiques and shopping arcades. Touts accost tourists with glossy ads and hawkers pull visitors aside to show them photos of fake Rolexes, all "high quality, low price."

ORIENTATION

From the Star Ferry concourse, **Salisbury Road** extends east-west past the Hong Kong Cultural Centre and the New World Centre into Tsim Sha Tsui East. Once tagged "Nathan's Folly" after the imprudence of the British governor who designed it, **Nathan Road,** the main avenue of Tsim Sha Tsui, runs north-south, intersecting Salisbury Rd. near the Space Museum. The luxurious Peninsula Hotel reposes at the intersection. To the west of Nathan Rd. lies **Kowloon Park.** The Tsim Sha Tsui MTR station has exits all along Nathan Rd. Smaller streets running perpendicular to Nathan Rd. house many of Tsim Sha Tsui's renowned shops and restaurants.

ACCOMMODATIONS

A towering ramshackle warren of bargain-priced guest houses, **Chungking Mansions** stands on 36-44 Nathan Rd., next to the red columns of the World Trade Plaza. The A1 airbus stops a mere 10m from Chungking. The so-called "mansions" is essentially a 14-16 story hulk of a building that has been subdivided repeatedly into six- to eight-room guest houses. Despite its dim interior, hidden fire escapes, and rat population, Chungking remains a popular establishment with backpackers. Within this ramshackle behemoth, there are decent guest houses that come close to Chungking's motto: 'very clean, very quiet, very cheap.'

Welcome Guest House, A5, 7th Fl. (tel. 2721 7793). Welcome is a local favorite, and the traveler should be aware that many people lie and say they are from Welcome, only to take the weary tourist's money; don't pay until you have arrived at the reception desk. Also has 15th-floor accommodations with cheery, pastel sheets. A/C and TV provided. Singles HK$140-160, with bath HK$170-200. Doubles HK$170-200, with bath HK$200-300. Visas for China arranged.

Peking Guest House, A2, 12th Fl. (tel. 2723 8320). Funky patterned bed linens boost spirits in this clean and jovial spot. A/C and TV provided. Diminutive singles HK$160, with bath HK$200. Doubles HK$220, with bath HK$260-35.

Beyond the Mansions

Victoria Hostel, 2nd Fl., 33 Hankow Rd., Tsim Sha Tsui (tel. 2376 0621). A right off Peking Rd.; look for blue-and-white sign. Go through Cheung Kee Watch Co. to the stairs in the back. Budget rates make dim chambers tolerable. Hot water and A/C in every room. Single sex dorms HK$80, no visitors allowed. 4-bed dorm HK$150. 6-bed dorm HK$120. Discounts for longer stays. Lockers free the 1st day, HK$25 per day thereafter. HK$50 key deposit. MC and Visa (3% surcharge).

Star Guest House, Flat B, 6th Fl., 21 Cameron Rd. (tel. 2723 8951), Tsim Sha Tsui MTR station (Cameron Rd. exit). Half a block after Carnarvon Rd., across from the Crocodile Shop. Cut through Perfect Jewellery Co. to the elevator. Upscale if small-ish rooms with phone, A/C, lockable drawers, and carpeted walls. Arranges visas for China and tours to China and Macau. Singles HK$290, with bath HK$360-380. Doubles HK$310, with bath HK$400-420. 24-hr. reception.

FOOD

Prices here are somewhat higher than in other parts of the territory, but don't let a little inflation burst your gastronomic bubble. The small streets west of Nathan Rd. harbor good restaurants. The rather grim stalls on the first floor of Chungking Mansions offer good food at inexpensive prices (often for under HK$20).

Nanjing Kitchen, 98 Canton Rd., ground Fl. (tel. 2317 6201). From the Star Ferry, take a left onto Canton Rd. and keep walking; it's across from the Harbor City Shopping Arcade. Amazing selection of appetizers: noodles mixed with anything—chicken or sour wontons (HK$20-28, up to HK$40 for seafood). 10% surcharge. English menu. Open Mon.-Thurs. 11am-midnight, Fri.-Sat. 11am-1am.

Taj Mahal Club, 3rd Fl, Block B, Chungking Mansions. Outspoken decor with natty pink-and-baby blue striped walls and all the decadence of three air conditioners. For 25 years, it's been a favorite among locals who gossip over tangy plates of chicken *tikka masala* (HK$40) and hot *naan* (HK$5). Open daily 11:30am-4pm and 6pm-11:30pm. English menu.

The Sweet Dynasty, 88 Canton Rd., ground Fl. (tel. 2375 9119). From the Star Ferry, take a left off onto Canton Rd. 3 stores before Nanjing Kitchen. Charming café with traditional tables and low round stools. Specializes in *tong shui*, sweet soups traditionally served after meals (HK$17). *Congee* (HK$30-110), rice (HK$28), and noodle dishes (HK$18-55) also available. English menu. Open Sun.-Thurs. 11:30am-midnight, Fri.-Sat. 11:30am-1am.

SIGHTS

Tsim Sha Tsui breaks from the temple-and-street market rut with ultra-modern museums. The **Clock Tower,** a lonely remnant of the old railway station, is to the right as you step off the ferry. Next door is the **Hong Kong Cultural Centre** (tel. 2734 2009), a huge, beige complex. Its Grand Theatre offers a variety of shows, from *The Phantom of the Opera* to members of the Texas Girls' Choir. Upcoming events are posted in the middle of the hall (9am-9pm). The adjacent **Space Museum,** 10 Salisbury Rd. (tel. 2734 2722), in the shape of a bisected golf ball, features hands-on exhibits. The Planetarium screens three Omnimax films each weekday (except Tues.) and ten on Sat.-Sun. and holidays. (Open Mon.-Fri. 1-9pm, Sat.-Sun. and holidays 10am-9pm; admission HK$10, students and seniors HK$5.) The Space Theatre has one daily sky show in English; headphones are provided for the other shows. (Admission HK$28, students and seniors HK$14; free on Wed.) Behind the Science Museum, the **Hong Kong Museum of Art** (tel. 2734 2167) guards Chinese antiquities, as well as contemporary Hong Kong art. (Open Mon.-Sat. 10am-6pm, Sun. and holidays 1-6pm; admission HK$10, students and seniors HK$5, free on Wed.)

Kowloon Park lies west of Nathan Rd. (MTR: Tsim Sha Tsui, A1 exit). The entrance is behind you. Weary road warriors can chill among fountains, pink flamingos, swimming pools resembling island lagoons, sculptures, and those dogged *tai chi* enthusiasts. (Open 6am-midnight. Games hall open 7am-11pm; free. Pools open 6:30am-10pm; admission HK$18, children and seniors HK$9.) The **Museum of History** (tel.

2367 1124), on the west side of the park, contains historical photographs and arti-facts. (Open Mon.-Thurs. and Sat. 10am-6pm, Sun. and public holidays 1-6pm; admis-sion HK$10, students and seniors HK$5, free Wed.)

If the Space Museum whetted your appetite for ultra-modern gadgetry, then try the **Hong Kong Science Museum,** 2 Science Museum Rd. (tel. 2732 3232), MTR: Tsim Sha Tsui, Cameron Rd. exit. Go right to Granville Rd., then turn right. Get on the pedestrian overpass near the Chatham Rd. intersection, and follow the red and white signs. A delight for budding Einsteins and their parents, the museum tweaks the cere-brum with interactive media. (Open Tues.-Fri. 1-9pm, Sat.-Sun. and public holidays 10am-9pm; admission HK$25, children, students, and seniors HK$15, free Wed.)

ENTERTAINMENT AND NIGHTLIFE

Bars and pubs bum around as well, particularly in the oddly shaped polygram formed by Carnarvon Rd., Cameron Rd., Chatham Rd., and Mody Rd. Tsim Sha Tsui is packed with bars, pubs, and dance clubs, including **Ned Kelly's Last Stand** and the **Old Hero Pub and Café.** For a brief foray into the rarified elegance of Hong Kong's elite, try **Felix** (tel. 2366 6251), the roof-top restaurant/bar at the Peninsula Hotel. The avant-garde chic and spectacular night views of Victoria Harbor are definitely worth dropping by for a late-night cup of coffee (HK$40) or dessert (HK$85). Don't miss the bathrooms; they're the talk of the town. (Open nightly 6pm-2am; major credit cards accepted).

■ Near Kowloon

Wong Tai Sin Temple, named after a legendary healer, is dedicated to Taoist and Buddhist deities, as well as to Confucius. Disembark at the Wong Tai Sin MTR station exit. Built in 1973, the structures are awash with gaudy, vibrant colors. Modern-day mystics stare into your future, finding ways to change bad destiny into good. Negoti-ate first or you're fated for an unpleasantly large bill. (Open daily 7am-5pm.)

Moving north into **Yau Ma Tei,** two MTR stations away or a 20-minute walk up Nathan Rd., tourists are entertained in street markets, cafés, and shops. The **Jade Market,** a chief attraction, is at the intersection of Kansu St., Reclamation St., and Bat-tery St. Leave the Jordan MTR station (Jordan Rd. exit) and walk down Nathan Rd. past the Eaton Hotel; Kansu St. is the first street on the left. Reclamation St. is the fourth. The bazaar is under the overpass behind an outdoor fruit market. Jade are carved into various images and knickknacks. The cheapest dainties cost about HK$5. Shop around and bargain for the best deals. (Open daily 10am-3:30pm.)

The area behind the market is transformed at night into the **Temple Street Night Market.** Fortune-tellers crowd the alley just outside the temple, hoping for a chance to feel the bumps on your cranium, or to coax their oracular parakeets into picking out an appropriate fortune. The damage for a basic palm reading is about HK$200. (Open daily, around 8-11pm.)

Lined with songbirds in delicate teak cages, the **Bird Market** on Hong Lok Rd. is both fascinating and grotesque. Stall owners sell live grasshoppers, popping them into plastic bags for you. From the Mongkok MTR station (exit C) take a left, pass a large Chinese movie theater, and take the first right. The Bird Market is about a block farther—just follow the chirps.

HONG KONG ISLAND

■ Central District

During the day, the financial and government center crawls with filofaxed business-men scrambling from one high-rise to another through endless crowds, cars, and trams in a stream of traffic that defies the narrowness of the streets. Older, upscale tourists flex Platinum Cards in the infinite number of boutiques selling Yves St. Laurent, solid gold bars, and other 24-carat emblems of conspicuous consumption. By 7pm the streets are deserted. Only the expat-barfly-haven of Lan Kwai Fong, and the Star Ferry concourse, where noodle vendors set up to intercept folks rushing home, scrimmage with action-packed intensity well into the night.

ORIENTATION

Let the Star Ferry concourse be your guiding light. Stationed at the northern edge of the neighborhood, this complex shares the district's chief thoroughfare, **Connaught Road Central,** with the low-rising general post office and Jardine House, a metal-clad round-windowed office tower. **Des Voeux Road Central** and **Queen's Road Central,** the area's two other main streets, run south of and parallel to Connaught Rd.; **Pedder Street** and **Ice House Road** connect all three roads.

Central is a veritable Valhalla of landmarks. The Hong Kong and Shanghai Banking Corporation Headquarters Bldg., a steel and glass monstrosity, stands beside the Bank of China, both bordered by Des Voeux Rd. to the north, Queen's Rd. to the south, and Ice House Rd. to the west. Alexandra House looms over Des Voeux Rd. across from the landmark. The few alleys at the southern end of D'Aguilar St. cutting across Queen's Rd. constitute the expat haunt known as **Lan Kwai Fong.**

FOOD

Hong Kong's business district favors fast-food and full-service over colorful eateries and vendors. It is easy to feast frugally in the basements of major office buildings. **Maxim's** and **Café de Coral** are options for those seeking cheap Chinese fast food. For more fare, wander around **Wellington St.** and **Stanley St. Pedder St. Central Market** has three floors of meat, fish, and vegetable stalls in the belly of a concrete building on the corner of Queen's Rd. Central and Queen Victoria St. The smell is fierce but prices are low and the food undeniably fresh.

Vegi Table, 1 Tun Wo Lane, ground fl. (tel. 2877 0901). Take the hillside escalator from Central Market to the Lyndhurst Terrace exit. Tun Wo Lane is just to the left down the stairs. All the tea, soup, and rice you can eat with the daily set meal (usually under HK$40), or a selection from the menu. It's hard to be a glutton for those constrained with chopsticks, so be sure to ask for cutlery. Reservations recommended for lunch. Open Mon.-Fri. 11am-3pm and 6-9pm, Sat. 11am-3pm.

SIGHTS

Some of Hong Kong's most tranquil gardens provide an herbal oasis in the midst of Central's parched urban desert. **Statue Square** is a popular spot. From Star Ferry, enter the pedestrian underpass; a blue sign for Statue Square is on the left. Part of the square lies across Chater Rd., where the statue of Sir Thomas Jackson, one of Hong Kong's beloved capitalists and chief manager of the Hong Kong and Shanghai Banking Corporation, happily surveys the landscape of lucre.

Across Des Voeux Rd. Central from Statue Square is the futuristic flagship of the **Hong Kong and Shanghai Banking Corporation,** the fourth headquarters to be located on this site. "The Robot Building," completed in 1985, states in crystal-clear terms that Hong Kong won't yield its iron grip on capitalism without a fight. The interior workings of the escalators and elevators are completely exposed, as are the offices, which are open to the interior atrium and glass-walled on the street side.

Hong Kong Park, a 10-hectare modern landscaping marvel on the east edge of the Central district, is a requisite stop for any visitor. Follow the sidewalk from the Hong Kong Hilton as it turns onto Garden Rd. Watch for Peak Tram signs; the park's main entrance is up a staircase across the street from the tram souvenir shop. An aviary, conservatory, and visual arts center roost in the park. (Park open daily 7am-11pm; aviary 9am-4:30pm, varies with season; conservatory Mon.-Fri. 9am-5pm, Sat.-Sun. and holidays 9am-6pm.) The visual arts center (tel. 2521 3008) has mostly modern art exhibits (open Wed.-Mon. 10am-6pm).

The **Zoological and Botanical Gardens** are just off Garden Rd., a 10-minute walk from the Hong Kong Hilton past St. John's Cathedral. The main entrance is at the intersection of Garden Rd. and Upper Albert Rd. An arch commemorates the Chinese who died fighting for the Allied cause. Winding paths crisscross the garden, perfect for visitors to squawk along with the early birds and break the zombie-like concentration of folks doing *tai chi.* (Open daily 6am-7pm.)

ENTERTAINMENT

Central nightlife is slightly classier, some say pretentious, than in the rest of town; many trendy pubs and clubs are on **Lan Kwai Fong,** an L-shaped lane off D'Aguilar St. The city-slicker-material-girl-disco-demimonde-regulars often provide enough entertainment to justify the upwardly mobile cover charges and bar tabs. **Club YES,** 19 Lan Kwai Fong (tel. 2877 8233), blasts the loudest music on the block. Mon.-Thurs. the HK$100 cover includes five drinks, Fri.-Sat. only two (open Mon.-Sat. 9pm-4am). Across the street, **Club 97** draws a slightly hipper clientele, discouraging style-lacking budgeteers with its HK$97 cover and no-nonsense pair of supermodel "bouncers" at the door. Popular bars along Lan Kwai Fong are recognizable by their tendency to spill out onto the street. Prices remain fairly constant (a bit pricey) and all establishments are within walking distance of each other. You can't go wrong.

Petticoat Lane, 2 Tun Wo Lane (tel. 2973 0642), near the Lyndhurst Terrace exit. Tun Wo Lane is an obscure alley to the left of the stairs. Petticoat Lane is at the end, behind a *faux* topiary hedge. Elegant and seductive, Petticoat captures a cosmopolitan mix of the gay, bi, and straight. Opulent brocade couches wrap themselves around the small single room establishment. Oils in gilt frames glow in the dim light of two poppy-red lamps apparently purchased at a Dr. Suess estate sale. Beer HK$38. Dinner served at the Pavilion Restaurant next door. Provides information on local events. Open daily noon-3am. Major credit cards accepted.

■ Sheung Wan

Just west of Central Market is Sheung Wan, where the Royal Navy dropped anchor for Britannia in 1841. Once inspiring enthusiastic comparisons to old Shanghai, the now-anemic district is surrendering to the bulldozers. The **Macau Ferry Terminal** reigns over the north edge of the district. **Western Market,** an Edwardian building converted into a tourist mall, slouches on New Market St. Farther south, at the corner of Ladder St. and Hollywood Rd., looms **Man Mo Temple,** where the lovelorn shake fortune-telling sticks to check on the state of their star-crossed destinies. Dedicated to the Taoist gods of literature and war, Man and Mo, the temple also houses a number of shrines to the city god and the 10 Divine Judges (open daily 7am-5pm).

■ Wan Chai

Wan Chai will probably never shake off its infamy as the setting for Richard Mason's novel, *The World of Suzie Wong.* Although the film was shot in Sheung Wan, Wan Chai remains linked in the imagination with brothels, bars, and furloughed sailors. In reality, much of northern Wan Chai has been transformed into a business district, where white-shirted executives close deals on their cellular phones during lunch. The southern part, however, retains some of the old red-light-district seediness, hosting topless bars interspersed among tattoo parlors and smoky pubs.

ORIENTATION

Between the harbor and **Gloucester Road** is reclaimed land which is overrun with elephantine office skyscrapers including Hong Kong's Immigration Towers and New

Convention Centre. Three streets, **Jaffe Road, Lockhart Road,** and **Hennessy Road,** run parallel to each other south of Gloucester Rd. and comprise "old" Wan Chai. They are cut perpendicularly by **Penwick Street, Luard Road, O'Brien Road,** and **Fleming Road,** which in turn meet **Johnston Road** where the tram tracks run. Forage for Wan Chai chow south of Gloucester Rd.; small cafés and restaurants, including some fast food shops, slink about Hennessy Rd. South of Johnston Rd., Spring Garden Lane gurgles with tropical fish and flowers, while nearby Lee Tung St. and Tai Yuen St. host **street markets** and **food stalls.**

FOOD

Vegetarian Garden, 128 Johnston Rd. (tel. 2833 9128), at the intersection of Johnston and O'Brien Rd. Look for the large neon sign. Ground floor is take-out; the restaurant is downstairs. Local clientele. *Dim sum* (HK$10 per basket) is ordered from a list. Superb vegetarian *shumai* (open-faced ravioli). English menu. Take-out counter open 7:30am-11pm. Restaurant open daily 11am-11pm.

Kublai's, 1 Capitol Place, 3rd Fl., 18 Luard Rd. (tel. 2529 9117). The entrance is on Jaffe Rd.; walk up Luard Rd. and turn right before La Bamba pub and disco. Kublai and Ghengis never had it so good; nor have most who flock to this Mongolian eatery. For HK$118 (children HK$98), fill your bowl as many times as you like. Select from an amazing array of veggies, meats, and fish; top it off with sauces and garnishes, and hand it to the army of cooks, who will have it ready in 10min. Incredibly tasty, a fantastic bargain, and fun for groups. Newly opened cybercafé (the first in Hong Kong). Reservations recommended. Open daily 12:30-3:30pm and 6:30-11:30pm. Other locations at 55 Kimberly Rd., Tsim Sha Tsui (2722 0733) and 1 Keswick St., Causeway Bay (2882 3282).

Quality Herb Tea House, 84 Hennessy Rd., MTR Wan Chai (Alliance Française exit). Corner of Luard Rd. and Hennessy Rd., across from Broadway Seafood Restaurant. Potent potables from golden teapots with dragon's head spouts. Chinese herbal brews HK$5-9 a bowl. Little blue stickers explain each tea's special properties. Open daily 10am-11pm.

ENTERTAINMENT

The Wanch, 54 Jaffe Rd. (tel. 2861 1621). MTR Wan Chai (Lockhart Rd. exit). Follow Jaffe Rd. west, just past the Fenwick St. intersection. The Wanch is on the left, with a Japanese flag sign. An intimate ode to Hong Kong pop culture, it's designed like a Star Ferry. Part of the outside is a tram and tram seats serve as booths; posters from *The World of Suzie Wong* plaster the dim interior. Open Sun.-Thurs. 11am-3am, Fri.-Sat. 11am-4am. Live music every night.

Carnegie's, 53-5 Lockhart Rd. (tel. 2866 6289). The "Spirit of Rock" heats up at night and goes wild on weekends. Cocktails HK$40-150. Happy hour 11am-9pm daily. Wed. is Ladies' Night; free cocktails for women served by topless waiters. Mon.-Thurs. 11am-2am, Fri.-Sat. 11am-4am, Sun. 5pm-2am.

Joe Bananas, 23 Luard Rd. (tel. 2529 1811), at the corner with Jaffe Rd. "International" club with road signs, Beatles posters, and a portrait of Martin Luther King, Jr. No t-shirts, hats, or shorts after 6pm. Fri. and Sat. after 9pm, HK$100 cover includes 1 drink. Wed. nights it's 2 for 1 drinks. Happy hour 11:30am-9pm. No dress code on Sun. Open daily 11am-5am.

■ Causeway Bay

The glare of neon-lit camera shops and hip western bars is subdued by dozens of clothing shops and old-style open-air night markets. Residential as well as commercial, Causeway Bay boasts innumerable "mansions" and apartment units squeezed between department stores. *Tai chi* dominates the crack-of-dawn in Victoria Park; early risers drop into Maxim's for *dim sum* breakfast and good conversation.

HONG KONG

ORIENTATION

Causeway Bay is divided roughly into north and south by the broad swath of **Hennessy Road** which becomes **Yee Woo Street** as it runs east. **Gloucester Road** runs parallel to and north of Hennessy until it hits Victoria Park and makes a sharp right-angle turn, crossing Hennessy Rd./Yee Woo St. Before that intersection, **Paterson Street** connects the two. South of Yee Woo St. is a cluster of small streets lined with clothing stores, herbal medication, dried-food shops, and inexpensive restaurants. The Causeway Bay MTR station has six exits. One emerges onto **Great George Street** near Daimaru department store. Another comes out next to Sogo department store. Two more appear farther west at Causeway Bay Plaza on Yee Woo St., and another pops up near the mouth of Jardine's Crescent. A final exit is in the Times Square shopping complex, east of Jardine's Bazaar and Jardine's Crescent.

FOOD

Maxim's Chinese Restaurant, Hong Kong Mansion, Yee Woo St. (tel. 2894 9933). Directly cross from the Causeway Bay MTR station (Daimaru exit). Ditch your beauty sleep for *dim sum;* show up at 7:45am and savor tasty dumplings, *congee,* soup, and free hot jasmine tea, HK$15-32 a basket. Good-sized breakfast under HK$45. Maxim's also serves standard Chinese fare at reasonable prices. Open daily 7:30am-midnight. *Dim sum* 7:30am-5pm. English menu.

SIGHTS

Escape the mundane realm of the Causeway Bay MTR (Times Square exit) and you'll find yourself at the pearly gates of shopping. A 13-level mall organized around themes such as "Suit and Dress," "Home Sweet Home," and "Dante and Virgil," **Times Square** showcases upscale designers and trendy specialties with other-worldly prices (open daily 10am-10pm).

Opposite Times Square on Russell St., a heated **outdoor market** throbs from 8:30am-7pm selling fresh meat along with inexpensive trinkets and juicy mangos, papayas, and star fruit. The booming **outdoor market** at **Jardine's Bazaar** and **Jardine's Crescent** testifies to the presence of a market economy. As you emerge from the Causeway Bay MTR station (Jardine's Crescent exit), the Crescent is the small tunnel of clothing stalls to the right of the Giordano store. The Bazaar is the next street on the left, with cheap eateries, whose tables spill out onto the sidewalk with inexpensive noodles, spring rolls, dumplings, and other snacks. Peddlers offer traditional herbal medicines, preserved bean curd, tea, and clothing up and down the street. The alleyway under the red sign for the **Yat Pun Henn Restaurant** connects the Bazaar with the Crescent; duck in for popular outdoor dining, cold juices, and grilled squid from 9am on.

The **Noon-Day Gun** squats near the harbor, across from the Excelsior Hotel. Catapulted to fame in Noel Coward's 1924 song *Mad Dogs and Englishmen* ("In Hong Kong they strike a gong and fire a noon-day gun"), the 1.5kg gun is still fired daily.

Victoria Park lends lushness to the gold and silver of the shopping district. Enter on Gloucester Rd., opposite the Park Lane Radisson. A roller-skating rink, bowling green, and swimming pool can be enjoyed for a fee, but free jogging trails are surrounded by spacious lawns, an aviary, and a topiary garden. The park is home to a large flower fair during Chinese New Year and hosts local families who come to eat lotus-seed cakes and gaze at the moon during the Mid-Autumn Festival. (Open daily 7am-11pm.) A single footbridge in the northwest corner of Victoria Park, along the path from the Model Boat Pool, leads to **Causeway Bay Typhoon Shelter** where countless floating homes bob next to sleek yachts. Look for a sign that says "passenger carrying sampan" in English (about 30min., HK$150). A good time to visit is during the Chinese New Year, when vessels swarm to the harbor.

■ Near Hong Kong

Ma Wui Hall Youth Hostel, Mount Davis Path, (tel. 2817 5715) is the closest hostel, albeit still a trek. Take A2 airbus to the Macau Ferry Bus Terminal and then a cab (HK$50). A cheaper alternative is the shuttle bus service the hostel has recently set up. Buses arrive in front of the Macau ferry terminal at 10am, 5, and 8pm (HK$10). Details are still being worked out, so it's best to call ahead for the exact schedule and room availability. Quiet cubicles offer a superb view of the harbor. Dorms for HI members are HK$50, overseas non-members HK$75. There is a limit of three consecutive nights. Reception is open 7am-midnight. Kitchen and locker storage are available. No visitors are allowed. The gate is locked at midnight.

Compared to the city below, **Victoria Peak,** the former home of the British governors, is significantly cooler and a century back in time. The tram is the fast and scenic way to the top (every 10-15min., 7am-midnight, HK$14, HK$21 roundtrip. Children under 12 HK$4, HK$7 roundtrip). A free double decker bus departs from Star Ferry on Hong Kong Island to the tram station (every 20min., Mon.-Sat. 10am-8pm; every 10min. Sun. and public holidays). Once part of the governor's lodge, the **Peak Gardens** are a great place to view the serene outlying islands and the frenetic skyline below. Follow Mt. Austin Rd. up the mountain from Peak Tower near the tram station for about 25 minutes.

One of Hong Kong's top draws, **Aberdeen** is a curious hybrid of run-down *sampan* and floating restaurants. Take bus #70 from Exchange Square, Central (A/C bus, every 5-10min., HK$4.50) or bus #72 from Causeway Bay (A/C bus, every 10-20min., HK$4.50). Trawler operators may ambush tourists for harbor tours (about HK$40), or you can hop on a floating restaurant's ferry to the eatery. It's a thrilling sight at night when the restaurants wink brazenly at customers in the darkness.

Ocean Park and Water World playfully romp just east of Aberdeen. **Ocean Park** (tel. 2555 3554), which modestly declares itself "the largest and most spectacular theme park in Southeast Asia," promotes the usual nerve-wracking, stomach-dropping roller coasters plus a goldfish pagoda, a shark aquarium, and a dolphin university. The Middle Kingdom, a theme park-within-a-theme park showcasing 17 Chinese dynasties, is near the back of the park. (Open daily 10am-6pm; admission HK$130, children 3-11 HK$65.) **Water World,** however, doesn't make any attempt at intellectual pretensions. Who needs high-brow when there's a giant aquatic playpen full of slides, pools, and tanned teenagers? (Open June-July 1, daily 10am-6pm; July 2-Aug. 31, daily 9am-9pm; Sept.1-mid-Sept., 10am-6pm; mid-Sept.-mid.-Oct. weekends and holidays only, 10am-6pm. Day admission HK$65; evening HK$40.) Take bus #70 from Exchange Square, Central (A/C bus, every 5-10min., HK$4.50) or bus #72 from Causeway Bay (A/C bus, every 10-20min., HK$4.50). Get off at the first stop after the Aberdeen Tunnel and walk up the hill. Cross the street and turn left where blue arrows point to Ocean Park.

For some powdery bliss, romp to **Repulse Bay's beaches.** In addition to two large statues of Kwun Yum and Tin Hau, traditionally revered as protectors of local fishermen, there are sturdy nets anchored offshore to ensure no unwanted sea life come for a morning *dim sum.* Just take bus 6 or 6A from Exchange Square in Central (HK$8, half-fare for children) or bus 260 (HK$10). Buses run every 15-30 minutes, and will drop passengers off on Repulse Bay Rd., where you can cross to the beach.

Perhaps the most intriguing aspect of Hong Kong is that its dense urban fabric is positioned within an almost untouched topography of sweeping hills. Over 40% of the Territory has been set aside for public parks, most of which are tattooed with an intricate network of excellently maintained trails. The "Magic Walks" series is available in most bookstores and covers most hiking options (HK$45-65) within the area. Happy trippers should bring sunscreen, proper shoes, and lots of water.

HONG KONG

INDONESIA

Indonesia's national motto, *bhinneka tunggal ika,* translates to "unity in diversity." The country's diversity is readily apparent; over 350 ethnic groups have absorbed centuries of peaceful and imperialistic influences from home and abroad. Having celebrated 50 years of independence in 1995, a younger generation with no memory of this heritage knows a nation held together by its benevolent dictator, President Soeharto and his military New Order government. While Indonesia's diversity is a source of pride for nearly all its people, tenuous unity is often maintained through political repression and unspoken threats of violence. The resulting stability has brought increased prosperity: foreign investments keep rolling in as per capita income rises and growth rates run at a yearly clip of 6-7% or higher. Visitors to Indonesia are justly rewarded for their perseverance in a country where little English is spoken and independent travel can be frustrating. With a few words of Bahasa Indonesia to help, the observant traveler to Indonesia will not only be captured by a kaleidoscope collection of cultures, stunning landscapes, and historical legacies, but also be touched by the spirited laughter, deep tolerance, and muted sorrows of a people moving through everyday life in this vast, provocative nation.

ESSENTIALS

■ Geography

An astounding 17,508 islands are within Indonesia's great wingspan, making it the world's largest archipelago, although only about 6000 are inhabited. The country spans the seas between the continents of Australia and Asia, dividing the Indian (or what they call the Indonesian) and Pacific oceans at the Equator. Measuring 5150km from east to west, it is well-endowed with a range of natural resources from petroleum to jewels. Many of the islands have volcanoes—active, extinct, or dormant—and large regions of dense jungle.

■ When to Go

When you come to Indonesia will depend on whether you like it dry or wet. While areas near the equator receive consistent amounts of rain year-round, other regions have pronounced wet and dry seasons. Dry weather comes with the East Monsoon from June to September; the West Monsoon from November to March brings rain (varying amounts in different regions). The humidity (75-100%) and the temperature remain fairly stable and warm year round, although higher altitudes can get much colder. Please see the Climate Chart in the **Appendix** on page 737 for more specific information on the areas you are planning on visiting. You may also want to plan your trip to either avoid or coincide with festivals and holidays (see below).

■ Money Matters

US$1=2347.00rupiah (Rp)
CDN$=Rp1716.13
UK£1=Rp3524.94
IR£1=Rp3575.19
AUS$1=Rp1739.36
NZ$1=Rp1422.98
SARand=Rp658.33

Rp1000=US$0.426
Rp1000=CDN$0.583
Rp1000=UK£0.276
Rp1000=IR£0.280
Rp1000=AUS$0.575
Rp1000=NZ$0.703
Rp1000=SARand1.519

The Indonesian unit of currency is the **rupiah.** Coin denominations are Rp25, Rp50, Rp100, and Rp500; notes come in Rp100, Rp500, Rp1000, Rp5000, Rp10,000, Rp20,000, and Rp50,000. The US$ is the most readily accepted foreign currency (both cash and traveler's checks). Traveler's checks can be changed at banks, money changers, and some hotels. Only major hotels, restaurants, and travel agencies accept credit cards. While ATMs are nowhere near as common as in western countries, they can be found in some major cities. The traveler should not, however, rely on the anticipated presence of ATMs as a bail-out. Money from home can be obtained through handy credit card advances, or such services as Western Union (see the **Essentials** section for more information).

Bills at major hotels usually include a 10% service charge. **Gratuity** is not expected, but a 5-10% tip is always appreciated. Tips for taxi and hire-car drivers are not necessary, but for satisfactory service Rp1000 is appropriate for a taxi, and a bit more for a hire-car. At the airport, porters should be given Rp2000 for a small bag, Rp3000 for one that weighs more than 20kg.

■ Getting Around

Any entry and exit without a special visa must be made through specific gateways: by air at Jakarta, Denpasar, Manado, Biak, Ambon, Surabaya, and Batam; by sea at Semarang, Jakarta, Bali, Pontianak, Balikpapan, Tajung Pinang, and Kupang.

BY PLANE

Air travel is the easiest, most comfortable way to get around Indonesia. National carriers **Garuda** and **Merpati** run to all provincial district capitals. Other domestic airlines include **Sempati, Bouraq,** and **Mandala.** Airport tax for international flights is Rp21,000; for domestic travel tax varies but averages about Rp8000.

BY BOAT

Government-owned PELNI ships serve all main points in Indonesia (bi-weekly) with A/C but spartan accommodations, basic food, slow journeys, and mediocre prices. Reserve ahead. To smaller ports, PELNI operates less comfortable Pelayran Perintis, with deck class only. Ferries also run between islands. Alternatively, with a letter of permission from your embassy and a willing schooner, you may sometimes be able to hop on a boat for free.

BY TRAIN OR BUS

Trains run only in Java and parts of Sumatra, and are often slow and delayed, but are sometimes your best bet for long trips. Reserve in advance. Most locals get around by bus; although often slow, overcrowded, and unpredictable, buses are cheap. You can even buy a bus ticket that gets you from one island to another. Overnight buses *(bis malam)* are usually faster but arrive at inconvenient hours.

BY CAR, TAXI, OR MOTORBIKE

You can hire a car with or without a driver; the former (mostly available in major cities) are Rp75-120,000 per day, and the latter about Rp8-10,000 per hr. (more for out-of-town). Catch taxis, metered in large cities, around busy public places. On major routes, share-taxis carry five passengers. Except for metered taxis, bargain for the fare before you hop in. Registered taxis, minibuses, and hired cars have yellow license plates (private vehicles have black plates, government vehicles have red). The government warns you to stick with registered taxis and drivers. Motorbikes and motorcycles run Rp12-25,000 per day.

OTHER LOCAL TRANSPORTATION

Other forms of transport include the **becak** (bicycle rickshaw), **bajaj** (orange motorized three-wheeler), **bemo** (minibus), **oplet** (a larger form of *bemo*, a.k.a. **daihatsu, angkutan, angkot, microlet, sudako,** or **colt**), **ojek** (motorcycle taxis), and **andong** (horse-drawn carts). Some of these can be hired as well for private use (with the driver). Investigate average rates for the town you're in, then bargain away!

■ Keeping in Touch

Indonesia's postal service is not terribly reliable—**register important mail.** Check **Practical Information** listings to see if its post office holds *Poste Restante*. Indonesia extends over three time zones: Eastern Indonesia Standard Time (Maluku and Irian Jaya) is nine hours ahead of GMT; Central Standard Time (East and South Kalimantan, Sulawesi, Bali, and Nusa Tenggara) is eight hours ahead of GMT; Western Standard Time (Sumatra, Java, Madura, and West and Central Kalimantan) is seven hours ahead of GMT. For **telephone calls,** medium to large towns have Perumtel or *wartel* offices, which often also send faxes. Major cities and several hotels in Bali and Jakarta have IDD. HCD numbers are: British Telecom, 001-801-44; Canada Direct, 001-801-16; New Zealand Telecom, 62-178-6400; Telecom Australia, 008-0161; AT&T, 001-801-10; MCI, 001-801-11; and Sprint, 001-801-15. Long-distance calls within Indonesia can be direct-dialed (0 + city code + destination number). Telephone codes are listed in the **Practical Information** section of each town.

■ Staying Safe

On all the islands, you can call the **police** at 110 and an **ambulance** at 118 in case of emergency. Although Indonesia is generally safe and violence is rare, young single women should be cautious. Western women in particular are often seen as easy targets for harassment. Be alert, and don't give the harasser(s) the reaction he (or they) wants. Beware of pickpockets, particularly on public transportation and at large tourist attractions; carry all valuables in a moneybelt and avoid toting large amounts of cash. Also watch out for the scams prevalent in tourist areas—be skeptical of limited-time-only "bargains" and other touts.

BISEXUAL, GAY, LESBIAN TRAVELERS

Homosexual acts in Indonesia are legal, and some men maintain sexual relationships with other men. Public displays of affection are not advisable for *any* couples, straight or gay. Defying categories assigned by the west, Indonesia has its own alternate gender, known as *waria*, which is defined as a man with the soul of a woman. While not wholly accepted by Indonesian society, *waria* participate in a subculture of their own, and knowledge about *waria* among the Indonesian population is growing. Although no laws deal specifically with AIDS or HIV, affected persons may be denied entry or even quarantined under certain other restrictions. For more information on Indonesia's gay and lesbian scene, *waria* communities, and AIDS activism in Indonesia, pick up a copy of *GAYa Nusantara,* a magazine published in Surabaya. Their offices are at Jl. Mulyosari Timur 46, Surabaya Timur (tel. 593 49 24).

■ Hours and Holidays

Generally, businesses are open 8am-4pm or 9am-5pm, breaking for lunch between noon and 1pm; many are closed on Saturday. Government offices are open Mon.-Fri. 8am-4pm. Although normal banking hours are Mon.-Fri. 8am-2:30pm and Sat. 8am-noon, some branches in hotels have longer hours. Department stores and supermarkets in the large cities are typically open 9am-9pm, with shorter hours on Sunday. Shops in smaller cities may close 1-5pm.

When planning a trip, you may want to keep in mind public holidays and festivals. Due to the range of ethnic groups and religious faiths represented in Indonesia, there are a wide variety of holidays the traveler should be aware of. Some can be an inconvenience, while others can be a boon; experiencing Nyepi, the day of stillness in Bali, is an unforgettable experience. Dates for 1997 events are listed below. Call or write the Indonesian Tourist Bureau (see the **Essentials** section on page 1) to get a 1997 Calendar of Events, along with their handy dandy Travel Planner.

January 1: New Year's. Celebrated with the most fervor in Christian areas.
February 7 & 8: Imlek (Chinese New Year). Businesses close for 2 days or more.
February 20-21: Idul Fitri. The end of the Muslim fasting month of Ramadan.
March 21(spring equinox): Nyepi, Balinese Saka New Year, a day of total stillness. The day before, sacrifices are made and priests chant mantras; at night families bang cymbals and parade with torches to excise the demons of the old year.
March 28: Wafat Isa Al-Masih (Good Friday).
April 14: Idul Adha. (Muslim Day of Sacrifice). Commemorated with mass prayers, animals are sacrificed and the meat given to the needy.
April 21: Kartini Day. Birthday of Raden Ajeng Kartini, pioneer of the fledgling women's rights movement in Indonesia. Women dress in national dress; husbands and kids are supposed to pamper them.
May 16: Kenaikan Isa Al-Masih (Ascension of Christ).
May 19: Tahun Baru Hijriyah (Muslim New Year).
May 21: Waisak Day (Anniversary of the birth/death of Buddha). Monks carry flowers, candles, fire, and images of the Buddha from Candi Mendut (outside Yogyakarta) to Borobudur.
July 28: Maulid Nabi Muhammad (Birthday of Muhammad).
August 17: Indonesian Independence Day. The most important national holiday, marked by dancing, processions, and other festivities.
October 1: Hari Pancasila. Celebrates Soekarno's five principles (see page 130).
December 8: Isra Mi'raj Nabi Muhammad (Ascension of Muhammad).
December 25: Hari Raya Natal (Christmas Day).

LIFE AND TIMES

■ The People of Indonesia

With a population surging past 190 million, Indonesia ranks as the fourth most populated nation in the world, with 350 ethnic groups and 250 spoken languages. Over 60% of the people live on Java and Bali, although they represent only about 8% of Indonesia's total land mass. Such population pressures have led to a government push for family planning through the Keluarga Berencana (KB) program. The program has succeeded in lowering the nation's fertility rate from six in 1965 to 3.3 in 1985. Indonesia's family planning efforts have received international recognition and have served as a model for other nations facing similar population pressures.

ACEHNESE

The Acehnese live in the northernmost part of Sumatra. Their ancestors were probably originally the people of Champa (present-day Cambodia and south Vietnam), who settled in Aceh, and then later became cut off from the rest of their kingdom. Later, Indians, Arabs, Turks, and the Chinese came to Aceh, assimilating with the inhabitants and giving rise to today's native Acehnese. They have their own language and a writing system modified from Arabic. Although predominantly Muslim, their lifestyle incorporates other influences. They were also the leading fighters against the Dutch, and for that Aceh Province has been named a "Special Province" and given greater freedom in governing itself.

BALINESE

Tolerant and friendly hosts of Indonesia's largest tourist destination, the Balinese have withstood innumerable characterizations by publications like this one. Bali is the most concentrated outpost of Hinduism outside India, and 90% of its inhabitants adhere to Balinese-Hinduism; the remaining 10% are Buddhist, Muslim, or Christian. The Balinese are known for their flourishing arts, which have been subject to the best and worst influences of the consumer tourism glut.

BATAK

Living in the mountain valleys of north-central Sumatra, the Batak are descended from wandering Karen tribes of Thailand and Burma, who were forced to migrate south 1500 years ago by expanding tribes from the north. These people mingled with Indians trading in Sumatra and adopted several aspects of early Hindu civilization. Today, the Batak are roughly divided into six tribes: the Karo, Pak Pak, Simelungun, Toba, Angkola, and Mandailing. Some tribes are Muslim, others are Christian, but despite nominal affiliation, many still adhere to various animist traditions.

BIMANESE

These people of East Sumbawa are the descendants of 18th century sultanates, the Dou Donggo, as well as immigrants from other islands in the archipelago. They are darker-skinned than their western neighbors, and have a reputation for strong adherence to Islam. Ruled by the Gowa Kingdom of south Sulawesi from 1616 until their subjugation by the Dutch in 1667, the Bimanese remained under the strong influence of the north for many years to come.

BUGIS

One of the four primary ethnic groups on Sulawesi, the Bugis inhabit the southern part of the island. Historically known as traders, the Bugis were masters of the sea and the most feared pirates of their time. In fact, the modern word "boogeyman" is derived from the name of this people. Today, the Bugis still work with the sea as fisherman and *perahu* (square-bowed boat) builders. The Bugis follow Islam, but only to the extent that it does not conflict with the more entrenched and ancient traditions and ideals of their pride-based culture.

CHINESE

Records show contact between China and the Indonesian archipelago as far back as the 5th century, but Chinese migrants didn't settle en masse in Indonesia until the Dutch brought them in as laborers early in the colonial era. Eventually they were utilized as middlemen between the Dutch and the Indonesian populations, and thus became the merchant class in colonial society. Today, the Chinese comprise only about 2% of the population of Indonesia, but own more than half of all businesses. Historically, they have been scapegoated by ethnic Indonesians, so that urban unrest almost invariably degenerates into violence directed at the Chinese community. Because of the stigma attached to the 1965 coup and Soekarno's close ties with Beijing back in the PKI heydays, all publications in Chinese characters are banned, Chinese languages are not spoken in public, and all Chinese-Indonesians must take indigenous Indonesian surnames.

JAVANESE

The Javanese penchant for being polite, respectful, and accommodating to others borders on a parody of itself at times, and has become the butt of many jokes by other ethnic groups in Indonesia. Even simple conversations are formalized to express humility and respect for one's position in society. Javanese people live throughout Central and East Java, though the heart of Javanese culture lies in the royal courts of

Yogyakarta and Surakarta in Central Java, where Javanese manners are at their most refined. The culture, customs, and language of the Javanese—the largest and dominant ethnic group in Indonesian society—pervade all the other islands, if not through the Javanese-dominated central bureaucracy, then through the Javanese transmigrants being moved throughout the archipelago.

MAKASSARESE

The Makassarese share many similarities to the Bugis, with whom they share southern Sulawesi, although they adhere to the area around Ujung Pandang. During precolonial days, the Makassarese were very concerned with social rank and status, a preoccupation which has remained in some form to the present day; among the upper classes social structure and norms are rigidly observed. Like the Bugis, the Makassarese both observe Islam and their native traditions and beliefs. They were also traditionally seafarers, often in great rivalry with the Bugis.

MINANGKABAU

Matrilineal and staunchly Muslim, West Sumatra's Minangkabau people manage to combine their two seemingly irreconcilable traits without conflict. As the fourth largest ethnic group in Indonesia, the Minang have contributed much to Indonesia's national character. While women control family households, inheritance rights, and marriage proposals, young men are expected to leave the house, make a living for themselves, and return home as desirable bachelors. This explains the huge representation of Minang people in Jakarta, and the high educational standards they set for themselves. Minang figures were instrumental in the nationalist movement and continue to rank among the leading intellectuals and authors of Indonesia.

SASAK

The Islamic Sasak inhabit the eastern part of Lombok, and are significantly poorer than the Balinese whom they share it with. Descended from overland Indian and Burmese settlers, they are a hill tribe with dark skin and some Caucasian features. Although Muslim, they are divided between the secular and less devout **Waktu Telu** (Three Prayer Islam) and the **Waktu Lima** (Five Prayer Islam). The Waktu Telu revere huge images in the ground and, as indicated by their name, pray only three times per day. Both groups have adopted something of a caste system, complete with language codes reserved for addressing those of differing social status.

SUMBAWANESE

The predominantly Muslim Sumbawanese inhabit the western half of Sumbawa and speak a language incomprehensible to that of their Bimanese neighbors. The Sumbawanese share many customs of the Sasaks of Lombok, and are taller and lighter-complexioned than the Bimanese.

SUNDANESE

The Sundanese are the dominant ethnic group of West Java outside Jakarta. They speak their language with a lilting, sing-song intonation that contrasts with the Jakartan dialect. In general, the Sundanese are more dedicated Muslims than the Javanese, but otherwise they have much in common with their neighbors.

TORAJANS

Torajans have inhabited the highlands of Sulawesi for ages, practicing a culture that has been attracting tourist dollars in the recent decades. Dutch colonialism proved to have lasting repercussions on Torajan life, adversely dismantling family and religious structures. Today, most Torajans claim adherence to Christianity, but the native *adat* is still strong and vivid, particularly visible in their funerary ceremonies.

■ History

Fossils discovered at Trinil, Mojokerto, and Sangiran in the past century have distinguished the region of Central Java as one of the earliest sites of hominid occupation outside of Africa. Discoveries of similar fossils in East Asia and Africa confirmed that **Java Man**—with a characteristic low-vaulted, thick-walled skull and large brow-ridges—is within the species *Homo erectus*. While it is generally agreed that *Homo erectus* is an evolutionary predecessor of modern humans, it's not true that Java Man evolved into today's Malay peoples. Rather, *Homo erectus* probably died out in Java about 350,000 years ago, while modern humans evolved from hominid populations in Africa and migrated in waves to repopulate Java Man's former home.

EARLY HINDU-BUDDHIST KINGDOMS

The earliest and perhaps most significant polity of pre-colonial history was the maritime kingdom of **Srivijaya.** Most scholars agree that Srivijaya's seat of power was around Palembang in Southern Sumatra from the 7th to 14th centuries. This prosperous empire comprised all of Sumatra, the Kra peninsula, West Java, and parts of Borneo. Its language and courtly culture spread out over the islands roughly at this time, bringing Sumatra, Malaya, the Riau archipelago, and the coastal regions of Indonesia's other islands into the same linguistic and cultural sphere.

Outside Srivijaya's control, a succession of neighboring kingdoms in Central Java gained prosperity through intensive agriculture. From the 8th through 10th centuries, the Mahayana Buddhist kingdom of **Sailendra** ruled in Central Java. This dynasty—descended from Funanese migrants who fled south Vietnam and Cambodia at the rise of the Chenla kingdom—is responsible for the magnificent **Borobudur,** the world's largest Buddhist monument. At its height, Sailendra re-conquered parts of Indochina, ending the Chenla dynasty there.

Contemporaneous with Sailendra, the **Hindu** kingdom of **Sanjaya** also ruled out of Central Java. Known for its own gargantuan Shaivite monuments (such as the temples of **Prambanan**), Sanjaya attained its wealth through control of international trade routes. Disputes over control of the Straits of Melaka brought Sanjaya into conflict with Srivijaya, which led to its complete destruction in 1006.

Central Javanese dominance and its prodigious architecture came to an abrupt halt at the beginning of the 10th century, most likely due to a violent eruption of Mt. Merapi. Sanjaya degenerated into a series of short-lived and divided dynasties. Indonesia's last great Hindu-Buddhist kingdom was the **Majapahit Empire,** centered at Trowulan in East Java. It reigned from 1292 until 1478 and spanned most of the archipelago—including the Malay peninsula—with contacts throughout mainland Southeast Asia. Majapahit is remembered and honored by modern Indonesia as the kingdom that unified the archipelago under one rule before the arrival of the Dutch. Majapahit's greatest rulers, **Hayam Wuruk** and his Prime Minister **Gajah Mada** are memorialized for fostering Java's Golden Age, the height of Indonesian arts and power. Majapahit's glory was ultimately usurped by the Sultan of Melaka, and the weakened kingdom fell to the Sultan of Demak. The royal court fled to **Bali,** which remains the last outpost of Indonesia's Hindu-Buddhist traditions.

THE RISE OF ISLAMIC SULTANATES

As early as the 7th century, the Indonesian archipelago was introduced to **Islam** through contact with Arab and Indian Muslim traders. The first Muslim communities, however, did not appear until the 13th century, when records show the existence of sultanates along the north coasts of Sumatra. These small trading communities soon became centralized beneath the state of **Aceh,** a staunchly independent sultanate whose capital city of **Banda Aceh** rose to prominence in the 17th century as an international trading port and learning center.

From Northern Sumatra, Islam spread to Java and as far east as Maluku and the southern Philippine islands. The spread of Islam on Java is associated with the legendary **wali songo** (nine saints) who brought Muhammed's teachings to the island. A series of sultanates arose along the north coast of Java during the 15th and 16th centuries, but spread more slowly in inland areas. Islam successfully penetrated inland Java with the rise of the **Mataram Kingdom** between Surakarta and Yogyakarta. Ruling the last of the Java's great kingdoms, **Sultan Agung** (1613-1645) united nearly all of Java except the prosperous trading port of Batavia (Jakarta), where the Dutch had begun to establish themselves. Islam became a curious syncretism of pre-existing Hindu-Buddhist and Javanese traditions with a Muslim veneer.

THE COLONIAL ERA

In 1511, the **Portuguese** arrived in Indonesia searching for lucrative spices and spreading the good news of **Catholicism.** They were primarily interested in trade, and today the Portuguese legacy consists merely of a few fort ruins in the eastern islands of Maluku, the incorporation of some vocabulary into the Malay language, and a few pockets of Catholic communities such as those in Flores and Timor.

The first **Dutch** ships arrived in 1596 in search of trade prospects. In 1692, private investors organized **Vereenigde Oost-Indische Compagnie (VOC)** to monitor and regulate Dutch trade interests in the archipelago. Within 10 years, through military force and exploitative diplomacy, the VOC gained a monopoly on all trade in the region. The Dutch were brought in to settle disputes between local dynasties, creating power imbalances and a local aristocracy increasingly dependent on Dutch "favors" in line with their strategy of "divide and subjugate."

The corrupt VOC went bankrupt in 1799 and the government stepped in to pursue an official colonization of the **Dutch East Indies.** A whole bureaucracy and administration was set up, along with a caste system which kept the "natives" separated from the Dutch ruling elite. Local rulers willing to comply with Dutch policies served as middlemen between colonial officials and the masses slaving away on plantations. Colonial rule was centralized on Java; complete control over the outer islands took longer, especially in rebellious areas such as Aceh and Bali.

At the dawn of the 20th century, collective Dutch guilt led to the creation of the **Ethical Policy,** under which the Dutch implemented educational and public health reforms and intensively invested in the outer islands. The Ethical Policy worked only too well in bringing Indonesians closer to European ideals; educated Indonesians, particularly the Javanese and Minangkabau, started organizing among themselves on the basis of religious or ethnic identity and political ideology. Trade cooperatives, communist parties, and various other organizations became vehicles for political action. Yet their special interests frequently conflicted with each other, and no united nationalist movement emerged at this time.

REVOLUTION AND INDEPENDENCE

The stage was set for the rise of the **Partai Nasional Indonesia (PNI).** This nationalist party was founded in 1927. Headed by **Soekarno,** who espoused an ideology that subordinated all others to that of a united and independent Indonesia. To foster an even greater unity, a national language, **Bahasa Indonesia,** was adopted in 1928.

During the Great Depression, the Dutch were no longer willing to keep the terms of their Ethical Policy, and oppression became their renewed pastime. Japan invaded Indonesia to take advantage of its rich petroleum deposits. The Dutch surrendered to Japan on March 8, 1942, bringing an end to 350 years of Dutch rule over the islands. Most Indonesians welcomed the Japanese for liberating them from the Europeans, but soon discovered that Indonesia's incorporation into the Greater East Asia Co-Prosperity Sphere was a fate worse than Dutch rule had ever been. After three and a half years of the most brutal colonial regime to occupy Indonesia, the Japanese surrendered to the Allies on August 15, 1945, leaving behind a highly politicized nation unwilling to tolerate the demands of colonialism any longer.

Soekarno had collaborated with the Japanese in order to ensure the survival of Indonesian nationalism. Anxious to take charge before the return of the Europeans, he declared independence on August 17. The Dutch returned hoping to restore their former colonial empire, and were surprised to confront a mobilized and chaotic population willing to go to war for the newly declared **Republik Indonesia.**

The **Indonesian Revolution** lasted from 1945 until 1950 and unified the nation against the Dutch, but did little else. The fledgling republican government was plagued with internal disputes, especially between the **Indonesian Communist Party (PKI),** the Nationalists and their ragtag military, and a variety of Islamic parties. By the fifth anniversary of Soekarno's declaration of independence, the Dutch—embarrassed by the continued conflict in which the international community sympathized with the Indonesians—officially transferred sovereignty.

Soekarno wrote the **Pancasila** (Five Principles), which has been the ideological basis of the Indonesian constitution ever since. The five principles are: belief in God, nationalism, humanitarianism, social justice, and democracy. From 1950 to 1957, Soekarno tried to form a government based on representative democracy. Those years were the most politically free period in Indonesia's history, but in a largely poor and illiterate nation, the result was corruption and stagnation.

By 1957, after several regional rebellions and the onset of a failing economy, Soekarno announced his new concept of **Guided Democracy,** which gave the president more dictatorial powers. It accomplished nothing, but kept Soekarno in the center spotlight. In the early 60s, the masses were riled up for the "liberation" of **West Irian** from the Dutch. Without an honest vote of self-determination, sovereignty over the west half of New Guinea was transferred to Indonesia on May 1, 1963 and the province was renamed **Irian Jaya.** In January of 1963, Soekarno launched his **konfrontasi** campaign against Malaysia, in response to the country's supposedly neo-colonialist arrangements with the British. Troops were deployed in the Malay territories of Borneo and skirmishes waged against the British and Malaysian armies. By the 1960s, the aging Soekarno had become a decadent caricature of himself, a master *dalang* (puppeteer) precariously balancing the characters of a *wayang* theater the size of an entire island nation.

THE NEW ORDER

Soekarno's balancing act collapsed tragically on September 30, 1965, when a failed coup, supposedly perpetrated by the PKI and involving the murder of six high-ranking generals, resulted in a right-wing **military backlash** throughout the nation (see **Human Rights,** below). Soekarno was implicated in the events of that night and his leadership was effectively de-legitimized. In the aftermath of these events, **Major General Soeharto** emerged as the commander in charge of the situation. Over the next year and a half, Soeharto systematically dismantled Soekarno's presidential powers and replaced the Guided Democracy with his **New Order** government, retaining only Pancasila from Soekarno's original ideological basis for the Indonesian state. A broken Soekarno lived under house arrest in Bogor until his death in 1970.

Soeharto's New Order was born upon Indonesia's most violent historical event, a massacre of Communist Indonesians by other Indonesians. This event brought an end to political activism, leaving a fear-inducing military in control over the state. Soeharto's first measures included banning the PKI, ending the *konfrontasi* campaign and making peace with Malaysia, and encouraging relations with the west.

The past thirty years under the New Order have brought stability to the government, impressive economic growth, and major improvements in infrastructure, public health, and education, at the expense of free speech and individual human rights. In 1975 **East Timor,** newly independent from the Portuguese, was on the verge of forming its own government when civil war broke out. Claiming that the Timorese posed a Communist threat to the region, the Indonesian army invaded on December 7, 1975 and made East Timor the 27th province of Indonesia, thus rounding out the national borders of Indonesia to include the entire archipelago.

> ### Bung Karno/Pak Harto
>
> Indonesianists have noted the radical difference between Indonesia's first and second presidents, but it doesn't take a linguistic anthropologist to see that the characters of Soekarno and Soeharto are easily distinguished in the terms commonly used by the Indonesian people. The moniker "bung" is a shortened form of the word *abang* which means "older brother" or "dear friend," while the term "pak" is a shortened form of *bapak* which means "father." While Soeharto might prefer to be called *"Bapak Presiden Soeharto,"* a title that reinforces concepts of hierarchy and power, Bung Karno relished the brotherly relationship he cultivated with his nation's people. Known also as *Penyambung Lidah Rakyat Indonesia* (Voice of the Indonesian People), Soekarno is remembered for his powerful oratory, a skill he often used to inspire Indonesians to carry out his Revolution. In contrast, Pak Harto speaks through his ministers, as it is Javanese custom for the *bapak* to remain a silent figure of respected authority.

■ Indonesia Today

Observers of the New Order discern two characteristic trends: stability and rapid development set against human rights violations. While successful social welfare programs have won praise from the international community, Indonesia's military government has perpetrated terrible crimes against its people. Today, an oppressive military induces a climate of violence and fear in areas of civil unrest such as East Timor, Irian Jaya, and Aceh.

A 74-year-old Soeharto with reported kidney trouble adds to the perception that Indonesia seems on the brink of disorder. Fears about his health have wreaked havoc with the Indonesian economy as **succession** is not yet settled. Soeharto has not named a successor, and as his legitimacy and influence wanes with his health, anxiety over Indonesia's future increases as major players from the military and presidential cabinet jockey for power in anticipation of Soeharto's imminent passing.

Beyond the prominent figures of **Vice President Try Sutrisno** and **Minister of Technology Habibie,** is the daughter of the late president Soekarno, **Megawati Soekarnoputri.** As the former head of the **Indonesia Democratic Party (PDI),** it looks like the government is considering her to be a serious threat: in June, 1996 she was usurped from party leadership. The government and military then backed a break-away faction of the PDI, who then elected a new chairman, Suryandi. Without being a member of one of the three officially recognized parties she cannot run for president in the 1998 elections. Megawati's threat lies in the government's fears of a rebirth of a fiery Soekarnoism. Rather than inspiring the reactionary and xenophobic fervor her father did, her outspoken criticism of the military and the existing system represents the true challenge to the current administration. As she says, "People want change. Globally, democracy is an idea whose time has come."

HUMAN RIGHTS

In its move toward developed nation status, Indonesia has had to confront international scrutiny of its less-than-stellar human rights record. The harsh means by which the New Order came to power have become those by which it maintains relative stability amid the rich amalgamation of ethnic groups and belief systems Indonesia encompasses. Amnesty International estimates that between 500,000 and 1,000,000 people were killed, and countless others jailed and harassed during the massive purge of communist and Soekarno-ist forces after the 1965 coup instituted by the government. From this harsh beginning, the government has continued to maintain an iron fist in its dealing with its people.

Today, Pancasila is the sole official ideology, required to be accepted and upheld by all political parties. Although freedom of expression is technically protected under the Indonesian constitution, the media is under tight government control, and harsh censorship is constantly exercised. Although Soeharto promised greater freedom of the press in early 1994, the prominent national publications *Tempo, Editor,* and *Detik* were closed down for covering stories that came close to exposing government-opposed factions. In June, 1996 the Supreme Court ruled that Information Minister Harmoko acted lawfully in revoking *Tempo*'s license. Harmoko justified the press crackdown by claiming that such openness of the press was counterproductive to national unity.

The government has also taken personal action to enforce the one ideology ideal. The Indonesian labor movement has been a particularly sore spot with the government. There is only one nationally sanctioned labor organization. On May Day, 1995, over 1000 marchers launching a national campaign to raise the minimum wage from US$3 to 4.50 per day were beaten and arrested on the street, sparking student protests in Jakarta, Semarang, Yogya, and Solo.

Most serious of all, however, have been the Indonesian government's actions to suppress local culture and movements for freedom in East Timor, Irian Jaya, and Aceh. It is estimated that in Aceh alone, 2000 people were killed between 1989 and 1993. Even more sobering is that since Indonesian incorporation in 1976, over 200,000 people in East Timor have been killed or died of disease or starvation.

The foundations of Indonesia's government allow such atrocities to go unchecked. Executive power is nearly total: Soeharto is essentially dictator for life, and there are few checks on his power. Working hand in hand with this is the overwhelming power of the military and police. In response to international pressure, Soeharto established a National Human Rights Commission in 1993. Yet despite the overtures made toward improving Indonesia's human rights record, the reality of change is questionable. The government has yet to accept international standards for human rights, believing that such standards should only be implemented to the extent to which they agree with national culture and history.

■ The Arts

ARCHITECTURE

The ancient monuments *candi* (ancient shrines) of Central and East Java testify to Indonesia's legacy of architectural grandeur. Among the achievements of the first millennium are the great monuments of Borobudur and Prambanan. In Bali, temples are known as *pura,* of which the island has over 20,000. Of these, the largest and most sacred is Pura Besakih on Gunung Agung. With the arrival of Islam on Java, mosques, rather than temples became the new vogue in construction. The *kraton* palace complexes of Yogyakarta and Surakarta are examples of the blend of Islamic and Hindu-Buddhist architectural traditions. A common Javanese structure used in the *kraton* as well as in Javanese households is the *pendopo,* an open-sided pavilion with a raised floor and wooden pillars supporting a roof of wooden beams that slope upward to meet in a point at the center. A classic example of a *pendopo* is at the grand mosque of Yogyakarta in front of the *kraton.* Every region of Indonesia has its own *rumah adat* (customary house), such as the Minang wooden houses, whose roofs slope up at the ends like buffalo horns, or Batak longhouses, built on piles with spaces reserved for storing ancestors' bones.

BATIK

This world-renowned textile art of producing intricate patterns through a series of waxing and dyeing has been most developed on Java. Batik has, however, become common throughout Indonesia and the rest of Southeast Asia. Originally done by hand, batik *tulis* is made with a *canting,* a tool that holds a small amount of liquid wax. The wax pours from a spout and is used like a pencil to create designs on fabric. The cheaper batik *cap* is made with pre-patterned metal stamps dipped in wax and then pressed repeatedly onto fabric. Batik shirts are the common dress for men on formal occasions, and women often wear batik sarong instead of skirts. In the past 20 years or so, batik paintings have become a popular art form. The best and cheapest batik paintings are found around the tourist areas of Yogyakarta; many of these galleries also give visitors a chance to make their own paintings.

DANCE

Particularly in Java and Bali, Indonesian dance traditions are highly developed. Javanese dance—meditative, deliberate, meticulous, and extremely challenging—is difficult for foreigners to follow. The Javanese, however, appreciate the muscle-cramping postures, limber movements, contemplative pauses, and distant stares that mark a good dancer. Balinese dancing shares the meticulous and detailed maneuvers of Javanese dance, but is differentiated by quick and jerky movements accompanied by the explosive Balinese *gamelan*. Traditionally, Balinese dancers kept all limbs and joints in constant motion, right down to darting eye glances and fluttering fingers. Dances may take place on almost any occasion, and usually narrate stories from ancient Indian epics or everyday life. The most popular dances are the *Barong*, depicting a battle between good and evil, and the *Kecak* (a.k.a. monkey dance), which reenacts a scene of the *Ramayana* around flame torches while 100 or more men sit in concentric circles shouting and chanting in rhythm. In the much simpler Sumatran dances, only single women are allowed to dance. Other less renowned dances are performed everywhere on the village level.

DRAMA

Modern drama was never developed to any extent outside Java. *Ludruk* is an all-male performance medium in which the roles of women are humorously, if somewhat derogatorily, rendered on stage. *Kethoprak* is grounded in the classic epic stories and myths of India and Java, but usually with a contemporary twist. *Ludruk* and *kethoprak* are very popular throughout Java in both rural and urban communities, and the government sponsors traveling troupes and televised performances as a means to disseminate various aspects of state ideology.

MUSIC

The *gamelan* orchestra—a sophisticated ensemble of gongs, metallophones, drums, a few vocalists, and string and wind instruments is unique to Java and Bali. Sundanese, Javanese, and Balinese each have their own variations of *gamelan*. Javanese *gamelan* is trance-like and difficult for western ears to follow. The Balinese version, however, is fast-paced, dramatic, and grabs attention. The discernible melodies of the Sundanese variety are the most tuneful for western ears. *Gamelan* accompanies many events, among them dance and *wayang*.

Indonesia's popular music traditions are diverse, drawing upon outside influences and musical traditions across the islands. There is the lilting *kroncong* music with its Portuguese influence and *dangdut* music with its Indian and Arabic rhythms. The Batak of North Sumatra are famed for their beautiful voices and their melancholy tunes, which frequently involve unabashed sobbing by the vocalists; the uninitiated find it hilarious. There is also a somewhat insipid top 40 scene, whose sounds are borrowed straight from Euro-American pop music.

WAYANG

The ancient Javanese art of shadow puppetry probably has its roots in ancestor worship, and, the *dalang* (puppeteer) is considered a conduit of spirits. Today he is highly respected for the ability he must have to manipulate several puppets at once, conduct the *gamelan* orchestra behind him, know an entire pantheon of characters and their historical context, and keep it all going non-stop from 9pm to 5am. The stories are drawn from episodes of the *Ramayana* and *Mahabharata* Indian epics, as well as from a number of indigenous stories. *Wayang* is a common medium used to disseminate state ideology in popular format. On the other hand, it's also a forum where state ideology is subtly mocked for hilarious and critical effect. *Wayang kulit* is the original shadow puppet art form, but it has been built upon by a number of subsequent traditions throughout Java and Bali. *Wayang golek* shows, more common in West Java, are similar, but their puppets are wooden three-dimensional figures and no screen separates the puppets from the audience.

Java

One cannot ignore the importance that Java has held over the rest of the archipelago. From the Sanjaya and Sailendra dynasties responsible for Indonesia's largest ancient temples, to the classical Majapahit Empire which united the archipelago before the arrival of the Dutch, to the sophisticated court cultures of the Yogyakarta and Surakarta sultanates, and finally to the powerful military government centered in Jakarta, Java has almost always taken center stage across island Southeast Asia.

Java's vast rice fields and innumerable mosques provide nutritional and spiritual sustenance for more than 100 million inhabitants. Rich volcanic soils have provided well, but swelling urban centers filled with increasing numbers of landless poor, and huge numbers of transmigrants pouring out to other Indonesian islands reflect the precarious balance in which the Javanese live. Outside the cities, many still live as they always have. The market is still the focus of the town, even after supermarkets appear. Women hold hands crossing the streets, and men walk along with an arm around one another at the end of a day's work.

Time spent on buses is an excellent way to get a deeper feel for the island. Landscapes can be as lush and mountainous as the Puncak or Dieng Plateau, quilted with tidy grass stairs and dotted with small villages, while lowland cities such as Jakarta and Surabaya ramble with reckless, maze-like urbanity. As the bus pulls into the next stop, it becomes apparent that the Javanese landscape is almost as crowded outside the bus as it was inside. The sheer numbers of people on Java alone are its signature feature. No other Indonesian island claims such high density; it's the cumulative centripetal effect from being the central linchpin of the archipelago for centuries.

■ Jakarta

The capital city of the fourth most populous country in the world is inseparable from its traffic. The city exists and expands because it is the magic portal for people who want to get somewhere else, but instead they spend a great deal of time locked in traffic jams. Sputtering orange *bajaj,* pastel taxis, scooters, and soot-begrimed buses roar and honk like Jurassic beasts. It isn't pretty at first sight, but there are grace and art at work here.

Construction is continuous, from back alleys to office blocks. On smaller buildings, bamboo and plank scaffolding looks like an engineer's drunken fantasy. The colored, mirrored glass of new skyscrapers reflects surly tropical skies and looks out over a maze of *kampung,* where most of the population barely scrapes by.

Tourists typically detest Jakarta, and leave for other parts of the archipelago soon after arrival. The visitor who chooses to linger will discover, however, that every major ethnic group of Indonesia is well-represented in the neighborhood *kampung.* It can be difficult to decipher all the various cultural influences that shape and decorate the city, but it's in these *kampung* where the soul of Jakarta lies. The myriad uniformed workers who run the basic operations of every business and government office come from there each day and take to the streets on Jakarta's enormous public transportation network while expats, Chinese merchants, and government bureaucrats who have made the system work for them come and go from the outskirts of the city, hidden behind the tinted windows of imported luxury vehicles. These mov-

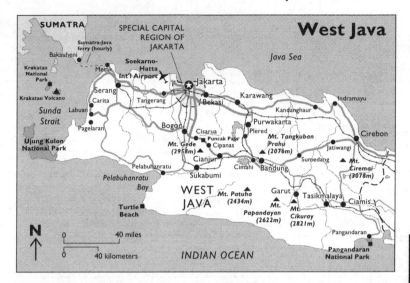

ers and shakers finding their way to work each day will shape Jakarta's future, just as it shapes them, but as the city grows and groans beneath its millions, Jakarta's dichotomy between affluent and destitute remains constant; one wonders if this is too high a cost for "getting somewhere."

GETTING THERE AND AWAY

By Plane

International flights arrive at **Soekarno-Hatta Airport,** northwest of the city. Outbound flights are subject to a departure tax of Rp21,000. Flights around Indonesia leave from the domestic terminal. Planes leave to: **Yogyakarta** (6 per day); **Surabaya** (every hr., 6am-8pm); **Bandung** (every 1-2 hr. 7am-4:30pm); **Denpasar** (2 per hr., 9am-10pm); **Medan** (5 per day); and **Batam** (6 per day). A/C buses go into Gambir Station in Jakarta (Rp3000). A taxi will set you back Rp25,000.

By Train

Gambir Station in central Jakarta, east of Merdeka Square, is the most convenient station, as it is a short 15-minute walk from budget-friendly Jl. Jaksa. Trains arrive here from other cities, and are rarely on time. Locals might help travelers figure out the cryptic announcements. In order to arrange a ticket, go to the station master, preferably a day in advance. There are student discounts, but not for the deluxe overnight express trains (the *Bima* and *Mutiara* to Surabaya).

By Bus

Buses are the best means of public transportation in Jakarta, but trains are preferable (more comfortable and reliable) for trips beyond the city. Buses to large cities close to Jakarta, such as Bogor, Bandung, and Banjar, generally leave from **Kp. Rambutan Terminal** (take bus #P16 or P10). Other long-distance buses leave from the **Pulo Gadung Terminal** to cities such as Surabaya, Yogyakarta, and Denpasar (take bus #P54). Buses to West Java leave from **Kali Deres Stasiun** (take bus #P78). Check terminal location when you book your ticket. Each terminal is located outside Jakarta and takes one to two hours to reach by public transportation. Seats on chartered buses cost more. The travel agencies on and around Jl. Jaksa hire buses to many cities. These buses are generally air-conditioned, non-stop, and leave from Jl. Jaksa or another central point within Jakarta.

By Boat

The state-run **PELNI Company** (tel. 421 19 21) has a fleet of seven ships that wind their way between major harbors throughout the country. PELNI ships provide spartan accommodations, basic food, slow journeys, and bi-weekly schedules at not-so-cheap prices. For ticket sales, their office is on Jl. Angkasa, Kemayoran.

GETTING AROUND

There's no easy, quick way to get around Jakarta. For short distances, leg it. **Bajaj** (orange motorized three-wheelers) can be a convenient mode of transport through the less-busy areas of town. Passengers should negotiate a price before setting off. **Taxis** (Rp900 base fee, Rp450 per km) offer air-conditioned comfort. City **buses** around Jakarta can be caught outside McDonald's on Jl. M.H. Thamrin—on the same side if you're going south, or take the overpass if you're going north. Buses run 6am-8pm (Rp500 and 700, A/C buses Rp1700). Small minivans called **microlets** have set routes and charge according to the distance (Rp300-500). **Rental cars** charge by the hour within the city (Rp10-15,000 per hr.) and by distance beyond Jakarta. There are several desks at the airport. In the city, inquire at **Avis,** Jl. Diponegoro 25 (tel. 314 29 00), **Blue Bird,** Jl. Mampang Prapatan Raya 60 (794 44 44), or **National** at Kartika Plaza Hotel, Jl. M.H. Thamrin 10 (tel. 333 423).

ORIENTATION

The focus of Jakarta is **Merdeka Square.** In the center of it is the **Monas,** the national monument. To the east is **Gambir Station;** to the north is the **Mesjid Istiqlal** and **Istana Merdeka** (the Presidential Palace); to the west is the **National Museum;** and south is **Jalan Jaksa.** North toward the harbor is **Glodok** (Chinatown), and farther north, around **Kota Station,** is the **Old Dutch District.** Near here is **Sunda Kelapa** where schooners dock. **Jaya Ancol** is northeast, along the harbor of **Tanjung Priok.** The **Ragunan Zoo** and **Taman Mini** are south of the city.

PRACTICAL INFORMATION

Tourist Office: Jl. M.H. Thamrin 9 (tel. 314 20 67), on the corner with Jl. Wahid Hasyim. From Jl. Jaksa walk south (away from Monas), and then turn right on Jl. Wahid Hasyim. Entrance is along inside hall of Djakarta Theatre building. Helpful staff offers free maps and information not found in the brochures. Open Mon.-Fri. 8:30am-4:30pm, Sat. 8:30am-1pm.

Tours and Travel: Many Jl. Jaksa establishments can book bus tours and transportation, but Jl. Jaksa and K.H. Wahid Sahim budget travel and holiday offices cover the travel spectrum. Most offer spaces on chartered buses to Pangandaran, Yogyakarta, and other desirable destinations at fair prices.

Embassies and Consulates: Australia, Jl. Rasuna Said Kav. C15-16 (tel. 522 71 11). Bus #P11 to Kunigan Plaza. Open Mon.-Thurs. 8:30am-1:30pm, Fri. 8:30am-noon. **Canada,** Wisma Metropolitan I, 5th Fl., Jl. Sudirman Kav. 29 (tel. 525 07 90). Bus #P1, P10, or P12 to the Metropolitan I. Open Mon.-Thurs. 7:30am-4:15pm, Fri. 7:30am-1pm. **Laos,** Jl. Kintamani Raya C-15 No. 33 (tel. 520 26 73). Bus #P11 to Mulia Centre. **Malaysia,** Jl. H.R. Rasuna Said Kav. X/6 No. 1-3 (tel. 522 49 47). Bus #P11 to Jl. Prof. Dr. Satriol. Open Mon.-Thurs. 8am-1pm and 2-4pm. **New Zealand,** Jl. Diponegoro 41 (tel. 330 680). **Singapore,** 2 Jl. H.R. Saruna Said Blok X/4 (tel. 520 14 89). Open Mon-Fri 8:30am-12:30pm, and 1:30-5pm. **Thailand,** 74 Jl. Imam Bonjol (tel. 390 42 25). Walk southwest from the Jl. M.H. Thamrin/Kebon/Kacang Raya traffic circle on Jl. Imam Bonjol. Open Mon.-Fri. 8:30am-3:30pm. **UK,** Jl. M.H. Thamrin 75 (tel. 330 904), a short walk from Jl. Jaksa. Open Mon.-Thurs. 7:45am-4pm, Fri. 7:45am-12:45pm. **US,** Jl. Merdeka Selatan 5 (tel. 360 360), between Gambir Station and Jl. Jaksa. Open Mon.-Fri. 7:30am-4pm. **Vietnam,** Jl. Teuku Umar 25 (tel. 310 03 58), a short walk southeast of Jl. Jaksa. Open Mon.-Sat. 9-11:30am and 1:30-4pm.

Currency Exchange: Various bank desks at the airport offer decent rates without a commission. City banks, offering slightly better rates, are everywhere, yet many do

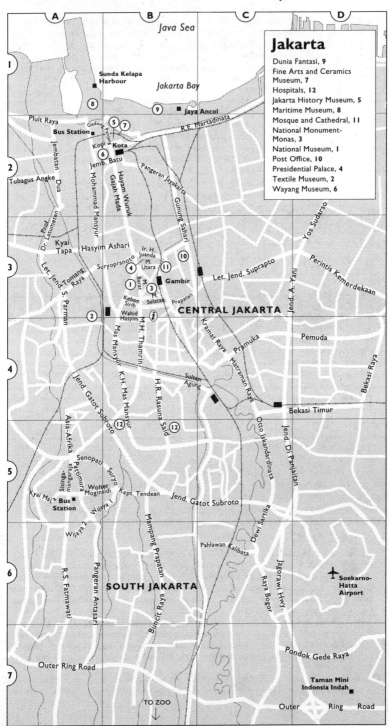

Jakarta

Dunia Fantasi, **9**
Fine Arts and Ceramics Museum, **7**
Hospitals, **12**
Jakarta History Museum, **5**
Maritime Museum, **8**
Mosque and Cathedral, **11**
National Monument-Monas, **3**
National Museum, **1**
Post Office, **10**
Presidential Palace, **4**
Textile Museum, **2**
Wayang Museum, **6**

Java Sea

Jakarta Bay

Sunda Kelapa Harbour

Jaya Ancol

Pluit Raya

Bus Station

Gedong Panjang

Kota

Kopi

Jemb. Batu

R.E. Martadinata

Tubagus Angke

Jembatan Dua

Prof. Dr. Latumeten

Mohammad Mansyur

Kyai Tapa

Hasyim Ashari

Hayam Wuruk

Gajah Mada

Pangeran Jayakarta

Gunung Sahari

Let. Jend. S. Parman

Let. Jend. Tomang Raya

Suryopranoto

Ir. H. Juanda

M. Utara

Gambir

Let. Jend. Suprapto

Yos Sudarso

Jend. A. Yani

Perintis Kemerdekaan

Kebon Sirih

Barat

M. Selatan

Prapatan

CENTRAL JAKARTA

Wahid Hasyim

Mas Mansyur

M.H. Thamrin

K.H. Mas Mansyur

H.R. Rasuna Said

Sultan Agung

Kramat Raya

Matraman Raya

Pramuka

Pemuda

Bekasi Raya

Jend. Gatot Subroto

Asia-Afrika

Senopati

Pattimura

Prapanca

Wolter Moginsidi

Kyai Maja

Bus Station

Wijaya 1

Wijaya 2

Suryo

Kapt. Tendean

Jend. Gatot Subroto

Otto Iskandardinata

Dewi Sartika

Jend. DI Panjaitan

Bekasi Timur

R.S. Fatmawati

Pangeran Antasari

Mampang Prapatan

Buncit Raya

Pahlawan Kalibata

SOUTH JAKARTA

Jagorawi Hwy.

Raya Bogor

Soekarno-Hatta Airport

Outer Ring Road

Pondok Gede Raya

Taman Mini Indonsia Indah

TO ZOO

Outer   Ring   Road

not change traveler's checks. On Jl. M.H. Thamrin, **Bali Bank** (tel. 323 807), around the corner from the tourist office, changes both cash and traveler's checks. Open Mon.-Fri. 10am-3pm. **Bank Surya** (tel. 230 29 33), across the street and 50m south, offers the same services. Open Mon.-Fri. 8am-3pm. In a pinch, there's always Jl. Jaksa, where many hotels and travel offices change money. **Sarinah Dept. Store,** across the street from the tourist office has a cash-only exchange desk. Open daily 8am-7:30pm.

American Express: Jl. Rasuna Said Block X/1 Kav. (tel. 521 61 06).

Luggage Storage: At the airport. Rp3000 per day. Open 24hr.

English Bookstores: Times, on the lower level of the **Plaza Indonesia Shopping Centre** beneath the Grand Hyatt on Jl. M.H. Thamrin. Open daily 10am-9pm.

Markets: Pasar Baru, northeast of Monas and across the river from the post office, has the typical market atmosphere with *warung* and fruit mixed in with a modern plaza of fast food restaurants.

Pharmacies: Apotik Melawai, Jl. Salemba Raya 59 (tel. 315 05 89), by RS St. Cardus. Open 24hr. **Gambir Apotik,** Jl. Kebon Sirih 77A (tel. 331 389), close to Jl. Jaksa. Open Mon.-Sat. 8am-9pm. *Supermarkets* have good selections as well.

Medical Services: MMC Kuningan, Jl. Rasuna Said Kav. C21 (tel. 522 52 01), is a general hospital, as is **RS Jakarta,** Jl. Sudirman Kav. 49 (tel. 573 22 41). **Ufar Madica Clinic** (tel. 310 30 47), next to Gambir Apotik on Jl. Kebon Sirih. Open Mon.-Sat. 8am-10pm.

Emergency: Police: tel. 110. **Fire:** tel. 113. **Ambulance:** tel. 118. **City Health Service:** tel. 119.

Police: Jl. Sudirman 45 (tel. 525 01 10). Open 8am-midnight.

Post Offices: GPO, Jl. Pos 2, Pasar Baru (tel. 344 69 88). Entrance is on Jl. Senen Raya, off Jl. Pos around the corner. Open Mon.-Sat. 9am-8pm, Sun. 9am-4pm. Take bus #P12. *Poste Restante* at counter 55 (tel. 361 561, ext. 232). Stamps at counter 47. **Warpostel,** Jl. Jaksa No. 2 (tel. 390 45 01). Open daily 8am-midnight. May not be as reasonable for airmail prices. **Postal code:** 10000.

Telephones: Coin (blue) and card (gray) phones are on virtually every street block, but are for local use only and don't filter out traffic noise well. For better connections, try the phones found in shopping centers and public buildings. **Indosat** offers **HCD** service from phones at the **airport** and the **Public Phone Office,** Jl. M.H. Thamrin 9 across from the tourist office. They have dozens of carpeted booths and a Jakarta yellow pages in English. Open 24hr. **Telephone code:** 21.

ACCOMMODATIONS

For better or worse, Jl. Jaksa is the backpacker's haven in Jakarta. Running north-south, this 0.5km-long stretch lies a few blocks south of the Monas monument—about a 15-minute walk from Gambir Station. Places to sleep range from the seedy to the more luxurious, with very little in between. Shop around, and make sure the room has a fan and good screens to keep out mosquitoes. Front doors generally close at midnight. The following listings are organized by street; Jalan Kebon Sirih Barat and Timur I are just off of Jalan Jaksa to the east and west respectively.

Jalan Jaksa

Nick's Corner Hostel, Jl. Jaksa 16 (tel. 314 19 88). Look for the stained white refrigerator-like building to chill you through your stay in steamy Jakarta. Rooms are medium-sized, but the A/C jacks up the prices. The hotel lobby atmosphere makes this hostel feel relatively secure. Doubles with double bed Rp32,000, with 2 twin beds Rp37,000. Triples Rp45,000. Some rooms have private baths. Safe deposit box Rp1000 per day. Open 24hr.

Djody Hostel, Jl. Jaksa 27-29 (tel. 314 17 32). Rooms (slightly larger than most) are white, boxy, and well-kept. Some rooms have better screens than others, however, so be discriminating in your choice. Breakfast included with all rooms. Singles Rp15,000. Doubles Rp22,000. Triples Rp35,000. All with shared *mandi* and fans. Safe deposit boxes available.

Djody Hotel, Jl. Jaksa 33-35 (tel. 390 59 76), offers very similar accommodations to its counterpart hostel next door. Some rooms have A/C and private baths. Doubles with shared *mandi* Rp35,000, with private bath Rp45,000. Breakfast included. Safe-boxes available. Open 24hr. MC, Visa.

Norbek Hostel, Jl. Jaksa 14 (tel. 330 392). The woman in charge runs a very tight ship and demands customers to follow her rules. Signs posted all over will inform you of her expectations. To reserve a room, pay in advance. No visitors who haven't paid for a room are allowed inside. Such tight security is generally considered desirable in Jakarta, so don't be turned off too quickly. Small doubles with fan Rp10,000, larger room Rp16,000, squeeze in another person Rp21,000, with A/C and private *mandi* Rp30,000. Triples Rp35,000.

Wisma Delima, Jl. Jaksa 5 (tel. 337 026). The first accommodation you encounter coming from Gambir Station, with its old AYH sign out front. Facilities are adequate. Screens are secure. All rooms have fan and shared *mandi*. Singles Rp7500. Doubles Rp15,000.

Hotel Tator, Jl. Jaksa 37 (tel. 323 940). Out of place on Jl. Jaksa, Hotel Tator's sleek black and white tile make it as shiny and manicured as a Marriott. For a slightly higher price, you can get clean rooms, a big comfortable bed, bright lights, a private bath, and free breakfast. Single with fan Rp27,500. Doubles with fan Rp42,500, with A/C Rp50,000, with hot water and phone Rp55,000.

Yusran Hostel, Jl. Jaksa 9 (tel. 314 03 73), a faded sign points you to the end of a lush, garden-lined alley. Friendly management and a distance from the street are in its favor, even though the clean rooms are small and lack amenities. All rooms have a fan, decent screens, and shared *mandi*. Doubles Rp16-17,000. Triples, Rp25,000. Quads Rp30,000.

Jalan Kebon Sirih Timur I

Bloem Steen Hostel, Jl. K.S. Timur I 174 (tel. 323 002). Even with the elevated prices, this place is the best deal around Jl. Jaksa. The newly renovated rooms and shared *mandi* are inviting. The singing birds on the front terrace add to the freshness of this little non-showy oasis. Rooms with double beds Rp20,000.

Kresna Hostel, Jl. K.S. Timur I 175 (tel. 325 403). Watch out for the stairs (sorry, no handrails), slippery tiles, and steep incline. The management is generally friendly and will hold mail for guests. Books for sale. Small doubles Rp15,000, with private *mandi* Rp20,000 (worth the extra cash).

Jalan Kebon Sirih Barat

Bintang Kejora Hostel, Jl K.S. Barat Dalam 52 (tel. 323 878). The laid-back, friendly management will keep rooms clean and do whatever they can for guests. Rooms upstairs have nice windows and lots of light. Travel office on premises. Singles Rp15,000. Doubles Rp20,000. Fans and shared *mandi*. Breakfast included.

Borneo Hostel, Jl. K.S. Barat Dalam 35 (tel. 320 095). This large, impersonal hostel feels more like a motel with its busy lobby and attached restaurant. Each room is relatively spacious and has its own sink. Dorms Rp10,000. Doubles with fan and shared *mandi* Rp20-25,000, with private bath Rp30,000. Prices rise about Rp5000 per room in high season. Safe-deposit boxes available.

FOOD

In Jakarta, you are never more than a block away from a *warung* any hour of the day. Nice restaurants are not exorbitant and offer precious air conditioning. Cheap backpacker menus cluster on Jl. Jaksa. *Sate* and Padang food are specialties of the *warung* while fancier local and international cuisine lines Jl. H. Agus Salim, a block west of Jl. Jaksa. Concentrations of restaurants also abound around the shopping areas of **pasar baru** and Blok M, and in Glodok. For market food, meander through **pasar jaya** (traditional market) behind Gondagia Station on Jl. Srikaya, about two blocks east of Jl. Jaksa, where all the *bajaj* are parked.

Jalan Jaksa

Angie's Café, Jl. Jaksa 15 (tel. 326 224). Caters to the backpacking crowd with a wide variety of foods at good prices. Try the icy banana juice for a cool treat. Great

INDONESIA

breakfast food for Rp1-2000. Don't be fooled by the "no alcohol allowed" sign in front—Angie's serves up Bintang with a smile.

Borneo Café, Jl. K.S. Barat Dalam 35 (tel. 320 095). Has good Indonesian food, including an extra spicy *gado-gado* which will leave you howling like Val.

Memories Café, Jl. Jaksa 17, across from Norbek Hostel. Offers the same menu as Angie's but plays the tunes of Eric Clapton, the Rolling Stones, and Nirvana over and over and over, making for a great stroll down memory lane.

Senayan Satay House, Jl. K.S. Barat 31A (tel. 326 238), at the head of Jl. Jaksa. Has A/C, funky wood carvings on the walls, and slightly higher priced fare. Small but interesting Indonesian menu offers some local delicacies. Seafood and Indonesian entrees, Rp3-6000. Open daily 10am-10pm.

Jalan H Agus Salim

Paradiso 2001, Jl. H Agus Salim 30 (tel. 390 58 26). Esther presents a wide selection of excellent vegetarian dishes. Try the veggie *sate* in peanut sauce. Most dishes Rp2-6000. Open Sun.-Thurs. 10am-10pm, Fri. 10am-5pm, Sat. 6-10pm.

Hot Pot Garden, Jl. H Agus Salim 16A (tel. 334 438). Choose from a variety of seafood and vegetables displayed in a refrigerated case in the back, and create your own soup. A bit pricey but the fresh food is well worth it. Meals are generally Rp5-15,000. Open daily 10:30am-2:30pm and 6-9:30pm.

SIGHTS

In the center of **Medan Merdeka** is **Monas,** the national monument. Often the first sight to be seen upon arriving in Gambir Station, Monas makes a good point of reference. Also known as Soekarno's Last Erection, this intentionally phallic monument represents the fertility of the nation. Standing 137m high, the torch is coated with 35kg of gold. The entrance is behind the statue of **Diponegoro,** north of the monument. A trip to the top guarantees a good view of Jakarta. Beneath Monas is an enormous room with dioramas on all four walls representing important moments in Indonesian history. (Monument and museum open daily 8am-5pm; admission for museum Rp500, students Rp250.)

On the west side of the square is the **National Museum,** which houses sculptures, artifacts, ceramics, textiles, and numerous maps from all over the archipelago. They offer multilingual tours, with English ones are Tues.-Thurs. at 9:30am. (Open Tues.-Thurs. and Sat. 8:30-2:30pm, Fri. 8:30-11am, Sun. 8:30-1:30pm; admission Rp200, students and children Rp100, with cameras extra Rp100.) Those who have taken a particular liking to textiles should go to the **Textile Museum,** Jl. K.S. Tubun 4, a few blocks southwest of Jl. Jaksa, which displays over 300 types of fabric. (Open Tues.-Thurs. 9am-2pm, Fri. 9-11am, Sat. 9am-1pm.) The **Istana Merdeka** (Presidential Palace) dominates the top of the square. Surrounded by some magnificent old trees, it's used only for formal functions by Soeharto. Northeast of the square is the dome of **Mesjid Istiqlal,** the largest mosque in Southeast Asia. Visitors are welcome, but should avoid noon prayer. The entrance is on the north side on Jl. Veteran.

Lying just northeast of Kota Station is **Fatahillah Square,** surrounded by Dutch buildings. The former Batavia Town Hall with teal shutters is now the **Jakarta History Museum** (tel. 692 91 01). Unfortunately, it's a fairly disorganized museum in need of a curator and a little light. (Open Tues.-Thurs. and Sun. 9am-3pm, Fri. 9am-2:30pm, Sat. 9am-12:30pm; admission Rp1000, children or students Rp500.)

The **Wayang Museum** (tel. 678 560), on the west side of the square, houses an extensive collection of *wayang kulit* (leather) and *wayang golek* (wooden) puppets from across Indonesia and a few other countries. The diversity of the collection allows for the unconventional, such as Adam, Eve, and Christ *wayang*. Modern-image puppets include a collection of bureaucrats (you always knew someone was pulling their strings). Visually satisfying displays, but more descriptions would be helpful. (Open Tues.-Thurs., Fri. 9am-2:30pm, Sat. 9am-12:30pm, Sun. 9am-3pm; admission Rp1000, children Rp300, Sun. Rp500.)

The **Fine Arts and Ceramics Museum** (tel. 676 090) is in a big classical building on the east side of the square. With no descriptions for guidance, visitors can merrily interpret the preponderance of war and family paintings as a reflection of the national psyche. The ceramics are mostly modern *kreatif* pieces, but there are interesting, eerily carved tree-trunk totems in the south courtyard. As with the other museums, this one could also use a curator with inspiration. Displays of fragile ceramics in department store cases and unlit, knee-high cabinets distract from the pieces themselves. (Open Tues.-Thurs., Sun. 9am-3pm, Fri. 9am-2:30pm, Sat. 9am-12:30pm; admission Rp1000, children Rp300, Sun. Rp500.)

Sunda Kelapa, the old harbor, lies a few blocks north of Fatahillah Square. The neighborhood takes on a maritime feel, with sails being sewn and ropes and chains sitting in big heaps. Head past the old **watchtower** and down Jl. Pasar Ikan to get to the oldest part of the city. The **Maritime Museum** (tel. 669 05 18), located in the old storehouses of the Dutch East Indies Company gives a good sense of old Batavia, as well as some good views of the area today. (Open Tues.-Thurs., Sun. 9am-4pm, Fri. 9am-3pm, Sat. 9am-1pm; admission Rp500, children and students Rp300.) They offer tours in Dutch and English. Meander through the alleys toward the big tile-roofed building to reach **Pasar Ikan** (fish market); it runs from 10pm to 2am. Across the wood bridge (Rp100) is the oldest part of Jakarta.

For a different view of Jakarta, take bus #P64 or P65 from Kota, or microlet #15 from Sunda Kelapa to **Jaya Ancol,** an enormous complex with resort facilities, a public 18-hole golf course, an amusement park, art market, and aquarium. To enter the area pay Rp2500 (on weekends Rp3000) and then take your pick of the offered activities for additional charges. **Dunia Fantasi** (tel. 682 000), a scaled-down Disney World complete with many Indonesian counterparts to American cartoon characters, has a roller coaster, ferris wheel, and other rides and games geared toward children. (Open 10am-9pm; admission Rp23,000 for access to all rides on weekends; Mon.-Fri. Rp19,000.) **Pasar Seni** has many small shops with Indonesian arts, like woodcarvings and paintings, and a stage with free local music. (Open daily 10am-9pm; admission Rp2000.) **Sea World** (tel. 641 00 80) aquarium just opened and boasts a wide selection of over 5000 aquatic animals from Indonesia and other tropical waters. (Open Sun.-Fri. 9am-8pm, Sat. 9am-9pm.)

South of the city, you can see some of Indonesia's unique fauna at **Ragunan Zoo** (tel. 782 975). To get there take the #P19 bus. (Open daily 9am-6pm; admission Rp1500.) The zoo is beautifully landscaped with lush shrubbery to resemble the natural habitats of its dwellers. In the southeast corner of Jakarta "you can see all of Indonesia in a day" at **Taman Mini Indonesia Indah** (tel. 840 92 29). Here, 27 pavilions with several full-scale houses from each province. Unfortunately, much of the history and function of the designs are lost on the tourist, and most buildings serve merely as shaded resting places for families. This extensive complex also includes museums, botanical gardens, an IMAX theater, and a small waterpark, each carrying an additional separate charge. On Sunday mornings there are free dance performances in the pavilions. (Open daily 8am-5pm; admission Rp2000, children Rp1000.) Take bus #P10 or P11 from Sarinah, or bus #P15 from Blok M, then either take a microlet or walk the last 500m.

ENTERTAINMENT

For cheap beer, nothing beats Jl. Jaksa, where travelers and expats trade war stories or chat it up with the infamous local blow-dart gun sellers. There are abundant discotheques in Jakarta with typically expensive cover charges and pricey beer. Two very popular nightclubs are at Jaya Ancol complex: **The Hailai International Executive Club** (tel. 689 868) and **Samrocks** (tel. 683 969). Other well-known hot spots are the **Tanamur** at Jl. Abang Timur 14 (tel. 380 52 33) and the **Music Room** at the Borobudur Intercontinental Hotel (tel. 380 55 55). For restaurants with local live music and dancing, check out **The Blue Note,** Standard Chartered Bldg., Jl. Sudirman Kav 33A Lt. Desar (tel. 573 28 83), **Green Pub** (Mexican food), at Jl. M.H. Thamrin 9 (tel. 315 93 32), and **Café Batavia,** in Fatahillah Square. Many luxury hotels and big banks also have fancy restaurants and nightclubs—search the yellow pages or the street advertisements for your choice of atmosphere.

East Timor: Jakarta's Failure

In the past decade, the New Order has come under increasing international pressure over the issue of **East Timor,** a former Portuguese colony occupied by Indonesia since 1976. The United Nations has never recognized Indonesia's sovereignty over the area, and since the end of the Cold War the "Communist threat" of an independent East Timor no longer justifies the occupation of the tiny destitute province. In 1991, the Indonesian military opened fire on hundreds of peaceful protesters in Dili, causing international uproar that persists to this day. In July of 1995 **General Herman Mantiri,** the nominee for ambassador to Australia, was asked to step down because of the Australian public's outrage over his support of the Dili massacre. Although events such as the "Mantiri affair" underscore the importance the western world has placed on the rights of East Timorese, the front lines are not at the U.N. or in the province itself. The real war seems to be happening among power brokers in Jakarta unwilling to admit that their policies in East Timor have failed. And until the New Order begins to work in the best interests of the East Timorese, international diplomacy and activity within East Timor are likely to go nowhere.

■ Labuan and Carita

These twin towns, in close proximity to Jakarta, are favorite weekend destinations for Jakartans and other Javanese city-dwellers. Carita Beach, just 10km north of the fishing village of Labuan, is particularly popular. A few inexpensive guest houses have access to the stretch of surf and sand, although several large resorts are imposing upon the area a more glamorous—and commercial—flavor. Perhaps the best reason for the adventurous traveler to stop in these small towns is to enjoy a resting point en route to the Ujung Kulon Reserve, where jungles, wild animals, and miles and miles of beach can be enjoyed for a much less taxing price.

ORIENTATION

Whether coming from the northwest via Merak, or the west or northeast via Bogor or Jakarta, one main road passes through both Labuan and Carita, changing names frequently along the way. Major buses stop in Labuan, directly next to the minibus and *angkot* station in the middle of town. **Jalan Sudirman** runs through Labuan toward the west, and turns into **Jalan Printis Kemerdekaan** at the market just past the bus terminal, where the road makes a sharp turn. Carita is 10km north, where guest houses line the street, now **Jalan Raya Carita.** In the hills behind Carita is a **waterfall** at Curug Gendang, perfect for a jump to the pool below. Buy tickets (Rp1500) at the entrance, next to the Maya Kantin Restaurant.

PRACTICAL INFORMATION

Tourist Offices: PPA Office, Jl. Printis Kemerdekaan 51, Labuan (tel. 817 31). Tickets and insurance to Ujung Kulon and Krakatau, as well as helpful maps and information about solo travel. Open Mon.-Thurs. 7:30am-3:30pm, Fri. 7:30-1pm.

Tours and Travel: Tour agencies are springing up everywhere, including **Mega Indonesia,** Jl. Perintis Kemerdekaan 290, Labuan (tel. 810 41) and **Tourist Information Black Rhino** (tel. 810 72), on Jl. Raya Carita next to the Sunset View Losmen. Tours to Ujong Kulon (US$150 for 3 days) and Krakatau (Rp200,000 just for the boat ride). The best way to cut costs is to gather a group. Reservations can be made directly with boat captains in Labuan, but be sure to choose a seaworthy boat and trustworthy crew, as the journey is rather rough.

Currency Exchange: BRI, Jl. Sudirman 156, Labuan (tel. 812 14), the big white building before the bus terminals, exchanges US$. To cash traveler's checks, take a 90-min. minibus ride north to **Cilegon,** where there are many banks.

Buses: The **bus terminal** in Labuan is next to the market. Buses run to major cities, and minibuses connect to nearby smaller towns. Buses leave to **Jakarta** (every hr.,

4hr., Rp4000) and **Bogor** (every hr., 6hr., Rp5000), stopping in **Rakasputung,** where connections to other cities can be made. **Cilegon,** a 1½-hr. minibus ride north (Rp2000), is also a major hub, with buses to **Merak** (Rp1000).

Local Transportation: The usual swarm of **becak** tool around Labuan, but to get to Carita take a **colt** (Rp500) or **ojek** (Rp2000). Pick up colts along the road or at the bus/*angkot* station.

Rentals: Aci Dive Shop, at Km10, next to the Black Rhino, rents scuba/snorkeling equipment, bikes (Rp5000 per day), tents, and sleeping bags.

Markets: The **market** is at the corner of the road just past the bus terminal. The nearby **Super Bazaar Supermarket,** Jl. Sudirman 21 (tel. 813 18), is essential for food and water supplies for Ujung Kulon treks. Open daily 9am-9pm.

Pharmacies: Apotik, Jl. Sudirman 145 (tel. 817 28), across from the bank. Open Mon-Sat. 7am-10pm.

Medical Services: Clinic, Jl. Sudirman 8 (tel. 810 09). By the green cross sign at Puskesmas Labuan, between the police station and the bank. Open 24hr.

Police: Jl. Sudirman 176 (tel. 811 10), next to the bus terminal and across from a big dirt road. Helpful staff. Open 24hr.

Post Offices: GPO (tel. 813 91), in Labuan, 1km beyond the terminals, beyond the bridge toward Carita. Open Mon.-Sat. 8am-2pm. **Postal code:** 42264.

Telephones: A **wartel** is next door to the GPO, a little farther up. International phones and fax service. Open 24hr. **Telephone code:** 0253.

ACCOMMODATIONS

Labuan

Although there is not much to do in Labuan itself, it is a convenient place to spend the night before heading out to Ujung Kulon early the next morning.

Citra Ayu Hotel, Jl. Printis Kemerdekaan 27 (tel. 812 29), about 200m toward Carita past the market. Run by an English-speaking, kind host. A local gathering spot for talking and card playing late into the evening. Beware of the mosque across the street, which send loud frequencies into rooms at ungodly hours. Simple, medium-sized rooms with private *mandi* and fan Rp22,500.

The Hotel Carigin, Jl. Printis Kemerdekaan 20 (tel. 813 88), is farther up the road toward Carita, across from the post office. The rooms are virtually empty (besides the beds) but cheap and they look out onto a simple courtyard garden. To escape the noise of local gossip and worshipping, and enjoy a fan and free breakfast, come here. All rooms are doubles with private *mandi* Rp15,000

Hotel Rawayana, another 0.5km toward Carita, is even more remote from town and a bit off the main road past the shell fountain with green water. Small bungalows with big beds, fans, and private *mandi.* Doubles Rp25,000 (Rp30,000 on weekends), with A/C Rp50,000. Although a good km from town, Hotel Rawayana at least guarantees a quiet night for sleeping—maybe the best place to crash after a few hard days trekking in the national park. Tea and coffee included.

Carita

For a good four km, beginning about 10km from Labuan, hotels and guest houses flank both sides of the street, offering accommodations ranging from mildly inexpensive to luxurious. Quarters more in line with backpackers' needs are mainly situated along a 300m stretch between Km10 and Km11. The **Sunset View Losmen** (tel. 810 75) is the guest house of choice, if they have space available. The wicker motif throughout the place is comforting, and adds an artsy touch to the spacious, furnished rooms. The restaurant in front is welcoming, as is the steady buzz from patrons. Cook up your own *nasi goreng* in the kitchen available for guest use. Doubles go for Rp20,000, triples for Rp30,000, all with private *mandi,* but no fans.

If the Sunset is full, there are a few cheap rooms to be had among the more posh bungalows with fans, screens, and clean bathrooms. The **Gogona,** a few houses down, has some dimly-lit super-cheap doubles for Rp12,500 that are close to the busy family quarters and road, but do have a private *mandi.* The other rooms in this hotel seem refreshing and delightful in comparison, with white-tiled floors, big comfy beds, and bright bathrooms for Rp50-65,000, depending on the floor. Weekend rates for all the guest houses seem unnecessarily high, so travelers should try to hit Carita on a weekday where hotel owners are more desperate for customers and will lower prices accordingly.

FOOD

Labuan has no restaurants geared toward tourists, but its slew of *padang* restaurants and *warung* offer great, authentic Indonesian food for low prices. Carita also has a few *warung* along the road, as well as a few small, cheap restaurants with Indonesian menus. **Rumah Makan Diminati** and the **Maya Kantin Restaurant** a few meters away from each other on each side of the Sunset View are open daily 7am-10pm, with dishes from Rp1500 to Rp6000. They both sell convenience store goods, like snacks, drinks, and toiletry items.

■ Near Labuan and Carita

UJUNG KULON NATIONAL PARK

In Labuan tickets, information, and advice on the park are available from locals who have worked there. It's home to about 60 seldom-seen Javan rhinos, along with lots of creatures. Admirably, there is no intention of making access easier: as a UNESCO World Heritage site, the park is to remain as preserved and protected as possible. Permits allow only one-week access to the park.

Near the coast and on the beaches some effects of the 1883 **Krakatau** explosion and ensuing 40m-high tsunami can still be seen (see **The Wrath of Krakatau** on page 325). The spectacular and secluded beaches of the south coast are untamed. Ujung Kulon is a well-kept secret among nature and wildlife enthusiasts and requires effort and planning, but is unquestionably well worth it.

Tourist agencies in Labuan and Carita offer expensive package tours that are easy to pass up; the PPA office in Labuan can help map out solo routes. The park is about four hours south of Labuan. Load up on food and water before leaving, as it's cheaper at the supermarket than down by the preserve, and leave bags at your hostel. Take a minibus to **Sumer** (Rp5000, 3hr.), then an *ojek* to **Tamanjaya** (30min., Rp5000). A **PPA office** at Tamanjaya sells tickets (Rp2000, plus Rp7000 insurance) and helps arrange for **guides,** required on any trip (Rp10,000 per day, plus food) and porters. Request an English speaker to learn more about the jungles, but don't worry, the beauty of Ujung Kulon speaks for itself. Porters are helpful for three-day outings—trails and dodgy bridges are difficult to navigate with a large water supply strapped to your back. While beautiful beaches and stretches of jungle can be reached without a boat, the best wildlife hangs out in the least accessible areas, around **Pulau Handeleum** and **Pulau Peucang** (Rp100-200,000 for a boat from Tamanjaya). For overnights in Tamanjaya, there are **bungalows** with electricity and *mandi* (US$30) and some space at **homestays** (Rp10-15,000) with no electricity and shared *mandi*. Both of these options serve meals. Along trails within the park some **rooms** are available at guideposts (Rp10,000), as well as some nicer lodgings (at steep prices) on the islands. Camping with a mosquito net and waterproof groundpad is also feasible. Hiking boots are good to trek with, but sneakers or rugged sport sandals are adequate. Bring insect repellent, tweezers, and disinfectant.

■ Bogor

Virtually a suburb of Jakarta, Bogor is cosmopolitan enough to satisfy any traveler's longings for creature comforts—from American movies and pirated Japanese video games to a surplus of donuts). Yet Bogor's true heart and soul are the world-renowned Botanical Gardens, nourished by the highest average rainfall in West Java. Though Bogor is easily navigated, travelers should try to get an early start, since rainy afternoons are frequent. It may be preferable to stay in Bogor and explore Jakarta rather than vice-versa, but beyond the Botanical Gardens, Istana Bogor, and the Gong Factory, there's more here for the anthropologist than the tourist.

ORIENTATION

Bogor is built around the **Botanical Gardens,** home to many plant species as well as **Istana Bogor** (Presidential Palace). The gardens are bounded by **Jalan Ir. H. Juanda** on the west, **Jalan Otista** to the south, and **Jalan Raya Pajajaran** on the east. Big buses from the Puncak and major cities drop off at the southeast area of this road, while minibuses from the Puncak stop east of the gardens, on the road parallel to Jl. Raya Pajajaran. Jl. Raya Pajajaran continues to the Puncak and Bandung, with a toll-road turnoff to Jakarta as well. Leading away from Jl. Ir. H. Juanda is **Jalan Kapten Muslihat,** which leads to **Jalan Dewi Sartika,** home to the market area. Following Jl. Kapten Muslihat past Jl. Permas, and beyond the train tracks, the next major intersection is with **Jalan Mayor Oking** turning to the right and **Jalan Palendang** to the left. Most of the backpacker joints sit along the Jl. Mayor Oking/Palendang stretch.

PRACTICAL INFORMATION

Tourist Offices: Jl. A. Yani. Open Mon.-Fri. 9am-3pm.

Tours and Travel: Travel Bureau Mulia Rahayu, Jl. Mayor Oking 18-20 (tel. 324 150), books bus, plane, and PELNI tickets. Open daily 8am-6pm. **Kantor Cabang Tours and Travel** (tel. 338 361) offers similar services. It's on Jl. Kapten Muslihat, in the beige and brown hat-shaped building at Taman Topi, north of the train station. Open Mon.-Fri. 8am-7pm, Sat. 8am-4pm, Sun. 9am-1pm.

Currency Exchange: Bali Bank, Jl. Kapten Muslihat 17A (tel. 312 990), near the railway station. Has an **ATM.** Open Mon.-Fri. 8am-3pm. **Bank BNI,** Jl. Ir. H. Juanda 52 (tel. 311 446), at the corner of Jl. Palendang. Open Mon.-Fri. 8am-4pm.

Air Travel: Garuda Indonesia (tel. 338 436). Open Mon.-Fri. 7:30am-5pm, Sat., Sun. and holidays 9am-1pm. **24-hr. reservations:** tel. (800) 217 47.

Trains: The **train station** (tel. 324 529), is west of the Botanical Gardens, on Jl. Permas, off Jl. Kapten Muslihat. To **Jakarta** (every hr., 7am-8pm, economy 1½hr., Rp1200; 1st class 1hr., Rp3-4000) and **Surabaya** (Rp1000). Make a reservation.

Buses: The **terminal** is southeast of the Botanical Gardens off Jl. Raya Pajajaran. To: **Jakarta** (every hr., 1½hr., Rp1200-3000); **Bandung** (every hr., 3hr., Rp3000-4000); and **Sukabumi** (every hr., 1hr., Rp1200). Local tourist offices also book private minibuses to most major cities.

Local Transportation: Angkot swarm the roads at fixed rates (Rp300). **Delman** (pony carts) can be found near the gardens, and **becak** are everywhere.

Markets: Pasar Kebon Kembang on Jl. Dewi Sartika has the usual maze of little stalls. **Pasar Baru,** Jl. Suryakencana 3, is near the gate to the Botanical Gardens behind the Bogor Plaza Shopping Centre.

Medical Services: RS Salak, Jl. Sudirman 8 (tel. 324 678). Pharmacy next door (tel. 320 496), and a doctor available 24hr. **Apotik RB Dr. R. Soekojo,** Jl. Palendang 29 (tel. 324 209), has a 24-hr. clinic and pharmacy.

Emergency: Police: tel. 110. **Fire:** tel. 113. **Ambulance:** tel. 118.

Police: Jl. Kapten Muslinat 16 (tel. 341 073). Open 24hr.

Post Offices: GPO, Jl. Ir. H. Juanda 5, across from where Jl. Palendang intersects the road around the gardens. The orange overhang is the giveaway. Open Mon.-Sat. 8am-6pm. *Poste Restante.* **Postal code:** 16124.

Telephones: Wartel Exotica, Jl. Pengadilan Blk. 14 (tel. 312 211), at Taman Topi, has **international phones, fax,** and telegrams. Open 24hr. At the entrance to the Botanical Gardens is another **24-hr. wartel,** with **HCD** phones and telegram services. **Telephone code:** 0251.

ACCOMMODATIONS

Abu Pensione, Jl. Mayor Oking 15 (tel. 322 893), ask a local for help if necessary. Abu caters to the eager traveler, offering a full range of rooms (some with views), comfortable verandas, a restaurant, and a travel agency. Dorms Rp7500. Singles with shared *mandi* and fan Rp10,000. Doubles with the same Rp20,000. Hot water, private bath, and A/C nearly double the price. Safe box available.

Puri Bali, Jl. Palendang 50 (tel. 317 498), southeast of the gardens. Run by the venerable octogenarian I. Made Tawan. Large rooms are a bit dim, but have high ceilings. Colorful paintings and artwork dandify the walls. Dorms Rp7500. Doubles Rp20,000. Rooms have fan and shared *mandi.* Free tea and coffee.

Firman Pensione, Jl. Palendang 48 (tel. 323 426), next door to Puri Bali, with more of a backpacker's atmosphere. Travelers can hang with the friendly, hospitable family. The open living area makes a great gathering place, more than compensating for the smallness of most of the rooms. Front rooms tend to be noisy. Generous portions of home-cooked meals. Dorms Rp7500. Singles Rp10,000. Doubles Rp15-18,000, with private *mandi* Rp20-30,000. Triples Rp25-30,000.

Wisma Mirah I, Jl. Martadinata 17 (tel. 333 520), a long walk from the town center (or a short ride on *angkot* 12 from the train station). Far, but allows some escape from the traffic noise. A bit upscale, Mirah offers a pleasant garden and big rooms, although they're a bit dim for the price. The chirping birds in the garden may suffice for those who miss the city noise. Doubles with shared *mandi*, fan, and sink Rp29,000-34,500. Extra bed Rp12,000. VIP rooms with A/C and TV cost more.

FOOD

All day and into the night, **warung** line up along Jl. Dewi Sartika. Those by the railway station are seedier, but they make many great varieties of *martabak.* **Bakeries** are part of almost every supermarket; particularly noteworthy is **Singapore Bakery** at the corner of Jl. Kapten Muslihat and Jl. Mayor Oking. For great Sundanese food, try **Mirah Sari,** Jl. Merdeka 18 (tel. 314 727), which is open daily 8am-9pm. Taman Topi also has a slew of restaurants; one of them, **Rumah Makan 88,** serves cheap Sundanese and Indonesian food, as well as yummy Chinese food and seafood for Rp2500-8000. *Warung* and great market food can also be found around **Pasar Baru.**

SIGHTS

A sprawling, verdant 100 hectares in the middle of Bogor, **Kebun Raya** (Botanical Gardens) puts most city parks to shame. For roughly Rp10,000, visitors can hire a guide to give them the scientific scoop on the 15,000 plants from around the world. The solo person will also appreciate a few hours' stroll. The traveler should be cautious, however; this domesticated jungle is also a haven for fat bugs that prey on human blood—wear plenty of bug spray. (Open 8am-4pm; admission Rp2000 Mon.-Sat., Rp1000 Sun. and holidays.)

Getting admitted to **Istana Bogor** is a bit trickier than the gardens. Tours can be arranged through the tourist office, but the "no t-shirt" rule may require donning loaner duds. Despite the skimpiness of the guide's descriptions, Indonesian history buffs will easily detect Soekarno's influence in the inordinate number of statues and paintings of nude women. These women, along with his four wives, surely helped to brighten up Soekarno's house arrest here from 1967 to 1970.

Those who seek nature of a more inanimate variety should check out the stuffed animals and skeletons at the **Zoological Museum** (tel. 322 177), left of the garden

---

The Life of Sir Stamford Raffles: Part the Fourth

Perhaps realizing that Indonesia would one day be the fourth most populous nation in the world, Sir Stamford Raffles, eventual founder of Singapore, had the perspicacity to plot the conquest of Java from the Dutch and served as Lieutenant-Governor from 1812 to 1816. His wife Olivia died during this tenure, but she, like Raffles, was so loved by the locals that her spirit lives on through her statue in the Botanical Gardens in Bogor. On his return to England, Raffles, the most popular man in the commonwealth, married a second wife, Sophia, and published the definitive two-volume *History of Java.* One wonders when this illustrious hero slept. (To read more about Sir Stamford's adventures, see page 320.)

entrance. (Open 8am-4pm; admission Rp500.) A little farther, near the GPO, is the **Ethnobotany Museum,** Jl. Ir. H. Juanda 5 (tel. 322 035). Dedicated to the interaction of the people and plants of Indonesia, the fledgling museum bestows upon visitors a renewed appreciation of tropical flora. (Open 8am-4pm; admission Rp500.)

Leaving nature's wonders behind, tourists can visit the **Gong Home Factory,** Jl. Pancasan 17, which is a veritable workshop of Thor. Take *angkot* #02 or 03 to the factory. (Open Sat.-Thurs. 8am-noon and 1-4pm.) Zig-zag back to the adjacent alley to visit another cottage industry—a **kerupuk factory.** The dough is kneaded, spun into cakes, dried, and dropped into hot oil daily 6am-3pm. To get there, take *angkot* 02 to catch a Ciapus-Rancamaya *angkot* by Pasar Baru. *Angkot* 02 also goes to a nearby **batutulis** (inscribed stone) on Jl. Batutulis, dating from the reign of the second Hindu kingdom here in the 16th century. It records the rule of King Surzawisesa, and was erected by one of his sons. (Open 8am-4pm; donations requested.)

■ Near Bogor

Escape from the city to **Pelabuhanratu,** a coastal town to the southwest, takes four hours by share-taxi or an indeterminate time by *angkot* or bus (Rp3000). The beach is nice, but currents render it unsafe for swimming. Although it gets crowded on weekends, there are plenty of places to stay. A one-hour minibus ride leads to **Cisarua,** a small town on the outskirts of Bogor which hosts seven **Air Terjun Cilember** (Cilember Waterfalls). The initial entrance fee comes to Rp1500, and guides can be hired for roughly Rp5-10,000 to take visitors through the area along a less-traversed path. The red clay trails are tough going, but the falls are worth the effort. **Taman Safari** (safari park), with roaming wildlife, a swimming pool, and other assorted entertainment, is also easily accessible from Bogor, and makes an interesting half-day trip. Take *angkot* 02 to Terminal Sukasari, and then a short minibus ride to Cisarua (Rp750)—tell the driver to stop at the Safari.

■ The Puncak

Meaning "mountain" in Bahasa Indonesia, the Puncak seems an understatement for the gorgeous mountain pass connecting Jakarta and Bogor to Bandung. The Puncak is a cool retreat from the heat of the larger western Java cities. Tea plantations stretch for km on either side of Route 2 (Jl. Raya), which winds through the towns of Cisarua, Cipanas, and finally up a steep hill to the town of Cibodas, the Puncak's backpacker's paradise. From any patio up this hill, terraced rice paddies are visible, and if the sky is clear, the peaks of Gunung Gede and Gunung Pangrango. The entrance to Gede Pangrango National Park and the Cibodas Botanical Gardens lies at the top of Jl. Raya Cibodas. Beyond the broad gates the avid trekker can find rigorous hikes, breathtaking views, and an incredible variety of wildlife.

GETTING THERE AND AWAY

Public buses have trouble navigating Rte. 2 (Jl. Raya) on weekends, when traffic is snarled, gnarled, and generally unpleasant. Otherwise, they run almost every 30 minutes from Jakarta, Bogor, and Bandung. Just hop on a bus indicating a route via the Puncak. The trip should cost Rp4000 during the week and double on the weekend. It is also possible to travel from Bandung to Cianjur by bus, then by *angkot* the rest of the way to Cibodas. Catch minibuses from the Bogor side on Jl. Raya. To go to Bandung, hop on a bus on Jl. Raya Cipanas by the *angkot* station, or simply flag one on the road—if the bus has empty seats, it will stop (2hr., Rp3-6000).

ORIENTATION AND PRACTICAL INFORMATION

Most of the guest houses are a few km up Jl. Raya Cibodas, toward the Botanical Garden at the top of the hilly road. To leave Cibodas for the post office, *wartel*, bank, or anything else, take an *angkot* to the bottom of Jl. Raya Cibodas and continue right a few km toward Bandung. This busy street has virtually all you may need.

Bank BNI, Jl. Raya Cipanas 167 (tel. 512 022), a few hundred meters up the road toward the Pass, cashes up to US$2000 in traveler's checks per day. (Open Mon.-Fri. 8am-3pm.) Another five minutes via *angkot* toward Bandung, **Bank BCA,** Jl. Ruko Pendawa A3 (tel. 513 089), is visible from the main road on the right. (Open Mon.-Fri. 8am-1:30pm, Sat. 8am-noon.) The Cipanas **angkot station** is up the street, next to the post office and past the **market.** There is a **24-hour emergency clinic** (tel. 512 465) at the intersection of Jl. Raya Cibodas and Jl. Raya Cipanas; the clinic has a **lab** and **pharmacy** on the premises. The **post office** (tel. 513 466) is at Jl. Raya Cipanas 109; it is open Mon.-Thurs. 8am-2pm, Fri. 8-11am, Sat. 8am-1pm. **Postal code:** 43253. Right next door is a **24-hr. wartel** which handles international calls, telegrams, and faxes. **Telephone code:** 0255.

ACCOMMODATIONS AND FOOD

Without a doubt, the Puncak cannot be fully appreciated without a one-, two-, or even three-night stay at one of the perfectly situated accommodations in Cibodas that overlook the beautiful cultivated valley. Away from the hustle and bustle of the main intercity route, these lodgings are within a 10-minute walk to the base of both the Botanical Gardens and Gunung Gede. To reach the following places, take a *bemo* several km up Jl. Raya Cibodas from the junction at Jl. Raya (Rp500).

Freddy's Homestay (tel. 515 473) is 100m short of the tall admission gate to the Botanical Gardens. Freddy and his wife offer small rooms with spectacular views and comfortable beds. English-speaking guides frequent the place and share local tidbits as well as lead tours. Dorms cost Rp10,000, doubles Rp15-20,000. All rooms have shared *mandi,* breakfast, and tea. Freddy and his wife also cook cheap, fantastic lunches and dinners, and will prepare picnic lunches.

Just beyond the admission gate to the right is the **Pondok Pemuda Hostel** (tel. 512 807) for the hardy, the hard-pressed, or the hard-up. Although the 12-person "dormitories" could use a little more attention, they come with a blanket and shared *mandi* for a bargain Rp5000. Next door is the **Wisma Jamur** (tel. 512 413), behind an unusually shaped white-washed main building. For stupendous views of the Puncak, a neat fish pond, shared *mandi,* and free breakfast, guests pay Rp15,000 per person for single, double, or triple rooms. More establishments can be had up the exhausting hills. The **guest house in the Botanical Gardens** is about a 15-minute walk from the main gates. All rooms are very spacious, sleeping three comfortably for Rp35,000. The guest house has free breakfast, and shared *mandi.*

Numerous *warung* settle all around the front gates of the park, and seem to be open all the time. The fresh fruit stands along the gate offers refreshing post-trek energy. The guest houses mentioned above also serve food. About 25m before the gates to the Botanical Gardens lies **Rizkah's,** a *padang* restaurant run by fluent English speakers eager to help misguided travelers find their way. Travelers who want a nice setting and hearty food but don't mind the relatively higher prices should try the **Valley View Restaurant,** Jl. Cibodas 13-15A (tel. 512 051), about mid-way between the Botanical Gardens and Jl. Raya Cipanas. Drinks and snacks cost Rp2500-5000, entrees Rp8-15,000. (Open daily 9am-9pm.) For those who must venture out of the Cibodas area, Jl. Raya Cipanas in both directions is flanked with fancy hotel-restaurants, cheaper *padang* joints, and omnipresent *warung.*

SIGHTS

The walk up Jl. Raya Cibodas is a sight unto itself. Residents participate in the nursery business, and *bonsai* and flowering plants line the whole 4-km stretch, all set amidst the awe-inspiring mountains. The **Kebon Raya Cibodas,** an extension of the Bogor Botanical Gardens, is 1km beyond the Jl. Raya Cibodas accommodations. Home to thousands of high-altitude species, the area is a bird-watcher's paradise. The land is well worth a long morning stroll and exploration. (Open daily 7am-5pm; admission

Rp2200.) The gardens spread out on the lower fringe of **Gede Pangrango National Park,** one of the more impressive pieces of a volcanic range that extends from Sumatra through Java. This large, protected area is home to numerous plant and wildlife that can be studied and enjoyed from the park's trails. To enter the park, go right of the Botanical Gardens gate to the Wisma Cinta Alam Visitors Centre to obtain a visitor's pass. For Rp4000 visitors can walk roughly 30 minutes to waterfalls, or another 90 minutes to a gushing, steamy hot spring. A roundtrip day hike to the summit of Gunung Gede costs Rp6000. Those who are properly equipped with tent and sleeping bag can spend the night on the summit of **Gunung Pangrango**. The path is rigorous but ends in a stunning outlook over the rest of Java.

En route from Bogor to Cibodas (or vice versa), travelers can stop at the **Gunung Mas Tea Factory** (Gunung Mas Pabrik Teh). From the gates of Gunung Mas, walk about 10 minutes up the street to the tea factory, passing a café and gift shop. While the overwhelming beauty of the plants stretching along the hills can be appreciated on your own, a closer look at the people who hand-pick the tea from these steep ranges can result in a deeper understanding of the rigorous process of tea making. A guided tour of the factory is available for Rp10,000. (Open daily 8am-noon.)

■ Bandung

Once known as the "Paris of the East Indies," Bandung was a favorite destination for Dutch vacationers from the late 19th century until World War II. Planning to make Bandung the capital of Indonesia, the Dutch tried to enhance the city's beauty with Art Deco buildings from some of Europe's foremost architects. Bandung now resembles industrial cities in most countries with the accompanying pollution, traffic, and noise. The capital of the province of West Java, Bandung is something of an intellectual capital as well, with upwards of 50 schools and universities. The traffic aside, the people of Bandung will gladly spend a few hours showing tourists around in exchange for some good English practice. Bandung's easy-going feel and cool climate make for a pleasant transition between Jakarta and the smaller cities and country towns to the east, and a springboard to nearby volcanoes and hot springs.

ORIENTATION

A sense of location is more important than one of direction for Bandung's angular layout. **Jalan Asia-Afrika,** a busy central street, runs west through the center of town by the **alun-alun** (town square), BRI building, and the Hotel Savoy Homann, with **Jalan Otto Iskandardinata** located perpendicularly south to north, ending at the Governor's Mansion. **Jalan Kebonjati** changes to **Jalan Sunjaraja** in front of the train station, and then runs parallel to Jl. Asia-Afrika. **Jalan Braga,** once the Dutch and Art Deco heart of town, runs north-south by the **Museum Asia-Afrika.** The north suburbs sport tree-lined boulevards, and volcanic peaks rise around Bandung on all sides. Street signs are placed perpendicular to the road they name.

PRACTICAL INFORMATION

Tourist Offices: Tourist Information Centre (tel. 420 66 44), at the northeast corner of the *alun-alun*. A rather useless map is available, as well as a dated but thorough information book, and a monthly guide to cultural events in the city. Tours in and around Bandung can be booked here. Open Mon.-Sat. 8am-4pm. Also a branch at the railway station.

Tours and Travel: Pacto Tours and Travel (tel. 420 47 39), in the Savoy Homann Hotel, Jl. Asia-Afrika 112. **American Express** agent here. Open Sun.-Fri. 8am-5pm, Sat. 9am-2pm. **Sari Holiday** (tel. 420 77 37), north of Jl. Asia-Afrika on Jl. Tamblong. Open Mon.-Fri. 8am-8pm, Sat. 8am-1pm. Most hostels book tours around Bandung, as well as express buses to major Indonesian cities.

Currency Exchange: Bank Nusantara Patahyangan, Jl. Sudirman 30-32 (tel. 420 20 88). Says Devisa on the doors. Exchange on 2nd Fl. Open Mon.-Fri. 8am-4pm, Sat. 8:30am-2pm. **Golden Money Changer,** Jl. Lembong 36 (tel. 420 55 34), next to the Army Museum. Another location at Jl. Otto Iskandardinata 180 (tel. 438 438). Open Mon.-Fri. 8:30am-4:30pm, Sat. 8:30am-2pm.

Air Travel: Husen Sastra Airport (tel. 615 871), 5km west of the city, a short trip by minibus to the gate. Many daily flights to Jakarta, Surabaya, Denpasar, and Semarang, and with less frequency to smaller cities. **Garuda/Merpati,** Jl. Asia-Afrika 73 (tel. 441 226), across from the Savoy Homann Hotel. **Sempati,** Jl. Merdeka 2 (tel. 420 16 12). **Bouraq,** Jl. Ciampelas 27 (tel. 437 896).

Trains: Terminal Stasiun, behind the *angkot* station on Jl. Stasiun Barat, right off Jl. Kebonjati. To: **Jakarta** (every hr., 2hr., 2nd class Rp15,000, 1st class Rp 25-30,000); **Surabaya** (3 per day, 12 hr., 2nd class Rp10-40,000, 1st class Rp21-60,000); and **Yogyakarta** (4 per day, 8hr., 2nd class Rp7-37,000, 1st class Rp35-50,000). All prices depend on type of train.

Buses: Inter-city buses traveling to western destinations leave from **Leuwi Panjang Terminal** on Jl. Soekarno-Hatta, a few km out of town. Take bus Ledeng-Leuwi Panjang or an *angkot*. Buses to the east leave from **Terminal Cicaheum** on Jl. A. Yani, a few km from town. Take bus Cicaheum-Kebon Kelapa. To: **Jakarta** (every 15min., 5hr., Rp12,5000, A/C Rp18,000); **Bogor** (every 15min., 3½hr., Rp7000, A/C Rp12,000); **Yogyakarta** (6 per day, 10hr., Rp20-45,000); **Surabaya** (6 per day, 14hr., Rp45,000); and **Denpasar** (bus line Simpatik, 1 per day, 18hr., Rp50,000).

Local Transportation: City buses (Rp250) have north-south and east-west routes. **Angkot** ply the city streets for Rp400 and surrounding regions (prices vary with distance). The major terminals are located in front of the railway station and at Kebon Kelapa (the old inter-city bus terminal). **Becak** also are scattered about, but probably best left until evening, when traffic dies down. **4848 Taxis** (tel. 434 48 48) are available throughout the city, and can be chartered as well.

Luggage Storage: Locker Office, at the railway station. Rp750 for less than 24hr. Rp1500 per day. Open daily 5am-6pm.

Markets: Manufactured goods line the sidewalks downtown all day long. **Pasar baru** offers textiles and clothing within and fruit outside on Jl. Otto Iskandardinata, near Jl. ABC. **Pasar malam** (night market) is mostly *warung,* off the northeast corner of the *alun-alun.*

Pharmacies: Kimia Farma 12, Jl. Ir. H. Juanda 1 (tel. 420 07 11). Pharmacies all over town open daily 8am-8pm.

Medical Services: Hospital RS Kebonjati, Jl. Kebonjati 152 (tel. 614 058).

Emergency: Fire: tel. 113. **Ambulance:** tel. 118.

Police: tel. 110. Main station on Jl. Merdeka (tel. 658 314).

Post Offices: GPO, Jl. Asia-Afrika 49 (tel. 431 050). International phones and telegrams available. *Poste Restante.* Open daily 8am-8pm. **Postal code:** 40111

Telephones: International phones available at the **GPO** and *wartel* all over town. Near the railway station is a **wartel,** Jl. Sunjaraja 119 (tel. 420 79 58). Open daily 8am-11pm. **Telephone code:** 022.

ACCOMMODATIONS

A bustling backpacker scene has given rise to cheap accommodations around the railway station. Most of these have simple restaurants and are good places to talk to the young Indonesians who semi-cooperatively run the hostels and local tours. They are perhaps the best source of information on mundane and touristy matters.

The New Sakadarna, Jl. Kebonjati 55 (tel. 421 85 53). Don't be intimidated by the long and winding alley—a clean and upbeat room is the light at the end of the tunnel. Eager and helpful staff offer breakfast and pleasant conversation on a small deck with a limited view. Dorms Rp7000. Singles Rp10,000. Doubles Rp13,000. Triples Rp17,000. Breakfast and fan included.

Hotel Surabaya, Jl. Kebonjati 71-73 (tel. 436 791). A very impressive building where colonial history lingers in the pictures and posters, colored-glass window, and the furniture of the deluxe rooms. All rooms are spacious and have wardrobes and bedside tables. Free tea and coffee. Economy class rooms: singles Rp11,500; doubles Rp20,000; triples Rp30,000; and quads Rp35,000. Standard class rooms have towels and blankets for about Rp2000 extra.

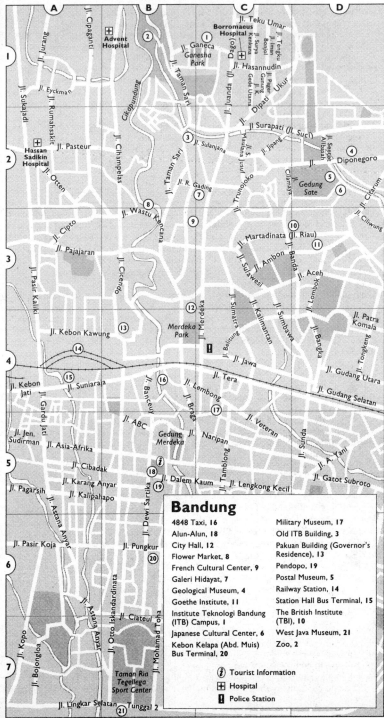

INDONESIA

Bandung

4848 Taxi, 16
Alun-Alun, 18
City Hall, 12
Flower Market, 8
French Cultural Center, 9
Galeri Hidayat, 7
Geological Museum, 4
Goethe Institute, 11
Institute Teknologi Bandung (ITB) Campus, 1
Japanese Cultural Center, 6
Kebon Kelapa (Abd. Muis) Bus Terminal, 20

Military Museum, 17
Old ITB Building, 3
Pakuan Building (Governor's Residence), 13
Pendopo, 19
Postal Museum, 5
Railway Station, 14
Station Hall Bus Terminal, 15
The British Institute (TBI), 10
West Java Museum, 21
Zoo, 2

ⓘ Tourist Information
✚ Hospital
❗ Police Station

Le Yossie Homestay, Jl. Kebonjati 53 (tel. 420 54 53). Look for the pastel green shutters to find this American-owned establishment. Though the lobby is a bit dark and the bathroom cave-like, rooms here are clean and bright enough. A single bathroom serves an entire floor. Rooms have fan and free breakfast. Dorms Rp7000. Singles Rp10,000. Doubles Rp13,500. Triples Rp16,500.

Hotel Maware, Jl. Pangarang 14 (tel. 420 49 34), a few blocks south of the *alun-alun*. A quiet alternative to the hotels in the railroad area or near the heart of the city. Down a few stairs off the quiet lane, Maware offers standard rooms at reasonable prices overlooking a pleasant tropical garden landscape. Singles Rp8500-12,500. Doubles Rp15,000. Breakfast included.

The Old Sakadarna, Jl. Kebonjati 50 (tel. 439 897). A little ways back from the busy street, it's nonetheless loud at most hours. Although well-worn, Sakadarna has a friendly feel thanks to Yeddi and the wonderful smells emanating from the kitchen. An upstairs terrace compensates for the small rooms. Singles Rp7000. Doubles Rp10,000. Triples Rp20,000.

FOOD

An awful lot of travelers seem to fall ill in Bandung, but it's difficult to avoid tempting *warung* smells; stick to well-frequented **warung** that look clean. *Bakso*, a noodle soup with balls of meat and *tahu* (tofu), are available everywhere, and the area around Pasar Baru offers a fabulous array of fruit. *Bandrek*, made of ginger, and *bajigur*, made of coconut milk and brown sugar, are local specialty drinks. There are a number of **bakeries** with tasty-looking European-influenced treats as well.

Sidang Reret, Jl. Naripan 9 (tel. 420 34 40), at the intersection with Jl. Braga. Sundanese food offered at tables or alternatively, on floor mats. There's a huge puppet stage and a life-size *golek* in one corner. *Wayang golek* shows on Saturday night (7-9pm); fills up for performances (free with dinner).

Queen Restaurant, Jl. Dalem Kaum 79 (tel. 420 45 61), a block east of the southeast corner of *alun-alun*. A popular, rather pricey Chinese/Cantonese restaurant with an extensive menu and huge portions (Rp8-25,000). Entertaining decor with slithering ceiling moldings surrounds the spacious vinyl seating area. Open daily 10:30am-2:45pm and 5:30pm-9:30pm.

Braga Permai Bakery, Jl. Braga 58 (tel. 433 778). Shelves upon shelves of chocolate desserts as well as baked goods with an Indonesian twist tempt the traveler in this European-style café. Menu offers Sundanese and Chinese specialities as well, and the outside tables provide great people-watching. Sweets cost about Rp500, meals Rp15,000. Open daily 10am-10pm.

SIGHTS

Bandung's architecture can be difficult to appreciate when you're weaving between the parked cars. An Art Deco movement swept through here in the 30s, courtesy of the architects Wolf Shoemacher, A.F. Aalbers, and F.W. Brinkman. Curious visitors can take one-hour tours (Rp15,000; book through the tourist office) or contact the **Bandung Society for Heritage Conservation** at their office in the Hotel Savoy Homann, Jl. Asia-Afrika 112, room 213 (open Mon.-Sat. 9am-5pm). This smooth, radio-esque building faces the less dramatic, but also art deco **Gedung Merdeka,** which houses the **Museum Asia-Afrika** (tel. 438 032). The museum has a display of pictures, headlines, and memorabilia from the 1955 Non-Aligned Movement Conference in Bandung, where 29 African and Asian nations identified themselves as a collective power, and agreed to pursue noninterference policies during the Cold War. (Open Mon.-Sat. 8am-4pm; free.) The **Army Museum,** Jl. Lembong 38, (tel. 420 33 93) is above Jl. Braga, entered from an interior courtyard of a clearly military building. Military buffs might be interested in comparing the older weapons and tanks to the more modern devices on display. (Open Mon.-Thurs., Sat. 9am-1pm, Fri. 8-10:30am; free, but a donation is requested.)

A few blocks south off Jl. Pangarang is A. Ruchiyat's **wayang golek factory** (tel. 420 13 35), a cottage industry on Jl. Pangarang Bawah IV. Follow the alley as it turns right, then left. Tourists are welcome to take photos of the crafting of these traditional, intricate puppets. The factory sells puppets and other *wayang golek* paraphernalia at fixed prices of Rp2500-85,000. (Open Mon.-Fri. 8am-7pm, Sat. 8am-2pm.) About 2km south is the **Museum of West Java,** Jl. Otto Iskandardinata 638 (tel. 510 976). It's Rp1500 for a look at Sundanese history, artifacts, and tradition.

A minibus from Kebon Kelapa goes to a **kerupuk factory** at Jl. Kopo Gang Pak Sahdi 27, across from Immanuel Hospital. Made from flavored and colored tapioca dough, *kerupuk* is deep fried for crispy eating. (Open Mon.-Sat. 8am-4pm.) Aspiring Julia Childs may want to check out the **Yun Sen Tofu Factory** and learn how the locals turn soy beans into *tahu* (tofu). The smell of tofu extract flows through the air all over the area. (Open daily; ask a factory worker if you may watch.)

North of the city, on Jl. Kebun Bintang stands the **Bandung Institute of Technology (ITB),** an impressive art deco building. Take an *angkot* to Kebon Kelapa, then take one headed in the Dago direction and get off at ITB. Also in the north suburbs is the **Geology Museum,** Jl. Diponegoro 37 (tel. 774 705), which has lots of mundane rocks, but some fantastic fossils—including an enormous elephant, a Komodo dragon, and **Java Man's skull.** (Open Mon.-Thurs., Sat. 9am-2pm, Fri. 9-11am; free.)

ENTERTAINMENT AND NIGHTLIFE

Bandung has a very active nightlife, if you know where to look. In the evening the city is a bustling home to karaoke clubs, discotheques, and late-night movies. The **North Sea,** Jl. Braga 82 (tel. 420 89 04), "Bandung's only real bar," is set like a ship, complete with water running between panes of glass. Dutch-owned, the bar offers weekend afternoon movies, free pool table, and sturdy Dutch bar food. (Open Mon.-Fri. 5pm-1am, Sat. noon-2am, Sun. noon.-1am.) Just a block farther is the decadent **Caesar's Palace,** Jl. Braga 129 (tel. 433 291). Be prepared to part with Rp20,000 up front. (Open nightly 10pm-3am.)

Just north stands the big BRI building at Jl. Asia-Afrika 57-59. On the 15th floor is the **Polo Room Discotheque** (tel. 420 53 25), where you can dance the night away with a stunning view of the city. (Open 10pm-2am, Sat. 10pm-3am; cover Rp10,000, weekend Rp20,000.) Next door at **Canopy Karaoke Lounge** (tel. 420 55 17), partygoers can sink into leather sofas and enjoy the karaoke stage acts. (Open 8pm-2am; cover Rp15,000.)

O'Hara's Tavern stands farther down, where Jl. Asia-Afrika becomes Jl. Sudirman, on the ground floor of the Hotel Perdana Wisata at No. 66 (tel. 438 238 ext. 181). The wood paneling here seems more reminiscent of a Wild West tavern than a pub from the Isles. There's live music nightly, generally top 40 and rock (Rp15,000 for the first drink).

Slightly more cultured entertainment is available on Saturdays (7pm-9pm) at **Sindang Reret,** in the form of a *wayang golek* performance. **Pak Udjo's workshop,** Jl. Padasuka 118 (tel. 771 714), puts on *angklung* (hand-held bamboo chimes) performances when at least 20 people come. Take an *angkot* toward Cicaheum, then walk up Jl. Padasuka. The shows start at 3:30pm and cost Rp10,000. **The Institute of Fine Arts (ASTI)** puts on performances as well; ask about the current offerings and the monthly schedule of events at the tourist office.

SHOPPING

As Yogyakarta is to handmade goods, so Bandung is to manufactured ones. The sidewalks of the old **Chinatown** area around Pasar Baru are like a feeding frenzy of shirts, shoes, socks, shorts, snapshots of stars, and vegetable peelers. **Pasar Baru** along Jl. Otto Iskandardinata near Jl. ABC, is an immense maze of textile and shoe shops, as well as the more traditional dried foods, fish, meat, and fruit stands. Behind *pasar baru* on Jl. Pasar Selatan and nearby streets, you can get a taste of the frivolity that makes the jean shop storefronts on **Jeans Street** (Jl. Cihampelas) so amusing. Neon colors and enormous statues of pop-culture heroes (James Bond, Batman) are worth a look and maybe a picture. Get there by *angkot* to Jl. Pasir Kaliki, then walk west to

Jl Cihampelas. Malls have flooded the city, most highly concentrated off the south-west corner of the *alun-alun* on Jl. Dewi Sartika and Jl. Cidabak. **Plaza Bandung Indah,** Jl. Merdeka 56 (tel. 407 10), is the fanciest and most expensive mall in town. It has big-name western stores, a discotheque, a playland (with bumper cars), and a six-screen theater. (Open daily 9am-9pm.)

■ Near Bandung

In Bandung, tourists can take self-guided tours of the sights, or hire local guides through hotels or the tourist office for day-long circuit tours of the southeast region (Rp35,000). On such tours, a quick look at a silk factory is followed by a stop at the **Candi Cangkuang temple** to Shiva, the oldest Hindu temple on West Java, dating from the 8th century AD. From the temple, another hour or so in the tour minibus leads to **Papandagan Volcano,** an impressive crater-packed mountain covered with sulfurous yellow crystals. Many visitors cover their nose and take a dip in the **Tarogong Hot Springs** which lie at the base. Leave a day for this leisurely and delight-ful tour, and escape the fitful traffic and stifling smog of the city.

The town of **Lembang,** a 30-minute, Rp1000 *angkot* ride from the railway station, offers an alternative refuge from the busy town. In Lembang, travelers can trek to **Tangkuban Prahu,** the "capsized boat" crater. Those who have the time should get off at Jl. Jayagiri in Lembang and head straight up, paying Rp800 to climb through a pine, then tropical forest. It's slick when rainy, and a solid 15-km hike. At the lower carpark and gate, the forest trail emerges and everyone must pay Rp1250. There are *warung* at the lower lot, and *bemo* to the top. The big gray caldera of **Ratu** sits and bubbles up sulphur and steam. Although one can imagine an impressive view of Bandung, clouds inevitably block any clear sights of the city. A path leads to the smaller **Domas Caldera** from the lower lot (get a guide for this route). At 1830m, Ratu is spectacular, and makes a wonderful escape from many of the tourists and hawkers. Those who have had their fill of vistas can head back down to the main gate and take an *angkot* toward Subang. After winding through tea plantations, get off a few km away at the top of the road to the "Air Panas Crater," the **hot springs** at **Sari Ater Resort,** Jl. Taman Sari 72 (tel. 200 319). Many visitors settle in here for a thera-peutic hot bath in the natural pools and waterfalls (Rp3000). It's best to go in the evening, around 9pm, to avoid the crowds. (Open 24hr.)

■ Cirebon

On the north coast of Java, Cirebon lies at the Sundanese/Javanese cultural crossroads where West and Central Java meet. With few major sights or tourist attractions, Cire-bon is not a typical tourist destination. Rather, it's a city where foreigners come to catch a glimpse into everyday Indonesian life, and a sacred pilgrimage sight where Javanese gather to witness and honor the tomb of Sultan Gunung Jati. With wide uncongested streets and an unbelievable number of *becak,* Cirebon presents a lei-surely and stately appearance, enforced by a large military presence. Cirebon is also a center for both *kerupuk* (shrimp crackers) and Daihatsu production, an odd cultural collision that seems somehow fitting for this small Indonesian city.

ORIENTATION

Cirebon stretches along the coast, with the heart of the city bound on the southwest side by train tracks. **Jalan Siliwangi,** the major thoroughfare, divides the city into two long strips. **Kali Sukalila,** a narrow channel, and **Jalan Gudang/Pasuketan** run almost parallel northeast to southwest, further dividing the length of Cirebon. **Jalan R.A. Kartini/Veteran** is the next busy east-west street north of the channel. The train sta-tion, town hall, and most of the hotels lie north of the channel, while the markets, stores, malls, and dense traffic are farther south. The harbor, GPO, and major banks are east of it. Street signs are often missing or vague, so don't hesitate to ask a local for help. *Angkot* G5 and G6 run up and down Jl. Siliwangi.

PRACTICAL INFORMATION

Currency Exchange: Banks line Jl. Siliwangi and Jl. Yos Sudarso by the post office. **Bank Niaga,** Jl. Siliwangi 110 (tel. 206 981). Open Sun.-Fri. 8:30am-2:30pm.

Air Travel: Pelabuhan Udar Penggung Airport (tel. 207 085) lies 5km to the southwest of the city and offers domestic flights to major cities. Take *angkot* GC or GG05 to get there.

Trains: Stasiun Cirebon (tel. 202 400), on Jl. Stasiun off Jl. Siliwangi. Express to: Jakarta (3 per day, 3hr., Rp12,500); **Yogyakarta** (1 per day, 6hr., Rp6-8000); and **Surabaya** (1 per day, 12hr., Rp12-16,000). Cirebon is a stopping point for most non-express trains running between Jakarta and other major cities on Java.

Buses: Terminal, 5km from town. Take *angkot* G8 (Rp1500). Expect a Rp1000 tariff upon entrance into bus terminal. Buses to: **Jakarta** (every hr., 4hr., Rp7000); **Pangandaran** via Banjar (every hr., 5hr., Rp12,000); and **Yogyakarta** (3-4 per day, 7-9hr., Rp4000).

Local Transportation: Angkot, the nickname for *angkutan kota* (city transport), have set rates: Rp400 around town, Rp1500 to the bus terminal and airport. Take a more leisurely ride on a **becak,** about Rp1000 per km, but be sure to bargain.

Markets: Pasar Kanoman lies in front of the Keraton Kanoman, and **Pasar Pagi,** sprawls under and behind the Mandala Cinema building on Jl. Karaggetas.

Pharmacies: Kimia Farma Apotek, Jl. Parujakan 12 (tel. 208 954). Open 24hr. Closer to the train station and hotel area is **Apotek Garuda,** Jl. Siliwangi 65 (tel. 204 442). Open daily 7:30am-9:30pm.

Medical Services: RS Gunung Jati (tel. 202 444), on Jl. Kesambi. Take an *angkot.* Or try the local hospital, **RS Sumber Kasih,** Jl. Siliwangi 135 (tel. 203 518). Pharmacy open daily 8am-11pm, 24-hr. emergency service.

Emergency: Ambulance: tel. 118. **Police:** tel. 110. **Fire:** tel. 113.

Post Offices: GPO, Jl. Yos Sudarso 9 (tel. 161 234). Coin and card phone. No official *Poste Restante,* but they hold packages in back. Open daily 8am-8pm. Also a branch in the center of town next to the new Yogya mall on Jl. Karanggetasblo (tel. 206 329). **Postal code:** 45100.

Telephones: For international calls, go to an upscale hotel, or the **wartel,** Jl. Kartini 7 not far from town hall. **HCD** and **fax** service. Open daily 6:30am-2am. **Telephone code:** 0231.

ACCOMMODATIONS

Most accommodations, both budget and upscale, cluster around the train station. Check-in is whenever you arrive. Check-out is 2pm.

Hotel Baru, Jl. Kali Baru Selatan 3 (tel. 201 728). From the train station, turn right onto Siliwangi, cross the bridge; it's about 200m down. Those who brave the walk are rewarded with this cheap, clean, and friendly hotel. Offers a wonderfully chatty, if sometimes noisy, atmosphere. Doubles with fan and bath Rp15-20,000, with A/C, TV, and hot water Rp35,000. Extra bed Rp7500. Breakfast included.

Hotel Priangan, Jl. Siliwangi 108 (tel. 202 929). Offers a multitude of options, ranging from cheaper roadside doubles to posh VIP pads complete with minibar. Inside, the Chinese garden pool with large fish lends a feeling of decadence, even to the penny-pinching traveler. Doubles with fan and *mandi* Rp22-24,000, with A/C Rp33,000. Triples with A/C, TV, and *mandi* Rp45,000. Quads similarly bedecked Rp48,500. VIP room with the works Rp58,000. 10% service charge.

Hotel Slamet, Jl. Siliwangi 95 (tel. 203 296), has a convenient shop in the hotel. Each room has 2 separate beds, and a loud TV. All rooms have bath. Doubles with fan and TV Rp27,000, with A/C Rp38,500. Extra bed Rp1100. Breakfast included.

New Land Grand Hotel, Jl. Siliwangi 98 (tel. 208 867). If only for the pleasure of sitting on the vinyl couch covers in the hotel lobby and observing wild and exotic tropical fish in their tank, the traveler should check this place out. The rooms have a 70s feel to get you in the mood for the discotheque next door—free passes for hotel guests might make the higher room rates worth it. Doubles go for Rp38-58,000 with varying degrees of amenities; A/C and *mandi* are standard.

FOOD

Cirebon offers up plenty of authentic Western Javanese food. All restaurants, *warung* and markets serve fresh fish and shellfish. Other Cirebon specialties such as *nasi lengko* (rice with bean sprouts, onion, cucumber, and *tempe*) and *nasi jamblang* (rice in dried teak leaves) are best right off the food carts on Jl. Siliwangi. Travelers might wish to explore the food stands in the **Pasar Kanoman** or **Pasar Pagi**. Most shops shut down by 4pm. **Warung** on every block offer a shaded seat and cheap dishes. Hours vary, but most *warung* open until late evening.

Restaurant Salebarang, located right over the bridge where Jl. Siliwangi turns into Jl. Karaggetas, has a diner-style layout and a light menu. Hungry for lunch and eager to escape the sweltering streets, the traveler can have soup, *nasi,* and other meals next to a fan and in front of the TV for Rp2-5000. Open daily 8am-9pm.

Restaurant Pujaneka, Jl. Siliwangi 105 (tel. 205 411), is diner-esque too, with vinyl chairs and a checkerboard floor. Catering to a young crowd, Pujaneka hangs colorful cartoon caricatures of food on the walls and boasts a "wonderland" playroom in the back. Indonesian food costs Rp2-5000. Open daily 10am-midnight.

Marina Seafood Restaurant, Jl. Karanggetas 64 (tel 210 033), located on the 4th floor over the New Yogya Department Store. Marina has fantastic views over Cirebon and the sea. Spacious seating in front of a stage that hosts live music and dance performances on Saturday nights. Big menu offers varying-sized portions ranging (Rp4-40,000). Open Mon.-Sat. 10am-10pm, Sun. *dim sum* 8am-noon.

SIGHTS

There isn't much to see in Cirebon, but it does have one claim to fame: the **Tomb of Sultan Gunung Jati**, considered one of Java's holiest sites. Sultan Gunung Jati, one of the first Islamic missionaries to Java, is revered for pushing out the Hindu kingdom of Pajajaran and conquering the Cirebon kingdom. In November devout Muslims pour in to celebrate the anniversary of the sultan's birth. To reach the tomb, take *angkot* GG or G6 to Makam Gunung Jati. Walk down the lane to the end and turn right. A small donation (Rp500-1000) can get a tour of the grounds.

At the eastern end of Jl. Gudang/Pasuketan, overlooking the harbor, is the Chinese temple **Klenteng Thiaw Kak Sie,** which serves the Chinese residents of Cirebon (about 15% of the population). Built in 1658, Thiaw Kak Sie is the oldest Chinese temple, as well as one of the most beautiful, in Indonesia. Inside, intricate frescoes adorn the walls and the scent of incense filters through the temple.

Head away from the harbor in a southwesterly direction and you will come to **Kraton Kanoman** (tel. 206 605), on Jl. Dalam Kraton Cirebon beyond Pasar Kanoman. Built in the 17th century, this palace opened in 1670. Inside the *kraton* stands the magnificent Paksi Naga Liman (elephant-serpent-bird) coach, so-called because of the three mythological creatures depicted on it. (Open 8am-4pm; admission Rp1000.) Farther south you will see the greenery of the *alun-alun.* At the southwest corner is another palace, the **Kraton Kasepuhan** (tel. 204 001), built in 1677. The museum features an odd collection of 16th century objects: *gamelan,* cannons, chests, armor, and knickknacks from faraway places. There is also a stable with several carriages, and another interesting coach, the Singa Barong carriage (elephant-serpent-*garuda*). (Open daily 8am-4pm; admission Rp1000.) Just across from Kraton Kasepuhan is **Mesjid Agung,** which dates back to 1480. To the north of the mosque is yet another *kraton* on Jl. Lawanggada, **Kraton Kacirebonan,** but you can only stare at it, as the royal family still lives here.

About 4.5km southwest of town is **Taman Sunyaragi,** housing Cirebon's botanical gardens in an odd, red brick structure. First built in the 15th century as a resthouse for the royal family, Sunyaragi has since gone through many changes. It has been a country palace (complete with waterfalls), a weapons armory, and a rebel base during the colonial wars (according to rumors). To get there, take *angkot* G2 to the Jl. Bypass and walk to the right.

■ Pangandaran

An increasingly popular coastal resort, Pangandaran dangles from the south coast of Java like a mango, milking its status for all it's worth. With beaches, dense forests, and decent surf all nearby, it is a favorite destination of Jakartans as well foreigners. There's late night entertainment and plenty of places to eat fresh seafood. Although the weekends can draw a crowd, Pangandaran's usually empty beaches and quiet streets can be a welcome change from some of the more commercial beach resorts in Indonesia. You'll have plenty of opportunities to explore lush forests and waterfalls, wander through the market outside the main gates, and visit surrounding villages. Most people, however, come to Pangandaran just to relax.

ORIENTATION

From the bus terminal, turn left and enter the big, red main gates, where guards request a Rp1000 entrance tariff for tourists entering for the first time. This palm-lined, well-lit boulevard follows directly into the smashing waves of Pangandaran's main swimming area, the west beach. Running perpendicular at the boulevard's end, **Jalan Pamugaran** stretches north and south, parallel to the water. **Jalan Kidang Pananjung,** home to many restaurants, hotels, and billiard halls, also runs north-south, although it is set farther back from the west beach; it begins just before the main gates and ends at the entrance to Pananjung National Park. Busy **Jalan Bulak Laut** connects Jl. Kidang Pananjung to Jl. Pamugaran.

PRACTICAL INFORMATION

Tours and Travel: Tourist offices all over town sell standard package tours, maps, and other tourist services. Most open daily 8am-10pm. Many hotels also offer tourist services. Although Pangandaran National Forest is technically closed, guides will lead eco-friendly tours (4-6hr., Rp15,000). Green Canyon Tours (all-day, Rp30,000). They also book buses to: **Yogyakarta** (Rp12,500); **Wonsobo** (Rp12,500); **Jakarta** (Rp17,500; with A/C Rp30,000); **Bogor** (Rp17,500); and **Bandung** (Rp10,500; with A/C Rp13,500).

Currency Exchange: Bank Rakyat Indonesia, Jl. Kidang Pananjung 212 (tel. 639 288), by the intersection with Jl. E. Jaga Lautan, offers reasonable exchange rates. Open Mon.-Fri. 8am-2pm. Outside the main gates behind the main market on Jl. Merdeka is another branch with slightly better rates (tel. 639 081). Open Sun.-Fri. 8am-2:30pm. Most tourist offices also change money at higher rates.

Trains: No train line runs directly to Pangandaran. In **Banjar** there is a train station with service to Jakarta and other cities.

Buses: Bus terminal, 50m from the main gates. To: **Bandung** (5 per day, 5-6hr., Rp6500); **Bogor** (4 per day, 8hr., Rp11,500); **Jakarta** (2 per day, 10hr., Rp10,000); and **Banjar** (7am, 1½hr., Rp4000).

Local Transportation: *Becak,* motorbikes, and bicycles rule the roads.

Rentals: Rent **bicycles** (Rp5000 per day) and **mopeds** (Rp15,000, Rp10,000 from the *ojek* stand opposite the main market) at the many specialized rental offices and tourist offices. Most hotels also offer free or rental bikes.

Markets: The **Main Market** lies outside the main gates beside the bus terminal. Open Wed. and Sat. 7am-5pm. Look for the new **Art Market** to open up in the future, replacing the old one that burned down a few years ago.

Pharmacies: (tel. 639 574), in back of the main market. Open daily 7am-8pm. There are also many shops with toiletry items along the outskirts of the market.

Medical Services: Hospital, Jl. Parapat 1 (tel. 639 118). A small hospital with an ambulance. Open 24hr. for emergencies.

Police: Jl. Merdeka 285 (tel. 639 075), located behind the main market. Some police are also stationed at the main gate 24hr.

Emergency: Police (tel. 110).

Post Offices: Jl. Kidang Pananjung III 129 (tel. 639 284). *Poste Restante.* Open Sat.-Thurs. 8am-2pm, Fri. 8-11am. **Postal code:** 49396.

Telephones: Telkom office, Jl. Kidang Pananjung 5 (tel. 639 333). Open 24hr. **HCD,** fax, telex, phone cards. Coin and card phones abound on the streets and at accommodations for local calls. Adam's Homestay on Jl. Pamugaran also has international phone services daily 8am-10pm. **Telephone code:** 0265.

ACCOMMODATIONS

Pangandaran has numerous places to stay, most of which are concentrated on the west beach road and inland. Small hotels and cottages cater primarily to Javanese tour groups and families, and lack international phones and English-speaking hosts. Bungalows close to the water, or a room in a peaceful *losmen* on the outskirts of town are often the best of the lot.

Pondok Cocobana, on the north side of town off Jl. Pamugaran. At the end of the boulevard to the west beach, about 75m. Well-traveled and well-spoken Agus offers 7 clean rooms with a porch area overlooking a tropical garden. Relaxing seclusion to the grooving tunes of Bob Marley. Big, tasty breakfast included. Tourist services and safe boxes available. All rooms have fan, *mandi,* and/or shower. Singles Rp7500. Doubles Rp22,500. Triples Rp22,500.

Delta Gecko, Sindang Laut Rt. 01/02, up the west beach. With 30 rooms, it's village unto itself, removed from the tourist scene. No phones or electricity. Take the bus past Pangandaran terminal to Jl. Pamugaran, Cikembulan (Rp500 extra), and then take an *ojek* (Rp1000). Or follow Jl. Pamugaran 5km north and look for it on the right. **Vegetarian restaurant,** arts and crafts, tours, library, and free bikes. Less than 100m away is an empty, unlittered beach. Eco-groovy Aussie Kristina and her animal friends make great company. All rooms include breakfast and *mandi.* Dorms Rp7500. Singles Rp10,000. Doubles Rp17,500-30,000. Family houses Rp25-30,000. Kristina gives free room and board in exchange for 6hr. of work per day; just write her beforehand.

Holiday Beach, Jl. Buka Laut 50 (tel. 639 285), at the upper end of the beach. If your bones are still chattering from a long, tense, bouncing ride to Pangandaran, you might want to pay the few extra rupiah and sink into a mattress above firm box-springs here. If your wallet is more sore than your back, climb the creaky stairs to the old section and settle in for less. Singles Rp7500. Doubles Rp10-20,000. Restaurant, tourist service, and safe deposit box available.

Hotel Mini, Jl. Kidang Pananjung 207 (tel. 639 296). Don't let the name throw you—there's nothing mini about this place except for its prices. Rooms have enough space for the big beds they house, and even include a hearty breakfast and fan. Tourist services and safe deposit boxes available. Hotel also rents bikes, mopeds, cars, and snorkel gear at a 30% discount for hotel guests. Singles Rp8000, with *mandi* Rp10,000. Doubles Rp12,500, with *mandi* Rp15,000.

FOOD

In addition to the restaurants associated with many of the accommodations, Pangandaran's food scene consists of large seafood places to smaller well-hidden roadside **warung** to busy cafés on Jl. Bulak Laut. Eateries are inexpensive (about Rp1500-7000 per meal) and generally open daily 8am-11pm. The **Fish Market,** on the east beach road, is possibly the best place to eat in town, and is open daily from 7am until all the customers leave (usually around 11pm). Prices range depending on weight and type of seafood. The area which locals refer to as the old center of town, the southern end of Jl. Kidang Pananjung, houses many restaurants and drinking hangouts.

Cilicap "Chez Mama," Jl. Kidang Pananjung 187 (tel. 639 98), offers the standard Chinese and Indonesian fare in an open-air, large room with light music in the background. Rp1-5000 per plate; seafood is a bit more.

Rumah Makan Simpati, Jl. Kidang Pananjung 220 (tel. 639 626). This "Sympathy Café" has a similar, but larger menu than "Chez Mama," and boasts a staff that speaks Indonesian, Dutch, German, French, and English.

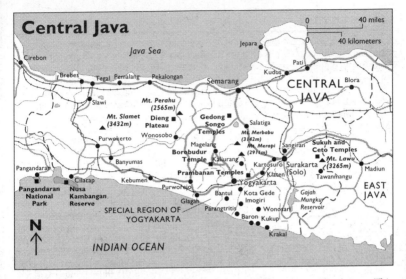

Central Java

Java Sea

Jepara

Cirebon

Pati

Brebes   Tegal Pemalang Pekalongan   Semarang   Kudus

CENTRAL   Blora

Slawi   JAVA

Mt. Perahu
(2565m)

Mt. Slamet   Dieng   Gedong   Salatiga
(3432m)   Plateau   Songo
Temples   Mt. Merbabu
Purwokerto   Wonosobo   (3142m)
Mt. Merapi Sangiran   Sukuh and
Magelang   (2914m)   Ceto Temples
Banyumas   Borobudur   Surakarta   Mt. Lawu
Pangandaran   Temple Kaliurang Kartosuro   (Solo)   (3265m)   Madiun
Prambanan Temples   Klaten Tawanmangu
Cilacap   Kebumen   Purworejo   Yogyakarta   EAST
Pangandaran Nusa   Kota Gede   Gajah   JAVA
National   Kambangan   Bantul Imogiri   Mungkur
Park   Reserve   Wonosari   Reservoir
SPECIAL REGION OF   Glagah Parangtritis
YOGYAKARTA   Baron Kukup

N   Krakal

INDIAN OCEAN

0   40 miles
0   40 kilometers

Bunga Laut Restaurant, on Jl. Bunga Laut, the new happening area of town. This restaurant changes its menu depending on the season to adapt to the different tourists' palates. The chatty proprietor will keep your ears full as you eat and take in the local artists' work that decorates the restaurant.

Francisco Brillo, just next door to Delta Gecko, puts Italian genius into his varied cuisine. Try his pineapple pizzas, pasta salad, or mixed BBQ for Rp6-9000. Franciso also offers rooms with fantastic views of the water (Rp12-15,000).

SIGHTS

For those who prefer to sweat from exertion rather than from lazing under the sun, Pangandaran has two major sights: Penanjung Park and Green Canyon. For a Rp1500 fee, travelers can enter **Penanjung Park** and glimpse white sand beaches with the hint of great snorkeling. Although the rest of the park is technically closed, guides in town or associated with most of the hotels will charge about Rp15,000 for an eco-friendly six-hour trek. You can expect to see limestone caves, the enormous and smelly Rafflesia flower, bats with two-meter wingspans, lizards, monkeys, deer, and, if you are lucky, porcupines. **Green Canyon** is about 30km away; the dock is accessible by minibus or moped, and then hire a boat to take go 15 minutes down the river. The water's lovely jade color gives the sight its name.

■ Yogyakarta

In 1755, Prince Mangkubumi built Yogyakarta's royal *kraton* and named himself Sultan Hamengkubuwono, meaning "the universe on the lap of the king." Despite the name's pomp, his lineage has survived until today, ten sultans later, due in part to Yogyakarta's combined respect for tradition and tradition of respect. As well as being the geographical hub of "Yogya," the *kraton* complex encapsulates what Yogya is most famous for: its history, crafts, and tourism. Through museums, classical arts, and daily interactions, Yogyakartans demonstrate pride in their city's semi-autonomous status and history of resistance against colonial powers. Yet, Yogya's residents achieve a curious balance of character, weaving pride with humility. Whether they're describing an intricate batik design, offering transport, or bargaining for durian, Yogya's locals are eager to help and quick to smile, making Yogya a hospitable and culturally rich destination for travelers of all persuasions.

ORIENTATION

Lying 603km southeast of Jakarta (10hr. by train), Yogyakarta rests at the base of **Gunung Merapi** (2911m). With Solo, its sister city to the northeast, Yogya is the tourist hub and cultural heart of Central Java. The city is built around the 1sq.km fortress of the **kraton complex** and the two square fields on the north **(Alun-alun Lor)** and south **(Alun-alun Kidul)** sides of the complex. **Jalan Malioboro (Jalan A. Yani** at its south end) is Yogya's main north-south boulevard. The *kraton* is on its south end and Tugu Train Station on **Jalan Pasar Kembang** crosses Malioboro at its north end. Jl. Malioboro, north of the train station becomes **Jalan Mangkubumi** which ends at the phallic **Tugu Monument.** The monument stands in the middle of another major intersection with **Jalan Diponegoro/Sudirman/Sumoharjo/Solo/Adisucipto.** This road leads east to the **airport,** and eventually Prambanan and Solo. Budget accommodations line **Jalan Sosrowijayan,** which branches west off Malioboro, and **Jalan Prawirotaman,** southeast of the *kraton.*

PRACTICAL INFORMATION

Tourist Offices: Jl. Malioboro 16 (tel. 566 000), southward on Malioboro past the modern Mutiara Hotel on the left. Brochures, maps, tickets, and tours. International phone service. They have a complicated train schedule which the staff can explain in English. Open Mon.-Fri. 8am-7:30pm, Sat. 8am-noon.

Tourist Police: Jl. Malioboro 14 (tel. 377 777), next to the tourist office. Go here with theft reports and complaints.

Immigration Offices: Jl. Laksda Adisucipto Km10 (tel. 586 130), near the airport. Good luck getting visa extensions. Open Mon.-Fri. 9am-4:30pm.

Currency Exchange: In the Sosrowijayan and Prawirotaman areas there are plenty of banks and money changers. Bring passport or a photocopy of it to change traveler's checks. Banks open Mon.-Fri. 8:30am-2pm, Sat.-Sun. 8:30-11am. **Bank of Jakarta** (tel. 562 398), on the corner where Pasar Kembang and Jl. Malioboro intersect, and **Lippo Bank** (tel. 564 523), attached to the colonial-style Natour Garuda Hotel, offer cash advances on MC and Visa for a Rp3000 fee.

American Express: In the **Natour Garuda Hotel,** Jl. Malioboro 60 (tel. 565 345). Air travel services including purchase and confirmations. Open Mon.-Fri. 8:30am-7pm, Sat. 8:30am-2pm.

Air Travel: Airport (tel. 565 840), 8km from the center of Yogya on Jl. Adisucipto. Take a taxi or catch a bus from Umbulharjo Terminal. Several Indonesian carriers, including: **Garuda,** Jl. Mangkubumi 56 (tel. 514 400); **Sempati** (tel. 511 612), in Natour Garuda Hotel; and **Merpati,** Jl. Panglima Sudirman 63 (tel. 514 272). To **Jakarta** (Rp170,000).

Trains: Tugu Train Station, Jl. Mangkubumi 3 (tel. 512 612), on Jl. Pasar Kembang. Trains to: **Jakarta** (13 per day); **Bandung** (6 per day); **Surabaya** (9 per day); and **Surakarta** (4 per day). Prices vary dramatically. For Jakarta, prices go as low as Rp25,000 and as high as Rp70,000. Tourist info staff can help demystify the schedule. Arrive 1hr. ahead of time to buy tickets.

Buses: Umbulharjo Terminal, Jl. Veteran (tel. 377 834), southeast of the city. To get there, take buses #1 and 14 from the Malioboro and Prawirotaman areas. Buses go all over Java, Sumatra, and Bali. Schedules and fares available at ticket agencies on Jl. Mangkubumi, Sosrowijayan, and Prawirotaman.

Local Transportation: City buses (Rp300) run north-south between Umbulharjo Terminal and Gajah Mada University along Yogya's main streets. Flag down buses at any point along the route. Route maps are hard to find; ask bus drivers if they pass by your destination. Buses are less frequent after 5pm. Metered **taxis** (Rp650 per km) can be hailed easily. **Becak** are slow, but the best to tour the city with. Agree on a price before boarding (Rp5000 per 5km is standard). **Andong,** horse-drawn carriages, are also available for hire.

Rentals: Cars, bikes, and **motorbikes** can be rented from many locations on Jl. Pasar Kembang, Malioboro, Prawirotaman, and Sosrowijayan. **Fortuna Rental,** Jl. Jlagran 20-21 (tel. 564 680) is 50m to the right of Tugu Station. Bikes Rp5000 per

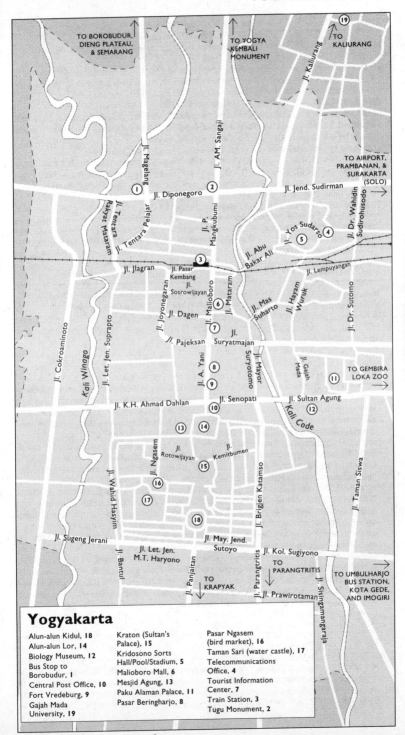

INDONESIA

Yogyakarta

Alun-alun Kidul, 18
Alun-alun Lor, 14
Biology Museum, 12
Bus Stop to
Borobudur, 1
Central Post Office, 10
Fort Vredeburg, 9
Gajah Mada
University, 19

Kraton (Sultan's
Palace), 15
Kridosono Sorts
Hall/Pool/Stadium, 5
Malioboro Mall, 6
Mesjid Agung, 13
Paku Alaman Palace, 11
Pasar Beringharjo, 8

Pasar Ngasem
(bird market), 16
Taman Sari (water castle), 17
Telecommunications
Office, 4
Tourist Information
Center, 7
Train Station, 3
Tugu Monument, 2

day, motorbikes Rp20,000 per day, and cars Rp75,000 per day. No age restrictions for car rental; bring a license (IDP preferred) and a passport.

Luggage Storage: Tugu Station stores baggage at Rp2000 for 6hr., Rp4000 for 24hr. No time limit. Counter open 24hr.

Markets: Yogya has several **public markets** *(pasar)* that warrant a visit for their spectacular value alone. **Beringharjo Market,** at Jl. A. Yani and Jl. Pabringan. Open daily 5am-4pm, but activity slows down mid-afternoon.

Pharmacies: Kimia Farma, Jl. Malioboro 123 (tel. 514 980). Open 24hr.

Medical Services: Rumah Sakit Bethesda, Jl. Saluran 6 (tel. 562 246). **Ludira Husada Tama Hospital,** Jl. Wiratama 4 (tel. 513 651). Open 24hr. Makes hotel/ guest house calls. Both have English-speaking doctors.

Emergency: Ambulance: tel. 118. **Fire:** tel. 113. **Police:** tel. 110.

Police: Kapolresta (tel. 512 940) on Jl. Reksobayan. Locations throughout the city.

Post Offices: GPO, Jl. Senopati 1 (tel. 515 800), at corner with Jl. A. Yani. *Poste Restante* held for 2 weeks. Money changer and tourist info. Open Mon.-Fri. 8am-8pm, Sat. 8-11am. **Postal code:** 55121.

Telephones: Wartel can place international calls (no credit cards). Cash calls can be made at **Tourist Information Centre,** on Jl. Malioboro 16, the **airport,** and **Airlangga Guest House,** Jl. Prawirotaman 6-8 (tel. 378 044). For credit card and collect calls, go to **Natour Garuda Hotel,** Jl. Malioboro 89. **IDD** phone available. **Telephone code:** 0274.

ACCOMMODATIONS

Yogya is one of the best cities in Indonesia for quality budget accommodations. Places of note cluster around Jl. Sosrowijawan and Jl. Prawirotaman. Many accommodations in the Sosrow area are located in the small *gang* (alleys) which connect the parallel streets of Jl. Pasar Kembang and Jl. Sosrowijawan. Accommodations elsewhere are often both pricier and of lower quality.

Bladok Losmen, Jl. Sosrowijayan 76 (tel. 560 452), just past Gang II. Offers 12 bright, immaculate, tastefully decorated rooms (wicker, batik, and natural wood) which face either a courtyard garden or balcony. German/Indonesian owners direct a professional, friendly, English-speaking staff. Rooms have fan, private *mandi* with cold shower, towel/soap, and drinking water. Free breakfast and safety locker. Singles Rp20,000. Doubles Rp30,000. 24-hr. reception. Attached restaurant offers pricey but high-quality European fare (Rp5-8000).

Sartika Homestay, Jl. Prawirotaman 44 (tel. 372 669). Bus #2 or 15 from Umbulharjo Terminal. Popular with young European couples, Sartika offers spacious, airy, and clean rooms. All rooms with fan and private bath (cold shower). Free breakfast. Singles Rp15-20,000. Doubles Rp25,000. 24-hr. reception.

Vagabond Youth Hostel (HI), Jl. Prawirotaman MG III/589 or Jl. Sisingamangaraja 28B (tel. 371 207). Bus #2 or 15 from Umbulharjo Terminal. The place is well-located and basic but reasonably clean and very friendly. Communal shower stalls and flush toilets. Free breakfast. Safety box but no padlock. Café and useful library. Good place to meet fellow travelers. Dorms Rp5000. Singles with fan Rp6500 for HI members; extra Rp1000 for non-members. 24-hr. reception.

Ghandi Losmen and Art Gallery, Jl. Sosrowijayan Wetan Gang II/75 (tel. 512 841), at the end of an alley running between Jl. Pasar Kembang and Jl. Sosrow. Ghandi has decent rooms for the price. Communal bathroom. Furnished, nicely maintained common sitting area with English language reading material. Free tea and coffee. Singles with fan Rp4000 (no extra charge for double occupation).

FOOD

Inexpensive restaurants in the areas surrounding **Jl. Sosrowijayan** and **Jl. Prawirotaman** have uniformly broad menus of western, Chinese, and Indonesian entrees (Rp2-5000). Locals usually dine at any one of the *warung* in the upper levels of the **Pasar Beringharjo.** After 9pm, hungry folks can go to the sidewalk restaurants along **Jl. Malioboro,** food stalls at the northeast corner of the **Alun-alun Utara,** and the market at the western end of Jl. Prawirotaman. Most dishes here cost Rp1000. Brave visitors can savor Yogya's culinary specialty, *gudeg*, a sweet jackfruit and coconut-based dish with chicken, boiled egg, and chili peppers for condiments.

Ayam Goreng Nyonya Suharti, Jl. Laksda Adisucipto Km7 (tel. 515 522), just outside of Yogya. You can't miss the huge sign on the highway to the airport. Ayam has some of the best Indonesian fried chicken (half-chicken Rp8500) anywhere. Ibu Suharti's special blend of herbs and spices catapulted her from mobile street seller to restauranteur, with branches in Jakarta, Semarang, and Denpasar.

New Superman Restaurant, Jl. Sosrowijayan Wetan GT 1/71 (tel. 513 472). The sign on Pasar Kembang can direct Superman-seekers into the right *gang*. A favorite among backpackers worldwide. Clean and uniquely situated in an Indonesian-style *pendopo* (pavilion). Options are vast, ranging from hot dogs to *nasi goreng*. Entrees about Rp3000. Western desserts. Open daily 8am-11pm.

Lotus Garden, Jl. Prawirotaman MG 3/593A (tel. 377 649). Another tourist-eatery, but distinguished by its arbored courtyard and high quality traditional dance and music performances (Tues., Thurs., and Sat. 8pm, Rp3000 cover). Western, Chinese, and Indonesian entrees Rp2-6000. Open daily 9am-11pm.

Colombo, Jl. Letjen Suprapto (tel. 589 442), on the large boulevard parallel to Jl. Malioboro. A longtime local favorite for Chinese food. Simple rice and noodle dishes (Rp3000), seafood, and meat (Rp7000). Excellent noodle soups. Rare non-smoking section in spacious, clean environs. Open daily 8:30am-10pm.

Mama's, Jl. Pasar Kembang 71, 100m left side of the train station. *Warung* food (*gado-gado* is a specialty) in a safe, clean venue at near-*warung* prices (Rp1500-w2000). English menus. The superb quality of the food is accompanied by the surly service of Mama who has been running this road-side eatery for over 20 years. Open daily 8am-9pm, but hours vary according to Mama's disposition.

Jagung Bakar, Jl. Tentara Pelajar 4B. Take Jl. Pasar Kembang past Tugu Station for 0.75km; turn right onto Jl. Tentara Pelajar at the street light. A local hotspot, its specialty is roasted corn on the cob with salty, sweet, or spicy flavored butters (Rp1000). *Roti bakar* (toasted bread) and *pisang bakar* (cooked bananas) are also served with strawberry, chocolate, pineapple, or cheese toppings. The menu and clientele are Indonesian, but the traveler should not be intimidated. Take off your shoes before sitting on the mats. Open daily 7-11pm.

SIGHTS

Many of Yogya's historical and cultural sights are found within the fortress walls of the *kraton*. The **Sultan's Palace** sits at the center, and is open in selected areas for visitors. Multilingual guides lead visitors through the grounds, pavilions, and museums owned by Yogya's past 10 sultans. Although additions have been made over the years, the ornate, richly symbolic original palace buildings were built in 1755. Hamengkubuwono X, the current sultan, is active in the government and resides in the *kraton* with his family. Most Javanese accept that his role is largely ceremonial but still hold him in very high esteem. To reach the main entrance of the *kraton*, walk down the west side of the Alun-alun Lor to Jl. Rotowijayan, and continue south for another block and then turn left. (Open Sun.-Thurs. 8:30am-2pm, Fri.-Sat. 8:30am-1pm; admission Rp1500, with camera Rp2000.)

A short walk west down Jl. Rotowijayan, and then a left turn on Jl. Ngasem leads to **Pasar Ngasem**, the bird market. Exotic birds from all over the archipelago are bought and sold here, among the more numerous are doves, pigeons, chickens, and roosters. A flurry of market activity, Pasar Ngasem fascinates both the naturalist and the anthropologically minded visitor.

From the front of Pasar Ngasem, the crumbling ruins of **Taman Sari** can be seen behind it. Taman Sari means "fragrant garden," although the Dutch referred to this complex as the "water castle." Built shortly after the *kraton*'s construction, Taman Sari was used only for a brief period as a pleasure garden for the sultan and his family before it fell into disrepair. There is a network of underground tunnels to explore, ruins to climb which afford views of the city (best seen early in the morning, when Gunung Merapi is still visible), and a deteriorated underground mosque. Local legend holds that the tunnels reach all the way to Parangtritis Beach 27km south of the *kraton* (see **Parangtritis,** page 167). The tunnels have been blockaded so as to prevent people from getting lost or trapped. Parts of Taman Sari have been restored, and for Rp300 tourists can see the pools that were used by the sultan and his family.

Mesjid Agung, the grand mosque of the *kraton,* stands at the southwest corner of the Alun-alun Utara. A beautiful example of Javanese architecture, the mosque was built in a *pendopo* supported by intricately painted columns and cool tiled floors.

For over two centuries, the yearly **sekaten** festival has been celebrated in honor of the birth of the prophet Muhammed. *Sekaten* lasts roughly a month, during which time the Alun-alun Lor is filled with amusement-park-style fun and games, exhibitions, and hordes of hawkers selling sweet snacks. *Sekaten's* schedule changes each year, but it is held sometime between June and September. You'll know it is *sekaten* time when you see circus tents.

Every year during June and July, Yogya also hosts an **arts festival.** Location and exact dates change every year; contact the Tourist Information Office for details regarding *wayang*, dance, music performances, and open studios and galleries.

SHOPPING

The most rupiah-friendly way to spend an afternoon in Yogya is, ironically, to go shopping. Without buying anything, a traveler can have an educational, entertaining, and cultural experience. **Pasar Beringharjo,** on the south end of Jl. Malioboro, is the largest and most convenient market in Yogya. A kaleidoscope of activity, the multistory indoor *pasar* sells pork chips, parkas, and everything in-between. It's best to go early in the morning. (Open early morning until 4pm.)

On the west side of Jl. Malioboro lies an informal market lined with stalls that sell Yogya's handicraft claims to fame: **batik, leather,** made into *wayang kulit* puppets, bags, lampshades, and souvenirs; and **silver.** Those looking for higher quality craftwork should visit specialized workshops and their sales rooms, many of which are found within the walls of the *kraton.* Ask at the tourist office for recommended shops. Javanese handicrafts can also be purchased through **Yakkum Craft,** Jl. Kaliurang, Km13.5, Desa Besi (tel. 953 86), where bags, carvings, and decorations are made by physically disabled adults. (Open Mon.-Fri. 8am-4pm, Sat. 8am-12:30pm.) **Kota Gede,** to the southeast of Yogya, is renowned for its silver. Jl. Kemasan is lined with shops, many of which take orders for brass, copper, and silver work.

ENTERTAINMENT AND NIGHTLIFE

Wayang kulit, shadow puppet theater, is an original Javanese art form. Ornate, two-dimensional puppets are played by a *dalang* (puppeteer) in front of a lit screen. The puppet's shadows and the *dalang's* voice enact Javanese myths and fables. The tourist office has a list of performances throughout the city. Also check the center for a list of *Ramayana* **ballets** at hotels and theaters in Yogya, and also at Prambanan during the full moons of summer. **Cultural performances,** including *gamelan* and *wayang golek,* are held daily in the *kraton's* Golden Pavilion. Check the tourist office for the most up-to-date schedules. Admission to the performances is free save for the *kraton* entrance fee.

If you find yourself around Jl. Malioboro after dark, you may run into a troupe of fire-eaters at the south end of Jl. Malioboro/A. Yani. Otherwise, stroll or *becak* it 0.75km to **Alun-alun Kidul,** south of the *kraton.* A popular hangout for young Indonesians, the attraction here is as fun as it is cheap: bring a bandana (or rent a blindfold for Rp250), wear it, and try to walk 100m in a straight line from the road to the passage between two enormous trees in the center of the yard. Success, which is reputed to bring good luck, is surprisingly difficult, particularly if you begin walking off the well-trodden path and on to the grass.

Late-night **dancing queens** can head over to **Mix Club** at the Yogya Century Hotel, Jl. Laksa Adisucipto 38 (tel. 564 272). A rather timid, local crowd haunts this night spot, writhing to the beat of techno-pop and bathed in the music-syncopated colored lights of the dance floor. The hefty Rp20,000 cover charge includes a free drink. (Open Sun.-Fri. 10pm-2am, Sat. 10pm-3am.)

■ Near Yogyakarta

Agencies which offer package tours to the sights around Yogya are ubiquitous. Sightseers may want to avoid tours that include shopping, which usually means little time spent at the actual sights and plenty of hours at batik factories and silver workshops instead (where prices are jacked up). Many travelers choose to go the cheaper route by eschewing agencies altogether and taking public transportation.

BOROBUDUR

Touted as one of the wonders of the world, **Borobudur** is the largest Buddhist monument in the world. Built between 778-856AD during the Sailendra dynasty, the temple sits on a hill overlooking the surrounding fields. Borobudur consists of seven levels, topped by a 40-m stupa. Made of andesite stone, the monument reflects a fierce dedication to the Mahayana Buddhist philosophy and remains a testament to the back-breaking labor of five generations. Lying 40km northwest of Yogya, Borobudur can be reached by local buses from Umbulharjo (Jl. Veteran) and Pingit (Jl. Magelang), which take tourists to Muntilan; here, buses to Borobudur can be caught. The tourist offices clustered around Jl. Sosrowijayan and Jl. Prawirotaman offer package tours, some of which take tourists early enough to see the sunrise.

Before scaling the height of the monument, visitors might want to go to the Audio Visual Centre to see an informative 35-minute video (in English and other languages, Rp4000). Many tourists, foreign and local alike, try to improve their luck by reaching into the stupas to touch the stone Buddhas' hands and navels (the right hand please, as the left is considered unclean). Make the pilgrimage early and during the week if possible; Borobudur attracts thousands of visitors every year and its considerable grandeur can be hard to appreciate when spending your time dodging out of high schoolers' group photos. For a breathtaking view of the surrounding area, go to the hills behind the monument. (Open daily 6am-5pm; Rp5000 for non-Indonesians, Rp2500 for non-Indonesian students with ID.)

Nearby stand two other historically significant monuments, **Mendut** and **Pawon.** Pilgrims from as far away as China have walked across Java to visit and attain enlightenment from Borobudur via Mendut and Pawon. Many visitors find themselves overwhelmed by the entreaties of hawkers, rather than the details on the bas-reliefs. Admission includes entrance to the **Archaeological Museum,** which exhibits test tubes of the fungi that suck on Borobudur's volcanic rocks as well as photos of the monument's impressive reconstructions.

PRAMBANAN

Seventeen km to the northeast of Yogya are the **Prambanan temples.** From Yogyakarta, take a bus from Umbulharjo Terminal or an intercity bus heading toward Solo (approximately 30min.). When passengers get off the bus, they should be able to see the peaks of Gunung Merapi and the main Prambanan temple. Maps are available at the **tourist service** (open Mon.-Sat. 7am-5pm), across the street from the intercity bus drop off to the far east (left if your back is to the temple) side of the *pasar.* Those who are planning to see more than just the main Prambanan temple can do so by bike (Rp2000 per day). Built in the 9th century during the Hindu Sanjaya dynasty, the Prambanan complex consists of a series of temples dedicated to Shiva, Vishnu, and Brahma. The heaping rubble in the area are the remains of the temples destroyed by Gunung Merapi's eruption in 1006. (Admission to the complex Rp5000, for students with ID Rp2500; includes a camera pass, English-speaking guide, free access to toilet, museum, and intercom.) The Prambanan park holds *Ramayana* ballets in an outdoor theater (May-Oct., 7-9pm; tickets Rp15-35,000) several days a week. The Prambanan tourist office has a schedule.

Those who aren't worn out from temples yet need not fear, since plenty more are within easy walking distance: **Candi Lumbung, Bubrah, Sewu,** and **Sojiwan.** Monuments to the north **(Candi Plaosan, Banyunibo, Sari, Kalasan,** and **Sambisari)** are best visited by bike or *becak* from Prambanan. Standing 2km south of Prambanan, **Kraton Ratu Boko** offers a splendid panoramic view of the countryside. It you've rented a bike, ride south along the road to the west of the market (the side closest to Yogya). Signs to Kraton Boko lead the way to the main gate (admission Rp250), where maps are available. The mysterious palace consists of a series of stone foundations built on plateaus overlooking the trees and valleys below. There's a gorgeous view of the plain from the northern side of the *kraton*.

For **accommodations** near Prambanan, **Ny. Murti Guest House** (tel. 961 03), is opposite the entrance to the Prambanan temple. Singles with bath cost Rp15,000, doubles with bath Rp17,500.

GUNUNG MERAPI AND KALIURANG

Gunung Merapi erupted in November 1994, killing thousands. It's now closed, although guides still offer to take visitors up with enthusiastic assurances that it's safe. While hiking up Merapi to within 2km of the top and seeing live lava can be exciting, this form of recreation is risky. Travelers do it, and guides are available, but be forewarned: **hiking an active volcano is dangerous!**

The occasionally active **Gunung Merapi** rises 2920m above sea level and is 30km north of Yogya. The best view of Merapi is from the observatory of **Plawanga,** an hour's hike from Kaliurang. From Selo, north of Merapi, the brave can hike up the volcano (with or without a guide) and reach the top in four hours. From Yogya, take a bus to Kartosuro, then to Boyolali, then to Selo. Or, from Kaliurang, walk to Selo in one hour. Start at 1am to reach the summit in time for sunrise. Dress warmly, but be prepared to shed protective clothing after daybreak. A spectacular sunrise makes up for the sleep deprivation.

For a tamer (and lava-less) adventure, stick around **Kaliurang,** 28km north of Yogya on the slopes of Merapi. From Yogya, take the bus from Umbulharjo or the Terban Terminal on Jl. Simanjuntak. Kaliurang is cool and tourist-friendly, with several cheap hotels, a campground, and a youth hostel. The hostel, **Vogels Homestay,** Jl. Astamulya 76, is off the main road. It's in a rather run-down area, but is cheap (small doubles Rp5000 for HI members or students). Even cheaper dorm-style accommodations are also available. The Kaliurang **market** is dominated by bananas, but look out for Kaliurang's specialty, sweet, brown-red *tempe* or *tahu bacem* and the mild *jadah,* made from glutinous rice.

To explore the town's hiking paths, head to **Telaga Putri,** a walkable but significant distance away from the youth hostel. Hike on bricked paths under gigantic trees and cool off by clambering up to the observatory for a view of the valley. The gates shut at 4pm; if you get locked in, its an easy climb across the fence.

IMOGIRI

The **Imogiri Royal Cemetery,** 17km south of Yogya, houses the deceased members of the Royal Houses of Yogya and Surakarta (Solo), including Yogya's last sultan, Hamengkubuwono I. Imogiri is less touristed than other famous sites and affords a rare opportunity to witness the solemnity of ancestor worship and the regard which most Yogyakartans retain for members of royalty. Buses to Imogiri leave from Umbulharjo bus terminal. Built in 1645 by Sultan Agung, the cemetery is comprised of three distinct courtyards. To the left, rests the royalty of Solo, to the right, the sultans of Yogya, and at the center, the ancient Mataram kings (the collapse of the Mataram in 1755 created the independent states of Yogyakarta and Solo). All visitors are expected to wear formal Javanese clothing in the tombs: after climbing the 345 steps which lead up the hill top cemetery, discard your sweaty garments and rent more

It's Not Easy Being Green

At Parangkusumo, about 1km west of Parangtritis, there is a shrine which commemorates the mythical romance and consummation between Sultan Senopati of the Mataram kingdom, and Nyai Loro Kidul, Queen of the South Seas. Forever heartbroken over the sultan's decision to return to Mataram, Nyai Loro Kidul has been known to kidnap and drown anyone who wears her favorite color, green, along her beaches. Rumor has it that the tunnels beneath Taman Sari in Yogyakarta once reached all the way to Parangtritis Beach, so the Yogya Sultanate could perpetuate the mythical belief that Nyai Loro Kidul was associated with Yogya's royal house after the Mataram Kingdom was divided into the Yogyakarta and Surakarta sultanates. Locals at Parangtritis offer prayers and offerings to the angry goddess each week, and to this day the old clothes, hair and fingernail clippings, and assorted other offerings from the Sultan himself are sent out on a raft to appease her. Visitors are forewarned to leave something for her at the shrine and leave green clothes at home.

appropriate attire (Rp1000). Men should wear a sarong, long-sleeved shirt, and hat. Women are less modestly dressed in a sarong and batik halter top. The tombs are best visited with a guide, but maps are available at the dressing station for those on their own. In each room, enter quietly, make a donation (Rp100 will do), and kneel by the cool marble. After paying your respects to the more recent royalty, be sure to visit the sacred burial chambers of Sultan Agung and Hamengkubuwono I near the top of the hill. A climb up to the hill behind the tombs can be cool and refreshing after the steamy burial chambers. (Open Mon. 10am-1pm, Fri. 1:30-4pm.)

PARANGTRITIS

Parangtritis Beach, 27km south of Yogya, can be reached by public bus from Umbulharjo Terminal or by minibus and horse-drawn carriage from Jl. Parangtritis at the southeast corner of the *kraton*. As a daytrip, visitors enjoy the smell of salty waters, drink *es kelapa muda* (young coconut milk) from its freshly axed shell, and klip-klop up and down the black sand in horse-drawn carriages. Dramatic cliffs to the east shelter secluded coves and caves. The desert-like landscape of this beach, however, is hardly ideal for swimming or surfing, since the undertow of the Indian Ocean is strong and deadly. Local lore has it that yearly victims are abducted by Nyai Loro Kidul, goddess and Queen of the South Seas—made jealous by those foolhardy enough to wear her favorite color green to the beach. Not a Bali-esque resort beach, are plenty of *losmen* in the village); the pale seascape and insistent wind do well for contemplative souls in need of some peace.

■ Surakarta (Solo)

Ask the Solonese what's special about their city and they'll probably provide a knee-jerk response along the lines of "Solo is the cultural heart of Java." Solonese seem to be fed this kind of city pride even before they're weaned onto *nasi liwet*. And with good reason, too: Solo boasts two *kraton*, a host of classical art to support them, the second oldest museum in Indonesia, and a successful batik industry. The city's history began when Sultan Pakubuwono moved his Mataram Kingdom to the city in 1745. Solo is quiet, walkable, and sustains comparatively mild interest in multi-story mall complexes and other facets of the McDonaldization occurring elsewhere in Java. Although these neon-adorned shopping plazas are not scarce, community life still centers around the public markets and the areas surrounding traditional palace walls. A clean, friendly city with artsy energy, few tourists, and plenty of cheap accommodations, Solo is worth a couple of days' attention from travelers.

ORIENTATION

Jalan Slamet Riyadi is the city's main boulevard, cutting east-west through town, and is conveniently traveled by Solo's double-decker buses. The tourist office is on the west side of Jl. Slamet Riyadi, with the post office and telephone office on **Jalan Sudirman,** off the street's east side. Many of Solo's restaurants and *warung* cluster on streets off the center of Jl. Slamet Riyadi, with the **Puro Mangkunegaran Kraton** at their north edge. Homestays can be found off both sides of Jl. Slamet Riyadi: to the north, on **Jalan A. Dahlan,** and to the south, far down **Jalan Gatot Subroto.** The **Kraton Surakarta** and the **batik market** is southwest and the **Tirtonadi/Gilingan Terminal** and **Balapan Train Station** are north of the city center.

PRACTICAL INFORMATION

Tourist Offices: Dinas Pariwisata, Jl. Slamet Riyadi 275 (tel. 711 435), on the far west side of Solo's main boulevard. Free city map, tourist brochures, and a calendar of events. Open Mon.-Fri. 8am-5pm, Sat. 8am-1:30pm.

Tours and Travel: High-priced tours can be purchased along Jl. Slamet Riyadi at any of tour agency. Most *losmen* or homestays can find cheaper city and bike tours. Try Warung Baru Restaurant or Solo Homestay, both on Jl. A. Dahlan.

Currency Exchange: Bank Central Asia (BCA), Jl. Slamet Riyadi 3 (tel. 422 25). Accepts traveler's checks and transfers money from MC, Visa, and AmEx without charge. Open Mon.-Fri. 8:30am-2pm, Sat. 8:30-11am. **INTA Tours and Travel,** Jl. Slamet Riyadi 96 (tel. 540 10). Provides the same services as BCA but credit card cash transfers incur a 3% fee. Open Mon.-Sat. 8am-4pm.

Air Travel: Adi Sumarmo Airport (tel. 324 88), 10km northwest of the city. Carriers: Garuda, Sempati, Bouraq, Merpati, Mandala. Service to **Jakarta, Denpasar,** and **Singapore.** From the airport, the cheapest ride to town is by bus which picks up on the main road outside the airport. Take a blue minibus to Kartosuro Terminal (Rp300) and then a double-decker down to Jl. Slamet Riyadi.

Trains: Balapan Railway Station (tel. 714 039), on Jl. Monginsidi. To: **Jakarta,** (7 per day, economy Rp8000); **Surabaya** (9 per day, 4½hr., economy Rp7500); **Semarang** (2 per day, 3½hr., economy Rp1300); and **Yogyakarta** (7 per day, 1hr., economy, Rp2000). All trains through Solo stop in Yogya.

Buses: Tirtonadi (tel. 717 297), on the north side of town on Jl. A. Yani. The main inter-city bus terminal. Seats on the special overnight buses (A/C, toilets, and videos) have to be booked in advance. **Raya,** Jl. Sutan Syahir 13 (tel. 635 838). Near Tirtonadi is the **Gilingan Terminal** where inter-city minibuses or "travels" depart to Yogyakarta, Semarang, Malang, and Surabaya.

Local Transportation: Becak are cheap, plentiful, and relaxing. **Taxis** are less easily hailed but can be found at all major hotels. Double-decker buses travel along Jl. Slamet and Jl. Veteran only (every 10min., 5am-8pm, Rp250). Orange minibuses travel along more diverse routes, ask if they're going your way.

Markets: Pasar Triwinder, the antique market, lies near the Mataram Palace. Open daily 8am-4pm. **Pasar Klewer** is the batik market, near the Kraton Solo. Inside market open daily 8am-4pm; the outside fruit market and *warung* open past dusk. **Pasar Gede,** diagonally across from the GPO, sells fruits, vegetables, and spices. Open daily 8am-4pm. **Pasar Bladek** is an outdoor aviary on the outskirts of town near Gilingan Terminal. Open daily 8am-4pm.

Pharmacies: Address over-the-counter needs at any streetside *apotik* (pharmacy). The supermarket on the top floor of the Matahari Department Store on Jl. Gatot Subroto sells western-brand medicines. 24-hr. pharmacy at **Rumah Sakit Kasih Ibu Hospital,** Jl. Slamet Riyadi 404 (tel. 714 422).

Medical Services: Expats swear by the **Klinik Prodia Laboratorium,** Jl. Ronggowarsito 143 (tel. 414 34), a 24-hr. modern hospital. 24-hr. hotline tel. 445 44. MC, Visa, AmEx. Also the **Ruman Sakit Kasih Ibu Hospital** (listed above).

Police: Jl. Slamet Riyadi 376 (tel. 712 332), and other posts all over town.

Post Offices: GPO, Jl. Sudirman 8 (tel. 472 39), off the east end of Jl. Slamet Riyadi. *Poste Restante* held for 1 month. Open Mon.-Fri. 8am-7pm, Sat. 9am-1pm. **Postal code:** 57100.

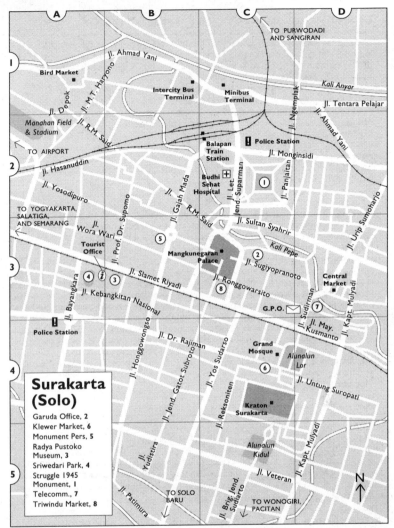

Surakarta (Solo)

Garuda Office, 2
Klewer Market, 6
Monument Pers, 5
Radya Pustoko
Museum, 3
Sriwedari Park, 4
Struggle 1945
Monument, 1
Telecomm., 7
Triwindu Market, 8

Telephones: Jl. Mayor Kusmanto 1 (tel. 486 00), across the street from the GPO. 24-hr international service. There are *wartel* all over town. Ask for the nearest one at your hotel. The Kraton Solo has **HCD. Telephone code:** 0271.

ACCOMMODATIONS

Accommodations in Solo are of comparable or better quality to those found in Yogya, but go for less. Quality *losmen* cluster around Jl. A. Dahlan and the *gang* which connect Jl. Gatot Subroto and Jl. Yos Sudarso. Most places offer bike rentals and highly rated bike tours.

Warung Baru Homestay, Jl. A. Dahlan 23 (tel. 563 69). One of the best deals in town, it's clean and extremely secure. Furnished rooms include fan and shared *mandi* and shower. Singles Rp7500. Doubles Rp12,500. Free breakfast. Go first to the restaurant on Jl. A. Dahlan. Employees there will cheerfully take you on the 3-min. walk to the homestay. Batik course offered.

Cendana Homestay, Gang Empu Panuluh III 4 (tel. 461 69), on a *gang* off Jl. Gatot Subroto, just before the Matahari Dept. Store. Turn in at the ADA textile sign. Beautifully maintained place with 8 large, clean rooms. Singles with shared *mandi* Rp8500. Doubles Rp11,500. Breakfast included.

Joyokusuman (Hendra Guest House and Painting Studio), Gajahan 7 Rt. 2/3 (tel. 548 42). One of Solo's oldest and most beautiful homestays, it is also the most secluded and hard to find. Look for a *becak* driver who knows the way near the Alun-alun Kidul. Rose-tree archways, courtyards, gardens, porches, and meditation platforms. Singles with private *mandi* and fan Rp20,000. Doubles Rp25,000.

Remaja Homestay, Jl. Cockro 1 Kauman (tel. 477 58), off Jl. Yos Sudarso. Remaja's *gang* is opposite the Batik Keris store. An undiscovered bargain offered by an exuberantly friendly family who stuffs you with full, big breakfasts. Basic singles with fan Rp5000. Doubles Rp8000. Doors are closed 2-7am.

Happy Homestay, Jl. Honggowongso Gg. Karagan #12 (tel. 712 449). Turn onto Honggowongso from Jl. Slamet Riyadi. Slightly removed from Solo's central activity, Happy is a true homestay as common areas are shared with the owner's family. Colorful, well-kept, and one of the most money-friendly places in town. Singles with fan Rp6000. Doubles Rp8000. Breakfast, tea, and coffee included. Discounts for long-term guests.

Relax Homestay, Empu Sedah 28, Kemlayan (tel. 464 17). From Jl. Slamet Riyadi, go south onto Jl. Gatot Subroto. Turn left into the *gang* opposite the Singer sewing machine shop. Modest rooms face a garden and fish pond. English-speaking Manggus, the friendly owner, works at the tourist office and is an invaluable source of info about Solo, and Indonesia in general. Singles with fan and large bed Rp8500. Doubles Rp11,000. Breakfast Rp1000. Camping allowed for Rp2000.

"Westerners"/Pak Mawardi Homestay, Kemlayan Kidul #2 (tel. 331 06), just opposite the Paradise. One of the oldest and most heavily-trafficked homestays, the Westerners is "for Westerners/foreigners only." Frequently full, it ends up supplying business for neighboring homestays. Basic rooms in *kampung* family-style environment. Dorms Rp6000. Singles Rp7000. Doubles Rp7000. Breakfast Rp2000. Free tea and cold water.

FOOD

Nasi liwet is the representative dish in Solo. *Warung* are particularly dense at night along Jl. Gatot Subroto and Jl. Teuku Umar. **Ibu Mari's** on Gatot Subroto across from Linga Furniture and **Bu Wongso Lemu's** place in the middle of Jl. Diponegoro are local favorites. Tourist restaurants concentrate along Jl. A. Dahlan. Sugar-lovers who have had one too many banana pancakes can find sweet alternatives at the **American Bakery** at Jl. Slamet Riyadi 90 (tel. 326 07; open 8:30am-8:45pm) or the **Holland Modern Bakery,** Jl. Slamet Riyadi 135 (tel. 324 52).

Warung Baru, Jl. A. Dahlan 28 (tel. 563 69), off Jl. Slamet Riyadi. Famous and rightfully so. Solo's beacon for foreign travelers and expats. Warung Baru is always abuzz with activity. Customers enjoy good cheap food, including homemade bread and a large selection of pizzas. Staff counsel about tours and travel. Entrees Rp1-4000. Open daily 7am-11pm.

Malioboro Ayam Goreng, Jl. Diponegoro 14. Follow Jl. Gatot Subroto toward Jl. Slamet Riyadi and it becomes Jl. Diponegoro. Fried chicken's the name and its the only game available at this very family-oriented restaurant. The chicken is hot, crispy, and spicy (Rp1700).

Bakmi Surabaya, Jl. Gatot Subroto 265 (tel. 410 14). Far down south on Jl. Gatot Subroto. Fantastic rice and noodles in clean, fanned environment. Strangely, also a showroom for Harley-Davidson paraphernalia. Open daily 9am-10pm.

Gamelan Restaurant, Jl. A. Dahlan 28 (tel. 416 40). A notable breed of the general tourist restaurant species. Across the street from the Warung Baru and largely unpopulated during the day, Gamelan comes alive at night with freshly prepared western and Indonesian dishes and lots of beer and romantic lighting. Entrees Rp1-2500. Open daily 8am-11pm.

SIGHTS

The presence of Solo's two *kraton* focuses and perpetuates Solo's classical arts and embodies important historical and architectural features of Solonese culture. All this aside, they are visually unimpressive, particularly compared to Yogya's *kraton*. The smaller **Mangkunegaran Palace** is home to the current prince and his family. Built during the latter years of the 18th century, the *kraton* is intimate and well-maintained. Visitors can see the ornate *pendopo,* which houses a first-rate *gamelan* orchestra (rehearsals Wed. 10am-noon), peek into the private gardens of the prince, and wonder at the regal but largely undecipherable holdings of the palace museum. English-speaking guides are available. (Open Mon.-Sat. 9am-2pm, Sun. 9am-10pm; admission Rp1500.) The **Kraton Surakarta,** lying in the southeast section of town, was built in 1745 by Pakubuwono II. It's currently home to the present sultan, 73-year-old Pakubuwono XII, and his six wives and 38 children. Partially restored after a devastating fire in 1985, the *kraton* limits visitors to the main receiving hall and the palace museum, which more closely resembles a royal yard sale of sorts. The tower rising above the palace's main gates in rumored to be the secret meeting place of Solo's kings and Nyai Loro Kidul, Queen of the South Seas (see **It's Not Easy Being Green** on page 167). English-speaking guides are available. (Open Mon.-Thurs. and Sat.-Sun. 8:30am-2pm; admission Rp1000.) On Sundays, free dance performances go from 9-11am and 3-4pm.

The **Museum Radyapustaka,** beside the tourist office on Jl. Slamet Riyadi, is the second oldest museum in Indonesia and exhibits Mataram kingdom artifacts, including a collection of *wayang* puppets, *keris* daggers, statues, and ancient Javanese philosophical texts. (Open Tues.-Thurs. 8am-noon, Fri.-Sun. 8-11am.)

ENTERTAINMENT AND NIGHTLIFE

Quality performances of traditional *wayang orang* dance can be viewed from 8 to 11pm every night except Sunday at the **Sriwedari Park,** beside the tourist office on Jl. Slamet Riyadi. **Gamelan Performances** are held nightly in the lobby of the Kusuma Sahid Hotel, 5 to 8pm. *Keroncong* music is performed Thursdays 8 to 9pm. For a small city, nightlife is surprisingly plentiful, with five major discos and numerous billiard halls. **Nirwana,** next to Pasar Gede, has the best music (cover charge about Rp6000 on weekends). Shooters can play dirt cheap pool at **Contesa Billiards** near the Matahari Department Store on Jl. Gatot Subroto (Rp400 per game).

■ Near Surakarta

Targeting sights around Solo provides inspiration to get off the *losmen's* cushy lawn furniture. Getting to these sights is half the fun and usually more than half the time. Travelers can test their patience at Solo's two most highly hyped excursions: Sangiran Museum and Sukuh temple. Fifteen km north of Solo, **Sangiran** is where the fossil skull of *Pithecanthropus erectus* (a.k.a. "Java Man") was discovered by a Dutch paleontologist in 1936. The discovery of Java Man, now considered a subspecies of *Homo erectus,* revamped theories about early humans' migration patterns. Excavations are still proceeding at Sangiran, and a small museum there showcases ancient pig and hippopotamus teeth, a glassed-in diorama of home on the prehistoric range, and some staggering mammoth bones. To get to Sangiran, take a minibus from Gilingan Terminal toward Purwodadi or Kalijambe, and ask to get off near Sangiran, where *ojek* can haul visitors up the hill (Rp1000) to the museum. (Open Mon.-Sat. 8am-5pm; admission Rp1000.) To return to Solo from the *ojek* stand, hop on a large bus with BERSERI printed on its front (Rp400 to Jl. Slamet Riyadi).

If you trust the official tourist office's instincts, **Sukuh Temple** (admission Rp300) is "the most erotic temple in the world." Standing 34km northeast of Solo, Sukuh is commonly believed to have been carved with the intent of providing sex education to adolescents in the 15th century. With the exception of one or two panels, the carvings around the temple are hardly X-rated, but they are well-preserved and detailed. In truth, the temple is less about romance and more about mystery—the exact function and builders of the Hindu monument remain unknown, and its Maya-esque structure, unusual for Javanese architecture, has confused archaeologists for decades. Resting on the slopes of Gunung Lawu, Sukuh is not easy to reach, but worth it for the views from the temple's roof. To get there, catch a double-decker bus from Jl. Slamet Riyadi (Rp200) and ride until Palur. From Palur, ride a big bus heading for Karang Pandan (30min., Rp500), then take a minibus to Sukuh (20min., Rp300). Unless visitors travel on a market day, the minibus will dump them off at the bottom of a hill; they can either pay Rp1500 for an eagerly waiting *ojek* ride to the temple, or walk up the steep hill (about 30min.).

A 2½-hour hike can be taken from Sukuh along a clearly marked path that ends at **Tawangmangu,** a rather skimpy 100-m waterfall. Tawangmangu can also be reached directly by bus from Solo. The last bus from the waterfall to Karang Pandan leaves at 4:30pm. **Candi Ceto** is 7km north of Sukuh, from where *ojek* can whisk sight-seers (for Rp9000) up the steep path (unless they're up for a 3-4hr. hike). Built in 1470, Ceto, also Maya-like, is higher than Sukuh and offers better views, but the stone carvings are less impressive and not nearly as "erotic."

■ Semarang

Much has changed since Semarang was considered "the best town in Java" by 19th-century Dutch colonialists. Notable cultural sites are few and appropriate accommodations for budget travelers even fewer. The fact that this industrial port city still rates "better than Jakarta" by visiting businessmen is not a ringing endorsement—particularly when uttered by those who can hide from Semarang's smog and undecipherable traffic patterns in its many glitzy hotels. Excepting travelers who have a particular interest in the colonial Dutch architecture that dominates several downtown streets, or those fascinated by busy Javanese cities, visitors on a budget use Semarang only as a departure point to nearby picturesque sites.

ORIENTATION

The capital city of Central Java province, Semarang is on the north coast, accessible by air, bus, and train from most points in Java. The airport, harbor, train tracks, and **Tawang Railway Station** border the northern edge of the city. **Jalan Haryono,** running north-south on the east side of the city, and **Jalan Pandanaran/A. Yani,** running northeast-southwest through the city center, insulate the commercial areas from the more residential southside. At the heart of activity are three rotaries: at **Simpang Lima** (the main square), **Tugu Muda** (the monument commemorating Indonesian youths' battle against the Japanese), and the north end of **Jalan Pemuda,** near the giant Metro Grand Park Hotel called the **Johar Complex.** The streets linking these points form a triangle and offer exhaustive shopping and eating opportunities. Other areas that may interest tourists—particularly architecture buffs—are **Chinatown,** to the south of **Jalan H. Agus Salim,** and the ritzy colonial-style hills of **Kintelan** district, southwest of downtown.

PRACTICAL INFORMATION

Tourist Offices: Semarang Regency Tourist Office (tel. 921 424), on the 1st floor of the Matahari Dept. Store at Simpang Lima Square. Open Mon.-Fri. 8am-3pm. **Central Java Provincial Tourist Office,** Jl. Madukoro Blok BB/PRPP Complex (tel. 607 184). More of a booth than an office. From Tugu Muda, take a bus away from town (west) on Jl. Sugiopranoto and ask to get off at PRPP or Jl. Amjasmoro. From the bus stop, cross the street and find a *becak* to take you to the "Kantor Pariwisata" (about Rp1000). Inconveniently located but an excellent source of info and advice on all of Central Java. Open Mon.-Fri. 8am-3pm.

Currency Exchange: Banks are generally open Mon.-Fri. 8am-3pm, Sat. 8-11am. **BDNI,** Jl. Pemuda 175A (tel. 553 920), at Tugu Muda, exchanges traveler's checks and advances cash from AmEx.

Air Travel: A. Yani Airport (tel. 544 735), on Jl. Siliwangi 5km west of town (Rp5000 by taxi). To: **Jakarta** (7 per day), **Surabaya, Denpasar,** and **Singapore.**

Trains: Tawang Railway Station, off Jl. Merak, has trains to: **Jakarta** (8 per day); **Surakarta/Yogyakarta** (4 per day); and **Surabaya** (2 per day). Schedules available at the station and the tourist office on Jl. Madukoro Blok.

Buses: Terboyo (tel. 581 921), on Jl. Kaligawe, has buses running to Yogyakarta, Surakarta, Surabaya, Jakarta, Denpasar, and Sumatra. **Bus Patasnusantara,** Jl. Dr. Cipto 108C (tel. 545 417). Buses have A/C, TV, and toilet between Semarang, Wonosobo, and Solo. Inquire at terminal for schedule and fares.

Taxis: Puri Kencana Taxi, Jl. Imam Bonjol 144 (tel. 511 761). **Indra Kelanan Taxi,** Jl. Pemuda 83 (tel. 542 570).

Local Transportation: Semarang's small orange buses, alternately called **colts,** travels, or minibuses, and its large **bis kota** (city buses) have overlapping, inefficient routes. Minibuses generally cost Rp200—pay this until you are asked for more, or ask a local (other than the driver) what the *harga biasa* (usual price) is. Stand expectantly by the road and shout out the name of your destination when bus workers lean out of the doors. Minibuses become scarce after 9pm. Large, intercity buses cost Rp250 (for all distances) and stop running after 9 or 10pm. **Becak, ojek,** and **andong** can be hailed, but cannot run on busy streets.

Rentals: Metro Hotel, Jl. Salim 2 (tel. 547 371), rents **cars** with drivers. Rp8000 per hr., minimum 2hr.

Pharmacies: Kimia Farma, Jl. Pemuda 135 (tel. 543 646). Open 24hr.

Medical Services: Tlogorejo Hospital (tel. 413 305), on a small road north of Jl. Panjaitan that runs parallel to the river.

Police: Central station, Jl. Dr. Sutomo 19 (tel. 311 390).

Emergency: Fire: tel. 113. **Police:** tel. 110. **Ambulance:** tel. 118. **Red Cross:** tel. 311 891.

Post Offices: Jl. Pemuda 4 (tel. 161 for postal info). No *Poste Restante.* Open Mon.-Sat. 6:30am-8pm, Sun. 8am-4pm.

Telephones: International **wartel** are all over town, but credit card calls cannot be made on them. **Wartel II,** Jl. Alun-alun Timur 2, behind the GPO. Fax service. Open daily 7am-8:30pm. **Telephone code:** 024.

ACCOMMODATIONS

Semarang is a businessman's city, and the high prices of hotels will keep it that way. Much of the budget accommodations in Semarang are not nice places to visit, much less spend the night—managers can be hostile and beds dirty.

Hotel Rahagu, Jl. Imam Bonjol 35 (tel. 542 532), halfway between the post office and the railway station. Most *becak* drivers know Rahagu by name. Rooms are not spotless and noise from the bustling hallways carries easily, but compared to budget hotels near the city center, Rahagu is a furnished, spacious oasis. Rooms have private *mandi* and fan. Tea included too. Doubles Rp17,500.

Hotel Candi Indah, Jl. Dr. Wahidin 112 (tel. 312 912), on the south side of town, just past the intersection of Jl. Sultan Agung and Jl. Wahidin near the Candi Gold Course. Remote location, but Candi Indah has clean rooms with modern furnishings and radios. For Rp12,000 per person, you can sleep the night away in "driver rooms," dorm-style accommodations in tight, bunk-bedded closets. Singles Rp30,000, with A/C Rp50,000. Doubles with A/C Rp50,000. MC and AmEx.

Hotel Candi Baru, Jl. Rinjani 21 (tel. 315 272). Take an intercity bus heading to the Kintelan area and get off at the Grasia Hotel on Jl. Parman. With your back to Grasia, cross the main road and walk straight for 200m. Candi Baru is on a hill overlooking the harbor. The cheapest rooms are adequate and cost Rp30,000. Breakfast and snack included. Attached restaurant. MC, Visa, and AmEx.

FOOD

Semarang is teeming with **restaurants, outdoor stalls,** and **mobile carts,** particularly along the south end of Jl. Gajah Mada and the north end of Jl. Pahlawan by the Citraland Mall and Simpang Lima. Meat is usually present in food; vegetarians may find themselves eating *gado-gado* and *nasi goreng* time and again.

Nusantara, Jl. Pandanaran No. 6 Ruko 11 & 12 (tel. 411 801), just past the Tugu Muda intersection on the left. Meaty options galore, displayed in bowls in the window. Mostly precooked but tasty dishes over hot rice. Fried chicken (Rp1300) and fried shrimp (Rp6000). Open 24hr.

Toko Oen, Jl. Pemuda 52 (tel. 541 683). Expat stronghold. Large, colonial-era restaurant with stained-glass windows opened to the busy street. Dutch food is the specialty but also offers Indonesian and Chinese fare, and a good selection of ice cream. Most entrees Rp3-7000.

Pringgading, Jl. Pringgading 54 (tel. 516 991). An A/C oasis in the midst of tropical heat. Extensive menu focusing on Chinese-style seafood, served with fancy folded napkins by hovering, pink-uniformed waitresses. Good vegetarian options. Specialties include *babi goreng kering* (fried pork, Rp9000), *mie sup* (noodle soup, Rp7000), and *ayam mente* (chicken with cashew nuts, Rp10,000). Open daily 9am-2:30pm and 5-9:30pm.

■ Near Semarang

GEDONG SONGO

The **Gedong Songo Temples** are at least a day's trip from Semarang, but are well worth the long and sometimes crowded voyage. Buses from Semarang's Terboyo Terminal for Bandungan leave regularly (Rp1000, plus extra if your bag is large). With stops, the ride takes roughly 90 minutes winding along terraced valleys, rivers, and ravines. Passengers must ask to get off at Bandungan's Pasar Joho. Walk up the hill with the *pasar* to the left. Several *losmen* summon travelers, including **Losmen Muria,** on Jl. Gintungan, which has very modest rooms and shared *mandi* for Rp9000. **Wisma Gaya** is up the hill from Muria and has beautiful views and pricey rooms at Rp40,000 (MC accepted). The best way to get from Bandungan to Gedong Songo is by *ojek* for Rp3000 (15 min.); car rides go for Rp20,000. Once inside the Gedong Songo area, visitors can hike on their own (4hr.) or ride on horseback (Rp8000) around the temples. On weekends the place is crowded with college-aged kids camping, smoking, playing guitars, and feeling very cool. Camping is allowed. (Open daily 6am-8pm; admission Rp350.)

DIENG PLATEAU

The site of sacred Hindu temples built on a highland plateau, **Dieng Plateau** is accessible from Semarang (119km northeast), Yogyakarta (107km southeast), Bandungan, or Wonosobo. From Bandungan, the trip takes two hours through Ambarawa market and Secang. The trip from Semarang via Bandungan takes about four hours. Dieng is 45 minutes from Wonosobo, which makes it an ideal base from which to explore the temples. **Losmen Jawa Tengah** on Jl. A. Yani, near the intersection of Jl. Pasman has simple but clean single rooms with shared *mandi* for Rp8000, doubles Rp10,000. The **tourist office** next to the bus terminal stores luggage for daytrippers (open daily 7am-3pm). Visitors should try to get to the plateau as early in the day as possible. Buses (Rp2000) leave constantly from the Wonosobo bus terminal (open 7am-3pm). A two-hour walk meanders through hot springs, temples, and one of the nicest views in Central Java. Guides are not necessary but can be hired for Rp10,000. From the Wonosobo bus terminal, find connections to **Magelang** (every 10min., last bus at 4pm, 1½hr.) where connections can be made to **Yogyakarta, Semarang** (every hr., last bus at 6pm), and **Surakarta** (last bus at noon).

■ Surabaya

On the heels of Jakarta, Surabaya is the second largest city in Indonesia, a fact which is hard to ignore. The city boasts six-lane streets, a formidable skyline, and at least five major indoor shopping complexes the size of small towns. There is noticeable economic disparity among the residents of Surabaya, many of whom do not share in the city's concentrated pockets of wealth. A major manufacturing center and seaport, Surabaya is a wholeheartedly commercial town where travelers seeking the elusive "authentic Java" may be put off by the city's glitz and restless modern pace. Surabaya connects to every island in the archipelago by ferry, and is a major bus hub, with connections to Bali and other destinations in Java. Most travelers use the city as a transit point and an opportunity to enjoy the big city luxuries not to be found in other parts of East Java.

ORIENTATION

Surabaya is a sprawling harbor city with a river that snakes between and under its more popular spots, making it a challenge to navigate. The huge Tunjunan Plaza is where the two main commercial streets, **Jalan Tunjunan** and **Jalan Pemuda,** intersect each other. **Jalan Yos Sudarso** and Jl. Pemuda meet in the approximate center of town. **Gubeng Train Station** is at the end of Jl. Pemuda after the Delta Plaza. Southwards, at the end of **Jalan Raya Darmo,** is the Surabaya Zoo. Following the river north is **Jalan Peneleh,** where travelers can find a cluster of reasonably priced accommodations. Still upriver is the **GPO, Kota Station,** Arab Quarter, and Chinatown. **Jalan Tanjung Perak** and the river eventually head to sea, to the **Madura Ferry Terminal,** and to Surabaya's harbor.

PRACTICAL INFORMATION

Tourist Offices: (tel. 853 18 14), on Jl. Wisata Mehanggal, toward the airport. Lots of info on the city. Open Mon.-Fri 8am-2pm, Sat. 8am-1pm. **Branch office,** Jl. Pemuda 118 (tel. 524 499), across the street from Surabaya Plaza. From Gubeng Station, walk left on Jl. Gubeng Pojok and then right on Jl. Permuda. English spoken. Open Mon.-Sat. 8am-4pm.

Tours and Travel: Linda Jaya, Jl. Ngagel Jaya 30 (tel. 583 093), and Jl. Panglima Sudirman 70-1 (tel. 407 43).

Embassies and Consulates: Australia, d/a World Trade Centre, Jl. Pemuda 27-31 (tel. 519 123). **UK,** d/a Hong Kong Bank, Jl. Basuki Rakhmad 33. **US,** Jl. Dr. Sutomo 33 (tel. 582 288). New passports in 24hr.

Currency Exchange: Bank Duta, Jl. Pemuda 12 (tel. 512 126). AmEx traveler's checks only. MC, Visa advances. Open Mon.-Thurs. 8am-3pm, Fri. 8-11am and 1-3pm. **Bank Bumi Daya,** Tunjungan Plaza (tel. 511 303). MC, Visa advances. **24-hr. ATM** at **Bank Bali,** Jl. Tunjungan 52. Visa, AmEx, Cirrus.

American Express: Pacto, Jl. Basuki Rachmad 106-128 (tel. 526 385), next to the Hyatt Regency. Open Mon.-Sat. 8am-4pm.

Air Travel: Juanda Airport (tel. 831 831), 18km south Surabaya. To: **Denpasar** (several per day, Rp92,900); **Yogyakarta** (1 per day, Rp65,400); and **Jakarta** (1 per day, Rp85,000). Taxis (Rp15,000) and Damri airport buses (Rp2500) shuttle visitors into town. *Bemo* can be caught 3km away as well (Rp350). Ask drivers about your destination. **Garuda,** Jl. Basuki Rahmat 124 (tel. 511 234).

Trains: Surabaya's 3 main train stations are: **Gubeng,** Jl. Gubeng Pojok (tel. 400 80; reservations tel. 535 39 93); **Kota/Semut,** Jl. Stasiun Kota; and **Pasar Turi** (tel. 450 14), on Jl. Semarang. Trains traveling through Gubeng stop at Kota/Semut and vice versa. Trains to Pasar Turi—usually to or from north Java—are a separate line. From Gubeng to: **Malang** (7 per day, 7:25am-5pm, 2-5hr., economy Rp2000); **Banyuwangi** (3 per day, 7hr., economy Rp3500, business Rp7000); **Jakarta's Gambir Station** (12:15pm, economy Rp10,000; 3pm, business Rp26,000; *Bima* night train, 4pm, 15-16hr., executive B Rp44,000, executive A Rp58,000); **Yogyakarta/Surakarta** (5 per day, early morning-5pm, economy Rp7500, business Rp14-18,000); **Bandung** (5:40am, 5, and 7:10pm, Rp13,000); **Ketapang** (8:10am,

1:50, and 10:10pm, Rp8000); and **Malang** (12 per day, 7am-11pm, Rp2000). Buy tickets 7 days in advance. Reservation charge Rp1500 for executive and business class; Rp1000 for economy, but reserving is unnecessary. From Pasar Turi, trains go to **Jakarta's Pasar Senen** (5 and 6:30pm, economy Rp10,000; *Mutiara* night train, 4:30pm, 11hr., Rp36-58,000). Both trains go to **Semarang** (economy Rp7500, business Rp27,500, special Rp52,000). Ticket office open daily 8am-1pm. The executive ticket office is on the left side of Pasar Turi if you are facing the platform; business and economy tickets are sold on the right side, from a separate office, open daily 8am-2pm.

Buses: Bungurasih/Purabaya Terminal, 10km south of town. **Executive/deluxe buses** (A/C, video, reclining seat, toilet, meal, snacks) to: **Bandung** (every hr., 4-8pm, 13hr.); **Jakarta** (every hr., 3-8pm, 16hr.); **Denpasar** (every hr., 4-8pm, 12hr.); and **Singaraja** via **Lovina** (every hr., 5-8pm, 11hr.). Buy executive bus tickets at least 1 day in advance from the terminal or any travel agent. **A/C buses** to: **Surakarta/Yogyakarta** (every hr., 6am-3pm, 6-7hr.); **Malang** (every hr., 6-8pm, 2hr.); and **Banyuwangi** (every 2hr., 6am-8pm, 6hr.). Pay on the bus; no reservation needed. Economy buses are slower, more crowded, and leave when full.

Ferries: PELNI office, Jl. Pahlawahan 112 (tel. 210 42). Several ships dock at Surabaya; look for the *KM Kerinci, KM Rinjani, KM Umsini,* and *KM Awu.* The port is 100m from Tanjung Perak Terminal. Open Mon.-Thurs. 8:30am-3pm, Fri. 8:30-11am and 1-3pm. If ships leave Sunday, the office is open the preceding Saturday 8:30am-noon. Purchase tickets at least 3 days in advance for 1st, 2nd, and 3rd class. Cash only. Economy class to: **Jakarta** (Rp29,000), **Medan** (Rp82,000), and **Bali** (Rp26,000). There are also ferries running to **Kamal,** Madura (every 30min., 30min., Rp350). **Kalla Lines PT,** Jl. Perak Timur 158 (tel. 341 203), a private company, sells tickets to some other destinations.

Taxis: Base fare of Rp900 for the first km and approximately Rp450 for each additional km. **Taxi Super,** Jl. Ngemplak 20 (tel. 420 96).

Local Transportation: Joyoboyo Terminal, on Jl. Joyoboyo by the Surabaya Zoo, is the main local bus terminal. Two useful **city bus** routes to know are those of buses marked C or P-1. From Bungurasih Terminal, city buses C (Damri, Rp200) and P-1 (Patas, Rp400) run by the zoo, Tunjungan Plaza, Toko Nam on Jl. Embong Malang, Pasar Turi Station, the PELNI office, the GPO, PELNI to Kalimas harbors, and the ferry station to Madura, ending at **Perak Terminal.** Buses begin running at 6am and peter off at 9pm. There are also 37 different **bemo** routes weaving through the city; almost half use Joyoboyo Terminal as a base. The best way to ride *bemo* is to ask locals or attendants if they are heading to your destination. Yellow **anguna** (unmetered taxis) can be flagged down off main streets.; agree on a price first. **Becak** are limited to one-way roads, so they take circuitous routes.

Rentals: Toyota Rent-A-Car, Jl. A. Yani 210 (tel. 819 999). **Cars** rented Rp90,000 first day, Rp80,000 thereafter. Must have IDP or hire a chauffeur.

Luggage Storage: at Pasar Gubeng (Rp1000 per day).

Markets: Pasar Kayun, on Jl. Kayun, is a daily flower market lined with restaurants from 9am to 10pm. **Pasar Genteng,** on Jl. Genteng Kali, is a fruit and miscellany market by day, and a food market by night. **Pasar Pabean,** off Jl. Rajawali, is a traditional meat and vegetable market. Open early morning to 5pm. **Pasar Baluran,** the gold market, lies on Jl. Baluran, at the end of Jl. Embong Malang.

Pharmacies: Kimia Farma, Jl. Raya Darmo 2 (tel. 577 777) and **Apotik Pusura Clinic,** Jl. Yos Sudarso 9A (tel. 507 334). Both open 24hr.

Medical Services: Dr. Sutomo General Hospital, Jl. Dharmahusada 6 (tel. 400 61). **William Booth General Hospital,** Jl. Diponegoro 54 (tel. 576 133). **St. Ventcentius (RKZ),** Jl. Diponegoro 51 (tel. 577 562).

Emergency: tel. 110. **Fire:** tel. 113. **Ambulance:** tel. 118, 119, or 334 030.

Police: 3 offices: Jl. Raden Saleh 1 (tel. 420 94), Jl. Dukuh Kupang Barat XV 1/6-8 (tel. 579 040), and Jl. A. Yani (tel. 838 258).

Post Offices: GPO, Jl. Kebonrojo 10. Open 24-hr. *Poste Restante.* Mail counters (tel. 342 200) open daily 7:30am-10pm. **General postal information:** tel. 101. More convenient **branch** at Jl. Pemuda, just past the General Soerjo Statue on the left. Open Mon.-Thurs. and Sat. 8am-2pm, Fri. 8-11am. **Postal code:** 60175.

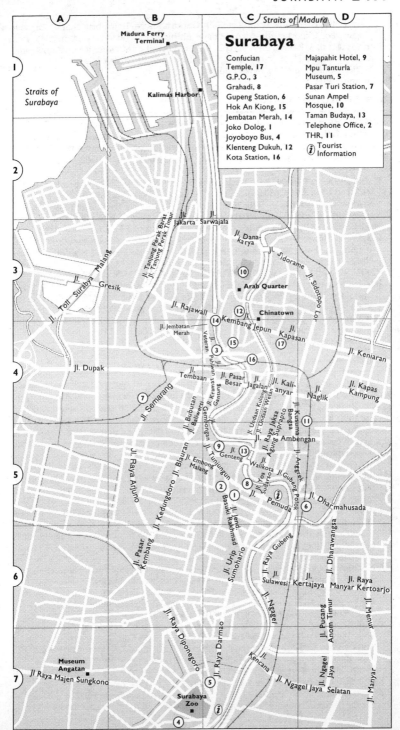

Surabaya

Confucian Temple, 17
G.P.O., 3
Grahadi, 8
Gupeng Station, 6
Hok An Kiong, 15
Jembatan Merah, 14
Joko Dolog, 1
Joyoboyo Bus, 4
Klenteng Dukuh, 12
Kota Station, 16

Majapahit Hotel, 9
Mpu Tanturla Museum, 5
Pasar Turi Station, 7
Sunan Ampel Mosque, 10
Taman Budaya, 13
Telephone Office, 2
THR, 11
i Tourist Information

INDONESIA

Telephones: The **24-hr. wartel** at **G.D. Gapura Surya,** Jl. Jambrut Ntara 1 (at Tunjungan Plaza), and **Juanda Airport** have international, collect, telegram, telex, fax. **Indosat** (tel. 512 003), on Jl. Kayun, has credit card calls. Other international *wartel* at **Surabaya Mall,** Jl. Kunsuma Bangsa 116, and **Komplex Darmo Park,** on Jl. Mayjen Sungkono. Most *wartel* do not accept credit card calls. Cash only. **Telephone code:** 031.

ACCOMMODATIONS

For such a large city, Surabaya has very few quality budget accommodations. Bamboe Den is the only place in town that caters to backpackers. Aside from a few out-of-town locations, the only other option is a group of cheap but dingy hotels clustered in the Peneleh area (generally Rp20,000/Rp25,000 for singles/doubles).

Bamboe Denn Hostel, Jl. Ketabang Kali 6A (tel. 403 33), west of the intersection with Jl. Yos Sudarso, toward the river. Most *becak* driver in town know Bamboe. Modest environs but specifically for travelers, offering free drinking water and travel tips. Bunk beds in 2 large rooms Rp5000. Singles Rp6000. Doubles with shared *mandi* Rp12,000. Bring mosquito repellent and a lock for the lockers.

Hotel Paviljoen, Jl. Genteng Besar 94 (tel. 434 49), near the intersection with Jl. Tunjungan. Enter into a long hallway with a high ceiling and padded bamboo chairs. Clean rooms come complete with accessories—soap, towels, furniture. Doubles with fan Rp23-27,500. Breakfast included.

Roleen Homestay, Jl. Ngagel Jaya Utara 117 (tel. 574 063). Owned by RObert and kathLEEN Augustin, Roleen is on the south side of town, near Ubaya University. Not a bargain or in a convenient location, but a true homestay (with only 5 rooms) in a nice house located in a quiet residential neighborhood. Friendly family of fluent English speakers. Rp35,000 for 2 beds with 2 fans and bath. Rp45,000 for a double with A/C. Breakfast included.

FOOD

Some of the best places to find good, cheap food are in the **riverside restaurants** along Jl. Kayun, and in **warung** and **night stalls** lining Jl. Genteng Besar. **Kayun Park** is also bordered by small, cheap eateries that serve excellent seafood, as well as the typical Indonesian and Chinese fare. Local specialties include *ular* (fried snake). Several Indonesian restaurants cluster in the **Siola** (the name of a department store) area, one street farther along Jl. Tunjungan after Jl. Genteng Besar. Shopping centers in Surabaya all have fast food courts but are pricier than most.

Mie Tunjungan, Jl. Genteng Kali 121, just past the intersection and the Siola Department Store. Specializes in delicious *mie pangsit* (chicken noodles with wonton) for Rp2500. Open Mon.-Sat. 9am-9pm.

Sri Reejeki Ayam Goreng, Jl. Genteng Kali 158 (tel. 516 20), across the street and down from Siola. Fried chicken for all occasions. Feel your cholesterol levels skyrocket and try the unique *pempek Palembang* (Rp2500), a hard-boiled egg inside a condensed rice and batter-fried exterior. Open Mon.-Sat. 8am-4pm and 5-11pm, Sun. 8am-midnight.

Café Venezia, Jl. Ambengan 16 (tel. 430 91), one street parallel north and across the river from the Siola area. Long menu, high prices, and questionable decor, but the food is surprisingly good and you can get away from the heat and bustle. Specializes in steak (sirloin Rp9900) and ice cream, but also has Indonesian and Japanese food, omelettes, and hot dogs (Rp4200). Open daily 10am-11pm.

Pengampon, Jl. Kusuma Bangsa 128, on the same side of the street and close to Surabaya Mall and THR complex. The enormous Hong Kong-esque restaurant has a hefty menu of Indonesian and Chinese food, including pig's bowels soup (Rp7500), as well as vegetarian dishes. Mixed vegetables with rice go for Rp4500. Tables all face a stage, used for a live band and karaoke. Open daily 10am-2pm (lunch, karaoke) and 5-10pm (dinner, band).

Metro Café, Jl. Tunjungan 101 (tel. 443 51), opposite Tunjungan Plaza at the base of the elevated stairway. Lace curtains over windows, and Indonesian food with tempeh and tofu on request. Sanitized A/C-cooled environs. Try the *nasi pecel* (rice with veggies in peanut sauce) Rp3200. Open daily 9:30am-9pm.

Benny's Gelati, Ice Cream and Donut/Istana Buah Restaurant, Jl. Tunjungan 88 (tel. 511 172), down the street from the plaza; look for the big red apple. Australian owner has created a hip and glossy café interior. Ice cream (Rp2000) and sandwiches (Rp5-6000). Serves beer. Open daily 9am-9:30pm.

SIGHTS AND ENTERTAINMENT

Surabaya's most fascinating features are not its sights in the traditional sense, but its commercial activity, which is nearly impossible to avoid. Even if you don't usually find yourself in malls, Surabaya's are worth strolling through, if only to gawk at their enormity and enjoy some soft ice cream and a refreshing A/C-pick-me-up. **Tunjungan Plaza** (open daily 9am-9pm), in two interconnected sections, is particularly impressive, and is reputed to be the largest mall in Indonesia. The **People's Amusement Park (THR)** is behind the THR Mall (schedules available in the tourist office). It's open Thursday and Saturday nights 8pm-midnight. Cheap thrills offered include a ferris wheel, mini rollercoasters (Rp800 per ticket), and traditional dance and music performances.

Visitors to the **Surabaya Zoo** (Kebun Binatang), in the south of town at the end of Jl. Raya Darmo, should be prepared to feel not just sympathy, but empathy as well for the animals; there's a current debate as to whether the animals or the tourists are the real attraction (even the giraffes stare). To reach the zoo from the Tunjungan area, catch a Damri or Patas bus from the bus stop by the Simpang Hotel; tell the attendant you're heading to the "Kebun Binatang" (15min.). Heading back from the zoo, ask to get off at "Toko Nam" to end up near the Tunjungan area. The zoo is quite extensive and worth an afternoon's browsing, with collections of birds, reptiles, restless elephants, white tigers, some chubby jaguars, an adorable long-nailed sloth bear, and a Komodo dragon. Every second and fourth Tuesday of the month, they string up a live goat and people congregate from all over the city to watch the dragon go at it. (Open daily 7am-6pm; admission Rp1500.)

The **Arab Quarter** of town and the **Sunan Ampel Mosque,** the oldest mosque in East Java, can be seen within an afternoon as well. The mosque was built by Sunan Ampel, one of the *wali songo,* nine Muslim holy men, who initiated the spread of Islam in Java. To get there, take any *bemo* (*bemo* 10 is ideal, as it passes along Jl. Walikota Mustajab, the east end of Jl. Genteng Besar) to Jembatan Merah Terminal and then a *becak* (Rp1000) or walk 15 minutes northeast to Sunan Ampel. To head from the mosque back to the Simpang Hotel bus stop, take city bus P-1 (Rp400) or C (Rp200) and ask for "Simpang." Also worth a stroll is the old **Tanjung Perak/Harbor area,** which can easily be reached by Damri or Patas city buses.

NIGHTLIFE

Tequila Willies, Jl. Kayun 62 (tel. 527 138), across the street from the restaurants lining the river. Dark. Pinball. Dark wood bar stools. Mostly expats. Serves hearty fare, such as burritos (Rp6500) and crab and asparagus soup (Rp4000). No cover. Draft beer Rp5000. Live music nightly 10pm-2am and canned disco until 3am. Restaurant open nightly 7-10pm.

Studio East Discotheque, at Andhika Plaza, a 5-min. walk from Bamboe Denn. Diplomats mix with backpackers and upwardly mobile Indonesians. The dancing is nothing to write home about, but at least it's lively. Ladies get in free on Fridays. Beer Rp5000. Rp10,000 cover. Open nightly 11pm-3am.

■ Near Surabaya: Pulau Madura

Pulau Madura lies 3km off the East Java coast. On the up side, Madura's rock and sand landscape is beautiful and the island is remarkably untouristed. On the downside, Madura is not yet hospitable to tourists. It has limited accommodations, poor and unexciting sights (by Javanese standards), aggressive locals, and practically no one speaks English. **Women should not visit here alone.** The main reason to make the journey here is the island's famed **bull races** *(kerapan sapi)* held between August and October. The final race accompanies a festival of *gamelan,* dancing, and parades. Before the race, the bulls are led about town wearing bejeweled head-dresses, yokes, flowers, ribbons, and parasols, followed by an entourage of handlers and musicians. For details about the times and places of the races, contact the tourist offices in Surabaya or the **Madura Tourist Information Office,** Baparda Sumenep, Jl. Dr. Cipto 33, Sumenep (tel. 216 10).

Madura has three main cities, between which colts run and offer a low-budget way to tour the low, shallow side of the island near the port to Surabaya. A two- to three-hour colt ride east of **Bangkalan** is **Pamekasan,** the capital, in the south-central part of Madura. South and slightly west of the capital is **Camplong,** a swimming beach. The best beaches can be found near **Sumenep,** the most popular destination on the east side of the island. Siring Kemuning Beach, in **Tanjungbumi,** competes with Salopeng Beach at **Ambunten,** on the north shore, for being the most beautiful and untrammeled. Accommodations can be found in Bangkalan, Kamal, Sampang, Camplong Beach (bungalows), Pamekasan, Sumenep, Kalianget, and Pasongsongan. The **Losmen Bahagia** (Bapak Taufik Rahman), on Jl. Trunjoyo in Pasongsongan, has singles for Rp8000 and doubles for Rp10,000. In Sumenep, **Losmen Wijaya I** and **II,** near the bus terminal, have singles for Rp5000 and doubles for Rp8000. **Bapak Kamila House** on Siring Kemuning Beach has Rp15,000 doubles, including three meals per day. Prices island-wide go up during bull racing season.

Madura is easily reached from Surabaya. Ferries from Surabaya's port of Tanjung Perak leave every 30 minutes between 4am and midnight for Kamal Port on Madura. At Kamal, take colt minibuses to see the island or ride *becak,* which are available in the three main cities. Be sure to change money before you arrive.

■ Malang

Malang is a city of simple charms, with small-town hospitality, cool temperatures, conscientious cooking, carefully maintained public gardens, and a view of the mountains from downtown. Sadly, most travelers rush through this provincial, tree-lined town at break-neck speed to catch sunrise at Gunung Bromo instead. A transition point between the sweaty mosquito-traps to the west and the pristine nature sites to the east, Malang is a good place for the travel-weary in need of pleasant evening walks and a taste of Java's best apples.

ORIENTATION

Malang lies 90km south of Surabaya, bordered on three sides by volcanoes: **Gunung Butak** (2868m) to the west, **Gunung Arjuna** (3339m) to the north, and **Gunung Semeru** (3676m) and **Gunung Bromo** (2329m) to the east. The city is entirely walkable by foot and centers on two public spaces—**Tugu Monument** and the **alun-alun.** Tugu serves as a traffic rotary and is surrounded by government buildings and Malang's major hotels. From Tugu, the **train station** can be seen directly to the east. The *alun-alun* is south of the Tugu Monument and is bordered on all sides by the city's busiest shopping areas and the GPO. There are three bus terminals on the outskirts of the city; **Arjosari Terminal** to the north is the most heavily trafficked.

PRACTICAL INFORMATION

Tourist Offices: Along the Tugu Monument rotary. Provides bus and train schedules. Friendly, but better city maps and information on neighboring sights can be obtained at the front desk at larger hotels. Open daily 8am-1pm.

Currency Exchange: Banks are generally open Mon.-Fri. 8:30am-2:30pm, Sat. 8:30-11am. **Bali Bank,** on Jl. Basuki Rakhmat, back from the street next to a McDonald's. Accepts traveler's checks. **24-hr. ATM** accepts MC, Visa, Cirrus. Open Mon.-Fri. 8:30am-7pm, Sat. 8:30am-1pm.

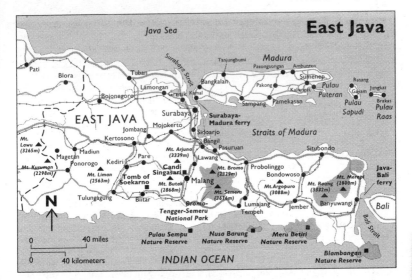

Air Travel: Abdul Rakhman Saleh Airport, 6km east of Malang center. Daily flights to **Jakarta** and **Yogyakarta.** To get to town from the airport, hop on an airport *bemo* to Blimbing (Rp500), then change to a *bemo* heading toward town (Rp350). **Garuda** (tel. 365 914), at Lippo Bank on Jl. Merdeka Timor.

Trains: Station, on Jl. Trunojoyo, visible from Tugu. Trains to: **Surabaya** (4 per day, Rp1500); **Jakarta** (9:06am); **Surakarta** (10:46pm); **Yogyakarta** (12:53am); and **Blitar** (11 per day, 7am-9pm). Buy tickets at the station daily 8am-6pm.

Buses: Arjosari, the main terminal north of the city. Buses leave frequently for Jakarta, Probolinggo, Denpasar, and Surabaya. To **Gunung Bromo,** take a Patas A/C bus from here to **Probolinggo** (8 per day, 6:35am-4:10pm), and then catch a *bemo* for the final leg of the trip. Non-A/C buses leave whenever the driver feels like it. **Gadang Terminal,** about 5km to the south, has buses going to the beach communities to the south. **Dinoyo,** on the west side of town, sends buses to **Batur** and **Seleta.** Complete schedules can be viewed at the tourist office. Book seats on **A/C buses** at any travel agency. There are no schedules for public buses—they leave at all hours, whenever the bus is full.

Local Transportation: Becak are widely available. **Bemo** (Rp300) have routes between terminals labeled on the *bemo* as follows: **A-D,** Arjosari to Dinoyo; **A-G,** Arjosari to Gadang; **D-G;** Dinoyo to Gadang; **D,** Gadang to Dinoyo; **E, F, or G,** Dinoyo to Arjosari.

Taxis: Rp800 flag fare, plus Rp300 per km. Can be hailed from hotels along Tugu Monument or call for pick up. **Citra Taxi** (tel. 495 105).

Luggage Storage: Next door to the train station. Open daily 4am-9pm. Also free storage at **Riche Tourist Info.**

Markets: In the evening, the **alun-alun** bustles with *warung,* merchants, and families. The **night market** lies just over the river by Jl. Kahuripan, and gets going around 7pm; there's also a 24-hour **flower market** here. During the day this is the site of the bird and fish market, **Pasar Burja.** Open daily 8am-5pm.

Pharmacies: Located in all the large shopping plazas along Jl. Angus Salim.

Medical Services: Concentrated along Jl. A. Yani. Two to try are **Ruman Bersalin Pan Balai Pengobatan** (tel. 493 059) and the super-modern **Prodia Laborto-rium Klinik,** Jl. Achmad Dahlan 7 (tel. 666 04). With your back to Hotel Toseri, walk right 25m. Open Mon.-Fri. 7am-8pm, Sat. 7am-4pm. MC, Visa, AmEx.

Police: Polresta (tel. 666 444), on Jl. Slamet Riyadi.

Emergency: Police: tel. 110. **Fire:** tel. 113. **Ambulance:** tel. 118.

Post Offices: GPO, Jl. Merdeka Selatan 5 (tel. 362 254). Open Mon.-Sat. 8am-8pm, Sun. 8am-7pm. No *Poste Restante.* **Postal Code:** 65119.

Telephones: 24-hr. wartel next to Toko Oen Restaurant on Jl. Basuki Rakhmat. Accepts credit cards. **Telephone code:** 0341

ACCOMMODATIONS

The recent closing of Malang's **Bamboo Denn Homestay** marked the end of a budget accommodations dynasty in the city. Owners claim they will reopen in December 1996 under the name of Tridaya Pertiwi Homestay on Jl. Mundu, near the Amsterdam Restaurant. Fret not, however, as bargains can be found clustering around the Tugu Monument area. Malang may force budgeteers to splurge a little, but in return, there's excellent service and mosquito-free sleep.

Helio's Hotel (tel. 362 741), on Jl. Pattimura, near the train station. One of the cheapest in town. From the train station, walk to the Tugu rotary, and follow it to Jl. Suropati. Make a right; it's 2 blocks down, in a quiet, residential area. Front desk gives travel info and arranges bus tickets. Clean doubles with shared *mandi* Rp14,500. Breakfast included.

Hotel Pelangi, Jl. Merdeka Selatan 3 (tel. 365 156), next to the *alun-alun* by the GPO. Centrally located, full-service hotel. Price includes buffet breakfast. 24-hr. restaurant. Free safety lockers for all rooms. Economy rooms with shared *mandi* Rp20,000, with hot shower Rp30,000. Add on 10% tax. MC, Visa, AmEx.

Splendid Inn, Jl. Majapahit 4 (tel. 366 860), along the Tugu Monument, next to the very classy Tugu Park Hotel. Inexplicably, its front gate says "Hotel $." True to its name, this splendidly landscaped hotel has splendid rooms: huge and furnished with color TV (including CNN) and private bathrooms with hot water. Swimming pool, billiards, free breakfast, tea, afternoon snacks and *gamelan* performances (Sat. only). Doubles Rp46,000, tax included. MC, Visa, AmEx.

FOOD

Malang has excellent food, reasonable variety, and tame prices. Many of the nicer hotels along Tugu Monument have attached restaurants with large selections of the Indonesian-western-Chinese hybrid variety. The casual **Bromo Café,** attached to the Montana Hotel on Jl. Kahuripa, is open 24 hours and packs lunches for daytrips. Sandwiches and Indonesian basics cost Rp2-4000. **Warung** (often called *depot* in Malang) are abundantly situated on roadsides (Rp1-2000) and in the **food bazaars** attached to the major shopping centers (Rp1500-3500). Three such mall-side bazaars face one another on Jl. Angus Salim.

Toko Oen, Jl. Basuki Rakhmat 5 (tel. 364 052), across the street from McDonald's. Westerners come to chat up while sipping on fresh fruit shakes (Rp2300) and sampling traditional Dutch fare (Rp4-10,000) in this colonial-era relic. Bakery and tourist office with tours to Bromo attached. Open daily 8am-9pm.

Gloria Restaurant, Jl. K.H. Angus Salim 21-23 (tel. 324 893). Gloria's high-quality Chinese food transformed what was once a humble roadside stall into a big, shiny banquet hall with an unfortunate color scheme. Fortunately, the noodle soups are some of the best this side of the Huang River (Rp3000). Tasty seafood and meat dishes are also available (Rp6-10,000). Open daily 8am-2:30pm and 5-10pm.

Melati Pavilion, Jl. Tugu 3, attached to the Tugu Park Hotel facing Tugu. This beautifully decorated, open-air restaurant presents the opportunity to put on a clean shirt and enjoy innovative, carefully prepared dishes. Tuna salad in papaya (Rp5500). The ambiance created by the carved teakwood and fresh flowers is by itself almost worth the high price for its western dishes. Indonesian basics for Rp3000. 10% government tax not included. Open daily 6am-midnight.

Jack's Café, Jl. Kahuripan 11A (tel. 320 623), away from the monument over the bridge. The only place that serves espresso (Rp1500). Live music Sat. 10pm-2am. Western and Indonesian food. Open Sun.-Fri. 11am-10pm, Sat. 11am-2am.

SIGHTS

As the well-trafficked stopover for travelers en route to the majestic Gunung Bromo, Malang offers few true sights of its own. The **Eng An Kong Chinese Pagoda,** at the intersection of Jl. Gatot Subroto and Jl. Zainul Zakse, is a colorful, powerful dose of Chinese Buddhist culture in the midst of a bustling Indonesian city. The intricate carvings, enormous archways, candles, incense, and shrines add to the quiet mystery of the place. (Open daily 6am-8pm; free.) Malang's other highly hyped sight, **Brawijaya Museum,** Jl. Besar Ljen 25A, consists of two main halls with photographs, weapons, and other memorabilia associated with the 5th Brawijaya Division, the third of Java's KODAM, or military area commands. Good for fans of military relics, but Indonesian labeling and a lack of English-speaking guides make the displays difficult to appreciate. (Open daily 7am-3pm; donation requested.)

■ Near Malang

CANDI SINGOSARI

Malang is a convenient base from which to visit several nearby Hindu temples, including Jago and Kidal temples to the east, and Singosari, 12km to the north. From Arjosari bus terminal, **Candi Singosari** can be reached by public bus to Lawang or Singosari town (20min., Rp300). Ask to get off at the *candi*. The temple was built between 1268 and 1292 in honor of the King Kertanagara, the last ruler of the brutal Singosari dynasty; his ashes, according to locals, are buried here. Two heads of Kala hang over the entrance to the unfinished temple, but only one of them has the intricate detail typical of Javanese carvings. Most of the stone figures that once guarded the six chambers around the *candi* have been shipped off to museums in Holland. The figure of Agastya, a student of Shiva, remains, peering over his distended belly that is said to contain the sea water he devoured in a fit of rage. During school holidays, English-language students loiter near the temple and offer to give tours. (Open daily 7am-5pm; donations accepted.)

BALE KAMBANG BEACH

Twenty-five km south of Malang, **Bale Kambang** is a stretch of sea backed by dense forest. Three offshore islands, accessible by bridges, provide some altitude and spectacular views of the ocean. More impressive is the motorcycle ride from Batur to Bale Kambang—12km of terraced fields, villages, and thick forest lands. Hikers can explore nearby cliffs and the village paths that extend from the main road to Batur. From Malang center travelers can take any G *bemo* to Gadang Terminal (Rp400). From Gadang, *bemo* go south toward Batur—some go directly while others change at intervening villages. Make sure the *bemo* driver knows where you are going. If he won't take you all the way to Batur, he'll put you on one that will. Expect to pay Rp1500 total from Gadang to Batur (1½hr.). At Batur, *ojek* go to the beach for Rp3000. The beach can be crowded, so those looking for some quietude should come only on weekdays, preferably before noon. *Ojek* drivers and young men loitering on the beaches will most likely harass women traveling alone; a mask of hostility can usually dissuade them.

■ Gunung Bromo

Despite the throng of visitors who hike to Bromo's summit at sunrise, Gunung Bromo (2923m) manages to deliver one of the most magnificent sights in all of Indonesia. Bromo generally refers not only to the ash-gray, semi-active crater named after the Hindu god Brahma, but to an entire cluster of active and dormant volcanoes set in an enormous 40km-wide crater, the Bromo-Semera Massif. The views are, as they should be, indescribable. Not much time, however, is needed to enjoy the Bromo area—

there is nothing to do here but stare at a beautiful mountain. Time set aside for an overnight stay and a five-hour day hike after sunrise is time aplenty.

GETTING THERE AND AWAY

Gunung Bromo, East Java's most popular travel destination, is located 50km east of Malang. It is most commonly accessed through the town of **Probolinggo.** From here, take a *bemo* to **Cemoro Lawang,** the stop for the Gunung Bromo area (last *bemo* at 6pm, 2hr., Rp2500). Travelers who miss the last *bemo* will have to park their packs in Probolinggo (not recommended, since some of the merchants are rumored to moonlight as highwaymen) or charter a taxi up the steep hills to Cemoro Lawang for Rp30,000. Alternatively, Bromo can also be approached from its northern edge through the coastal town of **Pasuruan.** From Pasuruan, minibuses run to Tosari, where visitors can then walk or hire a jeep for the crater.

To leave the Bromo area, head to the Probolinggo bus terminal by *bemo* (the last one leaves Cemoro Lawang at 4pm) where travelers can make connections to any city on Java or Bali. Long distances can be traversed by expensive A/C buses. These buses, usually overnight, leave at scheduled times and tickets should be arranged a day in advance. Tickets can be purchased at the Probolinggo terminal or at travel agencies in Cemoro Lawang (up to Rp30,000) for: **Jakarta** (1:15pm); **Yogyakarta/ Surakarta** (1:30, 10pm); **Denpasar** (7:30, 8pm); and **Ketapang** (ferry site to Gili Nan-ule and Bali, every hr., 10am-2pm). Public buses also go to all major destinations, including **Surabaya** (every 15min.) and **Malang** (every hr.).

ACCOMMODATIONS AND FOOD

Probolinggo bus terminal is located between Surabaya and Banyuwangi; the town itself doesn't merit a stop on the itinerary, but guest houses are available here to shelter stranded travelers. **Hotel Victoria** on Jl. Sudirman and Jl. Suroyo has acceptable singles for Rp10,000.

Cemoro Lawang, the village closest to the crater, provides the best quality accommodations in the area—most even have a spectacular view of the nearby volcanoes. *Bemo* drivers are paid a commission by several of the homestays to drop customers on their doorstep. *Losmen* are close together and travelers can benefit from shopping around. **Café Lava Hostel** (tel. (0335) 234 58), has clean, comfortable rooms and incomparable service for the cheapest prices in the village. Dorms cost Rp4000, singles Rp6000, and doubles Rp8000. Discounts are available with student ID or and ISIC card. All rooms share two very clean *mandi*. Lava's management is friendly, English speaking, and can give copious, unbiased travel advice. If Lava is full, the **Cemara Indah,** just 10m up the hill, has acceptable singles for Rp7000, doubles Rp10,000. All rooms include breakfast.

Food of the *warung* type is easy to come by on village roads (Rp1000) and even easier in tourist-oriented restaurants (Rp3-5000). **Puri Lava Restaurant,** connected to the Café Lava Hostel, bustles with Bromo-bound backpackers.

CLIMBING BROMO

Bromo and its surrounding peaks can be climbed at any point during the day (given the area's cool air, even during high noon). But a 4am reveille is necessary to join the pre-dawn pilgrimage to higher ground to catch the magnificent, crimson-red sunrise over Gunung Bromo. Two vantage points both provide worthy views. The first is a trek through the "sea of sand," the ascent to Gunung Bromo itself (about a one-hour walk/climb), and a view of the sunrise from the crater's edge. Alternatively, **Gunung Penanjakan** provides views of Bromo and the surrounding peaks from higher altitudes. The hike to Gunung Penanjakan takes two hours and is the less common route. Lava Hostel provides free maps of the trail and can take you halfway by jeep for

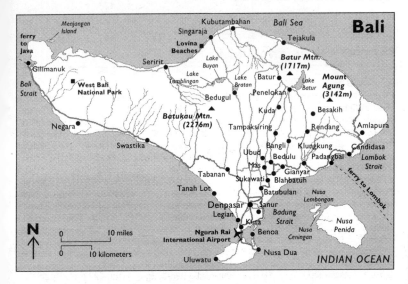

Rp6000. Either way, ask the hotel manager to wake you at 3:30-4am. Trekkers should dress warmly, bring a water bottle, and, if going the Gunung Penanjakan route without a guide, bring a flashlight.

After sunrise, the crowds magically melt away and you are left alone with promising hiking possibilities. If staying past sunrise, bring breakfast and dress to shed layers. If you went up Bromo during the wee hours consider climbing Gunung Penanjakan later in the morning. Facing Cemara Indah Homestay, walk right, and in about an hour, you'll hit the trail leading up to the 3000m elevation.

Bali

Guidebooks, brochures, and word of mouth have settled on a handful of clichés to gloss the most heavily visited island in Indonesia: Bali—Magical Isle of Paradise; Bali—Island of the Gods; Bali—Morning of the World; Bali—Land of 10,000 Temples; and Bali—Destroyed by Tourism. Indeed, Bali, an island of three million people on 5700sq.km, plays host to a hefty one million tourists per year. In its most touristed areas, spaghetti wins out over Balinese *lawar* and the population of braided, beach-bronzed Europeans seems to outnumber the mosquitoes. Such large-scale tourism, however, has mostly been contained in the south and a few areas on the east and northern coasts.

Although it is now fashionable to put down Bali for its crowds, consistently good weather, idyllic beaches, and colorful cultural traditions continue to make Bali a satisfying destination. Watersports and fresh seafood abound, but Bali's hottest commodity is its culture and, in general, the Balinese enjoy showcasing it. In Sanur, Kuta, Ubud, and other hot spots, visitors can buy tickets to see Balinese dance, *gamelan* orchestras, cremation ceremonies, temple rituals, and more. Although these shows are worth at least a few evenings' time, one of the fastest ways to get to the heart of Bali is through the public markets, *warung,* and family homestays—low budget ways to be spoon-fed Bali without the canned aftertaste. Leaving the postcard images of

Bali for the racks and noticing the less advertised details of Bali is good medicine for the "Bali is overrun by tourists" plague.

GETTING THERE AND AWAY

By Plane

Ngurah Rai International Airport (tel. 751 011, 24-hr. info tel. 164) lies immediately south of Kuta 15 minutes by taxi or direct shuttle. Money changer, baggage storage, and an ATM (Cirrus and AmEx) are available. There's an international departure tax of Rp20,000 per person which must be paid in cash. The domestic departure tax is Rp7700. Flights go to: **Jakarta** (7 per day, Rp222,000); **Medan** (Rp457,000); **Yogyakarta** (3 per day, Rp122,000); and **Mataram** (Rp55,000).

Beware of porters who may try to carry your luggage without being asked and then demand Rp500 per piece. From the airport, taxis with fixed rates take passengers to **Kuta** (Rp6500), **Sanur** (Rp15,000), **Denpasar** (Rp11,000), or **Ubud** (Rp40,000). Public **bemo** and **chartered transport** vehicles linger outside the airport area on the main road and are invariably cheaper than the taxis.

By Bus

Overnight buses leave regularly for Java from Bali and vice versa. Tickets can be bought through any tour agencies in Bali such as **Bali Buana Artha,** Jl. Diponegoro 131A, Denpasar (tel. 227 370) or Jl. Hasanudin 97, Denpasar (tel. 222 663).

By Ferry

Ferries run between **Gilimanuk** (on west tip of Bali) and **Ketapang** (on East Java) (every 40min., 24hr., Rp1000). Ferries to **Lombok** leave from **Padangbai**, on Bali's east coast (every 2hr., 4hr., Rp5500). **Express boats** to **Lembar,** Lombok leave from **Benoa Harbor** in south Bali (2hr., economy class Rp29,500). Tickets can be bought at the PELNI offices at Benoa Harbor (tel. 228 962) or at Jl. Diponegoro 165 in Denpasar (tel. 234 680), as well as at the **Mabua Express** office at Benoa (tel. 261 212). *Bemo* to Benoa leave from Suci Terminal in Denpasar. To get to Padangbai on public transport, catch a *bemo* from Batubulan. Alternatively, explore one of the "shuttle bus" services, such as Perama, or others offered through tour agencies.

GETTING AROUND IN BALI

Metered taxis have recently made their appearance on Bali. Make sure the fixed-rate meters are set to Rp800 at the beginning of the ride and insist on metered rates, since bargaining is usually more expensive. Taxis do not stop where *bemo* or local drivers are parked, so flag one elsewhere. **Ojek** congregate at key intersections where *bemo* do not run. **Dokar** are still used in Denpasar.

Public **bemo,** identified by their yellow license plates, are best caught in the early morning and generally stop running after sundown. *Bemo* can be privately **chartered.** Denpasar is the hub of *bemo* activity for the south part of Bali between terminals and to other parts of the island. Five terminals service the island:

Batubulan, 6km northeast of Denpasar. *Bemo* east to Bangli, Padangbai, Candi Dasa, Amlapura, and Tirtagangga, and north to Ubud via Kediri and Penelokan.

Kereneng, on the east end of Denpasar off Jl. Hayam Wuruk. Has connecting *bemo* to the other terminals.

Suci, near the corner of Jl. Hasanudin and Jl. Diponegoro. Serves Benoa Harbor.

Tegal, on the west end, near the intersection of Jl. G. Willis and Jl. Imam Bonjol. South to Kuta, Legian, Ngurah Rai Airport, Sanur, Nusa Dua, and Uluwatu.

Ubung, north of Denpasar on Jl. Cokroaminoto. Trips north and west, including Singaraja, Bedugul, Tanah Lot, Gilimanuk, and points in Java.

■ Denpasar

Once upon a time, before the days of large-scale tourist development, Denpasar was Bali's traveler hub, providing the island's only accommodation and easy access to the southern beaches. Today, with the establishment of separate resort enclaves in Sanur, Kuta, and Nusa Dua, it's no more than a daytrip on most itineraries, offering big city conveniences and the comprehensive Bali Museum. Denpasar has none of the features of an idealized Bali paradise—impossibly congested traffic can frustrate even the most serene vacationers—but it's a fascinating testament to the resilience of Balinese culture. Despite the obvious signs of westernization and changing material values, the customs of Balinese Hinduism have continued unabated. Women weave in and out of nighmarish traffic patterns, placing carefully crafted offerings on the ground, which are promptly flattened by passing 4x4s and *bemo*.

ORIENTATION

In the north of Denpasar, the dense market area lies between the two major parallel east-west streets **Jalan Hasanuddin** and **Jalan Gajah Mada,** which are connected by **Jalan Sulawesi.** Jl. Gajah Mada becomes **Jalan Suprapati** to the east, which then changes to **Jalan Hayam Wuruk** farther on. East of the markets, between the same streets, is **Puputan Square.** In the south of town are the Central Post Office and the Bali Government Tourist Office, both near **Jalan Raya Puputan,** the road leading east to Sanur. In the ritzy Renon area also on the south side are **Udayan University** and the massive **Duta Plaza Shopping Centre;** they border **Jalan Diponegoro,** which heads north toward the market area.

PRACTICAL INFORMATION

Tourist Offices: Dinas Pariwisata, Jl. Suropati 7 (tel. 222 387), across from the Bali Museum. The friendliest and most informative on the island. Free maps, brochures, and schedule of events for all of Bali. Staff will cheerfully help you decipher *bemo* routes. Open Mon.-Thurs. 7am-3pm, Fri. 7am-noon.
Tours and Travel: Gapura Jaya Tours, Jl. Hayam Wuruk 74 (tel. 228 460). Options are not as plentiful as in the Sanur or Kuta areas.
Embassies and Consulates: Australia, Jl. Moch. Yamin 1, Renon (tel. 235 092).
Immigration Office: Jl. Niti Mandala, Renon (tel. 227 828). With your back to the GPO, walk left and take the first left. Visa extensions and problems handled. Open Mon.-Thurs. 7am-2pm, Fri.-Sat. 7-11am.
Currency Exchange: Big banks cluster on Jl. Gajah Mada between Bandung Market and Puputan Square. **Bank Duta,** Jl. Hayam Wuruk 165 (tel. 226 578), just beyond Puputan Square. Accepts MC and Visa for cash transfers. Open Mon.-Fri. 8am-noon, Sat. 8-11am. **ATM: Bank Bali,** on Jl. Diponegoro where it hits Jl. Teuku Umar, near the telephone office, across the street from Bandung Market on Jl. Gajah Mada. MC, Visa, Cirrus.
Air Travel: Ngurah Rai International Airport (see **Getting There and Away,** above). **Garuda,** Jl. Melati 61 (ticketing tel. 225 245, reconfirmation tel. 234 606). **Merpati,** Jl. Melati 57 (tel. 235 358). **Bouraq,** Jl. Sudirman 19A (tel. 223 564)
Markets: Pasar Badung, the largest and oldest market in Bali, selling everything imagineable. Just across the river stands **Kumbasari Art Market,** of similarly lively activity. Abutting these markets is Jl. Sulawesi, the heart of Denpasar's **fabric district.**

Pharmacies: Kimia Farma 34, Jl. Diponegoro 125 (tel. 227 812), at the intersection with Jl. Teuku Umar. Open 24hr.

Medical Services: Sanglah Public Hospital, Jl. Kesehatan Selatan 1 (tel. 227 911). **24-hour clinic: Manuaba Clinic,** Jl. Cokroaminoto 28 (tel. 226 393).

Emergency: Police: tel. 110. **Ambulance:** tel. 118.

Police: (tel. 234 928) on Jl. Gunung Agung, or (tel. 225 456) on Jl. A. Yani.

Post Offices: GPO (tel. 223 565), on Jl. Raya Puputan in Renon, way to the south. *Poste Restante.* Open daily 8am-9pm. **Branch,** Jl. Kamboja 6, outside Kereneng Terminal. Both open daily 8am-9pm. **Postal Code:** 80235.

Telephones: Wartel offering cash international calls are scattered about town. The **phone office,** Jl. Teuku Umar 6, near the intersection with Jl. Diponegoro offers international, collect, or calling card calls from booths. Calls can also be made from hotels. **Telephone code:** 0361.

ACCOMMODATIONS

Few tourists stay for more than a few hours in Denpasar; this is probably both the cause and the effect of the few quality budget accommodations available. Many cheaper hotels and *losmen* in Denpasar will turn away western wanderers by explaining that their suspiciously quiet rooms are "full." This usually means that the managers want to avoid the hassle of filling out the police report required for foreign visitors. If you find a particularly good deal and will be staying in Denpasar for a few days, offer to make the report in person; the hotel may allow you to stay. The procedure is simple: bring your passport, dress conservatively, and explain that you wish to file a report on behalf of your accommodation.

Nakula Familiar Inn, Jl. Nakula 4 (tel. 226 446), on the same street as the popular Adi Tasa Hotel, about a 5-min. walk to Bandung Market. The best budget accommodation in the city. Huge clean rooms with private bath, porch, and ceiling fan. Singles Rp20,000. Doubles Rp25,000. Breakfast and drinking water included.

Adi Yasa, Jl. Nakula 23B (tel. 222 679), about 50m from Nekula Familar Inn. Popular with westerners and domestic tourists. The rooms are worn and musty but the service is earnest. Singles Rp12,500, with bath Rp15,000. Doubles Rp15,000, with bath Rp20,000. Breakfast included, but their other food is best avoided. The neighbor's pet monkey can elevate noise levels considerably.

Two Brothers Losmen, on Jl. G. Wilis near the Tegal *bemo* station. Convenient if coming from or going to Kuta. With your back to the station walk left and take a left onto Jl. G. Wilis. Pleasant, *losmen* set-up, with rooms around a central garden. Singles Rp10,000, with bath Rp15,000. Doubles Rp15,000, with bath Rp20,000. Breakfast included.

FOOD

Few tourists and the widespread presence of minority groups means good news for cheap dining options. Jl. Sumatra/Diponegoro is flanked with cheap, clean, casual eateries. Excellent *nasi campur* and *mie ayam* (Rp2000) can be found anywhere along the street. A **night market** behind the Bandung Market offers Rp1000 *warung* dishes (open daily 6pm-midnight). Another night market comes to life on Jl. Diponegoro near the **Kertha Wijaya Shopping Centre,** and there are **warung** set up throughout the day at Kereneng *bemo* terminal. Denpasar's **supermarkets** and surprisingly good **food courts** can be found in all the shopping centers; **Dewata Ayu Supermarket** (open daily 8am-midnight) is at the intersection of Jl. Teuku Umar and Jl. Sudirman, the **Tiara Dewata Supermarket** is at the north end of Jl. Sudirman, and the Kertha Wijaya Complex with a **Matahari Supermarket** is on Jl. Diponegoro 98, within walking distance of Jl. Hasanudin and Denpasar's market area.

Pondok Indah, Jl. Diponegoro 134 (tel. 327 85). A mostly Balinese menu with English translations of various fish, frog, and steak entrees (Rp3-7000). Tables are set up outside on the concrete, barely sheltered from the multi-laned Jl. Dipone-

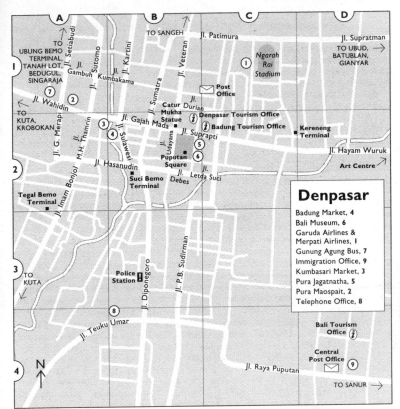

Denpasar

Badung Market, **4**
Bali Museum, **6**
Garuda Airlines &
Merpati Airlines, **I**
Gunung Agung Bus, **7**
Immigration Office, **9**
Kumbasari Market, **3**
Pura Jagatnatha, **5**
Pura Maospait, **2**
Telephone Office, **8**

goro. Also a choice spot for trying the Balinese food you've curiously eyed in less tourist-friendly hangouts. Fried carp with sweet and sour sauce (Rp7500). Divine *es teler* (sweet iced coconut and avocado drink/dessert, Rp1250).

Rumah Makan Betty, Jl. Sumatra 56, 1 block east of Jl. Sulawesi. One of several small, low-budget eateries on Jl. Sumatra that cater to Indonesians. Betty is a large, glassed-in, cafeteria-like joint specializing in East Javanese food and is unique for its popularity with expats. Very good. Popular *sop buntut* (soup) with pork Rp3000. Some vegetarian options. Open daily 7am-9pm.

Warung Nasi Bali, Jl. Hayam Wuruk 69A (tel. 223 889). Walk east (left) from the Kereneng *bemo* station, on Jl. Hayam Wuruk. It's on the left, 350m before Jl. Nusa Indah (the locale of several other small restaurants). The *warung* has no menu, but offers well-prepared Balinese delicacies like *lawar* and *babi guling* (braised suckling pig) at unbelievably good prices (Rp3000). Open daily 7:30am-6pm.

SIGHTS

East of Puputan Square on Jl. Mayor Wisnu stands Denpasar's primary attraction, the **Bali Museum.** Arranged around airy courtyards, buildings resembling different forms of traditional Balinese architecture house artifacts that provide newcomers with an introduction to Balinese society and history. Unfortunately, the museum does not have English-speaking tour guides or detailed labels. Wandering through the well-maintained courtyards and rooms informs and educates nonetheless. The tourist office offers an English-language brochure on the museum. (Open Tues.-Thurs. and Sat.-Sun. 7:30am-2:30pm, Fri. 7-11:30am; admission Rp200.)

The unusual Hindu temple of **Pura Jaganatha** reposes next to the museum. A tall, intricately carved steeple headed by a gold Hindu figurine is surrounded by two square levels and a lime-green moat. Tourists can walk around the exterior of the moat only. The temple is crowded in the afternoons and the evenings of *purnama* (full moon) and *tilem* (dark moon), when Balinese bring offerings and prayers to the moon. *Wayang kulit* begin on *purnama* or *tilem* at approximately 9pm.

Puputan Square, outside the museum and Pura Jaganatha, is a large, clean, grassy field with a monument, fountain, and benches at its north side. The monument depicts a family prepared to enter battle, commemorating the solemn, suicidal *puputan* of 1906, when the last king of Badung followed by family, court, and followers refused surrender and marched into the bullets of invading Dutch soldiers.

Every June and July, Bali holds an **art festival** with dances, music, and exhibits at the **Werdi Budaya Art Centre** (tel. 227 176), at the corner of Jl. Hayam Wuruk and Jl. Nusa Indah. The tourist office provides a schedule of events. The Art Centre also holds a nightly *kecak* performance, unique to Bali, from 6:30-7:30pm (admission Rp6000). *Kecak* is a dance and musical event characterized by the percussive, monkey-like chattering and "chak-chak-chak"-ing of the male chorus.

■ Near Denpasar

PURA ULUWATU

Pura Uluwatu overlooks cliffs on the southwest tip of Bukit Peninsula, the mushroom shaped area south of Denpasar and Kuta. Uluwatu is one of the *Sadkahyangan,* the six most important temples in Bali. The temple's construction, thought to date from the 11th century, is associated with the Hindu saint Danhyang Nirartha, who explored Bali in 1500 BC. Nirartha is reputed to have achieved *moksa,* or unity with God, at Uluwatu. The temple itself is relatively modest but perches at the very edge of dark, vertical cliffs that fall 70m into waves crashing at the rocks below. Visitors who wish to pray may enter the temple's inner court. Uluwatu is also popular with **surfing** enthusiasts; the Kuta tourist office has information on board rentals.

Reaching Uluwatu can be a challenge via public transportation. *Bemo* leave for Uluwatu from Denpasar's Tegal Station in the morning only. From Kuta, pick up the *bemo* from Tegal by waiting on the road heading away from the Duty Free Shop, near the gas pump on Jl. Raya Kuta. *Bemo* may run all the way to Uluwatu or may drop you at Pecatu on the Bukit Peninsula, from where you can hire an *ojek* (about Rp1000) to the temple. Private transport can be hired from Kuta for Rp20,000. The distance from Kuta to Uluwatu is bike-able (20km), but the roads near the temple are excruciatingly steep. (Open 5am until the last visitors have left; admission Rp1000, children Rp500; sarong and sash rental Rp500.)

■ Sanur

Despite its half-hour proximity to Kuta, Sanur hosts an entirely different scene than its lascivious neighbor. The dominant creatures here are middle-aged package tourists sustaining varying levels of sunburn, slowly treading Sanur's 3km stretch of clean, quiet, and safe beach. Although less obvious a presence, a large number of Hindu priests from Brahmin families also call Sanur home. These residents are concerned with placating the powerful spirits which inhabit the ocean and managing the cultural damage brought by large-scale tourism. Although the price of living in Sanur is noticeably higher than in surrounding areas, it's not a hopeless cause for the budgeteer—there are a few reasonably priced places to stay and the rupiah-conscious can entertain themselves by sneaking into hotel pools and accessing the beach through air-conditioned lobbies.

ORIENTATION

Strictly speaking, Sanur is a part of Denpasar, but it's a self-contained area from a tourist's perspective. The area can be divided into three parallel strips. Along the beach is an almost continuous boardwalk, dominated mostly by large hotels, restaurants, and water sport rental establishments. Parallel to the boardwalk and about 50m inland is **Jalan Danau Tamblingan (Jalan Tanjung Sari** at its south end). Here are the resorts, most of Sanur's restaurants and tourist-oriented boutiques, postal agents, craft shops, and tour agencies. Parallel to Jl. Danau Tamblingan and about 150m inland is the busy thoroughfare of **Jalan Ngurah Rai Bypass** (also known as **Bypass Road**) where the supermarket is located. The grounds of the Bali Hyatt dominate the south end of Sanur while the grounds of the even bigger Bali Beach Hotel dominate the north. The northernmost cross street is **Jalan Hang Tuah** which becomes **Jalan Sanur** on its way to Denpasar. Farther south is **Jalan Segara,** which becomes **Jalan Danau Buyan** as it heads west, after crossing Bypass Rd.

PRACTICAL INFORMATION

Tourist Offices: The nearest official office is in Kuta, but hotels and tour operators provide info and copious offers to take travelers wherever they might want to go. Private tour and travel offices are plentiful on Jl. Danau Tamblingan.

Embassies and Consulates: US, Jl. Segara Ayu 5 (tel. 288 478), on a small street just south of the Bali Beach Hotel. Denpasar proper has other foreign consulates.

Currency Exchange: Money changers on Jl. Danau Tamblingan and the beach boardwalk have better rates than hotels (except for the bank offices in the Bali Beach Hotel). Bali Bank **ATM** at the supermarket accepts MC, Visa, and Cirrus.

American Express: Representative office in the **Bali Beach Hotel** (tel. 288 449). Card holders can buy traveler's checks. The office does not hold packages but holds letters if addressed c/o PACTO (AMEX), Hotel Bali Beach, Sanur, Denpasar. Open Mon.-Fri. 8:30am-4:30pm, Sat. 8:30am-12:30pm.

Air Travel: Bali's **Ngurah Rai Airport** is about 40min. away by taxi (Rp12,000), or take a blue *bemo* to Tegal Station. The Bali Beach Hotel has an entire wing dedicated to airline offices where numerous international airlines are represented. Offices are open Mon.-Fri. 9am-5pm, Sat. 9am-noon.

Inter-city Transportation: To **Denpasar,** take a green *bemo* to Kereneng Station. Blue *bemo* go south to Tegal Station, where there are connections to Kuta and the airport. Private shuttle services to destinations all over Bali are available from tour offices. Taxis are plentiful and always waiting at hotel entrances.

Local Transportation: Flag down a **bemo** going your way (Rp300 for short distances within Sanur). The *bemo* terminal is at the end of Jl. Danau Tamblingan.

Rentals: Wirasana, Jl. Danau Tamblingan 126 (tel. 288 706) and Jl. Ngurah Rai Bypass 545x (tel. 286 066), opposite the police station. Cheapest cars Rp40,000 per day with insurance. Motorbikes Rp15,000 per day. MC, Visa.

Medical Services: Bali Beach Hotel has a **clinic** (tel. 288 511, ask for the clinic). Open Mon.-Sat. 7am-8pm, Sun. 10am-6pm. Call anytime in case of emergency.

Emergency: Police: tel. 110. **Ambulance:** tel. 118.

Police: (tel. 288 597), on Bypass Rd., at the edge of the golf course.

Post Offices: GPO, Jl. Danau Buyan. *Poste Restante* should be sent to: GPO, Banjar Taman. Open Mon.-Fri. 1-5pm, Sat.-Sun. 9am–noon. **Postal code:** 80228.

Telephones: Local, collect, and cash international calls can be made at the *wartel* near where Jl. Segara crosses Bypass Rd. Another *wartel* is located across from The Watering Hole on Jl. Hang Tuah. The **Bali Beach Hotel** has a 24-hr. **HCD** phone which accepts credit card calls (located behind the south lobby, between the main tower and cottage wing). **Telephone code:** 0361.

ACCOMMODATIONS

For its small size, Sanur has a fair number of reasonably priced accommodations, although none are low-budget in the true sense of the word. For Rp20,000, however, travelers can comfortably hit the hay near the beach and feel smug: those paying 20 times more can't be having that much more fun. The cheapest rooms are in three hotels, sitting side by side on Jl. Danau Buyan: **Hotel Sanur-Indah, Hotel Taman Sari,** and **Hotel Rani.** For a more isolated, less institutional feel the three side by side homestays on Jl. Danau Tamblingan offer similarly priced rooms: **Coco's Homestay** (tel. 287 391), **Luisa** (tel. 289 673), and **Yulia's** (tel. 288 089).

The Watering Hole, Jl. Hang Tuah 35 (tel. 288 289). Fronted by a restaurant of the same name, The Watering Hole is very pleasant, with fastidious and amiable owners. Well-kept rooms around a central garden. Singles Rp20,000. Doubles Rp26,000, with A/C Rp35,000. Discounts for longer stays.

Ananda Beach Hotel, Jl. Hang Tuah 43 (tel 288 327), north of the Bali Beach Hotel. Fantastic beachside value. Most of the 2nd floor rooms have a view of the water. Most singles Rp20,000. Doubles Rp25,000 and up. There are also 2 rooms for Rp15,000 that are acceptable, if rather dingy. If you want these rooms, the management may try to persuade you otherwise; be insistent about finding out if these rooms are full.

FOOD

Most restaurants, like everything else in Sanur, are tourist-oriented and overpriced. There are many elegant looking spots on Jl. Danau Tamblingan, which have breakfast buffets for Rp2500 and dance performances during dinner. **Bali Moon** serves Italian food worthy of its prices (pasta Rp9-12,000). For cheaper eats, many local restaurants serve *padang* food—there are several on Bypass Rd. and a very popular one next to the Ananda Hotel. A full plate runs about Rp2000. **Warung** carts serving *bakso* (Rp1000) and roasted corn (Rp500) scatter along the north end of the beach and are plentiful at the **night market** on the north end of Jl. Danau Tamblingan.

Choice Bakery and Coffee Shop, Jl. Danau Tamblingan 150 (tel. 288 401). Health-conscious food and homemade baked goods for great prices. Brown bread with papaya jam, Rp1500. Try the Thai *tom yam sai* (chicken, mushrooms, veggies, chili, and coconut milk, Rp4000). Open daily 7:30a.m-9:30pm.

Warung Lesse'an, Jl. Danau Toba 10B (tel. 286 343), across the street from the large Istana Garden Restaurant. Fantastic Indonesian dishes, artfully presented and at prices that tempt travelers to order half of the small menu. *Nasi liwet* dinner Rp3200. Wide variety of neon fruit juices Rp1000.

Rumah Makan Sanur, to the left after the entrance to Sindu Market. One of the least expensive places for a sit-down dinner. Bright lights and not much ambiance, but the large glass windows provide endless hours of people-watching. *Nasi campur* Rp2000. Open daily 7am-10pm.

SIGHTS

There is an invisible line along the northern side of Sanur's beach, dividing the rocky dark shore from the tan sandy beaches. This is also the de facto separation point between local beach-goers and foreign tourists. To the north, locals come to bathe, fish, and fly kites. An almost audible hush occurs as you walk south to the serene beaches at Sanur's resorts where reddening foreigners in various stages of undress quietly sunbathe and sip fruity drinks. Sanur's only non-beach related sight is the **Museum Le Mayeur.** The entrance is beach-side on Sanur's north end. Facing the beach with the Bali Beach Hotel's pool at your back, walk left. The former home of Belgian artist Le Mayeur (who lived in Bali during 1930-60), the museum houses the artists's work. (Open Tues.-Thurs. and Sun. 8am-2pm, Fri.-Sat. 9am-noon; admission Rp200.) During low tide, one can explore the reef teeming with sea creatures at the beach outside the Bali Beach Hotel.

ENTERTAINMENT

Nightlife in Sanur exists in the technical sense—there are a couple of discos along Jl. Danau Tamblingan. **Subec** and the **No. 1** are the most popular (Rp10,000 cover). **JJ's Bar** on the same strip is open until 2am. Activity here tends to assume the form of pleasant conversation. For real nightlife, head to Kuta.

Check restaurants for schedules of evening Balinese dance and *gamelan* performances. The **Sanur Beach Hotel** (tel. 288 011), at the far south end of the main drag, has a Frog Dance performance on Sundays, Legong dance on Mondays, and *Ramayana* ballet on Wednesdays. (Performances run 7:30-11:30pm; admission Rp47,000 with buffet dinner, Rp10,000 without.) **Swastika Restaurant II,** Jl. Danau Tamblingan 124, near the art market, has Frog Dance performances on Thursdays and Legong dances on Sundays, both at 8:30pm.

Sanur is considerably more lively during the day, when a range of water sports are available (for a price). The **Kantor Jelati Willis** booth on Sanur Beach, where Jl. Segara runs into the sand, offers the largest range of rental and activity options, including a traditional sailing boat with driver (1hr., $10), windsurfing (1hr., $15), snorkeling equipment (1hr., $3), waterskiing (15min., $15), parasailing (once around, $10), and scuba diving (see instructors).

■ Near Sanur: Nusa Lembongan

Boats leave for Lembongan Island between 8:30 and 9am right outside the Ananda Hotel (1½hr., Rp15,000). White sand, blue waters, and hardly a tourist in sight—Lembongan is a well-kept secret of surfers who brave the three large breaks over its reef. The few places for food and accommodation are in the northwest corner of the island, about 1km north of where the boat drops you off (with the water to your back, walk left). The **Main Sa Inn and Restaurant** offers Rp15,000 rooms with incomparable views on the second floor as well as good information about the island. Next door, **Agung's Lodge** has basic Rp5000 rooms and a very good budget-friendly restaurant. A 2½-hour walk around the whole island is pleasant, and the island's views of the water at dusk are superb. The only way to get off the island is the way you came; boats leave for Sanur between 10 and 10:30am.

■ Kuta

One thing about Kuta is for certain—everyone has an opinion about it. The various attitudes held about the most infamous tourist destination in Bali can be approximated into three general categories. In the first is contempt and disdain; many a visitor to Kuta has promptly run in the opposite direction, desperate to get away from the scantily dressed crowds, and aggressive merchants. Second is bemusement; Kuta is one of the few places where the tourists have themselves become an attraction. Third, and last, is pure, unadulterated love. Kuta is a hectic international scene of cheap restaurants and accommodations, bustling markets and crowded nightspots—all along a beautiful, surfable, sandy beach. Those looking for surf, sun, beer, and social interaction at all levels (with all orientations) will not be disappointed.

ORIENTATION

Kuta refers to an area of dense tourist development—one that continuously grows in all directions along the southwest tip of Bali Island; it now incorporates Legian to the north and Tuban to the south of Kuta proper. Most of the action still takes place in central Kuta's three streets: **Jalan Legian, Jalan Melasti,** and **Jalan Pantai Kuta.** Along with the beach boardwalk they form a rectangle which contains most of the activity. Small *gang* cut through the rectangle (mostly connecting Jl. Legian to the beach) and offer innumerable cheap room and food options. The most popular is **Poppies Gang**

I which can be entered either on Jl. Legian or Jl. Pantai Kuta. **Bemo Corner** is located where Jl. Legian and Jl. Pantai Kuta intersect. The **Ngurah Rai International Airport** is 15 minutes south by taxi, in Tuban.

PRACTICAL INFORMATION

Tourist Offices: Bali Government Tourism Information Centre (tel. 754 090), in Legian's Century Plaza on Jl. Bensari. **Kuta Tourist Information** (tel. 755 424) is more centrally located. Open Mon.-Fri. 7am-5pm. Look around the nicer shops for a free copy of the very helpful *Bali Plus Tourist Guide.*

Tours and Travel: Agencies spill out of every street and alleyway.

Immigration Offices: Jl. I Gusti Ngurah Rai, Tuban (tel. 751 038).

Currency Exchange: Money changers and **banks** galore line Jl. Legian and Jl. Pantai Kuta. Glance at a few of the exchange boards as rates can differ dramatically. Money changers offer rates at least a few rupiah lower than banks, but are more convenient and stay open until 9pm. Banks close by 2pm on weekdays and by noon on Sat. Banks and most money changers are closed on Sun. **24-hr. Bali Bank ATM** in Kuta Square Shopping Centre on Jl. Pantai Kuta. MC, Visa, Cirrus.

Air Travel: Ngurah Rai Airport, 15min. by taxi, bargain for a price before getting in (about Rp6000). **Garuda,** Natour Kuta Beach Hotel, Jl. Pantai Kuta 1 (tel. 751 179). **Singapore Airlines,** Ngurah Rai Airport (tel. 751 011, ext. 2119). **Sir New Zealand,** Kartika Plaza Beach Hotel, Kartika Plaza (tel. 753 593), **KLM,** Wisti Sabha Building, Ngurah Rai Airport.

Local Transportation: Bemo run from **Bemo Corner** along Jl. Pantai Kuta to the beach and to Legian. You can catch *bemo* going to Denpasar's Tegal Station on Jl. Tanjung Sari. *Bemo* can also be chartered. Private shuttle schedules for destinations on Bali and Java on street corners everywhere. Airport shuttle Rp5000.

Rentals: Cars go for Rp35,000 per day at most tour and travel agencies. One to try is **CV Wisata Motor Co.** (tel. 751 474) on Jl. Imam Bonjol.

Medical Services: 24-hr. Natour Clinic (tel. 751 361), at the beach end of Jl. Pantai Kuta. English-speaking staff does surfing injuries and beyond. Also **Kuta Clinic** (tel. 753 268), on Jl. Raya Kuta.

Emergency: Police: tel. 110. **Ambulance:** tel. 118 or 279 11.

Police: (tel. 751 598), on Jl. Raya Tuban, across from Bank Duta.

Post Offices: GPO (tel. 754 012), on Jl. Raya Tuban south of central Kuta. From *Bemo* Corner, head south on Jl. Bunisari, turn left on Jl. Kartika Plaza/Bakungsari, and a right onto Jl. Raya Tuban. The GPO is opposite the elementary school. *Poste Restante.* Open Mon.-Fri. 8am-4pm, Sat.-Sun. 8-11am. More conveniently located is **Ida's Postal Agent** (tel. 751 574), on Jl. Legian Kuta at the intersection with Poppies Gang II. *Poste Restante.* Open Mon.-Sat. 8am-8pm. **Postal code:** 80361.

Telephones: International **wartel** are all over, including one centrally located at the Kuta Square Shopping Centre. There's a **HCD** booth on the 1st floor of the Matahari Department Store in Kuta Square. A **24-hr. HCD** booth stands on the beach, directly across from the Bali Anggrek Inn. E-mail receiving/transmitting is available at Wartel Kambodiana in Kuta Square (tel. 753 330; e-mail kambodiana@denpasar.wasantara.net.id). **Telephone code:** 62361.

ACCOMMODATIONS

Finding a relatively inexpensive place to stay in Kuta is easy-cheesy; just stand on any street corner with a pack on your back and before long someone will holler "Room?! Need room!?" Even the cheapest *losmen* have flush toilets, showers, and fans. Prices usually include breakfast: fruit salad and a jaffle or pancake with tea. If you've got your sights set on the quieter Legian area, look for *losmen* on Jl. Melasti and Jl. Padma. Any more north and you'll be in mid-range, package tour territory. In central Kuta, low-budget places to crash cluster in the Poppies Gang I and II area. Bargain everywhere, particularly if things seem quiet.

Puri Agung, on Gang Bedugul. Turn onto Poppies Gang I from Jl. Legian, then take the first right; it's a short way down on the right. The rooms could stand to be rein-

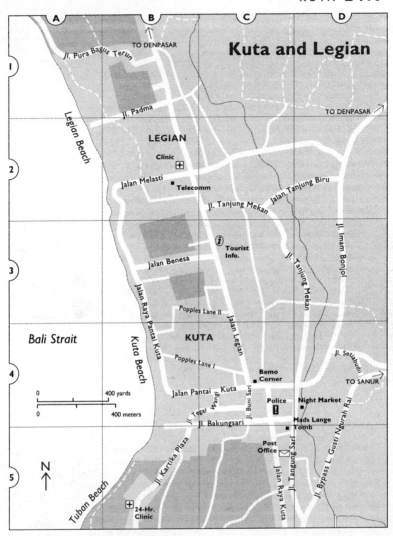

Kuta and Legian

TO DENPASAR

Jl. Pura Bagus Terun

Jl. Padma

TO DENPASAR

LEGIAN

Legian Beach

Clinic

Jalan Melasti

Telecomm

Jl. Tanjung Mekan

Jalan Tanjung Biru

(i) Tourist Info.

Jalan Benesa

Jl. Tanjung Mekan

Jl. Imam Bonjol

Popples Lane II

Jalan Legian

Bali Strait

Jalan Raya Pantai Kuta

KUTA

Kuta Beach

Popples Lane I

Jl. Setiabudi

Bemo Corner

TO SANUR

0   400 yards

0   400 meters

Jalan Pantai Kuta

Jl. Tegal Wangi Kuta

Jl. Buni Sari

Police

Night Market

Jl. Bakungsari

Mads Lange Tomb

Jl. Bypass I. Gusti Ngurah Rai

Jl. Raya Kuta

Jalan Raya Kuta

N ↑

Jl. Kartika Plaza

Post Office

Jl. Tanjung

Tuban Beach

✚ 24-Hr. Clinic

carnated but they're about right for the price and central location. Close to the action, but generally out of earshot. Singles Rp15,000. Doubles Rp20,000.

Taman Ayu, opposite Puri Agung on Gang Bedugul. 15 rooms clustered around a compound. Rooms are comparable to Puri Agung's, but smaller. Singles with fan and bath Rp10,000. Doubles Rp15,000.

Suci Bungalows, Jl. Pantai 25 (tel. 753 761), halfway down the street on the left if your back's to the beach. Each room has its own little porch, overhead fan, and bamboo lounge chair facing a well-manicured garden. Some rooms have reminders of their age, but they're generally attractive. Suci couldn't be more in the heart of things, which makes it convenient, but not necessarily desirable. Singles Rp15,000. Doubles Rp20,000. Rates are seasonal.

FOOD

It's easy to find spaghetti, burgers, and pizza in Kuta but hard to find Balinese cuisine. If you want to get away from the **food emporium** above the McDonald's has reliable fare in a fast-food setting. To join the ruckus, follow the crowd to the most tourist-friendly **night market** in Indonesia. Prices are a few hundred rupiah higher than usual but menus are in English and no one will stare. From Jl. Pantai Kuta, walk away from the beach and take your third right. The market is 100m down on your left. **Warung** are sparsely scattered on Jl. Pantai Kuta but roasted corn sellers (try it with the chili butter) cluster along the beach boardwalk at sunset (Rp1000). Restaurants without bars close at 11pm.

Warung Kopi (tel. 753 602), near the intersection with Jl. Padma. It lives up to its reputation of excellent Indian-inspired cooking and friendly service. South Indian pumpkin curry Rp7000. A very popular Indian buffet on Wednesday evenings after 7pm (Rp10,000)—make a reservation. Open daily 8am-11:30pm.

Bamboo Corner, on Poppies Gang I. Clean and pleasant despite its very budget-friendly prices. Unfortunately, the noisy *gang* makes itself known. Only dine at the sidewalk tables if you're looking to buy a watch, perfume, or a couple of hours with a prostitute. Chicken curry Rp35000. Open daily 8am-10pm.

Warung Murah, on Jl. Legian, even more northward than Warung Kopi on the beach side of Jl. Legian past Jl. Bagus Teruna. *Murah* means cheap and it lives up to its name, with Chinese and Indonesian-inspired seafood and soups, all Rp2000-2500. Be communal and share the long picnic-like table with other bargain-seeking customers. Open daily 8:30am-11pm.

TJ's, on Poppies Gang I, on the side nearest Jl. Pantai Kuta. *The* Mexican restaurant in Bali. Legendary for its *fajitas,* margaritas, and chocolate diablo cake. Worth the likely wait (especially after 7pm) and steep-ish prices. Dinner runs about Rp10,000, including a small beer.

ENTERTAINMENT AND NIGHTLIFE

With more organized forms (although rarely orderly) of entertainment than even Aussie schoolboys know what to do with, Kuta boasts no less than four **bungee-jumping** towers, a **waterslide park,** several **billiard halls** (although pool is free all day at Casablanca's Bar on Jl. Buni Sari), and a couple of **arcades.** Surfboards are available for rent on the beach by the hour (pay no more than Rp4000). **Waterbom Park** (tel. 755 676), on Jl. Kartika Plaza in Tuban is a five-minute walk southwards from *Bemo* Corner. Waterslides, tubing, and an electric-generated wavepool. For better or worse, you'd hardly know you were in Indonesia. (Open daily 9am-6pm; standard Rp15,000; MC and Visa.) Bungee-jumping packages are available at: **A.J. Hackett** (tel. 730 666), next door to Double Six Nightclub; **Adrenalin Park,** near McDonald's on Jl. Legian; **Bali Bungy Co.** (tel. 752 658), on Jl. Pura Puseh; and **Bungee in Bali** (tel. (0361) 758 362), 30 minutes away in Gianyar. These packages start at US$45 including hotel pick-up, t-shirt, and a photo of your jump. Bungee in Bali jumps customers over a waterfall, while the others do it over a pool.

Kuta's nightlife turns on hours after visitors to Bali's other hot spots are dreaming of tomorrow's fried prawns. Unless you have Solid Gold technique you may not want to start shaking your booty until after 2am when the crowd faucet turns on full force. Two of the most popular clubs in Kuta are owned by the same person and alternate nights. **Gado-Gado** (tel. 730 955), off Jl. Dhyana Pura in Legian, and **Double Six,** slightly south of its sibling, are popular clubs with a spectrum of nationalities, sexes, orientations, and services. (Gado-Gado open Tues., Wed., and Thurs. 11:30pm-4:30am; Double Six open Mon., Fri., and Sat., at the same time; Rp10,000 cover for both, includes one drink). Other clubs and bars cluster along Jl. Legian. **The Bounty Club,** a pirate ship-cum-restaurant/bar/disco with no cover and nearby **Peanuts**

Disco attract the highest concentration of raging surfer types. Peanuts hosts a Pub Crawl (Tues. and Sat.). The Rp3000 ticket price includes transport, any entrance fees, and participation in its drinking contests. When all is said and done, they will deposit you on the steps of your homestay. Kuta's Alcoholics Anonymous chapter (tel. 751 442) is not an altogether surprising development. As a general rule, the scene in Legian attracts more Europeans and has a significant gay presence. The bars and clubs in Kuta are Australian-dominated and cater to a younger set.

■ Near Kuta: Tanah Lot

The walk from Kuta Beach to **Tanah Lot,** the most photographed sea-side temple in all of Bali, is a 4½-hour barefoot hike across deserted beaches. En route, those who avoid the expensive shuttle tours to Tanah Lot will be rewarded with rice paddies and dramatic rock formations. The path is simple—just get on the beach at Kuta, with the water to the left, and keep walking. You can eye ball the distance from Kuta, rather symbolically, by watching the A.J. Hackett Bungy Jumping Tower slowly disappear. Cliffs or rock reefs occasionally force walking off the beach, but the paths around them are obvious. The only real challenge comes 100m before Tanah Lot, where a massive hotel/golf resort is being erected. The staff there can point out where the cleanest path through the rubble. Bring plenty of water and sunscreen. From Tanah Lot (in and of itself not really worth seeing), it's a long circuitous *bemo* trip back to Kuta: take a *bemo* from Tanah Lot to Kediri (20min., Rp500) to catch a *bemo* to Denpasar's Udang Terminal (Rp500). From there, take a *bemo* to Tegal Station (Rp400) where large minibuses constantly leave for Kuta (Rp700). Alternatively, you can find a tour bus in the Tanah Lot parking lot going to Kuta and try to convince the driver to let you hitch a ride. Make sure to get to Tanah Lot before 4pm, since *bemo* run unpredictably after then. The trip can also be done in reverse—*bemo* it to Tanah Lot and walk along the water back to Kuta with the advantage of getting the sun on your back.

▒ Ubud

Most travelers to Ubud end up staying days, months, or years longer than they'd planned. A European yuppie enclave an hour's bus ride north of Denpasar, Ubud is no less developed than Kuta, but most find Ubud's galleries, craft shops, and international cafés tasteful and the pace of life relaxing. Home to artist cooperatives, meditation centers, vegetarian-friendly restaurants, and hundreds of permanent visitors from the west, central Ubud is literally steps away from rice fields, isolated temples, and traditional villages. Those intent on raging nightlife or avoiding tourists should look elsewhere, but most find something to love about Ubud: the food is good, rooms are cheap, and there is no shortage of culturally oriented activities.

ORIENTATION

Ubud's main drag, **Jalan Raya Ubud,** runs north-south until it reaches the town's most touristed area, where it turns and heads east-west. Most other major roads are perpendicular to it. South of Jl. Raya Ubud on the west side of town, **Jalan Monkey Forest** runs alongside the market to Ubud's monkey forest. There it U-turns and becomes **Jalan Hanoman,** which leads back onto Jl. Raya Ubud, east of the market. Farther east, parallel to Jl. Monkey Forest and Jl. Hanoman, are **Jalan Sugriwa, Jalan Jembawan, Jalan Tebe/Saya/Sukma,** and, at the top of the hill, **Jalan Raya Peliatan,** which heads south and then east, where it intersects the road to Denpasar. North of Jl. Raya Ubud, Jl. Raya Peliatan becomes **Jalan Raya Andong/Tegalalang,** which runs past the police station and the **Telkom office** toward Kintamani. North of Jl. Raya Ubud, from west to east, are **Jalan Kajang** (bordering the Museum Puri Lukisan), **Jalan Suweta** (opposite Jl. Monkey Forest), **Jalan Sri Wedari** (opposite Jl. Hanoman), **Jalan Sandat** (opposite Jl. Sugriwa), **Jalan Tirta Tawar, Jalan Jerogandung,** and Jl. Raya Andong/Tegalalang.

PRACTICAL INFORMATION

Tourist Offices: Ubud Tourist Information (tel. 962 85), on Jl. Raya Ubud. Provides performance schedules, workshop info, a partial listing of nearby accommodations, and a free message board. Open daily 8am-9pm. Many **private tourist information centers** offer private transport, car/bike rentals, guides, and other services. For events like cremations, it is highly recommended that you have a guide. The tourist office and the Pondok Pekak resource center can help.

Currency Exchange: Money-changers all over the city give rates slightly lower than banks but are open until 8pm. Banks can do money transfers from credit cards. **Bank Danamon,** on Jl. Raya Ubud. Open Mon.-Fri. 8am-2pm, Sat. 8-11am.

Local Transportation: Bemo hang in front of the market from before dawn until dusk. Brown *bemo* head south to **Batubulan,** half-way to Denpasar (Rp1000). From there it is Rp800 to **Denpasar,** Rp700 to **Sanur** and **Kuta.** Batubulan is also the major connection point for *bemo* heading to eastern destinations. The last *bemo* from Batubulan to Ubud leaves between 4 and 5pm. Orange *bemo* head east to Gianyar (not a convenient location to make further connections). **Taxis** can be found along Jl. Raya Ubud and Jl. Monkey Forest. **Shuttle bus** services are offered by tourist info centers, travel agencies, and some homestays. Times and fares are listed on storefronts. To: **airport/Sanur/Kuta** (Rp7000); **Kintamani/Lovina** (Rp6-11,000); and **Candi Dasa/Padangbai** (Rp8000).

Rentals: Most tourist offices rent cars, bikes, and motorbikes. Prices are negotiable. Sedans are about Rp40,000, with insurance Rp50,000; motorbikes Rp10,000, with insurance Rp15,000; push bikes Rp3-5000. (All prices for 12hr.)

Markets: At the corner of Jl. Raya Ubud and Jl. Monkey Forest. Sales of fruits and vegetables begin before dawn. Livestock sold every 3 days. Clothes, hardware, handicrafts, and more. Stalls open 7am until evening, some until 11pm.

Pharmacies: Ubud Farma (tel. 974 214), on Jl. Raya Ubud, opposite the post office. Open daily 8am-10pm. Their clinic open Mon.-Sat. 5-7pm.

Medical Services: Ubud Clinic, Jl. Raya Ubud 36 (tel. 974 911), toward Campuhan. English-speaking service. Also makes housecalls.

Police: (tel. 975 316), opposite the Telkom office on Jl. Raya Andong.

Post Offices: on Jl. Jembawan, off Jl. Raya Ubud. *Poste Restante.* Large envelopes and packages filed separately. Open Mon.-Thurs. 8am-noon and 1-4pm, Fri. 8-11:30am and 1-4pm. **Postal code:** 80571.

Telephones: 24-hr. HCD booths at the post office, the main Ubud market, and the Telkom office opposite the police station. **Nomad Telecommunication Service,** Jl. Raya Ubud 33x (tel. 975 520), next door to Nomad Restaurant on the 2nd floor, is quieter but charges a fee for credit card and collect calls. Fax service. Open daily 8am-11pm. **Information:** tel. 118. **Telephone code:** 0361.

ACCOMMODATIONS

Ubud provides the best selection of rooms on the island. Rooms typically come with a fan, private bath, porch, traditional garden, and breakfast. Signs on the main road and on Jl. Monkey Forest direct travelers to several dozen such high quality, low price places. The quietest, most secluded rooms can be found on Jl. Jembawan.

Anom Bungalows, on a small lane off of Jl. Monkey Forest. The turn-off to Anom is across the Bank BNI. Large bungalows with ceiling fan and mosquito netting. Singles Rp10,000. Doubles with private bath Rp12,500.

Rice Paddy Bungalows, Jl. Hanoman 55, at the end of Jl. Hanoman away from the main street, diagonal from Three Brothers restaurant. Rooms have hot showers and a large bed. Singles Rp15,000. Doubles Rp20,000.

Taman Indah Homestay, on Jl. Sandat. Follow signs on Jl. Raya Ubud: "Taman Indah, in rice field, very peaceful." Indeed, it is set back from Ubud's main hustle and bustle. Check yourself in if the owner is not around. Rooms have fans and mosquito nets. Singles Rp10,000. Doubles Rp15,000.

Parnama Accommodation, at the end of Jl. Hanoman heading toward the Monkey Forest. The most luxury possible in a budget room with a hot shower and a private, luxuriously furnished veranda. Singles Rp25,000. Doubles Rp30,000.

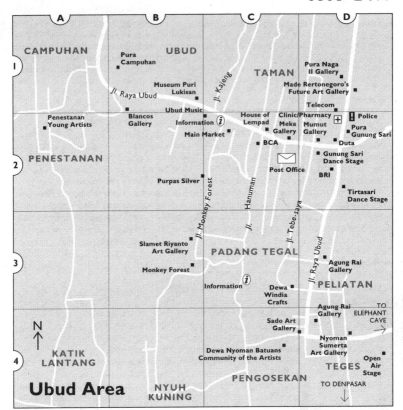

Ubud Area

FOOD

Ubud is considered to have the best food in all Bali. Mexican, Italian, Japanese, among other cuisines, are all done with care and imagination. Unfortunately, the food culture in Ubud has become so highly evolved that mid- to upper-range eateries have displaced many true bargains. Renowned **Café Wayan** has a good selection of baked goods, probably the only things you can afford in this place. Dirt cheap food can still be obtained in the *warung* on the side of the market and in *padang* restaurants geared toward locals. **Tino's,** near the tourist information center on Jl. Raya Ubud, provides supermarket necessities. (Open daily 8am-10pm.)

Dewa Warung, on Jl. Sugriwa. From Jl. Raya Ubud with the market on the right, turn right onto Jl. Hanoman and take the first left onto the end of Jl. Jembarawa (not the narrow alley). After 100m, turn left onto Jl. Sugriwa. Dewa Warung is on the right, with long tables where westerners and locals rub elbows. Excellent, dirt-cheap food in a casual, fun atmosphere. Indonesian entrees Rp1000-1300. Try the coconut pie (Rp1000).

Shadana Vegetarian Restaurant (tel. 975 630), on Jl. Raya Ubud, opposite the intersection with Jl. Hanoman. A few dimly lit tables share space with a handicrafts store. Prices to tempt even carnivores. Vegetable curry, tempeh, and tofu entrees Rp2-3000. Passionfruit milkshake Rp1500. Open daily 8am-9pm.

Casa Luna (tel. 962 83), on Jl. Raya Ubud. 3 floors of tables serving the best salads and baked goods in Bali. Imaginative entrees can get pricey (Rp8000). If you don't want to splurge, eat at a road-side *warung* and come here for coffee and chocolate cake (Rp2500). The atmosphere alone is worth a couple thousand rupiah.

Three Brothers (tel. 975 525), toward the end of Jl. Hanoman, past the intersection with Jl. Jembawan, on the left. More atmosphere than other dives with similar prices: woven bamboo walls, high A-frame ceiling with hanging palm leaf decorations, Japanese-style floor seating, soft music, and food served in baskets. *Pepes Bali* (grilled chicken with rice and coconut wrapped in a banana leaf, Rp2000). Live reggae music Wed. and Sat. Open daily 7:30am-11pm.

SIGHTS

The most popular tourist sight in Ubud is the **Monkey Forest Sanctuary**—an attractive path leading around dense forest to Ubud's **Pura Dalem** (Temple of the Dead). The place is filled by about 200 monkeys who search pockets for edibles. (Admission Rp1100, plus Rp500 for a camera.) At many points along the path, dirt trails extend out, leading into rice paddies or the nearby carving village of **Nyuhkuning.** Choose what feels right—it's easy to backtrack or get back to Ubud's central roads.

Ubud also features two beautifully landscaped museums. The entrance to **Museum Puri Lukisan** (tel. 975 136) is on Jl. Raya Ubud, diagonally across from Ubud Tourist Information. Several pavilions around a garden house permanent and rotating exhibitions of traditional and contemporary Balinese art. (Open daily 8am-4pm; admission Rp2000.) The privately owned **Neka Museum** (tel. 975 074) features the works of Balinese artists, as well as foreign work inspired by Bali. (Open daily 9am-5pm; admission Rp2500.) To get there, follow Jl. Raya Ubud up to Campuhan; the museum is all the way up the hill.

Green rice paddies, grazing cows, the Ayung River rapids, and small village life are all within a kilometer of Ubud's most crowded streets. Almost any street leading away from the main drag will reward the explorer with exceptional scenery. The following three- to four-hour hike going high on the hills of Ubud is rarely done and very satisfying. The beginning of the path is hard to find, but is clearly marked through hills, rice paddies, artist communes, and villages. The path starts behind the Cucu Café on the west side of Jl. Raya Ubud (toward Campuhan). On the left side of the restaurant is a small sign: "Goin' to the Hill." That should be the hiker's clue. Follow the steps toward the river, where a dirt path winds around the temple. After 1½ hours or so, the road forks at a sign which points toward the rice fields of Keliki village. Follow this for a flat hike. For more hills, take the other path, which eventually empties out at the main road in Campuhan. Seasoned bikers will find this to be a challenging but do-able ride.

Several organized **white water rafting** companies offer tours of Ubud's Ayung River. A day's trip includes transportation and a meal (about US$60). Brochures are available at private tourist information offices across town. Or call **Sobek** (tel. 287 059), **Ayung River Rafting** (tel. 238 759), or **Bali Adventure Tours** (tel. 751 292).

ENTERTAINMENT

Gamelan, dance, and other performances are held nightly at temples and stages throughout Ubud. The Ubud Tourist Information Centre has a comprehensive list of performances (7 or 7:30pm, tickets Rp7000, sold at the info center, tour agencies, or on the street). Transport services pick up the audience at 6:45pm if the performance is on a village stage. Particularly worthwhile are the Legong dance, *wayang kulit,* and the *kecak* performance.

The Ganesha Bookstore (tel. 963 59) on Jl. Raya Ubud has **gamelan lessons** Tuesdays from 6-7:30pm for Rp15,000. **Balinese dance courses** are offered at Dewi Sekar Ayu 26, on Jl. Hanoman. With your back to Jl. Dewi Sita, at the intersection with Jl. Hanoman, turn right and walk 100m; it's on the left. **Batik courses** and materials can be explored through the **Crackpot Gallery** on Jl. Monkey Forest. With the football field on the left, the Crackpot is 100m beyond the field on the left. Design your own t-shirt or cushion cover for Rp25,000. (Open daily 9am-8pm.) The **Meditation Shop,** on Jl. Monkey Forest, 400m from the Monkey Forest on the right from the football field, offers **free meditation workshops.** Stop by for details or join the evening meditation daily 6-7pm. (Open daily 5-9:30pm.) Casa Luna Restaurant offers **Balinese cooking classes** (Rp20,000, includes a meal).

Nightlife, as such, does not really exist in Ubud—yuppie couples linger over candlelight and cappuccino until the restaurants close at 11pm. Casa Luna and Coconut's Café on Jl. Suweta show movies nightly at around 7pm.

■ Near Ubud

The road that connects Ubud to Denpasar via the village of Batubulan links a string of **craft villages**—Mas (wood carving), Sukawati (windchimes and baskets), Celuk (silver), and Batubulan (stone carving). Sukawati is also the site of a colorful early morning produce market. Brown *bemo* pass through these villages, offering views of artists working on open verandas. Alternatively, it is an easy downhill ride by bike (bring some string to tie the bike down the *bemo* ride back to Ubud).

The most famous sight hereabouts is **Goa Gajah** (Elephant Cave), really a stone carved cavern that has nothing to do with elephants. Enter this 11th-century structure through the mouth of a demon into a large cave featuring phallic representations of Brahma, Vishnu, and Shiva. Paths behind the cave allow travelers to clamber down to the Petanu River and surrounding rice fields. (Admission Rp1100, plus Rp500 for a camera.) It is a short *bemo* or bike ride from Ubud. Take a brown *bemo* and get off where Jl. Raya Peliatan intersects the turn-off for Denpasar. Walk along the turn and the cave is just ahead. About 1km from Goa Gajah are the less-touristed stone carvings of **Yeh Pulu.** The attraction here is as much the *sawah* you encounter along the way as the carved cliff itself. From the road with the entrance to Goa Gajah, walk away from Ubud; the way is clearly marked by signs on the road.

Gunung Kawi, in Tampaksiring village, is a temple, hewn from rock in the 11th century, with a mysterious complex of tombs. The area to the left of the stone archway is thought to be the burial site of King Anak Wungsu's four concubines. Opposite these tombs across the river, are royal tombs, of the king and his four wives. On the far side of the river beside the royal tombs lies a courtyard and a series of caves and rock passages. Even better than the caves is the walk behind them through fields and jungles to a waterfall, a popular bathing spot. Gunung Kawi is best seen in the light of the late afternoon (4pm) or early morning (7am). To get from Ubud to Gunung Kawi, take an orange *bemo* to Gianyar (Rp300) and get off at the intersection where the *bemo* turns right (heading south). Then take a second *bemo* or walk up the hill to Gunung Kawi (Rp400). Alternatively, tourists can also bike to the temple. With the market to the right, go straight down Jl. Raya Ubud until it intersects another wide thoroughfare. Turn right and follow this street as it veers left (avoid the turn-off to Denpasar). Soon after the entrance to Goa Gajah a large road extends on the left. Take this road up all the way to Tampaksiring. The ride is almost entirely uphill and takes about one hour. Appropriate dress can be rented here. (Admission Rp1050, kids Rp550; plus Rp1000 for video; camera Rp500).

■ Singaraja

Singaraja, the capital of the Buleleng Regency on the north coast of Bali, is not a tourist hot spot but rather serves as the public bus connection to and from the popular Lovina beaches. Just 10 minutes from Lovina by *bemo,* Singaraja provides big city necessities and a few diversions for the over-beached. Once a major shipping port of the Dutch and the only entry point to Bali for foreigners, Singaraja remains a tidy, hospitable, trading-port town which has seen plenty of foreign faces pass by, but encounters few who actually stop.

ORIENTATION

Jalan A. Yani is the main street, running parallel to the harbor. The **bus terminal** (Banyuasri Terminal) where *bemo* stop from Lovina is at the west end of Jl. A. Yani. The main commercial activity is on its east end, at the intersection with **Jalan Dipone-**

goro and **Jalan Imam Bonjol.** All other points of interest, are on the south side of town on **Jalan Veteran.**

PRACTICAL INFORMATION

Tourist Offices: Dinas Pariwisata, Jl. Veteran 23 (tel. 251 41), where the road crosses Jl. A. Yani on the city's south side. From Banyuasri terminal, take a yellow *bemo.* Free maps and brochures. Open Mon.-Fri. 7am-3pm.
Currency Exchange: BCA Bank (tel. 237 61), on the south side of Jl. A. Yani. Cash from MC, Visa (Rp5000 charge). Open Mon.-Fri. 8am-2pm, Sat. 8am-noon.
Air Travel: Garuda, on the north side of Jl. A. Yani, just west of the river, for flights out of Denpasar.
Local Transportation: Banyuasri Terminal, on Jl. A. Yani on the west edge of town. To **Lovina** (Rp500). **Regular minibuses** leave for **Gilimanuk** (Rp2500) and **Denpasar. Sangket Terminal (Sukasada),** at the south end of Singaraja, has buses to: **Denpasar** (Rp3000); **Bedugul/Danau Bratan** (Rp1500); and **Gigit Waterfall** (Rp1000). **Penarukan Terminal,** on Jl. Surapati on the east side of town, has buses to: **Amlapura** (Rp3000); **Kintamani** (Rp3000); **Klungkung** (Rp3000); and **Yeh Sanih** (Rp1500). *Bemo* shuttle between Singaraja's bus terminals (Rp500): Banyuasri to Sangket is yellow, Sangket to Banyuasri is red, Penarukan to Sangket is blue, Penarukan to Banyuasri is green or brown. Buses and *bemo* die out after 6pm.
Markets: Buleleng Market, at the corner of Jl. Veteran/Semeru and Jl. Gajah Mada/ Mayor Metra, sells fruit and housewares.
Pharmacies: Wijaya Kusuma Apotik, Jl. Ngurah Rai 23 (tel. 228 90). Open 24hr.
Medical Services: Kertha Usada, Jl. A. Yani 108 (tel. 223 96).
Emergency: Police: tel. 110. **Ambulance:** tel. 118.
Police: on Jl. Pramuka (the north end of Jl. Ngurah Rai), just south of Jl. A. Yani.
Post Offices: Jl. Gajah Mada 156, at the intersection with Jl. A. Yani. *Poste Restante.* Open Mon.-Fri. 7am-4pm, Sat. 7am-1pm. **Postal code:** 81113.
Telephones: Wartel Kopegtel, Jl. Gajah Mada 154. Collect or cash international calls. Open 24hr. Phone booth right outside has an **HCD** phone that accepts credit card calls without charge. **Telephone code:** 0362.

ACCOMMODATIONS AND FOOD

Overnight visitors to Singaraja are usually domestic businessmen. Most travelers stay in Lovina, where the competition between hotels keeps prices down for tourists. **Losmen Duta Karya,** Jl. A. Yani 59 (tel. 214 67), is a 10-minute walk from Banyuasri down the street from Hotel Gelar Sari. The basic rooms face a garden of sorts, and are comfortable, despite the loud street sounds. Singles with bath and fan cost Rp12,000, doubles Rp15,000. Better rooms can be found at **Wijaya Hotel** (tel. 219 15), on Jl. Sudirman. Cross the street onto Jl. Sudirman from Banyuasri, then walk 100m to the hotel. It offers a large range of room quality. Decent standard rooms go for Rp15,000, doubles Rp20,000. MC and Visa are accepted.

Singaraja's best food options are on Jl. A. Yani. Near the Banyuasri Terminal is **Gajuk Café,** a hang-out for local students eager to offer travel advice in exchange for English practice. The café serves Indonesian basics and a smattering of western food (Rp1500-3000). Or try **Pasar Senggol** (night market), on the small road opposite the police station on Jl. Pramuka/Ngurah Rai. (Open daily 7-11pm.)

SIGHTS

Singaraja's **Pura Dalem** (Temple of the Dead), on Jl. Gajah Mada, is at street level, below the crematorium. The *pura* displays a wall of fantastic reliefs depicting Balinese *sorga* (heaven) and *nraka* (hell) and the earthly behavior associated with each. The scenes of *nraka* are graphic: people getting their arms sawed off, tongues pulled out, and being otherwise tortured. (Open daily 8am-4pm.)

The **Gedong Kertya,** Jl. Veteran 20 (tel. 226 45), next door to the tourist office, keeps the world's largest collection of palm leaf manuscripts on its crowded and dusty shelves. Hindu priests, scholars, and students come to the library to consult its volumes of ancient Balinese literature and drawings. It represents a bit of culture for those tired of mindless beach thrills. Visitors can examine the stylus tools used to inscribe the *lontar*, books made of strips of palm tied between two ruler-like pieces of wood. (Open Mon.-Fri. 7am-noon; donation requested.)

■ Lovina

Village is to city as Lovina is to Kuta. Lovina remains a quiet, relaxed resort area where Balinese village life has yet to be taken over by the touristically inclined. A refuge for beach-seekers who would rather leave the crowds of southern Bali behind, Lovina offers clean water, great snorkeling, cheap accommodations, and technicolor sunsets. This northern strip of beach, however, is not without its challenges: the beach is narrow, lava black, and while the beach-patrolling youth of Lovina are significantly more benign than the in-your-face hawkers of Kuta, attaching yourself to a Walkman will not stop them from lifting an earphone to ask whether or not you want to see Lovina's dolphins.

ORIENTATION

Lovina is used loosely to describe an eight km stretch of beach along the Bali Sea. The road that runs parallel to the beach is **Jalan Singaraja** and the restaurants and hotels sit in between. This strip includes several villages. From east to west, **Pemaron, Tukadmungga Anturan** (Happy Beach), **Kalibukbuk, Kaliasem** (Lovina), and **Temukug**. Along this stretch, the tourist activity centers around the village of Kalibukbuk, roughly located in the middle. Jl. Singaraja heads east to (where else?) **Singaraja** (a 10-minute *bemo* ride). Westwards, it heads to the ferry point of **Gilimanuk** (2hr.) and the Bali Barat National Park (1hr.).

PRACTICAL INFORMATION

Tourist Offices: On the main road in Kalibukbuk. Helpful staff provides maps and suggestions for daytrips. Also the office of the tourist police. Open Mon.-Sat. 8am-8pm, but actual evening hours oscillate.

Currency Exchange: Several money changers along the road offer rates slightly better than Singaraja's banks. Most are open daily until 5pm.

Buses: Public transport only goes as far as Singaraja where connections are available to anywhere in Bali. Several private transport agencies in Lovina offer direct shuttles to popular locations. To: **Denpasar/Kuta** (Rp15,000); **Ubud** (Rp15,000); **Gunung Batur** (Rp12,000); and **Candi Dasa** (Rp15,000).

Rentals: Motorbike (Rp10,000 per 12hr.) and **bicycle** (Rp5000 per 12hr.) rentals are widely available.

Post Offices: (tel. 413 92), on Jl. Singaraja. Open daily 8am-6pm. Many of the shops along the road also serve as postal agents where travelers can buy stamps and send packages. No *Poste Restante*.

Telephones: There are several **wartel** along the Lovina stretch which are open until midnight. The one by Wina's Restaurant accepts credit card and collect calls for a Rp4000 fee. **Telephone code:** 0362.

ACCOMMODATIONS

Lovina covers limited, relatively homogeneous land, making for a situation of near-perfect competition for hotels. As a result, quality and prices in budget accommodations are remarkably uniform. Expect a large room, double bed, fan, partially open-air private *mandi* with cold shower, covered porch, and breakfast, all steps away from the beach. Rooms average Rp10-15,000 (low season Rp8-10,000). The highest concentration of budget lodgings is on Jl. Laviana, a dirt road leading toward the beach off the main road in Kalibukbuk. Here, **Hotel Janur** (tel. 410 56), **Mas Bungalows** (tel. 417 73), and others offer comfortable rooms facing quiet gardens at competitive prices. This street is popular with backpackers and offers lodgings only a short walk from the beach. **Pondok Wisnu Cottages,** directly off the main road, offers rooms of comparable quality at slightly cheaper prices, but the live band at nearby Wina's Bar makes sleeping before midnight quite a challenge. **Note:** Lovina has almost as many mosquitoes as it has amorous, long-haired gigolos—consider getting a mosquito coil (Rp1000) from one of the many road-side vendors. Unfortunately, the gigolos are harder to get rid of.

FOOD

Restaurants crowd Lovina both road-side and beach-side. Prices tend to be mid-range (about Rp4-7000) and menus more or less the same, but the ubiquitous grilled tuna fish steaks are always fresh, the fried calamari piping hot, and the gourmet pizzas surprisingly good. **BU Warung** is a stand-out: cheap, cheap, cheap Rp1-2000 meals with quality better than most. It's road-side, a few doors east of Wina Bar and Restaurant. If you find yourself at Malibu's, you've gone too far. The Balinese grilled tuna slices in banana leaf are exceptional (Rp2000). Fresh squeezed orange juice is Rp800. The Australian-run **Sea Breeze Café and Restaurant** (beach-side) is tremendously popular for its desserts, cappuccino, faithful rendition of western dishes, and nightly performances of Balinese dance.

SIGHTS AND ENTERTAINMENT

As travelers quickly find out from any local, Lovina offers pre-dawn boat rides to see the dolphins and day excursions for snorkeling. Pay no more than Rp10,000 for the dolphins (a miraculous sight if they show, odds are about 80%) and Rp5000 for snorkeling (includes equipment and boat ride). The **snorkeling** is some of the best in Bali and shallow waters make it safe for beginners and children. Nearby waters also offer exciting **scuba diving** possibilities; the **Malibu-Lovina Diver Centre,** attached to the Malibu Bar and Restaurant (on the main road), offers dives for any experience level. All instructors are native English speakers and PADI certified. An all-day introductory course costs US$85 (includes two dives, all equipment, and meals). MC, Visa, and AmEx are accepted.

In the evening, several of the larger restaurants in Lovina show popular **English-language movies** on big screens for no cover. **Wina Bar and Restaurant** and **Malibu Bar and Restaurant** are the most popular. Both are road-side in Kalibukbuk, 15m apart. Both places also have **live band performances** following their movies. Malibu hosts a reggae band, while Wina's plays top 40. On Saturday night, Malibu also has a disco open until 3am (Rp5000 cover includes a beer).

■ Near Lovina: Yeh Sanih

10km east of the Lovina area, along the northern coast, is the small resort area of Yeh Sanih (also called Air Sanih). There's not much of a beach here—the main draw is a natural pool complex set inside an attractive garden along the coast. The pools are clean, relaxing, and deserted during the week. On weekends, this popular local site is crowded with cheerful families (admission Rp500 to enter the pool complex, free if you're staying inside the complex). **Puri Sanih Bungalows** offer accommodation inside the complex. Budget bungalows on stilts are Rp15-20,000. The *warung* across the street are a much better bet than the hotel's restaurant, as is the elegant **Archipelago Restaurant. Warung Seges** has good *nasi campur* and *soto ayam* (Rp1500). There are no tourist facilities here. *Bemo* to Yeh Sanih leave all day from Singaraja's Penarukan Station (Rp1000). Flagging a *bemo* east from Lovina leads to Singaraja (Rp700) and, if you're lucky, directly to Yeh Sanih (Rp1500). Heading back to Singaraja/Lovina, flag down any *bemo* going west.

■ Gunung Agung

For the Balinese, Gunung Agung is the center of the universe—the holy vantage point from which the gods observe the human preoccupations of Bali and beyond. The belief that Agung represents strong forces is not without factual basis. Roughly 3000m high and dominating the landscape of eastern Bali, geologically energetic Gunung Agung blew its top most recently in 1963, killing thousands and significantly altering the surrounding topography. Sitting 1000m on the slopes of Agung, Besakih, "the mother temple," is the mountain's corresponding religious monument. The most sacred temple in all Bali, Besakih is an enormous structure comprised of 30 separate temples, each representing a Hindu god and district in Bali. Travelers not visiting during one of its colorful holidays, or just uninterested in Balinese religion may be disappointed by the temple complex and the oft cloud-obscured Agung.

PRACTICAL INFORMATION

Tourist facilities are minimal; travelers come almost exclusively on package day tours from Ubud and Kuta, but **guides** for the climb to Gunung Agung are available at the few *losmen* outside the temple's entrance. Be wary of guides at the temple who attach themselves to you and ask to be paid exorbitant amounts after a five-minute "tour" of the complex. Be firm and direct about whether you want a tour (one is not necessary). If you do, a price should be agreed upon ahead of time. The entrance ticket to Besakih is Rp1000. In addition, you are requested to make a donation and rent a sash (Rp1000) if you intend to pray. Besakih can be reached by public *bemo* from the main *bemo* terminals in Klungkung (7am-6pm, Rp1000) and Amlapura (Rp1400). From Ubud or Batubulan, take a *bemo* to Gianyar and another to Klungkung. The *bemo* from Klungkung to Besakih may stop/change at Rendang. Package tours are plentiful at all the tourist hubs—they run about Rp20,000 and usually include a quick stop at all of East Bali's sights.

CLIMBING AGUNG

Climbing Gunung Agung is exhausting and in its steeper portions even dangerous. But it's a satisfying experience for those who crave aerobic stimulation and want the best possible seat from which to view Bali—provided you arrive at the summit before the clouds do. Climbers must spend the night in the area and can choose one of two paths—the popular route from the Besakih temple itself is a four- to five-hour, 6km ascent. The shorter climb departs from the village of **Selat,** south of the summit. From Selat, transport of some form or another takes hikers up to within 2km of the summit. Both routes, however, require that travelers leave well ahead of time to catch the view (well before daybreak in the case of the longer hike). In either case, a guide should be hired (Rp20,000), as the trails are ambiguous at parts; make arrangements a day in advance. Basic *losmen* setups (Rp18,000 per night, no breakfast) are easily found right outside the Besakih temple and in Selat. *Bemo* run regularly between Besakih and Selat (Rp500). Wear sturdy shoes, warm clothing, and bring a flashlight—it's a long climb.

■ Gunung Batur

The Gunung Batur area is a crater complex—a cluster of volcanic cones and a lake set inside an enormous crater. The serene beauty of Lake Batur and the mountain villages which hover around the crater's edge veils the area's volcanic volatility. Gunung Batur's 1917 eruption killed 1000 and destroyed 65,000 homes and 2000 temples. Ensuing eruptions in 1926 and 1963 forced villagers within the crater area to permanently relocate to its outer edges. Such destruction exists alongside ethereal beauty—the views are superb and the sunrises from the tip of Gunung Batur are not to be missed. Like many mountain regions, however, the Batur area offers little more than its physical beauty. Merchants are aggressive, the price of accommodation is relatively high, and the food unremarkable. Most travelers only stay a day.

GETTING THERE AND AWAY

Bemo arriving in the Gunung Batur area stop in **Kintamani** where connections can be made to other villages. Taxis and *ojek* also pick up passengers at the *bemo* stop. *Bemo* run between villages but at no set schedule. The best plan, except chartering a private vehicle, is to walk on the road (there is only one) and flag down a *bemo* when it comes by. To leave the Batur area, public bus connections leave from Penelokan to other island destinations. Morning departures (7-9am) are most frequent. Alternatively, travelers can arrange for a direct shuttle connection through any of the many transport agents along the main road in Toyabungkah (also known as Tirta). Tickets run between Rp10-15,000 for direct connections to Denpasar, Kuta, Ubud, Candi Dasa, and Singaraja. Visitors should change money before coming to the area, as rates are low.

ORIENTATION

The Batur area is located on the northeast corner of Bali. The villages of **Penulisan, Kintamani,** and **Penelokan,** which rest on the western edge of the crater, are at the highest elevations, and offer spectacular views. Lying along Lake Batur, **Kedisan** and **Toyabungkah (Tirta),** on the east side of the crater, are at lower altitudes but provide easy direct access to Gunung Batur.

ACCOMMODATIONS AND FOOD

Toyabungkah is the most convenient departure point for Batur's sunrise and, accordingly, plays host to many *losmen*, travel information centers, and restaurants. Everything is visible from the main road. Most places offer bungalow-type arrangements with a private bath and a hot shower for Rp5-10,000 extra. Near the village marker is **Darma Putra Homestay,** where singles go for Rp8000, doubles Rp12,000. **Arlina's** has singles for Rp10,000, with hot shower Rp20,000. An attached restaurant serves some decent and reasonably priced food. **Awanjja Bunglows** has less well-kept rooms but offers lake views. Singles here cost Rp8000, with hot shower Rp15,000. Doubles are Rp10,000, with hot shower Rp20,000. Penelokan and Kintamani are not recommended for overnights; although the entire Batur region is known for unpleasant locals, here they can be downright hostile.

Food preparation in Batur is lackluster at best, but the region's specialty—grilled or fried lake fish with garlic and ginger—is always fresh and probably the best bet at Rp4-8000. **Amertina's** in Toyabungkah has nice views of the lake, but is expensive.

SIGHTS

Before settling in for the night at Toyabungkah, travelers should visit Bali's highest temple, **Pura Tegeh Kuripan,** at an elevation of 1745m in the village of Penulisan, just north of Kintamani. The Rp1500 admission fee buys breathtaking views of both Gunung Batur and Bali's north coast. Assuming no cloud cover, it is one of the more satisfying temple experience in Bali. *Bemo* from Kintamani cost Rp1000. Impressive mountain views can be seen from the otherwise lackluster villages of Kintamani and Penelokan. If heavy clouds can be seen covering the top of Gunung Batur, don't bother making the trip. The crater lake of **Lake Batur** and surrounding sights can be visited by chartering a boat from the harbor in Kedisan (2½hr., Rp40,000 for seven people). The common route is from Kedisan to Trunyan village on the opposite side of the lake, along the lake to the Trunyan cemetery, across the lake to Tirta, and then back to Kedisan. Trunyan is a Bali Aga village—inhabited by aboriginal Balinese (most present-day Balinese are descendants of those fleeing the collapse of the Hindu Majapahit kingdom on Java). Their nearby **cemetery** displays one of the more distinctive characteristics of the villagers of Trunyan. Instead of cremating or burying their dead, they simply lay them out to decompose. The road between Kedisan and Tirta passes through the remains of what was once a fully developed village in 1963—now just cooled lava over hilly terrain. *Bemo* run frequently on this route and it is a pretty, if solemn, 1½-hour hike.

CLIMBING BATUR

Most people climb Batur before dawn to be rewarded with sunrise breaking over the crater. Trekking up lava for two hours in the dark can be frustrating, and although the sunrise looks warm and fuzzy, it won't necessarily make you and your scratched knees feel that way. If you have a flashlight and the desire to rise at 4am, hike pre-dawn. If not, you'll miss a once-a-day spectacular sight, but will gain a better appreciation for Batur's unique terrain. All *losmen* in Toyabungkah offer guide services and typically give a choice of short, medium, or long hikes. All hikes go up Gunung Batur starting at 4am, but the longer hikes take travelers past neighboring craters after sun-up. Prices fluctuate with the seasons, anywhere from Rp30,000 to Rp90,000. Wear sturdy shoes and bundle up; the climb is very steep in parts and is cold throughout. Gunung Batur can easily be climbed during the day without a guide and even in the dark, with a strong flashlight. If in doubt, pause for a bit and wait for a guided group to head your way.

To begin hiking from where the lake laps Toyabungkah's main drag, face the mountain and walk left to the yellow sign for Toyobungkah on the side of the road. The sure-fire path is by these road signs at the entrance to Toyabungkah. If it forks, take the most trodden branch through gardens and corn crops until you hit the woods, where a temple stands on the right. One hundred meters farther, the path crosses a smaller one; turn left, off the wide path. After turning left, stick with the path for about 45 minutes until the trees stop and the terrain turns to volcanic rock, sand, and ash. From here, there are no real "paths," so don't worry too much about following other groups. The way to go is up. After 8 or 9am, the place is deserted, but a start after 9 or 10am will leave travelers without a view.

■ Amlapura

Amlapura is a small, sleepy enclave of unhurried commercial and social activity, where everyone seems to know each other and the liberal use of pony-propelled transportation does not appear to strike anyone as inefficient. Although the main town of the east coast, Amlapura is not a convenient stopover for travelers. Nonetheless, it is a pleasant and friendly respite from nearby coastal tourist meccas.

ORIENTATION

The main road in Amlapura runs north-south at the town's very east end and unfortunately disguises itself with many names. From its north to south end: **Jalan Sultan Agung** becomes **Jalan Teuku Umar** which turns into **Jalan Gajah Mada** and finally (on its way to the Ujung Water Palace) ends up as **Jalan Bhayangkara**. The Jl. Gajah Mada section of the street is the center of town—a rectangle of market and social activity. The *bemo* stop is here, as are the banks and most places to eat.

PRACTICAL INFORMATION

Banks near the *pasar* are open Mon.-Fri. 8am-2pm, Sat. 8-11am, and exchange currency but not traveler's checks. The **post office** is near the entrance of town, on **Jalan Hasanuddin** after it crosses the river (open Mon.-Fri. 8am-4pm). There's no *Poste Restante*. A more centrally located postal agent is on **Jalan Sultan Agung** in the market area. The **police** station is just south of the market on the road to the Ujung Water Palace. *Bemo* from the **main terminal** in the market area leave for **Denpasar's** Batubulan (via Candi Dasa, Padangbai, Klungkung, and Gianyar) and **Singaraja** (via Tirtagangga, Culik, Tulamben, and Yeh Sanih). Blue *bemo* near the *warung* across from the terminal go to the **Ujung Water Palace** (Rp500).

ACCOMMODATIONS AND FOOD

Amlapura has very slim pickings—most travelers prefer to stay in Candi Dasa or Tirtagangga (both a 20-minute *bemo* ride). The extremely modest **Losmen Lahar Mas** is just at the entrance of town, before the post office, on Jl. Gatot Subroto. Basic rooms with bath go for Rp10-15,000. Food is largely limited to the *warung* in the *pasar*. A **night market** sets up next to the blue *bemo* at 5pm, but usually closes by 8pm. **Sumber Rasa,** on Jl. Gajah Mada, is one of the few sit-down establishments in Amlapura, and the only one with English menus (entrees Rp1-3000).

SIGHTS

Visitors to Amlapura can stroll through what remains of the once prosperous Karangasem Kingdom. The **Puri Agung,** also known as the Puri Kanginan, the former residence of the last Karangasem king, his wives and dozens of children, is open to the public. On weekends, one of the king's sons is on hand to cheerfully show off his childhood home. Notice the evidence of Dutch artwork and furniture—the Karangasem held on to their power in the kingdom long into the 20th century because of their collaboration with the Dutch. The *puri* is located north of the *pasar* along Jl. Sultan Agung. (Open daily 8am-6pm; admission Rp1500.)

The **Ujung Water Palace,** a somewhat more modest version of what the Karangasem king built in Tirtagangga, is just south of town. Blue *bemo* leave constantly from the market (Rp500). The best view of the water garden's pools, fountains, and overall design is from an elevated vantage point—climb surrounding hills to get a better look. Built in 1921, it was, like the Tirtagangga complex, built as a private retreat for the Karangasem royal family. Ujung is also accessible by *dokar*.

■ Near Amlapura

TIRTAGANGGA

By most accounts, Tirtagangga (Water of the Ganges) is the prettiest place in all Bali. Lying 10km northwest of Amlapura, Tirtagangga has one main attraction: the pool gardens built by Amlapura's *rajah* in 1947 as a private weekend retreat for his family. Situated on the lower slopes of Gunung Agung, the stunningly beautiful, multi-tiered **water garden** mimics the surrounding rice field-dominated landscape. Completely restored after being battered by the 1963 eruption of Gunung Agung and the earthquake of 1979, the pool complex retains a hushed, secret-garden feel. It's perfect for picnics and conversation (open daily 7am-6pm; admission Rp2100, includes use of changing rooms). The **Tirta Ayu Hotel/Restaurant** is the beautifully kept former residence of the *rajah*. Singles cost Rp25,000, doubles Rp35,000. The price includes breakfast and unlimited use of the pools. Cheaper accommodations and food can be found right outside the garden gates on the main road. **Rijasa Homestay** is directly across from the pools. Singles here are Rp10-12,000, doubles Rp12-20,000 (breakfast included for both). All rooms are clean and have a private porch. Superb views of surrounding rice terraces can be most cheaply had at **Prima Hotel.** To get there, follow the main road as it climbs up, past the Kusumajaya Inn. Singles go for Rp15,000, doubles Rp20,000, both with breakfast included. *Bemo* run between Amlapura and Tirtagangga (every 20min. until 6pm, Rp800), and Tirtagangga is also serviced by Perama shuttles. Tickets to destinations all over the island can be purchased at the **Good Karma Restaurant,** 50m up the main road from the pools. The **money changers** and **postal agent** are at the pool gates. The main road from Tirtagangga, leading away from Amlapura to Culik (20km) passes some of the most beautiful scenery in all Bali (many Bali postcards get their images from this road). *Bemo* run between Tirtagangga and Culik all day (Rp1000); tired travelers walking along the road can just flag one down.

AMED AND UPAH

Along the main road going north from Amlapura/Tirtagangga, *bemo* pass the village of **Culik.** At this stop is the turn-off for the coastal villages of **Amed** and **Upah.** Amed and Upah boast some of the most stunning coastlines of the island. Their quiet and relaxing air is reminiscent of what Bali must have been like 30 years ago. *Bemo* run from Culik to Amed until 11am. After that, transportation to the villages can be had by hiring an *ojek* (Rp2000 to Amed, Rp3000 to Upah). From Amed it's 4km along the coast to Upah. Amed is used exclusively as a dive-off point; all accommodations are in Upah. **Kusumajaya Beach Inn** and **Vienna Beach Prima Bungalows** are the cheapest, with singles for Rp30,000 and doubles for Rp40,000. Breakfast is included. Both hotels have counterparts in Tirtagangga that can help arrange transport to Upah. One local dive shop has branches at all the hotels and in Amed. Two dives off Upah cost US$45; it's US$55 for the very worthy dive off Tulamben to explore the sunken wreck of the **USS Liberty** (prices include transport, lunch, and tanks). Gear rental is another US$20 (MC accepted). There is nothing in these villages but a few hotels, restaurants, and dive shops—make sure to change money and buy basic necessities before arriving.

■ Candi Dasa

A few years back, the quiet beach-side village of Candi Dasa was a well-kept secret among expats and long-time travelers. Today, hundreds of visitors and several new hotels later, Candi Dasa remains a pleasant, laid-back seaside getaway with cheap food and budget ocean-view rooms. The story of Candi Dasa's beach, or lack thereof, however, is a sad allegory about the dangers of rapid tourist development. The removal of coral from around Candi Dasa's water for construction purposes has resulted in the beach's erosion. Today, you can only walk along a narrow strip of dark sand during low tide, and cement walls have been built to keep the waves from washing away beach-side bungalows.

ORIENTATION

Candi Dasa is a 1-km strip of beach on the east coast of Bali which runs along the Klungkung-Amlapura road. With your back to the water, Klungkung is to the left (west) and Amplapura is to the right (east). The slime-covered Candi Dasa Lagoon is sea side of the main road at its east end. Candi Dasa's local temple is directly across the lagoon. The waters of Amuk Bay border Candi Dasa on the south; hill rice terraces are at its north. If you are sitting on the sand, the big land mass straight ahead is Nusa Penida.

PRACTICAL INFORMATION

Tourist Offices: No official office, but private tourist information centers offer tours, rentals, and shuttle services.

Currency Exchange: No banks, but several **money changers** along the main road stay open daily until 8pm. Compare rates—they can vary significantly.

Local Transportation: Bemo run regularly on the main road until 6pm. With your back to the water, *bemo* going right are headed to **Amlapura** (connections to Tirtagangga and Singaraja). Those to the left go to **Padangbai** and **Klungkung** (connections to **Gianyar, Besakih, Penelokan,** and **Batubulan**). **Private shuttle** tickets can be purchased anywhere along the main road for direct service to destinations on Bali and Lombok. Daily morning departures to: **Denpasar/Kuta/Sanur/Airport** (Rp10,000); **Ubud** (Rp7500); **Lovina/Singaraja** (Rp15,000); and **Penelokan/Kintamani** (Rp15,000). Open tickets allow you to stop off in any city on the shuttle's route as long as you'd like before resuming your trip.

Rentals: Many accommodations and tour agents rent **bikes** and beach equipment. **Dewa Bharata Bungalow's** tourist info service (tel. 410 90) rents push bikes for Rp5000, motorbikes for Rp15,000, and snorkel equipment for Rp10,000.

Police: tel. 110. At the west end of the main road, on the north side, where the road runs along the bay.

Post Offices: Several **postal agents** on the main street, including Asri's Convenience Store. Open daily until 9pm. The nearest **post office** is 20min. away in Amlapura. **Postal code:** 80854.

Telephones: Wartel at the center of town on the main road. International cash calls only. Open daily 8am-11pm. **Telephone code:** 0363.

ACCOMMODATIONS

Budget beach-side bungalows run the whole length of Candi Dasa, but the quieter ones cluster at either end of the village. If you're coming from the east, before the road runs into the bay, several comfortable Rp10-15,000 bungalow-type establishments extend from the same dirt path. **The Flamboyant, Pelangi Inn,** and **Terrace Bungalows** all offer bars, mosquito nets, and private terraces. Terrace Bungalow's front units sit practically on the water. On the far west side of the beach road (where it suddenly turns sharply) another dirt path leads to a several bungalows comparable both in price and comfort, including **Barong Beach Inn.**

Geringsing Homestay (tel. 410 84), near the police station and the Perama bus service. Romantic, bamboo-lined rooms with *ikat*-woven curtains are joined to partially outdoor *mandi,* some with views of the mountain rising in the background. The most comfortable for its price range. Singles Rp8-9000. Doubles Rp12,000. All have mosquito nets and baths. Breakfast included.

Dewi Bungalows, on the Amlapura side of the slime-infested lagoon. Despite slightly ominous "silence is the best time for our brain" signs posted around the grounds, Dewi Bungalows is attractive, airy, and managed by friendly employees who solicit group participation for yoga practice. Individual bungalows with their own porch and *mandi.* The light comes through tiny holes in the woven bamboo walls in the mornings, and each bungalow faces a yard/garden area. Singles Rp7000. Doubles Rp10,000. Breakfast included.

Lilaberata, a few hundred meters before the raunchy lagoon (on the west side). Some of the cheapest rooms in Candi Dasa are here, but investigate closely before you dive under the itchy, scratchy covers. Benefits: rooms are large and close to the beach (you can hear the waves from bed). If you're modest (or a female alone), don't change in front of the flimsy curtains. Doubles Rp6000.

FOOD

From the road, the food scene doesn't look like much, with only a couple of run-of-the-mill Kuta-esque cafés, but get away from the road toward the water and several formidable, pavilion-topped-with-linen-and-separate-wine-lists kind of places all of a sudden pop up. Those hoping to spend less than Rp8000 for dinner can find a very good *nasi campur* or *soto ayam* family-type establishment on the side of the main road away from the beach (entrees Rp1500-3000). Cheaper tourist-oriented restaurants also face the street and have prices advertised. Seafood is always fresh and the cheapest non-vegetarian option. The more expensive places work hard at their service and atmosphere—they are worth a visit for affordable desserts or appetizers. **Lotus Seaview** beyond Amuk Bay has a high tea special (cakes and coffee or tea) for Rp5000 from 3-5pm. **TJ's** (of TJ fame in Kuta) has cheese nachos for Rp2500 and discounted drinks between 6-8pm. **Raja's Bar and Restaurant** shows nightly American movies at 7:30pm. **Luribang Bali Restaurant** has free nightly Balinese dancing with dinner (set Rp6500 dinner includes appetizer, main course, and dessert). The **Reggae Bar/Restaurant** is open late until 1am and has a high concentration of gigolos and related activities.

Warung Srijati, across from the Gandhi Reading Room and by the mucky lagoon. Minimal atmosphere but the only place in Candi Dasa that specializes in Balinese cuisine. The coconut-based vegetable *urap* and chicken *lawar* are excellent. Entrees Rp1500-3000. Open daily 8am-10pm.

Astawa, on the ocean side of the street on the Amlapura side of the filthy lagoon. The most presentation you'll get on a budget. Artfully arranged *nasi goreng* (Rp3000) and satay are served on indi·idual charcoal burners (Rp5000). Candlelight in the evening. Open daily 3am-10pm.

Candi Dasa Restaurant (tel. 411 07), opposite the Geringsing Accommodations on the west side of the road. As straightforward as its name: no frills but the seafood is fresh and cheap. The garlic shrimp (Rp3500) is highly recommended.

■ Near Candi Dasa

TENGANAN

A traditional Bali Aga (native Balinese) village 3km north of Candi Dasa, **Tenganan** is a walled-in rectangular community where little has changed in the last 300 years. There are no vehicles within the compound—only the sound of chickens, cows, and basic commerce. The road leading up to the village extends up from the main Klungkung-Amlapura road just before Candi Dasa. *Ojek* wait at the turn-off to take you up to the village entrance (Rp1000), but it's a pleasant two-hour walk (or one-hour bike ride). It's uphill all the way but the incline is slight. Visiting Tenganan is something like being inside a diorama and once the tour buses start rolling in, some visitors get the unpleasant sense that they are in a human zoo. Come early (before 9am) to avoid other gawking tourists. This is a very conservative village that has retained distinctive traditions, architectural styles, and forms of community organization in the face of Hindu predominance and the rapid changes brought by large-scale tourism (donation requested, Rp1000). The three-day-long **Udaba Sambah Ceremony** in June includes ritual trance fights between men armed with spiky whips. Another yearly ritual, Kawin Pandan, requires a young man to throw a flower over a high wall; he must then marry whoever catches it.

■ Klungkung

For several hundred years before Dutch occupation, Klungkung—the seat of the powerful Gelael Kingdom—was home to Bali's most highly regarded royals. Now, at a time when tourist dollars determine the relative wealth of Balinese cities, this sleepy eastern town is far past its days of court opulence and military might. The city's proudest products are its clean air and unhurried lifestyle. Tourists do not venture far past the former palace grounds and over-beached travelers will find a clean, pleasant town with colorful traditional markets. There is very little here designed to entertain you, foreign traveler, but that may be the point.

ORIENTATION

Klungkung, despite its historical importance and present-day role as a major transportation hub, is tiny, and walking around the city center can be done lickety-split. Klungkung's central landmark is its traffic rotary, where the main east-west thoroughfare, **Jalan Diponegoro,** runs into north-south **Jalan Gajah Mada/Puputan.** From the rotary, the big phallic **Puputan Monument** is visible, as are the old palace grounds (Island Gardens or Taman Gili). Across from the Puputan Monument is the **bemo stop.** Going east on Jl. Diponegoro (right if the palace is to the left) is the main commercial area and the very limited accommodation options. South from the rotary along Jl. Puputan, the main *bemo* terminal is on the right (1km from the rotary). Next to the terminal is Klungkung's enormous **pasar.**

PRACTICAL INFORMATION

Tours and Travel: No local facilities. Tourists almost exclusively come on tours from the more popular coastal areas.

Currency Exchange: Several **banks** along Jl. Diponegoro change money and transfer cash from MC and Visa. **Bank Danamon** provides both services (Rp10,000 fee for money transfers). Open Mon.-Fri. 8am-2pm, Sat. 8-11am.

Inter-city Transportation: Bemo (6am-6pm) to **Amlapura** (Rp1000) via **Padangbai** and **Candi Dasa;** and **Batubulan** (Rp2000) via **Gianyar** and **Besakih.**

Local Transportation: The yellow **bemo** at the main terminal goes 1km to the city center (Rp200). Pony-propelled **dokar** are still commonly used.

Markets: The **pasar** is in the south end of town, across from the main terminal.

Medical Services: Hospital (tel. 211 72), on Jl. Flamboyan on the outskirts of town. Very minimal English spoken. Or go to Ubud or Kuta's 24-hr. clinic.

Police: On Jl. Diponegoro to the far west, past the post office.

Post Offices: GPO, on the west side of Jl. Diponegoro. No *Poste Restante.* Open Mon.-Thurs. 8am-2pm, Sat.-Sun. 8-11am.

Telephones: 24-hr. **wartel** just east of the rotary on Jl. Diponegoro. **HCD** booths allows you to make collect and credit card calls. **Telephone code:** 0366.

ACCOMMODATIONS AND FOOD

Few foreign visitors stay in Klungkung more than a few hours. Those who come without the help of package tours usually base themselves in nearby Padangbai or Candi Dasa, where options are more plentiful. As a result, of the few rooms available, most are hardly bearable, even for the most resilient budget traveler. Standing at the rotary with the palace at your back walk straight ahead on Jl. Diponegoro. Right before the road bends sharply left is the **Loji Ramayana Hotel,** home to the only decent rooms in town. For Rp20,000 you get clean doubles but no frills. Rooms with shared *mandi* cost Rp10,000. Breakfast is included. If the Ramayana is full, the **Bell Inn,** across the street is the most bearable of the unbearable. Bare bones doubles go for Rp8000. Finding decent cheap food is a decidedly more satisfying venture. The local speciality *soto babad* (tripe in spicy broth served with rice) and the usual *warung* fare is widely available (Rp1-2000) but notably concentrated at the large *pasar* abutting the big *bemo* terminal. Try the fire-hot *nasi campur.*

SIGHTS

Sightseeing in Klungkung is unlikely to present itself as a challenge—all sights are near one another. The draw for most visitors is **Kerta Gosa,** the Court of Justice, a pavilion set in the northwest corner of the Taman Gili compound. Here the powerful Gelael king sat in conference with the high priests, handing out judgement on matters beyond the jurisdiction of village courts. There are 267 painted panels on the inside of the roof, which form a continuous concentric mural depicting the story of Bhima Swarga, Indonesia's very own Dante. In his journeys, Bhima Swarga traveled through the various levels of *paradiso* and *inferno*—the latter was graphically and gruesomely depicted as a warning to defendants who appeared before the judges of the Kerta Gosa. Also in the Taman Gili complex is the large **Bale Kambang** (Floating Pavilion), which was impressively restored by the Dutch during the early 20th century (open daily 7am-6pm; admission Rp2000, includes the museum). In dynastic times, the *bale* was the formal receiving area for important guests. The detailed and restored paintings on the inside of the *bale's* roof depict traditional Balinese folklore and astrological symbols. The **museum** has fascinating black and white photographs of the *rajah* and royal residence, but nothing is labeled in English. Across the street is Klungkung's **Puputan Monument**—the tallest structure in the city (free). The base of the monument contains carefully constructed dioramas with English labels—a visual crash course in Balinese history.

▓ Bangli

Of the three former eastern kingdom seats—Amlapura, Klungkung, and Bangli—Bangli is generally thought to be the most pleasant. Friendly, laid-back, and surprisingly cool, Bangli has much to offer those who do not mind the lack of beach or any semblance of nightlife. Superb night market fare, clean, uncrowded streets and one of the most beautiful temples on the island more than compensate for the lack of tourist facilities and the town's decided provinciality.

ORIENTATION

Bangli, long and narrow north-south, is about 40km north of Denpasar. The main east-west thoroughfare, **Jalan Kusumayuda**, crosses the main north-south street **Jalan Nusantara/Merdeka**. Most points of interest are in the general area of this main intersection—the **bemo terminal** and the Artha Sastra Inn are across from each other just south of it. The **night market** is just south of the *bemo* terminal. If you walk along Jl. Kusumayuda with your back to the **day market,** you will pass the **banks,** the **post office,** and the **hospital.**

PRACTICAL INFORMATION

Tourist facilities are non-existent, but money can be changed at the big banks, including **Bank BPD,** on Jl. Kusumayuda (open Mon.-Fri. 8am-2pm, Sat. 8-11am). The **post office,** also on Jl. Kusumayuda, is open Mon.-Fri. 8am-4pm (no *Poste Restante*). There is a **telephone office** offering cash international calls south of the day market on Jl. Nusantara (open until 9pm). Regular *bemo* run to and from **Batubulan** (Rp1200), **Klungkung** (Rp500), **Gianyar** (Rp500), and **Kintamani** (Rp100).

ACCOMMODATIONS AND FOOD

The **Artha Sastra Inn,** on Jl. Nusantara, is falling apart but, as a former palace residence, in a rather charming manner. The least decrepit singles are Rp10,000 and doubles are Rp15,000, including breakfast. The **Adnyana Homestay** has more modern rooms for the same price (breakfast is included). Going south on Jl. Nusantara from the main intersection, make a right after the telephone office and it's to the right. Food is cheap, excellent and readily accessible in the market areas along Jl. Nusantara, but things tend to shut down by 7pm (earlier on Sunday).

SIGHTS

Bangli's one true sight is the beautiful **Pura Kehen** at the northern edge of town. Walk north on the main road, about 1km from the town center, and signs will point to a turn-off on the right. Crumbling and battered, the 11th century temple still retains its essential features and detailed ornamentation.

■ Padangbai

For a tiny, modest port village, Padangbai has much to offer. Set alongside a semicircle of narrow beach, the village is a quiet pocket of colorful outriggers, cheap seafood, and humble fishermen. Padangbai is also the ferry port to Lombok and, once upon a time, was only used by travelers going or coming from there. Increasingly, Padangbai's ocean view, hassle-free living, budget-friendly bungalows, and fresh grilled prawn dinners are making it a travel destination in its own right.

ORIENTATION

Padangbai is about 50km northeast of Denpasar, off the main road between Klungkung and Candi Dasa. It takes all of 10 minutes to walk around every street in Padangbai. If you stand facing the water, the **ferry port** and **bemo station** are on the right side of the inlet and the beach-front **accommodations** are on your left. **Travel agencies, money changers, postal agents,** and tourist-oriented restaurants face the water. The two small streets leading away from the water have roadside food stalls and homestays. To get to the main road, walk with the water on your left until you reach the harbor gate. Then walk right, away from the water.

PRACTICAL INFORMATION

Tourist Offices: There is no official info center, but several private tourist services offer tours, rentals, and shuttles. **Nominasi Travel,** next door to the Equator Dive Shop, stays open until 8pm and can reconfirm airline tickets for Rp5000.

Currency Exchange: Several **money changers** along the beach change at rates slightly lower than Kuta and Candi Dasa and stay open until 8pm.

Air Travel: Bali's airport is 2½hr. away. There's no direct shuttle service from Padangbai but you can get one to Kuta and then take a taxi (15min.). Nominasi Travel sells plane tickets.

Buses: Private **shuttle buses** whisk travelers to several destinations on Bali, Lombok, and Java. Prices include ferry fees. Tickets can be purchased anywhere along the water. Several per day to: **Ubud** (Rp6500), **Sanur** (Rp10,000), **Kuta** (Rp10,000), **Kintamani** (Rp15,000), and **Carita** (Rp20,000). To Lombok: **Mataram** (Rp10,000), **Senggigi** (Rp12,000), **Bangsal** (10am, Rp15,000), **Gili Air** (10am, Rp17,5000), **Gili Meno** (10am, Rp18,500), and **Gili Trawangan** (10am, Rp20,000). Overnight buses: **Jakart**a (Rp58,000), **Yogyakarta/Surakarta** (Rp36,000), **Probolinggo/Surabaya** (Rp24,000), and **Malang** (Rp24,000).

Ferries: Ferries run to **Lombok** (every 2hr., 4hr., Rp5500). On some ferries you can also buy an A/C VIP ticket for Rp10,000.

Local Transportation: Bemo are in the parking lot by the ferry port. Between 7am-6pm *bemo* leave continuously to **Klungkung** and **Gianyar** (blue, Rp1000); **Candi Dasa** and **Amlapura** (orange, Rp1000). Large **public buses** leave during the same time period for **Batubulan** (Rp3500). After 6pm, you may be able to flag down a *bemo* on the main road.

Rentals: Snorkel equipment available everywhere for Rp4000 per day. **Motorbikes** (Rp15,000 per day) and **cars** (Rp35,000 per day) are available through Hotel Puri Rai and Kerti Beach Inn.

Medical Services: The closest **hospital** is 20min. away in Klungkung.

Police: Station at the entry gate of the ferry port.

Post Offices: A couple of **postal agents** face the water and stay open until 8pm. The real **post office** is not far off. With the water to the left walk until you can walk no more, turn right, then take the first left. Open Mon.-Thurs. 8am-2pm, Fri.8am-noon. No *Poste Restante.* **Postal code:** 80872.

Telephones: There's a **24-hr. wartel,** on the street leading away from the harbor gates toward the main road to Candi Dasa. International calls and faxes. Cash only. **Telephone code:** 0363.

ACCOMMODATIONS

As you walk away from the ferry harbor area along the water, the road bends left. To the left are several cheap, clean homestay options (Rp8-12,000). In this area **Parta Homestay** is the best maintained. The **Bagus Inn** has rooms with ceiling fans and mosquito nets. For a bed closer to the water, continue to walk away from the ferry port along the beach. **Hotel Puri Rai** (formerly Rai Beach Inn) is the most conspicuous and offers Padangbai's only rooms with A/C and hot water at US$40. By Indonesian standards, they grossly overcharge for their standard/economy rooms.

Topi Inn, facing the beach, it's the farthest you can get from the ferry port. The cheapest beds in Bali (Rp3000 for a communal loft). Safety locker provided. Private rooms with fresh water *mandi* and mosquito nets. Singles Rp10,000. Doubles Rp15,000. Breakfast included. Balcony provides great ocean views.

Kerti Beach Inn, next door to Hotel Puri Rai. Basic, clean bungalows and a pleasant staff. Rooms are a bit cramped, and you can hear the neighbors as if they were standing in your *mandi*. Singles Rp8000. Doubles Rp12,000. Breakfast included.

Padangbai Beach Inn, between Kerti and Topi Inns. Modest bungalows are not in the best condition, but they're spread out and face the water. Singles Rp10,000. Doubles Rp15,000. Breakfast included.

FOOD

The seafood is exceptional—prawns and shark are the local specialties and they are served with generous amounts of garlic. Prices are pretty uniform: Rp4-5000 for fresh seafood dinners, Rp2-3000 for Indonesian rice or noodle standbys. The cheapest prices for the most Balinese food are found away from the water and hotel-attached restaurants. **Warung Pantai Ayu,** across from the Hotel Puri Rai sits on the sand and provides customers with the best views and garlic shrimp in Padangbai. The restaurant attached to Topi Inn has Balinese dance performances on Wednesday nights (Rp6000, includes dinner). Restaurants close between 10 and 11pm.

SIGHTS AND ENTERTAINMENT

For its small size, Padangbai offers a surprisingly large range of water recreation options. The local CAMS-certified dive shop, **Equator,** offers US$50 full-day dives in nearby waters (lunch, transport, and equipment included; cash only). All-inclusive snorkeling packages to Nusa Penida cost US$25. You can get to Penida on your own; motorboats make the 30-minute trip in the morning for Rp4000 per person (with a full boat). The last boat leaves for Penida at 2pm. Snorkeling gear rental is Rp4000 per day. Boats are also available for deep sea fishing.

Just beyond the grassy cliff which shelters Padangbai's beach on the water's left side is an isolated, perfect inlet beach, **Pantai Kecil** (Little Beach). Sandy, white, immaculate, and almost always deserted, Pantai Kecil can be reached in 10 minutes by walking up the road which extends from Topi Inn. Follow the well-paved road until it ends definitively at a cement pathway. The path will step down and turn right. At the turn, go left on to a narrow dirt path. The path, a little overgrown and steep at points, clearly leads to the beach. Wear something sturdier than flip-flops for the climb. If you take instead the right path and follow the cement stairway, you will find yourself at a dramatic **lookout point** with good wave action, but no beach. There is nothing at Pantai Kecil but the ocean and sand. Bring water, snacks, and snorkeling gear—you'll want to stay awhile.

Lombok

Much can be said about the breadth of Lombok's diversity, all of which is concentrated onto one relatively small island. Two centuries ago the English botanist Alfred Russell Wallace postulated that the strait between Bali and Lombok was something of a line between the flora and fauna of Asia and that of Australia. Wallace's theory has since lost scientific credence and rigidity, but it has left a legacy of paradoxes. Culturally, the island harbors two very different traditions between the Balinese Hindus and the animist Sasaks gone Muslim. Geographically, the terrain is one of wet, tangled jungles and dry, flat outback. And finally, there's the discrepancy between the well-trodden tourism meccas and virtually unblemished and obscure villages.

Freshly paved roads, busy construction sights, and a surprising number of English speakers characterize Lombok's growth as a tourist destination. For the moment, the island's transitional state is an unqualified blessing, with the means, mechanisms, and amenities of easy travel in place but, for the most part, minimally used. All the frenzied activity, however, portends a new era for Lombok. Nothing stands between Bali's motley madhouse and Lombok's thorough peace. Tourists are already trickling in, and inevitably they will surge through the countryside. With this expected increase of visitors, there's no better time to visit than now.

INDONESIA

GETTING THERE AND AWAY

By Plane

Lombok's commercial **Selaparang Airport** marks the northern edge of Mataram, the official capital. The airport is served by **Garuda-Merpati** (tel. 237 62), **Bouraq** (tel. 273 33), as well as **Sempati**. Each offers a similar array of destinations at roughly similar prices. Flights to: **Jakarta** (2 per day, Rp311,000); **Denpasar** (8 per day, Rp56,500); **Ujung Pandang** (3 per week, Rp241,700); **Surabaya** (3 per day, Rp124,700); and **Sumbawa Besar** (2 per week, Rp73,000). Taxis are available in front of the airport, but a short walk to the road out front will put the traveler in sight of passing *bemo,* which charge at most a tenth (Rp300) of private rates.

By Ferry

Ferries cross from **Lembar,** Lombok to **Padangbai,** Bali (12 per day, starting at 6am, 3½-7hr., Rp5500). A similar ferry system operates between **Labuhan Lombok,** Lombok and **Poto Tano,** Sumbawa (every hr., 7am-7pm, 1½hr., Rp2000). First class tickets cost more. Bicycles, motorbikes, and cars can be taken aboard for extra rupiah. The ferries have snackbars, but food and water are cheaper ashore.

By Boat

Travelers can also reach Lombok by a more circuitous route. Ships dock at Lembar and move on as follows. The KM *Kelimutu* leaves Lembar every Monday for **Bima, Waingapu, Ende, Kupang, Kalabahi, Maumere, Ujung Pandang** and back. The KM *Sirimau* leaves Lembar every Friday and Sunday for **Ujung Pandang, Surabaya, Sampit, Cirebon, Pontianak,** and **Tanjung.** Inquiries about prices and specific times should be made at the ports themselves, as they are subject to change. Also available between these same ports are **catamaran services,** which are faster and fancier than ferries; business, however, appears to come and go with the quirks of the local economy. Inquiries can be made at Lombok Perama offices (see **Practical Information** below) and at the ports themselves.

GETTING AROUND ON LOMBOK

Bemo are lord in Lombok and run almost anywhere the visitor wishes to brave. They cost less than taxis. Beware of empty *bemo,* as drivers will assume the vehicle is being "chartered," and therefore charge the unsuspecting traveler more. *Bemo* terminals:

Suweta, on the eastern side of the greater Mataram hub. Suweta is Lombok's transportation hub and the place to begin almost any venture. *Bemo* run to Narmada, Praya, greater Mataram, Bangsal, Bayan, Kuta, Lembar, and Labuhan Lombok.
Ampenan, just north of the city's main intersection (near the market). Serves as the apogee in Mataram loops from Suweta, with *bemo* running north to Senggigi.
Praya, in the center of town. Serves points south: Sengkol, Sade, and Kuta.
Narmada, in the center of town. Serves central Lombok, including Masbagik, Pomotong, Suranadi, Tetebatu, and points east of greater Mataram.

Buses run from Suweta, too; they cost less than *bemo* and run to most of the same places, but entail more waiting around. **Taxis** run in greater Mataram (and will take you elsewhere if you pay enough), but aren't particularly common, and well near unheard of outside the city. **Ojek** (read: boys on motorbikes) have a way of cropping up at crossroads; they save time but never money.

■ Greater Mataram

The major urban hub of Lombok consists of four cities between which the traveler— and in all likelihood the native—would be hard pressed to draw lines. Ampenan is the ragtailed port, Mataram is the administrative capital, Cakranegara (or Cakra for short) is the home of traditional craftwork, weaving, and basketware, and Suweta is the cen-

Lombok, Sumbawa, and Flores

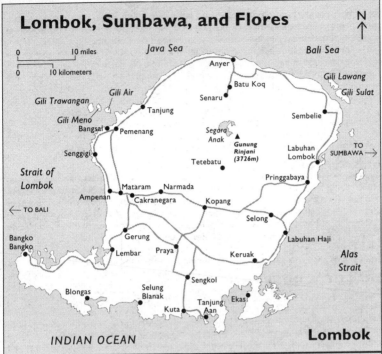

Lombok

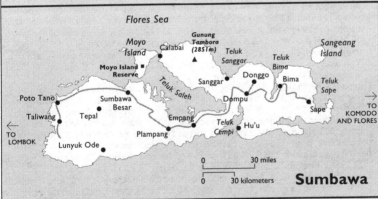

Sumbawa

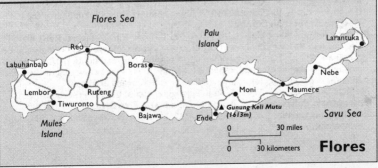

Flores

ter of transportation on Lombok. Strung out along 10km of one wide main street, these four cities constitute the burgeoning commercial locus of Lombok as it expands, repaves, and air conditions to bolster itself for tourism.

The greater Mataram area is generously endowed with spectacles for the visitor and it serves best as a gateway to the rest of Lombok. No glory of the seashore itself, Ampenan is only 12km south of the increasingly popular Senggigi Beach. A plethora of villages offer themselves as cheap and scenic daytrips from Lombok's capital of commerce and administration. The Greater Mataram area is more than a stepping stone; travelers should take note of the Museum Negeri as well as the cockfights of the Mayura Water Palace. Likewise, the Suweta Market is a sight with which to reckon, and the backstreets of northern Ampenan hide lucrative antique shops, a fine view of the ocean, and a temple painted inexplicably like a barber pole.

ORIENTATION

Traffic canters and careens through the greater Mataram area on two roughly parallel, one-way thoroughfares. *Bemo* make the circuit relentlessly with terminals at either end. From west to east **Jalan Yos Sudarso** changes to **Jalan Langko**, then **Jalan Pejanggik,** and finally **Jalan Selaparang.** Running east to west one block south is **Jalan Tumpang Sari,** which becomes **Jalan Panca Usaha, Jalan Pancawarga,** and finally **Jalan Pendidikan**. The hospital, governor's office, main square tourist office, and Mataram University are all along the Jl. Pejanggik section of the road in Mataram.

PRACTICAL INFORMATION

Tourist Offices: Provincial Tourist Service Nusa Tenggara Barat, Jl. Langko 70 (tel./fax 378 28), at the far western end of Mataram in the outskirts of Ampenan. Across the street from the branch post office. Good maps and pamphlets in English. Open Mon.-Thurs. 7am-2pm, Fri. 7am-11am, Sat. 7am-12:30pm.

Tours and Travel: Almost every hotel and *losmen* offers some kind of service, and the eastbound thoroughfare has no shortage of options. Tours will cost exponentially more than a similar self-crafted trip, but will ease the mind of travelers. One sure place is **Perama,** Jl. Pejanggik 66 (tel. 227 64), a few doors east of the hospital. More of a commercial connection than the government office.

Immigration Offices: (tel. 225 20) on Jl. Udayana a few hundred meters north of Jl. Pejanggik on the way to the airport. Regional Office: Dept. of Justice, W. Nusa Tenggara, Jl. Majapahit 7, Mataram (tel. 218 19).

Currency Exchange: There are numerous banks along the Cakra section of Jl. Pejanggik. **Bank Diamond,** Jl. Pejanggik 117 (tel. 356 49). **Bank Pembangunan Indonesia,** Jl. Pejanggik 109-113 (tel. 340 49). All are open in the morning and early afternoon. **Money changers** abound at the main intersection in Ampenan, along Jl. Pejanggik in Cakra, and across from the Suweta bus terminal on Jl. Sandubaya. Hours are longer but still not great; plan ahead.

Air Travel: Garuda (tel. 237 62), on Jl. Yos Sudarso. **Bouraq,** Jl. Pejanggik 43 (tel. 277 353). **Merpati** (tel. 322 26), on Jl. Pejanggik.

Local Transportation: Bemo run along the two main streets, stopping at terminals in Suweta and Ampenan. One fare (Rp300) for any distance, although they may try to charge you more. Watch what the locals pay and follow suit. *Bemo* also run to the airport along Jl. Udayana and to Senggigi along Jl. Saleh Sungkar. Please see **Getting Around on Lombok,** above.

Rentals: Rinjani Rent Car (tel. 214 00), on Jl. Bung Karno. **Metro Rent Car,** Jl. Yos Sudarso 84. Services also available at the airport. **Motorcycle** rentals can be found anywhere. Standard rates are Rp15,000 for 8hr. excluding petrol (Rp1000 per liter). **Note:** road safety, especially within cities, is far below that of the west. *Let's Go* does not suggest two wheels as the safest means of transit.

Medical Services: (tel. 213 45), on Jl. Pejanggik, east of the Governor's Office.

Emergency: Police: tel. 110. **Ambulance:** tel. 114. **Fire Brigade:** tel 114.

Police: In **Ampenan,** Jl. Langko 17 (tel. 337 33) and in **Suweta** (tel. 226 82), on Jl. Selaparang.

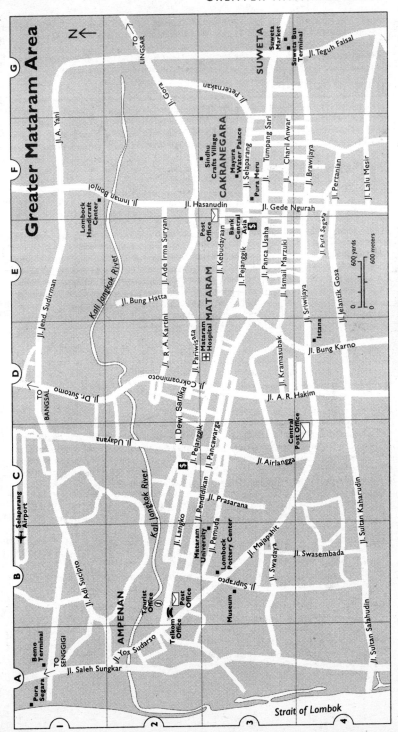

Greater Mataram Area

TO LINGSAR

SUWETA

Suweta Market

Suweta Bus Terminal

Jl. Teguh Faisal

Jl. A. Yani

Jl. Peternakan

Jl. Imam Bonjol

Jl. Goa

Lombock Handicraft Center

CAKRANEGARA

Sindhu Crafts Village

Mayura Water Palace

Pura Meru

Jl. Selaparang

Tumpang Sari

Charil Anwar

Jl. Brawijaya

Jl. Pertanian

Jl. Lalu Mesir

Jl. Hasanudin

Jl. Gede Ngurah

Post Office

Jl. Kebudayaan

Bank Central Asia

Jl. Pejanggik

Jl. Panca Usaha

Jl. Ismail Marzuki

Jl. Pura Segaya

Jl. Ade Irma Suryani

MATARAM

Kali Jangkok River

Jl. Jend. Sudirman

Jl. Bung Hatta

Jl. R. A. Kartini

Jl. Pariwisata

Mataram Hospital

Jl. Sriwijaya

Jl. Istana

Jl. Jelantik Gosa

600 yards

600 meters

0

0

Jl. Cokroaminoto

Jl. Kramasubak

Jl. Bung Karno

TO BANGSAL

Jl. Dr. Sutomo

Jl. A. R. Hakim

Selaparang Airport

Jl. Udayana

Jl. Dewi Sartika

Jl. Pejanggik

Jl. Pancawarga

Central Post Office

Jl. Airlangga

Jl. Langko

Jl. Pendidikan

Jl. Prasarana

Jl. Adi Sucipto

Mataram University

Jl. Pemuda

Lombock Pottery Center

Jl. Majapahit

Jl. Swadaya

Jl. Swasembada

Jl. Sultan Kaharudin

Bemo Terminal

TO SENGGIGI

Tourist Office

Telkom Office

Post Office

AMPENAN

Museum

Jl. Suprapto

Jl. Yos Sudarso

Jl. Saleh Sungkar

Pura Segara

Jl. Sultan Salahudin

Strait of Lombok

Post Offices: GPO, on Jl. Majapahit. *Poste Restante*. Open Mon.-Sat. 8am-2pm, Fri. 8am-11am. Other **branch**: Jl. Langko 21, Ampenan. Open Mon.-Sat. 7:30am-2pm, Fri. 7:30am-12pm and 1pm-2pm.
Telephones: Small *wartel* dot the greater Mataram area. The big **Telkom office** is at Jl. Langko 23 (tel. 370 00) and has a **HCD** telephone. **Telephone code:** 0370.

ACCOMMODATIONS

Lodgings are cheapest and most plentiful in Ampenan, but amid greater noise and hardier dust than some of Cakra's better backwaters. Mid-range accommodations are more common than *losmen* in the greater Mataram area. Many of the "pricier" (US$6 instead of US$4) places include breakfast and, like *losmen*, spare you the tax.

Inap Keluagra Oka (Oka Homestay), Jl. Repatmaja 5 (tel. 224 06), 200m south of Jl. Pejanggik in Cakra. Well-placed on a sidestreet between the two main thorough-fares. Shady, expansive courtyard and decent, if slightly dog-eared, *losmen*-quality rooms. Breakfast included, but no restaurant. Singles Rp10,000. Doubles Rp12,500.

Wisata Hotel and Restaurant, Jl. Koperasi 19 (tel. 269 71), 100m east of Ampenan's main crossroads. Just opened; clean and new with a pleasant terrace and friendly staff. Its proximity to a mosque may daunt the light or late sleeper. Some rooms with A/C. Singles Rp12,500. Doubles Rp15,000.

Chandra Hotel, Jl. Caturwarga 55 (tel. 239 79), south of the Governor's office right in the heart (and heat) of the greater Mataram area. "Bread and Egg every morning," says their literature. More of a western feel with hallways and interior reception desk, but nonetheless flavored by Lombokese proprietorship. Economy singles Rp12,500. Doubles Rp15,000. Triples and A/C rooms cost more.

Shanti Puri Hotel and Restaurant, Jl. Maktal 15 (tel. 326 49), about 100m south off Jl. Pejanggik in eastern Cakra. Comfort enticingly exceeds price with singles starting at Rp7000, doubles Rp9000.

Orindo Hotel and Restaurant, Jl. Teguh Faisal 11 (tel. 249 00), on the main north-south road through Suweta, less than 1km south of the bus terminal. Far from the center of town but convenient to the bus terminal. High-ceilinged, newly and nicely constructed. Breakfast included. Singles Rp20,000. Doubles Rp25,000. Some "suites" are more expensive and have A/C.

FOOD

Despite the proliferation of the hybrid hotel-and-restaurant, the greater Mataram area does have its constituency of *warung*. Lombok's Chinese and Arab communities offer cheap and simple restaurants in Ampenan. For those on the go or on a budget, Cakra's main strip offers good bakeries, as well as some American fast food, and the markets in Suweta and Ampenan sell everything for close to nothing.

Timur Tengah, Jl. Koperasi 22, near downtown Ampenan. Top-notch Middle Eastern, Indonesian, and western food. No main course more than Rp2000. Portions are conservative, but most dishes cost only Rp1000 and sampling is a joy.

Rumah Makan: Aroma, Jl. Palapa I 2, in west Cakra, south of Jl. Pejanggik. Clean, quiet, and cool. Chinese seafood of generous portions. Plenty of non-sea options also available. Main dishes from Rp2000-5000.

Cirebon, Jl. Pabean 113, west toward the sea from Ampenan's main intersection. Cirebon has a petite but promising menu of Chinese and Indonesian fare. Friendly management, local clientele, and prices starting at Rp1750.

Kafe Mira, Jl. Yos Sudarso 124, across the street from and closer to town than Cirebon (in Ampenan). Exhaustive menu of Indonesian food, with main courses as low as Rp500. Ginger coffee is a delectable finish to the meal.

Putri Duyung, Jl. Algenka 4 (tel. 375 78), south of Jl. Pejanggik in central Cakra close to the Suweta bus terminal. Spacious and quiet courtyard with wicker chairs. Plenty of choices, all Indonesian. Main courses Rp3-10,000.

SIGHTS

To escape the helter-skelter honking *bemo* and dull rows of government offices, try stepping into the **Mayura Water Palace,** one of the world's very few Hindu-court-of-justice-gone-civic-parks. Fighting cocks now cluck, ruffle, and strut as Balinese courtiers did when the palace was built in 1744. The park's main attraction is a large pavilion in the center of a monumental rectangular reflecting pool which used to house the court. The pavilion is curiously contrasted by western playground equipment for the youngsters. (Admission Rp500.)

Right across the street (Jl. Pejanggik) stands **Pura Meru,** Lombok's *grande dame* of Balinese temples. Although it too is a fine spot for evading the activity of the main street, size seems to be the temple's only real bragging point. Commissioned by Anak Agung Made Karang of the Singosari Kingdom in 1772, Meru honors the holy trinity of Brahma, Vishnu, and Shiva. Despite its holy gratuity, its 33 shrines, and three towering pagodas, the temple is rather plain and unexciting.

The better temple is **Pura Segara** on the north side of Ampenan. Painted to rival the jocund-colored fishing boats which line the beach before it, Segara is at the northwest corner of a well-shaded and quiet neighborhood, adjacent to a fascinating cemetery. It makes a pleasant and refreshing morning promenade.

Other points of interest include the **Museum Nusa Tenggara Barat,** on Jl. Panji Tilar Negara in southeast Ampenan, which displays 1239 ancient palm-leaf Indonesian manuscripts and a couple of exhibits in English.

SHOPPING

The greater Mataram area has a share of Lombokese Antique Shops, the better part of which can be found in Ampenan. **Gecko Silversmiths and Antiques, Ryan Antiques,** and **Hary Antiques** all are on Jl. Saleh Sungkar north of downtown. The ambitious customer can buy *ikat* cloth and hand-crafted sarong direct from one of Mataram's weaving factories. There are a number of them, including **Rinjani Hand Woven,** Jl. Pejanggik 44, across from the Cilinaya Shopping Centre, and **Selamat Riady,** on the Mataram side of the Water Palace off Jl. Hasanuddin. The surest bet for practical and otherwise hard-to-find merchandise is the **Cilinaya Shopping Centre** on Jl. Pejanggik east of the bend at Mataram. Inarguably the best and cheapest places to shop are greater Mataram's local markets. There's one in Ampenan (on the north side of town near the *bemo* terminal) and one in Suweta (east of the bus terminal), the latter being the largest and most noteworthy.

■ Near Mataram

SENGGIGI

North of Ampenan, miles of sand are at your disposal for the Rp300 price of a *bemo* ride. Northbound *bemo* are easily hailed on Jl. Saleh Sungkar or a few meters north past the *bemo* terminal. A well-paved stretch, Jl. Saleh Sungkar is easily navigated by motorbike. Mataram dissipates quickly into a series of ridges and beaches, some with far more palm trees than cows or locals, and some with the hubbub of international resort construction, tour buses, and myriad non-budget *turis.*

Senggigi is the paragon of the latter. Mid-range and upscale accommodations abound. Jl. Raya (or Main Street) is pockmarked with sidewalk construction and bedecked with signs proclaiming forthcoming luxury, and almost everything is twice as expensive here as in Ampenan. As unappealing as this may sound, Senggigi's beaches are awfully nice, and the town offers a rare pocket of nightlife on an otherwise sleepy Lombok. Furthermore, Senggigi has all the conveniences and amenities of Mataram, although at higher prices.

A two-dimensional coastal town, Senggigi is small enough that all of its services are easy to find along the main road: two **Telkom offices, postal service, money chang-**

ers, a supermarket, bars, **Blue Coral Diving, PADI training** (tel. 930 02), a noteworthy **night market,** some restaurants, and plenty of pricey lodgings.

There is, however, a pleasant niche for those on a budget. **Bumi Aditya Cottages** are cheap and painstakingly landscaped. They sit a few hundred meters off the main road; the driveway is just to the south of the first of Senggigi's two small bridges. Singles start at Rp10,000, doubles at Rp15,000. **Surady Homestay** has about the same prices for less polished, more spartan rooms. It hides behind the supermarket; look carefully, since its path and sign are rather inconspicuous.

With Senggigi as a home base, there are a number of directions to go. Within walking distance to the south is **Pura Batu Bolong** (Hole-in-the-Rock Temple). Built by the Balinese, Batu Bolong faces west across the strait to Bali's revered Gunung Agung—sundown is truly a glorious time here. Batu Bolong's precarious crags make it one of Lombok's prettier Balinese temples. Rumor has it that the Balinese once hurled virgins from Batu Bolong into the raging sea; fortunately, they don't seem to be doing that anymore. (Admission Rp500.)

On the far side of Senggigi, to the north, the spectre of tourism wanes. There are some hotels and ritzy bungalows around Mangsit, but by Setangi, any signs of bulldozers and fake thatch have given way to bovines and a nearly empty road. Much of the beach from Mangsit to Setangi is easily accessible from the road, and, on the outskirts of Setangi, is fringed by grazing cows, grass, and palm trees. More often than not you'll be the only bather. The distances are long enough that motorized transportation is advised; *bemo* run sporadically, and most rental motorbikes can manage the hills. The views from the tops of the ridges become increasingly grand, in inverse proportion to tourist services. Be forewarned that even roadside snack stands become rare from the north side of Setangi until the Pemenang/Bangsal area.

NARMADA

Bemo run from the Suweta terminal eastward for Rp300. In Narmada on the south side of the road there is a **water palace** (it's hard to miss—Narmada is no metropolis) that thrice exceeds Cakra's Mayura. **Pura Kalasa,** named after India's Kalasa River, is a temple of three pools of ascending hill-side levels. The highest pool, traditional, rectangular, and ornamental, was constructed to simulate Gunung Rinjani's Segara Anak for the King of Karang at the beginning of the 19th century. Legend has it that Kalasa, in addition to placating the King's religious needs—he had grown old and could no longer climb Rinjani—also placated his old-man lust; the Balinese monarch would peep down at the village virgins as they cavorted in the pool.

The next pool down has rounded stones and spring-fed water. With western floor lettering and lane lines, the pool is a popular swimming hole for local schoolboys. Tourists can join in the splashing fun if they ask first and pay a nominal fee (in addition to the temple's Rp500 admission). The third, lowest, and largest pool has duck boats aplenty and is often strewn with fishing lines. Local women often come here to do their laundry.

A combination of Sasak, Balinese, and Islamic architecture, Kalasa provides a good number of terraces, corners, shady trees, and gardens in and under which to sit and stroll. There are some *warung* inside (more expensive than those outside) and often a great number of local kids—especially if you visit on the weekend. Expect to be as much of a spectacle to them as the water palace is to you. On the north side of the main road is Narmada's market and *bemo* terminal. The former is large enough to be worth a look—a slightly more rural flavor than Suweta or Ampenan. The latter is the crossroads and point of departure for the sights of central western Lombok.

LINGSAR

North of Narmada but south of Lingsar itself is a temple complex in the middle of a flat rice field. Take a *bemo* from Narmada (Rp300), and chances are the driver will recognize you as a tourist and stop before the gate (there's not much else to see in Lingsar). **Pura Lingsar** is actually the grounds of two temples: the Islamic **Kemaliq** and Hindu **Pura Gaduh**. These two temples symbolize the peaceful co-worship of the Balinese and Sasak faiths with their complementary architecture. This peace is affirmed by the annual **Perang Ketupat,** held sometime between October and December. In addition to celebrating religious harmony, the ceremony is an occasion for prayers for rain and luck.

Within the Kemaliq section of Pura Lingsar is an eel pool fed by the spring water of Gunung Rinjani. Legend has it that if an eel surfaces to eat the egg of those who drop them, it is a symbol of luck. The eels' appetites, however, depend on the size of their stomachs, and thus their promise of fine fortune is only good for the eggs of the first few rounds of tourists. For the blessings of the gods arrive by mid-morning. Eggs are sold in the parking lot for Rp200. (Admission Rp500.)

SURANADI

Suranadi is a low-key and wholly satisfying prize for the exceptional *turis* who is looking to penetrate Lombok's central, jungle-ridden core. *Bemo* run north from the Narmada terminal to the Suranadi intersection for Rp300. Be aware that *bemo* running north from Narmada also go to Lingsar; you should ask the driver or read the destination sign above the windshield. Passengers who request Suranadi will be dropped at a fork in the road; the *bemo* then continues down one prong and Suranadi proper begins 250m down the other.

Suranadi offers two places to stay. **Taman Wisata** or "Hotel Suranadi" is conspicuously set at the road's sharp and upward bend, kitty-corner from the town's temple. The hotel boasts air conditioning, tennis courts, two swimming pools, and a bar and restaurant. The physical plant centers around a converted Dutch administrative building and prices are given in American dollars. Expect to pay US$20-48 for rooms or cottages. The pools, however, are available for use by non-tenants and the swim is well worth the nominal fee.

The cheaper and more thorough Suranadi experience is found at the **Surya Homestay.** Surya is not so easy to find—inquiries at Suranadi's small circle of *warung* (to the right of the main road) will be met warmly and quickly. Surya charges Rp25,000 per night, but that price includes breakfast, lunch, and dinner served up—in generous and artfully garnished portions—from the *warung*. Visitors will be fed until full. The price also includes, though not officially, admission to village life; guests are surrounded by babies, roosters, farmers, dogs, and women doing laundry. The two rooms are on the squalid side of friendly, but comfortable enough.

Those who opt out of a night in Suranadi may still enjoy visits to the nearby sights. **Pura Suranadi** is a temple which contains no fewer than five spring-fed pools. Visitors may bathe, but ask first and make the appropriate donation. Pura Suranadi is one of Lombok's oldest temples and, like those farther west, is built in Balinese-style architecture. Before the temple on the main road to the left is **Hutan Wisata Suranadi,** a neglected wildlife reserve. A ticket desk exists, but there is no fence or limiting entryway, so admission seems to be contingent upon the presence or absence of a tickettaker. The preserve is a case study in the environmental misfortune and tragedy of Lombok. Apparently until about 1982 the jungles surrounding Suranadi had a preponderance of black monkeys—a preponderance that has since been pared to well near nothing by bird-hunters from Mataram. The forest in Hutan Wisata is still relatively full of gray monkeys brachiating, but their swart cousins have yet to repopulate. Even if the visitor can't catch sight of a critter of significant genetic proximity to himself, Hutan Wisata is an easy, quick, and safe place to feel deep in the tropical underbrush.

■ Kuta

Once upon a time, Princess Putri Mandalika, distraught by her unmitigatable position between six courting local princes, cast herself seaward from one of Kuta's dramatic volcanic bluffs. Ever since then, the coy, slippery, and tragic maiden is reincarnated every year as the *nyale,* a snake abundant in the waters off southern Lombok—or so legend has it. The tale of Mandalika is responsible for the name of Kuta's beach—Putri Nyale—as well as the annual Bau Nyale ceremony (February or March) in which multitudes of local Sasaks camp on the beach, *nyale* are caught and cooked, and young folks play tag in boats on the water. Tourists abound for the annual Bau Nyale, but that's not to say they're scarce the rest of the year. Kuta is the staple stop for surfers, sunbathers, and budget travelers in southern Lombok. The majority of services in Kuta are rock-bottom cheap. Kuta offers close proximity to tremendous solitude, arid air, and, even when Mandalika is a far-off February memory, a bustling beach alive with net-mending, line-casting, crab-catching fishermen.

ORIENTATION AND PRACTICAL INFORMATION

The area is popular enough that *bemo* sometimes run from Lembar to Kuta—inquiries can be made in the crowd of *bemo* drivers at the Lembar ferry terminal. The trip shouldn't cost much more than Rp1000. From Suweta, buses run to Praya, Sengkol, and eventually Kuta for Rp1500; *bemo* make the same run and are slightly cheaper. **Perama** and other tour companies arrange buses from the greater Mataram area, and even from Senggigi, but charge nearly 10 times more than public transportation. Boats sail from Ekas to Awang, where *bemo* occasionally run to Kuta.

Kuta suffers from a dearth of street names and telephone numbers, but its size and character excuse this: the visitor probably won't get lost. The bulk of tourist services are concentrated on the beachfront road. There is a **police station,** the Wisma Segara Anak **postal agency/Perama office,** and **money changer/warung hybrids.** Kuta has no hospital, but Doctor A.A. GD. Raka B. lives on the main north-south drag (the road to Sengkol) about 1km from the beach. Kuta has no *wartel.* **Emergency number:** 110. **Telephone code:** 0364.

ACCOMMODATIONS AND FOOD

The bungalows along the beachfront are of similar quality and price. In the off season prices are exceptionally low and decent singles begin at Rp5000, doubles at Rp7,000. Note that prices may double in July and August when business really picks up. **Sekar Kuning (Yellow Flower) Wisma** has a wide selection of room choices, and its garden is better groomed than the competition. **Anda Cottages** also has good shade and prices. Travelers can haggle with the beach-front proprietors easily enough on their own, but there are a couple of nicer (though more expensive and less scenic) places off the beach. **Lamancha Homestay** charges Rp15,000 a room, but is a bit more polished than the main row cottages. A congenial family runs the show here and cares for the well-swept garden. Lamancha is on the eastern end of the beach-front road (after it has turned inland, away from the water). Even farther from the beach, better-tended, and higher-priced is the **Matahari Inn** (tel. 548 32). Low season singles begin at Rp15,000, doubles at Rp20,000. They have just added 12 newly built air-conditioned rooms which go for Rp80,000. Best of all, Matahari is intricately landscaped, with an elaborately decorated restaurant. The "International Library" looks like loads of fun.

Most accommodations in Kuta have their own restaurants, but the half dozen waterfront *warung* are cheaper and closer to the peddling activity of the main street. The **Bamboo Restaurant** offers food less grill-greasy than most other Kuta establishments, but costs more. Main courses cost Rp5000, with seafood for up to Rp10,000. The sign boasts a 125-item menu, but that variety seems contingent upon market day in Praya.

SIGHTS

Kuta's main sight is, obviously, its beach; Putri Nyale is scattered with coral, sand remarkably like birdseed, clumps of craggy rock, and local children selling sarong. While Putri Nyale is too rocky and shallow for good swimming, it does have varied sands, fishermen, a particularly good stroll, and rocky pockets. The changing clouds and shadows of dusk and dawn are worth investigating as are the rocks and bluffs to the west which tumble forth with long trails and vivid lookouts. Kuta also houses two rather petite bookshops and a market on Sunday and Wednesday. Surfing throughout the region is supposedly very good, and boats can be chartered to choice spots—check at the Perama office.

■ Near Kuta

SOUTH COAST BEACHES

Although **Putri Nyale** beach itself is too popular, rocky, and shallow to satisfy the wistful hopes of a paradise-intent tourist, such fulfillment is not far away. Selong Blanak, Tanjung Aan, and Gerupak all offer more swimmable and secluded beaches, and all are within day-tripping distance of Kuta.

Selong Blanak beach is worth the trip for the drive itself; the road ascends the coastal volcanic foothills and affords some pretty spectacular ocean vistas, and it also winds through valleys of pre-modern Sasak agriculture.

If your map shows no direct route from Kuta to Selong Blanak, it's out of date. The road is all paved now—more or less—although *bemo* are a rare sight along the 10-12km stretch and require patience and an early start for optimal use. The easiest way to make the trip is by motorbike; travelers who stay in Kuta can rent one from their *losmen* for as little as Rp12,000 per day. Petrol is available at a number of beachfront *warung* for Rp800 per liter. Bicycles can also be rented for around Rp5000 per day, but are recommended only for the fittest of the fit, given the dramatic topography of the area. From there it's a matter of heading west, veering to the left (whenever you have a choice of paved roads) and following any signs.

When you reach the intersection with a sign for **Selong Blanak Cottages,** turn left to reach the water. This establishment is 1300m from the beach and one of a few places to stay in southwestern Lombok. Singles and doubles both cost Rp15,000 in the low season; in the high season (July and August) single prices rise to Rp20,000 while double prices increase to Rp25,000. Rooms are clean and well-decorated with wicker and bamboo, but there isn't much—other than the beach—to keep the traveler busy. An isolated span of crabs, black rocks, and sallow sand, Selong Blanak provides good swimming and plenty of sun. There's a village hidden among the shoreline vegetation at the eastern end, but the rest of the unoccupied beach (at least a kilometer) permits privacy and peace.

In contrast to the arid, mountainous, outback-esque drive to the west, the beaches east of Kuta—Tanjung Ann and Pantai Gerupak—appear at the fringes of flat coastal coconut groves. Much of these groves are undeveloped and the density of trees approaches that of a forest. **Tanjung Ann** is a cove of Gumbang Bay east of Kuta. It's not hard to find—just always veer right (onto paved roads) along the eastbound road out of Kuta for about 6km. Known for its swimming and surfing, Tanjung Ann is not the place to head for seclusion and frolic *au naturel*. It is, however, a somewhat happening and thoroughly gorgeous stretch of beach. Although undeveloped presently, a Lombok Tourism Development Centre sign seems a harbinger of impending hotels and crowds. Tanjung Aan may well be Lombok's next Senggigi.

Gerupak, on the other hand, sits firmly in the hands of fishermen. Continue east on the road which runs to Tanjung Ann, and it'll eventually turn to dirt, and finally to the sand of a beach bedecked with fishing boats. There is no place to stay in Gerupak (and little place to park) but it offers a winding, wanderable coastline, a market on Tuesday, and, if you inquire among the right batch of seafarers, a boat across Gumbang Bay to Bumbang. For the most reliable transport, make the trip early in the day (Rp500). As with Selong Blanak, motorbike can be a fine way to beach-hop. Here, because of the flat terrain, a bicycle will also do fine.

SASAK VILLAGES

The road down to Kuta (or back to Praya) takes the traveler through the dry and dusty hand-tilled heartland of Sasak culture. Although any Sasak village which pro-

INDONESIA

nounces hawks itself is, by that very act, somewhat suspect, there are some quasi-commercial stops in southern central Lombok which hold on to their traditions.

Sade is the best known, and thus the most bilingual and commercial. Here, tourists can glean a sense of Sasak architecture, pace of life, and agriculture if they don't focus too intently on the craft booths. One way to mitigate the tourist-consciousness of Sade is to look behind the stands of goods for sale, where the products are produced. A similar, and perhaps slightly less affected village, is **Rembitan,** 2km north of Sade. Rembitan also comes complete with ambitious young guides, but has the additional attraction of **Mesjid Kuno,** one of Lombok's oldest (and most thatched-roofed) mosques. Farther north yet is **Sengkol,** a market center for outlying villages. Sengkol is also a stop between Kuta and Suweta if you take public transportation; if you have to transfer, you might want to check out Sengkol's market. From Sengkol, *bemo* run northwest to Penunjak and Sukara, centers of traditional pottery and fabric making, respectively. The hard-core shopper will probably find cheaper prices at these loci than at the middlemen dealers of Suweta and Ampenan. The most traditional Sasak villages are the small ones, as yet unplumbed and unwired, still cultivating with cows and back muscles. A *bemo,* bus, or motorcycle trip over any southern-central back-road will show you the true stuff.

■ Gunung Rinjani

Rising 3726m smack dab in the center of the northern coast, Gunung Rinjani is the biggest hit of the island, serving as a splendorous backdrop to almost all of Lombok's views. This hulking heap of rock and dirt sends water rushing seasonally to the far-thest corners of the island and governs the clouds as they twist and churn from north to south. By the very nature of its preponderant size, Rinjani is the holiest site on Lombok. Worshipping it as a volcano akin to Bali's sacred Gunung Agung, local Balinese Hindus make an annual journey to Rinjani's top to chuck goldfish and jewelry into Segara Anak, the crater lake. The Sasak Muslims often climb for the convalescent promise of the hot springs. Even many foreigners regard Rinjani as a glorious and awe-inspiring stop on the tourist circuit and subsequently make their own pilgrimage to the summit.

For travelers inclined toward the outdoors, climbing Rinjani is one of the most exhilarating experiences to be had on Lombok. Commercial trekking services are plentiful and affordable; there's no excuse for missing the volcano altogether. There are plenty of ways to skim Rinjani's slopes, both in terms of point of departure and method. The summit can be reached from nearly all sides—from Tetebatu, Saesot, Sembalun Lawang, or Torean—and inquiries about trips and guides may be made in respective towns. The most established, and possibly most scenic route, however, is by way of Batu Koq and Senaru, two villages located on the same road on Rinjani's northern foothills.

GETTING THERE AND AWAY

Due to the popularity of Rinjani treks, transportation to Batu Koq or Senaru can be arranged as part of a package tour through a Perama office. Standard three-day pack-ages run about US$110. Needless to say, self-fashioned expeditions cost less and can be undertaken easily. *Bemo* or public vans to Bayan can be caught either at the Suweta Terminal or anywhere on the road stretching along the northwest coast. These stop in Pemenang, Tanjung, and any of the smaller towns along the way. Fare is about Rp2500 from Suweta to Bayan. Although Rinjani is a popular destination, it is also far from any Lombok's commercial hub. After Bayan, people along the way may try to convince travelers there isn't regular public transportation; there is. *Bemo* run from Bayan to Batu Koq and Senaru for Rp1000. Batu Koq and Senaru can also be reached from Labuhan Lombok or Pringgabaya, but as this is a less frequented route; transportation is not as direct or reliable.

ACCOMMODATIONS AND FOOD

The villages of **Batu Koq** and **Senaru** lie 1km apart along the same road. Although Senaru is the smaller of the two, it is a closer and more scenic point of departure, as it is nestled farther up Rinjani's foothills. Senaru may be a tiny town, but the swarm of potential trekkers overrunning the area has ushered in numerous tourism services, which, fortunately, have not compromised the village's endearingly untainted backwoods appeal.

All of the accommodations in Batu Koq and Senaru offer services and rent equipment for trekking at competitive prices. Staying in a particular *pondok* does not bind a guest to use that *pondok's* guides and sleeping bags. That being said, trekkers should choose a room they like and then shop around before hitting the slopes. A *pondok* is more likely to give better deals to guests who are checking the competition down the main road.

Segara Anak Restaurant and Homestay, on the north side of Senaru (left off the road for those driving in from Bayan), offers excellent service, as well as a magnificent view of Senaru's rice-terraced river valley. Singles cost Rp7500, doubles 10,000. Breakfast is included. This homestay runs a van (free for customers) to the trailhead. Be forewarned, however, that prices in Senaru (and Batu Koq as well) can inflate outrageously during the high season. **Pondok Guru Bakti Senaru** is about 500m up the hill from Segara Anak Homestay, closer to the trailhead. For similar prices as Segara Anak, travelers can get nicer rooms but less remarkable views.

The cheapest option is the **Pondok Batu Koq Cottages,** farther north down the hill. Singles go for Rp5000, doubles Rp8000. Since it's on the west side of the main road (instead of east like Guru Bakti and Segara Anak), this *pondok* lacks the elevated vista of tropical mesh, resulting in rather dark rooms. The service, however, is helpful, and their trekking fees, are relatively cheap. Even those who don't stay may wish to consider a package trek here.

CLIMBING RINJANI

Travelers who find their own way to Batu Koq or Senaru opt for package deals from local *pondok.* These three-day packages with guide, tent, sleeping bag, sleeping mat, and water run for about US$80 per person. This is rather steep, but prices per person drop dramatically with more people, so you might want to bring or make some friends. Packages are well worth the money just to have a knowledgeable guide. Unless potential hikers are in top shape the climb is challenging, and waking to hot coffee and fried bananas is far nicer than rising to an empty stomach and cold, match-fumbling fingers. Those who shun the package deals, thrive on the Hemingway-esque existence, or already have some of the supplies can expect prices to break down as follows (estimated for three-day trips): tents rent for Rp12,000, sleeping bags Rp5000, sleeping mats Rp2500, porters Rp15,000 per day, and guides Rp20-25,000 per day. Porters speak less English than guides, don't cook, and don't lead—essentially they carry equipment. Due to fluctuating exchange rates, travelers can get better deals if they pay in rupiah.

Rinjani has three levels, each of which takes varying lengths of time to climb. In two days and a night, hikers can make it to the "first rim." From here a 45-minute sunset and the uncanny crater lake of Segara Anak can be observed. In another day, hikers can venture down into the crater, swim in the lake, and bask in the simmering, murky, supposedly medicinal hot springs. When going down into the caldera, travelers should watch their step; past hikers have fallen to their deaths stepping on loose rocks. The volcanic cone within the crater is an even rougher climb and most visitors are content to view it from a distance. With one more day and an extra dose of stamina, hikers can mount all 3726m of Rinjani. Whatever the duration and route, trekkers will witness surprisingly varied scenery; sunset from the first rim consists of about six different views, all of which alone would be nothing shy of majestic. Rinjani is an amazing escape (but also includes passage through) from the predominant tropical heat and foliage of most of northwestern and central Lombok.

INDONESIA

Here are some caveats that trekkers may want to keep in mind. First, travelers should not expect the climb to be easy. Those in relatively good shape will manage, but Rinjani is a mountain which, for those who haven't climbed extensively, is something akin to eight hours of stairs. Second, Rinjani's rims can be downright cold at night; water won't freeze but feet will. Be sure to have plenty of warm clothes, especially socks; sleeping bags will not provide enough warmth. Third, many hikers are indiscriminate about where they throw their trash and where they move their bowels, so watch where you walk and try to be an exception.

■ Tetebatu

As the arid southern Lombok plain begins its arch upward into Rinjani's alluvial slopes, the land becomes fertile from the benefit of the mountain's runoff and cool beneath Rinjani's daily nimbus of cloud. Tetebatu sits on the cusp between foothills and farmland, blending the misty and temperate weather of the former with the fertile horticulture of the latter. *Pondok* and *losmen* are islands amidst intricate fields of rice and tobacco; the best reason to visit is for unadulterated peace. The fields are yours to wander (greet the farmers and don't crush the crops) as far as the black monkey forest to the north and the jungle waterfalls to the east and west. If after a day or two placid Tetebatu loses its draw, a circuit trip of local craft villages can be made by *dokar,* bicycle, or motorbike.

ORIENTATION AND PRACTICAL INFORMATION

Bemo run from Suweta to Narmada for Rp300; from the latter, another *bemo* runs to Pomotong for Rp1000. Those coming from the south can catch a *bemo* from Praya to Kopang and then Kopang to Pomotong. However the traveler gets there, Pomotong is the turn-off for Tetebatu, and *bemo* run all the way there for about Rp1500. In Pomotong, motorbike drivers offer direct passage to Tetebatu.

Tetebatu has northern and southern concentrated areas separated by 1km along the main road. *Losmen* are located in two clusters, one between the two centers of Tetebatu, and the other on the eastbound side road which springs from the southern center. The monkey forest is north of the northern hub. Tetebatu has few formal services for the tourist beyond food and lodgings. A **Perama office** is part of Lentera Indah or Green Orry Inn on the south side of the eastbound road from lower Tetebatu. The only other answer to tourist services is at the bizarre but helpful shop of **Usman Ali** in the neighboring village of Kembang Kuning which is about 1km down the eastbound road past the city gate. Ali **changes money,** exhibits his personal art gallery, sells **postage stamps,** and arranges **treks** to the surrounding forests, fields, and Gunung Rinjani for reasonable prices.

ACCOMMODATIONS

The accommodations in Tetebatu are south of the town center on the main road. It is quite likely that a *bemo* driver will stop in front of the one which his cousin owns but travelers need not feel obliged. The array and quality of bungalows in Tetebatu are perhaps its best attribute. The tourist is likely to be in Tetebatu for a view of the fields, and as such, outlook is the foremost criterion for choice *losmen.*

Mekar Sari Homestay is one of the gems of this village. Rooms surpass mere cleanliness with their artful simplicity, handsome, checkered pillows, toilet paper, and a restaurant bedecked with Sasak masks, hats, and Balinese wind chimes. Rooms run Rp7500-10,000 during low season and include a generous breakfast. Fine jewelry is available from **Taswin Silversmith,** part of the compound. Mekar Sari is located in the cluster of accommodations between Tetebatu's two hubs. In the same clump as Mekar Sari stands **Wisma Diwi Enjeni,** which has an equally magnificent view, with rooms as cheap as Rp6-8000 in the low season. The landscaping is nicer than the rooms, but they are worth the price.

Cendrawasih Cottages, in the southern clump of lodgings off the eastbound road, are ornately Sasak almost to the point of Byzantine. They cost a little more, but for the Rp11-16,500 you get hyper-clean rooms, *mandi* with potted plants, a hammock, and breakfast in their elevated view-laden gazebo restaurant.

The rock-bottom best bargain solely in terms of quirkiness per rupiah ratio is **Ali Lombok Gallery and Inn** in the village of Kembang Kuning about 1km down the eastbound waterfall road. This place offers rooms for free, provided that visitors buy breakfast (Rp4000 for one person, Rp6000 for two). Ali's rooms may be sparse, but he promises free entertainment, whatever that entails.

FOOD

Tetebatu is not well-trodden enough to support anything of a restaurant industry. All the inns and homestays offer some kind of dining: **Diwi Enjeni's restaurant** has cheap prices, as does **Pondok Tetebatu** next door. Even if you don't stay at Mekar Sari, you may wish to try a meal in their restaurant. The food reflects both some professional culinary training and influence from Holland. On the south side of Tetebatu's northern cluster is *warung* Harmoni's universal menu.

SIGHTS

Locals seem not to mind the meandering tourists, and their tolerance and hospitality are what make Tetebatu the placid retreat it is. The expansive and occasionally labyrinthine fields are the foremost sight in these parts, and the visitor can spend an afternoon or full day wandering around. The countryside is an end unto itself, but offers resplendent walkways to a waterfall to the west, a waterfall and natural pool to the east, and a black monkey forest to the north. It would be difficult for visitors to find the back routes here unaided; local guides, however, offer half-day service for about Rp5000. Main roads go as far as the eastern waterfall and the monkey forest. For the former, follow the signs along the eastbound road out of Tetebatu's southern hub; the path is well-marked. To reach the monkey forest follow the main road north until it veers sharply to the right. A dirt road marked by a park sign (look for the word *hutan,* which means forest) continues north at that point. Local boys often gather here to offer their services as guides.

■ Near Tetebatu

The rural towns of Lombok are ripe with local textile arts and, far from being an exception, the region around Tetebatu may best exemplify the island's simple and ingenious crafts. Tetebatu has become aware of its proximity to these sights, thus *ojek* drivers and bungalow owners alike will offer tourists various packages and means to get around the handicraft loop. The **Green Orry Inn** and the **Pondok Bulan Homestay** both rent bicycles (and include useful, hand-drawn maps) for about Rp6000. The area is flat enough that biking is possible, although the stretches along the main east-west road (Pomotong to Masbagik) are busy enough to require equal parts level head and luck. Motorbikes are initially offered for Rp15,000 per day (excluding petrol), but negotiation may yield a cheaper price. Public transportation is the budget option; *bemo* and *dokar* cover all destinations, and as long as travel is conducted early they shouldn't be hard to catch. The frugal can walk to some of the nearby villages. Regional maps can be acquired at local inns.

Three km directly south of Tetebatu is the craft center of **Kotaraja.** While not the ideal stop, Kotaraja is a productive village where the crossroads of trade overlap. Another walkable 3km south of Kotaraja is the petite weaving village **Loyok.** Here, locals produce traditional cloth in the back of their homes and sell them in the front. On the main street there is a "handicraft center," but residential shops are more interesting to browse through. Visitors who ask to see where the weaving is done will likely make some friends and get a lesson in bamboo-ring making.

While in Loyok, the tourist might as well walk the 500m to neighboring **Rungkang,** where the locals sell earthy burnt-sienna pots which resemble over-baked grecian urns. **Masbagik,** however, is considered the center for the sale and production of ceramics. Lying east of Pomotong along the main drag, Masbagik has a large market on Mondays, as well as telephone and postal services. Travelers may want to flag down a *bemo* at this point, as Masbagik is a long walk from Tetebatu. **Pringgasela** lies farther from Masbagik (go east toward Rempung and then veer north off the main road), but worth the trip as it offers Lombokese weaving at its finest.

NORTHWEST GILI

Gili Trawangan, Gili Air, and Gili Meno could well be the three bears to the Lombokese traveler's Goldilocks; their slightly ascending sizes and common attributes of glorious reefs, good beaches, and motor-free roads aside, the three *gili* vary enough to offer visitors hot porridge, cold porridge, and porridge just right—though which island is which depends on the disposition and proclivities of the visitor. Unfortunately, all three islands are, to some degree, tourist magnets. Prices average at least Rp500 more than the mainland's, and the accommodations, especially during the high season, can cost twice as much. Tourists get miles of beach and fathoms of coral but pay a somewhat hefty price.

GETTING THERE AND AWAY

> Because of poor exchange rates on the *gili,* tourists should try to change enough money on the mainland before embarking to the islands.

A tour of the three *gili* can be arranged through a Perama office anywhere on Lombok. Such packages cost upwards of US$100. The do-it-yourself tour is far cheaper and not at all difficult to do. From the Mataram area, public vans and *bemo* run from the Suweta Terminal (Rp1500). Drivers stop at Pemenang where *dokar* drivers cluster about waiting to take new arrivals to the harbor town of **Bangsal,** 1km away (Rp500). Bangsal offers little more than the boats to the *gili,* and is thus lacking in tourist services. The only option for accommodation is the pricey but almost elegantly furnished **Taman Sari Guest House and Café,** halfway between Pemenang and Bangsal. Taman Sari charges Rp15,000 for a single, Rp20,000 for a double and has flush toilets. Breakfast and tax are not included.

The **ticket office** for transportation to the islands is next to the Perama office. Facing the water, it's on the right hand side. A sign clearly indicates prices. **Public boats** are the best way to go, but leave only when there are enough passengers. This usually isn't a problem and you should not have to wait more than an hour. Prices are: Rp1350 to Gili Air, Rp1650 to Gili Meno, and Rp1750 to Gili Trawangan. It's best to arrive in Bangsal before late afternoon. **Shuttles** run at 10am and 4:30pm and cost Rp3000 to Gili Air, Rp3500 to Gili Meno, and Rp4000 to Gili Trawangan. The ticket office also **charters boats** to Gili Air for Rp15,000, Gili Meno for Rp18,000, and Gili Trawangan for Rp21,000. From the same batch of seamen, tourists can charter themselves a boat for the day (this is also easily arranged once on one of the islands). Folks offer prices of Rp60,000, but there's always room for bargaining.

Similar transportation exists between the three *gili.* **Inter-island shuttles** run twice per day, usually mid-morning and mid-afternoon; specific times are available at ticket offices close to the landings. Boats between Air and Meno and Meno and Trawangan cost Rp3000, between Air and Trawangan Rp4000.

The boat trip is the high point (among many) of the visit to the *gili.* Despite the motor at the back of the boat, the motions, faces, and colors seem centuries old or utterly foreign. It would be wise to take off your shoes or wear those ugly Tevas, as your feet will surely get soaked. The men who pilot these crafts are barefoot themselves, laid back, and seemingly oblivious to the water.

■ Gili Trawangan

Gili Trawangan is the biggest and by far the most popular island. Even in the low season, it's bustling with young backpackers who come for the bars, the American movies, and the meager price of a hip and happening otherworldly beach resort. Contributing to the college dorm-like activity are the government's chainsaws and bulldozers; in 1992 some establishments were pressured and even forced to shut down or move from the west side of the island. Most of the cheap accommodations, currently Trawangan's only kind, are crammed into a narrow strip along the east coast. At the north and south ends of the strip, however, there are some places with respectable elbow room, and crowd-weary travelers can (at least during the low season when rooms are available) find some peace. A main draw of Trawangan for some social and anti-social folks alike is the *gili's* big hill, on which Japanese fortifications from World War II left traces. In addition, the government's alleged aggression has, for the present, kept the west side an expansive, underdeveloped stretch ripe for solitary wandering.

ORIENTATION AND PRACTICAL INFORMATION

Almost everything on Gili Trawangan is on the east coast. The boat landing is at about the midpoint of the east coast. Trawangan has a **Perama office** a little to the south of the landing. **PT Anjani Tours and Travel** is a couple of doors south, and **PT Wannen Tours** (tel. 311 77) is north of the landing. Prices are competitive, and all three can arrange tours and trekking throughout Lombok. **Money changers** dotting the main drag offer low rates. Do not be deceived by the postal service signs—they only indicate places which sell stamps; there is **no post office.** The **Telkom office** is a shanty, shortly north of the boat landing. **Dokar** and walking will suffice for transportation, although **bicycles** can be rented for a little more (at least Rp5000 per day). Trawangan hosts a generous share of **diving outfits** and is probably the best of the three islands at which to bargain shop. **Snorkeling** costs Rp3000 per day, but lower prices should be argued for. There is **no hospital and no police.**

ACCOMMODATIONS AND FOOD

In the most crowded neighborhoods there isn't much to suggest or rank; lodgings typically cost Rp10-15,000 for singles and doubles. Some scrappier rooms cost less, and each inn has a bar/restaurant, usually equipped with MTV and laserdisc movies. The more varied accommodations, however, are on the northern and southern fringes. Trawangan's restaurant/bungalow combos have cornered most of the culinary market, and the best answer to eating out is the string of beachfront **warung** north of the landing. These offer lower rates, a breeze good for warding off voracious flies, and cheaper prices than their competitors.

Rainbow Cottages, at the southern end of the strip about 1km left from the landing. This place fits the typical mold but has a little more elbow room. All rooms with electricity, showers, and breakfast. Low season singles Rp10,000. Doubles Rp12,000. Tax included.

Mawar I Bungalows, to the south of Rainbow. Offers everything you need, more isolation, and no frippery or garnish. Reasonable prices year-round. Singles Rp5000. Doubles Rp8000.

Alex Homestays, hidden in the village behind the strip. Walk 200m south from the landing and keep an eye open for the signs. Their price includes everything and a hammock. Singles Rp5000. Doubles Rp8000.

Sudi Mampir Cottages, north of the landing. All cottages face the ocean. Despite the peculiar, non-Euclidean lean of their bungalows, Sudi offers the standard package of electricity, shower, and breakfast. Singles Rp5000. Doubles Rp8000.

■ Gili Air

Gili Air is just right for those of mild sensibilities. Trafficked enough to be growing, but growing slowly enough to retain its lazy afternoon placidity, Air is a moderate average of its neighbors. Slightly more lush than its two counterparts, the island is forested by coconut groves and trodden by cloven beauties. The villagers are friendly, having resolved themselves to the blooming tourist trade, but not yet having grown Trawangan's sharp incisors of capitalistic smarts.

ORIENTATION AND PRACTICAL INFORMATION

Gili Air is almost entirely convex and its layout is quite simple. A main road traces the perimeter of the island with a few roads cutting through the village in the middle. Almost all of the tourist services are on the beachfront. The boat lands on the southern side of the island. The circumference of the island can easily be walked in a couple of hours. The southern and eastern coasts are the most crowded with bungalows and services.

The **Perama office** is located in front of the Hotel Gili Indah; from here, **tours** can be arranged all over Lombok, and glass-bottom boat trips are available for the immediate area. Air has no banks but **money changers** are in abundance. Air also has **no post office,** so those wishing to contact the outside world must use the **wartel** at the Hotel Gili Indah. There's a service charge of Rp5000 for collect calls. Once off the boat, there are three means of **transportation.** *Dokar* can take tourists anywhere on the island for Rp500. Feet serve just as well, although those in a hurry may opt for a bicycle rental (no more than Rp5000). **Scuba equipment** can also be rented and a number of places offer trips and training (about US$50 and US$250, respectively). **Snorkeling equipment** rents for about Rp3000 from almost any bungalow. Gili Air has **no hospital or police,** but there's a **health clinic** (Puskesmas) on the south side in the village.

ACCOMMODATIONS

The island is small enough to be quickly canvassed, and it won't take long to notice the uniformity of bungalows on Gili Air. All offer mosquito nets, *mandi,* and breakfast, with the variable luxuries being electricity, shower, inclusion of the 10% government tax in the price, hammock, and, of course, location. Count on adding Rp2-10,000 to the following prices during the high season in July and August (and don't count on finding a room easily). Gili Air lodgings tend to have an earlier checkout time (10am) than other spots on Lombok. Those looking for mid-range accommodations find their way to either **Hotel Gili Air** (tel. 223 11), at the far opposite from the boat landing, or **Hotel Gili Indah** (tel. 363 41), a short ways west of the landing.

Salabose Cottages, to the left of the landing in the southwest corner of Gili Air, offers the best combination of quality and price. Salabose faces west toward the mainland, Gili Meno, and, most importantly, the setting sun. All rooms include hammock, shower, breakfast, and tax. Singles Rp7000. Doubles Rp10,000.

Safari Cottages Bar and Restaurant, next door to Salabose. Safari is run by an Indonesian native who spent 28 of his 30 years in Holland; as such, Safari makes a successful effort to be a little hip with a Bohemian flavor to the decor, forthcoming live music, and daily evening buffets (with music and drink) for Rp4000. Rooms have no electricity but brand-new bathrooms. Includes breakfast and tax. Singles Rp12,000. Doubles Rp15,000.

Gili Kesuma Gardening Cottages, close to the boat landing (head straight inland after you disembark). Among Air's very cheapest finds. Has electricity but no showers. Kesuma Garden is more integrated with the village than most of Air's accommodations and thus has a casual-homestay feel. Singles Rp6000. Doubles Rp8000. Prices don't go up significantly in the high season.

FOOD

Almost without exception, each set of bungalows has a restaurant (and often times a *warung*). Worth looking at, if not patronizing, is Air's **Il Pirata,** located west and inland from the landing, which serves Italian entrees from Rp7-9000. Fantastically enough, it is constructed in the shape of a giant pirate ship. Enjoy your pasta amidst a fake Spanish caravelle with jibs and mainsheets of bamboo, cannons of coconut trunk logs, and colors of Indonesian red, yellow, and black.

■ Gili Meno

Gili Meno, in the middle, is the baby of the trio—and mildly destitute at that. Perhaps on account of a bad and somewhat fallacious mosquito rap, its briny tapwater, or sheer happenstance alone, Meno is the least visited and, consequently, least visitor-friendly of the three *gili*. During the low season Meno seems to operate at half-speed; all the bungalows rent to the traveler, but their restaurants usually close down. The lack of traffic can be a blessing, however, as Meno's grubby serenity can be part of its charm. The north of the island is empty and dry in a seductively covert way that would behoove the agendas of Butch Cassidy and the Sundance Kid. Although far too lively for misanthropes, the southeast shore is equally entrancing and considerably better groomed.

ORIENTATION AND PRACTICAL INFORMATION

Boats arrive at the southeastern side, and most of the tourist facilities are around, or just north, of the landing. Except for the Good Heart Restaurant on the northwest side, the western side of the island is undeveloped. It hosts a salt lake which allegedly serves the procreative needs of mosquitoes in the rainy season.

Meno offers the traveler even fewer resources than Air. Indonesia's endemic **Perama offices** have their Meno outpost near the boat landing; **tours** throughout Lombok can be arranged, as well as local glass-bottom boat trips. There are no banks but **money changers** are available, concentrating thickly around the landing. There is **no post office,** but the **wartel** is south of the landing at the Gazebo Meno Hotel. Although Meno is blessedly free of internal combustion engines, **dokar** transport those in a hurry for Rp500-1000. **Scuba diving trips** run about US$50 per day (including two trips); training is available for more. **Skin diving** is as cheap as you bargain, but at most Rp3000 per day. There is **no hospital or police.**

ACCOMMODATIONS

The middle, least populated, and smallest island, Meno has the barest offering of good food and lodgings. On both accounts, the area south (left) of the boat landing has the most to offer. The southeast corner boasts the most swimmable and sea-trinket ridden stretch of Meno's beach and is, consequently, the most populated. For bargain prices, head inland from the boat landing to Rawa Indah or Fantastic Cottages. In the low season, singles run about Rp6000, doubles Rp10,000. You get what you pay for: clean, simple bungalows in a grubby, rural cow plot.

Kontiki Cottages, south of the landing. A little on the expensive side, but the high-stilted, quasi-Sasak thatch domes are fun and well-shaded by Meno's abundant conifers. The bungalows have their own *mandi,* but share a central set of showers. Tax included. Singles Rp10,000. Doubles Rp15,000. Expect an Rp8000 increase during July and August.

Mallia's Child Bungalows, next door to Kontiki. Offers the same low season prices year round. Breezy outlook and golden sands will tempt the weary traveler. Singles Rp10,000. Doubles Rp15,000.

Blue Coral, 1km north of the boat landing. This dive is for the traveler seeking blithe isolation. The bungalows are simple. There are more fisherman on the beach than tourists, and Blue Coral's northern location makes both sunset and sunrise visible with a short stroll. Singles Rp10,000. Doubles Rp15,000.

FOOD

Most of the accommodations on Meno seem to have restaurants, but take note: during the low season they may be serving from a limited menu or not at all. Meno has two clean, friendly, and moderately priced *warung,* **Rust** and **Taro,** either of which can bring out uncooked fish for the potential diner's inspection. A trip to the **Good Heart Restaurant** on the far northwest side of the island is a good excuse for walking the island's perimeter. Good Heart affords a great view of the evening's setting sun. The food is a little cheaper than that in town and at least as good.

Sumbawa

Sumbawa is a rugged place with a rugged history, yet the arid, mountainous, and disaster-prone island's denizens have managed to weather the hardships with charismatic fortitude. The island consists of two ethnic and linguistic hemispheres—the Sumbawanese on the west who resemble the Sasaks of Lombok and the Bimanese on the east who favor the Florinese. These two former kingdoms are believed to have been Hindu until they succumbed to Islam, which was ushered in by Makassarese seafarers who plundered the northern coast. Although today Islam is the official religion, it's suffused with traditional animism still practiced by the locals, more so in the east than in the west. Indeed, visitors traveling from one end of the island to the other will notice the slight differences between the two regions:

Beyond the native cultural challenges the island has faced; outside forces have conspired throughout its history to provide ever-greater hurdles to surmount. From as near as Celebes to as far as the Netherlands, intruders have attempted to introduce their faiths, languages, and cultures to Sumbawa. Yet the difficulties of the island have not only been human. Mother Nature has proved a force to be reckoned with, bestowing the island's farmers with a dry climate, and wreaking destruction with the eruption of Gunung Tambora in the early 19th century. Sumbawa's trials have been reflected in the tenor of the island today—from the locals' indomitable spirit to the landscape—and this can be a draw for the visitor.

GETTING THERE AND AWAY

By Plane

Sumbawa Besar's **airport** lies 300m south of the river on Jl. Garuda at the western edge of town. Sumbawa is only served by **Merpati.** There are flights to Sumbawa Besar from **Denpasar, Bali** (5 per week, Rp100,000) via **Mataram,** Lombok (Rp69,700). Connections are also available to **Yogyakarta, Semarang,** and **Surabaya.** Bima's airport offers additional flights to Java, Flores, Timor, and Sulawesi.

By Ferry

Ferries run between **Labuhan Lombok** on Lombok's east coast to **Poto Tano** on Sumbawa's west coast (every hr., 8am-6pm, 1½hr., Rp2300). Tickets can be purchased at the pier. On the other end, ferries shuttle between **Pelabuhan Sape,** Sumbawa to **Labuhanbajo,** Flores (8am, 7-9hr. depending on weather, Rp11,5000), stopping at **Komodo** along the way. Bicycles, motorbikes, or small automobiles can be taken aboard ferries for an additional fee. Be wary of companies offering bus-ferry packages; it would be wise to investigate before paying.

By Boat

The **Bima PELNI Office,** Jl. Pelabuhan 103, runs ships from Bima to points on Timor, Flores, and Lombok, and dock every two weeks. Most of Nusa Tenggara's cities have PELNI offices; stop in for a schedule.

GETTING AROUND ON SUMBAWA

A fully paved main eastward road runs from Taliwang on the west coast to Sape on the east, going through Sumbawa Besar and Bima, the island's two transportation centers. Both have airports, but the traveler can't fly from one to the other. Instead Sumbawa is traversed almost solely by buses. From Sumbawa Besar to: **Taliwang** (5hr., Rp3000); **Poto Tano** (5hr., Rp2000); **Dompu** (5hr., Rp5500); and **Sape** (Rp10,000) via **Bima** (6hr., Rp7000). Local *bemo* can run to more distant and less populous destinations.

■ Sumbawa Besar

Although a small city, Sumbawa Besar is the second largest on the island. Despite its dearth of markets and crafts, Sumbawa Besar is still somewhat of a cultural center. The government often brandishes its power with parades and ceremonies, including the unveiling of the austere New Palace. An orderly city of relative wealth, Sumbawa Besar makes a pleasant layover between more spectacular sights east and west. Although there are few services for tourists and nary a soul speaks English, the locals are friendly and more than happy to give befuddled travelers a hand.

ORIENTATION

Jalan Diponegoro begins at the airport but soon changes to **Jalan Yos Sudarso** and again to **Jalan Setia Budi.** The local *bemo* station is on the northeast corner of the intersection of Jl. Setia Budi and **Jalan Urip Sumoharso. Jalan Dr. Wahidin** is the beginning of the westbound, riverside road. Jl. Dr. Wahidin soon becomes **Jalan Hasanuddin,** which follows the river west until it joins Jl. Diponegoro to become **Jalan Cendrawasih.** Residential neighborhoods lie to the north and some establishments of commercial import lie to the southeast of the loop along **Jalan Kartini.**

PRACTICAL INFORMATION

Tourist Offices: Perama office, Jl. Hasanuddin 48 (tel. 225 41), at the intersection with Jl. Kamboja. Offers standard pricey tours.

Currency Exchange: Banks are scattered along the southern branch of the main loop. Most are small with short hours. The traveler's best bet is **Bank Rayat Indonesia,** on Jl. Wahidin across the street from the government headquarters.

Air Travel: Merpati has a ticket desk at the airport (tel. 219 99) and at the Hotel Tambora, Jl. Kebayan 2 (tel. 215 55), near the convergence of Jl. Cendrawasih and Jl. Garuda. See **Getting There and Away,** above.

Local Transportation: Bemo run through the city loop and along the route from the airport and the GPO. **Dokar** also available. Standard fare for both is Rp300.

Markets: A market sets up near the *bemo* station. Another one opens intermittently by the bridge to the airport.

Pharmacies: Apotik Dinasty, Jl. Garuda 4 (tel. 220 33), across the street from the hospital and around the corner from Hotel Tambora.

Medical Services: Rumah Sakit, Jl. Garuda 5 (tel. 210 78), just east of the bridge to the airport, across the street from the T-intersection with Jl. Kebayan.

Emergency: Police: 110. **Ambulance:** 118.

Police: Jl. Hasanuddin 105, at the triangle intersection with Jl. Yos Sudarso.

Post Offices: GPO, 1km west of the airport, across the river from most of the city. *Poste Restante.* Best to take a *bemo.* A **branch office** is on Jl. Yos Sudarso, halfway between the main bus terminal and the *bemo* terminal. No *Poste Restante* here. Both are open Mon.-Thurs. 8am-2pm, Fri. 8-11am, Sat. 8am-2:30pm.

Telephones: Telkom office, Jl. Yos Sudarso 6 (tel. 210 00), across the street from the branch post office. Open 24hr. *Wartel* also dot the streets.

ACCOMMODATIONS

The better portion of Sumbawa Besar's lodgings are for Indonesian businessmen and soccer teams. Frills such as mosquito nets, private bath with shower, and complimentary breakfast are often not available.

Losmen Taqdeer (tel. 217 96), on Jl. Kamboja, a short walk south of the main bus terminal. A hallway of rooms, some private, some for rent, all clean without being barren. Writing desks available. Singles Rp6000. Doubles Rp12,000.

Losmen Mekar Sari, Jl. Hasanuddin 10, 1 block west of Losmen Taqdeer on the nameless side street parallel to Jl. Kamboja. Equal and generous shares of space, cleanliness, and quietude. Singles Rp10,000. Doubles Rp15,000.

Hotel Tambora, Jl. Kebayan 2 (tel. 215 55), offers some frills for travelers. Fans (Rp16,500-22,000) and A/C (Rp27,500-35,200) cost a bit, but some clean, if institutional, economy rooms go for Rp8250-11,000. Travel/tour/airline resources available. Decent but pricey restaurant.

Hotel Suci (tel. 215 89), on Jl. Hasanuddin. Walk 2 blocks south of the bus terminal on Jl. Kamboja, then turn right on Hasanuddin. Look for the sign. With lush tropical flora, it falls somewhere between the local *losmen* and the tourist-geared hotels. Rooms range from Rp7500-11,000 and include tea and breakfast snack.

FOOD

English-menu tourist restaurants are numerous here, but many of the *rumah makan* offer similar prices and quality. Local restaurants cluster along Jl. Diponegoro near the bus terminal, and food carts line the perimeter of the terminal itself.

Cirebon 2, Jl. Kebayan 4 (tel. 220 03), up the street from Hotel Tambora. Decorated with strands of beads and seashells. Gigantic menu with good prices (Rp3-5000). The original farther up the street has the selection and price, but not the snazzy bamboo look of its winning sequel.

Aneka Rasa Jaya, on Jl. Hasanuddin, 2 blocks south of the bus terminal and to the east (left) about 200m. A markedly Chinese *rumah makan* with a lot of seafood. The real mark of distinction is its market-like selection of seldom-seen western produce and pre-packaged food. Meals Rp3-6000.

SIGHTS

Sumbawa Besar's best sight is the old sultan's palace, **Dalam Loka,** located on Jl. Sudirman a couple of blocks east and south of the *bemo* terminal. It is one of the largest buildings made solely of wood, built at the end of the last century and recently refurbished. Two blocks west of the palace stands the new palace, built in the style of its predecessor.

The Balinese temple **Pura Agung Giri Natha** is a little out of place, both geographically and demographically. Cramped and awkward next to the post office on busy Jl. Yos Sudarso, Giri Natha is a Hindu temple that once served a dominant but now scant Hindu population. Painted silver and Pepto Bismol pink, and decorated with ample swastikas, the *pura* is hard to miss. (Rp500 donation requested.)

■ Hu'u

Perched on the coast of aquamarine Cempi Bay, Hu'u is where surf-lovers come to roast themselves and stay. In 1990, some Aussies came from down under, to the crashing waves of Hu'u their surfboards plundered. Since then, visitors have come from far and near, bringing with them lots of fun, MTV, and beer. A strip of bungalows near the waters have arisen, surrounded by bountiful greenery and some of Sumbawa's best scenery. From March to August, the waves are most robust, the number of buff and tumbling riders are greater, and the rough and rumbling parties go on 'til later. Those seeking private tides and coral should remember: the waves hide and spiral down between October and December. Die-hard culture-vultures need not skip town, as local children can wipe away many a frown. Sunbathing and spearfishing offer enough to do, but travelers lay wishing for more stuff in Hu'u.

ORIENTATION AND PRACTICAL INFORMATION

A bus runs directly from **Bima** to Hu'u (8am, 2½hr., Rp3000). Frequent buses from **Bima** (1½hr., Rp2000) and **Sumbawa Besar** (4-5hr., Rp5500) stop in **Dompu** first. Travelers should try to arrive in Dompu early, as buses going south are rare in the afternoon. Buses stop at a station north of Dompu proper, far enough that *bemo* (Rp300) are recommended to get into town. Once in Dompu, *dokar* (Rp300) go to the station (3km south of town), which sends two or three buses throughout the morning, fewer in the afternoon, to Hu'u. It's only 35km from Dompu to Hu'u, but the trip can take a couple hours. Many foreigners prefer to ride on top, which is less safe, but more pleasant. The bus stops at a station in **Rasabau,** from which a *bemo* can take travelers the 11km south to Hu'u.

Once you arrive in Hu'u, orientation is easy. The town is sandwiched between the main road (to the east) and the ocean (to the west). All the accommodations cluster south of the village, accessible by *bemo*. There are **warung,** roadside stands, and a **police station** along the main road. **Local transportation** consists of a few *bemo* which run along the main road, more often in the morning than in the afternoon. The nearest **medical services** of any kind are 35km north in Dompu. Periscope Bungalows (see **Accommodations and Food** below) **changes money** and traveler's checks, but at low rates. Intan Lestari **rents bicycles** and **snorkeling gear,** each for Rp5000 per day; inquire at other establishments for competitive prices.

ACCOMMODATIONS AND FOOD

The Hu'u bungalow standard is well above tolerable, and food and lodgings are often one and the same. Some places have more attractive vistas than others, but competition keeps all reasonable. **Intan Lestari's** restaurant has perhaps the best clubhouse/bar charisma, with roaring MTV. Out front, a gnarled tree provides a shady canopy for enticing hammocks. The rooms are fine, but don't face the beach (Rp7500-12,000, with private *mandi* Rp10-15,000). Breakfast is included. **Monalisa Bungalow's** restaurant doesn't have quite the view, but their range of room and board options compensates, ranging from singles (Rp4000) to deluxe doubles (Rp25,000), with a slew of options in between. The other noteworthy place is **Periscope Bungalows,** 2km north of the main cluster of establishments. The paths are lined with half-buried beer bottles (intentionally—it's rather chic) and the isolation suggests hard-core surf culture. Rooms with a view go for Rp10-15,000, while those in back are Rp7500-10,000. Periscope also changes money and traveler's checks. Additionally, there are some **homestays** in the village geared toward Indonesian travelers. Due to the steady stream of surfers, the locals have an increasingly unfavorable perception of tourists; for this reason, it might be good (although possibly difficult and weird) for westerners to patronize said homestays.

■ Bima

The historical rivalry between the Bimanese and Sumbawanese sultanates is long gone in an age of standard language, unified religion, and singular government. Comparisons between the two cities, however, still exist. If Sumbawa Besar is the tidy, mild-mannered, soft-spoken one, Bima is the feisty sibling. The city is no less congenial than its western kin, but its amiability has spice, sharpness, charisma, and a sprinkling of the bawdy. Whether it's in the vendors of the night market, the horses before the *dokar,* or the dancers in front of the old sultan's palace, Bima unfurls its vim on a daily basis without ever stopping for breath.

INDONESIA

ORIENTATION

Bima sits between two rivers. The airport and bus terminal are south of the southern river. **Jalan Terminal Baru** runs north from the airport into the city, where it becomes **Jalan Kaharnuddin,** the main street. The first street it hits is **Jalan Karantina/ Sukarno Hatta,** the main east-bound road leading to the **police,** the **Telkom office,** the **hospital,** and, ultimately, Raba. After that, it crosses **Jalan Sumbawa,** which runs into the hulking complex of the Sultan's Palace sitting in the middle of the city. The next important east-west street north is **Jalan Pompa/Hasanuddin/Diponegoro.** Services and resources are clustered within approximately 1sq.km.

PRACTICAL INFORMATION

Tours and Travel: Pt. Fajar Bima (tel. 428 10), on Jl. Sukarno Hatta, and **Pt. Grand Komodo,** Jl. Salahuddin 11 (tel. 420 18), offer tours and tickets to major sights. **Perama office,** on Jl. Lombok near Hotel Lila Graha, arranges tours as well. The staff at **Hotel Lila Graha** likewise arranges trips to Komodo.
Currency Exchange: Bank Rayat Indonesia, on Jl. Sumbawa. Open Mon.-Fri. 7:30am-noon, Sat. 7:30-11am. **Bank Danamon,** at the intersection of Jl. Sultan Kaharnuddin and Jl. Tongkol.
Air Travel: Bima Airport, 17km south of town. Regular buses run to and from Bima (Rp400). Daily flights to major cities on the larger islands. **Merpati,** Jl. Sukarno Hatta 60 (tel. 426 97).
Buses: Kumbe Terminal, a few km down Jl. Sukarno Hatta in Raba. To: **Sape** (every 30min., 7am-4pm, 1½hr., Rp1500); **Sumbawa Besar** (Rp6500); and **Dompu** (2hr., Rp2000).
Ferries: Travelers can inquire at the harbor for boats, ferries, and cargo ships to other port cities. Regular boats to **Labuhanbajo,** Flores and **Lembar,** Lombok. The *KM Kelimutu* stops in Bima on its circuitous route. Some cargo ships will take passengers to **Surabaya,** Java, although that can be a grueling experience.
Local Transportation: Dokar abound and **bemo** buzz between Bima and Raba along Jl. Sukarno Hatta and Jl. Sultan Hasanuddin (Rp300).
Emergency: Police: 110. Ambulance: 118.
Medical Services: Rumah Sakit Umum Daerah, Jl. Langsat 1 (off the Raba end of Jl. Sukarno Hatta). 24-hr. emergency unit (tel. 431 42).
Police: (tel. 430 26), on Jl. Sukarno Hatta.
Post Offices: GPO, on Jl. Gajah Mada, the eastern extension of Jl. Hasanuddin/ Diponegoro. A branch office also on the same road, but closer to town.
Telephones: 24-hr. **Telkom office,** east of town on Jl. Sukarno Hatta. No IDD phone. **Wartel Remaja Bima,** on Jl. Lombok. There's also a *wartel* near the bus terminal and a phone at the Hotel Lila Graha. **Telephone code:** 0374.

ACCOMMODATIONS

The wise visitor will shop around: a higher price doesn't ensure a better room. Most of the accommodations are conveniently close to each other in the dusty rectangular heart of downtown Bima.

Hotel Lila Graha, Jl. Lombok 20 (tel. 427 40), in the center of town. Take Jl. Kaharnuddin north toward town; Jl. Lombok is on the right. An Indonesian hotel in name and form, but fortunately not price. Singles and doubles with shared *mandi* and fan Rp8-12,000, with private bath Rp15,500-16,500. Includes breakfast. Telephones on the premises, and the owners can help organize trips to Komodo.
Losmen Kartini, Jl. Kaharnuddin 11 (tel. 420 72), 50m before the T-intersection with Jl. Hasanuddin. Dark, but a drier, better-swept, almost peaceful lack of city glare. No frills means no big prices: singles with shared *mandi* Rp5-10,000.
Losmen Para, Jl. Sultan Salahuddin 29, just south of the bus terminal. Proximity to the bus terminal is not, as one would expect, a drawback. More garden than most city *losmen,* with 3 types of room (the cheapest of which are fine). Singles/doubles Rp8-20,000. Nicest rooms have fans and private *mandi.*

Wisma Komodo (tel. 420 70), on Jl. Sultan Ibrahim between the museum and Jl. Hasanuddin. Prime location on the periphery of downtown's busiest core is the draw to this sparsely decorated place. Patronized mostly by Indonesian lower-level civil-servicemen. Singles/doubles Rp7500, with private *mandi* Rp13-15,000.

FOOD

If, from a general consideration of good health, you've been abstaining from the delights of street food, Bima may well be the place to give in to such cheap temptations. Food carts abound while restaurants do not, and the competition seems to do good things for their general upkeep. A dinner from Bima's night market is perhaps the best answer to eating out. If you can't quite shirk those bacterial inhibitions, there are plenty of indistinguishable *warung* and *rumah makan*. **Minang Jaya,** on Jl. Sumbawa and **Pemuda,** on Jl. Sulawesi seem among the better kept. As for restaurants, the best candidate is the one attached to Hotel Lila Graha, which has reasonable tourist-oriented food.

SIGHTS

Bima's main attraction is its **sultan's palace-gone-museum.** Like its counterpart in Sumbawa Besar, it has recently been refurbished after prolonged disrepair. Inside are haphazard displays of history: spears, skulls, boats, genealogies, traditional sultanesque garb, flags, and simulated royal bedrooms. There are a few signs in English but on the whole the museum is fascinating—if at all—for form rather than content. A small donation is expected.

■ Sape

Though an energetic port town, Sape has barely enough people to support its post office, bank, and "Billyard Centre." The port village of Pelabuhan Sape, 4km east along the main road, is a point of scenic, albeit transitory, interest for those headed east. While the village is a vision of briny mud during low tide and clear flood water during high tide, its larger upland sister is always high and dry no matter what the sea level. Although there's not much to see in either town, they represent passing through at its oceanic best.

ORIENTATION AND PRACTICAL INFORMATION

All of interest in both Sape and Pelabuhan Sape lies along 6km of west-east road. Pelabuhan Sape is at the point farthest east to the water and the main road ends conveniently at the gates of the ferry landing, where tickets may be purchased the morning of the crossing. West of Pelabuhan Sape is 3km of tidal lowlands and farm fields, followed by a 3-km stretch of Sape. The **bus terminal** is on the east side of Sape, just at the beginning of the fields. One *losmen*, two *rumah makan*, and the **ferry** are in Pelabuhan Sape, but the majority of services line the Sape proper stretch of the main road. Sape offers a handful of restaurants, a few *losmen*, a **police office,** a **Bank Rayat Indonesia** (which does not change money), Doctor Suparyanto, and a small **post office.** There are **no telephones.** Between Sape and Pelabuhan Sape is a park with information about the Komodo dragon which offers some literature.

ACCOMMODATIONS AND FOOD

The limited number of options for lodging in greater Sape does not necessarily indicate poor quality. **Losmen Mutiara,** Sumbawa's easternmost commercial establishment, immediately adjacent to the ferry landing at the Sape end of the road is one of the best deals around. Although prices run a little high (singles Rp10,000, doubles with shared toilet Rp15,000), the waterfront location compensates. **Losmen Friendship** in town makes up for its distance from the ferry landing by including breakfast, private *mandi*, and snazzy green plastic windows for a standard Rp10,000. Also in town is **Losmen Ratna Sari,** with little to praise, but also little to criticize (rooms cost Rp5-10,000).

While Sape has a small market scene, it's not a great place to scrounge for a meal— either in terms of variety or cleanliness. Sape and Pelabuhan Sape do have a smattering of *rumah makan,* but they don't offer many options. The **Sape Café** is cheap and serves shrimp crackers with fried rice, while the **Bougenville,** a few hundred meters east of Sape on the way to Pelabuhan Sape, is promisingly apart from the dust and bustle of downtown.

■ Near Sape: Komodo Island

Komodo Island is home to some big reptiles. *Varanus komodoensis,* the **Komodo dragon,** king of the monitor lizard family, can grow to over 6m long, do horrible things to warm and cold-blooded prey alike, and gross as much money for Sumbawa and Flores as all their beaches combined. Ferries run to Komodo from Sape (Rp10,000) or Labuhanbajo (Rp4000). A small boat plucks visitors from the ferry landing and conveys them to Komodo's actual shores (Rp1500). On Komodo, the national park runs accommodations in the only village of **Loh Liang.** Singles cost Rp10,000, doubles Rp15,000. There is no food service, but there are basic cooking facilities. Travelers might want to purchase groceries before going to Komodo. (Admission to both costs Rp2000 per person.) Those wishing to go anywhere beyond Loh Liang are required to hire a guide for safety precautions. Walking guides to dragon hot spots charge their first three customers Rp3000 each, and each additional person Rp1000 (up to 30 people). Guides are government trained and, despite what it may seem, worth the money. Komodo dragons have wicked tails, swimming proficiency, and a record (albeit presumed) of having eaten those who have disappeared from Loh Liang.

Before making the trip to Komodo or Flores, travelers should buy food. The trips are long and the locals know it. Try to avoid buying food on the ferry and even a desperate morning scramble for biscuit in Pelabuhan Sapa—they'll charge you for it.

Flores

Although Flores has been prime stomping ground for western fans of Jesus since the Portuguese arrived in the mid-1500s, the basic animist nature of these people hasn't changed. Christianity is not the only import of the western world that has met with resistance on Nusa Tenggara's most populated island; rugged Florinese mountains seem to defy modern paved roads, making interior travel long and difficult. This island of volcanic origin is indeed of an extreme topography and, like the spirit of its people, does not easily blend, mold, or convert.

Flores is far more primed for tourists than its western neighbor of Sumbawa. Without all the tabloid bells, beer, and whistles of mainstream Indonesia, Flores offers a path to the traveler that, although bumpy, is lined with friendly people, decent *losmen,* and peaceful towns. The stream of foreigners, however steady, is light, and tourists are welcome guests whether retreating to the cool of Ruteng and Bajawa, touring the *ikat*-laden interior villages, or gazing at the tri-colored spectacle of sunrise over Keli Mutu.

GETTING THERE AND AWAY

By Plane
Ende Airport, on Jl. A. Yani, is on the water at the far southeastern side of town. There are flights to: **Denpasar** (6 per wk., Rp200,000); **Kupang** (6 per wk., Rp88,000); **Mataram** (5 per wk.); and **Bima** (6 per wk., Rp87,000). Less frequent

flights also service **Labuhanbajo** and **Bajawa. Maumere Airport,** south off Jl. Kelimutu, 3km east of town, flies to **Surabaya, Kupang,** and **Ujung Pandang.**

By Ferry

Ferries connect Flores with Timor, Sumba, Sumbawa, and some of the smaller islands in between. The ferries from **Sape,** Sumbawa to **Labuhanbajo** and vice versa run once per day (8am, 8-10hr., Rp11,500). Bikes may be brought aboard for an additional fee. In addition, a Rp200 harbor tax may be collected by the ticket takers before boarding the boat. Both boats stop to let passengers off at Komodo along the way (see **Near Sape: Komodo Island** on page 240). One ferry per week leaves Ende, stopping at **Kupang, Waingapu,** and **Sawu** (Tues. evening). Ferries also run from **Larantuka** to **Kupang** (Thurs. and Sun., returning Tues. and Fri., 12 hr.). **PELNI** boats dock at Labuhanbajo, Ende, Larantuka, and Maumere about every two weeks. Each city has a PELNI office where schedules can be picked up.

GETTING AROUND ON FLORES

Buses run from one end of the island to the other. There's one flight per day to Denpasar which stops in **Bajawa** (Rp45,000) and **Labuhanbajo** (Rp100,000). The cheapest way to travel on the island is via Flores's nearly 700-km serpentine mountain highway. Buses go from Labuhanbajo to **Ende** (Rp15,000) and **Ruteng** (Rp5000) and from Bajawa to **Ende** (Rp5000) and **Ruteng** (Rp5000). Fares usually indicate approximate length of travel; Rp1000 is equal to one hour. Foreigners should expect to pay more. *Bemo* are thick everywhere (Rp300-500).

■ Ende

Once a major port and favorite city of the Dutch, Ende is palpably the thriving center of Flores, both geographically and politically. To the east and west of the city is the ocean, while to the north and south are verdant volcanic heaps. But the natural wonders don't stop there; Ende is the gateway city to Flores' mystical Keli Mutu. Exemplifying the dichotomy that is Flores, Catholics, Protestants, and Muslims co-exist in Ende with their respective hybrid animist faiths.

ORIENTATION

Ende stretches across the neck of a peninsula, with **Ende Harbor** to the west and **Ipi Harbor** to the southeast. **Jalan Mesjid, Jalan Hatta,** and **Jalan Mahon/Sukarno** run north-south parallel to each other from Ende Harbor. **Jalan Kartini/Pahjawan** is the northernmost thoroughfare, running northeast past the Protestant and Catholic churches and the hospital. **Jalan Katedral/A. Yani** bounds the city on the south, forking near a cluster of *losmen;* one prong continues east while the other, renamed **Jalan Adisucipto,** continues southeast toward the ferry office and Ipi Harbor. On the east side of town, **Jalan El Tari** runs northwest-southeast through Jl. Pahjawan past Jl. A. Yani and ends at the **airport.** From the intersection of Jl. El Tari and Jl. A. Yani, **Jalan Kelimutu** extends northwest past the *pasar malam* to the telephone office. Running north and parallel to Jl. Kelimutu is **Jalan Nangka.** The narrowest area between Jl. Pahjawan and Jl. Katedral forms downtown Ende.

PRACTICAL INFORMATION

Tourist Offices: No official tourist office. Try contacting the manager of Hotel Ikhlas for official maps and regional brochures.

Tours and Travel: PT Kelimutu Permai Tour and Travel (tel. 213 55), on Jl. Nangka. Shares office with Merpati and keeps the same hours (see below).

Currency Exchange: Bank Rayat Indonesia, on Jl. Yos Sudarso (in the Dwi Putra Hotel). Best rates on Flores. Open Mon.-Fri. 7:30am-noon, Sat. 7:30-11am.

Air Travel: Merpati (tel. 213 55), on Jl. Nangka. Open Mon.-Tues. and Thurs.-Sat. 8am-1pm and 4-5pm, Sun. and holidays 10am-noon.

INDONESIA

Buses: Ndao Bus Terminal, on Jl. Mesjid north of the city proper. Buses go once per day to: **Bajawa** (4hr., Rp4000); **Labuhanbajo** (14hr., Rp13,000); and **Ruteng** (10hr., Rp9000). **Wolowana Terminal,** on Jl. A. Yani, east of town. Several buses leave daily to: **Moni** (2hr., Rp2000) and **Maumere** (6hr., Rp5500).

Ferries: PELNI office, Jl. Kathedral 2 (tel. 210 43), in the thick of downtown. Has schedule information for the KM *Kelimutu*.

Local Transportation: Bemo run the along the main streets (Rp400).

Rentals: Istana Bambu Restaurant and Hotel Ikhlas rent both.

Medical Services: Hospital, on Jl. Pahjawan, past the intersection with Jl. El Tari.

Emergency: Police: 110. **Ambulance:** 118.

Police: Located on Jl. Polisi, overlooking the town from the east.

Post Offices: GPO, Jl. Basuki Rahmat 15 (tel. 212 03), on the northeast side of town, near the Pahjawan-El Tari intersection. Open Mon.-Thurs. 7:30am-2pm, Fri. 7:30-11am, Sat. 7:30am-2pm. **Branch office,** Jl. Yos Sudarso 4, in the downtown area, across the street from Dwi Putra Hotel. **Postal code:** 86318.

Telephones: Telkom office, Jl. Kelimutu 5. **24-hr. branch,** Jl. Yos Sudarso 1.

ACCOMMODATIONS

Ende's accommodations are both cheaper and more tourist-friendly than most other places in Flores. The nicest digs are east of the town's thickest sector, but even the farther ones aren't a bad walk from the crowded sea-front streets.

Ikhlas Hotel (tel. 216 95), on Jl. A. Yani, just past the fork in the road near the airport. Not only the best bargain in Ende but perhaps in all of Flores. A range of rooms from those closer to the street (Rp3500-6000) to rooms with private bath, fan, and sitting room (Rp10-15,000). Cheap and friendly service from the in-house restaurant. Ende's best answer to a tourist office and a *wartel*.

Hotel Safari (tel. 216 95), on Jl. A. Yani, just next door to Ikhlas. Masterfully cultivated courtyard, with live tropical birds. Singles Rp15,000. Doubles Rp20,000. All rooms have private bath.

Nurjaya Hotel (tel. 212 52), on Jl. A. Yani, closer to town center. Amidst Ende's titanic hotels, Nurjaya is an anomaly for its small size. Chances are there will be only a few lucky guests. Singles Rp5500. Doubles Rp11,000. Breakfast included.

Dwi Putra Hotel, Jl. Yos Sudarso 27-29 (tel. 206 85), at the northeast corner of the downtown area. One of Ende's fanciest hotels, with high ceilings, flush toilets, and very little dirt. Most budgeteers could probably only afford economy class rooms (Rp20-25,000). Breakfast included.

FOOD

The restaurant scene in Ende isn't exactly spectacular, but the capital's proximity to the ocean ensures a good amount of seafood at many places. Travelers can also sample the ubiquitous and popular Padang food from local *rumah makan*. **Simpang Lima,** on Jl. A. Yani near the airport, is run by a Sumatran who loves to engage his customers in conversation. **Rumah Makan Kelimutu,** Jl. Kelimutu 26 (tel. 220 18), on the east side of town, wins the grand prize for cheap food and its classy decor. Ende's closest thing to a western restaurant is **Istana Bambu,** Jl. Pasar 39 (tel. 214 80), in the heart of downtown. In addition to a sizable menu of Chinese and Indonesian food, Bambu provides tour assistance in limited English, German, and Japanese. Fancy Bambu panels and candles in the evening provide some ambiance. Finally, the restaurants in **Dwi Putra** and **Ikhlas** hotels are relatively cheap and provide the quasi-western fare of toast, pancakes, and chips. Dwi Putra offers more and safer seafood than most Endean restaurants.

■ Near Ende: Christ in Detusoko

On the road to Moni, three-quarters of the way from Ende, on the outskirts of the village **Detusoko,** is the **Wisma Franciscus,** a streetless retreat operated in conjunction with other missionary doings: church, school, and clinic. For the respectable sum of

Rp30,000 (for two people), a nun hosts travelers for the night, providing clean beds, generous portions of dinner and breakfast, and a taste of Christ in the countryside. The rugged country is stitched with places to walk and travelers can take in the scenery, good food, and silence. Many travelers prefer to arrive Saturday afternoon. That way, they can walk around, enjoy dinner, and arise the next morning to attend an impressive local service. Detusoko is accessible via the Ende-Maumere bus—just tell the driver your stop (and don't pay more than Rp2000). Alternatively, you can get there by public *bemo*, or try to charter one. Moni lies just 10km up the road. A *bemo* should make the run sometime during the day, the visitor may just have to wait for some hours.

■ Moni

A standard jumping off point for the Keli Mutu pilgrim, Moni is a charming town as beautiful as any other cool, hillside Florinese backwater. The homestays that have cropped up like mushrooms in the town to service the constant tourist flux are a boon to the traveler, providing good travel onwards and a comfortable stay in town. Indeed, the fabulous views, local hot springs, and waterfalls make two days at this town at the base of Keli Mutu as pleasant and entertaining as the usual one. Despite the steady tourist trickle, Moni has retained its amiability and its nature as a pleasant stopover en route to the nearby peaks and tri-colored crater lakes.

ORIENTATION AND PRACTICAL INFORMATION

Moni is about 50km from Ende and about 100km from Maumere on the road between the two. Buses run regularly from both ends (Rp2000 and Rp5000 respectively) although, as always, mornings are the best bet. Moni lies along 2km of a road that winds along sloping hills and rice plains; those coming from Ende will be going downhill and those from Maumere will be going uphill. From Ende, the road winds up along the narrow sides of a jagged ravine and over bridges at which the traveler may blink. The brevity (at most two hours) and drama make the journey interesting. The road up to **Keli Mutu** is just farther uphill on the Ende side of town. Although replete with homestays, Moni makes little other provision for its guests. There's a **Telkom office** at Restaurant Kelimutu, but whether it works or not is iffy.

ACCOMMODATIONS AND FOOD

Moni breaks away from the traditional Florinese *losmen*. Homestays are notably cheap, ranging from Rp3500-10,000. Every place provides mosquito nets and breakfast, and most offer the welcome pampering of moms and grandmothers. The majority of the homestays sit in the middle of the village, all of comparable quality and price. Some of the farther establishments are just as good, sometimes even better, considering their relative isolation and wondrous vistas. **Wisata Homestay** is in the middle of the mountain flat (downhill from the market) and offers a complete panorama of jungled slopes. Singles cost Rp4000, doubles Rp8000. Farther from town in the same downhill direction and off a side road (look for the sign) is **Palm Homestay.** Singles go for Rp5000, doubles Rp10,000. The higher price gets seclusion, a charming family, a private cottage with attached *mandi*, and ample tourist resources. With signs near Palm's, but on the main road, is **Ankermi Restaurant and Accommodations,** which has the benefits of stylish architecture, a restaurant, and proximity to the village's rushing stream. Again, its perks cost a bit more than usual at Rp5-10,000.

As for food, Moni has some of the best on Flores. For a cheap Rp2500, a number of places serve food of both quantity and quality. Some to try are **Palm, Amina Moe,** and **Maria.** One of the culinary highlights on Flores can be found at **Chenty Restaurant and Pub,** in the center of town. Travelers rave about the Moni Cake, a fried concoction of mashed potatoes, meat, and vegetables all covered with cheese.

■ Near Moni: Keli Mutu

Of course the reason Moni now has the trappings of a tourist town is its stones-throw proximity to Flores's grandest and easiest-to-access natural wonder, the three crater lakes of three colors. The mountain Keli Mutu is a volcanic hulk with basins of hue-changing water. Presently one crater is turquoise and the other two (unfortunately for those who make the sales pitch) are similar shades of black. For a long time the lakes were green, black, and turquoise and, before that, they were maroon, blue, and black. Locals consider the pools the resting place of spirits, where color acts indicates morality; in line with their own legends, the recent changing of the green pool to black does not bode well for the purity of the Florinese dead.

A public truck now runs up Keli Mutu on a daily basis to accommodate the steady audience of foreigners. The truck ride up, beginning at 4am, costs Rp3000, although halfway there the truck stops and visitors are asked to pay another Rp1500 to enter the park. The ride back down leaves at 7pm, for another Rp3000. Those who wish to walk around the lakes beyond the truck's departure time can walk the breathtaking, if long, 13-km route (3hr.). The road is fully paved except for the last 500m. Alternatively, *bemo* linger about to be chartered. If you take the public truck up, you will probably share your Keli Mutu sunrise with a goodly number of fellow westerners. Misanthropes who prefer to gape in solitude can walk, bike, or *bemo*-charter at another time of day; be forewarned, however, that clouds obscure the vista by mid-day almost without fail.

■ Labuhanbajo

Labuhanbajo offers a volume of services disproportionate to its inauspicious fishing-village size. The town is a major crossroads for Indonesians and western tourists alike. The inhabitants seem to do all right by the preponderance of visitors in their sleepy small town but, on any given day in the high season, the main street holds twice the traffic of the average place this size. While Labuhanbajo is most often used as a point of departure to Rinca, Komodo, and Sumbawa, it holds water as a destination unto itself. Almost all of the accommodations boast a view of the bay which, for its horizon of desolate, weathered islands of rock, as well as its clutter of bobbing and lamp-lit fishing boats, makes for a spectacular sunset. While there is no beach in town, a 15-minute walk south yields a fine stretch of sand and the beach hotels—isolated (and often cheap) resorts, on islands or mainland beaches north of town by boat—fulfill the promise of their name.

ORIENTATION

Labuhanbajo is a simple costal crescent with a major ferry landing at the northern end. The vast majority of services lie south of the landing along **Jalan Soekarno/Yos Sudarso/Pelabuhan,** the main road. The town isn't any more than 1.5km from stem to stern, and everything is easily found. While Labuhanbajo hosts no bus terminal, it's a major stop for **buses** bound for Ruteng. These buses can be caught throughout the day along the main road; check with hotels for times and they may even arrange for a bus to come to the door.

PRACTICAL INFORMATION

Tourist Offices: The national parks have an **info booth** about Rinca and Komodo, 200m south of the ferry landing on the ocean side of the road. The main office is farther south on the outskirts of town, but the booth has English brochures.
Tours and Travel: Almost every hotel arranges snorkeling trips, island treks, and boats to Komodo and Rinca. As always, tours are cheaper in groups. **Perama Office** (tel. 410 58), another 100m south and across the road.
Currency Exchange: Bank Rayat Indonesia, 0.5km south of the ferry landing. Open Mon.-Thurs. 7:30am-noon and 1-3pm, Fri. 7:30-11:45am and 1-3:30pm. Rates

for any currency except US$ are wretched; accepts traveler's checks only from Bank of America, AmEx, Thomas Cook, and Citibank.

Ferries: The **PELNI office** burned down in summer 1996. Look for it at the pier. The KM *Kelimutu* docks in Labuhanbajo every couple of weeks. Please inquire for actual schedule.

Rentals: The national parks take visitors diving for US$95 per day, and local rentals are similarly pricey. There's a **scuba shop** adjacent to the Hotel Bajo Beach and another scuba place at the PELNI office. Snorkeling equipment can also be obtained for Rp3000 per day from most of the hotels.

Post Offices: 0.75km south of the ferry landing on the road's east side. Open Mon.-Thurs. 7:30am-3pm, Fri. 7:30-11am, Sat. 7:30am-1pm.

Telephones: Telkom office, on the south side of town near the main park office. From the ferry landing, walk about 1km south, take the first left after the bridge, and then the first significant right. **Telephone code:** 0385.

ACCOMMODATIONS

Labuhanbajo is popular enough to have frills; complimentary breakfast goes without saying, and fans are common. In addition to the following listings, Labuhanbajo has offices for the beach hotels—which take tourists for free to the seclusion of their bungalows. Most of the pamphlet-waving men accosting newcomers are merely trying to get business, but travelers should still be wary of suspicious-looking touts.

Chez Felix, Jl. Prof. Dr. Johanes (tel. 410 32), 0.5km south from the ferry landing on an uphill road. Formerly a homestay, now billing itself a hotel. Fortunately it still has a familial atmosphere. A wonderful place to watch the hustle and bustle the street without the actual noise. Rooms with shared *mandi* Rp6-8000, with private *mandi* Rp8-10,000, with fan Rp10-15,000.

Gardena Bungalows and Restaurant, 100m south of the ferry landing. Set on one of the hillside's steeper slopes, Gardena is forested enough to escape the street's hub-bub, but not so much as to lose its view. Restaurant has an extensive and notably cheap menu. Bamboo wicker bungalows with shower, mosquito nets, porches, and view. Singles Rp7000. Doubles Rp10,000.

Mutiara Beach Hotel (tel. 410 39), 100m south of the ferry landing. Great location in front of the ocean, but also more in the thick of things. Some of the town's cheapest rooms (Rp5000-8000), with fan and private *mandi* Rp7500-12500.

FOOD

The numerous *rumah makan* don't seem to be patronized by tourists, but that doesn't mean they shouldn't be. The restaurant at Gardena Bungalows has a better than decent atmosphere and the prices are among the best in town.

Borobudur Restaurant, a couple doors south of Gardena Bungalows, offers a big menu of fresh seafood captured in the bay right outside. Plenty of Chinese and Indonesian selections. Meals cost about Rp2-6000.

Restaurant Dunia Baru, on Jl. Yos Sudarso across the street from Gardena. Fried rice lovers can thrill in the four different options. Some good Chinese and Indonesian fare. Meals average Rp2-5000.

Sunset Restaurant, on the main street between the road and the water, 500m south of the landing. Limited menu, but what they make is good and where they make it is great. Go for dinner and play along with their name. Rp3000-6000.

■ Ruteng

Although traversing Flores's circuitous and inconsistently-paved interior can be an arduous task, persistent travelers will be rewarded with cool days spent in highland market towns. Ruteng is one of these. Ruteng is a logical, easy, and not wholly uninteresting stopover for the traveler who prefers five hours of jarring bus rides to 10. Indeed, the surrounding scenery is worth exploring, as are the nearby caves and traditional Manggarai villages. Hotel proprietors and other locals can offer guidance to these sights and may be able to arrange for a *caci* (traditional whip fighting) demonstration for tourists. Trans-Flores travelers will find in Ruteng the sweet luxury of a night's sleep in a pleasant, if not spectacular, settlement.

ORIENTATION AND PRACTICAL INFORMATION

Most of Ruteng is conveniently laid out in rectangles and distances are short. The **bus terminal** is on the west side of town. The town center is up the hill and most accommodations are on the far side of downtown. The **airport** lies 1km to the northeast. For currency exchange, **Bank Negara Indonesia,** on Jl. Kartini (next to the Telkom office), has the best rates. (Open Mon.-Fri. 7:30am-12:30pm and 1:30-4:45pm, Sat. 7:30-11:30am and 1:30-4:45pm.) **Merpati** (tel. 211 47) is to the northeast between the town and the airport. The **emergency number** is 110; for an **ambulance** try 118. The **police station** (tel. 211 10) is on Jl. Bhayangkara, across from the soccer field, not too far from the bus terminal. The **post office,** Jl. Dewi Sartika 6, is on the south side of town near the former king's house. **Postal code:** 86511. The **Telkom office,** Jl. Kartini 8-10 (tel. 218 88), is also on the south side of town near the government offices. (Open 24hr.)

ACCOMMODATIONS AND FOOD

Isolated in the rugged hills of Flores, Ruteng is an exhilaratingly cool retreat from the tropical heat. Unfortunately, its slow traffic means that there are few establishments for the traveler to choose from and prices are often higher than in more touristed towns. Perhaps the best place to stay is **Hotel Sindha,** Jl. Yos Sudarso 26 (tel. 210 80). Aside from the various ghastly tri-color combination paint jobs, Sindha offers clean rooms, a free (if small) breakfast, and a decent Chinese restaurant. Singles and doubles with shared bath cost Rp7-10,000, with private bath Rp10-15,000. **Hotel Manggari,** Jl. Adi Sucipto 6 (tel. 210 08), and **Hotel Dahlia,** Jl. Bhayangkara 18 (tel. 215 77), are less decorated and more expensive, but cater to a similar crowd. **Losmen Agung I** (tel. 210 80), is a few hundred meters north of town on Jl. Motang Rua. Economy rooms (Rp7-10,000) face a lily-padded fountain and a view of Ruteng. More expensive, bigger rooms (Rp15-20,000) offer just as splendid an outlook.

Ruteng's dining options are rather skimpy, but the food is hearty. Tourists may want to buy water downtown, as restaurants tend to mark up prices significantly. Smaller independent eateries are the most affordable. **Bambooden Restaurant,** Jl. Motang Rua 30 (tel. 215 89), serves a plethora of chicken and egg variations. The other tourist favorite in town is **Dunia Baru,** Jl. Yos Sudarso 10 (tel. 216 90). Chinese-owned, Dunia has a large menu of rather pricey dishes.

SIGHTS

Golo Curu is a hill north of town from which Ruteng and much of its environs can be surveyed. It's enough of a climb to give a good view, but not so much of one to take a great deal of time, preparation, or fortitude. Follow Jl. Motang Rua north out of town—Golo Curu can be seen straight ahead. About 1km north of the center of town, the road crosses a bridge and immediately thereafter veers to the left. A smaller road forks at the same time to the right; follow this smaller road through a neighborhood as it winds up the side of Golo Curu. Travelers should try to stay on the paved pathway which passes by some graves. As the hill steepens, a series of gaudy Jesus reliefs begin and, as you ascend the hill, so does he, bearing a cross, shrugging off Roman guards, and eventually rising to heaven. Golo Curu is crowned by a shrine to the Virgin Mary, and the entire climb is a fascinating glimpse at Indonesian Catholicism. Morning and late afternoon are good times to climb.

▨ Bajawa

This market town of the Ngada people has weathered its transition into the modern world with atypical grace. Although Bajawa's hotels are seldom empty, life goes on undisturbed and the town's clean streets have avoided the tension so rife in other Indonesian tourist towns. There are plenty of warm greetings and the town accommodates guests with an ingenious and refreshing brand of hospitality. Perhaps this will change, but for now Bajawa wears the clothes of tourism well.

ORIENTATION

Little runs precisely north, south, east, or west. That said, it's really not a tough place to navigate and is small enough to walk anywhere. **Jalan Soekarno-Hatta,** on which the **bank, post office,** and **Telkom office** are found, marks the north side of town. Perpendicular to it, **Jalan Gajah Mada** runs south, by the **bemo stand,** the **market.** To the west of Jl. Gajah Mada are about half of Bajawa's accommodations; to the east is the downtown area, as well as **Merpati** and the other lodgings. The **airport** is 25km north on the country road into which Jl. Gajah Mada turns, and the **bus terminal** lies 3km uphill to the east.

PRACTICAL INFORMATION

Tours and Travel: Locals can supply hand-drawn maps and regional tour plans. Any hotel can produce such a person, often without a request.

Currency Exchange: Bank Rayat Indonesia (tel. 210 24), on Jl. Soekarno-Hatta on the north side of town. Offers good rates. Open Mon.-Fri. 7:30am-4:30pm. **Bank Pembangunan Daerah,** Jl. Basuki Rahmat 17 (tel. 211 21).

Air Travel: Bajawa airport, 25km north near Soa. Reachable by a Merpati shuttle or *bemo*. **Merpati** (tel. 202 12), at the center of town near the market. Two flights per wk. to **Kupang** (Rp120,000) via **Ende** (Rp43,000) and **Bima** (Rp87,000). All flights leave on Tues. and Fri.

Buses: Watujaji Terminal, 2km east of town, a Rp300 *bemo* ride away. Hotels can buy tickets for their guests and arrange a pick up in the morning. To: **Ruteng** (4hr., 4500); **Ende** (4hr., Rp5000); and **Labuhanbajo** (8-10hr., Rp8500).

Local Transportation: Bemo gallivant throughout the city (Rp500).

Emergency: Police: 110. **Ambulance:** 118.

Medical Services: Conspicuously off Jl. Haryong on the west side of town.

Post Offices: Jl. Soekarno-Hatta, on the north side of town. Open Mon.-Thurs. 7:30am-3pm, Fri. 7:30-11:30am, Sat. 7:30am-1pm. **Postal code:** 86415.

Telephones: Telkom office (tel. 210 00), on Jl. Soekarno-Hatta, across the street and east of the bank and the post office. Open 24hr. **Phone code:** 0384.

ACCOMMODATIONS

For a town of only 12,000 people, Bajawa has a surprising number of good places to stay. Prices and quality are becoming standard as more travelers flow into Bajawa. Travelers can't go wrong in picking any hotel that strikes their fancy.

Hotel Elizabeth (tel. 212 25), on Jl. Inerie. Recently opened, Elizabeth offers enthusiasm, hospitality, cleanliness, and an afternoon snack—perhaps it's the next Bajawan hotspot. Simple rooms with shared *mandi* Rp7-10,000, with shower and mosquito nets Rp10-15,000.

Hotel Sunflower (tel. 212 36), on Jl. Hayam Wuruk, on the west side of town, east side of Jl. A. Yani. Snazzy bed linens and hillside vantage draw a crowd. The best rooms are in front (insist on the red and yellow sheets). Rooms include private *mandi*. Singles Rp7000. Doubles 10,000.

Hotel Ariesta (tel. 212 92), on Jl. Diponegoro. Hidden far on the town's east side behind the hospital. One of the quietest and cleanest places in Bajawa. Flush toilets. Manager speaks English. Singles Rp15,000. Doubles Rp20,000.

FOOD

The town's center sells a variety of cheap, fried, oddly shaped sweets. *Rumah makan* are scattered all over the city. For more ambiance, the traveler can eat at **Hotel Anggrek** or one of the following prime spots.

Restaurant Kasih Bahagia, on Jl. Gajah Mada just north of the center of town. A Chinese restaurant serving typical favorites in generous portions. Cheap and flavorful. Meals Rp2-5000.

Restaurant Carmellia, Jl. A. Yani 82 (tel. 214 58), on the west side of town. Highly acclaimed for their spring rolls. Tempeh is as good as it gets, and their milk-egg drinks can be ordered with ginger. Entrees Rp2-6000.

SIGHTS

The east side of town is replete with towering **totem poles,** which can be classified as *ngadhu* (male) or *bhaga* (female). These bizarre totems are reputed to contain generation upon generation of ancestral ghosts, who protect Bajawa from evil spirits. To see more of these poles, as well as traditional Ngada architecture, monoliths, hot springs, and sarong (for sale), go to any of the surrounding villages. Local teenagers often swarm tourists to offer their services as guides. In general, they can be trusted, but travelers should still take the usual precautions. *Bemo* can also take tourists to these villages, but then they're on their own. Hotels have maps to help guests plan excursions.

South Sulawesi

Contorted squid-shaped island that it is, Sulawesi seems to have as much coastline as land. Nowhere is this wealth of seafront life as conspicuous, rich, or textured as in the ports and fishing villages of South Sulawesi Province, which is populated by Bugis, Makassarese, and Torajans. It is the histories and activities of the former two that characterize the predominantly Islamic and ocean-dependent cities of the south. The larger cities—Ujung Pandang, Parepare, Watampone (Bone), and Polewali—attract, by merit of their coastal positions, large and transient populations of immigrants, sailors, and fishermen from throughout the greater region. In past times, Ujung Pandang was the seat of the Makassarese, while Bone was the home to the Bugis; today this division has been almost fully effaced by the comings and goings of the two populations, first under colonial rule, then under a unified state.

The landscape of the south begins with the arid palm/cornscapes of the land below Ujung Pandang. As travelers move north, the peninsula becomes increasingly lush, and rice replaces maize as the crop of choice. The transition from coastal plain to coastal mountain is exaggerated and sharp here, as flat fields stretch to the base of mountains without ever sloping. Farther north in Tana Toraja the contrast between flat and steep gives way to the labyrinthine topography of tight and winding mountain valleys. The Torajan people were for a long time driven to the hilltops by perennial invasions of the Bugis, but have come down to refill the vales.

GETTING THERE AND AWAY

By Plane

International flights fly into both **Hasanuddin Airport,** which lies 23km northeast of Ujung Pandang on the road to Maros, and **Sam Ratulangi Airport,** 6km from Manado. There's an international airport tax of Rp20,000 and a domestic one of Rp8500. The following are Merpati quotes to: **Jakarta** (Rp396,400); **Surabaya** (Rp247,900); **Denpasar** (Rp185,200); **Mataram** (Rp234,000); and **Maumere** (Rp163,000). Mandala has cheaper fares than other domestic airlines.

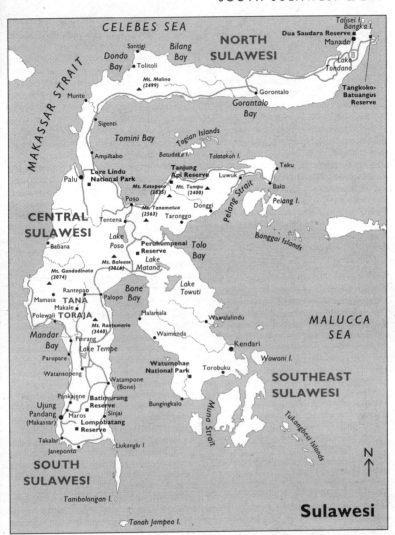

Sulawesi

By Boat

At least nine PELNI ships dock in Ujung Pandang on their 14-day tours of eastern Indonesia's major ports. Inquire at the PELNI office near the harbor for exact schedules. Fares may be cheaper than traveling by plane, but travel time is much longer. First, second, third, fourth, and economy classes are available. Some of the destinations of the ships are **Jakarta, Surabaya, Denpasar, Banyuwangi, Bima, Labuhanbajo, Cirebon,** and **Lembar.**

GETTING AROUND ON SULAWESI

By Plane

Sulawesi's three most popular destinations—Ujung Pandang, Toraja, and Manado— are far apart enough to warrant air travel. The plane from Ujung Pandang to

Rantepao (Rp90-115,000) actually lands at the small airport located half-way between Rantepao and Makale. Flights also go to: **Gorontalo** (Rp263,000); **Palu** (Rp116-153,000); and **Manado** (Rp290,000).

By Bus

The cheaper way to get around Sulawesi is by bus. The **Trans-Sulawesi Highway (Transul)** connects Ujung Pandang in the south to **Manado** at the very northern tip of the island. Supposedly one should allow 60-100 hours to travel between the two cities. Few travelers, however, go straight from one point to the other but choose instead to make stops along the way in towns like Palu, Poso, Donggala, or Gorontalo. **A/C buses** run from Ujung Pandang to: **Parepare** (3hr., Rp7000); **Rantepao** (8hr., Rp16,000); and **Mamasa** (10hr., Rp15,000). The **bus terminal** is inconveniently located in Panaikan; go to the *bemo* station and then take a *bemo* to the terminal. Travelers should try to buy a ticket at least one day in advance, and request a front seat for more comfort. **Liman Express,** on Jl. Timor, is highly recommended.

■ Ujung Pandang (Makassar)

A teeming city of cluttered ethnic *kampung,* corrugated tin roofs, waterfront bars, shady esplanades, floating *perahu,* and friendly, eager-to-learn-English residents, lively Ujung Pandang defies description. In the old days, Ujung Pandang was just one of a series of forts erected by the Gowa kingdom to protect its strategic port of Makassar. By the 16th century, Makassar had become the link between the islands of the archipelago. Indeed, Makassarese seafarers traveled far and wide, shuttling the lucrative spice trade through their waters. The city was already a melting pot of Bugis, Mandarese, and Makassarese cultures, but trade ushered in even more ideas, customs, and people from as far away as the Middle East and Europe.

After establishing hegemony over Manado to the north, the Dutch realized that they needed to secure Makassar as well in order to monopolize the spice trade. Using classic imperialist schemes, the Dutch manipulated local rivalries to their own end; they aligned themselves with Bone, a once-powerful kingdom that had been subjugated by Gowa, to capture Makassar in 1667. The fort of Ujung Pandang was renamed Fort Rotterdam, and from here the Dutch strategized the final conquest of Gowa. Proving that they could not be defeated so easily, the Makassarese continued to revolt against Dutch rule, resulting in the complete destruction of Makassar. A treaty expelled all other Europeans from the city and it literally became a ghost town, bereft of any traces of its former population and glory.

It wasn't until the 19th century that Makassar began to reclaim its previous role in trade and, once again, such goods as nutmeg, cloves, copra, sandalwood, pearls, and precious oil passed through Makassar. Consequently, the city's economy picked up and people flocked to the new capital of "The Great East." Present-day Ujung Pandang, which became the official name of the city in the 1970s, is no longer just a historic commercial center but a still-vibrant city.

ORIENTATION

Although the clamor of Ujung Pandang seems to reach as far as the airport, some 20km to the east, the heart of the city is relatively compact. **Jalan Rajawali/Penghibur/Ujung Pandang/Martadinata** runs along the coast, passing by **Fort Rotterdam** at its northern end. Running roughly parallel to Jl. Rajawali/Penghibur to the east is **Jalan Slamet Riyadi/Hasanuddin/Cendrawasih. Jalan Cokroaminoto/Sudirman/Dr. Ratulangi** runs nearly straight through the geographic center of the city, forming the eastern border of **Karebosi Square,** and ending near the **Pasar Sentral** and the **bemo station** at its northern end. The next major thoroughfare to the east is **Jalan Yos Sudarso/Andalas/Latimojong** which runs south from near **Paotere Harbor,** passing the **Mesjid Agung. Jalan Bandang/Veteran** bounds the concentrated area of the city on the east. Stretching east-west along the southern boundary of Karebosi, dividing the city in half lengthwise is **Jalan Kartini/Bawakaraeng/Urip Sumiharjo** which eventually leads to the airport. **Jalan A. Yani/Bulusarung/Masjid Raya** starts from near the fort and runs east, forming the northern limits of Karebosi. The area north of Jl. A. Yani along **Perahu** and **Main Harbors** is the commercial center of the city. Maps are handed out freely at many hotels.

PRACTICAL INFORMATION

Tourist Offices: Government Tourist Office (tel. 211 42), on Jl. Andi Pangeran Petta Rani, an unfortunate 4km southeast of the center of town. More convenient, if less helpful, options include the staff at Legends Hostel, Ft. Rotterdam, and the bigger hotels who can provide maps to the traveler.

Immigration Offices: Jl. Seram Ujung 8-12, in the north of town, near the harbor.

Currency Exchange: Jl. A. Yani is the place to go. Among its residents are **Bank Rakyat Indonesia** (with a 24-hr. **ATM**), **Bank Rama, Bank Danamon,** and perhaps the most helpful, **Bank Central Asia,** which has longer hours (open Mon.-Fri. 8am-2pm, Sat. 8am-noon), has an **ATM,** and accepts credit cards and traveler's check at good rates. The **money changer at the airport** offers the same rates as the banks in town.

American Express: Jl. Sudirman 56 (tel. 853 906). Open Mon.-Sat. 8am-1pm.

Air Travel: Merpati, Jl. Bawakaraeng 109 (tel. 442 471), has flights to more cities in Indonesia than its competition. **Garuda,** Jl. Slamet Riyadi 6 (tel. 322 705). **Sempati,** Jl. Sudirman 24 in Hotel Victoria (tel. 311 612). **Mandala** (tel. 324 288), in Latanette Plaza on Jl. Sungai Saddang.

Local Transportation: The **bemo station** is on Jl. Cokroaminoto, northeast of Karebosi. *Bemo* (known here as *pete-pete*) go anywhere in town for about Rp400. **Becak** travel anywhere as well (Rp500-1000). Agree on a price before boarding, and make sure your driver really knows where he's going. Taxis can also be hired for about Rp95,000 per day from most accommodations.

Pharmacies: Several **Apotik Kimia Farma** are in town, including the 24-hr. main store, Jl. Hasanuddin 46 (tel. 324 442), just south of the supermarket.

Medical Services: Rumah Sakit Akademis Jaury (tel. 320 280), on Jl. Akademis, just off Jl. Bulusarung.

Emergency: Police: tel. 110. **Fire:** tel. 113. **Ambulance:** tel. 118.

Police: Jl. Hasanuddin 3 (tel.325 850), next door to Hotel Marannu.

Post Offices: Jl. Slamet Riyadi 10 (tel. 323 180), 1 block south of Jl. A. Yani. *Poste Restante* at window #15. **Postal code:** 90111.

Telephones: Scattered throughout town. **Wartel** at Jl. Kajaolaliddo 2G-4, Jl. Balaikota 2, and Jl. Veteran 28, and on Jl. Sulawesi and Jl. Nusantara. Perhaps most convenient are **HCD** phones found in the biggest hotels. Try Hotel Marannu or Legends Hostel. **Telephone code:** 0411.

ACCOMMODATIONS

Plenty of upscale hotels advertise themselves boldly in Ujung Pandang's skyline, but budget haunts seem to have hidden themselves from the masses.

Legends Hostel, Jl. Jampea 5G (tel. 320 424), north of the intersection with Jl. A. Yani. It has clean, cheap dorm beds (Rp5500) and reasonable rooms (Rp12,500), free coffee and tea, bike rentals (Rp4000 per day), an aquarium, common books for shared travel advice, IDD phone, roof-top terrace, and restaurant. Unfortunately, it's close to some noisy karaoke bars and has only 3 bathrooms.

Ricardson Homestay, Jl. Sawerigading 21 (tel. 320 348), 2 blocks east of the intersection with Jl. Penghibur, near Bundt's Orchid. While not a great price for lone travelers (rooms have a flat rate of Rp25,000), it's the best deal in town for pairs. Rooms are beyond clean and tasteful, perhaps even elegant. There's an immaculate white tile balcony, stained-glass windows, breakfast, and sometimes lunch. Top notch massage is Rp5000 per hr.

Hotel Riantira, Jl. Ranggong 10 (tel. 324 133), a few blocks in from the waterfront, north of Bundt's Orchid. You shouldn't judge a hotel by its exterior, or you'll miss Riantira's charm inside. Economy rooms with breakfast, flush toilet, and fan Rp20-

25,000, with A/C and TV Rp35-45,000. Guests can also request the "emergency" room, where beds go for Rp15,000.

FOOD

Ujung Pandang displays a stunning assortment of food that provides a welcome relief from the limited menus of provincial towns, and serves up seafood like no other place on Sulawesi. Be sure to try the *ikan bakar* (fish grilled over charcoal). In the evening, a motley crew of **food carts** span well over a km along Jl. Penghibur—a nightly gastronomic feast known as **Pantai Losari.** Other non-restaurant options can be savored at **Pasar Sentral,** across from the *bemo* station. In addition, there's also a legion of *rumah makan.* The **corner diner** next to the Toko Cahaya Food Market on Jl. Sulawesi offers quality food and local bustle, while the **warung** beside Legends Hostel does some wacky things to the sandwich.

Rumah Makan Malabar, Jl. Sulawesi 264 (tel. 319 776). Trying to choose from their fantastic selection of Indian dishes can be downright distressing: should you go for mutton or chicken curry (Rp7000)? Better yet, goathead soup (Rp5000)? No—how about a *martabak* pancake (Rp5000)? Decisions, decisions.

Restaurant Ujung Pandang, Jl. Irian 42. The place to sup on seafood, as well as tasty Chinese fare. Everything imaginable from the sea: shrimp (Rp7000), cuttlefish (Rp5000), and their famous freshwater crab (Rp20,000). Vegetables and chicken also come in various concoctions.

Café Uchang, on Jl. Sudirman, just south and across the street from the cinema. Since coffee is bad everywhere else in town (even though it's grown in abundance on Sulawesi), this is *the* place to get your caffeine high. Sorry, no food, but drink up, admire the murals, take in live music, and chat with the friendly staff.

SIGHTS

Once known as Fort Jumpandang (from where Ujung Pandang take its name), the structure that stands near the waterfront on Jl. Penghibur has long abandoned its military trappings and now houses a **museum** and **cultural center** (open Tues.-Sun. 7:30am-4pm). After overpowering the Makassarese the Dutch claimed the fort as their victory prize and renamed it **Fort Rotterdam.** During the colonial era, the fort became the Dutch administrative headquarters in the south, presiding over a small town that was rebuilt to replace old Makassar, which had been razed to the ground. The fort has been renovated and is a beautiful specimen of red-shingled, white-stuccoed Dutch architecture. Former cargo-halls now hold the **La Galigo Museum,** a collection of ethnographic exhibits (admission to the fort Rp500 on the first day, Rp200 to the museum thereafter, free on Sun.).

Scattered north of the fort are a number of Chinese temples which can be viewed in a short amount of time. The first one the visitor encounters is at the corner of Jl. Sulawesi and Jl. Serui, one block north of Jl. A. Yani. Known as the **Temple of the Heavenly Queen,** this one is dedicated to the Chinese goddess Tian Hou Gong, who protects sailors. Walk farther up Jl. Sulawesi to Jl. Bali, where the **Temple of the Dragon Apparition** (Long Xian Gong) stands. Built in 1868, this temple houses three altars, of which the central one celebrates Xian Mu, the mother of immortals.

Venturing even farther north leads to the Javanese-style **Tomb of Diponegoro,** at the corner of (where else?) Jl. Diponegoro and Jl. Andalas. Alas, the mystery of the elusive Diponegoro (a name that no Indonesian city can do without) has been solved. This much-loved prince of Yogyakarta boldly led Indonesian forces against the Dutch in the Java War of 1825-30, only to be taken and imprisoned in Makassar until his death in 1855.

South of the fort, just of Jl. Penghibur is **Bundt's Orchid Garden,** Jl. Mochtar Lufti 15 (tel. 322 572), an unlikely extravagant collection of flora in the center of town. Bundt is dead now, but the legacy of horticultural prowess lives on in this delightful garden museum (free admission).

Farther south, near the limits of Ujung Pandang proper is **Sutera Alam,** Jl. Onta Lama 47, a silk weaving center in an inconspicuous white building on a small side street running east off Jl. Sudirman. A shop sells various garments, but be sure to get a look at the upstairs, where visitors can see the intricate silk-making process, from the first dye to the final weave.

■ Near Ujung Pandang

MAKASSAR BAY

Several small islands of emerald jungle ringed with white sand dot the waters of Makassar Bay, beckoning travelers to sample the excellent swimming, diving, snorkeling, and sunbathing opportunities they have to offer. This area is also home to some of the finest coral reefs in this part of the world. Unfortunately, the reefs closest to the coast have been nearly destroyed due to explosives and careless snorkelers. Underwater adventurers must go out at least 10km for the live stuff. **Samalona** is the jewel of the bay, and has bamboo huts on the beach for rent (Rp35,000). For diversions of a quieter nature, head to **Kudingarang Keke,** a nearly deserted oasis even farther out from the coast. The reefs are as spectacular as can be here, but sewage threatens the idyllic beauty of the place. Divers who really want to head out as far as possible can go two hours out to the island of **Kapoposang,** where the sea drops dramatically and underwater fauna flourish peacefully among the fishes, including white-tip reef sharks. Try to get to Kapoposang early to get in a couple of dives before 1pm and head back to the mainland; otherwise you'll have to stay overnight with the friendly Bugis locals.

Boats headed to the islands can be chartered at **Tumba Kayu Bangkoa Pier,** just south of the intersection of Jl. Pattimura and Jl. Penghibur, and can fit six people. All prices depend on distance and travel time: **Lae Lae** (Rp6000); **Samalona** (30min., Rp35,500); **Barang Caddi** (1hr., Rp59,000); **Barang Lompo** (1hr., Rp59,000); **Kudingarang Keke** (1hr., Rp59,000); and **Bone Tambung** (1½hr., Rp70,500). To get to the more touristy **Kayangan,** join the locals on boats that depart from the pier across the street from the fort (15min., Rp2350, Sat. Rp3000, Sun. Rp4200).

Sporting goods lining Jl. Somba Opu sell and rent snorkeling gear. For diving, try the **Makassar Diving Centre,** Jl. Ujung Pandang 3, across from the fort, which offers mask, snorkels, and fins on a per day basis. Package tours are also available: one day diving with boat, weights, tanks, and guide (US$50, minimum 2) and three-dive overnight trips to beautiful Kapoposang (US$150 per person, minimum 4).

MAROS CAVES

Proving once again that Southeast Asia is the land of water, waterfalls, temples, and caves, Sulawesi has its own Mesolithic wonders for cave aficionados. With over 55 caverns, Maros is a caveman's wonderland of winding paths, running streams, and painted walls. Deer, pig-deer, and other four-legged creatures make up the interior decorating of the caves, all believed to be 5000-10,000 years old. To get there, catch a *bemo* from the central station in Ujung Pandang to Maros (1hr., 40km, Rp500).

BANTIMURUNG WATERFALL

An easy 1½-hour northeast bound journey allows one to escape the hub-bub and hustle of urban Ujung Pandang. Nestled among limestone cliffs and thick vegetation, the 12m **Bantimurung Falls** are swimmable, and thus extremely popular with the local people (admission Rp2000). Take the path to the left of Bantimurung proper to reach some smaller falls and **Stone Cave,** a 15-minute walk away. A flashlight will make explorations infinitely easier and guide-free. Another cave to the right of the falls and river is **Goa Mimpi** which has installed lights, but a flashlight may be necessary. Numerous food and trinket booths line the entrance way; be sure not to miss the gigantic monkey gate. To get to the Bantimurung Falls, take a bus (Rp700) or a *bemo*

(Rp700-1000) to Maros (1hr.). From here, take another *bemo* to Bantimurung (Rp500). On the way to the falls, you will pass by the Maros Caves.

GOWA

The remains of the great kingdom of Gowa lies just 7-11km south of Ujung Pandang, stretched out along the Jeneberang River. There are three major sites that visitors may want to see. It's best to visit these by car, otherwise you'll have to rely on several modes of transport. The first is the fortress of **Sombaopu,** situated at the mouth of the river, which was the southernmost and strongest of the string of forts that defended Makassar. The kings of Gowa ruled from here, surrounded by impenetrable 3m-thick walls. Since 1989, Indonesian archaeologists, guided by two ancient maps, have been excavating the site, resulting in some interesting finds, including bricks inscribed with an unknown script. During the third week of July, the annual **South Sulawesi Cultural Festival** is held here. To get to the fort, take a *bemo* from the central station and get off at Tangul Patompo (Rp1000). From here, hire a boat across the river; Sombaopu lies 0.5km away.

The second site lies farther east where the Jeneberang River bends south. This area is considered to be **Old Gowa,** where ancient mosques, royal tombs, and legendary coronation stones remain. At the northwest section stands the **Tomb of Syech Yusuf,** the most sacred in South Sulawesi. A religious scholar-turned-resistance fighter, Syech Yusuf (1626-94) is credited with bringing Islam to the Muslim communities on Sri Lanka and in South Africa, where he was exiled by the Dutch.

A road on the south side of the tomb runs southeast to **Katangka Mosque,** the oldest mosque on Sulawesi, allegedly built in 1605, shortly after Islam became the official religion of Gowa. Archaeologists are doubtful of the exact date of the mosque's construction, however, as it contains several architectural innovations from as late as the 18th century. Massive royal tombs surround the mosque.

Continue down the road and make a sharp right 300m down from the mosque. When you hit another road, turn right again to reach **Batu Pelantikan** (Coronation Stone). This higher ground is known as Tamalate, and was the site of the Gowa palace over three centuries ago. Batu Pelantikan rests on the highest point of the ground where Tumanurunga, the celestial maiden, reputedly married Karaeng Bayo, thereby granting him rule by divine right as the first king of Gowa. It was on this sacred stone, then, that all the kings of Gowa were coronated. Next to the stone is the **Tomb of Hasanuddin,** the celebrated 12th king of Gowa, who led a long struggle against the Dutch before he was finally defeated in 1660.

Bis kota run from the central bus terminal to Old Gowa (Rp500). If you want to start at the mosque, ask to get dropped off there and you can walk around the area. *Becak* in the vicinity can take you around as well. Alternatively, if coming from Sombaopu, you can walk the 3km to Old Gowa; just follow the Jeneberang River east.

West of Gowa lies another group of tombs which are not part of the Gowa dynasty. Here, the **Tomb of Aru Palakka** remains, instead, as a taunt to the Makassarese. The Bugis leader from Bone, Aru Palakka joined forces with the Dutch to vanquish Gowa (his revenge for Bone's defeat at the hands of Gowa in 1644). He was crowned king of Bone, which, as the ally of the Dutch, grew rich off the spoils of war. At his death in 1696, Aru Palakka requested to be buried in the land that he conquered rather than in his homeland. Needless to say, the Makassarese despised him and left his tomb to the creepy crawlers of the jungle. Fortunately for Aru, his Dutch friends stepped in to maintain the tomb's present state.

Head back to the main road and continue south to reach the royal palace of **Sungguminasa,** now known as **Muzium Balla Lompoa** (open Mon.-Sat. in the mornings, closed Sun. and holidays). The current structure was rebuilt in 1936 and rests on stilts, reachable by stairs which lead up to the reception area. Notice the five wooden gables on the roof, an indication that this traditional home has of the rank of royalty. The palace houses the treasures of Gowa's royal family, which are kept locked up. The treasure room is only open to the public once per year on Idul Adha (April 14, 1997). If you miss that grand day, have a good reason ready and beg at the *bupati*'s office. Some of the highlights of the collection include: the crown supposedly worn by Tumanurunga when she descended from heaven; the gold chain believed to have been brought by the heavenly queen as well, used to foretell the kingdom's prosperity or misfortune; and a *keris* (dagger) studded with gems, perhaps a gift from the powerful Sultan of Demak. *Bemo* run from Ujung Pandang (30min., Rp500) or you can walk the 2km from Old Gowa.

TALLO

The Makassar kingdom actually consisted of two kingdoms—Gowa and Tallo. Both royal families, however, belonged to the same house; Tallo was founded by a Gowa prince in the 15th century on a spit of land 3km north of Ujung Pandang, at the mouth of the Tallo River. While Gowa provided the king of Makassar, Tallo's king acted as the chancellor of the state. In fact, it was one of these chancellors, Sultan Awal-ul-Islam (1593-1636), who introduced Islam to Makassar. There isn't much left of Tallo except a 2-km sea wall, which practically encircles Tallo. The northernmost of the line of forts once stood here. Several royal tombs scatter in the area, many of which were only begun to be restored in the late 70s. There is one tomb in the northwest corner of Tallo that is claimed to be the tomb of Karaeng Matoaya (a.k.a. Sultan Awal-ul-Islam), but his tomb has already been identified among the Gowa ruins. Getting to Tallo can be hellish, since public transportation is unreliable. It's best to drive or hire a *bemo*.

■ Parepare

Parepare lies midway between Ujung Pandang and Tana Toraja. The second largest city in South Sulawesi Province, and a significant port unto itself, Parepare seems much akin to its southern behemoth of a brother, Ujung Pandang—without the interminable parades of blaring *bemo* and the endless maze of backstreets, however. Although more placid and quiet, Parepare is still large enough to warrant a day or two of a traveler's time. The town boasts no fewer than three markets and offers magnificent sunsets from its esplanade, unmarred by badgering hawkers. As a hub for buses running north and south, Parepare is also a convenient base for trips along the northwest coast of the province and east to Senkang and Watampone (Bone).

ORIENTATION

Parepare fits into a corner of land constituted by a western coast which dips inland at the northern boundary of the town. **Jalan Lasinrang** runs northeast-southwest along the northern shore of water until it meets **Jalan Hasanuddin,** which runs north-south along the western coast, changing names to **Jalan Matirotasi.** Smaller streets form a simple grid inland from these two streets. Pare Pare has a couple of commercial clusters, one along the coastal north-south roads, and one along Jl. Lasinrang. Although the **bus terminal, night market, banks, post office, Telkom office,** and most of the hotels are in the southern part of town, the northern half is the thickest part of Pare Pare and has the better of its two day markets. The main port is on the west coast, but smaller passenger boats dock at the port to the north.

PRACTICAL INFORMATION

Tours and Travel: Lantari Tour and Travel, Jl. Bau Massepe 578 (tel. 239 59). **Pt. Abadi Polacitra Mandiri,** Jl. Bau Massepe 361 (tel. 243 20).

Currency Exchange: Bank Negara Indonesia, Jl. Veteran 41. Open Mon.-Sat. 8am-2pm. **Bank Rakyat Indonesia** (tel. 213 95), on Jl. Bau Massepe. Open Mon.-Fri. 7:45am-4:45pm, Sat. 8am-3pm.

Buses: Terminal, 3km south of town. Regular buses to and from **Ujung Pandang** (3hr., Rp4000) and **Rantepao** (4-5hr., Rp5000), and a few times per day to **Polewali** (2hr., Rp3000), **Sengkang** (2hr., Rp3000), and **Watampone** (2hr., Rp2000).

There's an occasional direct bus to **Mamasa** coming from Ujung Pandang, in late morning (7hr., Rp7000), although chances are it will be filled.

Ferries: PELNI Office, Jl. Andi Cammi 96 (tel. 210 17), near the harbor.

Local Transportation: Bemo run from the terminal in the center of town to points north along Jl. Lasinrang, to points south along the north-south road, and to the bus terminal in the south.

Emergency: Police: tel. 110. **Fire:** tel. 113. **Ambulance:** tel. 118.

Medical Services: Dokter H. Haeruddin Pagarra and **H. Chaerani Haeruddin** can be found at Jl. Bau Massepe 296.

Post Offices: Jl. Karaeng Burane 1. **Postal code:** 91111.

Telephones: Telkom office, Jl. Bau Massepe 262 (tel. 223 21). **Wartel** at Jl. Dg. Parani 25 and Jl. Bau Massepe 306. All 3 are open 24hr. **Telephone code:** 0421.

ACCOMMODATIONS

Hotel Gandaria, Jl. Bau Massepe 395 (tel. 210 93). A garden, moderate restaurant, spiral staircase, and surprising degree of quietude for its city hotel feel. Clean range of rooms from smaller ones with fan (Rp15,000) to larger ones with A/C (Rp36,000). Rooms each have a set price, regardless of the number of guests.

Hotel Gemini, Jl. Bau Massepe 451 (tel. 217 54). Clean as a hotel can be with a dirt road down the middle. While the management guards absolute prices like they're top secret, rooms with shared *mandi* seem to run Rp5-7000, and those with private bath Rp10-12,500.

Wisma Rio, Jl. Pinggirlau 10, across the street and a few steps north of the western port. While serving the local traffic that comes and goes on PELNI boats, Rio seems happy enough to put up western land lubbers. Dark, primitive, friendly rooms cost a flat rate of Rp8000.

Ashar Hotel, Jl. Hasanuddin 9 (tel. 217 06). All the ambiance of America's best car wash. Fortunately, however, rooms are as clean as one would expect from such a theme. Light sleepers, beware: it's close to a mosque. Singles begin at Rp15,000 with fan. Doubles begin at Rp10,000.

FOOD

Nobody in Parepare has made an effort to cook up good food, especially for tourist types. But most do all right by the food already in the making for local folks. Jl. Panggir Laut offers cartfood, vistas, and friendly locals. Parepare's two day markets abound with the standard sumptuous offering of fruit.

Rumah Makan Padang Raya, Jl. Bau Massepe 389, a door or two south of Hotel Gandaria. As the name suggests, Padang food here is fresh and flavorful. The fried chicken and spinach greens warrant unqualified praise.

Restaurant Asia, Jl. Baso Daeng Patompo 25 (tel. 214 15). Nothing of note decorwise, but a slew of Chinese food selections available. Higher prices than most hole-in-the-wall joints with entrees ranging from Rp6-20,000.

MARKETS AND SIGHTS

Aside from the beautiful surrounding scenery, the open ocean, and the ships dotting the harbor, there's only the markets to go to for sightseeing action. The world has hidden its foremost bounty of used clothing in the **night market** of Parepare. Endless piles of dresses, pants, shirts, and loud ties often exceed the stamina of all but the most seasoned used-clothes hound. Although something less of an occasion, the **day market,** in the northern of two commercial hubs, is a winding landscape of merchandise. The day market in the southern commercial center sits inconspicuously in the center of the block—watch the alleyways for signs of hidden commerce. On the southwest corner, men sell basketware and other woven goods.

■ Mamasa

Sometimes called West Toraja because of its cultural and linguistic similarities with the Torajans, Mamasa presents, in all respects, a less ostentatious show of Torajan tradition. There are fewer fellow tourists, fewer slaughtered buffalo, less *bemo* traffic, and less conspicuous tour groups. You won't, however, find such a grand or bloody show of death. In place of all the pomp and spectacle, Mamasa offers something almost a shame to advertise: unspoilt rural calmness and friendliness. The only traffic of outsiders to Mamasa Valley comes from visitors who come for the sake of seclusion and end-of-the-road beauty. There are places to stay, endless daytrip and trekking possibilities, and a handful of local guides who see enough business to have learned some English. Locals are on the delightfully shy side of hospitable, and the place feels like your own when—as is often the case—tourist business is slow. Mamasa brandishes its mix of Christianity with the sweet lull of morning and evening choirs, as well as a crop of hillside churches which contrast sharply with the abundance of buffalo-beheaded *tongkonan* (traditional houses). Expect plenty of sunny mornings, but be prepared for the rainy afternoons.

ORIENTATION AND PRACTICAL INFORMATION

Mamasa straddles the river which runs through the valley. The town's few streets follow the quirks and contours of the land. Mamasa's attractiveness is due in part to its haphazard layout, but fortunately its size limits the confusion.

As the hours of interminable mountain curves and bumps continue without end, turn back to this page and read this sentence again: *the trip to Mamasa is worth it.* Buses run from **Polewali** (at least 3 per day, 5hr., Rp3500) and **Pare Pare** (at least 1 per day, mid-morning, 7hr., Rp7000), which originate in **Ujung Pandang** (10-12hr., Rp10,000). If the bus in Pare Pare is full, take a bus to Polewali, then catch one to Mamasa from there. Buses leave Mamasa in the morning, while *bemo* make the trip to Polewali several times per day. *Bemo* cost the same as buses, but are not recommended for the faint of heart or stomach.

Mamasa's **banks do not change money.** Bring plenty of money with you. Mamasa has a **hospital** in the center of town with an overwhelmingly pink roof. The **wartel** stands across the street from Losmen Marampan.

ACCOMMODATIONS AND FOOD

Mamasa boasts a disproportionately large number of places to stay, given its size and isolation. **Losmen Marampan** goes so far as to cover the traveler with a grand traditional *tongkonan* roof. Rooms here, as with most in town, are rented per room and not per lodger. *Mandi*-less rooms on the cozy side of small cost Rp7500, with private bath Rp10,000. The **Toraja Mamasa Church** runs a guest house with singles for Rp5000, and doubles for Rp7500. All rooms have their own *mandi* and toilet, as well as fine wood interiors. **Mantana Lodge** is new, as evidenced by its quasi-traditional ceiling beams, its up-to-date tourism info, its white and sparkling tiles, and its slightly higher room rates. Singles start at Rp10,000, doubles at Rp15,000. Larger carpeted rooms cost Rp20-25,000. At night these are, perhaps, the coziest rooms in town, but during the day (when Mamasa is without electricity), some rooms are too dark—a flaw redeemed by an upstairs porch. **Losmen Mini** is right in the thick of town with innocuous enough rooms for the flat rate of Rp7500, with *mandi* Rp10,000. While some of these lodgings offer restaurants, the cheapest and most savory fare is served at a few *warung* downtown for Rp2000. The luxury option for room and board is an impressive complex 3km north of Mamasa proper called **Mamasa Cottage.** Singles here cost US$55, doubles US$62.50. The restaurant serves buffets at matching prices, and perks include A/C, swimming pool, and basin for a natural hot spring.

HIKING AND TREKKING AROUND MAMASA

The traveler would have to search long and hard to find a mountain valley as conducive to walking around as the Mamasa Valley—of course, the traveler has to search long and hard to find the Mamasa Valley to begin with. Hiking excursions and treks above a couple of hours may require a guide (standard rate Rp60,000 per day), available through most accommodations (guides are available for shorter walks as well). There are routes of various length, requiring anything from one day to three days. Horses are available at Rp25,000 per day to carry packs. As with any guide, personal recommendations from fellow travelers may be the most reliable and trustworthy. For multi-day hikes, villagers in any of the small villages you visit can put you up for the night; just inquire with the village head. The road past the hospital leads to the right and eventually turns into a path which leads to the village of **Tusan,** a small cluster of traditional houses. The path continues on to **Tondok Bakaru,** another traditional village. After Tondok Bakaru, **Kole** is to the left and once through Kole the path meets up with the main road out of Mamasa. Take a right heading south and a 45-minute walk brings you back to Mamasa; or turn north and head to **Rante Buda,** which features one of the 300-year-old well-preserved traditional houses. The Tusan-Tondok-Bukarno-Kole-Mamasa loop takes approximately two hours.

■ Rantepao

How much travelers enjoy Rantepao will depend entirely on how "authenticity" is defined. If it means remoteness, seclusion, and practically employed roof-weathered houses, the "tourist capital" of Tana Toraja will be a disappointment. If, however, your definition is real ceremonies, refurbished *tongkonan* houses, and the public clamor of a town bearing its traditional colors, then Rantepao is the right place. The sole seat of the Toraja tourism boom, Rantepao is, as such, bedecked with all the bells and glossy whistles of a place geared toward the affluent outsider. Luxury hotels stand where a generation ago electricity was a pipe dream; tour buses buzz the roads of bewildered rice farmers, and "traditional houses" are every year touched-up with fresh acrylic paint of the region's colors. The town's restaurants and homestays cater to western sensibilities, and local guides and proprietors think they know exactly what you want to see.

Rantepao, however, offers tradition at its best, albeit executed with an eye toward the interests and pocketbooks of a foreign audience. Although locals organize and guide each tourist through the landscapes and ceremonies of their peculiar culture and home, that culture and that home (except for the flourishes of paint) have remained almost wholly unscathed. Tana Toraja jumps to accommodate those who come to see it, but not at the price of making itself a cartoon. The region is fascinating and rife with peculiar rites and, despite what it may seem ahead of time—when the prospective guide tells you that the funeral ends tomorrow and only he can help you find it—none of the ceremonies are put on for tourists. As soon as you arrrive at a funeral, wedding, or house ceremony, you'll feel precisely what you are: a foreigner privy to one of world's neatest and most private happenings; such events have, would, and will happen without you. Dress appropriately, snap your pictures, bring some gifts, and take note that you're lucky as hell.

ORIENTATION

Rantepao is defined by its main north-south drag which enters town from the south as **Jalan Pong Tiku,** changes to **Jalan Pao Pura** as the town begins to happen, becomes **Jalan A. Yani** in the center of town, metamorphoses to **Jalan Mappanyuki** as it nears the northern curve of the river, and leaves the north of town as **Jalan Pahlawan.** Most services and amenities lie along this main road or between it and the **Sadang River** to the west and north. Some of the better accommodations, however, hide on the northwest side of town, across the river, on **Jalan Suloara,** off the main road (when it is Jl. Pahlawan). The **airport** is 24km to the south, near Makale. Rantepao's **market** is in the center of town, but there's no *bemo* terminal.

PRACTICAL INFORMATION

Tourist Offices: Pusat Informasi Wisata, Jl. A. Yani 62A (tel. 212 77). Free xeroxed maps and listing of ceremonies. Many eager guides solicit visitors here.

Tours and Travel: Lantari Tours and Travel, Jl. Mappanyuki 114 (tel. 231 85). **Tikulembang,** Jl. Mappanyuki 69 (tel. 231 42). **Toraja Highland Tours and Travel,** Jl. Diponegoro 12 (tel. 230 35).

Currency Exchange: Bank Rakyat Indonesia, Jl. A. Yani 96 (tel. 211 06). **Bank Danamon** is across the street. For longer hours, try the 2 **money changers** near the intersection of Jl. Mappanyuki and Jl. Diponegoro.

Air Travel: Merpati Air (tel. 214 85), on Jl. Pao Pura. Rather unreliable flights to **Ujung Pandang** (1 per day Mon.-Fri., 2 per day Sat., Rp115,000).

Buses: The number of buses depends on the number of passengers. Buy your tickets in advance from **Liman Express, Erlin, Alam Indah,** and **Fa Litah,** all of which are on Jl. Mappanyuki, north of the traffic rotary. To **Ujung Pandang** (7am, 1pm, and 7pm, 9hr., Rp12,000) with a rest stop in **Parepare.** Buses also pick up passengers at the traffic circle to **Palopo** (starting at 9pm, 3hr., Rp3000).

Local Transportation: Bemo ply the streets. There's no main terminal, but flag down any *bemo;* just make sure it's going where you want to go.

Rentals: Motorbikes and **bicycles** available for rental. Prices are Rp30,000 and Rp7500 per day respectively.

Pharmacies: Perpustakaan Tongkonan, Jl. A. Yani 55-57.

Medical Services: Rumah Sakit Elim, Jl. A. Yani 68 (tel. 212 58).

Emergency: Police: tel. 110. **Ambulance:** tel. 118.

Post Offices: Jl. A. Yani 111, across the street from the bigger of two Bank Rakyats. Open Mon.-Thurs. 8am-2pm, Fri. 8-11am, Sat. 8am-1pm, Sun. and holidays 9am-noon. **Postal code:** 91831.

Telephones: Telkom office, next to the post office. *Poste Restante.* **HCD** phone available. **Wartel** are everywhere as well. Open 24hr. **Telephone code:** 0423.

ACCOMMODATIONS

The giant boom in tourism two years ago resulted in plenty of rooms in Rantepao. Since then, the flow of tourism has ebbed slightly, leaving more than enough accommodations for tourists. Establishments in Rantepao span the spectrum, from cheap to luxury; the best bet for bargain-hunters are probably homestays.

Wisma Malita, Jl. Suloara 110 (tel. 210 11). Go north on the main road through town until you cross the Sadang; take an immediate left on Jl. Suloara and look for Malita on the right, 400km west. While the 0.5km walk to town may seem undesirable, the quiet location is your reward. The gardens are well-maintained and the tiles are clean. Rooms Rp10-12,500, with a flush toilet Rp18-20,000.

Zella Homestay, Jl. Suloara 113B (tel. 236 05), just one door west of Malita. A homestay in the literal sense of the word: travelers pay Rp12,000 or Rp15,000 (private bath and hot water) to share the family's space. Breakfast served. Prodigious library provides endless hours of junk reading.

Rapa Homestay, Jl. Pembangunan 56 (tel. 215 17), in the heart of town without seeming so. A long walk and a grand total room count of 3 ensures a satisfying degree of privacy and quiet for your Rp15,000. Breakfast included.

Pia's and Poppie's Hotel, Bar, and Restaurant, Jl. Pong Tiku 27A, south of central Rantepao, about 1km on the main drag to Makale; look for signs west of the road. A charmingly ill-contrived hodge-podge of architecture, with tiles, fieldstones, and random ornamental antlers. The bathtub alone may well be worth the price. Singles Rp20,000. Doubles Rp25,000.

Wisma Sarla, Jl. A. Mappanyuki (tel. 21167). Sarla's main street location means more noise, but you get spacious balconies, common rooms, and rooms for rent. In addition, your rupiah buys friendly proprietors and breakfast. Singles Rp7500. Doubles Rp12,000. Triples Rp17,500.

Mace Homestay, Jl. Tengko Saturu 4 (tel. 218 52), across the street from Zella on the river's far side. A higher price buys the guest a smidgen of elegance, with milk in the coffee, flowers in the yard, and two banana pancakes in the morning. Small and far enough to escape the tourist mob. Singles Rp20,000. Doubles Rp25,000.

FOOD

The cuisine at Rantepao's tourist-oriented restaurants has suffered a bit from the onslaught of foreign visitors. The local specialties of bamboo-tube-cooked meats *(pa' piong),* black rice, and palm wine have, in general, been reduced to tasteless Epcot-Center-contrived food. Fear not, however, as small restaurants and *warung* still serve up *pa' piong* the old-fashioned way. *Balok* (palm wine) is cheapest in the markets, but taste it before you buy.

Rumah Makan Indo Grace, on Jl. Mappanyuki. Entrees on the cheaper side of touristy. Decor is a mild plus: red checkered table cloths, blue tile floor, yellow paneled ceiling. Mostly Chinese food, but some respectable Torajan fare.

Restaurant Sarlotha, Jl. Mappanyuki 109. A *rumah makan* that changed to a restaurant recently enough that good food and low prices still seem made and decided in someone's private kitchen. Good *nasi,* good *mie,* and some of Rantepao's cheaper *pa' piong.*

Rumah Makan Rima I, on Jl. Mappanyuki. Perhaps too popular, Rima is a prime spot to eat pancakes or survey the hippest European travelers currently in town. If, by some horrendous fluke of travel, you have not yet been accosted by a local guide-to-be, Rima is the place to find one.

SIGHTS

Despite the influx of tourists into Rantepao, just a short walk out of the city will land travelers in the middle of nowhere, in hills and vales less trafficked, if at all, by foreigners. The rolling hills, watery rice paddies, and endless sea of greenery harbor small villages which can provide visitors with the opportunity to be immersed in local culture, if only for a day. It's usually better to simply walk around than to suffer bone-jarring rides along bumpy, unpaved roads. The best time to go **trekking** is from March to May and from mid-July to mid-October. The end of the dry season is preferred, as clouds ushering in the wet season can protect trekkers from the harsh sun. Avoid trekking in the wet season, when downpours turn most roads into mudslides and leeches are aplenty. Guides are highly recommended for multi-day trips, but are not needed for daytrips. If you feel better having someone to mediate your interaction with the locals, then hire a guide (Rp60-95,000 per day). Porters can also be hired (Rp15-24,000 per day).

If you plan on multi-day excursions, be sure to bring some equipment. We suggest you take sturdy footwear, rain gear, a blanket or sleeping bag, a small knapsack, a flashlight, a first-aid kit, sunscreen, long pants, and long-sleeved shirts. Bring water, but food is not needed, as rest stops equipped with food are available along the more popular hiking routes. Some nice *losmen* can be found deep in Torajaland, but if there isn't one where you go, you can stay in *tongkonan* houses or with the villagers. Just be sure to give the owner of the house Rp8000 for food. Many villages around Rantepao have entrance fees of about Rp1000.

Sumatra

Straddling the equator, the enormous island of Sumatra baffles visitors with its bustling cities, isolated islands, and remote villages. Notorious for its long distances, poor roads, and fickle climate, travel through Sumatra takes time. As the western flank of Indonesia, and one of the largest islands of the nation, Sumatra plays second fiddle only to Java in politics and economics. The Malay communities of the island, such as

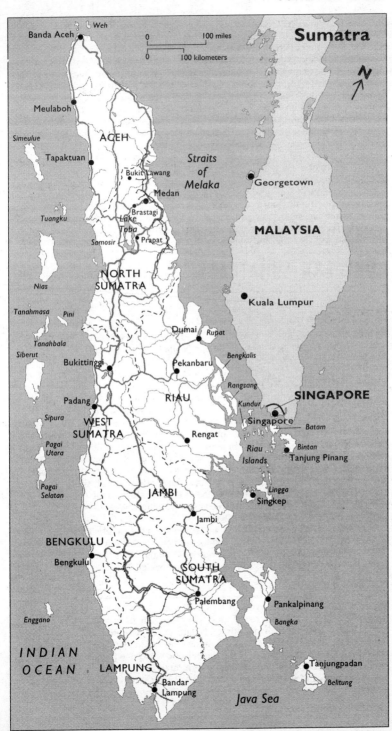

the Minangkabau of West Sumatra and Orang Melayu of the east coast, have donated their native languages to the rest of Indonesia, helping to mold the archipelago into a unified nation under Bahasa Indonesia.

Sumatra is decidedly top-heavy in terms of sights. After suffering Medan, the adventurous might head north to the staunchly Islamic province of Aceh, but most make their way south to magnificent Gunung Leuser and the refreshing Lake Toba region. Hikers head to Bukittinggi in West Sumatra Province to immerse themselves in the heart of Minang culture. Continuing south requires perseverance and a penchant for exploration, although a stop in the backwater provincial seat of Bengkulu is warranted for even the most amateur Soekarno-philes. Bandar Lampung, at the southern tip of Sumatra, welcomes travelers en route to Java.

Dubbed *"Suma Tera"* (Black Earth) by the first Europeans to colonize the island, Sumatra is one of the few Indonesian islands to retain its colonial name. The island has changed much in spite of its lingering moniker, but Sumatra still poses many challenges to foreigners who visit. Many regions prove to be inaccessible for even the most determined, and women traveling alone may experience acute harassment. But aside from the uncomfortable journeys and bellicose locals, Sumatra still offers exciting destinations and a variety of traditions. For the intrepid traveler willing to explore, this "black earth" frontier-land awaits.

NORTHERN SUMATRA

◼ Medan

Poor Medan. Few Southeast Asian cities are as maligned by travelers, many of whom look forward to three days in Medan as they might to a 72-hour root canal. The city's choking pollution, perpetually snarled traffic, and extortive taxi and *becak* drivers are all strikes against her. Nevertheless, as North Sumatra's gateway city and chief transportation hub, Medan is an inevitable stop on any itinerary. Those who venture into the city, away from the noxious fumes of the main thoroughfares, are rewarded with warm Indonesian friendliness and curiosity, as foreigners are scarce here.

This metropolis of two million souls is anything but dull. Under the Dutch, Medan, strategically situated on the Straits of Melaka, grew from a backwater town to an industrial center. Immigrants from across the archipelago and beyond flocked to Medan to share in its prosperity. Today the population is a vibrant mix of coastal Malay, Batak, Indian, and Chinese. Its accordingly rich religious heritage accounts for many of Medan's most intriguing sights, from the fanciful Mesjid Raya (Grand Mosque) to the colorful Candi Hindu (Hindu Temple). Much to the delight of budget *gourmands,* this ethnic diversity also ensures that cheap, delicious, and varied cuisine abounds.

Aside from their frenetic traffic habits, Medanites maintain reluctantly relaxed lifestyles. If the fumes become overwhelming, remember that within a few hours you can be swimming in Lake Toba's blue water, or hiking the rainforested volcanoes of Brastagi, to name but a few of North Sumatra's many delights.

ORIENTATION

Medan rambles with little rhyme or reason. Like many Indonesian cities, the streets shed monikers quicker than Zsa Zsa sheds hubbies. The main north-south thoroughfare changes names more than six times. It starts out as **Jalan Putri Hijau** and changes to **Jalan Balai Kota** at the Deli Plaza Shopping Centre. After passing **Merdeka Square,** it becomes **Jalan A. Yani.** South of the intersection with **Jalan Palang Merah,** it briefly becomes **Jalan Pemuda** before changing to **Jalan Brigjen. Katamso,** passing the **Istana Maimun** and several travel agencies. Jl. Palang Merah, which leads west from Jl. A. Yani (and quickly becomes **Jalan H.Z. Arifin**), passes through the Chinese and

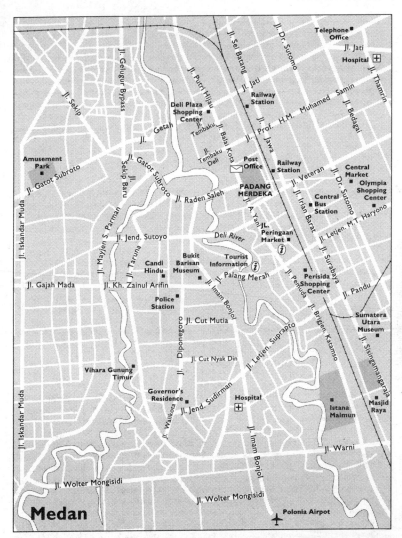

Medan

Indian area of the city. A number of cheap *warung* and delicious bakeries line Jl. H.Z. Arifin. The other important road for travelers to learn is **Jalan Sisingamangaraja,** which roughly parallels Jl. Pemuda/Brigjen. Katamso, passing the **Mesjid Raya** and **Bukit Barisan Hero's Cemetery.** A number of hotels catering to every budget can be found in the vicinity of the Mesjid Raya. Medan's two bus terminals, **Stasiun Pinang Baris** and **Stasiun Amplas,** are unfortunately located on the inconvenient western and southern edges of the city, respectively.

PRACTICAL INFORMATION

Tourist Offices: Provincial Tourism Office of North Sumatra, Jl. A. Yani 107 (tel. 538 101). Just north of Jl. Palang Merah on the right. Eager staff has useful maps of Medan. Beware: map is not to scale. Leave packs here for a day of sightseeing. Open Mon.-Thurs. 7:30am-4:15pm, Fri. 7:30-11:30am.

Tours and Travel: Most agents line Jl. Brigjen. Katamso south of Jl. Letjen. Suprapto. **Trophy Travel and Tour,** Jl. Brigjen. Katamso 33DE (tel. 555 666), is Medan's largest travel agency. Open Mon.-Sat. 8am-8pm, Sun. 8am-1pm. All major credit cards. **Pacto Tours and Travel,** Jl. Brigjen. Katamso 35G (tel. 510 081), arranges treks through Gunung Leuser Park (6 days, US$520, all expenses included, min. 2 people) and Alas River rafting (6 days, US$630 per person, min. 2 people). Trips leave on fixed dates. Open Mon.-Fri. 8am-4pm, Sat. 8am-1pm.

Embassies and Consulates: Malaysia, Jl. Diponegoro 43 (tel. 531 342). Open Mon.-Thurs. 8am-1pm and 2-4pm, Fri. 8-11:30am and 1:30-4pm. **Singapore,** Jl. Tengku Daud 3 (tel. 513 366). Open Mon.-Fri. 8am-12:30pm and 1:30-4:30pm. **UK,** Jl. A. Yani 2, 3rd Fl., (tel. 519 992). Open Mon.-Fri. 7:30am-1:30pm.

Immigration Offices: Jl. Binjei 268A (tel. 852 112). Several km north of town; take a *damri* bus from Jl. A. Yani and ask to get out at "Kantor Imigrasi." Open Mon.-Fri. 8:30am-4:15pm.

Currency Exchange: Sumatran rates outside Medan are very bad. Most banks are along Jl. Palang Merah, and Jl. Pemuda/A. Yani. **P.T. Delimegan Valutindo Money Changer,** Jl. A. Yani 94 (tel. 513 535). Open Mon.-Fri. 9am-5pm, Sat. 9am-3pm. **Bank Dagang Negara,** Jl. A. Yani 109 (tel. 536 800). Open Mon.-Fri. 8:30am-3:30pm. **ATMs** can be found at Deli Plaza Shopping Centre, most centrally located banks, and hotels. Cirrus, Visa, MC.

Air Travel: Polonia International Airport (tel. 538 444), 3km south of town at the end of Jl. Imam Bonjol. The international terminal lies directly behind the main gate, while the domestic terminal is about 300m to the right. From town take a *becak* (Rp3000) or metered taxi (Rp5000). **Garuda,** Jl. Suprapto 2 (tel. 515 869). Branch office (tel. 516 400) in Dharma Deli Hotel, Jl. Balai Kota 2. **Merpati,** Jl. Brigjen. Katamso 72/122 (tel. 514 102). Book tickets through Garuda. **Sempati,** Jl. Cut Meutiah 1 (tel. 551 612), on the ground floor of Tiara Convention Centre. **SMAC,** Jl. Imam Bonjol 59 (tel. 537 760). **Bouraq,** Jl. Brigjen. Katamso 43 (tel. 552 333), often have cheaper flights than the competition. **MAS,** Jl. Imam Bonjol 17 (tel. 514 300), on ground floor of Danau Toba Hotel. Open Mon.-Fri. 8:30am-4:30pm, Sat. 8:30am-2pm, Sun. 9am-1pm. All major credit cards. **Silk Air/Singapore Airlines,** Jl. Sudirman 14 (tel. 537 744), on ground floor of Polonia Hotel. Open Mon.-Fri. 8am-5pm, Sat. 8am-1pm, Sun. 8am-noon. All major credit cards. There's at least one flight per day to major destinations: **Banda Aceh** (1hr., Rp145,500); **Jakarta** (2hr., Rp416,200); **Denpasar** (3hr., Rp561,400); **Padang** (Rp151,200); **Singapore** (1½hr., US$140); **Kuala Lumpur,** Malaysia (1hr., US$77); and **Penang,** Malaysia (45min., US$74).

Buses: Ticket prices depend on the degree of comfort; fares are approximate as they vary between companies. Cheapest are rattle-trap **public buses** with no A/C and no guarantees. For these you pay the fare on the bus. Locals can direct you to the correct bus, although it's wise to ask several people. Tickets must be purchased in advance for the more expensive but faster **private buses.** Most locals avoid the bus terminals entirely and purchase tickets directly from individual bus companies found along Jl. Sisingamangaraja. Buses for reserved ticket holders pick up passengers at the company office before heading to the main terminals. **Amplas Terminal,** 6km south off Jl. Sisingamangaraja, services the south. To: **Prapat** (every 10-15min., 6am-5pm, 4hr., Rp4000, A/C Rp10,000); **Bukittinggi** (every hr., 8am-4pm, 12hr., Rp22,000, A/C Rp22-45,000); **Jakarta** (8am-7pm, 48hr., Rp65,000, A/C Rp75-145,000); and **Padang** (Rp22,000). Tourist info booth open Mon.-Sat. 8am-4pm (tel. 714 101). **Pinang Baris Terminal,** 8km west on Jl. Pinang Baris, services points north and west of Medan. Entrance fee Rp100. To: **Bukit Lawang** (every 30min., 7am-5pm, 2½hr., Rp1500); **Brastagi** (every 15min., 7am-5pm, 2hr., Rp1500); and **Banda Aceh** (every hr. 8am-9pm, 12hr., Rp20,000, A/C Rp27-45,000). For those who wish to avoid Medan's bus terminals, **Antar Lintas Sumatera (ALS),** the island's largest bus company, has its office at Jl. Amaliun 2A (tel. 719 959). Take a *sudako* down Jl. Sisingamangaraja to the Mesjid Raya (Rp350); Jl. Amaliun is on the left before the mosque. A/C buses to: **Jakarta** (4 per day, Rp73,000, with toilet Rp95,000, VIP Rp145,000); **Bukittinggi** (3 per day, Rp22,000, with toilet Rp25,000, VIP Rp45,000); **Padang** (3 per day, Rp22,000, with toilet Rp28,000, and VIP Rp35,000); and **Prapat** (2 per day, Rp10,000, with toilet Rp15,000).

Ferries: Leave from **Belawan,** 26km north of Medan. **Penang Ekspress Bahagia,** Jl. Sisingamangaraja 92A (tel. 720 421). Open Mon.-Sat. 7:30am-5pm. Sells ferry tickets to **Penang,** Malaysia (Tues., Thurs., and Sat., 10am, 5hr., Rp95,000). Visa. Cash only for same-day purchase. Includes bus to Belawan at 7am from Pacto Tours and 7:30am from Jl. Sisingamangaraja. **Selesa/Perdana/Langkawi Ekspress,** Jl. Brigjen. Katamso 35D (tel. 545 306) also goes to **Penang** (Wed. and Fri., 1pm and Sun., 10am, 5hr., Rp95,000). Includes bus from office Wed. and Fri. at 10am and Sun. at 7am. Open daily 7am-6pm. To **Lumut,** Malaysia (Tues. and Thurs. 2pm, 3½hr., Rp95,000). **PELNI,** Jl. Kol. Sugiono 5 (tel. 518 899), connect to major domestic ports. To **Jakarta** (Mon., 36hr., economy Rp116,500). Tickets go on sale the Tues. before. Cash only. Open Mon.-Fri. 8am-3pm, Sat. 8-11am.

Local Transportation: Yellow-and-blue **sudako** (minibuses) careen along set routes; major destinations are usually written on the windshield but check with the driver first. *Sudako* leave from the Central Market for **Amplas** (Rp350). To **Belawan,** take a *sudako* marked "Morina" from Jl. A. Yani or Jl. Sisingamangaraja (Rp700). To **Pinang Baris** take **bis damris** or *sudako* marked "P. Baris" which run along Jl. A. Yani/Balai Kota (Rp300-500). *Sudako #64* travels between the bus terminals via Jl. Palang Merah (Rp700). **Becak** and **becak misin** (motorized) also prowl the streets (within downtown Rp2500). Metered **taxis** start at Rp4100 and Rp1000 per km; it may be wiser, however, to bargain a set price, as meters may be inaccurate. From airport to downtown Rp5000, from Amplas Rp8000.

English Bookstore: Gama Utama Book Centre, Jl. Sisingamangaraja 12 (tel. 741 125). Guide books and maps of Indonesia and Sumatra, including Medan and Lake Toba (Rp8000). Bahasa Indonesia phrasebooks. Open daily 8am-10pm.

Markets: Pasar Sentral (Central Market), located off Jl. Sutomo, just east of the Sambu *sudako* station. **Perniagaan Market,** on Jl. Perniagaan, sells fabrics by the meter. Both markets are open 8am-6pm.

Pharmacies: Apotik Kimia Farmia, Jl. Palang Merah 32. Open 24hr. **Contact Lens Supplies: Optik Lichin,** Jl. A. Yani 102 (tel. 556 266). Open Mon.-Sat. 9am-8pm, Sun. 11am-4pm.

Medical Services: St. Elizabeth Hospital, Jl. Haji Misbah 7 (tel. 544 737), near the Polonia Hotel. English-speaking doctors. Considered the best facility in Medan, **Klinic Specialis Banda,** Jl. Sisingamangaraja 17 (tel. 715 772), is closer to downtown. Private clinic with English speaking doctors. Open 24hr.

Emergency: Police tel. 110. **Ambulance** tel. 118.

Police: Jl. H.Z. Arifin 7 (tel. 538 077).

Post Offices: GPO, Jl. Bukit Barisan 1 (tel. 511 477), at the intersection with Jl. Balai Kota, opposite Merdeka Square. *Poste Restante.* EMS. Open Mon.-Sat. 8am-7pm. **Postal code:** 20111.

Telephones: Indosat central office, Jl. Perintis Kemerdekaan 39 (tel. 524 972). IDD, HCD service. Only place that accepts calling card calls. Open 24hr. All major credit cards. Some *wartel* place collect calls, others accept only cash. **Wartel Tiara,** Jl. Imam Bonjol 15 (tel. 530 398), just north of the Jl. Palang Merah intersection near the Irama Hotel. Open 24hr. **Telkom branch** in GPO (tel. 565 777). Open Mon.-Sat. 8am-7pm. **Telephone code:** 061.

ACCOMMODATIONS

There is no shortage of cheap beds. Several cheap *losmen* act as backpacker clearing houses, where travelers shack up for a night before heading to the country. The more popular ones fill up quickly; it is best to arrive early. Most medium- to high-end hotels are clustered along Jl. Sisingamangaraja near the Mesjid Raya.

Wisma Yuli, Jl. Sisingamangaraja, Gg. Pagaruyung No. 79B (tel. 719 704). Gg. Pagaruyung is directly opposite the Mesjid Raya; look for the sign near the end of the alley on the right. Light sleepers beware: the mosque's massive speakers are an effective alarm clock—at 4:30am. Near the Belawan shuttle bus stop. Doubles with fan, writing desk, and shared *mandi* Rp12,500. Swish rooms with fan and western bath Rp25,000. Prices include breakfast and fan. Staff will help with bus and ferry reservations. HCD phone (Rp6000). Check-out 2pm.

Sarah's Guest House, Jl. Pertama 10/4 (tel. 743 783). From the Mesjid Raya, head south on Jl. Sisingamangaraja. Take a right before the large Toyota dealership, a left 100m later, and then a right onto Jl. Pertama about 200m down. Sarah's, on the right of this quiet side street, is the best cure for the Medan blues. The manager will make Medan as painless as possible and pick up hapless travelers at no extra charge. Dorms with fan Rp3500. Doubles with fan Rp10,000, and bath Rp15,000. Good, cheap Asian and western food (Rp1-3000). Books ferry, bus, and plane tickets at no extra charge. Free transport to the airport or ferry office.

Losmen Irama, Jl. Palang Merah 112S (tel. 326 416). From the intersection with Jl. Pemuda, head west and cross a small river to a traffic triangle with a sculpture of a violinist. Irama is on the next small street to the right. Perhaps the most popular backpacker dive, it fills up fast when the afternoon boats from Penang get in. Can be stiflingly hot at night without a fan. Helpful staff; some speak excellent English. Dorms Rp5000. Doubles Rp10,000. Triples Rp15,000. Fan Rp2500. Windows in front rooms. Shared *mandi*. HCD phone. Door is locked at midnight.

Shahiba Guest House, Jl. Armada 1A/3 (tel. 718 528). Head south on Jl. Sisingamangaraja; at the far end of Bukit Barisan Hero's Cemetery turn right onto Jl. Armada. Shahiba is 20m down on the left. Run by an affable Toba Batak family; the distinctive red, black, and white stenciling on the walls is a dead giveaway. Probably the finest dorm in Medan. Rooms from Rp12-25,000. Doubles with private bath Rp25,000. Dorms Rp6000. All prices include breakfast and fan.

FOOD

The traffic may be abominable, the touts relentless, and the dust suffocating in Medan, but at least you can feast on cheap, delicious food. **Warung** and tiny hole-in-the-wall restaurants abound. Medan's chief culinary specialty is Padang food, West Sumatra's spicy regional specialty. During the evening, cheap Chinese *warung* fill Jl. Semarang, two blocks east of Jl. Surabaya (open 6pm-midnight). Sample a multicultural selection of these at the **Perisida Shopping Centre** between Jl. Pemuda and the railroad tracks. A number of cheap *warung* and delicious bakeries line Jl. H.Z. Arifin. The **Seri Deli Recreation Garden,** on Jl. Mesjid Raya, opposite the Mesjid Raya, has a large number of stalls surrounding a small man-made pond. (Open 4:30-11pm.) Proving yet again that Southeast Asia is where bad fast-food joints go to die, the Deli Plaza boasts three, count 'em, **three fried chicken outlets!**

G's Koh-I-Noor Meal House, Jl. Mesjid Raya 21 (tel. 513 953). Turn left onto Jl. Perdana from Jl. A. Yani, then right onto Jl. Mesjid Raya. G's is on the right. A favorite of Medan veterans, the scrumptious North Indian food reduces experienced travelers to orgasmic blubbering. The cheerful owners, Mr. and Mrs. Singh, are full of candid travel advice. Large portions of mutton curry (Rp4000), vegetable curry (Rp2500), and sweet fruit *lassi* (Rp2000). Pre-order for *tandoor* chicken. Open daily 9am-9pm.

Rumah Makan Famili, Jl. Sisingamangaraja 21B (tel. 321 285). From the Grand Mosque head north on Jl. Sisingamangaraja. It's about 2 blocks up on the right, next to the Ibunda Hotel. Very popular Padang food, heavy on the chili and coconut milk. Filled to the gills at lunchtime. Signature dishes include goat curry and intestinal stuff cooked in coconut. Dishes Rp1-3000. You can also ask for "Padang food," and get 6 or 7 different dishes including chicken, mutton, veggies, and seafood. You're only charged for what you eat. Great for groups (Rp15-25,000).

Tip Top Restaurant and Ice Cream Palace, Jl. A. Yani 92 (tel. 244 42). North of the Jl. Sukamulia-Palang intersection, on the left before Merdeka Square. Tip Top opened when Sumatra was still Dutch. A hangout for travelers and expats alike; most just come for a beer on the patio but there's a large menu of Chinese, European, and Indonesian food. Most dishes Rp3-8000. Beer Rp2250-5500. Ice cream Rp1350-2750. Open daily 9am-11pm. HCD phone.

Tahiti Bakery and Cake Shop, Jl. Taruma 70-72 (tel. 519 692), just north of Jl. H.Z. Arifin near the Jl. Cik Ditiro intersection. As you enter and the intoxicating smells emanating from the kitchen hit your nostrils, ask yourself this question: why are the world's best Boston Creme donuts (Rp900) in Medan? Indonesian sweets Rp4-700. Ice cream, fresh bread, and pudding. Open daily 7:30am-10pm.

SIGHTS

Aside from its curious people, the city's chief crowd-pleaser is undoubtedly its impressive architectural legacy. Nothing else epitomizes this tradition more than the majestic black domes, brilliant turquoise tiles, and towering minaret of the **Mesjid Raya** (Grand Mosque), at the corner of Jl. Sisingamangaraja and Jl. Mesjid Raya. Built by Sultan Mahkmun Al-Rasyid, the mosque was actually designed by a Dutch architect and constructed in 1908, with materials from all over the globe. Several past sultans and their families are buried in the surrounding garden. (Open daily 7am-6pm; donation of Rp500 requested.)

Not far from Mesjid Raya on Jl. Brigjen. Katamso is the **Istana Maimun**. This large, low palace has been the home of the Deli sultans since its construction in 1888 with money gleaned from the lucrative tobacco trade. The 12th Sultan of Deli and his family still live here. Only the throne room is open to the public. (Open daily 8am-5pm; Rp1000 donation requested, includes tour.)

The **Vihara Gunung Timur,** a Buddhist temple sacred to Medan's influential yet low-profile Chinese community, stands on Jl. Hang Tuah off Jl. Cik Ditiro. The ceiling of the sanctuary is covered with red prayer lanterns and a large glass case contains many Buddha images of various styles and sizes. (Open during daylight hours; photography prohibited.) Standing across from Jl. H.Z. Arifin 128, is the **Candi Hindu,** a Hindu temple decorated with hundreds of brilliantly colored and life-size statues of gods, heroes, and mythical creatures. (Open during daylight hours.)

Of Medan's two museums, by far the more interesting is the **Museum Sumatera Utara,** Jl. H.M. Joni 51 (tel. 716 792), whose large collection documents the geological, natural, and cultural history of the province. (Open Tues.-Sat. 8:30am-5pm; admission Rp200, with camera Rp250 extra.) To get to the museum take *sudako* #01,04, or 64. From the south end of the Bukit Barisan Hero's Cemetery, Jl. H.M. Joni is on the left, and the museum is 700m down the street on the right. A second museum, **Museum Bukit Barisan,** Jl. H.Z. Arifin 2 (tel. 326 927), lies near the police station. The entrance is flanked by cannons, indicating its military focus. It mainly documents North Sumatra's role in the struggle against Dutch colonial forces, and consists of a single room crammed with weapons of every size and description. Traditional Batak houses stand in the rear courtyard surrounded by jeeps and motor scooters. (Open Mon.-Fri. 8am-1pm; donations requested.)

■ Pulau Bintan

A tiny island in the middle of the 3000 even tinier islands that form the Riau Archipelago, unassuming Pulau Bintan has become a major transportation hub. A stay here is common on most itineraries (Marco Polo even paid a visit in 1202), but most travelers make it as brief as possible. Still, if trapped for a few days waiting for the next boat to adventure, discover Bintan's oft-overlooked charms.

The bulk of travelers passing through this transit point are Indonesian laborers bound for plantations and construction sites in Malaysia, the balance being backpackers en route to or from Sumatra and Singaporean weekenders, for whom this is the cheapest and most convenient island retreat. Tanjung Pinang's touts are assertive but not desperate, and visitors can find much of interest on the wharves and in the large day market which sprawls near the waterfront. Not a scintillating destination on the absolute scale, it's not bad in comparison to other gateways.

ORIENTATION

Tanjung Pinang is the largest city on Pulau Bintan, and much of the city's activity focuses on the wharves. Most travelers arrive at the **main pier** on the east end.

INDONESIA

Straight down the pier and past the dock offices the first road is **Jalan Merdeka.** This is the main drag and runs roughly east-west, from the large arch near the pier to the **fruit market.** Walking straight through the Merdeka intersection leads to the intersection with **Jalan Bintan.** The next parallel street east is **Jalan Teuku Umar,** home to the passable **night market. Jalan Pos** begins opposite Jl. Bintan close to the **post office** and curls along the fringe of the wharves for a short distance. The **police station** is outside of town and **Pulau Penyenget,** that dollop of archaeological joy, floats off-shore to the west of the city.

PRACTICAL INFORMATION

Currency Exchange: Bank Negara Indonesia, Jl. Teuku Umar 630 (tel. 214 32), opposite the taxi stand. Cashes traveler's checks. Open Mon.-Fri. 8am-5pm. **Lippobank,** 11 Jl. Merdeka (tel. 279 47). Accepts Visa and MC with a 4% surcharge. Exchange counter open Mon.-Fri. 8am-2pm. There are also **money changers** near the Jl. Pos and Jl. Merdeka intersection, but rates are not great.

Air Travel: Kijang Airport lies 20km east of the city. **P.T. Pinang Jaya,** Jl. Bintan 44 (tel. 212 67), just past Hotel Surya. Merpati to: **Jakarta** (Tues., Thurs., Sat., and Sun. 2:20pm, Rp288,000) and **Pekanbaru** (Tues., Thurs., Sat., and Sun. 11am, Rp138,000). **Sempati,** Jl. Bintan 9 (tel. 213 77). To: **Jakarta** (1pm, Rp262,000) and **Pekanbaru** (Tues.-Thurs., Sat-Sun., 9:45am, Rp138,000).

Buses: Terminal, 7km outside of town, reached by a Rp500 minibus ride. From here, buses circle the island every 2hr. until 3pm, chugging past the beaches to the east (Rp2000) and heading north to **Tanjung Uban.**

Taxis: Bargain hard at the fruit stand on Jl. Merdeka for fares to: **airport** (Rp10,000 per car); **Kijang** (Rp6000-30,000 per car/bus); and **Trikora Beach** (Rp5000 or Rp25,000 per car).

Ferries: Schedule varies with season; expect routine delays. **Toko,** Jl. Merdeka 77, sells tickets from the main pier to: **Singapore** (3 per day, 10:30am-4:20pm, 2hr., Rp54,000); **Dabo Singkep** (noon, Rp25,000); **Jakarta** (11:45am, Rp30,000); **Sekupang** (11:45am, Rp12,000); and **Tanjung Balai** (2pm, Rp21,000); **Telaga Pungur** (every 45min., Rp9000); and **Pasir Gudang,** Malaysia (1pm, Rp55,000). **P.T. Netra,** Jl. Pos 2 (tel. 213 84), has tickets to: **Belungkor** (noon, Rp50,000); **Pekanbaru** (7:45am, Rp37,000); **Tanjung Batu** (1pm, Rp16,500) continuing to **Moro** (Rp23,000); **Lingga, Tanjung Kelit,** and **Pemuba** (Mon., Wed., and Sat. 9:30am); and **Belakang Padang** (Sat., 7:45am, Rp13,000).

Boats: To **Pulau Penyenget,** walk down Jl. Pos toward the waterfront and continue to the end of the small jetty—small wooden motorboats cost Rp500 one way. Oar-driven *sampan* to **Senggarang** across the harbor depart two piers over (Rp500 per person); motorized transport (Rp1000). **Pulau Batam** speedboats leave from the main pier (every 30min. until 4:30pm, Rp9-10,000) and from Tanjung Uban, north of the city (Rp6-8000).

Local Transportation: Honking **minibuses** abound. Within the city Rp300, past the Km5 mark Rp500. **Motorcycles** take to the streets for Rp300.

Medical Services: Along Jl. Sudirman, in the south of the city. Malaria is supposedly prevalent, especially during the rainy season (which varies from year to year). Start medication before arrival.

Markets: Day market, sprawling carnival of innumerable varieties of citrus fruits, bananas, and vegetables, as well as seafood. Follow the crowds from Jl. Merdeka away from the jetty and veer left at the fork in the road onto Jl. Gambir. The first left on Gambir leads to the building which houses the market. The **night market** next to Bank Dagang Negara on Jl. Teuku Umar is infinitely more fun.

Police: (tel. 211 10), at Km5. **Police box,** at the corner of Jl. Merdeka and Jl. Ketapang, east of Jl. Teuku Umar.

Post Offices: On Jl. Katamso about 3km out of town. *Poste Restante.* Open Mon.-Thurs., Sat. 8am-2pm, Fri. 8am-11pm. **Branch,** at the corner of Jl. Pos and Jl. Merdeka. About 100m through the west arch and on the left. Open Mon.-Sat. 8am-8pm, Sun. 8am-1pm. **Postal code:** 29111.

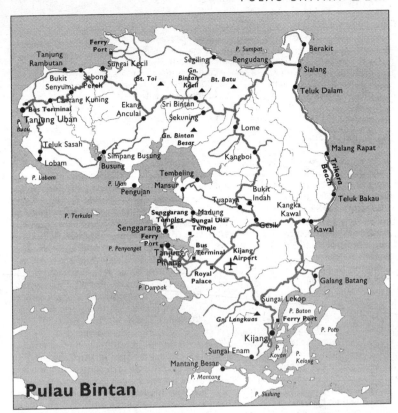

Pulau Bintan

Telephones: Telkom office (tel. 217 77), on Jl. Hang Tuah, the road to your right from the main pier, near a large waterfront statue of a seashell. Long distance available 24hr. **Telephone code:** 07111.

ACCOMMODATIONS

There are plenty of cheap dorms available in Tanjung Pinang, three being located on Lorong Bintan II. To get there, take the first right off Jl. Merdeka as you are walking into town from the jetty. Lorong Bintan is just an alley on the left immediately before the Sempurna Jaya Hotel. **Rommel's Westerner** is the first guest house on the left; continue down the alley and turn left at the end—on the right and not immediately visible are **Bong's Homestay,** Lorong Bintan II 20 (tel. 226 05), and **Johnny's,** Lorong Bintan II 22. All offer dorms for Rp5000 and all are friendly establishments with light breakfasts included. Of the three, Bong's is the best equipped with backpacker amusements and has private rooms for Rp10,000. All have dipper baths and no sinks. For an actual hotel, heat to **Hotel Sri Bintan,** Jl. Plantan 1 23 (tel. 245 06), with A/C, TV, and showers. Turn left from Merdeka on Jl. Pos, follow it as it curves right, then turn left toward the waterfront on Jl. Plantan 1, immediately on the left. Standard doubles go for Rp46,200 (1st floor) and Rp57,700 (2nd floor).

FOOD

Tanjung Pinang's offerings are lacking somewhat for variety. *Bak kut teh,* the poor man's simmered pork from Fujian is also common in restaurants by the waterfront.

The night market is next to Bank Dagang Negara on Jl. Teuku Umar and has about 30 stalls—don't worry, ice is made from boiled water.

Ayam Goreng 88, Jl. Pos 50, beside the Sanno Hotel. *Halal* chicken in all forms, insect and smoke-free environment, and Elvis hits of the 70s make this a neutral, A/C retreat for those days when you don't feel like having a cultural experience. Chicken burger Rp2600, ice cream Rp1500. Open daily 10am-9pm.

Bintah Indah 99, next to Ayam Goreng, this is a clean coffee shop serving up good *kuey teow* Rp1700, BBQ fish, *bak kut teh,* and satay. Open daily 8am-9pm.

■ Island Sights

PULAU PENYENGET

Diminutive Pulau Penyenget (2.5sq.km), just off Tanjung Pinang, was the seat of the Riau *rajah's* far-flung kingdom for hundreds of years. History has tattooed its slopes and shores with a collection of crumbling forts, palaces, and royal tombs. The last remnant of a culture considered to be the seed of Malay civilization, Penyenget has residents who still speak pure Bahasa Melayu. To get to the island catch one of the motorboats moored half-way down the main pier (10min., Rp500). The boats drop anchor at Penyenget jetty, where you must pay an additional Rp500 entrance fee.

Just beyond the jetty shines **Mesjid Raya Sultan Riau,** a 178-year-old mosque which locals claim is held together with egg-white mortar, although its tangy yellow and green walls, domes, and minarets look like they were painted with Hi-C Citrus Cooler. The library houses a rare collection of antique tomes and manuscripts including five hand-written copies of the Qur'an, but is not usually open to the public. Tourists should avoid visiting on Fridays, when special ceremonies take place.

To tour the other historic sites, exit the mosque and pass through the arch to the left, turning left down the small concrete path. A small path on the right, about 100m down leads to the **tomb of Rajah Abdurrachman.** A short walk up the hill behind the tomb leads to the very scanty remnants of the **island fort,** the highest point on the island. The path then winds through the quietly moldering shell of **Rajah Ali's palace,** which was abandoned only this century. Farther down the track which forks to the left are the ruins of an old house and the **tombs of Rajah Jaafar** and **Rajah Ali Ibni.** From the original path, a stroll to the end of the road, followed by a turn right leads to the **modern Riau palace.**

Pilgrims travel here to venerate the royal internments along these paths including those of **Rajah Ali Jajai,** writer of the first Malay grammar, who received the isle as her dowry. She ruled until her death in 1844, and members of the royal scion still live along the south shores.

TRIKORA

About 36km from Tanjung Pinang, Trikora is a desolate strip of beach where nothing ever happens. As such, it is very relaxing and the beach is clean—snorkeling and powdery sand is to be had at **Pulau Bralas** (about 20min. by small boat). Local fishermen have built fishing platforms in the shallow water off-shore. The only time to avoid Trikora is monsoon season (Nov.-Mar.).

Yasin's Guest House (tel. 267 70) is a collection of ramshackle huts on stilts varying widely in desirability, all with mattresses on the floor. A tiny hut for one person costs Rp17,000; extra people can squeeze into these huts but must pay Rp17,000 for meals, since other dining options in Trikora are limited. Huts are also equipped with dipper baths, but go outside for the toilets. Yasim will take you snorkeling (get your own equipment before coming) at Bralas for Rp25,000 per boat. From the bus terminal in Tanjung Pinang, buses run to the east coast until 3pm (every 2hr., Rp2000). Tell the driver you want to get off at Yasin's. Shared taxis leave when full from Jl. Teuku Umar until noon (Rp3000 per person, 5 people per taxi). To rent a private taxi after noon costs Rp13-30,000 per car.

■ Brastagi

On the surface, this former Dutch hill station is nothing but a dusty drag on the tourist bus route south to Lake Toba. More active folks, however, find Brastagi, set against the ethereal beauty of North Sumatra's cool mountainous hinterland, a veritable garden of outdoor delights. Founded in the early 1900s as a retreat for plantation owners and colonial officials, Brastagi's dark, fertile volcanic soil yields a cornucopia of succulent fruits, including the luscious marquisa passionfruit, famed around the world for its tastebud-titillating flavor. Yet, aside from its vibrant markets, Brastagi offers little to detain the adventurous traveler headed off to nearby sights.

The area around Brastagi is sometimes known as the Karo Highlands, as it is the site of many traditional Karo Batak villages. Climbers of all ages can tackle steaming Mt. Sibayak, which dominates the northern approaches to town and appears perpetually on the verge of another eruption. For die-hards, there's regal Gunung Sinabung, 30km south of town, whose lower slopes are cloaked in damp, dense jungle.

ORIENTATION

Downtown Brastagi consists of a single divided thoroughfare, **Jalan Veteran.** At the north end of Jl. Veteran stands a tall columnar **war memorial** where Jl. Veteran forks. The left branch becomes **Jalan Gundaling** which leads up the hill past the fruit market toward **Mt. Sibayak,** while the right branch leads downhill out of town, eventually becoming the **Brastagi-Medan Highway.** The tourist info center, post office, and *wartel* cluster near the memorial. Heading south, Jl. Veteran passes the bus terminal and **central market,** on the left before forking in two again. The left-hand road continues 12km to **Kabanjahe** while the right-hand road, **Jalan Udara,** leads to **Gunung Sinabung** and the Karo village of **Lingga.**

PRACTICAL INFORMATION

Tourist Offices: Tourist Information Centre, Jl. Gundaling 1 (tel. 910 84), at the north end of town just to the left of the war memorial. Friendly staff and excellent info on transport. Check here for upcoming Karo ceremonies. Guides for climbing Mt. Sinabung and Mt. Sibayak. Organizes rafting and/or trekking trips in Gunung Leuser National Park. Open Mon.-Sat. 7:30am-8pm, Sun. 9am-8pm. **Sibayak Guest House Losmen** and **Wisma Sibayak Guest House** are also excellent sources. Blackboards in *losmen* list travelers assembling groups for ascents of the volcanoes or trekking/rafting.

Currency Exchange: Bank Rakyat Indonesia, Jl. Veteran 84 (tel. 912 32). Open Mon.-Fri. 8am-3pm. **P.T. Pura Buana,** Jl. Veteran 55 (tel. 911 50). MC, Visa advance (10% charge). Open daily 7am-midnight. Also a *wartel* and travel agency.

Buses: Station is in front of the central market on Jl. Veteran. To: **Medan** (every 10min., 4:30am-8pm, 1½hr., Rp1200); **Pangururan** (every hr., 9am-2pm, 5hr., Rp4000); and **Kutacane** (every 30min., 9am-4pm, 5-6hr., Rp5500). Faster **minibuses** to **Kutacane** (every hr., 8am-8pm, 4hr., Rp6000) from Cv. Karisma, Jl. Veteran 51 (tel. 919 66). To **Tapaktuan** (every 30min., 6-9pm, 12hr., Rp8500). Take a *sudako* from the market to **Kabanjahe** (Rp300). To **Prapat,** take a bus from Kabanjahe to **Siantar** (every 90min., 7:30am-5pm, 3hr., Rp2000), then take a bus coming from Medan to Prapat (last bus 5pm, 2hr., Rp2000). To **Haranggaol** from Kabanjahe (Mon. and Thurs., 9am, 3-4hr., Rp4000) and meet the ferry to **Ambarita** (Mon. and Thurs., 1pm, 4hr., Rp4000). **Tourist buses** provide the only direct service to Bukit Lawang and Prapat, passing through Brastagi at about 1pm, but there's no guarantee of a seat. To **Prapat** (4hr., Rp15,000) and **Bukit Lawang** (6hr., Rp15,000). Book at least 1 day in advance. Purchase tickets at tourist office and most guest houses.

Markets: Pasar Sentral (central market) is on Jl. Veteran behind the bus terminal. Open daily 8am-8pm. A better place to sample Brastagi's famous fruit is, the **fruit market** on Jl. Gundaling behind the tourist office. Open daily 8am-8pm.

Pharmacies: Dharma Bakti, Jl. Veteran 49A (tel. 913 21). Open daily 8am-8pm.

Medical Services: Public Health Centre, Jl. Veteran 36 (tel. 910 28).

Police: Brastagi sector, Jl. Perwira 161 (tel. 911 10).
Post Offices: Jl. Veteran 4, next to the tourist office. *Poste Restante.* Open Mon.-Thurs. 8am-2pm, Fri. 8-11am, Sat. 8am-2pm. **Postal code:** 22156.
Telephones: Telkom office, Jl. Perwira 1 (tel. 911 08), next to the post office. HCD phone. Open 24hr. **Telephone code:** 0628.

ACCOMMODATIONS

Brastagi boasts some of the best and most professional guest houses in North Sumatra, with great food and excellent information services. Many also organize trekking and rafting expeditions in Gunung Leuser National Park. Most of the *losmen* and cheap hotels are concentrated along Jl. Veteran near the war memorial.

Sibayak Guest House Losmen, Jl. Veteran 119 (tel. 911 22). From the war memorial head south on Jl. Veteran; the guest house is about 200m down on the left. One of the most popular guest houses in North Sumatra. Lots of info on the area's attractions, as well as Karo culture and rituals. Organizes rafting, climbing, and trekking groups. Warm staff keeps the rooms tidy. Dorms Rp2500. Singles Rp3000. Doubles Rp6000, with bath Rp7500. Triples with bath Rp9000. Good restaurant and small bookshop on ground floor.

Wisma Ikut Guest House, Jl. Gundaling 24 (tel. 911 71), just past the fruit market off Jl. Veteran. This rambling old wooden hillside mill once served as a restaurant and dance hall for colonial soirees. The towering ceilings and creaky floorboards remain, not to mention stunning views of Mt. Sibayak. Dorms Rp2500. One nice single Rp3000. Doubles Rp3000. Large doubles with private porch Rp7,5000-10,000. Shiny *mandi* outside.

Wisma Sibayak Guest House, Jl. Udara 1 (tel. 916 83). From the bus terminal, head south on Jl. Veteran. The guest house is set back from the road where Jl. Udara branches to the left. The same unparalleled info and maps as the Sibayak Losmen, but quieter and slightly more relaxed. Dorms Rp3000. One single Rp4000. Doubles Rp6000-7500. Triples Rp9000. Outside bathrooms.

Ginsata Hotel and Guest House, Jl. Veteran 27 (tel. 914 41), across the street from the tourist office; lobby is behind the Irfan Padang Restaurant. Basic hotel (singles Rp7500, doubles Rp10,000 with bathroom) but the jewel is the guest house in an old villa around the corner from the hotel, removed from the hubbub of Jl. Veteran. Endearing, homey atmosphere. Manager speaks fluent English and organizes excellent rafting and trekking expeditions in Gunung Leuser National Park. Singles Rp3500-4000. Doubles Rp5000-7500.

FOOD

Aside from the fruit, the eating in Brastagi isn't stellar. The best and most competitively priced food can probably be found in the kitchens of guest houses. The **Sibayak Guest House Losmen,** in particular, has a lengthy menu of local and western favorites served in mammoth portions. **Muslimin,** Jl. Veteran 128 (tel. 912 03), next to the bus terminal, dishes up cheap, delicious Padang food to a bustling local crowd. *Ikan gulai* (fish with vegetables) is Rp1500, *guam gulai* (complete chicken meal with rice and tea) is Rp2500. A number of inexpensive fruit juices are available as well (marquisa passionfruit juice for Rp600). (Open daily 7am-2am.)

HIKING THE MOUNTAINS

Brastagi has been a tourist town since its founding in the early 1900s, when even colonial officials from British Malaya would come here to golf, ride horses, and attend lavish dinner parties. Today, most visitors come to Brastagi for more invigorating pursuits—chiefly, hiking the volcanoes which make the landscape so spectacular. Most popular is the 1880m **Gunung Sibayak,** whose lopsided summit appears to be smoking, an illusion created by the very active sulphur steam jets on top. An exceptionally well-maintained trail, complete with concrete steps, winds up the west slope of the volcano. The lower of the two summits is fenced off and cannot be reached. The route to the higher summit is very dangerous and should only be attempted with a guide. A second route down the east slope of Sibayak to Semangat Gunung hot springs slants away to the right from the lip of the crater. Despite being inlaid with steps, the trail is quite steep and during the wet season can be slick and treacherous. To climb this way, it's wise to begin from Semangat Gunung and hike up, saving the easier western route for the way down. The trail starts directly behind the large drilling operation at Semangat Gunung. A northerly "jungle" route winds up from the Brastagi-Medan Hwy. and should only be attempted with a guide (Rp64,000 for 2 people). *Bemo* run between Pasar Sentral and Semangat Gunung (Rp800). To reach the west route, go north on Jl. Veteran, bearing left at the war memorial onto Jl. Gundaling. Turn right at the end of the soccer field just before the large Sibayak Multinational Hotel. Follow the road uphill for 30 minutes or so, passing the Karo Hill Bungalows, and turn left onto a dirt road where the paved road turns sharply to the right. (Admission Rp500.)

Gunung Sibayak can be climbed in 2½ hours. Start early in the day to avoid the early afternoon clouds, which can ruin a lovely vista. A guide is not necessary to climb Gunung Sibayak via the western route. It's unwise to climb alone, but those who do should have no problem attaching themselves to a group. The weather can change dramatically in a matter of minutes; you might want to pack a rucksack with water, fruit, and a sweater, since it can be chilly on top.

There are two sets of hot springs northeast of Brastagi near the foot of Sibayak: the **Lau Debuk-debuk Hot Springs,** 12km from Brastagi, and the **Semangat Gunung Hot Springs,** 2km farther down the road toward the volcano. Lau Debuk-debuk is the larger of the two, with several bathing pools allowing you to soak comfortably in the sulphurous waters. You can get there by minibus from Pasar Sentral (Rp800) or hike down from Sibayak. (Open during daylight hours; admission Rp500-2500 depending on the depth of the pool.)

Serious hikers who wish to climb a more pristine, more challenging peak can try **Gunung Sinabung** (2454m), 27km west of Brastagi. It's higher than Gunung Sibayak, more remote, and should only be attempted by experienced climbers in good physical condition. The trails on Gunung Sinabung are crude and completely devoid of markings. There have been several fatalities on Sinabung over the last few years. For all these reasons, it's highly advisable that travelers who wish to climb Sinabung heed the advice of the tourist office and guest houses and **hire a guide** for around Rp80,000 per day. Make sure your guide is licensed by the HPI. Most hikers begin at the village of **Sigaranggarang** and end at **Lake Kawar** for a post-climb swim. Much of the hike is spent in unspoilt jungle. The final few hundred meters to the summit is over loose volcanic rock. The climb should take three hours on the ascent, and the earlier you begin, the better the chances of a view. On a clear day it is possible to see shimmering Lake Toba, 30km to the south. Chartering a *bemo* from your guest house is the best way to ensure getting an early start (Rp10,000).

VISITING KARO VILLAGES

The highland region around Brastagi is the heart of Karo Batak country and there are a number of Karo villages that can be reached in a day. Obviously, the farther from town you venture, the less heavily touristed the village will be, although these days entrance fees (Rp300) and hawkers are the norm.

Closest to town is the small village of **Peceren,** about 1.5km past the war memorial, on the road to Medan. Karo dwellings, complete with buffalo horns and thatched roofs, stand side-by-side with modern, concrete houses topped with satellite dishes. Although guest house operators decry it as "impure," Peceren is a much more realistic look at Karo life than other artificially "traditional" settlements. The best time to visit is in the evening when the souvenir sellers have packed up.

There are several other Karo villages a bit farther away, including **Barusjahe** (20km from Kabanjahe), with houses more than 200 years old, **Serdang** (23km from Kabanjahe), and **Dokan** (23km from Kabanjahe). All can be reached by minibus from Kabanjahe, although Serdang is only a 3-km walk from Barusjahe. Check with the tourist office for details. The Sibayak Guest House Losmen has mapped out a three-hour walking tour from Brastagi through several smaller villages, then to the larger, tourist-oriented village of **Lingga.** Check at their office for details.

GUNUNG LEUSER NATIONAL PARK

The 850,000 hectares enveloping the natural fault lines of the Alas and Kluet River Valleys constitute the largest national park in Southeast Asia. Established as Indonesia's first national park in 1980 from a series of smaller reserves, this ASEAN heritage site remains largely untouched by human's presence. Since the Gayo and Alas people have migrated up the valleys into the mountains, most of the park has never been inhabited by people. The Gayo, who live primarily in the hilly highlands, grow tobacco, rice, and coffee, and raise water buffaloes. The Alas people, who have moved up the Alas River Valley, cultivate the fertile rice *sawah* of the ancient Danau Alas. Most of the park lies at altitudes of 1000-25000m. The Alas and Kluet River Valleys comprise lowland forest with vines, spiny palms, and the malodorous Rafflesia, the world's largest flower, while the higher altitudes are meadows of alpine flowers. Over 325 species of birds, including colorful hornbills, reside in the park. Macaques and orangutans abound in places, while Sumatran tigers, elephants, and the very rare Sumatran rhino are few and far between. Most visitors come for its abundant trekking and rafting opportunities. While the park lies largely in Aceh Province, parts of its expanse extend into North Sumatra, where hikers head in from the tourist town of Bukit Lawang. The more adventurous head to Ketambe and Blangkejeren for less-traveled treks and rafting expeditions.

TREKKING IN GUNUNG LEUSER

Trekking is the most popular activity in Gunung Leuser National Park. The smaller the group and the more obscure the area, the more likely are wildlife sightings. Prices vary substantially, with the most exorbitant treks being those arranged in Medan. In general, the closer you are to the starting point, the cheaper the hike. Nearly every tourist office and guest house in nearby towns organize treks. Prices for these usually include food and drink, camping equipment, necessary permits, a guide, and transport to the start of the trek. Most guide services can help arrange transportation from the finish point to the next destination. It's usually best to pay in rupiah rather than U.S. dollars to avoid low exchange rates.

The best guides are licensed with the **HPI** (the Indonesian Guide Association); the PHPA office in Bukit Lawang has a list of all the guides approved to work in the area. English-speaking abilities and genuine interest in the jungles may also be qualities to look for. Browsing through the comment books of guest houses may give you a feel for the different trek opportunities, as well as the outstanding guides.

Most trekkers start their trips in **Bukit Lawang.** Standard HPI prices are Rp30,000 for one-day treks, Rp50,000 for two days, and Rp75,000 for three days; group size is usually a minimum of three people. Treks to Brastagi start in **Marike,** about 30km from Bukit Lawang in an area with many cocoa plantations. Your luggage will be sent to Brastagi by tourist bus. The route can be completed in three days (around Rp100,000 per person, minimum 4 people) or in five days on a different route (around Rp250,000 per person). The more adventurous can traverse a mountain range on a six-day trek to **Kutacane** (about Rp300,000 per person).

Those wishing to escape the tourist traffic can start out of **Ketambe.** Prices tend to be similar to those in Bukit Lawang, and guides generally do not require a minimum group size. Most treks organized in Brastagi actually begin in Ketambe, but you may want to compare the trekking companies in Kutacane if you are planning a longer expedition. Six-day treks to the mountains **Gunung Bendahara** and **Gunung Kemiri** cost about Rp1,000,000 for one person to Rp440,000 per person for five people. Make sure that your guide wants to climb these mountains; many dislike even the thought of the long, cold climb. A good indicator is how many times he has ascended the mountain or been to the place before. Trekkers to higher altitudes should prepare for temperatures which may dip below freezing at night.

Treks out of **Blangkejeren** are even cheaper and more personal than those out of Ketambe, and leeches rarely bother you on these seldom-trodden trails. Several guide services operate out of town, which is the closest base for treks to the towering twins **Gunung Leuser** (3119m) and **Gunung Loser** (3404m). The trip takes seven to 10 days depending on the route, and it would be wise to choose a guide with experience in the mountains. Treks to these peaks cost Rp300-400,000 depending on the length of the trip, the number of people involved, and the experience of the guide. The Sinebuk Green Bungalows, near Kedah Village, can arrange trips to the twin peaks (Rp1-3,000,000).

RAFTING IN GUNUNG LEUSER

Rafting expeditions are another popular activity, ranging from the boisterous water park-like feel of the **Bohorok River** in Bukit Lawang to multi-day adventures down the **Wampu River** near Ketambe. Rafting often services advertise Class II rapids on the **Alas River**, but the bulk of the "rafting" is more like a float down the river. Rafting tends to be more expensive than trekking and, as with trekking, prices include all expenses. From Bukit Lawang, rafting trips down the Wampu River average Rp75,000 per person per day for one to four-day trips. In the Kutacane area, rafting trips down the Alas River start in Ketambe and head toward Gelombang. The most competitive rates can be found from tour services in Kutacane. One-day floats from Ketambe to Kutacane cost as little as Rp30,000 per person (minimum 3 people). Three- or four-day adventures cost about Rp60,000 per person per day, although prices can be lowered for larger groups. Offering a taste of two worlds, the popularity of **combined rafting/trekking trips** is on the rise, and these can be arranged in the Bukit Lawang or Kutacane/Ketambe areas. Three days rafting and two days trekking can be organized out of Kutacane for Rp225,000 per person. A two-day combination trip out of Bukit Lawang runs about Rp80,000.

Practically every guest house has **inner tubes** for use on the Bohorok River (Rp1000 per day). While loads of fun, tubing can also be dangerous—nasty injuries caused by the unseen rocks or submerged logs are common. During the dry season (Feb.-June), the water level may be too low to float safely. Check with the visitor center first. It is possible, although perhaps a bit chilly, to float to **Bohorok** village, a distance of about 6km (2-3hr., depending water level). Frequent local buses can ferry the drenched back to Bukit Lawang (Rp500).

■ Bukit Lawang

Technically, Bukit Lawang is not really a town at all, but a tourists' colony carved out of the rubber and cocoa plantations northwest of Medan. In terms of sights, Bukit Lawang is largely a one-horse—or rather, one-ape—town. Its *raison d'être* is the Bohorok Orangutan Station where the gentle primates, illegally kidnapped from the Sumatran rainforest and sold as pets all over the world, have been reintroduced to their natural habitat. The sight of a mother orangutan, child on her back, swinging out of the jungle canopy to share a meal of bananas a few meters from your camera lens is a truly unique and exhilarating experience.

Beyond attending a few orangutan feedings and reveling in the rapids of the Bohorok River, there is little, and most travel south to Brastagi or Lake Toba or north to Banda Aceh. Not surprisingly, resourceful guest house operators have done all they can to make Bukit Lawang a sort of mini-Club Med with great apes. Tubing down the Bohorok River, hiking through the park, or more ambitious rafting trips on the nearby Wampu River are popular diversions. On weekends Medanites flock to Bukit Lawang by the hundreds, and the river resembles one long water park.

ORIENTATION

The Visitors Centre, PHPA office, and tourist office cluster near a dirt lot bus **"terminal."** The path leading upriver from the bus stop is sometimes referred to as Jalan **Orang-utan.** About 500m upriver is an elaborate gate marking the entrance to a **public campground;** many of the most popular guest houses are beyond the campground along the river. The **Bohorok Orangutan Centre** is about 1km upriver from the Visitors Centre on the opposite bank. The Visitors Centre and Tourist Information Centre put out a helpful map of the guest houses and major attractions.

PRACTICAL INFORMATION

Tourist Offices: Bukit Lawang Visitors Centre (tel. 544 491), on Jl. Orang-utan opposite the bus terminal. Organizes treks and rafting trips. Open daily 8am-3pm. The **PHPA Ranger Station** (tel. 542 574) is next door to the Visitors Centre. Organizes treks and nature walks with a ranger or local biologist. Questions about safety or permits answered here. Tickets to see the orangutans should be purchased here (but if you arrive late they can be bought at the feeding station). Rp4500 per person, good for 2 days (4 feedings). Open daily 7am-5pm. The **Tourist Information Centre** is down a path, left of the Visitor's Centre. More for tours than for info. Organizes treks, rafting, and float tube trips downriver to Bohorok. Open daily 8am-10pm.

Currency Exchange: In a pinch, traveler's checks can be cashed at the *wartel* kiosk, **Brastagi Tours and Travel**, and some guest houses at decent rates.

Buses: The **bus "terminal"** is near the Visitors Centre. To **Medan** (every hr., 5:30am-5pm, 3hr., Rp1500). Tourist buses leave daily at 7:30am to **Brastagi** (5hr., Rp15,000) and **Prapat** (10hr., Rp25,000). Book at least 1 day in advance. Purchase tickets at Tourist Information, the Visitor's Centre, or a guest house.

Medical Services: There is a tiny polyclinic next to the PHPA office.

Police: The nearest station is a few km down the road in Bohorok.

Post Offices: No post office, use letter collection boxes. **Postal code:** 20774.

Telephones: Telephone kiosk on the left, soon to be upgraded to *wartel* status, off the path to the Bukit Lawang Cottages behind the tourist information center. Rp2000 service fee for international collect calls, or pay with a credit card (5% fee). Open daily 8am-7pm. **Telephone code:** 061

ACCOMMODATIONS

When the orangutan rehabilitation center was established in 1973, Bukit Lawang boasted one grubby *losmen*. Today, there are over 25 with more on the way. Room quality varies greatly; you may want to see the room and *mandi* first before laying down your money. The popular places fill up quickly, so come early for the best selection. There is a small **campground** about 500m upriver from the PHPA office just beyond a tall entrance gate. It's used almost exclusively by Indonesian students. There are bamboo tent frameworks and little else. No reservations are needed. A flat rate of Rp200 covers clean-up costs.

Ariko Inn (formerly the "Beverly Hills Resort"), about 800m beyond the orangutan rehab center. The path is long and a bit treacherous. Set amidst a bamboo grove surrounded by forest (with the nearest neighbors almost 1km away), Ariko's as close to a tropical Shangri-La as Bukit Lawang gets. Excellent swimming hole, and the jungle teems with wildlife. Charming, simple bungalows—all constructed with local materials—along the river for Rp4000. Attentive staff organizes treks.

Jungle Inn, about 400m beyond the campground entrance gate, is conveniently located near the orangutan center. Bills itself as "simple but sweet." This Bukit Lawang institution has a 2-story restaurant decorated in true jungle style, complete with bamboo chairs and gnarled, twisting vines. Cheapest doubles are skimpy but clean with mosquito netting (Rp3000). Slightly larger rooms with *mandi* Rp6000. Rooms built over the river are some of the nicest in town—one of them has a large tree growing through the middle of the private *mandi* (Rp10-25,000). Well-established trekking/rafting service.

Eden Inn, right before the campground entrance gate on the left, a short walk from the center of "town." Amiable place with clean and inexpensive, if slightly worn, rooms. Offers excellent, well-established treks and rafting trips. They only employ HPI-licensed guides and post a list of those who can work in the Bukit Lawang area. Doubles with private balcony overlooking the rapids and shared *mandi* Rp3000. Concrete bungalows on the river Rp5000 with private *mandi.* Inexpensive restaurant. Check-out 12:30pm.

FOOD

There are cheap *warung* and *padang* joints along the river near the bus terminal.

Goa Restaurant, just beyond the PHPA office. One wall of this fabulous restaurant is formed by a large river-weathered rock. Postcards sent to Goa's congenial owner from all over the world testify to its popularity. Curries are the name of the game, cooked to order and served in mammoth bowls. Vegetable curry with rice is a don't-miss (Rp1500). Chicken curry with noodles (Rp3500). *Gado-gado* and rice (Rp1500). A number of fruit juices. Open daily 7am-midnight.

Jungle Inn Restaurant, part of the Jungle Inn Guest House, near the river crossing to the orangutan rehab center. Even travelers staying elsewhere come to this renowned restaurant. A large menu of "jungle cuisine": *gado-gado* (Rp2500), *chapati* (Rp1800), and the mysterious "jungle food" (Rp2000). But this place's reputation was built on their titanic fruit salad of passion fruit, papaya, bananas, watermelon, and half a pineapple. Gasp at the size, laugh at the price (Rp2000). Fruitshakes (Rp1800), "exotic herbal tea" (Rp1200). Open daily 7:30am-midnight.

SIGHTS

Bukit Lawang's most famous guests are not backpackers but *pongo pygmaeus abelli,* the orangutans who live in the town's best known guest house—the **Bohorok Orangutan Station.** The station was founded in 1973, with grants from the World Wildlife Fund and the Frankfurt Zoological Society, to reintroduce orangutans who had been illegally captured back into their natural habitat. The entire process from the time they are brought to the station to the time they are released takes about three years. Since 1973, the orangutan rehabilitation project has successfully returned more than 140 animals to therainforest. For more information on the orangutans and the rehab project, the Bukit Lawang Visitor's Centre shows an informative film on the subject every Monday, Wednesday, and Friday at 8pm. Please refer to **Any Which Way But Loose** on page 438 for specifics on rehabilitation centers and visitor behavior.

The station is about 1km upriver from the Visitor's Centre on the opposite bank. Visitors are allowed to observe the two daily feedings (8am and 3pm). Two-day permits (four feedings) can be purchased at the PHPA office or at the station (Rp4500).

A series of caves lurk south of town, including a superb **Bat Cave,** 2km south of town. Take the trail that begins behind the Wisma's main lodge; it winds through a rubber plantation before turning right to the cave (there are signs). The cave itself is quite dramatic. To reach the entrance, partially obscured by hanging vines, you must first clamor up a series of rickety wooden ladders. The dark (a flashlight is essential) cavern is filled with...bats. A narrow corridor leads from the back of the cavern some 600m into the hillside. (Admission Rp500.) About 1km beyond the Bat Cave is the **Swallow Cave,** named for its chief inhabitants.

■ Kutacane

There's little to detain travelers in this one-street Muslim town at the heart of the Alas River Valley, capital of the Aceh Tenggara region. Most shack up for a night on the way north toward Ketambe and Blangkejeren or south toward Brastagi. The giant volcanic explosion which created the present day Lake Toba 75,000 years ago deposited enough ash in the Alas River Valley to create a dam and the subsequent Danau Alas (Lake Alas). Legend maintains that Acehnese war heroes broke the dam, and the subsequent draining of the valley left an incredibly fertile expanse of land between two opposing mountain ranges.

For those arriving from the south, Kutacane is a welcome to the Special Province of Aceh, which is strongly Muslim, and maintains more autonomy than other provinces in Indonesia. All travelers, especially women, should dress modestly. It's a very good idea to have at least a cursory knowledge of Bahasa Indonesia, as locals will be more likely to be friendly.

ORIENTATION AND PRACTICAL INFORMATION

Kutacane boasts one main drag, **Jalan A. Yani,** which heads north to Ketambe and Blangkejeren, and south in the direction of Sidikalang and Brastagi. Most services are located along a 500m section of the road. Buses leave from the **bus terminal,** at the north end of town on Jl. A. Yani, to: **Medan** (every hr., 4am-1pm, 8hr., Rp4000); **Brastagi** (4hr., Rp6000); **Blangkejeren** (every hr., 7am-4pm, 4hr., Rp4000) via **Ketambe** (1hr., Rp1500); and **Sidikalang** (every hr., 6-10am, 3hr., Rp4000). **Currency** and traveler's checks can be changed at awful rates at Wisma Rindualam. Stock up on malaria pills at **Apotik Sari,** Jl. A. Yani 4 (tel. 210 87). The **hospital** (tel. 210 11) is located 5km north of town on the road to Blangkejeren. The **police station,** Jl. A. Yani 108 (tel. 210 17), is directly across from the post office. The **post office** is at Jl. A. Yani 91 (tel. 213 66), opposite the bus terminal (open Mon.-Thurs. 7:30am-3pm, Fri. 7:30-11:30am, Sat. 7:30am-1pm). **Postal code:** 24611. Next door is the **24-hour telephone office,** Jl. A. Yani 62 (tel. 210 04). **Telephone code:** 0629.

ACCOMMODATIONS AND FOOD

Wisma Bangun, Jl. Rajawali 86-8 (tel. 210 56), has clean airy doubles (Rp5000) and dorms (Rp2500) with shiny *mandi* and friendly staff on a quiet side street. From the bus terminal, 300m south on Jl. A. Yani, take a right on Jl. Rajawali and then a left onto a side street after 30m; Bangun is on the left. **Wisma Rindualam,** Jl. A. Yani 7 (tel. 212 89), maintains a stronghold on the traveler's market with its helpful staff, park and trekking information, and free transport to the Pondok Wisata Guest House in Ketambe. The prices are great (dorms Rp2500, doubles Rp5000), but the walls are thin. The odiferous outside *mandi* features numerous cracks in the walls. Nicer, more expensive rooms are available at the **Wisma Maroon,** Jl. A. Yani II 15-17 (tel. 210 78). Doubles with no windows (and little circulation) are Rp7500, with windows and shared *mandi* Rp10,000. Nicer doubles with *mandi* are Rp25-45,000. Same directions as to Wisma Bangun, but take a right onto the side street after 30m; Maroon is on the right. Padang food abounds in **warung** on Jl. A. Yani. Try some of the local fruits, such as the *nangka* which grows in the fertile valley. Villagers flock to the weekly **market** on Saturdays (7:30am-2pm) behind the bus terminal.

■ Ketambe

Situated at a natural bottleneck where the mountains close in upon the rice fields of the Alas River Valley, Ketambe offers a tranquility which visitors to Bukit Lawang only dream about. Home of the Ketambe Research Station (off-limits to tourists) and the Gurah Recreation Forest, the few travelers who make it to Ketambe come to relax, take day hikes to hot springs, or plan more serious trekking and rafting trips in the area. Because of its lack of visitors, travelers are quite likely to see a much larger range of wildlife, including gibbons, macaques, and orangutans.

ORIENTATION AND PRACTICAL INFORMATION

Hardly a town, Ketambe is made up of the guest houses which lie along the **Kutacane-Blangkejeren Road** and the **Ketambe Research Station,** which is situated on the other side of the Alas River. Permits (Rp2000 per day) can be purchased at the **PPA Guesthouse** (open Sat.-Thurs. 8am-6pm), at the **Gunung Leuser National Park Headquarters** (tel. (0629) 213 58) in Tanah Merah, 2km north of Kutacane (open

Mon.-Thurs. 8am-3pm, Fri. 7:30-11:30am, Sat. 8am-12:30pm), or from Mr. Maraeng-gan, the owner of **Wisma Rindualam** in Kutacane. Guides are required for all over-night treks in the park and they can arrange the necessary permits. To get to **Blangkejeren** (every hr., 8am-5pm, 3hr., Rp3000) or **Kutacane** (every hr., 9am-6pm, Rp1500), flag down a bus. Most guest houses provide maps.

ACCOMMODATIONS AND FOOD

Most accommodations are located on the 300-m stretch south of the park gate. Guest house kitchens provide the only available meals, except on Sundays, when several food vendors set up (ask around to find out where they are). All the guest houses pro-vide trekking and rafting services. **Pondok Wisata Ketambe,** Jl. Kutacane-Blangke-jeren Km31 (tel. (0629) 212 89), stands on the east side of the road 300m south of the park gate. It has excellent but pricey food, detailed area maps, and extensive informa-tion about the park and North Sumatra. Cramped doubles on stilts with netting and shared *mandi* cost Rp3000. Doubles with *mandi* in wooden bungalows on the ground go for Rp10,000. **PPA Guesthouse** is off the main road toward the river, 1km north of park gate; bear right after 150m and the guest house is 100m ahead. Doubles (Rp15,000, includes meals) overlook the Alas River. **Wisma Sadar Wisata,** 30m north of Pondok Wisata Ketambe, sits among the rice fields of the local village. Bam-boo-constructed rooms are only 10m from the road. Newer wooden bungalows with attached outside *mandi* and flush toilets are near the river and off the road. Singles are Rp5000, doubles Rp7500. The spacious open-air restaurant rests on stilts above a rice paddy and features satellite TV.

■ Near Ketambe: Gurah Recreation Forest

The **Gurah Recreation Forest** is one of four special areas set up in Gunung Leuser National Park to allow visitors to experience the park for a picnic, day hike, or over-night trip. Permits (Rp2000 per day) are needed to enter the park, and overnight trips require a local guide. Hiking trail maps are available at all guest houses. The seemingly simple trail system can be confusing, as there are no trail markings in the forest itself. It's easy to miss trail turn-offs without a guide, and some tracks are not marked on the map. Guest houses can also arrange guided overnight trips to **Gurah Hot Springs,** a three-hour hike up the Gurah River from the road, which offer seething comfort. The forest tends to be quite wet, and along with all that water come bloodsucking leeches. To ward off these bugs, guides recommend wearing long pants and a long-sleeved shirt, tucking your pants into your socks, and soaking your socks in tobacco juice. The slower you walk and the less you talk, the greater your chances of seeing wild animals, which tend to stay close to the rivers.

■ Blangkejeren

Barely more than a large village, this cool mountain town offers little to the traveler other than a taste of Gayo culture and a base for trekking. Very few people speak English; some knowledge of Bahasa Indonesia will make one's presence more endear-ing to the residents. The bus ride from Kutacane, slow and windy, offers spectacular mountain scenery and a snapshot of village life, although the Blangkejeren Valley itself has been largely deforested. The center of town is marked by a phallic, half-peeled corncob-like monument which greets new arrivals with its tall wooden form thrusting into the air. Wayward cattle, sheep, and other random livestock wander "downtown" in search of a lost meadow.

ORIENTATION AND PRACTICAL INFORMATION

From the center of town, marked by the phallic monument, **Jalan Kutacane** heads south to Kutacane, **Jalan Rikit Gaib** runs northeast toward Takengon, and **Jalan Kuta-panjang** goes north and eventually west in the direction of Terangon. Because the streets have confusing names and often overlap, it's easiest to ask locals for directions to a specific place. **Buses** depart from bus company offices along Jl. Rikit Gaib to: **Takengon** (3 per day, 8-10am, 6hr., Rp10,000); **Kutacane** (every hr., 6am-3pm, 4hr., Rp4000) via **Ketambe** (3hr., Rp3500); and **Terangon** (4 per day, 8am-4pm, 3hr., Rp3000), with connection to **Blangpidie** (5hr., Rp20,000) on the west coast highway. The **tourist information center,** with useful posted maps, is next to Rina restaurant, 30m west of the monument on Jl. Kutapanjang. It is open at the whim of the proprietor. There's **no official currency exchange** available. The simple pharmacy **Toko Obat "Taufik,"** Jl. Rikit Gaib 156 (tel. 210 22), is open daily 7am-9pm. A spartan **clinic** on Jl. Kutapanjang rests next to the post office (open Mon.-Sat. 8am-1pm). The **police station,** Jl. Kutacane 5 (tel. 211 10), is 20m south of the monument. The **post office,** Jl. Kutapanjang 84, stands 200m north of the monument (open Mon.-Thurs. 7:30am-3pm, Fri. 7:30-11:30am, Sat. 7:30am-1pm). **Postal code:** 24653. The **telephone office,** Jl. Kutacane 25 (tel. 210 00), is 700m south of the monument (open 24hr.). **Telephone code:** 0642.

ACCOMMODATIONS AND FOOD

As in Kutacane, it may be wise to check out the privacy of the *mandi* in your *losmen* before deciding to stay. **Losmen Mardhatillah,** Jl. Rikit Gaib (tel. 210 10), 50m north of the monument, offers high ceilings and light rooms with windows. The large and secure *mandi* and friendly staff can make you feel at home. Rooms are Rp5000 per person. English-speakers will be in paradise at **Rahmad,** Jl. Ra. Tartini 200 (tel. 210 23), conversing with the super-friendly and English-proficient owner. It is about 50m up an alleyway north of the monument between Jl. Kutapanjang and Jl. Rikit Gaib. Low-ceilinged rooms have windows and are relatively quiet (Rp3000 per person). The curfew is 10pm.

Most *losmen* do not have a restaurant, forcing travelers to venture out and try the streets. **Rina,** Jl. Kutapanjang 19 (tel. 210 57), 30m west of the monument, cooks up a spicy *mie goreng* for Rp1000 (open daily 7am-midnight). **Lina** (tel. 212 73), on Jl. Rikit Gaib across from the monument, dishes out Padang specialties for Rp1-2000 (open daily 6am-10pm). The **market,** to the east of Jl. Rikit Gaib, offers little to the traveler save fruits and batik fabrics (open daily 8am-2pm).

■ Near Blangkejeren

Travelers can temporarily forget the deforestation in the Blangkejeren area and lose themselves in the jungle paradise near **Kedah Village.** Situated on the bank of a mountain stream, the **Sinebuk Green Bungalows** are nestled in arboreal splendor, a 45-minute hike in from the nearest road in Kedah. Friendly staff tries to ensure that your stay is most satisfactory. Accommodating wooden bungalows with thatched roofs are spaced among a garden of beautiful yet mysterious plants (Rp10,000 per person, including 3 meals). The food here is simple yet deliciously filling. The easiest way to find the bungalows is to ask for Mr. Jali, the jolly proprietor, whom everybody seems to know. **Minibuses** depart frequently from the market in Blangkejeren to **Kutapanjang** (30min., Rp500). From there, minibuses run to **Kedah Village** (Mon. and Thurs., 15min., Rp500). *Becak* (Rp2500) also take passengers to Kedah. Otherwise, it's only a 5-km walk from Kutapanjang. Sinebuk Green arranges treks (Rp25,000 for 2 days, includes food) to a working **tobacco hut.**

> The land around Takengon and Blangkejeren blooms some of the cheapest and strongest marijuana in the world, much to the chagrin of the Indonesian government. Travelers are advised not to take up offers of smoking with locals; the government's efforts at quelling this industry are serious and foreigners (especially backpackers) will not be treated leniently if caught with the drug.

ACEH PROVINCE

■ Takengon

Dominated by the serene 20km-long Danau Laut Tawar (Lake Tawar), refreshing Takengon, at 1000m altitude, is a spicy, sprawling market town, the capital of the Aceh Tengah region, and the heart of Gayo culture. The disconcertingly strong military presence in the town attests to the political instability in Aceh Province, and propaganda reminding locals of Indonesia's independence is plastered on gates, signs, and fences throughout the region. The hills around Takengon play host to numerous coffee plantations and take on a mystical air as threatening rain clouds drape over the shoulders of their summits. Travelers will find sleepy fishing villages, bat-filled caves, soothing hot springs, and cliffs suitable for rock climbing.

ORIENTATION

Any approach to Takengon heads down toward the caldera lake on narrow, winding mountain roads. The town centers around its two markets, **Pasar Petani** and **Pasar Inpres**. A sparkling, new red-tile monument lies next to its fallen predecessor and marks a six-way intersection at the center of town. Heading uphill from the monument, the divided **Jalan Lebe Kader** is home to the **post office, Telkom office,** and **police station.** Going clockwise, the next streets are **Jalan A. Yani, Jalan Laut Tawar, Jalan Malem Dewa, Jalan Sudirman,** and **Jalan Mahkamah. Jalan Pasar Inpres,** the first left 50m down Jl. Laut Tawar from the monument, plays host to the thriving Pasar Inpres, and nearly all the shops in town. The **bus terminal** lies at the other end of Jl. Pasar Inpres. The other important street, **Jalan Yos Sudarso,** which heads toward Isak, is 200m up Jl. Lebe Kader from the monument. Lake Tawar is 500m from the city center.

PRACTICAL INFORMATION

Tourist Offices: No tourist office in town, and maps are hard to come by.
Currency Exchange: Bank Rakyat Indonesia, Jl. Yos Sudarso 281 (tel. 212 94). Exchanges U.S. dollars and traveler's checks. Open Mon.-Fri. 8am-4pm.
Buses: Buses depart from the **bus terminal** at the intersection of Jl. Pasar Inpres and Jl. Terminal. To: **Banda Aceh** (7-8am, 8pm, 10hr., Rp10,000); **Blangkejeren** (8-10am, 6-9hr., Rp10,000); **Medan** (7-8pm, 12hr., Rp12,000; with A/C Rp16,000); and **Bireuen** (every hr., 7am-7pm, 3½hr., Rp3500).
Local Transportation: Most **sudako,** which go by the name *labi-labi,* depart from Pasar Petani when full. Some *labi-labi,* including those to Bintang, depart from the bus terminal. Fares are Rp200-1000.
Markets: Pasar Inpres, the main market in town, encompasses many alleyways and stalls, which lie on the lake side of Jl. Pasar Inpres about halfway to the bus terminal. The smaller **Pasar Petani,** sprawling between Jl. Laut Tanar and Jl. Yani, is a bit skimpier in offerings but more user-friendly to individual buyers.
Pharmacies: Apotik Pesangan Baru, Jl. Lebe Kader 17 (tel. 215 75). Open Mon.-Sat. 8am-10pm, Sun. 8am-noon, 4-9pm.
Medical Services: Jl. Kebayakan (tel. 213 96), 2km from town; by *becak* (Rp500).
Police: Jl. Lebe Kader (tel. 210 71), across from a small clock tower.
Post Offices: Jl. Lebe Kader 4. Open Mon.-Thurs. 7:30am-3pm, Fri. 7:30-11am, Sat. 7:30am-1pm. **Postal code:** 24512.
Telephones: Telkom office, Jl. Lebe Kader 3 (tel. 217 99). Open 24hr. **Telephone code:** 0643.

INDONESIA

ACCOMMODATIONS

Losmen are surprisingly few in a town of Takengon's size. Several cluster next to the bus terminal, while most are near the monument. The only accommodation on the lake is **Hotel Renggali** (rooms Rp55,000 and up), 2km from town.

Penginapan Bintang Ruang, Jl. Mahkamah 7 (tel. 215 24). From the monument take Jl. Mahkamah 100m to the cinema. The *losmen* is directly to the left of the cinema. Friendly, helpful, English-speaking owner can help you navigate Takengon's sea of possibilities. Clean *mandi.* Spacious and clean doubles Rp6000. Triples Rp9000. Quads Rp12,000. Wake up to an acoustical cacophony of roosters.

Losmen Parawisata, Jl. Terminal 301 (tel. 213 22). The only inexpensive *losmen* near the bus terminal. The charming family who runs this *losmen* offer clean, secure *mandi.* The entrance and lounging area are a bit dark and cramped but the rooms are nice. Rp6000 per person with shared *mandi.* Singles with *mandi* Rp10,000. Doubles with *mandi* Rp15,000.

Losmen Libraindah, Jl. Yos Sudarso 267 (tel. 210 11), a bit far from town, 300m up Jl. Yos Sudarso. The peaceful Dutch building surrounds a well-tended garden and offers some relief from the town's noise. Basic doubles with outside *mandi* Rp10,000. High-ceilinged doubles Rp17,500. Triples with lovely green walls, TV and large inside *mandi* (flush toilets) Rp25,000.

FOOD

Rumah makan cluster near Pasar Petani and next to the bus terminal on Jl. Terminal, serving up similar fare, including Padang food. Although seemingly impossible, Aceh is even spicier than traditional Padang food. A sure tastebud enhancer is **Rumah Makan Arena Jadi,** on the corner of Jl. Terminal and Jl. Pasar Inpres, which serves delicious *mie goreng* (Rp700) and *nasi padang* specialties. (Open daily 6am-11pm.) The *warung* on Jl. Terminal or Jl. Pasar Inpres has *martabak telur* (spicy fried eggs, Rp50 per egg) and delicious *pisang goreng* (fried bananas, Rp50).

SIGHTS

Placid **Danau Laut Tawar** stretches 20km to the east of Takengon, and tourists come just to admire the water resting next to the cliffs of the caldera or to swim in its cool blue waters. Those short on time can catch a good view of the lake and "urban" Takengon from the old Dutch mansion, **Buntul Kubu,** which rests on a hill protruding up from **Jl. Malem Dewa,** just 100m from the town's central monument. To catch the true splendor of the lake warrants an excursion by *labi-labi* or minibus along the precarious shore roads. *Labi-labi* run from the bus terminal to **Bintang village,** on the other end of the lake (5 per day, 8am-5pm, 1½hr., Rp1000) on the northern shore road, and return by the same route. *Labi-labi* departing from Pasar Petani only run about halfway to Bintang village on the southern shore road (every hr., 8am-6pm, Rp500-800, ask for ones heading toward Loyang Kuru). Other alternatives include canoes (Rp3000 per hr.) or bicycles (Rp5000 per day). The southern shore road is particularly nice for biking, although it is narrow in places and occasionally steep. For both options, inquire at Penginapan Bintang Ruang Guest House.

Those who haven't seen a hot shower in ages may want to head over to the **Simpang Balik Hot Springs,** 14km north of Takengon on the road to Bireuen. Most locals frequent the lower set of pools, which are comfortably hot and soothing (Rp500). About 100m uphill lies a second pair of pools, which are painfully hot and depressingly shallow. Buses run frequently from the bus terminal to Simpang Balik (every 30min., 7am-4:30pm, Rp500). The pools start about 100m from the entrance gate on the main road labeled "Wih Pesam."

■ Banda Aceh

Situated strategically at the northern tip of Sumatra where the Indian Ocean clashes with the Straits of Melaka, Banda Aceh remains the heart of Islamic Acehnese culture, as well as an affluent market city in its own right. About 99% of the population adheres to Islam and mosques seem to be at every street corner. Nearly all the women who roam the streets wear the *jibab* (head and shoulder covering), although remarkably few men sport *peci*. Banda Aceh's independent form of strictness seems to bespeak the strong autonomy of its people, whose trials and tribulations are enshrined in the city's many monuments.

After the arrival of Islam in the 13th century, Banda Aceh flourished into a commercial, religious, and intellectual center. For the next four centuries, the sultanate of Aceh increased in power and importance, reaching its zenith during the reign of Sultan Iskandarmuda (1607-1636). After several unsuccessful attempts, the Dutch succeeded in conquering Aceh in 1873. The continued resistance of the Acehnese, however, resulted in a 45-year guerilla war which eventually enfeebled the Dutch, who were finally driven from Sumatra's shores with the help of the Japanese in 1942. Aceh became a part of Indonesia three years later, although civil upheaval persisted, an indication of the province's lack of patriotism to the nation. To help appease this unrest, and as a reward for its pivotal role in fighting off the Dutch, Aceh was designated a "Special Province" with considerable lassitude in forming local government policies. For those travelers who don't mind the noisy streets and relatively expensive accommodations, Aceh is a unique area with friendly locals, thriving markets, and traditional Islamic culture unseen elsewhere in Indonesia.

ORIENTATION

The **Aceh River** divides Banda Aceh roughly in half. On the southwestern side of the river, the impressive Mesjid Raya Baiturrahman dominates the center of town, next to the bustling Pasar Aceh. From the mosque, **Jalan Balai Kota** heads south, turning into **Jalan Teuku Umar** before reaching the **Seutui Bus Terminal**. Just across the river is **Simpang Lima**, a five-way intersection from which spins **Jalan Pante Pirak,** running southwest across the river; **Jalan Sri Ratu Safiatuddin,** heading northwest for the night market; **Jalan Panglima Polem,** heading north; **Jalan T. Nyak Arief,** going northeast toward the Telkom office, the police station, the tourist office, and the hospital, and **Jalan Kota Alam** curving east to the post office.

PRACTICAL INFORMATION

Tourist Offices: Aceh Tourism, Jl. T. Chik Kuta Karang 5, off Jl. T. Nyak Arief. Helpful English-speaking staff offers numerous brochures, maps, and information for all of Aceh Province, and most other parts of Indonesia. Open Mon.-Thurs. 7:45am-2:15pm, Fri. 7am-12:15pm, Sat. 7:45am-2:15pm.

Tours and Travel: P.T. Krueng Wayla Travel, Jl. Sri Ratu Safiatuddin 26 (tel. 220 66). Open Mon.-Sat. 8am-5pm, Sun. 8am-noon. **P.T. Artabu Tour and Travel,** Jl. Mohd. Jam 40 (tel. 236 30). Open Mon.-Sat. 8am-6pm.

Immigration Offices: Jl. T. Nyak Arief 82 (tel. 237 84). Foreigners arriving in Banda Aceh directly from abroad can only receive a 1-month visa (US$30).

Currency Exchange: Outside Medan, Banda Aceh has the best rates. **Bank Central Asia,** Jl. Panglima Polem 38-40 (tel. 338 87). Open Mon.-Fri. 7:45am-3pm. Sat. 7:45am-noon. **Bank Dagang Negara,** Jl. Diponegoro 47. Open Mon.-Fri. 8am-3:30pm. Both accept major foreign currencies and US traveler's checks.

Air Travel: Sultan Iskandarmuda Airport (tel. 331 14), 17km east of town in Blang Bintang. From Jl. Diponegoro take *labi-labi* #01D (30min., Rp1500) or a taxi (Rp15,000). **Garuda,** Jl. Panglima Polem 127 (tel. 325 23), in Hotel Sultan. To: **Medan** (2 per day, 1hr., Rp145,500). Open Mon.-Thurs. 7am-noon and 2-4:45pm, Sat.-Sun. 9am-1pm. **Pelangi Air Malaysia,** Jl. T. Nyak Arief 163 (tel. 217 05). To **Kuala Lumpur** (2hr., US$125) via **Penang** (Mon., Wed., and Fri., 1hr., US$85). Open Mon.-Fri. 8:30am-5:30pm, Sat. 8:30am-2pm.

Buses: Long-distance buses depart from the **Seutui Terminal,** 3km south of town on Jl. Teuku Umar. Take any *labi-labi* #03 at Jl. Diponegoro and ask for *terminal bis* (Rp250). Tickets can be purchased in advance at one of the many bus company offices on Jl. Mohd. Jam, as well as at the terminal. To: **Medan** (every hr., 8am-midnight, 10hr., Rp19,000, A/C Rp25,000, A/C with toilet Rp30,000); **Takengon** (every hr., 6am-8pm, 10hr., Rp10,000); **Tapaktuan** (every hr., 6am-8pm, 12hr., Rp13,500) via **Calang** (4hr., Rp3000) and **Meulaboh** (7hr., Rp7500); and **Bireuen** (every 30min., 7:30am-9pm, 5½hr., Rp6500). Buses to Bireuen also depart from the Beurawe Shopping Centre (10am-5pm), on the north side of the Aceh River on Jl. Syeh Abdul Rauf.

Ferries: Leave from **Malahayati Harbor** in Krueng Raya, 35km northeast of Banda Aceh. *Labi-labi* #02H departs from Jl. Diponegoro every 30min. to the harbor (Rp1500, 1hr.). To **Pulau Weh** (2:30pm, 2-3hr., Rp4250). Purchase tickets at the ticket booth next to the entrance gate at Malahayati the day of departure.

Local Transportation: *Labi-labi* (minibuses) zip along set routes. They all depart from behind Pasar Aceh on Jl. Diponegoro. To **Krueng Raya** or **Malahayati Harbor** (#02H, every 30min., 6am-6pm, 1hr., Rp1500) and **Lhok Nga** (#04E, every 30min., 6am-6pm, 30min., Rp1000). Fare within downtown is Rp250-300. **Taxis** in the downtown area Rp2000. **Becak misin** also putter around.

Pharmacies: Kimia Farma, Jl. Diponegoro 8 (tel. 215 59). Open 24hr.

Medical Services: Umum Dr. Zainoel Abidin (tel. 226 51), on Jl.T. Nyak Arief 600m past the police, on the right. 24-hr. pharmacy. English-speaking doctors.

Police: Polres Aceh Besar (tel. 216 41), on Jl. T. Nyak Arief, at the corner of Jl. Syiah Kuala 600m up from Simpang Lima.

Post Offices: GPO, Jl. T. Angkasah 33 (tel. 214 25), about 50m from the tourist office. *Poste Restante.* EMS. Open Mon.-Thurs. 8am-6pm, Fri. 8-11am and 2-6pm, Sat. 8am–2pm. **Postal code:** 23121.

Telephones: Telkom office, Jl. T. Nyak Arief 13 (tel. 200 28). International collect calls. **HCD** phone. Open 24hr. Several **wartel** also dot the city, offering **IDD** and collect calls: **Telephone code:** 0651.

ACCOMMODATIONS

Inexpensive rooms are difficult to come by in Banda Aceh and *losmen* tend to fill up quickly. *Losmen* and hotels cluster in the area of the mosque along Jl. A. Yani in Peunayong (Chinatown). A room in the back can be a respite from loud street noise.

Hotel Raya, Jl. Mesjid Raya 30 (tel. 214 27), about 250m down Jl. Mesjid Raya, on the right. Well-kept former colonial house in a more affluent part of town. A newer addition behind the house packs most of the rooms, which encircle a blaring TV; try to get a room away from it. Spacious doubles with fan and shared *mandi* Rp12,500. Luxurious doubles Rp17,500. Triples with attached *mandi* and fan in the old house Rp20,000. Breakfast included.

Losmen Rasa Sayang, Jl. Cut Meutia 26E (tel. 221 24), about 100m up from the *labi-labi* "starting gate" on Jl. Diponegoro. The cheapest *losmen* in town, and the closest to Pasar Aceh. Dark rooms with thin wood walls and screen partitions. Lots of street noise. Doubles Rp8000. Triples with shared outside *mandi* Rp12,000. Often full.

Losmen Aceh Barat, Jl. Khairil Anwar 16 (tel. 232 50), near the intersection with Jl. Panglima Polem. Combines value, relative quietude, and location amid the excellent culinary delights of Peunayong. Friendly staff oversees a spacious living room with TV. All rooms have high ceilings. Doubles with fan Rp12,500, with attached *mandi* Rp16,000, with A/C and TV Rp40,000. Triples Rp18,750. Quads with shared *mandi* Rp25,000.

Hotel Prapat, Jl. A. Yani 19 (tel. 221 59), at the end of Jl. Sri Ratu Safiatuddin in Peunayong, 200m from Simpang Lima. If the cramped dark rooms of the *losmen* are getting to you, Hotel Prapat is a nice step up from the rest. A bit motel-esque, but all rooms come with a spacious *mandi* and complimentary sandals. Doubles with fan Rp27,500, with A/C Rp27,500, with TV Rp33,000.

FOOD

Considering Banda Aceh's relative affluence, there are surprisingly few choice restaurants in town. *Warung* and small, cheap restaurants abound, particularly in the area around Pasar Aceh (open daily 7am-6pm). The **night market** (open daily 8pm-2am), at the junction of Jl. A. Yani, Jl. Safiatuddin and Jl. Khairil Anwar in Peunayong, is also a good bet (Rp1-2000 per dish). The **Rindang Café,** between Jl. Balai Kota and Jl. Mesjid Raya, across from the Kuala Tripa Hotel, offers several stalls and variety in a nice park behind Banda Aceh's water tower.

Rumah Makan Asia Utama, Jl. Cut Meutia 39-41 (tel. 232 36), about 200m from Losmen Rasa Sayang. Some of the best seafood, served up in traditional Acehnese style (similar to Padang). Specialties include *kepiting* (crab, Rp10,000), *ikan goreng* (fried fish, Rp700), *udang* (shrimp, Rp2500) or *ayam Aceh* (Rp2000). Pay only for what you eat. Open daily 7:30am-10:30pm.

Restaurant Aroma, Jl. Cut Nyak Dhien 18 (tel. 327 79), near the intersection with Jl. Khairil Anwar. Specializes in Chinese seafood. Try *ikan udang sambul* (shrimp with chili sauce, Rp6000). Vegetarians rave about the *capcai* (mixed veggies, Rp4000). Expensive if dining solo. English menu. Open daily 9am-10pm.

Restaurant New Tropicana, Jl. A. Yani 90 (tel. 214 42). The glistening white tile floors and bright lights are a bit of a shock coming off the dim street, but locals in search of a step above Banda Aceh's tiny restaurants flock here for delicious, if a bit expensive, Chinese and Indonesian food. Try the shark fin soup with crab meat (Rp7000). Rp10,000 for a main course. Mild starfruit juice (Rp2500). English menu. Open daily 10am-3pm and 6-10pm.

MARKETS

Banda Aceh's markets lie near transportation points around the city, all serving up traditional market delights from imitation designer shoes to squirming fish products. All markets are open daily 7am-6pm. Undoubtedly the best market is **Pasar Aceh,** which encompasses the area between Jl. Diponegoro and Jl. Perdagangan behind the mosque. If you're looking for something in particular it's best to ask around. Acehnese jewelry and gemstone shops cluster on Jl. Perdagangan next to the mosque. All the traditional Acehnese souvenir items can be found in the corner of the "shopping center" building directly at the corner of Jl. K.H.A. Dahlan and Jl. Diponegoro. Traditional *bordir Aceh* (Acehnese dress) is Rp39-55,000. Batik *Aceh* goes for Rp12,000 and traditional Acehnese daggers are Rp7000-100,000.

The **Pasar Peunayong** packs a number of separate markets on both sides of Jl. Supratman on the eastern side of the Aceh River in Peunayong. The other parts of this sprawling market are stocked high with clothing and food, with a less aggressive atmosphere than Pasar Aceh.

SIGHTS

A jewel of impressive architecture dominating the center of town, the **Mesjid Raya Baiturrahman** (Great Mosque) marvels visitors with its five crisp, black domes, two towering minarets, and vaulted arches. The current mosque replaced the first mosque, built by Sultan Iskandarmuda in 1612, which was burned down in 1873 when the Dutch stormed Banda Aceh. As an offering of peace (which turned out to be short-lived), the Dutch constructed a new mosque on the site, completed in 1881. Non-Muslims are requested not to enter the mosque itself, although they are welcome to tour the grounds which include a long pool and a tower at the far end of the grounds. The tower can be climbed daily 4:30-6pm for Rp1500 to catch some excellent views of the mosque and the city environs.

A 15-minute walk from the Mesjid Raya Baiturrahman is the **Aceh State Museum** (tel. 210 33), on Jl. Mahmudsyah. Anyone with even a mild interest in the traditions and culture of Aceh Province will find this museum fascinating, with its diverse collections and exhibits. Directly across the bridge, the **Rumah Aceh** is a traditional Acehnese communal longhouse, raised high on stilts with a thatched roof and painted in shades of reds and greens. A three-story **museum** building lies to the left of the Rumah Aceh. Pass up the history of life on the ground floor and head upstairs for tools, traditional clothing and jewelry on the second and third floors. (Open Tues.-Thurs. 8am-6pm, Fri. 8-11am and 2:30-6pm, Sat.-Sun. 8am-6pm; admission Rp200.) In front of the building sits Aceh's very own Liberty Bell; this one is a tall Chinese bell called **Cakradonya,** presented to Sultan Pasai by Cheng Hoe in 1469, which was used to gather citizens for important directives of the sultan. Next to the museum lies the **Grave of Sultan Iskandarmuda,** who ruled the Acehnese Sultanate during its heyday. The entrance to the grave complex is flanked by rusting cannons, guns, and bombs used to fight the Dutch.

A short walk west on Jl. Iskandarmuda past the Pendopo (Governor's House) is the strange **Gunongan**—a pleasure garden and 10m-high "mountain" built by Sultan Iskandarmuda for his Malaysian wife. She and other members of the royal family would "climb" the curving arches of this whitewashed mountain to enjoy the view. Gunongan stands next to **Kandang,** a 20m-square walled cemetery where several sultans are buried, and also looks out over **Pinto Khop,** a similar, but smaller white-washed structure where the sultan bathed. To climb Gunongan, ask the guard at the Jl. Teuku Umar gate to unlock the door (open daily 8am-6pm).

Head west on Jl. Iskandarmuda 300m and take a left to the entrance for **Kherkof,** the cemetery home to over 2000 graves of Dutch soldiers killed between 1873-1927. The cemetery itself feels like an oasis of serenity, detached from the buzz of the streets nearby. Fading white stone graves lie amid well-tended paths and the utter silence leaves one feeling sympathy for all the Dutch who may not have known what they were getting into when they waged war on Aceh. North and east of the Pinto Khop, **Kandang XII Cemetery** contains more tombs of sultans.

■ Pulau Weh

Dubbed Indonesia's Golden Island, Pulau Weh was a thriving port in the early 20th century, but the rise of Singapore soon eclipsed Sabang, Weh's major city, which is actually more of a somnolent fishing village. In the 1970s, Indonesia planned to create a duty-free port to revive Weh's former status, but these plans never materialized and the island was left to remain the golden treasure it is today. Undoubtedly, the island's natural wonders are its primary attraction, with steamy volcanoes and mounds of rolling jungle rising sharply from the crystal waters of the sea.

A lively mix of Acehnese, Javanese, Minangkabau, Batak, and Chinese populate the island. Although only a three-hour boat ride from Banda Aceh, Pulau Weh lacks the religious conservatism of the mainland. Gays find a more liberal atmosphere, lone women travelers are less likely to be badgered, and all visitors find the island a welcome source of relaxation, whatever the weather might be.

GETTING THERE AND AWAY

The island can be reached by ferry from Malahayati Harbor, 35km northeast of Banda Aceh (2:30pm, 2-3hr., Rp4250). The ferry makes the return trip in the morning (8:30am, Rp3900). Catch *labi-labi* #02H, heading for Krueng Raya, which shuttles between Jl. Diponegoro in Banda Aceh and Malahayati Harbor (every 30min., 1hr., Rp1500). A newer and larger ferry with safety features, such as life-jackets, has replaced the old ferry which sank in January 1996, killing hundreds of passengers. *Labi-labi* to Sabang (30min., Rp1500) and occasionally Iboih/Gapang Beaches (1hr., Rp3500) meet the ferry in **Balohan.** From Sabang, pick-up trucks go to Iboih/Gapang (30min., Rp2000). *Labi-labi* depart Sabang every morning at 7:30am and pick-up trucks leave Iboih and Gapang at 7am to meet the return ferry.

ISLAND ORIENTATION

Most of Pulau Weh's 24,413 inhabitants live near **Sabang,** leaving the rest of the island nearly deserted. The weather on the island is fickle, and long (or short) periods of sun or rain can set in at any time of the year. Luckily, the winds follow a more regular pattern; waves crash in from the west during the west monsoon season (June-November) and bear down from the east in the east monsoon season (December-May). Good roads access most of the 154 sq.km island. From Sabang, in the northeastern peninsula of the island, a coastal road curves around clockwise, passing **Kasih, Tapak Gajah, Sumur Tiga, Ujung Kareung,** and **Anoe Itam Beaches,** which line the east coast. Heading south from Sabang, roads run to **Balohan Harbor** and **Paya Keunukai Beach** on the southwestern coast, passing a waterfall and a steaming volcano along the way. The other main road heads across the northern edge of the island to **Gapang** and **Iboih Beaches,** and the wild **Iboih Recreational Forest.** Local boats (Rp5000) ply the bay for 7km between Iboih and Sabang. Most of the west coast is only accessible by boat and lies untouched.

PRACTICAL INFORMATION

Tourist Offices: No official tourist office. **Harry's Coffee** (tel. 211 48, open daily 7am-1pm and 4pm-midnight), and **Stingray Dive Centre** (tel. 212 65, open daily 8am-noon and 4pm-9pm), both at the corner of Jl. Teuku Umar and Jl. Perdagangan offer maps of the island, information, and other services.

Currency Exchange: Bank Rakyat Indonesia, Jl. Perdagangan 123 (tel. 210 31), has poor rates for US$ and traveler's checks. Open daily Mon.-Fri. 8am-5pm.

Taxis: *Ojek* can be arranged to pick you up at a certain time from your destination. Inquire at Losmen Pulau Jaya. To **Sumur Tiga Beach** (Rp2000).

Local Transportation: One or two pick-up trucks run daily to **Gapang** and **Iboih Beaches** (4-6pm, Rp2000) and to the hot springs near **Bango** on the southwest coast (9am, Rp1000). A market boat departs Iboih at 7am and leaves Sabang at 11am for the return trip (Rp5000 each way for foreigners).

Rentals: Motorcycle rentals at **Losmen Pulau Jaya** and **Harry's Coffee.** Standard rate Rp25,000 per day with petrol.

Pharmacies: Sabang Farma, Jl. Perdagangan 3 (tel. 21140). Good for such a small place. Also sells souvenirs. Open daily 8am-1pm and 5-10pm.

Medical Services: Hospital, on Jl. Teuku Umar (tel. 21310), 1km north of town. English-speaking doctors. Tourists can also be admitted to the **Navy Hospital** (tel. 211 15), on Jl. Kilat 1.5km east of town.

Police: Polsek Sukakarya (tel. 21052), on Jl. Perdagangan next to the Telkom.

Post Offices: Jl. Perdagangan 66 (tel. 212 67). Open Mon.-Thurs. 8am-2pm, Fri. 8-11am, Sat. 8am-2pm. **Postal code:** 23512.

Telephones: Telkom, Jl. Perdagangan 66 (tel. 211 08). **HCD** phone. Open 24hr. **Telephone code:** 0652.

ACCOMMODATIONS

Losmen Pulau Jaya, Jl. Teuku Umar 17 (tel. 213 44). Clean, basic rooms with fan and outside *mandi* packed into a classy white building. Ask for a room in the back and relax in the breeze of the silently whirring fan. Ever-smiling staff has detailed maps of Sabang. Singles Rp4000. Doubles Rp7500. Triples Rp10,000.

Losmen Irma, Jl. Teuku Umar 3 (tel. 211 48), at the corner of a lively intersection. Rooms with big windows catch all of Sabang's evening sounds. Sunbathe, barbecue, or check out the swell views over Sabang and the rest of the island. Marvelous English-speaking staff can help arrange your stay on the island. All rooms have fan and outside *mandi*. Singles Rp4000. Triples/quads Rp3500 per person.

Holiday Losmen (tel. 211 31), down an alley off Jl. Perdagangan, about 50m from Losmen Irma. Compared to similarly priced establishments in Banda Aceh, this friendly *losmen* is a real treat. Towels, soap, and sandals accompany every room to complement the gargantuan *mandi*. A welcome relief from the cacophony of street noises. All rooms come with a fan, but be sure it doesn't rattle before taking the room. Singles with shared *mandi* Rp7500. Doubles Rp15,000, with inside *mandi* Rp25,000, with A/C Rp40,000. Triples Rp30,000.

FOOD

Various *rumah makan* line Jl. Perdagangan, offering fried noodles, rice, and other Indonesian dishes. Travelers will find it hard to find food during the 1-5pm *siesta*.

Perkasa Utama, Jl. Perdagangan 1557 (tel. 211 85), about 200m past the Telkom office on the left. A quiet restaurant frequented by locals, who may divert their attention from the street scene in order to watch you eat. Broiled *ikan tonkol* (tuna, Rp500) or *ikan rambai* (fish with special sauce, Rp1000) are good dishes to try. Open daily 7:30am-10pm.

Restaurant Sabang, Jl. Perdagangan 27 (tel. 211 81). Slightly expensive, but delicious Chinese seafood specialties. Indulge yourself with the *udang asam manis* (sweet and sour prawns, Rp12,500) or save your wallet and try the *ikan tauco goreng* (fried taucoh fish, Rp4-6000). The amiable cook often comes out of the kitchen to cook up *mie rebus* at a nearby *warung* (Rp1200). Open daily 6-11pm.

GAPANG AND IBOIH BEACHES

Of Pulau Weh's two major beaches frequented by travelers, **Gapang Beach** is the nicer choice. Its 150m-long stretch of snow-white silica, fringed with skinny palms, curves around a stunningly clear bay with views of Sabang and Pulau Rubiah. Only about 30 bungalows are set back in the trees and up on a nearby hill, leaving Gapang pleasantly uncrowded. Most bungalows are Rp5000, but ask to see several as they vary in age and quality. Rp10,000 pays for a view over the ocean and the mountainside. The one restaurant here serves cheap, appetizing food.

Three km north, Gapang's more popular neighbor, **Iboih Beach,** packs in a more festive atmosphere. The beach itself is not that impressive, being only about 60m long, hemmed in by dark towering trees and a steep hillside rising behind. Nearby Pulau Rubiah blocks off the only views of the ocean beyond. Despite this, however, travelers continue to bypass Gapang and descend upon Iboih instead, where they find the proximity of Pulau Rubiah and the company of fellow travelers more appealing. There are five restaurant-based groupings of bungalows, each offering similar thatched A-frame wooden huts with no electricity for Rp3000 (singles) or Rp5-6000 (doubles). Each establishment serves a family-style dinner of traditional Indonesian food for Rp2000 at a set time. **Mr. Razali Bungalows,** about a 200m hike north of the beach, earns high marks for the bubbly and friendly staff that makes excellent doughnuts (Rp400) daily. **Fatimah Bungalows,** right before Mr. Razali's, has a nice view from the restaurant, and monkeys seem to frequent the trees in the area. **Mama's Bungalows,** on the left side of the beach when looking out at the ocean, cooks up delicious and filling dinners.

Snorkeling and **diving** are the two primary allures of Gapang and Iboih Beaches. Crystal clear water offers good visibility up to 25m during calm weather. Live coral and scores of tropical fish line the shoreline from Iboih to Gapang Beaches. The **Rubiah Sea Garden,** which rings Pulau Rubiah 200m offshore from Iboih Beach, has been designated a special nature reserve and houses scores of spectacular coral and tropical fish. Boats to Pulau Rubiah can be chartered for Rp10,000 per boat (for 15 people). Snorkeling equipment at all bungalows rents for Rp2000 per day for snorkel and mask and Rp3000 per day with fins.

Those who want a deeper experience can join a **scuba course. Stingray Dive Centre,** on Iboih Beach, with an office in Sabang, Jl. Teuku Umar 3 (tel. 212 65), offers a PADI open-water course for US$260 and an advanced course for US$200 or both for US$440. Introductory dives for beginners are US$30 for the first dive and US$25 for the second. Certified divers can join in a day of guided diving (two dives with lunch) for US$40 (minimum of three people) or rent equipment and dive on their own (two dives Rp63,000). Night dives cost US$30. They can also arrange dives in other areas.

Salt-logged divers on coral overload can opt to check out the wonders of the seldom-visited **Iboih Recreational Forest,** which encompasses the northwestern tip of the island. Dense jungles dominate the area, with roaming wild boars and monitor lizards, cousins of the Komodo dragon. Hike up the volcano behind Iboih or rent a motorcycle (Rp25,000 per day) to explore the road which heads up to the end of the island. Bungalow owners are eager to help you plan an excursion to the forest, and can help advise you as to whether or not you will need a guide.

THE WEST COAST

The west coast of the island remains relatively untouched; most of it is accessible only by boat. One set of bungalows, **Irma Bungalows,** lies on the shores at **Wind Long Beach.** Accessible by car from Sabang (Rp2000), these eight bungalows are Pulau Weh's utopia of relaxation (open Oct.-May.). Singles are Rp3000, doubles Rp5000. Inquire at Irma Losmen in Sabang to stay at their bungalows. The coast offers up its delights during the east monsoon season. Dolphins are a common sight and several caves, mainly accessible by boat, wait to be explored. The bat cave is only a 30-minute walk from Wind Long Beach.

THE EAST COAST

The most picturesque and least visited beaches are found on the east coast. When the west coast comes under the throes of monsoon season (June-Nov.), head east. A 2-km walk from Sabang up Jl. Teuku Umar leads to **Pantai Kasih** (Love Beach), where Sabang's couples come for romantic views of the sunset. Two km east is **Pantai Tapak Gajah** (Elephant Step Beach), which can also be reached by a more direct 3-km route from Sabang. Continuing down the coast, **Pantai Sumur Tiga** is 3km farther, with its long stretch of blinding white sand and excellent coral. Limestone rocks hollowed by seawater abut **Pantai Ujung Kareung** (End of Rock Beach). **Anoe Itam Beach,** another 4km down the coast, rounds out this beautiful stretch of beaches. There is an old Japanese WWII fortress nearby. There are no bungalows along the east coast, so most people resort to running day excursions from Sabang or perhaps roughing a night on the open beach in good weather. The easiest form of transport to the beaches is renting a motorcycle (Rp25,000 per day) which can accommodate two people. Taxis with drivers can be chartered for Rp40-50,000 per day. *Ojek* also go to any of the beaches and pick up passengers at a designated time, as well. Inquire at Losmen Pulau Jaya.

■ Island Sights

Nature lovers will get their fill with the hiking, hot springs, and underwater exploration which surround the island. Sabang itself, however, doesn't offer much in terms of sights. The **Keuneukai Hot Springs** are off the road on the southwestern coast, 15km south of Sabang, accessible by pick-up truck (9am, Rp1500), although there is no organized transportation back. Visitors can walk or try hitching back to Sabang. A steaming **volcano** rises up next to Balohan Harbor, although it's not nearly as impressive or tall as its cousins on mainland Sumatra. **Harry's Coffee,** below Irma Losmen, organizes **island tours** by minibus (Rp15,000 per person, minimum four people) and **boat tours** around the island (Rp200,000 per boat, maximum 10 people). The island bus tour lasts a full day, with stops at all the major beaches, hot springs, and volcanoes, and finishes up with snorkeling off Iboih Beach.

■ Lhok Nga

On weekends, locals flee Banda Aceh to these marvelous beaches, which are only a short 14-km hop from the city. The rest of the week most visitors have the beaches to themselves, with cheap rooms and glorious sunsets as a welcome relief from the nearby frenzy of the city.

ORIENTATION AND PRACTICAL INFORMATION

The small town centers around the **Pasar Lhok Nga,** about 200m west of the **Banda Aceh-Meulaboh road,** where most shops and services are found. *Labi-labi* shuttle between the *pasar* and **Banda Aceh** (6am-5pm, 30min., Rp500). Longer distance buses and minibuses should be flagged down on the main road, across from the road to the *pasar.* Buses go to **Tapaktuan** (every 30min., 7am-8pm, 10hr., Rp19,000) via **Calang** (3hr., Rp5000) and **Meulaboh** (5hr., Rp8000). **Vita Farma,** a skimpily stocked pharmacy, stands at the center of the *pasar* (open daily 8:30am-9pm). A Puskesmas **polyclinic** with 24-hour emergency radio contact is on the left side of the road to the *pasar* about 50m from the highway (doctors available Mon.-Fri. 8-11am, Sat. 8am-noon). Heading away from Banda Aceh on the highway, the **police station** (tel. 440 27) is 100m down on the left before the bridge and houses a local **telephone** booth. **Telephone code:** 0652. Crossing the bridge, the **post office** is 200m down on the right, across from a sizeable military complex (open Mon.-Thurs. 7:45am-3pm, Fri. 7:45am-noon, Sat. 7:45am-2pm). **Postal code:** 23353.

ACCOMMODATIONS AND FOOD

Several homestays and a beach resort make for slim but sweet pickings. **Homestay Darlian** has whitewashed walls, sparkling floors, and a friendly, honest family. The Double or triple rooms charge Rp6000 per person. Ask the *labi-labi* driver to let you off at "Padang Golf Seulawah," and the homestay is the white house directly across from the golf course entrance. The beach is 300m from the homestay. **Homestay Mami Diana,** next to Darlian's, has cheaper doubles (Rp5000 per person) in a wooden building on stilts with a thatched roof.

   Pantai Cemara Restaurant is 400m off the main road just over the bridge. Travelers need not be daunted by the expensive accommodations, as the food is fortunately on the cheap end (open daily 8am-11pm). Enjoy the radiant colors of the sunset from the oceanside patio or karaoke the night away inside. Try their specialty, *nasi goreng aceh pantai cemara* (Rp3000). The homestays don't serve food, so head for the *pasar,* a 200m walk away. Several *warung* serve up *martabak telur* (egg omelette, Rp500) and fried noodles and noodle soup (Rp700). Most *warung* are open daily 7am-9pm.

SIGHTS

The swimming off the west coast is potentially treacherous. Locals almost always tell visitors that the water is "safe" for swimming, but treat this advice skeptically. Hard-to-see rocks lie scattered just below the surf and most beaches have steep slopes and a strong undertow. Be prepared for the worst and never swim alone. Some beaches are more protected than others, so it's wise to ask for advice concerning which beaches are *safer* than others.

Unless you want to look suspicious snooping around Indonesia's military compounds, head for the two beaches which Lhok Nga has to offer to land-weary folk. The **golf course beach,** 300m from the homestays, is accessible by walking to the end of the road, and climbing over a small wall to the beach. Although the strip of sand appears to be the property of the golf course, Darlian assures that it is open to the public. **Pantai Cemara** feels a bit less private, yet pleasantly quiet during the week. (Rp1000 fee on weekends.) The waves can get quite high, making the swimming potentially dangerous, but the surfing is excellent.

■ Calang

The white-sand beaches of the west coast continue around this town and some are in sheltered bays, offering some protection from the evils of the Indian Ocean.

ORIENTATION AND PRACTICAL INFORMATION

One **main street** runs from the **Banda Aceh-Meulaboh road** west 400m to the center of town. **Minibuses** leave from the center of town for **Banda Aceh** (every hr., 8am-midnight, 3½hr., Rp6000) and **Tapaktuan** (every hr., 8am-1am, 7hr., Rp8000) via **Meulaboh** (2hr., Rp3000). Bigger **buses,** which are Rp1000 cheaper than minibuses, can be flagged down on the main road (noon-1am to Tapaktuan, 2pm-1am to Banda Aceh). The **police station** (tel. 211 10) is on the right side of the main street 400m from the highway. Heading up the street on the left side of the police station and taking a left 40m later leads to a small **polyclinic,** 30m down this street on the left (open Mon.-Sat. 9am-2pm). For emergencies, locals can lead you to the doctor's house. The **pharmacy** is on Jl. Kejematan, off the main street about 300m from the highway (open daily 8am-9pm). The **post office** (tel. 210 02) stands to the right of the police station (open Mon.-Thurs. 8am-2pm). **Postal code:** 21002. The **24-hour Telkom office** (tel. 210 10) is a 2-km trek, on the right side of the road to Meulaboh. **Telephone code:** 0654.

ACCOMMODATIONS AND FOOD

There is only one *losmen* in town, but it's fine and very friendly. **Penginapan Sari Jaya** (tel. 210 49), at the end of the main street across from the post office, has simple doubles with shared *mandi* for Rp6000. Several *warung* and cheap restaurants serving up local fish specialties line the main street. The *ikan tonkol* (fresh tuna) is prepared in several delicious fashions (Rp500-1500). **Rumah Makan Bahari** (tel. 210 55) serves up excellent local fish dishes as well (open daily 8am-9pm).

Bungalow-style treehouses are the norm at **Camp Europa,** 15km north of Calang. Guests enjoy the marvelous beach and accommodations, all of which include four meals a day of good Indonesian/German food. Prices range from Rp17-30,000 per person (including meals) for the treehouse and bungalow-style rooms. Minibuses and *labi-labi* heading north from Calang drop passengers at the Camp Europa sign on the main road; the camp itself is a 500-m hike in from the sign.

Another 2km north up the road is the spectacular **Lhok Gelumpang** peninsula, home of the fantastic **Pondok Gelumpang Raya Kampung Kuala Jubet Bungalows.** From the highway, walk 700m from the entrance to Lhok Gelumpang and take a right after the bridge. The bungalows are 50m ahead. Perhaps the finest digs in all of Sumatra, the bungalows are constructed of bamboo stalks and thatch with artistic detail (doubles Rp25,000). There's no restaurant yet, although one is scheduled to open soon. For now, head to the small town of **Lageun,** 2km north on the main road, for Indonesian food. The manager often drives guests to town at no charge.

SIGHTS

Lhok Gelumpang is the home of a protected beach in a horseshoe-shaped bay just in front of the bungalows. Minibuses run from town (Rp1000) to this isolated cove. There's no charge for public use during the week, although a Rp1500 beach fee applies on weekends. Calang town is close to a nice beach running 200m between two buttresses of sharp black rocks which the waves crash over. The beach is a 1-km walk north (take a right) from the back of the soccer field behind the post office.

■ Meulaboh

As the administrative center of West Aceh Province, Meulaboh is little more than that. It's a dusty, lackluster market town, serving as a base for jaunts to nearby beaches or the ferry to Pulau Simeuleu. Touts often accost travelers in the bus terminal, vendors hawk along the streets, and locals may eye foreigners with suspicion.

ORIENTATION AND PRACTICAL INFORMATION

Lying 245km south of Banda Aceh, Meulaboh is at the edge of a coastal plain which boasts numerous rice paddies and coconut trees. The main street in town, 700m-long **Jalan Teuku Umar,** runs between a monument dedicated to Teuku Umar, and a monument which looks like a large bullet at the junction of the Banda Aceh-Tapaktuan road. **Jalan Nasional,** the main highway, starts where the street turns at the bullet. Most official government services are on **Jalan Merdeka,** which runs right from the Teuku Umar monument.

The **bus terminal** is 100m down Jl. Singgah Mata, left off Jl. Nasional 100m from the bullet. Buses and minibuses leave from here to **Banda Aceh** (every hr., 8am-8pm, 5½hr., Rp8-12,000) via **Calang** (2hr., Rp3000) and **Tapaktuan** (every hr., 8am-8pm, 5hr., Rp7-8000). **SMAC,** Jl. Teuku Umar 21 (tel. 211 47), flies to **Sinabang,** Pulau Simeuleu (Rp92,000), and **Medan** (Rp134,500) every Tuesday, Thursday, and Sunday at 9am. Flights leave from **Cut Nyak Dhien Airport,** 21km south of town. The airplane fare includes the taxi, which picks up passengers from their hotels at 7am. Reconfirm flights one to two days in advance with the SMAC office (open Mon. 9am-noon and 2-3:30pm, Tues.-Thurs. and Sat. 10am-noon and 2-3:30pm). **Ferries** depart from Ujung Karang Harbor, 4km from town (Rp1000 by *becak*), to **Sinabang** (6pm, Mon., Wed., Fri., 13hr., Rp9500); purchase tickets two hours prior to departure. Currency exchange is available at poor rates at **BRI,** on the corner of Jl. Merdeka and Jl. T. Chik Ditiro across from the post office. It accepts U.S. dollars in cash and traveler's checks as well (open Mon.-Thurs. 8am-4pm, Fri. 8am-noon and 2-4pm). **Apotik Melati** is 200m down from the bullet (open 24hr.). The **Cut Nyak Dhien Hospital** on Jl. Gajamada (tel. 21118), 1km from town left off the road to Tapaktuan, has an emergency room (open 24hr.). The **police station,** Jl. Nasional 10 (tel. 210 96), is 50m past the pharmacy. The **post office,** Jl. T. Chik Ditiro 2 (tel. 211 64), stands 200m up Jl. Merdeka on the left (open Mon.-Thurs. and Sat. 8am-5pm). **Postal code:** 23612. The **24-hour Telkom office,** Jl. Merdeka 59 (tel. 216 66), stands in the shadows of the red and white communications tower which dominates town. The handy **Wartel Aneka Usahajasa,** Jl. Singgah Mata 142 (tel. 221 00), is next to the bus terminal (open 24hr.). **Telephone code:** 0655.

ACCOMMODATIONS AND FOOD

Accommodations of varying quality and price abound and cluster in the area of the two monuments. **Losmen Mestika,** Jl. Nasional 78 (tel. 210 33), next to the police station, is a nice whitewashed building surrounding a colorful garden. A restaurant serves up local food (Rp2000 for a hearty breakfast with tea). Clean, small doubles cost Rp7500, more spacious ones with fan and private *mandi* Rp15,000. Deluxe rooms include A/C and TV for Rp35,000. **Hotel Mutiara,** Jl. Teuku Umar 157 (tel. 215 31), about 30m from the bullet, offers a wide array of clean rooms, set back from the busy street. The restaurant serves up basic rice and noodle dishes for Rp1-2000. Singles, doubles, and triples with fan and inside toilet are Rp7500, Rp12,500, and Rp15,000 respectively. The rooms are a bit close to the blaring TV. It's more peaceful in the back, although the wood-constructed rooms are older, smaller, and share a *mandi.* Singles go for Rp3500, doubles Rp5000, and triples Rp6000. Luxurious rooms with toilet, A/C, and TV are Rp25-40,000.

There are several decent restaurants in town to try. **Rumah Makan Singgalang,** Jl. Teuku Umar 232 (tel. 231 14), serves up excellent local fish specialties, including fish in chili sauce for Rp750 (open daily 8am-10pm). Head over to **Rumah Makan Minang Elok,** Jl. Merdeka 28 (tel. 211 51), for local seafood cooked up the Minangkabau way, such as *ikan tonkol chabe* (chilied tuna, Rp500), *pejek udang* (fried shrimp cakes, Rp500), and *hati ayam,* a mushroom/mussel/chicken specialty. The hot and crowded market, **Pasar Bina Usaha,** 100m down Jl. Nasional, offers local fruits and typical market fare (open daily 6am-6pm).

SIGHTS

Catch your fill of sublime beaches here, as they are much nicer than those farther south. **Pantai Kuala Tua** is 2km north of town (Rp700 by *becak*), a bit close to the highway, but long and tranquil nevertheless. Another lovely beach can be found at **Ujung Karang Harbor,** as well as the **Karang Sutra Restaurant,** which serves some tasty food. **Pantai Lhok Bubon** lies in scenic seclusion, about 17km north of town (Rp1000 by *labi-labi,* 7am-6pm).

■ Tapaktuan

The rice fields of the coastal plain end at this laid-back town, where steep green mountains meet the crashing of the sea. The atmosphere is one of the friendliest in all of Sumatra: smartly dressed school children wave cheerfully to wayward travelers and local men battle out intense games of dominoes over dark coffee in the afternoons. Meanwhile, waterfalls and caves offer fascinating forays into the surrounding mountains for travelers.

ORIENTATION AND PRACTICAL INFORMATION

The road from Banda Aceh, known as **Jalan Sudirman,** winds through town. The **bus terminal** and **market** are off Jl. Sudirman at the base of a steep hill. **Jalan A. Yani** bears to the right at the first monument coming from Banda Aceh. **Jalan Merdeka,** the main street in town, starts where Jl. A. Yani hits the sea and heads 300m back to the second monument on Jl. Sudirman. **Indonesian Guides Association (HPI),** at the Flamboyant Juice and Coffee Bar, Jl. Merdeka 237, has superb **tourist information** and maps for the Tapaktuan and Pulau Banyak areas (open daily 8am-1am). U.S. dollars can be exchanged at poor rates at **BRI,** Jl. Nyak Adam Kamil 42 (tel. 210 38), left off Jl. Sudirman between the two monuments (open Mon.-Thurs. 8am-3pm, Fri. 8-11:30am, Sat. 8am-1pm).

Minibuses head for **Subulussalam** (6:30am-6pm, 4hr., Rp6000) with connections there for **Singkil** (7am-10pm, 4hr., Rp6000) and **Sidikalang** (7am-6pm, 2hr., Rp3500). Buses in Sidikalang head to **Panguraran,** Lake Toba (every hr., 7am-3pm, 2hr., Rp400) and **Brastagi** (7am-6pm, 3hr., Rp4000). **Night buses** also make the trip to **Medan** (5-8pm, 12hr., Rp13,000), following the Subulussalam-Sidikalang-Brastagi route for cheaper fares than the minibuses. There are also buses to **Banda Aceh** (7am-8pm, 12hr., Rp18,000) via **Meulaboh** (5hr., Rp7000) and **Calang** (7hr., Rp10,000). The **police station** (tel. 213 13) and **24-hour hospital** (tel. 210 13) face each other on Jl. Sudirman across the bridge from the second monument and the intersection of Jl. Merdeka. The **post office** (tel. 210 18) is another 100m down Jl. Sudirman on the left (open Mon.-Thurs. 8am-3pm, Fri. 8-11:30am, Sat. 8am-1pm). **Postal code:** 23711. The **24-hour Telkom office** (tel. 211 08) lies 1km past the post office on the left. **Telephone code:** 0656.

ACCOMMODATIONS AND FOOD

A bunch of *losmen* and hotels cluster around Jl. Merdeka and behind Jl. Sudirman. **Losmen Jambu,** Jl. A. Yani 77 (tel. 213 65), is 150m from the first monument. Attas Tanjung, the manager, can help make stays in town a pure delight; he advises on sights and helps out with transportation arrangements. Rooms are pleasantly removed from the hubbub and come with mosquito coils. Doubles cost Rp6500, with fan Rp10,500, with *mandi* Rp15,000. Triples with fan go for Rp12,500, with *mandi* Rp17,500. **Losmen Kanada,** Jl. Merdeka 52 (tel. 212 09), has a balcony which is actually over the water. Spartan doubles with rickety wood construction are Rp5000.

With very few restaurants in town, most visitors head to the **pier** in front of Losmen Bukit Barisan on Jl. Merdeka instead to mingle with locals and enjoy cheap but good standard fare in the cool of the setting sun (open daily 8-11pm). For Acehnese specialties, travelers can try **Rumah Makan Kiah,** Jl A. Yani 75, next to Losmen Jambu,

INDONESIA

which serves an excellent buffalo meat stew (Rp1500), as well as a plethora of fish dishes (open daily 7am-9pm). **Rumah Makan Family,** Jl. Merdeka 84 (tel. 213 10), offers up good fried shrimp and tuna (open daily 6am-9:30pm).

SIGHTS

A journey into the mountains to explore foaming waterfalls and Delphian caves is a welcome alternative to the not-so-spectacular beaches in the area. The falls of **Tingkat Tujuh,** 7km south of town, crash seven levels into clear pools, which provide satisfying swimming opportunities cloaked in jungled canopy. *Bemo* shuttle from town to the village of Patuk Itam (7am-4pm, Rp200), where locals can point to the trail leading to the waterfall. The paved road narrows to a cart path after 200m and then down to a trail, which heads another 500m up to the falls (admission Rp500 on weekends). The **Air Dingin** waterfall, 17km north of town (Rp500 by *bemo*), also offers warm waters for macerating below the 20m-high cascades. Those who miss the sand can relax at the beach across the road; the traffic, however, is quite bothersome. A quieter beach is **Pantai Tui lhok,** 1km north of Air Dingin, which also boasts a waterfall, though smaller. **Lapangan Terbang Cut Ali Beach,** 17km south of town next to the little-used airstrip, is a beautiful secluded black sand beach with small waves. Minibuses (Rp1000) drop passengers off at the airport road and the beach is 1km down on the other side of the airstrip.

Only a few km upstream from town, a 50m-long stream-carved tunnel-cave, known as **Goa Kalam,** awaits serious investigation; a good light and guide are recommended for the trip. Jungle trekking daytrips can be organized around **Panton Luas,** 15km from town, and in the **Sikabu** area, 20km north of town. Treks into the coastal tongue of **Gunung Leuser National Park** run out of **Bakongan,** 60km south of town at the base of the Kluet River Valley. Tourist information provided by Flamboyant Coffee Shop lists guide services (Rp20,000 per day) for the area.

■ Pulau Banyak

Sumatra's newest island paradise dishes out heaps of tropical specialties to those travelers venturesome enough to endure the tortuous road and boat travel to these less-trafficked isles. Legend maintains that the 99 islands were formerly one that was broken apart by the slap of a dragon's tail. Only three are inhabited, leaving plenty of room for exploration up jungle rivers or seldom-seen coral reefs.

GETTING THERE AND AWAY

The islands are theoretically accessible by boat from **Singkil, Teluk Jamin** (75km south of Tapaktuan), **Sibolga,** and **Gunung Sitoli** on Nias Island. The only regular service, however, is from Singkil, and the best bet to avoid long unplanned stays on the mainland is to head here. Regardless, boat travel still depends on the tides, weather, and demand. To reach Singkil from **Medan** take a bus from Pinang Baris terminal to **Subulussalam** (6hr., Rp6000) via Brastagi and Sidikalang, and then change to a minibus bound for Singkil (4hr., Rp6000). Direct minibuses from Medan usually depart around 10am (Rp15,000) from the Singkil Raya Restaurant, Jl. Bintang 81 (tel. 321 074), near the bird market. From **Tapaktuan** minibuses run to Subulussalam (6:30am-6pm, 4hr., Rp6000), where they change for Singkil. From **Pangururan,** Lake Toba, take a bus to Sidikalang (8am-3pm, 2hr., Rp4000) and change to a minibus to Subulussalam (7am-6pm, 2hr., Rp3500). From Singkil boats to **Balai Village** on Banyak leave at 8am and sometimes at 5pm (3-5hr., Rp5500). Boats also depart from Teluk Jamin to Balai in the morning (2 per wk., 6-8hr., Rp10,000). For exact departure times, contact the **Indonesian Guides Association** at the Flamboyant Coffee Shop in Tapaktuan, or ask for Pak Ambrin in Teluk Jamin. Boats depart from **Sibolga** (2 per wk., 10-14hr., Rp15,000) and **Gunung Sitoli** (1 per week, usually midweek, 8hr.). Boats return to the same locales on roughly the same schedule. Without phones on this island, departure information is a bit sketchy and you may find yourself staying the night in Balai.

Transportation to the accommodations, which mainly lie on the other islands, is arranged from Balai and the cost depends on the length of the journey (30min. to Pulau Ujung Batu, Rp2000; 1½hr. to Pulau Palambak Besar, Rp5000).

ACCOMMODATIONS AND FOOD

Most accommodations on the islands are bungalow-style and many have no electricity. Four islands currently have bungalows, and two islands have *losmen* in the villages. It is worthwhile to be aware of current food and lodging prices before committing to one establishment. The **Nanda Restaurant,** at the boat landing in Balai, has updated information on all available accommodations. **Pulau Palambak Besar** hosts **The Point, Bina Jaya,** and **Pondok Asmara Palambak (PAP)**. Singles go for Rp4-6000, doubles are Rp6-7500, and three meals per day cost Rp6000 at The Point and Bina Jaya. **Pulau Ujung Batu** has the **Jambu Kolong Cottages, Pulau Panjang** has the **Jasa Baru Cottages,** and **Pulau Rangit Besar** has **Coco's.** *Losmen* on Balai include **Daer's Retreat** and **Lei Kombih.** Inquire for **Lukman** at the Puskesmas (health center) for lodging and trekking to **Haloban Village** on **Pulau Tuangku.** During bad weather, food choices may be grim, as supply boats can't reach the islands.

SIGHTS

Powdery white sand beaches beckon sun-lovers, while offshore coral promises rewarding excursions for many a traveler. Most bungalows rent **snorkels** and masks for Rp2000 per day. **Scuba diving** is possible out of **The Point** on Pulau Palambak Besar (for beginners first dive US$25, second dive US$20). Most accommodations offer free **canoes** for paddling, but be aware during long crossings that swimming is the only option if the boat sinks. The islands are perhaps best known for the **green-and-leather-back turtles** on Pulau Bangkaru, whose numbers have dropped precariously low due to egg poaching. The Turtle Foundation lobbied to successfully establish Bangkaru as a national park, and visits to the island to see the turtles are only arranged once per week to let those endangered creatures have their peace. Three-day trips depart on Saturdays. The entire trip is Rp100,000 (profits go to the Turtle Fund), and includes transport, guide, food, water, and sleeping arrangements in a local hut. The foundation is based in Balai Village and trips should be booked from there. While private boats are not allowed to visit Bangkaru, they can go practically anywhere else, including exploring the jungle, snorkeling, or staying in one of the fishing villages on the larger islands.

DANAU TOBA (LAKE TOBA)

Few changes are as dramatic as those which take place during the 180km drive south from Medan to Danau Toba. Gone is the muggy, oppressive heat of the Sumatran coastal plain, replaced by cool, invigorating air. The shift from pancake-flat rubber and palm oil plantations to soaring volcanic cliffs is just as swift, and startling enough for first-time visitors to question whether they are on the same island.

Southeast Asia's largest body of fresh water, Danau Toba is widely regarded as one of the region's most beautiful and unique areas. The steep, craggy slopes that ring Toba form the rim of an ancient volcano, whose cataclysmic eruption some 75,000 years ago created the lake and may have even triggered the last Ice Age. In addition to being the largest crater lake in the world, the 590-m Danau Toba is also one of the deepest. In good weather, the water gleams a deep blue, contrasting brilliantly with the evergreen forests which line the shore. When the skies are overcast and clouds spill over the surrounding cliffs, Danau Toba's beauty becomes almost surreal.

Unseen by western eyes until the 1850s, Lake Toba was then, as it is now, the home of the Toba Batak, largest of the five principal Batak groups who inhabit the interior of North Sumatra. The Toba Bataks are considerably less friendly than their other Sumatran neighbors. Many locals depend on tourism for their livelihood, but business with tourists seems more like a necessity to them than a choice. In the face of tourism and development, the Toba Bataks have stubbornly clung to traditional ways of life. The towering, crescent-moon-shaped roofs of brightly painted *rumah adat* (customary houses) are frequent sights in many lakeside villages, still governed by traditional laws. For travelers, Danau Toba offers something for everybody and every energy level—from swimming, trekking, or biking to simply lounging about with a gratifying book, and wallowing in the natural splendor.

■ Prapat

Nestled at the foot of a series of high, rolling hills on the eastern shore of Danau Toba opposite Pulau Samosir, Prapat enjoys the sort of picture-book location tourism developers salivate over…which is precisely why the village is now experiencing a prolonged frenzy of hotel construction. These days finding a square meter of undeveloped land is difficult. Even the picturesque hills that rise in the middle of town, once topped only by quaint Batak churches, are now encrusted with boxy concrete hotels and hokey *faux*-Batak bungalows.

Visit Prapat on a weekday, when 90% of the rooms are empty, and you'll wonder how anyone, even rapacious tourism promoters, could justify such an orgy of construction. On weekends and holidays, caravans of buses from Medan roll into town, unleashing hundreds of weary urbanites escaping the insolubilities of their home city. Most backpackers feel uncomfortable in Prapat and her grossly overpriced hotel rooms, and stay in town only long enough to leap on a ferry bound for Samosir. A night in Prapat still beats one in Medan, however, and the excesses of tourism have not yet managed to eliminate the spectacular natural setting.

ORIENTATION

Jalan Sisingamangaraja is the main road, swinging roughly west-to-east through town, passing the **police, wartel,** and **post office,** as well as the **bus terminal** before heading toward Bukittinggi. **Jalan Kol. TPR Sinagara** (formerly Jl. Pulau Samosir) branches off Jl. Sisingamangaraja at a large Welcome Gate along the lake, follows the shore before crossing a small ridge, becoming **Jalan Haranggaol** at the Natour Prapat Hotel, and leading downhill to the Samosir **Tiga Raja Pier.** Countless souvenir stalls are along Jl. Haranggaol near the ferry launch.

PRACTICAL INFORMATION

Tourist Offices: Jl. Kol. TPR Sinagara 1 (tel. 411 11), beneath the Welcome Gate. Will likely direct transportation inquiries to a travel agency. Supposedly open daily 8am-9pm, but so few tourists come here that it's not always staffed.

Tours and Travel: As there have been some reports of ripped-off tourists, the safest bet is to buy services from established travel companies. **Andilo Nancy Travel Service,** the largest, has 3 offices: the bus terminal (tel. 412 76; open daily 8am-10pm); Jl. Sisingamangaraja 76 (tel. 414 33; open daily 8am-10pm); and Tiga Raja Pier (tel. 415 34; open daily 6am-6pm).

Currency Exchange: Rates in Prapat are poor, so plan ahead. **Sejahtera Bank Umum (Bank SBU),** Jl. Kol. TPR Sinagara 8 (tel. 417 03), on the grounds of the Toba Hotel. Exchanges cash and traveler's checks for most major currencies. Open Mon.-Fri. 8am-4pm. Several **money changers** also line Jl. Haranggaol.

Buses: Purchase tickets at the terminal or through a travel agency for the safest, most comfortable alternative. Book in advance, particularly for distant locales. Public buses and most private coaches leave from the terminal on Jl. Sisingamangaraja, 1km east of the police station. The following approximate fares are for non-A/C public buses. To: **Medan** (every hr., 5am-2pm, 4hr., Rp4000); **Bukittinggi** (noon, 20hr., Rp23,000; A/C noon, 2, and 4:30pm, Rp30,000); **Sibolga** (every hr., 10am-noon, 5hr., Rp9000); **Padang** (1pm, 22hr., Rp25,000; A/C noon, Rp32,000); and **Jakarta** (noon and 2pm, 48hr., Rp62,000; A/C noon and 2pm, Rp95,000). To **Brastagi,** take a bus to **Pemangtangsiantar/Siantar** (every hr., 1hr., Rp2000), switch to **Kabanjahe** (every 1½hr., 3hr., Rp2000, last bus 5pm), and go the rest of the way by *sudako* (Rp300). Tourist buses depart to **Bukittinggi** (6am, 15hr., Rp27,000) and **Bukit Lawang** (7am, 10hr., Rp25,000) via **Brastagi** (5hr., Rp15,000). Book tickets for tourist buses at travel agencies.

Ferries: Passenger ferries to **Pulau Samosir** leave from Tiga Raja Pier. Separate boats go to Tomok, Tuk-Tuk, and Ambarita on the eastern shore, dropping passengers off at the accommodation of their choice. To: **Tuk-Tuk** (every hr., 9:30am-7:30pm, 40min., Rp1000); **Tomok** (every hr., 9:30am-7pm, 40min., Rp1000); and **Ambarita** (every hr., 9:30am-5:30pm, 40min., Rp1000). A rusting car ferry shuttles back and forth between Ajibata Pier (south of Tiga Raja) and Tomok, following roughly the same timetable.

Local Transportation: Spiffy *oplet* follow Prapat's maze of winding streets counterclockwise, usually from Tiga Raja Pier to the bus terminal, down Jl. Sisingamangaraja and then down Jl. Sinagara/Haranggaol back to Tiga Raja (Rp300).

Markets: There is a **Batak market** every Tues. and Thurs. at Tiga Raja Pier (6am-1pm), and a **larger market** on Sat. (6am-6pm). Come early for the best deals.

Medical Services: Prapat Public Hospital (tel. 413 32), on Jl. Rumah Sakit, about 800m past the bus terminal off Jl. Sisingamangaraja.

Police: (tel. 415 71), on Jl. Sisingamangaraja next to the large Welcome Gate.

Post Offices: Jl. Sisingamangaraja 75 (tel. 414 88). Open Mon.-Thurs. 8am-3pm, Fri. 8am-noon, Sat. 8am-1pm. **Postal code:** 21174.

Telephones: Telkom office, Jl. Josep Sinaga 28 (tel. 411 08). From Tiga Raja Pier, most *oplet* follow Jl. Josep Sinaga uphill toward the bus terminal. The office is next to the communications towers. **HCD** phone. Open 24hr. **Wartel RTO,** Jl. Sisingamangaraja 72 (tel. 411 58). Collect call service, must pay for 1st min. Open daily 7am-midnight. **Telephone code:** 0625.

ACCOMMODATIONS

Despite the number of hotels in tiny Prapat, there are surprisingly few decent budget accommodations. The glut of pricier hotels, however, means that during mid-week, it may be possible to extract bargains. Cheaper hotels and *losmen* cluster along Jl. Haranggaol and the lower portion of Jl. Sisingamangaraja.

Pago Pago Inn, Jl. Haranggaol 50 (tel. 413 13). From the Natour Hotel, about halfway (100m) down Haranggaol, toward the pier, on the right. Laid-back atmosphere and well-kept rooms. Pleasant, hardwood-floor rooms upstairs, with a lounge and a balcony overlooking the lake and Samosir. Nice shared *mandi*. Singles Rp7000. Doubles Rp10,000. Triples Rp12,000.

Singgalang Hotel, Jl. Sisingamangaraja 52 (tel. 412 60), 50m past the police station. Conveniently located near the bus terminal and inexpensive restaurants, but a bit removed from the tourist strip at Tiga Raja. Large and slightly worn, but very clean rooms, each with 3 or 4 beds. Rates increase with the number of bodies—Rp7500 for 1, Rp15,000 for 2, Rp25,000 for 3, Rp30,000 for 4. English spoken. Squeaky clean shared *mandi*. Popular Chinese restaurant downstairs.

Wisma Purnama, Jl. Haranggaol 85 (tel. 416 63), 50m up from Tiga Raja Pier. A basic Sumatran *losmen*, with solid wood construction, although the whole place is a bit dark. Communal *mandi* are sparkling clean. Owners don't speak much English, but are eager to please. Doubles Rp7000.

FOOD

A number of restaurants line Jl. Sisingamangaraja, including a cluster of overpriced Chinese spots near the water; prices drop farther uphill, where cheap *padang* dives abound. A **small fruit market** sets up daily near Tiga Raja Pier.

Rumah Makan Yose, on Jl. Haranggaol, adjacent to the Pago Pago Inn. A wide range of curries and *soto* (soups). Delicious veggie curry and rice costs less than a cup of coffee in the Big Apple. For the more extravagant, there's shrimp in chili paste or fried lake fish. Most dishes Rp1-3000. No English menu, so learn the names of a few dishes or let your fingers do the talking. Open daily 9am-9pm.

Hong Kong Restaurant, Jl. Haranggaol 9/11 (tel. 418 95), near the crest of the hill opposite a string of souvenir stalls. Popular with travelers, but more expensive than smaller *padang* shops (Rp3500-6500). *Gado-gado* rivaling the Kansil family secret recipe (Rp3000). Spicy prawns Rp6500. Open daily 9am-10pm.

Hidangan Khas Minang, Jl. Sisingamangaraja 108 (tel. 414 61), about 100m past the Singgalang Hotel on the right. One of a gaggle of cheap *padang* joints on Jl. Sisingamangaraja. The cleanliness and English menu set it apart from the crowd. All your *padang* favorites, including chicken curry soup (Rp3000), *rendang* (Rp2500), octopus chili (Rp2500), and *nasi goreng* (Rp1750). Fried fish straight from Lake Toba (Rp3500). Open daily 6am-midnight.

■ Pulau Samosir

Samosir Island is, in fact, not really an island at all but a large mushroom-shaped peninsula jutting into Danau Toba; it officially became an "island" when the Dutch dug a canal across the peninsula's narrow neck at the town of Pangururan. Whatever its geographical circumstance, Samosir is an inevitable stop on most traveler's itineraries. There can be no denying the island's physical beauty, particularly along the eastern shore. On Sundays, Batak hymns drift over the rolling fields, adding an almost ethereal soundtrack to the natural beauty of the setting.

Sadly, Samosir is no longer the little-known backpacker's retreat of 10 years ago. Tuk-Tuk peninsula has grown thick with guest houses, souvenir stalls, and restaurants. Furthermore, many locals, even those who make their livings off the tourist trade, have grown tired of the hordes of foreign visitors and make little effort to conceal their dislike. Nevertheless, Samosir remains an ideal spot for a respite from the grind of travel in rural Sumatra. Take advantage of the unparalleled swimming, trek through the unspoiled hinterland, or simply swap traveler's tales with your comrades-in-Tevas over cool banana *lassi* in one of the lakeside cafés.

ORIENTATION

Roughly 40km long and 20km wide, Samosir covers approximately 650sq. km. The largest town on the island is **Pangururan,** the seat of local government, on the western shore. A single **perimeter road** circles the northern half of the oval-shaped island, connecting Pangururan with **Tomok** on the eastern shore. At the northern tip of the island is the pleasant village of **Simanindo.** Most visitors stay on the **Tuk-Tuk Peninsula** about 4km north of Tomok. The **Tuk-Tuk Ring Road** branches off the main road to the right about 3km north of Tomok at a small benzine station. After 2km, at the southern neck of the peninsula, the short-cut to the small village of **Ambarita** branches off to the left, and guest houses start to proliferate on the right. The narrow strip of pavement, scarcely wider than a broad sidewalk, follows Tuk-Tuk's gold coast of guest houses and *warung* for about 2km, joining the short-cut at the northern neck and continuing along the shore to **Ambarita,** 3km up the coast. About 8km inland from Ambarita is the tiny hamlet of **Partokoan,** a popular stopover point for hikers on the Ambarita-Pangururan traverse.

PRACTICAL INFORMATION

Tourist Offices: There's no official tourist office on Samosir but a number of restaurants in Tomok and Tuk-Tuk bill themselves as tourist information centers. But you'll probably get better info and advice from your guest house.

Tours and Travel: A few tiny travel agencies in Tuk-Tuk sell tourist bus tickets, ferry tickets from Medan to Penang, and even airline tickets. Most guest houses also sell tourist bus tickets. Beware of frauds; make your travel plans at a reputable travel agency in Prapat. **DWI Lucky Tour Service,** on Tuk-Tuk, near the Carolina Cottages Resort, is in the process of becoming a full-fledged travel agency. Sells tickets for the tourist coach to Bukittinggi, Brastagi, and Bukit Lawang. Open daily 7am-7pm.

Currency Exchange: Most guest houses provide exchange services at abysmal rates. Change your money in Medan.

Buses: Pangururan has the only bus terminal on Samosir. To: **Medan** (4 per day, 8am-3pm, 6hr., Rp6000) via **Brastagi** (3½hr., Rp4500); **Medan** via **Prapat**, crossing at **Tomok** (8 and 11am, 6hr., Rp6000); **Tarutung** (8am, 3hr., Rp4500) for **Bukittinggi** (15hr.) and **Sibolga** (2hr., Rp2500); and **Sidikalang** (8am-3pm, 2hr., Rp4000) for **Tapaktuan** (6hr., Rp9500) and **Singkil** (6hr., Rp8500), both via **Subulussalam** (2hr., Rp2500).

Ferries: To **Prapat** (7am-4pm, Rp1000) from Tomok's public landing. Ferries to **Tuk-Tuk** (every hr., 7am-4pm, Rp1000) and **Ambarita** (every hr., 7am-3pm, Rp1000) leave from along the shoreline, passing the guest houses en route; wave from your pier to flag one down. From Tomok to **Ajibata** car ferry (every 3hr., 7am-7pm). From Simanindo to **Tigaras,** north of Prapat (every hr.). From Pangururan to: **Haranggaol** (Mon.-Tues., 7-8am, 3½hr., Rp4000); **Balige** (Tues., 1pm, 3½hr., Rp4000); **Ambarita** (Sat., 8am, return 6pm, 3½hr., Rp4000); and **Simanindo** (Sat., 8am, return 6pm, Rp4000).

Local Transportation: Buses shuttle between **Pangururan** and **Tomok** (every hr., 5am-5pm, Rp2000), tracing the north shore. To **Simanindo** (Rp1500).

Rentals: **DWI Lucky Tour Service,** Tuk-Tuk. Bikes (Rp6000), motorscooters (Rp20,000), motorcycles (Rp25,000), and minibuses (Rp125,000). Most guest houses rent bikes/motorbikes for about the same rates.

Medical Services: A small **health center** in Tuk-Tuk near the Mafir Guest House with a live-in doctor who speaks English. A slightly larger **clinic** in Ambarita, 200m beyond the bank. In an emergency, return to Prapat or Medan.

Police: Main station, opposite a football field on the road to Tuk-Tuk. Open 24hr. **Police post** on Tuk-Tuk near the Carolina Cottages. Open Mon.-Sat. 8am-2pm.

Post Offices: Ambarita, Jl. Raya 39 (the main road). Open Mon.-Thurs. 7:30am-3pm, Fri. 8-11:30am, Sat. 8am-2pm. **Postal code:** 22395.

Telephones: Overseas collect and calling card calls can be made from most guest houses on Tuk-Tuk and in Ambarita (Rp6000 per call). **Telephone code for Ambarita, Tuk-Tuk, Tomok, and Simanindo:** 0625. New **Telkom office** (tel. 201 08) in Pangururan, on Jl. Dr. Fl. Tobing, on the west side of the island, 800m past the intersection with Jl. Sisingamangaraja. Collect calls and domestic direct dial services only. Open 24hr. **Telephone code for Pangururan:** 0626.

ACCOMMODATIONS

As the premier tourist destination in North Sumatra, there is no shortage of cheap guest houses in Tuk-Tuk and Ambarita, and, as a result, the services are among the best. These days guest houses crowd the shore all the way to Ambarita and beyond. The density decreases away from Tuk-Tuk and it's possible to feel a bit more isolated. Most accommodations offer bike and motorcycle rental, and food. With the exception of the best-known guest houses, there are no fixed room rates; prices depend on the proprieter's whim and your bargaining acumen.

Tuk-Tuk

Bagus Bay Stayhouse (tel. 414 81), on the south neck, just after the Ambarita shortcut road at the beginning of the string of guest houses. A large, popular guest house, run by a Batak and his Australian wife, on a placid inlet great for swimming; guests are free to use the canoes and windsurfer. Simple, if impersonal, singles and doubles Rp5000, with *mandi* Rp10,000. Bungalows in split-level Batak-style cottages with private bath Rp10,000. Indonesian and western food at the central lodge. Batak music every Wed. and Sat. night.

Samosir Cottages (tel. 410 50), on the northeast shore of the peninsula, 50m off the perimeter road. Freshly scrubbed rooms boast fabulous views, privacy, and tranquility. Simple motel-style rooms with picture windows, terraces, and private baths: Rp8000 for 1, Rp10,000 for 2. Larger doubles with hot shower Rp15,000. Typical *faux*-Batak bungalows by the water Rp10,000. If you catch a big fish in the pond, the kitchen will cook it up the Batak way (Rp3000). Satellite TV and VCR. Cross-island treks and rafting expeditions.

Reggae Guest House, on the extreme north tip of the peninsula before it begins to narrow again. Pleasant all-wood rooms would have Bob wailin'; all rooms have private bath but travelers can take a morning dip in the clear water 1m away. Singles Rp3000. Doubles or Batak-style bungalows for two Rp5000. The open-sided Nelson Vugo Restaurant is a great spot for sunset gazing.

Ambarita

Timbul Bungalows (tel. 413 74), about 500m south of town off the road to Tuk-Tuk. Built on a mini-peninsula with lake views in 3 directions, it's as isolated as Ambarita gets these days. Most rooms are individual cottages which afford privacy and superb views. Basic bungalows Rp5000. Larger rooms with flush toilet and shower Rp8-12,000. Batak houses built on hills take first place for view and privacy (Rp6000). International collect call service from restaurant.

Barbara's Guest House (tel. 412 30), about 3km north of Ambarita village on the road to Simanindo; the Ambarita ferry stops here. On the grassy, windswept coast with stunning views of the lake and the Samosir highlands. Jovial staff and an array of services, including overseas collect calls. Excellent swimming spot. Dorms Rp2000. Rooms for 1 Rp5000, for 2 Rp7500. Spacious doubles with private bath (flsuh toilet, shower) Rp10,000 (for 1 person Rp7500), with hot water and springy mattress Rp15,000. Satellite TV.

FOOD

Most travelers eat at their guest houses, whose kitchens offer a wide range of food. There are throngs of *warung* and small restaurants in Tomok and Tuk-Tuk, many proudly offering Magic Mushroom Omelettes. Be aware that visitors have reported getting sick from these hallucinogens.

Tabo Vegetarian Restaurant and Bakery, Tuk-Tuk, on the south neck of the peninsula, 70m east of Bagus Bay. Run by a German-Indonesian couple, Tabo offers a funky atmosphere and great vegetarian food. Guests sit in swanky wicker chairs at tables hewn from tree trunks or on cushions at low tables. Sandwiches made with freshly baked bread. Tofu, tempeh, and veggie burgers Rp3000. Most dishes Rp2-3500. Open daily 8am-11pm.

No Name Pizzeria and Bookshop, Ambarita, about 4km north of town on the road to Simanindo, past Barbara's and Sibala. Although owned by a Neopolitan, it's the Balinese chef who dishes up 'squisito pizzas with imported ingredients from Italy. 7 kinds of pizza (Rp5000-65,000), from vegetarian to the "Diablo." Pasta (Rp5-6000) and salads (Rp3000) available. Free transport back to your guest house if you're staying in Tuk-Tuk or Ambarita. Open daily 10am-11pm.

SIGHTS

Most travelers come to Samosir for the chance to spend a few lazy days splashing in the lake, mix with fellow wanderers, and take advantage of the rock-bottom prices. Nevertheless, for slightly more active and cultural pursuits, the island boasts worthwhile attractions, mostly along the east shore, within 20km of Tomok. Motorcycles and bicycles are far and away the best way to get around Samosir. The only roads which are safely navigable by motorcycle are the northern coast road from Tomok to Pangururan (passing through Ambarita and Simanindo) and the Tuk-Tuk Ring Rd.

There are several **megalithic tomb complexes** in Tomok near the landing. The refrigerator-sized coffins, adorned with highly stylized and enigmatic faces, were built to house the remains of local Batak kings, the Sidobutars (whose descendants still live in Tomok). From the pier, head west across the main road. The first complex is on the right a few meters up, surrounded by bamboo trees. There are a number of stone chairs and statues of humans and animals as well, all hewn from single blocks of stone and now overgrown with moss and lichen.

Continuing down the path past the first set of tombs leads to the **Museum of King Sidobutar,** in a small, traditional Batak house. The collection consists of a random assortment of Batak artifacts. Farther uphill is the **tomb of Rajah Ompu Soributu**

Sidobutar himself, which lies beneath the bows of a *hariam* tree. The king's tomb is now encrusted with souvenir shops. For the best deals, come early. (Open during daylight hours; admission by donation.)

A more interesting, and slightly less commercialized megalithic site, **Siallagan village,** lies 8km up the road in Ambarita, behind the post office and near the town harbor; the Tuk-Tuk road leads right to it. Hidden behind a row of well-preserved Batak houses is a collection of stone chairs, a stone table, and what appears to be a stone sofa (it's only missing the stone TV set to make the perfect Flintstone living room). It was here that village honchos would arbitrate quarrels; if the offense was grievous enough, the loser would be led to the second set of stone furnishings, where he or she would be cooked and eaten.

North of Ambarita, the island perimeter road passes through peaceful farmland, and the cliffs behind Tomok and Tuk-Tuk gradually recede into rolling hills, dotted with Batak shrines. Some 20km later it reaches the village of **Simanindo,** on the northern tip of the island. Simanindo is home to the **Huta Bolon Museum,** famed for its performances of **traditional Toba Batak dance.** The show takes place in "Huta Bolon Village," a small well-preserved Batak village (now strictly a museum show piece) surrounded by a 1m-high stone wall. Most interesting of the traditional buildings is the large *rumah rajah* (king's house),. Helpful sheets explaining the village and each dance routine are provided as part of the Rp3000 admission. The actual museum consists of a single *rumah adat,* but the collection of Batak tools and handicrafts, including some fine carvings, is clearly explained. (Open daily 9am-4pm.) Dance performances are held Mon.-Sat. at 10:30am and 11:45am, Sun. at 11:45am; each lasts 45 minutes.

Those who get stuck in Simanindo can spend the night at the **Bintang Restaurant,** which has several basic rooms for Rp3000 per night (outside *mandi*). Off Simanindo is the small resort island of **Pulau Tao,** where nice private bungalows can be had for about Rp50,000 per night. To get there, hire a boat from the public pier, at the end of the dirt road that passes Huta Bolon Museum.

Pangururan is Samosir's largest town, and rather uninspiring at that, although it does provide scenic forays into the hills on the mainland. The **Mt. Belirang Hot Springs** (Rp500) offer healing sulphurous comfort only 4km west of town. Motorcycle enthusiasts can take a trip up **Mount Tele,** which is actually the steep ridge on the mainland. Beware of oncoming fast-moving buses careening downhill. Visitors who find themselves stranded in Pangururan can stay at the friendly **Barat Accommodation,** Jl. Sisingamangaraja 66 (tel. 200 53), in the center of town. Basic rooms with communal *mandi* cost Rp4000, doubles Rp7000. The restaurant downstairs serves basic backpacker fare. Mr. Barat, the friendly Batak owner, speaks English well and is an excellent source of info on Batak culture, history, and lore. Maps of town, the hot springs, and cross-island hiking trails are also available.

Kurt Stüttecker and his wife run **rafting and trekking trips on the Sahan River,** 30km south of Prapat, in Parhitoon. Herr Stüttecker has 11 years' experience leading trips all over the world, and many budget travelers find his trips quite safe (US$55 for 2 days). Trips are offered for all skill levels; Stüttecker estimates his most challenging float, the "most extreme whitewater trip in Asia," to be class V rapids. They also organize treks, overnights in highland villages, or combined trekking/rafting trips. Inquire at Bagus Bay Stayhouse or Tabo Vegetarian Restaurant in Tuk-Tuk, or at the Andilo Nancy Travel Service in Prapat.

HIKING ACROSS PULAU SAMOSIR

The best cure for claustrophobia is an invigorating hike across the breadth of the island for a glimpse of modern Batak life less tarnished by tourism. The nicest route runs from Ambarita west to Pangururan or vice-versa. Either way, it's possible to complete the hike in a single day if you start early and go fast; hiking from west to east is generally regarded as the faster route. Well-marked trails wind around isolated Batak villages, which have not been prettied up for the tourist trade, and numerous coffee, clove, and tapioca plantations; at certain times of the year, the air is heavy with the rich aroma of roasting coffee beans.

A better way to fully appreciate the interior is to stay the night in one of several villages with homestays. Hikers setting out from Ambarita (the preferred route) pass tiny **Partokoan**, home of two guest houses, **John's** and **Jennie's.** From Partokoan, a rocky cart path heads 9km up to the larger village of **Roongurni Huta**, where it meets up with the road left to Tomok (24km) or right to Panguraran (16km). The latter winds down the gentle slope to town, arriving at **Sidihoni Lake** after 6km where **Weny Guest House** puts up hikers for Rp1000 per night on the shore of the lake. The last 10km down to Panguraran offers stunning views of the steep crater walls and **Gunung Pusuk Buhit** on the western mainland.

From Ambarita (38km from Panguraran), the path begins opposite the Bank Rakyat Indonesia office; look for the large sign advertising John's Guest House in Partokoan. From Panguraran, the dirt road to Roongurni Huta branches off to the left off Jl. Dr. Tobing, opposite a Catholic church. Less ambitious hikers may choose to hike only part of the way up from Ambarita, where lovely views and colorful sunsets can be seen. Another trail leads from Tuk-Tuk to the narrow waterfall that cascades down the jungle-covered cliffs opposite the tiny peninsula. The trail begins next to the small benzine station at the intersection of the main road and the Tuk-Tuk perimeter road (2km). A pleasant alternative route from Tuk-Tuk to Ambarita begins here as well. Follow the waterfall path for about 200m and then take a right. The narrow dirt road leads through several small villages, past churches and across rice fields before rejoining the main road near Ambarita.

PULAU NIAS

Tiny Pulau Nias, only 5600sq.km, packs in quite a variety of experiences within its rolling verdant hills and palm-lined shores. Long celebrated as one of the premier surfing spots in Indonesia, Nias is blessed with swirling waves and powdery sand. Recently, however, the traditions of the Niah people have become a prime attraction. The aggressive but friendly people of Nias present a bit of a mystery to historians. The ancestors of the Niah people are believed to have been proto-Malays, perhaps Bataks, who arrived on the island over 7000 years ago. However, they display physical characteristics of the Mongoloid people of northern Asia and speak a wildly distant language. Some of their art forms and styles resemble those from civilizations as far away as India and as close as Vietnam. Despite what appears to be early contact with outsiders from both Asia and Europe, the Niah people have remained relatively isolated. As a result, their culture is unique among the indigenous ethnic groups of Sumatra.

European vessels "discovered" the island in the late 1600s, and Dutch occupation of the north ensued, lasting for two centuries. The south, on the other hand, bitterly resisted the Dutch. Consequently, the cultural differences that already existed between the two halves of the island were further reinforced. Ironically, the unoccupied south developed a more distinguished architecture, such as the *rumah adat* (traditional houses), which derive their style from the European ships that landed on the island. Since many Niah traditions were well-preserved into this century, including human sacrifices and head-hunting, Nias presents an extraordinary destination for travelers looking for a calm yet intriguing locale to luxuriate in history.

GETTING THERE AND AWAY

The primary transit point to Pulau Nias is the town of **Sibolga**, a short ferry ride away. The town does not have too much to offer, other than the usual horde of hustlers at the ferry and bus terminals. **Buses** connect the terminal on Jl. Sisingamangaraja in Sibolga to **Prapat** (8-10am, Rp7000, minibuses every hr., 8am-8pm, Rp9000) and **Bukittinggi** (8am and 4pm, 14hr., Rp12,500). Sibolga also has the standard services: a **police station,** Jl. Tobing 35 (tel. 218 12), **hospital** (tel. 215 59) on the same street, a

post office, Jl. Sutomo 40 (tel. 221 62) with *Poste Restante,* and decent exchange rates at **Bank Dagang Negara,** Jl. Katamso 43 (tel. 217 22). There is a **Telkom office,** Jl. Tengiri 15 (tel. 230 09), with **HCD** as well. **Postal code:** 22500.

If travelers end up stuck in Sibolga for a night, there are a few accommodation options. **Hotel Mutiara Indah,** Jl. A. Yani 20 (tel. 216 81) has economy rooms for Rp7000, and doubles with fan and *mandi* for Rp12,500, triples Rp15,000. **Anugrah Hotel,** Jl. Suprapto 112 (tel. 214 72) is rather noisy but has fabulous sunsets. Triples with shared *mandi* are Rp15,000, with private *mandi* Rp25,000. **Losmen Surya-baru,** Jl. Horas 164 (tel. 213 86) is a bargain with doubles for Rp5000, with *mandi* Rp10,000. Satisfy your hunger at *warung* along Jl. Suprapto. Or, try **Rumah Makan Bunga Tanjung,** Jl. Katamso 40 (tel. 212 02). (Open daily 9am-9pm.)

Overnight ferries ply from Sibolga to Gunung Sitoli and Teluk Dalam while the island is connected by plane to Medan and Padang. **PT Simeulue** sails from **Sibolga** to **Teluk Dalam** (Tues., Thurs., and Sat., 8pm, 10-14hr., Rp12,050 deck, Rp17,050 cabin). The Saturday boat continues from Teluk Dalam to **Pulau Tello** (Sun., 10am, 7hr., Rp2500 extra from Sibolga, Rp7000 from Teluk Dalam) and returns from Pulau Tello on Mondays. The boat returns from Teluk Dalam to Sibolga (Mon., Wed., and Fri., 8pm) at the same rates. The same company also runs boats for **Gunung Sitoli** (Mon.-Sat., 8pm, 9-10hr., Rp8500 deck, Rp13,500 cabin). Return boats from Gunung Sitoli to Sibolga also run Mon.-Sat. at 8pm. Buy tickets at the PT Simeulue office before it closes at 6pm; tickets purchased at the harbor are subject to an administrative fee, usually Rp3000 extra. **PT ASDP** operates a much larger, faster, and safer-looking solid metal car ferry to Gunung Sitoli, which is highly recommended if the weather is rough. Ferries regularly depart from both Sibolga and Gunung Sitoli to the opposite destination (Mon.-Sat., 8pm, 8hr., Rp11,600 deck). Tickets can be purchased at the harbor until the time of departure at no penalty.

PELNI ships arrive every other Saturday from **Padang** to **Gunung Sitoli,** continuing to **Sibolga** (Rp17,500), returning to Padang (Rp48,000) the next morning, and **Jakarta** (Rp118,500) two days later. All fares are economy from Gunung Sitoli.

SMAC, Jl. Lagundi 46 (tel. 210 10; open Mon.-Sat. 7am-4:30pm, Sun. 8am-1pm), has flights to **Medan** (Mon., Wed., Sat., Sun., 9:20am, Tues., Thurs., Fri., 11:50am, 1hr., Rp125,800) and **Padang** (Wed., 8:30am, 1½hr., Rp119,700). **Binaka Airport** lies 20km south of Gunung Sitoli. Taxis there from Gunung Sitoli can pick up travelers at their hotels (Rp3500). Flights should be confirmed one day before departure.

▨ Gunung Sitoli

A sizable town and the capital of Nias, Gunung Sitoli serves as an excellent base for forays to northern Niah villages, beaches, and nature reserves in the untouristed north. Unfortunately, hustling *becak* drivers lurk around the ferry and bus terminals, ready to overwhelm visitors with their services. Outside the terminals, the town is friendly and noticeably more prosperous than most Niah villages. Locals who practice Islam (about 6% of the population) live on the outskirts of town.

ORIENTATION AND PRACTICAL INFORMATION

The main north-south thoroughfare is **Jalan Sirao,** which starts where it branches off **Jalan Gomo/Yos Sudarso** at the Hotel Wisata at the north end of town. Heading south, **Jalan Lagundi** branches off to the left after 250m. After another 250m, **Jalan Sudirman** heads to the right and Jl. Sirao crosses over the river on a newly-constructed bridge, turning into **Jalan Diponegoro,** which heads south to Teluk Dalam.

The **tourist office,** Jl. Sukarno 6 (tel. 215 45), across the main square from the Hotel Wisata, stocks brochures and maps of Nias. (Open Mon.-Thurs. 7:30am-4pm, Fri. 7:30am-noon.) **Bank BNI,** Jl. Imam Bonjol 40 (tel. 219 46), 150m south of the telephone office, offers bad rates for cash and traveler's checks. (Open Mon.-Fri. 8am-4:15pm.) **Pharmacy Mira Ling,** Jl. Sirao 179 (tel. 217 79), just north of the bridge, is expensive but well-stocked. (Open daily 8am-9pm.) The **hospital,** Jl. Dr. Ciptomangunkusomo 15 (tel. 214 74), is the best on the island, 100m from the phone office. The Nias regional **police office**, Jl. Melati 5 (tel. 215 58), can be found 100m south of the bus terminal, off Jl. Diponegoro. The **post office**, Jl. Hatta 1 (tel. 214 40) stands next door (open Mon.-Thurs. 8am-2pm, Fri. 8am-noon., Sat. 8am-3pm). **Postal code:** 21800. The **Telkom office**, Jl. Hatta 3 (tel. 210 55), on the south side of the main square, offers an **HCD** phone (open 24hr.). **Telephone code:** 0639.

Buses and *oplet* to the south depart from the **bus terminal,** 300m south of the bridge on Jl. Diponegoro, going to **Teluk Dalam** (every hr., 7am-2pm, 4hr., Rp6000). Buses and *oplet* to the north also depart from the terminal, but pass through the center of town along Jl. Gomo. **Ferries** depart from the harbor, 3km north of town, off the main road (Rp500 by *oplet*, Rp1000 by *becak*). For ferry tickets, try either **PT Simeulue,** Jl. Sirao 23 (open Mon.-Sat. 8am-6pm) or **PT ASDP,** Jl. Yos Sudarso 191 (tel. 215 54), in the Hotel Wisata (open Mon.-Sat. 8am-6pm). **PELNI,** Jl. Lagundi 3 (tel. 218 46), also operates ferries (open Mon.-Fri. 8am-3pm). Inquire about transport to **Pulau Banyak** at the fishing boats along the river.

ACCOMMODATIONS AND FOOD

The **Gomo Inn,** Jl. Gomo 148-150 (tel. 219 26), opens out to Jl. Sirao on the back side, about 50m down from Hotel Wisata. Clean, simple doubles with fan and *mandi* are packed down a narrow corridor and away from the raucous street (Rp11,000). The VIP room with A/C and TV costs Rp30,000, but is rather musty. **Losmen Banuada,** Jl. A. Yani 21 (tel. 218 78), stands on Jl. Gomo down the hill. Basic rooms with shared *mandi* go for Rp2000 per person. It's on a nice street which leads to the market. By the bus terminal, **Losmen Hidayat,** Jl. Diponegoro 131 (tel. 217 09), puts up the road-weary in accommodating triples (Rp10,000), although the street noise is loud. A nice, cheap restaurant bustles downstairs.

Warung and cheap restaurants proliferate, along with some nicer establishments. At **Rumah Makan Beringin,** Jl. Lagundi 1 (tel. 217 01), you can chat with the super-friendly owner over some tasty *ayam gulai* (chicken curry, Rp1800). (Open daily 6am-9pm.) Catch Chinese seafood specialties at **Restoran Bintang Terang,** Jl. Sirao 10 (tel. 210 34), such as tangy fried cuttlefish (Rp5000). (Open daily 6am-9:30pm.) At **Rumah Makan Nasional,** Jl. Sirao 87 (tel. 216 29), watch the fans with colorful streamers keep flies off the food as guests sample *udang petai* (an Indonesian shrimp specialty, Rp2000) or the wide variety of fish. (Open daily 7am-9pm.)

SIGHTS

Several traditional northern **Niah villages** are close to town. The houses differ considerably from those in the south, and are characterized by their large oval shape and a thatched roof soaring up to 10m. It's possible to stay several nights in some villages, and traditional dancing and music can be arranged. Compared to the south, few tourists visit these villages and it's wise to be respectful of local customs, such as wearing long pants or a long skirt. Perhaps the best preserved is **Saiwahili-Sihare'ö,** 5km west of town. Minibuses run to the village from the bus terminal (7am-6pm, 30min., Rp500). **Hilimbawödesölö,** 14km south of Gunung Sitoli, is another remarkable village to visit. Catch a bus south to Km12 and then take a motorcycle (Rp1000) or walk the last 2km to the village. The village of **Dahana** is only 3km west of town. No buses run there, but it can be reached by motorbike or by walking up Jl Sudirman/Pancasila. Perhaps the nicest way to experience the local culture is to walk to the villages. Heading to **Tögi Ndrawa Cave** (5km) and then over to Saiwahili-Sihare'ö and back to town makes an enjoyable promenade.

Bountiful beaches for secluded sun-soaking lie within easy reach of town. Lovely **Pantai Olora** awaits visitors north of town at Km10, while the **Muara Indah Recreation Forest,** just past Km14, boasts a nice lake, beach, and a meandering estuary to the ocean. Heading south, sand enthusiasts can run amok on **Pantai Laowömaru** at Km7. All can be reached by minibus from town (Rp500).

▓ Teluk Dalam

Most visitors to this pleasantly compact port town find themselves in transit, either waiting for the ferry to Sibolga, stocking up on supplies, or preparing for excursions to Niah villages. As in Gunung Sitoli, the touts accosting weary sack-rucking travelers off the night boat from Sibolga are particularly unfriendly and aggressive. Aside from those at the pier, most of the other residents in town are friendly and helpful. A copra oil plant lends an intoxicatingly delicious smell to the town.

ORIENTATION AND PRACTICAL INFORMATION

The main street is **Jalan A. Yani,** which starts at the **Simpang Raya** intersection, changing to **Jalan Imam Bonjol** 150m down, where **Jalan Pelabuhan** heads left to the harbor and **Jalan Yos Sudarso** veers right. Ferry tickets can be purchased at **PT Simeulue,** Jl. A. Yani 41, on the day of departure. **Buses** to **Gunung Sitoli** (7am-2pm, 4hr., Rp6000), **motorcycles** to **Lagundi Bay** (Rp2000) and **oplet** to local villages all depart from the Simpang Raya intersection. **Currency exchange** is available at poor rates at **Bank BPDSU,** Jl. A. Yani 48 (tel. 213 02). (Open Mon.-Fri. 8am-3pm, Sat. 8am-1pm.) The sizeable **Puskesmas 24-hour clinic** is on Jl. Kartini. From Simpang Raya, follow Jl. Diponegoro 400m and bear left on Jl. Kartini; the clinic is 150m up the hill. The **police station,** Jl. Mohammed Hata 1 (tel. 211 10), is off the road to Lagundi, 150m up from Simpang Raya. The **post office,** Jl. Imam Bonjol 2 (tel. 211 30), sits at the corner of Jl. Pelabuhan (open Mon.-Thurs. 7am-5pm, Fri.-Sat. 7am-3pm). **Postal code:** 22865. The **Telkom office** (tel. 211 08), on Jl. Imam Bonjol, stands 50m down from the post office on the right (open 24hr.). **Telephone code:** 0630.

ACCOMMODATIONS AND FOOD

All the budget accommodations are within 100m of the center of town. **Lagundi Losmen,** Jl. A. Yani 97 (tel. 212 18), stands at the corner of Jl. Pelabuhan. To get to the simple triples upstairs (Rp5000), visitors have to navigate the dark, smoky kitchen and steep wooden ladder. Dark shared *mandi* are clean, and there's a cheap restaurant downstairs. **Hotel Jamburae** (tel. 210 47) is on Jl. Pelabuhan, next to the pier, and offers more spacious, if pricey, doubles (Rp11,000, with *mandi* Rp16,000). **Losmen Cari Nafkah,** Jl. Yos Sudarso 9, is 50m up from Jl. A. Yani on the right, directly across from the copra oil plant. Quieter rooms are a bit cramped and have wooden bunk beds. The outside shared *mandi* is decent. Singles cost Rp2500, doubles Rp4000.

Cheap **warung** line Jl. A. Yani and Jl. Diponegoro. Stock up on fresh fruits at the **market,** on Jl. D. Panjaitan, which parallels Jl. A. Yani, one block away from the harbor. (Open daily 8am-8pm.) **Rumah Makan Simpang Raya,** Jl. Saonigeho 7 (tel. 210 43), serves up excellent local fish and chicken specialties (open daily 6am-midnight). Delve into the crispy *ikan bakar chabe* (chilied grilled fish) or feast on the titillating chicken curry (Rp2000). **Rumah Makan Andalas,** Jl. A. Yani 7 (tel. 210 34), ladles out Padang delights. Try the *ikan tonkol* (tuna) for Rp1000 or spice out on their fish and chicken curries (Rp500-2000).

▓ Lagundi Bay

Only 12km west of pushy Teluk Dalam, this semi-circular bay draws a thriving surfing culture, with its classic undisturbed waves peeling off the sharp coral reef which rings much of the firth. Neophytes wallow in the warm waters of the long sandy Lagundi Beach, while hard-core surfers head up to the closely-packed *losmen* at Sorake Beach, where the swells break just off shore. When the surf is flat, excursions to nearby traditional Niah villages offer a pleasant interlude.

ORIENTATION AND PRACTICAL INFORMATION

Coming from Teluk Dalam, the road arrives first at **Lagundi Village,** at the top of the south-facing bay, home of **Lagundi Beach** and more peaceful waves. Guest houses and bungalows stretch around the beach for about 300m from Yanti's to Sibayak, at the western end. A **24-hr. Puskesmas polyclinic** (tel. 212 02) is on the main road behind the Lagundi Holiday Cottages. A **police office** is just off the main road, about 50m west of the polyclinic. A road junction lies just across a steel trestle bridge 150m west of the police office, where the road to Gunung Sitoli heads north, the road to **Botohilitanö Village** climbs west, and the **Sorake Beach Road** charges south. A **postal agent** (tel. 212 09), 50m down the Sorake Beach Rd. on the right, sells stamps, sends packages, and also helps organize traditional dancing in Botohilitanö (open Mon.-Sat. 8am-5pm). Heading down Sorake Beach Rd. with the bay on the left, the string of *losmen* starts 600m past the postal agent, continuing for about 1km before the road terminates at the exorbitant Sorake Beach Resort. A three-story **judging tower** with unparalleled views of the ocean dominates the beach near the middle of the strip of *losmen.* The **Seabreeze Losmen,** 50km north of the tower, has **currency exchange** at poor rates, as well as an **HCD** and card phone next door.

Motorcycle drivers roaming the beaches can take you to Teluk Dalam for Rp2000. The adventurous can **rent motorbikes** for Rp5000 per hour, but be warned that most roads are in poor condition. Before hopping on any motorbike or bus, be sure to agree on a definite price, making clear what exactly you want. It's common practice for motorcycle drivers to exaggerate distances to extract a higher price. Minibuses to **Binaka Airport** (4hr., Rp40,000 per person, although drivers often try to extract more) can be arranged. Local buses to **Gunung Sitoli** can be caught at the road junction next to the postal agent (7-8am, 4hr., Rp6000).

ACCOMMODATIONS AND FOOD

Most *losmen* around the center part of Sorake Beach are closely packed and intimate with their neighbors. On either end of the main beach action, guest houses are more comfortably spaced with an increasing number of more private bungalows, most with attached *mandi.* Along Lagundi Beach, accommodations are set back a bit from the beach under the coconut palms, and most rooms have private *mandi.* Prices per night are amazingly cheap (Rp500-2000 in the communal *losmen*), but food prices tend to be on the higher end. To prevent getting ripped off, be careful about choosing your guest house. Ask other travelers for advice. Many of the central *losmen* on Sorake Beach have no locks on the doors and theft by locals is an occasional problem. It's generally safer to stay at *losmen* with plenty of other guests, especially if you can't lock your door.

Marlynto's, run by "Mama" and "Papa" Marlynto, offers superb meals and cheap rooms, snuggling amid a tight row of *losmen,* 150m south of the judging tower. The six rooms in the hut offer little privacy, but it's well worth it for the camaraderie, delicious food, and proximity to the waves. Rooms cost Rp500 per night, and less for longer periods of time. Meals cost more than other *losmen* on Sorake Beach, but they're worth the extra rupiah. Catch up on world news from the satellite TV at the Marlynto's house. A bit more isolated, **Niuraya** catches a nice breeze with comfortable bungalows off the point about 200m down from Marlynto's. The friendly proprietors serve up tasty fare at a gazebo restaurant, pleasantly removed from the beach. Bungalows are Rp2000.

The older *losmen* on Lagundi Beach sport higher room prices that compensate for the cheaper victuals. **Magdalena,** considered to have the best cook at Lagundi by some, has nicely spaced bungalow-motel style accommodations. The *losmen* is directly behind the white lighthouse off the beach. Rattan and thatch-roofed doubles with nice attached *mandi* cost Rp5000. **Risky,** 70m east of Magdalena, maintains neat thatch-roofed huts (doubles Rp4000) and good, cheap food.

Nearly every *losmen* expects visitors to eat most of their meals at the *losmen,* with similar menus of occasionally monotonous *mie goreng,* fruit salads, banana pancakes, and the like. For dinner, local fish specialties, such as tuna, snapper, or shark, are quite tasty and put the other offerings to shame. Fishermen roam the beach, selling fresh fish which your *losmen* owner will cook up for you. Roving children peddle stalks of bananas, coconut (Rp200), and banana rolls (Rp200), as well as fresh doughnuts (Rp200).

SIGHTS AND ENTERTAINMENT

Competition class **surf** draws wave-riders from around the world to the solid right-hand barrels which pummel down off **Sorake Beach**. Between June and September, sets often reach 3m, with the occasional 4m waves rolling in. The waves off Sorake are not for beginners and should be treated with respect—one wrong turn will have novices thrashed upon the sharp coral reef. **Lagundi Beach** is a pleasure for swimming, and bodyboarders play on the smaller waves. Surfboards are readily purchased along Sorake Beach, and rent for Rp3000 per day.

VISITING TRADITIONAL NIAH VILLAGES

The hilltops on southern Nias are home to numerous **Niah villages,** many of which can now be visited as a daytrip from Lagundi Bay or Teluk Dalam. Many *rumah adat,* with their ship-like wooden construction, are along the stone-paved streets of the villages, in two facing rows. Large carved stone benches, many weighing several tons, line the streets, once used for laying the deceased on, but now just for drying laundry. The houses are tightly packed with virtually no space between them. Different types of wood are used for the different parts of the house, with the raised living area resting on solid pillars. Sadly, corrugated steel roofs have started to replace the decaying thatch roofs, although the rest of the houses are quite intact in most villages. At the center of each village is a large square, in front of the chief's house, where village meetings are held in an oversized gazebo, and traditional dancing, including the world-famous stone jumping, is performed. Upon arriving at any village, head first for the chief's house to pay your respects. Usually he will ask for a Rp2000 donation. After visiting the chief, visitors are free to roam about the village. Always ask before taking photos of people, as some do not like to be photographed and others may ask for money.

Considered the origin of Niah culture, **Gomo Village,** 40km north of Teluk Dalam, boasts numerous stone megaliths and chairs, along with several original *rumah adat.* The stones are engraved with intricate carvings, whose significance is still a mystery. Some of the menacing megaliths are over 2000 years old, including the hissing creatures whose oversized melons greet intruders. Gomo is most easily reached by motorbike (Rp20,000 roundtrip), and guides in Teluk Dalam and Lagundi offer their services for another Rp10,000.

Bawömataluo, about 12km from Lagundi and Teluk Dalam, is one of the largest and best-preserved villages, towering 300m above the ocean. The stone steps leading up to the village are flanked by the stone lizard monsters with bulging eyes, and huge fangs. The chief's house, with a 20m-high roof, is an architectural wonder, raised on thick wooden poles. The interior contains numerous wood carvings of monkeys, serpents, and village scenes on the walls and poles supporting the house. The chief's throne rests on a raised bench overlooking the village square. A 3m-long megaphone-like drum aims out at the square, hanging from the crisscrossing wood beams above. If the chief is not home, leave a Rp2000 donation in the small wood box on the wall. Outside, a fantastic number of **stone megaliths** line the streets, clustering around the chief's house. While Bawömataluo is more impressive to visit than nearby villages, the large number of tourists who flock here have jaded many of the local people. Irregular *oplet* run from Teluk Dalam (Rp500). Alternatively, you can ride the back of a motorcycle (Rp3000).

Hiliameta is a friendlier but smaller village within walking distance of Lagundi Bay. Nautical houses line the main street similar to Bawömataluo, although the chief's house is hardly distinguishable from the rest. Much of the woodwork on the *rumah* *adat* is quite intricate and it's a marvel to observe the construction which has no artificially connected joints. The village is 500m up a concrete walkway which turns into stone steps, starting off the main road about 1km east of Lagundi village. The village is just above the Catholic church, which is visible from the bay. The turnoff is about a 45-minute walk from Sorake Beach, and motorbikes can take you there for Rp700. Another Niah village, **Botohilitanö** rests on the hill only 1km west of Sorake Beach. It's a 10-minute walk from the crossroads next to the postal agent, or up the road across from Seabreeze on Sorake Beach.

While the Niah are now a peaceful lot, their war dances are a spectacular sight. Most performances include the famed stone-jumping, where young men launch themselves from a small stone onto a two-meter high platform. The cheapest way to view this uniquely Niah feat is to take a look at a Rp1000 note. Visitors at Lagundi Bay can arrange to see a full performance by contacting *losmen* owners. Performances are staged in Botohilitanö village (Sun. 2pm, Tues. 8pm for a flat fee (regardless of number of people watching, Rp100,000, including stone-jumping Rp125,000).

It's possible to make day hikes through several villages, which are connected by well-marked stone walkways. A nice route from Orahili to Hilisimaetano passes through seven villages, including Bawömataluo. Hikers can arrange for a motorbike to pick them up at the terminus. A better way to experience village life is to stay the night in one of the villages. Many villages put up visitors for Rp4000 per night (including meals). Try to take as little money, goods, and valuables along as possible; there have been occasional reports of thefts in the villages.

CENTRAL SUMATRA

▨ Bukittinggi

An oasis of toned-down tourism, Bukittinggi (elevation 1000m) is the heart of Minangkabau culture, represented in the architecture, food, and performing arts of the region. Tourists overrun the town, as the crowded cafés attest, to take in all that Bukittinggi has to offer—from being fully immersed in Minangkabau life to seeking thrills in the volcanic cones of Gunung Singgalang or Gunung Merapi to teeming markets. Bukittinggi's many rewarding activities keep visitors well-occupied, especially after the multi-hour vehicular nightmare it takes to reach the region.

ORIENTATION

The hills in the center of town result in curvaceous roads and tricky navigation. **Jam Gadang,** the famous clock tower built by the Dutch, dominates the center of town, across from the **Pasar Atas** (upper market). On the left side of the Pasar Atas, **Jalan A. Yani** heads north (downhill), kinking right at a four-way intersection and continuing downhill past abundant *losmen* and cafés and under the towering footbridge which connects the **zoo** and the old Dutch **Fort de Kock.** From the four-way intersection, **Jalan Teuku Umar** climbs uphill (west) to **Jalan Yos Sudarso,** changing names to **Jalan Tengku Nan Renceh,** and drops downhill toward **Panorama Park** and **Ngarai Sianok Canyon.**

PRACTICAL INFORMATION

Tourist Offices: Jl. Lenggogeni 1 (tel. 224 03), next to Jam Gadang. Friendly and organized staff, with information on local sights and events; can help find qualified guides. Open Mon.-Thurs. 8am-2pm, Fri. 8-11:30am, Sat. 8am-1pm.

Tours and Travel: Everywhere on Jl. A. Yani. Arranges air, bus, and taxi travel; rents motorbikes and safeboxes; changes money, and offers a variety of tours. **Tigo Balai Tour,** Jl. A. Yani 100 (tel. 319 96), arranges transportation and treks to Pulau Siberut. Open daily 8am-8pm. **P.T. Randy Tours,** Jl. A. Yani 70 (tel. 228 36) specializes in excursions and treks in the area. Open daily 8am-7pm.

Currency Exchange: Bank BNI, Jl. A. Yani 126 (tel. 225 78), offers competitive rates and cashes traveler's checks. Open Mon.-Fri. 8am-4pm. **Bank Nasional,** Jl. Yani 83 (tel. 336 42), has slightly better rates for cash and offers MC and Visa cash advances. Open Mon.-Fri. 8am-2pm.

Buses: Tickets for long-distance jouneys should be purchased from a travel agent or directly from the bus company. **City bus terminal,** at Aur Kuning. Buses to: **Padang** (every hr., 7am-6pm, 2-3hr., Rp2000); **Prapat** (noon, 13hr., Rp22,500); **Sibolga** (4pm, 12hr., Rp12,500); **Medan** (noon and 2pm, 18hr., Rp23,000); **Pekanbaru** (8am, 6hr., Rp5000); **Danau Maninjau** (every hr., 8am-6pm, 1½hr., Rp1000); and **Solok** (every hr., 7am-6pm, 2hr., Rp1600). A **tourist bus** departs to **Prapat** with stops at the equator and a hot spring (7:30am, 13hr., Rp27,000).

Local Transportation: Angkot run around town following a roughly clockwise route up Jl. Sudirman, Jl. A. Yani, Pasar Baurah (lower market), and Aur Kuning bus terminal (Rp300). Horse-drawn **dokar** clop around (fares around Rp1000 in town), while 3-wheeled fumigating **bemo** are being phased out.

Markets: Two expansive markets; **Pasar Atas** (upper market) and **Pasar Bawah** (lower market) ensure that finding what you want may take a bit of time. The Pasar Atas has clothing, fabrics, batik, etc., while Pasar Bawah packs in *warung*.

Pharmacies: Apotik Al-Kautsar, Jl. Kesehatan 17 (tel. 312 34), just past the bottom of Jl. A. Yani and to the left. Open 24hr.

Medical Services: Rumah Sakit Dr. Achmad Mochtar, Jl. Dr. Rifai (tel. 213 22). From the bottom of Jl. A. Yani, bear left onto Jl. Kesehatan. It's 150m down.

Police: Jl. Sudirman 23 (tel. 214 50), 500m south of the post office on the left.

Post Offices: GPO, Jl. Sudirman 75 (tel. 213 15), 500m south of the Jam Gadang on the left. EMS. *Poste Restante.* Open Mon.-Sat. 8am-2:30pm, Fri. 8am-noon and 1-5pm, Sun. 8am-noon. **Branch office** by the tourist office. **Postal code:** 26116.

Telephones: Telkom office, Jl. M. Syafei 16 (tel. 321 09), near the intersection with Jl. Sudirman. Open 24hr. **HCD** phones at the public phone bank next to Jam gadang and at the Rendezvous Coffee Shop (bottom of Jl. A. Yani on the right, Rp2000 per call).**Telephone code:** 0752.

ACCOMMODATIONS

Drab, inexpensive accommodations cluster along the lower end of Jl. A. Yani, while nicer, more expensive rooms are up the hill on Jl. Yos Sudarso.

Aisha Chalik Hotel, Jl. Cindur Mato 101 (tel. 352 60), near the entrance to the zoo. From the 4-way intersection on Jl. A. Yani, head up the stairs; the hotel is on the left. The best combination of quality and value. Nice high ceilings in a pleasant Dutch colonial house up on the hill. Good tourist info and organizes daytrips in the area. Singles Rp1000. Doubles Rp8-10,000. All with shared *mandi.*

Hotel Murni, Jl. A. Yani 115 (tel. 355 69), at the bottom of the hill on the left. Clean, airy rooms and common spaces, especially on the second floor, distinguish this establishment from its uphill cousins. Good tourist info on the area educates a lively backpacker crowd. Singles Rp4000. Doubles Rp8000. Triples Rp12,000.

Hotel Nirwana, Jl. A. Yani 113 (tel. 320 32), next to Hotel Murni. Clean wooden rooms are nice and quiet with windows out back. The porch has a good view for people-watching. Room rates are flexible, so try bargaining. Average rates: singles Rp7000; doubles Rp8000, with *mandi* for 2-4 people Rp20,000.

Just Tropical Homestay, Jl. Yos Sudarso 19 (tel. 349 46), near the intersection with Jl. Teuku Umar. Off the bustle of Jl. A. Yani, in an old wood house with high ceilings and good-sized rooms. Nice outdoor patio for relaxation. Singles Rp8000, with *mandi* Rp12,500. Doubles Rp10,000, with *mandi* Rp15,000.

FOOD

Tasty Minangkabau food dominates the culinary spectrum at local restaurants and *warung*. The cheapest meals can be had on big market days, amid the maze of stalls in **Pasar Bawah.** *Warung* hawk their treats around **Pasar Atas** and on Jl. A. Yani at almost any hour. Backpacker cafés cluster at the bottom of Jl. A. Yani.

Simpang Raya, Muka Jam Besar 45 (tel. 225 85), across from Jam Gadang, and Muka Mesjid Raya 95 (tel. 219 10), across from the cinema behind Pasar Atas. A veritable chain of *padang* restaurants which pump out delicious Minangkabau food to a ravenous local crowd. Choose from spicy chicken, fish, beef, or veggie delights. Their *mie goreng* (Rp2000) is especially hearty, topped off with hot-pink *kerupuk* (crackers). Both open daily 7am-9pm.

Asean Restaurant, Jl. A. Karim 14, up from the 4-way intersection at Jl. A. Yani, 100m on the left. Hot, tasty Chinese food served up in a simple, echoing banquet hall. A bit lonely, except when big local parties pack the place. Stock up on vitamins with the heaping *cap cay* (vegetable plate, Rp3000), or go for an excellent sweet and sour chicken or pork (Rp6500). Open daily 9am-10pm.

SIGHTS

Towering above the marketplace, the charming face of **Jam Gadang,** a big Dutch-built clock with Minangkabau roof, oversees the activity. To the north, on the hillside east of Jl. A. Yani, the city **zoo,** another disharmonious Dutch innovation. The park surrounding the zoo connects by the footbridge above Jl. A. Yani to the site of the Dutch **Fort de Kock,** of which little remains save a few small cannons. Romantic Indonesian couples occupy the gazebos which overlook the town, a rare display of public affection in this country. (Open daily 7am-6pm; admission Rp1000.) Also in the park, housed in a traditional Minangkabau *rumah gadang,* is a **museum** full of interesting psychological and religious commentary on Minangkabau culture (open Sat.-Thurs. 8am-5pm, Fri. 8-11am and 2-5pm; admission Rp300). From Jl. Panorama, which runs from the bottom of the hill south of Jam Gadang to Jl. Tengku Nan Renceh, you can reach **Panorama Park** which has panoramic views of **Ngarai Sianok Canyon,** as well as entrances to the **Japanese tunnel system,** where many Indonesians died from forced labor by the Japanese during the WWII occupation (admission Rp300, Rp500 extra to the tunnels). Across from Jl. Panorama is an **Army Museum** with military relics and disturbing photos (open Sat.-Thurs. 8am-5pm, Fri. 8-11am and 1-5pm; donations requested).

If you long to meander through Ngarai Sianok Canyon, hike to **Kota Gadang,** a silver-working town across the canyon. Orient yourself at Panorama Park—the path to the village heads up the stairs on the other side of the canyon. To get to the path, follow Jl. Teuku Umar/Tengku Nan Renceh down past Jl. Panorama and take a left at the fork in the road. Take the trail behind a coffee shop at the first big switchback. At the coffee shop, inquire after Rev—his knowledge of flora and fauna makes him an invaluable guide for the curious. The trip runs about 5km.

Two volcanoes, **Gunung Singgalang** (2878m) and **Gunung Merapi** (2891m), dominate Bukittinggi's skyline. The climb up Singgalang (9hr. roundtrip) is invigorating, but not too difficult. A guide is still recommended as the trail may be hard to find. Merapi last erupted in 1979, but it's still considered dangerous and is officially closed to climbers. Guides offer their services to thrill-seekers, who make the arduous climb up to the steaming ash and cinder volcanic core. Guides for both peaks run about Rp20,000 per person, with a minimum of four people.

Pandai Sikat is a handicraft town, specializing in carvings and *songket* weavings. Take a bus to Koto Baru (Rp500), then catch an *angkot* or walk the last 2km. **Pariangan** is a traditional village which can be reached by bus from Padang Pajang (Rp600). At **Lima Kaub,** 5km from Batusangkar, try to decipher the old Sanskrit stones which rest here. Buses also run to **Batang Palupuh,** a nature reserve for the Rafflesia flower To the northeast is the beautiful nature reserve, **Harau Canyon.** Buses run from Bukittinggi (Rp1000).

ENTERTAINMENT

Bukittinggi hosts nightly traditional Minangkabau **dance performances** at a small theater down the hill behind the tourist office. A different local dance group performs each night, making for a healthy competition between the groups. It's a lively cultural introduction, chock full of different dances celebrating the varying aspects of

What's Up with the Horns?

The people of West Sumatra, now known as the Minangkabau, earned their moniker from their cunning defeat over their enemies, in the same manner that the Greeks conquered Troy. In this case, however, the West Sumatrans were the defenders of their land against mighty invaders who threatened their way of life. Realizing that they had no chance in combat, the West Sumatrans suggested that the battle be settled by a bullfight. The invaders agreed and returned with an enormous, strong bull which was a champion fighter. The clever Sumatrans, on the other hand, brought a tiny buffalo colt separated from its mother and tied sharp knives to its fledgling horns. The enemies sneered at this, sure that victory was at hand. To their surprise, however, the colt immediately rushed over to the large bull to suckle, thereby slicing the bull open with the knives, effectively winning the battle. In tribute to their ingenuity in the face of danger and the colt who saved the people, the West Sumatrans called themselves the "Minang" (Winning) "Kabau" (Buffalo), and thereafter designed their roofs and ceremonial headdresses in the shape of buffalo horns.

Minangkabau life. It's well worth the Rp7500 for the two-hour performance. Purchase tickets at travel agents, the tourist office, or the door. **Buffalo fighting** is also a popular activity. Tuesday evenings, duels are staged at **Air Hangat,** 14km from Bukittinggi, and Saturdays at **Batagak,** 9km away. Both matches start at 5pm (Rp1000), and are accessible by bus from Aur Kuning terminal (Rp500), but the last bus to town may return as early as 6pm.

■ Near Bukittinggi: Danau Maninjau

An extinct volcanic crater lake 36km west of Bukittinggi, Maninjau's relative isolation has drawn traveler's seeking solitude. Over the west side, the land dips sharply down to the Indian Ocean. Spectacular weather patterns around the lake create mists, freak downpours, and dramatic sunsets. The last section of the descent from Bukittinggi involves 44 numbered hairpin bends. There's a jungle path down from **Lawang,** which takes about two hours (watch out for ground-dwelling leeches in wet areas), and heads down to **Bayur** village on the northeast coast of the lake. Catch a bus to Matur (Rp800) and hike, or take a bus (Rp200) 2km up to Lawang.

A number of beach-front bungalows have sprouted just north of Maninjau village, and just past Bayur, 4km north of Maninjau. The immensely popular **Febby Homestay** is only 400m up from the Maninjau village, right on the beach. There's plenty of room and chill music for lazing around. Cozy doubles costing Rp5000 cluster together, offering little privacy. Up 1km past Bayur on the left, **Rizal Beach Homestay** (tel. 614 04) packs in a trendy traveler's crowd on a nice beach with ample space and great views of the lake. The cheap restaurant cooks up tasty fare and excellent local fish dishes. Dorms cost Rp4000, singles Rp5-6000, doubles Rp7-8000. Bungalow doubles are Rp12,000. All rooms have shared *mandi.*

■ Padang

Whether you approach by ground or air, arrival in the seat of West Sumatra's provincial capital involves a dramatic descent from the Bukit Barisan range to the coastal lowlands. Eager to join the rush of capitalistic fervor, Padang enjoys a growing prosperity, although its residents are careful to preserve their proud Minangkabau heritage. By phasing out *bemo* and *becak misin,* city planners have managed to avoid the pollution which plagues other Indonesian cities, at least for the time being. Aside from roaming the Pasar Raya, there's not much to do in town, but offshore islands offer excellent opportunities for beach frolicking. Padang's catch-22 weather, however, complicates any travels: when the sun is out it's too hot to wander for long, but when it rains (which it often does), it deprives the vistas of their colors. Logically enough, the city is also *the* place for Padang food; if it gets too spicy, reach for a bowl of bananas.

ORIENTATION

The coast runs from north to south along Padang's west edge. The **bus terminal** is on **Jalan Pemuda,** one block in (called **Jalan Diponegoro** south of the terminal). The main street is **Jalan M. Yamin,** which runs east to west and intersects at the south corner of the bus terminal. Moving east, Jl. M. Yamin runs past the **microlet station,** the **market,** and the unmistakable Matahari Plaza. Three hundred meters later, the tall Minangkabau-roofed **post office** is at the intersection of **Jalan Aziz Chan/Sudirman** where Jl. M. Yamin continues east as **Jalan Proklamasi.**

PRACTICAL INFORMATION

Tourist Offices: Regional Tourism Service of West Sumatra, Jl. Sudirman 43 (tel. 342 32), 800m up from the post office on the left. Helpful brochures with maps of West Sumatra and a good map of the city. English spoken. Open Mon.-Thurs. 7:30am-2:30pm, Fri. 7:30-11:30am, Sat. 7:30am-1pm.

Tours and Travel: Hotel Cendrawasih, Jl. Pemuda 27 (tel. 228 94), across from the bus terminal. Organizes 7-10-day treks to Pulau Siberut and daytrips (US$8) to offshore islands. **PT Natrabu Travel,** Jl. Pemuda 29B (tel. 330 08). Deals mostly with airline tickets and minivan rental (Rp125,000 per day). Open daily 8am-6pm.

Immigration Offices: Jl. Khatib Sulaiman (tel. 551 13), 500m north of the Telkom office.

Currency Exchange: Bank Bumi Daya, Jl. Sudirman 2A (tel. 338 40). Open Mon.-Thurs. 7:30am-3pm, Fri. 7:30-11:30am and 1:30-3pm. **Bank BNI,** Jl. Dobi 1 (tel. 319 42). Down Jl. Hiligoo from the monument on Jl. M. Yamin. Open Mon.-Thurs. 8am-4pm, Fri. 8am-noon and 1:30-4pm. Both accept traveler's checks. **Money changers** are on Jl. Pemuda, but banks offer better rates.

Air Travel: Bandara Tabing Airport, 9km north of town. Catch *bis kota* #14A up Jl. Sudirman (Rp300) or microlets up Jl. Pemuda (Rp500). Taxis to the airport (Rp5-6000). Departure tax is Rp8800 domestic, Rp20,000 international. **Merpati,** Jl. Gereja 34 (tel. 320 01), flies daily to **Jakarta, Medan, Batam,** and **Palembang,** and 3 times per wk. to **Singapore** and **Pekanbaru.** Open Mon.-Sat. 8am-5pm, Sun. 8am-noon. **Garuda,** Jl. Juanda 79 (tel. 584 89), **Sempati,** Jl. Juanda 79 (tel. 516 12), and **Mandala,** Jl. Pemuda 29A (tel. 327 73), all fly daily to **Jakarta. Pelangi,** Jl. Gereja 34 (tel. 381 03), flies daily to **Kuala Lumpur** and 3 times per wk. to **Johor Bahru,** Malaysia. Open Mon.-Sat. 8am-3pm. All fares are standardized between airlines: **Jakarta** (Rp290,800); **Medan** (Rp165,400); **Batam** (Rp144,500); **Singapore** (US$121); **Kuala Lumpur** (US$123); **Johor Bahru** (US$104); **Palembang** (Rp172,000); and **Pekanbaru** (Rp65,300).

Buses: Terminal, on Jl. Pemuda just west of Pasar Raya. To: **Bukittinggi** (every hr., 7am-6pm, 2½hr., Rp2000); **Medan** (10-11am, 20hr., Rp25,100, A/C Rp30,100); **Jakarta** (10am-3pm, 30hr., Rp34,000, A/C Rp70,100); **Bengkulu** (1pm, 17hr., Rp17,500); **Sungai Penuh** (10am, 4-5pm, 10-13hr., Rp7500); **Jambi** (3-5pm, 14hr., Rp13,000); **Palembang** (noon, 18hr., super executive Rp45,100); **Bandar Lampung** (noon, 24hr., Rp28,500, A/C Rp62,500); and **Pekanbaru** (8-9am, 3-8pm, 8hr., Rp8500, A/C Rp11,000).

Ferries: Muara Harbor, on Jl. Batang Arau, at the southwestern corner of town. *Bemo* shuttle from Pasar Raya to the harbor irregularly, or catch *bis kota* #14A heading south on Jl. Sudirman. **PT Rusco Lines,** Jl. Batang Arau 88 D/11 (tel. 219 41), 30m down an alley from the Minolta Photocopies sign on Jl. Arau. Open Mon., Wed., and Fri. 8am-6pm, Tues., Thurs., and Sat. 8am-4pm. All ferries leave Padang at 7:30pm from Muara Harbor (deck Rp11,500, cabin Rp16,000, between islands Rp16,000). Mon. to **Muara Siberut,** Pulau Siberut (arrives 6am, Tues.), departing at 1pm for **Muara Sikabaluan,** Pulau Siberut (arrives 4pm), and at 8pm for Padang (arrives 6am Wed.). On Wed., the ferry follows the same timetable with the reverse route. On Fri. ferries leave to **Sioban,** Pulau Sipora (arrives 6am, Sat.), departing at 1pm for **Tua Pejat,** Pulau Sipora (arrives 3pm), departing at 8pm for **Padang** (arrives 6am, Sun.). **PELNI** (tel. 616 24) has ships departing from Teluk Bayur to

Jakarta (Sun., noon, Rp81,500) and **Sibolga** (Fri., 1pm, 26hr., Rp50,000). Open Mon.-Fri. 8am-3pm, Sat. 8am-2pm, Sun. 8-11am. Two other harbors, **Bungus** and **Teluk Bayur,** run ferries to similar destinations.

Local Transportation: The usual array of city buses, taxis, microlets, *bemo,* and *dokar.* Catch local transportation at Pasar Raya.

Markets: Pasar Raya encompasses several whole blocks of buildings east of the bus terminal. Open daily 7am-6pm. The **night market** along Jl. Permindo at the western edge of the *pasar* extends to 9pm.

Pharmacies: Apotik Al Azhar, Jl. Proklamasi 54 (tel. 326 14), 100m east of the post office, next to several pharmacies. Open 24hr.

Medical Services: Rumah Sakit Dr. M. Jamil, (tel. 223 55) on Jl. Kemerdekaan, 500m east of Jl. Sudirman.

Police: (tel. 223 17), on Jl. M. Yamin next to the post office.

Post Offices: Pos Besar Padang, Jl. Aziz Chan 7 (tel. 278 15). *Poste Restante.* Open Mon.-Sat. 7:30am-8pm, Sun. 7:30am-6pm. **Postal code:** 25000.

Telephones: Telkom office, Jl. A. Dahlan 17 (tel. 506 42), 2km up Jl. Sudirman/ Aziz Chan from the post office on the right. **HCD** phones. Open 24hr. **Wartel CV Ria,** Jl. Belakang Tangsi 3 (tel. 376 90), south of Jl. M. Yamin between the Pasar Raya and Jl. Pemuda/Diponegoro. Fax, international calls and collect calls. Open 24hr. **Telephone code:** 0751.

ACCOMMODATIONS

Budget *losmen* cluster along Jl. Pemuda near the bus terminal, while quieter places scatter about town.

Sriwijaya, Jl. Alang I/15 (tel. 235 77). Head right 100m east of the post office on Jl. M. Yamin/Proklamasi, down Jl. Alang Lawas I; it's 70m on the right. Economy rooms come with a fan and porch area in front. Singles Rp10,000, with *mandi* Rp15,000. Doubles Rp14,000, with *mandi* Rp18,000. Triples Rp18,000. Quads Rp22,000. A/C rooms range Rp20-30,000. Small restaurant.

Hotel Benyamin, Jl. Aziz Chan 19 (tel. 223 24), down an alley behind Femina Hotel, just up from the post office. Well worth braving the heat and venturing beyond the bus terminal. Upstairs rooms get a nice breeze and it's clean and pleasant. Breakfast included. Singles Rp15,000. Doubles with fan and *mandi* Rp24,000. Triple suite with TV Rp35,000, with A/C Rp43,000.

Hotel Tiga Tiga, Jl. Pemuda 31 (tel. 226 33), across from the bus terminal. Many clean, mosquito-free rooms, although, because of the area, peace and quiet are a bit lacking. Tiny restaurant, but good common areas. Singles Rp10,000, with fan and *mandi* Rp20,000, with A/C Rp25,000. Doubles Rp15,000, with fan and *mandi* Rp26,000, with A/C Rp33,000. Triples Rp20,000, with fan and *mandi* Rp32,000, with A/C Rp41,000.

FOOD

For the less daring, Padang restaurants have more than your average spicy Padang food. **Lunch warung** are at the bus terminal and just east toward Pasar Raya. At night, Jl. M. Yamin and Jl. Permido on the western edge of the *pasar* are alive with culinary activity and *warung* are also set up along **Pantai Padang,** where Jl. M. Yamin ends. There's an A/C food bazaar on the second floor of **Matahari.**

Simpang Raya, Jl. Bundo Kandung 3-5 (tel. 264 30), south from Matahari, 50m on the right, and Jl. Aziz Chan 24 (tel. 248 94), across from the post office. A delicious chain of restaurants popular with tourists who come to savor Padang food. The various bowls are stacked precariously high, but yield excellent flavor. Fish with sauce (Rp1000), breaded chicken (Rp1500), *nasi soto* (Rp2200). Open Sat.-Thurs. 7am-9pm, Fri. 7-11:30am and 1:30-9pm.

Restaurant Tunpa Nama, Jl. Rohara Kudus 87 (tel. 266 87), 300m north of Jl. Permido on the western edge of Pasar Raya. An original "upscale" restaurant in Padang which serves quality fare at good prices. Outdoor and indoor seating; karaoke on

Saturday nights. *Rendang daging* (special beef, Rp1400), chicken curry (Rp1800), chicken satay (Rp500 per stick). Open Sat.-Thurs. 10am-10pm.

SIGHTS

Most "culture" in this city is pre-digested to some extent. The **Taman Budaya** (Cultural Centre), Jl. Diponegoro 19, stages traditional dances most evenings; go by to check the schedule. Across the street at Jl. Diponegoro 10, the **Museum Negeri Sumatera Barat** is located in a traditional Minangkabau house with two rice barns out front. The entrance gate is at the far end on Jl. Gereja, across from the Natour Muara Hotel. (Open Tues.-Sun. 9am-4pm; admission Rp250.)

Pantai Padang stretches up the western edge of town, hosting numerous vendors and *warung* during the evening along the southern part. The beach is a bit dirty, but the views of the ocean and the setting sun can be spectacular. **Air Manis Beach** is long, tame, and remarkably picturesque and home of the famous **Malin Kundang stone.** To get there, walk south along Pantai Padang until you hit the river—narrow boats ferry across for Rp200 per person. On the other side, the path leads past Japanese fortifications, through a Chinese cemetery, and eventually to the beach, about 4km down (on Sun., admission to the path Rp300, same for the beach). From the far end of the beach it's about 1km more to Teluk Bayur. Microlets shuttle every 30 minutes along the paved road from Air Manis to Padang (Rp500), or catch the frequent buses on the main road at Teluk Bayur. In the more distant waters there are coral-ringed islands for snorkeling; excursions run from the Cendrawasih Hotel (US$18 per day, or try to bargain to charter a fishing boat for less).

KERINCI NATIONAL PARK

Spanning four provinces, untouristed Kerinci is a magnificent enclave of Kerinci culture, highland agriculture, and mountainous jungle. Designated as a national park in 1982 and now an ASEAN heritage site, the park is dominated by 3805-m Gunung Kerinci, which rises from the highland valley. Pristine mountain lakes and dense jungle soar over crashing waterfalls which feed the tea and cinnamon plantations at elevations of up to 1500m.

The park is a model of Indonesia's genuine efforts toward conservation. The well-established World Wide Fund for Nature (WWF) has worked closely with local farmers to curtail illegal cultivation and animal poaching. Large tracts of jungle remain to be explored, home to an estimated 4000 species of plants, 37 species of mammals, 136 species of birds, and the mythical *orang pendek.* The Sumatran elephant, rhino, and tiger all make their home in the park, while bird-watchers flock to the area to marvel at such creatures as the bronze-tailed peacock pheasant, Schneider's pitta, and Salvadori's pheasant. The valley around Sungai Penuh and Danau Kerinci rests at 800m, allowing for pleasantly cool nights, while the villages in the Kayu Aro region, at 1500m, provide chillingly cold showers in the mornings. A genuine friendliness and respect for foreigners pervades the valley and, like the ecosystem of the park, respect for the region's people should be maintained.

■ Sungai Penuh

The capital of the Kerinci District lies among rice paddies and rolling hills, far removed from the provincial administration in Jambi. The town serves as a good base for planning trips and treks to the nearby countryside and mountains. Children are overjoyed by the presence of tourists on the streets, and often form a phalanx of bubbling smiles around the few ambling visitors who make it up here.

ORIENTATION

The town rests on a hillside, rising uphill to the south. The large square at the center of town helps orient the wayward, guarded by **Jalan Imam Bonjol** on the south side and **Jalan Sudirman** on the west side. The **bus terminal** and **market** are downhill 100m from the northeast corner of the square. **Jalan Martadinata** heads east, downhill from the eastern side of the square.

PRACTICAL INFORMATION

Tourist Offices: Kerinci National Park Headquarters, Jl. Basuki Rahmat 11 (tel. 222 50). From the northwest corner of the square, head west on the road toward Kayu Aro. The office is 100m uphill on the right, before the soccer field. A great place to get unbiased info on the park's sights and activities. Brochures and maps in English, as well as detailed information on the park's wildlife. Open Mon.-Thurs. 7am-2pm, Fri. 7-11am, Sat. 7am-1pm.

Currency Exchange: Bank BRI, Jl. Sudirman 3 (tel. 213 19), at the corner with Jl. A. Yani. Open Mon.-Thurs. 8am-3pm, Fri. 8-11:30am and 2-3pm, Sat. 8-11:30am.

Buses: Buses and minivans depart from the **terminal,** although it may be faster to catch minivans on the road out. To: **Padang** (10am and 5pm, 10-13hr., Rp7500); **Jambi** (10am and 4pm, 13hr., Rp8000); **Bengkulu** (noon, 18hr., Rp11,000); **Kayu Aro, Kersik Tua,** and **Pelompek** (every hr., 7am-6pm, Rp1000).

Local Transportation: Horse-drawn **bendi** race about town at a remarkably fast clip (Rp500-1000).

Pharmacies: Apotik Kerinci, Jl. Sisingamangaraja 27 (tel. 216 02), north of the square. Open daily 8am-8pm.

Medical Services: (tel. 210 18), on Jl. Basuki Rahmat, across from the park office.

Police: (tel. 21110), on Jl. Depati Parto. Head down Jl. Martadinata and bear right at the fork. It's another 800m down on the right.

Post Offices: Jl. Sudirman 1A (tel. 210 10), at the southwest corner of the square. Open Mon.-Thurs. 8am-5pm, Fri. 8-11am, Sat. 8am-3pm. **Postal code:** 37114.

Telephones: Telkom office (tel. 215 80), on Jl. Imam Bonjol, at the southeast corner of the square. **HCD** phone. Open 24hr. **Telephone code:** 0748.

ACCOMMODATIONS

Hotel Matahari, Jl A. Yani 25 (tel. 210 62). Head one block west of the post office; it's 150m uphill on the left. A step above the rest with spacious rooms overlooking town. Good tourist info posted and the proprietors are quite helpful. Singles Rp5000. Doubles Rp8000. Triples Rp12,000, all with shared *mandi.* Tack on a *mandi* for Rp6000 per person (2-6 people).

Losmen Anak Gunung, Jl. Agus Salim 43 (tel. 210 18), left off Jl. Martadinata, 70m from the square on the right. Close-packed rooms lend a tight feel with neighbors, but this is the norm for all the cheaper *losmen* in the area. The prices can't be beat though. Singles Rp3000. Doubles Rp6000.

FOOD

Warung and hole-in-the-wall establishments flourish around the north edge of the square, as well as down Jl. Martadinata and Jl. Muradi.

Rumah Makan Minang Soto, Jl. Muradi 4 (tel. 214 42), 200m down Jl. A. Yani from Hotel Matahari. The restaurant is a bit more expensive than local *warung,* but the thriving local crowd attests to its culinary excellence. As the name suggests, this is a great place to slurp down *minang soto,* a hearty beef stew served with white rice (Rp2200). Open daily 7am-11pm.

Restaurant Marantama, Jl. Depati Parbo 8 (tel. 214 43), down Jl. Martadinata, on the right just after the fork in the road. A popular, nice *nasi padang* joint that fills take-out orders. Run by a friendly Muslim family who will continue to refill your tea and water at no extra charge *ad eternitum.* Chicken (Rp2200), beef (Rp1500-2000), and fish (Rp700-1500) dishes. Open daily 5:30am-9pm.

SIGHTS

The graceful **Mesjid Agung Pondok Tinggi** is an old, pagoda-style mosque perched on the hillside in town up Jl. Sudirman, 200m from the post office. Built in 1874, the original mosque was constructed with no nails, although iron bolts appear to connect the rafters. The soaring interior is remarkably peaceful, with wooden planks and beams painted in bright colors. The mosque is locked, although an inquiry to the locals roaming about will produce the key. (Donation requested.)

Heading in the opposite direction, the **Semurup Hot Springs,** 12km north of town, soothe the hot-shower starved with their mildly sulfurous waters (admission Rp500). Communal *mandi* (separated by sex) disperse tolerably hot water in the long building directly before the springs. For true hot *mandi* revelry, shell out Rp500 for your own private room, but test the water temperature since it varies in the different rooms. To reach the hot springs, catch a minivan from the bus terminal; ask for "Air Panas Semurup." If you're lucky there might be one that's going directly to the springs (Rp600). Otherwise most buses can drop you off at the intersection of the main road (Rp400). From the intersection, it's a 2-km walk; bear right at the fork after 1km and then left after another 700m.

The Kerinci people perform **traditional dances,** including *asyiek,* which contacts the spirits of dead ancestors. Also unique to the area is Basikie music, a complex mix of various drum beats. Suling Bambu music involves bamboo flute, music, and singing. These ceremonies and dances are hard to come by, but you may be treated to one if spending several nights in a local village. Guides in Sungai Penuh also offer to arrange showings for Rp20,000 per performance.

■ Kayu Aro

As the bus putters uphill from Sungai Penuh to this region at the foot of Gunung Kerinci, hedge-like tea plantations roll out to cinnamon trees, which blush the hillsides a light rosé color. The region is collectively called Kayu Aro and is divided into three distinct towns: Bedeng VIII, home of the tea factory; Kersik Tua, 7km north and the starting point for treks up the mountain; and the larger Pelompek, another 10km up, the starting point for hikes to Danau Gunung Tujuh. The region hosts an interesting mix of cultures, as most of the workers on the tea plantation are descendants of the original Javanese workers originally imported to the area by the Dutch. The Javanese mingle with the local Kerinci people, who dominate the rest of the area. The homestays are heaven to travelers seeking solitude from the rush of tourism in other parts of Sumatra.

ORIENTATION AND PRACTICAL INFORMATION

Each of the three towns is an easily negotiated one-street affair. Buses and minivans shuttle between **Pelompek** and **Sungai Penuh,** and are easily flagged down at **Kersik Tua** or **Bedeng VIII** (every 30min., 7am-6pm, 1½hr., Rp1000). Buses to Padang can be flagged down (11:30am and 5-6pm, 10hr., Rp6000). Two small **PPA** huts lie at the entrance to the park 2km west of Kersik Tua and in **Sungai Jernih** village (2km east of Pelompek). Purchase permits at either of these huts (or the park headquarters in Sungai Penuh) to enter the park (Rp1500 per sight). There's no official tourist office, but **Eco-Rural Travel office** in Kersik Tua, directly across from the turn-off up the mountain, dispenses good information and offers guide services. If it's closed, head over to Subandi Homestay (50m south), and Subandi, who works for the tour company, can open it up. A small **police** post and **health clinic** are in each of the three towns. **Postal code:** 37163. There's **no telephone** service.

ACCOMMODATIONS AND FOOD

Bedeng VIII has no *losmen,* but five homestays are sprinkled along the road in Kersik Tua. Highly recommended is **Subandi Homestay,** 50m south of the turnoff to the mountain. The friendly family makes you feel at home. Guests can sip complimentary tea and breakfast on the porch overlooking the tea plantation and soaring Gunung Kerinci. Subandi is an excellent source of information on the area, and can help you arrange your activities of choice. Rooms cost Rp6000 per person.

Several *losmen* and restaurants dot Pelompek, but the real getaways are up the hill at the border to the park near Sungai Jernih village. **Solok Homestay** is 100m from the PPA hut (Mr. Solok is a ranger) and earns high marks for its peacefulness and friendly proprietor. Rooms are Rp6000 per person, Rp2500 per meal. The adventurous can hike 1.5km toward Danau Gunung Tujuh to the **KSNP Guesthouse,** which lies in the park. There's no phone or electricity here or at Solok, but you can bring your own food in from Pelompek or ask the ranger to cook for you.

SIGHTS

The sprawling 5000 hectares of the **PTP Nusantara-VI tea plantation** yield 18 tons of Aroma Tea daily, which is primarily exported to Europe. A combined force of 4000 workers collects leaves in the fields, which become tea in Bedeng VIII's factory—a mere 24 hours from picking to packing. The whole operation is tightly controlled, with considerable security. Complimentary tours are available when the factory is operating (Tues.-Sat., 7am-8pm; Rp2000 per person tip recommended).

Secluded **Danau Gunung Tujuh** is the highest freshwater lake in Southeast Asia at 1996m, surrounded by dense virgin jungle, solidly within the bounds of the park. Hike up from Pelompek to marvel at the seven mountains from which the lake takes it name, or take a dip in its refreshing water. It's a pleasant day hike from Sungai Jernih village (2hr.), and a guide is not necessary, despite what touts may claim. From the end of the asphalt road at Sungai Jernih (2km east of Pelompek), a large welcome gate marks the park's entrance. Buy your permit at the PPA office (Rp1500), and follow the path, which narrows to a clear trail past some houses. Remember to take a snack, water, rain gear, and a sweater, as it can be quite cool, especially when it rains. Just 4km up the main road from Pelompek in **Letter** village is the 50m-high **Telun Berasap Waterfall,** which cascades off the mountain into a fierce pool. Catch a northbound bus from Pelompek (Rp400); the waterfall is a 300-m hike from the village. Guides are available for all activities in the park, although it's wise to choose an HPI-licensed guide (check with the park headquarters).

CLIMBING KERINCI

A guide is highly recommended for the climb up Gunung Kerinci, which usually takes two days, even though the climbing time is only eight hours from Kersik Tua. As recently as 1992, three Javanese hikers who were climbing without a guide died on the mountain (one fell to his death, the other two got lost in the jungle and were never found). The first day of hiking is not too strenuous—about six hours through the tea plantation to the park boundary (Rp1500 permits at the PPA hut here), climbing up through the jungle to Camp 2, a shelter at 3000m with some fresh water. The final steep ascent to the summit can then be accomplished in the morning, when there's the greatest chance of no cloud cover. Sleeping bags can be rented in Kersik Tua for Rp4000 per night. Guides up the mountain run Rp30,000 per day, although a group of climbers can join with one guide. The weather at the high altitudes can be cold (down to freezing) and fickle (snow or hail possible), and climbers should take warm clothes and a sleeping bag for the night.

SOUTHERN SUMATRA

■ Bengkulu

A friendly, backwater provincial capital, Bengkulu will remind weary travelers why they love Indonesia. This city on the southwest coast of Sumatra is a pleasant surprise. It's a pilgrimage hot spot for both Soekarno devotees (his former house and cell are here) and Rafflesia hunters (the flower was "discovered" here by Sir Stamford Raffles in 1818). Although there isn't much to do in Bengkulu, it is a typical stop-over point on the journey between Padang and Bandar Lampung. Yet this very quality lends it charm; uncrowded, unspoiled, convenient beaches are easy to come by, and with a full range of accommodations nearby, Bengkulu can't be beat.

ORIENTATION

The main road into town runs southeast to northwest and changes names from **Jalan Parman** to **Jalan Suprapto** at the BNI Bank boat sculpture. At the **Mesjid Jamik** (the red-roofed central mosque) it changes names again to **Jalan Sudirman** and continues sinuously west as **Jalan A. Yani**. **Jalan Haryono** jets off northeast at the intersection by the Mesjid Jamik. The **beach** is on the southwest coast.

PRACTICAL INFORMATION

Tourist Offices: (tel. 212 72), on Jl. Pembangunan; take a yellow colt headed out of town. Travel agents in town carry the same brochures and local maps.

Currency Exchange: Not all the banks on Jl. Parman exchange. Try **BCA,** Jl. Suprapto 150A (tel. 217 04), downtown. Open Mon.-Fri. 8am-2pm, Sat. 8-11am.

Air Travel: The **airport** lies 14km east of the city, accessible via yellow colt or taxi (Rp10-15,000). To: **Palembang** (3 per week); **Jakarta** (daily); **Padang;** and **Bandar Lampung. Merpati,** Jl. Sudirman 246 (tel. 272 22), next to the Hotel Samudera Dwinka. Open daily 8am-5pm. **Garuda,** Jl. A. Yani 922 (tel. 214 16). Open daily 8am-5pm. Travel agents such as **C.S.H. 88,** Jl. Suprapto 88 (tel. 228 35), can also book flights. C.S.H. has a helpful, English-speaking staff.

Buses: Inter-provincial buses stop at the **Terminal Panorama,** 7km from town (a colt to town is Rp300), or at their local private stations in the city. For any long distance travel, don't deprive yourself of a basic level of comfort; take A/C or minibuses. **Citra Rafflesia** (tel. 203 13; open 24hr.) and **San Travel** (tel. 218 11; open daily 6am-6pm) are across the street from each other on Jl. Haryono. Both offer A/C, fully equipped buses to: **Jakarta** (2 per day, 22hr., Rp60,000); **Padang** (1 per day, 8hr., Rp27,000); **Palembang** (1 per day, 8hr., Rp27,000); and **Yogyakarta** (1 per day, 60hr., Rp80,000). Take a minibus to **Jambi.** Cheaper bus companies offering hellish rides for half the price can also be found on Jl. Haryono.

Local Transportation: Microlets cruise the streets in inconsistent paths for Rp300. Yellow ones go farther out of town, and any can be chartered to go to whatever destination you please. **Becak** and **dokar** also compete for passengers.

Rentals: Yudi Rent-A-Car, Jl. Sitikhadijah 93 (tel. 267 26), and the rental service at the **Horizon Hotel** rent **cars** for a steep price.

Markets: Pasar Minggu, a large horseshoe-shaped market, extends off Jl. Suprapto onto Jl. Abidin and curves around, petering out again at the main road. Mobile food carts also cruise the scene.

Pharmacies: Apotik Purnama, Jl. Suprapto 4 (tel. 422 86). Open daily 8am-9pm.

Medical Services: RS Jiwa (tel. 229 88), on Jl. Bakti Husada.

Emergency: Ambulance: tel. 211 18.

Police: (tel. 221 10), across from the governor's mansion on Jl. A. Yani.

Post Offices: GPO, on Jl. Parman III, far away. Take a yellow colt headed out of town. Open daily 8am-4pm. Try the closer **branch,** Jl. A. Yani 38, near Ft. Marlboro. Open Mon.-Thurs. and Sat. 8am-3pm, Fri. 8-11:30am. **Postal code:** 38225.

Telephones: **Telkom office,** Jl. Suprapto 132 (tel. 200 00). International and collect calls. Open 24hr. **Telephone code:** 0736.

ACCOMMODATIONS

Bengkulu has dirt-cheap *losmen* with friendly, laid-back atmospheres. It's hot and muggy everywhere, so it's worthwhile to invest in a fan and some mosquito coils. Check-in and check-out times are pretty standard, but negotiable. Travelers arriving late at night should just knock persistently; someone should eventually appear.

Hotel Vista, Jl. Haryono 67 (tel. 208 20), welcomes travelers with their cheerful and friendly management and bright, spotless, white rooms. The TV is loud, but no more than usual. A room in the back at least takes you away from traffic horns. Singles in the front of the hotel Rp6500. Doubles Rp7500-15,000, depending on location and amenities. The Rp12,500 rooms have clean, private *mandi* and fan.

Losmen Surya, Jl. Abidin 26 (tel. 213 41). Rooms tend to be dark and noisy, but try to get one in the back, preferably on the 3rd floor, for a great view of the market below and a decent breeze. The shared *mandi* could use some cleaning. Singles Rp6000. Doubles Rp8000. Treat yourself to a fan (Rp1000).

Losmen Damai, Jl. Abidin 18 (tel. 229 12), across the street from Losmen Surya. Has virtually no amenities to speak of and the rooms are dark, but you get what you pay for (in this case very little). Singles Rp3000, with private *mandi* Rp6000. Doubles Rp4000, with private *mandi* Rp7500. Fans Rp1000.

Nala Seaside Cottages, Jl. Pantai Nala (tel. 218 55), next to the Hotel Horizon. A bit more pricey, but in prime location about 50m from the ocean and an empty beach. The cozy pink quarters are straight out of a cotton candy fantasy. Soft mattresses, showers, and A/C. Singles Rp30,000. Doubles Rp36,000. An extra bed Rp7500. Breakfast and tax included. Restaurant on premises. AmEx.

FOOD

Padang restaurants with a large variety of meat, chicken, fish, and tempeh have sprung up all over Bengkulu. **Warung** seem less abundant than usual, but can be found, especially around the market. A string of four seafood restaurants have very good (although similar) menus of fresh seafood, just northwest of the mosque on Jl. A. Yani. **Bakeries** on Jl. Suprapto serve the bread-starved well, but beware of the chocolate gook that seems to sneak itself into every loaf. The yummiest, stickiest, most buttery *martabak* in Indonesia can also be had right here in Bengkulu.

SIGHTS

Rumah Bung Karno (Brother Karno's Home), on Jl. Soekarno-Hatta, on the southern part of town, is the house where Indonesia's first president, Soekarno, served in exile from the Dutch from 1938 to 1941 (open daily 8am-5pm; admission Rp200). It's fairly modest, but not a bad place to serve time. To the northwest of Soekarno's house, at the convergence of Jl. Sudirman and Jl. Suprapto, is the stately **Mesjid Jamik,** which was designed by the engineer-turned-politician Soekarno during his exile. Also near the house to is the **Bengkulu Museum,** on Jl. Pembangunan. (Open Sun.-Thurs. 8am-2pm, Fri. 9-11am, Sat. 8am-noon; admission Rp200.) It's in an impressive building, but houses an insignificant collection.

Heading west from the famous house leads to Jl. Hasan. Go north a bit and at the intersection with Jl. Sentoso is the **Hamilton Monument,** an obelisk memorial to a certain Mr. Hamilton who died for the British cause here. North on Hasan is downtown Bengkulu, situated on the promontory sticking out into the ocean. Go up to Jl. Berlian to the intersection with Jl. A. Yani where **Fort Marlborough** stands overlooking the sea. (Open Sun.-Thurs. 8am-2pm, Fri. 9-11am, Sat. 8am-noon; admission Rp200.) Reconstructed a few years ago, it's in good shape now. It offers a small caisson with historical pictures and good views of the sea and town. Abutting the fort to the west **Chinatown** *(Kampung Cina)* spreads out behind Pasar Barukoto by the sea, constituting the oldest part of the city (look for the red-roofed buildings).

INDONESIA

The Life of Sir Stamford Raffles: Part the Fifth

With fame and fortune secure in England after his highly important stint in Bogor, the Colonialist Wonder, Sir Stamford Raffles, relentlessly devoted to oriental exotica, returned to the archipelago as the administrative advisor in Bencoolen (present-day Bengkulu) in southwest Sumatra. Finding the Sumatrans too unruly even for him, Raffles (and some botanist named Arnold), discovered the world's largest flower, which he fittingly named after himself, *Rafflesia arnoldy*. (To uncover one of Sir Stamford's greatest achievements, see page 449.)

Bengkulu's beaches are accessible on foot through the Nala Seaside Cottages or with a Rp200 admission fee. The beaches are clean, wide, and virtually empty except for a few fishermen. Surf breaks on a rocky reef offshore by the cottages at **Pantai Panjang.** Farther south is **Pasir Putih Beach,** by Pulau Baai Harbor, about 19km away. The harbor is the departure point for weekly PELNI service to **Enggano Island,** home to a few villages that rarely see foreigners. To stay on Enggano contact the *kepala desa,* the village head, upon arrival. Enjoy the beaches, but watch out for the poisonous snakes in the jungle. The **Samudera Dwinka Hotel,** Jl. Sudirman 246 in Bengkulu, arranges boats to **Pulau Tikus** (Rat Island), which is visible from the beach. It has a lighthouse and makes a popular daytrip fishing spot.

A dried **Rafflesia** flower can be seen at the university campus, and the motif is found all over Bengkulu in many designs. Those hoping for the real thing should go first to the **PHPA office,** Jl. Mahoni 11, which should have hints about where to look (usually on the outskirts of Tabapenanjung and Kepahiang). Rafflesias typically bloom during July and August for a couple of weeks.

■ Palembang

The largest city in South Sumatra Province, Palembang is largely supported by Pertamina oil refineries. Its claim to fame is the legacy of the Srivijaya Empire, although very little remains now to show for it. Today, this small metropolis moves at a rate similar to busy parts of Jakarta, with its epicenter revolving around the large and noisome Musi River. The traveler may find the true interest in Palembang lies outside its scant museums and sights in the riverside fruit market.

ORIENTATION

Ampera Bridge connects the north and south areas of Palembang, although most facilities lie on the northern side of the river. **Jalan Sudirman** is the noisy, dusty main drag, running northwest from the bridge and the **Monpera Monument. Jalan Iskandar** runs east from the intersection at the **International Plaza,** and runs past **Jalan Kol. Atmo,** which roughly parallels Jl. Sudirman. Farther up, Jl. Sudirman crosses **Jalan Kapt. Rivai.**

PRACTICAL INFORMATION

Tourist Offices: Dinas Parawisata, on Jl. Benteng behind the Monpera Monument, ground floor of Museum Budaya. Brochures for Palembang and South Sumatra. Open Mon.-Thurs. 8am-4pm, Fri. 8-11am, Sat. 8am-4pm. The head of the office, Mr. Abi Sofyman, is extremely knowledgeable.

Currency Exchange: Bank BNI, Jl. Sudirman 142 (tel. 313 502). Open Mon.-Fri. 8am-3pm, Sat. 8am-1pm. **Bank Bali,** Jl. Kol. Atmo 479 (tel. 311 38), at the intersection with Jl. Iskandar. Open Mon.-Fri. 8am-4pm.

Air Travel: Sultan Mahmud Badarddin II (Talang Betutu) Airport, 12km north of town. By taxi (Rp12,500, 15min.) or by public bus. Take *bis kota* to Km12 (Rp400) and then another to the airport (Rp200). To: **Jakarta** (4 per day); **Semarang** (1 per day); **Yogyakarta** (1 per day); and **Denpasar** (1 per day). **Garuda** and **Merpati** offices (tel. 368 404) are in Hotel Sandjaya on Jl. Kapt. Rivai. Open Mon.-

Fri. 7:30am-4:45pm, Sat. 9am-1pm. Bouraq and Sempati serve **Bangka** and **Beli-tung Islands.**

Trains: Kerpati Station, across the river from the tourist office, about 4km west. Take any colt or *bis kota* going to Kerpati (mostly yellow vehicles). To **Bandar Lampung** (3 per day, 8hr., 1st class Rp27-31,500, 2nd class Rp15-21,500) and **Lubuklinggau** (3 per day, 1st class Rp23-26,500; 2nd class Rp13,500).

Buses: A rash of bus companies on Jl. Kol. Atmo, north of Jl. Iskandar, go every which way in A/C comfort. **ANS** (tel. 364 814), **PO Putra Remaja** (tel. 356 185), and **CSH 88** (tel. 357 107) are open daily until early evening. To: **Padang** and **Bukittinggi** (15hr.); **Malang** (24hr.); **Jakarta** (17hr.); **Bandung** (20hr.); **Yogyakarta** and **Surabaya** (22hr.); **Denpasar** (30hr.); **Medan** (34hr.); **Banda Aceh** (45hr.); and **Bengkulu** (10hr.).

Ferries: Ferry port, about 7km downstream from Ampera Bridge. To **Jakarta, Bengkulu, Jambi, Batam,** and **Bangka** and **Belitung Islands.** Arrange through travel agencies. **PT Musita,** Jl. Sudirman 616 (tel. 313 921). Open Mon.-Sat. 8am-5pm. **Lukuta Ltd.,** Jl. Kol. Atmo 609 (tel. 364 029). Open daily 8am-5pm.

Taxis: Taxis for hire roam town and congregate outside the International Plaza, at the intersection of Jl. Sudirman and Jl. Iskandar, and by Ampera Bridge. Or, call **Trans Ampera Taxi** (tel. 811 520).

Local Transportation: Big *bis kota* (city buses) run from Km12 outside of town on different routes: yellow go to **Kerpati,** red to **Plaju,** and random colors go to **Pusri** and **Lamabang.** All are clearly marked and cost Rp200-400. Smaller yellow colts parked outside the tourist office in from of Ampera Bridge travel a circuitous route around town and then go to the train station (Rp300).

Markets: The **Pasar 16 Ilir** has no clear boundaries and extends some distance by the bridge along the river, northeast of Jl. Sudirman. A few km up Jl. Sudirman is **Pasar Cinde,** north of the intersection with Jl. Jalmas.

Pharmacies: Apotik Rora, Jl. Sudirman 200 (tel. 350 086), opposite International Plaza. Open 24hr.

Medical Services: RS Caritas, Jl. Sudirman 809 (tel. 353 375).

Emergency: Police: tel. 110. **Ambulance:** tel. 118 or 354 088.

Police: Jl. Iskandar 35 (tel. 354 350), next to Bank Bumi Daya. Open 24hr.

Post Offices: GPO, Jl. Merdeka 3 (tel. 352 626), next to the Monpera. Open Mon.-Fri. 8am-7:30pm, Sat. 8am-6pm, Sun. 8am-7pm. **Postal code:** 30132.

Telephones: Many 24-hr. **wartel** are scattered around town, especially on Jl. Sudirman. The big **Telkom office,** Jl. Merdeka 5 (tel. 360 056), is next to the GPO. Fax, telegrams, telex, and **HCD.** Open 24hr. **Telephone code:** 0711.

ACCOMMODATIONS

Palembang has plenty of expensive hotels, a limited number of moderately priced ones, but no true budget accommodations. *Losmen* seem to have slipped out of existence here, if they ever existed at all.

Hotel Sriwidjaya, Jl. Iskandar 31 (tel. 355 555), down an alley on the south side of the street near the intersection with Jl. Sudirman. Clean rooms are well-furnished, but somewhat cramped. Choose between a room by a loud TV lounge or by the noisy street. Either way, the wake-up call is at 5:45am, when the hotel delivers breakfast to the rooms. Rooms have *mandi,* fan, and towel. Singles Rp18-21,000, with A/C and TV Rp30,000. Doubles Rp19-24,000, with A/C and TV Rp32,500. Breakfast included.

Hotel Nusantara, Jl. Iskandar 563 (tel. 353 306). Set off the street a bit, Nusantara has some quieter alternatives to the loud Palembang accommodations. Rooms are medium-sized with big, comfortable mattresses. Doubles with fan and private *mandi* Rp20,000, with A/C and other amenities Rp25-35,000.

Hotel Hasah As, Jl. Iskandar 636 (tel. 365 221). One of the cheapest places to stay in Palembang. Rooms are unusually bright with big windows and a small balcony. All rooms have fan and shared *mandi.* Singles Rp12,500. Doubles Rp15-17,500. Triples Rp20,000. Quads Rp22,500.

Hotel Sintera, Jl. Sudirman 38 (tel. 354 618). Enter from the Seman Bridge overpass or from the entrance below; it's set back from the street. Spacious lounges with leather chairs and fish tanks on each floor are nice hang-out spots, although many rooms also have small living areas of their own. Singles with fan and private *mandi* Rp20,000. Doubles Rp25,000 and Rp33,000, with A/C and living room Rp38,500 and Rp44,000. Breakfast included.

FOOD

Palembang has few mid-range establishments, but *padang* restaurants are every-where, offering a wide range of specialties. **Warung** congregate a block off the river, both by the GPO and east of Ampera Bridge. The local specialty is *pempek* (soft, eggy dough around chilis, eggs, veggies, and more), which is found in many Indonesian restaurants. **Pasar 16 Ilir** sells fresh fruit, including papayas for Rp500.

SIGHTS

The **Ampera Bridge,** built by the Japanese from 1962-65 as reparation for their destruction of Indonesia in World War II, is a good place to view life on the Musi River. To cruise the Musi, bargain with a captain at the **Boom Baru dock,** one of the ferry ports, and expect to pay Rp25,000 for four hours. Alternatively, talk to Mr. Sofy-man at the tourist office, who often leads tours of the river with a stop at Palembang's famous batik factory (Rp25,000 for a boat).

Next to the GPO, standing conspicuously north of the Ampera Bridge west of the major rotary is **Monpera,** a monument which looks like a huge origami experiment. It was erected in memory of a battle fought for five days and five nights against the Dutch in 1947. Across the street is **Mesjid Agung,** a mosque built in 1738. Behind Monpera is the **Museum Budaya** in an old, restored Dutch building, upstairs from the tourist office. Although the collection is skimpy, a talkative curator tries to prove oth-erwise (open Mon.-Sat. 8am-2pm). The **Museum Negeri Propinsi Sumatra Selatan** (tel. 411 382), located at Km6, has well-organized collections with Indonesian subti-tles. The textiles and traditional outfits are interesting, as are the *rumah lima* and statues out back (open Tues.-Sat. 8am-2pm). Take a bus heading for Km12 and get off at the museum turnoff. From there it's about 0.5km to the left. Farther up the main road, between Km6 and Km7, is the five-hectare public garden **Hutan Wisata Pun-tikayu.** In addition to a wide assortment of trees and flora, the garden is home to the usual monkeys, crocodiles, and deer.

Touted by locals as the "second Bali," **Pulau Bangka** and **Belitung,** accessible by ferry, lie in the waters to the east of Palembang, toward Kalimantan. Palembang serves as a good departure point for these fully equipped vacation spots, with cot-tages on unspoiled white sand beaches with fine diving spots. Contact tourist agents in Palembang for transport and accommodation information.

■ Bandar Lampung

The port city Telukbetung and its hillside neighbor Tanjungkarang comprise the urban region of Bandar Lampung. The capital of Lampung Province, the city is a nat-ural rest-stop for the weary backpacker in Sumatra and an excellent source of "ship cloth" tapestries and *tapi* sarong, distinct in their gold and silver embroidery. Back-packers are likely to end up in this transportation hub anyway; air, train, and bus routes pass through the city. Nevertheless, most of Bandar Lampung is necessarily laid-back due to the equatorial heat. Surrounded by beaches and islands, its most famous neighbor is the infamous Krakatau, the island-volcano that demolished Teluk-betung in 1883. Every July the people of Bandar Lampung commemorate this mass destruction with traditional Lampung dances and music, along with parades, races, car rallies, and a foot and boat biathalon around Krakatau.

ORIENTATION

Ferries from Merak, Java arrive in Bakauheni, 90km southeast of Bandar Lampung. Merak is served by buses from almost everywhere in West Java; the most frequent are from Jakarta's Kalideres station (3½hr.). **Bakauheni** is a crowded, Rp1700 bus ride from the Rajabasa bus terminal, 10km northeast of Bandar Lampung (1½hr.), or a Rp6000 shared-taxi ride with door-to-door service—not a bad deal for the extra comfort. The **Rajabasa bus terminal** and **airport** are both north of the city; the **train station** is down the road from most of the cheap accommodations on **Jalan Kotaraja,** which intersects **Jalan Kartini.** Jl. Kartini runs north-south, changing names a few times along the way. It is the center of administrative functions, but unfortunately has a frustratingly haphazard number system.

PRACTICAL INFORMATION

Tourist Offices: Department of Tourism, Post, and Telecommunications, Jl. Kotaraja 12 (tel. 251 900). Although not officially set up as a tourist info center, the office has eager, helpful English speakers divvying out Lampung and Bengkulu brochures. Open Sun.-Fri. 8am-4pm.

Tours and Travel: Femmy Tours and Travel, Jl. W.R. Monginsidi 143 (tel. 446 90), far south on the corner where Jl. Kartini becomes Jl. Monginsidi. Charters **minibuses** for up to 8 people (Rp200,000 per day). Open daily 8am-4pm. **Elendra Tours and Travel** (tel. 704 737), on Jl. Sultan Agung, and **Krakatau Tours,** Jl. Kartini 19-25 (tel. 263 625) offer similar services, including package trips to nearby sights for fairly hefty prices. Both are open daily 8am-4pm.

Currency Exchange: BCA Bank, Jl. Bukittinggi 18D (tel. 665 65). Bring a purchase agreement and passport for traveler's checks. Maximum on AmEx US$300 per day. Open Mon.-Fri. 8am-1pm. **Bank BNI,** Jl. Kartini 51 (tel. 55 202), farther south. Maximum US$300 per day. Open Mon.-Fri. 8am-4pm.

Air Travel: Branti Airport, 24km north of town. To get there, catch a public bus outside of the Merpati office. **Merpati,** Jl. Kartini 90 (tel. 632 26), on the corner of Jl. A. Yani, also sells Garuda tickets. To **Palembang** (Wed.) and **Jakarta** (5 per day, 50min.). Open Mon.-Fri. 7:30am-9pm, Sat.-Sun. 9am-4pm. MC, Visa, DC.

Trains: The **station** is at Jl. Kotaraja 1. Ticket office (tel. 628 854) open daily 10am-6pm. To: **Palembang** (4 per day, 8hr.); **Baturaja** (2-3 per day); **Kotabumi** (2-3 per day); and **Tanjungkarang** (2-3 per day). All fares depend on type of train (Rp5000 for slow economy to Rp28,000 for express, 1st class).

Buses: Rajabasa, main inter-city terminal, 20min. north via light blue *angkot* from the station by the railroad. To: **Palembang** (every hr., 6hr., Rp20,000); **Jambi** (overnight, 18hr., Rp70,000); **Padang** (overnight, 24hr., Rp40,000); and **Bengkulu** (overnight, 14hr., Rp50,000). Buses and share-taxis (Rp6000) go between Rajabasa and the ferry to **Java** (every 20min., Rp2500; A/C Rp3500).

Taxis: All over town. **Dynasty Taxi,** Jl. A. Dahlan 53 (tel. 456 74). For destinations outside the city, **Trans Bandar Taxi,** Jl. Kartini 68, offers set prices for chartered service all over Sumatra and to Jakarta. Open daily 8am-6pm.

Ferries: The 27-km ferry crossing from **Merak,** Java to **Bakauheni,** Sumatra is included in bus and share-taxi fares, but deprives travelers of the option of the small fast boat with A/C, TV, and comfy seats (4 per day, under 1hr., Rp6000). The bigger boats board cars and buses as well (every hr., 2hr., children Rp1500, 2nd class Rp2000, 1st class Rp3000).

Local Transportation: Multicolored **colts** loop around the city. Their main station is by the train station, at the central Tanjungkarang area.

Rentals: The **Sheraton Inn Lampung,** Jl. Monginsidi 175 (tel. 486 666), can arrange a **car** with driver (Rp175,000 per day). English speaker on request.

Markets: Bambu Kuning Plaza, between Jl. Bukittinggi and Jl. Imam Bonjol, is a market with fruit and veggie vendors outside. **Pasar Seni,** across the street from the Telkom office, has local artists' work and batik. Open daily.

Pharmacies: Apotik Tanjung Karang, Jl. Bukittinggi 112 (tel. 523 07). Open daily 8am-9pm. Many others abound throughout town.

Medical Services: RS Dr. H. Abdul Moeloek, Jl. Teuku Umar (tel. 702 445).

Emergency: Police: tel. 255 110. **Ambulance:** tel. 118.

Police: (tel. 253 283), at the intersection of Jl. Kartini and Jl. Imam Bonjol, by the pedestrian overpass. Open 24hr.

Post Offices: GPO, Jl. A. Dahlan 21 (tel. 253 014). Take a green *angkot.* Open daily 8am-8pm. There's small **branch** more centrally located at Jl. Kotaraja 12, next to the tourist office. Open Mon.-Thurs. 8am-1pm, Fri. 8-11am, Sat. 8am-noon, Sun. 9am-5pm. **Postal code:** 35111.

Telephones: Telkom office, Jl. Majapahit 14 (tel. 253 811). Open 24hr. Catch a green colt. **HCD** and collect calls. There are also **wartel** at the Telkom building on Jl. Bukittinggi, just past the police station. **Telephone code:** 0721.

ACCOMMODATIONS

Affordable accommodations cluster in the center of Tanjungkarang. From the bus terminal, take an *angkot* into town, and get off at the intersection of Jl. Kartini and Jl. Kotaraja. Small, dark bottom-end lodgings line Jl. Kotaraja; the pricier hotels off Jl. Kartini offer more creature comforts.

Hotel Ria, Jl. Kartini 79 (tel. 253 974). Spacious rooms have wardrobes, desks, chairs, and drying racks. Rooms with shared *mandi* and fan are Rp17,500, with private *mandi* and fan Rp27,500. Rooms with A/C, TV, and other luxuries run Rp35-45,000. Breakfast and safe deposit box available.

Hotel Gading, Jl. Kartini 72 (tel. 255 512). Look for the big red sign pointing prospective guests down a side street to Gading. Lots of little frills here: showerheads, nice patios, towels with racks, house phones, breakfast, and clean rooms. All rooms have private *mandi.* Rooms Rp20,000, with fan Rp30-40,000, depending on the floor. A/C also available.

Hotel Mini, Jl. Dwi Warna 71 (tel. 255 928), across the side street from Hotel Gading. Although the rooms are smaller and lack the extras, this is probably the best deal around. Plain rooms located away from the main street, but sociable locals in the lobby are just as disruptive as street noise. Nonetheless, for Rp22,000, travelers get cleanliness, private *mandi,* fan, and breakfast.

FOOD

Bakeries queue up along the lengths of Jl. Kartini and Jl. Kotaraja. More **warung** and *padang* restaurants are located off the main strip and along the side streets, especially by Gadang and Mini Hotels. Fruit and *martabak* stands are also plentiful around Bambu Kuning Plaza. One or two km south on Jl. Kartini is the **Garuda Restaurant,** Jl. Kartini 31 (tel. 252 109), which has a multitude of *padang* Indonesian plates (Rp2-8000), just in a restaurant atmosphere. The great juice bar has an assortment of delicious concoctions as well. (Open daily 7am-11pm.)

■ Near Bandar Lampung

Both Lampung Province and the city's environs boast many enjoyable sights and beaches. Unfortunately, getting to many of these places can be difficult and extremely tiresome by public transportation. The more comfortable and less frustrating way to travel around the area is through an expensive tour guide agency.

Out in Lampung Bay are several islands, including **Pulau Sebesi** and **Sebuku.** Sebesi is closest to Krakatau and is served by a morning and afternoon ferry (Rp3000) from **Canti,** a small town about 10km from the Bakauheni ferry port. There are accommodations available, and local boats can be chartered for the 3½-hour trip to Krakatau. Just southeast of Bandar Lampung is **Pasir Putih,** a small, pleasant beach looking out to **Pulau Condong,** a small island resort with pleasant beaches and pricey hotels.

A two-hour drive northeast of the city, **Way Kambas National Park and Elephant Training Centre** is home to Sumatran tigers and rhinos, along with plenty of smaller fauna. Camping is not allowed here. The nearby **Way Kanan River** is an ornithologist's paradise, as it shelters some of Sumatra's rarest, most exotic, and most colorful feathered friends. To the west, Bukit Barisan (Marching Hills) forms a spine on the coast; **Bukit Barisan National Park** begins at the southernmost tip at Tampang, and stretches up the coast. Travelers can explore the **Danau Menjukut** area by boat from Kota Agung to Tampang. There's a camping area near **Wonsobo.** Near the border

The Wrath of Krakatau

Krakatau earned its mark in history on August 27, 1883 when it erupted violently, leaving a trail of destruction felt around the world. The eruption weakened the foundations of the island and it crumbled, as water rushed into its lava interior, resulting in an even more violent explosion in which tons of debris were pitched 20km into the air. The explosion was heard in Australia, volcanic rocks scattered as far Madagascar, and ash encircled the earth for three years. Tsunamis rolled up into vicious 40m-high waves, which effectively devastated hundreds of villages along the Sumatran and Javanese coasts, and their effect could be felt all the way in Europe. The peak of Krakatau was all but destroyed, and, in its place, the explosions left a crater 400m below sea level. For nearly half a century, Krakatau seemed at peace. Then in 1927, from the depths of the crater, Krakatau started smoking again, as a plume of steam flared up unexpectedly. Continued action from below has already piled enough rocks and ashes together to create Krakatau Anak, which is now 150m above sea level. Indeed, it seems that the volcano was merely resting these past 100 years, as seismic activity was detected again in 1979. The question is not only whether Sumatra and Java can take another such eruption, but can the world?

with Bengkulu Province, **Krui**, a small coastal town, is close to some surfing beaches, and **Liwa** is a base for exploring **Danau Ranau**. Near Bandar Lampung there's also **Pugang Raharjo Archaeological Site**, which has megaliths from a Buddhist period in the 12th to 17th centuries; it can be reached from Talang Padian.

KALIENDA

Small, unspoiled Kalienda lies on a south Sumatran inlet, one hour from the ferry port of Bakauheni and about 1½ hours from Bandar Lampung. Kalienda serves as a great activity hub, offering a strenuous mountain climb, relaxing and isolated beaches, hot springs, and the cheapest trips to Krakatau, all within short reach of the eager traveler's fingertips. Although a few moderately priced hotels are beginning to sprout up around town, **Penginapan Beringin**, Jl. Kesuma Bangsa 75 (tel. 2008), remains the most convenient and cheapest place to stay. It's located right on the main thoroughfare in town, and features huge rooms, some with equally large private *mandi*, for Rp11,000. Access to **Way-urang Beach** is just across the street.

Perhaps Kalienda's best function, however, is as a starting point on the way to **Gunung Krakatau**. The Hotel Beringin sets up tours to the mountain-island area for roughly Rp35,000 per person (Rp200,000 for a boat of 6-8 people). The trip consists of a three- to four-hour boat ride to an island about 1km from Krakatau Anak (with a stop along the way for some decent snorkeling) where travelers spend the night in tents by the beach. Only a crater remains of Krakatau today, but Krakatau Anak (which means "Son of Krakatau"), the cone of ash and rocks, is now the active and exciting site. If your guide declares it safe, travelers can actually walk around Anak's base and get a closer look at the black smoke emerging from its crater, although *Let's Go* highly discourages this. As recent as 1993, Krakatau took a group of tourists by surprise, and two Americans were killed.

Access to and from Kalienda is easy. From Bandar Lampung or from Bakauheni, take a bus to Canti, about 3km away, then catch an *angkot* to Kalienda. Ask any local the direction to Hotel Beringin if you get lost. Kalienda does have a few *padang* and Indonesian stalls, a 24-hour **wartel** (tel. 0727) and a pharmacy, **Apotik Rajabasa** (tel. 2333; open Mon.-Sat. 7am-8pm).

DANAU RANAU

Danau Ranau (Lake Ranau), flanked by hills and **Gunung Seminung** (1900m) on the its south side, has yet to develop in any way that caters to tourists, so the area is largely unspoilt. Unfortunately, this also means that transport to Ranau will be an arduous six- to eight-hour bus ride from Bandar Lampung. Buses from the south stop in **Liwa,** a small town southeast of the lake, while those from the north stop in **Bandingagung,** on the northern tip of Ranau. Although both of these towns offer cheap lodging, the best bet is to hop on a colt to the **Danau Ranau Cottages** in Pusri, an isolated group of cottages that sit on the lake's eastern edge. Pusri is accessible from Bandingagung (45min., Rp3000) or Liwa (1hr., Rp2500), and lies between the two. The Cottages offers large, well-furnished rooms, all with porches that overlook the lake and mountain, costing a hefty Rp48,500 and up.

Pusri and Danau Ranau offer the ultimate retreat not only from the noisy, bustling cities, but from activity in general. There's not much to do around the lake but lounge on a rented canoe, enjoy the blissful scenery, and then take a dip in the refreshing water. A Rp25,000 chartered motorboat can take travelers across the lake to **Gemuhak Springs,** a walled-off pool of hot springs right on the lake and the base of Seminung. Exploring the foothills around the mountain can be exciting—wild pigs and monkeys often keep travelers company as they trek.

If you have the time, Danau Ranau, visited from Wisma Pusri, is a perfect and relaxing hideaway. Rent a car if at all possible, however; an attempt to leave from the area via public transport can ruin any glorious images you had developed. Buses come through both Liwa and Bandingagung at completely unpredictable times, and it's extremely difficult to get anywhere besides Bandar Lampung.

INDONESIA

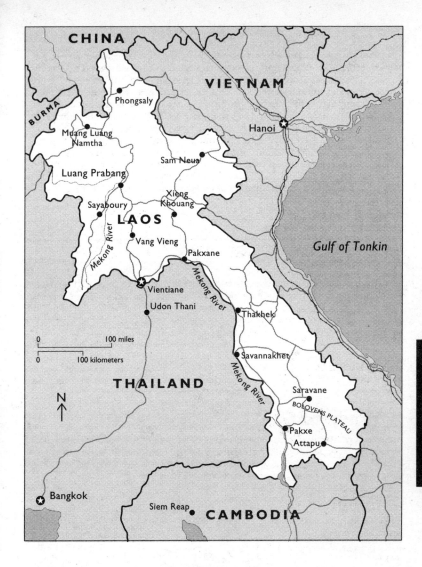

LAOS

Stepping into Laos is like traveling in time: the roads are unpaved, skyscrapers are non-existent, and bicycles outnumber cars. This mountainous, undeveloped nation seems desolate and lost among its neighboring countries who are vying for a piece of the capitalist pie. Sparsely populated with 4.5 million people, Laos is an open, wilderness country perched on the edge of the Southeast Asian frontier. The land remains relatively untouched, although it bears the scars from two million tons of bombs dropped by U.S. fighters during the Vietnam War.

Although Laos's doors are widening to the world, they are swinging open very slowly, with a good deal of starting, stopping, and squeaking of hinges. The country's leadership is anxious to avoid tumbling down the slippery slope of naked greed, drug abuse, rampant prostitution, and AIDS that it sees as by-products of the uncontrolled capitalist orgy across the Mekong. Nevertheless, the opening of the gigantic Australian-funded Friendship Bridge in 1993 was a step toward greater participation in the world community and visiting the country has never been easier.

Laotians harbor surprisingly little resentment toward foreigners considering their unfortunate involvement in the Vietnam War and, in fact, see learning English as their ticket to involvement in the world economy. Travelers are often approached by locals desiring practice and, more than in other Southeast Asian countries, these conversations tend to be genuine attempts at friendliness.

ESSENTIALS

■ Geography

Laos is a landlocked country which stretches 1000km north to south and is covered with a spiderweb of rivers and high, sloping hills. Mountains and plateaus cover over 70% of the terrain, making Laos an agricultural wasteland. Only 8% of the land is arable, yet it supports 85% of a population that engages in subsistence farming. All rivers and tributaries in the country flow into the Mekong River, which forms the country's borders with Burma and Thailand. The Mekong River Valley and its fertile flood plains make up all of the agricultural and wet-rice lands in Laos. The northern half of the country is topped almost entirely with steep-slope mountain ranges, with the highest peaks found in Xieng Khouang Province. Laos's largest mountain plateau, which rises 1200m above sea level, sprawls just north of here.

■ When to Go

Laos has a rainy season from the beginning of May until the end of September, and a dry season from October until April. During the rainy season, road travel through the country is more difficult. The best time to visit Laos is between November and February, when the temperature drops slightly and the rains subside.

■ Money

US$1=927.00kip	10kip=US$0.010
CDN$=677.822kip	10kip=CDN$0.015
UK£1=1431.752kip	10kip=UK£0.006
IR£1=1412.009kip	10kip=IR£0.006
AUS$1=687.000kip	10kip=AUS$0.017
NZ$1=562.040kip	10kip=NZ$0.020
SARand=260.024kip	10kip=SARand0.047

Laos' currency is the **kip.** Notes come in 20, 50, 100, 500, and 1000 denominations. *Let's Go* lists prices in both kip and US$, as the latter acts as a second currency. The kip fluctuates often, generally rising relative to other currencies. Along the border with Thailand, baht are widely used as well. While baht and US$ are readily accepted as payment in Vientiane, only kip is considered legal tender, so it is technically illegal to pay in anything else. **Tipping** in restaurants and hotels is not a common occurrence, and may even be returned. It is customary, however, to tip guides. **Bargaining** should be executed anytime a price is not indicated—especially in markets. The Lao tend to be fair in their bargaining practices, and a reasonable price can usually be agreed upon quickly and with minimal fuss.

■ Getting Around

Traveling beyond Vientiane Province is, in a word, hellish. Most of the roads in the country are unpaved. During the dry season they are dusty and pot-holed, yet passable, while during the rainy season they become rivers of mud. Road travel woes to the north are compounded by the fact that many of the highways in more remote regions have yet to be repaired since the Vietnam War.

While travel permits between provinces are no longer necessary, authorities require travelers entering a new province to register immediately with the immigration police. Travelers will be fined US$5 for every day they fail to check in. In the south of Laos, no one seems to care, or is even aware of this policy; travelers report never having to pay fines. Wherever possible, *Let's Go* lists the immigration offices for those who wish to be on the safe side.

BY AIR

During the rainy season, air travel is often the only way to reach more remote areas of the country. **Lao Aviation** has a comprehensive network of flights linking the capital with every region of the country from Luang Namtha along the Chinese border to Attapu in the south's "Emerald Triangle." Flights to more obscure points only go when enough people have purchased tickets. Fares are relatively inexpensive (see **Practical Information,** page 339 for listings). Confirm your flight at least one day in advance. Arrive at the airport at least two hours early no matter what the Lao Aviation desk clerk says. Some travelers have reportedly shown up at the airport terminal at the appointed time only to find that the seat had been unceremoniously re-sold to someone else. There is a 300kip tax on all domestic flights.

BY BUS

Laotian infrastructure is rapidly improving and buses now run regularly in most provinces. Bus travel still tends to be slow and difficult outside Vientiane Province. In the far north, bandit activity, horrible roads, and rain keep traffic to trucks.

BY BOAT

For centuries boat travel was the chief means of transportation within Laos (besides elephants, of course). A jaunt down the Mekong remains an intriguing option for those who have both time and patience. Most boats are commercial vessels hauling cargo from the capital to more isolated areas, but may take on passengers. There are no set fees; just agree on one with the captain before leaving. Don't expect a luxury cruise line; bring a sleeping bag and stock up on bottled water and dry provisions. During the dry season the water level drops considerably and boats may get stuck. The exact travel time is dependent upon a number of variables, including the river current, amount of cargo, and number of stops made along the way.

■ Keeping in Touch

Mail from Laos is somewhat reliable, although slow. Postage is quite cheap, but many travelers prefer to send overseas packages from Thailand. Receiving mail in Laos is possible through *Poste Restante* in Vientiane. Postal officers will inspect anything that's not clearly just a letter.

It's hard to come by **telephones** in Laos, especially in remote areas; during heavy rains, the phone system might shut down altogether! Phone numbers in the "urban" areas have six digits and those in the rural areas have either three or six digits. For

international phone calls, your best bet is in Vientiane (see **Practical Information** on page 339), since the country's telecommunications network is nearly non-existent. No collect or incoming calls. Most telephone services take only cash payments. Some hotels do accept credit card calls. The local time in Laos is seven hours ahead of Greenwich Mean Time (GMT).

■ Staying Safe

Laos has a low crime rate; nonetheless, travelers should always take precautions. The road between Vang Vieng and Luang Prabang is often attacked by **bandits.** If at all possible, stay away from road travel in this area. Be careful in the Golden Triangle area near the Thai-Burmese-Laotian border, known for its opium production. Locals are wary of foreigners and may give travelers a hard time. In Xieng Khouang Province, the Bolovens Plateau, and along the Ho Chi Minh Trail, watch out for **cluster bombs.** The process of clearing mines is expensive and several non-governmental organizations (NGO) have taken up that task, but some still remain. An average of 10 people, usually children, are killed or injured every month by these bombs.

■ Hours and Holidays

Businesses in Laos are open Monday through Saturday from 8am to noon and 2 to 5pm. Sundays and official holidays are rest days. Festival dates may vary by one day each year in accordance to the lunar calendar.

January 1: International New Year (official).
January 6: Pathet Lao Day (official).
February 6: Boun Maka Bucha (rice roasting ceremony).
March 8: Women's Day (official).
March 22: People's Party Day (official).
April 13-16: Lao New Year (official).
May 1: International Labor Day (official).
May 5: Boun Visaka Bucha (rocket festival).
June 1: Children's Day (official).
August 2: Boun Kao Padabdin (boat racing in Luang Prabang).
August 13: Lao Issara Day (official).
August 23: Liberation Day (official).
September 2: Boun Kao Salac (special food offering).
October 12: Freedom from the French Day (official).
October 30, 31: Boun Ok Phansa (end of Buddhist Lent).
November 26-28: That Luang Festival.
December 2: Independence Day (official).
December: Hmong New Year (around harvest time).

LIFE AND TIMES

■ The People of Laos

More than wars and foreign domination, the people of Laos are what have kept the country divided. When the country's borders were drawn, the 68 minority ethnic groups in Laos were not taken into account, a negligence which ultimately proved to be the divisive issue hindering the country's unification. Laos's chaotic terrain, absence of modern communication facilities, low levels of urbanization, low literacy rates, and brief national history have also hampered the attainment of national social cohesion. Although within the boundaries of an official state, many of the ethnic groups continue to live under self-rule, thereby bringing harsh reprisals from a government dominated by the Lao ethnic majority. The Lao further exacerbate ethnic tensions by excluding hill tribes from educational, social, and economic opportunities. In addition, Laos has suffered terribly from the loss of nearly a third of its former population since the end of the Vietnam War. The people in Laos are generally classified in three groups according to the altitude at which they live.

LAO LOUM

The **Lao Loum** make their homes in the rich, verdant Mekong River Valley. The ethnic Lao people began migrating into the region from southern China in the 8th century, driving out the Lao Theung already occupying the area. Today, this group constitutes one third to one half the population of Laos. The Lao have a more organized social and political system than any other Laotian group and are, moreover, the most highly educated people of the country. Consequently, the Lao control the government and dominate all trade and commerce which is not in foreign hands.

LAO THEUNG

Considered the highland Lao, the **Lao Theung** consist of 45 different tribes and are descended from the Mon-Khmers who have inhabited the region since 2000BC. The arrival of the Tai-Kadai peoples in the 8th century forced the Lao Theung to seek shelter in the hills where the newcomers would not venture. Called the *Kha* (a derogatory term meaning "slave") by the lowland Lao, the semi-nomadic Lao Theung live on the slopes of the Annamite Mountains and Bolovens Plateau. They practice slash-and-burn agriculture, shifting their villages every few years.

LAO SOUNG

The newest of the migrants in Southeast Asia, the Lao Soung began their southward movement into the region in the early 18th century. In Laos, they settled in the high mountains in the north which were uninhabited and similar to their former mountain homes in southern China. Unfortunately, the war displaced many of the Lao Soung and today they can no longer be found in one specific region of Laos.

The Hmong

The origins of the **Hmong,** perhaps the best known and most hated of Laos's hill tribes, has been an enigma for many scholars. Placing high value on independence (Hmong translates to "free men"), the Hmong have moved constantly in order to maintain their autonomy. From southern China to Southeast Asia, they have always settled in remote mountains, isolating themselves from neighboring tribes. Hmong men and boys were recruited by the CIA to battle Lao and Vietnamese communist forces in the "secret war" in Laos, intended to prevent North Vietnamese expansion into the country. When the communists won, however, the Hmong were forced to flee the country or risk being slaughtered due to their involvement in the war. Today, the Hmong live predominantly in Xieng Khouang and Luang Prabang provinces, and remain relatively removed from mainstream Lao society. A group of rebels continue to wage a war against the government by sabotaging roads and even killed tourists not long ago. The majority of the Hmong are uninvolved in this unfortunate situation, but they bear the suspicion of foreigners and the brunt of government crackdowns.

The Yao

Culturally and ethnically similar to the Hmong, the **Yao** are easily distinguished by their beautifully and elaborately embroidered dresses, black turbans, and red-ruffed tunics. A unique group in Laos, the Yao have a writing system based on Chinese characters. Like other hill tribes, the Yao recognize spirits and worship their ancestors; however, they also follow Taoism as it was practiced in 13th-century China. All of these indicators point to their origins in China, but traditional Yao legends say they came from "across the sea." They are skilled craftsmen, most notable for their intricate silversmithing. Most of the Yao today live in Luang Namtha Province.

Free Men

The Hmong pass on history and legends through their oral tradition. Over time, fact intermingled with fiction, leaving historians to separate the two. According to early Chinese records, the Hmong (called *Miao,* meaning "barbarian") had once lived in the Yangtze River Valley before being pushed out by the Chinese. Recorded as the "first enemies" of the Chinese, the Hmong resisted Sinicization and Chinese rule and, instead, retreated to the mountains of southern China (where 5 million live today). Even China's most brilliant generals could not overpower the Hmong in their mountain fortresses. Ultimate defeat came when the Chinese emperor falsely extended a peace treaty of a royal marriage to unite the two kingdoms. The Hmong King Sonom accepted, but he and his family were promptly executed. Other historians add that the Hmong are descendants of migrants from central Europe. Evidence of this is taken from the facial features of the people, many of whom bear striking Caucasoid characteristics, blue eyes and blond hair included. While those bearing Asiatic features were able to blend in, the Chinese proceeded to kill the Hmong who stuck out. Many others chose instead to migrate south into the high mountains of Laos, Vietnam, and Thailand to live as free men. The Vietnam War dispersed about one million Hmong refugees all over the world, from Great Britain and France to the U.S. and Canada to French Guyana and Australia.

■ History

In the first century AD, the region comprising present-day Laos belonged to the kingdom of **Funan.** Centered in northern Cambodia, Funan accepted the **Hindu** culture brought into the region by Indian merchants and theologians. In the 7th century, the kingdom of **Chenla,** also a Hindu dynasty, surfaced in southern Laos to displace Funan and dominated the area for two hundred years. Chenla extended its jurisdiction throughout the Mekong Delta until internal disputes divided the kingdom. In their weakened states the two kingdoms eventually became vassals to the expanding **Sailendra Empire** on Java.

Early in the 8th century, **Tai-Kadai** groups began to migrate from southern China toward the Mekong River Basin where they established independent principalities ruled by hereditary chieftains. The Lao, who belong to this ethno-linguistic family, settled in the Mekong River Valley of modern-day Laos. For the most part, migration had trickled down by the 10th century; three centuries later, however, the Mongol ascension to power in China drove another wave of Tai-Kadai peoples south.

The history of Laos as a unified nation began in 1353 with the founding of **Lane Xang,** the "Kingdom of a Million Elephants." Prior to that, Laos had been a mere vassal state to feuding empires like **Lannathai, Angkor,** and **Sukhothai.** With Khmer assistance, **Fa Ngum,** a Lao prince raised in the courts of Angkor and married to a Khmer princess, returned to his homeland and conquered the small states that make up Laos today. His father-in-law gave him a statue of a golden Buddha, called the **Pha Bang,** for which the royal capital of **Luang Prabang** was named after. For the next 20 years, Fa Ngum consolidated power by conquering Laos and the Khorat Plateau of northeastern Thailand. He brought missionaries from the weakening Khmer empire to introduce **Theravada Buddhism** as the state religion. Even though he was the founder of Lao nationhood, Fa Ngum was exiled by his own ministers in 1373 because of his excesses and his ruthless military commanders.

For the next 300 years, Lane Xang prospered. At its zenith, it stretched all across the north of the Indochinese peninsula. **Samsenthai** (1373-1416), Fa Ngum's son, aligned the empire with the Siamese, importing from them the construction method of wats, which sprung up all over their kingdom. He divided Lane Xang into administrative districts which lasted until 1975 when the monarchy was abolished. **Phothisarat** (1520-48) moved the royal seat from Luang Prabang to **Vientiane,** which became a religious and commercial center. The king's marriage to a Lannathai princess brought that kingdom under the rule of Lane Xang. **Setthathirat** (1548-71), Phothisarat's son, ruled over both kingdoms until 1570 when Lannathai was seized by the Burmese. He managed, however, to successfully defend Lane Xang against its encroaching neighbor. Today, Laotians venerate Setthathirat for bringing the **Emerald Buddha,** the most revered Buddha image in Thailand, from Lanna to Vientiane before Lanna's fall to the Burmese invaders. Under the reign of **Souligna Vongsa** (1633-94), Lane Xang saw its golden age. He was an enlightened leader who expanded the boundaries of Lane Xang to Yunnan to the north, Shan Burma to the west, Cambodia to the south, and Vietnam to the east. After the king's death in 1694, the kingdom erupted into chaos, while Vietnamese warlords, once allied with Lane Xang under Souligna Vongsa, menaced the land.

In 1713, three kingdoms emerged with divided loyalties to Laos's neighbors: the kingdom of Luang Prabang, ruled by Souligna's grandsons, was under the influence of China; Vientiane, under the rule of Souligna's nephew, sided with the Vietnamese empire of Hue; and **Champassak** aligned itself with Siam. The Siamese eventually overpowered all the kingdoms, annexing Vientiane in 1826, Champassak in 1846, and Luang Prabang in 1885.

At this time, the French, who had already established Vietnam as a protectorate, were seeking a way to stop the British forces in Burma from expanding eastward into France's jewel colony. The solution to that dilemma thrust Laos into the territorial struggle between the British and the French, who quickly moved to establish relations with Vientiane in 1886. Less than a decade later, Siam had officially recognized Laos as a French protectorate. **Annexation** was completed by the turn of the century; however, France paid little attention to this backwater country, whose mountains and rough land were not suitable to France's plans for colonial development. As a result, the French continued to invest in Vietnam and kept Laos as a buffer against the British.

The invasion of Indochina in 1941 by the Japanese marked the beginning of Laos's struggle for autonomy and independence. **King Sisavangvong,** at first reluctant to break with France, was pressured to declare independence for his country in 1945, with the support of the Japanese. France refused to accept Lao independence. As a result, several anti-French movements arose to counter French imperialism, including the **Lao Issara** (Free Lao) under the leadership of **Prince Phetsarath** and the **Pathet Lao** (Lao Nation), the communist movement founded by Phetsarath's half-brother **Prince Souphanouvong** in the 1950s.

The Lao Issara led the movement for formal independence from France, but when the time came for negotiations, dissent divided the organization. Phetsarath's faction refused to negotiate and insisted on complete independence. The second faction, headed by another half-brother **Prince Souvanna Phouma,** believed that negotiations with the French were necessary for the creation of an independent Laos. The third was under the leadership of Souphanouvong (known as the "Red Prince") who pushed for an alliance with Ho Chi Minh's **Viet Minh** to rid the region of all western influence. All three factions came to an uneasy agreement and formal independence was finally granted in 1953. The **Geneva Accords** in July 1954 established Laos as a neutral state.

The U.S. believed that Laos, as a neutral zone, was a buffer between the communists in Vietnam and the rest of Southeast Asia—the first "domino," according to Dwight Eisenhower. With the French no longer exerting control in the region, the U.S. increasingly involved itself in the conflict and sent special forces into Laos. In 1961 the Geneva talks reaffirmed Laos's neutrality and asked all foreign troops to withdraw, but both the U.S. and North Vietnam denied their presence, instead dragging the neighboring war into the isolated country.

The air war in Laos has left the country pockmarked with barren craters and unexploded bombs to this day. From their bases in northeastern Thailand, American fighters launched a **secret war** in Laos for nine years. More than two million tons of bombs were dropped on Pathet Lao strongholds in the north and the **Ho Chi Minh Trail** supply line that snaked through the eastern mountains, making Laos the most heavily bombed country in war history. So covert was the American operation that soldiers were dressed in civilian clothes and "Laos" was erased from all military records. The country became known as the "other theater."

After the American withdrawal from Southeast Asia, Laos finally fell to the Pathet Lao on August 23, 1975. In order to consolidate their power, the communists rid themselves of their opposition by abolishing the 600-year-old monarchy and sending many political prisoners and pro-Americans to their death in "re-education camps." Souphanouvong became president and appointed **Kaysone Phomvihane,** another communist, premier of the **Lao People's Democratic Republic (LPDR).**

After years of internal conflict, corruption, and foreign dominance, many Laotians welcomed the Pathet Lao, for in this group they saw the unity of the Lao people once again. A third of the people fled the country, however, and poured into Thailand, overflowing the refugee camps. Countless numbers, unfortunately, were ambushed and killed by Pathet Lao and Vietnamese soldiers who guarded the Mekong River, the Iron—or rather, Bamboo—Curtain of Southeast Asia.

■ Laos Today

Two decades after the communist victory, it appears as though economics and politics have come a full circle. Marxist economics have been replaced by free markets and Laos is slowly opening itself to the rest of the world. The hard-line stances of the Lao government are gradually giving way to democratic policies. In March 1991, the party voted for pro-market reforms and appointed new leaders dedicated to **"New Thinking."** By August 1991, Kaysone had urged the government to move toward a free-market economy, symbolized by the removal of the hammer-and-sickle from all state emblems. Later that year, the government ratified a national constitution and the U.S. agreed to repair relations with the country by sending an ambassador to Vientiane for the first time in over 15 years. **Nouhak Phoumsavan** succeeded Kaysone after his death in November 1991. A hard-line communist dedicated to carrying out his predecessor's visions, Nouhak earnestly supports free-market reforms and is working to re-establish Laos's relations with other countries

While the government is eager to acquire foreign aid and open its borders to international trade, it is equally determined to confine development and preserve the country's culture. Newly erected buildings in major cities have been principally constructed in the predominant French colonial style and, in some cities, the government has gone so far as to prohibit development in specific areas. Large infrastructure projects have, nonetheless, been planned for the coming years, including the construction of a 250km tollway across Laos, stretching from the Thai border on the west to the Vietnamese border on the east. The Lao government is eager to build more dams and exploit its potential for hydroelectric power plants. There is talk of damming the Mekong, which many Laotians feel is necessary since they are short on power. The environmental impact, however, would likely be catastrophic.

Since development has been largely confined to cities, the government fears that if rural areas remain underdeveloped, the economic gap between city and country could become too wide. Health and education programs are thus now being promoted outside urban centers in an attempt to bring prosperity to the countryside.

The last five years have seen Laos re-establish its ties with its Southeast Asian neighbors, in particular with Thailand, China, and Vietnam. While Thailand remains by far its largest trading partner, China might not lag behind for much longer. Increased exports, new businesses, and a growing tourism industry are paying off; despite harsh criticisms for the nation's one-party government and issues of human rights violations, Laos has managed to develop a stable economy with an annual GDP growth rate of more than 6%.

HUMAN RIGHTS

The LPRP has governed Laos since 1975 and strictly forbidden the establishment of other parties. In the late 1980s, an unofficial Social Democratic Club (SDC) formed and began criticizing the country's one-party system while advocating the transition to a multi-party system. Shortly thereafter, the prominent SDC members were arrested. The LPRP does not have a constitution, nor did it hold elections for a national legislature or the Supreme People's Assembly until 1989. Even when these elections occurred, the LPRP was the only party allowed to contest. The people of Laos have been warned that they will be arrested if they stage demonstrations demanding a multi-party system. Not only does the LPRP forbid the formation of other parties, but it is primarily concerned with the Lao ethnic majority.

■ The Arts

Lao art, though influenced by Thai, Burmese, and Khmer styles, is unique and expressive. Little is documented, however, as much of the country's artistic heritage has been lost or destroyed. Well-known for its extensive ornamentation, art in Laos is mostly inspired by the life of the Buddha and the *Ramayana,* which has become a vital force in Lao culture.

ARCHITECTURE

Due to a long history of constant war and foreign domination, Lao architecture never fully developed. Since many of the early structures were built of wood, little has survived time. The best examples of original Lao architecture exist in the wats that still stand. While not as ornate as those in Thailand, Lao wats, especially in Luang Prabang, are stunning.

The **Vientiane style** of architecture found in the capital city resembles the temples of southern Thailand, with high, pointed, and layered roofs. Main sanctuaries tend to be rectangular and some have a veranda around the temple. Wats in Vientiane have higher roofs, taller buildings, and more prominent entrances than those of the other two Laotian architectural styles.

Luang Prabang takes its architectural style from that of northern Thailand. Wats in this classic style have multi-layered roofs and gracefully sweeping eaves that nearly touch the ground, giving the impression that the temple is a part of the natural environment. The pillars narrow toward the top—an imitation of the tree trunks that had originally been used as columns.

A third temple style is **Xieng Khouang** which has, unfortunately, been irrevocably lost. During the war, Americans leveled the provincial capital city of Xieng Khouang, razing every building in sight and taking the city's architectural style with it. A few temples in a style similar to Xieng Khouang remain in Luang Prabang; they can be distinguished by their wide sloping roofs, although without the layers.

DANCE AND DRAMA

Classical dance and drama came to Laos from India via Angkor in the 14th century, but it was not until the 16th and 17th centuries that **classical theater** fully developed. Marked by the creation of a ballet, dance and drama were organized at the Royal Court and a grand orchestra consisting of xylophones, gongs, trumpets, tambourines, violins, and mandolins accompanied the dance. **Mimic dancers** wore rich and vibrant costumes with masks and diadems. Gestures and movements similar to that of Indian choreography depicted episodes from the *Ramayana.* Later in the development of classical theater, chanters accompanied the dancers, and ultimately, actors themselves began to talk and sing as they gesticulated and danced.

LAOS

MUSIC

Laotians possess a passion for music. Songs and music are indispensable accompaniments to all celebrations and feature heavily in everyday life. Live **mor lam** performances, involving singing jousts of Lao epic poems, can be seen at the markets or temple fairs. Listen for the haunting, hollow sound of the **khene,** which is at the center of Lao traditional music. A bamboo reed instrument much like Pan's flute, only bigger, the *khene* is played at celebrations and funerals. The Hmong are renowned for their *khene* players who usually display elaborate moves, steps, and jumps to the rhythm of the music at New Year festivals (December). A Laotian orchestra consists of the *khene,* the **so** (a two-stringed cello), the **khouy** (a bamboo flute without keys), and the **nang-hat** (a xylophone made of wood).

WEAVING

Once a common household craft, weaving has emerged as an art form in its own right. Because of Laos's isolation from the rest of the world, Lao weaving has remained free of outside influences. Exclusively performed by women, young girls are expected to learn the art of weaving cotton and silk with shimmering gold and silver threads (called **tdinjok**) into scarves, skirts, and other clothing. Her ability to weave is seen as an asset during courtship. Popular Lao products made from these cloths include the **pha sin** (Lao sarong), the **pha baeng** (Lao shawl), and the **sin,** a bridal skirt with an elaborately embroidered hem.

HILL-TRIBE ART FORMS

Although not the dominant culture in Laos, the hill tribes have their own artistic contributions to the country. The Yao and Hmong ethnic groups are renowned for their beautiful craftsmanship in **silversmithing.** Both these groups value silver greatly and assess their wealth in terms of family silver. They make heavy neckpieces etched with intricate designs, lock-shaped pendants, earrings, chains, rings, and bracelets which are worn with their traditional dress. The Hmong are the only people in Laos who make **batik,** where cloth is covered with wax or a resin-like paste so that it becomes resistant to dyes used to decorate it. The result is a mixture of vibrant colors and brilliant patterns. Indigo-dyed batiks make up the main panel of Hmong skirts, with applique and embroidery added to them. **Applique** is a craft form in which cloth is cut, layered, and turned inside out for a rich collage of contrasting colors and geometric shapes. Most hill tribes, such as the Akha, also make beautiful applique.

NORTHERN LAOS

■ Vientiane

To travelers and adventure-seekers from a bygone era, the name Vientiane conjured romantic images of an exotic, beguiling, and slumbering colonial backwater, where days melted into years and the pace of life remained as sluggish as the Mekong River's current. It was said that only Saigon and Phnom Penh could rival her in beauty or enchantment. Today, while hardly a cultural backwater, the "City of Sandalwood" retains a touch of that old mystique which so entranced visitors in years past. Time seems lethargic here, and travelers fresh from the reeling chaos of Thailand or Vietnam often welcome the slow and easy pace of life in this riverine capital.

Vientiane has been the product of a vibrant mix of cultural influences since King Phothisarat first established his capital here in 1526, when Laos was known as Lane Xang, the Kingdom of a Million Elephants. During the heyday of this period, Vientiane grew rich off trade with her neighbors up and down the Mekong. Since then,

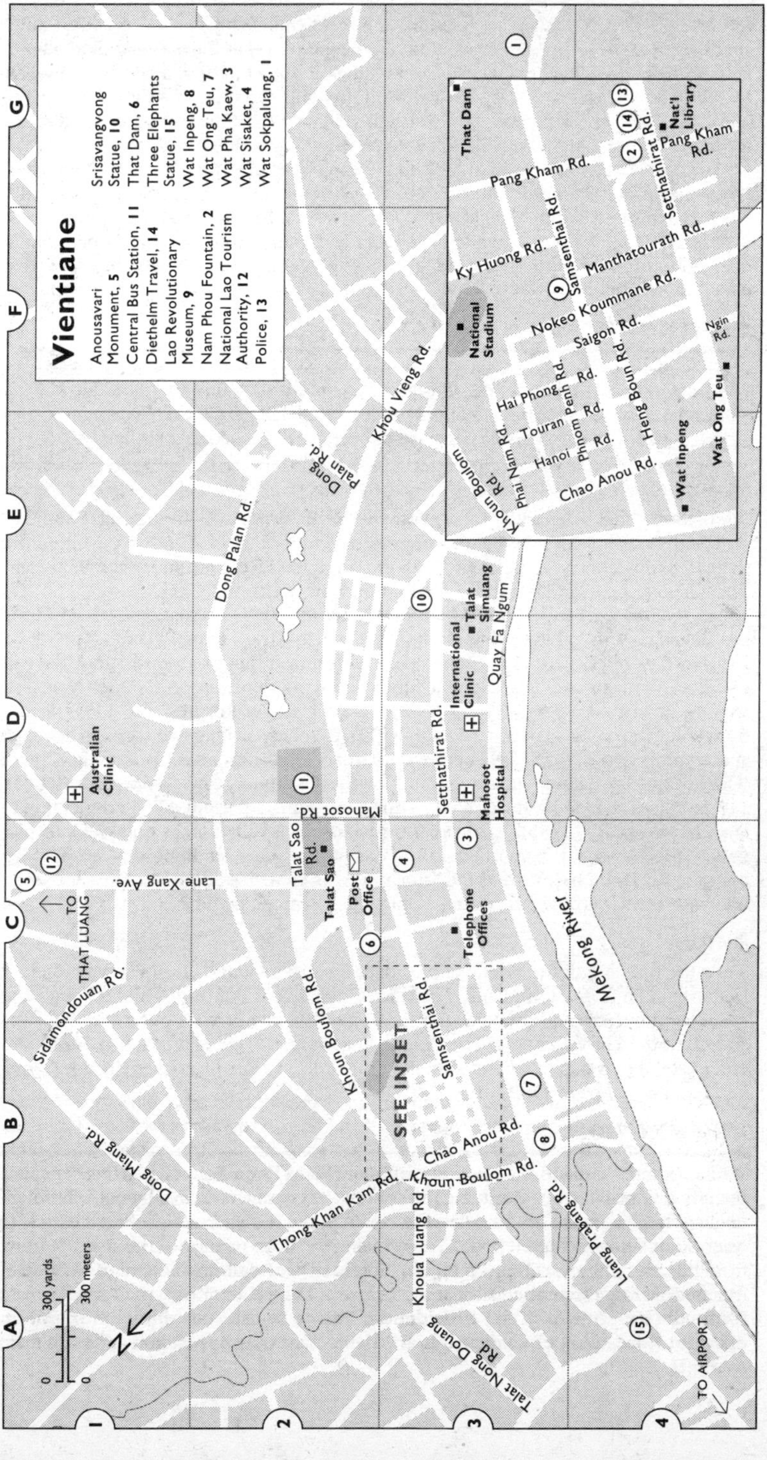

Vientiane

Anousavari Monument, 5
Central Bus Station, 11
Diethelm Travel, 14
Lao Revolutionary Museum, 9
Nam Phou Fountain, 2
National Lao Tourism Authority, 12
Police, 13
Srisavangvong Statue, 10
That Dam, 6
Three Elephants Statue, 15
Wat Inpeng, 8
Wat Ong Teu, 7
Wat Pha Kaew, 3
Wat Sisaket, 4
Wat Sokpaluang, 1

LAOS

Inset labels:

That Dam
Pang Kham Rd.
Ky Huong Rd.
Samsenthai Rd.
Manthatourath Rd.
Setthathirat Rd.
Nat'l Library
Pang Kham Rd.
National Stadium
Nokeo Koummane Rd.
Saigon Rd.
Hai Phong Rd.
Touran Rd.
Phai Nam Rd.
Phnom Penh Rd.
Hanoi Rd.
Heng Boun Rd.
Chao Anou Rd.
Khoun Boulom Rd.
Wat Inpeng
Wat Ong Teu
Ngin Rd.

Main map labels:

Khou Vieng Rd.
Dong Palan Rd.
Dong Palan Rd.
Australian Clinic
Sidamondouan Rd.
THAT LUANG
TO
Lane Xang Ave.
Talat Sao Rd.
Talat Sao
Post Office
Mahosot Rd.
Setthathirat Rd.
International Clinic
Quay Fa Ngum
Talat Simuang
Mahosot Hospital
Telephone Offices
Khoun Boulom Rd.
Samsenthai Rd.
SEE INSET
Chao Anou Rd.
Mekong River
Dong Miang Rd.
Thong Khan Kam Rd.
Khoun Boulom Rd.
Khoua Luang Rd.
Talat Nong Douang Rd.
Luang Prabang Rd.
TO AIRPORT

N
300 yards
300 meters
0

Chinese, French, Vietnamese, Russian, and most noticeably these days, Thai influences have all contributed to a cultural landscape that is at times quirky and always unique. Vientiane's individuality shows in things architectural, such as the Anousavari Monument, a rather incongruous Lao/Buddhist interpretation of the L'Arc de Triomphe in Paris, and culinary, with dishes like *khao jii pâté,* a breakfast sandwich of sliced cucumber, pâté, and chili sauce on fresh-baked French bread.

Vientiane is a city in transition, and some feared that the opening of the Friendship Bridge in April 1994 would unleash a torrent of western, consumerist influence that will force this jewel of the Mekong to go the way of other Southeast Asian metropoli. Rest assured, however, that while her sister cities to the south rush headlong into the neon sunset of the "modern" world, change will come to Vientiane at the city's own pace—slowly.

GETTING THERE AND AWAY

> In Laos, prices at many hotels, guest houses, and restaurants are quoted in U.S. dollars; in fact, some places will only accept U.S. dollars. *Let's Go* lists prices in both dollars and kip. It would be wise to keep small U.S. dollar bills handy.

By Plane

International flights land at **Wattay International Airport** (flight info tel. 212 066), on Luang Prabang Rd. about 3km from of the center of town. *Tuk-tuk* cost no more than 1000kip, taxis no more than 1500kip. There is a $5 departure tax for all international flights and a 400kip service fee for domestic flights.

Lao Aviation, 2 Pang Kham Rd. (domestic tel. 212 058, international tel. 212 051) has **international** flights to: **Bangkok** (5 per week, $100); **Hanoi** (Tues., 9am, $70); and **Ho Chi Minh City** (Fri., 7am, $125). Purchase tickets two to three days in advance. All major credit cards are accepted; cash only at the airport. (Open Mon.-Sat. 8am-noon and 2-4:30pm.) **Thai Airways,** 2 Pang Kham Rd. (tel. 216 143), flies to **Bangkok** (Thurs., Sat.-Tues., 12:55pm, $100). Purchase tickets one week in advance and confirm two to three days before departure. All major credit cards are accepted. (Open Mon.-Sat. 8am-noon and 2-5pm.) **Vietnam Airlines,** 62/5 Saylom Rd. (tel./fax 217 562) flies to **Hanoi** (Mon., Wed., Thurs., and Sun., 12:50pm, $75), connecting to **Ho Chi Minh City** ($155). A 30-day tourist **visa** costs $70; it takes one week to process. (Open Mon.-Sat. 8am-noon and 1:30-4:30pm.) **Lao Air Booking Co.,** 431 Setthathirat Rd. (tel. 216 761), has the same prices as Vietnam Airlines for fares and **visas.** All major credit cards are accepted. (Open daily 8am-noon and 2-5pm)

By Bus

Since the opening of the Friendship Bridge, the quickest and cheapest way to enter Laos has been from **Nong Khai,** Thailand. Once across the bridge and through Lao customs, travelers can hire a *tuk-tuk* (25฿) into the city or walk out to the highway and catch the Tha Dua bus (every 45min., until 5pm, 5฿) on its return trip. Buses also enter Laos at **Lao Bao** from Vietnam. For more information, please see **Border Crossing: Lao Bao** on page 358.

ORIENTATION

While central Vientiane—the area surrounding **Nam Phou Fountain**—is rather small, the city is actually large, spreading out for km. It is easily navigable by bike, although English street signs are few and far between in outlying districts. Most find it easiest to orient in relation to the Mekong. Three main roads run parallel to the river. Starting from the river, they are **Quay Fa Ngum, Setthathirat Road,** and **Samsenthai Road.** A number of smaller streets link these major roads. **Lane Xang Road,** the capital's main thoroughfare, runs from the **Presidential Palace** to the **Anousavari Monument. Mahosot Road,** also perpendicular to the river, passes the **bus station** and both main **markets.**

PRACTICAL INFORMATION

Tourist Offices: National Tourism Authority of Lao PDR (tel. 212 248), on Lane Xang Rd. Heading east it's on the right just before the Anousavari gate. Polite English-speaking staff distributes brochures with as much propaganda as info.

Tours and Travel: Signing with a tour company may be the best way to visit remote areas of the country, if you can afford it. The only international travel agency is **Diethelm Travel** (tel. 213 833) on Setthathirat Rd., in Nam Phou Sq. Open Mon.-Sat. 8am-noon and 2-5pm. **Inter-Lao Tourism** (tel. 214 832), on Setthathirat Rd. opposite Nam Phou, operates a very helpful info desk. **Lane Xang Travel Co.** (tel. 215 804), on Pang Kham Rd. near Nam Phou, is one of the largest agencies in the city. Open Mon.-Sat. 8am-5pm. **Vieng Champa Tour and Co.,** 255 Saylom Rd. (tel. 222 370), is a representative for Vietnam Airlines and provides visa services. Extends Lao visas ($2-3 depending on length of extension; takes one day) and procures visa for Vietnam ($60-70 depending on number in party; takes 4-7 days).

Embassies and Consulates: Australia (tel. 413 600; fax 413 601), on the corner of Nehru and Phone Xay Rd. Open Mon.-Thurs. 8am-noon and 1:30-5pm, Fri. 8am-12:45pm. Also handles the concerns of **British and Canadians. Cambodia** (tel. 314 952; fax 312 584), on Tha Dua Rd. Open Mon.-Fri. 7:30-11:30am and 2-5pm, Sat. 7:30-11:30am. **Thailand** (tel. 214 582), on Phone Kheng Rd. 1½ blocks past the Anousavari Monument on the left. Open Mon.-Fri. 8:30am-noon and 2-3:30pm. Tourist visas (500฿); allow 2-3 days to process. **US** (tel. 212 581; fax 212 584), on Bartholonie Rd., next to That Dam. Open Mon.-Fri. 8am-noon and 1-5pm. **Vietnam,** 60 That Luang Rd. (tel. 413 400). Open Mon.-Sat. 8-11am and 2-5pm.

Currency Exchange: Banque Pour le Commerce Exterieur Lao, 1 Pang Kham Rd. (tel. 213 200). Open Mon-Fri. 8:30am-3:30pm, Sat. 8:30-10:30am. MC and Visa cash advance. **Thipphachanch Vongxay Exchange,** 108/3 Samsenthai Rd. (tel. 217 504). Open daily 8am-7pm. Some banks also have exchange booths in the morning market.

American Express: Diethelm Travel is the Laos representative and issues traveler's checks. See **Tours and Travel Agencies** above.

Air Travel: Lao Aviation (see **Getting There and Away,** above) has domestic flights to: **Luang Prabang** (2 per day, $46); **Savannakhet** ($61); **Pakxe** ($95); and **Xieng Khouang** ($37). Cash only. Check first; the schedule is not fixed.

Buses: Central bus terminal (tel. 216 507), at the corner of Mahosot and Khou Vieng Rd., behind the morning market. To: **Vang Vieng** (7:15am and 1:30pm, 4hr., 1300kip); **Savannakhet** (7:30, 10, and 11am, 9hr., 7500kip); and **Pakxe** (11am, 17hr., 11,000kip). Buses link the capital with nearby towns. A flowchart lists departure times and fares in Lao and English; most buses leave early in the morning.

Taxis: Gather at the morning market. A day around the city is 23,400kip. Also run to **Tha Dua** (3300kip) and **Vang Vieng** (49,500kip roundtrip). Newer, more expensive taxis are at **Lang Xang Hotel** (tel. 214 102), on Quay Fa Ngum.

Boats: A viable and scenic mode of travel. Boats heading north leave from the **Kao Liaew Pier,** about 7km north of the city. Go there early and ask around. Boats do not leave every day, so you may have to wait. To **Luang Prabang** (5 days, 10,000kip). Boats to **Savannakhet** and the south leave from the commercial wharf, but may not run during the dry season.

Local Transportation: Tuk-tuk are omnipresent. The most efficient means of transport remains the trusty **bicycle.**

Rentals: Vientiane Motor, 35/1-3 Setthathirat Rd. (tel. 215 390), rents **4WD vehicles** for $80 per day and **motorbikes.** Open daily 8am-5pm. **Kanchana Lao Handicrafts,** 102 Samsenthai Rd. (tel. 213 467) has **bikes** for 1500kip per day. Many also guest houses rent bikes for 1000kip per day as well.

Pharmacies: Seng Thong Pharmacy (tel. 213 732), on Mahosot Rd. past the bus station and Khuadine Market, on the right. Friendly staff. English spoken. Recommended by Australian Embassy Clinic. Those headed for Luang Prabang or more remote areas should stock up on pharmaceuticals here.

Medical Services: Australian Embassy Clinic (tel. 413 603), on Nehru Rd. Serves only Australian, British, and Canadian nationals. Consultations Mon., Tues., Thurs., and Fri. 8:30am-12:30pm and 2-5pm, Wed. 8:30am-12:30pm. Initial consultation

$20 (US$ only). Excellent staff with Australian doctor. **International Clinic, Mahosot Hospital** (tel. 214 022), on Quay Fa Ngum. Doctors speak French and English. Cash only. Open 24hr.

Emergency: tel. 190 or 212 707. Don't expect English-speaking dispatchers.

Police: (tel. 212 706), on Setthathirat Rd., just south of the fountain, opposite Lane Xang Hotel. No English spoken.

Post Offices: GPO (tel. 216 425), on the corner of Khou Vieng and Lane Xang Rd. opposite the morning market. EMS shipping service. *Poste Restante* (300kip per letter). **Overseas telephone** and telegram service. **Postal code:** 0100.

Telephones: Central Telephone Office (tel. 214 470), on Setthathirat Rd. 1 block south of Nam Phou, next to the police station. No credit card or collect calls; cash only. **Fax** and telex services. Open daily 7:30am-10pm. For credit card calls go to Lane Xang Hotel. **Telephone code:** 21.

ACCOMMODATIONS

Even the cheapest rooms in Vientiane are still about three times as expensive as accommodations across the river in Nong Khai. The best option for travelers willing to shell out a bit more are the upscale guest houses, where spacious rooms in lovely colonial-style buildings complete with the conveniences of a hotel are the same price as a night in a middle-range Soviet-style monstrosity.

Say Lom Yen Guest House (tel. 214 246), on Saylom Rd. From the market or bus station, turn right off Khoun Boulom Rd. at the Shell station. Brand-new, with spotless rose-printed sheets, brilliant white walls, and always colorful fake flowers. Fills up quickly. Each room has a double bed and bath with hot water and flush toilet. Rooms with fan $8, with A/C $12.

Samsenthai Hotel, 15 Manthatourath Rd. (tel. 216 287), toward the river from Setthathirat Rd., on the right. Won't win any beauty contests, but the rooms are cheap and clean and the manager gets a gold medal for friendliness and patience. Upper floors sport expansive views of the river and Thailand. Singles with fans are $6 or $8. Doubles with A/C $12. MC, Visa, AmEx.

Phorn Thip Guest House, 72 Inpeng Rd. (tel. 217 239). Head down Chao Anou Rd. toward the river, pass through the intersection with Setthathirat Rd.; take a right immediately after Saysana Hotel and a left on unpaved Inpeng. Phorn Thip is on the left, near the end. An excellent deal and a realistic budget option in a rambling, colonial-style house with towering ceilings and wooden floors. Rooms fill up fast. Small singles with fan and shared bath $8. Doubles with private bath $13. With A/C additional $4. Entrance locked at 11:30pm.

Settha Guest House, 80/4 Samsenthai Rd. (tel. 213 241), between Pang Kham and Manthatourath Rd. Wooden floors, large windows, A/C, twin beds, hot showers, and flush toilets. Suites for 2 $16, for 4 $32.

Lani Guest House #1, 281 Setthathirat Rd. (tel. 214 919; fax 215 639), near the intersection with Chao Anou Rd., opposite Wat Ong Teu. It's set back from the road, so look for the sign. Quiet patio surrounded by bamboo and palm trees. Uniquely decorated rooms with hardwood floors have A/C, hot water, and telephones. Singles $25, for more floor space and a fridge $30. Doubles $30 and $35. Popular with aid workers and diplomats; make reservations 2-3weeks in advance by phone, letter (P.O. Box 58), or fax. MC, Visa, AmEx.

Syri Guest House (tel. 212 682), on Chao Anou Rd. From the Lao Revolutionary Museum, head away from the river on Nokeo Koummane Rd. past the tennis club; the guest house is on the right about 20m past the curve. Located in a spacious, colonial mansion that oozes old-world elegance. If you treat yourself to slightly finer lodgings, this is the place to do it. Singles with A/C, hot water, and TV $20. Doubles $25. Bike rental. Breakfast offered, as are cars to the airport.

Phanthavong Guest House, 69/5 Manthatourath Rd. (tel. 214 738). Go down Setthathirat Rd. with the river to the left and turn right 1 block after the fountain. The guest house is on the right, a few doors past the run-down but dirt-cheap **Ministry of Information and Culture Guest House.** Phanthavong's multi-lingual staff offers 2-bed rooms with green linoleum floors starting at $5, with private bath $8, with A/C too $10.

FOOD

For cheap eats head for **Heng Boun Rd.** and **Chao Anou Rd.,** where noodle shops and street vendors peddling savory yummies. Vendors also set up shop along **Quay Fa Ngum** overlooking the river, north of the Mixai Restaurant. Stalls are heavy on desserts and visitors can sample *lao khao* (rice whiskey), a national obsession, for about 500kip per shot.

Restaurant Ha-Wai, 74-76 Chao Anou Rd. (tel. 214 664), just east of the intersection with Heng Boun Rd. A culinary microcosm of Vientiane. For francophiles there's *filet mignon* (2800kip); for Vietnam aficionados, a wide assortment of *pho* (1500kip); and from China, grilled Cantonese duck (4000kip). Open daily 11am-2pm and 6-10pm.

Namphu Garden Restaurant (tel. 216 775). A pleasant beer garden with a monopoly on Nam Phou Fountain. Thankfully, food and drink are cheap. A variety of Indian, Chinese, and Lao food; most patrons just come for a beer by the fountain and head elsewhere for serious vittles. Beer Lao 1800kip. Mug of draft beer 600kip. Open daily 11am-11pm. Food served after 6pm.

The Taj, 75/4 Pang Kham Rd. (tel. 212 890), opposite Nakhorn Luang Bank, just near the fountain. Groove to the kickin' sitar music as you devour mouth-watering north Indian cuisine. Specialties include *tandoor* chicken 5500kip, *malai kofta* 3500kip, and *roti* 500kip. All-you-can-eat lunch buffet 3800kip. Open daily 11am-2:30pm and 6-10:30pm.

Vanh Mixay, 38 Nokeo Koummane Rd. (tel. 214 160). From Nam Phou head north on Setthathirat Rd., and take a left at the far corner of Wat Mixay, with the Banque Setthathirat on the other corner; it's on the right before Tai Pan Hotel. The miser's choice for Thai food. No froofy decor, but there are tables outside. Dishes 1200-1800kip. Open daily 10am-10pm.

Just for Fun, 51 Pang Kham Rd. (tel. 213 642), near the fountain, opposite the Lao Aviation office. This quirky eatery lives up to its name with a jovial white and lime-green color scheme, Richard Marx on the stereo, and Lao handicrafts for sale. Specializes in vegetarian food and herbal tea. Most dishes 1000-1500kip. Try sweet peanut curry with bean curd, or morning glory vines with rice (1400kip). Two-page list of teas (500kip). Lao coffee 400kip. Open Mon.-Sat. 9am-10pm.

Sweet Home Bakery, 109 Chao Anou Rd. (tel. 214 742). Heading toward the river, it's just beyond the Heng Boun intersection. Popular with locals and expats for its inexpensive and delicious pastries. Breakfast of Lao coffee and a pastry costs less than a dollar. Sidewalk tables provide excellent people-watching opportunities. Iced coffee 400kip. Ice cream 500-1000kip. Open daily 7am-10:30pm.

Thai Food, at the corner of Samsenthai and Khoum Boulom, is just that. Will satisfy the munchies for those itching to cross the river, or those who just have and miss it. If you can't order in Lao, the waiter can offer a few suggestions. You won't find better food for 1200kip. Open daily 10am-9pm.

MARKETS

As a rule, the production of merchandise with international appeal is not the forte of former Communist-bloc countries, unless you are in the market for busts of Soviet leaders or 15kg calculators. Vientiane, on the other hand, if not quite a shopper's wonderland, isn't a shoppers *gulag* either. Vientiane is an excellent place to purchase traditional *ikat* silk and cotton fabric.

Although night markets are rare in Laos, daytime markets are aplenty. **Talat Sao,** housed in a green-roofed building between Lane Xang and Mahosot Rd., is the all-day morning market. It has a substantial selection of Lao textiles, most of which lie farthest from the river. **Talat Khuadim** is on the opposite side of Mahosot Rd., just behind the bus station, and concealed from the street by storefronts. Plastic awnings rigged from central support columns shield vendors from the sun. Produce, toiletries,

LAOS

and packaged food dominate the array of goods available. Vendors selling fruit and *khao jii pâté* congregate just outside the market, along Khou Vieng Rd.

SIGHTS

Vientiane's featured attractions are all located within 1km or less of the **Nam Phou Fountain** and can easily be visited in a single day, especially with the aid of a bicycle. A number of temples and some of the best-preserved colonial architecture can be found along tree-lined Setthathirat Rd. and Quay Fa Ngum, near the Mekong River.

Vientiane's pre-eminent temple is **Wat Pha Kaew** (Temple of the Emerald Buddha) on Setthathirat Rd. The original temple was built in the mid-16th century by King Setthathirat to house the Emerald Buddha he brought from Chiang Mai (see **History** on page 332). Two hundred years later, in 1778, the game of musical Buddha continued when invading Thais reclaimed it. Sacked by the Thais in 1827, the wat was finally restored to its original grandeur (minus its namesake) in the 1940s. The two ornately carved wooden doors at the temple's north and south entrances are all that remain of the original structure. Inside, the temple houses a fine collection of statuary from all over Southeast Asia, including bronze Buddhas in the "calling for rain" stance (standing erect, hands at sides) and a replica of the Pha Bang, the most sacred Buddha image in Laos (the small gold figure in the middle of the room). (Open Tues.-Sun. 8-11:30am and 2-4:30pm; admission 200kip.) Photography is prohibited in the temple.

Across the street from Wat Pha Kaew, on the corner of Setthathirat and Lane Xang Rd., is Vientiane's other major wat, **Wat Sisaket**, built by King Anou in 1818. The temple was completed just 10 years before the Thais plundered the capital. In a display of sensibility not often seen in pillagers, the Thais spared Sisaket. Today however, nature and lack of funds are accomplishing what the Thais failed to do, and the wat is in desperate need of repair. The temple houses a small collection of Lao and Khmer statuary inside the cloister and the central sanctuary. (Open Tues.-Sun. 8-11:30am and 2-4:30pm; admission 200kip.) Photography is prohibited inside.

About 1km east of Wat Sisaket on the opposite end of Lane Xang Rd. is one of Vientiane's most distinctive landmarks, the **Anousavari Monument,** also called Pratuxai (Victory) Gate, today a popular hangout for Vientiane's teens. A fine view of the capital city can be had from atop the monument (open daily 8am-5pm; admission 200kip; 100kip more to park a bike).

Beyond the Anousavari Monument on That Luang Rd. is **That Luang,** the towering golden stupa that is one of the most important religious symbols in Laos. The statue in front of That Luang is of King Setthathirat, who built the temple in 1566. Twice raided during the 18th century (by the Thais and the Chinese), the shrine was refurbished by King Anou, who added the walls which currently encircle it. Originally four wats surrounded the stupa, one on each side, but today only the north and south wats remain. (Open Tues.-Sun. 8-11:30am and 2-4:30pm; admission 200kip.) At the far end of the parade ground opposite the stupa is the **Revolutionary Monument,** dedicated to the Pathet Lao soldiers who died during the war.

Another of Vientiane's important wats is **Wat Ong Teu,** a large religious complex at the north end of Setthathirat Rd., at the intersection with Chao Anou. The largest temple in the capital, it is home to one of the country's most prestigious Buddhist schools. A massive statue of the Buddha, weighing several tons, meditates within the main sanctuary. If the *sim* is locked, one of the young student-monks in residence may be able to open it in exchange for a few minutes of English practice.

L'Arc de Triomphe Oriental?

Inspired by Paris's famous monument, the former royal government erected Anousavari in memory of those who died during Laos's war for independence. When builders ran out of concrete, they used cement donated by the American military for the construction of Wattay Airport to complete the memorial in 1969. Thereafter the monument was known as the "vertical runway."

Wat Sokpaluang, a large forest temple south of the city center, is worth a visit for its traditional **Lao herbal sauna.** The saunas are built in elevated bamboo huts and steamed from beneath by a boiling water/herb mixture whose vapors rise up into the hut. The saunas are touted for their reputed medicinal value. Do not bathe for three to six hours after your sauna in order to allow the fragrant herbs to enter your skin. (Open daily; 1500kip donation expected.) Saunas last two hours. To get there, head south on Tha Dua Rd. past the concrete water tower, and take a left onto Khou Vieng Rd. After 700m take a right onto Sokpaluang Rd., and the wat is on the left.

Sightseers weary of wats can check out propaganda instead at the **Lao Revolutionary Museum** on Samsenthai Rd., northeast of Nam Phou. The hammer-and-sickle flag of the now-defunct USSR and the flag of the Lao PDR greet visitors at the entrance. The first floor highlights the Laos's natural wonders through photography while the second floor documents the struggle of Laotians, first against the French colonists, then against the American imperialists. (Open Mon.-Fri. 8-11:20am and 2-4:20pm, Sat. 8-11:20am; admission 200kip.) No photography is allowed.

ENTERTAINMENT

Vientiane boasts a number of excellent bars and beer gardens where Laotians and expats alike gather for cold beer and stunning sunsets along the Mekong River. There is little raucous nightlife here since bars and clubs must shut down at midnight. The Lao People's Revolutionary Party has **banned karaoke.**

Samlo Pub, 101 Setthathirat Rd. (tel. 222 308), near Wat Mixay. A wildly popular newcomer to the Vientiane night-scene. Abstract paintings by local artists decorate the ground floor. Hang out at the bar or shoot pool on the 2nd floor. A 3rd floor loft is stocked with pillows for those who have imbibed too much. Great western music. Bar is stocked with liquors you won't find anywhere else in Laos. Open Mon.-Sat. 5:30pm-midnight.

Mixai Restaurant, 31 Quay Fa Ngum. A large wooden open-air restaurant on the river. Popular with locals and expats. Most people just come to drink and watch the sunset, but the inexpensive Lao food is highly recommended: *tom yam* 2000-4000kip, *laap* 2000kip. Beer Lao 1200kip. Open daily 8am-10pm.

Salongsay Restaurant (tel. 214 114), a part of Lane Xang Hotel. Traditional Lao music and dance are performed nightly. The menu is pricey, but soda (300kip) and beer (600kip) are not. Performances nightly 7-9:45pm.

Friendship Club, across from the upscale Apollo Night Club. One of many drink and dance joints on Samsenthai Rd. past the intersection with Khoun Boulom Rd. Nurse a beer under the constellation of blinking holiday lights on the ceiling, or twist and shout to Thai favorites. Live music nightly 8-11:30pm.

■ Near Vientiane

THA DUA

Travelers who were entranced by the fantastical Wat Khaek in Nong Khai (see **Sights** on page 595) should pay a visit to **Xieng Khonane,** Wat Khaek's pre-1975 counterpart. The sculpture park was built by the same Lao monk/mystic who designed Sala

---

Floating Logs

At the tiny port on Nam Ngum you will notice the piles of massive logs and perhaps wonder where they came from. Nam Ngum Reservoir is the site of what may be the world's most unusual logging operation. Hurrying to complete the dam, no one thought to harvest the vast tracts of forest, which were soon covered in 20m of water. Lao loggers, with the help of Thais, developed special underwater chainsaws and lumberjacks quickly traded in their boots for flippers to get at the lucrative hardwoods.

LAOS

Kaew Ku before he fled Laos following the communist victory 23 years ago. Both temples feature the same unique combination of Hindu and Buddhist themes, although Xieng Khonane is not nearly as grandiose. Tha Dua is easily reached by bus from the central bus station (5 per day, 50min., 200kip).

NAM NGUM LAKE

Ninety km northeast of Vientiane, nestled in a valley surrounded by serpentine ridges and hardwood forests, lies **Nam Ngum Lake,** a vast man-made reservoir formed following the damming of the Nam Ngum River in the late 1970s. Today the dam's hydroelectric power plant supplies electricity to much of Laos, and large amounts to energy-starved Thailand. The natural setting is nothing short of spectacular. Nam Ngum is dotted with hundreds of emerald islets, some of which were used as prisons and political re-education camps during the early 1980s. Stories of attempted escapes from these Laotian Alcatrazes abound. One famous case involved a convict who escaped from his work camp, but was sucked under the dam by the current, only to turn up, in one piece, on the other side. Stupefied guards, convinced they had witnessed a miracle, let the charmed prisoner go.

Travelers seeking some voluntary solitary confinement of their own can find it on idyllic **Santipap Island,** site of a somewhat run-down but endearing government-owned **guest house.** Don't expect comforts like electricity and running water here; food is prepared over charcoal stoves and bathing water comes straight from the lake. Nonetheless, the scenery is breathtaking, and the clear, warm lake provides unparalleled swimming opportunities. Dorm beds go for 2500kip, doubles 3000kip.

To get to Nam Ngum Lake take a bus from the central bus station to **Ban Thalat** (7:10, 9, and 11am, 1½hr., 500kip). From Ban Thalat *songthaew* run to the lake for 400kip, passing the **dam complex** itself. Photography is strictly prohibited.

At the port, **Nam Ngum Restaurant** is worth a stop for lunch. It's to the left of the elevated pier, surrounded by ferns and potted plants. Fresh lake fish costs 2500-3000kip. Long-tail boats make the 30-minute trip to Santipap Island for around 5000kip. A convenient way to see the lake and spend a night on the island is to include it on a trip to **Vang Vieng.** Make arrangements for a long-tail to meet you the next morning to continue on to **Tha Heua** on the northern shore of the lake (3hr., 25,000kip) from which regular buses run to Vang Vieng (2hr., 500kip).

LAO PAKO

South of Nam Ngum Lake and about 50km north of Vientiane, hidden away on the bank of the Nam Ngum River is the small resort of **Lao Pako.** Billing itself as an "eco-tourism" lodge, Lao Pako consists of a central longhouse and individual bungalows. In the jungle on an isolated stretch of river accessible only by boat, Lao Pako caters to adventure-seekers. The Austrian owner, Mr. Pfabigan, organizes pfabulous treks, river-rafting expeditions, horse-back riding, and visits to nearby villages for the guests. Hammock lovers can enjoy less active pursuits, such as chess, checkers, and reading from the comfort of the main lodge's thatched-roof veranda, which affords great front-row views of the setting sun and Nam Ngum River. **Lao Pako Bar and Restaurant** is a popular watering hole for expats living in the capital. Rooms start at $6 for a bed in the dorm. Doubles with private bathroom are $19, bungalows $26. All rates are halved Monday through Thursday.

If you wish to "Enjoy your life at Lao Pako" as the fliers in Vientiane proclaim, stop by the **Burapha office,** 14 Quay Fa Ngum (tel. 216 600), to reserve a room; there is no telephone service at the resort. To get there, turn right at the end of Chao Anou Rd.; Burapha is one block up (open Mon.-Fri. 8am-noon and 2-5pm, Sat. 8am-noon). To reach Lao Pako, take a Pakxap-bound bus at the central bus terminal (6:30, 11am, and 3pm, 1hr.) and ask to get off at the village of Som Sa Mai. From the village take a long-tail to the resort (25min.).

■ Vang Vieng

As the bus leaves the flat plains of the Mekong River Valley behind and begins wheezing up steep mountain grades and swooshing down winding switchbacks, the scenery grows more beautiful with each passing km. Rolling foothills give way to jagged peaks inlaid with terraced rice fields; by the time the bus reaches the tiny district seat of Vang Vieng the view is awe-inspiring. Sheer limestone cliffs tower above the sleepy village on the west bank of the Song Nam River, like spikes on the back of some massive slumbering dragon. Locals call them Phou Daeng (Red Cliffs) in reference to the distinct pinkish tinge of the limestone. They're honeycombed with caves, some of which spread for km through twisting subterranean corridors. During the Vietnam War, this area was the stronghold of Hmong guerrillas, recruited by the CIA to fight a war against Lao and Vietnamese communists. Today there are many easily accessible Hmong and Yao villages near Vang Vieng.

ORIENTATION AND PRACTICAL INFORMATION

From **Kasi** it is possible to continue by road to **Luang Prabang.** The region between Vang Vieng and Luang Prabang is occasionally raided by bandits who rob and kill victims. Soldiers patrol the road to discourage would-be attackers. The trip, which normally takes 12 hours, can take twice that during the wet season. Trucks and buses run daily to Luang Prabang, 5000-9000kip.

From the **market,** where the bus from Vientiane drops off passengers, the **Song Nam River** is to the west, and beyond it is the sheer face of Phou Daeng. To the east is **Luang Prabang Road (Route 13),** Vang Vieng's main drag. A few hundred meters later the town ends and the road winds through the mountains past Lao and hill-tribe villages, reaching the town of **Kasi,** 70 bone-jarring km later. South on Luang Prabang Rd., about 50m from the market, is the **post office** (tel. 213 398), which provides **overseas phone** service for about 12,500kip per minute (open Mon.-Sat. 8-11am and noon-4pm). Opposite the post office is the rarely used **airstrip.** About 800m beyond the post office is the turnoff to the Vang Vieng Resort and **Tham Chang.** Heading south from the market along the river is the Phou Ban Guest House on the left and, 30m later, the turnoff to ford the river en route to **Tham Pourke.** The **district hospital** is also on this road.

Buses to **Vientiane** leave from the market (6 per day, 5:50am-1pm, 4½hr., 1300kip). Buses to **Kasi** also leave from here (11am-noon, 2hr., 800kip). **Bicycles** can be rented from a shop three doors up (toward Luang Prabang Rd.) or from the Siripangna Guest House near the market. Light is provided by generators and candles as there is no regular supply of electricity, although a new power station should come on line next year.

ACCOMMODATIONS AND FOOD

There are several adequate, inexpensive guest houses to choose from, the best of which is the **Phou Ban Guest House,** on the river road just south of the market. It's an ideal place to recuperate after a hard day's cave exploration. Rooms (all with two beds) are spacious with mosquito netting and fans (3000kip). Electricity is available between 6:30 and 10:30pm. The bathrooms behind the main house have squat toilets. Phou Ban also offers bike rentals and basic Lao dishes in its small restaurant. The guest book on the second-floor coffee table has helpful tips on exploring the caves and ethnic villages in the area.

On the opposite end of the market from Phou Ban Guest House, near Luang Prabang Rd. is **Siripangna Guest House,** the other popular backpacker hangout. Cramped but spotless rooms (all doubles) with concrete floors, private toilet, and shower go for 3000kip. The friendly proprietress speaks decent English and is a good source of information on the area. South of the market just off Luang Prabang Rd.

behind the post office is **Vieng Samanh Guest House,** in an elevated Lao house. Comfortable singles/doubles with mosquito netting and fans cost 3000kip. Bathrooms are outside the rooms.

Vang Vieng boasts a number of street-side noodle shops and a few small restaurants. **Nang Bat Restaurant** (tel. 213 514), opposite the market on Luang Prabang Rd., has a limited French and English menu with dishes for 800-1000kip. Yummy *laap kai* is 1000kip. This is also the place to meet Mr. Keo, a local guide who takes travelers to the caves and hill-tribe villages. (Open daily 6am-9pm.)

SIGHTS

Vang Vieng is a caveman's arcadia, with limestone caves riddling the cliffs outside town. With the exception of Tham Chang, the caves are largely unspoiled, so not only are they beautiful, but also difficult to find and easy to get lost in. Inexperienced adventurers should search out Mr. Keo at Nang Bat Restaurant, who takes small groups through the caves and to hill-tribe villages (5hr., 4000kip per person). Flashlights (88kip from the market) and sneakers are a must for cave explorations.

Closest to town is **Tham Chang,** an overpriced tourist trap on the grounds of the Vang Vieng Resort. Expect to pay 200kip to enter the compound and 2000kip more to see the cave lit up with cheesy colored lights. The view of the village and surrounding rice fields from the mouth of the cave is almost worth the price. Also west of the Song Nam River are Tham Pourke and Tham Phou Kham. **Tham Pourke** is closer to town. Head north from the market along the river and cross about 30m upstream. The cave is about 1km west of the river across several rice fields. To get to **Tham Phou Kham** (Cave of the Golden Crabs), head south from the market; the turn-off to ford the river is 50m down on the right. During the rainy season you may have to hire a fisherman to take you across (200kip). The cave is approximately 4km west (head for the small hill in front of the larger cliffs); the entrance faces town. Lucky travelers may catch a glimpse of the "golden crabs" which inhabit the subterranean pools. A **Hmong village** lies 3km west of the cave.

Twelve km north of town are the **Tham Xang** (Elephant Caves) off Rte. 13, near the village of **Ban Tham Xang.** To get there take a *tuk-tuk* heading north from the market (2000kip per person). Passengers will be deposited at the dirt access road leading to the caves. A few rice paddies later, villagers run an informal ferry service (200kip) across the river. The first elephant cave rises out of the rice fields in the center of the village like the dorsal fin of a huge shark. Inside the cave are numerous Buddha images, a footprint, and a stalactite bearing an uncanny resemblance to an elephant's head. Two larger caves lie at the foot of the cliffs, west of the village.

Vang Vieng's largest cave, **Tham Nang Phomhorm** (Cave of the Fragrant-haired Woman) is about 4km past Ban Tham Xang. Take the turn-off on the right at the village of **Ban Patthana.** The two-level cave is another 15km down this road, which passes **Ban Nam Yen,** a Yao hill-tribe village 3km before the cave entrance. Another Yao village, **Ban Samsavath,** is 6km north of Ban Tham Xang. South of Ban Tham Xang about 2km west of the bridge is a sprawling **Hmong village** of some 300 households, comprised of repatriated refugees from Thailand. The United Nations High Command for Refugees (UNHCR) oversees their reassimilation into Laos. Locals may not take kindly to photo-happy *farang.*

■ Luang Prabang

Luang Prabang is virtually synonymous with Lane Xang, the magnificent "Kingdom of a Million Elephants" that once stretched across northern Indochina. Substitute palanquins and pachyderms for bicycles and *tuk-tuk* and the city hasn't changed much. The graceful gold-leaf encrusted peaks of Luang Prabang's many wats glint through the canopy of palm trees that shelter the old quarter of the city. Monks, their saffron robes glowing like embers, add pinpricks of color to the scene.

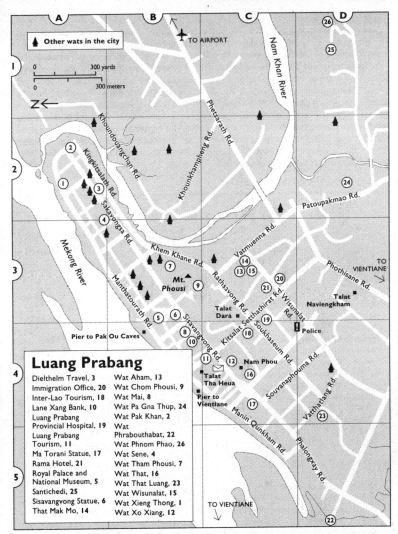

Luang Prabang

Dielthelm Travel, 3
Immigration Office, 20
Inter-Lao Tourism, 18
Lane Xang Bank, 10
Luang Prabang
Provincial Hospital, 19
Luang Prabang
Tourism, 11
Ma Torani Statue, 17
Rama Hotel, 21
Royal Palace and
National Museum, 5
Santichedi, 25
Sisavangvong Statue, 6
That Mak Mo, 14

Wat Aham, 13
Wat Chom Phousi, 9
Wat Mai, 8
Wat Pa Gna Thup, 24
Wat Pak Khan, 2
Wat
Phrabouthabat, 22
Wat Phnom Phao, 26
Wat Sene, 4
Wat Tham Phousi, 7
Wat That, 16
Wat That Luang, 23
Wat Wisunalat, 15
Wat Xieng Thong, 1
Wat Xo Xiang, 12

Luang Prabang was built by King Fa Ngum (1353-73), the unifier and first king of Lane Xang, on a rocky spit of land at the confluence of the Mekong and Nam Khan Rivers. The tiny city (present pop. 20,000) was lavished with gorgeous wats by the royal family, who maintained a palace there, even after King Setthathirat moved the capital to Vientiane in 1556. This shift proved to be a blessing for Luang Prabang, which remained largely isolated from the country and the world until well into the 20th century. As a result the city is widely regarded as the best-preserved in Southeast Asia. For travelers, Luang Prabang is a springboard for explorations of the remote northern provinces. With unspoiled natural and architectural splendor and unparalleled possibilities for adventures even farther afield, Luang Prabang will surely be the highlight of any visit to the land of a million elephants.

ORIENTATION

The main road, running roughly southwest-northeast from the soccer stadium to the **Nam Khan River,** is **Sisavangvong Road,** which becomes **Phalongxay Road** at the southwest end and **Sakkarine Road** at the northeast end. The **post office, tourist office,** and a number of important sights, including the national museum and Wat Xieng Thong are along this road. Parallel to Sisavangvong Rd. is **Manthathourath Road,** which runs along the **Mekong River. Boats** headed north and south leave from quays along the south end of this road. The main cross street, **Kitsalat Setthathirat Road,** runs away from the waterfront, through Tha Heua Market and the intersection with Sisavangvong Rd. It passes through Dara Market and the Provincial Hospital before intersecting **Wisunalat Road.** Lao Aviation, the **police,** the Rama Hotel, and several restaurants are on Wisunalat Rd.

PRACTICAL INFORMATION

Tourist Offices: Luang Prabang Tourism, 72 Sisavangvong Rd. (tel. 212 198). Friendly staff are good for practical questions. Arranges pricey tours to outlying sights ($40 average). Open Mon.-Sat. 8-11:30am and 2-5pm.

Tours and Travel: Most run non-budget trips to the caves and waterfalls. $70 and up for 1 person to **Pak Ou;** prices drop a little for groups. **Inter-Lao Tourism** (tel. 212 034), on Kitsalat Setthathirat Rd. opposite Dara Market. Open Mon.-Sat. 8am-noon and 2-5pm. **Diethelm Travel,** (tel. 212 277), on That Xieng Thong Rd., opposite Wat Sop. Open daily 8am-noon and 2-5pm.

Immigration Offices: (tel. 212 453), near the intersection with Kitsalat Setthathirat Rd., opposite Rama Hotel. Visas to Laos may only be extended in Vientiane. Open Mon.-Sat. 8-11am and 2-4pm. **Note:** Before leaving Luang Prabang by boat or bus travelers must "check-out" with the immigration authorities and pay a 300kip tax.

Currency Exchange: Lane Xang Bank, 90/8 Sisavangvong Rd. (tel. 212 185), near the Kitsalat Setthathirat Rd. intersection. Traveler's checks (3% charge), US$, and Thai฿. No credit cards. Open Mon.-Fri. 8:30am-3:30pm, Sat. 8:30am-noon.

Air Travel: Luang Prabang Airport (tel. 212 173), on Phetsarath Rd. Upon arrival register at the immigration desk and have the internal travel paper you received at the airport in Vientiane stamped. Flights to: **Vientiane** (2-3 per day, 40min., $46); **Houixay** (55min., $42); **Oudomxai** (40min., $24); and **Phonsavan** (Wed. and Fri., 35min., $30). Actual flight times are decided on a day-to-day basis, so inquire at **Lao Aviation** (tel. 212 172), on Wisunalat Rd. near the intersection with Kitsalat Setthathirat Rd. Purchase tickets (cash only) at least 1 day in advance. Re-confirm 1 day before. Open daily 7:30-11:30am and 2-4pm.

Buses: Buses run almost daily to Kasi (12-24hr., 9000kip) along the newly-paved Rte. 13. Trucks (about 5000kip) also ply the route and are less likely to be attacked by bandits. Vehicles leave downhill from Talat Naviengkham.

Boats: Boats leave from the dock behind the post office on Mahin Quakham Rd. to **Vientiane** (rainy season 3 days, dry season 5 days, 10,000kip, bring provisions). Check the quay early and often for vessels several days before you wish to depart. Be ready to leave on short notice, since there's no set schedule. Boats up the Nam Ou River to **Nambak** (8am, 5hr., 5300kip) leave from the concrete steps to the river behind the post office; speedboats (2hr., 20,000kip) can be hired at the quay behind the Royal Palace. From Nambak, pick-up trucks run to **Muang Sy.** To **Pakbeng** on the Mekong (8am, 9hr., 6000kip), continuing to **Houixay.** Tickets are sold at the bottom of the staircase to the left of Kitsalat Setthathirat Rd. from 7:30am and sell out fast. To **Pak Ou caves** (speedboat 1hr., slow boat 2hr., 15,000kip). Fishing boats run a continuous shuttle service to and from **Ban Chiang Man** across the river, gateway to Wat Long Khoune and Wat Tham (5min., 100kip). To **Ban Chan Pottery Village** (20min., 2000kip roundtrip).

Local Transportation: Songthaew and **tuk-tuk** can be hired from Talat Naviengkham to: **Khouang Si Waterfalls** (2hr., 8000kip); **Ban Phanom Pottery Village** (15min., 1000kip); **Ban Hat Hien** (10min., 500kip); and the **airport** (10min., 1000kip). **Bicycles** remain the best bet.

Rentals: Luang Prabang Tourism rents **cars** with drivers ($30), **motorbikes** ($10), and **bicycles** ($3) by the day. Many guest houses also rent bikes.

Medical Services: (tel. 212 123), on Kitsalat Setthathirat Rd. A few doctors speak French. Does not meet generally accepted standards of hygiene. In the event of a serious health emergency, return to Vientiane as soon as possible.

Police: Provincial Headquarters (tel. 212 151), on Wisunalat Rd. on the right before the Lao Aviation office. Some French spoken.

Post Offices/Telephones: (tel. 212 288), on Sisavangvong Rd., just north of Nam Phu on the left, in a large yellow building. **Overseas telephone** and fax service. Cash only, no collect. Open Mon.-Sat. 7:30-11:20am and 2-5pm. **Postal code:** 0600. **Telephone code:** 71.

ACCOMMODATIONS

Rama Hotel (tel. 212 247), near the Wisunalat-Kitsalat Setthathirat Rd. intersection. On the cheap end in town, but you'd never know it. Rooms are clean, spacious, and comfortable. What it lacks in intimacy it makes up for in quality. Rooms 7-8000kip (low season 5-6000kip), may include some combination of hot water, desk, and/or two beds. Unfortunately, it's next door to a noisy disco.

Viradesa Guest House, 13/2 Hoa Khoie Rd., past the Ma Torani statue and down a small lane to the right. A red, white, and blue sign points the way. Friendly family keeps their fledgling operation tidy. Dorms 3000kip. The best doubles (with bath and dazzling hot pink curtains) go for 7000kip. Arranges daytrips to the waterfall or Pak Ou Cave (includes a stop at a village known for distilling potent *lao khao*), both excellent values at around $20. Check-out 8am.

Vannida Guest House, 87/4 Souvanaphouma Rd. (tel. 212 374). With the river behind you, head right on Sisavangvong Rd. and turn left just past the Ma Torani statue. The guest house is 100m up on the right. Once the home of a Lao prince, now a clean, fresh establishment. Bright, pleasant doubles 9000kip, dark, brooding ones 7000kip. Summer discount 2000kip. Talk to owner about trekking.

Phounsab Guest House, 6/7 Sisavangvong Rd. (tel. 212 595), near the Royal Palace. Singles 6000kip, with private bath 10,000kip. Doubles 8000kip, with private bath 12,000kip. Friendly manager offers bikes (1500kip) and helpful touring tips.

Boun Gning Guest House, 109/4 Souvanaphouma Rd. (tel. 212 274), across a small side street from the Vannida Guest House. Take your breakfast on the lovely 2nd floor veranda. Shared bathrooms with hot water. Rooms (5-8000kip) vary substantially in size, but most have windows overlooking the backyard garden. Discounts to guests who stay 3 days or longer. Doors locked at 11:30pm.

FOOD

Fans of authentic Lao food will find Luang Prabang a garden of succulent and spicy culinary delights. Signature Luang Prabang dishes include watercress salad, *laap kai* (spicy chicken salad), and mountain-grown brown sticky rice. The budget-conscious should head for **Talat Tha Heua** (open early morning-8pm). A few noodle vendors and *khao jii pâté* sellers hang out at **Talat Dara** as well. Fresh fruits and vegetables are sold at **Talat Naviengkham** on Phothisane Rd.

Restaurant Luang Prabang (tel. 212 387), on Wisunalat Rd. opposite Wat Wisun. Sit on the sidewalk amid hanging plants or inside surrounded by Lao handicrafts. Wide selection of Lao, Chinese, Vietnamese, French, and vegetarian food. Large portions at moderate prices (1400-3400kip). Open daily 7:30am-10pm.

View Khaem Khong (tel. 212 471), on Manthathourath Rd. From the river bank behind the National Museum, it's about 50m upstream on the left. Boasts gorgeous sunset vistas. Popular with the city's fledgling yuppies. Menu is too hip to list prices, but most dishes cost a low 1000-2500kip. Open daily 7am-11pm.

Yong Khoune Restaurant, 145/1 Wisunalat Rd., across from Rama Hotel. This simple street-side eatery dishes up large helpings of savory Lao and Thai food at agreeable prices. Salivate over the Luang Prabang salad, a green salad topped with sliced eggs and crushed peanuts (700kip). Fried chicken in chili and basil leaves (1500kip). Most dishes 500-1500 kip. Open daily 6am-11pm.

Maylee Lao Food Restaurant, 5/6 Phou Vao Rd. From Talat Naviengkham, head south and take a right at the Shell station. The restaurant is beyond Muang Sua Hotel on the left. Delicious Lao food in a quiet setting. Signature dishes include *laap* (2000kip) and fried bamboo shoots stuffed with minced pork (1500kip). The gutsy can try cow viscera soup (1500kip). Open daily 6-10pm.

MARKETS AND SHOPPING

Luang Prabang has three major markets. **Talat Dara,** in the center of town at the intersection of Kitsalat Setthathirat and Rathsavong Rd., is the city's department store. Nearly one story above street-level on its tiered concrete foundation, Dara stands as a bastion of consumerism, overflowing with sandals, purses, watches, and electronic devices, most of which are of Thai origin.

Talat Tha Heua occupies the sidewalks of Kitsalat Setthathirat Rd. from the waterfront to Sisavangvong Rd. Frequented by many of the hill-tribe women, who present a colorful array of ethnic dress, Tha Heua is a good place to take breakfast of fruit and bread or *khao jii pâté*. The market runs from dawn to dusk.

In addition to its markets, Luang Prabang possesses a number of **handicraft and textile shops** that display the products of the region's long tradition of weaving excellence. Once patronized by the royal family and inspired by the array of ethnic styles scattered across the hills, the industry accounts even today for much of Luang Prabang's domestic exports. Most of the shops are clustered around Sisavangvong Rd. Embroidered fabric (starts at 5000kip per meter) and off-the-rack garments, such as the unmistakable blue-and-black Hmong vests, are available.

SIGHTS

The glory years of Lane Xang may have faded into the past, but Luang Prabang retains the trappings of a great capital, most notably in the vast number of wats, which remain the city's chief attractions. Many of the most important wats line Sisavangvong Rd. If you can only handle a few sights, be sure to visit Wat Xieng Thong, Wat Wisunalat, Wat Mai, Wat That Luang, Mount Phousi, and Wat Prabouthabat. Wats are often locked to prevent theft, but a polite request can usually open them.

Opposite the Provincial Hall on Phalongxay Rd. is the statue of **Ma Torani,** depicted as a young maiden washing her hair. According to Buddhist legend Ma Torani (Mother of the Earth) protected the Buddha from the demon Devarade by washing her hair, and the water swept the demon away. Her image can be seen stenciled on wats all over town.

On Sisavangvong Rd., craggy **Mount Phousi** (Marvelous Mountain) dominates the city. At the top stands **Wat Chom Phousi,** whose glittering gold stupa is visible for miles in every direction. In the evening there is no better spot from which to take in Luang Prabang's spectacular sunsets. A booth on the Sisavangvong Rd. side of the hill charges a 500kip admission fee. North of the tiny chapel, in a bizarre contrast to the peaceful wat, is the skeleton of an old anti-aircraft gun which no one seems eager to lug down. A narrow, partially overgrown path leads from the right of the A-A gun down the eastern slope to **Wat Tham Phousi,** whose entrance is framed by two American-made bomb casings that have found peacetime jobs as flowerpots. A jolly, rotund Buddha sits in a grotto next to the cave entrance inside of which is a large collection of Buddha images in varying stages of decay. Beyond the pavilion is a deep footprint of the Buddha.

Directly opposite Mount Phousi on the left side of Sisavangvong Rd. is **Wat Mai,** one of Luang Prabang's most beautiful temples. Seventy years in the making (finally completed in 1788), the temple was home to the sacred Pha Bang Buddha between 1894 and 1947. The entire north side of the wat is adorned with a gorgeous bas-relief covered entirely with gold leaf, depicting the story of Phravet, an incarnation of the Buddha. The Buddha image inside is one of the largest in the city.

Next door to Wat Mai is the **Royal Palace,** home to the National Museum. The palace was built by King Sisavangvong in 1904 (his statue stands on the front lawn). It remained the home of the royal family until the monarchy was abolished in 1975. One highlight of the collection is a copy of the **Pha Bang,** the golden Buddha that is Laotian Buddhism's most revered image. A gift to Lane Xang's first king from the Angkor court in the 1300s, the original is made of 50kg of pure gold and now resides in a Vientiane bank vault. Directly beyond the entrance hall is the grand throne room, marked by the distinctive seal of a three-headed elephant on the back of the throne. The elephant symbolizes the kingdoms of Luang Prabang, Champassak, and Vientiane which were unified under Lane Xang.

Head north on Sisavangvong Rd., which becomes Sakavongsa Rd., to get to the *grande dame* of Luang Prabang's many temples, **Wat Xieng Thong** (Copper Tree Temple), set amid a well-manicured tropical garden. Widely regarded as the crowning achievement of Lao religious architecture, the graceful temple was built in 1559 by King Setthathirat and lavished with money from the royal coffers until 1975, explaining its excellent condition. On the back wall of the temple is a mosaic depicting a copper tree. Just to the right of the gate as you enter is a large pagoda housing **King Sisavangvong's funeral chariot.** A 12m-high float surrounded by writhing golden *naga*, the chariot brought the king's funerary urn to the cremation site following his death in 1959 (open daily 8am-5pm; admission 250kip).

Another important temple, **Wat Wisunalat,** is on Wisunalat Rd. past the Rama Hotel on the left. Built in 1523, it was razed by Chinese mercenaries and then rebuilt at the turn of the 19th century. The towering *sim* houses a treasure trove of Buddhist art, watched over by the largest Buddha in the city. Stacked haphazardly along the walls are hundreds of Buddha images of various sizes and styles, some over 400 years old. To the right of the altar are several Sanskrit stelae.

Across Wisunalat Rd. from the temple is the Luang Prabang branch of the Lao Red Cross, which operates a **traditional Lao herbal sauna** similar to those at Wat Sokpaluang in Vientiane (open Wed.-Fri. 5-7pm, Sat.-Sun. 9-11am and 5-7pm; soak yourself for 1500kip). Bring your own towel. Also opposite the temple is the bulbous **That Mak Mo stupa,** sometimes referred to as the Melon Stupa because of its rounded top. Constructed in 1504, it once held many priceless Buddha statuettes now on display at the National Museum (open daily 8am-6pm; admission 250kip).

Heading south from the statue of Ma Torani on Phalongxay Rd., behind the soccer field is **Wat That Luang.** It's the final resting place of many royals, including King Sisavangvong, whose ashes are entombed in the golden stupa across from the entrance. The temple itself lacks the richness of other wats, but is beautiful in its austerity. A large gray stupa's corners are adorned with kneeling ascetics and lotus flowers. For sunset watchers, That Luang is surpassed only by Mount Phousi. Farther down Phalongxay Rd., on the right opposite a Shell station is **Wat Prabouthabat,** the crazy Aunt Matilda of Luang Prabang's temple family (open daily 8am-6pm; admission 250kip). Built in the 50s with money supplied by the local Chinese and Vietnamese communities, the temple gives the impression that it was designed by Walt Disney and colorized by Ted Turner.

■ Near Luang Prabang

ACROSS THE RIVER

For those hearty wat-goers who crave additional temples, the other side of the Mekong River boasts some other impressive structures. In terms of setting, few can match **Wat Long Khone's** location within a tranquil tropical garden on a high bank above the river. The temple dates from the 1700s and is in excellent condition thanks to recent renovation efforts. Behind the wat are several traditional wooden monks' quarters. Just 20m up the path from Wat Long Khone is **Wat Tham** (Temple Cave). This subterranean chapel is filled with Buddha images, many of them human-size. A labyrinthine passageway twists and turns some 50m underground, ending at a glittering quartz stalactite as thick as a tree trunk. A flashlight is necessary for exploring the cave; monks will gladly lead spelunkers through it, pointing out Buddha statues and rock formations along the way. To get to the opposite bank, take one of the fishing boats (100kip) that shuttle back and forth across the river when the small canoes are full. Boats leave from the second set of concrete stairs upstream from the Lao State Fuel Co. gas station.

CRAFT VILLAGES

Each of the three craft villages near Luang Prabang specialize in the production of a specific item: weaving, knives, and pottery. All make interesting excursions for visitors to view the village's industry from raw materials to finished products.

By far the most interesting is **Ban Phanom,** a weaving village roughly 4km east of the city. Located on the banks of the Nam Khan River, the 300-year-old village is inhabited by members of the Lu tribe, originally from southern China. Historically, Ban Phanom enjoyed considerable royal patronage, and many villagers served as the royal family's personal weavers and tailors. Partially as a result, Ban Phanom's weavings are of high quality and are sold in handicraft shops in Vientiane as well as Luang Prabang. (Open daily 8am-5pm.) It's best to come early, before the package tour groups arrive. To get to Ban Phanom by bicycle, head east on Vatniuenna Rd., passing over the river; the dirt turn-off to the village is about 10m past the entrance to Wat Pha Na Theup on the left. By *tuk-tuk* the trip costs 1000kip.

Well beyond Ban Phanom on the same dirt road near the Nam Khan River is the **grave of Henri Mouhot,** the French adventurer who stumbled upon Angkor Wat in 1860, only to die of malaria a year later in Luang Prabang. The grave is difficult to find (in fact, the grave itself wasn't "rediscovered" until 1990); ask a local to point it out, or risk a long, frustrating search.

About 5km northeast of town near the airport, the clanging of hammers against anvils in **Ban Hat Hien** announces that this is Luang Prabang's knife-making village. Some craftsman use old propellant canisters from American-made artillery pieces to make human-powered bellows that fan the coal fire. By bicycle, cross the bridge off Vatniuenna Rd. as if heading to the airport. The turn-off to Ban Hat Hien is on the right just before the old terminal. By *tuk-tuk* it's 500kip. Both Ban Phanom and Ban Hat Hien can be visited in a single morning.

South of Luang Prabang about 4km, on the opposite side of the Mekong, is **Ban Chan,** a pottery-making village. The entire village participates in the production of large *thong* (water jugs) and clay roofing tiles. Visitors can observe the entire process from the grinding of clumps of clay into fine sand to throwing the pots on hand-turned pottery wheels, and finally baking the pots and tiles in large, underground kilns. A visit to Ban Chan can easily be combined with an excursion to the temples across the river from Luang Prabang. Hire a boat from Luang Prabang or Ban Chiang Man (2000kip).

PAK OU CAVES

The **Pak Ou Caves,** an important religious site for 500 years, lurk at the confluence of the Mekong and the Nam Ou Rivers, 25km upriver from Luang Prabang. The two-hour boat trip passes through splendid scenery as the chocolaty Mekong snakes its way between rolling hills and craggy, serrated peaks soaring 60m above the water. The caves are buried on the left bank of the river, opposite the village of Ban Pak Ou. There are two caves, Tham Ting (the lower one) and Tham Phum (the upper one). Every April, during Phimai, the Lao New Year, thousands of devotees flock to the caves to pray, a practice once followed by the kings of Lane Xang dating back to the caves' discovery in the 1500s by King Setthathirat.

Tham Ting, featured prominently on many postcards and travel brochures, is packed with hundreds of Buddha images. **Tham Phum** is reached by a steep brick staircase leading from the river bank. Some of the Buddha images date back to the 16th century. (Admission 700kip for both caves.)

No river excursion is complete without a visit to **Xang Hai village,** famed for its *lao khao* (rice whiskey) distillation industry. Locals brew the potent firewater from sticky rice in large oil drums along the river bank. For 400kip, visitors can purchase half a bottle of still-warm moonshine. Village children delight in watching camera-clicking *farang* hop nimbly off the boat on arrival, and teeter back 10 minutes later.

Boats can be hired from the landing behind the Royal Palace for about $20 for a large boat with a roof (desirable, as the sun is brutal). Be sure to decide upon any additional stops beforehand. Long-tailed speed boats ($20) gather at the narrow concrete stairs just upriver of the Lao State Fuel Co. gas station.

KHOUANG SY WATERFALL

The waterfall is located 30km south of the city via a rugged dirt road which winds through rolling hills, their slopes notched with terraced rice fields, and increasingly rare teak groves, identifiable by their distinctive broad leaves and ram-rod straight trunks. A *tuk-tuk* can make the journey for 15-20,000kip. In terms of sheer grandeur, the falls are hardly Niagara-like, but swimming in the series of sapphire-blue pools below them is popular with Lao and *farang* alike. Steps cut into the clay slope run up the right side of the falls beneath the jungle canopy, to the first tier; here it is possible to cross the river and continue up a series of natural steps eroded by the water to the top. (Admission 700kip.)

■ Phonsavan

Geographically, Xieng Khouang Province, northeast of Vientiane along the Vietnamese border, is something of an anomaly. The terrain is a mix of rugged mountains and beautiful rolling hills, more reminiscent of Ireland than Indochina. Its high elevation ensures cool, at times down-right chilly, temperatures all year long. During November and December the mountains near the border are ablaze with poppy blossoms; opium, grown by the hill tribes, is the province's chief cash crop.

Historically, the province has been under Vietnamese hegemony, and the Vietnamese influence remains strong, although the population is equal parts Hmong, Khamu, and lowland Lao. To travelers, Xieng Khouang is best known for Thong Hay Hin (Plain of Jars), the mysterious collection of massive 3000-year-old stone vessels scattered across the region. More recently, Xieng Khouang was one of two Lao provinces most heavily bombed during the Vietnam War. Xieng Khouang City, the former provincial capital, was so hard hit that after the war the provincial seat was moved to Phonsavan, 36km to the north. The landscape is pockmarked with craters, and thousands of cluster bombs still litter the countryside, exacting a gruesome toll in lost lives and limbs from the local population. The skies over Phonsavan still scream with Soviet-made Mig-21 planes on training flights from the nearby airbase.

ORIENTATION

Finding your way around Phonsavan is easy. The town consists of two main streets. Running south from the Phudoi Hotel to the market is **Phonsavan Road** with a large **gold urn** in the middle. **Route 7** runs east-west and crosses the north end of Phonsavan Rd. like a "T" at the market. The budget hotels and guest houses line the east leg of Rte. 7. South of Phudoi Hotel, Phonsavan Rd. turns west, passing the **hospital** on its way to the **airport.**

PRACTICAL INFORMATION

Tours and Travel: Sodetour Travel (tel. 130), at the corner of Phonsavan Rd. and Rte. 7, organizes day trips with car, driver, and guide for about 30,000kip. English spoken. Hmong-run with highly praised tours of Hmong villages. Open daily 8-11:30am and 1-5pm. **Inter-Lao Tourism** (tel. 156), on Phonsavan Rd., on the left around the bend from the Phudoi. Rents Russian jeeps with driver 30,000kip, with guide 50,000kip. Arranges day-long tours. Only the director speaks English. Open daily 8am-noon and 2-5pm.

Currency Exchange: Aroun May Bank (tel. 187), at the south end of Phonsavan Rd., opposite Phudoi Hotel. Changes only US$ or Thai₿. No traveler's checks or credit cards accepted. No English spoken. Open Mon.-Sat. 8am-4:30pm.

Air Travel: Phonsavan Airport, 5km west off Phonsavan Rd. Consists of a single woven bamboo shed with immigration checkpoint. To **Vientiane** (40min., 35,100kip) and **Luang Prabang** (Wed. and Fri., 35min., 23,400kip). Arrive at least 2 hours before your flight to avoid being dropped from the flight list. **Lao Aviation** (tel. 284), on a dirt side street off Rte. 7. From the market head east on Rte. 7, and turn left at the Hay Hin Hotel; the office is on the left. Tickets must be confirmed one day before departure. Cash only. Open daily 7am-noon and 2-5pm.

Buses: Ramshackle buses and trucks to the rest of the province leave from the empty lot on Rte. 7, adjacent to the market. Buses to: **Ban Thatcho** (noon and 3pm, 1hr., 400kip); **Muang Kham** (noon and 4pm, 22km, 500kip); **Xieng Khouang** (36km); and **Nong Het** (120km).

Taxis: For hire at the bus stop next to the market on Rte. 7. During the dry season they can reach all three **Plain of Jars** sites (20,000kip), but during the rainy season travelers have to walk several km. To: **Tham Phyu Cave** (56km, 22,000kip); **Ban Nam Horn** (76km, 25,00kip); and **Ban Thatcho** (17,000kip).

Local Transportation: Tuk-tuk are plentiful and go anywhere in town for 300-600kip. To **Hay Hin I,** the first Plain of Jars site 10km west of town (5000kip) and **Ban Thatcho,** 24km east of town.

Rentals: Cars and 4WD can be rented from tour companies for 30,000kip with driver. No self-drive. Or, check at your hotel/guest house.

Markets: Phonsavan's **central market,** at the north terminus of Phonsavan Rd., opposite the post office. Open daily 5am-6pm. A small **Talat Vietnam** is on Rte. 7 north of town past the Vinh Thong Guest House.

Medical Services: Xieng Khouang Provincial Hospital (tel. 240), on Phonsavan Rd., southwest of town past the provincial hall on the right. Doctors speak some French and a little English and Russian.

Police: Xieng Khouang Provincial Police (tel. 141), on Phonsavan Rd., a 2-story concrete building in a field opposite the hospital. No English spoken.

Post Offices/Telephones: Post and Telegram Office (tel. 166), at the corner of Rte. 7 and Phonsavan Rd. across from the market. Open daily 8-11am and 1:30-5:30pm. **No overseas phone calls.**

ACCOMMODATIONS

Phonsavan has a number of cheap guest houses. Perhaps the only drawback is that Phonsavan only has electricity from 7-10pm.

Dok Khoune Guest House (tel. 162), on Rte. 7 near the market in a 2-story stucco building. A real house with hospitable owners. Decorated with an assortment of defused bombs in the corner of the lobby and expended cartridges posing as key chains. The 2-bed rooms are freshly painted and well-kept. Upstairs rooms 3000kip. Downstairs with bathroom and flush toilet 5000kip.

Vinh Thong Guest House (tel. 181), on Rte. 7, just past the Dok Khoune on the right. Not much from the outside, but the rooms are cheap and clean. Cluster bomb ashtrays in the lobby. Doubles 3000kip, with private bath 4000kip. Popular with backpackers. Convivial Vietnamese owner and his Lao wife have a go-any-where Land Rover and can organize tours for 10,000kip per day.

Phudoi Hotel (tel. 238), at the south end of Phonsavan Rd., opposite Aroun May Bank. The yellow Soviet-style building is an abomination; rooms are slightly more attractive, and clean and bright. Basic doubles with bathroom and flush toilet 7000kip. Triples 7000kip. Breakfast included. Friendly, English-speaking owner can arrange excursions.

FOOD

Don't expect much in the way of dining in a city with barely any electricity. The **food market** (open daily 6am-7pm) behind the post office sells fruit, vegetables, French bread, and some prepared snack foods. There are a few **noodle stands** here and across the street in the **main market.**

Sanga Restaurant, on Rte. 7 east of the market on the left before the Hay Hin Hotel. Serves cheap, basic Lao food, conveniently displayed on an English menu. Most dishes 1000kip: chicken curry, beef *laap,* and cucumber salad. Fried rice (700kip). Open daily 6am-10pm.

Inter-Lao Restaurant (tel. 156), on Phonsavan Rd, past Phudoi Hotel about 20m past the provincial hall on the left. Run by the manager of Inter-Lao Tourism, this joint is as chic as Phonsavan gets, with cloth napkins, clean glasses, and Lao music. French and decent Lao food (800-1500kip), but only the French menu is in English. Open daily 10am-8pm

■ Near Phonsavan

THONG HAY HIN (THE PLAIN OF JARS)

> While the areas immediately surrounding the jars have been cleared of land-mines, the rest of the countryside cannot be considered safe. Exercise caution and stick to well-trodden paths.

The principle sight around Phonsavan is, of course, the **Plain of Jars.** The romantic name conjures up visions of a vast rolling field littered with thousands of massive stone urns. Alas, reality is far less dramatic. The Plain of Jars actually consists of about 300 jars scattered across the countryside around Phonsavan in clusters ranging from 50 jars down to one measly urn. They are believed to be between 2500 to 3000 years old, although even this is debatable. A widely accepted theory holds that the jars are funerary urns used to inter bodies of the deceased. This hypothesis was strengthened by the discovery of human remains in one of the jars in 1963. Some archeologists believe the jars, which were hewn from solid stone, may have been made by ancestors of the Khamu people who, well into this century, continued to place the remains of their dead in jars.

Three groups of jars are readily accessible from Phonsavan. The first, **Hay Hin I,** is 12km west of town near the airbase and reachable by *tuk-tuk* (5000kip). The rather touristy site consists of about 50 jars on two levels (open daily; admission 1000kip). Next to the first group is a large bomb crater. Down the hill on the left is a cave used by Pathet Lao as shelter from those very bombs during the war.

The other two sites, **Hay Hin 2** (24km) and **Hay Hin 3** (32km) are accessible only by a thrill-a-minute car ride, and at times during the rainy season only by Russian jeeps. Although not as large a collection as #1, both 2 and 3 remain untouched by the hand of tourism and afford a sweeping view of the Lao highland landscape. The remote sites are certainly worth it if you can find enough people to make it economical. By taxi from the market it costs 17,000kip; during the rainy season it may be necessary to cover the final few km on foot. Off-road vehicles with driver can be rented from Sodetour or Inter-Lao Tourism for about 25,000kip.

There are several rarely visited **Hmong villages** in the region, including one at **Ban Dong Dan** near Hay Hin 2. Twenty-four km east of Phonsavan is the large Hmong village of **Ban Thatcho,** a frequent stop for package tour groups. It is easily reachable by *tuk-tuk* (8000kip), taxi (15,000kip), or bus (noon and 3pm, 400kip).

MUANG KHAM DISTRICT

Tham Phyu lies 56km from Phonsavan in Muang Kham District. During the Vietnam War the cave was used as a bomb shelter for civilians, until one day in 1968 when an unidentified aircraft fired a rocket into the cave, killing several hundred people. Most historians point to the Royal Lao Airforce, but the Lao government insists it was an American plane. Bone fragments are still scattered around the cave, a gruesome testament to the tragedy of war. Muang Kham District has achieved some degree of noto-

LAOS

riety for the local population's ingenious use of the flotsam of war—bomb casings, artillery shells, and scrap metal from downed aircraft—in their building projects. There are also several **Hmong villages** near Tham Phyu. For travelers who do not speak Lao but who want to get a good look at Hmong village life, it is best to go with a guide who can translate for you, as the villagers tend to be quite shy and suspicious of foreigners. The Phonsavan branch of **Sodetour Travel** is entirely Hmong-run. Their tours are highly recommended by travelers for the high degree of interaction between themselves and the villagers. A one-day trip to Tham Phyu and several Hmong villages costs around 27,000kip for car, driver, and guide. Sodetour also organizes three-day treks into the mountains near the Lao-Vietnamese border, where trekkers sleep in remote Hmong villages

SOUTHERN LAOS

■ Savannakhet

Savannakhet, or Savan, as it is locally dubbed, perches on the west bank of the Mekong River nearly 500km south of Vientiane. The commercial hub of the central Laotian panhandle, Savannakhet is a town on the make. The region is gearing up for an economic boom now that Laos and Vietnam are both in the process of opening the Pandora's box of capitalism. Savan, only a day's bus ride from Hue and Da Nang on the central Vietnamese coast, looks to take advantage of the expected boom. Among travelers en route to Vietnam or the splendors of the Emerald Triangle to the south Savan suffers from a not-entirely-fair reputation as an uninspiring pit stop. While the sights may not rival those in the enchanting deep south, there is a certain charm to the city's unabashed commercial atmosphere and narrow, cluttered streets. The population is far less reserved than those in northern cities, and visitors can expect plenty of cheerful *sabai-dee*'s and giggling children eager to clown around with the goofy *farang*. The streets are teeming with motorcyclists so eager to chauffeur pedestrian tourists that *tuk-tuk* are almost unnecessary.

ORIENTATION

Savannakhet lies on the banks of the **Mekong River** directly opposite the Thai city of Mukdahan. Savan's north-south layout keeps the river always to the west. Three main roads run parallel to the river: **Tha Heua Road,** along the bank, **Khanthabouli Road,** and **Ratsavongseuk Road.** They are linked by several streets running east-west, the largest of which, **Oudomsin Road,** passes the **market** in the north section of town. Five blocks south, **Simuang Road** begins at the immigration pier and runs away from the river. Several cheap restaurants and the Hotel Santyphab are clustered along its length. The **bus station** is on the extreme northern end of town and the **airport** the extreme south. Maps can be purchased at the Savan Banhao Hotel.

PRACTICAL INFORMATION

Tours and Travel: Savan Travel and Tour, in Savan Banhao Hotel, 644 Senna Rd. (tel. 212 202). Open Mon.-Sat. 8-11:30am and 2-4pm. **Lane Xang Travel and Tours,** 385 Ratsavongseuk Rd. (tel. 212 804), opposite the market. Package tours to Vietnam. Open Mon.-Fri 7am-noon and 2-5pm, Sat. 7am-noon. **Sodetour** (tel. 212 445), on Kanvoravong Rd. Organizes excursions to the dinosaur remains at Ban Namo, Phalan District. Open Mon.-Sat. 8-11:30am and 2-4pm.

Embassies and Consulates: Vietnam (tel. 212 418; fax 212 182). From the south end of the market head east on Oudomsin Rd., take the 1st right, onto Sisavangvong Rd; it is 1½ blocks down on the right. Visas issued for crossing at **Lao Bao** US$70; allow 3-5 days for processing. May demand payment in baht or kip. Open Mon.-Sat. 8-11:30am and 2-4:30pm.

Immigration Offices: At the pier. Unlike in the northern provinces, where travelers must register with the police in each province, such rules are not strictly enforced in the south. Try to get your passport stamped anyway.

Currency Exchange: Banque Pour le Commerce Exterieur Lao (tel. 212 722), opposite the market. MC, Visa, AmEx traveler's checks and cash advances. Open Mon.-Sat. 8am-3:30pm. **Exchange booths** near the market as well. Some offer discounted rates for traveler's checks. Most are open Mon.-Sat. until 5 or 6pm.

Air Travel: One airstrip and a rickety wooden "terminal," at the southwest end of town at the intersection of Makhavena and Sisavangvong Rd. To **Vientiane** (1hr., 47,000kip) and **Pakxe** (Mon. and Fri., 30min., 31,600kip). Again, schedule is erratic. Purchase tickets at least 1 day before and confirm. Cash only. **Lao Aviation office** (tel. 212 140), in the terminal. Open daily 7-11:30am and 2-5pm.

Buses: Bus station (tel. 212 140), at the intersection of Sisavangvong and Visouthat Rd., in the north end of town. Buses to **Vientiane** (5 and 11:30am, 8-12hr., 7000kip) via **Thakhek** (5hr., 2500kip) and **Pakxe** (4:30 and 6am, 6-8hr., 3200kip). Buses to Vientiane pass through in the afternoon and evening. One going to Pakxe comes by sometime after 6pm, but actual arrival and departure times are anybody's guess. To **Da Nang**, Vietnam (Mon., Tues., Thurs., Fri., Sun., 12:30am, 18hr., 17,500kip) via **Lao Bao** border crossing (7hr., 10,500kip) and **Hue** (16hr., 14,200kip). Arrive 1hr. early to guarantee a seat.

Ferries: The pier is next to the customs office, at the Simuang-Tha Heua Rd. intersection. Those entering Laos here must have a visa from the Lao embassy in Bangkok and must register at the customs office (1500kip). To **Mukdahan,** Thailand (Mon.-Fri., 5 per day, 9:30am-3pm; Sat., 4 per day, 9:30am-2:30pm; Sun., 1 per day which leaves when full, 20min., 1000kip).

Local Transportation: Tuk-tuk roam the streets in large numbers, but don't run between 10pm-4am, making it a challenge to catch midnight buses. Hail a motorbike with a 1000kip note or arrange a ride in advance. To **That Inheng** (40min., 4000kip roundtrip) and **That Phon** (2hr., 15,000kip).

Rentals: Phonepaseud Hotel (tel. 212 258), on Santisouk Rd., right off Sisavangvong Rd., has **bikes** for 1700kip per day. Also inquire at guest houses.

Markets: The fast-paced **day market** lies at the intersection of Oudomsin and Ratchavongseuk Rd., peddling fresh bread and bounteous heaps of goods.

Pharmacies: Pharmesco, 236/1 Ratsavongseuk Rd. (tel. 212 313), near the market. Carries French-made anti-malarial pills. Open daily 6:30am-6:30pm.

Medical Services: Savannakhet Provincial Hospital (tel. 212 131), on Khanthabouli Rd. 5 blocks south of Simuang Rd. on the right. Some English spoken. In case of emergencies get to Thailand as soon as possible.

Police: (tel. 212 212), on Khanthabouli Rd., 1 block south of the intersection with Simuang Rd., opposite the post office. Little English spoken.

Post Offices/Telephones: (tel. 212 296), on Khanthabouli Rd. From the intersection with Simuang Rd., the post office is 1 block south by the massive radio tower. Exchange booth (cash only) open during business hours. Cash only **overseas telephone** and fax service (open daily 7:30am-10pm). Post office open Mon.-Sat. 7:30-11:30am and 2-5pm. **Postal code:** 1300. **Telephone code:** 041.

ACCOMMODATIONS

Sayamungkun Hotel, 85 Ratsavongseuk Rd. (tel. 212 426), 1 block from the intersection with Simuang Rd.; look for the Guest House sign in front. Towering ceilings, hardwood floors, and lovely 2nd-floor patio. Owner speaks French. Clean doubles with fan and western bathroom 6000kip, with A/C 10,000 kip.

Hotel Santyphab (tel. 212 177), on Chaleunmuang Rd. 20m east of the French Food Restaurant. Savan's premier backpacker lodge. Dirt cheap rooms wouldn't pass Mama's white glove test. Great view of the river and Mukdahan. Rooms have shower and flush toilet. Doubles 3500kip, with A/C 5000kip.

Savan Banhao Hotel, 644 Senna Rd. (tel. 212 202), 2 blocks south of the market. Locals sometimes call it the Silan Hotel. It may look deserted, but the few who stay get clean, attractive rooms with A/C. Small rooms with double bed and shared bath 5000kip. Larger rooms with flush toilet 7000-8700kip.

That Phon

About 60km south of Savan on Rte. 13 stands a tall, white stupa that, while not overly awe-inspiring, is sacred to the Lao. Dating from the Angkor period, the story behind its construction is perhaps one of the most unusual Buddhist anecdotes. According to legend, the Buddha was in the middle of a particularly "moving" sermon when nature's call came on strong. Not content to use the local facilities and exercising the prerogative of a major deity, he had a *naga* build a toilet for him on the spot. That Phon's white spire now commemorates the site, proving that perhaps someone really can "shit bricks."

FOOD

Food is certainly one of Savan's bright spots; the city is practically afloat in *pho* due to the strong Vietnamese influence. One of the most popular shops is adjacent to the Hotel Santyphab. A large bowl is 500kip; add tea for 800kip. The market also boasts a large food section where vendors hawk *pho* (500kip), spring rolls (200kip each), and other Lao and Vietnamese snacks. Restaurants with English menus are surprisingly plentiful, given the dearth of tourists.

    Savanhlaty Food Garden, at the intersection of Simuang and Khanthabouli Rd., just east of Hotel Santyphab. Not exactly a night market, and not exactly a restaurant either, but it has the best meal deal in town. Sit at tables surrounded by a peaceful garden, while hawkers serve basic Thai and Lao food standbys such as fried rice (800kip), *pad thai* (800kip), and lots of savory noodle soups (600kip). Top it off with a fruit shake (300kip). Open daily 4-10pm.

    French Food Restaurant, 31 Chaleunmuang Rd. (tel. 212 792), at the corner with Tha Heua Rd. close to the immigration office. Owner and chef serves up excellent Euro and Asian dishes. Steak and fries 2500kip. *Sukiyaki* and Korean-style grilled beef also popular. Specialties include other-worldly *nem nuong* (grilled pork balls with starfruit, plantains, and veggies, 1500kip). Cannabis soup must be ordered in advance. Open daily 10am-9pm.

MARKETS AND SIGHTS

Savannakhet's **day market,** at the intersection of Oudomsin and Ratchavongseuk Rd., is surely one of its greatest attractions. Every morning, mountains of freshly baked *khao jii* feed hungry shoppers as they crowd the narrow lanes.

    The only wat of historical significance, **Wat Sayaphum** turned 100 years old two years ago. Standing on Tha Heua Rd., north of the pier, the complex contains two main *sim,* the largest of which is a gymnasium and is decorated on the inside with murals depicting scenes from the epic *Ramakien.*

    About 15km north of the city is **That Inheng,** the city's most revered religious shrine. The gray 25m-high stupa, adorned with ascetics and fanciful creatures, is all that remains of the ancient city of Sikhottabong. Women are not permitted to enter That Inheng's tiny chamber, which allegedly contains the Buddha's spinal chord. An empty, crumbling cloister surrounds the stupa on three sides, surrounded by a large religious community. The road is in deplorable condition and biking is not advised.

■ Border Crossing: Lao Bao

Nearly 200 buttock-bruising km east of Savannakhet along Rte. 9, which winds around the slopes of the Annamite Mountains, lies the border town of Lao Bao. Only recently opened to foreigners, it is the only overland route between southern Laos and Vietnam. The road is horrendous and the sleepless journey to the border may seem like an all-too-vivid nightmare. Passengers hold rags to their faces to avoid inhaling the thick red dust which covers everything, while the bus threatens to fall apart with each pothole. But the faithful will reach Lao Bao, where money changers assault foreigners with wads of Vietnamese dong and lousy exchange rates. Lao customs is usually just a formality, although travelers will have to show passports and pay a fine of $5 for each day they have overstayed their visa. Vietnamese immigration requires a visa stamped with the Lao Bao entry point. These can be obtained in Vientiane, Savannakhet, or Pakxe. The Vietnamese customs search takes three to five hours as the bus is combed for contraband. Some travelers advise taking the bus only as far as Lao Bao and passing through customs on foot to avoid the wait. These travelers usually catch a motorcycle taxi or hitch a truck to the next town. It is also possible to hop back on the bus, a $2 surcharge will be added onto the $4 fare from Lao Bao to Hue.

Perhaps the only redeeming quality of the hellish transit is the mountainous scenery on the Vietnamese side of the border—if it is still light enough to see. Most buses plying this route are bound for Da Nang. Those stopping in Hue, should ask the driver to let them off across the Perfume River, where budget hotels cluster.

▓ Pakxe

After traveling literally hundreds of km against a virtually seamless backdrop of rice paddies, and palm groves, the terrain begins to change near Pakxe. High, mesa-like hills, their slopes cloaked in verdant jungle, rise in the distance, marking the foothills of the nearby Bolovens Plateau. Here, in the region known as the Emerald Triangle (where Laos, Cambodia, and Thailand meet), the rugged natural beauty of Laos reaches a magnificent crescendo of remote mountain idyll, deep narrow gorges, and countless tiny islands populated by various ethnic groups. The gateway to these wonders is Pakxe, a quiet port city 680km south of Vientiane in Champassak Province. Historically, Vietnam and Cambodia have exercised an inordinate influence on the region, far more than Laos. In the 11th century, the Khmers built a grand temple city at Wat Phu, 40km south of Pakxe. From 1948 until 1975, Pakxe, at the confluence of the Mekong and Xedone Rivers, was the capital of the quasi-independent kingdom of Champassak. As the commercial and transportation hub of southern Laos, Pakxe makes an ideal base for forays into isolated Saravane and Attapu Provinces to the north and east, and the "land of 4000 islands" to the south.

ORIENTATION

The **Xedone** and **Mekong Rivers** border town to the west and south respectively. Most budget hotels, restaurants, and shops are clustered along several streets near the central market and waterfront. The main thoroughfare passes just north of town: **Route 13** runs from the **bus station,** 3km east of town, past the **evening market,** stadium, and Champassak Palace Hotel. Just north of Wat Luang, it crosses the Xedone River Bridge to the **airport.** *Tuk-tuk* rides are generally 300kip per person. All streets have numbers as well as names: **Roads 6, 5,** and **1** run parallel to Rte. 3 (east-west), with Rd. 1 closest to the Mekong. **Roads 10** and **12** cross perpendicularly. **Xedone Quay** runs on a diagonal from Rte. 13 to the **ferry pier** at the river confluence. The National Tourism Authority (NTA) publishes a helpful map of the city, available in Vientiane or at the Champassak Palace Hotel gift shop (2000kip).

PRACTICAL INFORMATION

Tours and Travel: Inter-Lao Tourism (tel. 212 226), on Rte.13 next to the Phonsavanh Hotel. Pick-ups that seat 4 people can be rented for $50 per day with driver. Open Mon.-Sat. 8am-noon and 2-5pm. **Sodetour** (tel. 212 122), on Rd. 8, past the gas station on the right, has 2-day package tours of the south ($500 for 2 people). Open Mon.-Sat. 8-11:30am and 2-4:30pm.

Immigration Offices: (tel. 212 000), at the police station. Open daily 8-11am and 2-4pm. English and French spoken.

Embassies and Consulates: Vietnam (tel. 212 658), on Rd. 24. Heading toward the Xedone River from Champassak Palace Hotel, Rd. 24 is just past Ketmany Restaurant on the right. Visas to Vietnam $70. Takes at least 5 days. Open Mon.-Fri. 7:30-11am and 2-4:30pm, Sat. 7:30-11am.

Currency Exchange: Banque Pour Le Commerce Exterieur Lao (tel. 212 770), at the corner of Rd. 10 and 5, opposite the market. AmEx traveler's checks. MC, Visa, and AmEx cash advances. Open Mon.-Fri. 8:30am-3:30pm, Sat. 8:30-10am. For higher exchange rates, a number of **jewelry shops** near the market exchange dollars for baht or kip (cash only).

Air Travel: Pakxe Airport, on Rte.13 about 1km west of the Xedone River Bridge. To **Vientiane** (1¼hr., $95) and **Savannakhet** (2 per week, 45min. $35). No set schedule, so inquire. **Lao Aviation office** (tel. 212 252), just before the airfield on the left. Purchase tickets at least 1 day in advance and confirm 1 day before (cash only). Open Mon.-Sat. 7-11:30am and 2-4:30pm, Sun. 7-11:30am.

Buses: Pakxe Bus Station (tel. 212 428), on Rte. 13 about 2km east of Champassak Palace Hotel, past the stadium. To: **Vientiane** via **Savannakhet** (4 per day, 7am-1pm, dry season 13hr., rainy season 16-24hr., 11,000kip); **Savannakhet** (4 and 6am, dry season 6hr., rainy season 7-10hr., 4000kip); **Champassak** (10am and 1pm, 1hr., 700kip); **Saravane** (6, 7am, and 1pm, 3hr., 1500kip); **Don Khong** (6 and 7am, 3hr., 2000kip includes ferry); and **Attapu** (6am, dry season 5hr., rainy season 12hr., 3000kip includes ferry). **Songthaew** leave frequently for **Pakxong** (1hr., 1000kip) as well. Catch the ferry and cross the river, where *songthaew* make the 45-min. trip to the **Vung Tao/Chong Mek** border crossing (660kip). **Share taxis** (1000kip per person) also make the trip.

Ferries: Ferries shuttle trucks and passengers **across the Mekong** (several per hr., 7am-6pm, 200kip without vehicle). **Boats** to **Don Khong** (8hr., 2000kip) via **Champassak** (2hr., 500kip) leave from the waterfront to the right of the ferry pier each morning around 8am.

Markets: The gargantuan **morning market,** just a block from the quay, overflows with everything a backpacker needs.

Pharmacies: Phone Souk Pharmacie, 33 Rd. 5 (tel. 212 440). Carries anti-malarial drugs. Open daily 8am-8pm. No English spoken.

Medical Services: (tel. 212 042; **emergency** 212 041), opposite the market. A small pharmacy to the right of the entrance. Open daily 7am-10pm.

Police: (tel. 212 145), on Rd. 12 across the street from the east end of the market.

Post Offices/Telephones: (tel. 212 056), on Rd. 8, at the intersection with Rd. 1. Open daily 8am-5pm. Cash-only **overseas telephone** (open daily 8am-10pm). **Postal code:** 1600. **Telephone code:** 031.

ACCOMMODATIONS

The pricey Champassak Palace Hotel (basic singles start at $40) and slightly more economical Sala Champ Guest House (doubles cost $22) cater primarily to package tourists. Budget options tend to be large, impersonal operations, but the situation may improve as they multiply.

Lao Travel Service Guest House No. 1, on Rd. 9. From the west side of the market, head south toward the Mekong, passing the hospital and crossing Rd. 1; look for the blue and yellow sign on the right. The reception desk is rarely staffed, so knock on the door to get the manager. Clean, attractive rooms have desks. Doubles with fan and shared bath 6000kip, with A/C and private bath 10,000kip.

Pakse Hotel, 112/113 Rd. 5 (tel. 212 131). It's the hulking yellow monstrosity in the center of town opposite the market. Cheapest rooms (5000kip) have distant shared toilets. A/C rooms have private bath (8500-12,000kip depending on size and other perks).

Phonsavanh Hotel, 294 Rte. 13 (tel. 212 842), on Rte. 13 at the intersection with Rd. 12. A basic backpacker's crash pad: cramped rooms were probably once clean. All rooms share a squat toilet. Spartan singles with fan 4000kip. Doubles 5000kip. Triples with sink and more elbow room 6000kip.

FOOD

Pakxe has the largest Vietnamese population in Laos and *pho* shops are everywhere. The **evening market** features a pavilion selling *kai ping, khao niaw,* fried fish, spring rolls, and noodle soups.

Dornsokdee Restaurant, 94/95 Rd. 6 (tel. 212 332), near the Rd. 10 intersection. Probably the most popular restaurant in Pakxe; the *sukiyaki* (6-9000kip, feeds 3-5) is in high demand. "Instant *sukiyaki*" is really just *pho* in disguise (1000kip). Basic Lao and Thai dishes 1000-2000 kip. Open daily 11am-2pm and 6-10pm.

Sedone Restaurant, 110 Rd. 5 (tel. 212 155), 2 shops down from Pakse Hotel opposite the market. A pleasant café-style restaurant. Tasty Lao, Thai, and Vietnamese dishes 500-1000kip for regular size portions, 1000-1500kip for bigger portions. *Tom yam plaa* 1000kip. Open daily 6am-10pm.

Ketmany Restaurant, 227 Rte. 13 (tel. 212 615), at the end of the long block west of Champassak Palace Hotel. As trendy as Pakxe gets—Ace of Base throbs on the stereo while teens eat ice cream and watch Thai-dubbed American movies. Check out the psychedelic Buddhist shrine above the door. Does brisk business in *pho* (500kip). Iced Ovaltine 300kip. Small bakery selection. Open daily 8am-5pm.

SIGHTS

Pakxe itself offers little in the way of attractions save the natural scenery. The city's principal wat, **Wat Luang,** erected on the east bank of the Xedone River in 1830, is worth a visit, if only as an example of renovation gone awry. The temple, which stands just south of the bridge, was refurbished in 1991, and the lovely carved original wooden doors and shutters are almost lost in a swarm of brightly painted, cartoonish reliefs and gaudy *naga*. A large golden Buddha dominates the interior, an island of serenity in a writhing mess of plaster kitsch.

At the top of a small hill on Rte. 13 in the middle of town is one of the most bizarre landmarks in Laos, the **Palace of Boun Oum,** former residence of the Prince of Champassak. Construction of the massive six-story palace began in 1969, and was not yet completed when the communists deposed the prince in 1975. Until recently the structure stood in its unfinished state; it now houses the Champassak Palace Hotel. Visitors can take the elevator to the top floor to take in the view of the Bolovens Plateau and the city spread out like a diorama below.

Lying 13km west of town off Rte. 13 is the weaving village of **Ban Saphay,** renowned for its *ikat* silk and *mat-mi* cotton cloth. The patterns are more complex, with brighter colors than northern weavings. You won't find the cloth in the local market, since most of it is sold wholesale, but two shops along the main road carry a large assortment of fabrics, sold by the meter, with a few ready-made garments. One is operated by the **Lao Women's Union,** but the privately owned **Lao Home-made Silk Skirt Shop** (nary a skirt in sight, however) carries a better selection. *Mat-mi* cotton begins at about 7000kip per meter, *ikat* silk at 3000kip per meter. To get to Ban Saphay, take a *tuk-tuk* from the central market (30min., 4000kip).

■ Near Pakxe: Wat Phu

The small town of **Champassak** lies 38km down river from Pakxe, sandwiched between the Mekong and a string of steep, craggy limestone hills. The town itself would hardly be worth a visit were it not for the ruins of an ancient Khmer temple 11km to the south. Known as **Wat Phu** (Hill Temple), or simply Muang Kao (Old City), the temple still has many structures in good condition, and it is considered one of the finest examples of Khmer art outside Cambodia (open 8am-4:30pm; admission 300kip, with camera an additional 700kip).

Archaeologists believe that the site might date back to the 6th century, during the Chenla period, but it was actually completed at the end of the 11th century by King Suryavarman II (1113-50) of Angkor. The temple bears many stylistic similarities to Angkor Wat, King Suryavarman's greatest architectural achievement, and may actually have served as a model or trial run for Angkor Wat. Following the fall of Angkor two centuries later, Wat Phu was abandoned to the jungle until a French expedition "rediscovered" the complex in 1866. (For more information, see **Cambodia: History** on page 59.) Today the temple is in desperate need of renovation; to this end

Curiosity Killed the King

In the early 11th century, King Khamatha of Champassak accepted a wager from an upstart rival to prove who could build a great temple more rapidly. While Khamatha set about the task of constructing Wat Phu, his challenger ordered the erection of Wat That Phanom (in present-day Thailand) by women. These female engineers pragmatically removed their shirts to work in the oppressive heat. When word reached the men at Wat Phu that That Phanom employed a topless construction team, the curious contractors abandoned their own site to observe the effort upstream. The dismayed Khamatha was powerless to stop the desertions and Wat Phu lay unfinished as That Phanom's triumphant spire was raised aloft. When the message came that That Phanom was completed, Khamatha, ashamed of his failure, took his own life. The voyeuristic builders returned to Champassak to find their king dead. Heavy with guilt, they constructed a stupa for their ruined leader, which still stands just a few hundred meters from Wat Phu. The temple itself remained in its unfinished state until the great Khmer king, Suryavarman II, completed it nearly a century later.

UNESCO is planning a major project. Be aware that some of the walls are not entirely stable, and exercise caution when poking around the ruins.

The temple access road skirts a large *baray* (man-made lake), which symbolizes the waters of the earth and also helped irrigate the surrounding rice fields. Originally visitors entered the complex by crossing a long causeway lined with *naga* balustrades, as at Angkor Wat. Today the causeway is fenced off. Two large rectangular galleries—the one on the right made of laterite, the one on the left of sandstone—stand on either side of the entrance.

At the top of a series of moss-covered laterite tiers is the small, almost delicate central sanctuary, an example of Khmer art and architecture at its best. Lithe *apsarases*, the celestial nymphs synonymous with Khmer sculpture, grace both sides of the entrance. Above it, a perfectly preserved lintel depicts Vishnu the Destroyer astride his trademark three-headed elephant. The temple has been reconsecrated to Buddhism and now a large, rather incongruous Buddha sits where the *linga* once did.

Wat Phu is easily visited as a daytrip from Pakxe via Champassak, which is accessible by bus and boat from Pakxe. The latter is by far the more relaxing and scenic of the two options as the Mekong passes picturesque hills and limestone cliffs. Boats bound for Champassak (2hr., 500kip) leave from the area just upriver from the ferry landing when they are full. Buses leave from the station on Rte. 13 as well (10am and 1pm, 1hr., 700kip). Both modes of transportation drop passengers off outside **Hotel Sala Wat Phou,** Champassak's one and only hotel with rooms going for $25-40; insist on big discounts during the low season. Motorized cyclos can be hired to go the rest of the way to Wat Phu for 4000kip roundtrip. The hotel rents bicycles, but plan on spending the night if you wish to bike to the temple. To get to Wat Phu, head south (downriver) along the main dirt road through Champassak and past several rice fields. The large reservoir and the gates of a more recent temple are visible to the right after about 11km. Ask a local for directions if you get lost.

The last bus to Pakxe leaves from the opposite bank around 4:30pm; boats heading upriver normally stop at the landing near Hotel Sala Wat Phou and about 1km farther upstream. The trip back upriver takes about 45 minutes longer and costs 500kip. The desperate can take a ferry across the river and hire a *tuk-tuk* for the 40-km ride (about 11,000kip).

■ Bolovens Plateau

Rising dramatically to the north and east of Pakxe is the rugged and isolated Bolovens Plateau. One of Southeast Asia's last frontiers, the region is still largely untainted by environmental desecration or tourism. Its natural splendors are unsurpassed; the region is laced with white-water rivers, steep, narrow gorges, and remote valleys. The plateau is also home to a plethora of ethnic minorities, many of whom were forced to flee their ancestral homelands in the Annamite Cordillera near the Laotian-Vietnamese border during American bombing campaigns in the 60s and early 70s. Among the larger groups are Ngai, Suk, Katou, and Alak, most of whom are animists and still practice shamanism in villages largely isolated from the modern world. The Bolovens Plateau possesses some of the world's most fertile soil, and is one of Laos's agricultural centers. Tea, coffee, fruit, and cardamom are grown in abundance on plantations founded by French *colons* at the turn of the century.

In the midst of this vast plateau, 113km northeast of Pakxe, lies the sleepy provincial capital of Saravane (pronounced Sarawan). Along its unnamed dirt roads, turkeys and cattle far outnumber bicycles, and cars are near unheard of. For travelers, the town offers the best base for further exploration of this remote region. Travel here requires time, patience, flexibility, and cash, as many towns with accommodations are used to only package tour groups and charge high rates for simple, at times rudimentary, rooms. Nevertheless, the rewards for those who come are more than worth the price. For now, the plateau remains a bastion of unsullied natural splendor ripe for discovery and adventure.

ORIENTATION AND PRACTICAL INFORMATION

Saravane, northeast of Pakxe, lies on the bank of the **Xedone River.** The newly-paved road from Pakxe passes the **bus station** and **airport** on the southwestern edge of town, then forms a ring around the town center. Daily **buses** go to **Pakxe** (5 per day, 4am-1pm, 3hr., 1500kip). Bi-weekly **flights** go to **Pakxe** and **Savannakhet.** The **market** is more or less the center of town, with the **post office** (EMS but **no phones**) and **bank** to the west and **hospital** and football field to the north. Saise Guesthouse, at the northeast corner of town near the river has a helpful map posted on the wall. *Tuk-tuk* from the bus station cost 500kip.

ACCOMMODATIONS, FOOD, AND SIGHTS

Saise Guesthouse offers a range of lodging options: fan rooms go for 4500-7000kip, with A/C 8000-10,000kip. Rooms here are as vast as the plateau itself, with baths to match. There are no English menus in town, but *pho* shops are aplenty and fruit from the market keeps the traveler from starving.

Inquire at Saise concerning exploration of the **Bolovens Plateau;** even independent travelers will appreciate up-to-date information on which bridges are out and which roads impassable. Others can enjoy the variety of trips which the guest house organizes. Visits to animist villages, waterfalls, archeological sites, and expeditions to the plateau towns of **Attapu, Tataeng,** and **Pakxong** (subject to road conditions) are among the options. Other opportunities include taking elephant rides and sampling *lao hai* in traditional drinking circles. Saravane itself has an interesting **market** which sometimes features rare animals from remote areas of the province.

■ Near Saravane: Thad Lo

Set amidst the stunning backdrop of the Bolovens Plateau, some 80km northeast of Pakxe, is idyllic Thad Lo. Built on a bend in the Xedone River, downstream from a series of tumbling waterfalls, it is downright utopian. Travelers can soak road-weary bodies in fantastic natural swimming pools, visit out-of-the-way villages, or just kick back in gorgeous but pricey bungalows, lulled to sleep by crashing waterfalls.

The handful of collapsing bamboo huts clustered along the main road between Pakxe and Saravane where the bus drops off passengers is unimpressive. About 1km down a dirt road (follow the signs) is charming **Thad Lo village**. Continuing through the village and bearing right leads to a small bridge just below Thad Heng Falls. **Thad Lo Resort** is down a path to the left of the bridge. It is a collection of bungalows grouped around a large main lodge. The eight-year-old government-run resort is in excellent condition and the location is enchanting. Two-bed bungalows (with electricity and western bathroom) start at 10,000kip. More lavishly furnished bungalows across the river, within spitting distance of the falls, cost 20,000kip. The open-sided lodge with high ceilings, wicker furniture, and bamboo bar is a classic tropical hang-out. The **Saise Guest House,** just across the bridge, is reserved for group tours from Saravane. Simple rooms run about the same as nicer ones at the resort.

The Thad Lo Resort has a Land Rover for exploring the surrounding countryside. A more exotic, if slightly hokey, option is to get around by elephant (3000kip per person per hr.). A one-hour trek on one of the slightly cantankerous pachyderms travels past Thad Lo, the upper falls, and across the river to an Alak animist village.

Thad Lo can be visited as a daytrip from Saravane or Pakxe, or seen as a lunch stop en route between the two. Buses go from Saravane to Pakxe (5 per day, 4am-1pm, 1hr., 500kip) and return (5 per day, 6am-1pm, 2hr., 1300kip). Be back at the junction by 1:20pm if bound for Pakxe or 2pm if bound for Saravane to guarantee a ride home, since travel time varies according to the number of pick ups the bus makes.

■ 4000 Islands Region (Sii Phan Don)

As the Mekong winds its way south from Pakxe it undergoes a Jekyll to Hyde transformation, from lethargic, mild-mannered river to raging, white-water torrent. At the extreme southern tip of Laos, 140km downstream from Pakxe, the Mekong widens to as much at 10km. Thousands of small islets, many of which are only above water during the winter, dot the complex web of branches and tributaries the Mekong becomes, earning the region its nickname. The larger, inhabited islands maintain a perceptible distance from affairs on either bank. Here, in the 4000 Islands region, the pace of life is dictated by the cycles of the river.

ORIENTATION AND PRACTICAL INFORMATION

The largest island, and the most logical starting point for explorations of the region, is **Don Khong.** There are several hotels in **Muang Khoune,** the island's main village. From Pakxe, take a **boat** (8am, 8hr., 2000kip) or **bus** (6 per day, 6am-1pm, 3hr., 2000kip) to Don Khong. The boat stops at Muang Sen, on the west side of the island; a *tuk-tuk* or motorcycle taxi to Muang Khoune costs 1500kip. The buses (except the first two, which end with ferry rides directly to Muang Khoune) stop in Ban Hat Xay Khoune, on the left bank of the Mekong. Skiffs run to the island when full (300kip per person). Lao Aviation has suspended service to Don Khong **airfield,** but charters both in and out are possible. Ask travel agents in Vientiane. There is a small **morning market** north of the Muang Khoune Pier.

ACCOMMODATIONS AND FOOD

Muang Khoune has three budget guest houses. The first, immediately in front of the ferry pier, has no name. The French-speaking proprietress offers singles for 5000kip and doubles for 7000kip, and cooks delicious meals. Bike rentals costs 2000kip per day. Thirty km past this guest house is the **Done Khong Guesthouse,** which is owned by the more upscale **Auberge Sala** downstream. Singles at the budget version go for 7000kip, doubles with private bath 9000kip. Bike rental is 2000kip here as well. A few hundred meters upstream (follow the sign "Room prices 3 to 30 dollars") is the **Souksun Guesthouse,** with the only dormitory in town (2500kip). Twin rooms with bath are also available for 8-29,000kip, though if you opt for A/C remember that it only works from 6-11pm. Bike rental is dearer than your dorm bed at $3 per day. An in-house restaurant serves Lao and Chinese food.

SIGHTS

Apart from relaxing amid a beautiful setting, the prime attractions of the 4000 Islands are the impressive waterfalls downstream from Don Khong. **Li Phi Falls,** on the southwestern tip of the island of Don Khone (do not confuse the two islands), is accessible by boat. Don Khone is notable as there is a small, 5-km railroad line (now inoperable) built by the French to bypass the rough stretch of rapids. Farther south, on the left bank, and just off Rte. 13, is **Khong Pha Phing,** the "Voice of the Mekong," a spectacular cascade that is the largest in Southeast Asia. Both waterfalls can be visited in a day with an early start. The owner of Souksun Guesthouse organizes trips: boat for six and skipper is 18,000kip for the day, add a picnic lunch for 3000kip per person. Since the final stretch of river is un-navigable, travelers have to take a motorcycle taxi to Khong Pha Phing (5000kip per person). This region is home to the only remaining population of the endangered **Irawaddy dolphins.**

LAOS

MALAYSIA

The beguiling scent of modernization fills the air and dusts the streets of Malaysian cities as the country flexes its economic muscles to leapfrog over its Southeast Asian counterparts into the 21st century. As Malaysia moves forward, however, it confronts the issues faced by so many other developing nations: how to do so without losing sight of its cultural heritage and religious devotion. To this conundrum Malaysia has not found an answer, nor has it determined how to deal with a rich mix of ethnicities under the rule of a Malay-dominated and oriented government.

Despite this confusion, however, the Federation of Malaysia remains one of the most intriguing destinations for the traveler in Southeast Asia. It has the same luxuries of fantasy beaches and intoxicating mountains found anywhere in the region, but possesses its own brand of cultural infusions. There are many stories to be recounted in this country, from the ancient legend of Mahsuri of Langkawi and the White Rajahs of Sarawak, to the not coincidentally Tolkien-esque landscape of Sabah. As Malaysia mobilizes to enter the cutthroat arena of developed nations, it is also poised to add to its already-bursting book of history.

ESSENTIALS

■ Geography

Malaysia's 13 states cover 329,750sq.km of land stretching from the isthmus of southern Thailand to the island of Singapore, just across the narrow straits of Melaka from the Indonesian island of Sumatra. The country then hops over and picks up the states of Sabah and Sarawak, which share the island of Borneo with Brunei and the Indonesian state of Kalimantan.

■ When to Go

Rain should be the primary concern in planning a trip to Malaysia, since temperature remains fairly constant. The rainy season in Malaysia differs from coast to coast. If you enjoy wearing a poncho, hit the east between November and February, and the west coast from May to September. Please see the **Appendix** for more specific climate information. Schools go on vacation from late February to early March, mid-May to early June, early August to mid-August, and late October to early December; popular tourist destinations tend to fill up quickly during these times.

■ Money Matters

US$1=RM2.50 (ringgit)	RM1=US$0.400
CDN$1=RM1.828	RM1=CDN$0.547
UK£1=RM3.861	RM1=UK£0.259
IR£1=RM3.808	RM1=IR£0.263
AUS$1=RM1.853	RM1=AUS$0.540
NZ$1=RM1.516	RM1=NZ$0.660
SARand1=RM0.701	RM1=SARand1.426

The legal tender for Malaysia is the **ringgit** (RM), and comes in denominations of RM1, 5, 10, 20, 50, 100, 500, and 1000. Each ringgit is divided into 100 **sen,** which are issued in coins of 1, 5, 10, 20, and 50 sen. There are also bulky RM1 coins. A 5% government tax is added to most bills and, in addition, a 10% service charge is automati-

Peninsular Malaysia

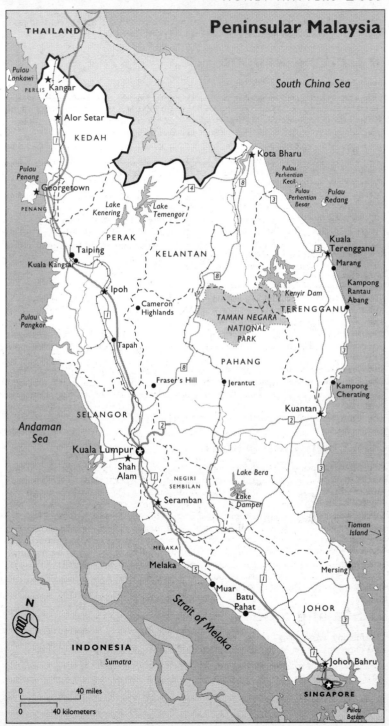

THAILAND

Pulau Lankawi

PERLIS ★ Kangar

★ Alor Setar

KEDAH

Pulau Penang

PENANG ● Georgetown

Lake Kenering

Lake Temengor

PERAK

● Taiping

Kuala Kangsar ●

Pulau Pangkor

★ Ipoh

● Cameron Highlands

● Tapah

KELANTAN

South China Sea

★ Kota Bharu

Pulau Perhentian Kecil

Pulau Perhentian Besar

Pulau Redang

Kuala Terengganu ★

● Marang

Kampong Rantau Abang

Kenyir Dam

TERENGGANU

TAMAN NEGARA NATIONAL PARK

PAHANG

Andaman Sea

SELANGOR

● Fraser's Hill

● Jerantut

Kuala Lumpur ✪

Shah Alam ★

NEGIRI SEMBILAN

★ Seramban

Lake Bera

Lake Damper

Kampong Cherating

● Kuantan

Tioman Island →

MELAKA

★ Melaka

● Muar

Batu Pahat

● Mersing

JOHOR

N

INDONESIA

Sumatra

Strait of Melaka

★ Johor Bahru

✪ SINGAPORE

Pulau Batam

0 — 40 miles

0 — 40 kilometers

MALAYSIA

cally added so **tipping** is not considered necessary. On the other hand, it's not considered rude, and might be in order for exceptional service.

■ Getting Around

BY PLANE

Airport tax is RM5 on domestic flights, RM20 on international flights. From **Subang Kuala Lumpur International Airport,** Malaysia Airlines (MAS) flies to 95 locations in Malaysia and worldwide. For flight info, call the airline directly.

BY BUS OR TRAIN

Both A/C and non-A/C **buses** run between major towns at reasonable prices. Fares are higher for express buses and vary with distance. **Malayan Railways,** or **Keretapi Tanah Melayu Berhad (KTM),** runs throughout Peninsular Malaysia, but service is much more developed for west coast travel. KTM railpasses allow unlimited travel on passenger trains in Malaysia and Singapore for 10 days (US$55, children 4-12 US$28) or 30 days (US$120, children 4-12 US$60). For those under 30 with an ISIC or Youth Hostel Card, a seven-day KTM pass is US$32. The **jungle train** from Jerantut to Wakaf Baru, near Kota Bharu, is a slow but scenic tourist option.

BY CAR

Inter-city **taxis** connect all major towns and cities. Due to fixed fares, it is most economical to share (and split fares four ways). Local taxis are often unmetered, in which case you should agree on a price beforehand—the driver will often quote a figure before you get in, giving you a chance to decline politely. Additional surcharges apply for taxis booked by phone, trips between midnight and 7am, and trips carrying more than two passengers.

To **rent a car,** you must have an international driver's permit (IDP) or a license issued by your government. In addition to rental companies, some hotels rent cars. Expect to pay RM240-350. Remember that driving is done on the left side of the road and that, by law, the driver and all front-seat passengers must wear seatbelts. Rains in the monsoon season may make east coast travel difficult.

■ Keeping in Touch

The Malaysian **postal system** does quality work. Airmail across the globe should take under one week, but larger parcels may take up to two weeks. Malaysia is eight hours ahead of GMT. This puts Malaysia one hour ahead of Thailand to the north and Sumatra to the south, which can be confusing for border crossings. *Let's Go* lists telephone codes in the **Practical Information** section of each city. Long-distance calls are usually easiest at card-phones; IDD is available at nearly all of them. Cards can often be purchased at local telephone offices or convenience stores. The most convenient card to get is the Telekom Malaysia card. Be aware that phone cards are not interchangeable with different phone companies. **HCD** numbers: Australia, 800 0061; Canada, 800 0017; New Zealand, 800 0064; UK, 800 0044; AT&T, 800 0011; MCI, 800 0012; and Sprint, 800 0016.

■ Staying Safe

Trafficking illegal drugs carries the death penalty. This warning, and similar ones, are plastered across Malaysian tourist literature for good reason—Malaysia does not take kindly to drugs. **The emergency number for Malaysia is tel. 999.**

BISEXUAL, GAY, LESBIAN TRAVELERS

A mere two years ago homosexual acts could bring up to 20 years in prison and/or whipping. While homosexuality is no longer a criminal offense in Malaysia, open displays of affection are not a good idea, and neither is discussing homosexuality; it's a taboo topic both in the media and in conversation. For Malays, legally subject to Islamic law, open homosexuality is even more difficult than for the traveler.

■ Hours and Holidays

Businesses are generally open 9:30am-7pm, but banks only stay open until about 3pm, and supermarkets and other large stores serve customers 10am-10pm. Government offices are open 8am-1pm and 2-4:15pm Monday through Friday, and 8am-1pm on Saturdays. In most parts of the country offices and businesses are closed on Sunday, and close at noon or 1pm on Saturdays. In Johor, Kedah, Perlis, Kelantan, and Terengganu, however, buildings are closed on Friday, and banks and government offices are often open half-days on Thursdays. Approximate dates for 1997 events are listed below.

January 1: New Year's Day.
January: Thaipusam, in honor of Hindu deity Lord Subramanian.
February 7 & 8: Chinese New Year, a 15-day lunar festival.
February 20-21: Idul Fitri. The end of the Muslim fasting month of Ramadan.
April 28: Hari Raya Aidil Adha (Muslim Day of Sacrifice).
May 1: Labor Day.
May 21: Wesak Day, commemorating the life of Buddha.
June 5: King's birthday. Celebrated in Kuala Lumpur with processions.
June: Awal Muharam.
April 18: Hari Raya Haj. Pilgrims celebrate the return from the Haj to Mecca.
July: Festival of the Hungry Ghosts. Candles with faces are burned on street altars.
July: Maal Hiraj, commemorating the first day of the Muslim calender.
August: Mooncake/Lantern Festival, marks the overthrow of the Mongols.
August 22: Maulid Nabi Muhammad (birthday of Muhammad).
August 31: Hari Kebangsaan, or National Day.
October: Kiew Ong Yeah, involves mediums supposedly possessed by spirits of the 9 emperor gods, and culminates with a fire-walking ritual.
October 31: Diwali, a Hindu festival of lights.
December 25: Christmas Day.

LIFE AND TIMES

■ The People of Malaysia

Malaysia has a population of just over 19 million, 15 million of whom live on the peninsula, while the rest inhabit Sabah and Sarawak to the east. There are distinctions between Malaysian, Malayan, and Malay. Malaysian is a political term, referring to a citizen of the country. Malayan denotes anyone from the peninsula, while Malay is a term for the ethnic Malay people, most of whom are Muslim. The similarity between these terms reflects the cultural biases inherent in the nation's structure.

BAJAU

The Bajau share Sabah with the predominant Kadazans and find their roots in settlers from the south Philippines. These immigrants were seafarers and famous pirates in the 18th and 19th centuries. Today they are the second-largest ethnic group in the state, strict Muslims, and renowned horsemen.

CHINESE

Constituting about one-third of the population, Chinese-Malaysians began arriving in the 1400s and the influx stepped up during the 1800s, as immigrants came to work for the colonial tin-mining industry. This direct connection to British business gave the Chinese an advantage in industrial dealings. Over the years, the Chinese have come to dominate Malaysian commerce while making political concessions to the Malay majority. Many early Chinese immigrants married Malay women, giving birth to the **Baba-Nyonya** culture, perhaps most easily recognized in *nyonya* food, a mix between Chinese and Malay styles. Today, the large Chinese population is among the most vocal for increasing the definition of National Culture to include other religious and ethnic traditions.

DAYAK

The Dayak are one of the ethnic groups inhabiting the state of Sarawak. The name in fact refers to a conglomeration of ethnic groups who live inland, each of which names itself after the rivers near which they are settled. All the Dayak people were head-hunters historically; taking an enemy's head was seen as a means of acquiring the good characteristics of that person. These heads were dried and displayed, and some can be seen today. Despite the changes brought by modernity, and the fact that most Dayak are professed and baptized Christians, their *adat* (culture) persists today, if only in a less violent form.

INDIAN

The next largest percentage of Malaysians (9%) are Indian-Malaysians, many of whom are descendants of Hindu Tamil laborers brought over by British rubber plantation owners earlier this century. The influence of Indian trade over the centuries, however, means that some Indian ancestry, however distant, is probable among many inhabitants of the peninsula. The status of the Indian culture and population as non-indigenous and non-national is perhaps more ironic than that of the more populous Chinese, due to the Indic influence found in Southeast Asia long before Islam and other cultural traditions left their marks. Indian-Malaysian communities are found in almost every decent-size city, particularly on the more cosmopolitan west coast, where almost every city has its own Little India.

KADAZAN

The Kadazans are the largest ethnic group in Sabah, and were known as Dusuns (peasants) until Sabah joined the Malaysian Federation in 1963. Like the Dayak, who also live on Borneo, the historical traditions of the Kadazan lie in head-hunting, although they are practicing Roman Catholics today. Despite this fierce background, they are now known for their peacefulness and honesty. They still speak their own language and share a rich cultural tradition. Among today's practices is the Magavau ritual, the Harvest Festival held in May. The festival includes offerings to the rice spirit, and the playing of traditional games.

MALAY

Ethnic Malays constitute 50% of the nation's population. Although many argue that their migration thousands of years ago puts their ancestry in China, the favored status granted to the Malay, called *bumiputra* (Sons of the Earth), qualifies them as indigenous Malaysians. Barely constituting a majority, the birth rate of the Malay people has been an important consideration in government planning. Attempts to create favorable conditions for large Malay families have been quite successful.

ORANG ASLI

The singular term **Orang Asli** (Authentic People), referring to the aboriginal Malays is misleading, as Orang Asli refers to a diverse set of predominantly animist tribes who inhabit the peninsula. The two major groups are the **Semang** (or Negritos) in the north, and the **Senoi** in the south, but many other small tribes exist within the interior. They are rarely seen outside of their remote rainforest and highland settlements, and comprise only a minute fraction of modern Malaysia's population.

■ History

PRE-HISTORY

For thousands of years the Malaysian peninsula has been criss-crossed by traders and navigators who left behind a unique conglomerate of cultures and a multi-layered ethnic diversity. The peninsula's first inhabitants, the aboriginal Malays, or Orang Asli, probably arrived more than 10,000 years ago. The **proto-Malays,** the ancestors of the ethnic Malays, came around 6000 years later, perhaps from southern China. Most of Malaysia's pre-history, however, is simply conjecture.

EARLY KINGDOMS

From as early as the first century AD, the Straits of Melaka linked China and India through trade. Control of these ports was a boon for local rulers on the west peninsular coast and Northern Sumatra, while the Orang Asli of the interior remained relatively isolated. Throughout the 4th, 5th, and 6th centuries Malaysia boomed from its gold and tin resources as well as its safety from overland pirates. Through these early years of trade, the northern states of the peninsula were loosely known as the **Langkasuka** kingdom. Subsequent contact with Indian traders brought strong cultural and religious traditions to the peninsula, including Hinduism, Buddhism, and Brahmin priests. The Sumatran state of **Srivijaya,** which encompassed Malaya beginning in the 7th century, spread this Indic influence throughout Southeast Asia.

After buttressing attacks from both India and Siam around the end of the first millennium, the Srivijayan empire weakened, leaving Malaya as fragmented states under the nominal rule of the Javanese **Majapahit Empire.** This regional subservience ended with the establishment of **Melaka** in early 15th century, and the factors of its founding reveal the complex stew of interaction within Southeast Asia. According to 15th century writings the prince **Sri Paremesvara,** was fleeing the wrath of Majapahit rulers in Java. He was driven north and founded Melaka in legendary style. Protected by its large neighbors to the northeast, Melaka quickly grew as a naval port and trading center, usurping the power of the Majapahit.

THE RISE OF ISLAM

As with any good story, the happy ending was just a beginning. Sri Paremesvara converted to **Islam,** and was renamed **Iskandar Shah** to accompany a marriage alliance with the Muslim ruler of the Sumatran state of Pasai. The spread of Islam among the Malay thus began with his reign. Conflicts after his death regarding whether Islam or the Indic influences would prevail in Melaka eventually led to the ascension of **Muzaffar Shah,** a devout Muslim. Under the leadership of his Prime Minister, **Tun Perak,** Melaka pushed the Thai vassals off the peninsula. By the reign of Melaka's last shah, **Mahmud Shah,** at the end of the 15th century, Melaka's domain included all of Peninsular Malaysia, Singapore, and parts of Thailand and Northern Sumatra

The western "age of exploration" brought the ever-diplomatic Europeans to the region. Although the **Portuguese** invaded in 1511, their presence did little to keep those of the peninsula from being faithful to the Shah dynasty. Instead, these people fled south and established the state of **Johor.** The Muslim Indonesian state of **Aceh** began vying for trade ports as well. In 1699, the last true heir of the Melakan ruling family was killed by his own court. Although he was a cruel ruler, the assassination was still considered a terrible act against God, and threw the Malay world into disarray throughout the 18th century. Chaos and piracy in the straits marked the next hundred years, and the lack of order attracted the Bugis from Sulawesi and the Minang from Sumatra and Sulawesi. These new forces set up powerful states on the peninsula and competed with both the Sultan of Johor and the **Dutch**, who had replaced Portugal in Melaka during the late 1600s.

COLONIAL RULE

The Dutch ceded the island of **Penang** to the **British** at the end of the 18th century. So began this stabilizing, but oppressive colonial presence in Malaya. The primary city of Penang, **Georgetown** absorbed regional trade quickly. Through political alliances and entrepreneurial maneuvering the British eventually moved into Melaka, Indonesia, and Singapore. It was only with this intervention that modern Indonesia and Malaysia became formally differentiated, through the famous **Anglo-Dutch Treaty of 1874.** The kingdom states of Malaysia fell under British eye, and Indonesia under Dutch. With the **Treaty of Pangkor** British power was strengthened, as the southern states acquired British "counselors" who dealt out indirect rule. By World War I, Malaysia had been divided into five federated and four non-federated states. More independent, but less developed, than the five federated states, the four states to the north politely declined counselors, after being nominally transferred to Britain by Thailand. In 1919, however, the last of these states, Terengganu, was compelled to accept a powerless, but symbolic, British General Adviser. Colonial occupation of Malaysia continued until World War II, and was marked by economic advances as well as uprisings and subsequent suppressions. More subtle anti-colonialist feeling was growing, and throughout the 20s and 30s the Malay press and intelligentsia began to increase political consciousness, creating small political organizations which educated individuals to anti-colonialist possibilities, especially as they related to current Islamic thought from the Middle East and Turkey.

FORGING A NATION

During **World War II** the Japanese moved into Malaysia, returning the northern states to Thailand and exploiting Malaya's resources and strategic location. With the end of the war a few years later, the British, who had turned tail and left the country defenseless, came back, but were unable to return the country to its former docility. Protests began from politically active movements in reaction to decades of direct outside interference as well as the Japanese's inspiring, if hollow, anti-colonialist rhetoric. In the late 1940s, the **United Malay National Organization (UMNO),** formed to combat the unacceptable British plan for refederation and forced a continuing dialogue. This led to an increasing frequency of local elections in the 1950s. The military arm of the **Malay Communist Party** added guerilla tactics and other violent forms of pressure which, although not politically popular, kept Malaya in a state of emergency throughout the decade and created incredible difficulties for the British. The steady movement toward independence culminated on **August 31, 1957,** with the establishment of the independent **Federated States of Malaya.**

The 1960s provided a roller coaster of excitement for the newly independent country. Joining with Singapore and the states of Sabah and Sarawak on Borneo, Malaya became Malaysia on September 16, 1963. This infuriated Malaysia's new international neighbors, as the Philippines were holding onto an ancient claim to Sabah, and Indonesia believed Malaya's action to be covert neo-colonialism under the auspices of the British. Indonesia's president, **Soekarno** declared **konfrontasi** (Confrontation), which supported protests and revolts in Malaysia's eastern states and border skirmishes between Sabah and Sarawak and Kalimantan. This led to extreme tensions, bordering on war, between the two until 1966.

Within Malaysia as well, ethnic tensions continued to grow. The diverse nation was home to a proud Malayan majority who dominated politically, but remained behind economically. The administrative attitude toward Singapore's predominantly Chinese population created more policy problems for the Malay-oriented government, which had established Islam as the official religion and Bahasa Malaysia as its language. As Singapore attempted to gain federal political footholds in the new nation, the peninsular government grew increasingly apprehensive, and by 1969 a teary-eyed **Lee Kuan Yew** withdrew Singapore from Malaysia, while Britain finally severed its deep ties. In May of that year, ethnic riots erupted in Kuala Lumpur after the Malay majority party, the **Alliance** (the joining of the UMNO with the conservative Malayan Chinese Association) lost a significant number of seats to non-Malay supported parties for the first time. Malay political leaders called mass meetings, and quickly lost control of the riled mobs, many of whom came armed. The ensuing riots left many dead and over 5000 Chinese homeless. **Prime Minister Tunku Abdul Rahman** was blamed for the riots by more militant Malay politicians and elites, such as **Dr. Mahathir Mohammed,** who was quickly thrown out of the UMNO for questioning Tunku Abdul's leadership. Malay response, in general, however, blamed the riots on concessions to non-Malay groups, rather than Malay racial attitudes, and the Prime Minister was supplanted by **Deputy Prime Minister Tun Abdul Razak** along with a temporary ruling council which ruled by decree. The council prohibited public discussion of issues such as Malay special status. These issues were deemed too "sensitive" for public discussion and continue to be censored.

Tunku Abdul retired in 1970, leaving Tun Abdul Razak to become Prime Minister with the dissolution of the ruling council. Under his rule, UMNO gained increasing power, and the country continued to pander to Malay interests. Further political alliances increased the status and political clout of Malay citizens and economic policies were implemented to support Malay business ownership. The old Alliance gained support from other parties and reformed as the **Barisan Nasional** (National Front). Malaysia continued to expand its international relations, especially to communist nations. In 1971 the status of Malay citizens was given a further boost through the creation of the **National Culture Policy,** which defined National Culture as indigenous tradition, informed heavily by Islam. Ironically, indigenous tradition referred only to that of the Malay people. It disregarded not only the Chinese and Indian traditions, which influenced Malaya before Islam, but also the Orang Asli, who had populated the region thousands of years before the proto-Malay. Policy makers insisted on education in Bahasa Malaysia alone and provided federal support for a "National Culture," which only included ethnic Malay art and literature. With Tun Razak's unexpected death in 1976, his deputy and brother-in-law, **Hussein Onn,** came to power with a small political base and poor health. Though the country's confidence wavered, he steered the nation toward greater development until 1981. Into Hussein's shoes stepped his unlikely deputy, Dr. Mahathir, who had slowly risen in the ranks since his original expulsion. Mahathir's administration began an increasing movement to Islamicize Malaysia. Islam became a part of Malaysian education, and Bahasa Malaysia words found in Islam, including those for God or religion, fell under a religious copyright and were only allowed to be used by Islam. Throughout the 1980s Mahathir pushed religious fervor along with rapid growth and industrialization. In 1987 Mahathir's re-election was surrounded by controversy which included the court's declaration that the UMNO was unconstitutional. Mahathir prevailed, however, organizing the **UMNO Baru** (New UMNO).

■ Malaysia Today

Today, with majority rule (a Malay-dominated government), the authorities are eager to see Malays take on an equitable share of the nation's wealth, formerly concentrated in the hands of the Chinese. Government propaganda assures the people that happy Malaysians are working together harmoniously in pursuit of mutual prosperity and development, while the grumbling about discriminatory policies and the old cultural-stereotyping continue.

The modern government is a constitutional monarchy similar to Britain's, with executive power resting with the Prime Minister and parliament. More distinctive to the Malaysian Government is the **Conference of Rulers** and the **Yang di-Pertuan Agong** (Supreme Ruler). The Conference of Rulers is comprised of the nine hereditary sultans of the region who determine 27 of the 63 senators, and select the country's titular monarch from among the senior sultans. The current Agong, **Ja'afar ibni Abdul Rahman,** was selected in April, 1994. Each Supreme Ruler is elected for five years, appoints Supreme Court Justices, and performs other governor-like duties.

Malaysia is a rapidly developing nation, and although not as advanced as Singapore, it provides more modern facilities for tourists than either Indonesia or Thailand. Under current Prime Minister Mahathir Mohammed's administration, the country has moved away from dependency on tin and rubber, and toward industrialization. Development fever has embraced the entire nation, and the people are mobilized to achieve developed nation status by 2020. Mahathir has several major projects in the works, among them rapid transit in Kuala Lumpur, a new international airport, a huge hydroelectric development, and even a new capital city. Internationally, his ambitions for the country also look toward development: financial restrictions have been relaxed to attract foreign investment, particularly from business displaced from Hong Kong.

His ambitious proposals have met with resounding support; his re-election victory in 1995 was the largest in independent Malaysian history. The downside of this is severe **environmental degradation.** Much of the land that is not protected or valued as a tourist attraction has been damaged. Bus rides are rarely scenic due to hills scarred by mining, huge monocrop plantations of rubber or palm, and wastelands of factories and construction sites. Environmental awareness has only recently gained popularity, but much of it is little more than rhetoric.

With rapid industrialization, some think Malaysia might become westernized, like so many other developing nations. This is only partially true. Dr. Mahathir has espoused a **"Look East" policy** when seeking foreign investment and trade. Even as Malaysia continues forward with **AFTA,** the new Asian Free Trade Agreement, and is an active member of **ASEAN,** the United States continues to be second only to Japan as a foreign investor. The Islamic party discusses implementing Islamic *hudud* laws to replace the secular courts and newspapers question the moral integrity of imported western TV programs. What all of this means is that western-style ads with rock stars and fast cars still work their mind-numbing magic, but are quickly removed or "edited" by the government's Censorship Board. For a small country with a high economic growth rate and an increasing international market, "Look East" often gives way to "Growth at any Cost." Ah, the best of both worlds.

HUMAN RIGHTS

In its quest for unity, the Malaysian government lays down a hard hand regarding freedom of expression, particularly in the media. This, as well as the country's use of capital punishment and restrictions on religion, have become ammunition for the human rights organization Amnesty International to criticize Malaysia's policies. The government works for unity within Islam by banning certain Islamic organizations. Actions against the Al Arqam Islamic Sunni sect have gained particular international attention. The Islamic Shiite movement is also viewed with suspicion by the government and may be banned. Malaysia's quest for a unified moral and religious front has become increasingly fervored, and the danger is that it might backfire if or when the Malaysian people wish to realize certain freedoms of religion and expression.

■ The Arts

DRAMA AND DANCE

Malaysian dance and drama are very closely related. This is exemplified with the **Ma'Yong,** a uniquely Malay dance-drama art form which gained prominence as a court tradition over 400 years ago. At the same time that Shakespeare was filling all his roles with men, the presenters of Ma'Yong were reserving all the roles for young women, except for the buffoon's role, which only a man could play. Without scenery or other conventions, attention is focused on the actresses' movements. The stories are romantic dramas, seemingly all the same type of hero story in which a boy saves a beautiful princess from an ogre.

The **Malay shadow play** is an ancient mix of puppetry and theater found across Southeast Asia. Although the shadow play almost certainly has its roots in Java, many of the Malay conventions are traced to the Khmer style, which may have been brought from Java by **Jayavarman II** (see **Cambodia: History** on page 59). The central story of the shadow play is the *Ramayana.* A *dalang* (puppeteer) sits behind a long cotton screen with two-foot tall figures brightly and ornately decorated. He gracefully moves these behind the screen in order to tell the story. Accompanying the production is a small orchestra led by the oboe.

Malay dance comes in many popular forms; most important for the Malay is the graceful movement of the arms and hands. Most famous of the court dances is perhaps the **Ashek,** a three-part dance with 11 young women, where the lead dancer weaves her way among the other stationary women. **Malay folk dances** revolve around crop production or the harvesting of fish and are open air dances used to appease spirits and bring in good crops. Most involve a female lead dancer and a chorus line of other young males and females.

MUSIC

Malay music takes some of its influence from Cambodia, India, and the Middle East, but its sounds are unique. Those instruments which are given greatest recognition are considered to have some connection to magic. Among the most widely recognized is the **rebab** (spike fiddle), an adaptation of a similar Middle Eastern instrument. It produces a very nasal sound, and leads the orchestra for the Ma'Yong. The Arabic **gendang,** large drums that usually come in pairs, provide tempo for most Malay drama and dance events, as well as for *silat* demonstrations. The Malay oboe, the **serunai,** has also achieved popularity and leads the orchestra for shadow plays.

Popular singing styles include **pantum,** an evolution of Islamic devotionals which consist of improvisational duets; **ghazals,** a mournful style, reminiscent of Islamic love songs; and the classical singing which accompanies the powerful, percussion-heavy **dondang.** The Europeanization of Malay music took place with **P. Ramlee,** the famous crooner of Malaysia, whose shorter romantic ballads and western instruments transformed the *dondang* style.

BATIK

The common Southeast Asian art form of batik is well represented in Malaysia. Within the country, the definition of batik applies more to the design than the process of its creation. Batik is considered an ethnic Malay art form, and is therefore given government support. As with many forms of traditional art, much of its production is centered in Kelantan and Terengganu. The Indonesian formal process of batik was probably first used in Malaysia in the late 18th century. Other forms came about even later. The traditional Malay pattern involves an abundance of tropical leaves and vines abstracted into curves and lines across the material, and is similar to those used on the ornamented Malay kites.

■ Recreation

Many sports are popular in Malaysia, from the traditional *sepak takraw* to soccer, hockey, and cricket. **Sepak takraw** is very similar to the Thai *takraw* (see **Thailand: Recreation** on page 467). **Kite flying** in Malaysia is almost an entirely different pastime than the western weekend activity most travelers have experienced. In Malaysia kites fill local legend, saving princesses and performing miraculous feats. Although the tradition no longer maintains the popularity it once did, it still flourishes in the eastern states of Kelantan and Terengganu. Kite flying contests are widespread and passionate. Most kites are about seven feet tall and six feet wide, and produce a distinctive humming sound when flown.

To compare western **tops** with Malay **gasing** is to compare Free Willy with Moby Dick. They may be the same animal, but the similarities end there. Adult men spend weeks fashioning perfectly balanced and proportioned tops, then put them in competition with others. The center of the top is a short steel spike with a rim of lead; finished products usually have the circumference of an Olympian's discus and weigh a bit less than a shotput. Contests continue all day, and even magic is called upon, in the form of "top doctors," to gain important victories.

The Malaysian form of martial arts, **silat,** supposedly originated in Sumatra, but has been changed and perfected on the peninsula for hundreds of years. Its creation occurred, as the story goes, when three Malay brothers traveled to Sumatra in the 13th century to study Islam. One of them, **Aminuddin,** was getting water from a pool at the base of a waterfall. As he watched the water he noticed a small flower riding the water's ripples. Encouraged by a mysterious voice, Aminuddin decided to form a style of self-defense from the flower's movements. *Silat* is a graceful art using crouches, rolls, hand blows, and kicks. It is often demonstrated in public, especially at wedding ceremonies. Many of the secrets of *silat,* however, are not allowed to be demonstrated, and its history is filled with stories of magic powers passed down from masters to promising students.

WEST COAST

■ Kuala Lumpur

Somewhere between its self-proclaimed splendor as the "Garden City of Lights" and its literal English translation, "Muddy River Mouth," lies the true capital of Malaysia, Kuala Lumpur. Visitors and residents tell tales of both extremes, and the city often seems to fit both descriptions. Despite its heavy traffic, teeming streets, and intense humidity, KL (as it's almost exclusively called) has somehow retained the appeal of a tropical metropolis. Its daunting monoliths of finance and exhaust-laden air are offset by the beauty of its lush vegetation and the green and the stunning mix of colonial and Islamic revivalist architecture.

Kuala Lumpur was just the muddy river mouth its name indicates until 1857, when 87 Chinese miners ventured up the Klang river in their search for tin. Stopping at the junction of the Klang and Gombak rivers because the water became too shallow for them to proceed farther, they found a vein of tin in today's Ampang with the help of a *pawang* (magician), and began to dig test pits, in which ground water pooled and Anopheles mosquitoes happily bred. One month later, all but 18 were dead of a strange fever. Despite the fear that gripped them at this deadly display of supernatural forces, the miners kept coming and KL was soon a frontier town of a few thousand, mostly Hakka Chinese. By all accounts, it was a filthy, disease-ridden hamlet, with an almost entirely male population, and gambling joints, opium dens, and brothels. Yet interest in controlling Kuala Lumpur's tin, liquor, and opium reserves grew and soon became the focus of the Selangor Civil War (1867-1873), of which the British emerged the only clear winners.

Somehow KL has survived its checkered past and grown into a sprawling metropolis with the time and money to maintain such niceties as parks and commons. So devoted is this town to progress and action that in mid-1994 the government declared war on *lepakking* (loafing). Yet the overriding government presence does not obscure the city's position as a cultural milieu. KL's dedicated denizens have produced a fascinating fusion of three rich heritages—Malay, Chinese and Indian. In this blend, Kuala Lumpur represents the consummate Malaysian experience.

GETTING THERE AND AWAY

By Plane

To get to and from the **airport** (tel. 746 1014) at Pekau Subang, take blue bus #47 from Klang Station; the same bus also travels into the city (RM2). Taxis take about 45 minutes to go from the city center to the airport (RM25). To: **Bangkok** (2 per day, RM770); **Hanoi** (1 per day, RM895); **Ho Chi Minh City** (1 per day, RM890); **Hong Kong** (1 per day, RM1093); **Jakarta** (4 per day, RM710 roundtrip); **Madras** (1 per day, RM1150); **Penang** (17 per day, RM109); **Phnom Penh** (1 per day, RM 850); and **Singapore** (30 per day plus a shuttle every hr., RM160).

By Train

The **railway station** (tel. 274 74 42) is on Jl. Sultan Hishamuddin, across from the National Art Gallery. Trains leave to **Singapore** (7:35am, 2:10pm, 1st-class RM68; 2nd-class RM34, 10:15pm, 1st-class RM68; 2nd-class RM40; 3rd-class RM30) and **Butterworth** (7:45am and 1:45 and 10:35pm, 1st-class RM67; 2nd-class RM30-40; 3rd-class RM30). From Butterworth to **Bangkok** (2:12pm, 2nd-class RM93.90).

By Bus

The long-distance bus station is the **Pudu Raya Station** on Jl. Pudu. Dozens of express bus companies sell tickets for destinations all over Malaysia. Their offices are either within the station itself or across the street near the 7-Eleven store and the Kuala Lumpur City Lodge. The **Ekspres Nasional** (tel. 230 33 00) has a counter inside the station, just above the pedestrian overpass. (Open daily 6am-11pm.) To: **Butterworth** (4 per day, 10am-11:30pm, RM17.10); **Kuantan** (9 per day, 9am-12:10am); and **Singapore** (9am, 10pm; RM17.80). The **Melaka-Kuala Lumpur Ekspres** runs at the same times.

By Taxi

Four different taxi companies handle service to various regions of the country from the floor above the buses. Lone travelers will most likely be sharing inter-city taxis with three others. Private cabs are more expensive. Stations:

> **Persutuan Kebajikan** (tel. 232 65 04). To west and south Malaysia. To: **Johor Bahru** (RM40, with A/C RM38); **Melaka** (with A/C RM17); and **Muar** (RM21).
> **Persutuan Pemandu** (tel. 232 50 82). To eastern Malaysia. To: **Kota Bahru** (RM40); **Kuala Terangganu** (RM160); and **Kuantan** (RM100).
> **Persutuan Teksi** (tel. 238 02 13). Runs to the north. To **Ipoh** (RM20, RM80 for the whole car, plus RM2 toll) and **Butterworth** (RM41 per person, RM164 for the whole car, plus RM6 toll).

GETTING AROUND

By Bus

Bus stops are everywhere in KL and usually labeled with the numbers of the buses that stop there. Fares are RM0.22. Pink **Bas Mini** are both the most reckless and plentiful, charging a flat rate of RM0.60 regardless of distance; they run shorter routes within the city. Routes are prominently displayed inside the front windshield. Silver **Interkota** buses run into town, as well as to satellite towns (flat rate RM0.90), and large red-and-white **Cityliner** buses reach the distant residential areas. The different

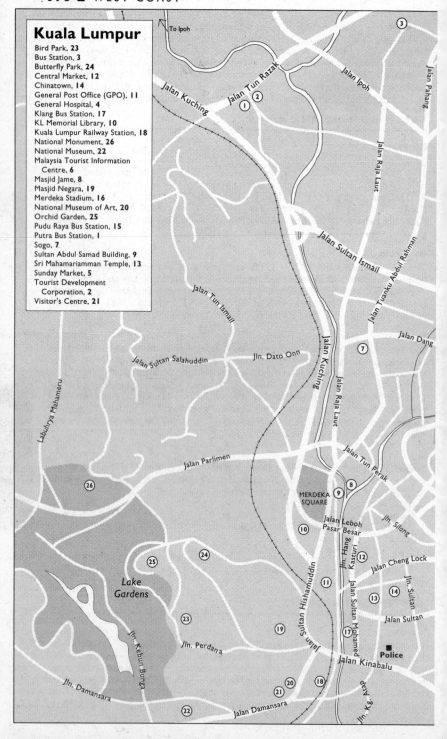

Kuala Lumpur

Bird Park, 23
Bus Station, 3
Butterfly Park, 24
Central Market, 12
Chinatown, 14
General Post Office (GPO), 11
General Hospital, 4
Klang Bus Station, 17
KL Memorial Library, 10
Kuala Lumpur Railway Station, 18
National Monument, 26
National Museum, 22
Malaysia Tourist Information
    Centre, 6
Masjid Jame, 8
Masjid Negara, 19
Merdeka Stadium, 16
National Museum of Art, 20
Orchid Garden, 25
Pudu Raya Bus Station, 15
Putra Bus Station, 1
Sogo, 7
Sultan Abdul Samad Building, 9
Sri Mahamariamman Temple, 13
Sunday Market, 5
Tourist Development
    Corporation, 2
Visitor's Centre, 21

To Ipoh

Jalan Kuching
Jalan Tun Razak
Jalan Ipoh
Jalan Pahang
Jalan Raja Laut
Jalan Sultan Ismail
Jalan Tuanku Abdul Rahman
Jalan Tun Ismail
Jalan Dang
Jalan Sultan Salahuddin
Jln. Dato Onn
Jalan Kuching
Jalan Raja Laut
Labuhrya Mahameru
Jalan Parlimen
Jalan Tun Perak
MERDEKA SQUARE
Jalan Leboh Pasar Besar
Jln. Silang
Jln. Hang Kasturi
Jalan Cheng Lock
Lake Gardens
Jalan Sultan Hishamuddin
Jalan Sultan Mohamed
Jln. Sultan
Jalan Sultan
Jln. Kebun Bunga
Jln. Perdana
Police
Jalan Kinabalu
Jln. Damansara
Jalan Damansara
Jln. Kg. Arab

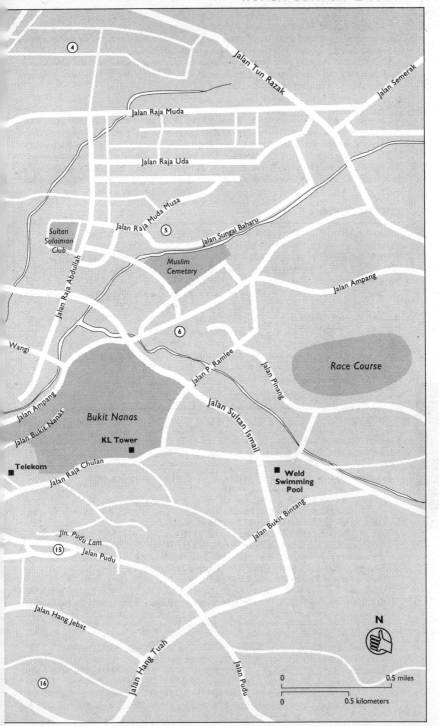

bus stops around town serve the following areas: Klang bus station (southwest, including airport and Petaling Taya); Bangkok Bank (north Bato caves); Lebuk Ampang (north, Taman Sari Gombak and Taman Greenwood); and Chow Kit Road (all directions, Petaling Jaya, Ampang, Bangsan, Kepong, and Gombak). The **Klang Bus Station** is in Chinatown, across the street from the Starlight Hotel on Jl. Hang Kasturi. Most minibuses stop at the Central Market.

Taxis

Taxis may or may not be metered. If unmetered, it's a good idea to agree on a price before getting in. Metered cabs start at RM1.50 and increase by RM0.10 per 200m. Additional surcharges apply for taxis booked by phone (RM10), trips between midnight and 7am (50%), and trips carrying three (RM0.20) or four (RM0.40) passengers. To book a cab by phone, call **Telecab** (tel. 211 12 11), **Kuala Lumpur Taxi Driver's Association** (tel. 221 52 52), or **Federal Territory and Selangor Radio Taxi Association** (tel. 293 62 13). (All open 24 hours.) Taxi hotline: tel. 255 33 99.

ORIENTATION

There is no method to the madness of Kuala Lumpur's streets. The best alternative is to remember certain major thoroughfares and peruse a city map before arriving with your first destination in mind. **Jalan Tuanku Abdul Rahman** and **Jalan Raja Laut** are the main six-lane thoroughfares running north-south. They are not pedestrian-friendly, but most Bas Mini routes travel on either of these two streets, connected in the north by **Jalan Chow Kit,** a busy market area. Jl. Tuanku Abdul Rahman and Raja Laut converge in the south to form **Jalan Sultan Hishamuddin,** east of which lies **Chinatown. Jalan Cheng Lock** bounds Chinatown to the north, and **Jalan Petaling** runs through its heart. Parallel to Petaling to the east is **Jalan Tun H.S. Lee,** which runs north into the financial center of town, ending at **Jalan Gereja,** which starts off westbound, then changes into **Jalan Ampang,** sometimes called Embassy Row, and heads northeast. Most sights are in the west half of the city, while the east contains many luxury hotels, malls, offices, and nightclubs.

PRACTICAL INFORMATION

Many offices close for lunch from 1-2pm. On Fridays, some offices—especially government bureaus—close for prayers, generally from 12:15-2:45pm. Banks and large shopping centers typically stay open.

Tourist Offices: Malaysian Tourist Information Complex (MATIC), 109 Jl. Ampang (tel. 242 39 29), after the intersection with Jl. Sultan Ismail. **MAS** office, an **Ekspres Nasional** counter, and a **Telekom office.** Open Mon.-Thurs. 9am-1pm and 2-5pm, Fri. 9am-12:30pm and 2:45-5pm, Sat. 9am-1pm. Information desk open daily 9am-9pm. **Kuala Lumpur Tourist Association,** 3 Jl. Hishamuddin (tel. 238 18 32), next to the National Art Gallery. Open Mon.-Fri. 8am-5pm, Sat. 8am-12:45pm. **Railway Station branch** (tel. 274 60 63), on Jl. Sultan Hishamuddin. On the same side of the station as platforms 1, 2, and 3. Open daily 9am-9pm. **Airport branch,** Terminal 1 (tel. 746 57 07). Open daily 9am-10pm.
Tourist Police: Police Tourist Unit (tel. 249 69 53), on Jl. Hang Tuah.
Tours and Travel: MSL Travel, 66 Jl. Putra (tel. 442 47 22), off Jl. Chow Kit, next to the Grand Central Hotel. Offers the Eurotrain Explorer Pass for unlimited travel on KTM-Malayan Railway (1 week, US$36; 21 days, US$60) or SRT Railway of Thailand (1 week, US$32; 21 days US$48). Discount travel passes and ISIC cards. Open Mon.-Fri. 9am-5pm, Sat. 9am-1pm.
Embassies and Consulates: Australia, 6 Jl. Yap Kwan Seng, 50450 (tel. 242 31 22, after hours 242 39 42; fax 241 44 95). Open Mon.-Fri. 9-11:30am and 1:30-3pm. **Canada,** 7th Fl., Plaza MBF, 172 Jl. Ampang, 50450 (tel. 261 20 00, after hours 261 20 31). Open Mon.-Fri. 8am-4pm. **Indonesia,** 233 Jl. Tun Razak, 50400 (tel. 245 20 11). Open Mon.-Thurs. 8:30am-1pm and 2-4:30pm, Fri. 8:30am-1:30pm and 2:30-4:30pm. **Laos,** 108 Jl. Damai (tel. 248 38 95). Open Mon.-Fri. 8am-noon and 2-

4:30pm. **New Zealand,** 193 Jl. Tun Razak, 50400 (tel. 248 64 22). Open Mon.-Fri. 8am-12:30pm and 1:30-4:30pm. **Singapore,** 209 Jl. Tun Razak (tel. 261 62 77). Open Mon.-Fri. 8:30am-1pm and 2-5pm.**Thailand,** 206 Jl. Ampang, 50450 (tel. 248 83 33; fax 248 65 27). Open Mon.-Fri. 9am-1pm and 2-5pm; consular section open Mon.-Fri. 9am-1pm. **UK,** 185 Jl. Ampang, 50450 (tel. 248 21 22; fax 244 77 66). Open Mon.-Fri. 8am-12:30pm and 1:30-4:30pm. **US,** 376 Jl. Tun Razak, 50400 (tel. 248 90 11; fax 242 22 07). Open Mon.-Fri. 7:45am-12:30pm and 1:15-4:30pm. **Vietnam,** 4 Persiaran Stonor (tel. 248 40 36). Open Mon.-Fri. 9am-noon and 2-4:30pm, Sat. 9am-noon.

Immigration Offices: Pusat Bandar Daman Sara (tel. 255 50 77), on Jl. Semantan, near the Road Transport Dept. Block I. Open Mon.-Thurs. 8am-12:45pm and 2-3:30pm, Fri.-Sat. 8-11:30am.

Currency Exchange: MayBank, 100 Jl. Tun Perak, 50936 (tel. 230 88 33), a short walk from the Pudu Raya Station, across from Metrojaya. RM5 plus RM0.20 per traveler's check. Open Mon.-Fri. 9:30am-4pm, Sat. 9:30-11:30am. **Hong Leong Bank,** 57 Jl. Hang Lekiu (tel. 232 32 11), opposite the Telekom office. 1% commission plus RM0.15 per traveler's check. Open Mon.-Fri. 10am-3pm, Sat. 9:30-11:30am. **Bank Simpanan Nasional** (tel. 238 83 77), at Pudu Raya Bus Station. About RM0.10 less for traveler's checks than for cash, plus RM5 commission and RM0.15 charge per check. Open Mon.-Sat. 9am-4pm, Sun. 9:30am-12:30pm. Most **ATMs** accept MC, Visa, and Cirrus or Plus (RM5 transaction charge).

American Express: 2nd Fl., MAS Bldg., Jl. Sultan Ismail, P.O. Box 12269, 50772 (tel. 261 00 00). Cardholder mail should be marked "client mail" and addressed to this office; held for 3mo. free. Open Mon.-Fri. 8:30am-5:30pm, Sat. 8:30am-noon.

Diner's Club: customer service tel. 261 10 55; emergency card replacement tel. 261 13 22.

Luggage Storage: Akijaya Enterprise (tel. 230 53 34), at Pudu Raya Bus Station, near the Ekspres Nasional counter. RM1 per bag per day. Open daily 8am-10pm. **Matang Luggage Service** (tel. 274 55 61), at the railway station on platform 4. RM2 per bag per day. Open daily 7am-10pm.

Pharmacies: All around Jl. Sultan/Cheng Lock. **Apex Pharmacy** (tel. 232 77 35), Metrojaya Sihar Kotak, on Jl. Tun Perak. Open Mon., Wed.-Sat. 11am-7pm.

Medical Services: Kuala Lumpur General Hospital, Jl. Pahang (tel. 292 10 44). **City Medical Centre,** 413-425 Jl. Pudu (tel. 221 12 55).

Emergency: tel. 999.

Post Offices: GPO, Jl. Sultan Hishamuddin 9 (tel. 274 11 22). *Poste Restante.* Open Mon.-Sat. 8am-6pm. **Postal code:** 56070.

Telephones: Pusat Telekom, on Jl. Raja Chulan. **Perkhidmantan Biro,** corner of Jl. Raja Chulan and Jl. Bukit Namas. Open daily 8:30am-9pm. **HCD** phones, fax, and telegram. **Assisted International Calls:** 108. **Telephone code:** 03.

ACCOMMODATIONS

Chinatown has many cheap Chinese hotels and dorms catering to backpackers, but most rooms are windowless and vary in quality. More spacious and pleasant places are on Jl. Tuanku Abdul Rahman between Jl. Dang Wangi and Jl. Tun Perak.

Backpackers Travelers Inn, 60 Jl. Sultan (tel. 238 24 73), off Jl. Cheng Lock, on the right; look for the red sign. Stevie, his wife, and the professional staff have turned this hostel into *the* place to stay in KL. Extremely clean. Nightly movies at 9pm in A/C lounge. Lockers and tour reservations. Dorms RM8, with A/C RM10. Singles/doubles RM25-40, with A/C RM50-70. RM2 buys luggage storage and a shower after you've checked out.

Kowloon Hotel, 142-146 Jl. Tuanku Abdul Rahman (tel. 293 42 46), across the road from the Globe Silt-Store north of Merdeka Sq. If you want it all—large room, A/C, TV with four video channels, bath, IDD phone, and mini bar—the Kowloon will give it to you for a good price. Standard rooms have a queen bed. Singles RM85. Doubles RM103. Superior rooms have two twin beds. Doubles RM120. Triples RM138. Quads RM156.

Ben Soo Homestay, 61B Jl. Tiong Nam, 2nd Fl. (tel. 291 80 96). Call Ben Soo upon arrival in KL, and he'll take you to his quiet family home north of town. Ben is a good-natured, and unassuming hotelier. The homestay's small size means that it is often full; book in advance. All rooms have fans, windows, separate baths, and free breakfast. Dorms RM10. Singles RM25. Doubles RM30. Triples RM35.

Kuala Lumpur International Youth Hostel (HI), 21 Jl. Kampung Attap (tel. 273 68 70), on the right at the very end of the street. Dorms have spring mattresses and spotless, pink-tiled bathrooms. Kitchen and TV rooms. Free linen and lockers. Dorms RM15 the 1st night, RM12 thereafter with an approved (6 stamp) HI card. HI cards RM30 for foreigners, RM15 for Malaysians. No alcohol permitted. Doors locked at midnight. Make reservations 1 month in advance. MC, Visa.

Riverside Lodge, 80 Jl. Rotan (tel. 201 12 10), off Jl. Kampung Attap, a 5-min. walk from Chinatown across Jl. Kinabalu. Secluded location means great sleep. Detailed city and travel information, and spotless rooms. Dorms RM8. Singles RM20. Doubles RM23. Doubles with balcony RM25. RM5 per additional person.

Twin Happiness Hotel, 44 Jl. Silang (tel. 238 76 67), just past the Traveler's Home. Newly renovated rooms with furniture and clean sheets. Free filtered cold and hot water on request. Central location and friendly, helpful proprietors. Dorms RM8. Doubles with shower and window RM40, with A/C and toilet RM48.

YMCA Hostel, 95 Jl. Radang Belia (tel. 274 14 39), inconveniently far south of the city center; take bus #33 or 46 or minibus #12. Fantastic facilities and comfortable rooms. Hotel-quality A/C rooms with TV, but non-A/C rooms have worn, brown motel blankets and no carpet. Singles RM38, with A/C and bath RM68. Doubles RM50, with A/C and bath RM78. Triples RM65, with A/C and bath RM90. Quads RM75. Non-YMCA members pay extra RM3 per person per week. Breakfast included. Restaurant open daily 7:30am-9pm. Transport to airport RM17. Unmarried couples may not share a room. MC, Visa.

YWCA Transient Hostel, 12 Jl. Hang Jebat (tel. 230 16 23), off Jl. Sultan on the left, past Jl. Wesley. Women and married couples only. Comfortable, hardwood-floored rooms are Puritan-plain. The airy lounges are a comfortable hangout, and there's an eclectic library on the first floor. Rooms have fans and separate baths. Singles RM30. Doubles RM50. Triples RM70. Quads RM80. 24-hr. check-in. Make reservations during the summer and December.

Tivoli Hotel, 136-138 Jl. Tuanku Abdul Rahman (tel. 292 41 08), near Kowloon Hotel, above the Ibramsha Nasi Kandar restaurant. The slightly musty, cement-floored rooms have something of a warehouse feel, but are spacious and high-ceilinged, with hard-to-beat prices. Singles with fan RM24. Doubles with fan RM30, with bath and A/C RM40.

FOOD

As far as the budget traveler is concerned, local street food might be the best reason to stay in KL for longer than one night. There's no shortage of good food; the mixing of cultures has produced a brilliant medley of cuisines. In the evenings, **Jl. Sultan** and **Jl. Hang Lekir** host an open-air carnival of steamboat restaurants, *sate* sellers, and exotic-fruit juice vendors, while the **Chinatown night market** rages along Jl. Petaling. **The Kampung Bahru Sunday Market,** located near the Muslim cemetery on Jl. Sungai Baharu in the northern part of the city, is another trusty place. The third floor of the **Central Market** also has a small hawker's center that is largely ignored and a few mid-range restaurants serving Malay, Indian, and Thai food.

The Kapitan's Club, 35 Jl. Ampang (tel. 201 02 42). Follow Jl. Gereja as it turns into Jl. Ampang on the right. This classy *nyonya* restaurant is surprisingly inexpensive. The walls are hung with photos of American icons. Here you can sup on Portuguese-style Red Devil Chicken (RM11.50), *sago gula melaka* (RM5), and finish with a real cappuccino. Open daily 11am-11pm, happy hour 4-8pm.

Restoran Insaf, 116 Jl. Tuanku Abdul Rahman (tel. 293 97 37), near Merdeka Sq., at the south end of the street on the left. Also at 158 Jl. Tuanku Abdul Rahman (tel. 291 28 06), farther down the same street. Stands out from the jostling crowd of Malay-Indian restaurants in terms of hygiene and friendliness. Enjoy beef *vendeng* (RM4), *biryani*, and *mee goreng* (RM2-3) in an A/C and insect-free environment. Open Mon.-Sat. 8am-9pm, Sun. noon-4:30pm.

Coliseum Café, 98-100 Jl. Tuanku Abdul Rahman (tel. 292 62 70), at the south end of the street. The grand old dame of KL, this legendary restaurant-bar has been serving hearty, western food since British colonials first chowed with fancy cravats and lace parasols. Sizzling steak RM23.90. Grilled fish RM6.30. Roast chicken, veggies, and chips RM7. Look for William, the genial waiter who's been around almost as long as the restaurant. Open daily 10am-10pm.

MARKETS

Each night in Kuala Lumpur provides a choice of residential *pasar malam* (night markets), the crowded streets of Chinatown, food stalls in Little India, or the tawdry lanes which make up **Chow Kit market,** just south of Jl. Chow Kit. The area immediately south of the Jl. Cheng Lock and east of the Klang River is the most lively place in Kuala Lumpur: **Chinatown.** At dusk, the central part of Jl. Petaling becomes a night market crammed with clothing, videotapes of recent box office smashes, pirated albums, and tourists. Food stalls and open-air restaurants roll their tables into the street on Jl. Hang Lekir and Jl. Sultan. **Little India** lies north of Chinatown on and around Jl. Mesjid India, which runs parallel to Jl. Tuanku Abdul Rahman north of Merdeka Square. There is no night market here, but food stalls abound. The largest gathering of food hawkers is at the **Saturday night market** on Jl. Tuanku Abdul Rahman between Jl. Tun Perak and Jl. Dang Wangi. The locations of the largest night markets during the week are: Mon., section 1 in Wangsa Maju (northeast of town in the direction of the zoo); Tues., Seri Petaling (south in the direction of Serembau); Thurs., Jl. Kaskas in Taman Cheras; and Fri., Taman Melati Gombak.

SIGHTS

Most of the big tourist attractions lie west of the railroad. The **Kuala Lumpur Railway Station** on Jl. Sultan Hishamuddin, built in 1900, is a magnificent jumble of domes, minarets, and archways that looks more like a sultan's palace than the hub of modern Malaysia's public transportation system. **The Malayan Railway Headquarters Bldg. (KTM),** across the street, is in much the same style.

Next door to the railway headquarters is the **National Art Gallery** (Balai Seni Lukis Negara), which has an assorted collection of impressive artwork by Malaysian artists. (Open Sat.-Thurs. 10am-6pm, Fri. 10-noon and 3-6pm.) From here, turn right down Jl. Sultan Hishamuddin and turn right again at Jl. Damansara to arrive at the **Muzium Negara.** This museum has the usual exhibits of weapons, dioramas of royal ceremonies, Orang Asli crafts and artifacts, and the obligatory dusty, stuffed wildlife. (Open daily 9am-6pm; admission RM1, under 12 free.)

The **National Mosque** is on Jl. Sultan Hishamuddin. From the National Art Gallery, turn left and the mosque is on the left past the intersection with Jl. Perdana. This modern, metallic center of the Islamic faith in Kuala Lumpur is a stark contrast to the Masjid Jame across the river. Built on two levels, the upper deck houses the main prayer hall and a reflecting pool. If travelers borrow a robe (and a scarf for women), they can explore them entirely, sliding around in their socks. (Open Sat.-Thurs. 9am-noon, 3-4pm, and 5:30-6pm, Fri. 3-4pm and 5:30-6pm.) Continuing up Jl. Sultan Hishamuddin in the direction of the large, white Dayabumi complex, Hishamuddin becomes Jl. Raja, a brick-paved road/walkway with **Merdeka Square** on the left and the **High Court** on the right. *Merdeka* means freedom, and this square was the site for Malaysia's Independence ceremonies in 1957. On Saturday evenings after 5pm, this section of Jl. Raja, as well as Jl. Tuanku Abdul Rahman directly to the north, is closed to traffic for a huge outdoor party.

On the western edge of the city is the 91.6-hectare **Lake Gardens,** an oasis of green just beyond Kuala Lumpur's congested freeways. From the National Art Gallery, turn left and walk up Jl. Sultan Hishamuddin, then turn left onto Jl. Perdana and follow it to the gardens. The complex features a planetarium, a dinosaur museum, war memorials, even an exclusive casino. The biggest draw is the **Taman Burung** (Bird Park), an outdoor aviary housing over 100 species of tropical birds, including the strange-look-

MALAYSIA

ing Malaysian hornbills. (Open 9am-6pm; admission RM3 adults, RM1 children.) Other attractions in the garden include the **Taman Orkid dan Bunga Raya,** the Orchid and Hibiscus Garden (open 9am-6pm; free). Boats can be rented on the lake in the gardens (tel. 298 32 53) for RM3 per hour.

Off Jl. Parlimen in the northern section of the garden is the **National Monument,** dedicated to Malaysians who died in the two World Wars and the Emergency of 1948-1960. The main sculpture was designed by Felix de Weldon, the sculptor of the Iwo Jima Memorial in Washington, D.C. The **Central Market** (tel. 274 65 42) occupies the corner of Jl. Cheng Lock and Jl. Hang Kasturi. Considered by many to be over-priced and tourist-infested, the market is probably better used as a point of reference than as a place for exploration. (Open daily 7:30am-10pm.)

The **Masjid Jame,** as curvaceous as the National Mosque is angular, stands on a lush island of palm trees at the confluence of the Kelang and Gombak Rivers behind Central Market. Built in 1907 on the site where the first settlers landed in Kuala Lumpur, the mosque is one of the most stunning sights in the city, with its meticulous lawn and multitude of grand domes and dainty minarets.

The nearby **Sri Mahamarlamman Temple,** a Hindu temple located in the heart of Chinatown, is often overlooked for its magnificent Islamic neighbors. From Central Market, take a left on Jl. Cheng Lock and turn right on Jl. Tun H.S. Lee—about two blocks down on the right. The temple is on the left. The focus of this 121-year-old temple is a silver chariot that occupies a prominent position in the procession to the Batu Caves during the Thaipusam festival. (Open daily 6am-9pm.)

ENTERTAINMENT.

A healthy yuppie population, droves of expats, and teens with disposable incomes have bestowed KL with many nightlife options. Discos, pubs, bowling alleys, and even cybercafés do a brisk business until about 2am on most nights. Despite the wide range of options, it may take Kuala Lumpur's nightlife some time to find itself. There is a small but growing interest in theater and dance, with major hotels hosting occasional performances. For information call MATIC (tel. 264 39 29), Auditorium DBKL (tel. 291 60 11), or Experimental Theatre (tel. 292 10 64).

The Jump, Wisma Inai, 241 Jl. Tun Razak (tel. 245 00 46). House music and junk shop regalia define this rather docile restaurant/disco. Performance bartending and Tex Mex food prevail; lunch RM12, dinner RM20. Kitchen open till midnight; dancing after 11pm. Open Sun.-Thurs. 11:30am-2am, Fri.-Sat. 11:30am-3am.

Boom Boom Room, 11 Lorong Ampang (tel. 232 69 06). From the 24-hr. Telekom office, turn right; it's the blindingly blue building set away from the street on the right. Boom Boom is known for its transvestite cabaret shows which vary in quality—Friday or Saturday is best, when the crowds are larger. The disco is large and oddly decorated, but uninspiring. Cover RM15 weekdays, RM20 weekends; includes one drink. Open Sun.-Thurs. 8pm-3am, Fri.-Sat. 8pm-4am.

Barn Thai Jazzaurant, 370B Jl. Tun Razak (tel. 244 66 99), beside the Micasa Hotel apartments on the east side of the city. This friendly, genteel establishment might be a bit too starched for its calling as jazz messenger. Weekly jam sessions, b.y.o. instrument. Good Thai entrees (RM8-18), but poor cocktails (RM12-29); stick to beer (RM8.50-14). Happy hour 5-9pm. Open Mon.-Thurs. noon-1am, Fri.-Sat. noon-3am, dinner only Sun.

Global Café, 1/F Taman Banggar, Bukit Bandaraya (tel. 284 47 17), a RM5 taxi ride to the southwest of central KL. Stay in touch with the electronic world while sipping a cuppa joe or beer. Get on a terminal for RM15 per hr., students RM12 per hr., 50% discount from 10am-noon daily. Open daily 10am-midnight.

Modesto's, Telawi Lima (tel. 284 24 46), in Banggar Bahru, and also located behind the Concorde Hotel in northeast KL on Jl. Perak (tel. 248 99 24). A jeans and t-shirt pub/Italian restaurant. Relaxed pool tables and dartboards. Good pizzas and pasta (RM12-25). Happy hour 5-9pm. Open daily 11am-1:30am.

■ Near Kuala Lumpur

The most famous attractions outside KL are the **Batu Caves** (tel. 689 62 84). Hundreds of Hindu devotees descend on the caves for the annual Thaipusam Festival, armed with hooks and needles, which they use to pierce their skin. For the rest of the year, the caves are open to the public and provide a home for a community of docile, wild monkeys. Visitors can climb the 272 steps to the main cave for free or pay RM0.50 to view the Gallery Cave's paintings of Hindu mythology. Take the #11 minibus from Central Market, Sri Jay Bus #349 from Lebu Ampang Bus Stand, or Len Omnibuses #68 or 70 from Jl. Gereja. (Open daily 7:30am-6:30pm.)

As befits the makers of the world's most famous pewter goods, the **Royal Selangor Pewter Factory,** 4 Jl. Usahawan Enam, Setapak Jaya (tel. 422 100), has the world's largest pewter tankard. Guides take visitors through the whole pewter production process, then serve cold drinks from the finished product, and hover attentively suggesting expensive goblet sets and tea services from their souvenir showrooms. (Open Mon.-Sat. 8:30am-4:45pm, Sun. 9am-4pm.) To get there, take buses W12 or W10 from the Lebuh Ampang bus stand (RM0.70). Taking bus #174 from the Lebuh Ampang bus stand (RM1) leads to the fascinating **Orang Asli Museum** (tel. 689 21 22), which houses exhibits relating to Malaysia's indigenous people. (Open Sun.-Thurs. and Sat. 9am-5:30pm; free.) Bus #170 from Lebuh Ampang (RM0.80) takes tourists to see **National Zoo and Aquarium** (tel. 408 34 22), home to 500 species of animals and fish. (Open daily 9am-5pm; admission RM5 adults, RM2 children.)

■ Melaka

Melaka was founded in the late 14th century by the wandering Sumatran Prince Sri Paremesvara. Over the next 500 years, Melaka grew into a major port, which subsequently became the center of Islamic influence and the most powerful military power on the peninsula. Then came the Portuguese in 1511, followed by the Dutch in 1641, and finally the British in 1795. Melaka is now the oldest and most culturally multi-dimensional of all Malaysian cities. Reminders of nearly 500 years of European rule, in the form of churches, government buildings, and graveyards, exist all over Melaka, but the legends and heroes of the pre-Portuguese days live on in popular imagination, as well as street names. Some of Malaysia's most unique mosques and temples are found in the historic area northeast of the river. Other colonial remnants lie south of the river, although this part of town might be a bit over-produced for the tourist's benefit. The town has no night market to speak of, street fare is comparatively scarce, and the nightlife mainly consists of pubs, karaoke clubs, and other venues featuring "talented female-vocalists." Nevertheless, Melaka offers perhaps Malaysia's happiest medium between small town lassitude, urban decadence, and historical aura.

ORIENTATION

The city sprawls across both sides of the **Melaka River,** which winds its way southwest as it empties into the **Straits of Melaka.** On the northwest side of the river's mouth are the Buddhist temples, antique shops, and Baba-Nyonya homes of **Old Melaka,** running along **Jalan Tun Tan Cheng Lock** and **Jalan Hang Jebat,** both parallel to the coastline. The **express bus terminal** is in the business district, just across the river from **Jalan Munshi Abdullah** and about a 30-minute walk from Melaka Raya, the hostel area in the southeast of town. Munshi Abdullah heads south from the river, intersecting with **Jalan Bendahara** (eastern section) and **Jalan Laksamana** (western section). Turning right on Bendahara leads to the town's historic center near the river's mouth. The southeast side of the river mouth is jam-packed with sights, easily recognizable by the bright red **Christ Church** and the **Stadthuys.** The traffic circle next to the river boasts the gateway to backpacker heaven—**Jalan Merdeka. Taman Melaka Raya** is a series of side streets off Jl. Merdeka which offers some of the best values for budget accommodations in all of Malaysia.

PRACTICAL INFORMATION

Tourist Offices: Melaka Tourist Information Centre (tel. 283 65 38), on Jl. Kota near the bridge connecting Jl. Laksamana and Lorong Hang Jebat, across from the clock tower. Limited selection of pamphlets, but pick up the silver *American Express-Melaka Heritage Trail* brochure, which maps out a guide to a number of monuments (especially for Old Melaka). Open Mon.-Thurs. 8:45am-5pm, Fri. 8:45am-12:15pm and 2:45-5pm, Sat. 8:45am-5pm, Sun. 9am-5pm.

Tourist Police: (tel. 270 32 38), on the "pedestrian mall" section of Jl. Kota, across from the tourist information center.

Tours and Travel: The tourist information center runs 45-min. boat tours on the Melaka River (RM6, children RM3). Check with the tourist office for a schedule.

Currency Exchange: OCBC Bank, 6 Lorong Hang Jebat (tel. 282 48 12), just over the bridge from the tourist office. Open Mon.-Fri. 10am-3pm, Sat. 9:30-11:30am. **MayBank,** 6 Jl. Hang Tuah (tel. 282 24 77), close to the bus and taxi stations. Turn left when emerging from the small street leading to the station; the bank is on the left. **ATM.** Open Mon.-Fri. 9:30am-4pm, Sat. 9:30-11am. **Bank of Commerce,** on Jl. Melaka Raya. Open Mon.-Fri. 9:30am-3pm, Sat. 9:30-11:30am.

Trains: The nearest train station (tel. 441 10 34) is at **Tampin,** 38km north of Melaka. To: **KL** (11:35am and 5:50pm, RM9); **Butterworth** (5am, 2nd-class RM42); and **Singapore** (6 per day, 2am-3:50pm, 2nd-class RM27).

Buses: Express bus station, on Jl. Tun Ali. Long-distance buses are run by private companies. The **Kuala Lumpur-Melaka Express,** 324 Jl. Kilang (tel. 282 25 03), has buses to **KL** (every hr., 8am-6pm, RM6.75). The **Johora Express** (tel. 282 52 01) runs to **Singapore** (8 per day, 8am-8pm, RM11). **Mayang Sari** (tel. 282 93 01) runs to **Butterworth** (9am, 2, and 9pm, RM25.40).

Taxis: On Jl. Tun Ali, at the opposite end of the road from the express bus station. Cabs to: **KL** (RM17); **Muar** (RM5); and **Batu Pahat** (RM10). To **Port Dickson** (RM45 per car), but the fare can be split with other passengers.

Local Transportation: The town is compact enough to cover on foot. **Trishaws** congregate around the tourist office. About RM5 per trip, RM15 per hr.

Rentals: Muhibbah Enterprise (tel. 283 06 31), on Jl. Munshi Abdullah, in the Intan Plaza Shopping Arcade. Bikes for RM5 per day. Open daily 10am-6:30pm.

Pharmacies: Guardian Pharmacy (tel. 282 94 99), on ground floor of Mahkota Parade. Open daily 10am-10pm. **Apex Pharmacy,** 83A Jl. Munshi Abdullah (tel. 282 52 96). Walk toward the bus station. Open Mon.-Fri. 9am-7pm, Sat. 9am-6pm.

Medical Services: (tel. 282 23 44). Take bus #19 from the local bus station.

Emergency: tel. 999. **Fire:** tel. 994.

Post Offices: GPO (tel. 283 38 60), on Jl. Bukit Baru. Take bus #19 from the local bus station. Open Mon.-Sat. 8am-6pm, Sun. 10am-1pm. **Pos 2020** (tel. 284 84 40), on Jl. Laksamana, behind Christ Church. Better for buying stamps and mailing letters and packages. *Poste Restante* must explicitly say this office or it will go to the GPO. Open Mon.-Sat. 8am-5pm. **Postal code:** Jl. Merdeka and the hostel area 75000; Old Melaka 75200; business district 75100.

Telephones: Telekom office (tel. 284 91 91), on Jl. Banda Kaba, just past the Dutch cemetery. Not a full-service office, but a booth on the left sells phonecards; nearby are cardphones. Open 24hr. **Telephone code:** 06.

ACCOMMODATIONS

An amazing number of clean and comfortable rooms are available. Inexpensive options are off Jl. Merdeka, just beyond Mahkota Parade Mall. There is another set of budget hotels on the small streets off Jl. Munshi Abdullah on the other side of town.

Malacca Town Holiday Lodge #2, 52 A,B,C Kampung Empat (tel. 284 69 05), close to the express bus terminal. Walking away from Jl. Hang Tuah on Jl. Kubu, turn right on Jl. Kampung Empat and stay left as the road forks. Located in the Wine and Spirits building, it's the only place with such large and inexpensive rooms. Singles RM12-15. Doubles RM15-18, with attached bathroom RM30-35, with A/C from RM40. Kitchen facilities and bike rentals available.

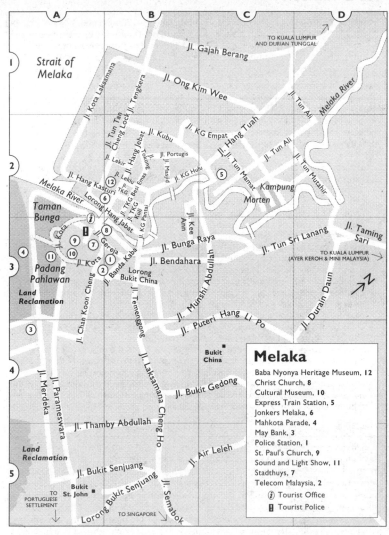

Melaka

Baba Nyonya Heritage Museum, 12
Christ Church, 8
Cultural Museum, 10
Express Train Station, 5
Jonkers Melaka, 6
Mahkota Parade, 4
May Bank, 3
Police Station, 1
St. Paul's Church, 9
Sound and Light Show, 11
Stadthuys, 7
Telecom Malaysia, 2

ⓘ Tourist Office

🛈 Tourist Police

Eastern Heritage, 8 Jl. Bukit China (tel. 283 30 26). Owned by a wealthy local Chinese family, this beautiful old house is teeming with well-behaved backpackers. The manager is an artist whose work decorates the walls of each room. The tiled dipping pool downstairs is a particularly welcome addition, as is the old, wooden bar. Dorms RM7. Singles with fan RM15. Doubles RM18. Triples RM24.

Sunny's Inn Guest House, 270A/B Taman Melaka Raya (tel. 283 79 90). Sunny is more than energetic; he's an astute businessman and an excellent host, having established one of the friendliest atmospheres around. Hot and cold showers, international telephone and fax service, kitchen facilities, and updated travel info, as well as bicycle, motorbike, car, and van rentals. Two recent movies nightly. Dorms RM6-8, with A/C RM9-12. Singles RM12-18, with A/C RM20-30. Doubles RM15-22, with A/C RM25-35. Triples RM24-32, with A/C RM34-40. Attached shower for RM10-20 more.

Melaka Youth Hostel (Asrama Belia Malaysia), 341 Taman Melaka Raya (tel. 282 79 15), sister to the youth hostels in KL and Port Dickson, this rather featureless dormitory of 80 beds is open to AYH and HI members. Common room with TV and dining room. Males and females sleep in separate rooms. Rooms with fan RM10, with A/C RM14 for the first night; RM7 and RM11 each additional night.

FOOD

Melaka's varied history has resulted in excellent food, including the speciality *sate celup,* a bubbling hotpot of spicy broth into which *sate* sticks are dipped. Although there are few **food stalls** around, some can be found on Jl. Kee Ann below Jl. Munshi Abdullah (open daily 5-10pm) and on Jl. Merdeka near the mouth of the river.

Rasturan San Pedro, 4D Aranjo Rd. Ujong Pasir (tel. 284 57 34). Turn right off Jl. Paremesvara/Ujong Pasir onto Jl. Albequerque, which leads into the heart of the Portuguese settlement. Good Portuguese seafood and the only view of the straits you're likely to get at a Melakan restaurant. Portuguese fried *sotong,* or honey-fried *sotong* RM8-10; prices for fish and crab vary with season and availability. Open daily noon-2pm, 5:30-10:30pm.

Restoran Veni, 34 Jl. Temenggong (tel. 284 95 70). A short distance up Jl. Temeng-gong from its intersection with Jl. Laksamana on the right. A genial and insect-free, banana-leaf restaurant proclaimed by locals to be the *crème de la crème* of south Indian food in Melaka. Plain *dosai* RM0.50, spicy mutton *varuval* RM3.50, and *biryani* RM4.50. Open daily 7am-9:30pm.

Restoran Vazhai Elai, 42 Jl. Munshi Abdullah (tel. 283 16 07), one of the best Indian joints in town. A short walk on Jl. Munshi Abdullah, heading toward the river from Jl. Bunga Raya. Enjoy the catchy Tamil music and the curious stares from children who wonder at western fork and spoon users. As authentic and delicious as it gets. More than you can eat costs less than RM5.

Jonkers Melaka, 17 Jl. Hang Jebat (tel. 283 55 78). From the tourist information center, cross the bridge and go down the road; the restaurant is on the left about 10 doors down. *Nyonya* and western cuisine served in a genuine *peranakan* house; tables are placed in a small, central courtyard within the building. Set of four *nyonya* dishes RM20. Also serves a weekend special, usually delicacies such as Portuguese baked fish. Open daily 10am-5pm.

SIGHTS

The town is almost unbearably hot between noon and 4pm, so the best time to see the outdoor attractions is before 11am. Across from the tourist information center, the bright-pink **Stadthuys,** built by the Dutch in the mid-1600s as the official residence of the Governor of Melaka, now contains the Melaka Ethnographical and Historical Museums (tel. 284 19 34). The **Ethnographic Museum** houses exhibits of porcelain, weaponry, stamps, medals, and coins used in Melaka over the centuries, as well as dioramas. One glass case holds the boxing gloves of Mohammed Ali. Upstairs, visitors can endure the non-A/C exhibits of the **Historical Museum** which trace Melaka's development. (Both open Sat.-Thurs. 9am-6pm, Fri. 9am-12:15pm and 2:45-6pm; admission RM2, children RM1.)

Christ Church, next door to the Stadthuys, was built by the Dutch in 1753 to memorialize their victory over the Portuguese. Services have never ceased since 1753—not even during the Japanese occupation. Some of the tombstones in the floor are even older than the church itself. The large stone in the center aisle attracts the most attention. It belonged to an Armenian merchant and bears a rather sentimental inscription in Armenian. (Open Thurs.-Tues. 9am-1pm and 3-5pm, Wed. 9am-1pm.) Continuing down Jl. Laksamana toward the river's mouth, a replica of a Portuguese galleon is on the right. This is not a hokey seafood restaurant but the **Maritime Museum,** which has three floors of ship models and exhibits on the history of Melakan sea trade and piracy. (Open daily 9am-9pm; admission RM5.)

Atop the hill in back of Stadthuys is **St. Paul's Church.** The small, stocky church, built by the Portuguese in 1521, is best known for the old tombstones propped up against its walls. The altar area is dominated by an open crypt which housed the body of St Francis Xavier, missionary extraordinaire, for nine months before he was sent to his eventual resting place in Goa, India. People have taken to tossing small change into the tomb for luck.

Down the steps through an English cemetery are the last remnants of the **Porta de Santiago,** one of the gateways leading to the now-demolished Portuguese fortress of **A Famosa.** The Dutch used the fort during their stay, but the British demolished it entirely in the early 1800s to ensure that Melaka would not be able to compete with Penang for dominance of the straits trade. The Porta de Santiago was saved only through the intervention of the young Stamford Raffles (see **The Life of Sir Stamford Raffles** on page 445).

Around the bend from the gate is the **Cultural Museum** (tel. 282 07 69), housed in a luxurious, wooden replica of the old Sultan's Palace. Dioramas depict the sultan's audience chamber and bedchamber. (Open Sun.-Thurs. and Sat. 9am-6pm, Fri. 9am-12:15pm and 2:45-6pm; admission RM2, children RM1.) The meticulously manicured garden in front of the palace is the site of the nightly **sound and light show,** a multi-media extravaganza depicting Melakan history. Shows take place at 8 and 9pm in Bahasa Malaysia and 9:30 and 10:30pm in English. During the month of Ramadan, there is one show in English at 8:30pm. (Admission RM5, children RM3; tickets sold at the Cultural Museum's ticket booth.)

Across the river from the historic European buildings is **Old Melaka,** a district of narrow, winding streets and homes of wealthy Chinese, many of which bear traces of their original Dutch construction. **Baba Nyonya Heritage Museum,** 48-50 Jl. Tan Cheng Lock (tel. 283 12 73), was constructed in the 1890s as a private residence of a prominent Baba Nyonya (Chinese-Malay) family and was converted into a museum in 1985. From the tourist information center, cross over the river and turn left on Jl. Kasturi; take the next right and the museum is on the right. (Open 10am-12:30pm and 2-4:30pm; admission RM7, children RM4.)

Located on the corner of Jl. Kampung Hulu and Jl. Masjid is Malaysia's oldest mosque, **Masjid Kampung Hulu,** which dates from 1748. Along with two other similar mosques in town, this one claims a pagoda-like minaret and a three-tiered roof, combining Sumatran and Chinese architectural styles in a way not seen elsewhere on the peninsula. (Open Sat.-Thurs. 9am-6pm.)

Cheng Hoon Teng Temple is located on Jl. Tokong just below the intersection with Jl. Lekiu and is the oldest functioning temple in the country, since 1673. This temple once served as the place of worship, city hall, and courthouse for Melakan Chinese. Farther away from the historic part of town is **Bukit China,** a hill originally designated as the residence of the hundreds of attendants that accompanied Princess Hang Li Poh to Melaka when she came from China to marry the sultan. At the foot of the hill is Hang Li Poh's well, built for her after she became Queen of Melaka. Legend has long held that anyone who drinks from the well is guaranteed to return to Melaka;

The Life of Sir Stamford Raffles: Part the Third

With the fundamentals of Colonialist philosophy under his belt, Stamford Raffles, the young stud of the civil service, moved from Penang on to Malacca where he promptly became Agent to the Governor-General of Malaya. During this time, through his unparalleled foresight and powers of persuasion, he single-handedly saved Malacca from complete destruction by the British. He was quickly, but not surprisingly, promoted to Secretary to the Governor-General. Never above mixing with natives, Raffles quickly learned the Malay language, which afforded him greater interaction with the local people. He even had friends among the Malay, one of whom, the Sultan of Sambar in Borneo, gave him a pet orangutan which Raffles dressed in trousers, a coat, and hat. Yes, good Sir Raffles was always trying to improve the lot of poor, unfortunate souls. (To hear what Sir Stamford did next, see page 131.)

the Dutch and the forces of the Johor Sultanate proved this wrong by poisoning the well during the wars of the 1500s-1600s to kill their enemies.

The **Portuguese Settlement,** south of the historic area, is hot and somnolent during the day; the main attractions are the seafood restaurants around the Medan Portugis (Portuguese Square). On Saturdays at 8:30pm, Portuguese dance troupes perform in front of the Restoran de Lisbon (tel. 284 80 67). Check with the tourist office for details about the **Festa San Pedro.**

■ Ipoh

This somewhat utilitarian capital city of Perak has historically been used as a transit point for the region's natural resources. As early as the sixteenth century, Acehnese marauders were drawn to the mineral wealth of the area around Ipoh, after which city denizens faced successive skirmishes with Portuguese, Bugis, Dutch, and Thai traders, pirates, and soldiers. The town, however, only took off when the British assumed control in 1874, bringing in a mass migration of English colonists, Chinese merchants, and Indian laborers. Tin mines sprung up in 1890, providing a new livelihood for its inhabitants, and by the turn of the century, both Ipoh's size and population had grown ten-fold.

Indeed, the bustle and light-industrial sprawl of Ipoh show it to be a city on the move. The city is no longer fueled by its role as a small village harbor or tin mining center. Rather, today's driving forces in this small metropolis include its hodge-podge of industries, modern mega-malls, and droves of fast food chains. Ipoh's riverine thoroughfares generate a certain amount of anxiety in the hearts of slothful trekkers, and many of them give it short shrift, as they race toward the country's offshore island paradises. Those who are prepared to dig a little, however, will discover several high-grade points of interest and a motherlode of delicious *gopi* food.

ORIENTATION

Ipoh is 205km north of Kuala Lumpur along Highway #1, about halfway between KL and Penang. The **Kinta River** runs north-south, splitting Ipoh roughly in half. Much of Ipoh's commercial activity takes place on the east side of town, while the **bus** and **train stations** are on the far west side of town. The **Central Market** takes up a whole city block bounded on the west by **Jalan Laksamanaar** and on the east by **Jalan Dato Onn Jaafar.** The city's main thoroughfares form a grid with six streets running north to south. From the bus station going east are **Jalan Panglima Bukit Gantang Wahab, Jalan Sultan Yussuf,** the Kinta River, Jl. Laksamanaar, Jl. Dato Onn Jaafar, **Jalan Raja Musa Aziz,** and **Jalan Raja Ekram.** The northernmost cross street is **Jalan Sultan Idris Shah,** and parallel to it is **Jalan Sultan Iskandar Shah.**

PRACTICAL INFORMATION

Tourist Offices: The **Perak Tourist Centre** (tel. 253 28 00), on Jl. Bandaraya/Tun Sambanthan near Padang Bandaran and the High Court provides maps. Open Mon.-Fri. 8am-12:45pm, and 2-4:15pm, Sat. 8am-12:45pm.

Currency Exchange: There are banks all over town where money can be changed for a surcharge. Near the Town Hall on Jl. Dato Maharaja Lela, **Hong Kong Bank** and **Standard Chartered Bank** have **ATMs** which accept MC, Visa, or Cirrus.

Air Travel: Sultan Azlan Shah Airport (tel. 312 47 70; 24-hr. reservation hotline 746 30 00), on Jl. Lapangan Terbang 7km outside town. Airport tax is RM5. MAS flights to **KL** (30min., RM66) and **Singapore** (90min., RM244). **MAS,** Lot 108, Bangunan Seri Kinta, Jl. Sultan Idris Shah (tel. 241 41 55, at airport 312 24 59). Open Mon.-Fri. 8:30am-5pm, Sat. 8:30am-3pm. Taxis to the airport cost RM10.

Trains: KTMB Ipoh (tel. 254 79 87), on Jl. Panglima Bukit Gantang Wahab. Trains to: **Kuala Lumpur** (express, 10:50am, 4:50pm, 4hr., RM18-22; mail trains, midnight, 1, 1:40am, RM18-22); **Singapore** (express, 10:57am, RM48); and **Butterworth** (express, 10:40am, 2:20, 5:40pm, and 12:28am, 3½hr., RM17-27).

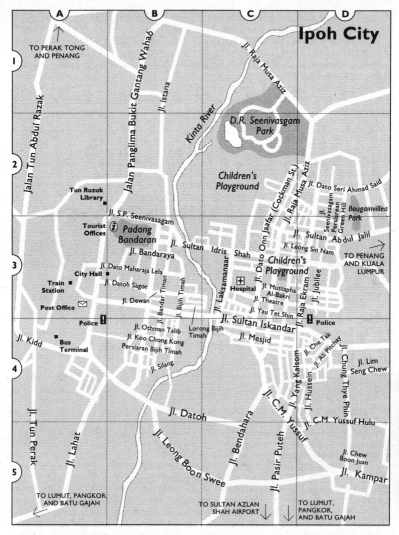

Ipoh City

TO PERAK TONG
AND PENANG

Jalan Tun Abdul Razak

Jalan Panglima Bukit Gantang Wahab

Jl. Istana

Kinta River

Jl. Raja Musa Aziz

D.R. Seenivasagam
Park

Children's
Playground

Jl. Dato Seri Ahmad Said

Jl. Raja Musa Aziz

Jl. Seenivasagam Perdaran Green Hill

Bougainvillea
Park

Tun Ruzuk
Library

Tourist
Offices

Padang
Bandaran

Jl. S.P. Seenivasagam

Jl. Bandaraya

Jl. Sultan Idris Shah

Jl. Dato Onn Jaafar (Cockman St.)

Jl. Sultan Abdul Jalil

Jl. Leong Sin Nam

TO PENANG
AND KUALA
LUMPUR

Jl. Dato Maharaja Lela

City Hall

Train
Station

Jl. Datoh Sagor

Jl. Dewan

Jl. Laksamanaar

Bandar Timah

Bijih Timah

Children's
Playground

Hospital

Jl. Mustapha
Al-Bakri

Jl. Theatre

Jl. Jubilee

Jl. Raja Ekram

Post Office

Police

Jl. Othman Talib

Jl. Koo Chong Kong

Persiaran Bijih Timah

Lorong Bijih
Timah

Jl. Yau Tet Shin

Jl. Sultan Iskandar

Jl. Mesjid

Police

Jl. Kidd

Bus
Terminal

Jl. Silang

Jl. Che Tak

Jl. Ali Pitchay

Jl. Chung Thye Phin

Jl. Lim
Seng Chew

Jl. Tun Perak

Jl. Lahat

Jl. Datoh

Jl. Leong Boon Swee

Jl. Bendahara

Jl. Pasir Puteh

Jl. C.M. Yussuf

Jl. Yang Kalsom

Jl. Hussein

Jl. C.M. Yussuf Hulu

Jl. Chew
Boon Juan

Jl. Kampar

TO LUMUT, PANGKOR,
AND BATU GAJAH

TO SULTAN AZLAN
SHAH AIRPORT

TO LUMUT,
PANGKOR,
AND BATU GAJAH

MALAYSIA

Buses: Medan Kidd Bus Terminal, on Jl. Kidd in the southwest corner of town. Buses going everywhere. To **KL** (every hr., 9am-6pm, RM9.50) and **Butterworth** (every 1½hr., 8am-2:30pm, every hr., 3:30pm-9pm, last bus leaves at midnight). Buses to **Lumut** (every hr., RM3.80) leave from the main terminal.

Taxis: The **taxi stand** for long distance travel is at the Medan Kidd Terminal. To: **KL** (RM22 per person) and **Penang** (RM21).

Local Transportation: Six **bus** lines ply the main drags, all ending up at the terminal on Jl. Kidd. Red, white and blue buses are A/C. **Taxis** around town usually costs RM5 (RM10-20 per hr.). **Radio Cab** (tel. 254 02 41) operates 7am-midnight.

Rentals: Avis Rent-A-Car (tel. (05) 312 65 86), at the airport. Open Mon.-Sat. 7:30am-7pm, Sun. 7:30am-5pm. **Hertz** (tel. 313 71 09).

Markets: The **pasar besar** (day market) is on the east side of town bounded by Jl. Laksamanaar and Jl. Dato Onn Jaafar. The 3rd floor is a hawker center with Chinese and Malay food stalls. Malay food is at its best at the **Pusat Penjaja Padang Kanak**

on the northern half of Jl. Raja Misa Aziz. The big **pasar malam** (night market) is usually about 5km outside of Ipoh, the location changes nightly.

Pharmacies: Apex Pharmacy, Lots 11-12, Yik Foong Complex, ground fl., Jl. Laksamanaar (tel. 253 86 55). Open 10am-9pm. *Farmasi* are everywhere.

Medical Services: (tel. 533 289) on Jl. Hospital, on the northeastern outskirts.

Emergency: tel. 999.

Police: (tel. 501 736), on Jl. Sultan Iskandar Shah.

Post Offices: Pejabat Pos Besar (tel. 548 555), next door to the train station. Open Mon.-Sat. 8am-8pm. **Postal code:** 30670.

Telephones: Telekom office, Jl. Dato Onn Jaafar (tel. 549 292, ext. 164), south from the central market. Open Mon.-Sat. 7am-10pm, Sun. 7am-1pm. Also on Jl. Sultan Idris Shah, near the Kinta River (tel. 253 77 88). Open Sat.-Thurs. 8:30am-4:15pm, Fri. 8:30am-12:30pm. Both have **HCD. Telephone code:** 03.

ACCOMMODATIONS

Cheap Chinese hotels dot the eastern part of town. Many establishments line the eastern end of Jl. Mustafa Al-Bakri, although the massage parlors here lend it a rather seedy quality. Or try the south end of the New Town on Jl. Yang Kalsom.

Grand Cathay Hotel, 88-94 Jl. C.M. Yussuf (tel. 241 33 22), at the intersection with Jl. Yang Kalsom. The endearing Chinese owner gives good advice on what to do in Ipoh. Singles/doubles with fan and shared bathroom RM23.10, with private bath RM29.70, with A/C RM45.

Golden Inn Hotel (tel. 253 08 68), on Jl. Che Tak. Take a left on Jl. Yang Kalsom after the intersection with Jl. Sultan Iskandar Shah. Cheaper than the Cathay and has better facilities. Doubles with bath and fan RM22, with A/C RM27.50.

YMCA of Ipoh, 211 Jl. Raja Musa Aziz (tel. 254 08 09). Nestled in the green countryside extending from D.R. Seenivasagam Park, this establishment offers everything from Tae-Kwon-Do to Jazzercize. Well-tended, spotless rooms. Dorms for 1-5 people RM15. Singles with phone, A/C, and bath RM43. Doubles RM51 and up. Temporary membership of RM1 per week is required for non-members.

The Majestic Ipoh Station Hotel (tel. 255 56 05), on Jl. Panglima Bukit Gantang Wahab. In a restored colonial building above the train station, this hotel is the expensive alternative. The reception desk is on the 3rd floor, presiding over an immense balcony with a view of the city and the mountains beyond. All rooms have A/C, TV, and IDD phones. Doubles RM120. Triples RM130. Deluxe 4-person room RM150. Western breakfast at the coffee house downstairs.

FOOD

The local food culture is based around *kedai gopi*, which generally have stalls serving everything from western breakfast to Hainan chicken rice. Good locations for *kedai gopi* are Jl. Bandar Timah and Jl. Dato Onn Jaafar. For Malay food and desserts, head for the Pusat Penjaja Padang Kanak on Jl. Raja Muser Aziz.

Kedai Kopi Kong Meng, 65 Jl. Bandar Timah, just below Jl. Sultan Iskandar Shah. Just one of the many excellent coffee shops along this street, Kong Meng has delicious *hao fen* (RM2), with beef or chicken and vegetables served either fried or as a soup. Open daily 8am-4pm.

Restoran Kader, 71 Jl. Sultan Yussuf (tel. 253 44 41), located at the south end of Jl. Sultan Yussuf. The specialty is *nasi kandar,* a spicy concoction of curry, chicken, fish, and vegetables served over rice. At lunchtime, see the suits come in and dig right into their lunch with their hands. It tastes better that way. *Roti canai* is served for breakfast and throughout the day. Open daily 7am-9pm.

Kix-S, 43-A Jl. Raja Musa Aziz (tel. 241 73 08), a hole-in-the-wall bar/restaurant near the Lido Theatre. A creepy, Hong Kong lounge-style place with comic book-esque murals. A pitcher of Guinness RM25 or local beer RM14. Salads and western entrees RM3-9, tea shakes and flavored coffee RM3. Open daily 3pm-1am.

SIGHTS

Ipoh's most significant sights are mainly architectural. Jl. Panglima Bukit Gantang Wahab has many impressive colonial buildings, including the train station and the Town Hall, surrounded by well manicured gardens. Next to the Town Hall is the bland **State Mosque.** Approximately 200m north of the Town Hall, on Jl. Panglima Bukit Gantang Wahab is the **Muzium Darul Ridzun,** a museum dedicated to the forestry and mining industries. Downstairs are photographs of old and modern tin mines and an amazing exhibit tracing the development of the steam iron. (Open Sat.-Thurs. 9:30am-5pm, Fri. 9:30am-noon and 2:30-5pm; free.)

The museum-weary might want to try a stroll in **D.R. Seenivasagam Park.** Covering the broad expanse between the YMCA and the traffic circle on Jl. Raja Musa Aziz, it offers soccer fields, gazebos, shady trees, and fish-filled ponds. The newly designed Japanese Garden adds flair to this somewhat characterless facility.

The limestone hills surrounding Ipoh are home to an extensive network of natural **caves.** The Chinese who immigrated into the region used the caves as Buddhist temples. North of Ipoh on the road to Kuala Kangsar is **Perak Tong,** a temple best known for its paintings and seemingly endless stairwell. (Open daily 8am-5pm; steps open 9am-5pm.) It can be reached on the Kuala Kangsar bus. Another cave temple of interest is **Sam Poh Tong,** 6km south of Ipoh on the main road, serviced by the Kampar bus. It is the oldest in the region, built 128 years ago, and shelters ponds brimming with hundreds of fish and turtles. (Open daily 9am-5pm.) Also reachable by the Kampar bus is **Kek Lok Tong,** just before Gunung Rapat. (Open daily 9am-5pm.) For spelunkers who are disappointed with the paved-over character of the Chinese cave temples, a solution may be **Lang Hill,** just south of Perak Tong, featuring beautiful limestone formations overhanging a central pond.

The road to **Lumut,** southwest of Ipoh, passes through countryside dotted with elaborate Chinese cemeteries, open-cast mines, and small mining towns gone bust. One such town is **Papan,** a fascinating piece of living history. Built as a mining town in the 1890s, Papan has become a near-ghost town since the demise of tin. Any uninhabited building is left to fall to pieces, reclaimed by the vegetation. A relic of Malaysian history, Papan should be seen before it disintegrates entirely.

About 45 minutes outside of town, accessible either by taxi or a short bus ride from Butu Gajah on the Gopeng bus is **Kellie's Castle,** the rapidly decaying remnant of William Kellie Smith, a wealthy Scottish planter who died during the building's construction in 1926. If you can scrounge RM0.50, take a quick peek at the castle's empty rooms, rubble walls, and narrow arches.

Getting to these regional sights may be difficult. Many travelers hire a taxi for RM10-20 per hour from the taxi stand at the bus terminal. Those with a bit more time to spare and fewer ringgit to spend catch buses from the terminal to all of the sights. Going this route takes a full day but runs only RM5.

■ Kuala Kangsar

Dwarfed by both its northwestern neighbor, Taiping, and the state capital of Ipoh to the southeast, Kuala Kangsar has remained a smaller and quieter town with majestic grace and royal dignity worthy of the Sultan of Perak himself. Indeed, since 1931, Muslim heads of state have inhabited the palace of Istana Iskandariah overlooking the Perak River on the outskirts of town. This has lent Kuala Kangsar its reserved and peaceful aura and perhaps prevented its capitulation to the forces of expansion and modernization. The city's few main streets capture Malaysia's distinct ethnic mix while its more distant gardens and sidewalks afford lofty river views and shady retreats. Although the sights in Kuala Kangsar can be seen within a few hours, their digestion begs infinitely more time from the visitor.

MALAYSIA

ORIENTATION

The several short streets that make up Kuala Kangsar's commercial center sprawls near the **clock tower** at the intersection of **Jalan Taiping** and **Jalan Kangsar**. The **train station** is on the northwest outskirts of town, approximately 2km from the center clock tower, or a 15-minute walk down either **Jalan Tun Razak** or Jl. Taiping. The **bus station** is located on **Jalan Raja Bendahara**. Following this road to the right leads to a traffic light and Jl. Taiping. **Jalan Daeng Selili** is Kuala Kangsar's main thoroughfare. The town's mosques, palaces, and museums are all found over the bridge and under the gate visible just behind the clock tower.

PRACTICAL INFORMATION

Tourist Offices: The police, train station, and post office can be helpful, but often one must look to friendly English-speaking residents for assistance.

Currency Exchange: UMBC, 6-7 Jl. Daeng Selili (tel. 776 17 62). Open Mon.-Fri. 9:30am-3:30pm, Sat. 9:30-11:30am. **Bank Bumiputra,** 39 Jl. Kangsar (tel. 776 52 20). Open Mon.-Fri 9:30am-5pm. Sat. 9:30am-1pm.

Trains: (tel. 776 10 94), on Jl. Stesyen about 2km northwest of town. To **KL** (10am, RM26; 4pm, RM22; 10:50pm, RM10; 11:50pm, RM 26; 12:30am, RM22) and **Butterworth** (11:30am, RM13; 5:40pm, RM9).

Buses: Bus station, on Jl. Raja Bendahara, between the intersection with Jl. Taiping and the traffic circle. To **Taiping** (every 30min., 6:40am-7:40pm, RM2.85) and **Ipoh** (every 10min., 6am-6pm, every 30min. 6-9:30pm, RM3). **Transnasional Ekspres** (tel. 776 10 33) runs buses to **KL** (5 per day, 10am-7:30pm, RM11.70).

Taxis: The taxi stand at the bus terminal has in-town and long-distance taxis.

Pharmacies: 29 Jl. Kangsar (tel. 776 41 57). Open Mon.-Sat. 9am-5pm.

Medical Services: (tel. 776 33 33), on Jl. Sultan Idris Shah, a right off Jl. Taiping.

Emergency: tel. 999

Police: (tel. 776 22 22), on Jl. Raja Chulan.

Post Offices: (tel. 776 45 55), on Jl. Daeng Selili at the clock tower. Open Mon.-Sat. 8am-5pm. **Postal code:** 33000.

Telephones: Telekom office (tel. 776 92 92), on Jl. Raja Chulan. Cardphones are located throughout the city and at the bus station. **Telephone code:** 05.

ACCOMMODATIONS

Double Lion Inn, 74 Jl. Kangsar, right on the traffic circle where Jl. Kangsar meets Jl. Raja Bendahara. The downstairs serves as a bakery/coffee shop; travelers awake to the delicious smell of baking bread. Open since the 40s, this spartan flophouse retains relics that give it a nostalgic feel. Singles with fan RM12. Doubles with A/C and attached bath RM35-40.

Rumah Rehat Kerajaan-Government Rest House (tel. 776 38 72), 100m from the bridge on Jl. Istana, perched on the hillside overlooking the river. While not quite the nearby sultan's palace, the Rest House provides choice accommodations in town. Doubles with A/C and clean bath RM50, with hot water RM60.

Hai Thean Hotel, 25 A Jl. Daeng Selili. Cleaner quarters than the Double Lion, but at the price of a sterile setting. From the clock tower, walk a short distance down Jl. Daeng Selili; it's on the right. Singles with fan RM17. A 2-3 person room RM25.

FOOD

Despite its diminutive size, Kuala Kangsar is brimming with gastronomic temptations in typical Malaysian style. Chinese and Indian/Muslim restaurants abound along Jl. Kangsar and in the market area between Jl. Kangsar and the bus station.

Restoran Choon Kee (tel. 776 18 04), on the left across from the hospital. A 1-km hike from the clock tower on Jl. Taiping. Worthwhile Cantonese seafood and cheap home-cooked food. No menu; ask for suggestions. Meal for two RM15-20.

New Kassim Restaurant, 25 Jl. Daeng Selili (tel. 776 73 09). A lively Muslim couple welcomes hungry customers. Let Maimun fuss over you like a mother, bringing forth plates of *mee goreng* or *roti*. Reliably delicious traditional Muslim fare for RM1-3. Open daily 7am-9pm.

SIGHTS

Thrusting its gold onion domes toward the sky along Jl. Istana, **Masjid Ubudiah** was commissioned in 1917 by Sultan Idris Murshidul'adzam Shah I, the 28th Sultan of Perak, as thanksgiving for his recovery from a chronic illness. Although its construction was plagued by difficulties it was finally completed and today remains an impressive landmark. Shortly before Masjid Ubudiah is **Sofee Villa,** a large wooden structure with Moorish arches, and the decrepit but impressive **Istana Kota.** Istana Kota was formerly the palace of Sultan Idris Shah. Now the huge white edifice is awaiting renovation and will theoretically be upgraded into a museum.

Continuing along the same road for about 10 minutes leads to **Istana Iskandariah,** the Sultan's Palace. Although barricaded by a wrought-iron fence, it is easily admired from the road which encircles it. The *istana* began serving as the royal home in 1933. Make sure to follow the road around to the front of the palace for a better photo of the building and a good view down the Perak River.

Past the palace and toward Jl. Istana, the **Royal Museum** is an apparent architectural *non sequitur* built without a single nail and in the shape of a sword. Inside visitors can trace the history of Perak's royal families, admire the royal regalia, and learn about the heyday of Perak state. Once known as Istana Kenangan (memory palace), this structure actually served as the home of the 39th Sultan, Iskandar Shah, as he awaited the construction of the present Istana Iskandariah. Remember to take off your shoes. (Open Sat.-Wed. 9:30am-5pm, Thurs. 9:30am-12:45pm; free.)

On the other side of the river stands an institution which certainly vies with Istana Iskandariah for historical significance and architectural merit. **Kolej Melayu** (Malay College) is a secondary school/junior college which has turned out many statesmen and business leaders during its 81 year history. Opened in 1905 by the British government, the school was the first to give Malays an English education, and to this day it maintains a strict policy of only admitting 100% Malays. Although used by the Japanese in World War II to disseminate their ideology (both as a school and later a concentration camp), these days, college wards receive more diluted forms of motivation such as the slogan "Academic excellence can only be obtained through a positive mental attitude." Studies are underway to see if this is actually the case.

■ Taiping

Like the names of many Chinese cities, Taiping (expansive peace), is a total misnomer. The wistful label was dubbed by Captain Ah Quee, Taiping's first Chinese *kapitan*. Disputes here over mineral rights and the opium trade had led to a full-scale civil war in 1874, giving the British an opportunity to impose the Treaty of Pangkor. Taiping is now a tranquil vacationland for the country's wealthy. The city's centerpiece is the lake gardens at the eastern edge of town, where limpid pools dwell in the shadows of hardwoods and venerable *samanea saman* trees. But perhaps Taiping's greatest charm, more than its low prices or verdant gardens, is self-possession. It is the sort of place where people live their whole lives without coveting the glitz and glamour of Kuala Lumpur or Singapore, perhaps cherishing the value of a *taiping* that was so hard-won.

ORIENTATION

The central part of Taiping is set up in a grid pattern. The main drags go east-west. To the east is where the government offices, lake garden, zoo, museum, and library are located. These roads, from south to north, are **Jalan Panggong Wayang, Jalan Kota, Jalan Pasar, Jalan Taming Sari, Jalan Barrack,** and **Jalan Stesyen.** Distances are short: it takes less than 10 minutes to walk from Jl. Panggong Wayang to Stesyen. The **taxi stand** is on **Jalan Iskandar** between Jl. Kota and Jl. Panggong Wayang.

PRACTICAL INFORMATION

Tourist Police: 293 Jl. Iskandar, next to the Express Bus/Taxi stand. Enthusiastically provides visitors with a sketch map of the city, directions, and advice.

Currency Exchange: Bank Bumiputra Malaysia Berhad, Jl. Kota (tel. 807 245), next to the pink clock tower. Open Mon.-Fri. 9:30am-4pm, Sat. 9:30am-noon. **Fulahm Touring Agency,** 25-E Jl. Kelab Cina (tel. 804 30 69), off Jl. Panggong Wayang. Open Mon.-Fri. 9am-6pm, Sat. 9am-1pm. **Maybank** on the eastern side of Jl. Taming Sari and **Standard Chartered Bank** on east Jl. Kota both have **ATMs** which accept MC and Visa.

Trains: Stesyen Keretapi Taiping (tel. 807 25 91), on Jl. Stesyen, 500m west from the downtown area. 2nd class to **KL** (9:25am, RM28; 3:26pm, RM24) and **Butterworth** (4am, noon, and 6:15pm, RM7).

Buses: The **Stesyen Bus,** at the west end of Jl. Panggong Wayang. To **Kuala Kangsar** (every 15min., 7am-6pm, RM2). The **express bus terminal** in Kemunting has buses to **Butterworth** (every 30min., 7am-8:30pm, RM4) and **KL** (every hr., RM13-14). Take a taxi to Kemunting (RM4).

Taxis: To the right of the express bus terminal. Share-taxis to other parts of Malaysia cost more than the buses.

Markets: The **day market** is in the center of town running from Jl. Taming Sari to Jl. Panggong Wayang.

Pharmacies: Farmasi Kota, 125 Jl. Taming Sari (tel. 806 32 66). Open daily 9am-9:30pm.

Medical Services: on Jl. Taming Sari (tel. 808 33 33).

Emergency: tel. 999.

Police: (tel. 808 22 22), on Jl. Taming Sari, uptown past Jl. Istana.

Post Offices: (tel. 807 75 55), uptown on the far eastern side of Jl. Barrack. Open Mon.-Sat. 8am-5pm. **Postal code:** 34000.

Telephones: Telekom office (tel. 808 92 92), next to the post office. Open Mon.-Fri. 8:30am-4:45pm, Sat. 8:30am-1pm. **Telephone code:** 05.

ACCOMMODATIONS

Peace Hotel, 30 & 32 Jl. Iskandar, on the corner with Jl. Panggong Wayang. An elderly but hyperkinetic Chinese gentleman runs a tight ship at this inexpensive and popular hotel. Stained glass windows and tiles on the outside of the building lend atmosphere. Singles/doubles with fan and sink RM12. Triples RM16.

Hotel Malaysia, 52 Market Sq. (tel. 807 37 33), in the heart of Taiping, next to the day market. Family-run hotels are usually the best bet for cleanliness and this one is no exception, having been in business for three generations. Singles with fan, bath, and phone RM20, with A/C RM30. Doubles with A/C RM32.

Rumah Rehat Baru (New Rest House), #1 Jl. Sultan Mansur Shah (tel. 807 20 44), continue east on Jl. Taming Sari out of town, turn right on Jl. Bukit Larut and take the first left. Another immediate left leads up a short drive to the rest house. Idyllic setting away from the city. Very popular with locals and foreigners alike; book in advance. Comfortable rooms with private bath. Singles/doubles with fan RM31.50, with A/C RM36.75. Triples with fan RM44.10, with A/C RM49.35.

FOOD

This Chinese-dominated city is a great place to fill up on those Cantonese and Hokkien treats you may have missed elsewhere. Try *sam leok kiew bak chang* (rice dumplings) or *po pian* (thin cake).

Bismillah Restaurant, 138 Jl. Taming Sari, at the intersection with Jl. China. Built and opened in 1900, this Indian-Muslim restaurant is a Taiping institution. Marble-topped tables, framed Arabic calligraphy, and colorful clientele give the place character. Enjoy *roti canai* for breakfast or *nasi biryani* on Mondays, before they run out (RM3). Other dishes cost RM2 or less. Open 6am-9pm.

Restoran Tom Yam Taiping/T. Brek Caterer, 120 Jl. Taming Sari (tel. 806 82 26). Muslim women glide among the tables at this recently opened Taiping favorite. Let them serve you one of the 10 dishes of *nasi* (RM2.50-4.50), *mee* (RM1.50-2.50), or *ayam* (RM2.50). If you crave something familiar, try a western dish (around RM9) such as steak, fish and chips, or lamb chops. Clean, air-conditioned, and loaded with choices. Open noon-10:30pm.

Kum Loong, 45-47 Jl. Kota (tel. 807 26 49), just east of the pink clock tower. At 60 years of age, this restaurant has emerged as the people's choice for *dim sum.* Come in the morning to hang with the old Chinese men who are lifelong customers. Endless tea and cheap bite-size goodies.

SIGHTS

Taiping has Malaysia's first museum, the **Muzium Perak,** built in 1883 on the site where British residential administrator J.W. Birch was murdered. It's about 1km from the center of town on the left of Jl. Taming Sari. A Vietnam War-era CAC Avon Saber parked outside, a gift from the Australian base at Butterworth. Inside are photos of old Taiping, exhibits of royal garb and accoutrements, and a large collection of Orang Asli tools, pottery, musical instruments, and clothing (with English subtitles). (Open Sat-Thurs. 9am-5pm, Fri. 9am-12:15pm and 2:45-5pm.)

The **Taiping Lake Gardens and Zoo** is one of the biggest and most beautiful parks in Malaysia. The road encircling the park is sheltered from the sun by ancient, Tolkien-esque *samanea saman* trees. The park, intentionally devoid of palm trees, might just as well be in a London suburb were it not for the occasional basking lizard. The zoo is not such a hit, however. (Open daily 10am-6pm; admission RM3.)

Malaysia's oldest hill station, **Bukit Larut,** formerly known as Maxwell's Hill, lies 1250m above sea level in the mountains that form Taiping's scenic background. It is popular for its cool temperatures and mountain greenery similar to the Cameron Highlands, but has the added attraction of seclusion and peace. The only way to get to Bukit Larut is by taking the government-operated Land Rovers which leave every hour, on the hour, 8am-5pm from the base in Taiping on Jl. Air Terjun, just past the northeast end of the Lake Gardens (RM2). Up in Bukit Larut accommodation is available at rest houses and bungalows (RM80-200). Some have cooking facilities, and most have simple western and Malaysian meals available. The tourist police recommend calling ahead to verify that the Land Rovers are making the ascent, as recent landslides have interrupted their schedules. For more information and to make reservations (best done in advance) call the officer in charge at the Bukit Larut Hill Resort, 34020 Taiping (tel. 807 72 43).

PULAU PENANG

Penang's moist island setting sealed its fate long ago, first by nourishing rubber and spice plantations, then by irrigating the creeping crud of beach overdevelopment, and finally by giving rise to fungal cardphones and ATM machines which today

---

The Life of Sir Stamford Raffles: Part the Second

Recognized as a shining star in his first years with the East India Company, Sir Stamford Raffles, the veritable savior of Southeast Asia, was appointed to his first overseas position as Assistant to the Chief Secretary in Penang. He arrived there in 1805 with reckless enthusiasm and his wife Olivia. A true renaissance man, Raffles once again astounded and outdid his peers by not only thriving in commerce and politics (his primary duties as a servant to the EIC), but by pursuing his passion for exotic Eastern philosophy, history, religion, art, linguistics, botany, and zoology. He also immediately developed a powerful paternal instinct to protect the natives under his empire's dominion; this would serve him well throughout his illustrious career. (To continue on the path of this consummate Orientalist, see page 389.)

MALAYSIA

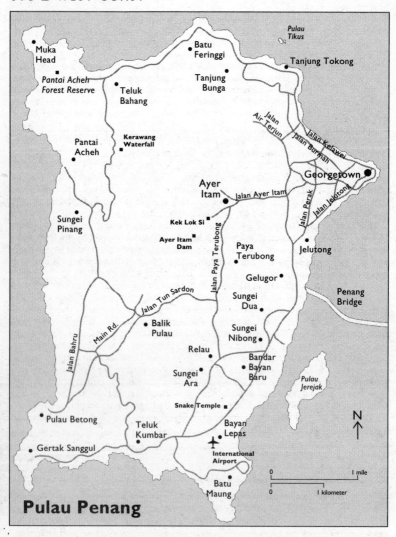

Pulau Penang

sprout spontaneously on any given vertical surface in Georgetown, the island's capital. Old Georgetown, nonetheless, preserves vast swaths of venerable Chinese houses, and more remote destinations like Taluk Bahang and Monkey Beach have yet to succumb to developer's folly.

Seemingly immortal moped drivers swarm the narrow streets of Georgetown. Their presence, however, is no indication of the pace of life in either the city or Penang as a whole. Never hurried, the island's people will often go out of their way to help disoriented tourists and will be happy just to chat for a while.

The years of British domination began when Francis Light and his British East India Company first set up shop in 1786 on what was then called Prince of Wales Island. The British named the island's capital after King George III, and it remained in their control until its incorporation into the Federation of Malaysia in 1957.

GETTING THERE AND AWAY

Penang is easily reached from Butterworth, which is, in turn, accessible by bus and train from all over Peninsular Malaysia. **Bayan Lepas International Airport** (tel. 834 411) lies 20km south of Georgetown. To get there, take yellow bus #83 (every hr., 6am-10pm). **Malaysian Airline System (MAS)** (tel. in town 262 00 11, at airport 830 811) runs flights to: **Singapore** (4 per day); **Bangkok** (1 per day); **Medan** (1 per day); and **Madras** (Wed.). Call MAS for schedule information. The **train station** is located at the ferry landing in Butterworth. Trains to **Kuala Lumpur** leave at 8am, 2, and 10:15pm. One train departs per day from Butterworth heading north to **Alor Setar, Padang Besar,** and across the Thai border to **Hat Yai** and **Bangkok** at 2pm. The **bus station** is also at the ferry landing in Butterworth. Almost every location on the western seaboard of Malaysia has frequent buses to Butterworth. **Ferries** run every 15 minutes around the clock between Butterworth and **Georgetown.** It costs RM0.40 to go to Penang, but a ride to the mainland is free.

ISLAND ORIENTATION

Getting around Penang Island on your own is easy—there are only a few main roads and they are well-marked. Travelers arrive in Georgetown, which takes up the northeast corner of the island. Heading west from there along the north coast, is **Gurney Drive,** a popular eating and relaxation spot off the main road. Several km farther loom the countless luxury beach resorts of **Batu Ferringhi,** an over-developed strip of coastline. Penniless pilgrims continue in pursuit of **Teluk Bahang's** budget accommodations and more laid-back atmosphere.

■ Georgetown

Georgetown is a clean but not glittering cultural and culinary mecca where livelihoods and demographics are divided along racial lines, making it an apt metaphor for the tensions which afflict the country as a whole. Narrow city streets and markets pulse with life late into the night, and aimless walks will reveal to the bemused traveler a collection of architectural styles which is surely one of Asia's most eclectic. Once a bastion of western influence, Georgetown today serves as Penang's seat of administration and as the commercial hub of the state. Situated too far north to accommodate naval dockyards, Penang's importance as a trading post declined steadily with the rise of Singapore to the south. The port's modern heirs have, however, parlayed Georgetown's location into a major hub for trade between Malaysia and other Southeast Asian countries. While its debris and screeching street noise seem to mar Penang's tropical-resort feel, Georgetown offers a fascinating cultural dynamic and affords the budget traveler the services only a major city can.

ORIENTATION

Georgetown sits on a peninsula jutting out on the eastern side of Penang. At the northeastern tip of the peninsula, guarding the city, is **Fort Cornwallis,** surrounded by a large expanse of grass. Bordering the fort's complex away from the coast is **Lebuh Light,** which twists and turns, changing to **Jalan Sultan Ahmad Shah** at the western end. The main street in southern Georgetown is **Jalan Macalister,** which becomes **Jalan Magazine** east of the traffic circle. From this traffic circle, **Jalan Penang** runs north toward the coast. **Pengkalan Weld Quay** runs along the southeastern coast of Georgetown, where the **ferry terminal** and the yellow and blue **bus station** can be found. Two streets west, nearly parallel to Pengkalan Weld, **Lebuh Pantai,** which straddles the length of Georgetown, is the center of the business district. Four blocks farther west, **Lebuh Pitt** cuts through the heart of Georgetown and morphs into **Jalan Masjid Kapitan Keling.** Just east of Lebuh Pitt/Jl. Masjid Kapitan Kling, **Little India** dominates a thin strip of blocks in the middle of Chinatown. Running northwest to southeast between Jl. Penang and Pengkalan Weld, **Lebuh Chulia** constitutes the central thoroughfare of **Chinatown.**

PRACTICAL INFORMATION

Tourist Offices: Malaysian Tourism Promotion Board, 10 Jl. Tun Syed Barakbah (tel. 262 00 11). Open Mon.-Fri. 8am-4:15pm, Sat. 8am-12:45pm. For maps and specific information regarding Penang go to the **Penang Tourist Association** (tel. 616 663), on Pesara King Edward. Open 8am-5pm. English spoken in both offices. The complimentary *Visit Penang* magazine has useful info, a good map, telephone numbers, and low-budget hot spots.

Tourist Police: (tel. 261 55 22).

Tours and Travel: MSL Travel Sd. Bhd., Ming Court Lobby, Jl. Macalister (tel. 237 26 55). Offers the Malay and Thai equivalents of the Eurailpass, available to students with an ISIC. Other packages also available.

Embassies and Consulates: Indonesia, 467 Jl. Burma (tel. 374 686). **Thailand,** 1 Jl. Ayer Rajah (tel. 379 484). **UK,** c/o Price Waterhouse, UMBC Building, Lebuh Pantai (tel. 625 333).

Currency Exchange: At any of the many money-changers on Lebuh Chulia or the major banks along Lebuh Pantai. Banks may take a small service charge, but their rates are slightly better. A **Maybank ATM,** close to Lebuh Chulia on Lebuh Campbell, accepts MC and Visa. Banks offering a full range of services, including **Hong Kong Bank** (tel. 262 30 00) and **Citibank** (365 888), are also available.

Ferries: To **Butterworth** (every 15min., 24hr., RM0.40, cars RM5). 2 express services operate out of the same building as the tourist offices. **KPLFS Company** (tel. 262 56 30) goes to **Medan** (Tues. and Thurs., 9am and 2pm, Sat., 10am, RM90, RM160 roundtrip) and **Langkawi** (8am and 6:15pm, RM35, RM60 roundtrip). **Ekspres Bahagia** (tel. 263 19 43) goes to **Medan** (Mon., Wed., and Fri., 10am) at the same rates as KPLFS.

Local Transportation: All **buses** pass through KOMTAR. Coastal buses leave just north of the ferry terminal on Pengkalan Weld. MPPP city buses leave from Gatot Lebuh Pasar. All buses headed away from the jetty on Chulia will take you to KOMTAR. There are 5 different bus companies in Penang: **Red** and **White** MPPP buses run into Georgetown and as far as Penang Hill; **Yellow** buses go to the Southeast; **Green** buses go to Air Itam; **Blue** buses cover the north shore; and **Minibuses** run from the jetty to western Georgetown.

Taxis: Are unmetered, so agree on a price beforehand. Taxis are not worth the extra money considering the convenience of the bus system and the ubiquity of **becak,** which offer a slower and more scenic way of seeing Georgetown, especially at night. A 1-hr. tour should cost RM10-12.

Rentals: IDP required for all car rentals. **Avis Rent-A-Car** has 3 outlets: E & O Hotel on Lebuh Farquhar (tel. 263 18 65), Rasa Sayang Hotel Lobby (tel. 881 15 22), and Bayan Lepas International Airport (tel. 839 633). **Kasina Rent-A-Car** (tel. 229 38 41) has vans and Landcruisers from RM236 per day, insurance included. **Ruhanmas Rent-A-Car,** 76-C-1 and 157-B Batu Ferringgi (tel. 881 17 60) has vans and 4WD starting from RM105 per day. Bike and motorbike rentals are along Lebuh Chulia. Motorbikes RM15 per day. Rates at Batu Ferringgi and Teluk Bahang aren't as good as those on Lebuh Chulia.

Markets: Penang's main **pasar malam** (night market) sets up far from the center of town and moves every few weeks. Ask around for current locations. One market that can't be missed for its sheer size and variety springs up every night around 7pm along **Jalan Macalister.** A **morning market** holds sway on Lebuh Carnavan between Lebuh Chulia and Lebuh Campbell until about 11am. **Ayer Itam** also boasts a large market which picks up at night.

Pharmacies: Guardian Pharmacy, Ground Fl., KOMTAR on Lebuh Tek Soon (tel. 263 11 19). Fully stocked with all necessities, as well as brand-name toiletries. Prescription counter. Open 10am-9:30pm.

Medical Services: General Hospital, on Jl. Hospital (tel 373 333).

Emergency: tel. 999. **Fire:** tel. 994. **24-hr. Information Hotline:** tel. 373 737.

Police: (tel. 999), on Jl. Penang.

Central Georgetown

Broadway Hostel, 15
Fort Cornwallis, 20
Green Planet, 5
Hard Life Cafe/Hostel, 9
Kapitan Keling Mosque, 8
Kuan Yin Temple, 13
MPPP Bus Station, 16
Malaysian Tourist Office, 18
Night Market, 2, 3
Penang State Museum
 and Art Gallery, 11
Penang Tourist Office, 19
Reggae Club, 6
Sri Mariamman Temple, 14
St. George's Angelican, 12
Taxi/Bus, 1, 4, 17
Wan Hai Hotel, 10
White House Hotel, 7

Post Offices: GPO Penang (tel. 619 222), on corner of Lebuh Downing and Pengkalan Weld. Open Mon.-Sat. 8am-6pm. *Poste Restante* open Mon.-Sat. 8am-6pm. **Postal code** (for the post office only): 10670.

Telephones: Telekom office (tel. 237 32 73), on Jl. Burma. It is on the left a few blocks down the road. Open 24hr. **HCD** service available here and on the ground fl. of Bangunan Tuanku Syed Putra (tel. 261 07 91) on Lebuh Downing. Open 24hr. **IDD** available from any card phone. **Telephone code:** 04.

ACCOMMODATIONS

Georgetown's many budget hotels are mainly located on Lebuh Chulia. Prices, if not quality, are constant from place to place. If the main backpacker dens are already full, don't fret. There are oodles of cheap and pleasant Chinese hotels along the side streets adjoining Lebuh Chulia.

Wan Hai Hotel, 35 Lorong Cinta (tel. 261 68 53). Lorong Cinta is about 300m down on the left, coming from Jl. Penang. Wan Hai is 50m up and makes its company not with the boisterous Chulia crowd but with Chinese *huiguan* (ceremonial halls) and a *mahjong* tile factory. This old Chinese shophouse has large, clean, and airy rooms with fans and sinks. Motorbike and bicycle rental, as well as travel services provided. Dorms RM7. Singles RM16. Doubles RM18.

White House Hotel, 72 Jl. Penang (tel. 263 23 85). Heading north on Penang Rd. past Lebuh Chulia, turn left on Jl. Sri Bahari. White House is immediately on the right. This mid-range hotel is a good value, even if the green tiles don't make for much of an aesthetic experience. Rooms have showers and phones. Singles/doubles RM25, with A/C RM 35.

Swiss Hotel, 431-F, Lebuh Chulia (tel. 620 133). Coming from the ferry terminal, the Swiss Hotel is down Lebuh Chulia past Jl. Masjid Kapitan Keling/Lebuh Pitt on the left. Set back from the road, but still fairly noisy. Rooms are smaller than average but each is equipped with its own shower. Swiss Hotel is popular with backpackers, but lacks the relaxed family feel of the older Chinese hotels in the vicinity. Singles/doubles RM17.50.

YMCA International Hostel, 211 Jl. Macalister (tel. 228 82 11), in the suburbs. City buses do go into town, though (RM0.50). Big, clean, and, despite its inconvenient location, often full; make reservations in advance. All rooms have telephones. Doubles with fan RM35, with TV RM45, with A/C RM45, with hot water RM60. Triples RM70. Non-YMCA members RM2 extra.

FOOD

The hybrid cuisine known as *nyonya* is one fortunate outcome of Penang's competing cultures. Some of the best food is found on the streets; Chinese hawkers ladle out sugar cane juice, *ais kacang* (shaved ice, sweet corn, sweet red beans, *saso,* and syrup), *chendol* (shaved ice with small noodles made of green pea flour, submerged in coconut milk and pandan syrup), and *bubur cha cha* (sweet coconut milk over ice with chunks of fruit, yams, and colorful rice gummies), among others. The regional dishes most often associated with Penang are *nasi kander,* a curry dish with chicken or mutton, and *laksa,* fish soup with rice noodles. Also try Hainanese chicken rice at any one of the open-air restaurants along Lebuh Chulia. Some great **food centers** are found at the west end of Gurney Drive (on the outskirts of town on the way to Batu Ferringhi) and at the west end of Jl. Tun Syed Sheh Barakbah.

Nyonya Corner, 15 Jl. Pahang (tel. 228 14 12). From KOMTAR walk out Jl. Macalister, turn left on Jl. Anson, and again on Jl. Pahang. Nyonya Corner is on the left, 50m down. Presided over by the personable Mr. Yong, Nyonya offers an excellent variety of *nyonya* and Malay dishes. Crowd-pleasers include the basil-garnished "curry kapitan" chicken, and beef *vendan.* Generous servings and attentive service are worth the average RM18 for a meal. 5% service charge automatically added. Open Tues.-Sat. 11:30am-3pm and 6:30-10pm.

Green Planet, 63 Lebuh Cintra (tel. 261 61 92). Look for the big green sign. The free hot showers, express mail service, travel services, and book exchange will endear you to this western-style restaurant. The pampering will also make you forget the above-market prices. A full meal costs about RM10. A new addition to the family business is the **Rainforest Restaurant** at 294 Lebuh Chulia (tel. 261 46 41). This restaurant has all the trimmings of its sibling plus a fax machine and internet access. Tickets to Langkawi or Medan sold here. Both open Mon.-Sat. 9am-2:30pm and 7pm-midnight, Sun. 7pm-midnight.

The Tandoori House, 34-36 Jl. Hutton (tel. 619 105), 2 blocks south of the intersection with Lebuh Chulia. Amble down to Georgetown's finest Moghul restaurant, where polished service, surroundings, and presentation will cure the bluest funk. Tasty chunks of mutton in a spicy, creamy sauce RM8. *Gulab jamun* (fried milk balls soaked in sweet syrup) make a good dessert (RM3). Service charge and government tax 15%. Open daily 11:30am-3pm and 6:30-10:30pm.

Reggae Club, 483 Lebuh Chulia (tel. 261 50 81), just off Jl. Penang. It is hard to see the club, but listen for the booming bass. Reggae Club serves up burgers, hot dogs, spaghetti, and fried rice, but most tempting are the iced beer mugs. Grab a booth, browse travelogues, and decide whether you'll dred those unkempt locks. Average meal RM10. Open daily 2pm-2am.

Restoran Kassim Mustafa, 12 Lebuh Chulia (tel. 263 45 92). From the ferry, Kassim is on a corner on the right side of the road before Lebuh Pitt. One of the better Indian Muslim coffee-shop-style restaurants in Georgetown. *Nasi kandor* or *roti canai* make scrumptious morning meals; later, fresh curries are ladled from huge saucepans onto plates of rice. Mr. Yasin, the owner, is reputed for his eponymous

© 1996 AT&T.

Someone back home *really* misses you.
Please call.

With **AT&T Direct**℠ Service it's easy to call back to the States from virtually anywhere your travels take you. Just dial the **AT&T Direct** Access Number for the country *you are in* from the chart below. You'll have English-language voice prompts or an AT&T Operator to guide your call. And our clearest,* fastest connections** will help you reach whoever it is that misses you most back home.

AUSTRIA● 022-903-011	GREECE● 00-800-1311	NETHERLANDS● ...06-022-9111
BELGIUM● 0-800-100-10	INDIA✖ 000-117	RUSSIA●▲♪ (Moscow).755-5042
CZECH REP▲ ...00-42-000-101	IRELAND 1-800-550-000	SPAIN ◇ 900-99-00-11
DENMARK.................8001-0010	ISRAEL...............177-100-2727	SWEDEN...............020-795-611
FRANCE...............0 800 99 0011	ITALY● 172-1011	SWITZERLAND● ..0-800-550011
GERMANY.................0130-0010	MEXICO 95-800-462-4240	U.K.▲ 0800-89-0011

Can't find the Access Number for the country you're calling from? Just ask any operator for AT&T Direct Service.

Photo: R. Olken

Greetings from LET'S GO

With pen and notebook in hand, a change of clothes in our backpack, and the tightest of budgets, we've spent our summer roaming the globe in search of travel bargains.

We've put the best of our research into the book that you're now holding. Our intrepid researcher-writers went on the road for months of exploration, from Anchorage to Angkor, Estonia to Ecuador, Iceland to India. Editors worked from spring to fall, massaging copy into witty and informative prose. A brand-new edition of each guide hits the shelves every fall, just months after it is researched, so you know you're getting the most reliable, up-to-date, and comprehensive information available.

We try to make this book an indispensable companion, but sometimes the best discoveries are the ones you make on your own. If you've got something to share, please drop us a line. We're Let's Go Publications, 67 Mount Auburn Street, Cambridge, MA 02138 USA (e-mail: fanmail@letsgo.com). Good luck and happy travels!

Yasin *teh-tarik*, the boiled milk tea that they pour from cup to cup to cool (RM0.60). No alcohol served. Most meals RM4-5. Open 5:30am-11:30pm.

SIGHTS

Walk along Jl. Macalister to get a glimpse of grand old colonial mansions, some of them in picturesque ruins and others converted into shops. A fit of nostalgia for the imperial past might take you to **Fort Cornwallis** at the northeastern tip of Georgetown. A small museum recounts founder Captain Francis Light's acquisition of Penang from the Sultan of Kedah in 1786. Of more interest, however, is the lore regarding the "Big Cannon" and "Floating Cannon," neither of which are associated with military merit but instead serve as the centerpiece of fertility rites. (Open daily 8:30am-7pm; admission RM1.)

From the fort continue down Lebuh Light away from the jetty. Making a left onto Lebuh Pitt leads to **St. George's Church,** on the corner with Lebuh Farquhar. In an uneasy coexistence with its tropical surroundings, the austere church represents the vanguard of Anglicanism in Malaysia. Sunday service is in English. (Open Tues.-Sat. 8:30am-4:30pm and all day Sun.) Next door to the church on Lebuh Farquhar is Dewan Sri Penang, a large modern behemoth which houses the **Penang State Art Gallery** (2nd floor), the **Penang Public Library** (3rd floor), and the **Penang State Museum.** The Art Gallery rotates exhibitions of photographs and paintings of local and international interest. The State Museum displays historic memorabilia and exhibits on Penang's social history. (Open Mon.-Thurs. and Sat.-Sun. 9am-5pm; free.)

Backtrack down Lebuh Farquhar and turn right onto Lebuh Pitt/Jl. Masjid Kapitan Keling. At the end of the block, on the corner with Lorong Stewart, stands **Kuan Yin Teng Temple,** the oldest Chinese temple on Penang. Built in 1800, this temple is devoted to the Buddhist Goddess of Mercy, who is also associated with fertility and good fortune. The courtyard in front is clouded with smoke from burning incense, "spirit money," and joss sticks, while inside, saffron-clad monks ring prayer bells.

Continue down Lebuh Pitt/Jl. Masjid Kapitan Keling to the back of the Hindu **Sri Mariamman Temple,** on the left just before the intersection with Lebuh Chulia. See the front of the temple one block over on Lebuh Queen. This temple reflects traditional South Indian architecture adapted to the present locale. Lord Shiva and his consort Parvati preside over this practicing temple, which also shelters the Shrine of the Nine Planets. **Masjid Kapitan Keling** is another must-see on the imperialist trail. From Sri Mariamman Temple cross Lebuh Chulia and walk one more block down Jl. Masjid Kapitan Keling. Built in the late 1700s by the troops of the British East India Company, it was the first mosque in Penang.

Walking farther down Jl. Masjid Kapitan Keling will bring you to **Khoo Konggi,** a Chinese meeting house/temple tucked away in an alley between Armenian Street and Lebuh Aceh. The Hokkien *Khoo* or Mandarin *Qui* clan *konggi* was originally built in 1835 for the worship of the Khoo's patron saint, Tua Sai Yeah, and to provide for the welfare of clan members recently arrived in Penang. The *konggi* is but one type of association hall: others include the *huiguau*, the *cháo*, and the *cí*, guild and surname associations which are found in great quantity in the northeast part of Georgetown. (Open Mon.-Fri. 9am-5pm, Sat. 9am-1pm; free.)

West on the main road to Batu Ferringhi is a peaceful, low-walled **cemetery** on Jl. Sultan Ahmad Shah, not more than 1km past the intersection with Jl. Penang. Georgetown's founder, Francis Light, is buried here along with countless other colonial officials. Out of walking distance but accessible by MPPP city bus #2 is **Wat Chayamang Kalaram,** a Thai Buddhist temple just off the main road to Batu Ferringhi on Lorong Burma (not to be confused with Jl. Burma). The reclining Buddha is the largest in Malaysia and reputedly the third largest in the world.

■ Teluk Bahang

Slightly beyond Batu Ferringhi lies Teluk Bahang, where the roosters are audible above the flatulent mopeds and the livestock outnumber the convenience stores.

Rickety piers extend far into the bay and fishing boats are a household item. The batik factory lays huge reams of cloth out to dry on the grass of the public park and the Butterfly Farm's collection of creepy crawlies and butterflies attract a large crowd. Tank up on water and walk along the coast to Pantai Acheh Forest Reserve or check out the Forest Park. Stay in Teluk Bahang for a few days and you will be on a first-name basis with most of its laid-back populace. To get there take blue bus #93 from Lebuh Chulia or KOMTAR (45min.).

ACCOMMODATIONS

Rama's Guest House, 365 Mk. 2 (tel. 885 11 79). Coming from Batu Ferringhi, turn right at the traffic circle in Teluk Bahang. Rama's is not easily visible, so keep an eye out for the faded "Guest House" sign about 100m down Jl. Teluk Awak. Rama's has shared bathrooms, showers, kitchen, 1 dorm (RM7), and 2 rooms (RM14). Groups or families might want to consider Rama's newest addition, a fully furnished 2-bedroom flat with bath, kitchen, and TV (RM60).

Miss Loh's Guest House, turn left at the Teluk Bahang traffic circle, continue for 500m and take the first right. Miss Loh's is immediately after the bridge on the left but has no sign. During business hours, contact Ms. Loh at her convenience store, Kwong Tuck Hing, 150 Jl. Teluk Bahang (tel. 885 12 27), right next to the bus stop at the traffic circle. Miss Loh has been in business for 21 years. Rooms lack fans but the surrounding garden's shade compensates. Common toilets and showers. Rates negotiable. Dorms RM9. Singles RM15-20. Cottages RM30-40.

FOOD

The main center for food is immediately before the traffic circle on Teluk Bahang as you enter town. Fare is simple but good and cheap with most meals under RM5. There is a collection of food stalls on Jl. Teluk Bahang about 500m through the traffic circle which has *koay teow* and *roti/martabak* for under RM1.50. Guests at Rama's or Miss Loh's who plan to cook can take advantage of a large market for fruits, veggies, and meat located on the left just beyond the public park on Jl. Teluk Bahang.

Sun Stall (tel. 885 14 69), on the right side of the main road just before the traffic circle. A Malay and Indian Muslim Restaurant serving *nasi biryani* (saffron rice, RM1), *chaw koay teow* (fried flat rice noodles, RM1.80), *ayam goreng* (fried chicken, RM2), as well as some "western" items. Plenty of curries to choose from; just point and eat. Open Mon.-Thurs. and Sat.-Sun. 7am-10pm, Fri. 7am-1:30pm.

Restoran Ibrahim, a Muslim restaurant just to the left of Miss Loh's store. Offers standard Malay dishes for low prices. Full meal of *roti/nasi, paying rendang,* and an iced Milo for about RM2.

Yellow Point Restaurant (tel. 885 16 68), directly on the traffic circle. A new addition to the local scene, this place serves up Chinese dishes in a moderate price range. Menu includes some "exotic" meals, such as black pepper venison (RM10), claypot bean curd (RM5), and the classic Taiwanese shark's fin soup (RM50). A wide range of seafood available at market prices. Draft and imported beer, mixed drinks. Open daily 11am-3pm, 6-9pm.

■ Island Sights

Heading west from Georgetown along the north coast, visitors will see signs directing them to the **Botanical Garden,** a pleasant forested park hugely popular with the locals for picnics and exercise. Trees from all around the world grow here, and there are special pavilions devoted to specific greenery. Monkeys roam, although visitors have recently been forbidden from feeding them. The park is generally crowded all the time but most people don't stray far from the entrance and the main paths; you might want to. Early morning or late afternoon are the best times to visit, as it is not too hot. Take MPPP city bus #7, or signs along the main road will lead you there easily if you're going solo.

Near Teluk Bahang are the Penang Butterfly Farm and the Pantai Acheh Forest Reserve. The **Penang Butterfly Farm** is at 830, Mk. 2, Jl. Teluk Bahang (tel. 811 253). Coming from Batu Ferringhi, turn left at the traffic circle and continue for about 1km. First on the left is the Butterfly Farm where tanks simulating natural habitats enclose a horrific variety of exotic creepy crawlies, including giant millipedes, giant black scorpions, and dragon-headed beetles. Yes, the emphasis is on the grotesque and deadly, but the large greenhouse garden also shelters hundreds of species of butterflies, frogs, toads, and ducks. (Open Mon.-Fri. 9am-5pm, weekends and holidays 9am-6pm; admission RM5.)

About 10km down the road toward Batik Pulau is **Air Terjung Kerawang** (Kerawang Waterfall), which is not a very impressive sight nor one easily accessible by bus. Durians and other fruits for picnics can be had at the **Durian Orchards** just a short walk away. The treasured spheres are supported by pink and green strings lest a gust of wind fell them prematurely.

Hard-core nature enthusiasts can satisfy sylvan urges at the **Pantai Acheh Forest Reserve.** The trail begins at the End of the World Restaurant. To get there, follow the road along the north coast in Teluk Bahang. From the trailhead, walk for about 30 minutes to a campsite with a wooden shelter near a swaying footbridge. At this campsite, the trail forks. To the right, it leads to a **lighthouse** at the northwest tip of the island; the left trail goes to **Keracut Beach,** where there are more camping facilities. You might want to consider bringing your own food if you plan to camp at any of the sites, which tend to be crowded with local campers.

The hike to the lighthouse is quite an adventure and often downright treacherous, but should take no longer than two hours. Those who take the hike should bring plenty of drinking water. Beginning at the campsite, the trail is pretty good until you reach the first beach, where there is a biological field station and a dock. In the next patch of forest, the path becomes dangerous: broken walkways traverse huge boulders and I-can-see-hell-at-the-bottom crevices. Twisting roots and hanging vines assist travelers in bridging these crumbling chasms. The most dangerous part of the trail has been marked with white squares of paper pointing out the best way to climb.

When the white squares end, the roughest part is over. The trail then spills out over more boulders onto an empty, undeveloped beach approached only by day-trippers on boats. The path resumes just beyond the abandoned bungalow at the end of the beach. A rusty, out-of-date Do Not Enter sign depicts a cop shooting a trespasser, but hikers now go up the crumbling asphalt trail to the lighthouse without crossing the law. The lighthouse keeper lives alone at the top; he'll let travelers in, give them water, and maybe even take them to the top for a view of the island.

From Ayer Itam, one can walk to **Kek Lok Si Temple,** the largest Buddhist temple in Malaysia and an impressive work of Chinese Buddhist architecture. The steps leading up to it are either surreal or annoying, depending on your mood and energy level. The peaceful sanctuaries here are nirvana compared to the mayhem passed en route. Remember to take off your shoes at the central sanctuary and do not take pictures of the monks, although other photography is permitted. In the stunning main sanctuary, thousands of Buddhas on individual platforms line the walls, and deities fly about the ceiling in colorful relief.

A funicular (every 30min. or 15min. in late afternoon, 6:30am-midnight) climbs 740m up **Penang Hill,** which offers great views of Georgetown, especially at sunset on a clear day. The trip up the hill may take 45 minutes, but you can stop halfway to take a gander at the estates of the rubber plantation owners of old. The Crag Hotel at the top, built by the Sarkies Brothers (who also built the Raffles Hotel in Singapore), is now a government-run tourist attraction. You can take red bus #8 from Ayer Itam, or walk five minutes to Penang Hill Station, where locals can direct you.

Although diappointing overall, you should probably see the **Snake Temple,** if only because in your travels in the rest of Malaysia everyone will ask you whether you went here while on Penang. Sleepy, defanged vipers are obviously a bit burnt out on the incense smoldering at the temple of the Azure Cloud. If it's any incentive, admis-

MALAYSIA

sion is free and snake vitality and population are said to vary by season. To get there, you can take yellow bus #66.

PULAU LANGKAWI

No longer a happy hunting ground for budget travelers, Langkawi is a sparsely populated island which has been subjected to the worst of all possible fates: a government policy to promote tourism. As a result, hulking resort hotels squat expectantly all over the island, their armies of personnel standing idle. Meanwhile, Thai, Bangladeshi, and even Albanian workers have been imported to complete the infrastructure deemed necessary to accommodate the expected torrent of incoming guests. Rapid development has changed Langkawians from farmers to cab drivers, but it has yet to have a significant impact on their relaxed attitudes toward life. Little wonder; the sultry climes and warm green waters skirting Langkawi have the ability to assuage the moral agency of even the most dedicated monkeywrencher.

Arriving at the jetty in Kuah, one's primary impression of the island is colored by what appears to be a gargantuan chickenhawk, actually the mythical *garuda* bird said to nest in the islands. Such a beginning makes it difficult for the tourist to swallow Langkawi's other "legends," many of which are blatantly contrived. The mainstay of local story telling is that about the lovely Mahsuri Bunti Pandala Mayak, daughter-in-law of the island's chieftan and representative to the Sultan of Kedah. Wrongly accused of adultery by her jealous mother-in-law and sentenced to death, she was tied to a tamarind tree and stabbed with her own spear. To the amazement of the spectators, white blood gushed forth from her body, symbolizing her innocence. In her dying breaths she uttered a curse banning prosperity from the island for seven generations.

Indeed, over the next 200 years the island was subject to Thai and Acehnese marauders, crop failure, and little economic activity...until now. With the seven generations now passed, Langkawi is undergoing a spectacular transformation from haunted fisherman's outpost to breathtaking island treasure. Although Langkawi's economy has boomed as a result of tourism, the increased traffic and environmental desperation brought on by development are now causing islanders to reassess their definitions of prosperity.

GETTING THERE AND AWAY

Kuah, Langkawi's main town, is accessible by boat from Kuala Perlis and Kuala Kedah on the mainland, and from Pulau Penang to the south. Boats also arrive at Kuah from Satun, the southernmost town on the west coast of Thailand. Kuala Perlis is reachable by **bus** from **Kangar,** on the mainland (every 30min., RM0.80), and **Butterworth** (11am, 2, 4, and 6pm, RM6.20).

Ferries run to Langkawi from: **Kuala Kedah** (7 per day, 8am-6:45pm, 1hr., RM15); **Kuala Perlis** (11 per day, 7:20am-6:20pm, 45min., RM12); **Penang** (8am and 6pm, 2½hr., RM35); and **Satun** (8:30, 10am, 2, and 5pm, 1¼hr., RM18). Other islands off Langkawi are accessible only from the main island and for a handsome price. If you get stuck in Kuala Perlis because you missed the last ferry over, the only place to stay is **Pens Hotel** (tel. (04) 985 41 22), on Jl. Kuala Perlis, the main road in town. Singles go for RM63-81, doubles RM75-93. A/C singles with bath are RM57-63.

MAS (tel. (03) 746 30 00) offers flights to **Kuala Lumpur** (6 per day, 8am-7:45pm), **Penang** (4 per day, 10:30am-6:40pm), and **Singapore** (9:30am and 12:15pm). Langkawi airport is at Padang Matsirat, about 20km from Kuah and 7km from Pantai Cenang. Flat taxi fare from the airport to Pantai Cenang is RM10.

ISLAND ORIENTATION

The Langkawi island group consists of 99 islands off the northwest corner of Peninsular Malaysia, only three of which are inhabited. The main island is Langkawi, and visi-

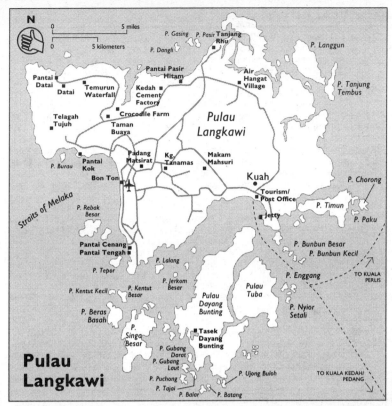

N

0   5 miles
0   5 kilometers

P. Gasing
P. Pasir Tanjang Rhu
P. Dangli
P. Langgun

Pantai Pasir Hitam
Air Hangat Village
P. Tanjung Tembus

Pantai Datai
Datai
Temurun Waterfall
Kedah Cement Factory
Pulau Langkawi

Telagah Tujuh
Crocodile Farm
Taman Buaya

P. Burau
Padang Matsirat
Kg Tanamas
Makam Mahsuri

Pantai Kok
Bon Ton
Kuah
P. Chorong

Straits of Melaka
Tourism/ Post Office
P. Timun
P. Paku

P. Rebak Besar
Jetty

Pantai Cenang
Pantai Tengah
P. Bunbun Besar
P. Bunbun Kecil

P. Tepor
P. Lalang
P. Enggang
TO KUALA PERLIS

P. Kentut Kecil
P. Kentut Besar
P. Jerkun Besar
Pulau Dayang Bunting
Pulau Tuba
P. Nyior Setali

P. Beras Basah
P. Singa Besar
Tasek Dayang Bunting

Pulau Langkawi

P. Gubang Darat
P. Gubang Laut
P. Puchong
P. Ujong Buloh
TO KUALA KEDAH/ PEDANG

P. Tajai
P. Balar
P. Batang

tors arrive at the port town of Kuah in the southeast corner of the island. The roads are excellent, making it easy to get around Langkawi on your own; motorbikes are an efficient choice. Every intersection is well marked with direction boards, so it is almost impossible to get lost. There are public buses trundling around the island, but they run very infrequently and almost never on schedule. Taxis are ubiquitous and their high prices are mostly fixed.

The popular beaches that host most of the accommodations are **Pantai Cenang** and **Pantai Kok** on the southwest corner and west side of the island, respectively. **Pantai Tengah,** immediately south of Pantai Cenang, also provides accommodations. On the north end of Langkawi, sights include **Teluk Datai, Air Terjun Temurun waterfall,** the **crocodile farm, Tanjung Rhu** beach, and the fabricated **Air Hangat Village. Mahsuri's tomb** is in the center of the island near Kuah, and **Telaga Tujuh waterfall** is near Pantai Kok.

■ Kuah

The town of Kuah lays claim to *chendol* hawkers, a duty-free Harley Davidson dealership, and Langkawi's only traffic light. Muddy streets clotted with traffic criss-cross Kuah, lined with endless rows of identical stalls selling loud t-shirts and chartreuse Garfield monstrosities. Astute travelers go west to Pantai Cenang and Pantai Kok which have almost all of the services offered in Kuah such as laundry, shopping, and money-changing. The taxi fare from the jetty to any part of Kuah is RM4.

PRACTICAL INFORMATION

Tourist Offices: (tel. 966 77 89), on Persiaran Putra. Coming from the jetty into Kuah, it's on the left side. Helpful staff. Open daily 9am-6pm.

Currency Exchange: Money changers can be found all over Kuah. There are banks on Jl. Pandak Mayah; turn right off Jl. Persiaran Putra, across from the taxi stand. Outside of Kuah, Padang Matsirat has money changers.

Buses: Langkawi's bus system is useless and schedules are never kept. The best way to get around is via motorbike. The bus station is across from the hospital on Jl. Kisap, the main road leading north. Ask around and maybe you'll get lucky. To **Pantai Cenang** (6 per day, 9:10am-4:40pm, RM0.70) and **Pantai Kok** (4 per day, 8:10am-4:40pm, RM1.70).

Ferries: To: **Kuala Perlis** (5 per day, 8am-6pm, 45min., RM12); **Kuala Kedah** (4 per day, noon-7pm, 1¼hr., RM15); **Penang** (6:30pm, 2½hr., RM35); and **Satun, Thailand** (9:30am, 12:45 and 3:30pm, 1hr., RM18).

Taxis: All fares are fixed. From the jetty to Kuah town is RM4. To **Pantai Cenang** (RM12) and **Pantai Kok** (RM16).

Rentals: Car rentals at most major resort hotels for about RM80-100 per day.

Markets: The big **pasar malam** (night market) on Langkawi changes location nightly, rotating between towns: Padang, Matsirat, Ulu Melaka, Kedawang, Kuah, Air Hangat, and Kuala Teriang. **Kualis hawker center** on Jl. Padang Matsirat near the center of town also transforms daily into a night market.

Pharmacies: MNY Multi-Pharmacy, 102 Persiaran Mutiara, Pusat Dagangan Kelana Mas (tel. 966 00 66). From the jetty, on the left side as you enter the detour to the left off the main road. Open daily 9am-11pm.

Medical Services: Hospital (tel. 966 63 33), on Jl. Leboh Kisap on the corner of the main road and Jl. Langgar Kisap.

Emergency: tel. 999

Police: (tel. 966 62 22), on Jl. Leboh Kisap across from the hospital.

Post Offices: (tel. 966 27 21), 500m before the tourist office on the right side of Persiaran Putra. The only one on the island. Open Mon.-Thurs. and Sat.-Sun. 8am-5pm, Fri. 8am-noon. **Postal code:** 07000.

Telephones: Telekom office, Jl. Pandak Mayah 6 (tel. 966 61 91), a few blocks off the main road. Open Sat.-Wed. 8:30am-4:30pm, Thurs. 8:30am-1:15pm. IDD calls from public phones. **Telephone code:** 04.

ACCOMMODATIONS

Budget travelers staying in Kuah must search long and hard for unremarkable rooms at about RM20. Kuah is not especially aesthetically pleasing—if possible, you might want to stay elsewhere on the island.

Hotel Langkawi, 6-8 Persiaran Putra (tel. 966 62 48). Clean, friendly, and near the tourist office, it's a convenient place to shack up for the night. All rooms have fan and separate bath. Singles RM20. Doubles RM30. Triples RM37. An attached bath, A/C, and TV costs RM45 for 2 single beds and RM55 for 1 double and 1 single bed.

Hotel Malaysia and Restaurant, 66 Jl. Mahsuri (tel. 966 62 98). Take Jl. Padang Matsirat out of Kuah and turn left after the Grand Continental Hotel. Cheap, clean rooms. Singles RM25, with A/C RM30. Triples RM35. Quads RM50. Branch at 39 Pusat Masmeyer (tel. 966 80 87), 100m down on the opposite side of Jl. Mahsuri.

FOOD

Few of Kuah's restaurants are worthy of special mention, and all charge inflated prices. The best and cheapest food is at the hawker center at the intersection of Jl. Ayer Hansat and Persiaran Putra, incidentally home to the famed traffic light.

Sari Seafood (tel. 966 61 92), on Jl. Putra. Attracting Langkawi islanders as well as droves of German and Japanese tourists, this seaside restaurant serves mostly Chinese seafood dishes in the middle price range (RM10-15). Local noodle dishes in the café go for RM2-3. Breezy open-air area location looks out on Kuah Bay. The

wide variety of dishes and extensive dessert menu make this Kuah's most worthwhile restaurant.

■ Pantai Cenang

Located in the southwest corner of Langkawi Island, Pantai Cenang achieves a balance between the dusty t-shirt stands of Kuah and the uniformly mediocre food and
lodgings of Pantai Kok. Among Pantai Cenang's inhabitants, the aimlessly wandering
cattle are the most dissatisfied with the unrelenting land development. Displaced
from their pastures by a runway extension and countless luxury resorts, these hapless
bovines have resorted to grazing by the roadsides. Savvy tourists courteously yield the
sidewalk to these vagrant lummoxes or face a displacement of their own. Accommodations and food are the best on the island, motorbike and car rentals abound, and
the town's location allows daytrips to every part of Langkawi. The beach itself is
pleasant and the water warm and green, if a bit murky. Exploring the mud flats and
sandbars that appear when the tide recedes in the late afternoon and at sunset makes
for a pleasant interlude.

ACCOMMODATIONS

Sam's Place (Dolphin Village Motel), 17 Rumah Sewa Haji Saad (tel. 955 52 60).
Coming from Kuah, continue past AB Motel for 500m and take the small paved
road which leads to the right. The friendliness and cleanliness found here far surpass most hotels in town and more than make up for the lack of beachfront. Dorms
RM8, only RM2 if you plan to stay for a month (pay in advance). Singles with fan
and bathroom RM30. The best rooms are in the old Malay house.

AB Motel (tel. 955 13 00), 1km from the intersection of Lebuh Pantai Cenang and
the road from Kuah. Wooden huts on the beach are clean but rather hot under
their metal roofs. Huts with fan and bath RM40. A/C huts across the street away
from the beach RM70. No alcohol allowed in the café, which has cheap Malay fare
for around RM3. Island hopping tours offered for RM30.

Twenty Twenty Chalet and Restaurant, Lot No. 2014, Jl. Lebuh Pantai Cenang
(tel. 955 28 06), 200m east of AB Motel, across from the road from the beach.
Immaculate huts have presentable carpeting and writing desks. Twenty Twenty
also remains the only budget hotel which offers authentic toilet paper and blankets. Dorm beds in the long house for 1 or 2 people RM25, for 3 RM35, for 4 RM40.
Huts with fan and bath RM35, with A/C RM70. Outside, the restaurant prepares
tasty Thai seafood dishes and a mean barbecued chicken (chicken *percik*).

Delta Motel (tel. 955 22 53), the last place on the beach before the rocky headland
dividing Pantai Cenang from Pantai Tengah. Restaurant, car rental, boat tours, and
motorbike rental all on the premises. Clean huts on the beach (with fan, shower,
and toilet RM35, with A/C and hot water RM65) and a longhouse with somewhat
cramped quads farther from the beach (with fan, toilet, and shower RM50).

FOOD

Bon Ton at the Beach (tel. 955 36 43), on Jl. Pantai Cenang, past Pelangi Beach
Resort on the way to Pantai Kok. Upscale restaurant and gallery serving *nyonya/*
New Californian cuisine. Cool open dining area with marble-topped tables and
cane chairs once offered a view of pristine beach but now looks out on the construction of an airport runway extension. Nonetheless, if you are looking for
scrumptious food and desserts, try the Langkawi Special: *nasi ulam*, chicken *percik*, spring roll, pumpkin in coconut curry, chicken *tom yam*, and mango *kerabu*
(RM28). Open daily for lunch 12-3pm, tea 3-7pm, dinner 7-10:30pm.

Cenang Seafood Restaurant (tel. 955 41 28). Cheap Chinese-owned seafood joint.
Framed lobsters the size of small dogs provide the only decor. The Pacific clams
with dry chili (RM18), black pepper chicken (RM10), and Cenang bean curd (RM7)
will compensate for the lack of ambiance with savory sauces and flavors all too
often missing from Chinese food on the island. Open daily 11am-3pm and 6pm-
11pm. Menu is in English, German, and Chinese.

Breakfast Bar (tel. 840 02 06). You won't really know Langkawi until you visit this popular morning hangout, about 100m from AB Motel in the direction of Pantai Kok. All local business owners and a sprinkling of expats gravitate here each morning to gossip and recover from last night's bender. Cheapest American breakfast in town (RM5) and brewed coffee.

The Tree (tel. 449 97 64), entrance to this German restaurant/bar located right next to Twenty Twenty Chalet. Set in a former cashew plantation and features a beautiful chainsaw-hewn bar. Famous for having the biggest and tastiest steaks on the island (RM21.50). Small but delectable menu may also include items such as Shark stew (RM17.50). Open daily 7pm-1am.

ENTERTAINMENT

Think duty-free liquor and your picture of Cenang nightlife will be complete. Anthropologists may leave their ledgers at home, for entertainment here comprises naught but canned beer and other such pre-packaged wantonness.

Oasis Bar and Restaurant (tel. 955 31 90), on Jl. Pantai Tengah. Turn right at the end of Jl. Pantai Cenang at its border with Pantai Tengah. The best-stocked bar in town and fancy mixed drinks for around RM7.50. Three food stalls also serve up food for about RM3. The management is friendly and proficient in the politics of land development on Langkawi. Come before the government turns it into a caddy-shack. Open daily approximately 6pm-2am.

■ Pantai Kok

Pantai Kok's small but beautiful beach, located in the western corner of Langkawi, is already showing signs of environmental degradation. Whether it was the curse of Mahsuri or the Sheraton Inn on a nearby hillside which brought catastrophe to this strip of sand, we may never know. Pantai Kok nevertheless remains one of Langkawi's most isolated beaches, separated from Pantai Cenang by a 30-minute motorbike ride or a RM16 taxi fare, and is definitely worth a day trip. To get there, follow the signs to Burau Bay and Telaga Tujuh.

ACCOMMODATIONS AND FOOD

Entrepreneurs in this village were quick in realizing the business potential of their backhoe-free environs and have accordingly built several inexpensive hotels to accommodate budget travelers. Unfortunately, little energy is expended on upkeep and prices continue to rise. Food is nothing to write home about and compares unfavorably with Pantai Cenang fare.

The best place in town is the **Last Resort** (tel. 955 10 46), on Jl. Teluk Burau. Thatch-roofed wooden huts on the beach are attractive but rather dank. Rooms in longhouse with fan are RM30. Single chalets with fan go for RM35-40, with A/C RM55. Huts for two to four people with A/C cost RM80. The attached restaurant/bar remains the most pleasant establishment on the beach. Right next to the Last Resort is **Country Beach Motel and Restaurant** (tel. 955 12 12), which is definitely a compromise in comparison. Rooms in longhouse with fan and separate bath cost RM18. Single chalets with fan go for RM30, with A/C RM65.

The Original Jungle Bar at the Beach, located behind the Mila Beach Resort, is the poor cousin of its counterparts in Pantai Cenang. Due to its status as the only beach bar on Pantai Kok, however, it has become a fixture of backpacker life here. Most beers cost RM2. The extensive menu ranges from peanuts to fried squid (RM1-6), fried eggs and chips (RM3), seafood *tom yam* with rice (RM7), and a broad selection or seafood and curry dishes (RM6-18).

■ Island Sights

There's little to see in Kuah, but the rest of the island is full of lovely beaches and waterfalls. Traveling around the island is simple, thanks to the excellent roads, signs, and minimal traffic outside of Kuah. Heading west from Kuah, one of the first sights of interest is **Mahsuri's Grave** *(Makam Mahsuri)*, on Rte. 118 off the main road from Kuah (Rte. 112), opposite the Langkawi Island Golf Club. After the turn-off, keep an eye out for the patch of road whose original marble pavement is intact. The grave of Mahsuri is quite a tourist event. Remove shoes before entering the mausoleum or house. (Open daily 8am-6:30pm; admission RM1).

Heading northeast from Pantai Kok, a left on the road leading to Teluk Datai leads to the **Crocodile Adventureland** (Taman Buaya) (tel. 959 25 59), about 2km up. Don't expect a touchy-feely natural habitat experience—the gift shop sells crocodile skins, oil, and sundry other croc products. The park, or rather, farm, houses 15 ponds of crocodiles of various species. Signs in several languages exhort visitors not to miss the "action" at the mating pond. (Open daily 9am-6pm; admission RM6.)

Continuing toward Teluk Datai will lead past **Pantai Pasir Tengkorak** and **Air Terjun Temurun** (Temurun Waterfall). This route affords excellent views of rocky beaches and a serene bay dotted with tiny breadloaf islands. **Teluk Datai** is home to a golf course (one of two on the island) and two large, highbrow resorts. A short drive after the golf course through the stands of primeval Dr. Seuss trees leads to a quiet spot where travelers can associate with their monkey brethren and follow a path down to the water's edge.

Northwest of Pantai Kok is **Telaga Tujuh,** the Seven Wells Waterfall. While the 20-minute hike is steep and dangerously dehydrating during the dry season, a splendid view of the waterfall can be found at its bottom, less than 300m from the starting point. For the more adventurous, the full hike affords spectacular views of Langkawi, refreshing swims in the fall's seven wells, and close contact with the monkeys. In Malaysia's dry summer months, however, the waterfall dries up and becomes a hangout for local ne'er-do-wells. Donkey rides are also available (RM10). (Parking charge: RM1 per car and RM0.50 per motorbike.)

The clearest water and best **snorkeling** are to be had on the smaller islands south of Langkawi. Many hotels along Pantai Cenang arrange four-hour island-hopping tours for RM30-45. Tours leave at 9:30am and 2:30pm, and feature snorkeling around Pulau Beras Basah, the wildlife park on Pulau Singa Besar, and the Lake of the Pregnant Maiden on Pulau Dayang Bunting. Snorkeling gear is provided. Many of the hotels also offer watersports such as water-skiing and jet-skiing. The northern shore, one of Langkawi's most secluded areas, offers a pleasant drive. Rocky outcrops, beaches, and untouched villages line this stretch of road.

CAMERON HIGHLANDS

The few cow towns that make up the Cameron Highlands have long provided a cool retreat for homesick Brits, and these days for natty local execs from the turbid atmosphere of low-lying Kuala Lumpur. Flocks of tourists, however, have not marred the lush vistas or hospitable personality of this remote corner of Pahang state. Named after William Cameron, a government surveyor who charted the region in 1885, the Cameron Highlands remain a cheap and convenient place for the burned out to recharge wanderlust and explore the surrounding jungle in relative isolation. Cool mornings and low humidity inspire jungle walks, which snake for miles around the hillsides of the Highlands. So enchanting are these woods that American silk tycoon Jim Thompson ventured for a stroll in 1967 and was never seen again (see **Missing: One Silk Magnate. Answers to Jim.** on page 487).

Outside the jungle walls, resourceful farmers have carved terraced vegetable and strawberry farms from the steeply contoured land, while vast tea plantations supply most of the pekoe tea consumed by the lowlanders. Land Rovers are the agricultural vehicle of choice, and farmers can be seen coaxing them along with loads of vegetables and fertilizer in tow. The overall effect is very nostalgic and one finds that recent construction of condominiums in the area is not as jarring as it might be, due to strict government regulations of the pace and character of new development.

There are three towns in the Cameron Highlands; in increasing distance from Tapah they are Ringlet, Tanah Rata, and Brinchang. Brinchang is the biggest of the three, but Tanah Rata is the main town with most of the facilities. Ringlet is the lowest and least convenient of the towns.

■ Tanah Rata

Nestled in the clouds 14km farther than Ringlet and about 8km before Brinchang, Tanah Rata is reached only by way of an infamously hair-raising ride along a steep and winding road. This same road becomes Tanah Rata's main drag, with a monopoly on the main facilities of the Cameron Highlands—many of which offer bargains to the budget traveler. The street can be busy and noisy, but things quiet down just outside the developed area in the environs of Tanah Rata's cozy guest houses.

ORIENTATION

On the right side of the road stand the **bus station** and numerous **Malay food stalls,** while the left side of the road fronts restaurants, hotels, and shops. Everything in town lies within a stone's throw of everything else. Past the main part of town the road continues up to Bala's Holiday Chalets 2km away and then onto Brinchang.

PRACTICAL INFORMATION

Tourist Offices: Tanah Rata Tourist Bureau, on the main road coming from Tapah, next to Tandoori Restaurant at the beginning of town. The small, white building has no identifying sign, but has a small library and plenty of information. Hours are arbitrary, especially during the off-season.

Currency Exchange: Hong Kong Bank, 31-32 main road (tel. 491 12 17). Open Mon.-Fri. 10am-3pm, Sat. 9:30-11:30am. **Maybank,** 20-21 main road (tel. 491 16 16). Open Mon.-Fri. 9:30am-4pm, Sat. 9:30-11:30am.

Buses: From the station halfway down the main road, the **Regal Transport Co.** (tel. 901 485) operates local routes. To: **Tapah** (9 per day, 8am-5:30pm, RM3.50, A/C RM3.70); **Boh Tea Estate** (10, 11am, 1:30, 5pm); and **Brinchang** (every hr., 6:40am-6:45pm, RM0.50). Express buses to **KL** (8:30, 10:30am, 1:30pm, RM10.10) and **Penang** (8:30am, 2:30pm, RM14.10).

Taxis: Next to the bus station. RM15 per hour (max. 2hr.). To **Brinchang** (RM3).

Markets: Both the **day market** and the **Saturday night market** are less than interesting. Coming from the bus station, go left on the main road and turn right at the Federal Hotel. The market is on the left.

Medical Services: (tel. 491 19 66), past the row of shops on the left side of the main road. During office hours (8am-4:15pm), patients should check in at the registration room. **24-hr. emergency room.**

Emergency: tel. 999

Police: (tel. 491 12 22), just past the hospital upon leaving the main part of town.

Post Offices: (tel. 491 10 51), on the shop side of the main road near the Oriental Hotel. Open Mon.-Sat. 8am-4:30pm. **Postal code:** 39000.

Telephones: There is no Telekom office, but Telekom cardphones are available all over town. **Telephone code:** 05.

ACCOMMODATIONS

The best bet in Tanah Rata is to choose among one of the many family-run, reasonably priced guest houses. Nearly all provide attractive services, including bus reservations to major destinations in Malaysia, international phone service, hot water (you'll need it up here), kitchen facilities, and tourist information.

Father's Guest House, P.O. Box 15 (tel. 491 24 84). Walk out of town in the direction of Ringlet, cross the small bridge, and take the first left. Stairs on the left lead up to this former monastic army barracks which now houses some of the most pampered backpackers in Malaysia. Free movies, hot showers, cheap meals, and information boards available. Dorms RM6. Large doubles RM16, with bath and shower RM25. Lower rates for longer stays.

Twin Pines Chalet, 2 Jl. Mentigi (tel. 491 21 69). Heading from the bus station in the direction of Ringlet, take the first left. Close to town, cheap, and clean, Twin Pines would be ideal were it not for the construction at its doorstep. All the usual guest house accoutrements, including a restaurant. All rooms have bath and toilet. Dorms RM6. Doubles RM16-30. Triples for RM8-10 per person.

Bala's Holiday Chalets, Lot 55 (tel. 491 16 60), 2km up the road from town (a sign indicates the turn-off). The distance is an inconvenience, but they shuttle guests to and from their lovely colonial-style house with fine Highland vistas. Give a call upon arrival in Tanah Rata for pick-up. Fresh roses on the tables, tea and scones in the afternoon, and a super dinner menu. International phone service, mail service, maps, travel info, hot water, bus reservations, and a small library available. Dorms RM7. Singles RM16. Doubles RM25-30, with bath RM50-88.

Rumah Rehat (Rest House) (tel. 491 12 54). Walk down the road branching off the main road opposite the hospital and take a right at the drive which precedes the vegetable sculpture. Classy but well-worn quarters house few backpacker brethren. The lights go out before 11pm most nights. All rooms have bathrooms. Doubles RM80. Triples RM100. Family rooms RM200. Reserve in advance.

FOOD

Good food at inexpensive prices can be found almost anywhere in Tanah Rata. Entering town, there are cheap food stalls on the right side of the road before the bus station serving standard Malay and Chinese fare. Several good Indian and Chinese restaurants are on the left side of the road. Guest houses have menus as well.

Restoran Thanam, 25 Main Rd. (tel. 491 16 45). This popular Indian-run restaurant on the left side of the road is open for breakfast, serving *roti* with fruit and fresh juices (orange, carrot, lemon, watermelon). Crowded with beer-swilling foreigners at night, making service a bit slow. Most of the rice dishes on the English menu cost under RM3. For dessert, slurp up a shake or ice cream. Beers are RM4 and RM8. Open daily 6:30am-10:30pm.

Ye Olde Smokehouse (tel. 491 12 15), by the golf course, about halfway between Tanah Rata and Brinchang. The Smokehouse is undoubtedly a unique example of English provincial architecture the like of which is not to be found in any other part of Malaysia. The suites (RM400-600) and the supper (RM40 and up) might be a bit rich for the common blood.

Warung Kek Rich Bake and Coffee House, 100m from the bus station heading toward Ringlet, on the left. Come in the morning for thick pancakes with strawberries or a *kaya* waffle (RM1.50-2.50) or later at night, when the only other place still open is the karaoke bar next door. Open daily 8am-midnight.

▓ Brinchang

Brinchang is only 5km and a short taxi (RM3) or bus (RM0.50) ride from Tanah Rata. In fact, it's so close that you might consider making it a daytrip. Visitors who stay here will find it more expensive and relatively colorless in comparison to its lower neighbor, although there are a few good restaurants in town.

ORIENTATION

There is no bus station in Brinchang—just a **bus stop** along the main road at the central square. In the square there's a playground, the **pasar seni** (art market), and **Malay food stalls.** West of the square, behind the Hong Kong Hotel about 20m is **Bandar Baru,** with the laundry, bank, and drugstore.

PRACTICAL INFORMATION

The **Public Bank Berhad,** MDCH 41-43 Bandar Baru (tel. 491 15 90), exchanges currency. (Open Mon.-Fri. 9:30am-3:30pm, Sat. 9:30am-noon.) The bus stop is on the main road next to the Hong Kong Hotel and Restaurant. Catch a **public bus** (RM0.50) or a **share-taxi** (RM3) from there down to Tanah Rata, where all other connections can be arranged at the bus station. The **day market** is held in Bandar Baru. The **night market** sets up there as well on Saturday nights and public holidays, and is larger and more interesting than the one in Tanah Rata. **Highland Health Shop,** 12 Bandar Baru (tel. 491 28 48), is the closest thing in town to a pharmacy. (Open Mon.-Fri. 9:30am-4pm, Sat. 9:30am-1:30pm.) The **GPO** is on Main Rd. (tel. 491 10 16) past the central square on the left. (Open Mon.-Sat. 8:30am-12:30pm and 2pm-4:30pm.) **Postal code:** 39100.

ACCOMMODATIONS

The hotel situation here is disappointing in comparison to Tanah Rata. Most of the cheapies are impersonal cubbyholes that you might find in any Malaysian city. All worthwhile hotels are located in the immediate vicinity of the central square.

Highlands Hotel, 29-32 Jl. Besar (tel. 491 15 88), close to Shal's Curry House. Carpet that's actually an improvement over the concrete beneath in spacious rooms with attached baths. Singles/doubles RM37. Quads RM42.

Hong Kong Hotel, No. 5 Main Rd. (tel 491 17 22), on the left hand side coming from Tanah Rata, right across from the bus stop on the corner. Clean rooms have two double beds with an attached bathroom. At RM35 a night, it's a real bargain if you are traveling in a group of 2 to 4 people. Restaurant downstairs has western breakfast, steamed buns, and the usual coffee shop Chinese food at low prices.

Chua Gin Hotel, 11 Main Rd. (tel. 491 18 01), two doors down from the Hong Kong. Clean rooms with attached baths. One double bed RM35. A quad with 2 double beds and 1 twin RM45. The same room for 5 is RM55.

FOOD

Brinchang's food is more promising than its lodging selection. Several Chinese and Indian restaurants offer filling food. The **Malay food stalls** are in the central square.

Shal's Curry House, 25 Main Rd. (tel. 491 24 08), on the opposite side of the square from the main road, it has a green sign with the logo of a fish head in a clay pot on a banana leaf. Definitely worth a try. Locals come here to sup on breakfast of *roti* and tea (RM1.20), and the deft dough maestro also whips up *roti* with peanuts and honey or butter and coconut. Vegetarian dishes aplenty. A full meal costs RM7-10. Open daily 7:30am-10pm.

Restoran Kowloon, near the Malay food stalls. Specializes in steamboat, but also has a wide variety of mid-range dishes, and clean tablecloths to boot. Steamboat costs RM13 per person, claypot spare ribs RM8. Some western dishes available. Open daily 11am-3pm and 5-11pm.

■ Cameron Highland Sights

The Highlands' best sights are agricultural: tea plantations and terraced vegetable, strawberry, and dairy farms are all unique to the Highlands and should not be missed. The butterfly farm and Buddhist temple, on the other hand, are not as interesting as their counterparts in Penang, Kuala Lumpur, or Melaka. While those who plan to stay for only a couple of days may opt for a 4½-hour guided tour (offered by most guest houses for about RM15 plus admission fees), it is also quite possible to get around on your own steam or by public bus.

Hiking is doubtless the traveler's favorite pastime while in the Highlands. Trail maps are available at most guest houses. Some trails are more difficult than others, but the maps have descriptions of each one, so you can choose accordingly. Don't overestimate your energy or endurance, however. Count on each hike being more difficult than its description. Equip yourself with water and comfortable hiking boots, and don't make the same mistake Jim Thompson made: bring companions.

Some jungle walks serve as shortcuts between towns and sights. Walk #9A, beginning at the end of the road which branches off the Tanah Rata-Brinchang road directly across from the hospital, provides an easy descent to a vegetable farm and the Mini Dairy Farm. Walking left up the road for about 2.5km leads to **Boh Tea Estate.** This is the oldest and best tea plantation in the Highlands and offers a splendid view. Visitors can have a cup of tea and homemade shortbread in the open café or take a free tour of the factory. (Open Tues.-Sun. 9am-4:30pm.) The bus to Boh leaves Tanah Rata at 10, 11am, 1:30, and 5pm. A good walk combination taking you to the top of **Gunung Berenban** (just under 2000m high) begins with walk #9, then branches left onto the more strenuous walk #8 after less than 1km. After three hours, hikers will reach the summit of Gunung Berenban. From there continue left and follow walk #7 back down to the Malaysia Agricultural Research and Development Institute (MARDI). The peaks of the Highlands are wooded and do not give great views but, as always, the process of getting there is the most enjoyable.

INTERIOR PENINSULAR MALAYSIA

■ Jerantut

Jerantut is relevant to traveler's itineraries only as far as it's the official gateway to the national park. The town, much like Valérie Valtz, is small, harmless, and a little disheveled. The increasing popularity of Taman Negara and the new highway running through town into the interior regions of Palang and Terengganu promise to transform Jerantut into a tourist nursery before long. One night here is plenty; get a good night's rest, pick up some supplies, and rise early the next morning to begin exploring Taman Negara.

ORIENTATION AND PRACTICAL INFORMATION

There are only two roads of significance: **Jalan Besar** and **Bandar Baru.** The **bus station** is on Bandar Baru. Hotel Chet Fatt and **MBF Finance Berhad** with **ATM** (MC, Visa, Cirrus) and **currency exchange** are both across the street. Turn left from the bus station, and the **post office** (tel. 266 62 01) is at the end of the street. (Open Mon.-Sat. 8am-5pm.) **Postal code:** 27000. Head right, past Hotel Chet Fatt, and turn left, and make the next right on Jl. Besar, facing the **police station** (tel. 266 22 22). The Emporium is on the right. Green Park Guest House is farther down on the left.

Taxis can be arranged by guest houses to go to Kuala Tembeling Pier (minibus RM4 per person), or you can take a bus. Boats leave from the pier to **Taman Negara** (9am and 2pm). Local **buses** run to: **Kuala Tembeling** (4 per day, 8am-5pm, 30min., RM1.20) as well as **Kuantan** (4 per day, 7am-3:15pm). There is an express bus to **Kuantan** (3pm, RM8.50). **Express buses** to **Temerloh** (RM3), **KL** (RM9), and **Klang** (RM10.70) are run by **Perwira,** all departing at 8:30, 10:30am, 2:30, 4, and 5pm. If the Jerantut station doesn't have your destination, try the station in Temerloh, a bigger town about an hour south. Buses go to **Temerloh** (every hr., 6am-6pm, RM3.80). The **train station** (tel. 226 22 19) is on Jl. Station. Trains run to **Wakaf Bharu** (near Kota Bharu; 5:30am, 6½hr., RM12.60) and **Singapore** (9:15pm, 9hr., RM14.80). **Taxis** zoom to **KL** (RM22 per person) and **Kuantan** (RM20 per person).

Upon arrival at the train station, turn right on the barren road and walk 100m to the intersection with Jl. Besar. To get to **Bandar Besar,** turn left. To get to the **hospital** (tel. 266 33 33) follow Jl. Besar out of town and turn at the last left. Keep to the right and follow the signs for about 0.5km.

ACCOMMODATIONS AND FOOD

A large overhead sign marks **Hotel Chet Fatt,** Lot 2755 Jl. Diwangsa, 2nd Fl., Bandar Baru (tel. 266 58 05), across the street from the bus station. The friendly Chinese owner manages immaculate rooms with flip-flops for the shower, towels, soap, soft pillows, and blankets. The front rooms are rather hot and noisy, and require passage through the TV room to access the shower. Doubles with fan are RM15. A/C rooms range from RM20-28. Chet Fatt is often full on weekends; reserve in advance.

The **Green Park Guest House,** Lot. 34 Jl. Besar (tel. 09 266 38 84), is on the last left heading out of town on Jl. Besar, about 30m before the mosque. The owner is a seasoned tour guide with a forestry degree, and is a veritable vault of knowledge. The spartan rooms have plenty of windows and clean shared baths. The staff can arrange transportation and accommodations in Taman Negara. Dorms (4 beds per room) are RM8 per person. Singles go for RM12. Doubles RM20. Triples RM27. The best of its ilk, **Jerantut Resthouse** (tel. 266 44 88) is located about 200m beyond the Green Path Guesthouse on the left. The staff have good information on the park. A large lounge area and café separate this from the town's more functional guest houses. Dorms (6 per room) are RM7, doubles with individual bath RM15-20. The minibus ride/plantation tour (RM23) is worthwhile. It stops at cocoa, rubber, and oil palm plantations, finally arriving in Kuala Tahan after 2½ hours; definitely a better alternative than the boat from Tembeling to Kuala Tahan (RM19).

Stock up on supplies for Taman Negara at either the **day market** next to the bus station or at the **Emporium** on Jl. Besar. The **night market** on Saturday nights behind the day market (just before sundown-10:30pm), sells somewhat unremarkable food. In other parts of town, *roti canai* stands are set up for late night snacks.

■ Taman Negara

A glance through the comment book in the small library of Taman Negara, Malaysia's first and largest national park, reveals that it is one of the world's best kept tropical rainforests, while simultaneously perching on the brink of ecological disaster. The new highway being blazed through the forests east of the park, as well as a proposed air strip fulfill the demand created by Taman Resort's ambitious marketing strategy which has increased the parks' tourist population exponentially in the last four years. Officially, the resort is confined to 15 hectares and so far only a tiny fraction of the park's area is accessible by trail. Fortunately, few of the park's visitors venture more than 2km from the resort and park headquarters, making it easy to dodge crowds and bask in the forest primeval.

Taman Negara was under government administration from 1937 until recently, when it was allowed to join the development frenzy. A combination of increased river traffic, land development, and noise pollution ensures that wildlife stays far away from the resort areas. Just before dawn is the best time to hike out and see the natural beauty of the place; the air is cool and the wildlife, especially the magnificent birds, are more likely to venture out. "Hides" around the park's salt licks allow guests to quietly observe larger animals. Diehard adventurers can make the nine-day trek to and from Tahan Mountain and the nearby four-tiered waterfall, but the planning and expense of the trek can prove even more daunting than the summit.

GETTING THERE AND AWAY

Taman Negara can be reached by privately arranged bus/taxi or by boat on the Tembeling River. The **boats** (9am and 2pm, RM19, returning at the same times) leave from the village of **Kuala Tembeling,** accessible by bus (RM1.20) or share-taxi (RM4 per person) from Jerantut. To make the 9am boat, renting a taxi (40min.) is the best bet, since the 8:15am bus from Jerantut often runs late. The boat ride up the river takes longer (3-3½hr.), while the trip back downstream is shorter (2-2½hr.). Keep your eyes peeled for monkeys, lizards, and colorful birds on the shores. For overland transport, which is preferable on the way to the park, see the Jerantut Resthouse.

Taman Negara

Legend:
- ▲ Peak
- ◗ Cave
- Railroad
- Trail
- State border
- Park border
- River

10 miles
10 kilometers

TERENGGANU

- S. Petang
- ▲ G. Padang
- ▲ G. Bewek
- G. Mandi Angin
- S. Pertang
- G. Cherlak
- K. Chamir
- J. Aur
- S. Tembeling
- S. Kembir
- ▲ G. Beldai
- ▲ G. Gagau
- ▲ G. Milong
- Bt. Milong
- S. Badong
- Melimau
- K. Koh
- **PAHANG**
- K. Klapor
- K. Keniam
- K. Trenggan
- Nusa Camp
- S. Perlis
- ▲ G. Penumpu
- ▲ G. Keniam
- Gua Besar
- K. Perkai
- S. Trenggan
- K. Tahan
- Sungei Tiang Airstrip
- K. Atok
- S. Koh
- S. Aring
- **KELANTAN**
- Bt. Hantu
- S. Relai
- ▲ G. Perlis
- Padang
- Bt. Remis
- National Park H.Q.
- S. Tenok
- S. Tahan
- S. Tembeling
- Bt. Guling Gendang
- S. Atok
- 4-Tiered Waterfall
- G. Tahan
- ▲ G. Gedong
- S. Teku
- Gua Tumpat
- Lime Stone Cliffs
- ▲ G. Ulu Kechau
- Gua Siput
- Gua Peningat
- S. Muntok
- S. Kepong
- G. Rabong (Sinting)
- Merapoh
- S. Relai
- Batu Lompat
- S. Tekai
- K. Toh

MALAYSIA

Visitors to Taman Negara should make reservations in advance for their boat ride (either with the resort or Nusa Camp) and accommodations, especially during weekends and holiday seasons. The forestry department requires all visitors to buy an entry permit (RM1), and photography (RM5) or fishing (RM10) permits if necessary. Put these in a safe place—you'll be asked to produce them when you leave. Now that the park is private, it stays open all year. Visitors, however, have a miserable time of it from November to January, as the rains prevent outdoor activity. Bring lots of water, fruit, and snacks to Taman Negara; snacks at the mini-market are more than three times as expensive as in the rest of Malaysia, and only slightly less so in the village across the river. **The Emporium** in Jerantut is a good place to stock up on goods before heading to the park.

ORIENTATION

Taman Negara has a total area of 4343sq.km. **Taman Negara Resort** is in **Kuala Tahan** on the left of the river; on the right is a village of cheap hostels and restaurants. **Boats** shuttle back and forth across the river for free. Upriver a few km is **Nusa Camp,** a cheaper alternative. Good maps with trails and points of interest are available at most tourist offices in Malaysia. Clearly marked trails and directional arrows make it difficult to get lost. Most local accommodations sell a more detailed book about the park and its paths for RM4. If you're undertaking a lengthy hike or are not particularly experienced in jungle trekking, you may consider hiring one of the many expensive, but congenial and knowledgeable guides.

PRACTICAL INFORMATION

Currency Exchange: Change money before going to Taman Negara. The reception desk at the resort will exchange money, but at terrible rates.

Trains: See **Jerantut: Practical Information.**

Buses: The 9am boat back to Kuala Tembeling arrives in enough time to catch the bus in Jerantut. The 2pm boat, however, does not, necessitating a RM4 taxi ride.

Boats: Nusa Camp runs **river bus** routes within the park that are much cheaper than private charters (RM30-290 per day). **Nusa Riverbus** routes go from Nusa Camp to **Kuala Tahan** (RM5), and **Kuala Trenggan** (RM5), and from Kuala Tahan to Kuala Trenggan (RM10), and Kuala Tahan to **Blau Yong Cave** (RM3) several times per day. Guests at Nusa Camp ride the riverbus from Nusa Camp to Kuala Tahan for RM3, but the boat stops running at 6pm.

Taxis: In Kuala Tembeling, fixed-price share-taxis go to: **Jerantut** RM16; **Kuala Lumpur** RM100; and **Kuantan** RM100. Max. 4 passengers.

Rentals: The resort office next to reception rents hiking and camping gear per day: binoculars RM10, fishing rod RM7, sleeping-bag RM3, nylon and rubber jungle boots RM2.5 (up to size 44 or US 9), flashlight RM2 (no batteries), small backpack RM3, large backpack RM6, canoes RM25, 2-person tent RM8, 4-person tent RM14, and bottle of fuel RM4.50.

Post Offices: The reception at the resort sells stamps. **Postal code** for Taman Negara environs (Kuala Tahan, Kuala Tembeling, Jerantut, etc.): 27000.

Telephones: Again, at the resort's reception desk (they'll rip you off some more).

ACCOMMODATIONS

Kuala Tahan's cheap accommodations are across the river from the resort. Ferries will go there for free from the resort's dock.

Teresek View Village (tel. (09) 266 30 65). Camp on their barren, parched field for RM2.50 per person, or rent a 2-person (RM12) or 4-person (RM14) tent. Hostel beds RM10. Rickety A-frames with attached bath RM30. Bungalows RM50-60. Mini-mart, equipment rental, prayer mats, and transport to Jerantut by jeep (2 hr., RM20 per person, min. 4 people).

Liana Hostel offers dorms for RM10 (4 beds per room), with limited bathroom facilities. Most rooms have a nice river view. The manager is the most senior jungle guide in the park and offers an amazing variety of tours, including the aborigine survival course (RM30 per person, 4 min.) in which travelers take to the hills with an Orang Asli family for 3 nights, with nothing but a bag of rice and a blowgun to bring down frogs and birds. Night safaris (RM20 per person, 6 min.) and river rafting (RM20 per person, 6 min.) are also offered.

Agoh's Chalets (tel. (010) 988 00 49) is on the embankment between Liana and Teresek, 50m to the right of Teresek with one's back to the river. Separate double huts with common bath RM30. Small restaurant's repertoire stops at *mee goreng.*

Taman Negara Resort, Kuala Tahan, 27000 Jerantut, Pahang Darul Makmur (tel. (09) 266 35 00). **Kuala Lumpur Sales Office:** Lot 6, 2nd Fl., Hotel Istana, No. 73 Jalan Raja Chulan, 50200 Kuala Lumpur (tel. (03) 245 55 85). Any of these numbers can be used to make advance reservations for the boat to Kuala Tahan and accommodations. For most of the year, call a few days ahead. During local holidays, reservations should be made farther in advance. The resort is the most expensive place to stay, but also the most convenient, with the most facilities. There's a range of accommodations: hostel with dorms RM20.70. A/C guest house rooms; singles RM120, doubles RM150. Double chalets range from RM200-290. Extra beds RM25. 10% service charge and 5% tax.

Nusa Camp, Jerantut Office, 16 LKNP Building, 27000 Jerantut, Pahang Darul Makmur (tel. (09) 266 23 69), at the Jerantut bus station. It poses as a tourist office. **Kuala Lumpur Office:** Express National Counter, Malaysia Tourist Information Centre, 109 Jl. Ampang, 50450 (tel. (03) 264 39 29, ext. 112). **Kuala Tembeling Office** (at the jetty): No. 5, Taman Negara Jetty, Kuala Tembeling, Jerantut, 27000, Kuala Tembeling (tel. (09) 266 30 43). Reservations for boats and accommodations can be made. Down-river from the Resort, Nusa Camp provides a complete package of facilities and activities, but at lower prices. Malay cottages RM60. A-frame chalets RM40. Dorms RM9. Restaurant serves set meals: breakfast RM5, lunch RM7.50, and dinner RM8.50. All rates subject to 5% tax.

Hides within the park are shelters equipped with mattresses and pillows. Open to all, inquire about locations and reservations at the Wildlife Department at the Resort. Lodges within the park are RM8 per person and can accommodate 8 people. Reserve at the Wildlife Department. Rats are rife in both forms of lodging—hang your edible materials (and bring duct tape to patch holes).

FOOD

Both Nusa Camp and Taman Negara Resort have their own restaurants, but prices are ridiculous. Even the "budget cafeteria" is expensive. Thankfully, several reasonably-priced restaurants line the river. The **Family Restaurant** on the shore opposite the resort is the least of all evils, with good noodle dishes, burgers, and other options for RM2.50-3. Open daily 8am-midnight. The **Floating Restaurant** next door is likewise satisfactory.

SIGHTS

Mother Nature's majesty is the park's *raison d'être.* The network of trails is clearly marked, so it's easy and safe to slip away from the resort in the early morning and surround yourself in virgin jungle. Spend a night at one of the many hides to spot wildlife. The large, nocturnal mammals such as elephants, tigers, rhinos, leopards and wild cattle rarely visit human-frequented areas of the jungle. Although only appropriate for those fit for the challenge, the **nine-day trek** to and from Gunung Tahan, Peninsular Malaysia's highest peak, and a nearby four-tiered waterfall is probably the best way to take in the diversity and ecological riches of Taman Negara. The trip requires massive planning. All food and camping materials must be bought in Kuala Tahan. Travelers must consult with park authorities beforehand, and hire a guide (RM500 per week, RM50 per day after the first week). The info desk at the resort often has postings from people willing to share the costs of a trek to the peak. Although not a problem on most paths, leeches can be a concern; locals recommend spraying BAYGON (in the green can) on shoes and socks.

For a fresh perspective, take a stroll on the recently-built **canopy walk** about 2km away from park headquarters (11am-3pm; RM5). Suspended by a web of woven ropes, wires, cables, and wooden planks along the tree-tops, the canopy walk is the longest (470m) traverse of its kind providing a tremendous view of the jungle, although the thrill of being so high above the ground would be enough in itself. Bring a camera. Authorities test the safety of the walkway daily (hence the short hours), checking stress points and the integrity of the delicate structure.

PERHENTIAN ISLANDS

The islands are one of Malaysia's newest marine parks. Fishing is prohibited within two nautical miles, as are spear-fishing, souvenir collecting of any sort, and littering. Do not touch or step on any coral. The exquisite but extremely fragile reefs have already begun to show signs of damage; one touch can destroy an entire branch. Items to bring for an extended stay include mosquito repellent, a flashlight, batteries, toiletries, toilet paper, and condoms. Accommodations (except Petani Beach House) are closed Nov.-Feb. due to monsoons.

Pulau Perhentian Besar (Big Island) and Pulau Perhentian Kecil (Small Island) are a pair of oceanic twins bathing in the tropical waters of the South China Sea. About 20km off the mainland coast, the 1½- to 3-hour boat ride to their shores provides plenty of eye candy for expectant travelers as the islands' smooth green contours and sparkling beaches come into view with agonizing slowness. Upon arrival, your first steps onto the beaches, whose sand does delightfully intimate things to bare feet will prove that these islands are no mirage. Word of the Perhentian's exquisite charms, however, is widespread in travelers' circles. Don't be surprised if during your trip the view is ominously eclipsed by mattresses, plastic chairs, and building supplies. Things are getting more crowded but, for many, these two isles still embody the tropical ideal.

GETTING THERE AND AWAY

The islands are reached by boat from **Kuala Besut.** From Kota Bharu, the best plan is to take a taxi (1½hr., RM20 per car, fits 4 people) but, if you can't find fellow passengers to split the cost, you can take a bus to Pasir Putih and from there catch another bus to Kuala Besut (total trip RM4.20). From Kuala Terangganu, take a taxi (2hr., RM40 per car, fits 4 people) or a bus to Jertih and then a bus to Kuala Besut (total trip RM8). The largest of the various boat services, 5P (Persatuan Pengusaha Pelancongan Pulau Perhentian, next to the jetty, beneath a large Information Centre sign (tel. (09) 691 91 89), has 16 boats that leave when they have 12 booked passengers (8am-5pm, RM30 roundtrip), but your best bet is to show up at 10am or 2pm where there's almost always a boat leaving for the islands. The tourist office in Kota Bharu sells tickets for **Tanjung Enterprise** (tel. (09) 691 01 89), which is to the left of the jetty for the same price. Boats leave the island at 8am and 2pm (2hr.); let your guest house owner know the day before you leave.

■ Pulau Perhentian Kecil

Currently the favored twin, Kecil owes its popularity to Long Beach, the island's most popular stretch of sand in which to snuggle for UV caresses. Its sandy bottoms are perfect for swimming, while its rocky edges blaze with coral. Some backpackers become so captivated with the island's charms that they end up staying for months, working part-time for the bungalows in exchange for food.

ISLAND ORIENTATION

Long Beach is on the east coast and moving counter-clockwise from south to north are the following accommodations: Rock Garden, Cempaka, Long Beach Chalets, Mata Hari, and Moonlight. Isolated D'Lagoon is on the next beach to the north and boasts some of the island's best coral, accessible only by boat. On the west coast, almost opposite Long Beach and reachable by a 15-minute jungle walk, is **Coral Bay,** a quiet beach whose waters are spiked with dying coral. Raja Wali, Au Beach Chalets, and Coral Bay Chalets shack up along these shores. Continuing farther south, in a **small cove** with a private beach, is Mira. A 30-minute walk farther south is larger **Petani Beach,** which houses Petani Beach House on its premises. **Perhentian village** is at the southeast tip of the island.

PRACTICAL INFORMATION

Currency Exchange: Moonlight or **Checkpoint.** Poor rates. RM5 service charge.

Local Transportation: Motorboats shuttle from Long Beach Chalets to: **Perhentian Besar** (RM10); **D'Lagoon** (RM10); **Mira** (RM15); and **Petani** (RM15).

Medical Services: (tel. (011) 971 14 23), behind the police station, across a small bridge to the right. Nurse performs routine care, more serious cases should go to the mainland. Open Sat.-Wed. 8am-4pm, Thurs. 8am-12:45pm.

Police: In a blue building along the beach behind a rusting fence. Its main duty is filing insurance claims. Open Sat.-Thurs. 8am-4pm.

Post Offices: Most guest houses will deliver mail to the post office in the village. **Mata Hari** sells stamps. For important missives, it's best to wait to return to the mainland. **Postal code:** 22200.

Telephones: Available at **D' Lagoon.** International calls RM10 per min.

ACCOMMODATIONS AND FOOD

Most travelers set their sights on the powdery charms of Long Beach, whose limited accommodations fill up quickly, so that by noon most have hoisted their red no-vacancy flag. If everything is full at Long Beach, hike to Coral Bay or hire a small motorboat to one of the smaller beaches or even Perhentian Besar. Many accommodations face water shortages during peak season (June-August).

Long Beach

Mata Hari (tel. (09) 697 76 12), the most coveted digs on the beach. Solid, spacious, well-crafted bungalows (RM18) set back from the dunes or sky blue bungalows with bath (RM40) are available. Hammocks sway from shady front porches. Shared bath with real showerheads. Restaurant (open daily 7am-midnight) serves such treats like as ginger beef (RM6) and chocolate shakes (RM3). No alcohol allowed. Snorkel trips (gear RM12 per day, RM7 per 3hr.).

Rock Garden, the cheapest lodgings on Long Beach. Active, cheap-fun attitude, with a penchant for recycling. Super-friendly waitstaff operates on a first name basis, hollering at people on the beach. Dorms RM5. Older A-frame huts RM10. Newer huts nearer to the bathrooms and beach RM12. Breakfast daily 8-11am, lunch 1-4pm, and buffet dinner 7:30pm (RM7) at their funky beachside restaurant. Boats to Perhentian Besar (RM5) and other destinations.

Moonlight (tel. (010) 982 81 35), isolated at the north end of Long Beach. Several thatched A-frames (RM15, with bath RM35) and larger bungalows (large bed RM22, family-size with 2 rooms and 2 beds, RM40). The restaurant (open daily 7am-very late) and surf-side deck are favorites among cocoa butter-drenched set in search of a fruit shake (RM3.50) or banana pancakes with chocolate syrup (RM3). Group meals (RM7.50) served by lamp light at 7pm. No alcohol allowed. Taxis go to Besar (RM12 roundtrip) and the village (RM10).

D'Lagoon (tel. (011) 970 631), in a placid cove on the isolated northeast tip of the island, accessible only by boat. Travelers willing to forgo Long Beach's social frolicking will be rewarded with a private beach facing one of the best snorkeling sites on the island. In the evenings try the 10-min. hike through winding jungle paths to the isolated west coast beaches for idyllic sunsets. Dorms RM10. A-frames RM15.

Rooms with bath RM40. The popular tree-house is a small hut 5m up in the arms of a giant tree (RM15). Camping RM5. Clean shared baths, with showers. Rents snorkeling equipment and offers batik lessons. Restaurant open daily 7:15am-3:30pm and 7-10pm. Group dinners (usually fish) for RM6.50.

Coral Bay

Aur Beach Chalets, right next to Coral Bay Chalets. Offers A-frame huts with mosquito nets and spacious shared baths with running water (RM15). To see iguanas, hike up the path toward Long Beach.

Coral Bay Chalets, a relaxed, family-run establishment on the north end of Coral Beach. A-frame huts with mosquito nets and well-water baths (RM15). Waitstaff at uninspired restaurant offer guests free fried bananas and fresh jackfruit, or a cup of tea and toast the morning they depart.

Mira (tel. (010) 982 93 89), reachable only by boat or by hiking for about 2hr. from Coral Bay Beach. A bohemian atmosphere, where a profusion of navel rings can be viewed. Hillside rooms surround a small stretch of sandy-bottomed beach and coral farther out. Twisted driftwood cots are set among wild ginger and banana trees. Malay longhouse with broad balconies RM15, larger rooms RM20. Camping space RM8. Restaurant open daily 7:30am-11pm. Steaming banana pancakes RM2.50. Set dinners RM6-10. Snorkel gear RM4-5 per hr., RM12 per day.

Petani Beach House (tel. (010) 881 24 44), sandwiched between Mira and the village. A meticulously landscaped affair, with pyrotechnic flowers and a sizable stretch of beach. 5 bungalows with bath (RM50, RM30 low season) and 2 "semi-detached" rooms with shared bath (RM30, RM20 low season) available year-round. Upscale rooms have lighting and fans. Restaurant specialty is fish (RM15 and up). Snorkeling equipment RM20 per day. Reservations recommended.

ENTERTAINMENT

"Old man, old boat, no teeth" is how locals describe Hamzah, a village fisherman. Amiable Hamzah often takes visitors on his boat to **the island's best snorkeling sites;** he'll even let you spend as much time as you like exploring. At RM15 per head (not including gear) it's a great deal compared to tours that race around the island at a break-neck pace. Ask for him at Mata Hari.

If floating above extraordinary coral gardens is not enough, consider a **scuba course.** The friendly and knowledgeable staff of **Coral Sky** (tel. (010) 910 963), next to Mata Hari on Long Beach, offers PADI courses, including open water certification. The four-day course (RM650) includes scuba theory, confined water training, and four dives and results in international certification. Other PADI courses offered are advanced certification, rescue, and dive master training. Qualified divers can explore local dive sites for RM120 for two dives or RM95 with their own equipment; discounts are available for three days or more of diving (MC, Visa, and traveler's checks). **Turtle Bay Divers** (tel. (60) 11 337 514) is also on Long Beach, next to Moonlight Chalets, and offers similar services and prices (MC and Visa).

Hikers yearning to scuff their boots might consider the **two-hour trek to the village.** The trail begins at the south end of Coral Bay just behind the half-finished frame of a wooden house on the hillside. The path disappears periodically, often winding haphazardly in what seems like the wrong direction, but will eventually deliver hikers to Petani. From Petani Beach House, the village is only 15 minutes away; you can take a boat back in clear weather. Trekkers should get an early start and bring plenty of water. For those too sunburned to contemplate any more UV, the **turtle hatchery** in front of Mata Hari allows travelers to admire newly hatched turtles as they make their moon-lit trek to the waves. Beginning in June, drop by at 11pm to see if they are being released (no noise, flashlights, or flash photography).

▓ Pulau Perhentian Besar

Balinese batik and Indian weaves wave cheerfully in the sea breeze, welcoming weary road warriors to Besar's shores. The larger island is a brief speedboat ride across the waves of the narrow channel separating the two islands.

ORIENTATION AND PRACTICAL INFORMATION

Most accommodations here concentrate along the talcum lengths of the west coast. Below the upscale resorts to the north, and isolated from other budget lodgings farther south by a tumble of large wave-swept rocks, is **Mama's Place.** Farther south beyond the rocks are **Coco Hut, Ibi's,** and **Abdul's.** Rounding the forested tip of the island, via a 30-min. walk, brings you to the south side fringe of beaches, inhabited by a few large establishments and the intimate **Seashell's Chalet.**

There is no official tourist office. Most places can answer basic questions and provide **postal service,** but Mama's Place is a good source of information and stamps, as well as **currency exchange** (RM5 service charge). **Check Point,** just past Coco Hut and before Ibi's, changes currency for similar rates and is the closest thing on the islands to a **store,** with a pricey selection of sunscreens, toiletries, and souvenirs. It also offer a book exchange, haircuts (RM5), and **boat trips** (roundtrip rates to: Mama's Place RM4, Resort RM8, Blue Lagoon RM16, Pelangi RM14, village RM4, Petani RM8, Mira RM14, Coral Bay RM16, and D'Lagoon RM16).

ACCOMMODATIONS

Pulau Besar boasts refined accommodations with plenty of bath water, amenities, and a budding nightlife. Managers are often willing to dicker discreetly over rates.

Mama's Place (tel. (010) 984 02 32). A perennial favorite. Thus, finding a room can be difficult. Pastel beachside bungalows with shared bath RM20. Prance through Mama's papaya patch to upscale digs with fan and attached bath RM30-45. Tiny restaurant serves dinner nightly at 7:30pm, but ask Mama first. No alcohol allowed. Small book exchange and some beach needs. Sea canoe rental (RM20 per day) and trips to Sasudara island (10am-5pm, RM25).

Abdul's (tel. (010) 983 73 03) offers intimacy but less coral on its beach. Acid green bungalows (RM12, RM15 for beachside) or wooden chalets with fan and bath (RM40). Electricity 7pm-8am. Restaurant has engaging view of the village (open daily 7am-11pm). Try their famous seaside fireball (deep-fried ice cream with strawberry sauce) for RM5. Snorkel gear RM10 per day. Snorkeling trips 10am-2pm, RM15 with gear. Overseas calls RM10 per min.

South Shore

Isolated from the west coast's social scene, the south shore picks up the trash from offshore fishing. Most hotel staff keep their areas clean, however, and the relatively undeveloped length is perfect for evening strolls. In the next cove is the famous spring that earned the Perhentian Islands their status as a stopping place for boats to fill up on fresh water.

Lazy Lizard stands all by itself. The very basic palm thatch A-frames with mosquito nets (RM10) share a common shower and bath, but most of the guests spend their days in the beach-side hammocks, stirring only to walk 10m for a burger (RM2.50) and beer (RM6) in a nook made from an old ship's prow. Camping space RM5. Multi-lingual manager. Snorkeling gear RM10. Inquire about trips to other islands or about renting the 2 larger motorboats. Plenty of water.

ENTERTAINMENT

For a touch of romance, pack your snorkeling gear and lunch for two and head to Blue Lagoon, a deserted beach on the north shore. Check Point arranges roundtrip transport for RM16. In the evenings, visitors can two-step to the country music and soak in the Wild West decor at the **Sea Horse Café** (tel. (010) 984 181), just behind Check Point. (Open daily 7:30am-2:30pm and 7:30pm-1am.) And, of course, who couldn't use a little tequila (RM4)? For entertainment of a different variety, there are several dive centers around the island as well.

Check Point (tel. (010) 980 57 04), rents sea canoes (singles RM20, doubles RM35), fishing rods (RM15), and snorkel gear (RM15). Also arranges group fishing tours for RM25 per person with one day notice. Snorkeling trips RM25, includes gear. Windsurfing RM15 per hr., RM60 for a day. Overnight stays can be arranged on **Rawa Island.**

A.N.D. Dive (tel. (011) 971 762), on the south beach at Pelangi Chalets. Two dives for RM80, with gear RM120. PADI certification (RM650), other courses offered as well. Open daily 8:30am-6pm. No credit cards.

Watercolours Dive Centre (tel. (018) 893 18 52), near Mama's Place. Offers PADI certification for RM650. Veteran divers can go for two dives RM90, with gear RM120. 10% discount for 3 or more days of diving. Sea canoes RM25 per day, RM15 half-day. Snorkeling gear RM12.

EAST COAST

■ Kota Bharu

Dubbed by many as the heart of traditional Malay culture, Kota Bharu is one of the most attractive urban centers in Malaysia. The capital of the Kelantan State, it is the largest city within a few hours of the Thai border and thus a sensible stopover if you're coming from or going to Sungai Kolok or Ban Taba in Thailand. Perhaps the local cultural pastimes have been slightly over-hyped and glossed up for tourists (top-spinning, kite-flying, *silat,* drum-beating, dancing, and puppeteering), but the various daily performances are certainly worth a visit. Just as memorable are the colorful and busy day and night markets held in the center of town. The city itself provides a good place for a few days of touristic distraction, not to mention the sights outside town. The fantastic selection of budget accommodations and restaurants are sure to make a stay here more pleasant.

ORIENTATION

Kota Bharu lies along the east banks of the **Kelantan River.** Running roughly north-south from the river are five major thoroughfares. **Jalan Post Office Lama** traces the river, running through **Padang Merdeka** (Independence Square). The next street east is **Jalan Sultanah Zainab,** which hits the southernmost street of **Jambatan Sultan Yahaya Petra/Jalan Hamzah/Pusir Puteh** at a traffic rotary. **Jalan Temenggong/Sultan Ibrahim** parallels Jl. Sultanah Zainab for a distance before veering southeast. **Jalan Kebun Sultan/Mahmud** stretches to the east and converges with Jl. Sultan Ibrahim at its south end. **Jalan Dusun Muda** bounds Kota Bharu on its far eastern side. The city center sprawls in the northern half of the city. Two streets divide the length of the city into rough thirds: **Jalan Tok Hakim/Padang Garong/Pengkalan Chepa** runs through the city center leading east to the airport and **Jalan Hospital** radiates eastward just north of a second traffic circle with a **clock tower.**

PRACTICAL INFORMATION

Kelantan State is Islamic, so most establishments are closed Friday instead of Sunday and some places close early on Thursday afternoon.

Tourist Offices: Tourist Information Centre (tel. 748 55 34), on Jl. Sultan Ibrahim in a bubble-gum pink building near the traffic circle with the clock tower.

Kota Bharu

N
↑

Jalan Merbau

TO PANTAI CINTA
BERAHI AND COTTAGE
INDUSTRIES AREA

Jalan Post Office Lama

Jalan Tok Semian

Jl. Majid

Jalan Sultan

Padang Merdeka

Jl. Hilir Kota

Jalan Tengku Besar

Istan Balai
Besar

Jalan Kebun Sultan

Jl. Hulu Kota

Jalan Pintu Pong

Jalan Pasar Lama

Jalan Post Office Lama

Shopping
Centre

Jalan
Tengku Chik

Buluth Kubu
Bazaar

New
Central Market

Kelantan River

Jalan Tok Hakim

Night Market

Open air
Eating Area

Taxi & Bus
Station

Jalan
Padang Garong

TO ROYAL THAI
CONSULATE AND
KOTA BHARU AIRPORT →

Jalan
Tengku'Petra Semerak

Jl. Temenggong

UMBC

Jalan Pengkalan Chepa

Jalan Sultanah Zainab

Jalan Hilir Pasar

Old Market
Jl.
Hulu Pasar

Telecom
Office

Malayan
Bankimg

Jalan
Che Su

Jalan Datok Pati

Jalan Doktor

Jalan Ismail

Jalan Mahmood

Jalan Gajah Mati

Jalan Hospital

Town Council

Tourist
Information
Centre

Sultan
Muhamad IV
Stadium

Jalan Zainal Abidin

Police Station

Open air
Eating Area

Post Office

Cultural
Centre

Jalan Bayam

Jalan Sultan Ibrahim

Jalan Bayam

Immigration
Office

Jalan Dusun Muda

TO KUALA TERENGGANU
& KUALA LUMPUR

Jalan Sultanah Zainab

Jalan Pasir Puteh

TO WAT PHOTIVIHAN,
THAI BORDER, AND EAST
WEST HIGHWAY (PENANG)

Jalan Hamzah

Malayan
Banking

Jalan Kuala Kerai

Express
Bus
Station

Jambatan Sultan Yahaya Petra

TO GUA
MUSANG

MALAYSIA

Very helpful staff; excellent English spoken. Brochures, maps, and souvenirs are available. Open daily 8:30am-12:45pm and 2-4:30pm; from Jan. until late Feb. or early Mar. (the end of Ramadan), open Sat.-Wed., Thurs. 8-11am.

Currency Exchange: Hong Kong Bank (tel. 748 14 51), on Jl. Padang Garong. Traveler's checks, MC, and Visa. Open Sat.-Wed. 10am-3pm, Thurs. 9:30am-11:30pm. **Azam Restoran/Money Changer/Guest House,** 1872-D Jl. Padang Garong (tel. 744 17 86). Good rates, sometimes better than the bank's. Open Sat.-Thurs. 7am-8pm. **Bank Simpanan National,** 61 Jl. Pintu Pong (tel. 748 44 66). The only bank open on Fri.—come here only if you need to, since rates are poor. AmEx traveler's checks and Visa cards, but no Visa checks. Open daily 9am-4pm.

Embassies and Consulates: Thailand (tel. 782 545), on the right side of Jl. Pengkalan Chepa on the way out of town toward the airport. Open Sun.-Thurs. 9am-12:30pm and 2-4pm. Closed on Malaysian and Thai holidays. Grants visa extensions, but requires 24 hr. to process; bring 2 photos.

Trains: The nearest train station is at **Wakaf Baru** (tel. 719 69 86), where the jungle trains depart for Malaysia's interior. It's a hassle to use this to get to Kuala Lumpur, but might be a good option for **Jerantut,** the launching point for Taman Negara National Park (6:20am, 8½hr; 3:45pm, 6½hr.). To continue on to **Kuala Lumpur** or **Singapore,** you must change at **Gemas Station. The Timuran Express** departs daily at 7:15pm direct to Singapore (13hr.).

Buses: The **local bus terminal** (tel. 744 01 14) is in the center on town on Jl. Padang Garong. To **Kuala Terengganu** (6 per day, 8:30am-5:30pm, RM7.40). The **Express Bus Terminal** (also known as Langgar Station) lies outside town on Jl. Pasir Puteh. To: **KL** (9am and 9pm, RM20, RM25); **Kuantan** (6 per day, 8am-11pm, RM15.80); **Singapore** (8pm, RM30); and **Penang** (9am and 10pm, RM19.40). It is best to make a reservation at least 1 day before departure, especially for long-distance journeys. Reserve at either bus station, regardless of destination. A network of regional buses also leave from the central station or within its vicinity. Heading for the **Thai-Malaysian border,** bus #29 leaves every hour from the central bus terminal to the border town of Rantau Panjang.

Taxis: The long-distance taxi stand is right next to the main bus station in the center of town. Taxis depart as soon as they've found 4 passengers, who split the fare to: **KL** (RM45 per person); **Kuala Terengganu** (RM12 per person); **Kuantan** (RM25 per person); **Butterworth** (RM35 per person); **Wakaf Bharu** (RM2.50 per person); and **Kuala Besut** (RM5 per person).

Local Transportation: Trishaws within Kota Bharu average RM2-3.

Rentals: Avis Rent-A-Car (tel. 748 44 57) operates out of the Perdana Hotel on Jl. Mahmud. Rates run RM150 and up per day. Weekly packages also available. Passport deposit and IDP required. Most guest houses rent **bicycles** for RM5 per day. Some other guest houses, such as Mummy's Hitec Hostel, will let guests use their bicycles for free.

Markets: The **New Central Market** is bounded by Jl. Pintu Pong, Doktor, and Tengku Chik. The ground floor is the "wet market." Fabrics, handicrafts, and spices are sold around the building. Fabrics and handicrafts can also be found at **Buluh Kubu Bazaar,** next to the Istana Balai Besar. Or try the top floor of the **Old Market** bounded by Jl. Dato Pati and Temenggong. The **night market** is located near the bus station and is definitely worth a visit. Vendors usually set up around 5pm and are open until the wee hours of the night.

Pharmacies: Kian Farmasi, 2981 B-C Jl. Padang Garong (tel. 748 39 06), in the center of town, across from K.B. Inn Guest House. Open Sat.-Thurs. 9am-10pm.

Medical Services: Hospital (tel. 748 55 33), at the end of Jl. Hospital.

Emergency: tel. 999. **Fire:** tel. 994.

Police: (tel. 748 55 22), on Jl. Sultan Ibrahim between the post office and tourist office. Some officers speak English.

Post Offices: GPO (tel. 748 40 23), on the left side of Jl. Sultan Ibrahim, south of the clock tower traffic circle. Open Sat.-Thurs. 8am-5pm. **Postal code:** 15670 (for post office only).

Telephones: Telekom office (tel. 744 66 09), on Jl. Doktor in the center of town, south of the intersection with Jl. Padang Garong. **HCD.** Accepts MCI, Sprint, and

AT&T, but no credit cards. Open Sat.-Wed. 8:30am-5pm, Thurs. 8:30am-noon. **Telephone code:** 09.

ACCOMMODATIONS

Mummy's Hitec Hostel, 439-B Jl. Pengkalan Chepa (tel. 744 47 60), opposite the Thai Consulate. It's a 10-min. walk from the center of town, but the management can pick you up for free if you call. You can also take bus #4 or 9 from the bus station. Mummy was a legendary party lover who opened the first guest house in KB in the early 70s. She passed away about 5 years ago and has since been succeeded by Boy the Dog and Asean, an old friend of Mummy's who keeps everything exactly the same, only cleaner. Free breakfast, tea, and coffee. Dorms RM5. Singles RM8. Doubles RM10. Guests have free use of bicycles.

K. B. Inn Guest House, 1872-D Jl. Padang Garong (tel. 744 17 86), next to the Azam Money Changer and close to the central bus station. Central location, but in the midst of street traffic. Nasron, the owner, is famous for his hospitality and wise travel advice. Enjoy views of the city from the rooftop. Rooms with fans are rather dim. Common room with TV and books aplenty. Shared bathrooms. Singles and doubles RM10-12. Free breakfast, coffee, tea, water, and cooking facilities.

Ideal Traveler's House, 3954 F-G Jl. Kebun Sultan (tel. 744 22 46), on a small paved road off Jl. Pintu Pong, just east of Jl. Kebun Sultan. In a peaceful neighborhood. Popular with backpackers and families alike. Airy, clean, and comfortable rooms with wooden floors. Breakfast available for a price. Books tickets to the Perhentian Islands. 2 single beds RM10. 1 double bed RM12. 1 double and 1 single RM18. Double bed with balcony and private bath RM25. All rooms have fan.

Town Guest House, 4959-B Jl. Pengkalan Chepa (tel. 748 51 92), located out of town one block past the Caltex gas station. Facilities galore: motorbike and car rental; plane, train, bus, and boat ticketing; book exchange; and safety box. Rooftop restaurant. Rooms have carpeting and fan. Dorms RM5. Singles and doubles without bath RM10. Rooms with bathroom RM12-15, and A/C RM20-25. MC.

FOOD

The place to eat in Kota Bharu is the **night market** which sprawls across the street from the main bus terminal (open nightly 6pm-midnight). Plenty of local specialties abound, including *ayam percik* (chicken grilled on sticks), and *nasi dagang* (coconut-based rice topped with tunafish cooked in a special sauce),. Most dishes run less than RM2. **Hawker stalls** set up at the river end of **Padang Merdeka,** the ground floor of the **Old Market,** and on the upper levels of the **New Central Market.** Several Chinese joints line **Jl. Kebun Sultan,** near Ideal Traveler's House. **Jl. Gajah Mati,** the road heading toward the river from the rotary, has many Indian eateries.

Qing Liang Vegetarian Restaurant, 3400-H Jl. Zainal Abidin (tel. 748 27 66), on a small side street that connects the main thoroughfares of Jl. Sultan Ibrahim and Jl. Sultanah Zainab. Not so fancy, this vegetarian restaurant offers good value for great food. All the food is on display in the back; just point and order. 3 toppings plus a beverage RM4. No English. A/C splendor. Open daily 11:30am-9pm.

Family Cake House and Restaurant, 1964-A Jl. Dato Pati (tel. 748 38 08), close to the Jl. Hospital intersection; look for the English sign. This A/C haven is quite popular with locals at lunch. The house specialty is *nasi dagang* with plenty of cakes. Open Sat.-Thurs. 11am-9:30pm, Fri. 11am-6pm.

Meena Curry House, 3377-G Jl. Gajah Mati (tel. 747 09 59), near the intersection with Jl. Sultanah Zainab. One of the "banana leaf" restaurants that dot Malaysia's landscape. Customers hunker down before a clean banana leaf and a bedrock of solid rice, which is then drenched with ladles of chicken and fish curry. Chicken RM3.50, fish RM2.80, or vegetarian RM2.50. Silverware is considered poor form; dig in with right hand. Open daily 11am-3pm and 6-9:30pm.

SIGHTS

Kota Bharu's sights are all within walking distance of each other and take a day or two to explore. The **Gelanggang Seni** (Cultural Centre), on Jl. Mahmud across from the Perdana Hotel, is a great place to witness local art forms and pastimes. From 3:30 to 5:30pm on Saturdays, Mondays and Wednesdays, visitors are likely to see top-spinning, kite-flying, drum-beating, and *silat* demonstrations. On Saturday and Wednesday nights (9-11:30pm), there are traditional performances of *wayang kulit* (shadow-puppet shows), dance, and traditional drama. Check with the tourist office to see what's on the schedule. All exhibitions and performances are free.

Padang Merdeka commemorates the Malay struggle against British rule. Tok Janggut, who organized rebellions against the colonial tax system in the early 1900s, was killed by the British and displayed here as a warning to other malcontents. The square is surrounded by monuments to the Malay heritage in Kota Bharu. At the east end of the rectangle, away from the river, is the **Istana Balai Besar,** a large wooden hall built in 1844. No entrance or photography is allowed here. Nearer to the river on the right side of the square are the **Royal Museum, Art and Handicraft Museum,** and **War Museum.** The surplus of museums, however, has somewhat diluted the quality of the individual collections. If you're in the mood, the **State Museum** next to the tourist information on Jl. Sultan Ibrahim is worth a gawk for its cultural exhibits. Most museums charge RM2 and are open Sat.-Thurs. 10:30am-5:45pm.

Outside Kota Bharu there are several places to visit. **Moonlight Beach** makes a pleasant excursion and has plenty of cheap accommodations and small restaurants (look for homes with signs that say *tempat penginapan, asrama,* or budget accommodations). The beach used to be named **Pantai Cinta Berahi** (Beach of Passionate Love), but the conservative Kelantan State decided that was just too suggestive. Most people still refer to it by the old name, however. To get to "PCB" take bus #10 (RM0.70), which departs every 30 minutes from in front of the Royal Museum.

A **river cruise** through the jungles and isolated villages surrounding Kota Bharu is available. Roselan "Fabulous" Hanafiah, an award-winning and cheerfully chatty guide leads a half-day tour through the canals and rivers of Kelantan (10am-1pm, 3-10 people, RM70). Check the tourist office for the specifics of the tour and meet Roselan for yourself. Travelers on a smaller budget can take their own cruise on a public river boat and then return to Kota Bharu by bus. Most boats depart from Kuala Krai, which can be reached by bus from the central terminal.

Visitors who want to fully immerse themselves can make reservations through Mr. Roselan to stay with a local family in their village through a program called **The Kampung Experience.** Visitors are allowed to choose the families they stay with (kite and batik makers, fishermen, potters, etc.), as well as learn about their profession and daily life in a Kelantan village. Three-day packages cost RM220 per person (children under 12 RM110, under 4 stay free). Reports have been glowing and it's the only program of its kind in Malaysia.

ON THE MAINLAND

■ Kuala Terengganu

Capital of a decidedly conservative Islamic state, Kuala Terengganu unfurls between the restless pounding of the South China Sea to the east and the brackish eddies of the Terengganu River to the west. Little more than a fishing village in the past, the city is once again turning to the sea with the discovery of off-shore petroleum deposits. Fed by oil, concrete air-conditioned high-rises loom over more picturesque, weathered structures from yesterday's economy. It's not a four-star destination, but burrowing for bargains in the Central Market, puttering about the boat yards of Duyong Island, and strolling in the expansive Istana Tengku Long Museum might be enough to distract beach-bound travelers for at least a little while.

ORIENTATION

Kuala Terengganu follows a basic scheme that's somewhat crumpled by sea and river at the edges. **Jalan Sultan Zainal Abidin** runs east-west along the seaward tip of the city. Its center is marked by the **express bus terminal,** across from which is the Seri Pantai Hostel. **Jalan Sultan Ismail,** the city's commercial spine, runs parallel to Jl. Sultan Zainal Abidin. Its west edge begins with the Hotel Terengganu, while to the east lie the **police station** and **immigration office. Jalan Dato Isaac** is sandwiched between these two streets. **Jalan Tok Lam** stretches from the city's center north to its shores and connects all three boulevards. Parallel and to the west is **Jalan Masjid Abidin;** travelers walking from Jl. Sultan Ismail successively encounter the **taxi station** and the **local bus station. Duyong Island,** in the waters of the west coast, is accessible by ferry from the west shores.

PRACTICAL INFORMATION

Tourist Office: Tourist Information Centre (tel. 622 15 53), on Jl. Sultan Zainal Abidin. City maps. Open Sat.-Wed. 9am-5pm, Thurs. 9am-12:45pm. **Tourism Malaysia,** 2243 Wisma MCIS Building, ground fl. (tel. 622 14 33). Open Sat.-Wed. 8am-4pm, Thurs. 8am-12:45pm.

Immigration Offices: (tel. 622 14 24), 2nd Fl. of Wisma Persekutuan Building, at the intersection of Jl. Pejabat and Jl. Sultan Ismail. Same-day visa extensions. Open Sat.-Wed. 8am-4pm, Thurs. 8am-12:45pm.

Currency Exchange: Bank Bumiputra (tel. 622 26 11), on the corner of Jl. Masjid Abidin and Jl. KG Dalam. MC, Visa, AmEx, traveler's checks. Currency exchange upstairs, next to the **ATM.** Open Sat.-Wed. 9:30am-5pm, Thurs. 9:30am-1pm.

Air Travel: (tel. 666 42 04), 13km out of town. **MAS,** 13 Jl. Sultan Omar (tel. 622 76 54). To **KL** (3 per day, RM109). MC, Visa, AmEx. Open Sat.-Wed. 8:30am-4:30pm, Thurs. 8:30am-2:30pm.

Buses: Local **buses** and **minibuses** leave from the **large terminal** at the intersection of Jl. Masjid Abidin and Jl. Syed Hussain. To: **Marang** (every 30min., 7:30am-6pm, RM1.20); **Rantau Abang** (every hr., 7am-6pm, RM3.30); **Duyong** (every hr., RM.50); and **Dungun** (every hr., 7am-10:50pm, RM4.20). **A/C buses** leave from the **Express Bus Station** near the Jl. Sultan Zainal Abidin and Jl. Tok Lam intersection. To: **KL** (3 per day, 9:30am-9:30pm, 8hr., RM21.70); **Kota Bharu** (5 per day, 8:30am-5pm, 3hr., RM7.50); **Mersing** (3 per day, 8:30am-9:30pm, RM16.10); and **Kuantan** (7 per day, 8am-4:30pm, 3½hr., RM9.20). Warisan Express to **KL** (9am, 8hr., RM20) and **Kuantan** (9pm, 3½hr., RM8). Bumi Express to: **Melaka** (10pm, 8½hr., RM20.10). Santanara Express to **Singapore** (8:30am and 9:30pm, 11hr., RM23).

Taxis: On Jl. Masjid Abidin, north of the Jl. Sultan Ismail intersection. To: **Kota Bharu** (RM48, A/C RM70); **Mersing** (RM120, A/C RM160); **Marang** (RM10, A/C RM15); **Kuantan** (RM60, A/C RM80); and **Kuala Besut** (RM40, A/C RM55)

Local Transportation: Trishaws ply the streets for RM2-3 per trip.

Pharmacies: Dew Ma, 10-D Jl. Tok Lam (tel. 622 02 00), near the north tip, with a large English sign. Open Sat.-Wed. 9am-10pm, Thurs. 9am-6pm.

Medical Services: The hospital, on Jl. Sultan Mahmud, south of the rotary.

Police: (tel. 622 22 22), on the corner of Jl. Sultan Omar and Jl. Sultan Ismail.

Post Offices: (tel. 622 85 55), on Jl. Sultan Zainal Abidin. Facing the river, it's about 100m left of Jl. Masjid Abidin. *Poste Restante.* Open Sat.-Thurs. 8am-5pm.

Telephones: Telekom office (tel. 623 15 84), on the corner of Jl. Sultan Ismail and Jl. Banggol. Overseas calls. No credit cards or calling cards. Open Sat.-Wed. 8am-5pm, Fri. and holidays 8:30am-noon. **Tourist Information Centre** has an international service booth. **Telephone code:** 09.

ACCOMMODATIONS

Awi's Yellow House, along the shores of Duyong Island. Accessible by boat from the jetty across from the tourist office or behind the Seri Malaysia Hotel on Jl. Bandar. Upon reaching Duyong, walk upriver until the sea wall stops. Cross the small bridge and continue along the shore until you reach a large boat yard. Awi's is four houses farther, past the batik shop on the left side. It's not yellow, but it does face a yellow house. Dorms RM5. Singles RM8. Doubles RM14. Family rooms for 6-7 people RM25. Cooking facilities. Boats to the city stop here around 6pm, but city buses stop at the bridge every hour until 11pm.

Ping Anchorage Traveler's Homestay, 77A Jl. Dato Isaac (tel. 622 08 51), just off the Jl. Tok Lam intersection; from the mosque it's on the right with a small English sign. Despite aloof staff, rooms are bright and airy. Roof-top café open 8am-10pm. Shared bath with sinks that leap off the wall and travel service. Dorms RM5. Singles/doubles with fan RM12-15. Rooms with bath RM30. Reception open daily 8am-10pm; gate locked at 10pm but don't worry, guests get keys.

FOOD

For a quick lunch try the cluster of cheap **food stalls** on the first floor of the local bus station on Jl. Syed Hussain. For late night excursions, the **night market** stacks up just around the corner at Jl. Tok Lam. Head to the shores of **Pantai Batu Buruk** on the east coast for similar fare in saltier, seaside settings.

Restoran Cheng Cheng, 224 Jl. Bandar (tel. 623 22 24), about 30m south of the Dragon Gate, next to a parking lot. Step up to an extensive buffet of Chinese dishes, including vegetarian selections. To calculate your bill, colored clothes pins are affixed to the edge of your plate, one for each entree, but managers often forgo this embarrassing, yet colorful ritual. Open daily noon-3pm and 5-8:30pm.

Restoran Zainuudin, 79C Jl. Tok Lam (tel. 623 37 79), near the intersection with Jl. Sultan Ismail. Plush, fuzzy blue menus. Managers say dishes are "Thai-inspired." Ginger chicken RM3. *Tom yam campur* RM4. Open daily 7am-11pm.

SIGHTS

West of the city at the intersection of Jl. Kota and Jl. Bandar, the **central market** entices visitors with hours of intrepid bargain-hunting pleasure. **Gelanggang Seni,** the cultural center, is on the east shore of Terengganu, off Pantai Batu Buruk. Locals stroll the beach in the evenings before wandering over to watch amateur troupes perform *silat* and traditional dances. Showtimes are Friday at 5pm and Saturday at 8:30pm, but schedules are erratic. Boats to restful **Pulau Duyong** depart from behind the pink and gray Seri Malaysia Hotel at the south tip of Jl. Bandar, as well as from the jetty across from the tourist office on Jl. Sultan Zainal Abidin (last boat 6pm, 15min., about RM0.50). Along these quiet shores locals still slowly construct boats of all sizes without plans or diagrams. Those with time and RM500,000 to spare can cruise home in their own custom-built yacht.

■ Marang

The photogenic visage of Marang, one of a dwindling number of coastal fishing villages that still makes its living off fishing, can be found on postcards throughout the peninsula. The picturesque, palm-fringed coastline with Kapas Island and the harbor nearby make this conservative community a relaxing getaway.

ORIENTATION AND PRACTICAL INFORMATION

In Terengganu State, Marang (not to be confused with Merang) is immediately south of Kuala Terengganu, the state capital. Marang can only be reached by the Marang or Dugan bus or shared-taxi by the Terengganu-Kuantan Highway. The **bus stop** is the highway; if you cross the bridge you've missed Marang. Most people get dropped off at the new 4-way intersection next to the giant statue of the lobster and cuttlefish in day-glo colors. When you leave town, find a place to sit with some locals and they'll help you flag down your bus. Also on the highway, on the side away from the shore, is the **post office** (tel. 618 22 15), open Sat.-Thurs. 8am-5pm. **Postal code:** 21600. The Marang **clinic** (tel. 618 22 16) is located between the two. Open Sat.-Wed. 8am-4pm, Thurs. 12:45pm-2pm. The main part of town pulses on **Jalan Lama,** the street parallel to the highway, running close to the river and beaches. It turns toward the highway at the southern end of town where the river starts to meet the sea. Jl. Lama ends at a small set of steps leading to the highway. The **police station** is at the very end of Jl. Lama on the highway side (tel. 618 22 22). Heading in the opposite direction on Jl. Lama will take you past the town's shophouses, two footbridges, and bring you to the better budget accommodations.

Offshore is **Kapas Island,** a popular resort spot. There are fine beaches here, but overdevelopment has destroyed most of the coral. Boats cost RM15 roundtrip, last boat 1pm. Last boat from Kapas is at 3-4pm. Guest houses and several agents in Marang can arrange your crossing, or you can just swim there; every year in July there is a 7km swim race to the island. First one on the beach lands RM2000.

ACCOMMODATIONS AND FOOD

There are plenty of places to stay in Marang, and most have their own eateries. Although the food situation here is not as attractive as the accommodations, there's an exciting Sunday and Wednesday **night market** which occupies most of Jl. Lama in the main part of town. For such a small town, Marang's market is big on activity and epicurean amazement.

Island View Resort and **Island View Inn,** Lot 1507 and 1506, Kg. Paya (tel. 09 618 21 81). North on Jl. Lama between the 2 footbridges, and across the street. Recently expanded, with a wider range of accommodations and a shiny veneer. The prices, however, have stayed the same. Open-air common space with TV. HCD phone. The restaurant has only a breakfast menu, but the Seafarer Restoran is nearby. Dorm beds RM7. Comfortable rooms with bath and fan RM15-18. Rooms with A/C and bath RM40, with TV and hot water RM50.

Kamal's Guest House, on Jl. Lama, just past Island View Resort toward the second footbridge. An older establishment that creaks around the joints, but friendlier and more lived-in than its neighbors. Wonderful, quiet courts and shady trees. Beds are outfitted with gloriously delirious *batik* sheets. Singles with fan and bath RM12. Private chalet RM15.

Seafarer Restoran, Lot 1507, Kg. Paya, Marang (tel. 618 28 54). Expensive, tourist-oriented, with great tropical fisherman decor. Limited selection of western and Malay dishes. Black pepper steak (RM20), *spaghetti bolognese* (RM8.50). Beef Redang and rice RM6. Fish comes straight from the docks. Four species of beer. Open daily 9am-1am.

■ Rantau Abang

Even smaller than Marang, Rantau Abang, another popular sun-and-surf destination on the east coast, hardly qualifies as a village. The east coast's shoreline stretches for hundreds of kilometers from Kuantan to Kota Bharu, and Rantau Abang would be only a blip on this lengthy stretch if it weren't for the giant leatherback turtles, which draw hundreds of tourists annually. As the currents, tides, and turtle instincts would have it, the roughly 5km stretch of beach at and around Rantau Abang is the favorite site of female leatherbacks, who come to lay their eggs between May and September, with the peak months being July and August.

ORIENTATION AND PRACTICAL INFORMATION

Rantau Abang's most visible landmark is the **Turtle Information Centre** (tel. (09) 844 169) to the left (beach side) of the highway if you are coming from points north. The highway is the only road in town. The center has decent exhibits on the turtles. There is a free video presentation (every hr., 9:30am-10:30pm). From May through August, the center is open Sat.-Thurs. 9am-1pm, 2-6pm, and 8-11pm, Fri. 9am-noon and 3-11pm. From September through April, the center is open Sat.-Wed. 8am-12:45pm and 2-4pm., Thurs. 8am-12:45pm. To leave Rantau Abang for the south, catch a **bus** to **Kuala Dungun** (RM1, last bus 5:30pm) and transfer to: Kemaman (every hr., RM3.20) and Kuantan (every hr., RM8) where you are more likely to find long-distance express connections. Practically any bus heading north will stop in **Kuala Terengganu,** where you can change buses.

ACCOMMODATIONS AND FOOD

Along the highway, there is a forlorn collection of **food stalls** next to the Turtle Information Centre. Here, the tortoise-loving backpacker will find the town's two guest houses right on the beach. Cross a boardwalk over a swampy area to access them. The only night market is in Dungun on Thursday nights; Awang's Beach Bungalows will take you there and back for RM5.

  Ismail Beach Resort (tel. (09) 843 293), has the nicest rooms, doubles with sink, fan, and satisfactory bath for RM12-15. Chalet-style structures, 1 single bed and 1 double bed, cost RM30, and 2 double beds cost RM50. The restaurant is better than the roadside food stalls but service is slow. Most meals RM2.50-5, good BBQ seafood. Open daily 8am-10pm, closed 3-6pm. Restaurant is closed 3-6pm.
  Awang's Beach Bungalows (tel. 843 500). The less decorous option; rooms are rough around the edges, baths have sandy cement floors and lack sinks. Doubles with fan RM10-15. More expensive rooms have nicer baths. Rooms with A/C RM60. Awang also arranges transportation to Kapas Island for RM15 and bike rentals are RM5 per day. Serve and dive at the beach volleyball net or putter at batik making (RM15-20). Restaurant serves Malaysian, Chinese, and western dishes. If you don't know by now, "sausage" refers to a warmed-over hot dog.

SIGHTS

Weighing up to 500kg and having a length of nearly 1.5m, the leatherback females lumber onto the beach past the high tide using their immense flippers to move about. On land, they dig a hole 60-80cm deep, lay 60-120 tennis ball-sized eggs in the nest, and bury them before returning to the sea to swim gracefully away. One female may do this 4-5 times in one season. The eggs hatch after about 55 days, with a success rate varying from 40 to 80%. A baby turtle's chance for survival to adulthood is about the same. Leatherback landings at Rantau Abang have dwindled to fewer than one-hundred. It seems clear that this drop in landings is a direct consequence of human disturbance of the leatherback's reproductive strategies. Crowds of up to 100 people gather around, shining lights and taking flash pictures, as the turtle makes her way up the beach to do her job. Some spectators have been known to sit on the turtle's back and the eggs are still considered to be a delicacy.

  The situation has improved significantly in recent years. The government has taken an active interest in the survival of the species and the preservation of Rantau Abang as a site for the turtles' egg laying. The wildlife department has set up different zones of limited or no access to visitors and eggs are collected from the sand and nurtured in hatcheries where their survival chances are much better. Unfortunately, tourists flagrantly ignore regulations prohibiting coming within 5m of a pregnant turtle, using flashlights, or flash photography. If violators are caught there is a fine of up to RM1000 or six months in prison. *Let's Go* recommends following these simple rules at the beach in Rantau Abang: Keep at least a 5m distance from the turtles; no lights; no flash photography; no campfires; no noise; and no litter.

  "Agents" patrol the beaches at night and when a turtle lands, bang on everyone's door to wake up interested tourists. Spottings RM3. If the turtle is more than a km away from where you are, rides will be offered and a total of RM6 will be charged to you for the ride and wake up call. You get trucked out to the living attraction and the exploitation begins. On the whole, it is probably both easier and cheaper to check with the turtle hatchery next to Awang's Beach Bungalows at night to see if they have any newly hatched baby turtles to release into the sea. The same strict rules apply, but the impact of the tourist is lower and the sight is inspiring.

■ Cherating

Lying prostrate on the parched shoulder of Rte. 3 is Cherating, the town the rest of Malaysia forgot. It doesn't lack foreign beach goers, however, who have set upon the village like flies. Its more attractive aspects include a windy beach (one of the world's top 10 windsurfing beaches), the occasional leatherback turtle (mostly July and August), and The Moon, one of Malaysia's best budget guest houses. Less titillating are the omnipresent beach-oriented tourists along with the mundane beach restaurants which contribute to their dissipation. Escape, however, is close at hand—just rent a bike and perambulate to the beach directly north of town or explore the back roads leading inland.

ORIENTATION AND PRACTICAL INFORMATION

Cherating is less than 50km north of Kuantan, accessible by bus (RM2.50). From **Rantau Abang** and other northern towns, public buses stop at **Dungun** and connections must be made to **Kemaman** (RM4.30). A bus from Kemaman going to Kuantan will make the Cherating stop (RM0.90), right on the highway.

The town itself has two main roads: the **Kuantan-Terengganu Highway** (running east west), and the road which runs along the beach and meets the highway at both ends. Cherating is contained within the borders of this rectangle. The eastern **bus stop** is about 100m up the road, at the intersection with the part of the road leading to The Moon. All along the beach road are guest houses and restaurants suited to varying budgets, as well as **Travel Post** (tel. 581 91 34), a de-facto **tourist office** offering **tours,** tips and packages, **international phone service,** and **currency exchange.** They may charge for its services. (Open daily 9am-10pm.)

ACCOMMODATIONS AND FOOD

A rather monotonous selection of guest houses and restaurants are packed like sardines along the beach road. They offer either A-frame style or small chalet-style huts (RM10-60). The restaurants cater to western patrons, and supply plenty of movie videos. Malay food is average-priced while western food goes for a bit more.

The Shadow of Moon at Half Past 4 (tel. 581 91 86), is located about 100m on the left when heading toward the beach from the eastern bus stop. Possibly the best reason to stay in Cherating, with its handmade wooden beds, friendly atmosphere, and nightlife at The Deadly Nightshade where you can laze on couches and browse through the polyglot library amidst skulls, and carvings. Rooms in the longhouse are RM15, chalets RM30. Weekly and monthly rates are available, or pick up a shovel and stay for free. The bar is open until 2am, beers are RM5.

Mah Long Teh Guest House (tel. 581 92 90), is on the highway behind the bus stop. Stilted bungalows with fans and mosquito nets are not glamorous but certainly up to backpacker standards. Guests are stuffed with amazing home-cooked breakfasts and dinners, included in the bare-bones price of RM12. Tea, coffee, and cool water are on tap. Rooms cost RM5.

Tanjung Inn (tel. 581 90 81) is on the road which runs parallel to the beach west of town. From the western bus stop walk toward the beach and take a right at the first and only intersection. Tanjung is 100m down on the left, featuring a well-landscaped courtyard complete with sun chairs, shaded picnic tables, and tidy bougainvillea. Well-built chalets with hardwood floors, screen windows, and trustworthy bedding (doubles) are RM20, with bath RM40. Quads RM65. Suites (max. 8) are RM400. A café is attached.

ENTERTAINMENT

Located surf-side, **Cherating Sports Centre**, a strange combination of bar and water-sports rental, offers a variety of equipment for rent. Wind surfboards are RM10 per hour, RM50 per day with instruction. Canoes are RM10 per hour, RM35 per day. Laser sailboats go for RM25 per hour, RM 80 per day. Bicycles are for rent at **Sara's Batik** at the western bus stop for RM6 per hour (RM10 per 12hr., RM19 per day). A bicycle may be necessary to reach the beach, judged by many as superior to the main beach, which lies approximately 2km to the east of Cherating. Take the highway in the direction of Kuala Terengganu. Daily volleyball matches at 5pm and nightly bonfires at 9:30pm.

■ Kuantan

From those coming from the east coast, Kuantan will seem refreshingly modern and cosmopolitan. There is a large Chinese community in town owing to its tin mining past. It is also surrounded by waterfalls, caves, and beaches that merit daytrips and its new State Mosque is one of Malaysia's most beautiful. Just 5km away is Teluk Chempedak, a pleasant beach resort with inexpensive accommodations.

ORIENTATION

The **express bus terminal** is on **Jalan Tun Ismail** in the northeast part of town. With your back to the station, proceed right (west) on Jl. Tun Ismail to **Jalan Bukit Ubi,** the town's main drag. A five-minute walk after turning left (south) on Jl. Bukit Ubi leads to the **State Mosque** and **Jalan Mahkota** where the **post office, tourist office,** and long-distance **taxi station** are located. The **local bus station** is on **Jalan Besar,** parallel to the river one block south of Mahkota.

PRACTICAL INFORMATION

Tourist Offices: (tel. 513 30 26), on Jl. Mahkota across the street from the Kompleks Terantun. Info on Taman Negara National Park, nearby sights and daytrips, and a map of Kuantan available here. Open Mon.-Fri. 9am-12:15pm and 2:45-5pm, Sat. 9am-1pm.

Immigration Offices: (tel. 521 373), on Wisma Persekutuan. Offers same-day visa extensions. Open Mon.-Fri. 8am-4:15pm.

Currency Exchange: ATM machines abound, but expect a RM5 surcharge. The **Maybank** across from the express bus station on Jl. Tun Ismail accepts MC, Visa, and Cirrus. **Hong Kong Bank,** 1 Jl. Mahkota (tel. 524 66 66), is about one block behind the mosque on the left. Accepts MC, Visa, and traveler's checks. Open Mon.-Fri. 10am-3pm, Sat. 9:30-11:30am. If banks are closed, try **Hamid Bros.,** 23 Jl. Mahkota (tel. 521 119), across from the mosque. Open Mon.-Sat. 9am-9pm, Sun. 10am-2pm. Don't confuse them with the Hamid Bros. Store down the road.

Air Travel: The **airport** (tel. 538 12 91) is west of town. Take the bus (every hr., 7am-5pm) from the local terminal or rent a taxi (RM15-20). **MAS** (tel. 515 70 55) on the ground floor of the Wisma Bolasepak Building on Jl. Gambut, has flights to **KL** (6 per day, 6:25am-10;25pm, RM74) and **Singapore** (Fri. and Sun., 6pm, RM190). Open Mon.-Fri. 8:30am-5:30pm, Sat. 8:30am-12:30pm. On Sun. and holidays call (03) 746 30 00. MC, Visa, AmEx, DC.

Buses: Local bus terminal, on Jl. Besar, about 1 block south of Jl. Mahkota. To: **Cherating** (every hr., RM2.50); **Jerantut** (7 per day, RM8); and **Kemaman** (every hr.). The new **express bus terminal** looms on Jl. Tun Ismail. To: **KL** (8 per day, RM11.90); **Melaka** (8am and 2pm, RM14.15); **Johor Bahru** (4 per day, RM16.50); **Butterworth** (8pm, RM14.15); **Kuala Terengganu** (8 per day, RM9); and **Kota Bahru** (3 per day, RM16). Luggage storage on second floor charges RM5 per hr. or RM 7 per day. Open daily 7am-12:30pm.

Taxis: From the **city taxi stand,** on Jl. Mahkota close to the pedestrian overpass, they go anywhere in town for RM4. **Share-taxis** also leave from the stand and travel the peninsula. Fare per car (max. 4 people) to: **KL** (RM100); **Jerantut** (RM80); **Kota Bahru** (RM120); and **Johor Bahru** (RM160).

Rentals: Hertz Rent-A-Car (tel. 528 041) at Samudra Riverview Hotel on Jl. Besar. Rates average RM150 per day and up; weekly packages also available. Open Mon.-Fri. 8am-6pm, Sat. 8am-3pm. Accepts major credit cards.

Medical Services: Hospital Besar Kuantan (tel. 513 33 33), on Jl. Tanah Putih. Head out of town on Jl. Besar (going southwest, away from Teluk Chempedak) and the road changes name to Jl. Tanah Putih. It's on the right.

Emergency: tel. 999.

Police: (tel. 513 22 22), on Jl. Mahkota.

Post Offices: Pejabat Pos Besar, (tel. (03) 521 032), on Jl. Mahkota at the intersection with Jl. Merdeka. Open Mon.-Sat. 8am-5pm. **Postal code:** 25670.

Telephones: Telekom office (tel. 513 92 92), next door to the post office. Especially well equipped with all imaginable services, fax (send/receive) included. Open Mon.-Sat. 8:30am-5:45pm, Sun. 8:30am-1pm. **Telephone code:** 09

ACCOMMODATIONS

New Capitol Hotel, 57-59 Jl. Bukit Ubi (tel. 505 222). Turn onto Jl. Bukit Ubi from Jl. Tun Ismail. Tiled rooms have two single beds with fresh linen and immaculate bathrooms, including small Malay cistern baths that are great for doing laundry in. Curious pedestal toilets squat 1m above the floor. Doubles RM18, with bath RM22-32 depending on size.

Kuantan Planet Hotel, 77 Jl. Bukit Ubi, 1st and 2nd Fl. (tel. 513 98 52). On the last side street on the left before the Jl. Tun Ismail intersection. Closets with bed RM11. Doubles RM18, with A/C RM30, with A/C and private bath RM38. 24-hr. check-in, and some of the best rates in town.

Hotel Crystal, 2/F, 59-61A Jl. Mahkota (tel. 526 577), opposite the Hong Kong Bank. For the A/C-oriented, this hotel has large doubles (common baths) with unspoiled blue carpeting and a choice of double or twin beds, all RM39. Spartan but soothing, with a spacious lounge area in the lobby.

FOOD

The **food stalls** are found on Jl. Mahkota near the State Mosque, behind Ocean Shopping Centre on Jl. Tun Ismail, and by the river behind the local bus terminal. Kuantan has few specialities to its name, but local chefs do a competent job with the usual Malay and Chinese dishes. Try shredded coconut with *gula melaka* placed inside a short bamboo cylinder and steamed (RM0.50). *Lemang* (rice and curry cooked in bamboo over an open flame) is also tasty and cheap (RM1).

Restoran Chan Poh, 52 Jl. Bukit Ubi (tel. 527 678), across from the cinema and a few stores down. A great place for late night *dim sum,* just ask to peek inside the miniature steamer trays out front. Tray of shrimp dumplings RM1.50, heaping plate of fried *mee* or *hor ten* RM2. Open daily 8am-1:30pm and 6-11:30pm.

Soo Sen Yen, 48 Jl. Wong Ah Jong (tel. 513 68 89). Jl. Tun Ismail become Jl. Wong Ah Jong after crossing Jl. Bukit Ubi, and Soo Sen Yen (Vegetarian Garden) is a block down on the right. Chili-oriented bean curd, gluten dishes, and claypots served in an often full, small, A/C dining room. Most dishes RM3-5. Open Tues.-Sun. 10am-3pm and 5:30-9pm, Mon. 10am-3pm.

Parvathy Restoran, 75 Jl. Bukit Ubi (tel. 514 31 40). Heading away from Jl. Mahkota it's 7 stores past the cinema on the left. Prepares a daily selection of vegetarian dishes and the old standbys: *thosai, roti, chapati,* and *nasi biryani,* plus a host of curry selections. Open daily 7am-11pm.

SIGHTS

The town's only noteworthy attraction is the **Masjid Negeri** which is more colorful and curvaceous than most mosques. Visitors are allowed inside if they are quiet and respectful, dressed appropriately (no shorts or bare shoulders), and do not walk on

MALAYSIA

the carpeted areas or onto the offices. No pictures allowed. Early morning is the best time to visit.

The most popular attraction around Kuantan is **Teluk Chempedak,** just 4km out of town on the east coast shore. Teluk Chempedak's sandy 2-km beach is bounded by rocky headlands. The developed part is at the north end, where a promenade passes by restaurants, souvenir shops, and a cheap food stalls. Walk over the bridge here and explore the trails through the forests. Past the rocks is another, much smaller, beach which offers a secluded respite from the crowd. Budget accommodations can be found at **Sri Pantai Resorts,** 2 Jl. Sim Lim (tel. 525 250), where rooms with fan (no bath) cost RM25. Rooms with bath and A/C start at RM60. MC, Visa, and AmEx. Get to Teluk Chempedak by taking bus #39 from the bus stop by the State Mosque on Jl. Mahkota (7am-9pm, RM0.60).

Also in the area are some sights worthy of daytrips. **Sungai Pandan Waterfall** is a 50m cascade with eight tiers and a large natural pool at the bottom. Take a bus (every 2hr., RM2.50) from the local bus station to Felda Panching (30km), from which point it's a 3.5-km hike to the falls. Nearby is the **Charah Cave,** a natural limestone cavern enclosing a statue of the reclining Buddha. Take bus #48 (to Sungai Lembing, RM3) from the local bus station to Panching. From the town it is a 4-km hike to the cave (admission RM1).

■ Mersing

Little needs to be said about Mersing, a small but well-off town whose name means something like *Ke* Tioman (to Tioman) to most travelers. A captive audience of bus-borne backpackers has never advanced the cause of courteous service. Food here is vastly superior to that on Tioman Island, even if the proprietors are perpetually crabby. Warnings about the conservative east coast are, for the most part, true. Women should avoid wearing shorts, and solo women travelers should expect a constant onslaught of stares, come-ons, blown kisses—the works.

ORIENTATION

The two main roads, **Jalan Abu Bakar** and **Jalan Ismail,** meet the road from Johor Bahru at a roundabout with a huge sculpture of two crossed swords. The **tourist office** and the **wharf** both lie along Jl. Abu Bakar. Next to the wharf is the blue-and-white tile **Plaza R&R,** a **tourist center** containing an **express bus terminal,** travel agencies, restaurants, and an information booth. **Taxis** and the **local bus station** are on **Jalan Selenium,** a short street one block north of Jl. Abu Bakar.

PRACTICAL INFORMATION

Tourist Offices: Mersing Tourist Information Centre (METIC) (tel. 799 52 12), on Jl. Abu Bakar. On the left from the rotary, about 100m before Plaza R&R. Friendly and knowledgable staff. Open Mon.-Fri. 8am-4:45pm, Sat. 8am-2:15pm.

Currency Exchange: Bank Bumiputra Malaysia Berhad, 4-5 Jl. Ismail (tel. 799 16 00), right next to the Embassy Hotel. **ATM** accepts MC, Visa, and Cirrus. Changes traveler's checks; RM2 charge. MC, Visa accepted (RM4 service charge). Open Mon.-Fri. 9:30am-4pm, Sat. 9:30am-noon.

Buses: Private express **long distance buses** depart and arrive either at the Restoran Malaysia or the Plaza R&R. Purchase tickets at either venue for daily buses to: **KL** (3 per day, noon-10pm, RM16.50); **Singapore** (12:30pm, RM15); **Melaka** (4 per day, 9:30am-4pm, RM11.20); **Kuantan** (1pm, RM9.10); **Kuala Terengganu** (11pm, RM18.90); and **Penang** (5pm, RM35).

Taxis: (tel. 799 13 93), on Jl. Suleiman. From the roundabout, walk down Jl. Abu Bakar. Take a left at the 1st intersection, then right at the end of the road.

Markets: Parkson Ria Supermarket, on Jl. Ismail next to the Mersing Inn. Open daily 10am-10pm.

Pharmacies/Medical Services: Kelinik Mersing, 16 Dato Muhammad Ali (tel. 799 12 70), fills prescriptions and performs exams. Open daily 8am-5:30pm; doctors

are in 10am-noon and 3-5:30pm. **Hospital Daerah** (tel. 799 33 33) is at the far end of Jl. Ismail, a 15-min. walk out of town; handles more serious ailments.
Emergency: tel. 999.
Police: tel. 799 22 22.
Post Offices: (tel. 799 10 31), on Jl. Abu Bakar. Open Mon.-Sat. 8am-5pm.
Telephones: On Jl. Dato Timor, has 6 cardphones and sells phonecards. Open Mon.-Fri. 8:45am-4:15pm, Sat. 8:45am-12:15pm. **Telephone code:** 07.

ACCOMMODATIONS

Omar's Backpacker's Hostel, on Jl. Abu Bakar, just beyond the post office if walking toward the pier. Spartan rooms, shared bath, and community kitchen. Dorms RM6. Doubles RM14. Congenial Omar also offers a tour of 3-4 islands on his boat for a bargain RM55 (including lunch, afternoon tea, and snorkeling gear; 4 person min., 12 max.). Also offers accommodations on Sibu Island, a bit farther from the mainland than Tioman. **Sheikh's** next door has more of the same.
Hotel Embassy, 2 Jl. Ismail (tel. 799 35 45), near the rotary by Bank Bumiputra. Impeccable bedding and firm mattresses at low prices. A bargain indeed. Doubles with common bath RM16, with private bath RM25, with A/C RM35.

FOOD

Small **open-air restaurants,** many specializing in seafood, abound along Jl. Abu Bakar. Try the **market** across the street from the taxi and local bus station on Jl. Suleiman for overflowing baskets of durian, bananas, mangoes and pineapples. **Loke Tien Yuen Restaurant,** 55-56 Jl. Abu Bakar (tel. 799 16 39), at the intersection with Jl. Dato Timor, has a fiercely loyal following among locals (English menu). *Charsiu* rice RM2.50. Open daily noon-9pm. **Restoran Ee Lo,** at the roundabout where Jl. Abu Bakar and Jl. Dato Mohammed Ali meet, is another popular seafood/chicken rice restaurant; it's open until midnight most nights. **Food stalls** on the main roundabout also stay open late and have average Malay dishes.

PULAU TIOMAN

Tioman is the Malaysian island paradise with perhaps the longest history as a tourist attraction. Hollywood was one of the first visitors when *South Pacific* was filmed here in 1958. It is, therefore, somewhat surprising that the island has seen little development and the tourist population is about 80% backpacker. The reason is political: Tioman is a Malay reserve area, meaning that all land is held by natives of the island. Since politicians stand to gain little from development, they have ignored the island, installing public street lights only this year. The island makes a pleasant retreat for the traveler: the sandy beaches are superb, undertow is minimal, and the water is almost perfectly clear to a depth of over 30ft. The beaches vary widely with the season: during public and school holidays, they are mobbed by city folk (high season comes in August) but during the annual monsoon season (Nov.-Jan.), the island is spurned by tourists and prices fall. June and July are probably ideal: the seas are calm, the crowds haven't arrived, but there's still enough company around to stave off boredom.

GETTING THERE AND AWAY

The most popular way to get to Pulau Tioman is by **boat** from Mersing. Boats vary widely in speed and comfort; inquire about such matters at the time of ticket purchase. The fare is RM25 for adults and RM15 for children. The best boats arrive at the first stop on Tioman 1½hr. after departure. **Do not buy a return ticket beforehand,** as it may not be honored by the ferry company that takes you back. Tioman Island's **airport** is located in Kampung Tekek. **Pelangi Air** (KL tel. (03) 262 44 53; Tioman tel. 414 71 07) has flights to and from **Singapore** (3 per day, RM196); **KL** (4 per day, RM146); and **Kuantan** (1 per day, RM84). MC, Visa, and AmEx accepted. **Tioman Air** (tel. (09) 414 78 30) makes the 15-min. flight to and from **Mersing** (2 per day, RM60) and a longer one to **Johor Bahru** (1 per day, RM105).

ISLAND ORIENTATION

Most of the popular beaches lie on the west coast. The ritzy **Berjaya Tioman Beach Resort** reigns over this side of the isle and is about midway between the north and south extremes. **Kampung Tekek** (Tekek Village), the largest village on the island, is about a 20-minute walk north of the resort. **Kampung Air Batang** is a budget haven. A smaller and more picturesque, though similarly crowded beach is at **Kampung Salang**, a 45-minute sea-bus ride from Air Batang. For some real solitude, seek out **Kampung Juara,** on the east coast of the island, where a half-dozen smallish hotels dot the largely deserted beach of firm sand. Juara is a two-hour sea-bus ride from Tekek (or a 2-hr. walk along a jungle trail). South of the resort, **Paya, Genting,** and **Nipah Villages** also boast fine beaches, but tend to be neglected by westerners. The south end of the island boasts two impressive natural formations: the **Asah waterfall** and **twin mountains** that have earned themselves the epithet "Mukut" or "grand-mother" for their resemblance to an old woman's face.

■ Kampung Tekek

Tekek, the fourth ferry stop on Tioman, is the first village with cheap accommodations. Travelers would do well to persevere, however, as this town's beach is nothing special relative to the rest of the island, and other than this the village's only remaining attractions are the airport, the mini post office, and large convenience stores. Although once a popular destination, Tekek is now avoided by tourists. The beach stretches on and on, but litter is a problem, and a new concrete embankment near the jetty has done little to improve the appearance. Yet despite this, the long expanse of white sand farther south is fine for swimming and sunbathing, and the rocky regions north of the jetty are good snorkeling spots.

ORIENTATION AND PRACTICAL INFORMATION

A bridge connects the jetty with the **airport-hotel road.** This road is actually a 2m-wide path leading to **Mango Grove/Marine Park** in the north. From there, a short bike over a hill takes you to another path which leads to **Nazri's Place** at Air Batang's north end (30min.) To the south, the road leads to the **B.T.B.R. Resort** (20min.). Coming from the jetty, the **Kompleks Terminal Kampung Tekek** is on the left, where the airline offices, mini-mart, **phones,** and **bank** are located. The **airport** is a few yards to the left of the plaza Kompleks.

There is no official **tourist office.** The Kompleks Terminal Kampung Tekek has a **money changer** which accepts only traveler's checks (no service charge). (Open Mon.-Sat. 9am-4:30pm.) On Sundays and after hours, catch the free resort bus from the airport to the cashier's counter in the Tioman Resort lobby. (RM5 surcharge for non-guests.) The **post office** is located 10 minutes south (right) of the jetty, just past the Sri Tioman signs along the road. **Telekom cardphones** are found on the jetty, at Kompleks, as well as on the road going south. (Open Mon.-Fri. 8:30am-12:30pm and 2:30-4:15pm, Sat. 8:30am-12:45pm.) **Telephone code:** 011. Just to the right of the jetty is the **clinic.** (Open Mon.-Thurs. 8am-12:45pm and 2-4:15pm, Fri. 8am-12:15pm and 2:45-4:15pm, Sat. 8am-12:45pm.)

Turn left as you get off the ferry for the **airport** (tel. 344 038). **Pelangi Air Office,** at the resort, is open daily 9:30am-12:30pm and 2:30-5pm. **Ferries to Mersing** (7:30, 8:30am, RM25, children RM15). Contact guest houses for tickets. Schedules vary. **Sea buses** sail to: **Air Batang (ABC)** and **Salang** (9:45, 11:15am, 2:15, and 4:15pm, RM3 and RM8); **Juara** (9:15am, RM55); and the **Resort** (5 per day, 9:15am- 4:15pm, RM3). Buy tickets on the boat or from the hotels. There are **bicycles for hire** at some guest houses in Mango Grove, north of Tekek for RM5 per hour. The **RND Mini Mart,** a 10-minute walk south, across the road from Liza Restaurant, stocks an impressive inventory, including the all-important flashlight for those pitch-black nights. (Open daily 7:30am-11pm.)

ACCOMMODATIONS AND FOOD

There are a few establishments at Mango Grove, located at the northern end of Tekek, a 20-min. walk away. Although they are mediocre, the beach here is quieter and cleaner than in the village proper. **Ramli's** (tel. (010) 716 673) is a cheap, if not altogether genial, establishment of clean bungalows with fans, double beds, and baths attached (RM15, RM10 for stays of a week or more). The beach in front is too rocky for swimming, but there's fine snorkeling off the coast. A double chalet is RM10-12, with bath RM20-40. The restaurant is open daily 8-11am and noon-10pm. Trips to Coral Island are available. **Sri Tioman Chalets & Café** (tel. 414 51 89). Turn right from the jetty and walk five minutes until you pass Liza Restaurant. Look for the sign on the right, the hotel is beach-side. Loose linoleum floor makes a good ant refuge—keep everything edible off your bed. Bathrooms are clean but lack sinks. Attached café is just average. Doubles with bath in the back of the compound are RM25, in the middle RM30, with sea view RM40. (Open daily 7:30am-10pm.)

SIGHTS AND ENTERTAINMENT

The best option here is an excursion to the talcum powder beaches of **Coral Island,** where reefs and abundant marine life invite snorkeling. The island is accessible from all three of the western beaches and is most cheaply reached from Salang. From Tekek, **Diveros** (tel. 352 776) offers a two-dive, five-hour trip to Lord Island for RM160 (equipment included) as well as equipment rental and five-day beginner courses for RM750. They are located on the beach next to Sri Tioman Chalets.

The **round-island sea bus** is a good way to combine swimming and snorkeling with sight-seeing. The boat leaves from the Tekek jetty at 9:15am and goes around the southern coast, passing the twin mountains known as Mukut (grandmother) and stopping at **Asah Waterfall,** which has been featured in many Hollywood films. The sea bus makes a lunch-stop at Juara, continuing on to Teluk Dalam for snorkeling. The trip takes an entire day and costs RM40 without equipment.

An excellent break from beach monotony is the surprisingly cool and insect-free trek (about 1½-2½hr., 4km) from Tekek to Juara. From the jetty, turn left on the cement path and walk for about 500m, taking a right on the paved path just before the mini mart. The trail is steep but well maintained—at the halfway point it becomes a smooth paved road. Once in Juara, take a sea bus (RM15) back to Tekek.

▓ Kampung Air Batang

Kampung Air Batang offers absolutely nothing other than backpacker accommodations, food, and souvenir shops. The beach is cleaner than Tekek's and social life is more varied than Salang's...slightly.

ACCOMMODATIONS, FOOD, AND ENTERTAINMENT

Air Batang Chalets (tel. 349 868), at the end of the road left from the jetty, is so famous that it is now usually known as ABC. The hotel is a lively place frequented by backpackers of all nationalities; their basketball court and restaurant, widely regarded as the best in all of Air Batang, are both constantly hopping. Doubles RM10, with bath RM15, with fan RM20. Bungalows on Bamboo Hill with a good sea view are RM40. The restaurant is open daily 7:30am-10pm, last orders taken at 9pm. Snorkel gear rental is RM10 per day.

Nazri's II (tel. 333 486), can be reached by turning left off the jetty and walking 10 minutes; Nazri's II directly precedes ABC. Spacious, widely-spaced chalets for two roost on the hillside and feature hardwood floors, mirrored dressers, and sparkling bathrooms. Hill-view doubles RM25-35. Sea-view doubles are RM35-45. Doubles with mountain views go for RM55. The excellent restaurant overhangs the hillside, offering set dinner specials. Jet ski rental is RM60 per half hour.

Nazri's Place (tel. 349 534), is at the far south end of the beach, past TC. Nazri's has rooms arranged in blocks and neat little flower gardens in front of each chalet. Rooms contain one double bed and one bunk, plus private bath, fan, and a large veranda (RM60). Rooms in the back lot have 4 bunks; doubles are RM30. Triples go for RM40. Quads RM50. Huts without electricity are RM10, A/C doubles RM30. The **restaurant** turns into a hopping hangout at night with mixed drinks (RM8-15). Open daily 7:30-11am and noon-3pm; drinks only 3-7pm and 7-11pm. Snorkeling equipment (RM12) and boat tickets available. Reception closes 11pm.

Ben's Dive Shop, north of the jetty, has four-day certification courses for RM650, full day excursions to Coral Island (2 dives) for RM150, and equipment rental for off beach dives (RM45 for one tank and equipment). Open daily 8:25am-6pm.

■ Kampung Salang

Salang, at the north tip of Tioman Island, is the last stop on the ferry from Mersing. The extra 20 minutes on the boat necessary to reach this small dreamy beach is well-spent. The town is crammed with foreigners and dive shops and is relatively pricey, but the seas are headier and the setting generally more attractive.

ORIENTATION AND PRACTICAL INFORMATION

The beach and budget accommodations stretch out on both sides of the pier. The right of the jetty is more popular with swimmers and sunbathers and has most of the restaurants and cafés. Most budget hotels offer **currency exchange** at mediocre rates. International (RM13 per min.) telephone calls can be made from the reception desk. **Telephone code: 011. Sea buses** set out at 8:30, 10am, 1, 3, 3:30 (except Fri.), and 5pm to: **ABC** (RM6); **Tekek** (RM8); and **round-island** (8:30am, RM35). **Ben's Diving Centre** (tel. 717 014) offers the same services as it does in Air Batang. Rental of scuba gear for off-beach dives is RM45 (one tank). One dive costs RM90 and two are RM115. All equipment is included. MC, Visa, and traveler's checks are accepted. **Fishermen Scuba Studio** (tel. 730 230), just to the left from the jetty, is well-equipped, and has professional guides. Two dives are RM140 (including lunch and guide); prices are reduced to RM110 for three or more people. A half-day is RM110, night dives are RM70. There is a reduced rate for multiple dives. Credit cards are accepted.

ACCOMMODATIONS AND FOOD

There are around half a dozen inexpensive hotels in Salang, all lined up along the beach. Most have restaurants which serve Malay, Chinese, and western seafood. **Salang Pustaka (Khalid's Place)** (tel. 953 421), on the right from the jetty (follow the signs), is set back from the beach across a wooden bridge. Dorms are RM10. Chalets with small porches and fan have fake stone floors. Doubles go for RM25. Quads RM70, with A/C RM96. Quints with bath are RM60, with A/C RM120. Trips to Coral Island are RM25 (snorkeling gear included). **Salang Sayang (Zaid's Place)** (tel. 719 820), is to the right from the jetty (follow the signs). This hotel has it all, even a tiny library (RM3 per book for 3 days; RM20 deposit). Rooms are compact with pink mosquito netting, towels, and soap. Doubles are RM50-75 depending on size and view, basic triples go for RM60. Family room (quad) is RM80. All have attached bath. Safety deposit box. Reservations recommended for August.

■ Kampung Juara

Juara, the island's lonely east coast town, was actually Tioman's original settlement. Before 1928 the island was completely unsettled with the exception of this close-knit community. Then, an outbreak of black magic in that year killed off about half the townspeople, after which many survivors fled to the west coast. Juara is the hardest

place to reach on the island, but is worth a stay, due to its excellent snorkeling, lower tourist concentration, and deserted beach that drops into indigo depths.

ORIENTATION AND PRACTICAL INFORMATION

Chalets spread out on both sides of the rickety jetty. The road is set back from the beach and the jungle trail to Tekek meets it south of the jetty. **Happy Café,** next to the jetty, will **exchange** traveler's checks and major currencies, but rates are unpredictable. Happy Café also sells ferry and sea bus tickets. The **ferry** departs for **Mersing** (8:30am, RM25) while the **sea bus** heads off to **Tekek, Air Batang, Salang,** and **Berjaya Resort** (3pm, RM15, to the resort RM20). The **Mini Mart** at Atan's Place is open daily 7:30am-11:30pm.

ACCOMMODATIONS AND FOOD

Atan's Place and Turtle Café (tel. (07) 799 23 09), to the left of the jetty, is an attractive dark wood chalet with blue and white tile baths (RM15). The restaurant is uninspiring. No alcohol is allowed. (Open daily 7:30am-11:30pm.) Their snorkeling and trekking trips are recommended. **Juara Bay Resort** is a 10-15 minute walk to the left from the jetty. Brand new chalets perch on the hillside over a small inlet at the southern end of Juara's main beach. The chalets have nice hardwood floors, porches, and tile baths. All are doubles, costing RM30, regardless of view. The deck/café down below is breezy and shaded and a good place to relax, a quality lacking in most other establishments on the beach.

SARAWAK

Sarawak earned its name when the Sultan of Brunei handed it over to James Brooke, the first White Rajah, with the simple words *"Serah kapada awak,"* meaning "I give this to you." For the next century, the Brooke family stood as the de facto rulers of Sarawak, attempting to control the excesses of the land and the unruliness of rival head-hunting tribes. After finally toppling the White Rajah and the British, Sarawak sought protection under the Federation of Malaysia in 1963.

The largest of Malaysia's 13 states, Sarawak is also the richest, due to its massive expanse of seemingly endless jungle. Since the frenzied logging industry boomed just over 30 years ago, loggers have left many barren tracts of land across the region. As the government welcomes the billions of ringgit rolling in, they have even less incentive to preserve Sarawak's rainforest. With over 60% of its jungles approved for logging, Sarawak is now the world's leading exporter of timber. Unfortunately, the state's 27 ethnic cultures as well as its wildlife are slowly being exposed and forced out of their homelands by the deforestation. Over the last few years, indigenous environmentalists, with the help of Swiss activist Bruno Manser, have criticized the Malaysian government for its lack of concern for the well-being of Sarawak's inhabitants. The flak that the government has taken for its support of the logging industry has made it wary of international travelers, and any trip into the wilds usually requires a permit. Despite whatever unpleasantness that this application process make evoke, rest assured that it is worth it to see the wonders of Sarawak, including the famed longhouses, fathomless caves, talcum beaches, and the stygian recesses and razor pinnacles of Gunung Mulu National Park.

■ Kuching

Kuching is East Malaysia's most enjoyable and dynamic urban experience. It's also the capital of Sarawak is the Federation of Malaysia's largest state. The peculiar mystery of its naming has slowly become the stuff of travel guide legends. Originally it was known simply as Sarawak. Later, the second White Rajah Charles Brooke inexplicably renamed it *Kuching* (cat). Some locals insist that the name was inspired by the Chinese word *kochin,* meaning harbor. Others retort that it was named after a tropical fruit tree, rather like a lychee that grows wild along the river's edge—the *mata kuching* (cat's eye fruit). Still others whisper in conspiratorial tones that the charming town owes its famous name to a spectacular case of cultural misunderstanding. When the Raja inquired about the name of the particularly attractive stretch of land along the river, his counselors instead thought he was pointing to a long cat on the shore, and replied *"kuching."*

Regardless of where it takes its name from, Kuching is, without a doubt, a multi-faceted city with unique appeal. Gleaming 15-foot tall statues of cats and examples of turn-of-the-century architecture jostle with some of the best museums in Southeast Asia. After an afternoon of perusing the best craft and souvenir shops in both Sarawak and Sabah, visitors might want to take some time promenading along the Iban-inspired mosaics and colored cobbles of the newly renovated waterfront esplanade. Farther afield are the Sarawak Cultural Village and the Semenggoh Wildlife Rehabilitation Centre. Bako National Park, the oldest in Sarawak, is only a brief two-hour bus and boat journey farther northeast.

ORIENTATION

Kuching proper unfolds along the southern banks of the **Sarawak River** and can be divided into three discrete districts: west, central, and east. The street running along the river connects these three areas. It begins in the extreme west of the city as **Jalan Gambier.** In this general vicinity are the **local bus terminals,** the mosque, and the **night market.** As the road travels east it becomes **Jalan Main Bazaar.** The venerable **Fort Margherita** stands across the river. A right before the courthouse leads to **Jalan Barrack,** while a right past the courthouse leads to **Jalan Tun Haji Openg.** The central district of Kuching commences past the souvenir shops on Jl. Main Bazaar, at a busy intersection presided over by the scarlet walls of **Tua Pek Kong Temple.** Turning right brings you down **Lebuh Temple** and to most of Kuching's budget accommodations. After entering the eastern section of Kuching, past the concrete wedge of the Hilton Hotel, Jl. Main Bazaar becomes **Jalan Tunku Abdul Rahman,** which eventually forks at a kitschy statue of regal felines. Jl. Tunku Abdul Rahman continues to the left, while to the right is **Jalan Padungan.** Travelers should exercise particular care while meandering Kuching's streets; there are few crosswalks and even fewer motorists sympathetic to pedestrians' concerns.

PRACTICAL INFORMATION

Tourist Offices: The **Ministry of Tourism** (tel. 410 944), on Jl. Barrack, across from the town playing fields and before the new wing of the Sarawak Museum, with a large English sign in front. The excellent staff can answer most questions and offers detailed information on transportation, sights, and local events. The **National Parks and Wildlife Office** (tel. 248 088) is in the same building. Come here to make reservations for accommodations in Bako National Park and arrange permits for both Bako and Semenggoh Wildlife Rehabilitation Centre. Open Mon.-Thurs. 8am-4:15pm, Fri. 8am-4:45pm, Sat. 8am-12:45pm. **Sarawak Tourist Association (STA),** along the esplanade, opposite the courthouse (tel. 248 620). Also has a small counter at the airport terminal. Provides good maps and brochures. A good place to look for postings from yachts seeking crews for journeys to other Asian ports. Open Mon.-Thurs. 8am-12:45pm and 2-4:15pm, Fri. 8-11:30am and 2:30-4:45pm, Sat. 8am-12:45pm.

Tours and Travel: Tropical Adventures Tours and Travel, 17 Jl. Main Bazaar, 1st. Fl. (tel. 413 088). A respected company offering trips to local longhouses and adventure tours to national parks. A 2-day trip to a longhouse runs RM600 for 1 person, RM250 per person for 5-10 people. Longer 5-day river and trekking packages cost RM1500 for 2 people to RM1100 per person for groups of 5-10. **Borneo Transverse,** 15 Jl. Green Hill (tel. 257 784), offers similar tour experiences and is recommended by STA. MC, Visa, AmEx accepted with a 3.5% charge.

Embassies and Consulates: Indonesia, 5A Jl. Pisang (tel. 241 734). Residents of most western nations no longer need apply for visas to cross into Indonesia at Pontianak or Entikong. 2-mo. visas are issued free at the border with a passport valid for at least 6 mo. and proof of a return plane ticket. Open Mon.-Thurs. 8am-noon and 2-4pm, Fri. 8am-noon and 2-4pm.

Immigration Offices: (tel. 245 661), 2nd Fl., Bangunan Sultan Iskandar, Jl. Simpang Tiga, Petra Jaya. Take the blue-and-white Chin Lian Long Bus #14A or 14B to Petra Jaya (20min., RM0.50). The office is in the gray 18-story building before the overpass. 1-mo. visa extensions take a few hours to process. There's a RM1 filing fee, and you must have a plane ticket out of the country when applying. Open Mon.-Thurs. 8am-noon and 2-3:30pm, Fri. 8-11am and 2-3:30pm, Sat. 8am-noon.

Currency Exchange: Hock Hua Bank, 28 Jl. Tun Haji Openg (tel. 417 922), directly across from the post office. Open Mon.-Fri. 9:30am-3:30pm, Sat. 9:30am-noon. **Bank Bumiputra** (tel. 236 809), next to Singapore Airlines on Jl. Tunku Abdul Rahman. Open Mon.-Fri. 9:30am-4pm, Sat. 9:30am-noon.

American Express: (tel. 252 400), 3rd Fl., MAS building on Jl. Song Thian Cheok. No check cashing services. Open Mon.-Fri. 8:30am-5:30pm. **Cardmember mail** can be collected form the **CPH Travel Agency,** 70 Jl. Padungan (tel. 426 025), just off the intersection with the cat statue.

Air Travel: Kuching International Airport (tel. 457 373), 10km south of the city. Sarawak Transport Company's bus #12A runs to town (every hr., last bus 6pm, 30min., RM0.90), or purchase a coupon for a taxi to the city center (RM16.50). **Storage lockers** available for RM3 per day. Convert your money before arriving at the airport, but save RM40 for the **airport tax. Singapore Airlines** (tel. 240 266), next to the Riverside Majestic Hotel on Jl. Tunku Abdul Rahman. To **Singapore** (Wed. and Sat., 6pm, RM267). Open Mon.-Fri. 8:30am-noon and 1:30-4:30pm, Sat. 8:30am-noon. **Dragon Air** (tel. 233 322), in the same building as Singapore Airlines. To **Hong Kong** (Wed. and Sun., RM1429). Open Mon.-Fri. 9:30am-12:30pm and 2:30-5pm, Sat. 8:30am-12:30pm. MC, Visa, AmEx. **MAS** (tel. 246 622), on Jl. Song Thian Cheok. Daily to: **Sibu** (RM72); **Bintulu** (RM117); **Miri** (RM164); **Kota Kinabalu** (RM228); and **Sandakan** (RM284). Morning flights to **KL** are cheapest at RM192; later in the day, RM267. Daily flights to **Singapore** (RM307) and **Hong Kong** (RM1162).

Buses: There are 3 main local bus companies in Kuching. **Sarawak Transport's (STC)** green-and-cream buses depart from the bus stop on the west end of the esplanade across from the courthouse on Jl. Java. Bus #6 goes to **Semenggoh**

Wildlife Centre, bus #12A to the **airport,** and buses #3, 3A, 9, 9A, and 9B all run to the **long-distance bus terminal** outside of town on Penrissen Rd. (6am-9pm, RM0.50). **Chin Lian Long's (CLL)** blue-and-white buses depart from in front of the mosque on Jl. Mosque. Buses #17 and 19 (RM0.70-1) service Bintawa Express wharf. **Petra Jaya's (PJ)** red, yellow, and black buses depart from Jl. Khoo Hun Yeang near the night market. Bus #6 runs to the wharf for boats to **Bako National Park** and bus #2B to the **cultural village** in Damai. Long-distance buses depart from the Penrissen Rd. terminal ouside of town. To get there, take STC bus #3, 3A, 9A, or 9B or a taxi (RM10). To **Miri** (12:30 and 1pm, 4 more 9-10pm, RM70), via **Sibu** (RM32) and **Bintulu** (RM52). Arrive early to ensure a ticket. **P.O. Mudah** runs a bus to **Pontianak** (1pm, RM34.50). **Biaramas Express** goes to **Pontianak** as well (7am and 12:30pm, RM34.50).

Boats: Boats are the most convenient way to Sibu. Express boats depart from the **Bintawa Express Wharf.** CLL buses #17 or 19 (30min., RM0.70) go to the wharf. **Ekspress Bahagia,** 50 Padungan Rd. (tel. 421 948), has one boat direct to **Sibu** (12:45pm, RM33-38) and one via **Sarikei** (8:30am, RM29-36).

Rentals: Pronto Car Rental, 98 Jl. Padungan (tel. 237 889, 24-hr. line (010) 887 04 68). Pronto Sages are RM140 per day; 4WD RM450 including insurance. IDP required. Also has a booth at the airport. Reservations requested. Open Mon.-Sat. 8am-5pm. MC, Visa, AmEx.

Markets: The not-so-impressive **daily market** converges on the western banks of the Sarawak River just off Jl. Gambier. More happening is the weekly **Sunday Market,** although it's actually at its best on a Saturday night. It sets up near the Jl. Jawa-Jl. Satok intersection in the southern part of town.

Pharmacies: PharmaCARE Medicine Shoppe (tel. 412 600) in the basement of the Riverside Majestic Shopping complex. Also stocks an extensive selection of western toiletries. Open daily 10am-10pm. MC, Visa, AmEx.

Police: (tel. 241 222), at the corner of Jl. Khoo Hun Yeang and Jl. Barrack. ·

Post Offices: (tel. 248 091), on Jl. Tun Haji Openg in an austere building with a grand façade of columns and friezes. *Poste Restante* in the room to the right of the main entrance. Open Mon.-Sat. 8am-noon and 2-4pm.

Telephones: at the GPO, including one that accepts credit cards. If these are broken or in use, try the night market. The airport also has credit card phones. Most of the major hotels can provide fax services.

ACCOMMODATIONS

Kuching Hotel, 6 Jl. Temple, 1st Fl. (tel. 413 985), next to Hong Garden. Exceptionally outgoing staff keeps track of everyone's name by logging them in on a chalkboard. Sturdy rooms with fan, sink, and shared bathrooms. Across from a construction site, so things can get noisy. Singles RM18. Doubles RM23.

Anglican Rest House (tel. 240 188), on Jl. McDougall. Enter via the driveway on Jl. McDougall and follow the road to the left as it forks to the back of the church compound. Perched on a small hillock, surrounded by verdant lawns and fragrant frangipani trees. Solemn, yet elegant interiors with polished wooden floors and unadorned, cavernous halls. Spartan singles with excellent views on the top floor RM18. Doubles RM23. Quiet cubbies on the first floor: singles RM20, doubles RM25. All rooms have fan and shared bathrooms. 2 small apartments with attached bath are also available for RM30, or RM35 for double occupancy.

B & B Inn, 30-I Tabuan Rd., 1st and 2nd Fl. (tel. 237 366), next door to the Borneo Hotel. Kuching's only hostel has plenty of tourist info, as well as daily newspapers and a small common area where tourists can lounge and exchange travel advice. Dorms RM14, light breakfast included. Singles RM22. Doubles RM30. All have shared bath and showers.

Orchid Inn, 2 Jl. Green Hill (tel. 411 417), past the Tiger Garden Restaurant and Rurama Lodging House. Spacious rooms are quiet if a bit dark, and come with the extra bonus of a bathtub to soak away those travel-induced aches and pains. All rooms have A/C, private bath, and TV. Singles RM40. Doubles RM45. Extra jumbo family rooms available for RM55. MC, Visa, AmEx.

FOOD

Inexpensive and delicious cuisine is everywhere in Kuching. **Vendors** cluster in the west end of town, just south of the terminus of Jl. Gambier. Also popular are the **stalls** opposite the Chinese temple on Jl. Carpenter. **Top Spot Food Court,** opposite Dragon Air on Jl. Padungan, has 36 food stalls atop a car park. The **open-air café** on the ground floor of the Beijing Riverbank Restaurant, across from the Riverside Majestic Hotel at Kuching's esplanade, also provides light refreshment. (Open 24 hours.) A Chinese-Muslim restaurant upstairs sometimes serves all-you-can-eat buffet specials. For dining with a view, head to **Menara Cafeteria** (tel. 234 369) atop the civic center tower on Jl. Budaya (open daily 10am-10pm). Follow Jl. Tun Haji Openg away from the river to the traffic rotary. The white tower is visible from here. On a clear day, Gunung Santubong and Serapi are visible from the observation platform.

See Good Food Centre (tel. 232 609), on the ground floor of Wisma Si Kiong, directly behind the MAS building. Uncontainable, See Good's festive green-and-red tables spill out into the parking lot and street. Round up a few friends for some of Kuching's tastiest and cheapest prawns, fish, crab, squid, and clams. A complete meal goes for RM9.50. Free bananas. Open daily 5pm-midnight. Closed the 4th and 8th of every month.

Zun San Yen Vegetarian Restaurant, Lot 165, Jl. Chan Chin Ann (tel. 230 068). Turn left off Jl. Tunku Abdul Rahman onto Jl. Chan Chin Ann at the Pizza Hut. Zun San Yen is halfway down, on the right. A/C restaurant with a buffet overflowing with savory sautéed fern fiddleheads and wild mushrooms with tofu. Price is by the gram; a generous self-serve selection of 2-3 dishes and a plate of rice run a meager RM3-4. Open daily 7:30am-2:30pm and 5:30-9:30pm.

Bismillah Restaurant, Jl. Khoo Hun Yeang. Down the street on the left from the police station across the intersection with OCBC Bank. A popular North Indian Muslim restaurant; it can be difficult finding a table in the mornings. The fire of their curries can only be smothered with heaping plates of *biryani* rice and *naan* (RM1.80) and numbing glasses of *lassi* (RM2). Open Mon.-Sat. 7am-6pm.

Caprila Ice Cream Café (tel. 422 057), on the first floor of the Sarawak Plaza. Probably your last chance for a cup of fragrant earl grey tea (RM1.60) or a frothy cappuccino (RM2.40) before plunging into Sarawak's profane world of lukewarm Nescafé and bitter local brews. Caffeine-conscious travelers also enjoy the café's robust A/C over dishes of ice cream. Open daily 10am-9:30pm.

SIGHTS

The streets of Kuching are spiced with unexpected confrontations with colonial architecture, which was spared the serious bombing during World War II that afflicted other eastern Malaysian cities. Located along the esplanade and Jl. Main Bazaar, the quiet white façade of the **courthouse,** built in 1874, conveniently fronts the Square Tower, built in 1879 as a fortress and prison. Across the river are the gleaming pavilions of the **Istana,** built in 1870 by Charles Brooke as a bridal gift to his new wife. The grounds, now the residence of the head of state of Sarawak, are closed to the public, but are beautifully illuminated every night. On Jl. Tun Haji Openg is the **Round Tower,** built in the 1880s as a hospital, and fortress if needed. **Bishop's House,** located within the Anglican Church complex, has the distinction of being the oldest accommodation in Sarawak. The simple, wooden structure was completed in 1849 for Dr. McDougall, the nation's first Anglican bishop. It's now a private residence and closed to visitors. The oldest Taoist temple in Sarawak, **Tun Pek Kong** stands on Jl. Temple, across the street from the esplanade.

The region's most comprehensive and engaging museums are ensconced within Kuching center and, best of all, each is free. Across the river the antique walls of **Fort Margherita** (1879), named after Charles Brooke's wife, have been restored to house a **Police Museum.** It's the only remaining fort in the state where visitors are permitted. Take the ferry from the esplanade across the river (RM0.20) and walk past the park on the right to the road beyond. Turn right and head up the hill. At the gate you

The Dynasty of the White Rajahs

In the 19th century, the term "White Rajah" struck the fancy of many Europeans, conjuring up exotic images of a princely dynasty ruling over savage head-hunters. In 1839, James Brooke, a wealthy Englishman, stepped in to settle some difficulties the Sultan of Brunei was experiencing with the Dayaks, Malays, and Chinese of present-day Sarawak (which had been under Brunei's control since the 15th century). In return for his assistance, the sultan bequeathed him the vast territory and Brooke named himself the *rajah*. Only five short years after this, Brooke attacked Brunei and demanded more land, specifically the island of Labuan. Despite the White Rajah's might, conflict persisted within his private fiefdom; pirates were an ever-present menace and Brooke, deeply embroiled in the head-hunting fervor, laid down hefty rewards for their heads.

Charles Brooke succeeded his uncle to become the second White Rajah in 1863. A pragmatic man, he had no qualms about using ruthless means to achieve his goals. The acquisition of land and consolidation of territories continued until his death in 1917, when his son Charles Vyner Brooke stepped up as the next *rajah*. The region's steady development continued under his direction until the Japanese invaded in the 1942. After World War II, Charles Vyner returned from Sydney, Australia and Sarawak was annexed a British colony on July 1, 1946. In response, Anthony Brooke, Charles Vyner's nephew and heir apparent, backed an anti-secessionist movement that ultimately climaxed with the murder of Sarawak's appointed British Governor in 1949. After this violent incident the heretofore peaceful movement began to lose its credibility and Anthony renounced his claims, while the British used the attack as an opportunity to forcefully crack down on remaining protesters. Following Peninsular Malaysia's independence in 1957, Sarawak, along with Brunei and Sabah, entered negotiations to join the Federation of Malaya and was formally incorporated six years later. Thus ended the dynasty of the White Rajah.

must surrender your passport and pick up a pass. (Open Tues.-Sun. 10am-6pm; free.) The **Chinese Museum,** a small butterscotch building along the esplanade, across from Tua Pek Kong Temple, traces the migration of Sarawak's Chinese community and its role in the town's history. (Open Tues.-Sun. 9am-6pm; free.)

The **Sarawak Museum,** on Jl. Tun Haji Openg, is not to be missed, it is reputed to be one of Southeast Asia's finest. Follow the road away from the river and past the town green. The pedestrian overpass to the new wing is clearly visible from the road; turn left and walk up the to the main entrance in the old wing. The original building's design was inspired by the town houses of Normandy, France. The downstairs of the old wing is mostly occupied by natural history displays and a small section on the role of the oil industry in Sarawak. The exhibits upstairs focus on Sarawak's 27 ethnic groups, with an Iban longhouse, tribal dwellings, and intricate Orang Ulu wood carvings. (Open Sat.-Thurs. 9am-6pm; free.)

The **Sarawak Islamic Museum** looms just behind the new wing of the Sarawak Museum. Its seven galleries are beautifully decked out with stunning examples of Islamic art from both Southeast Asia and abroad. Illuminated religious texts, mother-of-pearl inlaid furniture and lengths of gold-threaded textiles are part of a survey of the range of art inspired by this religion. (Open Sat.-Thurs. 9am-6pm; free.)

ENTERTAINMENT AND NIGHTLIFE

After the sodden heat of the afternoon has relented, most of Kuching's residents head to the newly completed **esplanade** along Sarawak River to people-watch and stroll in the evening breezes. Despite a rather eerie Disney-like feel, the dramatically-lit fountains, manicured drifts of flowers, and arabesques of Iban-inspired paving patterns offer a pleasing respite from the trials of city life at the end of a long day. Tourists can indulge in a bit of quiet nostalgia and hire a *sampan* from the docks for a leisurely cruise by moonlight (RM15-20 per hr.).

For a bit of nightlife, amble over to **De Tavern,** Lot G21, Taman Si Sarawak, Jl. Borneo, level 1 (tel. 419 723), across from the Hilton. Patrons can loll on one of the couches and watch unsuspecting visitors stumble in front of the dart board hung precariously close to the front door. Barflies can add *tuak* (rice wine) to more traditional malted options such as Carlsberg Beer for RM11.80 per bottle. (Open daily 4:30pm-1:30am; happy hour 4:30-8:30pm.)

SHOPPING

Kuching is absolutely the best place to buy East Malaysian crafts. Stores overflow with fierce Iban spirit masks, tapestries, Penan baskets, and blowguns. Most of the shops line up along Jl. Main Bazaar. **Unika Gallery,** 5 Jl. Wayang (tel. 413 282), off Jl. Main Bazaar, is worth a browse. Prices here are a bit higher, but so are the quality of goods and the wealth of expertise held by the English-speaking staff. (Open Mon.-Sat. 9:30am-5:30pm.) Pursuing Kuching's shops can be both overwhelming and disturbing; in addition to examples of modern craft, it seems a good part of the region's cultural heritage is for sale as well. As a result, travelers should exercise caution when making purchases. Be prepared to shop around and then bargain hard—a single piece of *ikat* weaving can easily run RM700.

■ Near Kuching

SARAWAK CULTURAL VILLAGE

The **Sarawak Cultural Village** is cultural voyeurism at its best. Unabashedly touristy and artificial, this self-styled "living museum" is more like a zoo. It's the best place in East Malaysia to gain a brief insight into the indigenous life-styles that are quickly becoming outmoded. Sprawling in the shadow of Gunung Santubong, the 17-acre village highlights seven reconstructions of Bidayuh, Iban, Penan, Orang Ulu, Melanau, Malay, and Chinese dwellings. Each is inhabited by a cast of English-speaking representatives from each culture, who engage in typical domestic activities and answer any questions visitors might have. Having an Iban woman patiently explain how she produces glittering lengths of *ikat* cloth from what appears to be a hopeless tangle of colored thread is much more engaging than seeing the finished product hanging on a museum wall. The buildings themselves are well worth inspection. The day culminates with tribal dancing and singing in the village theater. These are very contrived as dancers pop balloons with blowgun darts, but each scene is well-choreographed and the costumes are traditional ethnic dress. There are two programs daily. The first is from 9am-12:15pm, and the second from 1:30-5:15pm. Dances are staged at 11:30am and 4:30pm. Admission to the village (tel. 846 411) is a hefty RM45 for adults, RM22.50 for children under12. PJ bus #2B departs from Jl. Khoo Hun Yeang to Damai and the cultural village (7:30, 8:45, 10am, 1:30, 4:45, and 6pm, 45min., RM2.80). For the return trip, PJ buses depart from the rotary in front of the village entrance (8:30, 9:45, 11am, 2:30, 5:45, and 7pm). Sometimes the later buses fail to show, but it's still possible to catch one of the shuttle buses from the Holiday Inn at Damai to Kuching (10:05am, 1:50, 5:25, 7:25, and 9:30pm, RM10).

SEMENGGOH WILDLIFE REHABILITATION CENTRE

This is one of the best places to see the region's peculiar and alluring forest inhabitants up close. Established in 1976, conditions at the center are generally better than at most zoos in Southeast Asia. The center takes custody of wild animals and birds, many of them endangered, that have been injured or kept illegally as pets, and gradually rehabilitates them to the point where they can survive on their own.

The most popular residents of the center are the young orangutans, who return twice per day to receive handouts of fruit to supplement whatever they forage in the park's forests. The adult orangs who have failed to be reintroduced to the wild are kept in a large cage away from the rest of the animals. These surly old orangs spit sugarcane husks and throw banana peels at the visitors who peer too closely or disturb them with camera flashes. Displayed along a plank walk farther beyond are the cages of other species of animals, all in various stages of reintroduction. Residents usually include Proboscis monkeys, gibbons, honey bears, silvered langurs, bear cats, and several species of eagles, storks, and the famous hornbill.

Feeding times are at 8:30am and 3pm. Gifts of tropical fruit such as rambutan, jackfruit, and durian are much appreciated; leave them with the park officers when you arrive. Visitors are asked to never feed the animals, since it interferes with the rehabilitation program; in addition, they can bite and catch colds and other diseases easily from humans. Permits are required to visit the center and can be arranged at the government information center (tel. 248 088) on Jl. Barrack in Kuching.

A taxi costs RM30 one way to the Semenggoh. STC bus #6 departs from the bus stop at the west end of the esplanade on Jl. Gambier at 8:20, 10:300am, noon, and 1:30pm (45min.) and drops passengers off at the Forest Department nursery; from here it's a half-hour stroll along a plank walk through the forest to the feeding stations. Buses return from Semenggoh nursery at 9:20, 11:30am, 1:30, and 3pm. If you attend the afternoon feeding session, you must walk back to the main highway to catch STC bus #3, 3A, 9, 9A, or 9B. Bypass the boardwalk and follow the feeding center's access road back to the main entrance. Turn right and then walk a few hundred feet to the first road on the left. Turn here and follow the road for about a half-hour through Kampung Jawa. When it finally meets up with the main highway, the bus stop is a short walk to the right. Semenggoh is open daily 8am-4:15pm. Time your arrival and departure carefully; they tend to lock the gates around lunchtime (12:45-2pm) and promptly again at 4:15pm.

BAKO NATIONAL PARK

Created in 1957, Bako is Sarawak's oldest national park. Within its 27sq.km, trails lead through almost every vegetation type found in Sarawak, and eventually end up at cliff-lined beaches. The beaches themselves are shallow and the waters murky due to the output of local rivers from the mainland. Avoid the mud flats near the mangrove forests or you'll be bogged down in foul-smelling slop up to your knees. The rare Proboscis monkey can be glimpsed within the park boundaries during early mornings and late evenings. The mischievous troops of long-tailed macaques that loiter around park headquarters are ill-behaved but seldom hostile unless fed. The park is also a popular weekend destination for local residents, so be sure to make reservations for accommodations in advance. **Permits** are mandatory for trips to Bako. Pick these up while arranging accommodations from the tourist information center (tel. 248 088) on Jl. Barrack. Daytrippers can obtain a permit directly at the Bako jetty before catching their boat.

The **park office** is located over the small bridge to the left of the compound as you get off the boat. Here the local delinquent tribes of monkeys often introduce themselves by nabbing crucial travel documents. Drop by to check in and pay the RM3 entrance fee. There is also a RM5 permit fee for cameras and RM10 for video recorders. Lockers are available for RM3 per day. Next door is an engaging **interpretive center** with some amazing photos of Bako's trails, beaches, and wildlife.

Most of the **accommodations** cluster behind the canteen in the back of the park grounds. Lodges are rented by the room and are available with two, three, and five beds per room. The cost is RM40 regardless of the number of beds, or RM80 for the entire two-room house. Rooms in the hotel with two bunk beds and cooking and communal facilities cost RM10 per night. Unfortunately, during the dry summer months (July-Sept.) there is often a water shortage, so the showers might not work. If you have a tent, camping spaces are available for RM4 per night. A small **canteen** with a pleasant wooden porch serves up a basic repertoire of fried rice and noodles for about RM2 per plate (open daily 8am-10pm). There's also a limited selection of munchies and beverages (bottled water RM3.60).

PJ buses depart from Jl. Khoo Hun Yeang (every hr., 6:40am-6pm, 45min., RM2.10, RM3 roundtrip). Buses returning from the pier follow a similar schedule from 6:30am-

5:40pm. By taxi, it's a RM40 ride. Alternatively, travelers can split the RM30 cost of the 40-minute boat ride among themselves. Those traveling by boat should travel early in the day, occasionally low tides can interfere with transport; inquire at the National Parks Office. If you must get back to Kuching by a certain time, make arrangements through the park office to be picked up in the morning. Otherwise, just wait around and see if there's anyone else returning who can share the costs of the boat ride.

■ Sibu

Earlier this century, Sibu was settled by tenacious Foochow immigrants from southern China at the invitation of Sarawak's second *rajah,* Charles Brooke. Lying 60km upriver in the wilds of the Rejang basin, Sibu was, for years, left largely to its own devices. Over the decades the Chinese community has retained its vibrant trading heritage; a frenetic, capitalist energy pervades Sibu's narrow, auto-clogged streets and the cramped corners of its overstocked shops. As the principle municipality on the Rejang River, it's here that lumber wrested from the dense forests upstream is converted into scandalous quantities of hard currency. In recent years, this pervasive economic optimism has begun to consolidate throughout the city in an impressive collection of public works projects. All of this construction adds up to a bit of a headache for the traveler, although in the future, Sibu might entice foreign visitors to linger awhile before heading to Kuching, Kapit, or the glittering beaches and dank cave systems to the east.

ORIENTATION

Sibu lies on the banks of the Rejang River. Express **boats** heading downriver leave from the pier by the Tua Pek Kong Temple on the west side of town, while upriver express boats leave from the pier to the south, near the **bus terminal**. The city is bounded on the northwest by **Jalan Bintang,** which runs from the river to the **airport**. From the water, there are three traffic circles. Radiating perpendicular to Bintang at the first rotary is **Jalan Pulau,** which runs toward the waterfront. From the second rotary, **Jalan Kampung Nyabor** stretches past the **post office** and **police stations** and curves south at **Jalan Ki Peng,** finally ending when it hits **Jalan Mission** by a large rotary. From this third rotary **Jalan Lanang** radiates father south. **Jalan Exchange/Causeway** runs parallel to Bintang, linking Jl. Pulau and Jl. Kampung Nyabor. **Jalan Marshidi Sidek** runs southeast from Jl. Exchange/Causeway, hitting the north-south thoroughfare of **Ramin Way/Jalan Lintang** at an angle. The latter bounds the downtown area of Sibu with Jl. Kampung Nyabor to the east. From north to south four important streets are in the city center, all of which run perpendicular to Jl. Lintang: **Jalan Central, Jalan High, Jalan Market,** and **Jalan Channel.**

PRACTICAL INFORMATION

Tourist Offices: Frankie Ting of **Sazhong Travel,** 4 Jl. Central (tel. 336 017), across from the park, is the chairman of Sibu's Sarawak Tourist Association. Open Mon.-Fri. 8am-noon and 1:30-4:45pm, Sat. 8am-noon and 1:30-4:15pm.

Tours and Travel: Sazhong Travel, 4 Jl. Central (tel. 336 017). Arranges tours to longhouses (2-day, RM150 per person for a group of 2-4; 3-day, RM840). Also arranges domestic and international plane tickets. Visa, MC, AmEx. Open Mon.-Fri. 8am-noon and 1:30-4:45pm, Sat. 8am-noon and 1:30-4:15pm.

Currency Exchange: Hock Hua Bank (tel. 320 088), on Jl. Pulau, in a 12-story white building across from the Methodist Church. Open Mon.-Fri. 9:30am-3:30pm, Sat. 9:30-11:30am.

Air Travel: Airport, 6km outside of town, with plans to construct another soon to be implemented. Taxi RM20. The **MAS** office (tel. 326 166), on Jl. Tuanku Osman, just before it curves right to meet Persiaran Brooke. Open Mon.-Fri. 8am-5pm, Sat. 8am-4pm, Sun. and holidays 8am-12:30pm. Daily flights to: **Bintulu** (RM64); **Miri**

(RM112); **Kota Kinabalu** (RM180); **Sandakan** (RM218); **Kuching** (RM72); and **KL** (RM320).

Buses: Bus company offices are on Jl. Khoo Peng Loong, next to the upriver boat wharf, near the esplanade. Construction has begun on the new bus terminal in this area as well; until it's finished, inquire at the bus company offices for bus departure locations. Buses to **Bintulu** (every hr., 6am-6pm, RM16.50) and **Miri** (7:30am and 1pm, RM34). Tour buses go to **Kuching** (6, 9, 10:15am, 1, 1:15, and 8:30pm, RM32). Express boats are usually more convenient. Additional bus connections are possible farther south from Sarikei.

Boats: Ekspress Bahagia boats to **Kuching** depart from the downriver boat wharf near the Chinese temple (7:15am via Sarikei, 11:30am direct, RM29-38). Buy tickets at the wharf. Boats to **Kapit** depart farther upriver near the bus terminal and run until about noon (3hr., RM16). Most post departure times.

Markets: Plans are in place for a large indoor market that will run parallel to Jl. Channel. Currently, there's the **main market** on Jl. High and the **jungle market** behind the row of shop houses near the wharf to Kapit. Every evening Sibu's fervent capitalists converge on Jl. High to stage one of the most vibrant **night markets** in all of Sarawak. Things come to a grudging conclusion around 10pm.

Pharmacies: United Medical Hall, 34 Jl. Kampung Nyabor (tel. 310 166), in the small row of shop houses directly across from the entrance to the Premier Hotel. Open Mon.-Fri. 8am-8:30pm, Sat. 8am-noon.

Medical Services: Is it a resort or a hospital? Sibu's new pastel medical facilities (tel. 343 333) are a RM6-8 cab ride out of town toward the airport.

Police: (tel. 322 222), on Jl. Kampung Nyabor near the post office.

Post Offices: (tel. 332 198), on Jl. Kampung Nyabor. EMS mail services available next door. Open Mon.-Sat. 8am-5pm. **Postal code:** 96000.

Telephones: IDD public phones are along Jl. Tuanku Osman. The **Telekom office** (tel. 335 252) resides nearby on Persiaran Brooke; look for the communications tower. Telegram and fax services available. Open Mon.-Thurs. 8:30am-12:45pm and 2-4:45pm, Sat. 8:30am-1pm.

ACCOMMODATIONS

Sarawak Hotel, 34 Ramin Way (tel. 333 455), at the intersection with Jl. Wong Nai Siong, before the Sugar Bun outlet. An excellent place to get your fill of luxury before heading upriver. Friendly staff treats guests on every floor to a fresh bath towel and individually wrapped slivers of flower-scented beauty soap daily. Newly renovated rooms come with all the frills: A/C, TV, telephones, and attached baths with hot water. Singles RM35. Doubles RM40.

Rex Hotel, 32 Ramin Way (tel. 323 687), just behind the Sarawak Hotel; enter through the parking lot next to the Rex Theatre. Much like the Sarawak next door, although rooms are worn and a bit frayed around the edges. Best of all, every room is outfitted with a large bathtub perfect for stewing road-weary laundry and limbs. Singles RM35. Doubles RM40. Family-style lodgings RM48.

Hoover House, 22 Jl. Pulau (tel. 332 491), to the left of the Methodist church. A faded white structure with pasty blue trim and a tile roof. Rather stuffy rooms feature gleaming polished wooden floors, high ceilings, and western baths. It's not the most comfortable, but certainly a charming place. Check in with the caretaker in back. Fan rooms with bath RM10 per person for doubles, triples, and a single quad; RM5 for pastors and church workers. A/C rooms RM25-30 for visitors, RM20-25 for pastors and church workers.

FOOD

Café Palmelia, Jl. Kampung Nyabor (tel. 323 222), in the Premier Hotel. Offers a generous all-you-can-eat buffet spread of soups, breads, veggie stirfries, and seafood specialties. Save some room for fruit and dessert, including the chef's dessert of the month (RM4.50 plus tax). Oriental buffets served Mon.-Fri. RM15 for adults, RM8 children, Steamboat buffets Sat.-Sun. RM18 adults, RM12 children. 5% tax, plus a 10% service charge. Open daily 6:30-9:30pm.

Hock Chu Leu Restaurant, 28 Jl. Tunkang Besi (tel. 330 254). Follow Jl. Central to Ramin Way; it's just past the intersection, on the left with an English sign. It has been around Sibu for 42 years. The talkative manager has thoughtfully installed an astounding 9 ceiling fans for his patrons' comfort. An excellent place to sample one of Sibu's local dishes, foochow noodles. The thin noodles are steamed, then served in a broth of soy and oyster sauces with spring onions and shrimp. A small order and a fruit drink run around RM5. English menu. Open daily 10am-2pm and 5-9:30pm. Closed Chinese New Year.

All the Best Vegetarian Restaurant, 39 Jl. Tuanku Osman (tel. 349 195), just off Jl. Tuanku Osman as it curves to the right, with a red English sign. An open-air Islamic vegetarian restaurant with a quiet clientele. Just step up to the counter to select a dish, or sample a variety by ordering *nasi campur* (RM3). Open Mon.-Sat. 6am-5pm, Sun. 6am-2pm.

SIGHTS

Tua Pek Kong Temple, with its kaleidoscope tiles and pillars, stands on the river-bank offering an excellent view of the Rejang. The temple is usually overflowing with devotees, their hands full of flowers and incense sticks. It's possible to climb to the 7th floor to savor the cool evening breezes; just ask the caretaker for the keys. For a small donation he will also give visitors a brief tour of the temple's murals and explain its history. (Temple closes at 6pm.) The **cultural center** (tel. 331 315) houses a small, intimate clone of the Sarawak Museum in Kuching. Reconstruction of longhouses are on display with labeled tools and there is an exquisite collection of Chinese porcelains. It's a RM5 cab ride from Sibu. (Open Tues.-Sun. 10:30am-5:30pm; closed Chinese New Year; free.)

▓ Kapit

"Thus was completed amidst the click of cameras, the death agony of pigs, the screech of fowls, and the guttural sounds of the natives, a peace ceremony unprecedented in character…" reads a plaque placed in front of Fort Sylvia. It commemorates a monumental truce agreement negotiated by the White Rajah's minions in 1924 among the areas' local tribes. Despite all appearances that things have calmed down today, even a hundred years later Kapit is still not quite domesticated nor predictable. Foreigners will attract curious stares from local tribesmen in the market place. In the past, however, Kapit has been more popular with international travelers as a jumping off point for trips beyond the eroded rivers surrounding the logging camps and into the eerily serene jungles beyond for visits to Orang Ulu longhouses. The communities here certainly see less tourist traffick than around Kuching, but travelers may not consider the longhouses any more interesting. Using profits from logging, most of these longhouses have become thoroughly modernized and traditional dances and costumes are saved only for special holidays. Still, intrepid travelers with plenty of time, money, and a healthy tolerance for leeches can venture even father upriver into the heart of Borneo.

ORIENTATION

Most of the town's activity focuses on the eroded riverside and its two massive concrete **jetties.** Facing the Rejang River, speedboats and long-tail boats traveling east upriver to Pelagus Rapids and Belaga depart from the jetty on the left; longboats traveling westward and downriver to Sibu depart from the jetty on the right. Roughly between the two is Kapit's **town square,** surrounded by a grid of streets and alleys. Still facing the river, to the immediate right is **Jalan Tan Sit Leong;** the shop of the tour guide Tan Teck Chuan is located here. To the immediate left is **Jalan Court.** Beyond the rows of shops to the left is the Kapit **town market.** Immediately behind the town square is **Jalan Teo Chow Beng,** which is roughly parallel to the river, heading both east and west out of town. Following it upriver leads past the **Telekom office.** Clustered around an artificial lake beyond the bank are the **police station,** the

Resident's office, the Civic Centre, and, farther beyond, the Kapit public **hospital.** Following Jl. Teo Chow Beng downriver takes you past the popular town food court to the left on **Jalan Tiong Ung Hong,** then onward to the **post office. Jalan Airport/ Selinik** bounds the city on the south, stretching from the rotary on the west to the rotary on the east side of town.

PRACTICAL INFORMATION

Resident's Office: (tel. 796 425), on the first floor of the blue trimmed building in the State Government Complex, near the pond. Come here to get **permits to Semenggoh Wildlife Centre.** Open Mon.-Thurs. 8am-12:45pm and 2-4:15pm, Fri. 8-11:30am and 2:30-4:45pm, Sat. 8am-12:45pm.

Currency Exchange: Hock Hua Bank (tel. 797 677), at the east end of Jl. Teo Chow Beng, with a large blue-and-white sign. Open Mon.-Fri. 9:30am-3:30pm, Sat. 9:30-11:30am. **Maybank,** next to Meligai Hotel on Jl. Teo Chow Beng's west end. Open Mon.-Fri. 9:30am-4pm, Sat. 9:30-11:30am.

Air Travel: Airport, 4km south of Kapit, a RM10 taxi ride away. **MAS** (tel. 796 484), behind the row of shops on Jl. Tan Sit Leong. Open Mon.-Fri. 8:30am-noon and 1:30-5pm, Sat. 8:30am-noon, Sun. 8:30-11am. To **Sibu** (Sun., RM48) but frequently cancelled due to fog.

Boats: Boats to **Sibu** depart frequently until about 3pm (RM16 and up, 3hr.). Facing the river, they depart from the jetty to the right. There's usually a sign indicating the next departure. Boats upriver depart from the jetty to the left. During the wet season, express boats leave from Kapit or directly from Sibu to **Pelagus Rapids** and **Belaga** (5-6hr.). During the dry summer months (July-Sept.), only the speedboats can navigate in the shallow waters (2 per day, before 11am, RM50). Longboats can also be rented, although this runs upward of RM200 per day.

Markets: Situated on the western edge of Kapit, in a decrepit wooden structure.

Pharmacies: Teng's Pharmacy, 35 Jl. Court (tel. 797 399). Open Mon.-Sat. 7:30am-8:30pm, Sun. 7:30am-noon.

Medical Services: (tel. 333 418), east of town, past the Civic Centre.

Police: (tel. 796 222), just beyond the eastern rotary. Office hours for travel permits upriver Mon.-Thurs. 8am-12:45pm and 2-4:15pm, Fri. 8-11:30am and 2:30-4:45pm, Sat. 8am-12:45pm.

Post Offices: (tel. 796 332), on Jl. Teo Chow Beng. Open Mon.-Fri. 8am-noon and 2-4:30pm, Sat. 8am-noon.

Telephones: Public telephones stack up outside the gleaming white **Telekom** office at the east end of Jl. Teo Chow Beng. To send **faxes** or telegrams, wander behind the new office tower to the small house in the back. Open Mon.-Fri. 8:30am-4:15pm, Sat. 8:30am-12:30pm. **Telephone code:** 084.

ACCOMMODATIONS

In recent years, many of the budget hotels in Kapit town have degenerated into brothels. The result is an overabundance of pricey mediocre accommodations.

Rejang Inn (tel. 796 709), on Jl. Temenggong Jugah, across from the yellow MBF Finance Berhad sign. The best budget option in the city. The rooms are spartan but clean and rooms at the end of the hall have excellent vistas of the river. Friendly guitar-toting reception staff offers impromptu lessons. Fan-cooled rooms without bath RM15. Larger A/C rooms with private bath and showers RM20.

New Rejang Inn, 104 Jl. Teo Chow Beng (tel. 796 600). Walk upriver along Jl. Teo Chow; it's just behind Viking Fast Food on the left. Gleaming new facilities. Every room has a writing desk, comfortable beds, color TV, A/C, telephones, and sparkling baths with hot water on tap. Helpful managers can answer basic questions. Singles and doubles RM40. Larger family rooms RM48.

Dung Fang Hotel, No.116, Lot 510, 1st Fl., Jl. Temenggong Jugah (tel. 797 799), across from Meligai Hotel. Standard rooms with attached bath, A/C, and TV. 2nd floor doubles RM35, 3rd floor RM38. The few singles here (RM30-35) are incredibly small and without bath.

FOOD

Take advantage of Kapit's rustic culinary opportunities by sampling such local cuisine as *babi hutan* (wild boar) and *rusa* (venison). Overall, the best budget option in town is the **food court** on Jl. Tiong Ung Hong, a quiet place where only half of the stalls are open at any given time (open daily until 9pm). **Frosty Boy** (tel. 796 608) offers milkshakes (RM2.50) and pizza (open daily 9am-9:30pm).

> **Ling Tong Bakery** (tel. 796 721), directly across from the day market. The favorite morning stop for a cup of milo and a plateful of fragrant breads and rolls. *Pollo buno*, lotus seed, and red bean cakes all run about RM0.50 per piece; just point out with your thumb what you want. Open daily 6:15am-5pm.
> **Chuong Hin Café,** across from the Sibu jetty. Settle into a chair and order a lemon iced tea (RM0.70) as immense barges piled with logs drift past on the river below. Delicately arranged sweets on the table tops and steaming dumplings in the case in front will tempt any hungry stomach. Open daily 6am-5pm.
> **Tropika Restaurant,** 68 Jl. Tiong Ung Hong (tel. 797 639), just in front of the public food court, with a large, green-and-white English sign. A simple establishment that specializes in both Malay and Indonesian food. In the afternoon discuss longhouse etiquette with fellow travelers over *nasi campur* (RM3) and iced lemon tea (RM0.70), or over piles of fresh *roti* in the morning. Open daily 7am-9pm.

SIGHTS AND ENTERTAINMENT

There's not too much to do in Kapit town after the day's pyrotechnic sunset over the Rejang. Organized entertainment is rather tawdry and varies from the relatively inane karaoke clubs to the more insidious brothels staffed by Indonesian immigrants. Hotel Meligai has a small, air-conditioned **pub** that serves beer and often features Filipino bands of dubious musical skill (open Mon.-Fri. and Sun. 8:30pm-1:30am, Sat. and holidays 8:30pm-2am).

Fort Sylvia was built in 1880 and named after the third *rajah*'s wife. It was constructed as a visible sign of the government's intent to put an end to inter-tribe hostilities and head-hunting within the area. Today its silver-gray wooden walls house administrative offices and are closed to the public. The local **museum** is housed within the Civic Centre on the eastern edge of town. It's a pale shadow of the fabulous displays in Kuching, but worth a brief visit. There's an excellent topographic model of the upper Rejang River describing the various towns and longhouses along its shores. Supposedly, it's open Mon.-Fri. 9am-12:45pm and 2-4:15pm, Sat. 9am-12:45pm, but usually you have to hunt someone down to unlock the door. (Free.)

Visiting Longhouses

A longhouse is just that—one long dwelling that houses an entire community within its sturdy walls. Structures were constructed from rot-resistant ironwood and bamboo flooring, with the whole thing held together with sturdy rattan cord. The size of a longhouse was described in terms of the number of doors; some had hundreds of doors and were well over 1km in length. The entire building is raised to take advantage of cooling drafts and maximize safety from marauders, with livestock kept in pens below. All of this makes for a tightly knit community, presided over by a *tuai* (headman) who enforces a set of strict rules to maintain social harmony. Today, many modern communities have chosen to reinterpret the basic form of the longhouse in sturdy concrete and brick.

In the past, a visit to East Malaysia was not considered complete without a trip to the longhouse. Guests were traditionally greeted with excitement for the news they brought to the isolated communities and seen as an excuse to throw raucous parties where large quantities of *tuak* (rice wine) were swilled until daybreak. Tourists were understandably impressed and longhouse fame spread. As these communities became more affluent, they sought to improve their standard of living by building sturdier and more congenial tin-roofed cement structures, much to the dismay of many tourists. Longhouse dwellers, on the other hand, started to resent the increas-

Longhouse Etiquette

It would be wise for travelers to brush up on some etiquette before venturing to longhouses, so as to ensure a pleasant stay. The first step is to wait for an invitation to enter the longhouse and take off your shoes before doing so. At meals, be sure to sample any offered food to avoid offending your host. Otherwise, basic courtesy is the rule: do not touch anything, avoid taking pictures of anyone unless properly introduced and then quietly ask permission. The Orang Ulu, like any other people, will warm up to visitors once they are comfortable. To facilitate this, be sure to leave yourself open to a bit of silliness (you may be asked to perform a dance or song) and respect their customs. In particular, modesty in dress is very important. When bathing, men should keep their underwear on and women should use a sarong. Evenings usually culminate in a bit of a celebration with rice wine (be sure to take at least a small sip if offered) and plenty of dancing and music. Visitors are fully expected to contribute; your hosts will love it if you participate wholeheartedly, even if it means making a bit of a fool of yourself. It's certainly appreciated if guests bring gifts. Pencils and crayons for the children, balloons, practical clothing such as shirts and hats, as well as luxuries such as foreign cigarettes are welcome. It's also nice to bring some pictures of your family, postcards, coins, stamps, or a book about the country you come from. For instant and enduring fame, bring a Polaroid camera and lots of spare film. Nearly all gifts are appreciated, but avoid sweets and alcohol.

ingly frequent arrival of well-to-do foreign travelers on their doorstep expecting to be feted like a *rajah* in exchange for a mere box of cigarettes.

Unless you are fluent in the Iban dialect, most travelers require a guide to visit one of the area's longhouses. It's likely that tourists will also be approached in cafés and hotel lobbies by free-lance guides attempting to solicit business. Before signing on with any guide, check with the hotel staff or other travelers first. Mr. Tan Teck Chuan at the **Tan Seng Hin Shop,** 11 Jl. Tan Sit Leong (tel. 796 352), just off the town square, is one of the area's most reputable tour guides. His shop is open Mon.-Sat.7am-5pm, Sun. 7am-noon and his office is in the back (no credit cards). The mailing address is: P.O.Box 16, 96807 Kapit. He is fluent in Iban and has connections with local Penans upriver. Be sure to peruse his brochures and to ask to see his collection of slides. Two-day trips to an Iban longhouse cost RM495 for a group of two, up to RM900 for a group of five. Chuan can also coordinate trips farther upriver to visit some of the most remote settlements in Sarawak. For extensive treks into the extreme hinterlands, he asks for 1½-2 months advance notice, as he must send messages and organize things via boat and word of mouth.

The best time to visit the longhouse is in early June when each hosts its own celebration of the traditional Dayak Gawai (harvest festival), although the best weather is July-Sept. Things to bring include a plastic bag for cameras, rain gear, toilet paper, flashlight, sunscreen, mosquito repellent, motion sickness pills, aspirin, and other basic toiletries. If traveling into the deep jungle, be sure to obtain appropriate travel insurance and research any necessary health precautions (i.e., malaria pills need to be started a week before hand).

Permits are required for travel upriver from Kapit. It's a fairly innocuous process. First pick up an application at the resident's offices. Fill these out and then walk to the police station at the bottom to the hill. You will have to undergo an interview with an officer on the top floor before walking back to the resident's office and receiving the official stamp of approval. If you plan to travel farther upstream than Belaga, then you must report to the police there and file additional paperwork. Most guides can walk you through the process.

▨ Bintulu

As described by Bintulu's Development Authority, "The New Bintulu is a premier, well-planned, and environmentally attractive industrial town." The key word here is industrial; Bintulu is a rapidly expanding commercial center whose success is based primarily on the discovery of off-shore natural gas deposits in the 60s. But perhaps of more interest to the intinerant traveler is the city's tantalizing proximity to the polished sands of Similajau Park and the jungled depths of Niah National Park. On the whole, Bintulu is expensive and offers a poor value for both accommodations and food. Arrive early to make full use of its banks, supermarkets, and other services while there's still time to catch connections to more alluring destinations.

ORIENTATION

According to the *Guinness Book of World Records*, Bintulu has the distinction of being located closer to an airport than any other city in the world. In fact, the **airport** runway cuts down the middle of town, dividing Bintulu into two separate halves. North of the airport on **Jalan Tun Razak**, and accessible only by a long hot walk or a RM5 taxi ride, are the town's **police station, main post office,** and the **National Parks office.** Directly south of the airport is Bintulu's **long distance bus terminal.** With your back to the airport, directly to the right of the bus station is the intersection of **Jalan Somerville** and **Jalan Pedada.** Jl. Somerville runs parallel to the runway. Along its length is Hock Hua Bank, a small post office, and at its end the **Telekom office.** Jl. Pedada stretches directly from the airport to the waterfront. Along the way it intersects Bintulu's two major thoroughfares. As you walk toward the river, the first intersection is with **Jalan Keppel** to the right. To the left the street becomes **Jalan Abang Galau.** The next intersection is with **Jalan Main Bazaar** to their right, containing the **hospital, markets,** and a few restaurants. **Jalan Masjid** is directly to the left and contains the AA Inn and the MAS office.

PRACTICAL INFORMATION

Tourist Offices: Bintulu Development Authority (tel. 332 277), on Jl. Somerville; look for the white structure with the BDA sign. The BDA maintains a welcome center to the right of the main entrance. Open Mon.-Thurs. 8am-12:45pm and 2-4:15pm, Fri. 8-11:30am and 2:30-4:15pm, Sat. 8am-12:45pm.

National Parks Office: The booking office for accommodations at Similajau National Park is in the back of the complex of government buildings on Jl. Tun Razak. Reservations can be phoned in (tel. 331 117, ext. 50), which will save a long walk or cab ride (RM8-10 roundtrip from Bintulu). This, however, does not guarantee they'll phone the park to let them know you're arriving, so it's best to just drop by and fill out the forms to substantiate your claim in case of overbooking. Open Mon.-Thurs. 8am-12:45pm and 2-4:15pm, Fri. 8:30-11:30am and 1:45-4:45m, Sat. 8am-12:45pm.

Currency Exchange: Hock Hua Bank (tel. 331 433), on Jl. Somerville. Counter 14 changes traveler's checks. Open Mon.-Fri. 9:30am-3:30pm, Sat. 9:30-11:30am.

Air Travel: The **airport** is within walking distance a few minutes north of most hotels. **MAS** (tel. 331 554), on Jl. Masjid, next to Chef Fried Chicken. Daily flights to: **Kuching** (RM117); **Miri** (RM69); **Sibu** (RM64); and **Kota Kinabalu** (RM127). Open Mon.-Fri. 8:30am-4:30pm, Sat. 8:30am-3:30pm, Sun. 8:30am-12:30pm, holidays 8:30am-1pm. MC, Visa, AmEx.

Buses: Long distance bus terminal, in the north of town, near the airport. To: **Kuching** (5 per day, 6am-5:30pm, RM52); **Sibu** (every hr., 6am-6pm, 3½hr., RM16.50); **Batu Niah** (every hr., 7am-3pm, 3hr., RM10); and **Miri** (every hr., 6am-6pm, 5½hr., RM16.50, A/C RM18). **Midsar Express** (tel. 314 279) sends a single bus to **Sri Bandar Aman** (7am, 5hr., RM37.50).

Local Transportation: Local bus terminal, next to the markets on Jl. Main Bazaar, has some buses running the length of the city.

Markets: The twin cones of Bintulu's **day market** stretch skyward along Jl. Main Bazaar. The **Pasar Malam** settles around the local bus station nightly (7-10pm). Excellent selection of satay, grilled fish, chicken, and fresh fruit in season.

Pharmacies: L.T. Ling Pharmacy (tel. 335 996), near the bus terminal on Jl. Abang Galau. Open Mon.-Sat. 8:30am-9pm, Sun. 8:30am-12:30pm and 6-9pm.

Medical Services: Hospital (tel. 331 455). If you are traveling west out of town on Jl. Main Bazaar, it is on the left, across a small bridge.

Police: (tel. 331121), in the Government Complex on Jl. Tun Razak.

Emergency: 994.

Post Offices: GPO (tel. 339 164), on Jl. Tun Razak, outside of town. **Branch** on Jl. Somerville across from Hock Hua Bank. Open Mon.-Fri. 8am-5pm, Sat. 8am-1pm.

Telephones: Telekom office, on Jl. Lau Gek Soon, just north of the intersection with Jl. Keppel. International calls and faxes. Open Mon.-Thurs. 8:30am-12:45pm and 2-4:45pm, Fri. 8:30am-noon and 2:15-4:45pm, Sat. 8:30am-1pm.

ACCOMMODATIONS

Capital Hotel (tel. 331 167), on Jl. Keppel, above the Capital Café and Restaurant. Walk up the stairs, past the A/C restaurant; it's to the right. The reception desk is across from the Bintulu Town Social and Recreation Club. The cheapest beds in town. Well-worn rooms have a sink and desk, and either a ceiling fan (RM15) or a less-than-effectual A/C (RM20). Tawdry shared bathrooms. Overpriced rooms on the first floor with attached bath cost RM40.

AA Inn (tel. 335 733), on the corner of Jl. Masjid and Jl. Pedada, near a cluster of blue telephone booths. Reception is on the first floor. If not exactly fresh, the rooms are spacious and come with carpeting, TV, A/C and private baths. Singles RM32. Doubles RM32. "Family sized" rooms RM36.

Dragon Inn (tel. 315 150), just off the far east end of Jl. Abang Galau, across from the Plaza Hotel complex. Reception is within the powder-pink walls of the first floor. Small, box-like rooms with thin walls and carpeting. All rooms have A/C and a cramped attached bath with shower (RM30).

Kemena Inn, (tel. 331 533), facing the Chinese temple on Jl. Keppel, the entrance is in the rear of the building. Several grades above the others, friendly staff, clean rooms, and attached bath with hot water. Singles RM55. Doubles RM58.

FOOD

Marco Polo Grill, Lot A116, Shahida Town Extension (tel. 332 458), in the complex of shops on the far west of town, across from the hospital. An intimate wood paneled establishment afloat with plaid tablecloths and starched, gleaming white cloth napkins. Specialties include the Sarawak peppercorn steak (RM22) and the low-fat grilled fish (RM12). Round out the evening with apple pie *à la mode* (RM4). Fierce A/C. English menu. Open daily 11am-2pm and 6-10:30pm.

Popular Corner Food Centre (tel. 334 388), in the block of shops on the western end of Jl. Main Bazaar. Next to the Negeri Monument. By day it's a cafeteria-style establishment with well-prepared dishes and refreshing fruit juices. By night, its tables are moved outside. No English menu. Open daily 10am-1am.

Seaview Restaurant (tel. 334 499), next to the Riverfront Inn, on the eastern edge of the waterfront with a green and yellow English sign. It's a quiet, breezy respite from the manic streets. Drop by for a cup of java and watch red and green ferries drift past barges overflowing with logs being exported. Open daily 7am-7pm.

■ Similajau National Park

Some of Sarawak's finest beaches are a half an hour northeast of Bintulu, nestled within the developed bounds of Similajau National Park. Only 1.5km wide, the bulk of the park is composed of 30km of glittering silken beaches and austere coastal cliffs and crusted with heavy layers of orchids and pitcher plants. Excellent beaches front the park's accommodations, although the 9km of trails that snake through coastal forest lead to the even finer sands of Turtle and Golden Beaches. Along the way are the popular Sentunsur Rapids and the tannin-stained waters of Kolam Sebubong pool.

MALAYSIA

Although still relatively unheard of abroad, Similajau is popular with locals in the know and fills up during the weekends. Plan to arrive during the week, and with luck you may have the entire 30km to yourself.

GETTING THERE AND AWAY

There is no regular public transportation to park headquarters. This means the park is a hefty RM40, half-hour taxi trip from Bintulu. It's also necessary to arrange return transport with the taxi driver; this should cost no more than RM80 total. Transportation is the only major cost; accommodations and food are both reasonably priced at the park itself. Before the taxi pulls away, ask for a number where he can be reached; once you leave the parking lot and catch a glimpse of the smooth curve of glistening sand you may want to extend your visit.

PRACTICAL INFORMATION

The **park office** is located down a small walk way from the parking lot and to the right. Drop by here to pick up park brochures and maps (RM3), as well as to purchase permits for cameras (RM5) and video recorders (RM10). The office will assign guests a room if they do not already have a reservation, and can arrange transportation across the narrow Sungai Likau to the start of the forest trails. Next door is a small **visitor's center** with a vivid collection of photographs of the area's diverse flora and fauna. Although there's usually a ranger on duty, the best time to arrive is during office hours (Mon.-Thurs. 8am-12:45pm and 2-4:15pm, Fri. 8-11:30am and 1:45-4:45pm, Sat. 8am-12:45pm).

ACCOMMODATIONS AND FOOD

Two **hostels** have been recently constructed at the park. Every room sleeps four in bunk beds with sheets and blankets, and has a fan and cubbies for storing backpacks. Each hostel has cooking facilities with a stove, communal toilets, showers, and a large veranda swept clean by ocean breezes. A single bed costs RM10 per night, RM5 for children under 18. Closer to park headquarters are three **chalets,** each with two rooms sleeping four. These run RM120 for the entire chalet or RM60 per room. All accommodations stand along a clean stretch of fluffy white sand, set back in the surrounding vegetation. Shady camping areas nearby are also provided for RM4 per night. Reservations, especially for travelers planning visits on weekends, should be made in advance at the park's booking office in Bintulu.

There's a simple open-air **canteen** with such basics as fried rice (RM3) and welcome extravagances like chocolate-dipped vanilla ice cream bars (RM4). Dinner usually consists of a set menu of fresh fish and vegetable stir-fries. Snacks and bottled water are also available. For an extended stay, however, it's wise to stock your own supply. (Open daily 7am-9pm.)

SIGHTS

Many visitors are content to romp in the surf and loll on the generous sands directly fronting the chalets and hostels of the park. After the last rays of the sun have faded, however, the beach assumes a different character as the villainous flares of Bintulu's infamous gas refineries, located only a few miles off the coast, smoulder fiendishly through hazy clouds of salt spray, creating a rather breathtaking effect.

Farther afield are more secluded beaches, accessible only by hiking along well-marked forest paths. The trail begins on the far side of the radiant green waters of the Likau River, just to the east of the park office. These waters are also cruised by **saltwater crocodiles,** so it's best to arrange boat transport (RM4 roundtrip) at the park office. Be sure to arrange a pick-up time before 6pm, when the sky begins to darken and the trail becomes increasingly difficult to see. A boardwalk cuts a swath through mangrove root snarls and foul-smelling mud flats of the river bank, until the trail turns uphill into a mixed dipterocarp forest. The path has been cleared with a light hand (marked at intervals with slashes of red paint) so it's possible to see evidence of the park's 24 species of mammals, including primates, deer, squirrels, wild boar, Rhinoceros hornbills, and 185 other species of birds. After about an hour of walking the trail leads left to **Selunsur Rapids.**

Another 90 minutes of hiking leads trekkers to the edge of the park boundaries, and the source of the cool, rushing waters. Bypassing the rapids, it's another hour's trip to the quiet sands of **Turtle Beach.** Green sea turtles occasionally make their way here to lay midnight clutches in April and May. An hour farther past the beach are the glamorous lengths of **Golden Beach.** The sands here are tinted a rich buttery hue. Finally, half an hour beyond Golden beach is **Kolam Sebubong,** an isolated pool on the upper reaches of the swift Sebubong River. Over the years, its eddies have been tinted a jewel-like burgundy by tannic acid leaching from a soggy peat swamp nearby. The park can sometimes coordinate boat trips to the pool for afternoon picnics. To return to the park grounds just follow the forest trail back. If the sun has cooled a bit, however, it's also feasible to wander along the coast for a while, before rejoining the trail as it crosses one of the streams near the park offices.

■ Niah National Park

Niah National Park is best known for its expansive cave system which winds its way through the Park's crumbling limestone peaks. Despite its quiet grounds and decidedly backwater feel, Niah has had more than its share of controversy. In 1958 excavators discovered an intact human skull at the mouth of the Great Cave, which caused a furor in the scientific community. In nearby Painted Cave, archaeologists also unearthed a cache of Iron Age coffins carved like boats. Yet more controversy surrounds Niah over the lucrative collection of the fabulous swiftlet nests, which fetch up to RM1200 per kilo. Harvest involves shimmying up 30m-tall, rickety bamboo poles to the aerial heights of the caverns. Despite the overwhelming danger, collectors jealously guard the caves and bloody confrontations have long been a part of the cave's history. Park officials recently have become concerned about the collectors' effects on the swiftlet populations, and have closed the caves. It's wise to call before visiting to make sure the caves are open. Although its measurements are not as grand and its rock formations not as glamourous as the caves at Mulu National Park, Niah still presents an excellent spectacle as well as a great bargain for the budget traveler's time and money. Be sure to bring a flashlight, as the caves are unlit.

GETTING THERE AND AWAY

Batu Niah is a dusty village that serves as the gateway to Niah Park. Buses arriving from either Miri or Bintulu deposit passengers within walking distance of the town jetty on the Sungai River. The park itself is a pleasant longboat ride down this river (RM10 for 1-4 people, RM2 per person for more than 5). Along the way keep your eyes out for 2-m crocodiles sunning themselves merrily on the sandy banks. The 2km from Batu Niah can also be covered by hiring a taxi (RM10). It's best to arrive in Batu Niah early in the day to ensure transport to the park. Buses depart from Batu Niah square to **Miri** (every hr., 6:45am-3:30pm, RM8.50) and **Bintulu** (6 per day, 6am-3pm, RM10); some have A/C. Arrive early to buy your ticket on the bus.

PRACTICAL INFORMATION

The **Park's Reception Area** (tel. 737 450) is located a few hundred feet away from the river's edge in a handsome cluster of wooden buildings. If travelers don't have a reservation already, accommodations can be arranged here and paid for in addition to the park entrance fee (RM3); cameras cost an extra RM5, video recorders RM10. The office has basic literature on the caves, but the adjacent **information center** does a much better job. The exhibits are mildewed and faded, but still provide an excellent overview of the caves' venerable history of human habitation and the ongoing activities of guano and bird's nest collectors. The administrative office hours are Mon.-Thurs. 8am-12:45pm and 2-4:45pm, Sat. 8am-12:45pm.

ACCOMMODATIONS AND FOOD

The posh wood paneled room and sleek modern baths of the **hostels** are the second reason to visit Niah. The airy rooms are fan-cooled, and each has its own bathroom. If there aren't many visitors it's possible to ask for a room all to yourself. Each hostel has a quiet comfortably furnished common room. A single bed costs RM10 per night. Chalets sleeping four per room cost RM120, or RM60 per room, while deluxe accommodations in the **Park's Resthouse** are RM75 per night. There's a small open-air **restaurant** on the park grounds. It's popular with the locals as well as tourists, and provides the standard rice meals, with most dishes starting at RM4. Snacks and film are also sold. (Open daily 8am-10:30pm.)

SIGHTS

A RM0.50 boat ride across the river brings you to the start of the trail to **Niah Caves.** To the left is a small store selling snacks and water for the walk. It's a pleasant 3-km, 45-minute walk through the cool forest air to the caves. The plank walk, which can be slippery, makes hiring a guide unnecessary. Just 0.5km before you arrive at the entrance to the caves is a cluster of local Iban vendors with fresh fruit and cold beverages piled along the plank walk. The trail leads through a small passage known as the Traders Cave before arriving at the stunning 60m-high and 250m-wide mouth of the **Great Cave.** It was here in 1958 that Tom Harrison and his staff from the Sarawak Museum unearthed an intact human skull dated at over 40,000 years. Modern technology has since produced better aging tests, which have confirmed the skull's incredible age. The entire left side of the cave is covered with excavations, which disclosed a variety of stone tools and other human relics. The trail crosses through the **Cave of Bones, Beunt Cave,** and eventually leads to **Moon Cave.** After this point it's impossible to proceed without a flashlight or candles. After a brief walk through the midnight caverns of the "sleeping place," visitors emerge once again into the sunlight. The fern encrusted plank walk continues from here to the **Painted Cave.** This small cavern was used by Iron Age man as a cemetery. Originally it contained boat-like coffins stacked against walls bearing cryptic images painted in orange, which depicted the deceased's journey into the afterlife. The relics have since been removed for conservation, but the faded paintings are still visible to the right behind a locked gate. At dusk the cave's bats bestir themselves to swoop and circle before finally emptying from the cave in a stupendous black belch.

■ Miri

Shell's discovery of oil in 1910 has left conspicuous residue throughout Miri. By 1913 oil production had already topped 26,000 tons. Oil revenues, in addition to the recent addition of fabulous timber concession profits, have made Miri the largest city in Sarawak (pop. 400,000). Crowded auto-clogged streets display signs of wealth such as the town's newest, tallest, and biggest shopping mall/luxury accommodation, the Mega Hotel. Although many visitors stay just long enough to make travel arrangements onward to Mulu or Niah Caves, or beyond to Sabah, Miri offers a pleasing diversity of restaurants, markets, and even a bit of nightly intrigue. Given this, the Malaysian government has unveiled an ambitious scheme to transform "Oil Town" into "Resort City" by 2005.

ORIENTATION

The bulk and snarl of streets is crushed between the **Miri River** to the west and hills to the east. The heart of the old town is near the towering **Wisma Pelita Tunku** complex. On the other side of the Pelita building is the tree-lined **Jalan Kingsway** traveling north away from the Pelita. The **police station** is farther down, before the road merges with **Jalan Brooke,** which becomes **Jalan Sylvia** as it goes out of town, then **Jalan Gartak. Jalan China** stretches westward past the Peliata complex to the waterfront. **Jalan Bendahara** runs north along the water's edge, which leads to the soaring blue and white tower of the **Mega Hotel.** In its shadow stands Jade Centre and the Palos along **Jalan Yu Seng.**

PRACTICAL INFORMATION

Tourist Offices: Sarawak Tourist Information Centre, Lot 452, Jl. Melayu (tel. 434 181; e-mail Sarawak@po.jaring.my; http://www.Sarawak.gov.my/stb). From Wisma Pelita, walk through the bus terminal. It's just beyond in a small white building to the right, set in a small park. Outgoing friendly staff speaks excellent English, and provides maps and brochures of the Miri area. Come here to make reservations for accommodations in Lambir, Niah, and Mulu Parks. Open Mon.-Thurs. 8am-12:45pm and 2-4:15pm, Fri. 8-11:30am and 2:30-4:45pm. Sat. 8am-12:45pm. Sun. and holidays closed.

Tours and Travels: Tropical Adventure (tel. 419 337), in the lobby of the Mega Hotel. Offers 4-day packages to the Pinnacles in Mulu National Park RM765) and 5-day treks back via the Head-hunters Trail (RM930). Also provides a number of other tours in both Sabah and Sarawak. Visa, MC, AmEx. **Transworld Travel Services,** 2nd Fl., Wisma Pelita Tunku (tel. 422 277), offers similar packages in addition to cheaper local tours. 5-hour trip to Lambir Falls and an Iban longhouse for 4 people (RM70 per person). Open Mon.-Sat. 8:30am-5pm. MC, Visa, AmEx.

Immigration Offices: (tel. 442 108). Follow Jl. Brooke east until it changes into Jl. Sylvia at the post office, and then into Jl. Gartak. Turn left at Jl. Perseku Tuan. It's in the large pink building closest to the road, on the ground floor behind door 3. Free extensions (up to 2 months) take a few days to process. Open Mon.-Fri. 8am-12:30pm and 2-4pm, Sat. 8am-12:30pm.

Currency Exchange: Bank Bumiputra (tel. 420 371), on Jl. Indica, off Jl. Bendahara. Charges RM5.15 to change traveler's checks. Open Mon.-Fri. 9:30am-4pm, Sat. 9am-noon. **Bank Utama** (tel. 411 882), in a post-modern building on Jl. Nahoda Gampar. RM2.20 per check. Open Mon.-Fri. 9:30am-3pm, Sat. 9:30-11am.

Air Travel: Airport, west of the city limits. Taxis (RM12-15) and infrequent public buses (RM0.50) run into town. **MAS** (tel. 414 144), has an office on the corner of Jl. Yu Seng. To: **Gunung Mulu Park** (3-4 per day, RM69, airport tax RM5); **Kuching** (RM228); and **Kota Kinabalu** (RM104). Open Mon.Fri. 8:30am-5pm, Sat. 8:30am-4pm, Sun. 8:30am-12:30pm, holidays 8:30am-1pm.

Buses: Long distance bus terminal, directly behind Wisma Pelita on Jl. Puchong. To **Batu Niah** (every hr., 6:45am-4pm, 2hr., RM8.50) via **Lambir Hills National Park** (RM2) and **Bintulu** (every hr., 6:30am-4:30pm, 5hr., RM16.50, A/C RM18). Several private bus companies go to major destinations in Sarawak: **SYKT Express** (tel. 439 325) and **Rejang Express** (tel. 435 336) are next to each other on Jl. Malay; **P.B. Express** and **Biara Mas Express** are at the bus terminal. Between all of them, frequent buses run to **Sibu** (RM34) and **Kuching** (RM70).

Local Transportation: Local bus station, behind Wisma Pelita on Jl. Puchong.

Markets: Miri has several markets. The **Pasar Besar** (large market) is at the western end of Jl. Brooke, near the concrete, hornbill-festooned rotary. Smaller **stalls** are on Jl. Oleander near the Chinese temple.

Pharmacies: KH Wong Pharmacy, 28E Jl. Kingsway, ground floor (tel. 413 313), near the intersection with High Street. Open Mon.-Sat. 7:30am-8:45pm.

Medical Services: Hospital Umum Miri (tel. 420 170), on Jl. Cahaya, south of the city on the road to Bintulu.

Police: (tel. 433 766), 2 buildings down from the Resident's Office, on the corner of Jl. Kingsway and Jl. Chia Tze Chi. Interviews for permits to Gunung Mulu Park are conducted in Room #5, just off the central courtyard of the building during office hours. Open Mon.-Thurs. 8am-12:45pm and 2-4:15pm, Fri. 8-11:30am and 2:30-4:45pm, Sat. 8am-12:45pm.

Post Offices: (tel. 432 887), on Jl. Sylvia on the eastern fringe of town. Inquire at the counter for *Post Restante.* Open Mon.-Sat. 8am-5pm. **Postal code:** 98000.

Telephones: IDD phones cluster under the trees across from Wisma Pelita, on Jl. Puchong. **Telephone code:** 085.

ACCOMMODATIONS

Fairland Inn, 1st Fl., 21 Jl. Kingsway (tel. 413 981), across the street from the Resident's Office. Good value for the ringgit, but beware of the noise. Gate locked at 11pm. Singles with bath, hot water, and A/C RM30-32. Doubles with the same accoutrements RM35.

Tai Tong Lodging House, 1st Fl., 26 Jl. China (tel. 411 498), directly opposite the Chinese temple and up the blue staircase. Dorm beds (RM8) are stacked in the lobby; tenants must leapfrog backpacks to get to shared baths. 11 rooms are also available, but the walls are little more than flimsy partitions. Gate locked at midnight. Singles with fan RM27, with A/C RM36. Doubles with fan RM32, with A/C RM38, with bath RM42.

Mulu Inn, 1st Fl., Lot 2453, Jl. China (tel. 417 170), across the intersection from the Wisma Pelita. The better rooms are on the first floor, away from the intersection. Rooms on the second floor are large and boxy, with a shared toilet. The cheapest single is RM25, with A/C RM37. Doubles start at RM42.

Silverwood Inn, Lot 655, Jl. Bendahara (tel. 420 577), a few shops down from KFC. Walk up the grand stairs and turn left into the A/C reception area. Carpeting, phones, TVs, and large bathrooms with hot water are standard at Silverwood. Singles RM55-60. Doubles with bathtub RM65. MC, Visa, AmEx, DC.

FOOD

Pete's Deli, in Mega Hotel's in-house mall (tel. 411 680). Lovingly hung with images of music and movie icons; pick your own personal dinner companion. Cuisine includes chicken and mushroom pies (RM3.80) and fresh green salads (RM3). Toast the Beatles with a cappuccino (RM2.50) or a peach *lassi* made with homemade yogurt (RM2.00). A/C and English menu. Open daily 10am-9:30pm.

Sin Mui Pin 5 Jl. South Yu Seng (tel. 414 462). A popular, cavernous open-air restaurant on Jl. Yu Seng's southern end, across from Jade Centre. Just look for the golden roast ducks displayed at the restaurant's entrance. Take a chance and order the "chicken with Chinese herb in paper bag" or be content with sauteed prawns over rice (RM12.50). Open daily 10am-11pm.

Applebee Bakery (tel. 412 761), on the ground floor of Wisma Pelita. Freshly baked loaves of bread and an excellent selection of everything from spicy curry puffs to flaky apple strudel (RM1 per piece). Open daily 8:30am-9pm.

Bilal Restaurant, Lot 250 (tel. 420 471), in the midst of Jade Centre. Savory Indian cuisine several notches above other restaurants in the area. Point-and-eat options available, or dig into generous plates of chicken *tandoori* (RM7) and tender *rogani naan* (RM2) from the English menu. Open daily 6am-9pm.

NIGHTLIFE

Those who have endured Mulu's permitting process may opt for a quiet evening out. English movies are shown at the **Cathay Cinema** on Jl. China (shows noon, 2, 7:15, 9:15pm, RM4.60 and RM3.60). Visitors can walk out of town on Jl. Malay to the roundabout, where a right turn leads to the free ferry across the Miri River. Follow the road for 100m to Long Jelly, a narrow wooden structure extending far out into the waves, a perfect spot to catch Miri's colorful sunsets. Across the river, travelers can catch bus #1 to **Taman Selera** (last bus 9pm), a few km south of town. Here, you can enjoy a cheap dinner at the food stalls, then savor a moonlight stroll along the sandy beaches. Or hit the **Pot Black Snooker Hall** (RM9.60 per hour), which is past the Mega Hotel on Jl. Yu Seng. (Open daily 10am-3am.) Tourists who want to live it up before the big hike can do so at the **Ranch** (tel. 415 504), just off Pot Black, which blasts live English and Malay music favorites nightly (open 10:30am-3am). The Holiday Inn's **Clipper Bar** hosts more dancing fun (open nightly 7pm-2am); it's just before Taman Selera, on the right. On weekends there's a RM15 cover charge, as well as a dress code (no skin—long sleeves and pants).

MALAYSIA

■ Gunung Mulu National Park

Largest in all Sarawak, Gunung Mulu National Park encompasses a 544sq.km of peat swamp, heath, dipterocarp forest, moss thickets, and monfane vegetation. Over 3500 species of plants and 20,000 species of animals including eight species of the famed but reclusive hornbill, have been documented to date in the park's extensive wildlands. Most of the visitors who arrive, however, are attracted more by the park's geology than its inhabitants. Above-ground adventures include the ever-popular two-day sweat to the razor-sharp 50m-high limestone Pinnacles on the slopes of Gunung Api, as well as a three-day hike to the misty sandstone crags of Gunung Mulu's summit. Below ground lurks the park's renowned tangle of caverns. Exploration of this system began only 20 years ago and is still progressing. Unfortunately, visiting many of these sites also involves heroic monetary outlays. Majestic Gunung Kinabalu in Sabah, the tallest peak in Southeast Asia, and the historic cairns at Niah National Park offer similarly thrilling experiences and are much more viable budgeteer options in terms of both time and money.

GETTING THERE AND AWAY

By Plane

The airport lies a few km from park headquarters. There's usually a boatman waiting at the gate to ferry visitors directly to the park (RM3). The return trip to the airport may not be quite as smooth. Arrive at the dock early to arrange transport; many of the boatmen are commissioned to bring travelers to the caves and you may be able to hitch a ride before everyone leaves for the day. The parks office can sometimes find a motorcycle to drive you. If desperate, it's a 45-minute walk; cross the bridge, turn right at the intersection, and keep walking.

By Boat

Groups with more time, money, and patience may opt to return to Miri by boat. This involves an entire day (and possibly night) of traveling via longboat, starting with the trip to **Long Terrawan**. If there happens to be a boat inclined to go, the fee is about RM35. If there's no boat, charter one (RM150 for 1-4 people, RM35 for more than 5). To be sure they make the next connection, most travelers leave at 4pm the day before they intend to travel and arrange accommodation at the longhouses at Long Terrawan. The residents may let you sleep on their floor (no food provided) in return for a small gift or gratuity. Often the reception desk at the parks office can help arrange things. Alternatively, the boat leaves at 3:30am that morning from park headquarters (2hr.) and tries to arrive in time to catch the express (RM20) or speedboat (RM22) to **Marudi** (2 hr., 6:30am). From the Marudi jetty, transfer to either an express (2:30pm, RM18) or speedboat (noon, RM22) for the journey to **Kuala Baram** (3hr.). Finally, from Kuala Baram, there are taxis to Miri (RM20).

By Foot

A third option for leaving the park aside from boat and plane is by foot. After conquering the Pinnacles it's possible to hike from Camp 5 to the settlement of **Lubang Cina** on the Terikan River, following the path once taken by marauding Kayan headhunting parties. Travelers then travel by boat, with an overnight stop at the longhouse at **Bala Losong** to **Medamit.** From here, it's possible to catch a taxi into **Limbang,** where inexpensive sea and air connections are available into Sabah. Trekking down the head-hunters trail requires a great amount of coordination of transport and accommodation; it's best to go through a travel agent's package tour.

PRACTICAL INFORMATION

Getting **permits to Mulu** can involve an afternoon of pageantry and intrigue. The extravaganza begins at the tourist office. Prospective hikers should bring two copies of their passport and Malaysian tourist visa upon arrival in Miri to make reservations for accommodation at Mulu. Fill out two sets of forms before ambling over to the gray-trimmed **Resident's Office** (tel. 433 203) on Jl. Kingsway. (Open Mon.-Thurs. 8am-12:45pm and 2-4:15pm, Fri. 8-11:30am and 2:30-4:45pm, Sat. 8am-12:45pm.) Enter the second door to the left of the main entrance, and present the forms to the secretary in back, who will then direct you to the police station two buildings down. Look for Room #5 behind the main entrance and to the right of a small courtyard and present your forms, photocopies, and passport to the officer to get a stamp of approval, assuring a shining new permit, which can be picked up back at the Resident's Office. The entire process takes a few hours, so it's best to start early in the morning. When you reach Mulu, head first for the **parks office** (tel. 434 561), directly to the left of the boat dock. (Open daily 8am-4pm.) Pay for accommodations, park fees (RM3), camera (RM5) and video permits (RM10) here, and arrange guides and transportation for adventures within the park. There are no equipment rentals (try Mulu Resort downriver), but lockers for storing packs are available. The pleasant staff also sells badges, postcards, and a few interesting books on the caves.

ACCOMMODATIONS AND FOOD

Lodgings cluster near the parks office. A bed in the dorm is RM10 per night. There are rats around so store any food you bring carefully, away from your bed. A room with four beds in a chalet costs RM60 per night, a room with five beds in the resthouse is RM75, and a single room with three beds in the VIP suite costs RM90. Although there are over twenty beds in the hostel, these are often claimed by large tour groups; book accommodations as soon as possible. There's a dimly lit anonymous restaurant on the park grounds. Aside from tables and chairs there's also a snooker table, where most of the kitchen staff lounge when there are no customers. The menu consists of fried rice and noodles (RM4) and a limited selection of beverages, since most everything has to be flown in from Miri.

SIGHTS

Show Caves

The **Show Caves** are Mulu's most accessible and least strenuous attraction. All the caves have been fitted with boardwalks and dramatically lit to highlight the fluid rock forms and contorted passages. Experts estimate that over half of Mulu Park's caves still remain unexplored. Most visitors hire a boat to visit Wind Cave and Clearwater Cave in the morning, drop by the Batu Bungan Penan settlement on the way back to the park, and break for a quick lunch before heading onward to Deer Cave and Lang's Cave via the plank boardwalk in the afternoon.

You may want to bring a flashlight to examine the dark passages, a raincoat, and a plastic bag for cameras and video recorders. **Guides** are mandatory for all visits to the caves. Many are ardent spelunkers themselves whose insight and anecdotes are just as interesting as the surrounding rock formations. Guides and transportation must be arranged at the parks office. The following is a list of some standard fees for **guides;** the first price is for groups of 1-5 people, the second is for groups of 6-10 people (all prices are for one person only): Deer Cave and Lang's Cave (RM18, RM20); Garden of Eden (RM11, RM12); waterfalls (RM12, RM14); Wind Cave and Clear Water Cave (RM18, RM20); Turtle Cave (RM18, RM20); Langang's Caves (RM66, RM72); and Simon's Caves (RM66, RM72).

The **Clear Water Cave** and **Wind Cave** systems (open daily 9:30am-1pm) were first officially explored only 16 years ago by the Sarawak Royal Geographic Society expedition, who mapped a mere 25km of passages. Over the past decade exploration has continued, bringing the grand total to date of over 78km of cave passages.

The first stop is Wind Cave, up a wooden plank walk to the right of the boat dock. Wait at the entrance for your guide to meet you. It was here in 1996 that the importance of funds for maintaining the park's extensive system of walkways was made clear to the Chief Minister, various Assemblymen and their wives, as the rotting wood of the platform collapsed under the venerable weight of their combined tonnage.

Wind Cave takes its name from the cool drafts that can be felt as its passages constrict. The cave's most stunning passage is the **King's Chamber,** a collection of spectacular golden stalagmites.

Clear Water Cave is a five-minute walk farther along the river. A number of small pavilions have been built at the foot of the cave for picnickers to cool off in the nearby stream before tackling the 200 steps up to the entrance. Only the first 200m of the Clear Water system are accessible to the public. The path first goes through **Young Lady's Cave,** named after the shadow cast by some rock formations at its entrance, and eventually ends at a 50-m plunge into a murky chasm conspicuously littered with the bleached bones of wild boar who got lost in the caverns. Be careful about holding onto the hand rails, which are sticky with guano.

The caves are 1km away by boat (RM85 for 1-4 people). On the return trip, the boatman can stop at the Batu Bungan Penan settlement for those visitors who want to look at the handicrafts for sale. Alternately, it's possible to visit the caves on the boat ride to Camp 5, the jumping off point for hiking the Pinnacles.

The path into **Deer Cave** hugs the base of the mountain, slowly guiding visitors past tumbled piles of debris fringed with tufts of green palms and ferns. Deer Cave is the world's largest cave passage; at over 2km, even the shrill complaints of the 2 million horseshoe bats inhabiting it are lost in the vast passage. During thunderstorms spontaneous fountains cascade from the roof 200m above, glittering like silver streams in the subdued light of the cavern. The sight is absolutely breathtaking and compensates for the inconvenience of getting thoroughly soaked. The trail snakes relentlessly onward, past a rock silhouette referred to as Mr. Lincoln, and eventually leads up to a lone rock outcrop where visitors can inhale the green vision of the **Garden of Eden** a few hundred feet beyond. The entrance to **Lang's Cave** is a few minutes walk from Deer Cave. The cave itself is diminutive by comparison, but its intricate rock foundations are well worth a visit. The brief, 20-minute walk climbs past small streams, over clear pools, and flows of rock with such fanciful names as Eve's Shower and the Jellyfish.

A 3-km boardwalk has been built from the parks office to these two caves (open 12:30-4pm). The trip takes from 30 to 45 minutes, although it's certainly worth taking some time to enjoy the scenery along the way. The walk winds through a verdant landscape, under arches of roots buttressing giant trees and past rushing streams that mysteriously disappear into limestone crevices. Guides will meet you at the cave entrances. If water levels are low, it's possible to proceed to the Garden of Eden for an additional RM11 and 40 minutes of hiking.

Adventure Caving

If the Show Caves seem just too passive, travelers may want to try **adventure caving.** Guides will lead the daring into the stygian bowels of Mulu's lesser known passages to scramble over boulders, wade through subterranean rivers, and rapelle into deep, deep pits. **Sarawak Chambers,** the world's largest natural chamber, can accommodate 40 Boeing 747 jets and is the size of 16 soccer fields. Eight hours of romp and stomp through its midnight landscapes cost RM88 per guide for groups of 1-5 people. Other destinations include the **Drunken Forest** and the **Stone Horse Cave** systems. Most visitors arrange expeditions through tour operators in Miri, but this is only necessary if you need equipment. The park guides can round up all the necessary gear you need with a bit of prior notice, although prices are steep at RM20 day for a head lamp. Contact the park guides directly for more information.

Gunung Mulu

Rhinoceri were the first to enjoy Mulu's craggy summit, and the trail used by most trekkers today literally follows their now extinct foot steps. The journey usually takes four days for travelers in moderate fitness, although the experienced climber can probably conquer Mulu in just three days. Most visitors arrive at Camp 1 after an easy couple of hours of walk and spend the afternoon exploring the area's forests and searching for signs of wildlife. The second day out is a tough uphill battle. It takes about 10 leech-infested hours to reach camp 4 at an elevation of 1800m. The next day the most zealous of climbers are up before the sun rises, endeavoring to confront the dawn's first rays with their telephoto lenses. The journey up to the wind-scarred peak involves about 1½ hours of climbing, some of it using thick lengths of rope to steady wobbly legs. After capturing the sunrise and a spectacular panorama reaching all the way to Brunei Bay, most visitors return to one of the camps for a night's rest before trudging back to park headquarters on day four.

The Pinnacles

Over 5 million years old, the **Pinnacles** knife their way skyward from the arduous upper reaches of Gunung Api. The solemn 50-m towers have been etched out of the exposed limestone face of the mountain by constant weathering of rain drops. The trek begins with a scenic four-hour longboat ride from park headquarters to Long Berar. From here it's another 23 hours of trudging through the jungle to reach Camp 5, the Pinnacle's base camp, with basic lodging and cooking facilities, some 8km away. After a good night's sleep and some words of encouragement from their guide, trekkers tackle the steep hillside of Api. Although only 2.5km long, the trail is extremely steep and requires four hours to scale the vertical slopes; the last hour is especially brutal. If there's the chance of rain, or the guides feel the group is too fatigued to tackle the ropes and ladders near the top of the trail, they bring the party back down to Camp 5. For determined trekkers with wills of iron and buns of steel, the trek concludes at a narrow vantage point overlooking the surreal spires of the stone forest. The trail downhill is just as tricky as up, and takes three to four hours. Most visitors recover at Camp 5 for a night before returning to park headquarters the following morning.

The cost of hiring a boat to Long Berar, the first leg of the journey to the Pinnacles, for a group of one to four people, is RM300 for roundtrip journeys and RM200 one way. Guides are a pricey RM110 for the three-day/two-night trek for a group of one to five people. Fair weather is necessary for scaling the slope up to the Pinnacles, and if rain looks imminent, guides will postpone the hike.

SABAH

Known as the "land below the winds," Sabah was once rumored to be a storehouse of precious gems. Consequently, foreigners from as early as the 12th century found their way to Sabah's shores to reap the island's promised treasures. First came Kublai Khan in 1260, Chinese traders in the 1400s, the itinerant Ferdinand Magellan in 1521, and the ambitious Baron von Overbeck in 1865, who bought the 76,115sq.km territory from the Sultans of Brunei and Sulu for a mere US$12,000 and named himself the Maharajah of Sabah. Britain formally took over the administration of Sabah in 1888 and in general all remained relatively calm until New Years Day in 1942, when the Japanese invaded Pulau Labuan. After World War II, Sabah joined the newly formed Federation of Malaysia.

Somewhat of an anomaly among the Malaysian states, Sabah could very well be its own nation. Ethnic Malays constitute only 8% of the population, while indigenous ethnicities make up two-thirds of all Sabahans. Aside from these ethnic dissimilarities, Sabah also deviates from the rest of Malaysia by electing a Christian state government that frequently opposes the Islamic central authority. Nationalism is alive and well in here and, in the face of all these elements, it's no wonder that Sabahans agitate for sovereignty.

Unfortunately, for would-be seekers of Sabah's many treasures, the region is difficult to access. Travel connections are both more expensive and less congenial than on the peninsula; it's best to travel as a group where possible to lower costs. Overloaded logging trucks and the erosion of river embankments have left many of Sabah's roads in a state of disrepair. Yet the underdevelopment of the state has helped preserve vast emerald jungle paradises, teeming with fascinating wildlife and

---

Mt. Kinabalu or Mt. Doom?

The North Borneo Frodo Society was founded in 1969 by Neill McKee, a Canadian volunteer living in Sabah, and Peter Ragan, an American. Noting uncanny similarities in Sabah's geography, vegetation, and people with those of other ages, these two clever young men proposed the theory that Sabah is in fact the site of Middle Earth, the magical land of J.R.R. Tolkien's fantasy trilogy, *The Lord of the Rings.* As strange as this idea might seem, Tolkien himself joined the society, lending credence to the claim. So as you travel through Sabah, beware of the nasty Gollum, who still roams the area, known to locals as the "oily man." Those interested in joining should contact Neill McKee, P.O. Box 44145, Nairobi, Kenya. Members must have lived in Sabah, read the trilogy, or both, or neither.

---

vegetation. Sabah's claim to fame, however, lies in its mist-shrouded mountain, Gunung Kinabalu, the highest peak in all of Southeast Asia, which has become a near-pilgrimage site for many travelers.

■ Kota Kinabalu

Kota Kinabalu (known simply in these parts as KK) is a raw, big-boned city, resonating with the blows of jackhammers at construction sites and the groans of tractors at sea-side land reclamation projects. Despite the local's best metropolis-building efforts, few visitors can be enticed to linger after their first airplane glimpse of Mt. Kinabalu, Southeast Asia's highest peak. No perky skyline can rival the austere grandeur of the granite summit, and the city's hamburger-munching masses are still outnumbered by the carnivorous maws of scarlet pitcher plants winding their way through the dripping cloud forests of the mountain slopes. Still the often overlooked beaches of nearby Tunku Abdul Rahman Park Islands make for an excellent surf and turf combo, while visits to the House of Skulls and Sabah's State Museum provide hours of intrigue in between.

ORIENTATION

KK's town center follows a basic grid system, dominated by three important east-west avenues. **Jalan Tun Fuad Stephens** curves along the waterfront to the north of the city center. This street contains the **jetty** for boats to the islands, the **city market,** and the **Sabah Parks office.** Just around the corner on **Jalan 19** is the excellent Travelers Rest Hostel. **Jalan Tun Razak** is the city's central boulevard, and the site of the **GPO,** and the **local bus terminal. Jalan Tunku Abdul Rahman** borders the edge of the city to the south. The Backpacker Lodge, **police station, long-distance bus terminal,** and **immigration office** all line up here. Several km farther west, Jl. Tunku Abdul Rahman meets **Jalan Kemajuan** at a large intersection with the Kompleks Karamunsing and the Kompleks Kuwasa.

PRACTICAL INFORMATION

Tourist Offices: Tourism Malaysia (tel. 211 732), on Jl. Segunting, ground floor, Wing On Life Bldg. Friendly English-speaking staff with general info on all of Malaysia. Open Mon.-Fri. 8am-12:45pm, 2-4:15pm, Sat. 8am-12:45pm. **Sabah Tourism Promotion Corp.,** 51 Jl. Gaya (tel. 212 121; http://www.jaring.my/sabah), just across the street in the old post office. Pamphlets on Sabah's attractions in many languages. Comprehensive map of KK (RM2). Open Mon.-Fri. 8:30am-4pm, Sat 8:30am-noon. A small office also at the airport (tel. 223 767). Open Mon.-Fri. 9am-5pm, Sat.-Sun. and holidays 9am-2pm.

Tours and Travel: Eco Borneo Tours, Lot 49, Jl. Tengku Abdul Rahman (tel. 213 668), in the small block of shops next to the Shangri-la Hotel. Mailing address: P.O. Box 3, Likas, 89407, Kota Kinabalu, Sabah, Malaysia. Winner of both Green Globe and Most Visionary Green Incentive Awards. Attempts to reconcile Sabah's developing tourist economy with the fragility of its forests' ecosystems. Tour prices and

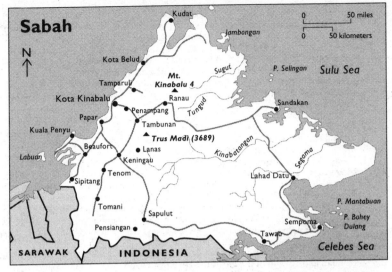

rafting trips start at RM180 and 2-day packages at **Sukau** (not including transport from KK) at RM367 for a group of 9. In an effort to control the spread of weeds choking nearby **Kenenanap Lake,** 1000 free nights of lodging have been set aside for groups of up to 20 people for 3 consecutive nights who volunteer to manually remove the weeds. The only cost is RM50 for food and transport and includes a free evening cruise to see the famed Proboscis monkeys. **Borneo Divers** (tel. 222 226; e-mail bdivers@po.jaring.my; http://www.jaring.my/bdivers), ground floor of Wisma Saba. A 5-star PADI dive center. 4-day open water certification course RM650-750. Everything from single dives (RM70) to unlimited dives (RM210). Tours to wrecks off **Pulau Labuan,** 100km south of KK (RM100-150 for 1 dive, RM185-235 for 2 dives), and **Pulau Sipidan,** with its famed 700m oceanic cliffs just 15m from the beach (2 days, US$675 per diver). Office open Mon.-Fri 8:30am-5pm, Sat. 8:30am-1:30pm. MC, Visa, AmEx.

Sabah Parks Office: Lot 3, ground floor, Block K Kompleks Sinsuran (tel. 211 881; fax 221 001; reservations fax 211 585), across from the Filipino market on Jl. Tun Fuad Stephens, in the north of the city. Polite, English-speaking staff. Mandatory stop for anyone wishing to book accommodations at Kinabalu Park Headquarters, Gunung Kinabalu, Poring Hot Springs, Tunku Abdul Rahman Park, Turtle Islands Park, Pulau Tiga Park, or Tawau Hills Park. Open Mon.-Fri. 8:30am-4pm and Sat 8:30am-noon. Reservations can be made up to a year in advance, and are highly recommended, as the parks are all extremely popular. Reservations can be made by faxing the above number or addressing correspondence to: The Director, SABAH PARKS, First Floor, Lot 1-3, Block K, P.O. Box 10626, 88806 Kota Kinabalu, Sabah Malaysia. A minimum of 10% of the accommodation fee (or RM10 if the fee is less than RM10) must be paid at the time of reservation via MC or Visa (no service charge) or in the form of a bank draft made out to Sabah Parks. Full payment must be received 1 mo. before the scheduled visit in order to confirm reservations. 10% charge for cancellations two weeks before the scheduled visit or changes in dates or numbers of visitors. All this said, it's possible to wander into the Parks office off the street. Despite the risk, many travelers arrange accommodations this way. If everything is full, however, try returning the next day in case someone has altered or cancelled a reservation. Park fees, insurance, guide, and porter fees where applicable are paid directly upon arrival at the parks.

Embassies and Consulates: Indonesia (tel. 218 600), on Jl. Kemajuan near Maybatik, north of the Jl. Tunku Abdul Rahman intersection. Issues 2-month visas; bring 2 passport photos. Open Mon.-Fri. 8am-4pm.

Immigration Offices: 4th Fl., Wisma Dang Bandang, Jl. H.J. Yaakob (tel. 216 711 ext. 116). 1-month visa extensions RM6; pay at counter 13 or 14. Open Mon.-Thurs. 8am-12:45pm and 2-4:15pm, Fri. 8-11:30am, Sat. 8am-12:45pm.

Currency Exchange: Maybank (tel. 254 295), at the corner of Jl. Pantai and Jl. 3. Open Mon.-Fri. 9:30-11:30am. **Branch** (tel. 268 906) cashes traveler's checks. RM5 per transaction, RM15 charge per check. Open daily 7am-10pm.

American Express: Lot 3.50 & 3.51, 3rd Fl., Kompleks Karamunsing, on Jl. Tuaran (tel. 241 200). Cashes personal checks but **no traveler's checks.** Holds mail for cardmembers. Open Mon.-Fri. 8:30am-5:30pm.

Air Travel: Airport (tel. 667 786), 6km outside the city center. Arrive at the gate early, as there are *no* boarding calls. **Buses** from airport must be caught outside the terminal on the highway. Catch the Putatan Bus (RM0.80) into town. **MAS** has an office at the airport in the departure hall (open daily 5am-7pm), as well in the Kompleks Karamunsing (tel. 213 555). Daily connections to **Jakarta, Hong Kong, Singapore** (RM544), **KL** (RM437), **Kuching** (RM228), **Miri** (RM95), and **Sandakan** (RM83). Open Mon.-Fri. 8:30am-5:30pm, Sat. 8:30am-4:30pm, Sun. 9am-1pm. **Dragon Air** (tel. 254 733), in the Kompleks Kuwasa. To **Hong Kong** (1 per day, RM940). Open Mon.-Fri. 8:30am-12:30pm. **Singapore Air,** 20 Jl. Pantai Tempahan (tel. 255 444), flies to **Singapore.** Open Mon.-Fri. 8:30-noon and 1:30-4:30pm, Sat. 8:30am-12:30pm. All airlines take MC, Visa, and AmEx. It's difficult to get cheap fares in KK—get it worked out before you arrive.

Buses: Long-distance bus terminal, in the middle of a field on Jl. Tunku Abdul Rahman in the south of the city. Buses to **Kota Belud** (2hr., RM5) depart when full until 3pm. Buses to **Gunung Kinabalu Park** (2hr., RM15) and **Ranau** (2½hr., RM18) depart until noon. Larger buses to **Sandakan** (6hr., RM15-25) leave most frequently in the early morning before noon. Arrive early for the best traveling weather. Touts offer to bring you to the bus. Don't pay anyone until you're sure it's reasonably full already; pay the driver directly to ensure a seat.

Taxis: A counter at the airport's arrival hall arranges taxis to the city center for RM10.20. Most rides within the city cost RM5. Look for taxis near large hotels.

Ferries: Tourism Malaysia recommends **Coral Island Cruises Ferry** service, which has safety equipment, to **Pulau Gaya** (Mon.-Fri. 10am, returning 3pm; Sat.-Sun. 9, 10, and 11am, returning 2pm and 4pm; RM16 roundtrip). Costs slightly more for trips to **Police Beach.** Locals also take visitors in their **speedboats.** To Gaya (RM10 one way). Boatmen will not want to leave unless full, so you may end up paying extra. Often they have snorkeling equipment for rent as well. It is advisable not to pay the boatmen until returning to KK, as there have been tales of tourists left stranded on the islands overnight.

Local Transportation: Local bus terminal, across from the post office on Jl. Tun Razak. The **Putatan Bus** (RM0.80) to the airport departs from here, as well as buses marked "Beach," which go to **Tanjung Aru Beach.**

Rentals: Trave Rent-A-Car, Lot 31, ground floor, Wisma Sabah (tel. 222 708). Prices start at RM60 per day without insurance. IDP required. Does not rent for trips over poor roads. Open Mon.-Sat. 8am-5pm. MC, Visa, and AmEx.

Hiking Supplies: Tong Hing Supermarket, on Jl. Gaya, past the tourist office heading east out of town. Snacks for hiking Gunung Kinabalu, toilet paper, and bug repellent. Open daily 8am-10pm. **Yao Han,** in the basement of Centrepoint Sabah, has a few pricey pieces of outdoor equipment, such as waterproof flashlights (RM27). Open daily 10am-10pm. MC and Visa.

Markets: The **market area** spreads out on the waterfront north of the city on Jl. Tun Fuad Stephens. Fresh fruit can be bought here. Open daily 8am-6pm. Next door is the **Filipino market,** where cheap souvenirs can be found. Every Sunday from 8am-noon there is a **street market** on Jl. Gaya as well.

Pharmacies: Pharmex, ground floor, lot 6, Block F Kompleks Segama (tel. 231 457). Open Mon.-Sat. 8:30am-7:30pm, Sun. 8:30am-1pm. **Syarikat Kara Mata** (tel. 258 589), next door, has contact lens supplies. Open daily 8:30am-6:30pm.

Medical Services: Sabah Medical Centre (tel. 424 333), Kingfisher Park, on Jl. Kuala Inanam.

Police: (tel. 221 191), south of town on Jl. Balai.

Post Offices: The **main post office** is at Jl. Tun Razak (tel. 210 855), next to the pedestrian overpass and the Kompleks Segama. *Poste Restante.* Open Mon.-Sat 8am-5pm, Sun. 10am-1pm. **Postal code:** 88806.

Telephones: Public telephones place collect calls and some accept foncards. A small **Telekom office** is in a row of shops behind the Kompleks Kuwasa off Jl. Tunku Abdul Rahman (accepts MC, Visa, and AmEx, with a 5% tax). Occasionally, it works. There is also a Telekom office at the **airport**. Open daily 8am-10pm. **Operator Assistance:** 108. **Telephone code:** 088

ACCOMMODATIONS

Travellers Rest Hostel, Block L, 3rd Fl., Lot 5&6, Kompleks Sinsuran (tel. 224 264), on the corner of Jl. 19 and Jl. Datuk Chong Thian Vun. A perennial favorite shouting distance from the Parks Office. Outgoing staff keeps well-furnished rooms squeaky clean. Luggage storage available. Inexpensive tours to Sukau and Turtle Island. Front door locked at midnight. Dorms RM15. Singles with fan RM25, with A/C RM38. Doubles with fan RM32, with A/C RM45.

Backpacker Lodge, 1st Fl., Lot 25, Lorong Dewan, Australia Place (tel. 261 495), near the rotary at Jl. Balai Polis; look for the black and white sign. It's isolated from the cacophony of construction that grips most of the city. The owner happily gives brochures and travel tips to her guests. Comfortable common area. Separate male and female 12-bed dorms with shared bath RM45 (includes light breakfast). A single 4-bed dorm is available for small mixed groups.

Hotel Bilal, No. 1, Block B. For those craving a bit more decadence. A profusion of plastic flowers in the small lobby. 10 doubles have A/C, sinks, and desks. Rooms with shared bath RM35, attached bath RM40. Attached Restoran Bilal serves some scrumptious *roti*. Open daily 7am-7pm.

Jack's B&B, No. 17, Block B, Jl. Karamunsing (tel. 232 367), on the outskirts of town, set back from Jl. Tunku Abdul Rahman and near the pedestrian overpass, past the intersection with Jl. Kemajuan. The management can pick travelers up from the airport, otherwise, take a taxi. From the city catch a Sembulan bus from the terminal (RM0.50) and ask to be let off at Jack's. Dorms with as many as 28 beds and as few as 2 available RM18. Breakfast included. Most have nightly A/C.

FOOD

The **Kompleks Sedgy,** just off Jl. Laiman Diki, is an open-air court that has the feel of a family reunion gone out of control. Also popular with the locals are the open walks of **Komplex Sinsuran.** Each shop shows its own video, so peruse the area before settling down for an evening's coffee and conversation. The food court in the basement of **Centrepoint** offers similar gastronomic bargains, but with cool A/C.

Port View Seafood Restaurant (tel. 221 753), on Jl. Haji Saman. Follow Jl. Tun Razak east out of town; look for the blazing neon sign. The simple open-air terrace lacks ambiance. Grab a pink plastic pail and snatch a lobster dinner from the tanks in back (1.5kg, RM80) or order a heap of steamed prawns from the menu (RM10-40). Arrive early to ensure a table. Open Sun.-Fri. 6pm-1am, Sat. 6pm-2am.

Restoran Sri Melaka, No. 9, Jl. Laiman Diki (tel. 255 136), across the street from the courtyard restaurants of Kompleks Sedco. The snappy silk frocks of the waitresses seem to be cut out of the same material as the mass of artificial foliage hovering over the kitchen. Green is everywhere here. Patrons rave over the Assam fish head (RM10-20), although the savory Redang Chicken (RM6-15) deserves praise as well. A/C and English menu. Open daily 9:30am-9:30pm.

Nan Xing Restaurant, 33-35 Jl. Haji Saman (tel. 239 388), on the ground floor of the Hotel Nan Xing, on the right heading out of town on Jl. Tun Razak. Excellent *dim sum* in A/C splendor every morning 7-10am (RM1-3 per basket), as well as an extensive selection of Chinese entrees for lunch (noon-2:30pm) and dinner (6pm-9pm). Cashew chicken RM8.80.

MALAYSIA

NIGHTLIFE

The cinemas at the intersection of Jl. Tunku Abdul Rahman and Jl. Laiman Diki often show movies in English. Shows are at noon, 2, 7, and 9pm; most seats cost RM5.50.

Tiffiny Discotheque, Block A, No. 9, Jl. Karamunsing (tel. 210 645), in front of Jack's B&B. Powder pink neon sign. Live music every night. 2-for-1 drinks as well (1-2am, except Sat. and holidays). Features a mix of Malay and English pop with a flashy light show. Open nightly 8pm-2am.

SIGHTS

In the southeast section of KK sits one of the few remaining relics of the city's association with the British North Borneo Chartered Company. Built in 1905, the solitary wooden column of **Atkinson Clock Tower** stands aloof on a small hill next to the police station off Jl. Balai Polis. The road to the right of the tower leads up to Signal Hill observatory for fine evening views of the ocean. Farther west along Jl. Tunku Abdul Rahman is a small stilt village, once fronting the ocean but now cut off by the Api Api Land reclamation project and a mammoth row of shop houses.

Sabah's **State Museum** is a good half hour's walk southwest from the city center along Jl. Tunku Abdul Rahman. Cross the large intersection with Jl. Kemajuan, and after the road crosses a small stream, turn left onto Jl. Penampang. There's a small gate 100m ahead on the left, which leads to the museum. The main building is a modern interpretation of the traditional Rugus Longhouses. Its cavernous interior houses exhibits on ethnography, natural history, ceramics, and archeology. (Open Mon.-Thurs. 10am-6pm, Sat.-Sun. and public holidays 9am-6pm; free.) Just beyond the main building is the **science and technology center,** which, strangely enough, houses a small art gallery with a few noteworthy works (open Mon.-Thurs. 10am-4:30pm, Sat.-Sun. and holidays 9:30am-5pm).

At the opposite end of the compound, past the artificial waterfall where tour groups queue up for pictures, is the newly completed **Kampung Warisan** (Heritage Village). Visitors can pose demurely in front of a traditionally constructed Bajau House, or hop from the dirt floor of a Chinese farm houses to the terrace of a Murut Longhouse in one pounce. (Open Mon.-Thurs. 10am-5pm, Sat.-Sun. and holidays 10am-5pm.) The compound lies within the environs of the **Ethno-botanic Gardens,** where plants used by Sabah's tribes for ornamentation, commerce, and medicine, vie fiercely for space and sunlight. Unfortunately, the few explanatory signs are vague and far between. Tucked away in a dark corner of the garden is a small **zoo.** Judging by the state of the handful of its worn and ragged inhabitants, it's more likely to become a staging area for future taxidermic endeavors of the museum. Deer, snakes, and even a rather perky hornbill can be seen here.

Farther afield, **Tanjung Aur Beach** is an additional 2.5km from the museum. The beach is pleasant, but is at its best on the weekends when locals arrive unrolling mats and ordering picnic lunches from nearby food vendors. For an afternoon of pleasant distraction, just take one of the buses across from the post office with a "Beach" or "Shangri-La Resort" sign.

■ Near Kota Kinabalu

MONSOPIAD CULTURAL VILLAGE

Monsopiad, famed warrior of the Kadazan, and his heroic achievements are still celebrated at **Monsopiad Cultural Village** (tel. 761 336), several km south of central KK in the small suburb of Donggonggon (admission RM15). Traditional performances of the Marut Warrior and Bamboo Dance are performed daily at 10:30am, 1:30, and 3:30pm. On Monday, Wednesday, Friday, and Saturday nights, performances are accompanied by a buffet dinner of Chinese, Malay, and traditional Kadazan cuisine (RM55; call for reservations). The enthusiastic proprietors are even willing to stage a

I, Monsopiad

Monsopiad began his life with an auspicious omen. When his mother became pregnant, the sacred bird Bugang built a nest and layed eggs on the roof of the family abode. As Monsopiad grew, so did the village's problems. The small settlement was beleaguered by a band of thieves. The young Monsopiad vowed to find and kill the robbers in exchange for a grand warrior's welcome. He set off with three boys on his search-and-destroy mission and after five weeks returned to a procession of song and dance from the villagers. Monsopiad was so taken by his welcome that he vowed to destroy all the enemies of the village, taking their heads as trophies to hang in his house and protect his family. The ever increasing pace and enthusiasm with which Monsopiad collected his trophies, however, began to alarm the villagers, especially those with particularly decorative cranii. Finally, after Monsopiad started provoking men into fighting with him, the village decided the aging hero had become a menace. A group of his friends banded together to end his life. He was buried with honor, having saved the village after all, with his head left intact out of respect. The skulls are still there in his house after three hundred years. Unlike many families who were convinced to bury their heirloom skulls by Christian missionaries, Monsopiad's descendents have kept this heritage and now make efforts to document and preserve the knowledge of their Kadazan culture.

Kadazan wedding complete with costumes, priestesses, and a village full of witnesses. A taxi from town costs RM15 one way, or call, and the owners will pick travelers up for RM10.

TUNKU ABDUL RAHMAN PARK

Tunku Abdul Rahman Park is composed of five small islands bobbing placidly only 3-8km from KK's bustling streets, making them the perfect daytrip before heading up to the mountain. The first inhabitants to enjoy the cool ocean waters and sandy stretches of these islands were part of the North Borneo Chartered Company's settlement, established on **Pulau Gaya,** the largest island, in 1882. Currently the island is home to a number of Filipino immigrants who have settled in the stilt village off its east coast. The island is etched with over 20km of trails through a mostly intact dipterocarp forest. The island interior is also home to the shy megapode bird *(megapodius freycinet),* whose call sounds like the meowing of a cat.

The trail from Park headquarters leads to a boardwalk through a dense thicket of mangrove, whose seeds germinate directly on the tree. Gaya has numerous beaches, although **Police Beach,** named because the local police recruits used to use the area for target practice, is the most secluded. It's on the island's north coast. **Pulau Sapi** (Cow Island), just off Gaya's southwest coast, is also popular, although its tiny 25 acres are overrun at times, and the beaches can be trashed as a result. The park headquarters is sited on **Pulau Manukan,** and **Pulau Mamutik** drifts nearby. Both have been accosted by pricey chalets that have claimed the long powdery drifts and beaches surrounding the two islands. **Pulau Sulung** is the least developed of the park's islands, and the extensive corals here are in much better condition. Here, parrot fish dart past snarls of staghorn coral, brain coral, and lettuce coral, making it a popular site for both divers and snorkelers. Since it is also the most remote of the park's islands, arranging transport can be problematic if traveling alone. (Admission to all the islands RM2.)

Camping is permitted on the islands for RM5 for adults and RM2 for those under 18. Written permission must be obtained from the parks office before setting out, and campers must provide their own food and equipment. Chalets are available on Manukan (rooms sleep 4 and cost RM200 on weekends and holidays, RM140 on weekdays). Similar accommodations are also available on Mamutik for RM250 weekends and holidays and RM180 on weekdays. Reservations must be made at the Park's office in KK.

KOTA BELUD

Kota Belud makes a pleasant distraction from the urban rhythms of Kota Kinabalu. Situated 75km north of KK on the coast, it's a pleasant, if butt-numbing, ride through fringes of rubber plantations and shaggy dipterocarp forests. The two-hour trip (RM5) passes quickly as the driver swerves to dodge kamikaze cows, and the rest of the passengers croon soulfully to the Malay love songs playing on the tape deck. Kota Belud is famed for its weekly *tamu* (market and trade fair), one of the largest in Sabah, held every Sunday morning about 7:30am-2pm. *Tamu* play an important role for the local Rugus and Kadazan people, as well as the large numbers of Bajau in the area. The Bajau, Sabah's famed cowboys of the east, are unlikely to be wearing their traditional brilliantly stitched garb unless it's a truly special occasion, such as the annual **Tamu Besar** (big market), held in November. The lucky might catch a glimpse of a mounted rider or two in the crowded *tamu* grounds.

Try to arrive in Kota Belud as early as possible. **Buses** leave from the long distance terminal on Jl. Tunku Abdul Razak (2hr., RM5) and drop passengers off on the highway in the city center. Get off, and look for the pink spires and gilt dome of the city mosque. Walk to it, and then bear right down Jl. Hasbollah. The *tamu* grounds are a five- to 10-minute walk out of town past the post office just off the large rotary. It's possible to spend Saturday night at the **Government Rest House** (tel. 976 128) just a few hundred meters beyond the *tamu* grounds (or a RM1 minibus ride from town), where immaculate, if tiny, singles with fan cost RM40. There are no restaurants in the area, so visitors must walk back to the city for dinner. Expect the sleepy hamlet to close up by 7pm. Buses back to KK depart when full from the Esso gas station (2hr., RM5, last bus 2-3pm); it's also possible to catch a bus coming from Kudat, if there are empty seats. Technically, it's also possible to charter a bus directly to Kinabalu National Park for RM40-50, but this might take some serious negotiating.

■ Gunung Kinabalu

Gunung Kinabalu is the world's youngest non-volcanic mountain and Southeast Asia's highest peak, as well as a huge magnet for Sabah's tourism industry. The mountain itself is composed of a solid core of congealed granite that began slowly pushing its way through the surrounding soft sandstone and shales less than one million years ago. Today, at a boggling 4101m above sea level, it continues to push skyward at a rate of 5mm per year. The mountain's seductive profile was first attempted by Sir Hugh Low in 1851, and later in 1856. Although the highest pinnacle has been named in his honor, he never quite made it that far. "Inaccessible to any but winged animals" was his appraisal of the peak as surveyed from the brink of the terrifying Lows Gully, a mile-deep chasm also named after this intrepid pioneer. Well, wouldn't you know it, John Whitehead, a zoologist with a special interest in birds was actually the first human to access the eerie heights of Kinabalu in 1888. Since becoming a national park in 1964, along with the completion of the 8.5km trail to the mountain top, Kinabalu has attracted thousands of visitors yearly. Despite being half the height of Mt. Everest, the summit is well within the abilities of anyone with good health, moderate fitness, and a determined will. Most travelers stay overnight at park headquarters, but it's also possible to walk up the slopes to Laban Rata and spend the night at its lodges. The ambitious then wake up at 3am, gather flashlights and cameras, and bustle into the cold morning air to arrive at the peak in time for the sunrise, before wobbling down the slopes to headquarters the same day.

GETTING THERE AND AWAY

The best time to climb the mighty mountain is in the dry season, between March and April, when the clearest views can be had. Regular buses from the long-distance terminal in Kota Kinabalu run to the park (2hr., RM15), as well as from the smaller town of Ranau. Buses to **KK** can be flagged down on the highway in front of the park entrance (2hr., RM10); service stops after about 4pm. Large A/C buses pass the park around 9am daily as well (4½hr., RM20-25). Alternately, minibuses are also available till noon. Transport to **Poring Hot Springs** can be chartered directly from the park (RM50-65) or transfer in Ranau. Catch minibuses to **Ranau** in front of the park's sign until 4pm (40min., RM5-10). Keep in mind that minibus service to Poring from Ranau (30min., RM5-10) stops at noon. There's a shop next to the reception office with an excellent selection of books on Sabah (open daily 7am-7pm).

PRACTICAL INFORMATION

Permits cost RM10 for adults and RM2 for children under 18. Climbers must also take out personal accident insurance for RM3.50. Porters may be hired for RM25 per day for the trip to Laban Rata, or RM28 to Sayat Sayat. Guides are mandatory for everyone scaling the summit, but not required of those climbing no farther than Laban Rata. They protect the park's interest by making sure no one carries out plants and other souvenirs or vandalizes the trails. They also make sure travelers stay safe, and offer words of encouragement during tough stretches of the trail. Groups with special interests can make requests for specific guides when they arrive (i.e., guides who speak fluent English or who have knowledge of plant species or an eye for birds). A guide for one to three people is RM25 per day, four to six people RM28 per day, and seven to eight people RM30 per day. Park officers will attempt to place independent travelers in groups to help minimize costs.

Warm clothes, sunscreen, insect repellent, a rain slicker/wind breaker, small flashlight, comfortable shoes (sneakers will do), toilet paper, aspirin, bandages, hard candy or chocolate for quick energy (it's a nice gesture to pack extra for your guide), and a water bottle are all recommended for the climb. Excess baggage can be stored at the park reception office, where lockers are provided free of charge for valuables. The **Visitor Centre** is located just past the hostels, before the access road loops back to park reception office. There is an intriguing, if small, exhibit of the park's flora and fauna upstairs. The theater in the basement hosts slide shows with informative dialogue about the park and the mountain trail itself (shows daily at 2pm, Fri.-Mon 7:30pm). Behind the Visitor Centre is the **Mountain Garden,** a botanical zoo that is worth a visit for any green thumb. Here a guide can point out many of the plants that linger along the mountain's trails. Plants endemic to the park have red labels, plants used medicinally are tagged blue, and more common species bear black tags. The garden has an especially beautiful selection of Gunung Kinabalu's 1200 orchid species, including the world's smallest flowering orchid. Its diminutive blossom is only the size of a pin head. The orchids are labeled with green tags, and some plants are likely to be blooming during any visit. (English tours daily 9am and 3pm; Malay noon.) Additionally, there is a guided tour through the local trails. This brief walk acquaints visitors with things that creep, crawl, and fly, as well as the sedentary flora. It lasts about an hour and departs daily from the Visitors Centre at 11am.

ACCOMMODATIONS

Just to the right of the park entrance, the reception office is the first stop for all visitors. (Open daily 7am-7pm.) The staff will then assign you to a room and give you a basic map of the park with directions to accommodations. If you have not made arrangements for lodging before arriving or wish to alter them, the staff will have to phone the offices in the city. If the offices have already closed or the computers are down, you're out of luck. Accommodations are a 10-minute walk down the curving one-way road to the left of the park entrance. A night in the dorms at the **Old Fellowship Hostel** (sleeps 46) and **New Fellowship Hostel** (sleeps 52) costs RM19, persons under 18 RM5. Cabin and basement doubles cost RM50, weekends and holidays RM80. Annex quads cost RM100, weekends and holidays RM160. Duplex six-person cabins and single story five-person cabins cost RM150, weekends and holidays RM200. A two-story seven-person cabin and the **Nepenthes Villas** quads cost RM80, weekends and holidays RM250. The **Kinabalu Lodge** octets cost RM270, weekends and holidays RM360. Camping is not allowed in the park.

In addition, plenty of accommodations are available on the mountains. The poshest digs are within the yellow-trimmed walls of the **Laban Rata Resthouse.** Dorm rooms (sleep 54) are still sparse and spartan, but they do have heaters, hot water, and electricity. Also available is a single room with attached bath that sleeps two (RM100), and a single room with bath for four (RM200). Laban Rata has a small canteen (open daily 7:30am-7:30pm and 2-3:30am) that sells a modest supply of provisions, and it serves hot meals at rather inflated prices (fried rice RM5.50, omelettes RM5, coffee RM1). The three other dorms in the area are **Gunting Lagadan Hut** (sleeps 44), **Panar Laban Hut** (sleeps 12), and **Waras Hut** (sleeps 12); all are unheated, but cooking facilities are provided as well as sleeping bags, free of charge. Rates are RM10 for adults and RM5 for persons under 18. The most basic accommodations (no electricity, heat, or access to the Laban Rata canteen, although cooking facilities are provided) are two hours of hard climbing up the Panar Laban Rock face at **Sayat Sayat Hut** (sleeps 10). Many visitors rave about the beautifully secluded locale of Sayat; the small accommodation certainly creates a sense of camaraderie. Groups gather in sleeping bags under the stars, talking well into the night. Boarders also don't have to get up as early to see the sunrise. Rare **Kinabalu rats** have also made appearances, and it can be bitterly cold (RM10, children under 18 RM5).

FOOD

The **Kinabalu Balsam Canteen** is located just below the park office, and offers excellent sunset views of the mountain from its veranda (open Mon.-Fri. 6am-10pm, Sat. and holidays 6am-11pm, Sun. 6am-10pm). Most dishes start at RM5, and there is a modest selection of snacks and other supplies at reasonable prices. **Liwagu Cafeteria,** part of the Visitor Centre complex, is stricken with a decor of orange and maroon table cloths (open daily 6am-9:30pm). Prices here hover at RM8 for entrees, although the quality of cooking is not much better than the canteen.

CLIMBING KINABALU

Travelers usually arrive at park headquarters the day before ascending the summit and spend an afternoon enjoying the cool climate and exploring the trails through the local forests. The next day, groups begin. Most choose to begin the ascent from the power station, a brief RM2 bus ride away, but it's possible to use the Liwagu trail (3hr.) as well. After an all-too-brief walk down to picturesque **Carson Falls,** it's all uphill along narrow but well-maintained trails. The climb is steady, but before long travelers arrive at the first of six rest shelters built along the trail. Pop-eyed tree shrews cautiously emerge from the shrubs here to frolic for handouts. As the trek continues higher, large tree ferns loom, and the iridescent purple flowers of the **Kinabalu balsam,** one of the parks unusual endemic plant species, unfold along the trail. In fact, over half of the plant species above 912m are found nowhere else in the world. As the day progresses and the km markers pass, the **pitcher plants** (*Nepenthes*) begin to appear. These freakish plants produce large pitcher-shaped leaves; insects are attracted to the liquid filled leaf, where they fall in and drown, their nutrients absorbed by the plants. There are nine species that grow in the park and the largest, *Nepenthes rajah,* can hold up to 2L of fluid.

Gradually, the trail steepens until climbers are scrambling over rocks and through increasingly barren landscapes. This is home of the friendly and rare **Kinabalu warbler** and the **mountain blackbird,** two bird species found only here. After about six to seven hours of walking, most trekkers arrive at Labah Rata for lunch. Those proceeding on to Sayat Sayat Hut stop briefly to eat and begin the assault of the Panar Laban rock face. The wooden staircases soon become steep ladders. Eventually, these give way to shelves of bare gray granite. **Panar Laban** (Place of Sacrifice) is where the Kadazan guides of the early explorers would offer sacrifices to appease the spirits of the dead. The tree line stops here, and the air is noticeably thinner. Ropes are available to haul tired limbs up the trail, and the entire trip to Sayat Sayat takes about two hours. Most choose to tackle this portion in the morning after a good night's rest and breakfast at Laban Rata, although it's even trickier at 3am (at which time you must climb in order to catch the sunrise at the summit).

From the basic facilities of Sayat Sayat, the one- to two-hour path is not particularly difficult or steep, but for those unused to such exertions in this air, the trip can be a test of will. As the trail winds ever upward, the guides point out the silhouettes of rock formations with such intriguing appellations as the "Camel" and the "Ugly Sisters." **Low's Peak,** at an altitude of 4101m, rises in a gentle curve from this austere landscape of wind swept granite. Tourists vie feverishly for the ideal vantage to capture the sun's first rays over Borneo, but quickly disperse after the sunrise. The trip back down takes only five to six hours. Extra caution should be taken, as the legs can be rather rubbery at this point.

Many pause for a quick breakfast at Laban Rata to fortify them for the final slog. Everyone who climbs the peak, or to Laban Rata, will have a handsome certificate of achievement waiting for them at the park office (RM1). It's best to stay overnight at the park, and catch buses to other destinations in Sabah in the morning, so try to make reservations for three days. Alternatively, a group can charter a bus to Poring if they want to go immediately to the hot springs after descending the mountain. In that case, go for two days at the park and one day at Poring.

■ Near Gunung Kinabalu

PORING HOT SPRINGS

The steaming sulphurous waters of **Poring,** 43km east of park headquarters, are a miraculous marinade for travel-weary legs fresh from the slopes of Kinabalu. The springs were first enjoyed by Japanese troops during WWII, but more recently the area has become the weekend haunt of locals from Ranau. The baths are across the river from the main gates (admission RM2, free for overnight guests). The 50-60°C (120-140°F) spring-fed waters are piped into open-air tiled baths for the masses through private pools; jacuzzis and small, unheated swimming pools are available for a separate fee. A brief walk past the baths leads to the **canopy walkway**—a series of suspended boardwalks quivering at some points 60m above the ground. The view of the lowland dipterocarp forest, different from the mountainous wilds of park headquarters, is enthralling, if a bit nerve-wracking, as the planks shimmy beneath one's feet. Entry is RM2 from 10:30am-3:30pm, an extra RM5 for cameras, RM30 for video recorders. Those intent on seeing wildlife eye to eye in the forest aerie can arrange special nocturnal visits, although it may take a bit of negotiating and fees are higher. Numerous trails meander through areas abundant with bamboo thickets (*poring* means "bamboo" in Kadazan) and past stale bat-infested caves. A 10-minute stroll to the right of the baths is **Kepungit Falls,** sporting a small chilly pool where travelers can take refreshing dips. Farther on is the graceful 150-m **Langanan Waterfall.**

Reservations for accommodations can be made at the park's offices in Kota Kinabalu or Sandakan. A double room in the three-bedroom cabins costs RM75, on weekends and holidays RM100. Doubles in the two-bedroom cabins are RM60, on weekends and holidays RM80. Triples in the Poring Chalets cost RM180, on weekends and holidays RM250. There are also two hostels (sleeping 24 and 40) costing RM10 per person and RM5 for persons under 18. There are cooking facilities available, as well as a few local restaurants.

RANAU

The spunky hamlet of **Ranau** is only of relevance to tourists traveling to Poring Hot Springs from Kinabalu Park headquarters, and then from the springs back to either KK or Sandakan. Although its citizens are friendly and engaging, it's best to avoid overnight stays in Ranau, as the two local hotels are somewhat pricey. The **Hotel Ranau** (tel. 875 661) is located just off the highway, next to the Bumiputra Bank. Dim singles are RM30, doubles RM40, with attached bath RM45, with A/C RM60, with hot water RM70. **Hotel Kinabalu** (tel. 876 028), behind Block A and with a blue and white English sign, is slightly more popular. Singles cost RM30, doubles RM45-50, with bath RM65. At the end of the street, **Restoran Seri Segut** serves basic dishes with an incredible view of the mountains to the east (open daily 7am-9pm).

Bumiputra Bank (tel. 875 271), next to the Ranau Hotel, just off the main highway in Block C, will cash traveler's checks for those strapped for cash, but at a heavy surcharge of RM10.55 per check (open Mon.-Fri.9:30am-4pm, Sat. 9am-noon). Large A/C tour **buses** to **Sandakan** stop from 8am-9:30am in the gravel parking lot behind Block E in the far west of town (RM15-30, 4hr.). **Minibuses** depart from here as well, but only when full, so get here early to ensure a ride. Across the street lies a **taxi** stand which dispatches vehicles to **KK** (2½hr., RM15 per seat, RM50 for taxi). Walking away from the highway from the taxi stand, the first left turn leads to the minibus stand for **Poring Hot Springs** (30min., RM3) in front of the Kedai Makan Mien Mien. Buses run daily until 1 or 2pm. At the far eastern edge of the city is a small **minibus** stand where buses leave hourly until the early afternoon for **KK** (every hr., 7:30am-2:30pm, 2½hr., RM18-20). The **post office** is on the highway toward Sandakan (open Mon.-Fri.8am-5pm, Sat. 8am-1pm). **Public phones** cluster near the bank.

◼ Sandakan

Grim and artless, the grid of numbered streets and heavy-handed concrete blocks of shops comprising Sandakan have all the efficiency of an army barracks. Aside from such basic tourist services as air and ground transport, there is little reason to meander into Sandakan proper. Instead, most travelers chose to alight at one of the guest houses outside of town, briefly breakfasting with the orangutans at the Sepilok Rehabilitation Centre before arranging inexpensive, no-frills tours to the proboscis-infested forests or Sandakan's hinterlands.

ORIENTATION

Navigating can be troublesome, since many of the streets in Sandakan have similar names, and street signs in general are rather scarce. **Jalan Tiga** is the town's main thoroughfare. At the extreme east end is the Wisma Koo Siak Chew building housing the **Sabah Parks office** and the **Telekom office.** Traveling west out of town leads to the **long distance bus terminal, the night market,** and the **post office** successively. Several km farther west is the Travellers Rest Hostel in Bandar Ramai-Ramai. South of Jl. Tiga, running along the waterfront, is **Jalan Pryer.** Buses to the Sepilok Orangutan Rehabilitation Centre depart from the **local bus terminal** here. The bulk of Sandakan proper is sandwiched between these two streets.

PRACTICAL INFORMATION

Tourist Offices: Outside of KK there are no official government tourist offices.
Sabah Park Office: 9th Fl., Wisma Khoo Siak Chew (tel. 273 453). Make reservations here for accommodations at any of the national parks. Open Mon.-Thurs. 8am-12:45pm and 2-4:15pm, Fri. 8am-11:30am and 2-4:15pm, Sat. 8am-12:45pm.
Currency Exchange: Banks cluster at the intersection of Jl. Tiga and Jl. Pelabuhan, at the Bulatan Merdeka roundabout. **Hong Kong Bank** (tel. 213 122) charges RM7 per traveler's check. Open Mon.-Fri. 9:30am-3pm, Sat. 9:30-11:30am. **Bank Bumiputra** (tel. 213 272), is across the street and charges RM2.15 per traveler's check. Open Mon.-Fri. 9:30am-4pm, Sat. 9:30am-noon.
Air Travel: Airport (tel. 667 786), 11km outside of town. **MAS office** (tel. 273 966), on Jl. Pelabuhan, on the ground floor of Sabah Bldg. Daily flights to **KK** (RM83) and other destinations. Open Mon.-Fri. 8am-5pm, Sat. 8am-1pm, Sun. and holidays 8am-noon. MC, Visa, AmEx, DC.
Buses: Large A/C buses depart from the **long distance bus terminal** on the west edge of town. Follow Jl. Tiga out of town, and turn left before the pedestrian overpass. **A/C buses** to KK (4 per day, 7-10am, RM20-25) and **Ranau/Park headquarters** (RM15-18). **Regular buses** to KK (3 per day, 6:30am-noon, RM15). 13-seat **minibuses** depart until 2pm. To **KK** (RM25) and **Ranau** (RM20).

Local Transportation: Taxis cost RM3-5 within a few km of the city center. A taxi to the airport costs RM15

Pharmacies: Borneo Dispensary, Lot 11-13, Block 28, Jl. Dua (tel. 218 758), on the corner with Jl. Lima. Open daily Mon.-Sat. 8am-5:30pm, Sun. 8am-12:30pm.

Medical Services: (tel. 212 111), on the highway to the airport.

Police: (tel. 212 22), on Lebuh Empat, north of town.

Post Offices: (tel. 218 167), on Jl. Leila across from the supermarket on the outskirts of town. *Poste Restante.* Open Mon.-Sat. 8am-5pm. **Postal code:** 90008.

Telephones: Cluster near the long distance bus terminal. No credit card phones. **Telekom office,** 7th Fl. Wisma Khoo Siak Chew (tel. 219 272), at the east end of Jl. Tiga. Open Mon.-Thurs. 8:30am-12:45pm and 2-4:15pm, Fri. 8:30-11:45am and 2-4:15pm, Sat. 8:30am-12:30pm. **Telephone code:** 089.

ACCOMMODATIONS

Most budget accommodations keep their distance from the city. Traveller's Rest is the closest, although still a 10- to 15-minute walk away.

Uncle Tan's (tel. 531 917), at Mile-17½ on Labuk Rd. Mailing address: PPM 245 Elopura, 90000 Sandakan. Ask bus drivers from KK to drop you off at the large red and white sign. From Sandakan, take a Batu 19 bus the 9km from the city (50min., RM1.70). Very basic rooms with mosquito nets and a tin shed that serves as a bathroom. Guests only stay long enough to arrange one of Uncle Tan's famous tours to Turtle Island or jungle adventure packages. The Sepilok Orangutan Rehabilitation Centre is only 10min. away by bus or take a bike. RM20 per night, includes 3 excellent meals. Reservations recommended.

Sepilok Bed and Breakfast (tel. 532 288), on Jl. Sepilok, off Mile-14 off Jl. Labuk. Picks up guests from the airport if they call. Otherwise, get off at the entrance to Sepilok Centre. From Jl. Labuk, walk or catch a Batu 14 bus down Jl. Sepilok toward the center. 2km later, when you reach a large wooden sign, turn right, and the B&B is 100m down. 15 acres of avocado, lime, jack fruit, and rambutan orchards. All longhouse-style rooms have baths, fans, and access to a large communal veranda. Dorms RM15. Doubles RM40 (includes breakfast). A café serves basics such as fried rice. Also offers tours. Reservations recommended.

Travellers Rest Hostel, 2nd Fl., Apt. 2, Block E, Jl. Leila (tel. 434 54), in Bandar Ramai-Ramai, is a rather grim collection of concrete apartment blocks. Near May-Bank Finance in the middle of the second block of apartments back from the highway, with a very small faded sign. Aside from the neighborhood, Traveller's Rest still offers a good deal with spacious rooms and comfortable communal areas. Dorms RM10. Singles RM18. Doubles RM24 (includes a light breakfast). The city center is a 10-15min. walk away, or take a local bus for RM.40.

FOOD

Used clothing stalls and stingray steak vendors vie for attention at Sandakan's **night market** located in front of the post office on Jl. Tiga, across from the Shop and Save supermarket. Dozens of point and eat options at every stand; if they don't have it, the next stall will. The action starts around 7pm and continues late into the night. There is another **market** on Jl. Pryer. Heaps of fried noodles cool at the vendor stalls on the second floor, where many locals catch a quick lunch during the week.

Fat Cat V, Block 38, Jl. Tiga (tel. 216 867), look for the large English sign. Very popular with Sandakan's younger crowd. Step into its A/C environs for a Nasty Adam burger, a hearty hamburger topped with an aesthetically carved hot dog and a dash of tomato sauce (RM3.70). The bakery next door stocks fresh bread and pastries. English menu. Open daily 9am-11pm.

Restoran Lock Yuen (tel. 210 879). The middle of three restaurants directly behind the long distance bus terminal. Directly on the water with a breezy balcony in back. Seabird calls replace the traffic noise of most places in the city, as ships glide placidly off shore. Sizzling prawns RM14, Carlsberg RM8.90. English menu but prices aren't listed; ask before ordering. Open daily 3pm-3am.

MALAYSIA

Supreme Garden Vegetarian Restaurant, Block 30, ground floor, Lot 2&3, Bandar Ramai-Ramai (tel. 213 292), off Jl. Leila in the fourth block of building in back, with a red-and-gold sign. Close to the Traveller's Rest Hostel. Grandma's bean curd (RM6) and some steaming seaweed soup (RM4) make an excellent meal, or queue up for the daily all-you-can-eat buffet from 11:30am-1:30pm (RM10). A/C and English menu. Open Mon.-Thurs. 9:30am-1:45pm, Fri. 9:30am-1:45pm, Sun. 8am-1:45pm and 5:30-8:45pm, holidays 7:30am-1:45pm and 5:30-8:45pm.

ENTERTAINMENT

Champion Bowl and Recreation Club (tel. 211 389). Large sign looms along Jl. Leila, just past the apartment complex with Traveller's Rest Hostel on the right. Games start at RM5 per person. Open daily 9am-1am.

SIGHTS

Sepilok Orangutan Rehabilitation Centre (tel. 215 189) is one of Sandakan's prime attractions, and also its cheapest (open daily 9-11am and 2-3:30pm; admission RM10 for foreigners, RM1 for Malaysian citizens, RM10 extra for video cameras). From Sandakan, catch one of the daily blue-and-white Sepilok Batu 14 buses (9, 11am, and 12:45pm, 23km, 45min.) from the terminal on Jl. Pryer. The bus should drop you directly in front on the center's front gate. The reception office is to the right of the entrance; a 40-minute documentary on the center's activities can be seen upon request. The center has a small gift shop where film and souvenirs are sold, and a **canteen** that serves refreshments (open daily 9am-9pm).

Upscale **accommodations** at the park are also available. A double room with bath and fan costs RM45, deluxe A/C rooms RM35, VIP suites RM65 (call 215 189 for res-

Any Which Way But Loose

So this is the umpteenth orangutan rehab center you've heard about in Southeast Asia, eh? Perhaps it's time for us to de-mystify the phenomenon of rehab centers. The process of re-introduction for adult orangutans usually involves treating any injuries and a mandatory quarantine period of three to six months to prevent the spread of infectious diseases among the center's other residents. Tuberculosis and malaria, both diseases contracted from human contact, are not uncommon. If they prove healthy, the animals may be released directly into the forests. Infant orangutans, however, present a special problem. Babies learn survival skills such as nest building, food gathering, and even how to climb from their mothers during the first year of their life, but stolen infant orangutans must be taught all these skills by humans in the nursery. They are encouraged to explore and develop their instinctive behaviors for one to three years. Even learning to climb may require hours of patient encouragement from the staff. Having mastered these skills, the youngsters are transferred to a forest location, usually known as Platform A, in an attempt to lessen their dependence on human care and emotional support. Here, they are free to explore the forests. Supplementary meals of milk and fruit are still given twice a day, but the diet is deliberately kept monotonous to encourage the animals to find their own food. Eventually, after showing signs of greater independence, the orangutans are led hand-in-hand by a park ranger to another site, often Platform B, even farther from the center's facilities. Food is limited to one feeding per day in an attempt to finally integrate the orphaned animals completely into their forest home.

There are a few simple rules that should be heeded at rehab centers: 1) do not leave trash anywhere; 2) don't smoke or wear insect repellent; 3) always maintain at least a 2m distance from the animals at all times; and 4) **never attempt to feed the orangs or any of the other monkeys on the trail.** They'll jump on your head, steal your camera, and drop it from a 30-m tree; better yet, they may even strip you butt-naked, as they did to a wayward visitor in 1995.

ervations). Sepilok was established in 1964 in response to concern over the threatened existence of the native orangutan in the wild. The center was proposed to help re-introduce infant orangutans taken illegally from their mothers into the forests of the reserve. Since the program's inception, over 100 animals have been released with varying degrees of success. Many still come back to the platforms, especially pregnant mothers seeking to supplement their diet. Platform A is open to visitors twice a day at the 10am and 3pm feedings. Here visitors can watch baby orangs scoop up messy handfuls of milk from plastic buckets and gleefully drizzle it into their open mouths.

The number of orangutan visitors depends on the availability of food to forage in the forests. Usually anywhere from four to 12 orangutans can be admired at work on their morning brunch. Afterwards, they congenially linger for pictures. Supervising staff can tell interested visitors each orang's name and are quick to disarm overly curious orangs by tickling them. Visitors are requested to leave all bags at the lockers in the visitors center, and to supervise children carefully. After the morning feeding the staff may invite visitors to see the center's Asian two-horned rhinoceros. The animal is part of the center's captive breeding program. Once so abundant that they stumble into Sandakan's streets from the forests, the rhino populations have in recent years suffered dramatically from habitat fragmentation and illegal poaching—the horn is believed to possess almost magical curative powers.

■ Near Sandakan: Turtle Islands Park

Less than 20 years old, Turtle Islands Park is composed of three islands—**Selingaan, Gulisan,** and **Bakkungan Kecil**—40km off Sandakan's coast. The parks were established to help protect declining populations of **Green** and **Hawksbill turtles** who come to the islands to lay their eggs. Both the eggs and the flesh of the turtles are considered delicacies and have been harvested for centuries by the local Cagayan people. As a result egg counts dropped from 700,000 in the late 60s to only 223,897 in 1987. The Green turtles (83% of all sightings) prefer to lay their eggs on Selingaan from July to October while the more elusive Hawksbills favor Gulisan from February to April. Especially during the full moon, turtles can be seen lugging their awkward bodies over the sandy stretches to the high water mark, where they take hours to dig a nest. The turtles then lay over 100 ping pong ball-sized eggs, each encased in a fungicidal goo. After covering the nest, the worn-out mother makes her way back to the ocean, streaming mucus tears to keep the sand from her delicate eyes.

Currently all the eggs laid in Selingaan are collected and resettled at the park's turtle hatcheries in an attempt to increase hatching survival. The individual clutches are carefully tagged and surrounded with wire mesh to prevent predation by monitor lizards and rats. After 50-60 days, the turtles emerge and are released into the seas. Over a 12-year period from 1977-1988, over 2.5 million hatchlings were reared in captivity and released, although it is estimated that only a mere 3% will survive, mate, and return to the islands. The Sabah Parks office in either Kota Kinabalu or Sandakan can arrange **accommodation** at the park's cabins on Selingaan. A room with two beds runs RM150 per night, and there is a **cafeteria** available at the visitor center. Unfortunately, the three-hour trip must be chartered—an expensive proposition for most travelers. Most visitors arrive as part of a tour, run by local guest houses. Although costs are much higher than similar turtle-watching beaches on the mainland, the chances of actually seeing a turtle are much greater here, as they come ashore almost nightly throughout the year. If a turtle is sighted, never flash a light in its eyes, or take flash photographs; be sure to give it plenty of space and remain respectfully silent.

KINABATANGAN RIVER

Most travelers come to Sandakan hoping to see wildlife; one of the densest concentrations of forest critters still remains along Sabah's **Kinabatangan River,** the largest river in the state. Proboscis monkeys routinely frolic in the thick canopies at the lower reaches of the river every morning and early evening. Other tree top denizens of the

MALAYSIA

Kinabatangan region include gibbons, macaques, and the occasional orangutan. On the ground, scaly aardvarks, porcupines, deer, and boar meander through the trees. In fact, a sleek leopard cat has become a nightly visitor to Tan's kitchen. The jungle scenery alone, however, makes a trip into the region worthwhile.

The laudable **Borneo Eco Tours** (see **Kota Kinabalu: Practical Information** on page 466) has numerous, if pricey, packages set in eastern Sabah which can be arranged from their offices in Kota Kinabalu. For budget tours of the region, travelers flock to **Uncle Tan's,** 29km outside of Sandakan (see **Sandakan: Accommodations** on page 477 for specifics). Transport to his jungle camp on the Kinabatangan River costs RM130. Single day/night trips to Turtle Islands run RM180, including transport, room, food, and fees. **Travellers Rest Hostel** maintains a similar camp near Sandakan. Since the biggest cost is transportation, it's best to stay several nights at the camps to get your money's worth and increase the chances of seeing wildlife. **Sepilok B&B** organizes all day cruises along the Kinabatangan River for RM160, but their other tour prices are less competitive.

SINGAPORE

Singapore has gotten a lot of bad press recently, especially from foreign observers who criticize its authoritarian state and Draconian penal code. The Singaporean majority has in turn criticized the high crime rates and lackluster economic performance of western nations. Only time can measure the success of the authoritarian way, but a few excerpts from a recent publication, *Things That Make Us Happy* may dispel many of the ominous illusions about the city-state: "Revitalizing National Day Speeches," "Songs with 'happy' in the title," "It makes me feel so glad when I pass my test, I will always do my best, I will be the best of the best," and, most importantly, "A great haircut which opens up so many new possibilities." In sum, Singaporeans have been co-opted willingly into a vision of bread and circuses where there is so much darn happiness swirling about that one can only gaze in wonder…and then get a haircut and go on a fish-meal diet. Other writings about Singapore make use of the usual Orwellian analogies, but it is quite possible to spend several days here without feeling any government intrusion into your personal life, simply enjoying the safety provided by Big Brother's secure embrace.

ESSENTIALS

▓ Getting There and Away

BY PLANE

Changi Airport (arrival and flight info tel. 542 12 34) is about 10km east of the city center. Two terminals are connected by the zippy **Skytrain**. There's a S$15 airport tax for which you can buy coupons ahead of time at hotels, travel agencies, and airline offices. Bus #16E runs to the airport in the morning and back in the evenings. The closest stop to the **Bencoolen St.** area is in front of the National Museum on Stamford Rd. To the airport, board anywhere on Bras Basah Rd. To the **Geylang Rd. area,** take #16 to the first stop on Penang Rd., then go to the Dhoby Ghaut Mass Rapid Transit (MRT) station, and take the MRT to the Kallang or Aljunied stops. To **Chinatown,** take #16 to the intersection of Stamford and North Bridge Rd.; from there, catch #174, 179, or 182 to the blue China Point building. **Taxis** are perhaps the most efficient means of transport (Bencoolen St., S$15; Chinatown, S$20 plus S$3 airport charge).

    Malaysia Airlines (MAS) (tel. 336 67 79) is cheaper than Singapore Airlines (SIA), but all of its international flights from Singapore are routed through Kuala Lumpur. The MAS office is in the Singapore Shopping Centre near the MRT stop on the corner of Penang Rd. and Clemenceau Ave. **SIA** (tel. 223 60 30) is in the airport, the DBS tower, and the Raffles City Plaza, just south of Raffles Hotel and flies to: **Kuala Lumpur** (20 per day, S$147; shuttle leaves every hr., S$170); **Penang** (4 per day, 8:30am-7:45pm, S$170); **Jakarta** (1 per day, S$640); **Bangkok** (3 per day, S$320); **Phnom Penh** (1 per day, S$505); and **Hanoi** (1 per day, S$540). **Silk Air** offers flights to many of these destinations, as well as to **Vientiane** (Tues. and Fri., S$720).

BY TRAIN

The **railway station** (tel. 222 51 65), on Keppel Rd., is on the south tip of the main island, 20 minutes from downtown by bus. (Open daily 6am-11pm.) **Buses** run every five to 15 minutes to and from the **Raffles Hotel** (buses #84, 97, 100, 131); **Selegie Rd.** (buses #97 and 131), **Chinatown** (buses #84 and 145), and **Little India** (buses #97 and 131). **Express trains** go to: **Kuala Lumpur** (3 per day, 7:50am-10:30pm, 1st class S$68; 2nd class S$34); **Butterworth** (3 per day, 7:50am-10:30pm, 1st class S$127; 2nd class S$60); and **Kota Bharu** (9pm). Buy tickets 60 days in advance (booking hours 8:30am-7pm). **Passenger trains** go to **Kuala Lumpur** (8:15pm) and **Johor Bahru** (4 per day, 8:20am-8:15pm). For trains to **Bangkok** (6:30pm), **Hat Yai,** and other international destinations, check with **Warita Express and Tours** or **STA Travel** (see **Budget Travel** on page 39).

BY BUS

Buses leave from the Golden Mile Complex on Beach Rd. From the bus stop at the intersection of Seah St. and Beach Rd. behind the Raffles Hotel, take buses #82, 100, or 181. **Warita Express** (tel. 292 36 04) has buses to: **Bangkok** (3:50 and 7pm, S$70-80); **Hat Yai** (3:50 and 7pm, S$30-40); **Kuala Lumpur** (4 per day, 9am-11pm, S$25); and **Alor Setar** (4-8:30pm, S$35-40), debarking point for **Langkawi** or **Thailand.** Most agents are open daily 8am-9pm and accept cash only. Other buses leave from the Lavender St. bus station in Little India.

BY FERRY

Most ferries dock at the **World Trade Centre,** on Keppel Rd., across from Sentosa Island, and cruise to Singapore's islands, Indonesia, and Malaysia. Ferry companies moor inside the center on the second floor. The center is served by buses from Bencoolen St. (#97 and 131), Bras Basah Rd. (#97 and 131), North Bridge Rd. (#61, 84, and 145), and Orchard Rd. (#143). **Ferrylink** (tel. 545 36 00) makes regular trips to **Tanjung Belungkor,** Malaysia (9am, noon, and 4:15pm; S$15, S$24 roundtrip). Indonesia-bound ferries are operated by **Auto Batam** (tel. 271 48 66) and **Dino Shipping** (tel. 270 22 28). Ferries go to: **Pulau Batam** (every hr., 7:50am-8:15pm, 30min., S$27 roundtrip); **Sekupang** (every 30min., 8:05am-6:05pm, S$27 roundtrip); **Pulau Bintan** (3 per day, 9am-2:55pm, 2½hr., S$49, S$63 roundtrip); and **Pulau Tioman** (8:30am, 3½hr., S$85, S$140 roundtrip). For all ferries, try to reserve ahead of time and arrive one hour before departure.

■ Getting Around

BUS

Local buses cover almost all of Singapore and run 6am-midnight. Snazzy yellow-and-orange-roofed stops brandish info boards listing buses by street, price, and destination. Downtown, fares are about S$0.50-0.70 (regular) and S$0.60-0.80 (A/C). State your destination when boarding and pick up your receipt from the machine. To master the bus system, pick up the Transit-Link Map or the map-less *Bus Guide* (S$1.40), also found in bookstores. **Farecards,** available at any MRT stop, are worth getting. Cards cost S$0.70, the smallest denomination is S$10, and you can add as much value as you wish. Cards work on buses and trains; when entering the bus, ask for the fare, insert the card facedown into the ticketing machine, and away you go. The **bus hotline** number is 1 (800) 287 27 27.

MASS RAPID TRANSIT (MRT)

Singapore's Mass Rapid Transit System (MRT) is the ultimate panacea for your transportation blues. Two main lines travel in air-conditioned comfort to virtually any destination (6am-midnight). A single-use fare card is S$0.60 for the three stops closest to where you board; S$0.70-1.20 for more. Better yet, buy a S$10 **Farecard.**

TAXIS AND TRISHAWS

With such a good bus and train system, there seems little reason use taxis. If you do, count on competent and honest drivers who speak English. Flag one down or head

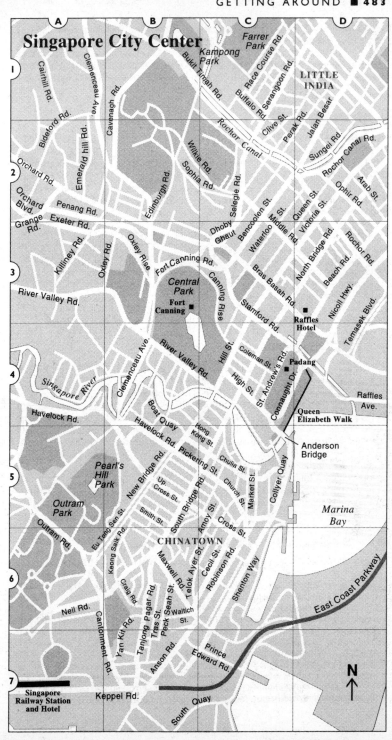

Singapore City Center

Cairnhill Rd.
Bideford Rd.
Clemenceau Ave.
Cavenagh Rd.
Emerald hill Rd.
Orchard Rd.
Orchard Blvd.
Penang Rd.
Grange Rd.
Exeter Rd.
Killiney Rd.
Oxley Rd.
Oxley Rise
Edinburgh Rd.
River Valley Rd.
Fort Canning Rd.
Canning Rise
Clemenceau Ave.
River Valley Rd.
Havelock Rd.
Boat Quay
Havelock Rd.
Pickering St.
New Bridge Rd.
Up. Cross St.
Smith St.
Eu Tong Sen St.
Keong Saik Rd.
Craig Rd.
Neil Rd.
Cantonment Rd.
Yan Kit Rd.
Tanjong Pagar Rd.
Tras St.
Peck Seah St.
Waltich St.
Maxwell Rd.
Anson Rd.
Prince Edward Rd.
Keppel Rd.
South Quay

Bukit Timah Rd.
Kampong Park
Farrer Park
Race Course Rd.
Serangoon Rd.
Buffalo Rd.
Clive St.
Perak Rd.
Jalan Besar
Rochor Canal
Rochor Canal Rd.
Sungei Rd.
Wilkie Rd.
Sophia Rd.
Selegie Rd.
Dhoby Ghaut
Bencoolen St.
Prinsep St.
Queen St.
Victoria St.
Middle Rd.
Waterloo St.
Arab St.
Ophir Rd.
North Bridge Rd.
Beach Rd.
Rochor Rd.
Bras Basah Rd.
Stamford Rd.
Hill St.
Coleman St.
High St.
St. Andrew's Rd.
Connaught Dr.
Hong Kong St.
Chulia St.
Church St.
Market St.
Collyer Quay
Amoy St.
Cross St.
Cecil St.
Robinson Rd.
Shenton Way
South Bridge Rd.
Telok Ayer St.

LITTLE INDIA

Central Park
Fort Canning ■

Raffles Hotel ■

Padang ■

Raffles Ave.

Queen Elizabeth Walk

Anderson Bridge

Singapore River

Pearl's Hill Park

Outram Park

Outram Rd.

CHINATOWN

Marina Bay

East Coast Parkway

SINGAPORE

Singapore Railway Station and Hotel

N

for the nearest taxi stand. The meter starts at S$2.40, and each additional 240m is S$0.10; most city fares cost S$3-7. From midnight to 6am, there's a late-night 50% surcharge. To order a taxi, call 474 77 07 or 481 12 11. Yellow cabs accept Visa. **Taxi Lost and Found:** tel. 450 53 49. **Trishaws,** parked at Bras Basah Park on Orchard Rd., are expensive and uneccessary for most sightseers. Call **Trishaw Tours** at the Waterloo Centre Car Park (tel. 545 63 11) for an official tour package

■ Money

US$1=S$1.414	S$1=US$0.707
CDN$1=S$1.034	S$1=CDN$0.967
UK£1=S$2.183	S$1=UK£0.458
IR£1=S$2.153	S$1=IR£0.464
AUS$1=S$1.048	S$1=AUS$0.954
NZ$1=S$0.857	S$1=NZ$1.167
SARand1=S$0.397	S$1=SARand2.522

Singapore's unit of currency is the Singapore dollar (S$), divided into 100 cents. Major credit cards are widely accepted, and ATMs can be found throughout the city. **Tipping** is officially discouraged, and is illegal at the airport. Clubs, bars, and classier restaurants and hotels label themselves either "plus" which means that you pay a 10% service charge, or "plus plus" where you pay 10% plus a 4% tax. There is now a 3% Goods and Services Tax (GST), but shops with "Tax Refund" signs give visitors a refund of the GST on all goods to be taken out of Singapore. **Bargain** in outdoor markets and at most shops in Chinatown and Little India, as well as for trishaw rides.

■ Orientation

The city can be divided roughly into six areas. **Bencoolen Street,** between Rochor Rd. to the north and Bras Basah Rd. to the south, is a backpacker-friendly area, as is **Little India,** across the canal to the north. The **Orchard Road** area is southwest of Bencoolen St., wholly contained in the space between Dhoby Ghaut and Orchard MRT stations. Around the City Hall MRT stop is the **Colonial District,** featuring the **Raffles Hotel.** Heading south on the MRT through Raffles Place leads into **Tanjung Pagar** in the heart of **Chinatown.** Most of the activity in this sprawling section of town is between **Eu Tong Sen Street** to the west, **Cecil Street** to the east, **Cross Street** to the north, and **Craig Road** to the south. The **Geylang Road** area lies east of the city center. A tourist office will provide a free map of Singapore, an indispensable aid to the budget pedestrian or, alternatively, blow S$5 on the best-selling **Transit-Link Travel Map,** which will help you to make full use of Singapore's excellent public transport system (available in most bookstores).

■ Practical Information

Tourist Offices: Scotts Branch, 02-02 Scotts Shopping Centre, MRT: Orchard (tel. 1 (800) 738 37 78). Cross Orchard Rd. to Scotts Rd.; it's in the 2nd complex on the right. Open daily 9:30am-9:30pm. **Raffles Branch,** 2-34, 328 North Bridge Rd. (tel. 1 (800) 334 13 35), in the Raffles Hotel Arcade. Free *Singapore Official Guide.* Ask for *Singapore Budget Hotels.* Open daily 8:30am-8pm.

Tours and Travel: STA Travel, 1 Tanglin Rd., 02-17 Orchard Parade Hotel (tel. 734 56 81). Student/youth-rate plane tickets, ISIC cards, and train packages for Thailand and Malaysia. Open Mon.-Fri. 9am-5pm, Sat. 9am-noon. MC and Visa (3% surcharge). **Singapore Comfort Travel Service,** 5001 Beach Rd., 01-11 Golden Mile Complex (tel. 294 94 50), on Beach Rd. at its northern end. International bus tickets. Open daily 8am-8pm. **Continental Travel,** 04-12 Peninsula Shopping Centre (tel. 338 89 20), downtown on the corner of Coleman St. and Bridge Rd. Open Mon.-Sat. 9:30am-6pm. Shop for international plane fares here.

Embassies and Consulates: Australia, 25 Napier Rd. (tel. 735 12 42). Open Mon.-Fri. 8:30am-4:30pm. Visas Mon.-Fri. 9-11:30am and 2-3:30pm. **Canada,** 80 Anson Rd. (tel. 325 32 00; fax 325 32 91), 14th-15th Fl., IBM Towers. Open Mon.-Fri. 8am-4pm. **Indonesia,** 7 Chatsworth Rd. (tel. 737 74 22). Open Mon.-Fri. 8:30am-1pm and 2-5pm. **Malaysia,** 301 Jervois Rd. (tel. 235 01 11). Open Mon.-Fri. 8:30-11:30am and 2:30-3:30pm. **New Zealand,** 391A Orchard Rd., 15-06 Ngee Ann Tower A (tel. 235 99 66, 738 67 00 for visas). Open Mon.-Fri. 8:30am-5pm. **South Africa,** 331 North Bridge Rd., 15-00, Odeon Towers (tel. 339 33 19). Open Mon.-Fri. 8:30am-5pm. **Thailand,** 370 Orchard Rd. (tel. 737 26 44). MRT: Orchard. Open Mon.-Fri. 9am-5pm. Visas 9:15am-12:15pm. **UK,** 325 Tanglin Rd. (tel. 473 93 33). Open Mon.-Fri. 8:30am-4:30pm. Visas 8:30am-noon. **US,** 30 Hill St. (tel. 338 02 51). Open Mon.-Fri. 8:30am-5:15pm. Visas Mon.-Fri. 8:30am-noon. **Vietnam,** 10 Leedon Park (tel. 462 59 38). Open Mon.-Sat. 9am-noon.

Immigration Offices: 95 South Bridge Rd. (tel. 532 28 77 or 1 (800) 538 54 00 for visa info), 7th-8th Fl., Pidemco Centre. Take bus #170 (every 15min., 35min., S$0.80) from the stop on Rochor Rd., near the head of Bencoolen St. Extensions. To avoid the hassle, some travelers go to Johor Bahru, Malaysia, and re-enter. Open Mon.-Fri. 8am-5pm, Sat. 8am-1pm.

Currency Exchange: Money changers offer marginally better rates than banks and hotels. Usually open daily 9am-9pm. **Banks** are generally open Mon.-Fri. 9:30am-3pm, Sat. 9:30-11:30am. **ATMs** are ubiquitous and most accept MC, Visa, Cirrus, and Plus. **American Express Bank,** 16 Collyer Quay (tel. 439 10 85), near Anderson Bridge. No cardmember services. Open Mon.-Fri. 10am-3pm. **Saj Drug Store Money Change,** 01-09 Raffles City Shopping Centre (tel. 339 17 23). Open daily 8:30am-9pm. **United Overseas Bank,** 11 Empress Pl. (tel. 338 93 93), in Victoria Concert Hall on the Raffles Hotel side of the Anderson Bridge. Open Mon.-Fri. 9:30am-3pm, Sat. 9:30-11:30am.

American Express: 3 Killiney Rd., 1st Fl., Winsland House (tel. 235 81 33). The rose-pink building is visible from the Somerset MRT stop. Mail held 1 month for card or traveler's check holders. Replaces cards and cashes personal checks for members. Open Mon.-Fri. 9am-5pm, Sat. 9am-1pm for member services; financial services Mon.-Fri. 9am-4:30pm.

Luggage Storage: Train Station, S$2 per day per piece. Open daily 7am-11:30pm. **Changi Airport,** S$3-4 per day. Follow the signs. Open 24hr.

Pharmacies: Every mall has a well-supplied pharmacy. **Guardian Raffles City Pharmacy,** Raffles City Shopping Centre #03-09, 252 North Bridge Rd., MRT: City Hall (tel. 339 21 37). Open Mon.-Fri. 10:30am-10pm, Sat. 10am-10pm, Sun. 10:30am-6:30pm for prescriptions.

Medical Services: Government clinics and hospitals have 24-hr. emergency rooms. **Raffles Medical Group Clinic,** Changi Airport Terminal 2 (tel. 543 11 18). Doctors available 8am-midnight. Open 24hr. for consultations (S$30).

Emergency: Police: tel. 999. **Ambulance:** tel. 995. **Fire:** tel. 995.

Post Offices: GPO (tel. 165 or 169), in the Fullerton Building on the corner of Fullerton Rd. and Collyer Quay. From Raffles Place MRT, turn right onto Battery Rd. It's across from the Hong Kong Bank skyscraper. Open Mon.-Fri. 8:30am-6pm and Sat. 8:30am-2pm. **Raffles City Branch,** in the Raffles City Shopping Centre, at the corner of North Bridge and Bras Basah Rd., MRT: City Hall. A Telecom office as well. Open Mon.-Fri. 9am-6:30pm, Sat. 9am-2:30pm. **Postal code:** 0106.

Telephones: Card phones and coin phones are everywhere and phonecard-vendors are similarly ubiquitous (try newsstands or post offices). Use the "Follow" button on cardphones to cut off your present call and make another. **Directory assistance:** tel. 161 or 100. **International access code:** 005. **International operator:** 104. **IDD prefix:** 001. **ComCentre** (tel. 169), on Exeter Rd. across from the MRT stop. Open 24hr. **HCD** at Telecom office. **HCD numbers:** British Telecom, 8000-440-400; Canada Direct, 8000-100-100; New Zealand Telecom, 65 1308 64 0000; Telecom Australia, 800-6100; Telecom Eireann, 800-353-353; Telekom South Africa, 8000-27-0270; AT&T, 800-0111-111; and MCI, 8000-112-112.

SINGAPORE

■ Health, Safety, and Specific Concerns

The **water,** as if you had any doubt, is safe. Also, not surprisingly, the medical facilities are modern and first-rate. Other than the heat, the intrepid traveler does not need to worry about any health risks. **Crime** is scarce in Singapore and for good reason. Big Brother doles out high fines, serious jail sentences, and the death penalty. You should still exercise caution, however, and wear a money belt. **Women traveling alone** find Singapore very safe, but going out in groups after dark is still recommended. Sexual harassment does rarely occur, but is mostly restricted to stares and less-than-subtle comments.

Singaporean law has no sense of humor, at least in the city center: do not jaywalk within 50m of a crossing (S$50 fine), import or sell chewing gum, litter, smoke in enclosed public areas, or eat or drink on the MRT. Most offenses carry hefty fines of S$500-1000. The rewards of importing **illegal drugs** involves some combination of rotting in jail, multiple caning lacerations, and death. Foreign embassies cannot intervene. For more information, contact any of Singapore's embassies or refer to the *Singapore Official Guide.*

Disabled travelers can maneuver around malls and office buildings easily, but Chinatown, Little India, and many hostels and little shops can be extremely difficult. Write The Singapore Council of Social Services (11 Penang Lane; tel. 336 15 44) for a guide to accessible attractions. **Homosexuality** is illegal in Singapore. Not surprisingly, homosexual acts face strict punishment—10 years to life in prison, although this is rarely enforced. There are some gay nightspots, but none are very "out."

■ Hours and Holidays

Banks are generally open 8am-4pm, shopping centers and large stores 9am-9pm or 10am-10pm, and smaller stores and businesses 9am-5pm. Holidays for 1997 are listed below; some are only approximate.

January 1: New Year's Day.
January 14: Ponggal, The Harvest Festival.
February 4: Thaipusam.
February 7 & 8: Chinese New Year.
February 9: Hari Raya Puasa.
March 28: Good Friday.
April 4: Qing Ming.
April 18: Hari Raya Haji.
May 1: Labor Day.
May 21: Vesak Day.
June 22 &23: Dragon Boat Race (celebrating the Dragon Boat Festival).
August 9: National Day.
August 14-September 12: Festival of Hungry Ghosts.
September 27: Mooncake Festival.
October 12-20: Festival of Nine Emperor Gods.
October: Navarathiri.
October: Thimithi (Fire Walking Festival).
October 12- November 10: Pilgrimage to Kusa Island.
October 31: Diwali.
December 25: Christmas.

LIFE AND TIMES

■ The People of Singapore

Although Singapore's population is one that has been migrating to the island since the 1300s, most Singaporeans are descendents of migrants from the British occupation in the 19th and 20th centuries. Only recently have the majority of Singapore's inhabitants been native-born. Singapore is over 75% **Chinese.** The **Malay** population hovers around 14% and has been living on the island the longest. **Indians,** the majority of whom are Tamil, were exported as laborers for the British, and make up 7%.

After its population explosion in the 1960s, the government worked toward getting all families, especially immigrant ones, to "Stop at Two." Now, however, Singapore has implemented "Go for Three" policies to maintain a high percentage of the Chinese population, and reach a healthy population of 4 million by 2020.

■ History

ISLAND COLONY

Although the modern history of Singapore begins with Sir Stamford Raffles, its existence far predates European incursion. The first known account of the island comes from the Chinese in the 3rd century, who called it **Puluochung,** "in the middle of the river's mouth." By the 14th century the island state of **Tumasik** (Sea Town) was established and already trading and warring with Siam to the north. Some legends say Tumasik was founded by a Srivijayan prince who claimed descent from Alexander the Great. According to another 15th century legend, the island was named by the son of the union between an Indian *rajah* and the daughter of the sea god. Believing he saw a lion on the horizon, the divine prince called it **Singhapura,** or "lion town." Raids by the mighty Southeast Asian empires of the time, as well as the Portuguese took their toll. When the Portuguese burned down a trading post at the mouth the Singapore River in 1613, the small island city reverted back to jungle, and sank out of the world's eyes for two centuries.

Although the Dutch and British struggled to control Singapore for its position along important trade routes, the island remained little more than a pirate's pit-stop, free of European intervention, until the 19th century. The first drastic changes came when that British errant, **Sir Stamford Raffles,** took an interest in Singapore and convinced the British government to support him. Raffles worked with the two local powers of the time, **Sultan Hussein** and Malay chief **Temenggong,** and transformed Singapore into a thriving port city central to the trade passing through Asia. He later was instrumental in bringing the "lion town" into the British empire.

The Life of Sir Stamford Raffles: Part the First

No mere mortal has contributed more to the history, politics, and knowledge of island Southeast Asia than the dashing Sir Stamford Raffles. The son of a slave trader, Raffles was born July 5, 1781 on a boat off Jamaica. Lay Raffles-enthusiasts are amused by the irony that the man who shaped the East Indies was actually born in the West Indies. Astute Raffles-historians point out, however, that Raffles' glory was destined all along, as his ancestry has been traced back to Sangiran, Central Java, where fossilized DNA residue of Java Man show unmistakable similarities to the Raffles' lineage. At the young age of 15, Raffles, the Mozart of Orientalism, received an incredibly important entry-level position with the East India Company (EIC) as an office clerk, but this was only the beginning…(Wait, I want to know more! Then see page 362.)

SINGAPORE

Waves of immigration followed, and the island developed the curious mix of Chinese, Indians, Javanese, Bugis, Arabs, Malays, and Europeans that characterizes it today. Piracy, intrigue, trade, exploitation, and prosperity waltzed through the area during the 19th century. As British expats strolled the *padang,* lacy parasols in hand, Chinese traders grew rich off Malayan exports, and indentured Indian convicts built St. Andrew's Cathedral and other local edifices. By the time Ngiam Tong Boon invented the **Singapore Sling** for the Euro-chic clientele of the Raffles Hotel in 1915, opium addiction had become a serious problem. The government, already intent on cleaning up Singapore by funding public works and improving social services, took on the drug problem by taking control of the opium market and cracking down on the subversive mafia-style activities of Chinese secret societies.

The Japanese turned the little colony into a living hell on **February 15, 1941,** when an inept British garrison was caught off guard by the invasion and quickly surrendered the colony. Europeans (including James Clavell, who wrote *King Rat,* which describes an internment experience) were carted off en masse to Changi Prison; the Japanese army raped, pillaged, and slaughtered the local Chinese population. The bloodbath is commemorated in the National Museum.

After the war, a battered Singapore fell into political disarray, welcoming the British back even as a new yearning for independence manifested itself. During the 1950s strikes and student demonstrations became prevalent as the populace began to agitate for self-determination. It was not, however, until the electoral victory of the left-leaning **People's Action Party (PAP)** and the subsequent rise of **Lee Kuan Yew** to Prime Minister in 1959 that Singapore embarked on its path to stabilization and modernization. The PAP sought to dissolve all ties to Britain and pursued an alliance with the strongly nationalist **Federated States of Malaya.** This uneasy partnership, however, culminated in a bitter divorce, and Singapore assumed its present form in 1965, fully independent from its much larger neighbor to the north.

SINCE INDEPENDENCE

The Cambridge-educated lawyer Lee became a *de facto* and then a *de jure* benevolent dictator, masterminding Singapore's miraculous transformation into a full-fledged, modern, city-state and an economic powerhouse with all the social service trimmings. In order to transform the swampy fishing villages of the island into an icon of modernity, Lee maintained that although democracy and free speech were important, they meant little to the individual with nothing to eat and nowhere to live. These freedoms have therefore become the price the people of the island have paid for the rewards of progress. The government's steely fist may be slowly unclenching: Lee stepped down in 1990, succeeded by **Goh Chok Tong,** whose administration re-admitted political exiles. Lee Kuan Yew remains active in the cabinet, however, and his popularity has waned little since his resignation. Although opposition parties continue to grow, many eye Lee's son, Lee Hsien Long, as a dynasty waiting to happen.

■ Singapore Today

On January 1, 1996 this island nation officially achieved developed nation status. Advanced technologically, Singapore has a plethora of social and material benefits for its citizens. Like many modern cities, Singapore places education, cultural pursuits, and economic growth as high priorities for the next millennia. Unlike other cities, however, Singapore's over-arching government has the power to establish and fund such programs.

Singaporeans and their government nurse a feeling of cultural superiority to other nations in the region, as well as to western nations, which they see as decadent and immoral. In school, tracking begins early and gifted children are grouped together throughout secondary school to encourage social networking and perhaps even marriage at a later date. Singapore has only one university and a few technical schools.

Students who don't distinguish themselves early have to be content with a secondary education or vocational certification.

HUMAN RIGHTS

Singapore's harsh stance on drugs and crime has been widely publicized internationally and, not surprisingly, come under fire from human rights groups such as Amnesty International. The press is under strict control, and the hand of the law is swift to descend and unyielding in its grip. The government regularly files (and wins) libel suits against its critics. In 1987, nearly 100 political activists were tossed into the slammer without a trial (legal under the Internal Security Act). Although not technically censored, only a few copies of newspapers critical of the government have been allowed into the country. In 1995, the *International Herald Tribune* was ordered to pay US$214,000 to former Prime Minister Lee Kuan Yew for articles that implied Lee used Singapore's courts as a tool of repression. The author was also ordered to pay libel damages to the tune of US$71,000.

■ The Arts

Specific cultural art forms aren't Singapore's strong point; rather, the city shines through the more permanent and modern medium of **architecture.** While many of its older regions, fishing villages, and bungalow-style *kampung* have undergone urban renewal, conservation has maintained some classic structures and neighborhoods, which often combine western, Indian, Arabic, and Chinese styles into unique and eclectic forms. Other buildings stick to one style, such as the Raffles Hotel, but are nonetheless extraordinary buildings. The skyscrapers of Singapore are more difficult to miss. Architect **I.M. Pei's** wizardry dots the landscape.

Other visual arts are predominantly modern, although certain genres are influenced by older Chinese styles, such as the traditional **pen and ink drawing.** Some other traditional forms from across the region can be found in local cultural presentations, including the Malay shadow plays and kite flying or the Chinese lion dance. Western and Chinese drama are both popular, but **films** take center stage. Western and Chinese action blockbusters can be found along with popular Malay and Indian films. For a more "cultural" evening, the Chinese opera, **wayang,** is one of your best bets, combining high (melo-) drama with elaborate costumes.

SLINGIN' AROUND SINGAPORE

■ Bencoolen Street

Herds of backpackers gather here to ward off the frenzied shoppers of nearby Orchard Rd. This land of small discount stores, vacant lots, and unremarkable coffeehouses stretches between the National Museum on Bras Basah Rd. and Rochor Canal, making it a convenient spot from which to explore the Little India, Raffles Hotel, and Orchard Rd. areas.

ACCOMMODATIONS

Goh's Homestay, 169-D Bencoolen St. 4/F (tel. 339 65 61). Homier than the other places on Bencoolen with a good-sized common room. Private rooms have nice sinks and tiled floors in good condition. Plenty of travel info. Bunk dorms (A/C at night) S$12. Singles S$34. A/C doubles (bunk with double bed on bottom) S$40-44. Triples S$52. Reservations recommended.

Lee Traveler's Club, 75 Beach Rd. #6-02 Fu Yuen Bldg. (tel. 339 54 90), 2½ blocks past Raffles Hotel. Look on the left for the polished brown elevator (6th floor reception). Come here for cheap dorms (S$6, with A/C S$8). Private rooms have cardboard walls and questionable bedding. Doubles S$25, with A/C S$35.

Peony Mansion Traveler's Lodge (Green Curtains), 46-52 Bencoolen St. (tel. 338 56 38), next to Bay View Hotel. On the 4th floor of Peony Mansion. Impersonal air with claustrophobic and spartan rooms. Common room with TV and in-house movies attempts to compensate. Light breakfast included. A/C dorms S$9. Singles with fan and sink S$25, extra person S$5. Small A/C doubles S$35, with shower S$40. Non-bunked triples with A/C S$45. MC, Visa for S$20 and up.

Sun Sun Hotel, Nos. 260A and B-262A Middle Rd. (tel. 338 49 11), in the classy old David Blias Bldg. A bit quieter, cleaner, and more spacious than those on Bencoolen proper. Clean attached baths. Fan singles, some with balconies S$40. Doubles S$48, with an additional person S$8. A/C singles/doubles S$55, with an additional person S$10. Nice Chinese bakery and the well-known Rochore Beancurd Restaurant downstairs for early morning munchies.

Shang Onn Hotel, 37 Beach Rd. (tel. 338 41 53), 1 block north of Raffles Hotel, left on the side street just past Beach Centre. This oft-overlooked hotel is fairly quiet, considering its location, and its tidy rooms are rather spacious. Singles S$30. Doubles S$34. Triples S$45.

FOOD

At night, many hawker courts change into open-air restaurants. The bigger the crowd, the cheaper the meal. The hawker center next to the National Museum is a clean and reliably palatable spot. (Open daily until midnight.) One set of these courts is in the alley next to **North Bridge Rd.** (across from the Lido Hotel and a few meters toward Beach Rd. on Middle Rd.). Tables stay out from around 6 to 10pm. **Bencoolen St. Market** unfurls from the red- and white-striped tents on Bencoolen St. all the way to Victoria St. The area around **Bugis St.** holds court at night, and all four blocks overflow with locals on Sunday afternoons. (Open daily 8am-10pm.) Sweets are the area's specialty. Treat yourself to peanut paste ball (S$0.50) and various Peranakan (Chinese-Malay) treats.

■ Raffles Hotel

The Raffles Hotel, built in the early 20th century by the Armenian Sarkies brothers, stands majestically on Beach Rd., and marks the beginning of a herd of government buildings, museums, and mission schools now converted into tourist attractions, including the National Archives and Parliament House. The City Hall MRT station and St. Andrew's Cathedral lie in wait farther south along Stamford Rd., as do the National Museum and Art Gallery and the National Library.

FOOD

Yet Con, 25 Purvis St. (tel. 337 68 19), 2 blocks north of the Raffles Hotel. Still going strong after 50 years, this is the wellspring of Hainanese cuisine in Singapore, dishing up the same chicken and *charsiu* roast pork (S$2) that earned it a fanatical following. The specialty is the Steamboat, where patrons cook their own food in a boiling pot. Vegetarian dishes available. Open daily 11am-9:30pm.

SIGHTS

The **Raffles Hotel,** a huge white behemoth, occupies the entire block between North Bridge and Beach Rd. along Raffles Blvd. The third floor of the hotel houses the **Raffles Hotel Museum,** which traces the history of the hotel from its founding in 1887 all the way through New Year's Eve 1993, with an emphasis on the golden years of the 1920s and 30s. (Open daily 10am-9pm.) **The National Museum** (tel. 330 09 71), on Stamford Rd. at the origin of Bencoolen St., mainly focuses on Singaporean history, but also boasts exhibits of Chinese porcelain and Aw Boon Haw's jade collection. (Open Tues.-Sun. 9am-5:30pm; admission S$3, children S$1.) The **Singapore Art Gallery** (tel. 336 16 40) is near the National Museum on the other side of Bras Basah

The Life of Sir Stamford Raffles: Part the Sixth

In 1819, Sir Stamford Raffles was between positions and had a little spare time on his generous hands, so he declared his intention to do something truly eternal. Thus was born the city of Singapore, which amassed a population of 5000 in just three months. Lacking the time to wait for approval from Europe, he returned to Bencoolen and made further foundational contributions in the fields of zoology, archaeology, and geology, among others. A witness to Raffles' brilliant forethought, Singapore grew in three years to over 10,000 people, with a booming economy exceeding Penang and Malacca combined. Pleased with his recent *magnum opus*, Raffles founded the Singapore Institution, where Malays could receive an Enlightened Western Education. A series of masterfully executed treaties with the Dutch ensured the survival of Singapore, the founding of the lordly Raffles Hotel, and a path through which the exotic riches of the Far East could be tapped. Hard times hit Raffles soon after, but amidst health problems, legal controversies, and the death of four of his children, Raffles still found the time to open the London Zoo and re-establish himself at the forefront of high society before he died on July 4, 1826, one day shy of his 45th birthday. An essential link in the transformation of the Far East, Raffles' reputation stands not just as the founder of one of Southeast Asia's largest cities, but also as the world's greatest humanitarian and natural scientist and as The Consummate Orientalist and Colonialist. Who can imagine what Southeast Asia would be like today without his efforts on the part of the West? (To return to the beginning of Sir Stamford's life, and follow his illustrious journeys, see page 487).

Rd. Housed in the former missionary school of St. Joseph's Institution, the gallery has a fascinating array of mostly modern multimedia works by Singaporean and regional artists. The lovely 128-year-old **Empress Palace Museum,** 1 Empress Place (tel. 336 76 33), near the southern mouth of the Singapore River, tries to compensate for Singapore's pitiful art scene with visiting collections from artsier China. (Open daily 9am-7pm; the art gallery, antique gallery, and Queen's Room on the first floor are free; the rest are S$6, children S$3.) Just off Arab St., about a 3-minute walk from the Bugis MRT stop, is **Sultan Mosque,** perhaps Singapore's most impressive. The mosque is Indian in inspiration, originally built with a S$3000 grant from the altruistic Sir Stamford Raffles.

ENTERTAINMENT

Sail away from nightlife on a **Chinese junk ride,** operated by **Watertours,** 3-A Clifford Pier (tel. 533 98 11). It docks at Kusa Island in the straits, so passengers can walk up to a "holy" hilltop with a view (pier departures 10:30am and 3pm; fare S$20, children S$10; dinner cruise leaves at 6pm, 2½hr., S$34, children S$17).

For some actual nightlife, visitors can try **The Long Bar,** on the 2nd and 3rd floors of the Raffles Hotel. This is the birthplace of the famed Singapore Sling (S$15), a fruity "lady's drink," and a must for every Singapore first-timer. Several lounge and cover bands entertain the peanut-shelling-happy crowd. A pitcher of margaritas costs S$30, Tiger S$27. (Open Sun.-Thurs. 11am-1am, Fri.-Sat. and eves of public holidays 11am-2am.) **The Billiard Room,** on the Beach Road side of Raffles, is an even swankier and more leisurely lounge with live jazz and a few snooker tables. Slump in a rattan chair, order a glass of red wine (S$12) and a fine Cuban cigar. (Open Sun.-Thurs. 11am-1am, Fri. and Sat. until 2am.)

■ Geylang Road Area

The city's northeast district is like a Malay noodle floating in Singapore's simmering broth of Chinese and Muslim-Indian ethnicities. The residential northeast section of town has guaranteed quietude and an atmosphere not too rich for backpacker blood. Although Geylang is reportedly a gangster hangout and houses a waning red-light district in its karaoke-intensive southern half, travelers usually do not feel any threat to their persons or morality, even at night.

ACCOMMODATIONS

Wads of guest houses (most around S$50) are stuffed between Geylang Rd. and Sims Ave. Tiny streets *(lorong)* cut across the two main roads and form the rungs of this ladder-shaped district. Watch your step around the idiosyncratic numbering system: odd numbers through 31 are between Geylang Rd. and Sims Ave., even numbers on the other side of Geylang Rd. The MRT stops at Lorong 1 (MRT: Kallang) and Lorong 25 (MRT: Aljunied).

Lai Ming, 432 Geylang Rd. #4 Lrg. 24 (tel. 744 20 38). Spacious A/C rooms with sink and shower in the corner and beds the size of plane runways. Singles could easily house 2, the doubles 3, 4, or more. Most importantly, Lai Ming is an escape from the surly service of other area hotels. Singles with shower and TV S$45, additional person add S$5. 24-hr. reception.

Yew Hua Boarding House, 44 Lrg. 25A (tel. 748 64 66). Exit the Aljunied MRT station, take a left, then take another left onto Lrg. 25A; it's on the left. The "Friendly Chinese" hotel is perhaps not quite that, but it's a pleasant place to snooze. Fastidious A/C rooms with showers tucked in the corners share hall bathrooms. Singles S$30. Doubles S$35. Triples S$40.

Hotel 81, 31 Lrg. 18 and 20 Lrg. 16. Brand spanking new, this is the Singaporean equivalent of a Super 8. Staff is copacetic and rooms have all the trimmings: A/C, TV with in-house video, IDD phones, bathroom, and shower. Singles/doubles with queen bed S$49, with 2 double beds S$59. Large deluxe doubles with queen bed S$69. Rates are hiked S$20 on weekends and there is a S$30 key deposit.

FOOD

Many a poor fish eventually flops its way to the seafood-rich beach area off **East Coast Parkway,** halfway between downtown and the airport. Take bus #14 from Bras Basah Rd. (S$0.60) to Mountbatten Rd. The **UDMC Seafood Centre** to the right and **East Coast Lagoon Food Centre** to the left, are known for the ocean views, squirming seafood, and pre-industrial Singaporean atmosphere. Geylang below Lrg. 16 is home to a rash of Eating Houses with *dim sum,* chicken rice, *nyonya* stews, and *doujiang* (soy milk) figuring in the mix.

Yong Lye Eating House, across from Lrg. 8 on Geylang Rd., look for the "24 hrs." sign. It may not look like much, but this rare *doujiang* restaurant is the island's most famous. Come here late at night to have a bowl of hot *dou hua* (sweet tofu porridge, S$1.20) or a *shaobing youtiao* (bean paste) and *doujiang* (griddle cakes, fried dough stick, and soy milk) set for S$2. Open 24hr.

San Yeu Cha, 362A Geylang Rd., on the corner of Lrg.20. Smaller and usually more crowded than the others. Serves up *nyonya* stews, and a mean chicken rice *(jifan)* with cilantro leaves (S$2). Open daily 8am-7pm.

Chang Ghiang Eating House, on the corner of Geylang Rd. and Lrg. 16. Follow your nose along the trail of exotic whiffs from this hectic open-air restaurant. Spiced pig's trotter S$3. Black mushrooms and chicken feet S$3. Culinary cowards can munch on *mee* and chicken rice. Open daily 7am-6:30pm.

▓ Orchard Road

Mobbed with shoppers, and an anathema to backpackers, the sidewalks of Orchard Rd. lead to pricey boutiques, five-star hotels, and mall after mall after huge A/C mall. Orchard Rd. caters to the caviar tastes of jet-setters who never leave its safe shores. Cultural attractions read like Ivana Trump's rolodex: Burberry's, Cartier, Chanel, Christian Dior, Ferragamo, Rolex, and Tiffany. You may feel poor as you drag your shaggy person down this tree-lined stretch of gleaming mega-malls and five-star hotels. Fashion victims everywhere bare their midriffs and look disdainfully at the gnarled toes peeping from your Tevas.

ACCOMMODATIONS

Given Orchard's residents, backpackers would be wise to find their beds elsewhere. If you really must hang with the jet set, try the **YMCA,** 1 Orchard Rd. (MRT: Dhoby Ghaut, tel. 336 60 00), in the Bencoolen St. area, across the road and visible from the National Museum. Its pricey but posh dorms have four bunk beds each, A/C, TV, private bath, and key lockers. The carpeted private rooms are equipped with the amenities of a major hotel. The reception is open 24 hours. Dorms cost S$25, singles S$85, doubles S$90. Family rooms are S$105, extra bed S$10. Reserve six weeks ahead (major credit cards; S$5 membership required of non-members).

FOOD

Most malls have A/C food courts. **Emerald Food Court,** in the basement of the Orchard Emerald Shopping Centre, serves Indonesian and Chinese fare (S$3.60). **Cuppage Road Wet Market** is just across Orchard Rd. from the Somerset MRT stop, down Cuppage Rd. (Open daily 7am-8pm.) **Perahakan Place,** directly west of Centre Point Mall, has food, as well as some pricey but worthwhile restaurant/pubs.

Olio Dome II, 6 Handy Rd. (tel. 339 85 11). Housed together with an artsy movie theater near the junction of Handy and Orchard Rd., this Italian restaurant introduced the concept of complimentary (homemade) bread to Singapore. Creative entrees S$12-17 (mango chicken S$14.50), *focaccia* S$7.50, good carrot cake, and great espresso S$4. Open Sun.-Fri. 10:30am-11pm, Sat. 10:30am-1am.

Maharani North Indian Cuisine, 5th Fl., Far East Plaza, Scotts Rd. (tel. 235 88 40). In the 4th building to the right as you turn from Orchard Rd. A small restaurant, but it is consistently voted one of Singapore's best. Delicious curries, *vindaloos,* and breads in a hushed setting. Set dinner S$29.50. Set lunch S$13.50. Mutton Moghlai S$5. Chicken *vindaloo* S$12.90. Open daily noon-10:30pm.

ENTERTAINMENT

Most clubs and bars are depressingly standard. In the way of discos, the best is **Velvet Underground,** 17, 19, and 21 Jiak Kim St., a fair distance south of Orchard Rd. off Kim Seng Rd. on the left. It's a mixed club with a mid-20s crowd, refreshingly lacking in lecherous expats and their SPG (Sarong Party Girl) hangers-on. Come on Monday and Tuesday for ambient/trip hop, Wednesday for 80s, and Thursday through Sunday for standard 150bpm thump thump. (Open daily 11pm-2am, until 3am on Fri. and Sat.; cover of S$25 gets you into Velvet, Zouk next door, and the adjoining MTV bar/pool room; 2 drinks included.) Next door, **Zouk** (S$18 cover) draws a younger, more spastic crowd, and has similar music, while the **Wine Bar** (tel. 738 29 88) is at a lower decibel level. **Ice Cold Beer,** on Peramakon Pl., has about the biggest selection of brew in town and a nice bare bones feel to it. A pint of Guinness draught is S$9. **Que Pasa** next door has good *tapas* for S$10 and a large selection of wine and cigars. (Both are open daily until 1 or 2am.)

■ Chinatown

Chinatown is testament to Singapore's pride in its new-found national heritage—the Chinese-colonial shophouses along its circuitous lanes have been gutted, refurbished, and repainted in bright pastels. The extension of the MRT through these parts has sent property values through the roof, which means that the bubbling coffee shops of old have given way to offices and classy boutique stores. You can still find a competitively priced stuffed bullfrog on these streets, however, which also host many of the city's religious sights and food centers. Landmarks include the **Pearl's Centre**

Mall along Eu Tong Sen St. and the **Maxwell Market Food Centre,** which is smack in the middle at the intersection of South Bridge and Maxwell Rd.

ACCOMMODATIONS

Metropolitan YMCA Singapore, 70 Palmer Rd. (MRT: Tanjung Pagar, tel. 222 46 66). Walk east from the station, turn right on Anson Rd., and then left on Palmer Rd. At the fork in the road, veer right and look for the Y. Not as upscale as the one on Orchard Rd., but it's in a quiet location and has a balcony. All rooms have A/C and IDD phones. Singles with common bath S$35. Doubles with attached bath S$65. Triples with bath S$75. Extra bed S$12. Attached nursery and restaurant.

Airview Hotel, 10 Peck Seah St. (MRT: Tanjung Pagar, tel. 225 77 88), across Wallich St. and up Peck Seah St. Well-ventilated rooms have A/C, TV, baths, and phone. Hall toilets. Doubles with cigarette-scorched carpets S$60. Triples S$75.

Chinatown Guest House, 325D New Bridge Rd., 5th Fl. (MRT: Outram Park, tel./fax 220 06 71), opposite Pearl's Centre Mall on the southwest edge of Chinatown. Go to Eu Tong St., cross the street and proceed left (this side of the street is New Bridge Rd.). Threadbare rooms smell like diesel. Free use of kitchen and lockers. Bath outside. Dorms S$10. Singles S$30. Doubles S$50. Open 24hr.

FOOD

Some of Singapore's biggest and best hawker centers roost here, as do some unique mid-range restaurants. **The Soup Restaurant,** 25 Smith St. (tel. 222 99 23), can be reached from the Outram Park MRT stop. Walk north up New Bridge Rd., take a right on Smith St. just after New Bridge Centre; it is on the right. This rare medicinal restaurant, located on two floors of an old rowhouse, is perfect for travelers seeking to improve everything from eyesight to sexual potency. Get a pot of Iron Goddess of Mercy tea to complement the experience.

As for hawker centers, Chinatown has some of the more varied. The **Telok Ayer/ Lau Pa Sat Centre** occupies both sides of Shenton Way, a five-minute walk south of the Raffles Place MRT stop. The more basic eastern half is cheaper and stays open all night. **Outram Park,** behind Pearl's Centre on Eu Tong St., overflows with the usual hawker specialities as well as some surprises, such as Northern Chinese *fa gao* (steamed cornbread and sweet coconut rice dumplings), which are sold for a pittance. **Murray Food Terrace** is well-known among Singaporean *hoi poloi* for its pricier restaurants, such as **New Indian Restaurant** (12 Murray St.), **Moti Mahal** (18 Murray St.), and **Moi Kong** (22 Murray St.). To get to Murray St., walk from the Tanjung Pagar MRT stop down Peck Seah St. toward Maxwell St., turn left, and left again before the Bank of China. **Maxwell Market Food Centre,** at the intersection of Maxwell and South Bridge Rd., boasts traditional Chinese fare and a startling supply of fish heads, duck, and durian. (Open daily 8am-10pm.) **People's Park Centre** is on Eu Tong Sen St. in Chinatown. Take buses #81, 83, or 103 from Bencoolen St. or the Raffles Hotel, or take the MRT to Outram Park and look for Eu Tong Sen St. The People's Park Centre is beyond the Pearl's Centre Mall. (Open daily 10am-10pm.)

SIGHTS

Singapore's Chinatown, beaming in pastels after a city wide face lift, doesn't leave much to the imagination. The **Chinatown Historic District** is designated as Telok Ayer St., a quiet avenue running parallel to Amoy St. Home to Chinese and Malay immigrants in the 19th century, this area became the Chinese commercial district and served as a hub for the slave trade due to its location on the original shoreline.

Three temples along Telok Ayer St. between Boon Tat St. and McCallum St. can be zapped in a jiffy, but only the Escher-like **Thian Hock Keng Temple,** or **Tian Fu Gong Temple** (Temple of Heavenly Happiness) merits more than a cursory pause (open daily 6am-5:30pm). The statue of Ma Cho Po, goddess of the sea, was installed in 1840. Sailors donated tile and ironwork, plus a spate of stone dragons who slink on the roof, the pillars, and the walls, much to the delight of Ma Cho Po.

At the southeast end of Temple St., the **Sri Mariamman Temple,** 244 South Bridge Rd., is an old Hindu temple which stokes up a 4-m pit for **Thimithi,** the **Firewalking Festival.** Hindu stalwarts wrap their toes with faith alone for the yearly October stroll. From the Outram Park MRT stop, follow Eu Tong Sen St. past Pearl's Centre and People's Park complex, then turn right onto Temple St. and walk to the end of the road. (Open daily 6am-12:30pm and 4-9:30pm.)

■ Little India

Scrubbed and purified in Singaporean fashion, this neighborhood's restaurants, shops, and overall panache have somehow maintained their vitality to a far greater degree than those of Chinatown. The district's two broad thoroughfares, Serangoon Rd. and Jl. Besar, run north-south, parallel to each other near the Raffles Hotel and the Orchard Rd. area. Zhujiao Centre, with its annexed food center and market, nibbles at the southern end of Serangoon Rd. Just north of the Bencoolen area, Little India provides the best compromise for the budget traveler; accommodations are reasonably priced, worthwhile sights are in easy reach, and inexpensive food is abundant. Jalan Besar Rd. forms Little India's eastern boundary while Serangoon Rd., beginning in the south at the Zhujiao Centre, defines the western edge.

ACCOMMODATIONS

Ali's Nest, 23 Robert's Lane (tel. 291 29 38). Heading north off Serangoon Rd., turn left across from Serangoon Plaza before Owen Rd. Accessible by bus #16 or 16E from the airport and #97 or 103 from the library. Communal kitchen, washers, free breakfast, coffee, tea, and a sun deck spice up the bargain. Dorms S\$7-8. Singles S\$15. Doubles S\$25. Free ride if you're lost.

International Hotel, 290 A&B Jl. Besar (tel. 293 92 38). A curious looking semi-circular building at the corner of Jl. Besar and Allenby St. Spacious rooms off the beaten track and as clean as Lee Kwan Yew's reputation. All rooms have A/C and bath, and common toilets. Singles S\$35. Doubles S\$40, extra person add S\$5. Relaxing coffeehouse downstairs.

Bencoolen Junction Travellers Lodge, 35A Jl. Besar (tel. 293 72 87), opposite the Sin Lim Tower; look for the "Budget Boarding House" sign. New, basic rooms with no frills, hallway bathrooms, and few windows. Doubles with fan S\$25, with A/C S\$35. Triples with fan S\$30, with A/C S\$40. Quads with A/C S\$60.

FOOD

Serangoon Rd. has plenty of possibilities for mouth-watering vegetarian Indian food. A string of restaurants, specializing in fish-head curry, *tandoor,* and other Indian recipes lie along Race Course Rd. **Zhujiao Centre** (Kangdang Kerbau Wet Market), on the corner of Serangoon Rd. and Bukit Timah Rd., is the place to go for your morning meals. (Open daily 7am-9pm.) Another mostly Chinese food center is on Jl. Besar, close to the International Hotel, and occupies two floors of a large complex between Rowell Rd. and Kelantan Ln.

Komala Vilas, 76-78 Serangoon Rd. (tel. 293 69 80), around the corner from Upper Dickson Rd. A cornucopia of south and north Indian vegetarian food. Use your right hand when eating. Try the *masala dosai,* a sassy mix of sauces (from coconut to chick pea) and spices, scooped up with a huge pancake rolled around a potato base (S\$1.60). Open daily 7am-10pm.

Bobby-O Claypot Curry, 35 Jl. Besar (tel. 298 38 76), at the southern end of the street, above Dunlop St. A diminutive A/C eatery where you scoop tasty curries from the standard metal trays. Claypot chicken S\$3.50, *naan* set meal S\$3. Open daily 7:30am-9:30pm.

Kamats, 102 Serangoon Rd. (tel. 291 79 30). A clean hometown favorite with friendly owners. Serves tasty *ghee masala dosai* and *biryani* (S\$2-3). Nice booths in the upstairs section open from 6:15pm. Downstairs open daily 9am-10:30pm.

SIGHTS

Like Bencoolen, Little India remains a low-rent district relative to Chinatown. Roughly bounded by a road-box made up of Bukit Timah Rd., Race Course Rd., Lavender St., and Jalan Besar Rd., the area's main events square off the six blocks northeast of the Rochor Canal between Clive St. and Race Course Rd.

Shops near Serangoon Rd. emit clouds of incense and freshly ground spices. Proprietors fuss with displays of jewelry, gold, *sari* (from S$8 up to S$3000 for those woven with gold thread), and Hindu gods resting on velvet. Around Upper Weld Rd. mayhem reigns as men haggle with a vengeance over second-hand treasures ranging from walkmans and foreign coins to jade figurines and bamboo bongs. **Sri Veerama Kali Amman Temple,** 141 Serangoon Rd. (tel. 293 46 34), at the corner of Belilios Rd., draws devotees of Kali, the multi-armed goddess of destruction (open daily 7am-12:30pm and 4-9pm).

At 397 Serangoon Rd., just after Perumal Rd., the **Sri Srinivasa Temple** (tel. 298 57 71) is a blue complex guarded by a thicket of barbed wire. The broken coconuts in the inner courtyard are for the elephant-headed Vinayagar, who is revered for his filial piety and worshipped first upon entering the temple. (Open daily 6:30am-noon and 5-9pm; Fri. and Sat. open until 9:30pm.) The temple is the launching pad for the **Thaipusam Festival.** At the beginning of the year, Hindus honor Lord Subramaniam with a pilgrimage from this temple to the Chettiar Hindu Temple. They carry a *kavadi* (metal cage) decorated with offerings, as well as hooks and spikes, which masochistic worshippers use to pierce their skin so the *kavadi* can hang freely from their flesh. But that's only the beginning—even more gruesome acts of self-mutilation are performed, but the zealots never bleed, a phenomenon thought to be due to their trance-like state. Check the newspaper a day ahead for the pilgrimage route (so you can pick another one).

Sakaya Muni Buddha Gaya Temple (Temple of 1000 Lights), 366 Race Course Rd., is popular with tourists but has little artistic merit (open daily 7:30am-4:45pm). Just across the street, the large complex of **Long Shan Ci** (Dragon Mountain Temple) has more impressive architecture, fountains, and a back room full of ancestral tablets of lineage groups that contributed to the temple's construction.

Labeled with Malaysian street names, the Muslim neighborhood around **Arab St.** unwinds east of Little India and north of the Bencoolen St. area. Plan ahead and pick up stocking-stuffers here, including batik, printed sarongs, baskets of all dimensions, jewelry boxes, and other crafts.

AROUND SINGAPORE

The **Singapore Zoological Gardens,** 80 Mandai Lake Rd. (tel. 269 34 11), are spacious and well-kept. Animals are enclosed by moats and hedges as opposed to metal bars, and the dirt patches common to most regional zoos are replaced by the flora of the animal's natural habitat. Many visitors like to come early in the morning for breakfast with orangutans or to share a scone with the friendly simians at high tea (breakfast 9am S$15, tea S$10). The zoo also has a rare collection of four **Komodo dragons,** which are publicly fed at 2pm, two Sundays per month, to the great delight of the audience and the carnivores themselves. Elephant rides are offered Mon.-Fri. from 1-4pm, Sat.-Sun. 1-2:30pm and 4-5pm. Travel there in luxury on the Zoo Express (tel. 292 23 88) from Orchard Rd. hotels. Or, take the MRT to Ang Mo Kio station and transfer to bus #138. (Open daily 8:30am-6pm; admission S$9, ages 3-16 S$4.) Most creatures are nocturnal; catch them at their loveliest on a **night safari** touring a patch of rainforest after dark glimpsing "pig bears," cervil cats, and rhinos. Take the tram (covering about 75% of the exhibit) or, for the truly tireless, walk. (Open daily 7:30pm-midnight; admission S$15.45, children S$10.30.)

Jurong Bird Park (tel. 265 00 22), on Jalan Ahmad Ibrahim, is also another popular site. (Open daily 9am-6pm; admission S$9, children S$3.) It contains over 450 species of birds, including the cassowary from Papua New Guinea, which is known for its startling ability to charge humans and rip their hearts out with its bare claws, and Antarctic penguins who are treated to cool water and man-made snow. For a more cheerful way to start your day, have **breakfast with the birds** (daily 9-11am, S$12, children S$10), and no, you don't have to eat what they eat (and hopefully they'll eat their heart out, not yours). Take the MRT to Boon Lay Station and transfer to bus #251, 253, or 255 at the bus interchange.

Singaporeans have a vicarious fascination with the crocodile, whose prehistoric savagery perhaps affords an escape from the bland technocratic harmony of the city-state. Come gape at the big, terrifying creatures at **Jurong Crocodile Paradise** (tel. 261 88 66), next to Jurong Bird Park, featuring crocodile wrestling at 11:45am, 2, and 4pm. (Open daily 9am-6pm; admission S$4.50, children S$2.50.)

The less lethal **Chinese and Japanese Gardens** at Jurong Park (tel. 264 34 55), on Yuan Ching Rd., are built on a pair of islands in Jurong Lake connected by an elegant, carved white stone footbridge. The Chinese garden features pagodas, gazebos, and structures with romantic names like "Moon Inviting Boat" and "Moon Receiving Tower," and other bits of Bernardo Bertolucci-esque sets that eclipse the ascetic Japanese garden. Take the MRT to the Chinese Garden station and follow the signs. (Open Mon.-Sat. 9am-6:30pm, Sun. and public holidays 8:30am-6:30pm; admission S$4.50, children S$2.)

■ Sentosa Island

Sentosa is a sprawling tourist complex where you can spend all day emptying your wallet considerably. The island is easily reached by walking over the 0.5km bridge behind the World Trade Centre. Admission to the island is S$5 for adults, S$3 for children; there's an extra charge for most worthwhile attractions. A free monorail loops around the island, bringing you to such attractions as: **Asian Village** (free) where children can enjoy amusement rides; **Underwater World** (S$12) where visitors can peer at 5000 species of fish through a submarine plexiglas tunnel; **Images of Singapore Museum** (S$5), more interesting than the National Museum, with many multimedia exhibits and dioramas; **Fantasy Island** (S$16), a vast water park with about 30 slides, wading pools and simulated white water rapids (closed Wed. and Thurs.); and the **Butterfly Park** (S$5), which will release you from any obligation to visit another butterfly park ever again. On Saturday nights **Siloso Beach** is hopping with expats and Singaporean *bumiputra* well into the morning at the weekly beach party. To get there, take buses #65 or 143 from Orchard Rd. For **camping** on the island make reservations (tel. 472 51 30) three days in advance. Four-person tents cost S$14, 8-person tents S$19.

THAILAND ประเทศไทย

The glossy pictures used to advertise Thailand's exotic beaches, temples, jungles, cuisine, and natural attractions have, according to the statistics, caught the eye of more than one passer-by; in the last decade, the number of tourists visiting Thailand has increased from one to six million per year. As the only Southeast Asian people never ruled by a western power, Thais possess a unique and independent cultural heritage which they have managed to maintain through the process of rapid industrialization and growing presence on the international economic scene. "The Land of Smiles" might be a trite title but is, in fact, remarkably accurate.

The country consists of six distinct regions: Bangkok, Central, East, North, Northeast, and South. Urbanites seek shelter in the capital's maelstrom of towering highrises and mammoth shopping complexes. Meanwhile, tourists devote days in the South and the East to soaking up tropical sun and frolicking on the beaches. The rugged head to the North on mountain treks to meet hill tribes who have inhabited the region for centuries. Archaeology buffs and fans of tranquility tour the Northeast and Central regions, picking through crumbling ruins and exploring the cradles of Thai civilization, which now repose in silent majesty.

ESSENTIALS

▓ Geography

Thailand (pop. 58.6 million) claims an area of 514,000 sq.km—about the size of Texas. The Chao Phraya River snakes through the fertile region, which extends from the rugged mountains bordering Burma to the northeast plateau. One of the world's major rice and fruit-growing areas due to the presence of the Chao Phraya River, the Central Plain thrives on a waterborne lifestyle of floating markets. Bangkok, the nation's chaotic capital, is also located here. Originally the cradle of Thai civilization, the North is charcterized by fertile river valleys and forested mountains. The East, rich in natural resources, provides a seemingly endless stream of bays and beaches, ending eventually at the Cambodian border. Bordered on the east by the Gulf of Thailand, on the west by the Indian Ocean, and on the south by Malaysia, the southern region is graced with tropical islands, palm-fringed beaches, coral reefs, fishing villages, forested mountains, wildlife sanctuaries, remote waterfalls, and mosques.

▓ When to Go

Thailand is generally hot and humid, with an average annual temperature of 28°C (83°F). The air is cooler in the mountainous north than in the tropical south. Three distinct seasons exist in Thailand. The cool season, October-February, brings high prices and high tourist density, but lower temperatures—especially in the north, where nighttime temperatures can dip to 11°C (52°F). The hot season, March-May, means summer highs near 38°C (100°F) throughout the country; traveling costs often plummet as tourism winds down. The rainy season, June-September, hits its peak in August when the rains just keep on coming. In May and October, heavy monsoons pummel the southern isthmus, making flooding an annual experience. Travelers come in greater numbers during this season, hoping to avoid the cool season's crowds and the hot season's unbearable heat.

THAILAND

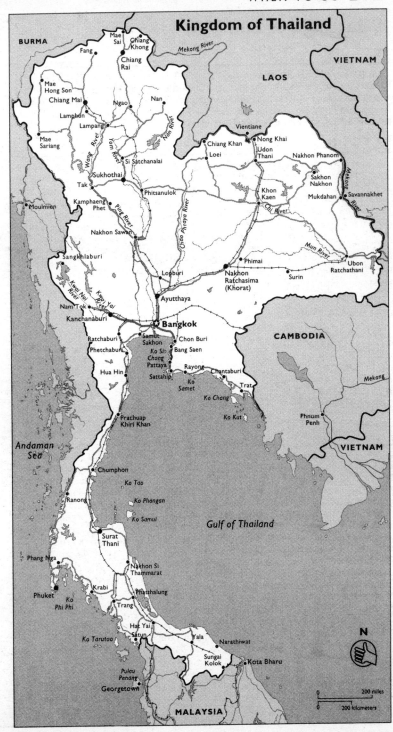

Kingdom of Thailand

BURMA

Mae Sai
Chiang Khong
Mekong River
VIETNAM

Fang

Chiang Rai

LAOS

Mae Hong Son
Chiang Mai
Ngao
Nan

Lamphun
Lampang

Vientiane
Chiang Khan
Nong Khai
Loei
Udon Thani
Nakhon Phanom

Mae Sariang

Si Satchanalai
Sukhothai

Sakhon Nakhon
Mukdahan
Savannakhet

Tak
Kamphaeng Phet

Phitsanulok

Khon Kaen

Chi River

Moulmien

Nakhon Sawan

Sangkhlaburi

Lopburi
Phimai
Mun River

Ubon Ratchathani

Nam Tok
Kanchanaburi

Ayutthaya

Nakhon Ratchasima (Khorat)
Surin

Ratchaburi
Phetchaburi

Samut Sakhon
Bangkok
Chon Buri
Bang Saen

CAMBODIA

Hua Hin

Ko Si Chang
Pattaya
Sattahip
Rayong
Chantaburi
Ko Samet
Ko Chang
Trat

Mekong

Prachuap Khiri Khan

Ko Kut

Phnom Penh

Andaman Sea

VIETNAM

Chumphon
Ko Tao

Ranong
Ko Phangan
Ko Samui

Gulf of Thailand

Surat Thani

Phang Nga

Nakhon Si Thammarat

Phuket
Ko Phi Phi
Krabi
Phatthalung
Trang

Hat Yai
Satun
Yala
Narathiwat

Ko Tarutao

Sungai Kolok
Kota Bharu

Pulau Penang
Georgetown

MALAYSIA

N

0   200 miles
0   200 kilometers

THAILAND

■ Getting Around

BY PLANE

Thai Airways holds a near-monopoly within Thailand and offers 17 flights from Bangkok to various destinations in the north, northeast, and south, plus flights within and across regions outside Bangkok. The only alternative to Thai is **Bangkok Airways,** a small start-up whose major routes are from Bangkok to Ko Samui and Phuket. Thailand has a 200฿ **airport tax** on international flights.

BY TRAIN

The Thai government, through the **State Railway of Thailand,** operates an efficient and inexpensive rail system that reaches many locales throughout the country. The four main train routes in Thailand start in Bangkok and run north to Chiang Mai, south to Malaysia and Singapore, northeast to Nong Khai, and east to Ubon Ratchathani. Minor routes connect Bangkok to Kanchanaburi and cities north of the eastern seaboard. For long rides (anything over three hours), third class is uncomfortable. Second class sleepers are still cheap and much more comfortable. They often sell out, however, so you would do well do reserve a few days early. **Sprinter trains** are the fastest, followed by **express trains. Rapid trains** are, ironically, the slowest. Only second and third-class are available. Reserve one to two days in advance; many guest houses can also book tickets.

■ Money

US$1=25.34฿ (baht)
CDN1$=18.529฿
UK£1=39.138฿
IR£1=38.600฿
AUS$1=18.779฿
NZ$1=15.364฿
SARand=7.108฿

1฿=US$0.040
1฿=CDN$0.054
1฿=UK£0.026
1฿=IR£0.026
1฿=AUS$0.053
1฿=NZ$0.065
1฿=SARand0.141

The Thai monetary system is based on the **baht** (฿), which is divided into 100 **satangs** (rarely used in transactions). All Thai currency has a picture of the King on it—don't deface any money unless you want to spend some time in a Thai jail. Thailand has a 7% VAT (value-added tax) on most items, including hotel rooms and food; it's usually tacked onto stated prices. VAT is rarely added onto the final bill; the menu, tariff sheet, etc. should specify if this is the case. **Tipping** is not customary. Some cab drivers will ask for a tip, but you needn't feel compelled to give one. Upscale restaurants often have a 10-15% service charge, but in nice restaurants without a service charge, it is appropriate to leave something (3-5%). Do not tip maids or service staff, especially in your guest house, but valets and luggage carriers should receive a small tip (5-20฿). As a foreigner, expect to pay higher entrance fees at certain places including beaches, museums, archaeological sights, and national monuments. Don't feel as though you are being cheated or treated with disrespect; the elevated *farang* price is the status quo throughout the country.

■ Keeping in Touch

The Thai **postal system** is extremely reliable and efficient for a country on the verge of becoming a Newly Industrialized Country (NIC). Airmail across the globe from Bangkok generally takes between seven and 10 days. Overseas mail from rural areas may take up to two weeks to arrive, but almost always makes it to its destination. For three-day overseas mail the postal service offers **Express Mail Service (EMS),** available at all post offices in Bangkok and many other post offices in the country. Thailand's **telephone country code** is **66. Home Country Direct numbers:** British Telecom, 001-99-944-1066; Canada Direct, 001-999-15-1000; New Zealand Telecom, 66 120 64 0000; Telecom Australia, 001-999-611-000; AT&T, 0019-991-1111; MCI, 001-999-2001; Sprint, 001-999-13-877. For domestic telephone information (including Malaysia and Vientiane, Laos) dial 101. *Let's Go* lists telephone codes in the Practical Information section of each city.

DATE AND TIME

Military time is widely used in addition to the standard western scheme. The cycle begins at 0001 hours (12:01am) and goes to 2400 hours (midnight). In the oral system, there are four base hours: 1 at night *(dee neung)* which corresponds to 1am in western time, 1 in the morning *(neung moang chao)* which corresponds to 7am, 1 in the afternoon *(bai moang)* which corresponds to 1pm, and 1 in the evening *(thoom neung)* which corresponds to 7pm. Thus, a meeting at "three in the morning" in the spoken language, will occur at 9am in western time. Finally, calendars in Thailand use the Buddhist Era to determine the year. To convert the year from the Christian Era to the Buddhist Era, add 543 years to the current year. Thus, 1997 is the year 2540 in the Buddhist Era.

■ Staying Safe

Travelers report that criminals in Thailand are often more clever and creative than direct and violent. As a result, scams abound. Taxi and *tuk-tuk* drivers, guest house operators, fellow travelers on trains or buses, and those friendly students at the museum have all been known to attempt various kinds of cons or outright thefts. We have heard stories about people who feign illness and lure a hapless good samaritan into a car to be robbed; English-speakers who start conversations with travelers in airports, waiting to be asked to watch their bags for a minute. Keep these warnings in mind, and talk to fellow travelers about their experiences.

Many of the larger Thai cities have separate **tourist police** forces which were established in 1982, in association with the Tourism Authority of Thailand, to provide safety for tourists. **Drugs** in Thailand are always illegal, regardless of what that guest house owner may say, and penalties can be very stiff—up to life in prison.

The emergency tourist police number for all of Thailand is 1699.

> One of the most common cons is the selling of gems. The most common line is that there is a one-week government special on gems, and you will not be charged tax if you buy today. There is no such special and there are no government export agencies.

BISEXUAL, GAY, AND LESBIAN TRAVELERS

Thai people, at least in Bangkok, seem to offer a benign but guarded tolerance of gay men and lesbians. There is no legally mandated discrimination against homosexuals, and Thailand seldom witnesses the grotesque hate crimes against gays and lesbians that plagues much of the west. People seem to feel that homosexuality is an individual practice that need not concern others, much less the state or society at large.

Still, sexual orientation is a taboo topic; most gays and lesbians remain more or less closeted. Public discussion and displays of affection or attraction are avoided by homosexuals and heterosexuals alike. In the home of the world's largest sex industry, Thais keep their sexuality buttoned up.

Although gay and lesbian nightlife does exist, much of it is closed to *farang*, who the Thais feel misrepresent their lifestyle by participating in the sex trade. Apart from de facto brothels, it is hard for *farang* to find a gay or lesbian bar or club scene.

THAILAND

■ Prostitution and AIDS

Thailand and prostitution are words which, for some, have unfortunately become synonymous. While most who visit Thailand have no intention of coming into contact with its sex industry, others might have only this on their itinerary. Today, the situation is both better and worse than it appears at a glance.

Women and children make up the majority of Thai prostitutes. Many are poor, lured into the industry with false promises of money, gifts, and respectable jobs in the city; others are kidnapped and forced to work for no pay. Countless more are sold into prostitution by their families to cover debts and escape abject poverty. Most prostitutes die young from disease or other causes related to their occupation.

Estimates on the number of women employed in prostitution range from 200,000 to 2,000,000. Understandably, prostitution has been illegal in Thailand since 1960 and carries stiff penalties (up to and including death). Nonetheless, tourism and the industry are mutually reinforcing. Two-thirds of all foreign visitors in Thailand are male. The U.S., Japan, Europe, Australia, South Korea, and Taiwan all have organizations that send sex tours to Thailand, but laws in many of these same countries now allow them to arrest their own citizens for sex crimes abroad. **Sexual offenders face one to seven years of prison in Thailand and fines of up to 140,000฿. Forced prostitution can bring a life sentence.**

AIDS is decimating workers in the sex industry and the population at large; estimates of HIV-positive prostitutes range from 15% to more than 50%. Every day 1000 Thais are infected, and the World Health Organization calculates that by the year 2000, 2-4 million Thais will have HIV. The Thai government's campaign against AIDS is now said to be the best and most progressive in Asia.

Recent years have seen a huge effort on behalf of the Thai government to increase awareness of AIDS and the potential hazards of having sex without contraception. The Thai government budgeted nearly US$45 million for AIDS education in 1993, and AIDS education has been placed on the public school curriculum. Thais now use condoms—known as *meechais*—in record numbers (as many as 80% of all brothel customers now use them, up from 20% in the mid-80s). While fewer Thai women are

---

Population and Community Development Association

Founded in 1974 by Meechai Viravaidya to pursue community development projects, mainly with refugees in the wake of the Vietnam War, the Population and Community Development Association (PDA) has become the largest—and possibly most successful—non-governmental organization in Thailand's history. Their unique and aggressive social action campaigns are refreshingly frank, using phrases such as "Make Love, not Babies" in radio, TV, and print ads. It has taken more than catchy slogans, however, to achieve the triumphant decrease in the average number of children per family: from seven to two in twelve years. By working to increase individual standards of living, PDA's comprehensive programs promote behavior beneficial to society as a whole. They have garnered several awards for their efforts, including a UN prize for being one of the most successful family planning programs in the world.

In the 1980s, PDA began to use its high-profile techniques in the fight against AIDS. In this vein, they opened the Cabbages and Condoms restaurant, with the goal of making condoms as easy to obtain as cabbages. Many of these programs are based in Northern Thailand, where a combination of less education and more prostitution (15 customers per night vs. 2 per night in Bangkok) has made AIDS a severe problem. Recently, PDA has further expanded their work to include environmental sanitation and occupational programs in rural villages and hill-tribe communities. Thai businesses have become involved through the Thai Business Initiative for Rural Development (TBIRD) program. These projects are tailored to village needs and vary from school lunch programs to promoting sustainable hill-tribe tourism.

entering prostitution, more and more Burmese women are being brought across the border to meet the demand of Asian and western males.

The AIDS crisis has put a damper on Thailand's sex trade; however, it has also pushed the business farther into the countryside, where it is believed the women are less likely to be infected and do not press for condom use. Hustlers for brothels in town now recruit from the hill tribes and the borderlands.

▓ Hours and Holidays

Many public holidays commemorate a royal event or recognize a Buddhist holy day. Banks, government offices, and firms close on these dates. Holidays often coincide with festivals, and all of them involve some sort of revelry. Chinese businesses generally close for the Chinese New Year (Feb. 7& 8, 1997), and some international firms close for Christmas. In general, government offices and banks are open Mon.-Fri. 8:30am-noon and 1:30-4:30pm. Regular shops usually stay open until 5, 7, or 9pm, depending on the size of the shop and the city. See regional listings for details on festivals. In 1997, the official holidays are:

January 1: New Year's Day.
February (full moon): Makha Bucha, Buddha's address to 1250 monks.
April 6: Chakri Day, marking the 1782 founding of the current Thai dynasty.
April 12-14: Songkran, the water festival, celebrating the Thai New Year.
May 1: Labor Day.
May 5: Coronation Day, honoring the 1946 coronation of the King and Queen.
May 10: Royal Ploughing Ceremony, kicking off the rice-planting season.
May (full moon): Wiskha Bucha, celebrating the life of Buddha.
July (full moon): Asanha Bucha, commemorating Buddha's first sermon and the beginning of Khao Phansa (the Buddhist Lent).
August 12: Queen's Birthday.
October 23: Chulalongkorn Day, marking the death of Thailand's revered leader.
November: Loi Krathong, cleansing of mind and spirit beneath the full moon.
December 5: King's Birthday.
December 10: Constitution Day.
December 31: New Year's Eve.

LIFE AND TIMES

▓ The People of Thailand

TAI

The word "Thai" is a political/geographical designation that refers to the citizens of Thailand, as the country has been known since 1939. Tai, however, refers to the ethnic Tai-Kadai people who speak Tai-based languages, many of whom live outside the borders of Thailand, in China, Laos, and Burma (where they were known as the Shan). Ethnically, Thailand is 75% Tai, and the word Thai is often used in its stead when referring to the people of Thailand. These people are divided into numerous sub-groups with somewhat different dialects and cultures. Prior to 1939, the country was known as Siam, from the Khmer name for the Tai people, Syam.

CHINESE

Ethnic Chinese make up only 10-15% of Thailand's population, yet their presence extends back for centuries. In fact, many scholars believe that the Tai people came from China. Assimilating more easily than some other ethnic groups, the Chinese

THAILAND

have a strong influence in Thailand, and their leadership in commerce is much greater than their small population would suggest.

OTHER ETHNIC MINORITIES

Malays constitute about 4% of the population; the rest is composed largely of Vietnamese, Mon, and Khmer. Thailand has traditionally been home to refugees—Burmese, Vietnamese, Laotians, and Khmer—fleeing political violence. Religious freedom, a relatively stable domestic situation, a growing economy, and a laissez-faire culture attract minorities to Thailand.

HILL-TRIBES

Over 550,000 hill-tribe people, or *Chao Khao,* live in north Thailand. The six major groups are the Karen *(Kariang or Yang),* the Hmong *(Meo),* the Yao *(Mien),* the Lahu *(Mussur),* the Akha *(Kaw),* and the Lisu *(Lisaw).* The Akha, Lisu, Lahu, and the Southern Chinese Mien all migrated from Yunnan Province in this century. Other small tribes include the Lawa, Khamu, H'Tin, and Yumbri *(Mlabri).* The Lawa, perhaps Thailand's oldest remaining inhabitants, are remnants of an ancient Mon-Khmer kingdom in Northern Thailand. Though the Shan people, or *Thai Yai,* have their own distinct language, they are not included among the hill tribes since they have never really been a nomadic people. Like the Karen, they have been struggling for autonomy from the Burmese government for years. The largest hill-tribe populations are in Chiang Mai, Chiang Rai, Mae Hong Son, and Tak Provinces.

■ History

PRE-HISTORY

There is some disagreement as to the origins of the Thai people. Some argue that the ancestors of the Thai people migrated from Mongolia or northern China. Driven by the Chinese, these peoples moved south to Yunnan, where the various tribes coalesced and established the kingdom of **Nanchao** in 651 AD. Counter-theorists, however, believe that the Thai people originated in what is now northeast Thailand. Recently discovered human remains in **Ban Chiang** (see **Near Udon Thani,** page 662) on the Khorat Plateau suggest that early farmers settled in the area around 4000 BC and lived there until the beginning of the Christian era. These tribes left for southern China in 651 AD, setting up Nanchao.

During the four centuries that followed the establishment of Nanchao, various tribes of the Tai-Kadai linguistic group moved farther south into the hilly, northern areas of Burma, Thailand, and Laos in search of greater independence from their powerful neighbor. These people, now known as the Shan, Thai, and Lao, eventually founded minor kingdoms and city-states. By 1000 AD, the Chinese had subjugated the original Thai group in Yunnan, and in 1253 AD, Kublai Khan conquered the remnants of the Nanchao lands and incorporated them into the Mongol Empire. Fifteen years earlier, two chiefs from the southern Thai tribes had moved into the central plains of what is now northern Thailand and quickly founded the new Sukhothai kingdom under the tutelage of neighboring **Angkor.**

SUKHOTHAI AND AYUTTHAYA

In 1275 **King Ramkhamhaeng the Great** ascended the throne. Under his active rule, **Sukhothai** reached its zenith in power and size, incorporating present-day Laos, Thailand, Singapore, and Malaysia. In 1283, King Ramkhamhaeng contributed to the cultural consolidation of the Thai people by introducing the **Thai alphabet** to his subjects. It remains, with relatively few changes, the alphabet used by Thais today. Other major accomplishments of Ramkhamhaeng's reign include the abolition of slavery (the first of a series of attempts), the codification of laws, and the introduction of **Theravada Buddhism.** His strength and compassion held the kingdom together, but his shoes proved too large to fill, and his Camelot crumbled within two generations of his death.

The son of a Sukhothai princess, **King U Thong**—later dubbed **King Ramathibodi I**—inaugurated the **Ayutthaya** period by founding the eponymous island city that served as the nation's capital for the next 417 years. Under **King Ramathibodi II,** two generations later, diplomatic relations with the Portuguese over the disputed territory of Melaka brought the first Europeans to what was then known as Siam; the Spaniards, Dutch, English, and French soon followed.

In 1584, after a 15-year period of Burmese occupation, **King Naresuan,** the son of a vassal-king, rose to become the greatest warrior-monarch in Thai history. Appointed by King Burengnong of Burma, Naresuan was given military training in Burma to prepare him to be a Burmese puppet ruler. Instead, Naresuan organized an army, ignited a revolution, and reclaimed the city of Ayutthaya.

Under **King Narai,** Ayutthaya reached its pinnacle with a population even greater than London's of that time. But in 1688, while the king was seriously ill, **Constantine Phaulkon,** your average Greek-adventurer-turned-Thai-Prime-Minister, was accused of conspiring to replace King Narai with a puppet-king loyal to France. The Thai nobility arrested Phaulkon and executed him. Relations with the French were cut off, and virtually all foreigners were expelled from the kingdom.

The trumpets of Jericho sounded for Ayutthaya in 1767. After laying siege for over nine years, the Burmese finally broke through and stormed the once-great capital. Everything was put to the torch, the king was killed, and mass slaughter ensued. Of a community of more than one million, only 10,000 people survived. **General Phraya Taksin** and a few hundred followers managed to escape the carnage. Regrouping on the east coast of Thailand, Taksin led an army of several thousand men to reclaim the nation and expel the Burmese. Within 15 years, he had achieved this goal and also captured Chiang Mai, Cambodia, and parts of Laos. It seems, however, his superhuman exertions drove him over the edge. Insanity struck the new **King Taksin,** who declared himself the reincarnation of Buddha.

Commander-in-Chief **Chao Phraya Chakri** found himself named king by the country's nobles and generals. He made his first two decrees in strict accordance with Siamese law. King Taksin was executed in royal fashion: he was placed in a sack and beaten to death so as not to spill royal blood. The general who had handed Chakri the helm was killed for committing treason against the former king. Not being of royal blood, he was swiftly beheaded. Chakri was given the title Rama I.

THE DYNASTY OF RAMA

Feeling that Thon Buri was too vulnerable, **King Rama I** moved the capital across the Chao Phraya River to the village of Bangkok. There he built the **Grand Palace** and the **Royal Chapel** (Temple of the Emerald Buddha) and consolidated the kingdom's various fiefdoms into a unified nation. He overhauled the Buddhist priesthood and created the "Law of the Three Seals," which set rules on economic, political, and military affairs.

The reign of King Mongkut, or **King Rama IV,** is probably one of the most significant transition periods in contemporary Thailand. Unfairly portrayed as a flippant and licentious monarch in Margaret Landon's novel, *Anna and the King of Siam,* Mongkut was actually a progressive and serious man. He anticipated the danger of western imperialism and met the challenge squarely with deft diplomacy and an active program of domestic modernization. In 1855, to strengthen the nation and to silence western critics, Siam negotiated a foreign trade treaty with the British—reversing 150 years of virtual isolation—and quickly imported western technologies. Mongkut's rule was cut short when, in 1868, he contracted malaria while leading dignitaries into marshy countryside to view a solar eclipse he had predicted. The reins of government fell into the able hands of his son, **Prince Chulalongkorn,** who was crowned **King Rama V.** His 42 years of rule were characterized by numerous reforms in Thai government and society, and a courageous foreign policy in an era of aggressive European colonialism.

The latter half of the 19th century witnessed Britain's seizure of Burma and the French colonization of Indochina. A showdown between the two powers over the fate of Siam was imminent. In 1893, after prolonged tensions between France and Siam in the northeast, two French gunboats shelled Siamese defenses at the mouth of the Chao Phraya River and sailed into Bangkok. Thanks to the swift diplomatic action of **Prince Devawongse,** the Siamese foreign minister who greeted the arriving ships and congratulated the captains on their prowess and skill, war between the two countries was narrowly averted. Siam was established as a buffer state, guaranteeing its independence. By the time of his death in 1910, King Rama V had become the most revered Thai monarch in modern history.

THE RISE OF THE MILITARY

During the Great Depression, the Thai treasury nearly went bankrupt from public works projects. Prominent academics and intellectuals demanded a **civil constitution.** On June 24, 1932, government workers and the military launched a bloodless coup. Proclaiming themselves the People's Party, the revolutionaries, led by **Major Luang Pibulsongkhram** and **Dr. Pridi Banomyong,** moved quickly to occupy high government posts. **Phraya Manopakorn Nitthada,** a former Supreme Court justice, became Thailand's first Prime Minister, and for the next three decades, Pibul and Pridi were the dominant forces in Thai politics. A 1933 attempt at counter-revolution was quickly suppressed.

Thailand did not enter World War II until December 1941, when Japan demanded entry into the country. Pibulsongkhram, then Prime Minister, gave in against strong opposition. When things went badly for the Japanese, Gen. Pibul resigned as Prime Minister and **Khuang Aphaiwongse** secretly allowed Allied forces into the country to help repel the Japanese. Thus, when the war ended in 1945, the U.S. resumed good relations with Thailand, declaring as void Thailand's earlier declaration of war.

The year 1946 was marked by gruesome royal intrigue. On June 9, King Rama VIII, **Ananda Mahidol,** who had returned from school in Switzerland just the year before, was found shot to death in his bed. Conspiracy buffs maintain that the king was a victim of a political design. Others remember the king as an avid gun collector and believe that he died when his favorite revolver accidentally discharged. Currently popular is the theory that he committed suicide. With the death of the young king, his younger brother, **Bhumibol Adulyadej,** ascended the throne, and Pibul returned to power. Thailand developed economically through the late 40s and early 50s and moved toward more democratic practices. Despite this progress, however, the government was riddled with corruption.

In 1957, the military seized an opportunity to stage a *coup d'état* during the general elections. **Field Marshall Sarit Thanirat** took over. The crooked police force was purged, drug dealers were executed, and communist propaganda was suppressed. By the time Sarit died in 1963, Thailand had become a staunch U.S. ally in Southeast Asia; under his successor, U.S. forces were permitted to build air bases in Thailand to support the war in Vietnam. In 1967, Thailand helped create the Association of Southeast Asian Nations (ASEAN), and in the next two years a new constitution was drafted, and the much-awaited elections were held.

Unfortunately, the elections proved to be generally meaningless. In June 1973, university students fed up with fifteen years of political repression led thousands of demonstrators into the streets, calling for a constitution to guarantee a truly democratic government. The more radical individuals left the cities to join the communist guerrilla forces. In October, the government responded, sending troops into Thammasat University to quell demonstrations, and more than 100 people were killed in what was called the **October Massacre.**

TOWARD DEMOCRACY

Before the October Massacre erupted into a full scale conflagration, **King Rama IX** intervened. Although he had no legal authority, he commanded great respect and loyalty among the people. Swayed by the king's reproach, **Prime Minister Thanom Kittikachorn** and other high-ranking officials went into exile. An interim government was established and soon drafted a new, democratic constitution. The tenth Thai constitution provided for national suffrage for men and women over the age of 20 and a certain amount of freedom of speech and religion.

Thailand's first general election in six years was held on January 26, 1975. After a year of political instability, however, the military and influential elites had come to see democracy as a dangerous experiment, and were determined to end it.

In a series of Reichstag fire-type maneuvers, the military and its conservative supporters reclaimed the government. Military leaders cited staged demonstrations as evidence of resurgent socialist and communist tendencies nurtured by democratic lassitude. A stand-off between students and police at Thammasat University, Thailand's favorite hot-bed of political activism, exploded on October 6, into another bloody assault on the campus. In the ensuing violence, scores of people were killed, and the military once again took control of the government.

After 16 *coups d'état* since World War II and long years of economic hardship, public dissatisfaction and shrinking military support led to the end of military rule and general elections in 1988. Peace and freedom from overt military domination, however, proved short-lived. The army launched a successful bloodless coup under the leadership of **General Suchinda Kraprayoon** in February of 1991. Citing general corruption in the government; he abolished the 1978 constitution, dissolved the legislature, and curtailed various freedoms, including the freedom of assembly.

While preparations were made for elections and constitutional revision, a military government of sorts was created under the title of the National Peace-Keeping Council (NPKC), and a civilian, **Anand Panyarachun,** was selected as the interim prime minister. Critics accused the army of influencing the framing of the constitution in order to institutionalize its rule. After a series of protests over this new constitution and the possibility of General Suchinda's leadership, thousands—including many members of the new middle class—took to the streets one more time on May 17, 1992. Suchinda ordered the military to clear them out, and between 100 and 1000 people died, many of them before Bangkok's Democracy Monument and western television cameras. King Bhumibol pushed Suchinda out of office and brought back Panyarachun to serve as a transitional prime minister.

▓ Thailand Today

On August 1, 1992, Anand fired the top four military officers in a bold move that signaled a new era in Thai politics. Their replacements promised to distance the military from politics. With the next prime minister, **Chuan Leekpai,** the leader of the Democratic party, the military still had substantial control over television, radio, and some state-owned industries. In July of 1995, Leekpai was defeated by **Banharn Silparcha,** head of the Thai Nation Party, a party long tied to corruption and vote-buying. Although the new party is pushing for a powerful six-party alliance, it's likely nothing will change, as there's little to no difference between the political stances of Silparcha and Leekpai, and although the latter may be more honest, the former is believed to be more competent. Most important, perhaps, is that the military finally kept its promise to stay out of the elections entirely.

Approximately two-thirds of Thais still work in agriculture, but more and more people are beginning to head for the cities in search of better jobs and higher wages. The general trend toward the prospering urban centers has resulted in a dramatic increase in Thailand's GDP per capita coupled with a surge in the population of Thailand's major cities. Many feel that the western and Japanese producers who sub-contract Thai work should be responsible for safety measures and regulations. But with the tourist industry reigning as the largest source of foreign money, the government is working to maintain its reputation in the international community. Child prostitution and environmental degradation have been nationally and internationally decried. Western countries have begun working with the Thai government to crack down, as

THAILAND

with the recent arrest of a Swedish tourist by his own government for sex crimes in Thailand (see **Prostitution and AIDS,** page 502).

HUMAN RIGHTS

Since 1988, when the Burmese military began a violent crackdown on the pro-democracy movement, thousands of men, women, and children have crossed the Burmese border to seek asylum in Thailand. Upon arrival in Thailand, officials have greeted the refugees with arrests, illegal immigration charges, and prison sentences. Clearly, Thai officials are reluctant to assume another country's burden, an attitude which has received condemnation from international human rights organizations.

Recent improvements have not gone unnoticed, in particular the construction of a so-called safe area camp in the Thai province of Ratchaburii near the Burmese border. The United Nations High Commissioner for Refugees (UNHCR) has established screening procedures for Burmese asylum-seekers and grants "person of concern" status to those who would be at risk of human rights violations were they to return to Burma.

THE MONARCHY

King Bhumibol Adulyadej is the longest-reigning living monarch in the world, the longest-reigning Thai King as well as the composer of the royal anthem (*Falling Rain*). He is not only revered for his dedication to the underprivileged but also for his role in resolving government conflicts, and his selfless commitment to the peace and unity of his country. **Travelers to Thailand must take special care never to insult the monarch in any way.** Stand when the Royal Anthem is played (usually before movies and other events); do not speak disparagingly of Royal Family members; and avoid defacing currency and licking stamps (both carry the King's portrait); in short, don't mess with the man, whose name means "Strength of the Land, Incomparable Power."

■ The Arts

ARCHITECTURE

During the early part of the Sukhothai period, Thai architecture was greatly influenced by the Khmer in the central and eastern parts of Thailand. Structures were covered with carved stone and held together with vegetable glue. Ornate thin gold sheets, mother-of-pearl inlay, and porcelain also covered the buildings.

The best examples of Thai architecture are found in Buddhist monasteries. Each age has contributed important structures to the monastery grounds. The *bot (ubosoth),* or main chapel, is a tall, oblong building with three highly sloped, superimposed roofs whose highest corners end in sharp points called *chofa.* These *chofa* represent swans, the carriers of Brahma. The *bot,* the most magnificent structure, houses the principal Buddha image and serves as the site of most ceremonies. The *wiharn* is similar in style to the *bot* but holds lesser Buddha images and is primarily used for meetings, meditation, and sermons. The *sala* is an open, gazebo-like structure used for meditaton and preaching.

Some monastic compounds contain a tower called the *phra chedi.* Derived from the Indian stupa, the *chedi* is a tapering, spire-like structure with a round or rectangular base that houses the possessions and cremated remains of important people: high priests, members of royalty, and Buddha. Phra Pathom Chedi rises 127m above the ground in Nakhon Pathom and is the largest *chedi* in the world.

DRAMA AND DANCE

Thai classical drama and dance are complementary. The three main types of dramatic media in Thai culture are the *khon,* the *lakhon,* and the *likay.* The first two forms are usually attended by the Thai upper classes, while the *likay* is a phenomenon among poorer Thais, making it the most popular form of the three.

The **khon**, or masked dance drama, is based on Indian dancing and ritual; its various stories come exclusively from the *Ramakien*. During the Ayutthaya period, it was performed only by men; women could not appear on stage until the middle of the 19th century. With the exception of the leading male and female characters, all actors wear elaborate masks. Similar to Greek drama, their verses are recited by a chorus that sits next to a small band. The *khon* is performed with a great deal of stylized action; the movements are suggested by motifs in the music. The original *khon* productions lasted over 20 hours; sleepy audiences and overworked actors prompted later playwrights to shorten their works to a mere three hours.

The **lakhon** is a less structured form of drama but shares some characteristics with the *khon*. Human characters in a *lakhon* do not wear masks, which are reserved for monkeys, demons, and other non-human, non-celestial creatures. Like the *khon,* the *lakhon* is derived from the *Ramakien,* but it also adds stories from Thai folk tales and Buddhist *Jakatas. Lakhon chatri* is a simple play usually performed at shrines for the benefit of gods. *Lakhon nai,* traditionally given by women, dramatizes romantic stories and focuses on gentle and graceful movements. The word *nai* means "inside" in Thai, and refers to the fact that performances occurred inside the palace. *Lakhon nok* (*nok* meaning "outside") were once performed by men only and took place beyond the palace walls. It is characterized by quick movements, fast-paced music, and humor. Today, men and women perform in both *lakhon nai* and *lakhon nok.*

In contrast to the *khon* and *lakhon* which are formal and highly stylized, the **likay** is bawdy and humorous. There are no masks, no exquisite costumes, and no tear-jerking scenes—just loud, sharp music, lyrics strewn with lewd innuendos, and on-the-spot improvisation by the performers. *Likay* is often performed at festivals, combining local and court stories to create a workable plot.

MUSIC

The Thais created unique musical instruments and gave them onomatopoeic names such as *krong, chap, ching, krap,* and *pia.* Simpler instruments were combined to create more complex ones. When Thai music assimilated elements of Indian, Mon, and Khmer styles, still more instruments were developed.

The oldest surviving Thai songs were composed during the Sukhothai period. One noteworthy tune, still well-known today, is *Phleng Thep Thong.* In the Ayutthaya period, music was decreed an official part of court life. Imperial expansion brought instruments and musical styles from neighboring regions such as Burma, Malaya, and Java into the court. During this period, the rules defining musical form were introduced. Songs were composed in a form called **Phleng Ruang,** literally a music story, but actually a suite of melodies.

After the fall of Ayutthaya, the growth of Thai music was halted, but the Bangkok period initiated a musical revival in which Thai literary masterpieces were translated into musicals, and poets added lyrics to music composed in the Ayutthaya period. Contemporary Thai music has taken all sorts of forms. Local and regional folk music, less studied than Thai classical music, is exceedingly common. One of the most popular styles is **luk thung,** Thai country music, which has developed into fast-paced electronic versions. The northeastern **mo lam** is a well-known folk style; it's fast-paced and features a male and a female vocalist who sing as if courting one another, accompanied by a *khene.*

PAINTING

Thai painting was once limited to murals inside the temples and palaces of Ayutthaya. Little of this work remains, however, as the city was torched by the Burmese in 1767. Thus, the vast majority of extant murals comes from the present Bangkok period. Thai murals are unsigned, and the artists remain unknown.

The scenes in murals are taken either from the *Jatakas* or significant events from contemporary Thai life. Figures are drawn in two dimensions without shadows, and the size of the character determines its relative importance in the story being told. Certain stylistic conventions designate social rank. Members of royalty and celestial beings are given peaceful, majestic forms and stately countenances, while the depiction of commoners is less flattering and more realistic.

■ Recreation

MUAY THAI (THAI BOXING)

Muay Thai was developed to keep Thai soldiers battle-ready in the 15th and 16th centuries. The first boxer to win historic recognition was **Nai Khanom Tom.** Captured by the Burmese, he won his freedom after dispatching a dozen Burmese soldiers in a boxing challenge. When word of his amazing feat reached Thailand, King Naresuan and his generals made *Muay Thai* a mandatory part of military training. Fights are full of ritual, music, blood, sweat, and violence. Every blow imaginable is legal with the exception of head-butting. Fighters go at it for five three-minute rounds, with the winner either knocking his victim into a dizzying malaise or taking the bout by points. Surprisingly, most bouts are decided in the latter manner. Fights are packed with screaming fans, many of whom have a financial stake in the match. While some provinces have venues, most of the best fighting occurs in Bangkok's Ratchadamnoen Stadium and Lumpini Stadium.

TRADITIONAL PASTIMES

Every year during the hot season, a strong southerly wind allows people to fly their handmade kites high over Bangkok. Kites are often shaped to represent animals such as serpents, fishes, and owls, and are sometimes flown against one another in games of aerial tag. **Kite fighting** is even patronized by the King.

In certain regions of the country, crowds watch and bet on **Siamese fighting fish.** The fish are extremely ill-tempered and, when let loose in a tank with another, will battle to the death in a flurry of fins and scales. The fish are so aggressive that they will often kill themselves trying to attack other fish in neighboring jars or tanks. Similar events are staged with cocks.

HILL TRIBES AND TREKKING

The flood of camera-toting tourists has changed many hill-tribe villages in North Thailand, turning them into bastions of commercialism. Be wary of tour guides advertising "newly discovered" or "non-touristy" villages. Ask around when picking a company and talk to fellow travelers; decent operation make reports from former customers available. Treks affiliated with guest houses are generally safer bets than the packages arranged by independent organizations.

In an effort to regulate this industry, the TAT publishes a list of trekking agencies, indicating those that use licensed guides (guides who have studied at the Tribal Research Institute in Chiang Mai). New TAT regulations also require that trekking companies, guides, and customers be registered with the tourist police. They will file a copy of your passport photo page before you set out. Reputable companies are also members of the Jungle Tour Club of Northern Thailand. Make sure your guides speak English and the languages of the villages on your itinerary.

Trek costs vary, depending on duration, destination, starting point, and the number in the group traveling. In Chiang Mai, a three-day, trek including elephant-riding and rafting cost around 1800฿. From Pai, the same trek could cost 900฿. As insurance becomes mandatory, prices may rise. Begin treks as close as possible to where you want to go. Pure hiking treks are the cheapest.

Most companies provide insurance, food, sleeping arrangements, transportation, and extra supplies like small backpacks, but **check beforehand.** Buy water along the way. Go in a group of eight or fewer, since smaller groups are less disruptive to the isolated social systems you will be visiting. If you can afford it, the best way to learn about hill-tribe culture is by hiring a personal guide (about 500฿ per day).

Health and Security

Try to gauge how rigorous the different treks are and bring a personal **first aid kit** (even if the company claims they provide it), sunscreen, a hat, mosquito repellent, and long clothing. Some regions contain malarial mosquitoes.

Before taking a trek, try to find a safe place to leave your valuables while you are gone. The TAT recommends that trekkers leave their valuables in a bank safety deposit box; there have been numerous reports of credit cards being lifted from guest house "security" boxes. **Bandits** have been known to raid trekking groups. Should this occur, it would be best to give your belongings to the bandits to avoid physical harm.

TAT discourages independent trekking. Unfriendly bandits, hill tribes, Kuomintang, and Shan United Army poppy cultivators get very angry when people wander into their fields. Not only that, but periodic border skirmishes are dangerous places for travelers. Some people have accidently wandered into Burma, and have had great trouble getting back out.

Trekking Etiquette

Don't expect to be welcomed into a village like a long-lost friend. Most villages have seen their fair share of foreigners, and many guides make no attempt to establish any sort of bond with the villagers. Hill tribes have no control over the organization and staging of treks, even though they are the main attraction. **Always ask before taking photographs.** Some people or even whole villages may object. Even if your guide says it's OK, ask permission of the specific people you want to photograph or record on video. Respect people, space, and things—particularly hill-tribe beliefs, and be careful about what you touch. For example, the gate at the entrance to Akha villages marks the point past which spirits may not enter; don't touch this. *The Hill Tribes of Northern Thailand,* which has a phrasebook section, is available at the Tribal Research Institute, and Lonely Planet puts out the useful *Hill Tribe Phrasebook.*

The hill-tribe societies are rapidly being integrated into Thai society. Their unique, centuries-old cultures are changing, and there's no question that tourism speeds the process. Many trails are littered with plastic water bottles and trash. If you want to be respectful, consider bringing bags to pick up after yourself and others.

When to Go

Of Northern Thailand's three distinct seasons, the cool season (Nov.-Feb.) is the best time to go trekking. The vegetation is at its lushest, and temperatures are usually in the mid-20s by day, falling to near freezing at night. In the rainy season (July-Oct.) the paths are muddy, and the raging rivers make rafting fun, but more dangerous. In the hot season (March-June) the land is parched and the air is dry.

CENTRAL THAILAND

The fertile central region of Thailand, also known as the Chao Phraya River Basin, stretches from Hua Hin in the south all the way up to Nakhon Sawan in the north. The people of the region speak the central Thai dialect, which is considered normal conversational Thai. As a region, its people are the wealthiest, in large part because Bangkok is its major metropolis.

Historically, the area has supported great cultures and civilizations with its fields of rice, but has also strained under the devastation of numerous wars. World War II and numerous conflicts with the Burmese have redefined borders several times and left ruins, both ancient and modern, strewn about the countryside. The area now seems to have entered a period of relative calm and prosperity. There is talk of opening the border between Burma and Thailand—an amazing leap of progress, considering the long tensions between the two. But in the shadow of high diplomacy, the Mon and Karen people wage an unacknowledged struggle for survival as their culture and existence continue to be eroded by political oppression, economic modernization, and, in the past decade, touristic invasion.

Ayutthaya constantly inspires awe with the magnitude of its temple ruins and monuments. Lush green landscapes fanning west of Bangkok are the background for Kanchanaburi, which attracts travelers to the banks of the River Kwai and the province's many national parks. Southbound buses and trains wind their way through the beginnings of peninsular Thailand, a teaser for the snady playgrounds of the south. Due to the proximity to Bangkok, the beaches here attract local travelers and are not overrun with *farang*. In the middle of it all, Bangkok serves as the region's, and the country's, hub—the massive brain, for the body that is Thailand.

■ Bangkok กรุงเทพ

Bangkok's Thai name, Krung Thep, means "City of Angels." Like its American equivalent, however, it often seems a few cherubs short of the celestial city. Whole showrooms of BMWs and Mercedes meet at each intersection, spewing carbon monoxide. Seething legions fight for territory on the sidewalks and protrude from every bus. The unsleeping, predatory heat and humidity reduce crisp clothing to saline sludge in seconds, coating exposed skin with a sweat-soot gel. When the umpteenth tout insists that your life will be incomplete without his ride, his Thai massage, or his sister, you'll be forgiven for imagining that Bangkok is just modernity gone haywire in a muggier climate.

Bangkok was not fashioned in a design studio under the careful gaze of planners; it was hewn from unsuspecting paddies by the double-edged sword of Thailand's burgeoning economy. In the past two decades, the standard of living has skyrocketed: Nintendo and Lexus have brought joy to the lives of millions of Thais, as have modern medicine, education, and technology. Yet, an ever-surging population of seven million saps resources from the countryside, swamps the inadequate infrastructure, and brutalizes the environment. Bangkok may be one of Southeast Asia's leading economic centers, but newly built high-rises must pierce a smoggy haze to find the sky.

The city's idiosyncratic modernization is something of a marvel. Wide-eyed *farang* witness trigger-happy Buddhist monks preserving Kodak moments with state-of-the-art camcorders, while well-heeled businessmen set aside cellular phones to pray at wayside shrines. As the permanent residence of the Royal Family, the government seat, and the nation's center of commerce and culture, it comes as no surprise that this tinsel town offers the most creature comforts anywhere in Thailand. The city's sights are impressive as well: an array of magnificent temples, historical sites, parks, monuments, and museums will stall your camera shutter. And in more serene moments, the open-minded observer will find the everyday fabric of the city worthy of thoughtful scrutiny.

GETTTNG THERE AND AWAY

> Be wary of touts offering free advice outside the station; there are rip-off artists everywhere looking for plump foreign wallets.

By Plane

Flights land at **Don Muang International Airport,** 25km north of the city center (tel. 535 12 54, 535 13 86 for departure info.). To find your way into Bangkok, wait for a ticket for a public taxi from an authorized vendor to the left of the left-hand exit (200-300฿ per car). A limousine counter to the right of the left-hand exit offers rides to any hotel (500฿ per person). For the thrifty, the right exit leads to the **bus stop.** A list of bus fares, destinations, and schedules is available at the **TAT (Tourist Author-**

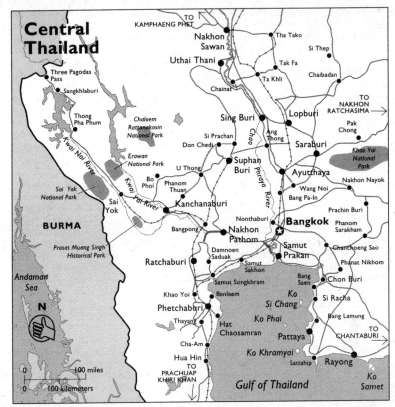

Central
Thailand

TO
KAMPHAENG PHET

Three Pagodas
Pass
Sangkhlaburi

Thong
Pha Phum

Chaloem
Rattanakosin
National Park

Erawan
National Park

Sai Yok
National Park

Sai
Yok

BURMA

Prasat Muang Singh
Historical Park

Andaman
Sea

N

0   100 miles
0   100 kilometers

Nakhon
Sawan

Uthai Thani

Tha Tako

Si Thep

Tak Fa

Ta Khli

Chaibadan

Chainat

TO
NAKHON
RATCHASIMA

Sing Buri

Lopburi

Pak
Chong

Si Prachan

Ang
Thong

Saraburi

Khao Yai
National
Park

Don Chedi

Suphan
Buri

Ayutthaya

U Thong

Wang Noi

Nakhon Nayok

Bo
Phoi

Phanom
Thuan

Bang Pa-In

Prachin Buri

Kanchanaburi

Nonthaburi

Bangkok

Phanom
Sarakham

Bangpong

Nakhon
Pathom

Samut
Prakan

Chanchoeng Sao

Damnoen
Saduak

Phanat Nikhom

Ratchaburi

Samut
Sakhon

Samut Songkhram

Bang
Saen

Chon Buri

Banlaem

Ko
Si Chang

Si Racha

Khao Yoi

Bang Lamung

Phetchaburi

Ko Phai

Thayang

Hat
Chaosamran

Pattaya

TO
CHANTABURI

Cha-Am

Ko Khramyai

Hua Hin

Sattahip

Rayong

TO
PRACHUAP
KHIRI KHAN

Gulf of Thailand

Ko
Samet

Kwai Noi River

Kwai Yai River

Chao Phraya River

ity of Thailand) **info center** (open 8am-midnight), the middle counter in the row near the exit. At bus terminal 2 you can take the new A/C airport bus (every 15min., 5am-11pm) to almost anywhere in town; ask for a bus schedule with a map. Across from the TAT counter are several currency **exchange booths;** the Thai Military Bank and Krung Thai Bank are open 24 hours. A **24-hour tourist police booth** near the right-hand exit offers English-speaking assistance. Flights out of Bangkok are subject to taxes of 250฿ for international and 30฿ for domestic.

By Train

All trains coming into Bangkok end at **Hualamphong Railway Station,** (tel. 223 70 10) on Rama IV Rd., which is a perpetual madhouse. The dearth of seating means that travelers sprawl on the floor. Inside, to the left of the main entrance, are a **police booth** and a **luggage storage center** (open daily 4am-10:30pm; 20฿ per day). To the right are newspaper stands and food stalls. There is an **info booth** in the center of the station by the platform with schedules in English and fares. Around the corner to the left is a Bangkok Bank **exchange booth** (8am-6:30pm) with a 24-hour ATM that takes Visa and American Express for cash advances. There is also a small **post office** outside the main entrance (open 8:30am-5pm).

Hopping into one of the numerous metered taxis or *tuk-tuk* waiting at the side entrance of the station is the best way to reach town. Otherwise, a walk down Rama IV Rd. (which begins at the station) will take you to a bus stop. A/C bus #1 and regular buses #25 and 40 go to Siam Square and continue down Sukhumvit Rd.; regular bus #23 goes to Banglamphu (Khaosan Rd. area).

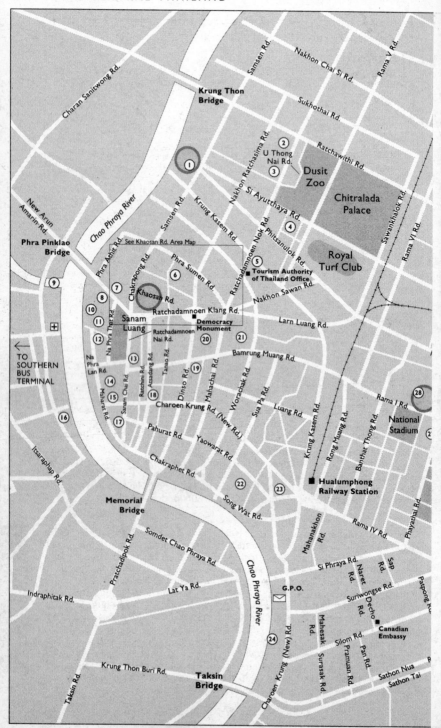

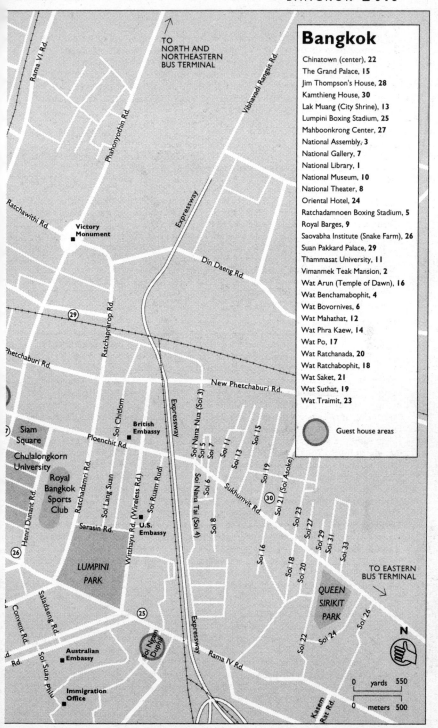

TO
NORTH AND
NORTHEASTERN
BUS TERMINAL

Bangkok

Chinatown (center), 22
The Grand Palace, 15
Jim Thompson's House, 28
Kamthieng House, 30
Lak Muang (City Shrine), 13
Lumpini Boxing Stadium, 25
Mahboonkrong Center, 27
National Assembly, 3
National Gallery, 7
National Library, 1
National Museum, 10
National Theater, 8
Oriental Hotel, 24
Ratchadamnoen Boxing Stadium, 5
Royal Barges, 9
Saovabha Institute (Snake Farm), 26
Suan Pakkard Palace, 29
Thammasat University, 11
Vimanmek Teak Mansion, 2
Wat Arun (Temple of Dawn), 16
Wat Benchamabophit, 4
Wat Bovornives, 6
Wat Mahathat, 12
Wat Phra Kaew, 14
Wat Po, 17
Wat Ratchanada, 20
Wat Ratchabophit, 18
Wat Saket, 21
Wat Suthat, 19
Wat Traimit, 23

Guest house areas

Rama VI Rd.
Phahonyothin Rd.
Vibhavadi Rangsit Rd.
Ratchawithi Rd.
Victory Monument
Expressway
Din Daeng Rd.
Ratchaprarop Rd.
Phetchaburi Rd.
New Phetchaburi Rd.
Siam Square
Chulalongkorn University
Royal Bangkok Sports Club
Henri Dunant Rd.
Ratchadamri Rd.
Soi Lang Suan
Soi Chitlom
Ploenchit Rd.
British Embassy
Witthayu Rd. (Wireless Rd.)
Soi Ruam Rudi
Soi Nana Nua (Soi 3)
Soi 5
Soi 7
Soi 11
Soi 13
Soi 15
Soi 19
Soi Nana Tai (Soi 4)
Soi 9
Soi 8
Sukhumvit Rd.
Soi 21 (Soi Asoke)
Soi 23
Soi 27
Soi 29
Soi 31
Soi 33
Soi 16
Soi 18
Soi 20
U.S. Embassy
Sarasin Rd.
Convent Rd.
Saladaeng Rd.
LUMPINI PARK
Australian Embassy
Immigration Office
Soi Ngam Duphli
Soi Suan Phlu
Rama IV Rd.
Expressway
QUEEN SIRIKIT PARK
Soi 22
Soi 24
Soi 26
TO EASTERN BUS TERMINAL
Kasem Rat Rd.

N

| 0 | yards | 550 |
| 0 | meters | 500 |

By Bus

The national bus transportation system is cheap and extensive. For virtually every destination, there is the choice of either A/C (blue) or non-A/C (orange) buses. Doing without A/C will typically halve the cost of traveling, but you will pay with your health. Fares listed are for A/C buses; non-A/C equivalents are approximately half. Outbound buses leave from four different terminals in Bangkok depending upon the destination. Beware of touts and other artful dodgers at bus stations, and safeguard your valuables.

Eastern Bus Terminal (for A/C tel. 392 92 27; for non-A/C tel. 391 25 04), on Sukhumvit Rd., before Soi 42. To get there take local A/C bus #1, 8, 11, or 13, or regular bus #2, 25, 38, 40, 48, or 98. Open 24hr. To: **Trat** (14 per day, 6-7hr., 140฿) and **Si Racha** (every 40 min., 5:40am-8pm, 2hr., 52฿).

Northeastern Bus Terminal (for A/C tel. 279 44 84, for non-A/C tel. 271 01 01), on Phahonyothin Rd. near Chatuchak Park. Take local A/C bus #2, 3, 9, 10, 12, or 13, or regular bus #26, 34, 39, 63, 104, or 112. To: **Nakhon Ratchasima** (every 15min., 7:15am-10:30pm, 5-6hr., 115฿); **Khon Kaen** (18 per day, 8-9hr., 193฿); and **Ubon Ratchathani** (7 per day, 9-11hr., 287฿; VIP at 8pm, 400฿).

Northern Bus Terminal, same location and phone number as Northeastern Bus Terminal. To: **Chiang Mai** (15 per day, 10-11hr., 352฿); **Sukhothai** (3 per day, 7hr., 218฿); and **Ayutthaya** (every 30min., 6am-6:30pm, 2hr., 40฿).

Southern Regular Bus Terminal (tel. 434 55 57), on Boromat Chonnani (Pinklao-Nakhonchaisi) Rd. To get to the terminal take regular bus #124 or 127. To: **Phuket** (4:50pm, 14hr., 380฿); **Phetchaburi** (every 45min. 6am-8:15pm, 3hr., 65฿); and **Kanchanaburi** (every 15min., 5:30am-8pm, 2hr., 65฿).

ORIENTATION

Bangkok's raw urban sprawl lacks any formal districting, making navigation a daunting challenge for the uninitiated. Tourists can make sense of the most important areas of the city, however, by using the Chao Phraya River, which curves in an "S" shape through the city, as a reference point. The bulk of Bangkok's sights, sounds, and commercial activity lie east of the river. Four bridges straddle the river from north to south: **Krung Thon, Phra Pinklao, Memorial,** and **Taksin.** East of Krung Thon Bridge is the **Dusit** area, home to the Dusit Zoo, government buildings, and Chitralada Palace, the residence of the Royal Family. To the southwest of Dusit, nestled in the top curve of the "S," is the **Banglamphu/Ko Rattanakosin** area, commonly known as the **old city.** Ko Rattanakosin refers to the southern half of the district, thick with palaces and temples, while Banglamphu describes the budget-travel-friendly **Khaosan Road** area near Phra Pinklao Bridge. Just south of Banglamphu and directly north of Memorial Bridge lies the **Yaowarat/Pahurat** area, otherwise known as **Chinatown** and **Indiatown.** Lying against the bottom curve of the "S" and just east of Taksin Bridge is **Silom,** or the **Financial District,** where jewelry stores and raunchy Patpong Rd. coexist side by side. Farthest away from the river to the east is the **Sukhumvit Road** area, a wealthy Thai neighborhood, where many pubs and clubs have sprung up, especially to the north along **Royal City Avenue.** Smack dab in the middle of all these districts is **Siam Square,** Bangkok's prime shopping district and home to many high-class hotels.

GETTING AROUND

Maneuvering in the city is a nightmare on wheels. Improvements are in the works but for now, every hour is rush hour, and visitors can expect to be bogged down in a vehicular morass even at 3am. The gaping jaws of the traffic monster can be avoided by traveling between 10am and 4pm during the day. Tangled tie-ups occur between 4pm and 7pm, when traffic moves at an average of 4km per hour and the fumes are so thick you can eat them. With the present construction of the rail system, expect traffic jams to last further into the evening.

By Bus

The shiny, happy bus system, run by the Bangkok Metropolitan Transit Authority (BMTA), supplies the most inexpensive and efficient means of transportation. Routes are extensive and usually serviced by a large number of buses, so there's minimal waiting time for the next bus. There are three types of buses: blue-and-white regular buses (no fan or A/C), red-and-cream regular buses (fan-cooled), and dark blue-and-white buses (A/C). The fare on the blue-and-white bus, which is slowly being phased out, is 2.5฿, while the more common red-and-cream bus charges 3.5฿. The fare on an A/C bus depends on the distance traveled (6-16฿). Pay all fares to the uniformed officer who walks through the bus.

The fiery orange-red and the pea-green buses (3.5฿ and 2.5฿ respectively), also run by the BMTA, are smaller, pernicious contraptions with no published routes. Since route numbers are often duplicated, make sure you get on the right type of bus, not just the right route number. Grrr. Airport buses run 6am-8pm; other buses run 5am-midnight or a bit later. Night services charge more, but they are few and far between.

It's best to sit (or, more likely, stand) near the front of the bus, as pickpockets can be more easily avoided. Since traffic travels on the left side of the road, sitting on the left (curb) side of non-A/C buses lessens the risk of asphyxiation. If you need help identifying the destination of the bus, ask the fare collector (not the driver). The following is a list of the major bus routes:

Regular Buses (Light Blue-and-White)

#1: Wat Po—Yaowarat Rd. (Chinatown)—General Post Office—Oriental Hotel.

#15: Banglamphu (Phra Athit Rd., Phra Sumen Rd.)—Sanam Luang—Democracy Monument—Wat Saket—Siam Sq.—Ratchadamri Rd.—Lumpini Park—along Silom Rd.

#18 and 28: Vimarnmek Teak Museum—Dusit Zoo—Chitralada Palace—Victory Monument.

#23 (formerly #53): Note that the #23 bus was the #53 in a past life; some buses still say #53, but #23 is the correct number. It runs Samsen Rd. (National Library)—Phra Athit Rd.—Sanam Luang—Wat Po—near Pahurat and Yaowarat.

#25: Wat Phra Kaew—Wat Po-Charoen Krung Rd.—Rama IV Rd. (near Hualamphong Railway Station)—Phayathai Rd.—Mahboonkrong Centre—Siam Sq.—World Trade Centre—Ploenchit Rd.—Sukhumvit Rd. to outer Bangkok.

#48: Sanam Chai Rd. (just east of Wat Po)—Bamrung Muang Rd.—Siam Sq.—all along Sukhumvit Rd.

#59: Airport—Victory Monument—Pahonyothin Rd. (American Express office)—Phetburi Rd.—Lanluang—Democracy Monument—Sanam Luang.

#74: Rama IV Rd. (outside Soi Ngam Duphli)—Lumpini Park—Ratchadamri Rd.—World Trade Centre—Pratunam-Ratchaprarop Rd.—Victory Monument.

#115: Silom—Rama IV Rd. (near Soi Ngam Duphli)—all along Rama IV Rd. until it meets Sukhumvit Rd.

#116: Sathon Nua Rd.—all along Rama IV Rd. (passes near Soi Ngam Duphli)—Sathon Tai Rd.

#204: Victory Monument—Ratchaprarop Rd.—World Trade Centre—Siam Sq.—Bamrung Muang Rd.

Air-Conditioned Buses (Dark Blue-and-White)

#1: Wat Po—Charoen Krung Rd.—Rama IV Rd. (near Hualamphong Railway Station)—Phayathai (Mahboonkrong Centre)—Siam Sq.—along Sukhumvit Rd.

#8: Sanam Luang—Bamrung Muang—Rama I—Ploenchit—Sukhumvit to outer Bangkok.

#10: National Assembly (Ratchawithi Rd.)—Dusit Zoo—Chitralada Palace—Victory Monument—Phahonyothin Rd. (American Express office)—Don Muang International Airport.

#11: Banglamphu Guest House Area (around Chakrapong Rd.)—Phra Sumen Rd.—Democracy Monument (Ratchadamnoen Klang Rd.)—Phetchaburi Rd.—World Trade Centre—Sukhumvit.

#15: Silom Rd. (corner of Silom and Charoen Krung)—Patpong and Bangkok Christian Hospital—Lumpini Park and Chulalongkorn Hospital—Ratchaprarop Rd. (near Victory Monument)—Din Daeng Rd.

By Taxi

Formerly, all fares were negotiable, but a 1992 law banned bargaining and introduced metered cabs (35฿ for 1km and 2฿ for each additional km and each minute spent stuck in traffic). Non-metered taxis are still around, but they are basically extinct. Unless you insist otherwise, taxi drivers may shut off the meter and attempt to bargain for a set fare; this can be particularly problematic for *farang*.

By Tuk-tuk

Like taxis, *tuk-tuk* (motor-tricycle) abound, and usually idle at the same locations as their four-wheeled brethren. *Tuk-tuk* can slither through dense traffic that brings taxis to a halt. Negotiation is key in using *tuk-tuk* and unless you are somewhat familiar with the going rate, you might fall prey to crafty drivers who will charge you twice that. Skillful negotiators, however, can get prices that are at least 30% cheaper than taxi fares.

By Motorcycle Taxi

Motorcycle taxis in Bangkok are usually identifiable by their drivers, who wear brightly colored vests. Located where taxis and *tuk-tuk* congregate, motorcycle taxis can zip through stand-still traffic and cost 10-25% less than *tuk-tuk*. Riding on a motorcycle taxi can be a risky affair, though. In theory, a helmet should be provided for the customer but this is not always done in practice. Tourists should insist upon one.

By Car

Travelers to Bangkok may want to avoid cars altogether, considering the ghoulish traffic and the perils of metro-motoring. A small sedan is typically 1000-1500฿ per day. Insurance is an extra 250฿. An International Driver's Permit and major credit cards are required. Rental agencies include **Avis,** 2/12 Witthayu Rd. (tel. 255 53 00), **Hertz,** 420 Sukhumvit Rd. 71 (tel. 391 04 61), and **National,** Maniya Building, 518/2 Ploenchit Rd. (tel. 255 68 37).

By Boat

The most convenient, expedient, and peaceful way to travel along the Chao Phraya River is by river-taxi—wooden boats along the back canals of the city. Boats run on a set route every 10 minutes from early morning until 7pm. Fares are 4-6฿ in most downtown areas. The main stops, from north to south, are: **Thewet** (for the National Library and Dusit guest houses), **Phra Athit** (for Khaosan Rd.-Banglamphu), **Rot Fai** (for Thonburi Railway Station and Royal Barges), **Chang** (for Wat Phra Kaew and Royal Palace), **Tiei** (for Wat Pho), **Ratchawong** (for Chinatown and Hualamphong), **Si Phraya** (for GPO) and **Oriental** (for the Oriental Hotel and Silom). Note that river taxis can easily be confused with smaller ferries that shuttle across the river from each landing for 1฿. A small sign identifies each pier (*tha*). Boat services also run to Nonthaburi and Ayutthaya. Ask at any pier for details.

PRACTICAL INFORMATION

The Latest Edition *Tour 'n Guide Map* to Bangkok available at tourist shops and guest houses, is a don't-leave-home-without-it map of the city (35฿). It includes all city bus and boat routes as well as important sights and landmarks.

Tourist Offices: TAT, 372 Bamrung Muang Rd. (tel. 226 00 60). Take regular bus #15 or A/C bus #8; get off as soon as it turns left onto Bamrung Muang heading away from Banglamphu. The office is at the intersection, inside the main courtyard below the water tower. A staff blessed with more enthusiasm than knowledge or resources hands out glossy leaflets. Open daily 8:30am-4:30pm.

Tourist Police: Division 1, Unico House, 4th Fl., 29/1 Soi Lang Suan, Ploenchit Rd. (tel. 652 17 20). Take regular buses #25, 40, and 48 to the corner of Ploenchit and Soi Lang Suan. English-speaking staff totals 500 and is vested with the same powers as the regular police. Also handles lost and found. Open daily 8am-4pm. **24-hr. booth,** opposite Dusit Thani Hotel in Lumpini Park (tel. 253 95 60). Regular bus #141, A/C bus #4, 5. **24-hr. booth,** Don Muang International Airport (tel. 535 16 41), 1st-floor lobby. Vans roam popular areas 24hr. **Emergency:** tel. 1699. **Tourist Assistance Centre:** tel. 282 81 29. Open daily 8am-midnight.

Tours and Travel: Many areas of Bangkok, especially tourist centers such as Khaosan Rd. and Soi Ngam Duphli, are replete with budget travel offices, which are often a part of or affiliated with a guest house. In Thailand, a truly legitimate "budget" travel agency, however, is as hard to come by. "VIP" tickets, often costing hundreds of extra baht, may actually only mean a spot at the front of the bus. **STA Travel,** Wall St. Tower, 14th fl.. 33 Suriwongse Rd. (tel. 233 25 82). Take regular bus #15 or A/C bus #5 to Silom Rd.; cut through Patpong Rd. to Suriwongse. Open Mon.-Fri. 8:30am-5pm, Sat. 8:30am-noon. **ETC Travel,** Royal Hotel, Rm. 318, 2 Ratchadamnoen Klang Ave. (tel. 224 48 00), near Atsadang Rd. Take regular bus #15. Member FIYTO. Open Mon.-Sat. 8:30am-5pm.

Embassies and Consulates: Australia, 37 Sathon Tai Rd. (tel. 287 26 80; fax 267 52 95). Regular bus #17, 22, 62, 67, 106, 116, 149. Open Mon.-Fri. 8:15am-12:15pm. **Cambodia,** 185 Ratchadamri Rd. (tel. 254 66 30). Consular services around the corner off Sarasin Rd. on the 1st *soi* on the left. Open Mon.-Fri. 8-11am. **Canada,** 11/F Boonmitr Bldg., 138 Silom Rd. (tel. 237 41 26; fax 236 64 63). Regular bus #115; A/C bus #2, 4, 5. Consular services Mon.-Fri. 7:30-11am. **Indonesia,** 600 New Phetchburi Rd. (tel. 252 3135). Open Mon.-Fri. 8:30am-noon and 1:30-3:30pm. **Ireland,** 205 United Flour Mill Bldg., 11th fl., Ratchawong Rd. (tel. 223 08 76). Open Mon.-Fri. 9am-noon and 1:30-4pm. **Laos,** Soi Rankapeng 39 Open Mon.-Fri. 9am-noon.Visa 300฿. 2-day processing. **Malaysia,** 15th Fl., Regent House Bldg., Ratchadamri Rd. (tel. 254 17 00). Open Mon.-Fri. 8:30-11:30am. **New Zealand,** 93 Witthayu (Wireless) Rd. (tel. 254 25 60; fax 235 90 45). Regular bus #13, 17, 62, 106. Open Mon.-Fri. 8:30-11:30am. **Singapore,** 129 S. Sathorn Rd., (tel. 286 21 11; fax 286 14 34). Open Mon.-Fri. 8:30am-noon. **South Africa,** 6/F Park Palace, 231 Soi Sarasin, Ratdamri Rd., (tel. 253 84 73; fax 243 84 77). **UK,** 1031 Witthayu (Wireless) Rd., 2nd Fl. (tel. 253 0191). Regular bus #13, 17, 62, 76. Open Mon.-Thurs. 8-11am, Fri. 8am-noon. **US,** 95 Witthayu (Wireless) Rd. (tel. 205 40 00; fax 254 29 90). Regular bus #13, 17, 62, 106. Consular services Mon.-Fri. 7:30-10am. **Vietnam,** 83/1 Wireless Rd., (tel. 251 72 02; fax 254 29 90). Open Mon.-Fri. 8:30-11:30am and 1:30-4pm. 3-4 day processing, visas 1200฿.

Currency Exchange: At least one exchange booth on every block in tourist areas; stiff competition keeps their rates almost equal. **Union Bank of Bangkok** is on Khaosan Rd. next to Grand Guest House. Open daily 7:30am-9pm. **Bangkok Metropolitan Bank Money Exchange** is at the corner of Suriwongse Rd. and Patpong 2 Rd. Open daily 1-11pm. **Bangkok Bank,** Soi 4 Sukhumvit Rd., is at the entrance of Nana Plaza. Open daily 7am-10pm.

American Express: IBM Building, 388 Pahonyothin Rd. (tel. 273 00 44) Open Mon.-Fri. 8:30am-5pm; **branch** and all **mail holding** at **Sea Tours Co. Ltd,** 128 Phayathai Plaza Bldg., 8th Fl. (tel. 216 57 83). Mail held for 60 days; no packages accepted. Open Mon.-Fri. 8:30am-noon and 1-4:30pm, Sat. 8:30-11:30am. Credit card authorization: call 273 00 22 (24hr.). **Lost traveler's checks:** call 273 52 96.

Luggage Storage: Hualamphong Railway Station, Rama IV Rd. (tel. 223 70 10). Open daily 4am-10:30pm. Also at most guest houses (for guests only), 5฿ per day; security may be iffy.

Pharmacies: A dime a dozen in Bangkok, but most are only open daily from 9am to 8pm. Plan ahead and stock up for medicinal or contraceptive needs. **New World Dept. Store (Banglamphu),** Krai Si Rd. entrance, 1st Fl. Open daily 8am-8pm. **Robinson Dept. Store (Silom/Financial),** Silom Rd., ground Fl. Open daily 10am-midnight. **Drug Store (Sukhumvit Rd.),** corner of Soi 21 (Asoke) Sukhumvit Rd. Open daily 8:30am-9pm.

Medical Services: The following have English-speaking doctors: **Bangkok Christian Hospital,** 124 Silom Rd. (tel. 233 69 81). Regular bus #115, A/C bus #2, 4, and 5. 24-hr. ambulance service. **Bamrungrad Hospital (Sukhumvit Rd.),** 33 Sukhumvit Rd. Soi 3 (tel. 253 02 50). One of the best private hospitals in Thailand. Open 24hr. **Chulalongkorn Hospital (Sukhumvit Rd.),** Rama IV Rd. (tel. 252 81 31), on the corner of Ratchadamri Rd. Ambulance service. **Siriraj Hospital (Thonburi),** 2 Pran Nok Rd. (tel. 419 70 00). Take regular bus #19 from Sanam Luang. Thailand's best and largest public hospital, it's the site of daily total chaos. **24-hr. ambulance service.** Cheapest vaccinations at **Red Cross Society's Queen Saovabha Institute** on Rama IV Rd.

Emergency: Tourist Police: tel. 1699. **Police:** tel. 191 or, for military police, 123. **Fire:** tel. 199. **Ambulance:** tel. 252 21 71.

Post Offices: GPO (tel. 234 95 30), on Charoen Krung Rd. next to Soi 32. Regular bus #1, 16, 35, 75, 93. **EMS** to Europe and North America. Open Mon.-Fri. 8am-8pm, Sat.-Sun. 8am-1pm. *Poste Restante* held for 2 months (Mon.-Fri. 8am-8pm, Sat.-Sun. 8am-1pm). **Packaging booth** (open Mon.-Fri. 8:30am-4:30pm, Sat. 9am-noon). **Branch offices: Banglamphu,** on the *soi* behind Sweety Guest House, parallel to Ratchadamnoen Klang Rd. Open Mon.-Fri. 8am-5pm, Sat. 8am-noon. Overseas telephone office on 2nd floor (open daily 7am-11pm). **Silom/Financial,** 113/6-7 Suriwongse Centre Rd., near Soi Than Tawan. Overseas phone. (Open Mon.-Fri. 8:30am-4:30pm, Sat. 9am-noon). **Sukhumvit Rd.,** 118-122 Sukhumvit Rd. (tel. 251 79 72), between Soi 4 (Nana Tai) and the Landmark Plaza. Another is at Soi 23, Sukhumvit Rd. (tel. 258 41 97), on the right. Both have EMS and overseas calls. Both open Mon.-Fri. 8:30am-5:30pm, Sat. 9am-noon. **Postal code:** 10500.

Telephones: To make **domestic calls,** look for "Fonepoint" (coin) or "Cardphone" (card) booths, usually in business and tourist centers. **International telephone calls** can be made at hotels, businesses, some guest houses, and some post offices. A sure place is the **Communications Authority of Thailand (CAT) Telecom** on Charoen Krung Rd., next to the GPO. Open 24hr. Fax and telex services. International phone cards (250฿ or 500฿) sold. **Telephone code** (including Nonthaburi, Samut Prakan, and Pathum Thani): 2.

ACCOMMODATIONS

The distinction between a classy guest house and a run-down hotel is a fine one. Whatever your quarters, confirm the price, know what it includes, and check the room carefully. In the summer, a fan is essential. Most decent, economical lodgings fill up quickly and often don't take reservations.

Banglamphu/Ko Rattanakosin

Every year thousands of travelers make a pilgrimage to the mecca of guest houses in Banglamphu, **Khaosan Rd.** Generally, the farther you move from Khaosan Rd., the more peaceful the area and the more regulations against alcohol, smoking, and prostitution. In terms of choice, accessibility, economy, and safety-in-numbers, Khaosan Rd. is where it's at.

Budget Accommodations:

Peachy Guest House, 10 Phra Athit Rd. (tel. 281 64 71). Airport bus #59 stops right across the street. Surrounding a pleasant courtyard, it offers the best value for A/C rooms with trimmings. Large, clean rooms and baths. Towels, toilet paper, and cable TV also available. Writing table, chair, and dresser in every room. Singles 85฿. Doubles 130฿, with A/C 200฿, and shower 230฿, with A/C and private bath 350-600฿. 50฿ deposit for key. Reserve during high season.

Merry V. Guest House, 33-35 Soi Chana Songklam. From Phra Athit Rd. take the alley across from the pier and then take a left. A new-looking red brick building with a restaurant serving some of the better food in Khaosan. This guest house lies peacefully next to a wat but just seconds away from the action in Khaosan Rd. Singles 100฿. Doubles 140฿. Triples 210฿.

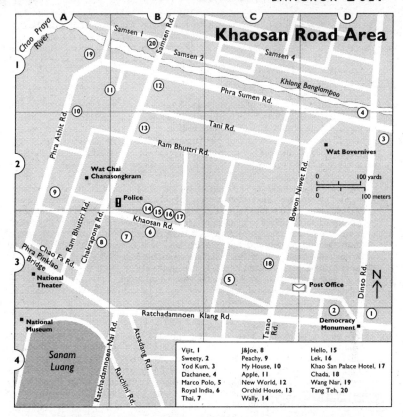

Khaosan Road Area

Vijit, 1	J&Joe, 8	Hello, 15
Sweety, 2	Peachy, 9	Lek, 16
Yod Kum, 3	My House, 10	Khao San Palace Hotel, 17
Dachanee, 4	Apple, 11	Chada, 18
Marco Polo, 5	New World, 12	Wang Nar, 19
Royal India, 6	Orchid House, 13	Tang Teh, 20
Thai, 7	Wally, 14	

J & Joe Guest House, 1 Trok Mayom, Chakrapong Rd. (tel. 281 29 49). Turn left from Khaosan Rd. onto Chakrapong Rd. and take the 1st alley left. Ideal, inexpensive digs for those seeking tranquility and cleaner air. Beautiful old teakwood house, tastefully decorated in pink and mauve, with frilly gingerbread trim. Singles 90฿. Doubles 150฿, with A/C 200฿. Breakfast 25-35฿.

Apple 2 Guest House, Trok Kai Chae, 11 Phra Sumen Rd. (tel. 281 12 19). Turn left from Phra Sumen Rd. into a narrow alley and walk 200m to the end. Lobby is the downstairs of a quiet, old, teakwood home. "Mama," though a friendly manager, is definitely in charge here, treating all her guests like family (she'll yell at you to turn off a light). Smallish but sanitary salons; common bathrooms are also well-scrubbed. Dorms 60฿. Singles 90฿. Doubles 120฿. Reservations recommended during high season.

Hello Guest House, 63-65 Khaosan Rd. (tel. 281 85 79). One of the original guest houses along Khaosan Rd. and one of the most popular. Strict management runs a tight ship despite throngs of backpackers and busy location. Singles 90฿. Doubles 120฿, with window 140฿. Bustling restaurant downstairs has movie marathons and is a good place to meet fellow travelers in Bangkok (dishes 35-80฿). No alcohol or smoking in room.

Mid-range Accommodations:

Marco Polo Hostel, 108/7-10 Khaosan Rd. (tel. 281 17 15), down the alley to the left of the Bank of Asia exchange booth. Spacious 2-tiered foyer houses a restaurant made popular by daily movie marathons (dishes 25-60฿). For ultimate temperature control, both fan and A/C are in all rooms, along with private bath. Singles 250-300฿. Doubles 250-300฿. Reservations during high season.

THAILAND

Khaosan Palace Hotel, 139 Khaosan Rd. (tel. 282 05 78). Take the alley to the right of Nita's Boutique.Curved columns and wooden oriental dragons in the lobby. Arguably the best digs on Khaosan Rd. Certainly the most expensive. Large private bath with hot water in each chamber. Singles 250฿, with A/C 400฿. Doubles 350฿, with A/C 500฿. Triples 500฿, with A/C 650฿.

Dusit/Government Centre

Home to various government ministries and agencies, as well as the Royal Family, the area has only limited accommodations for the proletariat. A cluster of friendly, offbeat, and clean guest houses offering much-needed quiet has popped up behind the National Library on **Si Ayutthaya Rd.** Since most are relatively new, they are generally in good condition. Management is more laid-back, blending well with the Dusit atmosphere.

Sawatdee Guest House, 71 Si Ayutthaya Rd. Soi 16 (tel. 281 07 57). Sawatdee means hello in Thai, and guests are certainly made to feel welcome here. Not only does the new green wallpaper make the place look attractive, but the low rates and friendly service will make it hard for you to say good-bye. Towels at front desk. Dorms (A/C when full) 40฿. Singles 60-80฿. Doubles 100-120฿. Family special 200฿. Overseas calling in lobby. No smoking or alcohol in rooms. Call ahead for vacancy info in the winter, but reservations are not taken.

Shanti Lodge, 37 Si Ayutthaya Rd. Soi 16 (tel. 281 24 97). Thrives on the 'make salad, not war' philosophy. Restaurant serves only veggie food, and all the staff are vegetarians. Aquarians will delight in the fish pond with turtles, while those seeking enlightenment can buy natural shampoos and conditioners made at the Buddhist temple of Santi Asoke. Perhaps to achieve universal harmony, only dorms are available (70฿). No smoking or alcohol.

Bangkok Youth Hostel (HI), 25/2 Phitsanulok Rd. (tel. 281 03 61), about 300m from the intersection with Samsen Rd. The only hostel in Bangkok, the fan-cooled building has acceptably sanitary dorm-style bunk beds (70฿) and spacious, pristine singles/doubles (250฿). The newer A/C building has awesome dorm-style, sex-segregated rooms (90฿), as well as narrow singles (250฿) and twin doubles (300฿). Private rooms have small, clean, personal baths, but only A/C rooms have hot showers. Go to the old building for singles/doubles, and the new one for dorms. Overseas calls. No smoking or alcohol. HI members only (non-members can buy a year-long membership 300฿). No reservations.

Chinatown/Pahurat/Hualamphong

Little has changed around here in the last few decades—still the same frenzied commerce, busy sidewalks, and ungodly population density. Guest houses and hotels line **Yaowarat, Pahurat, Chakraphet,** and **Rong Muang Rd.** Some are rip-offs, others make only Asians feel welcome, and many are what the Thais call "lizard hotels." Be forewarned that most of the few guest houses here are either really expensive, or dirty. Despite this, and the somewhat dangerous character of the neighborhood, there are some acceptable options.

TT2 Guest House, 516-518 Soi Sawang, Si Phraya Rd. (tel. 236 29 46). From Rama IV Rd. by Hualamphong, turn right on Mahanakhon Rd., then take the 1st left, and walk 10min. to the end of the *soi*. Set deep within a quiet residential neighborhood, it's the only exceptional place to stay in Chinatown. This place has achieved cult status among tourists, in part due to the signs plastered on each lamp post within a 1-mi. radius, but also for its spotless facilities and friendly management. Lobby doubles as a restaurant (open 5:30am-midnight). Dorms 90฿. Singles 160-180฿. Doubles (2 twin-sized beds) 200฿. Overseas calling and fax from the lobby. Reserve 2-3 wks. ahead in high season.

New Empire Hotel, 572 Yaowarat Rd. (tel. 234 69 90), near Ratchawong Rd. Convenient location, full amenities, and wheelchair access. Both staff and clientele speak more Cantonese than Thai. Pleasant lodgings offer telephones, A/C, and bathrooms with bathtubs. Singles and doubles 440-495฿, with TV 550฿. Triples 600-660฿. Fax service. Reserve 1 day ahead in high season.

Silom/Financial District

A couple of decades ago, Silom Rd. still charted its course through rice paddies, but the economic boom of the 80s made it the financial center of Thailand, with a pack of glitzy hotels in tow. The wallet-friendly guest house is still alive and well, but many are quickie crash pads renting rooms by the hour. Most budget establishments are located 2km from Silom Rd. along **Soi Ngam Duphli** and **Soi Si Bamphen,** which are off Rama IV Rd. near Lumpini Tower.

Sala Thai Daily Mansion, 15 Soi Sapankoo (tel. 287 14 36). Walking on Soi Si Bum-phren away from Soi Ngam Duphli, take the first *soi* to the left and then take a right. Sunny home run by a patient bibliophile. Rooms are smaller than the name implies, but have a desk, bookshelf, and wall-mounted fan. Sitting area with cable TV on each floor. Closes at 9pm. Singles and doubles 150฿. Larger rooms 200฿. Restaurant (dishes 25-40฿).

Lee Guest House #2, 12 Soi Sapankoo (tel. 679 70 45). Right next to Sala Thai Daily Mansion. This family-run establishment offers clean, tidy, fan-cooled rooms at a reasonable price. Singles 100฿. Doubles 150฿.

Anna Guest House, 21/30 Soi Ngam Duphli (tel. 286 8830), on the left-hand side of the road coming from Rama IV Rd. Rooms are fairly large and tidy; some have precipitous balconies, but nothing out of the ordinary. Colorful Anna, however, brightens up the place. Prices negotiable. Singles 80฿, for larger room 100฿. Doubles 120฿, with balcony 150฿, with bath 180฿.

ETC Guest House, 5/3 Soi Ngam Duphli (tel. 287 14 77), near Anna. Walk inside ETC Travel Centre to find the lodgings. Large, clean rooms with polished teak floors and small alarm clock. Hot showers. Singles 140฿, with A/C 220฿. Doubles 180฿, with A/C 280฿. Triples 240฿ (fan only). Free continental breakfast.

Siam Sq./Pratunam

Basking in the glow of Bangkok's biggest shopping malls, you'd expect the accommodations around the Siam Sq. area to deliver some luxuries. And they do: private baths, towels, toilet paper, soap, blankets, telephones (for overseas and local calls), dressers, writing tables, hot water, and sometimes even satellite TV and refrigerators with mini-bars. Most of the better lodgings are on **Soi Kasem San I** off Rama I Rd., across from the National Stadium Complex. Much quieter than Khaosan Rd. and practically tout-free, the *soi* claims a loyal following of travelers who swear they'd never stay anywhere else.

Pranee Building, 931/12 Soi Kasem San 1 (tel. 216 31 81). Another entrance is through the Wat Watana Yonta Co. on Rama I Rd., at the bus stop near Soi Kasem San 1. Springy feel with floral bedspreads and pictures in good-sized, pristine rooms. A/C rooms are much better value, since they have a balcony and western-style flush toilets. Singles and doubles 300฿, with A/C 350฿, with hot water and A/C 400฿. Doubles with twin beds, A/C, and hot water 500฿. Triples with 1 large and 1 small bed 600฿. No alcohol in rooms.

The Bed and Breakfast, 36/42-43 Soi Kasem San 1 (tel. 215 30 04). A family-run establishment—the kind of place that will lend you an umbrella when it rains. Swell ambience and a hushed location. Rooms are a bit small, but have A/C, telephone, and quaint trimmings. Satellite TV and complimentary continental breakfast in the bright dining room. Fax service. Lock up at 11pm; after that, rely on the night guard. Singles 380฿. Doubles (with 1 larger bed) 480฿, with twin beds 550฿. Triples 650฿. No alcohol. Call 3 days ahead for reservations Nov.-Feb.

Sukhumvit Rd. Area

Like Siam Sq., the Sukhumvit area has few guest houses and high prices, but the side *soi* off Sukhumvit Rd. bear many of Bangkok's trendiest nightspots. Everything is accessible from Siam Sq. or Banglamphu by A/C buses #8 and 11, and regular buses #25 and 48. You should consider staying in the area if you plan to take a bus down the east coast, since the Eastern Bus Terminal is at the Ekamai inter-

THAILAND

section, a few km down Sukhumvit Rd. and easily accessible by A/C bus #8 or regular bus #48.

S.V. Guest House, 19/35-36 Soi 19, Sukhumvit Rd. (tel. 253 06 06). One of the better deals in Bangkok; pleasant but subdued atmosphere. Each of the large, neat rooms sports a dresser, parlor area with mirror, flip-flops, firm springy bed, and a phone for local and overseas calls. Hygienic, tiled common bathrooms. Singles 250฿, with A/C 300฿. Doubles 300฿, with A/C 350฿. Triples with bath and A/C 400฿. Some French and German spoken. Call for reservations during high season.

Uncle Rey's Guest House, 7/10 Soi 4 (Nana Tai), Sukhumvit Rd. (tel. 252 55 65), on the left across from Nana Hotel. Follow the signs through the alley with the food vendors, then walk to the back left corner of the parking lot. Roomy chambers labeled with flower names include dresser, small wicker sitting area, well-kept bath with hot-water shower, and spine-tingling A/C. Phones for local and overseas calls in most rooms. Singles and doubles on 3rd and 4th floors 400฿, 1st and 2nd floors 450฿, with twin beds 550฿. Fax available. Reserve 2 days ahead.

FOOD

Everywhere in Bangkok, delicious victuals can be had at rock-bottom prices from street vendors and tiny, no-name restaurants. Learn the appellation of a few simple dishes, or point, and let your palate run wild. You can get streetwise experience in the low-pressure, A/C surroundings of supermarket food courts. The places we list aren't necessarily of better culinary quality, but provide variety, comfort, atmosphere, English-language menus, and (sorry) often higher prices.

Banglamphu/Ko Rattanakosin

This area is bursting with cheap eats, served up by both sidewalk vendors and restaurants. For good food stalls, stroll down **Soi Rambuttri, Krai Si Rd.** (in the evening), or **Phra Chan Rd.** (during the day) across from Thammasat University. On weekends, the area around **Sanam Luang** is also a popular hang-out for streetside peddlers of edibles. Nearly every guest house has its own restaurant, with varying degrees of menu selection. Khaosan Rd. has over 20 such restaurants with dishes running 25-60฿, or head to the eight floor of the **New World Department Store Food Centre,** at the corner of Chakrapong Rd. and Phra Sumen Rd., 8F. Open daily 8am-8pm. You will be rewarded with a great view of Bangkok, as well as Thai and Chinese dishes at prices so low (20-40฿) you'll almost feel guilty.

Khaosan Centre Restaurant, 80-84 Khaosan Rd. (tel. 282 43 66). In the middle of Khaosan Rd., it is the undisputed tourist favorite. This large restaurant, decorated with pots and voodoo statues, serves ample portions of Thai and American food at reasonable prices (dishes 30-60฿). Customers dine to the tunes of R&B, techno, or pop music pumping in the background. Try the fried rice with crab, or any of the fresh fruit shakes. Open 24hr.

Yod Kum, 365/1 Phra Sumen Rd. (tel. 281 71 86), across from Wat Bovornives. Strictly middle-class clientele in a shoebox-sized restaurant decorated with western memorabilia from the 20s and 30s. Ooh and ahh at the glass cabinet with crystal and old toys or the bottle cap collection. Hot-as-hell Thai curries, soups, and chili-paste dishes as well as some Chinese fare. Rice dishes 35-50฿. Curries 80-140฿. Beer and whiskey. English menu. Open daily 11:30am-11pm.

Tang Teh, 269-271 Samsen Rd. (tel 281 94 26), on the left at the 1st major intersection coming from Banglamphu. Airy, modern-artsy dining room, and dishes that will make your taste buds sing. Try *yam pla dook foo* (fried catfish with cashews and chili sauce 65฿). Stellar homemade ice cream (20฿ per scoop). English menu. Open daily 11am-2pm and 4:30-11pm.

Vijit Restaurant, 77/2 Ratchadamnoen Klang Rd. (tel. 282 09 58), by the Democracy Monument. No English sign, so look for café-style tables lining the sidewalk. The live music at lunch and dinner attracts locals who slurp on beer and whiskey. Chinese and Thai food knock the socks off Japanese and Vietnamese offerings.

Most dishes 40-80฿. Sour crab with coconut milk is popular (48฿). 10% service charge after 6pm. Open daily 11am-11pm.

Dusit/Government Centre

There are very few restaurants here, and they're generally sub-par. Start your search for cheap eats at the market packed with noodle stands on Si Ayutthaya Rd. across from the guest houses.

Thai Youth Hostel Association Cafeteria, 25/2 Phitsanulok Rd. (tel. 282 55 59). The sign on the door simply says "Thailand." Decor consists of carved-wood mirrors and national flags. Extensive menu loaded with various Thai dishes and a few western favorites of the soup/salad/sandwich variety such as "horse derves" and "chili fried hog." Dishes 30-60฿. English menu. Open daily 7am-11pm.

Chinatown/Pahurat/Hualamphong

Richard Simmons and Jenny Craig would go nuts in this gastronomically fixated part of town. Tiny, bustling Chinese restaurants crowd **Yaowarat Rd.** For Indian curries head to the **Prahurat** area. Food stalls are in **Hualamphong.** Not many places have English menus, so use your instincts.

White Orchid Coffee Shop, 409-421 Yaowarat Rd. (tel. 226 00 26), on the second floor of the White Orchid Hotel. The restaurant's claim to fame is its 120฿ lunch buffet (tax and service included) of mostly Chinese food. Workers from all over Chinatown rush in at lunchtime to feast on Thai and European offerings: curries, green salads, buttered fish with tartar, and deli meats. Beer, whiskey, and various cocktails. Open daily 11am-2pm for brunch. Friday dinner buffet 6-10pm.

Royal India Restaurant, 392/1 Chakraphet Rd. (tel. 221 65 65), through the small alley off Chakraphet Rd., between Saphan Han (the bridge) and Yaowarat Rd. The progenitor of the Royal India on Khaosan Rd., this is one of the best Indian restaurants in Pahurat. Extensive bread selection. Vegetarians will like the 14 meatless items (20-45฿). *Tandoori* chicken is popular, and the most expensive (110฿). Tasty *pakoras*—potatoes, peas, and mild spices in pastry. Open daily 9am-10pm.

Silom/Financial District

During the day, the neighborhood caters to the appetites of the business elite. Local noodle vendors, the original fast food dispensers, compete for lunch-time baht with their western counterparts. Look for local fare along **Convent Rd.,** and deep inside **Soi Ngam Duphli.** By night, **Silom Rd.** is flooded with street-side stalls. A steady stream of hungry souls flows through this district until the early hours (around 3am). Prices are generally higher than elsewhere in Bangkok.

Silom Restaurant, end of Silom Soi 15 (tel. 236 42 68). Huge, inexpensive Chinese and Thai dishes make this place a favorite with workers and families in the Silom area. Gorge on a large selection of fish and prawn dishes. Regular-sized (huge) dishes 60-90฿. The chicken curry (65฿) contains the most tender chicken imaginable. English menu. Open daily 11am-9:30pm.

Sukol Thros Bakery, 14 Silom Rd. (tel. 234 56 34), near Robinson Dept. Store. No English sign—look for a pointy 'S' logo. Popular with workers in the Silom area by day and couples by night. Decent selection of Thai hot and sour salads and delicious *pad Thai,* as well as some western fare. Dishes 25-90฿. In-house bakery makes a wide variety of cakes, meat pies, and Western/Thai/Chinese goodies. No reservations, but good luck trying to find a seat at lunch. Open daily 7am-9pm.

Thai Room (tel. 233 79 20), in the Plaza Bldg. on Patpong II Rd. At the entrance of the Pavilion Place Hotel take a right down the narrow corridor. Serving westerners coming out of Patpong bars for 28 years, the Thai Room is an institution among tourists, many of whom come back to see if it's still in business. The A/C interior is clean, with a slight lounge-lizard, 70s feel. Funky blue, green, and red lights adorn the walls. The English menu lists over 400 Mexican, Italian, Chinese, Thai, and American dishes (45-80฿). Open daily 10am-2am. All major credit cards.

Siam Sq./Pratunam

Finding food in this area is as easy as walking down the street. In the afternoon and early evening, food vendors hawk their goodies in front of the **National Stadium** on Rama I Rd., at the mouth of **Soi Kasem 1,** and along the network of *soi* weaving through **Siam Sq.** In Pratunam, vendors and sidewalk restaurants dot **Ratchaprarop Rd.** and **Soi Wattanasin** across from the Indra Regent Hotel. Western fast food places skirmish with regular restaurants as well as the food courts in almost every department store offering cheap eats (most dishes 35฿) and A/C.

UFM Noodle House, 230/17-18 Siam Sq. Soi 2 (tel. 252 71 87), on the same *soi* as the Kirin Restaurant. Other locations at 182-184 Siam Sq. Soi 1, in front of the Scala Movie Theater, and at Amarin Plaza, 4th fl. Sign says Noodle Shop with a pair of chopsticks. Young crowd flocks to this shiny, colorful place for Thai, Chinese, Japanese, and Italian noodle dishes made fresh daily (30-50฿). No alcohol. 5% service charge. Open daily 11am-9pm.

Dai Domon, 266/11-13 Soi 3 (tel. 251 32 74), across from Siam Sq. Young Thais hungry from shopping flock to this Japanese restaurant for its all-you-can-eat buffet (119฿) where customers can grill their own meat and seafood over a blazing gas fire. Buffet also comes with soup and *kim chee.* Open daily 11am-10pm.

Tota Restaurant, 63/12 Soi Lang Suan off Ploenchit Rd. (tel. 252 24 55). Regular bus #48 and A/C bus #8 pass by the *soi* on Ploenchit Rd. Pleasant A/C restaurant with pink walls, blue-tinted window panes, plants, and framed bird pictures. Serves spicy Thai cuisine. Most dishes 30-50฿. *Som tam* (25฿) and *yen tao fo* (30฿) are spicy specialties. Ice cream and fruit cool off tingling tongues. English menu. Open daily 10am-11pm.

New Light Coffee House, 426/1-4 Siam Sq. (tel. 251 95 91), next to the Hard Rock Café. With bizarre green mood lighting and a vinylized A/C ambience testifying to its 60s vintage, New Light lives on today with good international offerings. The menu covers lots of ground: Thai (60-80฿), Chinese (80-400฿), and European/American (40-150฿). Cheap and extensive sandwich selection. Open daily 8am-12:30am.

Sukhumvit Rd. Area

Along with Siam Sq. and Silom, Sukhumvit forms part of Bangkok's triumvirate of culinary powerhouses. Some of the best restaurants were set up by expatriate chefs trying to cook up a name for themselves on the Bangkok scene. Travelers with a hankering for Euro, Indian, Chinese, or simply good Thai cuisine will be satiated—but the price of satisfaction is usually steep. For those with less demanding palates, the **Ambassador Food Centre** (right side of the Ambassador Hotel parking lot near Soi 13 off Sukhumvit Rd., open daily 10:30am-11pm) serves a variety of Asian dishes (20-70฿) with some vegetarian options.

Cabbages and Condoms, 10 Soi 12 Sukhumvit Rd. (tel. 229 46 10), behind the Population Development Building. The brainchild of Dr. Vichit, a leading family planning advocate, the restaurant was established in 1986. All proceeds go to charitable organizations. Decorated with Thai wicker-work, condom brands from all over the world, and framed newspaper articles on the AIDS crisis. Decent Thai food; *gaeng nua* (beef curry) is a specialty. Pick up condoms in lieu of post-prandial mints. Most dishes 50-90฿, seafood dishes 100฿ or more. Open daily 11am-10pm. Reservations recommended on weekend evenings.

Bei Otto Bakery, Butchery, and Restaurant, 1 Soi 20 Sukhumvit Rd. (tel. 258 14 95). Bangkok's premier German restaurant and priced accordingly; those on a tight budget might want to sample from the bakery and deli instead. Good deals on cold cuts and home-made pastries, breads, and pickles. Load up on chicken or sausage pies (15฿ each) or sandwich fixings. Cold cuts include knockwurst and veal sausages (20-55฿). Sweets (5-45฿) and breads are baked daily. Bakery open daily 8am-midnight, restaurant open daily 11am-3pm and 6-11pm. English menu.

Thong Kee Restaurant, 308-312 Sukhumvit 14 (tel. 229 44 40), near Times Square Mall. Mouthwatering Cantonese seafood (dishes 80-150฿) served on beautifully polished wooden tables decorated with silver floral designs. Scrumptious fried rice dishes (30-40฿). Open daily 10am-11pm.

MARKETS

Markets are fundamental pillars of society for most Thais, serving both as sources of livelihood and of cheap food and clothing. Street markets are sources for knock-off designer watches, clothing (from Polo to Levis), pirated cassette tapes, and videos. With good bargaining, great deals can be found at the market. Also, while most department store wares (especially clothing and handicrafts) are also sold on the street, quality can be much lower.

The **weekend market at Chatuchak Park** is a bargain-hunter's dream. Hundreds of covered stalls form a labyrinth of shopping delight, selling everything from regular clothes to military surplus equipment. The weekend market is notorious for its adept pickpockets; guard your wallets and purses carefully. The market is actually open every day of the week from dawn to dusk, but the excitement and the vendors do not come out in full force until the weekend. Take regular bus #3 from Sanam Luang or A/C bus #2 from Silom. The bus ride could take up to three hours if traffic is grisly.

The **Banglamphu Market** branches out onto Chakrapong, Krai Si, and Tani Rd., while a more tourist-oriented street market can be found along Khaosan Rd. A mostly late-afternoon and early-evening market, the frenzied Banglamphu Market's best deals include food, leather products, and no-name clothing, in addition to Levis, Ralph Lauren, and Benetton spin-offs. It's one of the most convenient markets, with the widest range of products and the lowest prices. **Thewet Market** is on Krung Kasem Rd. near the pier; it's in the area north of Banglamphu next to Dusit and along the Chao Phraya River. Vendors hawk most of the usual market items, although it is best known for its flowers and plants.

In the Pratunam area, the lively **Pratunam Market** operates during the day along Ratchaprarop Rd., around and across the street from the Indra Hotel. Clothes are big here, although there is also a wide selection of knick-knacks, including toenail clippers, sunglasses, and fake braids.

In the **Silom** area, the street market scene is pretty sedate during the day. After nightfall, however, vendors set up stalls along **Patpong Rd.,** giving travelers a legitimate reason to go to Patpong. Fake designer clothing, lighters, pewter, wood carvings, counterfeit cassette tapes, and souvenirs can be found, among many other things. Prices are generally hard to bargain down because of the market's touristy nature.

SIGHTS

Banglamphu/Ko Rattanakosin

Wat Phra Kaew(Temple of the Emerald Buddha) and the **Grand Palace** (tel. 222 00 94, ext. 40) are the preeminent sights in Bangkok. Many buses find their way here and stop near the compound and across the street at Sanam Luang. The entrance gate is on Na Phra Lan Rd. (Open daily 8:30am-3:30pm; free for Thais, for foreigners 125฿.) A small guidebook and map are included with admission. Free tours are given in English daily at 10, 10:30am, 1:30, and 2pm.

In front of the entrance stands the Temple of the Emerald Buddha, originally the Royal Chapel of the Chakri Dynasty. It took three years to build, beginning in 1782 at the start of the Chakri Dynasty. Inside the main chapel building (*bot*) is the **Emerald Buddha,** the most sacred Buddha image in Thailand. Shoes should be taken off before entering the chapel. No photography is allowed.

The itinerant Emerald Buddha has passed through many halfway houses before finding a proper resting place. It was originally discovered in 1434, when lightning shattered a *chedi* in the northern city of Chiang Rai. An abbot found a stucco Buddha inside and later noticed the plaster flaking off, revealing a green substance. Curious, he sloughed off all the stucco, and *voilà*! the Emerald Buddha was found. Following the discovery, people flocked to worship the priceless statue. King Samfangkang of Chiang Mai yearned to possess the sacred object, and, being a monarch, summarily sent a royal elephant to transport it. At a fork in the road on the return trip, however, the elephant would only take the road leading to Lampang. The king sent three more elephants to do the job, but they, too, would only go to Lampang. Sensing divine forces at work, the king allowed the image to remain in the city of Lampang, where it was housed until 1468, when King Tiloka finally managed to relocate the hot commodity to Chiang Mai. Nearly a century later, the peripatetic figurine found its way to Laos, where it remained for 214 years until General Chao Phraya Chakri, the future Rama I, captured Vientiane and reclaimed it for Thailand. He carted off the statue to the capital of Thon Buri, where it was placed in Wat Arun. After he ascended the throne and moved the capital to Bangkok in 1782, King Rama I built the Royal Chapel, known as Wat Phra Kaew, for the Emerald Buddha, where it has remained ever since. Whew.

Next door to the temple is the **Grand Palace,** accessible through a gate connecting the two compounds. After turning right inside the gate, a stroll down the path leads past many important buildings on the left. The first is **Amarinda Vinichai Hall,** which once held important court ceremonies (open Mon.-Fri.). Next, **Chakri Mahaprasad Hall,** the residence of King Chulalongkorn, is a hybrid of European and Thai architectural design. Today, the reception areas and central throne hall are still used for certain royal ceremonies, although they are off-limits to ordinary folks. Farther on, **Dusit Hall** is a symmetrical building of Thai design whose audience hall houses a mother-of-pearl throne (open Mon.-Fri.). Admission to Wat Phra Kaew and the Grand Palace entitles the visitor to free admission to Vimarnmek Palace in Dusit with your admission slip.

After leaving the Grand Palace compound, a right turn past the gift shop leads to the **Wat Phra Kaew Museum.** The first floor contains relics and parts from buildings that originally stood in the compounds which have been replaced, as well as the bones from a white elephant, which are considered good luck. The second floor is air-conditioned and contains hundreds of Buddha images along with enamel and crystal wares. (Open daily 9am-3:30pm; free.)

From Wat Phra Kaew, a walk around the block (three left turns from the entrance) leads to **Wat Po** (Temple of the Reclining Buddha), which is the oldest and largest temple in Bangkok. Its grounds are split in two by Soi Chetupon: one side is home to the monastery, while the other contains temple buildings. Wat Po was built in the 16th century during the Ayutthaya period, when the area around present-day Bangkok was little more than a fishing village. King Rama I enlarged the temple's grounds and made improvements on its structures; his grandson, King Rama III, built the *wiharn* that houses the Reclining Buddha. The statue measures 46m in length and 15m in height; the feet alone are 3m long. (Open daily 8:30am-5pm; free.)

Famous for the variety and abundance of its Buddhas, Wat Po is home to Thailand's first university, a monastery founded a century before Bangkok to teach Thai medicine. In the past three centuries, it has developed into a world-famous school of traditional Thai massage. Today, this technique is still taught and administered on the temple grounds. In the eastern part of Wat Po is the **Medical Hall** where masseurs can be seen kneading their customers. Massages go for about 180฿ per hour, 280฿ with herbs. Those intrigued by this therapeutic massage can sign up for the 15-day course (3000฿).

To get to **Wat Arun** (the Temple of Dawn) from Wat Po, take a right from Chetupon Rd. onto Maharat Rd., and a left at Tani Wang Rd. This path goes to Tha Tien, a pier on the Chao Phraya River. From an adjacent pier, ferries make frequent crossings to the wat (1฿). The name of Thailand's second-most-famous wat is derived from Aruna, the Hindu god of dawn. Wat Arun was built in the Ayutthaya period and its Khmer architecture reflects the heavy influence of the neighboring Angkor kingdom. During King Taksin's short reign in Thon Buri, Wat Arun served as the Royal Chapel. Today, as a royal temple, Wat Arun is visited once a year by the King, who conducts a merit-making ceremony.

While Wat Arun is famous for its size and majesty, it was not until the reign of King Rama II that the idea of building a great *prang,* the steeple-like structure atop the *bot,* came into being. King Rama II, however, did not live to see his dream realized, since the wet Thon Buri soil delayed completion of the construction until the reign of King Rama III. Finished, the *prang* towered 81m over the temple grounds. Built in the Khmer style, it is inlaid with millions of ceramic tiles and porcelain, much of which was donated by villagers. It is an awesome sight to behold at sunrise, when solar beams make the temple glitter brilliantly and project its reflection onto the Chao Phraya River. The best view of the wat is from the Bangkok side of the river early in the morning, and the top of the prang affords a beautiful view of the water (open daily 8:30am-5:30pm).

The **Royal Barge Museum** (tel. 424 00 04), is a short bus or taxi ride away on Arun Amarin Rd. under the bridge over Khlong Bangkok Noi. Tourists can get there by regular bus #19. From the inconspicuous entrance, walk 300m along a winding path, following the arrows and signs through a riverside residential neighborhood, to get to the museum. The ferry goes from Tha Phra Arthit to Tha Phra Pinklao on the opposite bank (1฿). Take the first left on Phra Pinklao Rd. after the big school underneath the green arch. Follow the signs about 500m through the neighborhood to the museum. The most impressive barge in the museum is undoubtedly the **Suphannahongsa,** a 46m-long stiletto of a vessel reserved exclusively for the Royal Family. Its bow is carved into the shape of a mythical bird called the *hongsa.* Getting the Suphannahongsa moving in the water requires 50 oarsmen and a crew of 13 to transport the King and Queen in a royal procession. (Open daily 8:30am-4:30pm; admission 10฿.)

Walking through the small campus past the statue of Silpa Bhirasri leads to the university's side entrance. A left turn, followed by a right just down the road at Phra Chan Rd. brings you to Na Phra That Rd., with **Thammasat University** (tel. 225 75 17) on the left. Thailand's second oldest university, Thammasat is the country's premier institution of higher learning in political science and law, and the traditional hotbed of student activism. In the past two decades, the campus has been the sight of two of the bloodiest student demonstrations in Thai history. Today, campus activism has cooled down, but Thammasat maintains its reputation as one of the top universities in the nation.

On the right across from Thammasat is **Wat Mahathat,** an extremely old monastery, built before Bangkok became the nation's capital, also known as the Temple of the Great Relic. Mahathat houses a large sitting Buddha (open daily 9am-5pm). The wat was the home of King Rama I, who was an abbot before he did an about-face and took up military campaigns as a way of life. These days, the temple is known as a center of Buddhist teaching and the home of Wat Maha Chulalongkorn University, one of Thailand's two Buddhist colleges.

Back at Na Phra That Rd., across the street is **Sanam Luang,** the "national common" of Thailand. In the old days, criminals convicted of particularly heinous crimes were lined up here and shot. Although public executions have been discontinued, summer kite fighting contests are going strong, as competitors from all over descend upon the grass. The large kites are "males" called *chula,* while the smaller kites are "females" known as the *pukpao.* The goal of the *chula* is to catch the *pukpao,* and the goal of the *pukpao* is to avoid capture. For a few baht, you can satiate your testosterone-driven, kite-fighting urges and compete.

Farther away from Wat Phra Kaew on Na Phra That Rd. past Thammasat University stands the **National Museum** (tel. 224 13 96) in the compound to the left of the sidewalk. Look for that guard booth at the entry way. This Bangkok branch is the crown jewel of Thailand's national museum system, and the largest museum in Southeast Asia. In 1874, King Chulalongkorn started the museum when he opened a public showroom inside the Grand Palace to exhibit royal collections from the reign of his father King Rama IV. Smithsonian or British Museum devo-

THAILAND

tees, however, will sneer at the dusty, cluttered displays and hokey waxworks. Time-conscious travelers should take the free 90-minute museum tour given by English-speaking guides on Wednesdays and Thursdays at 9:30am (tours also offered in French, German, and Japanese). Guides specialize in various fields of Thai art. (Open Wed.-Sun. 9am-4pm, tickets sold until 3:30pm; admission 20฿).

Continue down Na Phra That Rd. until you reach Ratchini Rd. Take a left, walk under the Phra Pinklao Bridge, and turn onto Chao Fa Rd. The **National Theater** (tel. 221 01 71) is through the first gate on the left of Ratchini Rd. Dedicated in 1965, the National Theater has regularly scheduled drama and dance shows. On the second weekend of each month (Sat. and Sun.), *lakhon* is performed (10am and 2pm); *khon* is performed on the third weekend of each month (10am and 2pm). The last Friday of each month is reserved for a special cultural show at 5:30pm. The theater is also home to the **Thai National Orchestra,** which plays for the public the first Friday of each month at 5:30pm. When there are no state-sponsored shows, other performance companies may use the National Theater. Ticket prices run 40-80฿ for the regularly scheduled government-sponsored shows. The box office (tel. 224 13 42) is open Mon.-Fri. 8:30am-4:30pm, and one hour prior to performances.

On Chao Fa Rd., straddling eight lanes of traffic, is the **National Gallery** (tel. 281 22 24) which contains classical and contemporary works by prominent Thai artists, as well as the **National Film Archives**. The two air-conditioned rooms display paintings of scenes from epic stories (such as the *Ramayana*) and classical plays. One of the rooms shows four rare watercolors painted by King Rama VI. (Open Wed.-Sun. 9am-4pm; admission 10฿.)

A good 10-minute walk along the continuation of Chao Fa Rd., Ratchadamnoen Klang Rd. leads to the **Democracy Monument.** Commemorating Thailand's transition from an absolute monarchy to a constitutional monarchy in the Revolution of 1932, it was the site of bloody demonstrations in May 1992, when students and middle-class citizens took to the streets to protest the dictatorial rule of General Suchinda Kraprayoon. When the protesters refused to back down in a stand-off with the police, Suchinda ordered the army to attack. Dozens were mowed down by machine-gun fire. The general's move backfired, however, as the King and the public were outraged. Suchinda eventually resigned in disgrace and disappeared into exile before he could be arrested and put on trial.

On Worachak Rd. is **Wat Saket,** noteworthy for its **Golden Mount** soaring 80m into the sky. The mount was formerly the highest point in the city, and today its breezy, high location and 360° panoramic view make it a very popular place for the energetic. The nimble-limbed are rewarded with a tall golden *chedi* at the final destination (admission to the top 5฿). The main chapel stands within an enclosed set of corridors; the perfectly symmetrical design is stunning. The temple grounds provide a restful spot for contemplating the other 42 sights on your whirlwind itinerary. (Open daily 7:30am-5:30pm.)

Going down Worachak Rd. to Bamrung Muang Rd., **Wat Suthat** and its famous **Sao Ching Cha (Giant Swing)** lie to the right (accessible by A/C bus #8). In the past, Sao Ching Cha was the scene of Brahmin rituals, when a priest would swing high to try to catch money suspended 25m in the air in his *teeth!* Many priests lost their lives attempting this feat, and a law passed during the reign of King Rama VII prohibiting this exciting but dangerous ritual. King Rama I began construction on the temple, but it was not finished until King Rama III's reign. One of the largest wats in Bangkok, it is the only one without *chedi* or stupa. (Open daily 9am-5pm; free.)

A 10-minute walk to the left along Bamrung Muang Rd. will lead back to Wat Phra Kaew and Sanam Luang, right at **Lak Muang** (the City Pillar). Walk to Na Hap Phoei Rd.; the gate is on the right. Lak Muang was built by King Rama I at the founding of Bangkok to house the spirit of the city. Worshippers still come daily to pay their respects, bringing offerings of food and drink. (Open daily 5:30am-7:30pm; free.)

Wat Bovornives, on the corner of Phra Sawn Rd. and Bowon Nivet Rd. in North Banglamphu, is only a short walk from the Khaosan Rd. area. King Rama IV spent 27 years here as a monk and an abbot before ascending to the throne. The wat is also the home of the second Buddhist college in Thailand, **Mahamakut University.** If you want to flee the hordes of tourists, you can drop by and admire the main chapel's magnificent ornamental borders and Chinese-style stone guardian statues (open daily 9am-5pm; free).

Dusit/Government Centre

Bus #70 runs the entire lengths of Ratchadamnoen Nok Rd. and U Thong Nai Rd. and beyond, while bus #72 traverses the entire length of Si Ayutthaya Rd. Between the two, you can reach all the sights in this part of town.

Traveling north, away from the center of town from the point where Ratchadamnoen Klang Rd. and Ratchadamnoen Nok Rd. meet, the roads widen and traffic subsides. Trees spring up more frequently, and buildings fronted by security guards and the occasional armed trooper begin to appear. This is the Dusit area, the governmental center of the city and country.

Past the Si Ayutthaya Rd. light, Ratchadamnoen Nok Rd. opens into **Suan Amphon,** site of the revered **statue of King Chulalongkorn (Rama V).** This beloved king ruled from 1868 to 1910 and is remembered for abolishing slavery, modernizing Thai society, and fending off mad British and French colonialists.

Behind the statue, guarded by an iron fence and a well-kept garden, stands the former **National Assembly (Parliament Building).** This gigantic, venerable domed building was commissioned by Chulalongkorn in 1908 to replace his old residence. This new Royal Palace, called Anandasamakhom, was patterned after St. Peter's Basilica in Rome, which explains its white marble and Italian Renaissance construction. In 1932, revolutionaries ended the absolute monarchy in a bloodless coup and seized the palace from King Rama VII, designating it as the new National Assembly building. Today it is referred to as the "old Parliament building," since the Assembly has been moved to another location in Dusit.

Ratchadamnoen Nok Rd. bends around the Assembly building to the right and becomes U Thong Nai Rd. On the right side of the road is the **Dusit Zoo,** the largest zoo in Thailand. Regular bus #70 conveniently stops right across the street from the U Thong Nai Gate. There are also gates on Rama V Rd. (bus #5) and Ratchawithi Rd. (bus #18, 28, and 108 or A/C #10). Visitors to the Dusit Zoo are soothed by the verdant flora and tall trees, amused by the playfulness of the Malaysian sun bears, and relaxed by steering a paddleboat on an artificial lake. Zoomorphic signs help guide visitors to their animals of choice. (Open daily 8am-6pm; admission 20฿, seniors over 60 10฿, and children under 10 5฿).

Farther up U Thong Nai Rd. past Dusit Zoo is an entrance to **Vimarnmek Palace,** on the left. When a constitutional crisis is brewing (which is most of the time in Thailand), this gate is locked to keep out the protestors who threaten to bring the country to its knees by playing bad folk music and pounding the ground with empty mineral water bottles. Bus #70 stops near here. Vimarnmek was built during the reign of Chulalongkorn, and its L-shaped structure is made of golden teakwood; curators claim that it is the largest teakwood mansion in the world. It has 81 rooms on four floors—impressive enough, but the most remarkable feature of the building is that it was constructed without nails.

Vimarnmek Palace contains numerous pieces of ancient art from various countries. Tours of the palace are given in English every half-hour. (Open daily 9:30am-4pm, last admission 3pm; admission 50฿, for children 5-15 20฿, under 5 free.) Admission to Wat Phra Kaew (Temple of the Emerald Buddha) and the Grand Palace entitles the visitor to free admission to Vimarnmek Palace; keep your admission slip. There is a free display of Thai dancing daily at 10:30am and 2pm. Shorts or sleeveless shirts are not allowed.

Following the route of bus #72 down Si Ayutthaya Rd., shortly after it passes the Ratchadamnoen Nok Rd. intersection, the grounds of Bangkok's famous **Wat**

THAILAND

Benchamabophit (Marble Temple), will appear on the right. Its perfectly symmetrical architecture and pure white Carrara marble walls were built in 1899 by (who else?) King Chulalongkorn. Every morning, monks chant inside the main chapel. The cloisters of the courtyard are splendidly lined with 52 bronze Buddhas, representing the styles of Buddha images from different periods. After visiting the main chapel, it is possible to stroll around the garden and see the sacred turtles given to the temple by its faithful worshippers. (Open daily 8am-5:30pm; admission 10฿.)

Past Wat Benchamabophit and Rama V Rd. on the left is a walled compound protected by a moat and specially trained soldiers. The compound is **Chitralada Palace,** official home of the Royal Family, and the assault-rifle-toting blue-uniformed troops are the King's Royal Guard. The palace is not open to the public. Do not attempt to enter. You will be shot. May our fearlessly thorough researcher rest in peace.

Chinatown/Pahurat/Hualamphong

When Bangkok was founded in 1782 by King Rama I, Chinese immigrants came to settle in the area southeast of the royal center along the Chao Phraya River; this has remained home to the ethnic Chinese community for over two centuries. Today, this area is called **Yaowarat** (after the road which runs through Chinatown), or **Sampeng.** In Chinatown there are no sights in the traditional sense, but what the area does offer is a slice of life, seen through a lens unchanged for decades. Although modern conveniences have intruded, the lifestyle of the inhabitants has remained surprisingly unchanged.

Near Yaowarat, in an area marked by Pahurat Rd., Chakraphet Rd., and countless alleys around and in between, is the **Pahurat** District of Bangkok, the traditional home of the ethnic Indian population. While a bit smaller than Yaowarat, Pahurat's streets are no less chaotic, filled with lively sidewalk and street markets. Inexpensive clothing sold by Sikhs and Hindus is the big draw here.

The only major temple in the Chinatown/Pahurat/Hualamphong area is the famed **Wat Traimit,** home of the **Giant Golden Buddha,** a three-meter, five-ton, 100% gold Sukhothai-style statue. When the Burmese sacked Ayutthaya, the people of the ancient capital saved the statue by covering it with stucco, a cheap but successful trick. Its true identity remained a secret until 1955, when the statue slipped from a moving crane as it was being transported to Wat Traimit and cracks developed in the plaster, revealing traces of glittering gold. The stucco was removed, and—eureka!—the Golden Buddha, over 700 years old, was redis-covered. Today it is housed in a small room above a currency exchange booth and gift shops. A small sitting area next to the ticket office has a tape recording of the history of the temple and of the Golden Buddha played in English, Chinese, and Japanese. (Open daily 8:30am-5pm; admission for Golden Buddha 10฿.) The main entrance is on Yaowarat Rd. near the intersection with Charoen Krung Rd., but there is also a smaller entrance on the short Traimit Rd., accessible by bus #73.

Silom/Financial District

Believe it or not, the area around Silom Rd. offers more than just the moth-eaten-rag-tag-down-at-the-heel-sleazy-whore-houses-cum-go-go-bars which line Patpong Rd. **Lumpini Park,** the largest park in Bangkok, is an oasis of flora and foliage. Bordered by Ratchadamri, Rama IV, Sarasin, and Witthayu Rd., the park has man-made lakes, wide roads, and some of the largest trees in Bangkok. In the mornings, elderly Chinese do *tai chi.* For a little pseudo-exercise, rent a paddleboat and cruise along the lakes (20฿ per 30min.; boat rentals daily 7am-7pm). The park is accessible from Silom by regular bus #15, 77, and 115; from Siam Sq. or Bang-lamphu by regular bus #15; from Sukhumvit take regular bus #25, 40, or 48 to Siam Sq. and make the connection to #15.

One of the world's most famous hotels, the **Oriental Hotel,** 48 Oriental Ave.(tel. 236 04 00), is along the Chao Phraya River. Walk down Charoen Krung Soi 40 toward the river; it will be on the right. Founded in 1876 by two Danish sea captains, Evie Jarck and Buck Salje, the Oriental was a classy hotel from the start. H. N. Andersen built the original, grand Italianate building in 1887, and it still stands as the **Authors' Residence** wing of the hotel, which shelters some of the finest and most expensive rooms. The famous guest list of The Oriental includes: Joseph Conrad (1888), King Chulalongkorn (1890), Carl Fabergé (1912), and Prince Charles and Princess Diana (as their marriage was headed down the slippery slope in 1988).

Siam Sq./Pratunam

This area is famed for its munificent temples of conspicuous consumption, where faithful worshippers bearing credit cards or cold hard cash pay homage to the gods of Gucci. Some sights are worth seeing, but it will take time and patience to traverse this area, home to the city's most gargantuan traffic delays.

The most noticeable landmark on Rama I Rd., aside from the Mahboonkrong Shopping Complex and the Siam Sq. Shopping Centre, is the **National Stadium.** Anyone may freely enter the grounds and run about like a fiend or join a pick-up game of soccer or *takraw*.

Across from the National Stadium complex, at the end of Soi Kasem San 2 and to the left, is **Jim Thompson's House,** 6 Soi Kasem San 2 (tel. 215 01 22), which houses one of Thailand's best collections of Ayutthaya and Rattanakosin period art (open Mon.-Sat. 9am-4:30pm; admission 100฿, for those under 26 40฿). A one-hour English language tour is included in the admission. Guides discuss various ingenious architectural oddities found in Thai houses and show visitors a shallow cup designed to prevent people from getting drunk too quickly. Proceeds from ticket sales go to various Thai charities.

Farther along Rama I Rd. around where the street name changes to Ploenchit Rd. is the famous **Erawan Shrine,** built after several workers lost their lives in mysterious accidents during the construction of the Erawan Hotel on Ratchadamri Rd. Devotees flock to give offerings to the Brahma figure housed within the small, glittering display. This shrine is believed to house especially influential and powerful spirits. Thai dancers hired by grateful worshippers whose prayers were answered by the deity often perform around the shrine.

Missing: One Silk Magnate. Answers to Jim.

It can be argued that the mystique surrounding James H. W. Thompson, O.S.S. (the pre-C.I.A. American intelligence organization) officer, and the father of the modern Thai silk industry, draws more visitors than the house itself. Jim Thompson was born in Greenville, Delaware, U.S.A. in 1906 and was an architect before enlisting in the U.S. Army during World War II. He was stationed in Thailand at the end of the war, and loved the country so much that he left his wife in America for an extended stay. Intrigued by the hand weaving of silk cloth, he spent his time and money creating the modern Thai silk industry and making Thai silk famous around the world. Thompson's mansion, a testament to his financial success and great love for things Thai, was built in authentic Thai style and decorated with antique Thai art, including some of the oldest known Thai paintings. On March 27, 1967, Thompson disappeared while hunting tiger in Malaysia. Numerous theories, enough to keep Oliver Stone happy, have been advanced about his fate. The unimaginative believe he was eaten by a tiger, but others think that he was exposed as a C.I.A. operative and deep-sixed, or that he was involved in a shady business deal that got out of hand. In any event, Thompson left the legacy of the Thai silk industry, as well as a beautiful house.

Less than 2km away on Si Ayutthaya Rd. is **Wang Suan Pakkard** (tel. 245 49 34), otherwise known as Lettuce Farm Palace. No lettuce can be found here now, but five traditional Thai wooden houses set on teakwood stilt-like columns struggle to take the place of the impressive Lactuca Sativa. An immaculately kept garden with plants from all over the world surrounds the buildings. In the back of the garden is the Lacquer Pavilion, filled with porcelain, statues of Buddha, and painted pottery from Ban Chiang. Perhaps the biggest attraction at Wang Suan Pakkard, however, is the relative calm it offers those weary of the Bangkok heat and congestion (open Mon.-Sat. 9am-4pm; admission 80฿, for students 20฿). To get there, take regular bus #54, 73, or 204 from Siam Sq. past the Indra Regent on Ratchaprarop Rd. Get off near the corner of Ratchaprarop and Si Ayutthaya Rd., and turn down Si Ayutthaya. The palace will be on the left, behind a wooden fence.

One of the more arousing sights in Bangkok is the **Goddess Tuptim Shrine** (Phallic Shrine) near the Hilton International Hotel on Wireless Rd. The shrine is known for the large numbers of priapic objects around its spirit house, brought there by couples seeking help for infertility. According to history, when the hotel was founded, a spirit house was erected for the Goddess Tuptim, whose spirit was said to live in a nearby tree. Slews of people had come to the shrine bringing gifts and eventually someone hit on the idea of a phallic gift. Soon, worshippers with fertility problems began making the trip to the shrine with their own tubular offerings. To see this unusual shrine, take a *tuk-tuk* or taxi to the Hilton, or get on bus #76 from Silom to its farthest point on Witthayu (Wireless) Rd., and walk the rest of the way (5min.).

Sukhumvit Rd. Area

Sukhumvit Rd., with its overwhelming number of *soi*, restaurants, and tailoring shops, may not enthrall the tourist. One of the few real sights is **Kamthieng House,** at 131 Soi 21-Asoke (tel. 258 34 91), an ethnological museum and home to the **Siam Society,** a Thai cultural society supported by the royals. Built in the mid-19th century, the Kamthieng House was originally on the east bank of the Ping River in Chiang Mai, where it was owned by an ancestor of the wealthy and well-known Nimmanahaeminda family. The museum attempts to reconstruct the daily life of 19th-century Thais, with exhibits on tools, utensils, and other objects. (Open Tues.-Sat. 9am-5pm; admission 20฿, students 10฿.)

Those seeking a respite from the confusion of town without actually leaving Bangkok can go to the **King Rama IX Royal Park** on Soi 103 Sukhumvit Rd. Grab A/C bus #8 from Siam Centre to Soi 103 and take a taxi to the park. Here, the magnificently sculpted 200-plus acres dwarf the more natural Lumpini Park. The land was donated to the King by a wealthy lady during the mid-1980s; the king then donated it to the public, hence the name. Exhibits detailing the life of King Rama IX in his various roles—philanthropist, sportsman, family man, model, actor, etc.—line the perimeter of the octagonal building in the park center. Each weekend, families and couples converge to picnic and frolic among the smooth grassy hills, neatly arranged flower beds, and manicured foliage. Paddleboats on the man-made lake rent for 20฿ per 30min. A 20-minute trolley ride around the park is 10฿. (Open daily 6am-6pm; admission 10฿.) The best time of the year to come to the park is during the first 10 days of December, when flowers and decorations commemorate the King's birthday (Dec. 5).

ENTERTAINMENT

As the song from the musical Chess says: "One night in Bangkok makes the hard man humble. Not much between despair and ecstasy." Bangkok may be full of appalling and prurient opportunities, but pubs, discos, markets, and cultural shows are an active, if under-publicized, surrogate nightlife. Bangkok has impressive cabarets in the **Calypso Cabaret,** Ambassador Hotel, entrance on Soi 11 Sukhumvit Rd. (tel. 261 63 55 from 9am-6pm or 254 04 44 from 6-10pm), featuring well-costumed transvestite performers whose gender is betrayed only by their singing voices. Acts range from wistful torch singing to parodies of famous artists. Calypso is performed in a 200-seat theater and is Bangkok's longest running and most popular show of its kind. Reservations must be made the day of the show. Two 80-minute shows daily at 8:30pm and 10pm. Admission (390฿) includes one free drink. Additional drinks cost 80-180฿.

For entertainment ideas, check out the free *Guide to Bangkok* (available at many bars, malls, restaurants, and hotels, or call 390 19 46), a monthly magazine dedicated to Bangkok's nightlife. Included is a Beer-o-meter page listing the beer prices at many popular bars and clubs, a pink page devoted to Bangkok's gay scene, and a Gig page listing the upcoming live performances by international and local bands.

Bars and Pubs

In Thailand, "bar" generally designates an establishment connected to the sex industry. They come in three types. The first are the go-go bars, which continue to perpetuate the Thai prostitution industry. The second type are "hostess bars," where attractive women are hired by the management to serve drinks and sit with customers. Some of these bars are fronts for prostitution, while some aren't. Finally, there are "pubs," where people can get together and drink without participating in the skin trade in any way. Keep in mind that some reputable establishments are located in not-so-reputable entertainment areas. The nature of a particular bar may change overnight, however.

Bobby's Arms, inside the parking garage where the road curves slightly, Patpong II Rd. (tel. 233 68 28). Established in 1975, this is Thailand's oldest British pub. It has a wide following of English-speaking expatriate workers. Get a dose of cribbage, backgammon, darts, and other staple British pub games amid the warm wood tones and overwhelming British paraphernalia. Flight crews of many airlines come here and get bombed out of their minds. Laugh, and feel secure knowing that you won't be on their 6am flight the next morning. Beers and ales (including Foster's, Guinness Stout) 40-85฿. Spirits 55-75฿. Cocktails 65-95฿. Happy hour daily 5-7pm (15% off all drinks). Open daily 11am-1am. Live music Fri.-Sat. 8:30-11:30pm. Dixieland jazz Sun. 8-11pm.

Woodstock, 210-213 Nana Plaza, 2nd Fl., Soi 4 Sukhumvit Rd. (tel. 258 25 65). Yes, the owner was at Woodstock. Pleasantly seedy, this place packs graying ZZ-Top fans around pool tables in a haze of passive smoke. Established in 1984 as a go-go bar, the owner later changed his mind and made it into a rock 'n' roll bar paying homage to the 60s and 70s. Beers 60-90฿. Cocktails slightly pricier. Happy hour (11:30am-8pm) offers beers at 45฿ (all other drinks 20% off). Open daily 11:30am-2am. Free popcorn. Real food (80-160฿) includes burgers.

Jool's, 21/3 Soi 4 (Nana Tai) Sukhumvit Rd. (tel. 252 64 13), 175m down the *soi* on the left. This joint with a lively atmosphere and the choicest pub food competes fiercely with its cross-town rival, Bobby's Arms. The smaller Jool's is usually packed with Brits of both genders who find it easy to get to know each other in the scrunched surroundings. Getting a stool can take hours. Stucco walls and a ceiling made of wooden planks give the bar an underground feel. Beer 60-80฿ and cocktails, 80-100฿.

The Bar at Bei Ottos, 1 Soi 20 Sukhumvit Rd. (tel. 258 14 95), on the left about 200m down the *soi*. The cozy bar, pictures of Germany, beer mugs, and other *München* motifs can cure some expatriates' homesickness and create it for others. The sturdy black brown slab bar has cushy vinyl to protect the predominantly German customers' midsections as they imbibe. *Oktoberfest* celebrations here take chugging to a new level. Beers and ales include local brands, as well as Foster's, Guinness Stout, Carlsberg, and the German D.A.B. Beers (70฿-250฿). Cocktails 95-150฿. Open daily 2:30pm-2am.

Discos

The disco in Bangkok is what you would expect anywhere: a cavernous building for frenetic dancing, decked in gaudy decorations, a booming sound system, and flashing video screens. Throughout the night, music shifts between live bands and a DJ spinning Euro and American fad-ish music. Discos stay hot for about six months to a year before the crowds find a newer, cooler place. Take note that clubbing in Bangkok is an expensive venture: cover charges, drinks, and food can empty the fattest wallet.

Concept CM² (tel. 255 6888), in the basement of the Novotel Hotel on Soi 6. Decorated with chic post-modern art, this club is as classy as it gets. Bartenders doing tricks, the clientele, and of course the Harley Davidson motorcycle on display all lend their aura to the club's atmosphere. Dance to the beat of Thai and English techno, or dine in the restaurant area where the silk menu comes in a bamboo tub (dishes 150-300฿). Like other clubs in Bangkok, beer here is a hefty 140฿. Cover 100฿. Open daily 6pm-2am.

Phoebus Amphitheater Complex, 50 Ratchadapisak Rd. (tel. 643 01 04), opposite Yaohan Shopping Centre. Utilizing the monstrous size of the building, the owners of this club have turned this place into a spaceship equipped with its very own laser show (11:30pm) and crewmen dancing in gray spacesuits. The live band (10:30-11:30pm) warms up the crowd until the real dancing lifts off at 11:30 when the lights descend to the dance floor. Beer and cocktails are 120฿. Cover 500฿ includes 2 free drinks. Open Sun.-Thurs. 9pm-3am, Fri.-Sat. 9pm-4am.

NASA Spacedrome, 999 Ramkhamhaeng Rd. (tel. 314 40 24). It keeps going, and going, and going...the undisputed winner of the disco longevity award. It's been pumping out hits since Culture Club. An enormous dance floor allows all ages and backgrounds to work out life's frustrations under a cloud of billowing fog and flashing lights. Cover Sun.-Thurs. 200฿ (2 drinks), Fri.-Sat. 250฿ (2 drinks); 300฿ (2 drinks) when a hot band comes to play. Open daily 9pm-2:30am.

Live Music

First popping up in the mid-80s, live music bars have held Bangkok's attention by providing good bands in a low-pressure, festive atmosphere. They've become the entertainment of choice for most people, especially on Friday and Saturday nights. There are as many musical options as there are live music bars; ranging from Thai music, jazz, or country to heavy metal. Bands generally start around 8pm, but things get cooking around 11pm or midnight.

Old West, 231/17 Sarasin Rd. (tel. 252 95 10), near Brown Sugar. The premier spot to take in live folk and country music. Head into the saloon through the swinging doors where you can sip Jack Daniels or Jim Beam amidst Wild West kitsch such as saddles, cattle skulls, and pictures of cowboys and Native Americans. Beer 75-80฿. Cocktails 80฿. Small food menu (40-80฿). No cover. Two bands per night play rock and blues (8:30pm-closing time); check the schedule outside. Open daily 5pm-1am.

Brown Sugar, 231/19 Sarasin Rd. (tel. 250 01 03), opposite Lumpini Park. A Bangkok favorite, it plays the sweetest jazz and pulls in its well-dressed clientele even on weeknights. Pubby feel created by the heavy emphasis on brick and pictures of past performers. Famous past guests include Willem Dafoe, Gregory Hines, and Spyro Gyra. Some food (60-360฿, most under 100฿). Beer 120-150฿. Cocktails 150฿. Music every night from 9:30pm until closing time. Open Sun.-Thurs. 11am-1am, Fri.-Sat. 11am-2am.

Thai Classical Dance Dinners

The highlight of some people's visits to Bangkok is a night at a Thai restaurant with a classical dance show. Since the National Theater schedules infrequent performances of Thai classical dance, some restaurants have tried to fill the gap. Most Thai classical dance dinners put on half a dozen traditional dances in an hour-long show (the dinner lasts another hour). Shows usually include *khon* dances from the *Ramakien*. No shorts, sandals, or tank-tops allowed. Reserve at least a day in advance.

Ruen Thep, Silom Village, Silom Rd. (tel. 234 45 81). Better-than-average ambiance for a Thai classical dance dinner. Doors open daily at 7pm. Thai dinner served at 7:30pm amid pools of carp and turtles. Performance 8-8:30pm. Includes 7 dance styles (changed monthly). 350฿ per person. All major credit cards.

Muay Thai (Thai Boxing)

Muay Thai goes on every day of the week in Bangkok at one of two venues. On Sunday, Monday, Wednesday, and Thursday, the action's at the **Ratchadamnoen Boxing Stadium,** Ratchadamnoen Nok Rd. (tel. 281 42 05). Take regular bus #70 from Sanam Luang. Bouts usually take place in the evenings. Or try the **Lumpini Boxing Stadium,** Rama IV Rd. near Lumpini Park (tel. 251 43 03). To get there, take regular bus #115 from Silom Rd. Bouts start at 6:20pm. Tickets at both stadiums are sold at the gate. Prices run 180-800฿ depending on seat class.

SHOPPING

The Siam Sq. and Silom areas are packed with most of Bangkok's major department stores and shopping centers. Most open daily from 10am-9pm and remain open on most national holidays. The undisputed heavyweight of all of Bangkok's shopping centers is **Mahboonkrong Centre,** on the corner of Rama I and Phayathai Roads in the Siam Sq. area. A six-tiered shopping Goliath, Mahboonkrong houses the Tokyu Department Store as well as hundreds of other shops and restaurants. Across Phayathai Rd., **Siam Square** is connected to Mahboonkrong Centre by a footbridge over the street. Siam Sq., Thailand's first shopping center, spreads over a network of *soi,* housing two movie theaters and a hotel. Across Rama I Rd. from Siam Sq. is the **Siam Centre,** a self-appointed "House of Boutiques." These "shoppes" cater mainly to young, chic Thais. **Amarin Plaza** is farther up Rama I Rd. at the intersection of Rama I with Ratchadamri Roads. About 200m down Ratchadamri Rd. is the relatively small **Peninsula Plaza.** Up Ratchadamri Rd. toward Phetchaburi Rd. is the **Zen World Trade Centre,** vying for Mahboonkrong Centre's spot as the mama of all shopping centers, but offering more open space than anything else. In the Silom area, on the corner of Silom and Rama IV Roads, the **Silom Centre** prominently displays a large "R" (for Robinson Department Store). The **Silom Complex** is farther down on the left, sheltering the popular **Central Department Store.** Across the Pinklao Bridge is **Pata Department Store** where five flights of shops aren't enough: Pata products and food vendors surround the building in semi-market fashion.

■ Near Bangkok

SAMUT PRAKAN

The center of Thailand's leather industry, Samut Prakan is about 30km south of Bangkok toward the Gulf of Thailand. Besides its numerous unentertaining factories, the town holds two popular attractions, the **Samut Prakan Crocodile Farm** and **Muang Boran,** the Ancient City. To get to both, take regular bus #25 from Bangkok to Pak Nam, the boisterous and crowded shopping area of Samut Prakan. Get off at the first stop after **Wat Phichai Songkhram,** a major temple in the heart of Pak Nam. To get to the Crocodile Farm, walk forward from the bus stop, along with the one-way traffic, toward the next street-corner, where a line of light blue *songthaew* marked with a capital "S" waits to go to the Crocodile Farm (3฿). To go to Muang Boran from the bus stop, backtrack against the flow of traffic to the street corner at the Bank of Ayudhya. Along the side street, a row of *songthaew* lines up to go to Muang Boran (3฿).

The **Crocodile Farm** (tel. 703 48 91), is a small zoo with an emphasis on crocodiles. Young trainers taunt and tease the creepy reptiles, and much to the delight of the bloodthirsty crowd, one of them even places his head into a crocodile's mouth. This "wrestling" extravaganza takes place on the hour 9-11am and 1-4pm daily. On Saturdays, Sundays, and holidays, shows are added at noon and 5pm. Included in the admission is an elephant show in which audience members are invited to lie down on the stage while an elephant or two steps daintily over their bodies. Other exciting attractions include an aviary of exotic birds, snake pits, and tigers. (Open daily 8am-6:45pm; admission: 200฿, children 120฿, Thai citizens 30฿.)

Muang Boran (tel. 323 92 53), Km33 on the Sukhumvit Highway, is proudly described by its owners as the largest open-air museum in the world. Not counting ancient ruins, they are probably right, as Muang Boran covers hundreds of acres of land. The museum contains replicas of famous Thai historical monuments and some authentic structures laid out in the geographical shape of Thailand. The most striking sights at Muang Boran are the **Sanphet Prasat Palace,** the **Dusit Maha Prasat Palace,** and the **Khao Phra Wihaan,** the top of which has a spectacular view of the surrounding countryside and the Gulf of Thailand. Bring all your desert gear because Muang Boran is scorching-hot. (Open daily 8am-5pm; admission 50฿, children 25฿.)

NONTHABURI

One of the nation's oldest provinces, Nonthaburi is about 20km north of Bangkok, on both banks of the Chao Phraya River. The town of Nonthanaburi, on the east bank, is believed to have been part of the great Ayutthaya Empire; now it's known for its fruit and earthenware. On the west bank of the Chao Phraya, in Amphoe Bangkluai, stands a magnificent, newly renovated temple called **Wat Chalerm Phra Kliad Wora Wihaan,** known to locals simply as Wat Chalerm. The temple had been neglected for years and was deteriorating markedly when King Bhumibol donated 20 million baht of his personal cache to renovate it. When renovations were completed, the king and queen attended a re-dedication fête on January 12, 1993.

Chinese styles strongly influence the statues around the grounds, as well as the ceramics and flowering decorations adorning the temple. Inside the cool main chapel sits a large golden-colored Buddha in a sash given by His Royal Majesty. Chinese artists patiently handpainted the excruciatingly intricate designs on the walls. The rabbit on the doors outside the chapel is a sign that the temple was built by King Rama II for his queen, whose birth year was the year of the rabbit. The small artificial cave on the temple grounds has a path set atop the waterway and a *naga* head sticking through the hill above the cave. (Open daily 9am-5pm; free.)

The best way to get to Wat Chalerm is by the **Chao Phraya River Express ferry,** which ends at the Nonthaburi Pier. From here, take a ferry to the west bank of the river (1฿), then hire a motorcycle to Wat Chalerm (5฿). Convenient places to board the ferry (5-15฿) are Tha Chang near the Temple of the Emerald Buddha, Tha Phra Arthit near Banglamphu, and Tha Thewet by the National Library.

RATCHABURI

Damnoen Saduak Floating Market is one hour out of town, on the road to Ratchaburi. Catch bus #78 (15฿) at the bus stop in front of the Chinese headstone store 200m down on your left when you turn right out of the *chedi*'s south exit. From Damnoen Saduak town, grab a yellow *songthaew* (3฿) on the main road across from the post office to take you the 2km to the floating market. Upon arrival, locals quickly approach you about water-taxi tours costing 200฿. If you want to do the tourist thing, get a boat for 50฿. But you can get equally good pictures by walking along the canals. The market is only on one stretch of water, with unimpressive houses and boat-rocking speedboats along the other side. Peak activity in the markets is between 9am and 10pm, with its centers at the Hia Kui and Thom Khan markets. Head out early if you want to see all the loot-laden boats; they return home at noon after all the tourists have disappeared.

■ Ayutthaya อยุธยา

Ayutthaya's lengthy history and integral role in the development of Thailand have distinguished the town in the hearts of most Thais. The Ayutthayan empire was founded in 1350 by Prince U Thong and lasted more than four centuries. In that time, the capital city raised 33 kings to the throne, withstood 23 invasions by Burmese troops, and extended its rule as far west as Pego in Burma and as far east as Angkor in Cambodia. As the dominant power in Southeast Asia, the empire flourished in the arts, literature, trade, technology, and commerce.

In 1767, on their 24th attempt, Burmese troops succeeded in breaching Ayutthaya's defenses and, when they found they could not hold the city, burned it to the ground. They took scores of prisoners and destroyed the wats, palaces, libraries, and *chedis*. They melted Buddha images for gold and slaughtered the king along with many Thais. Forced to abandon the location, the remainder of the Thai military moved the capital to Bangkok, where it has been located ever since. For more information see **History** on page 504.

Many Thais still view the sacking of Ayutthaya as the greatest tragedy in the country's history. A re-enactment of the battle preceding the fall of Ayutthaya, complete with elephants, swords, and explosions, is staged annually to commemorate the event. After a day at the monuments, take a look at life behind the scenes of Ayutthaya's well-orchestrated tourist industry. Spinning ghost stories is a favorite pastime in this bone-dry town. When tour buses have headed back to Bangkok and *tuk-tuk* drivers have given up their zealous search for foreign fares, locals claim to hear the cries of fallen soldiers and their massacred families among the charred ruins.

ORIENTATION

Ayutthaya proper is located on a roughly oval-shaped island, about 3km across at its widest point, that sits at the intersection of three major rivers, the **Chao Phraya, Pa Sak,** and **Lopburi. U Thong Road** travels the island's circumference, intersecting at some point all the island's major roads which run north-south and east-west. **Buses** pull in from Bangkok and elsewhere next to the **Chao Phrom Market** at the corner of **Naresuan** (also known as Chao Phrom Rd.) and U Thong Rd. in the northeast corner of the island. Most budget accommodations can be found off Naresuan Rd. in this area. The train station is located east of the island near the **Pridi Damrong Bridge.** While Ayutthaya's array of sights is spread across the island, several of the major ones are centrally located near the **TAT office** on **Si Sanphet Road.**

PRACTICAL INFORMATION

Tourist Offices: TAT (tel. 246 076), on Si Sanphet Rd. Facing the Chao Sam Phraya Museum, it is on the left. English spoken. Open daily 8:30am-4:30pm.

Tourist Police: (tel. 242 352). Next to the TAT office on Si Sanphet Rd.

Tours and Travel: Long-tailed boats and **cruisers** can be hired at the Chantharkasem Palace pier, north of the post office on U Thong Rd. for a 1-hr. trip around the island. A long-tail boat holds up to 8 people (300-400฿).

Currency Exchange: Bangkok Bank (Hua Raw), 20 U Thong Rd. (tel. 252 652), across from the school near the Ayutthaya Post Office. **Krung Thai Bank,** 8-10-12 U Thong Rd. (tel. 245 364). **Thai Farmers Bank,** 6/24 Mu 4 Naresuan Rd. (tel. 423 791). All three banks open Mon.-Fri. 8:30am-3:30pm with **24-hr. ATM.**

Trains: (tel. 241 521), east of Ayutthaya proper on the mainland. *Tuk-tuk* go into town (30฿). Trains to: **Bangkok** (19 per day, 1:12am-6:21pm); **Chiang Mai** (4 per day, 8am-11:30pm); **Lopburi** (8 per day, 9am-12:30am); and **Saraburi** (10 per day, 9am-10:30pm). Baggage storage (pick-up 5am-10pm).

Buses: (tel. 335 304). From Chao Phrom Market, buses go to **Bangkok** (every 30min., 6am-7pm, regular 20฿, A/C 30฿) and **Saraburi** (every 30min., 6am-5pm, 2½hr., 27฿), connecting to points in the northeast. To **Kanchanaburi,** take a non-A/C bus to **Suphanburi** (every 30min., 6am-5pm, 17฿), and transfer at the station to bus #411.

Boats: Chao Phraya Express Boat (tel. 300 400) offers the most affordable cruise option. Boats leave from Maharat Pier (Sun., 8am, return 5:30pm, lower deck 190฿, upper deck 250฿) and include the Royal Folk Arts and Crafts Centre at Bang Sai. **Horizon Cruise,** River City Pier (tel. 538 34 91), offers cruiseboats for rent.

Local Transportation: Mini **songthaew** serve as buses on the island and travel all the main roads. Expect to pay 30-40฿ for most trips to the monuments. Hire a **tuk-tuk** (150฿ per hr.). The cheapest way to the train station is the **ferry** (2฿) from the intersection of U Thong and Horattanachai Rd., near Chao Phrom Market. A final option is to rent a **bicycle.**

Markets: Chao Phrom Market is the main day market. Located where Naresuan Rd. intersects U Thong Rd., near a small Buddhist shrine. Shelves upon shelves of local fruits. Open daily 7am-7pm.

Medical Services: Hospital (tel. 241 027), at the intersection of Si Sanphet and U Thong Rd. at the south end of the island.

Emergency: tel. 199.

Police: tel. 241 001, 241 663, or 241 608.

Post Offices/Telephones: 123/11 U Thong Rd. (tel. 251 233). Handles regular mail, EMS express mail, telegraph service, and overseas calls. Open Mon.-Fri. 8:30am-noon and 1-4:30pm, Sat.-Sun., and holidays 9am-noon. **Postal code:** 13000. Overseas telephone office, 2nd Fl. of the GPO. 30฿ service charge for collect calls or dial HCD for free. Open daily 7am-10pm. **Telephone code:** 035.

ACCOMMODATIONS

The key thing to remember when heading to a guest house in Ayutthaya is that *you* decide where you will stay—not the in-your-face *tuk-tuk* driver at the train station or bus terminal. One thing you don't decide is the room rate, which skyrockets during festival season (around December)—that is, if you can find one.

Ayutthaya Guest House, 16/2 Naresuan Rd. (tel. 251 468), across from the bus terminal at Chao Phrom market, near the end of the *soi.* Large, comfortable, and festively decorated eating area. Friendly manager loves to party and socialize with guests. Stellar central location, and the noise level is tolerable. Rooms have clean, well-lit, shared baths. Dorms 60฿. Singles 100฿. Doubles 120฿. Bike rental 50฿ per day. Office open daily 7am-10pm.

New BJ Guest House, 19/29 Naresuan Rd. (tel. 251 512), on the same road as Chao Phrom Market, to the right before ancient Wat Phra Mahathat and Wat Ratburana. Ring the bell if you come in late. Dorms 60฿. Rooms (1 large bed) 120฿. The restaurant area is great for meeting fellow travelers, picking up sight-seeing tips, and learning Thai-style checkers. About 40฿ for a full meal.

Ayutthaya Youth Hostel (Ruenderm YH), 48/2 U Thong Rd. (tel. 241 978), north of the Pridi Damrong Bridge, at the intersection of U Thong and Pathon Rd. The best-looking place in town, although street traffic and long-tail river boats make sleeping impossible. With only 5 rooms, the place fills up fast. All have double beds draped with lace canopies and mosquito screens, a fan, wooden floors, and high ceilings. Large, Downy-soft towels. Rooms 250฿, for IYH members 200฿. Office open 10am-11pm. Restaurant and main door close at 11pm; another entrance remains open 24hr. Check-out noon. Call for reservations. Visa.

U Thong Hotel, 86 U Thong Rd. (tel. 251 136). Enter on the right side of U Thong Rd. across the street from the post office. A 20-min. walk from Chao Phrom Market. The U Thong Rd. ruckus will probably keep you up late and wake you up early. Rooms with double bed, private bath, and TV 220฿, with A/C 300฿. Two double beds with bath and TV 280฿, with A/C 400฿.

FOOD

Restaurants in Ayutthaya cater more to those fed up with meats at the markets or guest houses than to passing tourists looking for inexpensive meals.

Ruanderm, 48/2 U Thong Rd. (tel. 241 978), north of the Pridi Damrong Bridge, where U Thong meets Pathon Rd. If the hostel's room prices are too much to swal-

TO THE
NORTH

TO
BANGKOK

TO AYUTTHAYA
HISTORICAL
STUDY CENTER

yards   110
meters   100
0   0

N

Train
Station

Pa Sak River

Pridi
Damrong
Bridge

13   U Thong Rd.

Lopburi River

Bank

11

Pier   10

Hua Raw
Market

Bus
Stop

12

Bus
Stop

Khlong Makhamriang Rd.

Pamaphrao Rd.

Chao Phrom) Rd.

Horattanachai Rd.

Bang Ian Rd.

Pa Thon Rd.

Rochana Rd.

9

8

7

6

5

Chikun Rd.

21

20

Naresuan

Beung
Phra Ram

25

22

23   24

Si Sanphet Rd.

26

27

23

U Thong Rd.

19

18

17

28

Phu Khao Thong-Paniat Rd.

Old Lopburi River

4

Khlong-Tho Rd.

3

Pa Thon Rd.

Ayutthaya-Pa Mok Rd.

Chao Phraya River

2

31

30

29

1

Chao Phraya River

32

33

low, at least treat yourself to a meal here. This floating restaurant on the banks of the Pa Sak River is a favorite among locals for its open-air atmosphere. Wagon wheels, lanterns, and private eating alcoves are assembled among antique furniture and tons of plants. The food is downright delectable, though a bit pricey (60-80฿ per entree). Bilingual menu. Open daily 10am-11pm.

Riverside Seafood Grill (tel. 944 9239), on U Thong Rd., 200m south of the post office across the street from the Rodeo Saloon. Chanup, the owner of this riverside restaurant, is armed with a devastating culinary weapon: special sauce. Pick a fish (priced by the gram) and they'll grill it up with the killer flavoring that will make you froth with pleasure. Open daily 4-11pm.

Thai House Restaurant (Ruenthai Maisuay Restaurant), 8/2 Mu 3 Klongsuanplu District (tel. 245 977), farther down the road from Wat Yai Chai Mongkhon, around the bend and on the right. A bit farther away (about 50฿ to get here), it's set atop stilts in an old-style, wooden Thai house. The restaurant serves up moderately priced traditional Thai food, including an assortment of *yams* (a salad with meat or seafood and a lot of spices) and curried soups (50-60฿). A good place to see Thai dancing during dinner on Fri. or Sat. Open daily 11am-10pm.

SIGHTS

Ayutthaya is renowned in Thailand for its rich history. Before you run off to see the ruins, take an educational trip to the **Ayutthaya Historical Study Centre,** the modern Thai building on Rotchana Rd. near the Chao Sam Phraya National Museum. This US$8 million research institute, funded by the Japanese government, has an excellent high-tech exhibit on the ancient city's domestic political developments, trade relations with foreign countries, and the traditional lifestyle of its inhabitants. The explanations are written both in Thai and in English. It's worth the trip to see the detailed miniature reconstructions of Ayutthaya at the height of its power, and for the Thai chants that greet you as you trip off hidden light sensors. (Open Wed.-Sun. 9am-4:30pm; admission 100฿, 50฿ with student ID.)

The **Chao Sam Phraya National Museum** is across the street and to the left about 100m. The two galleries here illustrate all you just learned at the Historical Study Centre. On the first floor of the main building is a collection of old wooden door panelings and pediments with high relief images of demons, deities, and religious events. Farther back you'll find delicate ceramic work and examples of ancient Thai lacquerware. The second floor is where the shiny and glittery stuff is kept. A vault-like room on the east side displays gold treasures found in an excavation of Wat Ratburana. This collection of valuables includes swords, scabbards, and delicately worked headgear worn by queens and other noble ladies. Relics from Wat Mahatat are on the western side of the second floor. In the second exhibition hall, you'll see maps of the trade routes from India to Southeast Asia and a funky fake wood stove ablaze. (Open Mon.-Sun. 9am-4pm; second exhibition hall open Mon.-Fri. 9am-4pm; admission 10฿.)

On the eastern side of the island next to the post office is **Chan Kasem Palace National Museum.** The artifacts here don't size up to the Indiana Jones-type findings at Chao Phraya, but if you're at the post office, you might as well inspect the offerings. (Open Wed.-Sun. 9am-noon and 1-4pm; admission 10฿.)

If you've only got an afternoon to blast through the ruins of Ayutthaya, there are three main locations to target. **Wat Phra Si Sanphet,** on the west side of the island, was the largest temple in Ayutthaya's heyday, as well as the king's palace (admission 20฿, also includes the Ancient Palace just north). The line of three large fire-charred *chedis* is the trademark image of this site. Now empty, they once held the bones of the successive Ayutthayan kings: Rama I, II, and III. Next to this site is **Wihan Phra Mongkhon Bophit,** which shelters one of Thailand's largest Buddha images. Look for sarong-wrapped *bodhi* trees. Locals place broken images of Buddha under these trees; it is unholy to keep damaged Buddhas at home. Halfway between Wat Phra Si Sanphet and Chao Phrom Market are **Wat Phra Mahatat** and **Wat Ratburana.** King Borom Rachathirat II (Chao Sam Phraya) had these two pagodas built after his two brothers (Chao Ai and Chao Yi) killed each other in a brawl atop elephants.

The second important site to visit is **Wat Yai Chai Mongkhon,** which is located southeast of the island. This temple is known for the big *(yai) chedi* visible from miles away. Built in 1357 by King Naresuan after winning a duel atop an elephant, *yai chedi* shows its age with an impressive tilt. If you climb up into the *chedi,* you'll enter upon an eerie scene of eight golden Buddhas serenely meditating in a circle around you. On the grounds of this temple stands a meditation garden where each tree is adorned with politically incorrect bits of food for thought like "to have a wife is the ultimate suffering; to have independence is bliss." (Admission 20฿.)

Ayutthaya is the site of one of the country's largest **Loi Krathong festivals** which usually take place in November or December on the full moon. Thais gather around **Beung Phra Ram,** the large lake in the center of the island, to see fireworks, watch *li-kay,* Thai folk dance-drama, and groove to Thai pop stars on stage. The traditional ceremony of the holiday, the *loi* (floating) of *krathong* (small, lotus-shaped paper boats with candles and incense on top), takes place at the **Chan Kasem Pier** across from the Chan Kasem Palace Museum and post office. Legend says that couples who launch their *krathong* together are destined to become lovers. Get moving.

ENTERTAINMENT

Late-night options in this town are fairly limited. Sneaking into the ruins after dark to drink and listen for ghosts from the past is highly recommended by locals; however, lone women may not be comfortable among the men there. A distant second are some of the local bars.

Moon Café, 10/30 Chao Phrom Rd. (tel. 434 50 94), across from Ayutthaya Guest House; look for the English sign. A stereo system substitutes for a band here. A great place to glean travel info from fellow travelers. Grab a beer during happy hour (6-7pm) for 40฿, or afterward for 70฿. Open daily (no particular hours).

Rodeo Saloon and Restaurant, 79/81 U Thong Rd. (tel. 251 616), across from the Riverside Seafood Grill just before the post office. Look for the Jack Daniels sign ready to take you on. The western bar in town, it boasts *Bonanza* decor, posters of Elvis, live music, and karaoke. Drink prices comparable to Moon Café, but a more extensive (and expensive) menu. Pepper steak 70฿. Open daily 5pm-midnight, but the band normally doesn't get jumping until 9 or 10pm.

Thai Massage (tel. 244 582), at the Chao Phrom Market bus station. Sample the "good taste" massage (2hr. of traditional Thai bodywork, 200฿). The masseuse will first wash your feet and give you a pair of satin slippers. Then you'll change into snazzy polka-dot pajamas and take your place in an A/C cubicle. Be prepared to be stretched out and have every muscle in your body firing by the end. Pamper yourself—this travel stuff is hard work. Open daily 10am-midnight.

■ Kanchanaburi กาญจนบุรี

Kanchanaburi, Thailand's fourth largest province, spreads over nearly 20,000 rather mountainous sq.km and borders Burma to the west of Bangkok. The provincial capital of the same name (known locally as Muang Kan) lies 129km to the northeast of Bangkok and was originally founded by King Rama I to serve as a first line of defense against Burmese attacks through the vulnerable Three Pagodas Pass area.

Both Thais and foreigners alike are drawn to the awe-inspiring natural beauty and low-key attitude of Kanchanaburi. Many services here are geared toward tourists and the TAT is a good place to start. Travel agencies hawk one- to three-day tours of the outlying sights, which are spread over the province, but guest houses are good sources of information for solo travelers.

ORIENTATION

Two daily trains follow the **southern rail line** from Bangkok to Kanchanaburi, but a more frequent jaunt is by bus (from Bangkok's Southern Bus Terminal). Kanchanaburi's main drag is **Saeng Chuto Road,** connecting the train terminal at the north

end of the city to the **Ban Noue Village** 2km away in the southeast—an area home to
the bus terminal, market, and TAT. The **Kwai River** also meanders toward the southeast, paralleling Saeng Chuto Rd. Most of the guest houses are situated along the river
(actually, many float on the river) close to the train station at the north end. The
bridge (yeah, the famous one) is 2km north of the train station, an easy walk or bicycle ride from most accommodations.

PRACTICAL INFORMATION

Tourist Offices: TAT (tel. 511 200), on Saeng Chuto Rd. A 5-min. walk from the
bus station: exit the front of the station, turn left and walk 2 short blocks onto
Saeng Chuto Rd.; the TAT is 100m to your left. From the train station: take a left
onto Saeng Chuto Rd. and walk 20min. or catch a *songthaew.* Friendly advice,
English-speaking staff, maps, and brochures. Open daily 8:30am-4:30pm.

Tourist Police: (tel. 512 795), next to TAT office. Speedy 24-hr. assistance in case of
emergency. You can also get cold water, use the toilets, or leave heavy backpacks
with them. English spoken. There are two tourist mini-stations: one near the stadium and conference hall on Song Kwai Rd. (open daily 8:30am-midnight), and one
on the near side of the Kwai River Bridge (open daily 8:30am-7pm).

Immigration Offices: (tel. 513 325), on Mae Nam Maeklong Rd. From TAT, follow
Saeng Chuto Rd. away from the Ban Noue Village area and turn right at City Hall.
Watch for the English signs on the 4-km trek. If you can't bear to leave Kancha-
naburi, this is the place to get a visa extension. Open Mon.-Fri. 8:30am-4:30pm.

Currency Exchange: The TAT recommends 3 banks for foreign exchange services.
The others also have exchanges and **ATMs,** which generally operate 7am-10pm.
Thai Military Bank, 160/35 Saeng Chuto Rd., Ban Noue Village (tel. 511 677).
Bangkok Bank, 2 U Thong Rd., Ban Noue Village (tel. 511 111). **Thai Farmers
Bank,** 160/80-2 Saeng Chuto Rd., Ban Noue Village (tel. 511 203). Banks open
Mon.-Fri. 8:30am-3:30pm.

Trains: Kanchanaburi Railway Station (tel. 511 285), on Saeng Chuto Rd. To:
Bangkok (#172 at 7:31am and #198 at 3:21pm, 3hr., 25฿) and **Nam Tok** via the
River Kwai Bridge (#353 at 6:10am, #171 at 10:55am, and #197 at 4:26pm, 2hr.,
17฿). Additional trains may make the Bangkok-Kanchanaburi-Nam Tok trip on
weekends and holidays when tourist demand is high; check with the TAT. For the
best view of the "Death Railway" section on the way to Nam Tok, sit on the left.

Buses: The **bus station** (tel. 511 182) is in the heart of Ban Noue Village. Proceed
quickly from the station area—peddlers and *samlor* drivers are good at spotting
farang. Locals say that the waterfalls are more conveniently accessible by bus (or
even *songthaew*) than by train. To: **Bangkok** (#81, every 15min., 3:30am-6:30pm,
3hr., 35฿; with A/C, every 15min., 4am-7pm, 2hr., 62฿); **Ratchaburi** connecting to
destinations in the **south** (#461, every 15min., 5:10am-6:20pm, 2½hr., 26฿);
Suphanburi connecting to **Ayutthaya** (#411, every 20min., 5am-6pm, 2½hr.,
25฿); **Sai Yok Noi, Sai Yok Yai** and **Thong Pha Phum** (#8203, every 30min., 1-
3hr., 18-39฿); and **Erawan National Park** (#8170, every 50min., 8am-4:30pm,
2hr., 40฿). To **Sangkhlaburi** (#8203, 4 per day, 6am-noon, 5hr., 70฿); **A/C minibus service** departs from behind the bus terminal (7 per day, 7:30am-4:30pm, 3
harrowing hr., 100฿ and a numb backside).

Local Transportation: Songthaew run up and down Saeng Chuto Rd. frequently
(10฿ or less). **Motorbike taxis** or **samlor** are 10-20฿ (from railway to TAT). A scenic way to get to Chung Kai Allied War Cemetery or Wat Tham Khao Pun is by
ferry (2฿), leaving the pier at the intersection of Lak Muang and Song Kwai Rd.
Smaller groups or individuals can rent a **canoe** from some guest houses (around
50฿ per hr.).

Rentals: Bikes are 20฿ per day. **Mopeds** go for 200฿ and less for 24hr.; you may
have to put down a passport and 500฿ deposit. Motorcyclists should be *very* careful on the roads. Inexperienced motorcyclists should stick with bicycles.

Luggage Storage: At the Tourist Police behind TAT. It's free!

Markets: Day Market, in Ban Noue Village. The place to buy fruit, *phrik kii nuu,*
clothes, or toiletries. Open early morning until roughly 6pm. **Food vendors,** on
the side facing away from the bus station, offer 15฿ rice dishes. Open daily 7am-

Kanchanaburi

1 Chung Kai Allied War
   Cemetery
2 Japanese War Memorial
3 JEATH War Museum
4 Kanchanaburi Allied War
   Cemetery
5 Lak Muang (City Pillar)
   Shrine
6 Wat Tham Kao Pun
7 Wat Tham Mongkon Thong

Kwai River Bridge

TO PRASAT MUANG SINGH, SAI YOK, AND SANGKHLABURI

India Rd.

Kwai Yai River

Mae Nam Kwai Rd.

Route 323-Saeng Chuto Rd.

Train Station

Donrak Rd.

Songthaews to Kwai River Bridge

Song Kwai Rd.

Pak Phraek Rd.

Chao Khunnen Rd.

Ban Nue Rd.

Thesaban Bamrung Rd.

Kratai Thong Rd.

Hiran Prasart Rd.

Market

Burakarnkosol Rd.

Prasit Rd.

Bovorn Rd.

U Thong Rd.

TO SUPHANBURI

Khu Muang Rd.

Ferry Pier

Lak Muang

Town Gate

Lak Muang Rd. Post Office

Municipal Office

Police Station

Bank

Telephone

Phasuk Market

Bus Station

TAT Office

TO BANGKOK

Kamphaeng Muang Rd.

Wisut Tharangsi Rd.

Mae Khlong River

Pak Phraek Rd.

Saeng Chuto Rd.

Phatthanakarn Rd.

TO KHAO PUN CAVE

Kwai Noi River

Ferry Pier

Pak Phraek Train Station

General Post Office

Sathani Rotfai Rd.

Route 323-Saeng Chuto Rd.

Soi Saeng Chuto 20

TO RATCHABURI

TO WAT THAM KHAO NOI AND WAT THAM SEUA

TO BANGKOK

Hospital

City Hall

THAILAND

dusk. The **night market** on Saeng Chuto Road is somewhat disappointing. Stop for a meal if you're nearby.

Medical Services: Paholpolpayuhasena Hospital (tel. 511 507), on Saeng Chuto Rd., 3km past the GPO when heading out of the city. **Thana Kan Hospital** (tel. 622 358), on Saeng Chuto Rd., 800m to the south of TAT. **Saeng Chuto Hospital** (tel. 621 129), 500m to the north of TAT. **24-Hr. Clinic:** From the guest houses on Song Kwai Rd. head south. At the tourist police box, take a left and go 3 blocks. The clinic is on the left.

Emergency: tel. 191

Provincial Police Headquarters: (tel. 511 540), across from TAT.

Post Offices: GPO (tel. 511 131), on Saeng Chuto Rd. From Ban Noue Village, 1km beyond TAT on the left. *Poste Restante.* Open Mon.-Fri. 8:30am-4:30pm, Sat.-Sun. 9am-noon. **Local branch** on Lak Muang Rd. at the corner of Phraek Rd. by town gate. From TAT head right, take your 1st left and walk about 500m. Open Mon.-Fri. 8:30am-4:30pm, Sat. 9am-noon. **Postal code:** 71000

Telephones: (tel. 511 131), 2nd Fl. of GPO. Long-distance and overseas calls. Open daily 7am-10pm. **Telephone code:** 034

ACCOMMODATIONS

When you arrive in town you will be accosted by many a *samlor* driver hoping to escort you to a guest house on the river. If you're too hot and bothered to walk, pay them no more than 20฿ (10฿ for a motorcycle taxi). Although the river guest houses offer the best views and opportunities to meet fellow travelers, they are also the most vulnerable to the intense booming beat of the floating discos on weekends.

River Guest House, 42 Rong Heeb Oil Rd. (tel. 512 491), is a 10-min. walk from the train station or a 15฿ *samlor* ride from TAT. Simple wood-box rooms are afloat on the river—a hazard for late night trips to raid the honor-system refrigerator, but a convenience for spur-of-the-moment River Kwai dips. A laid-back scene. Singles 40฿. Doubles 70฿, with fan, net, and bath 100฿.

Rick's Lodge, 48/5 Rong Heeb Oil Rd. (tel. 514 831), between P.S. and River Guest House. Run by a Thai and Australian husband-and-wife team who speak Thai, German, and English. Satellite TV will provide your CNN fix as you enjoy the western bath in a bi-level bungalow. Restaurant offers great food and the best river view of any guest house. Bungalows 280-300฿.

Nita Raft House, 27/1 Phra Phrak Rd. (tel. 514 521). A 10-min. walk to bus station. An occasional boat wake will lull you to sleep until the floating disco barges begin their nightly river circuit. Owner dispenses videos and sight-seeing info. Tasty victuals (rice with fried veggies 17฿). Shoebox singles with mattress on floor 40฿. Doubles 60฿. Add 10฿ for fan, 100฿ for bed frame. Two single beds with fan and private bath are a steal at 150฿.

Jolly Frog Backpacker's, 28 Mae Nam Kwai Rd. (tel. 514 579). Call and they might pick you up from the bus or train station. This 45-room guest house offers the best chance to find fellow westerners in town. Concrete and drywall singles 50฿. Doubles 90฿. 2 twin beds with private bath 130฿. Bicycle rentals.

FOOD

Near the bus terminal in Ban Noue Village, food stalls and simple open-air eateries are ubiquitous. Similar oases abound along Saeng Chuto Rd., but the highest concentration of restaurants is along Song Kwai Rd. Most accommodations serve good meals for about 25฿.

Mem (tel. 513 851), on the corner of Song Kwai and Burakarnkosol Rd. No English sign, but it's the first in a series of restaurants north of the tourist police booth and white convention center. Isaan specialties. Fried fish cakes go for 30฿, most salads 40฿. Open daily until midnight.

Jukkru (tel. 620 570), 3 restaurants up the street from Mem. Again, no English sign, but fab, spicy food makes it worth the extra effort to find. Individual rice and meat dishes 20฿. Super-spicy seafood plates 40-60฿. Open daily 4-11pm.

Mae Nam (tel. 512 811), is the floating restaurant closest to the ferry on Song Kwai Rd. Squid's the draw here (40-60฿), served up by sailor-garbed waitstaff. English menu. Afternoon and evening music. Open daily until midnight.

Aree Bakery (tel. 511 961), on Burakarnkosol Rd. between the conference center and the stadium. Take the 1st right on Pakpreak Rd.; it's 100m down on the left. Friendly couple used to work in the Thai embassy and speak great English. Apple pie *à la mode* 20฿. Coconut cakes 10฿. Open daily 7am-9pm.

ENTERTAINMENT

Sick of sipping Singha and watching pirated videos at guest houses? Don't worry, there are other options. The local favorites are on Song Kwai Road: **karaoke bars** line the eastern side while the infamous floating **discos** rest on the banks. Those who seek the camaraderie of fellow travelers would do well to go to either of the *farang* bars in the town, listed below. Both of these places rent bikes (30-40฿) and motorbikes (200฿), as well as exchange currency seven days a week and accept both traveler's checks and cash. This could be a lifesaver for the desperate traveler since there is nowhere else to change money after the banks close on Friday.

Ampai (tel. 513 182), just off Saeng Chuto Rd. to the left, about 150m north of the River Kwai Hotel. London-born proprietor Ron Davis offers his patrons A/C and satellite TV as they dine on budget meals (20-30฿). You'll find Ron and the *farang* clientele very informative. Open daily 8am-midnight.

Punnee Café (tel. 513 503), next to Ampai. Another English establishment, featuring a used bookstore and full bar. Danny, the proprietor, also organizes and guides 1- to 3-day treks. If you like the place you can also stay for the night. Doubles with fan 150฿, with A/C 300฿. Open daily 8am-midnight.

SIGHTS

Renting a bike is the easiest and most wallet-friendly way to take in all the sights. The **bridge over the River Kwai,** about 3km north of the train station, is Kanchanaburi's most well-known memorial to those who lost their lives here during World War II. The current tourist attraction is actually a reconstruction of the original "Death Railway Bridge," which was bombed by the Allies. It is disappointingly tiny for a bridge shored up by so much lore, blood, sweat, and tears. During the war, engineers predicted that it would take five years to construct the bridge, but the Japanese army, in its eagerness to dominate Asia, forced POWs and local laborers to complete the railway in 16 months. In the process, tens of thousands died from disease, starvation, torture, and exhaustion. Laborers were buried where they fell. The first (wooden) bridge was finished in February 1943. Two months later, a bridge of steel was completed, but construction on the railroad continued from both ends until they met just short of the Three Pagodas Pass by Sangkhlaburi. For 20 months, the Japanese moved supplies in and out of Burma and Thailand until the Allies destroyed the bridge in December 1945.

On the bridge's eastern approach, train aficionados can examine vintage steam locomotives and peculiar hybrid road/railcars at the **Railway Museum.** During the first week of December, a spectacular nightly sound and light show commemorates the Allied destruction of the hated Japanese bridge. Legions of tourists throng to the event; plan ahead to witness it first hand. (Open daily 8:30am-5pm; admission 25฿.)

Also near the bridge are the **Japanese War Memorial,** riverside restaurants, and handicraft and jewelry shops. **The Art Gallery and War Museum** (tel. 513 478), 50m toward town from the bridge, is an outstanding museum that illustrates the major leaders of World War II and unflinchingly examines wartime atrocities. Along the wall of the smaller buildings are hand-carved replicas of Hitler, FDR, and Churchill, among others. Inside the marble-floored building are well-preserved weapons, uniforms, photographs, and displays on archaeology, war, and stamps. Upstairs, visitors can ogle the mural of past Miss Thailand winners. Admission is 30฿. Artistically

THAILAND

impressive is the glass-encased **Tomb of the Unknown Soldier,** which contains the remains of 106 men who lost their lives working on the Death Railway.

On the other end of town along Lak Muang Rd. lie the **town gate** and **city pillar shrine** of this youthful provincial capital (founded in 1831). Less than 1km away down Pak Phraek Rd. is the **JEATH War Museum,** established in 1977 by the chief abbot of **Wat Chaichumphon (Wat Dai** to locals) to honor victims of the Death Railway Bridge, or as the entrance announces, "To Forgive But Not Forget." JEATH stands for Japan, England, America/Australia, Thailand, and Holland, the nations that met in battle at Kanchanaburi. The thatched detention hut with cramped bunks contains photographic, pictorial, and physical memorabilia, including items donated by several POW survivors. Most notable is a disturbing series of paintings that vividly underscores the inhumanity of war. Information sheets are available. (Open daily 8:30am-4:30pm; admission 20฿.)

For wat-lovers, there are three major sites in the area besides Wat Chaichumphon. **Wat Thavasatkhalam** on Jiao Naen Rd., in the middle of town, is an active temple that is the most frequented by townspeople. **Wat Tham Khao Pun,** 1km beyond Chung Kai Allied War Cemetery, boasts a cave and beautiful Buddha images. Finally, 4km across the river, **Wat Tham Mongkon Thong** (The Cave Temple of the Golden Dragon) is famous for its magnificent cave site and its renowned **"floating nun,"** a venerable old lady who can meditate while supine on water without sinking. People come here from all over Thailand to receive her blessings; early weekend mornings are usually the best time to catch her in action, coinciding with the arrival of the tour buses. Behind the *bot,* steep steps lead up the mountain side and into the limestone cave, affording spectacular views of the surrounding mountains and valleys. A white-bearded, camera-shy Chinese hermit sells old remedies in front of the cave.

■ Near Kanchanaburi

Gorgeous national parks, historical sites, and the area around Sangkhlaburi are what really make the trip to Kanchanaburi Province worthwhile. The parks contain waterfalls of all sizes, from the five-minute photo-opportunity **Sai Yok Noi Waterfalls** to the most popular, multi-tiered **Erawan Waterfalls** and **Huay Khamin Waterfalls.** Cave cravers delight in the grottoes scattered throughout the province, especially **Phra That Cave.** For animal lovers, the green valleys created by the Kwai Noi-Kwai Yai River system shelter diverse forms of wildlife. **Prasat Muang Singh** and **Ban Kao Museum** open a window to an ancient time, with some Neolithic artifacts. But the hidden gem is serene **Sangkhlaburi,** hours away from the floating discos of Kanchanaburi and the bedlam of Bangkok.

Rte. 3199 and 323 split the province and are good jumping-off points. Buses leave regularly from Kanchanaburi town along these two arteries (see **Practical Information** on page 544). Trains go nearer to Prasat Muang Singh than the buses and Ban Kao historical area, but usually run behind schedule.

Rte. 3199 is a well-paved passage to Erawan, easily traversed by motorbike as well as by bus. Those who wish to go beyond Erawan to Huay Khamin or Phra That Cave should plan to use their own transportation (durable motorcycle or pick-up truck); otherwise, find a group to split the cost of hiring a boat or minibus. Before exploring the region, make bank and phone stops in Kanchanaburi town. Currency exchangers are rare, and long-distance calls may be prohibitively costly on the road.

As Rte. 323 heads west to Sangkhlaburi and the border, lonely stretches and sharp curves wind ahead. The bus or minivan is the best option for wary motorists. If you do take your own wheels, drive during the day and keep a careful eye on the fuel gauge. Thong Pha Phum is the most commonly used pit stop before running to the border. Bring extra money—many visitors stay longer than expected once they discover the pleasant weather and beauty of Sangkhlaburi. It is also home to some of the country's best deals on jewelry, cloth, and hand-crafted wooden furniture.

ALONG ROUTE 3199

Bo Phloi

Blue sapphires and semi-precious stones such as onyx are extracted from the open cast mines here. Not many tourists make the trip; usually they are only allowed to see the gem market. Rather than risk your cash buying gems in a random market, invest in a gem from Bo Phloi Ltd., which comes with a certificate of authenticity to prevent your being ripped off as so many travelers are. Bus #325 from Kanchanaburi will bring you straight there (every 20min., 6am-6:30pm, 1½hr., 50km, 14฿) or you can follow the blue and white gem signs. Bo Phloi is on Rte. 3086, along the way to Chaloem Rattanakosin National Park.

Erawan National Park

If you can only see one place around Kanchanaburi, this should be it. The seven levels of **waterfalls** seem to have been landscaped by some master architect, but the cascading water, natural pools, and bamboo groves were there long before humans ever discovered this paradise. (Open daily 6am-6pm; admission for *farang* 25฿, for motorcycles 5฿, for cars 30฿.) The money goes to the upkeep of this very well-managed and beautifully maintained Eden.

Before setting off, check the **visitor center** for their English maps. They also offer a slide presentation in Thai if you happen to be there with a group of 10 or more. Lovely slides are set to a musical soundtrack and accompanied by a talk on the Kanchanaburi national parks and the increasingly influential environmental movement in the country.

The first three levels of the waterfalls are an easy five- to ten-minute walk from the trail head. Tourists often bring swim gear for a refreshing dip. The higher up the falls, the more challenging the trail. The payoff in climbing the steep concrete stairs and crossing the bridges is the clearer water and the 0.5m-long fish. Then there's the legendary eighth level. Only those that know the way can make it from level seven (one of the park rangers has only been there himself three times in four years). Tigers and monkeys cohabit the untouched jungle around this crystal-clear pool. Talk to the headquarters people if you're interested; maybe you'll be one of the handful of people who have experienced level eight. The other seven levels can be seen easily in a two-hour roundtrip, but do add on another two hours for frolicking in Erawan's waters.

In the park, re-energize at the **food stalls,** a short walk from the visitor center. A simple rice dish and drink costs about 20฿. Bathrooms are here as well as along the trail. **Accommodations** range from camping (bring your own tent, 5฿) to dorms (no beds and common bathroom, 10฿) to bungalows (with four beds and bath, 250฿).

The park makes a perfect daytrip from Kanchanaburi; use public bus #8170 (every 50min., 8am-4pm, 2hr., 65km, 19฿). The last bus returns to Kanchanaburi at 4pm. *Songthaew* that also make the trip pass by the river houses at 9am and return from Erawan at roughly 4pm (60฿ roundtrip).

In emergencies, make a bee-line for the **National Park Headquarters.** It's the building straight through the check-point where the bus drops people off. The park has an excellent safety record, considering it is the most popular park in Thailand. During the rainy season, the paths can be slippery but manageable. Peak season is November to January, when visitors fill the pools. New Year's Day and major holidays will also see hordes of (occasionally drunk) people. To continue on to **Huay Khamin Falls** in Sri Nakharin National Park or **Phra That Cave** in Erawan, get information on road and travel conditions from the headquarters or visitor center. You must have a private vehicle (and good directions from Erawan Headquarters) to reach these sights.

Phra That Cave, well-known for its monumental stalagmites, is the largest and most popular spelunking sight in Kanchanaburi. Lanterns are provided at the cave entrance; 5-10฿ is a reasonable donation. There is no regular transportation over the

10km to the cave. Groups can hire *songthaew* (around 300฿), or you can jam up there via motorbike.

Sri Nakharin National Park

This park is rather inaccessible, especially compared to Erawan, but those who brave the challenge emerge with tall tales. The park headquarters is 105km from Kanchanaburi, but it is best to visit the park and **Huay Khamin Waterfalls** on a daytrip from a base at Erawan National Park or the Sri Nakharin Dam area. The seven-level falls are the centerpiece of the 1532-sq.km area. A Disney menagerie of deer, elephants, and tigers are hidden in more remote areas. Three bungalows are available in the park at 100฿ per person. To get to the park headquarters, take a 40-km dry-weather road parallel to the reservoir; it is passable only by motorcycles, pickups, and four-wheel-drive vehicles. Alternatively, take a 45- to 70-minute boat ride from the **Tha Kradan Pier**, 24km northeast of the Sri Nakharin Dam, 5km past Mongatet Village. Groups can charter long-tail boats for 1000฿ and up.

Si Sawat

If you're looking to get away from it all and willing to sleep on the floor to do so, head for Si Sawat on the banks of the Sri Nakharin Reservoir, five to six hours from Kanchanaburi on Rte. 3199. In this sleepy fishing village you can probably crash at the temple; ask the English-speaking school teacher for assistance. For dinner, try fishing on the lake—you're sure to catch a whopper. To get there, take #8170 from Kanchanaburi (every 50min., 8am-4:30pm, 40฿). Or pick up the bus in the afternoon after an early morning trip to Erawan.

ALONG ROUTE 323

Prasat Muang Singh Historical Park

An archaeologist's dream, the walled City of Lions is along the Kwai Noi River and contains skeletal remains and artifacts dating back 2000 years. Dominating the four groups of ruins, Prasat Muang Singh (Tower of the City of Lions) is believed to have been the westernmost outpost of the Khmer empire. Art from Cambodia, as well as the Thai Dvaravati period, decorates the tower. Laterite bricks give way to the inner shrine where the four-armed Bodhisattva images were housed 800 years ago.

For more information, go to the **visitor center** (tel. 572 573) to the right of the main ruins upon entering. The chief English-speaking administrator has articles about Muang Singh's history. (Open daily 8am-5pm; admission 20฿.) **Trains** come closer to the park than the bus. The train goes from Kanchanaburi to Thakilen (the stop for Prasat Muang Singh, 6:10 and 10:55am, 1½hr., 10฿). From the train station, walk 1km to the main road and then walk another km to the right. Trains head back to Kanchanaburi at 6:26am, 2:20, and 4:31pm. Bus #8203 stops 7km from the park, and transportation for the extra leg may be hard to find. When it's time to head back to Kanchanaburi, buses on Rte. 323 are best caught before 5pm.

Sai Yok Noi Waterfall

This waterfall is small, a drip in the bucket compared to Erawan. It's right off Rte. 323, across the road from the market area where the bus stops. The cascades are best experienced during the tail end of the rainy season. They lie 60km away from Kanchanaburi and 30 minutes before the **Sai Yok Yai National Park** entrance. Trains leave from Kanchanaburi at 6:10 and 10:55am (17฿). Get off at the end of the line (Nam Tok) and walk or hop on a *songthaew* or motorcycle to the falls, 2km northwest of the station. The #8203 bus will cost about the same for a faster trip, but the train ride is more relaxing and rather scenic. Trains back to Kanchanaburi leave Nam Tok Station at 5:25am, 1:15, and 3:10pm.

Wang Badang Cave

For intrepid tunnelers yearning for serious adventure, head to this cave, a 3-km walk from the station, or 2km off Rte. 323. Turn right 100m south of Sai Yok Noi. Remember to bring a flashlight and good shoes; rubber thongs won't hold up here.

The Lawa Cave

The largest cave in the Sai Yok Yai National Park area, it is most accessible to larger groups. A 10- to 12-person boat can be hired (1000-1200฿) at **Pak Saeng Pier** in Tambon Tha Sao southwest of the Sai Yok Noi Waterfall. Boats also go by Sai Yok Yai Waterfalls and **Dao Wadung Caves** (4hr. roundtrip).

Sai Yok Yai Waterfall and National Park

Celebrated in Thai poetry and song, the Sai Yok Yai Waterfall dribbles unimpressively except between July and September, when the 500sq.km park has more to offer. Barking deer, blue-winged pittas, gibbons, limestone wren babblers, wild pigs, and wreathed hornbills inhabit the deciduous forests. Holy rodents, Batman! Some of the world's smallest mammals, the Kitti hog-nosed bats, live here in the **Bat Cave,** accessible by various trails. (Open daily 6am-7:30pm; admission 25฿.)

You can pick up English maps and leave your hefty gear at the **tourist center** desk. **Accommodations** are limited to camping (5฿) and rooms for one or two over the river (200฿); a better option may be the Sai Yok Noi-area hotels. Daytrips to the park include the **Hellfire Pass** and **Burma-Thailand Death Railway Memorial** along the connecting section of Rte. 323. There is a hiking trail along the original tracks which were constructed by the Allied POWs under the Japanese.

The actual National Park entrance is 30 minutes from the Sai Yok Noi Falls. Scramble onto any bus or *songthaew* heading north (about 15฿) and tell them where you are going. It will then be a 3-km walk or 10฿ motorcycle lift to the visitor center. Bus #8203 goes from Kanchanaburi (30฿); you'll still have to get a motorcycle taxi to the information center.

Hin Dat Hot Springs

These two sights don't garner an English road sign, but their turnoff is about 127km from Kanchanaburi and before Thong Pha Phum. The natural springs bubble away in a hollow 3km northeast of Rte. 323. One pool stays a constant 40°C, while the other fluctuates from 35 to 38°C—hot, any way you cut it. If you can haul yourself out of these pools of bliss, the waterfall (your basic tri-level cascade) is 10km ahead.

Thung Yai Sanctuary Park

This national park, a UNESCO World Heritage sight, is living proof of environmental groups' continued role in Thailand's future. The large area of forested mountains and high plains lying west of Sangkhlaburi is a safe harbor for protected wildlife species including tigers, elephants, bears, otters, tapirs, gibbons, and peacocks. Only four-wheel-drive vehicles can traverse the terrain, even during the dry season; special permission is required for entry. Contact the Kanchanaburi TAT Office (tel. 511 200) for road conditions, accessibility, and entrance requirements; or talk to Armin at the Burmese Inn in Sangkhlaburi for details and possible jeep-with-driver rental.

■ Sangkhlaburi สงคลาบุร

An escape for the tourist who yearns to escape from other tourists, Sangkhlaburi is situated about 225km northwest of Kanchanaburi, on the northern edge of the reservoir created by the Khao Laem Dam. The 70-km route from the dam to town runs parallel to the reservoir, passing raw limestone mountainsides, verdant valleys, and several raft complexes harbored among partially submerged trees. Visitors come mainly for the Three Pagodas Pass, Chedi Phuthakaya of Wat Wang Wiwekaram (say that five times fast), and the markets and villages along the border. During the dry season (November-April), Sangkhlaburi offers opportunities for swimming in waterfalls, adventuring along the border, or simply relaxing and enjoying the fresh air and countryside.

ORIENTATION AND PRACTICAL INFORMATION

A/C buses drop passengers off at the market in the middle of town. Regular buses arrive one block away from the market area with its many food stalls. The Sree Dang Hotel is nearby while the Burmese Inn and P Guest House are about 1km down the road to the right from the bus stop. If you're not in a walking mood, ask a motorcycle driver to take you (10฿).

Currency exchange can be handled at **Siam Commercial Bank** (tel. 595 076). From the bus stop, walk two blocks to your right, then take a left. (Open Mon.-Fri. 8:30am-3:30pm.) To get to the **post office** from the bus stop, head three blocks to your right. At the photo lab, take a left and walk two blocks. Turn left and the post office will be on the left. (Open Mon.-Fri. 8:30am-4pm, Sat. 9am-noon.) **Overseas telephone calls** can be made at the post office. P Guest House will also place your call for a 50฿ charge. The **day market** is located in the center of town; from Phornpailin Hotel (see **Accommodations and Food** below), walk one block to the left, take a left and the market is on the left. The **Mon market** is across the wooden bridge at the base of the *chedi*. While both of these are open from 7am to dusk, the day market is most active in the morning before noon, and the Mon market in the early afternoon. In case of medical emergencies, contact the **hospital** across from the Phornpailin Hotel (tel. 595 058). (Open 24hr.) The **Missionary Hospital,** 18km from Sangkhlaburi in Huay Malai, has a western doctor. The **police** can be reached at tel. 595 031. **Postal code:** 71240. **Telephone code:** 034.

ACCOMMODATIONS AND FOOD

Follow the signs to the two rival guest houses, 15 minutes apart on the same road. The **Burmese Inn** (tel. 595 146) is 1km to the right from the bus station. Armin (Austrian), Meo (Thai), and their lovely baby Alissa (Thaistrian) have built a clean, comfortable, bungalow-style guest house nestled amid wild orchids. Armin offers helpful and interesting information and maps of the border area. Motorbike rental is 180฿ per day. Singles with net are 50฿, doubles 80฿. Rooms with private bath, fan, and desk go for 120฿, doubles 180฿. The **P Guest House,** 81/1 Tambon Nong Loo (tel. 595 061), 1km beyond the Burmese Inn, is run by Duranee Yen Jai and her husband, who maintain a beautiful restaurant and garden overlooking the lake. The view of the Mon village, wats, and wooden bridge is unbeatable, although the single rooms are small and the mattresses thin. Multilingual Duranee organizes daytime boat, elephant, and raft tours for 700฿ per person, including a room for the night. Motorbike rental is 150฿ per day. You can make overseas calls for a 50฿ charge. A single cot is 40฿, double mattress 50฿. Rooms with private bath are 120฿. The third option in town is the **Phornpailin Hotel** (tel. 595 039), near the central market where the A/C minivan drops passengers off. The hotel is down the street to the right. Well-scrubbed rooms and hardwood floors compensate for the dearth of river views. Rooms with two single beds, fan, and private bath are 180฿, with A/C 350฿. Deluxe rooms with fridge, TV, carpet, and A/C are 700฿.

SIGHTS

One of Sangkhlaburi's two basic tour packages whisks you off to Three Pagodas Pass, the bridge, the temple, and the Mon market and village. The jaunt is occasionally guided in English and costs about the same as a do-it-yourself expedition (two days 750฿, three days 950฿), but eliminates the hassle of hailing *songthaew* and motorcycles. Jungle trekking tours inflict considerable wallet wounds, due to their inclusion of long-tail boat, elephant-back, and bamboo raft experiences. After two hours, expect the "seats" on the elephants to be uncomfortable and the romance of the jungle to become routine. Long clothing or sunblock are highly recommended. Tours organized in Kanchanaburi include transportation to and from Sangkhlaburi, visits to the sights, accommodations, and some meals.

THE MON VILLAGE

Across Khao Laem Lake, created by the dam near **Thong Pha Phum,** is the **longest wooden bridge in Thailand.** The Mon constructed this 400-m trestle bridge to connect their camp with the main part of the city. From this bridge one can behold a spectacular panoramic view of Sangkhlaburi. To get to the Mon village, take a motorbike taxi across the bridge for 20฿.

The Mon people are not quite refugees—they do not have Thai citizenship, but some have obtained work permits from immigration. Most of them have fled the shackles of slave labor in Burma. For years, the Mon have fought the Burmese for the right of self-determination, claiming land that now comprises the eastern states of Burma. The Mon people remain in Thailand under the protection of the elderly Luang Phaw Utama, who watches over the temples in the area. Today, 1000 households sit beneath the gaze of the two new temples. After crossing the bridge into the Mon Village, head straight back to the paved road; follow this road left until you reach the wat's gate. From here the *chedi* and handicraft market are to the left, opposite the glittery **Wat Wang Wiwekaram,** which is the center for Mon worship.

The Mon temple is architecturally derived from Indian, Burmese, and Thai styles. Constructed in 1985, *chedi* was modeled on the Mahabodha stupa in Bodhgaya, India. **Wat Somdet** (before entering Sangkhlaburi) and **Wat Si Sewan** (between Burmese Inn and P Guest House) are respectively the Thai and Karen temples.

■ Border Crossing: Three Pagodas Pass

One-day tours from local inns leading up to this sight often make the Three Pagodas Pass and the border area an emotional letdown. The diminutive **Three Pagodas** at the border sit benignly on a patch of grass around which vehicles turn around to head back. The location was in one of the rowdiest regions during the Thai-Burmese War. According to one story, as the war was concluding in the mid-1700s, the King of Thailand laid down the three stones to mark the border between the two countries (since that time, the border has shifted). The flanking stones represented Thailand and Burma, while the middle one signified unity and peace. Villagers later constructed the three pagodas (*Chedi Sam Ong*) over the original legendary stones, and the middle shrine has been used by monks to pray for peace.

Between 6am and 6pm, Burmese border control allows *farang* to enter the country for two hours (130฿). The money goes to support the Burmese regime, however, and certainly does not help the Mon or Karen people. Moreover, the black market on the other side isn't all that special; the market developing on the Thai side will soon have similar goods, and almost everything here is sold in the Mon market for comparable prices. Local guest houses can take you to **Takien Thong Waterfall,** the Mon Village, and the border for 100฿ (five person minimum). During the dry season, it would be wise to hire a jeep with driver (700฿ for up to six people) from the Burmese Inn to chauffeur you for the day. Alternatively, motorbikes can be rented to hit the road solo.

▓ Phetchaburi เพชรบุรี

Although the TAT tags Phetchaburi as the "little-known province on the way to Hua Hin," romantics might prefer its usual label, "The City of Diamonds," bestowed when gems were found nearby in the Chao Phraya River. Most *farang* don't bother stopping here on their way to the southern beaches—don't be surprised if people whisper to each other as you stroll along Phetchaburi's busy streets. The town (pop. 35,000) chugs along regardless of outsiders—people rush to work in the morning, school children in uniforms flood the streets at 5pm, and by 9pm, everyone is at home, hanging with the family unit.

ORIENTATION

Located 135km south of Bangkok, Phetchaburi (also known as Phetburi or simply Phet) can be reached by bus or train (2-2½hr.). Finding your way around Phetchaburi should be a simple task considering the town's small size and the roads' simple grid format. The center of town and a good reference point is **Saphan Chomrut** (Chomrut Bridge) where the **Phetchaburi River,** which runs north-south, intersects the town's main west-east thoroughfare, **Pongsuria Road.** Most of the other major roads run parallel to the river and intersect Pongsuria Rd. On the west bank (from west to east) are **Rachadamern Road** and **Damnernkasem Road.** On the east bank are **Punich Jaren Road, Suranluchai Road,** and **Matayawong Road.**

PRACTICAL INFORMATION

Tourist Offices: The town is served by the **TAT office** in Cha-am, but it has sparse information on Phet.

Currency Exchange: Siam Commercial Bank (tel. 425 303), on Damnernkasem Rd., is south of the GPO. **Thai Farmers Bank** is 1 block beyond Chomrut Bridge on the east bank, on the corner of Pongsuria and Suranluchai Rd. Both banks are open Mon.-Fri. 8:30am-3:30pm.

Trains: To **Bangkok** (6 per day, 2:10am-6:50pm, 54฿ 3rd Class, 91฿ 2nd Class). The bus is quicker and more convenient.

Buses: The **regular bus station** on Phetkasem Hwy. is on the opposite side of Mt. Khao Wang from downtown. There are 2 bus routes to **Bangkok** (old route every 20min., 4am-5:30pm, 3½hr., 43฿; new route every 25min., 4am-5:30pm, 2½hr., 36฿). From the station, motorcycle taxis ride into town (20฿). **A/C buses** use a terminal just east of the GPO on Ratwithi Rd. Two companies offer service to **Bangkok** (every 45min., 5am-7:30pm, 3hr., 65฿). To intercept A/C buses headed farther **south,** go to Phetkasem Hwy.; ask for help at either bus station first.

Local Transportation: Your feet should take you anywhere in the downtown area or take **samlor** (10฿) or **motorcycles.** The **tram** on the far side of Khao Wang saves you the hike up to the 2 peaks (20฿ adults, 10฿ children). To get to **Khao Luang Caves,** go to Ratwithi Rd. at the mountain base and hire a *rot lenk* (a small pick-up) or *tuk-tuk* (10฿). Taxis to **Cha-am** (white station wagons) run on demand for 20฿ per person, when more than 4 people need to go. Ask around.

Medical Services: Phetchaburi Hospital (tel. 428 082), on Rot Fai Rd. north of town.

Emergency: tel. 191.

Police: Phetchaburi Police Station (tel. 425 500), on Ratwithi Rd. near the GPO. 24-hr. mini station at the base of Mt. Khao Wang.

Post Offices: GPO, at the intersection of Ratwithi and Damnernkasem Rd. Open Mon.-Fri. 8:30am-4:30pm, Sat.-Sun. 9am-noon. **Postal code:** 76000.

Telephones: 2nd floor of the GPO for long-distance calls and other services. Open daily 7am-10pm. **Telephone code:** 032.

ACCOMMODATIONS

Room rates are higher than in Thailand's backpacker meccas, but fret not, the places listed below are happy to have a *farang* sign in their guest book.

Chom Kow Hotel (tel. 425 398), the first house on the left on the east bank with a white sign in Thai. Large clean rooms with queen size beds, sink, and mirror. Located near downtown. Each floor has a balcony with a view of the river. Owner speaks English. Singles/doubles 120฿, with hall bathroom 80฿.

Ratanaphakdi Hotel (tel. 425 041), 2 blocks west of Chomrut Bridge on Pongsuria Rd. Look for the golden letters in Thai above the door. Lovingly preserved wooden stairs lead to an upstairs hideaway. Blue tile bathroom with western toilet down the hall. Singles 100฿. Doubles 200฿.

Day King Long Hotel (tel. 425 023). From Chomrut Bridge, go east on Pongsuria Rd. At Thai Farmers Bank, turn right onto Suranluchai Rd. and take the first left. It's the 2nd to last entrance on the left, past the shoe store. No-frills lobby but chambers are luxurious (140฿).

FOOD

There's no such thing as low blood sugar in Phetchaburi. The usual Thai spread is complemented by delectable desserts created by local bakeries. Palm sugar abounds in Thailand's crown jewel of sweet-making. A cluster of stores sells pre-packaged sweets along Phetkasem Rd. at the base of Khao Wang, but vendors also walk the streets around the temples. A **market area** and bakeries, such as **Lamiet** and **Khodi,** lie downtown near the clock tower and Wat Ko Kaew.

Tourists can also try the food courts tucked on the side streets of Pongsuria or Suranluchai Rd. **Rabiang Restaurant,** just west of Chomrut Bridge, has a long menu of classic Thai plates and soups (40-80฿), and the chef will tone down typically psycho-spicy Thai meals for sensitive *farang* taste buds. The owner puts Santana, B.B. King, or Dire Straits on the stereo as customers sip banana/papaya shakes (20฿). (Open 10am-midnight.)

SIGHTS

Phetchaburi's chief tourist lures, **Khao Wang Historical Park** and **Phra Nakhon Khiri Palace,** lie west of the river. (Open daily 8am-5pm.) To get to the palace, walk up the hill where it meets Ratwithi Rd. Although the path is steep, it is paved and the view from the top is a definite reward for your sweat and aching hamstrings. If you really don't want to walk, take the **tram** from the west side of the mountain (20฿ roundtrip, 10฿ for kids). The tram runs between 8am-5pm.

Built in 1858 during the reign of King Rama IV (King Mongkut), this was the first hilltop palace in Thailand. Furnishings and architecture are a blend of Chinese, Thai, and European styles. Phra Thinang Phetphum Phairon Hall of the royal palace is now a **museum,** displaying art and antiques including the royal throne and materials used at the royal household. (Open 9am-4pm; admission 20฿.) The observation tower gives a stunning wide-angle view of the province.

The walk to the other peak takes you past a towering *chedi* between the temple and the palace. The temple is supposedly modeled after the Royal Chapel in Bangkok, and even shares the name **Wat Phra Kaew.** Climbing to the base of the smaller gray *chedi* affords spectacular views of Phetburi, which include the large *chedi* and palace in one direction and a glimpse of the Gulf of Thailand in the other.

Wat Yai Sawannaram, on the right-hand side of Pongsuria Rd., is a 10-minute walk east of Chomrut Bridge. The entrance can be found at the vanilla-colored arches. The large compound features some amazing examples of Ayutthaya art and architecture, dating back 500 to 600 years. Two wooden buildings demand special attention here, but keys are required to get inside; ask one of the monks.

The wooden red **Teaching Hall** was actually built in Ayutthaya and transported here by boat 300 years ago. Door panels feature elaborately carved intertwining floral designs; the great slash in them is believed to have been left during a Burmese attack. The two central window carvings represent the King and Queen.

The main *bot* sits in a courtyard rimmed with golden Buddha images; unusual and windowless, it has a locked door of its own. Inside, wooden rafters reveal the under-side of the tiled roof, and the murals depict humans and mythical creatures paying their respects to the large Buddha under the white *chat.* The inside panels of the doors show *farang* in awe of the power of Buddha. The *bot's* columns and the objects within it revolve around the number six. (There's even a Buddha with six toes on one foot.)

Continuing down Pongsuria Rd. and turning right before the train tracks leads to the 12th century **Wat Kamphaeng Laeng,** 500m past the Esso station. If the front gate is locked, turn right on the road just after the wat and enter at the gate on your right. The five laterite-block structures which house Buddha images are suggestive of the Angkor-style *bot.* If it's closed, ask for the key to peek inside. **Phra Khruu Yanwit-**

THAILAND

mon, who is *Luang Phaw Phet* (the venerable monk of Phetchaburi), resides here and is much revered in the province. The belief that he possesses healing powers draws many to pay respects and seek his blessing.

The **Khao Ban Da It Caves** are hidden beneath the three communications towers on top of the hill, about 4km west of town on the other side of Phetkasem Hwy. The entrance to the compound is on the right side of the road past the series of three ornate shelters which are maintained by the monks of Khao Ban Da It. Steps between the two gray elephant statues go to the entrance of the caves. A flashlight can help spelunkers explore this underground labyrinth and find the "thousand Buddhas" tucked away into crevices. A *rot lenk* or *tuk-tuk* from town should run about 20฿. (Open 8am-6pm; donations requested.)

Promoted by the TAT everywhere and over-run by tourists are the **Khao Luang Caves,** 4km to the north of town. They are best seen between 11am and 2pm, when sunlight filters through two openings at the top of the cave, illuminating the collection of golden Buddha images and the red-tiled floor. Take a 10฿ *tuk-tuk* or *rot lenk* ride from Ratwithi Rd.'s intersection at Khao Wang mountain and then follow the 500m path uphill. (Donations accepted.)

■ Near Phetchaburi

Thailand's largest national park, **Kaeng Krachan National Park,** stretches out on the western half of Phetchaburi Province. It envelops a whopping 3000sq.km of land between Burma and the Gulf of Thailand, most of which is steep and deep tropical rainforest. Because species from both continental Asia and the Malaysian peninsula mix here, plant and animal life are especially diverse. Since the park's opening in 1981, four white elephants, for centuries considered divine symbols of royal prestige and fortune, have been captured here and given to the current king. If you like shooting rapids, the Phetchaburi and Phanburi Rivers are good for **rafting.** Sometimes park rangers lead **three-day hikes** in the high season for a 200฿ per day fee (with food 352฿) for four people. Car-less folks may find transportation around the park too pricey; those who do often content themselves to hanging out at the headquarters on the 45-sq.km **Kaeng Krachan Lake.** Four-person bungalows are 300฿, tents can be pitched for 50฿. The restaurant also overlooking the lake features yummy food like fried rice and chicken (15฿) or sweet and sour pork (40฿). To get to the park, take a minibus from Phetkasem Hwy. at Tha Yang to the park headquarters. The trip should cost no more than 20฿.

Chao Samran Beach is a 10฿ *songthaew* ride. Minibuses leave from the station along Matayawong Rd. It's quieter than the bigger beaches to the south, but people pack the place when the weekend rolls around. *Songthaew* usually stop running around 6pm.

■ Cha-am ชะอำ

Picture a small road that runs straight for several kilometers. On one side, place a long beach overlooking wide-open water, dotted with an occasional boat or jet ski. Sprinkle some beach chairs, umbrellas, casuarina and pine trees, and mini police stations beside the road. On the other side, spread hotels, guest houses, bungalows, seafood restaurants, snooker joints, and gaudy beach-wear shops. That's Cha-am.

Thais flock to Cha-am to hide from the stress goblins of the city, work, and school. Most make the 173-km trip from Bangkok for a weekend of *hat* (beach), *phra athit* (sun), and the *sanuk* (fun). Cha-am remains a peaceful Thai style resort town with few tourists except for the weekends and holidays. Bikini-clad *farang* who let it all hang out may feel a bit out of place on the beach, but all in all, Thai vacationers are happy to share their slice of the good life.

ORIENTATION

About 3½ hours from Bangkok, Cha-am is easily reached by the southern bus and train lines. It's only a half-hour more to Hua Hin. The **TAT** is right along **Phetkasem Highway** (Route 4). A few streets run to the beach, but the **main intersection** is with **Narathip Road** which meets the beach at one end and the train station at the other. The post office and police station are between the train station and Phetkasem Hwy. Narathip Rd. runs to a T-intersection with **Ruamjit Road,** the beachside street. To the right (south) are many places to eat and stay. The street parallel to Ruamjit Rd. away from the beach is **Chaolai Road,** which also has some guest houses.

PRACTICAL INFORMATION

Tourist Offices: TAT, 500/51 Phetkasem Hwy. (tel. 471 502). From the train station, go to the highway and turn right. Has plenty of useful brochures and maps for the local area as well as surrounding towns. Open daily 8:30am-4:30pm.

Tourist Police: 24-hr. TAT (tel. 471 502).

Currency Exchange: Banks line Phetkasem Hwy. and are generally open Mon.-Fri. 8:30am-3:30pm. **Exchange booths** are at the intersection of Narathip and Ruamjit Rd. Most are open 9am-8pm.

Trains: The station (tel. 471 159) sits at the end of Narathip Rd., away from the beach. To **Bangkok** (6:30, 6:50am, and 2:50pm, 4hr., 40฿). Cha-am is a minor stop, so confirm times with station officials.

Buses: A/C terminal (tel. 471 654), the small blue building past Aruntip Bungalows on Ruamjit Rd. Open 7:30am-5pm. To and from **Bangkok** (every 2hr., 9am-4pm, 3hr., 82฿). On weekdays you can just buy a ticket and board, but on weekends and holidays buy at least 1 day in advance. **Regular** buses also run to **Bangkok** (5am and 4pm, 3hr., 45฿) and to **Hua Hin** (every 30min., 10฿). Flag these down on Phetkasem Hwy.

Rentals: Bike and moped rentals can be found along Ruamjit Rd. Rentals 40฿ per day. Mopeds should run about 200-250฿ per day.

Medical Services: (tel. 471 007), on Klongtien Rd. 200m north on Phetkasem Hwy. from the intersection with Narathip Rd. Klongtien Rd. is on the right where the highway bears left; the hospital is about 1km down the street on the right.

Emergency: tel. 191. **24-hr. Tourist Police:** tel. 471 502

Police: (tel. 471 321), on Narathip Rd. next to the post office.

Post Offices/Telephones: GPO (tel. 471 252), on Narathip Rd. midway between the train station and the main intersection. Open Mon.-Fri. 8:30am-4:30pm, Sat.-Sun. 8:30-noon. **Postal code: 76120. Telephone code:** 032.

ACCOMMODATIONS

Cha-am is a Thai family getaway so many of the crash pads are meant to be rented as two- or three-room bungalows (600฿ and up). Expect some prices to double during popular months and holidays.

Pratarnchok House, 240/3 Ruamjit Rd. (tel. 471 215). Make a left off Narathip Rd.; it's the 4th guest house down (look for the English sign). Friendly management. Subtle tan color scheme was no doubt inspired by Banana Republic. Singles/doubles 200฿, with A/C and private bath 300฿. Standard room 150฿ for stays of 4 nights or longer most of the year.

Nalumon Bungalows, Ruamjit Rd. (tel. 471 440). Make a right off Narathip Rd.; look for the English sign. Smooth wooden balconies shade each upstairs bungalow from the unrelenting sun while guests repose on large circular beds. Singles/doubles with king-size bed and western bath 250฿.

Cha-am Villa Hotel, 241/1 Ruamjit Rd. (tel. 471 086). Bold English sign proclaims this place, slightly north of Pratarnchok House. Each spacious room has a large and comfy bed with firm pillows, cable TV, and phones. Western toilet and Thai shower. Singles/doubles 300฿, with A/C 400฿, with fridge and hot water 500฿.

THAILAND

FOOD

Not only is Ruamjit Rd. lined with places to stay, but it is also a haven for epicures. At most of the food carts or **street vendors**, snacks are 15-20฿. Restaurants cost a bit more, but are worth it for their wide selection of seafood. Near the five-star Methavalai Hotel on the north end of the beach, there are several restaurants with seaside patios serving tasty victuals for about 50฿. The **mini-mart** just north of Pratarnchok House is open daily 8am-11pm.

SIGHTS AND ENTERTAINMENT

If you've come to Cha-am expecting to do anything more than kick back on the beach, you've made a serious mistake. Thai college students make MTV's Beach Party look like a Tupperware gathering with their non-stop action on Cha-am's beaches between April and May. The **Fisher Pub** on the north end offers **snooker.** To show your stuff at one of their six tables in the large A/C hall you'll have to shell out 80฿ per hour (open daily 6pm-midnight). It might be more pleasant just to sit back on the beach in one of the chairs across from a well-lit restaurant and watch the world go by. At sunrise or sunset, take the 1-km stroll up the north end of the beach to **Wat Neranchara.** Here you'll see the Buddha as you have never seen him before: he has six arms covering his face, ears, and lap. The Gulf of Thailand crashes before him and the cool breezes caress him, but he is blithely oblivious to it all; nothing interrupts his meditation.

■ Hua Hin หัวหิน

Long, long ago, before Phuket and Pattaya were launched into the international jet-set travel scene, Hua Hin was catering to the upper crust from Thailand and abroad. In the 1920s King Rama VII deemed the spot worthy of royal relaxation and ordered up a summer palace, Klai Kangwon (Far From Worries), still in use today. Soon after, the State Railway Co. laid tracks to Hua Hin for an opulent train service from Bangkok. The Thai nobility has since exchanged fan-toting servants for air-conditioning and afternoon tea for karaoke, but many Bangkok families with a few baht to burn still own estates along the coast to the south of Hua Hin.

The town itself caters to sun-seeking Thais and foreigners with slightly more proletarian incomes. Compared to over-developed, x-rated Pattaya, Hua Hin is a laid-back PG, gracefully welcoming both the worn-out backpacker and the expat golfer. With a long stretch of *clean,* white sand (increasingly rare in Thailand), reasonably priced accommodations, and some of the best seafood in the country, it's no surprise that a great variety of Bangkok-embattled beach-goers head to Hua Hin.

ORIENTATION

Hua Hin (head rock) lies 232km from Bangkok and is a popular stop on the route of buses and trains heading south. Both **Phetkasem Highway** and the train tracks run parallel to the beach. Three major streets cross the highway and head to the sand. From north to south: **Chomsin Road, Dechanuchit Road,** and **Damnoenkasem Road.** The roads that are parallel to the shore are (from the beach) **Naresdamri Road, Poonsuk Road,** Phetkasem Hwy., and **Srasong Road.** Most of the guest houses, bars, and restaurants line the *soi* that connects Poonsuk and Naresdamri Rd.

PRACTICAL INFORMATION

Tourist Offices: Tourist Information Service Centre, 114 Phetkasem Hwy. (tel. 511 047), on the 1st floor of the municipal building at the intersection with Damnoenkasem Rd. Open daily 8:30am-noon and 1-4:30pm.

Tourist Police: (tel. 515 995), in the little white building on the left side of Damnoenkasem Rd., just before the beach. Open 24hr.

Tours: Travel agents line Phetkasem Hwy. and cluster in the Damnoenkasem Rd. area. They arrange trips to sights around Cha-am as far as Phetchaburi.

Currency Exchange: Banks and associated **exchange booths** stay open until around 9pm. They are along Phetkasem Hwy. as well as at the intersection of Damnoenkasem and Naresdamri Rd.

Air Travel: Hua Hin Airport, 5km north of the city. To **Bangkok** (6pm, 1hr.). All flights through **Bangkok Airways,** which has an office in Hua Hin (tel. 512 083 for reservations). Open daily 9am-5pm. AmEx, MC, Visa.

Trains: (tel. 511 073), at the end of Damnoenkasem Rd. away from the beach. Tickets sold 30min. before departure, but reservations should be arranged in advance. Open for reservations Mon.-Fri. 8:30am-12:30pm and 1:30-4pm, Sat.-Sun. and holidays 8:30am-noon. Fares are listed for 3rd-class. To: **Bangkok** (8 per day, 5hr., 44฿); **Chumphon** (10 per day, 4hr., 49฿); **Phetchaburi** (9 per day, 1hr., 13฿); and **Surat Thani** (10 per day, 7hr., 74฿).

Buses: Regular bus station (tel. 511 230), on the corner of Dechanuchit Rd. and Srasong Rd. Open 24hr. Regular bus tickets to **Bangkok** (every 15min., 4hr., 51฿) can be pre-purchased or bought on the bus. During the day, regular buses stop at the station, but at night the orange buses will look for flag-stops by the bus station or clock tower on Phetkasem Rd. Check beforehand at the bus station. To **Cha-am** (every 30min., 10฿). Regular buses to the south: **Chumphon** (every 30min., 8am-midnight, 5hr., 66฿) and **Surat Thani** (16 per day, 12:35am-11:55pm, 8hr., 112฿). **A/C Bus Station** (tel. 511 654), 1st floor of Siriphetchkasem Hotel Building on Srasong Rd. near Dechanuchit Rd. Open daily 4am-8pm. Reserve seat in advance to: **Bangkok** (every 30min., 3am-9pm, 3½hr., 92฿) and **Cha-am** (every 15min., 30฿).

Taxis: From Phetkasem Rd., in front of Chatchai Market (roundtrip) to: **Khao Sam Roi Yod National Park** (600฿), **Krilas,** or **La-U Waterfall** (600-800฿).

Local Transportation: Samlor and **motorcycle taxis** serve the main part of Hua Hin (10-20฿). Hire only drivers wearing vests with identification numbers. Local green **buses** run from the regular bus station to **Krilas** and **Takiab Hills** (every 20min., 6am-5:50pm, 5฿).

Rentals: on Damnoenkasem Rd., opposite Hua Hin Bazaar. Bikes 50฿ per day. Motorbikes or mopeds 150-290฿ per day plus deposit.

Markets: Hua Hin's **Chatchai** and **night market** set up at the corner of Dechanuchit Rd. and Petchkasem Rd. all the way to the bus station.

Medical Services: Red Cross Institute (tel. 511 024), on Damnoenkasem Rd. next to the tourist information office. Open Mon.-Fri. 8am-4pm, Sat.-Sun. and holidays 8am-noon. For major medical problems, try the **Thonburi Hua Hin Hospital** (tel. 520 841), 4km north of town on Phetkasem Hwy. Open 24hr.

Emergency: tel.191.

Police: (tel. 511 027), on Damnoenkasem Rd. toward the beach off the highway. At this number, the police can radio the tourist police.

Post Offices: GPO (tel. 511 063), across from the police station on Damnoenkasem Rd. as soon as you turn off Phetkasem Rd. Open Mon.-Fri. 8:30am-4:30pm, Sat.-Sun. and holidays 9am-noon. **Postal code:** 77110.

Telephones: (tel. 511 350), next to the GPO. Handles international calls, fax, telex, and even sells stamps. Open daily 8am-midnight. **Directory Service:** tel. 13. **Telephone code:** 032.

ACCOMMODATIONS

The guest houses that flourish in the area between Poonsuk Rd. and Naresdamri Rd. are cheap, clean, and within spitting distance of sizzling seafood. During high season, places fill up quickly and prices may shoot up. Many guest houses are adjacent to rambunctious bars, so the traveler should choose wisely.

All Nations Guest House, 10-10/1 Dechanuchit Rd. (tel. 512 727). Look for the sign as you head toward the beach. Easily accessible guest house, popular with the international set. Each floor has 2 rooms which share a mammoth bathroom. Ground-floor restaurant and bar. Singles 130-150฿, with king-size bed 250฿.

Joy Guest House, 6/5 Soi Bintabart (tel. 512 967), 3 blocks from Dechanuchit Rd., off Poonsuk Rd. Dutch-run establishment featuring a first-class pool table, imported beer and liquor, and a front-row view of Hua Hin's nightlife. Singles/doubles 150฿, with breakfast 175฿. Large rooms 200฿. All have shared bath.

M.P. Guest House, 6 A/2 Soi Kaanjanomai (tel. 511 344). Make a left off Damnoen-kasem Rd. onto Poonsuk Rd. and then take the 1st right onto Kaanjanomai Rd., a quiet alley. Spacious rooms have shared bathrooms and queen-size beds for 1-2 people. Rooms 100-150฿.

Maple Leaf, 8/5 Poonsuk Rd. (tel. 533 757), near M.P. Guest House. Though owned by a Canadian, the front office is decorated with not only Canadian but Japanese, German, and French flags as well. Brown wallpaper-covered floors lead to large rooms with green beds and western toilets. Singles/doubles 150฿.

FOOD

Seafood reigns supreme here, and for good reason. Every morning there are fresh deliveries of a wide variety of seafood to the pier. One to try is **Chao Lay Seafood,** 104 Naresdamri Rd. (tel. 513 436), or any of the other oceanside establishments on the same street. The **Headrock Pub and Restaurant,** 1541 Naresdamri Rd. (tel. 514 002), provides MTV, A/C, and Aussie steaks. Look for the pot of gold at the end of their visually and physically stunning "Rainbow" cocktail. When the sun goes down, the doors open at several excellent family-run seafood shops next to All Nations, with 10฿ bowls of *khao tom* (rice soup), plus whatever seafood you desire (add 5-15฿ more). Across the way, a restaurant makes incredible *plaa biew-waan* (sweet-and-sour fish) as well as *plaa raad phrik* (fish cooked in semi-sweet chili sauce).

SIGHTS AND ENTERTAINMENT

Hua Hin Beach rolls along for kilometers in either direction from town. The daily catch arrives at the **fishing pier** (at the base of Chomsin Rd.) when most people are still asleep. The best swimming requires a 1-km walk south of the pier where it's less rocky and smelly. Folks wander the sand offering massages, food, and pony rides.

If you stroll north along the beach (past Melia Hotel and the pier), the **Klai Kang Won Palace** comes into view. Designed by one of the King's grandsons, the palace became a royal summer residence in the 1920s. Naturally, this residence is closed to the public, but the mere presence of royalty ensures that the area surrounding it remains clean and manicured.

At the southern end of the beach, surrounded by scenic grounds stands the imposing **Sofitel Central Hotel,** whose entrance is at the bottom of Damnoenkasem Rd. Originally the Railway Hotel, it was built in 1922 by Prince Purachatra (then Director General of State Railways). This place earned its 15 minutes of fame in the film *The Killing Fields,* playing Phnom Penh's leading hotel. Rooms here run 19,000฿. Tourists can come in for high tea and meander through the gardens where foliage has been skillfully trimmed to resemble elephants and peacocks.

South beyond **Wat Amphala** on Phetkasem Hwy. are the twin hills of Khao Takiab and Khao Krilas. If you don't go by motorbike (the most convenient way), snag a local bus from the Dechanuchit Rd. station (2฿ to Khao Takiab Village, 5฿ to the hill; last returning bus at 5pm). **Khao Takiab** (Chopsticks Hill) features a wat overlooking the sea, with a view of pine tree-lined **Suan Son Beach.** Farther south is **Khao Tao** (Turtle Hill), while inland is **Khao Krilas,** each with spectacular views.

Live rock 'n' roll is featured occasionally at the **Rock Walk Pub;** off Dechanuchit Rd. Along Poonsuk Rd., the **Muay Thai Garden** serves up Isaan dishes and holds **Thai boxing** matches several times a month (200฿ cover charge).

■ Near Hua Hin

The area between Hua Hin and the Thai-Burmese border boasts spectacular natural sights for the rambler. The **Tanao Sri range** forms the border and backdrop for **Pa-La-u,** an untamed jungle in the **Kaeng Krachan National Park** (see also **Near Phet-**

chaburi). Within the jungle are the twin waterfalls **La-u Yai** and **La-u Noi,** which merge to become **Pa-La-u Waterfall.** Pa-La-u consists of over nine levels of cascades; it takes three days to reach the source. A one-day trip brings trekkers to the first few levels. Longer stays require a guide (100฿ per day) and camping equipment (10฿ per night per person). The park rents out tents; bungalows are also available, starting at 300฿. It is best to come between November and April.

Overnight trekkers should contact the **Sub-Forestry Office** seven to ten days in advance by writing to: Kaeng Krachan National Park, Pa-La-u Hua Hin, Prachuap Khiri Khan 77110. A *songthaew* from Chomsin Rd. in Hua Hin takes travelers to Fa Prathan Village 53km away on local highway 3219 (20฿), departing at 11:30am, 1, and 3pm, and returning at 6:30, 8, and 9am. From the village to the Sub-Forestry Office you can make the 4-km hike or hire a *songthaew*. From the office to the first cascade, there is official transport for 10-20฿ roundtrip. Hiring a *rot lenk* from Hua Hin to the waterfall (700฿ per day) or renting a motorcycle are the best options if you want to make a one-day trip.

On the way to Pa-La-u on Rte. 3219, three caves lie 27km from Hua Hin near Nong-phlab Village. The **Dao, Lablae,** and **Kailon Caves** offer exciting spelunking possibilities. The Pa-La-u mini-bus goes there for about 10฿.

Khao Sam Roi Yot National Park lies 63km southwest of Hua Hin off Highway No. 4 to Prachuap Khiri Khan. Stunning limestone hills rise from the sea and marsh. Evergreens clump densely in the forest and surrounding coastal waters where porcupines, leopards, barking deer, dolphins, crab-eating macaques, dusky langurs, serow (a rare goat-antelope beast), and 300 species of birds make their home. Park bungalows sleep two to 20 people and cost 300-1000฿ per bungalow.

THE EAST COAST

Thailand has focused almost all its new industrial development in the "eastern seaboard" region within 150km of Bangkok. Shiny new oil refineries, power stations, and petrochemical plants line up along the coastline, and pipelines criss-cross the inland rice paddies. Along the highways, the air is thick with diesel grit from the streams of freight trucks shuffling goods between Bangkok and the deep sea ports at Si Racha and Rayong. Two hours south of Bangkok in the middle of all the hubbub, Pattaya sits on an astonishingly dirty beach rolling in bundles of sex-industry cash. Nowhere is the harried pace of Thailand's economic development more evident.

East of Rayong to the Cambodian border, the face of Thailand's coastline undergoes a striking shift back a decade or two in time. As the burger joint-and-smoke stack strips disappear and the main highway sheds several lanes, tradition becomes the rule and western holiday-makers the exception. To the north, jungled limestone hills rise suddenly out of the coastal plains. Groves of mangosteen, rambutan, and durian encroach on a few remaining patches of rain forest. Elusive gem-traders smuggle Cambodian stones through small border towns.

Off the coast of the far eastern province of Trat, the largely undeveloped island of Ko Chang lifts thick rain forest high above the calm cobalt waters. Closer to Bangkok but just out of reach of the sweeping industrialization, Ko Samet hosts a steady flow of sun-seekers. And in the middle of a fleet of freight ships and oil tankers off the coast at Si Racha, the tiny Ko Si Chang seems immune to changing times.

■ Si Racha ศรีราชา

Twenty years ago, Si Racha was a simple fishing village nestled on the Gulf of Thailand, 100km east of Bangkok. Then came the country's meteoric economic growth during the 1980s, bringing an oil refinery, an international port, and a ten-fold increase in population. With its characteristic orgiastic abandon, the tourist industry has also set Si Racha firmly in its crosshairs. From Wat Ko Loi, which sits atop a craggy islet now linked to the mainland by a causeway, Si Racha appears under siege: from land by glittering hotels and condominium towers, and by sea from squat, hulking oil tankers. Despite these changes, Si Racha has maintained something of her previous identity. Gaily painted fishing boats still depart every evening from the town pier. Take a stroll down Jermjompol Rd., with its pungent, bustling market and network of tiny *soi* twisting down to weathered houses built on stilts over the water, and you can almost recapture—for a moment or two—a bit of that small village charm.

ORIENTATION

Buses from Bangkok or points east pull up next to the Raemton Department Store on **Sukhumvit Road,** the principal north/south highway of the area. To get to the heart of the village and the ferries to Ko Si Chang, cross Sukhumvit Rd., and follow **Surasak Road** for 10min. until it runs into **Jermjompol Road,** Si Racha's main street. The whole of the Jermjompol Rd. downtown, bounded in the south by a market and a clock tower and in the north by a park and the causeway to Ko Loi, is less than 0.75km long. The hotels are over the water, down the tiny soi off Jermjompol Rd.

PRACTICAL INFORMATION

Currency Exchange: Siam Commercial Bank, 98/9 Surasak Rd. (tel. 311 813). 200m before the intersection with Jermjompol Rd.; facing the water, bank is on the left. Exchanges traveler's checks. Open Mon.-Fri. 8:30am-3:30pm.

Buses: Fan buses to **Bangkok** leave from the intersection of Sukhumvit Rd. and Surasak Rd. Buses to **Pattaya, Rayong,** and points east leave from the other side of the road. A/C and VIP buses leave from Raemton Dept. Store on Sukhumvit Rd.

Markets: Outdoor markets are on Surasak Rd., near the clock tower at the south end of Jermjompol Rd. Open 5am-6pm.

Pharmacies: Pramuan Bhesat Pharmacy, 147 Jermjompol Rd. (tel. 311 962), on the south side of town. Across from Soi 18 and two stores toward the clock tower (uphill). Open 9am-10pm.

Medical Services: Polyclinic, 135/10-12 Sukhumvit Rd. (tel. 312 288), on the other side of the Dunkin' Donuts in Raemton Dept. Store. Cash only. Open 24hr.

Emergency: tel. 191.

24-hr. police box: (tel. 311 111), at corner of Jermjompol Rd. and Soi 10.

Post Offices/Telephones: (tel. 311 202), near the road to Ko Loi at the north end of Jermjompol Rd., a 10-min. walk from the hotels. Telegrams, mail, parcels, and **international telephone** network (collect 30฿; cash). Open Mon.-Fri. 8:30am-4:30pm. **Postal code: 20110. Telephone code:** 038.

ACCOMMODATIONS

When the seas are rough, staying in an ancient wooden hotel on stilts over the water is hardly an experience to savor. All are about a 20-minute walk from Sukhumvit Rd. bus stop and five minutes to the left of the Jermjompol Rd. stop.

Siri Watana, 35 Soi Siriwatana (tel. 311 037), 1 block north of Soi 10. Catch spectacular sunsets from picnic areas. Surprisingly good food 20-30฿. The Ratanaliem family speaks English, creating a wonderfully chatty atmosphere. All rooms are spotlessly clean with a private shower and toilet. Singles 120฿-170฿. Doubles 220฿-260฿. Rooms closest to the sea are most expensive.

Samchai Hotel, Soi 10 Phulphiphat (tel. 311 800), at the end of the *soi,* across Jermjompol Rd. from Surasak Rd. A festive spot complete with swings, bunting, and a rickety split-level porch for prime sunset gazing. Caters chiefly to local tourists. All rooms clean and comfy, with A/C, TV, and western toilet. Singles with fan 140฿, with A/C 350฿. Doubles with fan 240฿, with A/C 450฿.

FOOD

Si Racha is famous for its fresh seafood, usually prepared in a spicy (some say tangy, but it's hot) sauce, which is the local specialty.

THAILAND

East Coast Thailand

Seaside Restaurant, (tel. 312 537) on Soi 18, all the way at the end of the pier. All three of Si Racha's Mercedes huddle in the well-groomed parking lot. As close as Si Racha gets to *haute cuisine*. Probably the only spot in town with steamed fish in plum sauce (95฿) or seafood curry soufflé (100฿). Ice cream sundaes for dessert (50-75฿). Open for coffee and tea 8-10am and for the whole mouth-watering she-bang 10am-10pm.

Hua Huat Restaurant, 100 Jermjompol Rd. (tel. 311 047), across from the Krung Thai ATM machine, a few doors south of Soi 10. A family-run establishment, they're justifiably proud of their delicious, moderately priced food. Over a dozen shrimp dishes (fried shrimp with garlic 70฿) plus a tantalizing assortment of crab, fish, and Chinese dishes. Open 9am-9pm.

Sri Racha Seafood Restaurant, 160-164 Si Racha Nakorn Rd. (tel. 770 818). From the Sri Watana Hotel, cross Jermjompol Rd. and go straight (away from the water); it's on the left about 100m up. A Thai interpretation of an intimate Italian restaurant, right down to the red table cloths and sluggish service. Menu prices run from 45฿ for crispy catfish to 180฿ for steamed white snapper in lime juice. Open 8am-10pm.

■ Ko Si Chang เกาะสีชัง

Make no mistake about it, Ko Si Chang isn't Ko Samet or Ko Chang. The island boasts only one sandy beach—crescent-shaped Hat Tampang on the rugged western shore. The rusting hulls of freighters moored off Si Racha dominate the eastern horizon, while wind and tide occasionally align to turn the shoreline into a wasteland of flotsam and murky green water. Despite this menacing threat of industrialization, Ko Si Chang has managed to retain greater local flavor than her more picturesque sisters. Fishing, not tourism, remains the island's principle economic enterprise. King Rama V built a summer retreat here in the later 19th century; its remains, as well as several eclectic Buddhist sights, are worth exploring. More of a spot for lovers of local color than for beach bums, Ko Si Chang can provide a welcome respite from the east coast's endless barrage of sun and fun.

GETTING THERE

Ferries for Ko Si Chang depart from Si Racha's main pier, at the end of Jermjompol Rd., Soi 14. Three ferry companies offer daily service to the island with boats leaving about every hour between 6am and 8pm. When the tide is low, boats depart from Ko Loi. Returning boats leave Ko Si Chang's Talang Pier or Ta Bon Pier when the tide is low (daily, first boat 6:30am, last boat 6pm). The trip takes 40 minutes unless the captain feels like picking up passengers from the freighters anchored off shore (20฿).

ISLAND ORIENTATION

Ko Si Chang boasts two piers. **Ta Bon Pier** at the northern end of town and **Talang Pier** at the southern end. The two are linked by **Atsadang Road,** Ko Si Chang's main street. At Talang Pier, Atsadang Rd. forks, continuing uphill to the Tiew Pai Guest House and paralleling the island's eastern shore to the marine research center at its southern tip. A new dirt road is being constructed linking Atsadang Rd. with several massive fuel storage tanks on the southwestern corner of the island. A narrow concrete road branches off this road before the tanks, winding down the island's rugged western coast to lovely **Hat Tampang.** The Tiew Pai Guest House restaurant has a handy map of the island, listing all of the major attractions.

PRACTICAL INFORMATION

Currency Exchange: Thai Farmers Bank, 9-9/1-2 Atsadang Rd. (tel. 216 132), on the main road near the center of town. Open Mon.-Fri. 8:30am-3:30pm.

Rentals: Motorcycles (and a little red motor scooter) can be rented for 250฿ per day at Tiew Pai Guest House. Helmets available for the conscientious.

Pharmacies: (tel. 216 086), on Atsadang Rd., between Talang Pier and Tiew Pai. Stocks most of the basic items. Try local remedies like pomegranate leaf tea for an upset stomach. Open 6am-9pm.

Medical Services: Hospital (tel. 216 461), on the northern continuation of Atsadang Rd. next to the Si Racha Palace Hotel. Cupids over the entrance. Open 24hr., emergencies only after 4pm.

Emergency: Police (tel. 216 192), about 0.5km south (uphill) on Atsadang Rd. from Tiew Pai Guest House, labeled Marine Police. They have a super speedboat to get to the mainland hospital in 15min.

Post Offices: (tel. 216 227), a white building at the north end of Atsadang Rd. (the main drag) near the Chinese temple. Open Mon.-Fri. 8:30am-4:30pm, Sat. 9am-noon. **Postal code:** 20120.

Telephones: At the post office. Pull up a stool and call collect for 30฿. **Tiew Pai Guest House** at the other end of town on Atsadang Rd. has **24-hr. telephone service** and offers operator rates for 70฿ collect. **Telephone code:** 038.

ACCOMMODATIONS

Tiew Pai Guest House (tel. 216 084), on Atsadang Rd. at the south end of town. Freshly painted and spacious rooms range from fan-cooled singles or doubles with shared bathroom (100฿) to deluxe A/C bungalows with bathroom and sitting room (500฿).

Benz Bungalows (tel. 216 091), on the road to Hat Tha Wong, 1km south of the pier, past Tiew Pai. Each bright green bungalow enjoys its own view of the off-shore freighter fleet. Single or double with private shower 400฿, with A/C 700฿.

Sripitsanu (tel. 216 034), 1km up an alley to the right, just past Tiew Pai. Continue straight when the path forks at the Development Spiritual Centre. Cluster of bunga-lows high above a secluded cove with clean water. Facilities and accommodations are sparse; you're paying for stunning sunset views. Bare, but well-kept rooms with double bed and squat toilet 500฿. Better equipped ones, up to 1200฿.

FOOD

Ko Si Chang's food won't earn four stars anytime soon, but you'll survive. A few food vendors of the folding-table-beside-the-road variety congregate around the piers and along Atsadang Rd. south of the town. **Tiew Pai Guest House** cooks up a tasty west-ern breakfast (40฿), the staple rice dishes (30-40฿), and a few scrumptious shrimp din-ners (80-100฿).

SIGHTS

Motorcycle *tuk-tuk* drivers will buzz you through the maze of roads and paths for a tour (set prices are 200฿ for a glimpse of the main sights, 300฿ with a few hours of swimming at Hat Tampang). To go on your own, study the wall map in the Tiew Pai restaurant. The east side's two beaches are the easiest to reach. From town, go south down the main road. Head through the gates to the Aquatic Resources Research Insti-tute and down to the water. The beach to the right is the narrow and rocky **Hat Tha Wong**, ideally situated to capture a variety of refuse from passing ships and barges. Nearby is the hillside site of **King Rama V's summer palace,** marked by cracked bal-ustrades and wall foundations. Best preserved is the elegant little swimming pool now filled with green ectoplasm slime. One of the few English public signs warns tourists not to take a dip.

Beautiful **Hat Tampang** is the west side's only sandy beach. It's accessible by a red dirt road that forks off Atsadang Rd. near Benz Bungalows. The beach has relatively clear turquoise water and only a modest audience of fishermen on fine days, but occasionally the tide deposits whole landfills of non-biodegradable junk beyond the reach of petroleum-laced waves.

The south end of the island has a confusing network of 10-ft. wide reddish dirt paths which end in spectacular panoramas, if nothing else. Anyone who endures the ferry ride and pesky taxi drivers deserves to wander around the blissfully isolated southern tip of the island. Keep an eye out for the **"white squirrel,"** a little yellow beast that lives only on Ko Si Chang.

The even more spectacular west and northwest coasts alternate between lush greenery and dramatic gray stone. Not accessible by motorcycle or most bicycles, it's one of the few areas to explore where you won't run into anyone.

The town itself is surrounded by several hillside sights you can't miss. The 10m-tall **Yellow Buddha** on the hill to the west is perched atop a maze of tunnels and caves inhabited by a group of monks. Ask politely and they may let you explore their lime-stone abode that inspired former researcher-writer John Schoellerman to proclaim, "Asceticism kicks ass!" The **Chinese Temple** overlooking the north end of the town receives throngs of pilgrims each New Year. Farther on is yet another **Genuine Bud-dha Footprint.**

■ Ko Samet เกาะเสม็ด

Ko Samet was once known as Ko Kaew Phitsadan, "island of amazing crystal," because of the squeaking sound the sugary sand makes when kicked. Less romantic folks renamed it after the indigenous Samet tree used in boat building. Not so long ago, this 6km splash of emerald jungle off Rayong Province was one of Thailand's best kept secrets. A handful of lucky *farang* would ride the creaky ferry from Ban Phe

THAILAND

for a few blissful days (or weeks) of cavorting in the turquoise water, lolling under the palm trees, and gorging on cheap spicy seafood.

The sand still squeaks, but the island is rapidly becoming one of the most popular budget travel destinations in the country. Bungalows and seafood joints line the northeastern shore cheek by jowl, while obnoxious jet skis buzz back and forth off the beach. Veterans may grumble that Ko Samet is going the way of Ko Samui, but the island has thus far managed to stave off the Pattaya plague of monolithic hotels and seedy bars. Farther down the eastern shore the concentration of bungalows thins considerably; some of the small beaches, such as Ao Nuan and Ao Kiu, are straight out of your wildest tropical dreams.

Unfortunately, those who tire quickly of the beach scene may find a dearth of options on Ko Samet. There is little local culture to observe as the island functions largely to cater to hedonistic fancies. It can, however, make an ideal springboard for explorations of the more remote provinces of Chantaburi and Trat.

GETTING THERE

There are three piers in Ban Phe with ferry service to Ko Samet. The largest is **Nuan Tip Pier,** which has the most ferries every day. With your back to the water, the other two piers are 200m apart to the left. Ferries do not operate on a particularly strict timetable; when a captain has sufficient passengers (usually 18 or more), he leaves. This means that there are far fewer boats making the trip in the low season (May-Oct.), but frequently more than a dozen per day during the high season. To: **Na Dan** (4 per day, 7am-5pm, 30฿); **Ao Wong Duon** (4 per day, 9:30am-6:30pm, 40฿); and **Ao Wai** (2 per day, 11am and 2pm, 50฿).

ISLAND ORIENTATION

From Na Dan, at the northeast corner, a dirt road leads south, slightly inland, along the east coast, where all but one of the island's beaches border the surf. Beaches are listed below starting from Na Dan and going clockwise around the island. They are, in order, the heavily developed Hat Sai Kaew, the quieter and cheaper Ao Hin Khok and Ao Phai, the slightly wan Ao Tup Tim (Ao Pudsa), the charming and secluded Ao Nuan, the squalid Ao Cho (Ao Tawan), the unspeakable Ao Wong Duan, the decent Ao Thian and Hat Lung Dum, the upmarket Ao Wai, and the deserted and pristine Ao Kiu. One beach graces the west coast for sunset-grubbers: the mildly run-down Ao Phrao, which can be reached by a spur which parts company with the main road just behind Ao Phai.

PRACTICAL INFORMATION

Tourist Offices: The **ranger station** on the road between Hat Sai Kaew and Na Dan Pier has park information and free maps. Open 6am-5pm. There is also a small station on Ao Wong Dong. Park rangers greet each boat upon arrival in order to collect 50฿ from all foreign vacationers. A small, dilapidated **visitor's center** just beyond the gate to Hat Sai Kaew offers helpful maps of the island; the staff can give directions to the various beaches. Open daily 8am-4pm.

Tourist Police: There is a small tourist police office at Nuan Tip Pier in Ban Phe. The helpful, English-speaking officers are well stocked with TAT maps and brochures for Rayong, Chantaburi, and Trat Provinces. Open daily 8am-8pm.

Tours and Travel: Rimtalay Express, at the beginning of the road to Na Dan Pier (another office on Ao Tup Tim at the Pudsa Bungalows Restaurant is open during high season). Offers domestic and international air ticketing, minibuses to the airport, Ko Chang, and Bangkok, and snorkeling trips to Ko Kuti and Ko Thalu (250฿). They also have currency exchange, stamps, aerogrammes, telegrams, and international phone service. Open daily high season 8:30am-6pm; low season 10am-5pm. **Sea Horse Tour** (tel. (02) 353 30 72), on Ao Wong Duan or, in Bangkok, 23/12 Si Ayutthaya Rd. (tel. (02) 280 26 43), offers the same services as Rimtalay Express, plus minibus rides to Chiang Mai, Phuket, Hat Yai, Surat Thani, Samui, Penang, and Singapore. Snorkeling trips 250฿. Open daily 7:30am-8pm.

Currency Exchange: For decent exchange rates, use the bank in **Ban Phe** (open Mon.-Fri. 8:30am-3:30pm). See travel agencies above for Ko Samet exchanges, or look for the clumps of them on Hat Sai Kaew and the road to Na Dan Pier.

Buses: Ban Phe bus station, across the street from Nuan Tip Pier. To **Bangkok** (every 2hr., 5am-5:30pm, fan 50฿, A/C 90฿). For buses to **Chantaburi,** first catch a *songthaew* to **Rayong** (30min., 10-15฿); from there, buses to Chantaburi leave every 30min. (4:50am-6:30pm, 30฿). To or from **Ko Chang,** the **Sea Horse Tour** (see above) has A/C minibuses and will ease you onto a connecting ferry. It's cheaper (but more of a pain) to catch a regular bus to Chantaburi, connect with a bus to Trat, and then take a ferry to Ko Chang.

Local Transportation: Songthaew from Na Dan Pier go to: **Hat Sai Kaew** (10฿), **Ao Phai** (20฿), **Ao Tup Tim** (20฿), **Paradise Beach (Ao Phrao)** on the west side of the island (30฿), **Ao Wong Duan** (30฿), **Ao Wai** (40฿), and **Ao Kiu** (50฿). If there are fewer than 10 people, a *songthaew* can be hired for 150-400฿. It's only a 0.5km stroll on a nice dirt road from Na Dan to Hat Sai Kaew. From Ao Wong Duan, walking to Ao Phai takes 30min. with a steep rocky part just before Ao Tup Tim.

Rentals: Room 63 Aladin, on the little road from the dock and on the right just before the gate. **Motorcycles** can go as far south as Ao Kiu, but the walk along the coast is stunning. Rental 100฿ per hr., 600฿ per day; passport deposit required. Open daily 7am-10pm.

Markets: Ban Phe's **market** has usurped the whole pier area. Open daily from 5am until the last boat's arrival.

Medical Services: Clinic, midway along the road between Sai Kaew and Na Dan Pier. Open daily 8:30am-4:30pm. People with a fever should get checked for malaria, although it's now extremely rare on the island. The doctor leaves the island at night. Emergency transport to Ban Phe can be dangerous; should you need urgent help on Ko Samet, the nearest bungalow reception (Hat Sai Kaew, Ao Hin Khok, and Ao Phai have the best English-speakers) can assist you.

Police: On the road between Na Dan and Hat Sai Kaew, next to a health center.

Emergency: tel. 191.

Post Offices: GPO (tel. 321 07 32) in Naga Bungalows, Ao Hin Khok, has *Poste Restante.* Open Mon.-Sat. 8:30am-3:30pm. **Postal code:** 21160-101.

Telephones: Most bungalows have **international phones** for cash (standard rate 100฿ per minute) or collect calls (50-100฿ service charge). Ao Phai Hut (tel. 353 26 44), between Ao Phai and Ao Hin Khok, has an international phone (collect 80฿; open daily 7am-10pm). Naga Bungalows offers the island's best fax rates (150฿ per page to send, 30฿ per page to receive). **Telephone code:** 01.

ACCOMMODATIONS

Accommodations are generally bungalows on thick cement bases or stilts with a front porch, complete with a broom to combat the sand. Private bathrooms, screens, fans, and beds (versus mattresses on the floor) elevate prices. Check the bathrooms before paying. Bungalows with functional shared bathrooms, floor mattresses, and mosquito netting (no screens) should run 80-100฿, with attached shower 100-150฿; proper beds, screens, fan (electricity only at night), and private shower will be 170-200฿. Prices fluctuate depending on the season and the relative age and condition of the bungalows. Reservations during public holidays could save you a sandy night on the beach. See **Beaches** below for specific accommodations listings.

FOOD

Every bungalow operation has a restaurant with the standard inflated Ko Samet prices. All are usually open daily 7am-10pm. Imported food costs about twice the mainland prices (water 10฿, meat dishes 30-80฿, Muesli with milk 30฿); bring food from Ban Phe or Rayong to skip the island rates. Samet's seafood merits serious, if not nightly, appreciation, as villagers drag in boatloads of shrimp, squid, and fish each morning. Lemon and mint seafood fondue (100-120฿) makes a divine aphrodisiac. Restaurants often do not advertise the catch of the day; consult the waitstaff. There is a grocery store near Na Dan, and a fruit stand near the pier sells premium-priced pineapples, bananas, and seasonal treats. In addition, the women who trudge along the beach with pots of noodles will happily fix you a meal for a few baht. See **Beaches** below for specific food listings.

ISLAND SIGHTS AND ENTERTAINMENT

Snorkeling trips to the "coral islands" of Ko Kuti and Ko Thalu run daily from most major beaches. Ao Phai Hut, Rimtalay Tours, and Sea Horse Tour Express do full-day tours for 250฿, which includes snorkeling equipment, lunch, drinks, and boat. Talk to them a day in advance; most trips leave at 9 or 11am. **Game fishing** swamps the budget at 2500฿ per day for a boat at Vong Duern Villa on Ao Wong Duan (tel. (038) 651 741). **Motorboats** hang out off Hat Sai Kaew and Ao Wong Duan (1500฿ per hr. to Ko Thalu). In Ban Phe, Ban Phe Travel, Sunkankhamai Rd. (tel. (038) 651 159), just 10m from the pier, rents speedboats with a driver for 200฿ per hr. and a 15-person boat for 1500฿ per day.

On the northeast corner of the island (just north of Diamond Beach Island Resort), an over-14m-tall concrete **sitting Buddha** dwarfs the more delicate black Buddha by his right knee. Neither are in danger of landing in the Louvre. To get there (to the enlightened ones, not the Louvre), go along the Na Dan Pier-Hat Sai Kaew road and take the dirt road that leads from the east side of the primary school, around the Pineapple Beach Bungalows.

You'll have to make your own **nightlife** on Ko Samet after the restaurants close at 10pm. Whiskey and Cokes on the beach are as wild as it gets among this rambunctious early-bird crowd. On weekends, the **Silver Sands Resort** on Ao Phai pulls out all the stops with a beachside disco showcasing forty-something slaves to the rhythm; on weekdays it reverts to bar status. Sip Singhas to the sound of the surf or, for slightly better prices, try **U Konīká,** just before the ranger station on the way to Hat Sai Kaew from Na Dan. Probably the only Czech-run establishment on Ko Samet, it offers beers (sadly not Czech) for 40-50฿, as well as food and rooms. (Open daily 9am-late.)

BEACHES

Hat Sai Kaew

A 10-minute walk from Na Dan Pier, Hat Sai Kaew—the widest band of sand between tree-line and sea—was Ko Samet's first bungalow, bar, and restaurant magnet. Although the famous sand stays litter-free, plastic bags and straws ride the slightly milky waves at respectable distances. Travel agents and vendors of beach paraphernalia cluster along the road running from mid-beach to Na Dan Pier. During low season, the 1km of beach has no more bodies per square foot than the smaller beaches as far south as Wong Duan, but its size gives it a less secluded feel.

Diamond Beach Island Resort (tel. 239 02 08), takes up serious acreage with well-spaced huts and very thirsty plantation-style gardens. A number of once-primitive bungalows have received facelifts, raising the quality and the price. Still simple, if dingy, bungalows with outside showers can be had for 100฿, with squat-style toilets and showers 200฿; larger beachside bungalows 500฿, with A/C 800฿. They will organize snorkeling expeditions (300฿ for 6 hours).

White Sand (tel. 353 25 66), is at the south end of the beach. Most of the huts closest to the beach (and the noisy restaurant) have been redone; nicely tiled rooms with attached shower and squat toilet 400฿, same room with A/C 800฿. Less-impressive wooden huts well removed from the beach with grungy showers go for 150฿.

The **White Sands Restaurant,** on the south end of the beach, barbecues scrumptious fresh seafood nightly (80-200฿). Try the seafood fondue (100฿)—it's orgasmic. (Open daily 8am-9pm.) The cavernous **Saikaew Villas Restaurant,** south of the road from Na Dan Pier, coats even the biggest stomachs with slightly greasy vegetable fried rice (20฿), meat curries (40฿), and seafood (60-100฿). Open daily 7am-10pm.

Ao Hin Khok and Ao Phai

A half-eroded relic of a cement mermaid graces the rocky point between Hat Sai Kaew and the smaller but equally stunning **Ao Hin Khok.** According to Sunthon Phu's epic, the irresistible prince Phra Aphaimani was forced to consort with a repulsive giantess until a lovely mermaid arrived and dragged him from his underwater prison up to Ko Samet's shores, where they lived happily ever after. Today, topless European sunbathers on Ao Hin Khok's beach keep the aquatic lady from feeling out of place. **Ao Phai,** just to the south, shares its neighbor's mellow, secluded tone, its Eurobathers, and its beauty. Seasoned backpackers' bargain radars will pick up some of the island's best value accommodations here. For bars, Hat Sai Kaew is a short walk away on the beach-side dirt road.

Naga (tel. 353 25 75) offers shady repose beneath rustling trees; home-made cakes and breads (15-25฿) silence the growling stomachs of famished guests. Pizza (small 85฿, large 150฿) is a Naga specialty as are the highly touted vegetarian dishes (30฿). Veteran British proprietor Sue will do anything for her guests, short of performing minor surgical procedures. Thatched bamboo huts march up the hillside on stilts. Mattresses sit unceremoniously on the floors, but intact mosquito nets and well-scrubbed showers with 24-hour water lure an international Anglophone clientele. The owners plan to add new huts with attached showers and possibly A/C in the following year. Huts are 80-150฿.

Ao Phai Hut (tel. 353 26 44) is behind the narrow rocky jetty separating Ao Hin Khok from southern Ao Phai. Little Buddhas sit complacently over the doors to the solid, bamboo-covered wooden huts which have shelf space, dark wood interiors with raised beds, private showers (24-hour water), and fans (electricity 5:30pm-7am). Porch-sitting enthusiasts rhapsodize about the bamboo chairs. The excellent restaurant offers the usual videos: morning BBC, afternoon MTV, a violent movie at night, and on special occasions, a Madonna extravaganza. Small bungalows cost 100฿, larger 150฿; all bungalows at least 300฿ in high season, with A/C 500฿. International phone service (collect 80฿, AT&T card and cash only), snorkeling trips (250฿, minimum 10 people), and books (10฿ for three days).

Little Hut, immediately south of Naga on Ao Hin Khok, shows a decent-by-Samet-standards movie every night at 6pm. Luxurious thatched wood huts with shelves and a sprawling raised bed keep the sand where it belongs. Little Hut also has separate showers and toilets, with 24-hour water (except for a few minutes when fresh water is being pumped in), and the cheapest restaurant around. Enjoy a papaya shake (15฿) at bamboo tables right on the beach. Price varies depending on size and distance from the beach: 100฿, 150฿, 200฿.

Sea Breeze, at the south end of Ao Phai, has fairly spacious thatched wood huts well removed from the sea but not from each other. They have separate showers and toilets. Huts with a mattress on the floor are 80฿. Sturdy, screened huts with private showers and knee-level bed are 150฿, with two double beds 500฿. The office boasts an extensive book collection (20฿ per week, 150฿ deposit) as well as a fax (250฿ to send, 30฿ to receive) and international telephone service (80฿ collect call, 100฿ per minute).

Ao Tup Tim (Ao Pudsa)

The formerly lush hillside has become a barren testimonial to the power of trampling feet. Sand and sea sparkle on, still undaunted by the slime and scum that has infested Ao Cho and Ao Wong Duan. An easy walk from the northern beaches, Ao Tup Tim is definitely a better place to picnic than to live. You can also find **Rimtalay Express 2** here, with the same features as the original on Hat Sai Kaew.

Tup Tim, the nicer of the two places to stay, has a collection of woven reed-walled bungalows with well-worn floor mattresses and mosquito nets for 100฿, with tacked-on shower room 200฿. Water flows round-the-clock; electricity 5pm-3am. White frame bungalows complete with shower, platform bed, and screens are a pricier 300฿.

THAILAND

Ao Nuan

A slip of powdery sand emerges from the headland between Ao Tup Tim and Ao Cho before the cove swings back into stone. Nuan is the only truly secluded beach left on the north half of the island. The rock path from Ao Tup Tim to Ao Cho has a seaward branch leading down to this charming spot's sole sleeping quarters.

Nuan Bungalows is a landscaper's masterpiece—complete with floating lily pads, a collection of folk masks hanging on the open-topped, rock-walled shower, and ferns aplenty. Rugged, picturesque wood huts with floor mattresses cost 100-200฿. Guests can sink into cushions in the *tatami*-matted restaurant (open 8am-9pm). Perfect for moon-gazing and meditating. Nothing but sea, sun, sand, stars, and the 10฿-per-week library to keep you company.

Ao Wong Duan

Recent commercialization has made the once-stunning piece of sand attractive only to the rich and lazy. Water supply hoses criss-cross the bay between ferry boats. Incredibly pricey "resorts" line the beach with bland little bungalows. Only one row of decrepit wooden shacks falls below 300฿.

Ao Thian and Hat Lung Dum

A sparse crop of *farang* squash into 40m of white sand. Check under trees and behind books for more. They occasionally refocus their eyes on the gulls hypnotically circling the rock island just off shore. Get here by the wide smooth path in back of the miniature golf course at the south end of Ao Wong Duan.

Candlelight Beach Bungalows (tel. 321 19 34) fills each bamboo hut with a king-size mattress. Thatched roofs accommodate the very tall or claustrophobic; practice for a Twister tournament by tackling the obstacle course of flimsy bamboo slats on the front porch. Relatively sweet-smelling toilets and showers on the hill behind the huts enjoy a sea view, but the owner is planning to add showers to every hut soon. Water flows 24 hours; electricity 6pm-6am (6pm-midnight low season). Huts cost 80฿ (high season 100฿); with bath 300฿ (high season 500฿).

The eccentric **Lung Dum Hut** (tel. (038) 651 810) is located on **Hat Lung Dum** (the south part of Ao Thian). Even more remote and mellow than its northerly neighbor, it is still on the well-beaten (and fairly well-lit) path to the bars of Ao Wong Duan. Choose either the "love shack" (the tree house on the beach) or one of the rainbow of cinder-block bungalows. There's 24-hour running water in the separate, rustic showers. Electricity zaps from 6pm-4am. You may want a fan. A hut for one costs 100฿, for two 150฿. Tents are available. There's a ferocious dried shark perched over the cashier's desk; if you're lucky, you won't meet his big brother.

Ao Wai

You can live out your Robinson Crusoe fantasies on Ao Wai. The translucent water and coral-strewn sand are worth every second of the 20-minute walk from Ao Wong Duan. To get there, take the path marked "To sunset" to the main road from the Candlelight Beach (or the main road from Ao Wong Duan). At low tide, you can scramble over the coastal boulders scarred by crystalline salt pockets, but it's nearly impossible to tiptoe around the razor-sharp shells cemented to the rocks at water level. The **Samet Ville Ferry** makes the trip to Ban Phe and back at least once a day in low season (50min., 50฿), and more often in high season. You'll have to ferret out the times at Ban Phe Pier or Bungalow Koa Kaew about 400m east of Ban Phe Pier on the coastal road. Otherwise, you can call the Bangkok information office (tel. (02) 246 31 96). The **Samet Ville Resort** (tel. 321 12 84) monopolizes the silvery beach and does not advertise on Khaosan Rd. Small bungalows come in 2-13-person dimensions ranging in price from 800฿ for a double to 4800฿ for a 13-person monster. Also offers an 800฿ per person package deal including meals and transportation to and from the island.

Ao Kiu

This ultimate Ko Samet beach makes even Ao Wai (just a 15-minute rock scramble away) look muddy. If you open your eyes under water, every grain of sand appears in relief. Shells and chunks of coral (including the brain variety) join the palms in decorating the otherwise naked beach with perhaps the snowiest sand around. Ao Kiu is situated on the skinny end of the island, so the west coast is across the lawn—just wade through the dogs and roosters. Farther along, **Ao Pakarang** (about 15 minutes over the rocks) has, literally, gone to the dogs. A few weathered men "tend" a couple of old wooden bungalows hidden amidst piles of discarded water bottles.

The women at **Ao Kiu Bungalows/Restaurant** (tel. 321 12 31) flash more smiles than you can keep up with, but don't speak a word of English. They may ask for exorbitant prices; bargain hard or take a swim and hike back to Wong Duan and catch a *songthaew* to the northern beaches. Bungalows with outside shower go for 400฿, with inside shower 600฿. Seafood is 80฿, pineapple 40฿, shrimp and rice soup 35฿. They are not likely to have many guests during much of the year; you might want to bring a book or a friend.

■ Chantaburi จันทบุรี

As buses from Rayong rumble toward Chantaburi, the unsightly factories and pell-mell construction that characterize the east coast's industrial belt give way to fruit orchards and small villages. Gentle Chantaburi has decidedly more rural character: its spectacular market bulges with fresh produce from the surrounding countryside, especially during May and June when durians, mangosteens, and rambutans are harvested. Although called the "City of the Moon," Chantaburi has nonetheless benefitted from an earthly bounty: most of Thailand's rubies and sapphires come from the mines outside of town. This lucrative trade accounts for the seemingly incongruous number of foreign luxury cars that cruise Chantaburi's narrow twisting streets. Not too far away from the heart of Chantaburi lie tracts of virgin rainforest sheltered in two densely lush national parks.

Chantaburi's charms are as much human as natural, however. Several waves of Chinese and Vietnamese immigration have increased the city's ethnic (and culinary) diversity. *Farang* are still enough of a scarcity that visitors can expect a much more congenial welcome than in the tourist meccas to the west. As locals will proudly tell you, *jai-dee* is still alive and well here. With its friendly atmosphere and small size, Chantaburi is ideal for aimless wandering. So shuck the pack, stash the guidebook, and hit the streets. You won't regret it.

ORIENTATION

Finding one's way around Chantaburi can challenge even the most experienced urban explorers. From the bus station turn left (east) onto busy **Saritidet Road.** After approximately a 10-min. walk, Saritidet terminates at **Benchamarachuthis Road** directly opposite the Kasemsan 1 Hotel. The two river hotels are located down the tiny lane to the immediate left of the Kasemsan. Turning right (downhill) at this intersection onto Benchamarachuthis Rd. will take you into the heart of Chantaburi: the **gem district** where Benchamarachuthis becomes **Si Chan Road.** One block to the right is the sprawling **market area;** one block to the left is **Sukhaphiban Road,** which runs along the river. Walking down Benchamarachuthis Rd. past the Bangkok Bank of Commerce, the second intersection is with **Kwang Road,** which runs west past several banks to **Taksin Park** on the outskirts of town. Street names have a habit of repeating themselves, just to keep things interesting.

PRACTICAL INFORMATION

Currency Exchange: Thai Farmers Bank, 148 Si Rong Muang Rd. (tel. 311 575), just before the market roundabout, in a modern new building. Open Mon.-Fri. 8:30am-3:30pm. **Bangkok Bank,** 18 Kwang Rd. (tel. 311 495), about 4 blocks west of the Si Chan Rd. intersection. Has a walk-by exchange window open Mon.-Fri. 8:30am-3:30pm. In a pinch you may be able to exchange cash (US$) for baht at one of the many gold shops.

Buses: Buses run every hour from the Saritidet Rd. terminal to: **Bangkok** (108฿); **Trat** (10 per day, 6am-4:40pm, 4½hr., 50฿); **Khorat** (last departure 2:30pm, 127฿); and **Buriram** (last departure 4pm, 102฿) via **Aranyaprathet** (57฿). Buses to **Bangkok** also leave from the private bus company on Saritidet Rd. directly across from the hospital (10 per day, 5am-7pm, 108฿).

Taxis: These small pick-up trucks with a single bench seat prowl the streets honking incessantly. Drivers congregate in the market area. Most in-town destinations 20฿, out of town trips run 150-200฿. To **Nam Tok Phliu** 150฿ and **Khao Kitchakut National Park** 200฿. *Songthaew* also leave from the market.

Pharmacies: 96 Si Rong Muang 2 Rd. (tel. 321 613). At the end of the row of shops on the north side of the roundabout. Stocks all the basics. Open daily 8am-6pm.

Medical Services: Chantaburi Ruampate Hospital, 16 Saritidet Rd. (tel. 321 378), is just a few meters toward town from the bus station. It's the enormous white building fronted by a blue Thai-lettered wall. Open 24hr. English spoken.

Post Offices: one block south of Kasemsan 1 Hotel on Benchamarachuthis Rd. A 2-story cement monstrosity marked with blue overseas telephone symbol. Money orders. Open Mon.-Fri. 8:30am-4:30pm, Sat.-Sun. 9am-noon. **Postal code:** 22000.

Telephones: on the 2nd Fl. of the post office. Collect (30฿) or cash calls. Telegrams. Open daily 8am-4:30pm. **Telephone code:** 039.

ACCOMMODATION

Kasemsan I Hotel, 98 Benchamarachuthis Rd. (tel. 311 100). At the end of Saritidet Rd., a 10-min. walk from the bus station. An excellent combination of location, quality, and price. All rooms are freshly painted and kept shipshape by the friendly staff; monogrammed towels and slippers add a touch of class. Rooms with 2 double beds, fan, and squat-style toilet 150฿, with A/C 250฿, add a TV for 400฿. Check-out noon.

Arun Sawat Hotel, 239 Sukhaphiban Rd. (tel. 311 082). From the bus station, turn left onto Saritidet Rd. When it ends, take the tiny lane just to the left of the Kasemsan 1. Take a left just before the river; the hotel is on the left a few doors down. (No sign.) Mercifully removed from the din of Benchamarachuthis. Rather spartan rooms with 1 double bed and blessedly clean sheets 120฿, with A/C 220฿.

Chantra Hotel, 248 Sukhaphiban Rd. (tel. 312 310). Directly across the street from the Arun Sawat Hotel. Not the cleanliest place in town but certainly one of the cheapest. The river view is its best feature. The gregarious owners will make you feel at home without a word of English. Rooms with 1 double bed 80฿, with private shower 120฿, with 2 double beds (but no shower) 140฿.

FOOD

Despite the herds of foreign luxury automobiles, Chantaburi's restaurant selection is rather plebeian by Thai standards. By far the best option is the market's many **food stalls** concentrated around the market round-about and the surrounding area (open daily 9am-1pm), which produce almost every Thai and Chinese dish imaginable. Delicate Chantaburi noodles, almost translucent white strips, are shipped all over Thailand. Noodle stalls set up daily around the edges of the market. For those who desire a (slightly) more formal dining experience, we suggest the following:

Khun Tim Foodshop, perched over the river at the very end of the tiny *soi* leading down to Sukhaphiban Rd. to the left of the Kasemsan 1 Hotel. Beware: the family will be so tickled at having a *farang* visitor, they will undoubtedly break out the Richard Marx or Boyz II Men tape at least once. Great view of the river and the peaceful east bank. Lean menu features basic rice dishes (15฿), noodle dishes (20฿), and soups. Open daily 8am-midnight, closed some Sun.

Vegetarian Home, 17 Kwang Rd. (tel. 350 652). At the intersection of Si Chan Rd. and Kwang Rd., turn toward the river; it's on the right, opposite the Chinese temple. Caters to the Buddhist crowd, hence the huge portrait of the Goddess of

Mercy on the back wall. A tasty array of vegetarian dishes but no menu or labels—just point and shoot, or ask the owners' daughter, who speaks English. 2 dishes served over rice 12฿. Open Mon.-Fri. 7am-4pm.

Sriwatana Restaurant, 511 Saritidet Rd. (tel. 350 491). About 50m toward town from the bus station (on the opposite side of the street), the chic pink tiling is unmistakable. Specializes in Chinese chicken and rice (*khao mun gai*), succulent strips of white meat served over rice with a thin soup and several spicy sauces; a welcome break from those rich, fiery Thai curries. Small dinner 20฿, Coke 7฿. Open daily 7am-4pm.

MARKETS

> Due to the widespread proliferation and abundance of gems, you should always be wary of fakes. Several of the larger shops have labs which can verify stones for a small fee.

Chantaburi's market is vast, but its approximate center is the roundabout one block west of Benchamarachuthis Rd. There is little in the way of handicrafts or souvenirs. Most fascinating of all is the food section, where you can buy anything that once crawled, swam, or slithered. Vendors scattered around the market sell prepared foods (see **Food** above). Open daily 5am-6pm.

Walk down Si Chan Rd. on a weekday and it's largely deserted. On Fridays, Saturdays, and Sundays, however, it jumps to life as the heart of Chantaburi's gem district. The city is certainly one of the gem capitals of the world, as 50-60% of the world's rubies and sapphires pass through Chantaburi. Some come from the mines outside town, but most are shipped (or smuggled) in from elsewhere in Southeast Asia and Africa to be cut, polished, and sold.

SIGHTS

Chantaburi has little to offer die-hard culture-vultures. The area around the river is lively and worth exploring. Go at night when everyone is home and you'll be greeted by a chorus of *"farang! farang!"* Just across the footpath near the south end of the river road, the **Catholic Cathedral of the Immaculate Conception** rewards visitors with a heavenly host of Chantaburi matrons mumbling the Thai rosary. Said to have been revamped last by the French in the late 19th century, it seems they forgot to bring an architect. They did import guns and soldiers though, and held the town hostage from 1893-1905.

ENTERTAINMENT

The recently opened **Diamond City Pub,** 2512 Phrayatrong Rd. (tel. 350 92 57), is one of the few nighttime hang outs in Chantaburi. Don't let the name fool you, this glittering, neon bedecked club holds a capacity of over 2500, and Friday and Saturday nights it rocks. Live acts perform on a massive state-of-the-art stage. Expect to make hundreds of inebriated friends. No cover, except when big-name Bangkok groups are playing. Kloster beer 150฿, Coke 70฿. Open daily 6pm-2am. You might want to take a taxi (20฿); it's a long walk.

■ Around Chantaburi

KHAO KITCHAKUT NATIONAL PARK

It seems as though no self-respecting Thai province is without at least one waterfall. **Krathing Falls,** the centerpiece of **Khao Kitchakut National Park** 30km north of town on Hwy. 3249, falls somewhere in between these two categories. Niagara it ain't; indeed it's more a series of rocky pools limited by small chutes than a single dramatic "fall." Still, the setting beneath the widest triple-canopy jungle of Mt. Khao Phrabat Phluangry is gorgeous. Hiking trails follow the stream up the slope. Twelve

THAILAND

streams originate near the mountaintop, although even experienced hikers should think twice before following them through the deep, dark, snake-infested jungle. If you visit only one of the parks near Chantaburi, this should be it.

Bring mosquito repellent and malaria pills to ward off the endemic disease. The park is open daily 6am-6pm; admission 15฿. Daily *songthaew* depart from the small soi off Benchamarachuthis Rd. opposite Bangkok Bank, just south of the post office (6am-4pm, 50min., 15฿). The *songthaew* will drop you off at the start of a 1.5-km access road leading to the **24-hour park headquarters** (tel. (039) 431 983). Park ranger Kittisak Rattandadas speaks excellent English and is a sage on the park. A small **"canteen"** stocks a few basic items (whiskey, batteries, and toilet paper), and will prepare simple rice dishes (most plates 15-25฿). (Open Mon.-Fri. 8am-5pm, Sat.-Sun. 8am-8pm.) On weekends and holidays, when scores of sightseers and picnickers descend on the falls, fruit stalls, open-air restaurants, and souvenir stands line the access road. For those who can't get enough of the bugs, there are four **bungalows** for rent: one for eight people (600฿), two for 12 (1000฿), and one for 14 (1200฿). During the week they usually stand empty; for weekend reservations call the Royal Forestry Department in Bangkok (tel. (02) 576 48 42; open Mon.-Fri.). **Camping** is also permitted near the park headquarters for 15฿ per person; an old two-person tent can be rented for 40฿. Free 24-hour public toilets and showers are nearby. In an **emergency,** go to the park headquarters. **Makham Hospital** is 5km from park headquarters on Hwy. 3249; ask the rangers for a lift.

NAM TOK PHLIU NATIONAL PARK

Nam Tok Phliu National Park, Chantaburi Province's other park, lies 15km south of town. Its 134sq.km of rainforest is completely inaccessible; you can, however, visit the park's four waterfalls. **Nam Tok Phliu,** the largest of the falls, first became famous over a century ago when the prince of Siam and his bride-to-be fell in love with it. After his ascension to the throne as King Rama V, the royal couple often visited their favorite spot. Years later, upon the death of his wife in 1876, the king had a *chedi* enshrining her remains, as well as a monument built in her memory by the waterfall. The falls still receive over 30,000 visitors a year, a quarter of whom come during the month of June, the height of Chantaburi's durian season. The other three falls, **Nam Tok Makok, Nam Tok Klong Nalai,** and **Nam Tok Nong,** afford a bit more privacy but are a royal pain to get to.

A narrow path leads to the top of the modest falls. The rest of the park is, however, sadly bereft of trails except for one rumored to connect Tok Nong with Tok Phliu (ask at the headquarters). The park is home to a diverse but invisible (to visitors) collection of wildlife. Wild hogs, tigers, leopards, Asiatic black bears, barking deers, and a handful of rarely sighted macaques and pileated gibbons are just a few of the critters you won't see. Bird-watchers can imagine finding Siamese fireback and silver pheasants, short-tailed greenpies, and mountain owls.

To get to the park, take Hwy. 3 (Sukhumvit Rd.) to km347, turn east at the brown wooden Thai sign, then go 2.5km more to park headquarters. From Chantaburi, *songthaew* leave the north side of the market's roundabout and travel along the park's west side for about 25km, stopping at the park gate (30 minutes, 25฿), the intersection of Hwy. 3 (Sukhumvit Rd.), and the 2.5km road to the park (8฿). Walk back to Chantaburi, or hire a taxi to Hwy. 3 and flag down a *songthaew* (8฿; they stop running at 6pm). (Park is open daily 6am-6pm; admission 3฿.)

The **Park Headquarters and Visitors Centre,** next to Tok Phliu, offers maps in English showing all the places you cannot go. The office can also give you directions to the other three falls which are more remote and not as spectacular.

■ Trat ตราด

Enshrouded in jungles far from the reaches of Bangkok, Trat is the least developed of the eastern provinces. The vast majority of the population subsists on agriculture (primarily fruit cultivation) and fishing. Trat's bustling municipal market overflows with examples of natural beauty. A military checkpoint on the way into town is a reminder that the ill-defined border with Cambodia lies just over the green hills to the east. Wily gem traders are said to brave the jungle and the landmines that blanket the Cambodian side of the border to smuggle precious stones into Thailand. Only four hours by boat from Sihanoukville, Trat could well become a major trading city when and if the unstable situation across the border works itself out. Until then, this laid-back frontier town remains content to cruise along in low gear. Too many travelers breeze through Trat on their way to Ko Chang without a second glance. Several fine guest houses and a raucous night market sweeten the deal for those who elect to drop anchor here.

ORIENTATION

Lying 400km from Bangkok, Trat is truly a frontier town. **A/C buses** from anywhere north or west of town shudder to a halt on the east side of **Sukhumvit Road,** the main drag. Some regular buses stop on a quiet street parallel to Sukhumvit Rd. From north to south, **Trat Hospital, the A/C bus stop,** the **night market,** and the **Municipal Market** squeeze into six blocks along Sukhumvit Rd. **Tat Mai Road** runs behind the market parallel to Sukhumvit Rd.; its narrow southern extension, **Tok Yai On Road,** leads to the town's three guest houses, clustered within shouting distance of each other. Tat Mai's northern end intersects **Wiwatana Road,** which runs east toward the post office.

PRACTICAL INFORMATION

Currency Exchange: Thai Farmers Bank, 63 Sukhumvit Rd. (tel. 520 569), across from the A/C bus stop, offers decent rates. Open Mon.-Fri. 8:30am-5:30pm.

Buses: To **Bangkok** (every hr., 6am-11:30pm, 5hr., 140฿) stopping in **Chantaburi** (1½hr., 50฿).

Local Transportation: *Songthaew* to **Laem Ngop** (10฿) leave from Sukhumvit Rd. just south of the Municipal Market next to the pharmacy. To go to **Bo Rai,** they wait up to an hour for 10 people, and are nestled against the market's front (north) corner in the little parking lot between the building and Sukhumvit Rd. (35฿). To go to **Khlong Yai,** they leave from the back of the market (30฿); last *songthaew* back to Trat leaves Khlong Yai at 5pm.

Taxis: 10-15฿, although almost everything's within walking distance.

Markets: The town's **Municipal Market** should not be missed. The market sets up behind the A/C bus stop. Also the site of the tasty night market. The Foremost Guest House occasionally runs trips to a **Cambodian market** on the border.

Pharmacies: 2 Sukhumvit Rd. (tel. 511 356), across Soi Sukhumvit from the Municipal Market, on the corner. Look for the sign which says "Chemist." Malaria pills sold. Owner speaks good English. Open daily 7am-10pm.

Medical Services: Trat Hospital (tel. 511 02 10), on Sukhumvit Rd., beyond the traffic light at the north end of town. Open 24hr. but expect to wait 2-3hr. A **clinic** (across the street and a few doors toward Sukhumvit Rd. from the Foremost Guest House) has an English-speaking doctor who is in and out all day until 7pm.

Emergency: tel. 191.

Police: (tel. 511 239) on Santhisuk Rd., at the corner of Wiwatana Rd. about a block past the turn-off for the post office on the right (across from the soccer field). Open 24hr.

Post Offices: On Tha Reua Jang Rd., 10min. from the Municipal Market. Turn left (north) onto the road in back of the market. Turn right where it ends in front of the gas station; walk 2 blocks to the 4-way intersection with traffic lights; turn left and the post office is 100m ahead on the right. Telegraphs, parcels, and *Poste Restante.* Open Mon.-Fri. 8:30am-4:30pm, Sat.-Sun. 9am-noon. **Postal code:** 23000.

Telephones: Located above the post office. Positively wired with telex, international calls (cash; collect costs 30฿), and a fancy selection of radio communications. Open daily 7am-10pm. **Telephone code:** 039.

ACCOMMODATIONS

Foremost Guest House, 49 Thon Charoen Rd. (tel. 511 923), has a house, complete with windows, inside another larger house. This mellow place works on the honor system. Walls are papered with info about Trat Province, Isaan, Cambodia, and Vietnam. Plentiful showers, including a hot one. Along with Patric, the congenial and well-informed French owner, A/C lobby, stereo, *Poste Restante* service, and self-serve tea/coffee/toast (7฿) contribute to an authentic homey feel. Safe-deposit box. Dorms 30฿. Singles 80฿. Doubles 100฿. Triples 120฿.

N.P. Guest House, 12 Tok Yai On Rd. (tel. 512 270). From the market head south on Tat Mai Rd. which narrows and becomes Tok Yai On Rd. N.P. is about 100m down on the left—you can't miss the sign. A newcomer to the Trat scene, not as informative as Foremost but rooms are freshly painted, clean, and cheap. Bathrooms clean enough to double as operating rooms. Dorms 40฿. Singles 80฿. Doubles 100฿. Basic menu (most dishes 15-25฿).

Windy Guest House, 63 Thon Charoen Rd., is just before Foremost walking from Sukhumvit. You'll feel like you've moved in with the family, since the house has only three guest rooms, and they'll insist that you use the TV, the stereo, and the single bathroom. Built on stilts over a small river. Single or double with fan 60฿, high season 80฿.

FOOD

There's no excuse for not eating in the **market.** During the day (5am-7pm) **foodstalls** set up on the first floor of the Municipal Market. They compete mightily for customers, so a hearty vegetable noodle soup costs just 5฿. Elaborate versions with meat or fish set you back 10-15฿; for fresh mussels, shell out 15฿; various rice dishes can be had for 10-25฿. Pastry, fruit, and dessert stands sweeten the meal deal. The whole operation moves to the open square two blocks north of the municipal market building for the **night market** (behind the A/C bus terminal), lasting 7pm-midnight. Those willing to sell their first born for a gasp of air conditioning might try **Restaurant Sunday,** on Wiwatana Rd. From the market, head north on Tat Mai Rd.; when it runs into Wiwatona Rd. turn right (as if heading to the post office). It's on the left about 50m down. Fairly small English menu—the Thai menu is three times the size; ask if you don't see what you want. Rainbow fried rice is 40฿, veggie salad costs 30฿, and very unusual (and delicious) Thai omelette costs 60฿. Open Mon.-Sat. 9am-1am, Sun. 8:30am-10pm.

SIGHTS AND ENTERTAINMENT

There is little to do in Trat aside from strolling off to the market or catching a flick at the Sukhumvit Rd. cinema. Groups solvent enough to shell out 3000฿ for a day's rental of a ten-person fishing boat can go to sea from the Municipality Pier *(Tha Reua)* 2km outside town on Tha Reua Jang Rd. For those of modest means, the Foremost and Windy Guest Houses run frequent **sight-seeing trips** in the high season involving a tour of the border market at Ban Hat Lek, a stop at a local beach, and a visit to a former Cambodian refugee camp, all for a reasonable 100฿.

■ Near Trat

LAEM NGOP

A sleepy seaside village with an increasingly chaotic pier, **Laem Ngop** is a fine place to spend the night or stock up on essentials before boarding the ferry to Ko Chang. Trat, however, is much hipper, and just a quick *songthaew* ride away (20min., 10฿). For visa extensions (30 days, 500฿) and the official line on **visiting Cambodia,** head for the **Immigration Office** (tel. 597 261). The office is on the ground floor of a white building on the right about a 15-minute stroll up the main road from Laem Ngop to Trat. Open Mon.-Fri. 8:30am-noon, and 1-4:30pm.

Thai Farmers Bank (tel. 597 04 56), 300m from the pier on the Trat-Laem Ngop Rd., is open Mon.-Fri. 8:30am-3:30pm. **Chut Kaew Guest House** (tel. 597 088), near the bank, offers a row of cement-floored rooms (1 shower serves 3 rooms). Singles cost 60฿, doubles 120฿. Unless you just can't bear to leave Laem Ngop, though, the accommodations in Trat offer much more. Chut Kaew's patio **restaurant** doles out Euro and Thai nosh (open daily 7am-10pm). On the pier, **Rimsapan Restaurant** provides a pleasant (though somewhat overpriced) dining diversion for prospective ferry-goers. A wee plate of fried rice costs 25฿. A daily ferry now connects Laem Ngop with **Ko Maack** (1pm, 150฿). Boats can be charted to explore the islands off southern Ko Chang from Laem Ngop, but expect to pay big baht (to Ko Kud 6000฿). Guest houses on Ko Chang organize excursions at more manageable rates.

The **tourist police** (tel. 597 255) is located a few meters from the pier. Open daily 8:30am-4:30pm. Remember, the last *songthaew* to Trat departs the pier area at 6pm, after that taxis will make the trip for 100฿.

■ Border Crossing

A few words of warning for those considering **crossing the border into Cambodia.** It is possible to take a ferry from the Thai village of Pak Klang to the Cambodia port of Sihanoukville (3hr., 500฿). You must obtain a Cambodian visa at the embassy in Bangkok first. The Thai government, however, does not recognize Pak Klang as an official border crossing and you will not receive an exit stamp on your passport, which means you have exited the country illegally. Several foreigners have been jailed, fined, and deported when they later attempted to re-enter Thailand. The same holds true for those who attempt to enter Thailand via Sihanoukville; you will not receive an entry stamp and will be considered an illegal immigrant even if you obtain a visa in Phnom Penh first. According to the Thai Immigration Office at Laem Ngop the regulations may be changing soon; inquire at the Foremost Guest House for the latest scoop.

This is the place to witness nature at her jungled best and perhaps spy on the lucrative gem and hardwood smuggling operations that lurk along the Thai-Cambodian border. Several hotels such as the **Seaview Resort** on Ko Chang's Kai Bai beach used to run daytrips to Cambodia during the high season. The legality of these excursions was fuzzy at best and always dependent on the current situation in Cambodia. As of June 1996, the Seaview had no plans to continue these trips.

■ Ko Chang เกาะช้าง

Until very recently, Mother Nature reigned supreme on Ko Chang. Eve's fabled garden had one serpent; Ko Chang is blessed with seven poisonous varieties. The island's rugged, malaria-infested interior remains largely impenetrable, but man is quickly making his presence known. A road encircles three-quarters of the island, electricity is scheduled to light the island by 1997, and bungalows line Hat Sai Kaow (White Sand Beach). These improvements have made the island the new budget-travel hotspot in eastern Thailand.

Thankfully, pessimists' complaints that development has already spoiled Ko Chang are a bit premature. The east coast's southern beaches remain quite secluded and the concentration of bungalows low. Unlike her sister islands up the coast, Ko Chang offers more than just miles of white sand and crystal clear water. Several waterfalls in the interior are accessible by hiking trails, increasing your chances of seeing some of the island's unique wildlife (and of catching malaria if you're not careful). Along the eastern coast, the perimeter road passes through spectacular strips of jungle, as well as rubber and fruit plantations.

Some 39 smaller islands are scattered across the Gulf of Thailand south of Ko Chang. Many of them are uninhabited or host only a fishing village or two. Not surprisingly, some of these islands have also proven unable to evade the long arm of the tourist industry. Bungalows can now be found on Ko Maak and Ko Kud.

GETTING THERE AND AWAY

To reach **Ko Chang,** take a bus to Trat, then a *songthaew* from the front of the Municipal Market on Sukhumvit Rd. to **Laem Ngop Pier** (25min., 10฿), and a ferry to the island. Make sure you board the correct ferry, as some drivers may be more interested in your fare than your intended destination.

Getting to your destination on Ko Chang from Laem Ngop Pier will cost 70฿. In the rainy season (May-Oct.), the trip consists of a ferry to **Al Saparot Pier** (40฿) followed by a jeep ride down the island (30฿) to the west coast beaches. In the high season, the west coast's waves peter out, allowing ferries from Laem Ngop to drop off travelers right on the beaches. Daily ferries depart year-round from Laem Ngop at 9am and every hour, noon-4pm. In high season the noon and 3pm ferries go directly to west coast beaches, and the 2pm goes directly to Hat Sai Kaow; the others go by way of Al Saparot Pier, as in the low season. There is also a daily ferry to **Ko Chang's east coast,** stopping at **Dan Mai, Than Mayon,** and **Salapet** (1pm, 70฿). Return ferries depart Al Saparot Pier daily at 7:30, 9am, noon, and 4pm; expect a jeep taxi to pass by each of the west coast beaches within an hour of the ferry's departure (30฿). Additional ferries may pick up passengers directly from west coast beaches in the high season; ask any bungalow crew for details. Remember, traveling to Ko Chang is still an inexact science; if you're the only one on the boat, don't expect it to budge.

ISLAND ORIENTATION

Shrouded in tropical rainforest, Ko Chang is oblong-shaped. Its rocky eastern shore parallels the mainland of Trat Province, but the best beaches line the western coast and are inaccessible to ferries during the stormy season (May-Oct.). During this time ferries from Laem Ngop will deposit you at one of several piers near the village of **Ao Saparot** on the island's northeast corner. From here a pick-up truck "taxi" will run you over the precipitously steep headlands at the northern tip of the island to the beaches along the west coast; the bungalow cluttered **Hat Sai Kaow,** and the more secluded **Hat Khlong Phrao** and **Hat Kai Bai.**

A perimeter road is currently being constructed to encircle the island; it now runs from Salapet at Ko Chang's southeastern extremity to Hat Kai Bai about three-fourths of the way down the western shore, hence its nickname "Horseshoe Road." The stretch of road from Ao Saparot to Hat Sai Kaow has been recently paved. The final stretch of road from Hat Kai Bai around the southern tip end will not be constructed for several years, if ever, due to the treacherously steep terrain. As a result, **Bang Bao** on the southwest coast (a 3-hour walk from the road) and **Hat Sai Yao (Long Beach)** are accessible only by boat. Several bungalow companies have maintained offices on and around the Laem Ngop Pier that may provide island information and maps, but beware of committing yourself to anything you have not seen first hand.

PRACTICAL INFORMATION

Tourist Offices: Ko Chang National Park Headquarters (tel. (039) 521 122) in Than Mayom, a town at the midpoint of the east coast, 20km from Hat Sai Kaow on Horseshoe Rd. These two wooden cottages stay open 24hr., displaying wildlife and coral and providing info.

Currency Exchange: Get your legal tender in Laem Ngop or Trat before leaving the mainland. Most bungalow operations on Hat Sai Kaow, as well as the Thor's Palace Restaurant, will exchange traveler's checks at a 3% commission but at abysmal rates.

Ferries: If you *really* need to leave the island outside of scheduled departures, fishermen will charter their boats (1000-1500฿). **Emergency trips to the mainland**

cost 1500฿ via speedboat from Ban Rung Rang Bungalows (tel. 329 04 64) on Hat Sai Kaow or 3000฿ from Sea View Resort (tel. 521 00 55) on Hat Kai Bai.

Local Transportation: Taxis, the misnomer for jeeps and motorcycles, drain your wallet and endurance. From Ao Saparot to Hat Sai Kaow 30฿, but remember that transport to any of the three main beaches is included in your 70฿ ferry ticket. Rides between the beaches should cost 30฿ but expect to pay more for "special trips" (that is, about 50฿ for a ride from one bungalow on one beach to another bungalow on another beach).

Rentals: Those with off-road experience and some extra baht can rent motorbikes at some resorts on Hat Sai Kaow, and from several roadside petrol stalls across the road from the bungalows. Expect to pay 60฿ per hour or 400-500฿ per day.

Markets: Buy food in Trat's bitchin' **municipal market** before departing the mainland to minimize the restaurant bills on the island. Ko Chang has no markets.

Medical Services: The government-run hospital in Trat handles Ko Chang's serious medical problems (See **Trat: Practical Information**). The island's four **clinics** do provide an important service: **malaria testing.** They are located at Khlong Phrao on the west coast, Khlongson in the north, Dan Mai on the east coast, and the southern village of Salapet. All open Mon.-Fri. 8:30am-4:30pm.

Post Offices: There is no official post office on Ko Chang yet, but that could change soon. Most bungalows will mail letters and postcards for you.

Telephones: International phone calls can be made at most of the bungalows on Hat Sai Kaow, including **Ban Rung Rang, Sunsai,** and **Phlamola Cliff Resort.** Standard rates are 100฿ per minute or 100฿ service charge for collect calls (most have 10 or 20min. max. time limit). **Magic Bungalows** on Hat Khlong Phrao offers the same services. **Telephone code:** 01 (for cellular phones *on* Ko Chang); 039 (for phones in Laem Ngop).

THE WEST COAST

The north end of the west coast is spiked with soaring cliffs rising from the water. The west's gorgeous beaches are the most heavily trafficked part of the island. Of the west coast's three principle beaches, Hat Sai Kaow (White Sand Beach) is by far the most heavily developed; bungalows crowd the sand like flies on durian. Unless you crave Ko Samet-style revelry, skip White Sand and make tracks for the more secluded and less crowded Hat Khlong Phrao and Hat Kai Bai. The ultimate stretch of silica is a 15-min. walk through the jungle from the cove at the south tip of Hat Kai Bai. It has no facilities (yet). During the low season (May-Oct.) these latter two beaches can seem downright deserted, which is great for travelers in groups or die-hard adventurers but single travelers should bring a good book or find a friend.

Hat Sai Kaow

Misnamed "White Sand Beach," the grey grit scatters along choppy surf on the northwest coast. Deserted at dawn, the beach gets congested in the afternoons during high season. Backpackers congregate on the porches of bungalows to watch the sunset and bemoan the big, bad encroachment of guest house VCRs. The concentration of bungalows decreases dramatically at the southern end of the beach where several nice bungalows and a great restaurant are located.

Just north of Sunsai is **Thor's Palace Restaurant** (pronounced "tor"). Diners sit cross-legged on *tatami* mats inside or at bamboo tables on the beach. Thor, the amiable owner, keeps visitors entertained for hours with stacks of paperbacks, decks of cards, and board games. The hippest menu on Ko Chang (fried veggies with tofu 35฿) and the source of some of the best curry in Thailand. (Open daily 9am-midnight.) The White Sand Beach Resort and its neighbor, a cement bungalow operation, swallow up lots of space, but aren't the only accommodations. **Ban Rung Rang** (tel. (01) 329 04 64) at the north end has typical Ko Chang budget digs of thatched bamboo bungalows. Rooms with private bathroom are 500฿ (300฿ low season), with shared bathroom 130฿ (80฿ low season). **Cookie Bungalow,** just to the south, offers the same amenities. Farther south, **Sunsai** (tel. (039) 597 078) is a bit more removed from the socializing. One of the friendliest and best-run operations on Ko Chang.

Canadian owner Dave can happily answer any question about Ko Chang. Simple bungalows are 100฿, with bath and fan 300-600฿ depending on size. Discounts are available in low season. At the southernmost point, **Phlamola Cliff Resort** (tel. (01) 323 01 64) has two rows of thatched bamboo huts perched over the rocky point just south of Hat Sai Kaow (600฿, 300-400฿ low season) in addition to more pricey concrete rooms with electricity in the evening and private bath (900฿, 700฿ low season).

Hat Khlong Phrao

More peaceful than Hat Sai Kaow, Hat Khlong Phrao is the least developed of the three beaches and practically hibernates during the rainy season. Bungalows here are spaced farther apart, making the population density of beach-goers seem lower even when the island is crankin' (although the density of angry dogs seems high year-round). The best bungalows lie along the southern section of the beach. Inland from Hat Khlong Phrao, a one-hour walk from **Horseshoe Road** brings you to a waterfall. Under the cascade, a pool too deep to fathom refreshes salt-water-logged beach bums.

Coconut Beach Bungalows, (tel. (01) 329 04 32), about 4km south of Hat Sai Kaow, at the north end of Hat Khlong Phrao, plants its huts on a spread of grassy lawn behind a rocky portion of the beach. Singles or doubles are 150฿, more substantial bungalows with bath 500฿; discounts in low-season. **K.P. Bungalows** (tel. (01) 327 02 25), located in the middle of the beach, is a 10-minute walk south of the river mouth that splits Hat Khlong Phrao—expect to ford some knee-deep water if you choose to walk down the beach instead of following Horseshoe Rd. K.P. offers standard grass-roof bungalows with mosquito nets and views of the beach through the palms (100฿, low season 60฿), larger bungalows with attached bath (150฿, low season 120฿), and nice bungalows (300฿ and up). K.P. also offers one of Khlong Phrao's only operational **restaurants** in the low season (fried rice or spicy soups 25-35฿). A full range of services are available, including overseas phone calls. You can rent tents (100฿) when bungalows are full. **Magic Bungalows** (tel. (039) 597 231) at the southern end of the beach has a bevy of well-maintained huts set on a lawn lush enough to host the Masters Tourney. Simple bungalows with common bath are 100฿ (low season 80฿), with bathroom 300฿ (low season 250฿). If you have brought your **camping** equipment, the management at most resorts will let you set up your tent nearby and use toilet/shower facilities for a small daily fee (150฿).

Hat Kai Bai

Some visitors to Hat Kai Bai bemoan its small rocky patches of swimming beach. Others call it Ko Chang's most beautiful length of coast, making it their island home for weeks or months on end. Like Hat Khlong Phrao, Hat Kai Bai virtually shuts down in the rainy season. Most bungalow owners are still happy to rent you a room, but don't look for much in the way of food or social life.

Nangnual Resort, near the north end of the beach, peers out from its fringe of vine-choked trees and hanging plants, although a new pier detracts from the vista. Myna birds and Thai TV provide the soundtrack. The bamboo huts are just a five- to 10-minute walk from the swimming beach (100฿, June-Oct. 50฿). Snorkel and mask rental costs 40฿ per day. The popular **Kai Bai Beach Bungalows** have recently joined the video brigade. Bamboo huts run 100฿, with shower 200฿ up to 1000฿ depending on the comfort level; June-Oct. 50฿, with shower 100฿. Kai Bai boasts a large, airy restaurant. **Siam Bay Resort** (tel. 213 69 23), at the south end of Kai Bai just before the sandy cove, has electrified stucco bungalows for 800฿, June-Oct. 500฿. Cheaper bamboo bungalows are 150฿ (low season 100฿), with bathroom 100฿ (low season 150฿). (Open daily 6pm-midnight.) As on Hat Khlong Phrao, most bungalow owners accommodate campers for a daily fee (10-20฿).

Hat Kai Bai also houses the **Wind Eagle School of Taiji.** *Farang* Jessy Boxer has studied and taught *taiji (tai chi)* as a form of meditation for 30 years, and offers both 2½-hr. (200฿) and one-month courses (3000฿) in a gorgeous wooden dance room.

A man named **Alpha** rents out a couple of **bamboo huts** (with showers 100฿, June-Oct. 50฿), **books,** and **hammocks** at the north end of the beach. He'll give you the low-down on the park's environmental disintegration at the **Comfortable Bar** (open 10am-2am), which is straight out of a Dr. Seuss book—the chairs are tilted to best observe the colorful ceiling. A sedated version of Hat Sai Kaow's social scene lurches along at this outlandish bar and the few restaurants.

THE EAST COAST

The picturesque east coast is short on beaches but long on scenic beauty. At the western end, colonnades of rubber trees alternate with rambutan orchards. Several waterfalls are accessible by trails that begin along the shore. While the falls themselves are nothing to write home about, the opportunity to catch a glimpse of the island's rugged interior should not be missed.

Ao Saparot

At the northernmost point of the east coast, Ao Saparot's crescent of gold is usually just an *hors d'oeuvre* for the west coast beaches. In monsoon season (June-Oct.), the ferry terminates in this tiny village, but most people pray for the good luck to survive the "taxi" ride (30฿) and head for even fairer shores.

The Central Area

Sai Thong won't slow you down much, but **Dan Mai** hides a path to **Tok Khonansi** (a waterfall), a 30-minute walk inland. **Than Mayom,** 4km to the south, has plenty of roosters but no beach, and is home to the **National Park Headquarters** (tel. (039) 521 122) which has little to offer, save a small visitor's center, **free public toilets** (bring your own tissue), and Thai-style **showers.** Nearby **Nam Tok Mayom,** a favorite of that waterfall buff King Rama V, still bears his initials. Freezing clear mountain water gushes over a 7m vertical coppery rock into a jungle pool.

Hat Sai Yao (Long Beach)

On the west side of the peninsula jutting from the southeast corner of the island, Hat Sai Yao is remote and remarkable. Check with the Information Office on Laem Ngop Pier for the current scoop on accommodations, and ask the captain of the ferry to Salapet to make a special trip, since there are no direct ferries.

Salapet

On the bay at the southeast tip of the island, Salapet is Ko Chang's most "energized" fishing village. Accessible by ferry (to Laem Ngop 6am, return 1pm, 70฿), it is also one place to charter boats to the southern archipelago; expect to pay through the nose (at least 2000฿).

■ Near Ko Chang

THE SOUTHERN ARCHIPELAGO

The isolated group of islands off Ko Chang's south coast is famous for fishing, coral, rock formations, bird nests, and bat guano. You can scuba dive at **Ko Rang.** The deep, flickering water is home to coral, tons of fish, and toothy sharks. To get there, charter a boat in Salapet or check at Ko Chang bungalows for scuba or snorkeling tours. Sunsai Bungalows on Hat Sai Kaow runs day trips to the islands of **Ko Loi, Ko Ngam, Ko Gia,** and **Ko Rang** during the high season. Trips leave at 8:30am and return at sunset (350฿ per person). Magic Bungalows on Hat Khlong Phrao is planning to organize three-day package tours stopping at Ko Rang, **Ko Kham,** and Ko Kud (min. 5, 1500฿ per person; price decreases as number of people increases).

Ko Wai, a less-remote version of Ko Rang, is surrounded by a necklace of coral, and the fishing is legendary. **Ko Bhrao** has an archetypal palm tree-studded beach with only group lodgings. **Ko Lao Ya,** now accessible during the low season, is known for its coral and clear water (sound like a trend?) and has some bungalows. There are two bungalow operations on **Ko Maak: Lazy Days** and **Alternative Guest House;** both are well within a backpacker's budget (basic lodgings beginning at about 80฿) but they virtually shut down during the low season. Check with guest houses in Trat for the latest information. A daily ferry runs between Laem Ngop and Ko Maak (1pm, 150฿) but only intermittently during the low season when the seas can get quite rough. There are also accommodations on far-flung **Ko Kud,** but these are pricey and there is no regular public ferry. Check in Trat for more information.

NORTHERN THAILAND

Confident and poised, Northern Thailand receives visitors with easy graciousness, inviting them to uncover what lies behind the commercialized caricature the country presents elsewhere. Once the home of the prosperous and independent Kingdom of Lanna, the land runs over heavily forested hills, which are interspersed with farms, rice paddies, and poppy fields. Many people share this space: hill-tribes predominate in certain regions, Chinese immigrants proudly display pictures of the Thai Royal Family in shop windows, and refugee camps swell with Burmese, escaping the repression of a military government back home. The unique dialect, cuisine, dance, and wat architecture of Northern Thailand owes much to the fusion of these ethnicities, which continue to enrich and expand the meaning of "Thailand."

Potential visitors are simultaneously drawn to serene border towns and repelled by the presence of rebel camps, involved in sporadic, often violent disputes just across the border. However, even travelers oblivious to the culture surrounding them cannot ignore the ineffable natural scenery and fresh, cool air. The mountains of the north are the lowest extremities of the Himalayan foothills, and the Mekong River forms the border with Laos, while the Salawin River flirts with Burma before eventually draining into the Bay of Bengal. The Ping River cuts through Chiang Mai and in earlier times connected the North with central Thailand.

Chiang Mai stands at the door to the north provinces, which fan out on all the major compass points from the city's central location. To the south is antique-laden Lamphun. The west province of Mae Hong Son borders Burma and is thick with forest and hill tribes. North of Chiang Mai is Chiang Rai, the traditional gateway to the opium-laced Golden Triangle. Finally, to the east, snuggling up next to Laos, is Nan, often-ignored, yet perhaps the loveliest province in the North, if not all of Thailand.

One way to see the north is to go overland on Hwy. 107 from Chiang Mai, north to Fang and Tha Thon. From Tha Thon, an excellent new road leads up to Mae Salong, a village whose inhabitants are a mixture of Yunnanese, hill-tribe, and Thai. Many people prefer to take a long-tailed boat trip on the Kok River from Tha Thon to Chiang Rai and then use Chiang Rai as a base for venturing into the Golden Triangle to see Mae Salong, Mae Sai, Chiang Saen, and Sop Ruak.

Another approach is to detour from Hwy. 107, taking Route 1095 to Pai and into Mae Hong Son, then back-track to Hwy. 107 and head up to Tha Thon. Some people loop south from Mae Hong Son to Mae Sariang, then go past Doi Inthanon National Park and back to Chiang Mai. Or head southwest from Chiang Mai along Hwy. 108 to Mae Sariang first, then on up to Mae Hong Son and around. These routes offer choice mountain scenery and assured contact with hill tribes.

Growing regional integration is continually increasing possible crossing points into Burma and Laos. Check with any immigration office for the latest details. A land route to China is in the works, and weekly flights connect Chiang Mai and Kunming.

■ Chiang Mai เชียงใหม่

Who would have thought that mice scurrying down a hole beneath a *bodhi* tree would lead to all this? But that was the omen that convinced King Mengrai in 1296 to

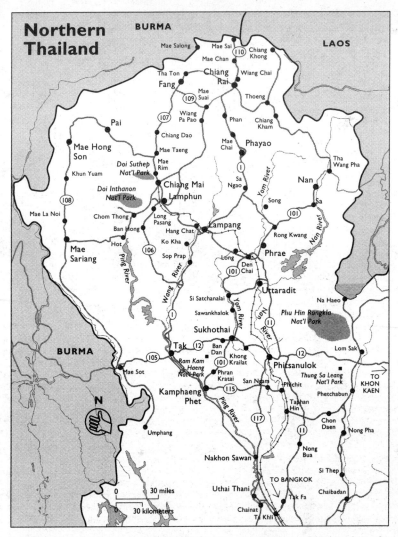

Northern Thailand

BURMA
LAOS

Mae Salong
Mae Sai
110
Chiang Khong
Mae Chan
Tha Ton
Chiang Rai
Fang
109
Mae Suai
Wiang Chai
Thoeng
107
Wiang Pa Pao
Phan
Chiang Kham
Pai
Chiang Dao
Mae Chai
Phayao
Mae Taeng
Mae Hong Son
Mae Rim
Tha Wang Pha
Khun Yuam
Doi Suthep Nat'l Park
Chiang Mai
Sa Ngao
Nan
Doi Inthanon Nat'l Park
Lamphun
1
Song
Sa
101
Mae La Noi
Chom Thong
Long Pasang
Lampang
Rong Kwang
Ban Hong
Hang Chat
108
Hot
Ko Kha
Phrae
Mae Sariang
106
Sop Prap
Long
Den Chai
101
Si Satchanalai
Uttaradit
Na Haeo
Sawankhalok
Phu Hin Rongkla Nat'l Park
Sukhothai
11
Tak
12
Ban Dan
Lom Sak
105
Ram Kam Haeng Nat'l Park
101
Khong Krailat
Phitsanulok
12
TO KHON KAEN
Mae Sot
Phran Kratai
Thung Sa Leang Nat'l Park
San Nam
Prichit
Kamphaeng Phet
115
Phetchabun
Taphan Hin
117
Umphang
Chon Daen
11
Nong Pha
Nong Bua
Nakhon Sawan
Si Thep
TO BANGKOK
Uthai Thani
Chaibadan
0 30 miles
0 30 kilometers
Chainat
Tak Fa
Ta Khli

N

Ping River
Wang River
Yom River
Nan River

BURMA

build Nopburi Si Nakhon Ping Chiang Mai as the capital of Lanna (the kingdom of a million rice fields). Contemporaneous with Sukhothai and Ayutthaya to the south, Lanna was a force to be reckoned with, and often clashed with them throughout the 14th and 15th centuries. In 1556, the neighboring Burmese vanquished Chiang Mai, then they marched on to besiege Ayutthaya. The city remained under Burmese suzerainty until 1775, when King Taksin led a Thai army to reclaim Chiang Mai.

Despite formal incorporation into Thailand, Chiang Mai retained a large measure of independence—commanding its own army, and great latitude in the governance of its people. Separated from Bangkok by 696km of mountainous terrain and dense jungle, the city could be reached only by an arduous river trip or a several-week-long elephant journey. Improved transport and communication systems in the 1930s finally brought all of Thailand firmly within the capital's reach. Although north and south have become one, denizens of Chiang Mai steadfastly cling to their distinct heritage,

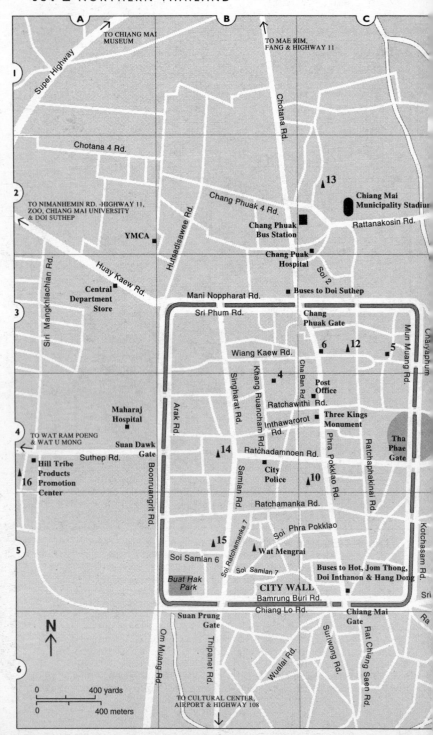

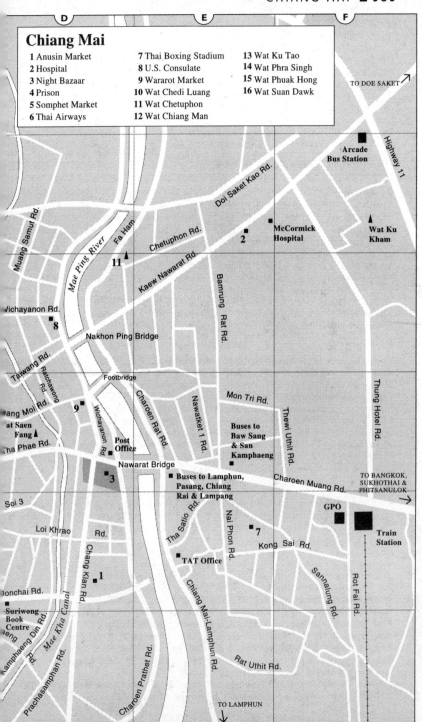

Chiang Mai

1 Anusin Market
2 Hospital
3 Night Bazaar
4 Prison
5 Somphet Market
6 Thai Airways
7 Thai Boxing Stadium
8 U.S. Consulate
9 Wararot Market
10 Wat Chedi Luang
11 Wat Chetuphon
12 Wat Chiang Man
13 Wat Ku Tao
14 Wat Phra Singh
15 Wat Phuak Hong
16 Wat Suan Dawk

TO DOE SAKET

Arcade
Bus Station

Highway 11

McCormick
Hospital

Wat Ku
Kham

Doi Saket Kao Rd.

Chetuphon Rd.

Fa Ham

Mae Ping River

Muang Samut Rd.

Kaew Nawarat Rd.

11

2

Bamrung Rat Rd.

Vichayanon Rd.

8

Nakhon Ping Bridge

Taiwang Rd.

Ratchawong Rd.

Footbridge

Mon Tri Rd.

Thewi Uthit Rd.

Thung Hotel Rd.

ang Moi Rd.

at Saen
Fang

ha Phae Rd.

9

Wichayanon Rd.

Charoen Rat Rd.

Nawatket 1 Rd.

Buses to
Baw Sang
& San
Kamphaeng

Post
Office

Nawarat Bridge

3

Buses to Lamphun,
Pasang, Chiang
Rai & Lampang

Charoen Muang Rd.

TO BANGKOK,
SUKHOTHAI &
PHITSANULOK

Soi 3

Loi Khrao   Rd.

Tha Satio Rd.

Nai Phon Rd.

GPO

Train
Station

7

Kong Sai Rd.

Chang Kian Rd.

1

TAT Office

Sannalung Rd.

Rot Fai Rd.

onchai Rd.

Suriwong
Book
Centre
aeng

Mae Kha Canal

Chiang Mai-Lamphun Rd.

Rat Uthit Rd.

amphaeng Din Rd.

Prachasamphan Rd.

Charoen Prathet Rd.

TO LAMPHUN

including their dialect, culinary specialties, and art and architecture, which exhibit Burmese influences.

Chiang Mai's status as Thailand's second largest city (pop. 250,000) belies its physical size, which is only a fraction of Bangkok's. Nevertheless, the international scene here is vibrant, infused with thousands of *farang* who venture up from the south drawn by the promise of adventure and a cooler climate. The enormous expansion of the tourism industry increases concerns that the stampede of tourists through certain mountain areas is eroding both hill-tribe culture and the natural environment. Trump-like visionaries with mountain condo fantasies and trekking entrepreneurs now clash frequently with local environmental and social action groups, but for now the Chiang Mai Valley is still accommodating everyone.

GETTING THERE AND AWAY

By Plane

Thai Air, 240 Pokklao Rd. (tel. 211 014), with additional branches around the city, handles all domestic flights into **Chiang Mai International Airport** (tel. 270 222), just 3km southwest of the city on Sanambin (Airport) Rd. Flights arrive from Bangkok's Don Muang and often sell out in advance (9 per day, 7:10am-10pm, 1hr., 1650฿ plus a 20฿ airport tax). From Chiang Mai flights leave to: **Bangkok** (13 per day, 7:15am-10:45pm, 1hr., coach 1650฿); **Chiang Rai** (7:40am, 4:55pm, 40min., 420฿); **Mae Hong Son** (5 per day, 40min., 345฿); **Phitsanulok** (1 per day, 1hr., 650฿); and **Phuket** (11:15am Fri.-Mon. and Wed., 2hr., 3455฿).

Thai Air runs a shuttle service to Chiang Mai (40฿), or try *tuk-tuk* (30-40฿). Cheaper still are the *songthaew* (15฿). Dirt-cheap rides are provided by bus #6 (5฿), which departs 200m away, on Sanambin (Airport) Rd.

By Train

The most popular means of shuttling between Bangkok and Chiang Mai, trains are safe, quick, and clean. Trains pull up at **Chiang Mai Railway Station,** 27 Charoen Muang Rd. (tel. 245 363), on the eastern outskirts of the city. *Samlor, tuk-tuk,* and the #1 west-bound bus can take newly arrived passengers into town.

Sleepers should be reserved far in advance. Lower berths are pricier but are ideal for the morning mountain view coming into Chiang Mai and for late-night toilet forays. Six trains per day run between Chiang Mai and **Bangkok:** third-class 121-171฿; second-class 255-305฿, with A/C 305฿; sleepers 355฿ and up. Expect a 30-80฿ surcharge on all tickets. Most of these trains also stop in **Phitsanulok** (7hr., 3rd-class 65฿, 2nd-class 136฿) and **Lampang** (2hr., 3rd-class 23฿, 2nd-class 48฿).

By Bus

To Chiang Mai from **Bangkok's Northern Bus Terminal,** the cheapest deal and the roughest ride are the four non-A/C buses (6, 6:30, 7am, and 5:30pm, 190฿). For more comfort, take an A/C bus (5 per day, 9:10am-9:30pm, 10hr., 242฿).

Buses going outside of Chiang Mai Province are based at the **Arcade Bus Station** (tel. 242 664), on the northeastern outskirts of town on Kaew Nawarat Rd. near the superhighway. *Tuk-tuk, songthaew,* or west-bound buses #1 or 3 can take travelers to the old city. To get to the station, catch an east-bound yellow #3 bus on Chiang Mai Rd. To: **Bangkok** (#18-orange, 12:30pm, 11hr., 190฿; A/C #18-blue, 12 per day, 237-470฿); **Chiang Rai** old route: (#148-green, every 30min., 6am-4:30pm, 6hr., 83฿), new route: (#166-green, 13 per day, 4hr., 57฿; A/C 3 per day, 79฿); **Mae Hong Son** via **Mae Sariang** (#170-orange, 7 per day, 6:30am-3pm, 115฿) via **Pai** (#612-orange, 6 per day, 7am-4pm, 115฿); **Nan** (#169-green, 4 per day, 6hr., 83฿; A/C 3 per day, 115฿); **Phitsanulok** (#155 or #623-orange, 5 per day, 6hr., 104฿; A/C 5 per day, 146฿); **Mae Sai** (#619-green, 5 per day, 5hr., 71฿; A/C 6 per day, 127฿); and **Lampang** (#152-green, every 30min., 6am-4pm, 2hr., 29฿).

Buses within Chiang Mai Province are served by **Chang Phuak Bus Station** (tel. 211 586), north of the old city beyond the gate on Chang Phuak Rd. South-bound bus

#2 goes within the moats. To get to the station, take bus #2 from Tha Phae Rd. To: **Bo Sang** and **Sankampang** (#225-red and white, every 30min., 5:30am-5pm, 20min., 5฿) and **Tha Thon** (#1231-orange, 5 per day, 4hr., 50฿).

Many private services offer discounted bus tickets between cities. You will usually get exactly what you pay for, and you may be expected to stay at an affiliated guest house upon arrival.

ORIENTATION

Chiang Mai, encircled by a **superhighway,** is easy to navigate. The heart of Chiang Mai is the **old city,** and within its square moat are winding streets and alleys. **Bamrung Buri Road** runs just inside the southern moat and has two gates, **Suan Prung Gate** to the west, and **Chiang Mai Gate** to the east. **Arak Road** runs along the western moat and has **Suan Dawk Gate**. **Sri Phum Road** follows the northern moat and has **Chang Phuak Gate**. **Moon Muang Road** follows along the eastern moat and has **Tha Phae Gate.** The gates, remnants of the city walls, are now undistinguished brick ruins. **Mun Muang Road** runs along the eastern moat. **Ratchadamnoen Road** bisects the old city east to west. Within the old city, the east-west *soi* numbers increase as you go north.

At Tha Phae Gate, Ratchadamnoen Rd. changes names to **Tha Phae Road** and courses 1.5km east to the **Ping River**. Tha Phae Rd. is rich with banks and currency exchange counters, as well as travel agencies. After crossing the Ping over **Nawarat Bridge,** Tha Phae Rd. becomes **Charoen Muang Road.** Tha Phae Rd. is intersected on the west bank of the Ping by **Charoen Prathet Road,** which runs north-south. Also intersecting Tha Phae Rd., and running roughly parallel to Charoen Prathet Rd. to the west, **Chang Klan Road** is home to the night bazaar, some banks, and more places to eat. The road running along the Ping on the river's east bank is **Charoen Rat Road** when it is north of Nawarat Bridge, and **Chiang Mai-Lamphun Road** when it is south of the bridge.

GETTING AROUND

Although not the sticky car jams of Bangkok, traffic here is still thick. Exploring the old city and the Tha Phae Gate area by foot is the most hassle-free option. For long-distance excursions, motorcycles or cars can be rented, but *songthaew, tuk-tuk,* and *samlor* can do just as well.

By Bicycle

Chiang Mai is a compact city and most sights are easily reached by bicycle. Random places in the Tha Phae Gate area have a few cycles—look for the row of bikes parked outside. The average bike goes for 30฿ per day, and rentals require a passport or a 500฿ deposit. **Jaguar,** 131 Moon Muang Rd. (tel. 419 161), has mountain bikes for the same price as the aged two-wheelers available elsewhere.

By Motorcycle and Moped

Many travelers opt for mopeds when exploring the area east of the river. Moped rentals cost 150฿ per day, and a motorcycle about 200฿. Insurance should be included in the price; a helmet is worth the extra 10฿. A passport or hefty deposit is required. Rental shops abound in the Mun Muang and Tha Phae Gate areas.

By Car

Traveling in a group, or farther outside Chiang Mai with a lot of gear may require a car rental (1000-1200฿ per day). Many rental shops on the streets are of questionable legitimacy, but there are two American car offices here: **Avis,** Orchid Hotel, 14/14 Huay Kaew Rd. (tel. 221 316) and **Hertz,** 90 Sri Donchai Rd. (tel. 279 474).

By Songthaew, Tuk-tuk, and Samlor

A *songthaew* safari beats any roller-coaster ride in terms of price (10฿) and hair-raising lurches. Tell the driver where you're going. If he shakes his head and speeds away, this means that your destination is not on his route. Don't fret, another one will come by soon enough. *Tuk-tuk* and *samlor* are omnipresent (20฿ for very short rides, 30฿ across the old city, and 40฿ across all of Chiang Mai).

By Bus

Local buses (3-5฿) service most places. Bus #1 runs east and west along Suthep Rd. and from Tha Phae Gate to the train station. Bus #2 runs north and south via Chang Phuak Gate. Bus #6 circles the city and goes by the airport. Bus routes appear on the **Tourist Map of Chiang Mai** (30-60฿ at many stores and at the TAT). Buses run 6am-6pm, and pass a stop every 15 minutes. They must be flagged down.

PRACTICAL INFORMATION

Get a copy of *Trip Info,* a comprehensive listing of virtually all traveler-oriented establishments in Chiang Mai (available at the TAT, restaurants, and guest houses).

Tourist Offices: TAT, 105/1 Chiang Mai-Lamphun Rd. (tel. 248 604), 0.5km south of Nawarat Bridge. Chock full of maps and brochures. The only other TAT office in the north is in Chiang Rai. Open daily 8am-5pm. TAT booths like the one at the airport are scattered around town.

Tourist Police: In the TAT building (tel. 248 974). Open daily 6am-midnight.

Embassies and Consulates: UK, 54 Village 2, Tambon Suthep (tel. 894 139). **US,** 387 Vitchayanon Rd. (tel. 252 665). Open Mon.-Fri. 8-11:30am.

Immigration Offices: 97 Sanambin (Airport) Rd. (tel. 272 510). Visa extensions require 500฿, 3 passport photos, and 2 copies of the passport photo page, visa page, and arrival/departure card. Open Mon.-Fri. 8:30am-noon and 1-4pm.

Currency Exchange: Plenty of places scattered around town. **Siam Commercial Bank** (tel. 273 171), on Chang Klan Rd. near the intersection with Tha Phae Rd. Open daily 8:30am-4:30pm. **24-hr. ATM** accepts all major credit cards.

American Express: Sea Tours Company, 2/3 Prachasamphan Rd. (tel. 271 441). Only AmEx connection in northern Thailand. Mail held for 3 months, free for check or card-holders. Open Mon.-Fri. 8:30am-4:30pm, Sat. 8:30-11:30am.

Luggage Storage: The train station has a cloak room with luggage storage (5฿ per day per piece for the first 5 days, 10฿ per day after that). Open daily 6am-6pm. Most guest houses store luggage for free, although safety can be dubious.

Markets: The **night bazaar** lies along the entire length of Chang Klan Rd. Geared toward *farang,* with lots of t-shirts and trinkets. Come early to get good deals. Open 6pm-midnight. For markets catering to the taste buds, see **Food** below.

Medical Services: McCormick Hospital, Kaew Nawarat Rd. (tel. 241 107). Some English spoken. **Maharaj Hospital** (Chiang Mai University), on Suthep Rd. (tel. 221 122). Both have ambulance service and **24-hr. emergency pharmacies. Malaria Centre,** 18 Bunruangrit Rd. (tel. 221 529), near Maharaj, just north of Suan Dawk Gate. Open Mon.-Fri. 8:30am-4:30pm.

Emergency: tel. 191.

Post Offices: (tel. 245 376), on Charoen Muang Rd., next to the Railway Station. Anywhere along Chiang Moi Rd., hop on bus #1 going east. Open Mon.-Fri. 8:30am-4:30pm, Sat.-Sun. 9am-noon. Telex and fax services. *Poste Restante* service open daily 8:30am-3:30pm. **Branch Office:** On Phra Pokklao Rd. just north of the intersection with Ratwithi Rd. in the old city. Open Mon.-Fri. 8:30am-4:30pm. **Postal code:** 50000.

Telephones: Red phones for local calls (1฿). Blue phones for calls within Thailand. For overseas calling card or collect calls, use **HCD phones** located at the night bazaar, the airport, the post office, Tha Phae Gate, the Thai Airways office, or guest houses (with a hefty surcharge). Overseas calls daily 8am-8pm in **telecommunications office** upstairs from the GPO. **Telephone code:** 053.

ACCOMMODATIONS

Mun Muang Rd., the southeast corner of the old city, Charoen Rat Rd., and Charoen Prathet Rd. teem with guest houses. Basic rooms are 60฿ and up. Cool season (Nov.-Feb.) and festival times increase prices by 20-50฿. Tour deals made in Bangkok often

stipulate that you trek with an affiliated guest house. Travelers should not store valuables in their guest houses while trekking; instead, leave them in a bank safety box.
The TAT office has a list of Chiang Mai Guest House Association lodgings, all of which
pay government taxes. These places may be slightly more secure.

Tha Phae Gate Area—Within Moat

Libra Guest House, 28 Mun Muang Rd. Soi 9 (tel. 210 687), near the northeast corner of the old city. This family-run guest house puts others in its price range to
shame. Freshly renovated, spacious, and spotless rooms, all with fan and private
bath tip the scale in Libra's favor. Gate locks at 1am, and the dogs don't take kindly
to fence hoppers. Singles 80฿. Doubles 100฿. Check-out 10am.

Moon Muang Golden Court, 95 Mun Muang Rd. (tel. 212 779). Above and beyond
the standard guest house, but still a decent deal for those weary of the usual dank
quarters. Rooms range from 150฿ (1 big bed, cold water, fan) to 300฿ (2 big beds,
hot water, A/C), with a variety of permutations in between.

Rose Guest House, 87 Ratchamanka Rd. (tel. 276 574), on the corner with
Ratchaphakinai Rd. The bamboo restaurant below promises more than the spartan
rooms with shared bath actually deliver, but consolation is the few baht saved by
staying here. Singles 60฿. Doubles 80฿. Check-out 9am.

Tha Phae Gate Area—Outside Moat

Daret's House and Restaurant, 415 Chaiyaphum Rd. (tel. 235 440), at Tha Phae
Gate. Enjoy fans and private baths in this condominium look-alike. Balconies on
each floor. Weight machines and a ping-pong table to pass the time. Singles 60฿.
Doubles 80฿, with shower 120฿. Check-out 10am.

Sarah's Guesthouse, 20 Tha Phae Rd. Soi 4 (tel. 208 271). Another guest house that
should not be lost among the horde. Spacious rooms with private cold shower and
common hot. Singles/doubles 100฿.

Ping River—East Bank

Pun Pun Guest House, 321 Charoen Rat Rd. (tel. 243 362), 1km north of the Narawat Bridge. Quiet, gaily decorated bungalows are raised on stilts over the river, and
have hot water for lots o' bathing fun. Singles with common bath 60฿, with private
bath 100฿. Doubles with bath 150฿.

Lanna River Hut, 75 Chiang Mai-Lamphun Rd. (tel. 241 016), near the TAT. Bamboo huts with mosquito nets and private baths set in a flowery garden lend flavor
to this guest house. The regular building has a spacious common area and hardwood floors. Dorms 50฿. Singles 40฿. Doubles 60฿.

FOOD

Chiang Mai has a tremendous number of restaurants, offering a colorful range of international culinary styles. Strong Chinese and Burmese influences imbue the hearty cuisine of Northern Thailand with a unique flavor.

The **Sompet Market** between Soi 6 and 7 on Mun Muang Rd., and the **Wahorat
Market** near the Ping River at the end of Chiang Moi Rd. offer the standard set of
grilled *saba*, fresh rambutan, sticky-sweet *roti*, and fried noodles. At night, the noc-
turnal **Anusarn Market,** between Chang Klan and Charoen Prathet Rd. just north of
Sri Donchai Rd., is an excellent snack zone. Fast food joints can also be found in the
Chiang Mai Pavilion or **Chiang Mai Plaza** on Chang Klan Rd.

For a serious culinary experience, try out a traditional *khantoke* dinner. In this formal northern meal, diners sit on the floor and use their hands to eat from bowls
placed on a low lacquer table. The dinner typically consists of glutinous rice, two
meat dishes, and two vegetable dishes. The well-frequented **Old Chiang Mai Cultural
Centre,** 185/3 Wualai Rd. (tel. 275 097), about 1.5km south of the old city from the
Chiang Mai Gate area, offers dinner accompanied by traditional northern dancing
from 7pm to 10pm nightly. Call ahead for reservations.

THAILAND

Tha Phae Gate Area—Within Moat

Vegetarian Food Restaurant, 65 Mun Muang Rd. (tel. 278 315), at Tha Phae Gate. Inconspicuous location, but delicious food. Sai Baba and his incredible hair preside over the operation. Dig into the northern curry (25฿), or the acrobatic Healthy Vegetable Soup (20฿). Open daily 8:30am-2pm and 5-9pm.

J.J.'s Bakery (tel. 211 069), under the Montri Hotel at Tha Phae Gate. A western transplant into the heart of the city. Start your day off right with ice cream, baked goods, and western breakfasts. A full meal goes for 60-150฿. Refreshingly air-conditioned. Open daily 6:30am-10:30pm.

Tiramisu, 142 Prapokklao Rd. (tel. 208 778). A combination Italian restaurant-bakery that shines brightly in Chiang Mai's dining circle. Their homemade bread (10-30฿) only whets one's appetite for the fresh pasta and *tiramisù* (45฿). Entrees 80-100฿. Open daily 8:30am-10:30pm.

Tha Phae Gate Area—Outside Moat

Croissant, 318 Tha Phae Rd. (tel. 252 418). Western food, coffee, and TV—a purist's nightmare, a homesick backpacker's dream. Espresso (30฿) with a buttery croissant will fortify *l'esprit* before the next excursion. Satellite TV airs everything from CNN to music videos. Movies shown daily. Open daily 7am-10pm.

Aroon Rai, 43/45 Kotchasarn Rd. (tel. 276 947). A local favorite for over 33 years. Wondrous array of Thai, Chinese, and Chiang Mai dishes. Schmooze with Thais and *farang* alike under the portraits of His Ubiquitous Majesty. Yummy chicken with coconut milk 30฿. Open daily 10am-8pm.

Near the Ping River

Riverside, 9/11 Charoen Rd. (tel. 243 239). Serving Thai and western food, this is *the* place to be seen in Chiang Mai. The food is delicious, as is the view, and there is western music every evening. Most entrees 50-80฿. Open daily 10am-1am.

The Whole Earth, 88 Sri Donchai Rd. (tel. 282 463), east of Chang Klan Rd. Promises "Heaven on Earth...at the Whole Earth," with its wholesome divine food. Aims to transform the world by means of the "same intelligence that creates a lotus from the mud." Also offers health education classes. Thai and Indian dishes available for carnivores, too. Entrees 50-200฿. Open daily 11am-2pm and 5-10pm.

Shere Shiraz, 23/25 Charoen Prathet Rd. Soi 6 (tel. 276 132), off of Chang Klan Rd., down the alley near Porn Ping Tower. Pakistani, Indian, Arabic, and Thai food. Everything is made from scratch, catering to individual tastes. This means extended preparation times, but the place is right in the middle of the Night Bazaar so passing time is no problem. Feast on a set meal of *tikki*, curries, *tandoor* chicken, breads, dessert, and tea (150-250฿). Open daily 9:30am-11:30pm.

SIGHTS

As in any other heavily touristed area, travelers in Chiang Mai must filter out the wretched yet prolific tourist traps. Although no spot has escaped the commercializing touch, Chiang Mai can still reward visitors with the precious gems of its long history and the 300-plus densely packed wats throughout the city. To maintain sanity, you could break with tight-wad tradition and hire a guide or take an organized tour.

Wat Chiang Man, the oldest wat in Chiang Mai, is in the northeastern part of the old city off Ratchaphakinai Rd., near Chang Phuak Gate. King Mengrai built this wat in 1296 when he founded Chiang Mai and made it his humble abode. With its extensive use of teakwood and its architectural harmony with the surrounding forest, the temple is a classic example of northern Thai design.

There is a *bot* inside the grounds, with huge teak columns and neighboring *wiharn.* The one on the right is home to two ancient and sacred Buddhist images. **Phra Sae Tang Kamani** (Crystal Buddha) is thought to have come from Lopburi about 1800 years ago. The second important Buddha image is **Phra Sila** (Stone Buddha), imported from India or Sri Lanka some 2500 years ago. (Open daily 9am to 5pm.) Rows of sturdy elephant buttresses support a *chedi* outside the *wiharn,* representing the mythical era of unity between man and animals.

Wat Phra Singh lies on the western side of the old city, near Suan Dawk Gate, at the end of Phra Singh Rd. Its chief attraction is the bronze **Phra Singh** in the finely decorated **Phra Wiharn Lai Kam.** Although locals will assure you otherwise, experts are not sure if this is the true Phra Singh Buddha—there are identical statues in Bangkok and Nakhon Si Thammarat. The image is the focal point of Songkran festivities each April 13-15.

Occupying the old city's southwest corner, **Buak Hat Public Park's** fountains and grassy stretches make a relaxing rest stop. To get there, walk down Mun Muang Rd. to the southern moat, take a right on Bamrung Buri Rd., and go 2km to the western moat. A rented mat can avoid those pesky grass stains. (Open daily 5am-10pm).

Continuing down Phra Singh Rd. to Phra Pokklao Rd. leads to **Wat Chedi Luang,** built by King Saen Suang Ma in 1401. The temple walls hold the remains of Chiang Mai's largest *chedi,* which once rose 86m above the ground. A *naga* staircase adorns the front porch of the *bot,* which houses the **standing gold Buddha** and 32 *Jataka* story panels depicting scenes from the Buddha's life. Legend claims that Wat Chedi Luang was home to the Emerald Buddha during its short stay in Chiang Mai. A nearby **sacred gum tree** supports the legend that as long as it stands, so will Chiang Mai.

Beyond the Old City

To venture into new territory, start at Chang Phuak Gate (White Elephant Gate) on the north side of the moat. From here, grab a west-bound *songthaew* or #3 bus. In the west part of town, **Chiang Mai University** sprawls over 600 acres just north of Suthep Rd. Serving the school's 12,000 students, the **university library** includes many English sources on all subjects. The **Chiang Mai Arboretum** is located 4km from the main entrance of the university, along Huay Kaew Rd. Studded with rare trees, it is a relaxing place to take a break from a hectic schedule. There's also an exercise park here. Next door, the **Chiang Mai Zoo** (tel. 221 179) houses thousands of animals in their natural habitat surrounded by hilly, forested terrain with lakes, waterfalls, and well-groomed gardens. (Open 8am-6pm; admission 20฿.)

On the southwest corner of the campus is the **Tribal Research Institute,** which has a small museum with excellent exhibits on the minorities inhabiting the mountainous area of northern Thailand. (Open Mon.-Fri. 8:30am-4:30pm.) Heading through the university gates from Suthep Rd., visitors will come upon a clock tower. A left turn, then a right, and another left leads to the institute. Those interested in learning more about the hill tribes can go next door to the **library** (open Mon.-Fri. 8:30am-noon and 1-4:30pm).

Farther along Suthep Rd., **Wat Ram Poeng** is the location of the **Northern Insight Meditation Centre** (tel. 278 620), where you can practice *vipassana* meditation. Saffron-robed monks, white-clad nuns, and lay practitioners quietly inhabit the grounds. Both wats are a bit off the beaten track, but can be reached by heading west from the city along Suthep Rd. After crossing the canal, take the third left, then follow the signs to Wat U Mong. Wat Ram Poeng is about 2km ahead.

Wat Chet Yot is 500m farther west on the superhighway. Inspired by the design of the Mahabodhi temple in Bodhgaya, India, King Tilokaraja built this shrine in 1455. Each of the *chedi's* spires represents one of the seven weeks that the Buddha spent in Bodhgaya, India after attaining enlightenment there. Wat Chet Yot also has important historical significance: in 1477, the Eighth World Buddhist Council met here to revise the *Tripitaka* scriptures of Theravada Buddhism. The two **Bo trees** are said to be descendants of the one the Big Guy himself sat under during his epiphany. The smaller *chedi* nearby reputedly holds the ashes of King Tilokaraja.

SHOPPING

Chiang Mai is Thailand's main center for handicrafts. Just strolling past stores on the street or shuffling through night markets will uncover a great variety of antiques, silver jewelry, hill-tribe embroidery, Thai textiles, pottery, and anything you could imagine for sale. The main hunting grounds are Tha Phae Rd. and Chang Klan Rd.

In Chiang Mai there are a couple of places that will satisfy any itch to buy hill-tribe wares. The **Hill Tribe Handicraft Project,** 1 Mun Muang Rd. (tel. 274 877), on the southeastern corner of the old city, sells audiotapes of Karen, Lisu, Akha, Lahu, Yao, and Hmong music, as well as quilts, bags, pullovers, shoes, and more. The administration hopes to shift tribal economies away from opium cultivation by providing another means of income. (Open Mon.-Sat. 8:30am-4:30pm.) The more well-known **Hill Tribe Promotion Centre,** 21/17 Suthep Rd. (tel. 277 743), is located next to Wat Suan Dawk. Also government-run, this is a bigger (and more expensive) place with a greater selection of traditional and innovative crafts. (Open Mon.-Sat. 9am-5pm.)

ENTERTAINMENT

The **British Council,** 198 Bamrung Rat Rd. (tel. 242 103), shows free British movies (Thurs. 7pm). **Alliance Française,** 1238 Charoen Prathet Rd. (tel. 275 277), shows French films subtitled in English (Tues. 4:30pm and Fri. 8pm; free to members, 10฿ for students, 20฿ for others). The **USIA/AUA,** 24 Ratchadamnoen Rd. (tel. 211 973), has free American movies (Sat. 7pm).

If you're sore from all the temple jaunts, luxuriate in a traditional Thai massage. Two centrally located options are **Suan Samoonprai,** 1/11 Chaiyaphum Rd. Soi 1 (tel. 252 706; open daily 9am-9pm), and **Garden of Many Herbs,** 2/2 Chang Moi Rd. Soi 3 (tel. 232 089; open daily 9am-9pm). Both offer seven-day courses (2000฿). The **Old Medicine Hospital,** south of the old city at 78/1 Soi Moh Shivaya Komarapaj (tel. 275 085), also garners praise for its relaxing massage. Some guest houses can arrange for a practitioner to pay a room call. A session usually runs 100฿ per hour.

NIGHTLIFE

Chiang Mai corners the market on bars and live music. Perhaps the most popular among *farang* and Thais alike are **Riverside** and **Brasserie.** Both offer live music and are located on the Ping's east bank by Narawat Bridge. Bars, bars, and more bars line Mun Muang Rd. and the Tha Phae Gate area. A popular place for Thai music is the **Ruan Come Garden,** 59 Kotchasarn Rd. (tel. 276 095; open daily 9am-1am). On some nights, the crowd joins in with the singing. **Linda's Bar and Snooker,** 3 Loi Kroa Rd., off Kotchasarn, has a few entertaining few games. (Open daily noon until "really late, sometimes all night.") **German Hofbrauhaus House** (tel. 821 273) is a beer and food joint near the night bazaar on the corner of Chang Klan Rd. and Loi Kroa Rd. They have a good menu in six languages. (Open daily 11am-11pm.)

TREKKING IN CHIANG MAI

Trekking is to Chiang Mai what gambling is to Atlantic City: it's what people are here to do. Although Mae Hong Son and Chiang Rai are closer to the action, the concentration of trekking companies in Chiang Mai has driven prices down. Most organized treks last from two to seven days, and provide transportation, food and equipment. Karen, Hmong, Akha, Yao, Lisu, and Lahu villages are all accessible from Chiang Mai. Most treks aim for the area northwest of Chiang Dao. In general, the farther one drives to begin a trek, the less touristed the area will be. Veteran travelers usually avoid treks which are only two hours or less out of the city, in favor of the ones which skirt the Burmese border. Treks to the Mae Tang River region and Mae Hong Son area are preferable to those to Chiang Rai, but all trails are well-trodden.

New TAT regulations require that trekking companies, guides, and customers register with the tourist police. They need to file a copy of your passport photo page before you set out. Companies should also be members of the Jungle Tour Club of Northern Thailand; look for guides who belong to the Chiang Mai Guide Association, and speak both English and the relevant tribal languages.

Some independent spirits choose to set out on their own in rented jeeps or motorbikes. This could lead to disaster or, conversely, the best experience of your life. In any case, check with the tourist police for the latest regulations. Potential trekkies should visit the Tribal Research Institute first (see **Sights**).

THAILAND

Not to be overlooked in the swarm is **The Trekking Collective,** 22 Ratchadamnoen Rd (tel. 419 080; mail to P.O. Box 142 Mae Ping Rd.), near Tha Phae Gate, which offers a variety of treks up to 10 days. Especially good for the experienced trekker, they're willing to break the "hike-bamboo raft-elephant ride" mold if you assemble your own group (5-6 people). Animal watching (deer, gibbons, wild elephants, boars, and birds) and bike tours as well as "survival" treks for the more adventurous. **Chiang Mai Green Tour and Trekking,** 29/31 Chiang Mai-Lampun Rd. (tel. 274 374), donates a portion of its proceeds to a conservation program, and the **Chiang Mai Youth Hostel,** 63 Bamrung Buri Rd. (tel. 276 737), gives medical supplies, educational materials, and haircuts to the hill-tribe people.

■ Near Chiang Mai

DOI SUTHEP AND DOI PUI

Wat Phra That Doi Suthep, seated majestically on Suthep Mountain, is unparalleled among the many excursions from Chiang Mai and remains one of the most sacred pilgrimage sites in the country. The centerpiece of the wat is a brilliant gold *chedi* visible from the city below. *Doi* (mountain) is a northern Thai word while *suthep* derives from the Pali word *Sudevoy,* the name of the hermit who inhabited the area before the shrine was built. *Phra That* refers to the Buddha's relics.

Buddha's *incus* (anvil, a teeny anvil-shaped bone in the middle ear) was discovered by a Sri Lankan monk in Thailand who was guided to it by a dream. A few years later, in 1383, while in the safe-keeping of King Ku Na the relic (so the story goes) spontaneously self-replicated. One was enshrined in Wat Suan Dawk, while the other was placed on the back of a white elephant that promptly made three trumpet-like noises and walked out of the city via the soon-to-be-named White Elephant Gate (Chang Phuak Gate). The beast climbed 100m to the wat's present location, trumpeted three more times, made three counter-clockwise circles, and knelt down. This omen convinced the king to dig a pit and place the stone-enclosed relic in the ground, along with other sacred objects.

Dress appropriately, as usual, to enter this sanctified spot. Complimentary loaner pants and skirts are available if you're guilty of a fashion *faux pas* (donations accepted). To participate more fully, purchase a flower with attached incense sticks and gold leaf paper (5฿); watch others to see what to do with it. If you can't handle the hike up the hill, take the trolley adjacent to the stairs (5฿). Conventional wisdom states that those who go to Chiang Mai without visiting Doi Suthep are no better than those who have never been to Chiang Mai at all.

The places around Doi Suthep are easily accessible; winding mountain roads are fun to navigate by scooter or motorcycle and the terrain and vistas are beautiful. *Songthaew,* leaving from Chang Phuak Gate and Chiang Mai Zoo, also ascend the mountain. To continue on to the village costs an extra 50฿ each way (130฿ total). Travelers can also rent a motorbike gaining freedom for 150฿, but be warned that this is can be dangerous. There are also sight-seeing tours offered by guest houses. Huay Kaew Rd. (Hwy. 1004) follows the mountain to the three main sights and is lined with turn-off viewpoints and waterfall routes. The monument on the left just before the road rising up the mountain is the **Kruba Srivichai shrine.** Kruba Srivichai was the monk who inspired thousands of volunteers to build the road to Wat Phra That in 1934. Pausing to pay respects, is believed to ensure a safe journey up and down the mountain.

Doi Suthep Pui National Park encompasses the entire area: a wide variety of plants, animals, and birds, plus waterfalls and the aforementioned sites. A project begun in 1987 by a professor from Chiang Mai University has so far collected 2062 species of vascular plants in the park, more than can be found in all of verdant Britain. Unfortunately, the park's flora and fauna are being edged up the mountain as Chiang Mai expands; teak trees, various legumes, and other commercially valuable trees have almost completely disappeared from the lowlands of Doi Suthep.

THAILAND

Spare some time for the drive to **Doi Pui's summit,** which rises 1685m and is only a few km past the Doi Pui village turn-off. Head right at the turn-off, follow the road on up, and bear left at the next branch-off for the short ride to the summit. The road will end and you'll have to hoof it the rest of the way to the peak. The top, surrounded by pine trees, is a good place to hike. Stop at the **park headquarters** (tel. 248 405) between the wat and the palace to get information before you set out on any long walks. Camping costs 40฿ per night. If you're with a group, you can rent a guest house at the park headquarters compound, complete with a grocery store and eating facilities. **Suan Son Guest House,** for example, can sleep 12 people for 1000฿ per night, and **Mon Tha** accommodates 45 for 2500฿ per night.

MAE SA VALLEY

Another possible day trip is an excursion to the **Mae Sa Valley.** The area's rural beauty barely compensates for the heavily tourist-oriented attractions here. Head north out of the city along Chang Phuak Rd. (Hwy. 107) and through the tiny town of Mae Rim. Right after the town (17km from Chiang Mai), there's a turn-off on the left onto Mae Rim-Somoeng Rd. (Hwy. 1096). At the **Mae Sa Elephant Training Centre** (tel. 236 069), the elephants and their riders put on a show daily 9:30-11:30am (admission 80฿). Post-show, there's an **elephant-back jungle tour** (250฿). Similar fun can be had at the **Mae Rim Elephant Farm,** 3km down the road, or **Pong Yaeng Elephant Training Centre** 9km farther.

Much of the Mae Sa Valley is also part of Doi Suthep National Park; in this end of the park there's another tribal village and some waterfalls. The best cascades tumble at the 10-tiered **Mae Sa Falls.** Only a few km from the Mae Sa Elephant Centre, the falls has a visitor center right before it, with a map of the area for further explorations. Entrance fee 5฿; 30฿ per vehicle. Touristy snake shows display the local deadly species. Slightly more genuine are the orchid and butterfly farms (10฿).

Bus #2 (3฿) can take you from Chang Phuak Rd. to Mae Rim District, where travelers can grab the rare *songthaew* (6฿) or a motorbike taxi (30฿) to Mae Sa Valley. Or, a *songthaew* can be caught right from the Chang Phuak Gate. Guest house tours to the valley are easy to arrange and often include stops at an elephant center, an orchid farm, and the falls (300฿).

DOI INTHANON NATIONAL PARK

The 188-km route from Chiang Mai to Mae Sariang along Hwy. 108 is ruggedly scenic. The drama picks up speed as the mountains huddle near **Chom Thong,** 58km away, a good place to stop for its access to **Doi Inthanon National Park,** home to **Thailand's highest peak,** is accessible from here. Blue buses from Chiang Mai leave the Chang Phuak Station (every 30min., 6am-6pm, 11฿) and also stop for about 15 minutes in the Chiang Mai Gate southern moat area. In Chom Thong (on the main road) the traveler can see **Wat Phra That Si Chom Thong,** which was first built in 1451 and expanded in 1516. The intricate, Burmese-style teak *bot* that is the temple's centerpiece is regarded as one of the most beautiful in the north. The altar holds the right side of Buddha's skull.

From Chom Thong, *songthaew* can be hired to the national park and Mae Klang Waterfall, an 8-km ride up to the Hwy. 1009 turn-off (10฿). A trip to the **summit of Doi Inthanon** is 50฿; band together and divvy up the 500฿ private rate. A summit-bound *songthaew* leaves the Mae Klang Waterfall area every two hours. But a motorbike can make the trip infinitely easier. Pick up some wheels for 120฿ per day at **N.P. Travel and Service** (tel. 341 220) in Chom Thong.

The 1-km path above the falls to the visitor center can also be reached by driving through the park's vehicle entrance, a few hundred meters past the Mae Klang turn-off (admission for motorcycles 10฿, for cars 30฿). **Mae Klang Waterfall,** with places to eat, swim, and picnic, is the only one of three falls worth seeing. Its big brother, Mae Ya Waterfall, a 28-km side trip, can be skipped. (Admission 25฿, children 15฿.)

Just above the eating spots, cross the bridge and take a left. After 1km, there's a driveway entrance into stunning gardens. The grounds are home to a branch of the Wittayalai Sung Kamphaeng San, the **Monk's College of Kamphaeng San,** based near Bangkok. It's up on a hill that commands a panoramic view of the surrounding mountains amidst meticulously maintained green grass, lovely flowers and trees, walkways, a fish pond, a temple, and lodgings for the seven monks who live there.

Just before the visitor center, a 1-km path leads to **Borichinda Cave,** which has a skylight to the surface in its sizeable entrance chamber. Guided tours can be arranged at the visitor center, which also has information and exhibits on local animal life, including the **nocturnal pangolin,** whose Gene Mazo-like tongue is 50% longer than its head and body, enabling it to consume 73 million ants per year.

Wachiratan Waterfall, the most powerful fall, is the next stop, at the 20.8km mark. Picnicking too close to the falls can result in the uniquely refreshing sensation of eating *pad thai* under a lawn sprinkler. At the 31km mark, the elegant cascades of **Siriphum Waterfall** appear to be sliding down glass. The lane leading to it winds through the park's Royal Project, which encourages local hill-tribes to replace opium production with strawberry and flower cultivation (unfortunately not as lucrative). The program also seeks to halt slash-and-burn agricultural methods, which have depleted the park's vegetation.

The road bids farewell at **Doi Inthanon's summit,** 48km from Chom Thong, which is usually shrouded under a misty blanket due to the monsoon climate. Nevertheless, the best time for viewing (and bird-watching) is the cool season. The average park temperature is 12°C (50°F)—bring a warm jacket and rain protection, especially if you intend to climb. The drive up the slopes looks out over lush terraced valleys. The park has **guest houses** available from 300-2000฿, and a **restaurant** at park headquarters just past Siriphum Falls.

■ Mae Sariang แม่เสรียง

Mae Sariang (pop. 7400), on the Yuam River near the Burmese border, promises a quiet retreat from the blaring percussion of more popular cities, and a proximate base for fearless adventurers. Surrounded by hill-tribe villages, this nondescript town is modernizing with its profits from border trade (both illicit and legitimate) throughout the southern part of Mae Hong Son Province.

ORIENTATION

Mae Sariang is bordered by the **Yuam River** to the west and **Hwy. 108** to the east. **Wiang Mai Road** lies between these two landmarks. **Laeng Phanit Road** runs parallel and closest to the river. One block to the east and parallel to it is **Mae Sariang Road** The highway is 1.5km from the river, and everything in town is situated between, with activity concentrated around the river.

PRACTICAL INFORMATION

Immigration Offices: (tel. 681 339), on Mae Sariang Rd. next to the police station. Open daily 8:30am-4:30pm.

Currency Exchange: Thai Farmers Bank, 150/1 Wiang Mai Rd. (tel. 681 339), between Laeng Phanit Rd. and Mae Sariang Rd. Open Mon.-Fri. 8:30am-3:30pm. **ATM** open daily 8am-10pm.

Buses: The **terminal** (tel. 681 347),100m north of Wiang Mai Rd., across from the gas station. To **Chiang Mai** (5 per day, 7am-1:30pm; A/C 3pm, midnight, and 1am, 4hr., 67฿) and **Mae Hong Son** (7 and 10:30am; A/C 5 per day, 1:30pm-1am, 4hr., 59฿). Buses to **Bangkok** depart from across the street at the gas station. **Yan Yong Tours** (tel. 681 532) offers shuttles (6pm, 15hr.; A/C 4 and 7pm, 13-14hr.).

Songthaew: To **Mae Sot** (every hr., 6:30am-12:30pm, 5hr., 150฿).

Pharmacies: 172/1 Wiang Mai Rd. (tel. 681 606), next to Renu Restaurant. Open daily 6am-10pm.

Medical Services: Hospital (tel. 681 027), on Wiang Mai Rd. 200m off Hwy. 108.

Emergency: tel. 191.
Police: (tel. 681 038), 200m south of Wiang Mai Rd. on Mae Sariang Rd.
Post Offices/Telephones: 31 Wiang Mai Rd. (tel. 681 356), 1km from the river. Has an overseas phone but no IDD. Open Mon.-Fri. 8:30am-noon, 1-4:30pm., Sat.-Sun. 9am-noon. **Postal code:** 58110. **Telephone code:** 053.

ACCOMMODATIONS

See View Guest House (tel. 681 556), off Wai Seuksa Rd. From the bus station, turn left and walk past the traffic light, take a right after the police station, walk across the bridge and take the first left. This concrete bomb shelter has large if dreary chambers with hot water. Great view of the giant Buddha across the valley. In the high season it has a restaurant and organizes treks. Singles in old teak house 80฿, in new building with private shower 120฿.

Riverside Guest House, 85/1 Laeng Phanit Rd. (tel. 681 188), 300m north of Wiang Mai Rd. Watch the river flow and the sun set over the mountains in simple rooms with common bath. Singles 100฿. Doubles 120฿.

FOOD

Renu Restaurant, 174/2 Wiang Mai Rd. (tel. 681 171), in the center of town, 50m toward the highway from the traffic light. Clearly marked with an English sign. A long-running favorite with long-running hours. Open daily 6am-midnight.

Intira Restaurant, across from Renu. Basically the same menu with slightly higher prices on some dishes, but for 5฿ here you can eat in the A/C dining room.

■ Near Mae Sariang

Because Mae Hong Son Province edges Burma, there are sometimes border skirmishes between Karen independence fighters and the Burmese army. December and January mark peak battle season. If you're planning to venture out of town, check with the police for the latest safety update and border status.

Mae Sariang is a great town to leave; use it as a base for semi-risky adventures in the country side. The lazy drudgery disappears in the surrounding border wilds. **See View** arranges excursions during the high season, but the area around Mae Sariang calls for an independent and intrepid spirit.

Cut-rate teak furniture crosses the Salanin River from Burma into Thailand at **Mae Sam Laep,** but the machine-gun-toting policemen and army commandos aren't there to turn back the piles of wooden chairs. About 46km west of Mae Sariang, Mae Sam Laep allows *farang* an insider's glimpse of the jungle-obscured action. Take a *songthaew* to Mae Sam Laep (50฿). Most Mae Sariang guest houses can arrange for one to pick trekkers up at a pre-arranged time on their daily route. Travelers can also snag one in the morning on the highway side of the bridge; there is a small field where they park. When one approaches, gesticulate like crazy. The first one leaves Mae Sariang at 6am, and the last returns in mid-afternoon, departing approximately every hour. Motorboats carry the multi-ethnic locals and trans-national trading goods up and down the river. **Sop Moei** lies 50km (2hr.) down the river. Boats cost 500฿ per day; stingier and braver souls risk the impossibly confusing and infrequent 30฿ passenger boats. The village headman operates a big guest house 100m from the river (rooms go for 100-150฿).

Beware of those offering to take a group over the border on a hush-hush spree. It may seem like the adventure of a lifetime, but once there, the traveler is at their mercy, and the return fare is often substantially higher. **Pha Ma Lo,** 3km east of Mae Sariang toward Chiang Mai, is a large White Karen village known for its reasonably priced hand-woven **fabrics.** *Songthaew* it both ways (50฿).

North of Mae Sariang, rural villages abound which can be visited on daytrips, or en route from Mae Hong Son, 160km away. Past the halfway point is **Khun Yuam,** about the same size as Mae Sariang (pop. 6500), where the bus stops for a welcome break.

Every November they host the **Bua Tong Blossom Festival** in celebration of the beautiful, wild sunflower blossoms that pop up everywhere. Just before the bus stop, signs indicate the direction of **Ban Farang Guest House.** There are other guest houses in this potential jumping-off point. South of Khun Yuam are the **Mae Ha Cave** and **Mae Na Hot Springs,** both worth a look if time permits. **Nam Tok Mae Surin National Park,** 30km from Mae Hong Son, contains the **Mae Surin Waterfall,** the highest waterfall in Thailand.

■ Mae Hong Son แม่ฮ่องสอน

A popular subject of postcards, Mae Hong Son's setting on the grassy banks of a quiet lake is ideal for practitioners of pastoral escapism. Nearby, unassuming wats combine Burmese and Thai architecture in a peaceful and fetching aesthetic, offering spiritual uplift to weary pilgrims. Yet, following the formula of any good Hollywood thriller, the idyllic scenery hides a more sinister side. Opium smuggling and other illegal border actions are never seen directly, but lurk within the shadows, often alluded to and mentioned in hushed tones.

According to local lore, Mae Hong Son was born out of an elephant *kraal.* King Puthawongse had sent out a party to capture wild elephants, and the hunters traveled all the way to this area before they managed to seize an adequate number. Not wanting to herd them back, the party built a *kraal* and a city eventually flourished. In the early part of this century, however, Mae Hong Son was converted into a city of exile, a *kraal* for criminals, recalcitrant officials, and other troublemakers.

Although modern-day residence is now voluntary, the town's past doesn't seem too far-removed. Efforts to promote tourism here have yielded excellent services and a beautiful town; it doesn't get much better than this.

ORIENTATION

Mae Hong Son is 348km from Chiang Mai via the southern route through Mae Sariang (on Hwy. 108) and 247km from Chiang Mai via the northern route through Pai (on Hwy. 107 and 1095). It is an easily navigable town. Buses stop on **Khunlum Praphat Road,** which runs north and south through the center of town. Turning left out of the bus station and heading south, the second street is **Singhanat Bamrung Road** (east-west). One block south, **Udom Chao Nithet Road** is dotted with guest houses and borders the lake. **Chamnansathet Road** runs south of the lake.

PRACTICAL INFORMATION

Tourist Offices and Tourist Police: 1 Ratchadamaphitak Rd. (tel. 611 812), on the corner of Singhanat Bamrung Rd. English spoken by some of the staff.

Immigration Offices: (tel. 612 106), on Khunlum Praphat Rd., 1km north of the bus station. Visa extensions need 2 photos and copies of photo and visa page from passport, and 500฿.

Currency Exchange: Bangkok Bank, 68 Khunlum Praphat Rd. (tel. 611 275). Open Mon.-Fri. 8:30am-5pm. **24-hr. ATM** accepts Visa, AmEx, and PLUS.

Air Travel: Mae Hong Son Airport, (tel. 612 057), on Nivit Pisan Rd. Go to the end of Singhanat Bamrung Rd. and turn left at the hospital. Transforms into an exercise park in the evening. To **Chiang Mai** (11:10am, 2, 3:10, and 4:40pm, 345฿). **Thai Air,** 71 Singhanat Bamrung Rd. (tel. 611 297), near Tourist Police. Open daily 8am-noon, 1-5:30pm.

Buses: 33/1 Khunlum Praphat Rd. (tel. 611 318). To **Chiang Mai** (4 per day, 8am-9pm; A/C 6, 9am, and 9pm, 9hr., 115฿) via **Mae Sariang** (same times, 4hr., 50฿) or via **Pai** (4 per day, 7am-12:30pm; A/C 8am, 3hr., 42฿, 8hr. to Chiang Mai).

Rentals: P.J. Motorbike, 28 Singhanat Rd. (tel. 611 291). 150-200฿ per day. Open daily 8am-6pm. For car rental, head to **Mae Hong Son Travel** or **Rose Garden Tour,** 7/1 Singhanat Bamrung Rd. (tel. 611 681), rents Suzuki 4-wheel drives.

Medical Services: Sri Sangwarn Hospital (tel. 611 378), at the very end of Singhanat Bamrung Rd. near the airport. Dr. Sunit Boonyasong operates a **small clinic,** 32

Khunlum Praphat Rd. (tel. 611 622), near the bus station. Open Mon.-Fri. 5-9pm, Sat.-Sun. 9am-9pm.

Emergency: Tourist Police: tel. 1699. **Ambulance:** tel. 611 378.

Police: Mae Hong Son Provincial Police (tel. 611 239, emergency tel. 191), south of the post office on the road to Mae Sariang.

Post Offices/Telephones: Mae Hong Son Post Office, 79 Khunlum Praphat Rd. (tel. 611 233). Open Mon.-Fri. 8:30am-4:30pm, Sat.-Sun. 9am-noon. **Overseas phone** (tel. 611 711), cash, collect, or **HCD** for calling card calls, telex, telegram, and fax. Open daily 7am-11pm. **Postal code:** 58000. **Telephone code:** 053.

ACCOMMODATIONS

Mae Hong Son Guest House, 295 Makasantee Rd. (tel. 612 510). Turn right out of the bus station, then left on the 1st street. Follow the signs. For those weary of the main town's frantic Bangkok-like pace, this friendly, family-run establishment features bungalows in a large garden setting. Helpful owner speaks English. Reputably good treks. Singles 50฿. Doubles 80฿, with private bath 200฿.

Jong Kham Guest House, 7 Udom Chaonithet Rd., northside of the lake. Take a left from the bus station, walk through the traffic light, take the 1st left after the light, and it will be 250m down on the right. Simple rooms surrounding a spacious lawn. Friendly staff. Rooms have common bath. Singles 70฿. Doubles 90฿. Bungalows 100฿, but the rooms are better.

Prince Guest House, 37 Udom Chaonithet Rd. (tel. 612 256), northside of the lake. Coming from town it's 100m beyond Jong Kham Guest House. Formerly the Cheer Pub. Has an expansive deck with a nice view over the lake and Wat Jong Klang, but there's nothing palatial about these digs. Singles 40฿. Doubles 60฿, with cold shower 80฿.

FOOD

Aladdin Home, on Khunlum Praphat Rd., across the street and just south of the bus station. Arguably the best restaurant in town. Their *khao soi*, a northern Thai coconut curry, is spectacular (20฿). Open daily 6am-10pm.

Sunflower Café, on Singhanat Bamrung Rd., 100m west of the traffic light. Small establishment run by friendly couple. Percolated coffee, homemade wholewheat bread, cakes, and pizza will satisfy any craving. Open daily 7:30am-late.

Fern Restaurant, 87 Khunlum Praphat Rd. (tel. 611 374). Runs the gamut from Thai to Chinese and European. Hanging plants, rattan chairs, and no-meat selections include pumpkin patties (40฿). Pai river fish 120฿. The cool napkins (5฿) are a great way to feel refreshed. Open daily 7am-2pm, 4:30-10pm.

Kai Muk Restaurant, 23 Udom Chaonithet Rd. (tel. 612 092). Excellent open-air place for Thai or Chinese food, served up by eager, uniformed youngsters. Tongue-scorching fried duck in crispy basil leaves is popular among locals (small 60฿, large 90฿), as is the late-night drinking. Open daily 10am-3am.

SIGHTS

Perched 474m above the town on a mountain peak is **Wat Doi Kong Mu,** the best place for a panoramic view of the city and environs. Built in 1874, this Shan-influenced temple is Mae Hong Son's most important wat. Two stupas contain remains of monks. The place is lit up like a Christmas tree in the evening. Get there by moving west on Udom Chaonithet Rd. and turn left at the end; continue until the wat road on can be seen on the right. The hike up is 1.5km. Another nearby shrine is **Wat Phra Non,** slightly north of the Doi Kong Mu turn-off road. The wat houses a 12-m reclining Burmese-style Buddha and the ashes of Mae Hong Son's kings.

Fitness buffs might enjoy the exercise track lining **Jong Kham Lake.** The small stand on the southwest shore sells bags of fish food for 3-15฿, great for stirring up a feeding frenzy among the athletic fish that somersault out of the simmering water. On the lake's south side, two wats draw scores of visitors. **Wat Jong Klang** is the one on the right, with glass paintings and wooden puppets brought from Burma about 100 years ago. Formerly a rest stop for journeying monks, it is now host to tourist pilgrims. (Open daily 8am-6pm.) Next door is **Wat Jong Kham,** built in 1827, so named because its gold leaf decorated pillars were originally silver-plated.

TREKKING IN MAE HONG SON

Some of the best trekking opportunities in Thailand awaits in Mae Hong Son. Indeed, many Chiang Mai-based treks come here. Surrounding hills support village after village of Lisu, Lahu and Karen tribes, in addition to Shan and Kuomintang (KMT) zones. The KMT are members and descendants of the nationalist party which was ousted from China by the communists. Other party hotshots went to Formosa and formed the Taiwanese government—these guys took a wrong turn and wound up in Thailand.

Most of the treks are hiking only and take you as far as Chiang Mai, although those including rafting and elephant riding are also available. The treks offered by **Mae Hong Son Guest House** have received favorable reports. Drop by their office in town at 20 Singhanat Bamrung Rd. (tel. 620 105). In the low season, Mae Hong Son hosts fewer travelers than Chiang Mai. This drop in regular business drives prices up and availability down. To get around this predicament, put your own group together and/or shop around. Numerous villages lie along roads accessible by car or motorbike. Pick up a map from the tourist police and roam if you want to.

■ Near Mae Hong Son

> Remember that quick trips across the border are illegal, dangerous, and a good way to pay big baht to get back into Thailand.

Border politics dominate outlying areas of Mae Hong Son Province. Directly across the border is the Red Karen state in Burma; just north of that lie various rebel camps. Uniformed policemen regularly stop and search buses for Burmese refugees.

Tourists should have no problem on the rural routes here, unless they are stashing drugs or carrying a Burmese refugee. In fact, almost no other city in Thailand makes it so easy to experience such an array of ethnic cultures and political backgrounds. A 150฿ motorbike ride provides access to Karen, Lisu, Hmong, and Lahu hill-tribe villages, Shan towns, and KMT camps, all of whom many tourists look upon as spectacles. Most guest houses and all trekking companies offer guided daytrips.

Most trekking companies also offer **rafting and boating trips.** From Mae Hong Son, most paddle (or motor) down the Pai River to the Burmese border (3-4hr.) where the Pai merges with the Salawin. Some head up to Pai, but it's more common for Pai folks to come the other way. Before leaving Mae Hong Son behind, you might want to visit the **Nam Hu Hai Chai Hot Springs,** 12km south of the city, which are very inviting in the winter.

There is no way a traveler in Thailand can make it as far as Mae Hong Son Province without hearing of the **Long-Necked Karens.** In addition to Hollywood-esque tour company billing, the faces of the long-necked women are often featured on tourist maps and guide books. Entering the touristy village costs 250฿, and the necks are not even stretched; the effect is achieved by squashing the rib cage and collar bone. A damper on sight-seeing comes with the realization that these people are Burmese refugees who are not allowed to own land and farm. Besides trinket sales and day labor, this is their only means of support. Those who have an inkling to see them may think of their baht as going toward a good cause.

HIGHWAY 1095 TO PAI

Some of Thailand's most stunning scenery adorns Hwy. 1095 between Mae Hong Son and Pai (111km). The road follows mountain peaks that crest above the sky and dive below cloudy waves. Twisting and turning the whole way, the views change, but the two constants are *suay maak* and nausea. About 35km from Mae Hong Son and

THAILAND

20km before the turn-off to Mae La Na, two great round-topped summits appear, shorn away from their brethren. Nearby reposes the **Sunnyata Forest Monastery**. A spectacular row of jagged tree-topped pinnacles juts up 15km later, at their base lies a village.

Heading out from Mae Hong Son on the left, a couple of km before the Fish Cave, is a road marked with numerous Thai signs. This lane leads through Shan and Hmong villages, a waterfall, mountain panoramas, and terminates at the KMT village of **Mae Aw**, 1½ hours from the Hwy. 1095 turn-off, which is situated along a mountain top right on the Burmese border.

Tham Plaa (Fish Cave), 20km north of Mae Hong Son, is a scenic daytrip that can be handled solo. Fish food sellers badger visitors at the entrance—you might as well capitulate and treat the sacred fishes to a snack of dried bugs. The Shan villagers who look after the fish never catch them, believing that the spirit of the mountain protects them from harm, and will hex violators. As a result of their protected status, the fish here have grown quite large (many more than 0.5m long) and round. Recently, a scuba-outfitted Australian camera crew penetrated the depths of the pool and discovered a waterfall and open air for several km. Among the knotty and twisted *taawon* trees stands a statue of the long-haired hermit who meditated here long ago. Local lore has it that Japanese soldiers retreating from Burma buried treasure in caverns throughout the mountain.

Including Mae Aw and the Fish Cave in one journey requires motorbike or car rental. A regular motorbike will suffice for most of the year, but in the muddy rainy season, a 4-wheel-drive or motorcross bike (and driving skills) are necessities. The Fish Cave is about a 30-minute drive and only takes a short while to enjoy, barring a nap on the grass at the lazy stream or a descent into the depths. To get there via public transportation, hop on a Pai-bound bus and signal the driver to stop at the cave. Don't pay the full Pai fare; the jaunt costs no more than 10฿.

SOPPONG

Midway between Mae Hong Son and Pai, the minuscule metropolis of Soppong provides a scaled-down version of both, with fewer services but some scintillating sights. Tham Lod is the main event here, but relaxation and excellent hiking are the real reasons to come. **Buses** run to: **Mae Hong Son** (5 per day, 8:30am-5pm, 2hr.) and **Pai** (6 per day, 9am-5:30pm, 1½hr.). All but the last two, which may not run during low season, continue to **Chiang Mai** (6hr.).

New Soppong skirts the highway, where the buses stop. Most guest houses are here, on or off the highway. Turning right from the bus station, old Soppong dozes along the road which branches off to the left. The best accommodations and a beautiful restaurant both fall under the **Kemarin Garden**. Turn right out of the bus station and then take another right. Bungalows with private bath and balconies with town views run 80฿ for a single, 100฿ for a double. Without private bath, singles fetch 50฿, doubles 60฿. Owner Udom doubles as a fantastic chef and triples as the best source of information on Soppong. He'll even provide a map, flashlight, and letter of introduction to the hill-tribes if you want to head out on your own. Lone travelers should pay the hill-tribe headman directly for accommodations and food; Udom doesn't get a cut. If you want to check other options, there are a handful of guest houses near the bus station with bungalows running from 50-100฿.

As an alternate hiking base, Soppong is in the immediate vicinity (10km radius) of several Lisu villages, and there are also Karen and Lahu villages nearby. North of town, a laterite road leads to **Tham Lod** 8km away, and beyond it to a Karen village. A river runs through Tham Lod; the cave is interesting to explore, although getting wet is unavoidable. Prehistoric remains have been found among its colorful stalagmites and stalactites. The kerosene lamps for rent are not only expensive (100฿), but harsh on the cave environment. Instead, bring a flashlight or try to get a loaner from your guest house. To get to the cave, catch a motorbike taxi (40฿). Or, make use of your bi-pedal power and walk. It's 1½hr. (9km) straight down the road from old Soppong.

▓ Pai ปาย

Pai's charm derives from a combination of high-country quiet and a booming tourist industry that has so far managed not to be too intrusive. The surrounding nature gushes with hot springs, waterfalls, and the Pai River which courses from the northern mountains. *Farang*, ethnic Thais, and a strong Muslim community contribute to Pai's cultural diversity. Regional day tours pass through KMT, Lisu, Shan, and Lahu villages. Accommodating and peaceful, Pai forms the halfway point on the easier and nicer route to Mae Hong Son. There is a sense of community among travelers here (actually Mae Sariang-Mae Hong Son-Pai is a route where travelers continually bump into the same fellow adventurers), and the warmth extends to the locals, who will give more smiles than the traveler may be accustomed to.

ORIENTATION

Pai lies 136km northwest of Chiang Mai and 111km from Mae Hong Son. Hwy. 1095 cuts through town, but most traffic is channeled away from the center of town and only skirts the western border formed by **Ketkerang Road.** At Pai's south end, the highway turns east and forms the southern border. The eastern border of Pai is naturally set by the **Pai River,** while the northern border is **Chaisongkhram Road,** more practically known as where the bus station is located. To the west, this road leads to the hospital, waterfall, and local hill-tribe villages. Within these borders, everything is fortunately easily accessible by foot, since there is a noticeable lack of public transportation. **Rungsiyanon Road** leads south from the bus station and crosses the east-west **Ratchadamrong Road** 200m down.

PRACTICAL INFORMATION

Currency Exchange: Krung Thai, on Rungsiyanon Rd. Open Mon.-Fri. 8:30am-3:30pm.

Buses: Pai Bus Terminal, on Chaisongkhram Rd., just east of the intersection with Rungsiyanon Rd. Because Pai is the center of the universe in this part of the world, buses to **Mae Hong Son, Chiang Mai,** and **Soppong** all leave at the same times: 7, 8:30, 11, and 11:30am; A/C 12:30, 2:30, and 4:30pm. To **Chiang Mai** (3½hr., 45฿; A/C 90฿) and **Mae Hong Son** (3hr., 42฿; A/C 84฿).

Rentals: For **motorbikes** try **Northern Green,** 87 Chaisongkhram Rd. (tel. 699 099). Honda Dreams for 100฿ per day. **Duang Guest House,** 5 Rungsiyanon Rd. (tel. 699 101), across from the bus station, rents mountain bikes for 30฿ per day. For the same price, the gears on the bikes at **Own Home** (see **Food** below) are supposedly better.

Markets: Both a **day** and a **night market** set up on Rungsiyanon Rd.

Pharmacies: Rungsiyanon Rd., near Ketkerang Rd. Open daily 8:30am-10pm.

Medical Services: (tel. 699 031), on Chaisongkhram Rd., 0.5km west of the bus station.

Ambulance: tel. 699 031.

Police: 72 Rungsiyanon Rd. (tel, 699 217), 0.5km south from the bus station.

Emergency: tel. 191.

Post Offices/Telephones: (tel. 699 208), on Ketkerang Rd., on the southwestern edge of town. **International telephone,** fax, and telegrams. Open Mon.-Fri. 8:30am-4:30pm, Sat. 8:30-11:30am. **Postal code:** 58130. **Telephone code:** 053.

ACCOMMODATIONS

Thanks to tourism, Pai has a plethora of cheap and comfortable accommodations—they're everywhere. Go straight, right, or left out of the bus station.

Mountain Blues Huts, 174 Chaisongkhram Rd., an 10-min. walk after a right from the bus station. Although the lake seems to exist for no other reason than to necessitate bungalows built on stilts, it nonetheless creates a relaxing aesthetic lost on most guest houses. With a stellar restaurant, pool table, and live music nightly 9pm-midnight, you'll never have to leave the property. Mosquito nets and hot water as well. Bungalows 50฿ per person. VIP 100฿.

PS Riverside Guest House, off Ratchadamrong Rd., near the Pai River, next to the bridge; follow the signs. A microcosm of Pai itself. Relax in a shady hut and let the soothing rhythm of the river carry your spirit to meditative nirvana. Mosquito nets and hot water in the cold season. Singles 50฿. Doubles 80฿.

Duang Guest House, 5 Rungsiyanon Rd. (tel. 699 101), across from the bus station. Convenient, clean, friendly, and cheap. Displays a superb wall map of the area. Mrs. Duang teaches a kindergarten class and offers money exchange, free tea, and even a party on Christmas. Dorms 40฿ and 50฿. Singles downstairs 50฿, upstairs 60฿. Doubles 70-100฿. Rooms with private shower 150฿.

Charlie's House, 9 Rungsiyanon Rd. (tel. 699 039), about 100m from bus station. Pleasant courtyard area. Hot water showers outside, spartan rooms inside. Sink into your super-soft mattress and let your cares drift out into space. Dorms 40฿. 2-bed singles 50฿. Doubles 80฿. Special lodgings: Romantic House, Sweet House I, and Sweet House II add private shower, fridge, and bigger bed, respectively.

FOOD

Chez Swan, 13 Rungsiyanon Rd. (tel. 699 111). Who would have suspected to find such an authentic French transplant right in the middle of Pai? *Quiche Lorraine* 50฿. *Camembert avec du pain* 45฿.

Own Home Restaurant, (tel. 699 125), on the corner of Rungsiyanon and Ratchadamrong Rd. The most popular with *farang,* but with good reason in this case. Outstanding Thai and western vegetarian menu. Lasagna 40฿. Homemade brown bread with cheese 20฿. Also has a book exchange. Open daily 8am-9pm

Thai Yai Restaurant, 12 Rungsiyanon Rd. (tel. 699 093). Bread made from whole wheat flour from nearby Shan (called Yai in Thai) village. Real coffee and butter. Brown bread with butter and honey 15฿. Peanut butter and banana sandwich 20฿. Carrot and ginger cake 15฿.

La Pet (tel. 699 162), in front of Happy Rabbit. Delicious Isaan dishes. Do you have the, uh, guts to try the oxen penis salad (30฿)? Roasted pig chin 30฿. Better than you might think. Really. May close in the low season.

■ Near Pai

Wat Phra That Mae Yen takes up residence on a hill complete with a penthouse view of the city. Rent a vehicle or take a very long stroll. Head east on Ratchadamrong Rd. and cross the Pai River; it's visible from the bridge. Cross the Mae Yen River; the stairs to the top are just ahead. It is 1km to the wat, then 360 stairs up. The stairs pose more of a nuisance than a struggle—they are about 5cm high and inconveniently spaced. It is faster to just walk alongside the staircase.

Despite its proximity to trekking areas, Pai doesn't entertain many trekkers. Most guest houses can arrange daytrips and longer treks. **No Mercy Trekking,** 9/1 Rungsiyanon Rd. (tel. 699 024), goes to the Soppong area on hiking trips, but also has rafting and elephant options. Groups cut costs in the low season.

Rafting along the Pai River is a staple ingredient of Pai treks. This waterway, the longest (180km) in Mae Hong Son, starts north of town, then turns west below Pai, and back-tracks north through Mae Hong Son, eventually emptying into the Salawin River on the Burmese border. River trips starting north of Pai usually take only a few hours, but there are multiple-day rafting treks from Pai to Mae Hong Son. The area between the Pai River and Hwy. 1095 is seldom charted on maps, but it's a network of interconnected Karen, Lahu, and especially Lisu villages.

North of Pai, there are also several Lisu, Karen, and Lahu villages. Some excursions are done in the Soppong-Mae La Na area, and Pai serves as an alternative stop to Mae Hong Son. The country northeast of Pai is rarely touristed, but it's possible to travel as far as **Ban Pang Luang** near the border, and south from there to **Wiang Haeng,** both sizeable by village standards. Alternatively, this area can be accessed via the more well-trodden roads from **Chiang Dao.**

■ Tha Ton ท่าตอน

Tha Ton is a departure point for boat trips down the Kok river to Chiang Rai. Although this sleepy town still seems a bit surprised by its popularity, local capitalists continue to provide services to accommodate the influx of tourism. The town, however, remains very hushed, interrupted only by boat traffic. Trekking opportunities and the Lisu, Karen, Lahu, Akha, and Yao villages nearby are unfortunately missed by most *farang,* who rush off to Chiang Rai.

ORIENTATION AND PRACTICAL INFORMATION

Buses leave for Chiang Mai from the lot on the northern side of the bridge (7 per day, 6:25am-3pm). The main road in Tha Ton is **Rte. 1089,** which continues across the river to Mae Chan, 62km away. Tha Ton is 43km from Mae Salong, 92km from Chiang Rai, and 175km from Chiang Mai. Along the river by the pier, shops sell souvenirs and clothes. A Buddha surveys his domain from a hill-top lookout point.

Long-tailed boats with huge propeller shafts depart for **Chiang Rai** (12:30pm, 3-5hr., 160฿). Along the way, the vessels stop at the villages of Phra That, Ban Mai, Mae Salak, Phatai, Jakue, Kok Noi, Pha Khang, Pha Keau, Hadwauodem, and Ruammit. Chartering a private craft (seats 8) costs 1600฿; the last boat leaves before 3pm as the ride becomes dangerous after dark.

There are no banks or currency exchange booths, but **Tha Ton Tour** near the pier may exchange a small sum. They also rent **motorbikes** for 200฿ per day, and cars with a driver for 1000฿ per day. The closest **hospital** is in Mae Ai, 9km south (tel. 459 036). In case of emergency, call your guest house or the tourist police (tel. 1699) for transportation to the hospital; they're faster than the ambulances.

A **tourist police box** is just before the pier. Sign in before leaving Tha Ton so they can keep precise tourist statistics. An officer is stationed there 24hr. The **post office** is on the main road near Thip's Traveler's House but it deals only in very basic postcard and letter service. Open Mon.-Fri. 8am-4:30pm, Sat. 8am-noon. There is **no overseas telephone. Postal code**: 50280. **Telephone code**: 053.

ACCOMMODATIONS AND FOOD

Guest houses and resorts are scattered along both sides of the river; higher-priced quarters reside on the north bank. The few places to eat in town are usually affiliated with the lodgings. **Thip's Traveller's House** (tel. 459 312), right by the bridge, organizes treks and is the closest to *songthaew* and bus drop-off points. Thips has cold private showers, hot common ones; elevated "King's throne" squatters can suit guest royally. Singles cost 80฿, doubles 100฿. The adjoining restaurant is a small-time hang-out on weekends. (Open daily 7am-9pm.) **Chankasem Guest House,** by the river past the pier, answers plenty of questions and arranges rafting trips. Glow-in-the-dark switches in downstairs rooms compensate for lack of natural lighting. Singles with cold showers cost 80฿, doubles 100฿, a common hot shower is 10฿. Upstairs, some 200฿ rooms come with hot showers, bookshelves, sinks, big bathrooms, and maps of the Golden Triangle. The restaurant, right on the water, serves basic sustenance. (Open daily 7am-9pm.)

Across the river, **Mae Kok River Lodge** (on a mini lychee and coconut plantation) provides an idyllic setting for a relaxing pre-trip lunch. Isaan dishes cost 50-75฿. Along the north shore of the river, the restaurant-*kap*-fancy hotel doubles as a reserve where jungle animals are re-acclimated for the wild.

SIGHTS

Wat Tha Ton showcases a highly visible Buddha—the 12m-tall white colossus sticking out of the hill. **Boat rides** to Chiang Mai are the main town industry. The Mae Kok River originates in the high mountains of the Shan states in Burma, enters Thailand above Tha Ton, and flows 200km to meet the Mekong River in Chiang Saen. In the past, bandits often assailed travelers; then armed guards began accompanying the

THAILAND

tourist freighters and such bravado decreased. No such incidents, however, have transpired since 1988. (See **Orientation** for boat info.)

Rafting up and down the length of the Kok gives a moving base for exploring riverside hill-tribe villages. Trips usually last two to three days (1400฿ per person, including meals and sleeping arrangements). In Tha Ton, contact Chankasem Guest House, Tha Ton Tour, or Thip's Traveller's House. **Mae Salak,** with a large Lahu population, is the largest village along the way and is the starting point for journeys south into the Wawi area, with its numerous Lahu, Lisu, Hmong, Akha, Karen, and Yao hill-tribe villages, waterfalls, and hot springs. **Phatai** is a Black Lahu village on the north bank and **Ruammit,** near Chiang Rai. Rafters at the end of their trips and tour groups at the beginning of shopping sprees gather here to enjoy the guest houses, elephant riding, and the nearby Temple Cave.

Some travelers favor road trips to **Mae Salong** from Tha Ton, lured by the well-conditioned pavement and exceptional scenery. Yellow *songthaew* depart regularly (7am-3pm, 1hr., 50฿) from near the police box; do not confuse these with the ones going to Fang. The best time to go is in the morning; in the afternoon, they only go about two-thirds of the way, to the junction of the road leading to Mae Salong and the road to Mae Chan (35฿).

■ Chiang Rai เชียงราย

Poor Chiang Rai. The provincial capital (pop. 70,000) has always played second fiddle to its southern neighbor of similar appellation. King Mengrai built the city in 1262, using it as command central for three decades before founding Chiang Mai and leaving his old pals face-down in the dust. The city today basks in the poppy glow of the Golden Triangle, the 60-sq.km convergence of Thailand, Laos, and Burma famous for its opium-producing activities. Chang Rai is a springboard for visiting this area, however, the Golden Triangle is but a daytrip in an area which merits weeks. Dozens of hill-tribe villages, primarily concentrated on the Burmese border, are options for daytrips or overnight stays. Several companies in Chiang Rai and throughout the province offer treks to the surrounding sights, and with both Burmese and Lao borders open, Chiang Rai could become a gateway city for international excursions. The guest house trekking and budget tour scenes are healthy, but alas, Chiang Mai remains *el número uno* in these (and most other) departments.

ORIENTATION

The **Kok River** flows west to east, forming the town's northern border. Accommodations can be found on the two big islands in the river. **Singhaklai Road,** site of the TAT office and guest houses, skirts the river. In the east, this street passes the **King Mengrai Monument** which hails visitors arriving from the airport. The active north sector of town lies between Singhaklai Rd. and **Banphraprakan Road,** 500m south and parallel to it. The town's most helpful landmark, the **haw nariga** (clock tower), occupies the middle of Banphraprakan Rd. **Jet Yod Road** (with lots of good food) leads south from there. **Phahonyothin Road** runs parallel, one block to the east with the bus station and the night market.

PRACTICAL INFORMATION

Tourist Offices: TAT, 448/16 Singhaklai Rd. (tel. 717 433). Border crossing and trekking information. English spoken. Open daily 8:30am-4:30pm.

Tourist Police: (tel. 717 779), at the TAT. English spoken. Open 24hr.

Tours and Travel: Chat House, 3/2 Soi Sangkaew Trirat Rd. (tel. 711 481). Day tours to **Doi Tung, Mae Sai,** and the **Golden Triangle** (600-1200฿ depending on group size). River boats, elephant rides, and overnights.

Currency Exchange: Thai Military Bank, 870/12 Phahonyothin Rd. (tel. 715 657), next to the bus station and Thai Airways. Open daily 8:30am-9pm. **Siam Commercial Bank,** 573 Ratanaket Rd., just south of Thanalai Rd. Open daily 8:30am-3:30pm. **ATM** accepts MC, Visa, Cirrus, and Plus. Open daily 6am-11pm.

TO MAE SAI & CHIANG SAEN

Highway 110

Highway 118

Phahonyothin Rd.

Kok River

Sriboonruong Rd.

Wat Sriboonruong ■

Telephone Office ■

Sigerd Rd.

Singhaklai Rd.

Utarakit Rd.

Hilltribe Education Center ■

Wisit

Wuang Rd.

Thanalai Rd.

Alliance Francaise ■

Phahonyothin Rd.

Bus Station ■

THAI Air Office ■

San Pannat Rd.

Prasopsuk Rd.

Phahonyothin Rd.

Library ■

TAT Office ■

Ratanaket Rd.

Police Station ■

Bank ■

Jet Yod Rd.

Dusit Island

Pier ■

Ruang Nakhon Rd.

Post Office ■

Market ■

Suksathit Rd.

Telephone Office ■

Itsaraphap Rd.

Sanambin Rd.

TO AIRPORT

Hospital ■

Trairat Rd.

Thanalai Rd.

Government Office and Town Hall ■

Ngam Muang Rd.

Telephone Office ■

Ratchadat Damrong Rd.

Utarakit Rd.

Banphraprakan Rd.

Ratchayotha Rd.

Soi 1

Soi 2

Winitchaikul Rd.

TO THA

THON

TO CHIANG MAI

0   yards   330
0   meters   300

N

Chiang Rai

Church, 9
Cinema, 7, 8
Clocktower, 11
King Mengrai Monument, 5
Mosque, 12
Wat Doi Thong, 1

Wat Jet Yod, 10
Wat Ming Muang, 13
Wat Ngam Muang, 2
Wat Phra Kaew, 3
Wat Phra Singh, 4
Wat Si Koet, 6

THAILAND

Air Travel: Chiang Rai International Airport (tel. 793 048). 9km out of town on Hwy. 110. To **Bangkok** (6 per day) and **Chiang Mai** (2 per day). **Thai Air office,** 870 Phahonyothin Rd. (tel. 711 179). Open Mon.-Fri. 8am-5pm, Sat. 8am-noon.

Buses: Chiang Rai Bus Station, Phahonyothin Rd., across from the night market. Regular and A/C buses (tel. 711 224). VIP buses (tel. 711 369). To: **Bangkok** (new route through **Phitsanulok,** 21 per day, 7am-7:30pm, 11hr., 189-525฿; old route through **Sukhothai,** 8 per day, 7:30am-8pm, 199฿); **Chiang Mai** (new route, 24 per day, 6am-5:30pm, 3-4hr., 57฿; A/C 102฿; old route via **Lampang,** every 20min., 5:20am-4:30pm, 6hr., 83฿; for Lampang, 5hr., 50฿); **Mae Sai** (every 15min., 6am-6pm, 1½hr., 17฿); **Chiang Saen** (every 15min., 6am-5pm, 1½hr., 17฿); **Chiang Khong** (every 45min., 4:45am-5:45pm, 3hr., 31฿); **Nan** (9:30am, 6hr., 104฿); and **Phitsanulok** via **Sukhothai** (5 per day, 6hr., 104฿).

Boats: To **Tha Ton** (10:30am, 170฿) from the pier near Dusit Island.

Local Transportation: The **songthaew** stand is 50m west of the post office. Fares within the city should be 2-5฿, 10-30฿ anywhere within a 10-15km radius. Across from the post office is a **samlor/tuk-tuk** stand.

Rentals: Practically every guest house rents the same motorbikes for the same prices (150฿ and up). Also try Teepee Hippie Happy (see **Entertainment**). **Chiang Rai Agency Centre,** 428/10 Banphraprakan Rd. (tel. 717 274).

Markets: Night market, alongside the Wang Come Hostel between Jet Yod and Phahonyothin Rd. Open daily 6-11pm. The **morning market,** across from the post office, is open all day. A **fruit market** is next to the bus station.

Medical Services: Overbrook Hospital, 444/3 Singhaklai Rd. (tel. 711 366), 150m west of TAT. **Chiang Rai Hospital,** (tel. 711 300), on Sathan Phayaban Rd., in the southern area near Jet Yod Rd. **PDA Clinic,** 620/25 Thanalai Rd. (tel. 719 167), at the Hill-tribe Museum. English-speaking staff. Open Mon.-Fri. 9am-8pm.

Emergency: tel. 1699 or 191. **Ambulance:** tel. 711 366.

Police: Chiang Rai Provincial Police Station (tel. 711 444), on Rattanakhet Rd. Near the Singhaklai Rd. intersection, 1 block east of the TAT. There is a **police box** on the corner of Rattanakhet and Banphraprakan Rd.

Post Offices: 486/1 Mu 15 Uttarakit Rd. (tel. 713 685), 150m straight south of the TAT; 250m north of the clock tower. Open Mon.-Sat. 8:30am-4:30pm, Sun. and public holidays 9am-noon. **Postal code:** 57000.

Telephones: Telecommunications Office (tel. 715 711), on Ngam Muang Rd. at the west end of town. Telex, fax, and **overseas calls.** Open daily 7am-10pm. The post office also offers telex, fax, and overseas calls. **Telephone code:** 053.

ACCOMMODATIONS

While lodgings are scattered all around town, the better ones dwell in the north end of town. All decent lodgings are five to 15 minutes from buses and shops.

Chian House, 172 Sriboonruang Rd. (tel. 713 388), east from TAT past the Rattana-khet Rd. intersection. Turn left, just past Wat Sriboonruang and follow the signs. 1km from the center of town. The pool here makes all the difference. Yes, a swimming pool and cheap rooms side by side. Private bath, sporadically hot showers, and self-serve drinks make the rooms an excellent value, but not the walk. Mountainbike rentals 50฿. Singles 60-80฿. Doubles 100-150฿.

Ben Guest House, 351/10 Sankhongnoi Rd. (tel. 716 775). Head south on San-ambin Rd., turn right onto Sankhongnoi Rd. then right onto Soi 4. Teak house with clean, comfortable rooms, and hot water. Amazingly friendly owner will constantly toss out the English colloquialisms he's picked up. Free lift to the bus station on your way out. Singles 60฿. Doubles 80฿, with private bath 120฿.

Mae Hong Son Guest House, 126 Singhaklai Rd., 100m east of TAT. Turn left (north) at the guest house sign. Like Chian House, a haven from Chiang Rai within the city limits. Achieves the effect by means of a shady garden and homey atmosphere. Its location by the river creates an entomologist's paradise. Bring bug spray and wreak havoc. Singles 60฿. Doubles 80฿.

Mae Kok Villa, 445 Singhaklai Rd. (tel. 711 786), west of TAT. The day market is located out front, but travelers need not worry about the racket, as it closes at dusk. Rather, backpackers should think of the market as a convenient lunch spot.

Not HI-affiliated, although the registration form gives this impression. Hospital-like dorms, only not as sanitary (40฿). Passable rooms with double bed and private bath 150฿. Gorgeous rooms with bathtub, western toilet, and vanity 190฿.

FOOD

For highest concentration of calories to store fronts, ramble on down to the neighborhood bounded by Jet Yod Rd., Banphraprakan Rd., and Phahonyothun Rd.

Rote Yiam, from the corner where Phahonyothin Rd. goes east-west and adjoins with Ratanaket Rd., head south and take the first right. Look for the picture of the soup bowl about 150m down. This small jewel serves up fantastic beef noodle soup (15฿), and offers a menu bursting with pictures.

Swiss German, on Jet Yod Rd., 200m south of the clocktower. A western restaurant with *gutes essen.* Hamburgers 40฿. Continental breakfast 30฿, pepper steak and salad 85฿. Open daily 8am-10pm.

Golden Triangle Restaurant, 590 Phahonyothin Rd. (tel. 711 339), on the section running east to west. Scan the clearly organized Thai food eating guide, and learn about *yam* (salads) and *tom yam* (soups) before you dig in. Tasty *gaeng kiaw wan* (green sweet curry) is 50฿. Open daily 7am-midnight.

Bierstube, 897/1 Phahonyothin Rd. (tel. 714 195), 200-300m south of Banphraprakan Rd. This beer joint delivers on its German promise. Hearty meat dishes. Not for the vegetarian or the kosher. *Schnitzel* 75฿. *Knockwurst* 85฿. Knuckles 105฿. Open daily 9am-midnight.

Cabbages and Condoms, 620/25 Thanalai Rd. (tel. 719 167), downstairs from the Hill-tribe Museum. Raising money and awareness for the anti-AIDS campaign. C&C cooks up a mean chicken curry (50฿). Open Mon.-Sat. 8am-midnight.

SIGHTS

Wat Phra Kaew, originally known as Wat Pa Yier, is on the west end of town across the street from Overbrook Hospital. When the stupa was struck by lightning in 1434, an **Emerald Buddha** inside was revealed. To commemorate the discovery, the wat was renamed Wat Phra Kaew (Wat of the Emerald Buddha). Today, the precious figurine sits in Bangkok's Wat Phra Kaew. Farther west is **Wat Ngam Muang,** on top of the similarly named hill. Its stupa contains King Mengrai's ashes and relics.

Although many trekking companies in Chiang Rai focus on daytrips to the Golden Triangle, the northern forests and many hill-tribe villages await in the vicinity. The TAT office distributes a useful guide to possible trekking itineraries, registered companies and appropriate prices (similar to Chiang Mai). Many tours follow the river, visiting the villages along its banks. The Lahu, Karen, Yao and Akha tribes dominate the area. Some companies offer trips into Laos, Burma, and even China. Before making the great leap forward, check the company with the TAT and/or Tourist Police.

Population and Community Development Association (PDA), 620/25 Thanalai Rd., 150m east of Phahonyothin Rd., offers treks and tours similar to other groups, but with the advantages of an exceptionally knowledgeable guide who has a relationship with the hill-tribes rather than traipsing through with gazing *farang*. Tourist money goes to the funding of rural development and AIDS education/treatment/prevention programs.

ENTERTAINMENT

Most of Chiang Rai's bars at least hint at sleaze. Take shelter from rented love at **Teepee Hippie Happy Bar,** 542/4 Phahonyothin Rd., south of Banphaprakan Rd. It doubles as an American West decor shop, and hosts an occasional acoustic blues band made up of self-termed "long-haired Thais." For some local know-how head to the expat bar **New Moon Café.** Run by two Londoners, this place is a great one to chat in and drain a few Carlsberg draughts (35฿). When Thais want to break loose, they head to the upscale **Par Club** at the Inn Come Hotel, 172/6 Rajbamrung Rd. (tel 717 850), southeast of the city center.

THAILAND

■ Mae Salong แม่สลอง

There is a lot of talk in the Golden Triangle these days about a land route opening up between Thailand and China. In a sense, though, one has already been pioneered. The village of Mae Salong sits on the western leg of the Golden Triangle, atop a mountain of the same name. Members of the Kuomintang, 93rd Division, who fled China after the 1949 revolution, settled here with their families after being driven out of Burma's mountains, where they had initially sought refuge. The few former KMT soldiers still alive in Mae Salong today are *very* old. Regardless, the Chinese identity of the village refuses to dissipate; Thai is taught in schools, but Chinese is the predominant language.

ORIENTATION AND PRACTICAL INFORMATION

Mae Salong can be reached from Tha Ton and Chiang Rai via Mae Chan and Ban Pasang. From Chiang Rai, take a bus heading east on Singhaklai Rd. or at the bus station to Mae Sai (every 15min., 6am-6pm, 1hr., 17฿) and get off 2km past the center of Mae Chan at Ban Pasang and the junction with Route 1130. From there, catch a blue *songthaew* (1hr., 50฿, 90฿ roundtrip) to Mae Salong. From Tha Ton, catch a yellow *songthaew* heading north from the police box (7am-3pm, 1hr., 50฿). *Songthaew* return until 3 or 4pm.

The **main road** through Mae Salong is a continuation of the roads from Tha Ton and Mae Chan. The town is roughly 3km long; the Tha Ton end is marked by the Khumnaiphol Resort, while the Mae Salong Villa marks the Ban Pasang end. The center of town, *songthaew* central, has some daytime **food vendors** and the **mosque,** not far from the guest houses. From before dawn until about 7am, all ethnicities mingle at the **morning market** near Mae Salong Guest House. The **Mae Salong Resort** (tel. 765 014) above the village may be able to **change money.** The **clinic,** 200m above the Mae Salong Guest House near the Thai flag, handles minor ailments. For serious treatment, the nearest hospital is in Mae Chan. A few part-time **police** have an unmarked spot, but in an **emergency,** try your luck with a local, or go to a resort so they can contact the police in Mae Chan. There are police boxes on the roads from Mae Chan and Tha Ton. The **telephone code** is 053, but there are **no overseas calls** in Mae Salong.

ACCOMMODATIONS AND FOOD

The guest houses are arranged harmoniously within 100m of each other on the hill. **Gold Dragon,** before the Shin Sane, off the main road, has pleasant bungalows with private hot showers and porches (200฿). Fireplaces in the larger upstairs rooms are comforting in the cold season (250฿). **Shin Sane Guest House,** just off the main road near the mosque, has pastoral sitting areas—an escape from worn, bare sleeping cells. Concrete chambers with shared bath go for 50฿ for a single, doubles 80฿. Nicer bungalows with private western facilities are 120-200฿ per person.

F-1 Minirestaurant (tel. 765 035), is on the second floor near the *songthaew* stop. It maintains a bit of a hospital cafeteria look, but its large windows allow for a view of the surrounding mountains. (Open daily 4-10pm.)

SIGHTS

The town is a sight for wat-weary eyes—witness the tea and coffee plantations and the fruit orchards cresting the mountain. Coming up from Ban Pasang, the three most visible structures on Doi Mae Salong are a radio tower, a pagoda, and a mosque. The dozen Chinese Muslim families in Mae Salong built their place of worship with Iranian funding. Each morning, the *mullah* mounts the minaret to give the call for a pre-dawn prayer, accompanied by a chorus of roosters and howling dogs. Hill-tribes in the area include the Akha, Lahu, and Lisu, and in smaller numbers, the Hmong and Yao.

Border Intrigue and Drug Lords

For Thais and foreigners alike, the Golden Triangle connotes one thing: opium. Geographically designated as the area where Laos, Burma, and Thailand meet, the region's reputation is well grounded in historical fact. While Thailand has been largely successful in controlling opium production within its borders, politics in the Golden Triangle continue to be dictated by the poppy. Drug money supplies the livelihoods of hundreds of impoverished hill-tribes and is the life-blood of nearby paramilitary organizations.

Increasingly, a new financial force has entered the *realpolitik* equation—tourism. The poppy fields are all well-hidden, but tour companies still manage to entice bus-loads of tourists here with the mere hint of the Hollywood-esque drug legends. Trekkers are led to villages and convinced that opium smoking is an integral part of tribal culture when it is actually considered as shameful among the young and healthy as it is in the West. The scenic river and majestic views of Burma make the area enticing nevertheless.

■ Near Mae Salong

In addition to the hill-tribe villages, pockets of Shan and KMT groups line the Burmese border and are interconnected by footpaths. Don't set out on your own in this area; drug dealings and clashes between Khun Sa's Shan United Army and the Wa National Army (as well as the Thai border patrols) make this a potentially perilous area. As recently as 1989, Khun Sa sent some of his troops to the northern slopes of Doi Mae Salong to abduct villagers because of opium smuggling conflicts.

The village of **Ban Hin Taek,** about 15km northeast of Mae Salong, was the headquarters of the Shan United Army and Khun Sa's home in the early 80s. Today the area has been renamed **Ban Thoed Thai** (Thai Independence Village) and is generally open for trekking; Khun Sa claims to have abandoned drug smuggling to concentrate on his political struggle.

■ Mae Sai แม่สาย

Mae Sai, the only land link with Burma, has both thrived and starved with the status of the border crossing. A recently discovered sapphire mine in the Shan State, however, has transformed it into one of the world's ruby trading capitals, rivalling even Chiang Mai's night market for golf ball sized gems. With luck, the burgeoning gem trade will stabilize border relations and continue allowing *farang* to cross. Despite showing great promise, Mae Sai's future is uncertain. Several factions of the now split MTA army continue to actively oppose the Burmese government, keeping most of surrounding hills a "No Man's Land."

ORIENTATION

Mae Sai is 61km from Chiang Rai, 68km from Mae Salong, and 35km from the Golden Triangle. Buses leave from **Chiang Rai** (every 15min., 6am-6pm, 1½hr., 18฿) and **Chiang Mai** (5 per day, 5hr., 71฿; A/C 5 per day, 4hr., 127฿). From Mae Salong, take a blue *songthaew* to Ban Pasang, and change there to a green one heading north (10฿), or flag a bus for the same price. *Songthaew* connect to Mae Chan.

The **bus park area** is too far south for convenience. The **border crossing** is 1km ahead, where Hwy. 110 terminates. In town, the highway is called **Phahonyothin Road** and basks in a carnival climate as *farang*, Thais, and Burmese browse, bargain, buy, and beg. **Silamjoi Road** jogs along the river; heading west from the bridge to the vicinity of many guest houses.

PRACTICAL INFORMATION

Tours and Travel: K.K. Guest House, 135/3 Silamjoi Rd. (tel. 733 055), arranges trips to Burma and Laos continuing to China, regional treks, and excursions to Doi Tung Sop Ruak. **Anada Travel,** 22 Mu 7 Phahonyothin Rd. (tel. 731 038), 500m from the bridge has tours to Keng Tung.

Immigration Offices: (tel. 731 288), on Phahonyothin Rd., near the hospital. Open Mon.-Fri. 8am-noon and 1-4:30pm. See **Near Mae Sai,** page 612 for border info.

Currency Exchange: Several banks on Phahonyothin Rd. **Krung Thai Bank,** 23 Phahonyothin Rd. (tel. 731 624), about 300m from the border, accepts MC and Visa. Open daily 8:30am-5pm. (US$5 is necessary to cross the border.)

Buses: Mae Sai Bus Park, 1km south of the bridge along Phahonyothin Rd. To **Chiang Rai** and **Chiang Mai** (14 per day, 6am-3:30pm, 33฿ to Chiang Rai, 71-127฿ to Chiang Mai). Several private companies around the bus park offer direct buses to **Bangkok** (200฿-500฿). Most depart early morning or late afternoon.

Local Transportation: Motorcycle taxis smother Mae Sai, and wear official numbered orange jerseys. **Songthaew** leave for **Chiang Saen** via **Sop Ruak** from Thai Farmers bank (30฿). **Tuk-tuk** and **samlor** too. 10-20฿ for anywhere in the city. Short distances make walking convenient, if not easier.

Rentals: Thong, on Silamjoi Rd., 150m from the bridge, rents motorbikes (Honda Dreams) for 150฿ per day. Open daily 7am-6pm.

Medical Services: Mae Sai Hospital, 101 Mu 1 Pomathalat Rd. (tel. 732 276), off Phahonyothin Rd. Turn-off near the Immigration Office, 2km from the bridge, before the post office. Some English spoken.

Emergency: tel. 731 444 or 733 616. **Ambulance:** tel. 731 300.

Police: Police Station (tel. 191), on Phahonyothin Rd., 200m south of the bridge.

Post Offices/Telephones: Mae Sai Post and Telegraph Office, 68 Phahonyothin Rd. (tel. 731 402), 2km south of the bridge. A long walk past the hospital and virtually everything else. Open Mon.-Fri. 8:30am-4:30pm, Sat.-Sun. 9am-noon. **Postal code:** 57130. Fax, telex, calling card, collect, and cash calls through the side door (tel. 731 727). Open daily 7am-10pm. More convenient are guest house phones and the small **telephone office** beneath the bridge on Silamjoi Rd. Open daily 8am-10pm. Both charge 50฿ service fee for collect or credit card calls.

ACCOMMODATIONS

King Kobra, 135/5 Sailomjoi Rd. (tel. 733 055). Uniquely decorated with bombs, a zebra skin, a stuffed King Cobra, and a whiskey bottle with centipedes in it. The American owner, Joe, can give the best border and travel info in the area. He also arranges treks to Northern Thailand, the Shan State, Laos, or Yunnan, China. Restaurant/bar overlooks Burma. Dorms 60฿. Singles with hot shower 120-250฿, with A/C 400฿. Doubles with hot shower 150-300฿, with A/C 500฿.

Mae Sai Guest House, 688 Wiengpangkam Rd. (tel. 732 021), at the end of Silamjoi Rd. about 1km. On the river and removed from urban jungle, spacious bungalows with back-friendly beds and hot water. Gate closes at midnight, or before, if the owner is tired. Singles 60-70฿. Doubles 100฿, with shower 150-300฿.

Mae Sai Plaza Guest House, 386/3 Silamjoi Rd. (tel. 732 230), about 350m down the river, west of the bridge. How this multi-level complex of colorful cottages remains affixed to the steep hillside remains a mystery to even the most astute *Let's Go* researcher. Rooms are a bit rough around the edges; opt for the private bath. All rooms are doubles 80฿, with cold shower 120฿, with hot shower 150฿.

FOOD

Get your vital nutrients at the **night market,** 200m south of the Thai Farmers Bank on the opposite side of Phahonyothin Rd.; it serves traditional Thai food from 7-10pm. Peek down the *sois* to catch market activity, then use your nose. Restaurant options are fairly bleak. Try your guest house or head to Mae Sai Riverside.

Jo Jo's, Phahonyothin Rd. (tel. 731 662), just north of the bus stop; big English sign. American breakfasts, Thai curries, and veggie selections. Extraordinary ice cream

Around the Golden Triangle

includes "Jelly Boys" (ice cream heads with jello hats, 25฿). Fried chicken on yellow rice 25฿. Rainbow Parfait 38฿. Open daily 6am-3pm.

■ Near Mae Sai

The best sights are away from the border to the south, easily accessible from the highway. Rented motorbikes are the optimal exploring companions, and allow for unobstructed eyeballing of the mountains as they rear up from the flat valley.

About 5km south of Mae Sai off Hwy. 110 lurks **Tham Luang** (Great Cave), 2.5km off the highway down a paved road. A well-run park, Tham Luang encompasses the Buddha Cave (a small formation predictably housing a Buddha) and the larger Royal Luang Cave (which is 7km deep). Bring a flashlight or rent a lantern from the park office. (Open daily 6am-6pm.)

Three km farther south, a road unfurls to **Khun Nam Nang Non** (Sleeping Lady Lagoon). The undulating rock formations resemble a reclining female figure. The only sign on the highway faces northbound traffic, so check over your shoulder for the brown English sign. (Open daily 6am-6pm.) The exit to **Tham Plaa** (Fish Cave) lies 1km south (13km from Mae Sai). Fresh water surges through the cave, also called "monkey cave" due to the proliferation of gamboling primates; hold onto your belongings. Bribe them with bananas (5฿).

■ Border Crossing: Mae Sai/Thachilek

A literal stone's throw from Mae Sai lies **Thachilek, Burma.** The status of the border, whether open or closed, can change from one day to the next. When it's open, you can obtain a one day pass to see Thachilek with multiple day passes available for traveling 168km to Keng Tung. This is not an official border crossing, meaning your passport does not get stamped and the crossing procedure can be uncomfortable. First, get US$5 to support the Burmese government, then head to the photocopy place to the left and underneath the bridge where you photcopy the info page of your passport, your visa stamp, and your disembarkation card (5฿). Bring your passport and the photocopies to the immigration booth on the bridge. Give you passport to the Thai official there and walk to Burma with the photocopies and the five bucks. These you give to the Burmese official in exchange for the thinnest and cheapest piece of paper you'll *ever* see. That piece of paper *is* your passport for all intents and purposes. **Hold on to it.**

Once in Burma you'll notice the market on your right just off the bridge. Perhaps the most interesting market in Northern Thailand, proffering the usual gamut of merchandise in addition to a selection of animal parts that surely must have added a few names to the endangered species list. Use common sense when you get that "one time offer," hold on to that paper. **The border closes at 5pm.**

▓ Chiang Saen เชียงแสน

This small town on the Mekong was founded in 1328 by the grandson of King Mengrai, King Saen Phu, who made it the capital of the Chiang Saen Kingdom. Scattered ruins, however, provide stone-faced testimony to the existence of pre-11th-century civilization. The city was destroyed in 1803 by Rama I to save it from Burmese subjugation and the district in distress did not begin to recover until the beginning of this century, when people started to resettle.

More visitors are scheduled for imminent arrival. Plans for regular passenger service along the Mekong between Thailand and China will bring *farang* and Chinese. As the Golden Triangle is being forced to sever its drug connections, the TAT steps up its aggressive efforts to push the region on tourists. During the day, Chiang Saen is extremely sedate, but at night the whole river boardwalk rages deliriously with food vendors, whiskey pit stops, guitar strummers, singers, and occasional dancers.

ORIENTATION

From Chiang Mai buses stop in **Chiang Saen** (6:30am and 2:30pm, 5hr., 73฿; A/C, 8am and 3pm, 130฿) on the way to Sop Ruak. From Chiang Rai, buses go through **Mae Chan** and **Mae Sai** (every 15min., 6am-5pm, 1½hr., 17฿). *Songthaew* also run to and from Mae Sai until 3pm (30฿). By car or motorbike it's more scenic to head east directly out of Mae Sai. Follow the sign 2km south of the Sai River that indicates Sop Ruak is 35km away.

The center of town is in the shape of a "T." The top is formed by **Rimkhong Road,** north to south along the **Mekong River.** Across the river to the east is Laos. The tail of the "T" is **Phahonyothin Road** which terminates at the river. Most sights and businesses are on Phahonyothin Rd. including the **bus park area,** 200m from the river.

PRACTICAL INFORMATION

Siam Commercial Bank, 116 Phahonyothin Rd. (tel. 777 041), exchanges currency and has a 24-hour **ATM** that accepts AmEx, Plus, and Cirrus. (Open Mon.-Fri. 8:30am-3:30pm.) J.S. Guest House has **bike rentals** (30฿). A nameless shop on the same road (Soi 1) south of Phahonythin Rd., rents **motorbikes** (150฿ per day). (Open daily 7am-7pm.) The **Chiang Saen Hospital** (tel. 777 017) stands 1km from the river. The **police** (tel. 777 111), on the corner of Rimkhong and Phahonyothin Rd., face the market. The **Post Offices/Telephones** (tel. 777 116) is 600m from the river. (Open Mon.-Fri. 8:30am-4:30pm, Sat. 9am-noon.) **Postal code:** 57150. There are no overseas telephone facilities. **Telephone code:** 053.

ACCOMMODATIONS AND FOOD

On the river, **Chiang Saen Guest House,** 45 Rimkhong Rd., 200m north of Phahonyothin Rd., has an admirable concern for the environment including wallpapering with "green" editorials. Singles are 60-80฿, doubles 100-120฿. Bungalows with cold shower go for 100฿ for singles, doubles 120฿. The **Siam Guest House,** 295 Rimkhong Rd., sits on the river, 300m north from Phahonyothin Rd. with a plush garden. They have great mosquito netting in otherwise sparse rooms and offer free maps of the area north of Mae Chan. Fanless singles are 60฿. Rooms with cold shower cost 100฿. Gate closes at 10pm. Decent Thai dishes and the best atmosphere can be found at riverside restaurants. Try **Sak Thai,** south of Phahonyothin (open daily 8am-11pm) or the **Mekong Riverside** just north (open daily 8am-10pm).

SIGHTS

At the entrance to the city from the Chiang Rai side is the **Chiang Saen National Museum,** a warehouse of artifacts from the Chiang Saen and Lannathai periods, in addition to hill-tribe clothes and tools. Some objects displayed date from the Neolithic period. Ancient ruins on the museum grounds are a taste of sites found in the province. (Open Wed.-Sun. 9am-4pm; admission 10฿.)

Next to the museum, a massive 13th-century brick *chedi* dwarfs **Wat Chedi Luang.** Back then it was the tallest Lannathai monument (58m). Today it's so overgrown with shrubbery that it looks like a hill. Off Rimkhong Rd., 3km north of the town entrance, is the uninspiring **Wat Chom Kitti.** The hilltop here offers a compelling view of the Mekong River and Laos.

■ Near Chiang Saen

SOP RUAK

Sop Ruak may be the official name of the village, but this place is better known by its 24-carat pseudonym, the **Sam Liam Tongkham (Golden Triangle).** Here, the narrow Sai River, separating Thailand from Burma, joins the Mekong. The wider Mekong sequesters Burma, Laos, and Thailand from each other; the triangle where the three countries come together is invisible, in the middle of the tributary.

This infamous town ranks with Woodstock '94 and Michael Jackson's *HIStory* as contenders for the Top Ten list of over-hyped, over-priced attractions. The river is spectacular, but capitalist inclinations have transformed the town into one immense souvenir shop. Relax on a Golden Triangle Boat Ride (300฿) after a night of tossing and turning at Golden Triangle Resort, where rooms fetch 2-12,000฿. Budgeteers can make a beeline for **PK House** (tel. 784 061) across from the "Golden Triangle" sign. Singles with cold showers are a bargain at 150฿. Doubles with hot showers start at 250฿. The few guest houses by the river have been bulldozed in anticipation of the economic boom expected to hit the region, now named the **Golden Quadrangle** (China has been added). Soon it may be possible to go to China via Thailand by boat; a land route through Mae Sai is being developed as well.

The **House of Opium** is a poppy museum with exhibits about various stages of production, as well as pipes, scales, and books. No samples are given out, but pipes are sold. (Open daily 8am-7pm; admission 10฿.) To reach Sop Ruak from Chiang Saen, go north 11km along the river, easily accomplished on a Mae Sai-bound *songthaew* from a stand across from the bus stop.

■ Chiang Khong เชียงของ

The tiny district of Chiang Khong, located on Thailand's northern boundary, has formerly garnered fame only for the *plaa beuk* (giant catfish) snared from the depths of the Mekong River. However, the recent opening of the border, allowing non-Thai foreigners to cross the Mekong into Laos and the trading port of Ban Houie Sai, now overshadows the aquatic felines as the main tourist attraction. There are also a number of Hmong and Yao villages nearby, but trek operators have yet to tap into this potential source of income.

ORIENTATION AND PRACTICAL INFORMATION

Chiang Khong can be reached by car or motorbike from Chiang Saen—just follow the river. There will be a fork at Ban Saew. **Route 1129**, on the right, is shorter, but going left is the scenic route along the river, around 15-20km longer. The trip can also be made by boat (1½hr., 1200฿) or by grabbing one of the green *songthaew* off of Rimkhong Rd., just south of Phahonyothin Rd. They leave whenever it suits the driver's fancy from about 8am to 2pm (2½hr., 40฿). **Buses** leave from **Chiang Rai** (every hr., 4:30am-5:30pm, 3hr., 31฿). From Chiang Saen, Rte. 1129 terminates at the town's main drag, **Saiklang Road,** which runs along the river. Turn right (southeast) to get to everything. Heading southeast, past the town center, Saiklang Rd. turns into **Route 1020,** where the bus stops. Out of the bus station, turn left to get to town. Once you're there, everything is in walking distance.

From the bus stop, heading northwest on Saiklang Rd., the **immigration office** (tel. 791 322) is first on the right. You'll need to stop here to get a re-entry visa if you intend to go to Laos and return to Thailand for longer than the allotted transit visa. Bring 500฿, two photos, and photocopies of your passport. Extensions are available as well (500฿); they'll tell you to go to Ann Tour for your Lao Visa. Next door is the **police station** (tel. 791 437). A few hundred meters farther is the **Thai Farmers Bank**, 416 moo 2 Saiklang Rd. (tel. 791 111) where to exchange money or get a cash advance off your MC or Visa. Farther north, past the wat, is the **post office** (tel. 791 325) which also has an **overseas telephone office**. (Open Mon.-Fri. 8:30am-4:30pm and Sat. 9am-noon.) **Postal code: 57140. Telephone code: 053.** At the northwest end of town is **Soi 1** which has the town's two guest houses. **Yooparach Hospital** (tel. 791 206) is 2km out of town on Rte. 1020.

ACCOMMODATIONS AND FOOD

Ban Tammila (tel. 791 350), off Soi 1, has simple bungalows with mosquito nets and outside, hot showers for 100฿. Nicer bungalows with private showers go for 150-400฿. The friendly owner speaks English and can arrange visas to Laos. Next door is the expensive **Ruan Thai Sopaphan** (tel. 791 023), with a lovely all teak sitting room overlooking the Mekong. Austere rooms with private hot showers and fans for 200-300฿. Bungalows on the river are 500฿. Negotiable in the low season. Near the intersection with Rte. 1129, the **Chiang Khong Hotel**, 68 Sai Klang Rd. (tel. 791 242) is near the pier and has basic, impersonal rooms with hot showers and fans for 120฿. There are several indistinguishable noodle and rice shops along Saiklang Rd. For a better view, dine at one of the guest houses or at one of the riverside restaurants, **Rinan** (open daily 8am-11pm) and **Rimkhong** (tel. 791 105; open daily 9am-midnight) between Sois 7 and 9. Nibble fishcakes (70฿) and fried rice (15฿) while gazing at the buildings in Laos.

■ Border Crossing: Chiang Khong/Ban Houie Sai

Ban Houie Sai across the river is now an official point of entry to Laos. A visa is simple to obtain. **Ann Tour**, 6/1 moo 8 Saiklang Rd. (tel./fax 791 218) near Soi 1 can arrange a 15-day visa in half a day (1700฿) with just your passport. For a better deal, get your visa application faxed from King Kobra Guest House in Mae Sai for 70฿. From there you can pick up the visa in Houie Sai for 1500฿. They also offer car and boat tours. You can take a ferry on your own from the pier north of the intersection with Rte. 1129 for 20฿. From here you can travel across Laos to Vietnam. Inquire at Tammila Guest House for details.

■ Nan น่าน

Less than 80km from the Laotian border, the hills conceal the charming town of Nan. Formerly called Woranakorn (Excellent City), the town was founded in the mid-13th century, contemporary with the establishment of Sukhothai. By the next century, Nan was one of the nine provinces of the early Lanna kingdom, and the architectural style of that era is evident in the town's wats and monuments.

During the 1960s and 70s, the region's isolation made it a safe haven for smugglers and the People's Liberation Army of Thailand (PLAT), communist rebels who periodically destroyed roads to keep the government at bay. While the PLAT's struggle failed dismally, their ghosts have nonetheless managed to fend off the capitalist vanguard of tourism for more than a decade. The surrounding province conceals a myriad of spectacular sights. Even the bus trip into Nan is beautiful, a magic carpet ride past small farming communities, lush green forests, and fog-covered mountains.

ORIENTATION

Buses (coming from the north) arrive at the station on **Ananthaworarittidet Road,** which runs roughly east-west through the center of town. A block to the south is **Mahawong Road,** which leads over the town's bridge and harbors the post office. Two blocks farther south is **Suriyaphong Road.** The **police station, City Hall,** and many sights flank this road. Four blocks east of the northern bus station is the **Nan River,** which forms the town's eastern border. **Sumonthewarat Road** is the town's main street and runs parallel to the river. Parallel and two blocks farther in is **Pha Kong Road. Nora Department store,** a useful point of reference, is on the corner of Ananthaworarittidet Rd. and Sumonthewarat Rd.

PRACTICAL INFORMATION

Tours and Travel: Fhu Travel Service, 453/4 Sumonthewarat Rd. (tel. 710 636), 1 block south and across the street from the Dhevaraj Hotel. English-speaking manager leads treks and tours starting at 1500฿ per person. Open daily 8am-8pm.

Currency Exchange: Thai Farmers Bank, 434 Sumonthewarat Rd. (tel. 710 248), just north of Mahawong Rd. Open Mon.-Fri. 8:30am-3:30pm.

Air Travel: Thai Air, 34 Mahaphrom Rd. (tel. 710 077). English spoken. To **Chiang Mai** (Mon., Wed., and Fri., noon, 510฿.) To **Bangkok** via **Phitsanulok** (1 per day, 1530฿ to Bangkok, 575฿ to Phitsanulok).

Buses: The bus station (tel. 710 027) is on Ananthaworarittidet Rd. To: **Chiang Mai** via **Lampang** (green bus opposite the station, 7hr.; regular, 8:30, 9, 11am, and 2pm, 83฿; 2nd-class A/C, 10am and 3pm, 115฿; 1st-class A/C, 8am, noon, and 10:30pm, 148฿); **Chiang Rai** (blue bus, 6-7hr.: 9am, 97฿; A/C, 9am, 136฿). Government buses to and from **Bangkok, Phitsanulok,** and **Sukhothai** arrive and depart from the station on Kha Luang near the river, 1 block north of Ananthaworarittiket Rd. The old route to Bangkok passes through **Sukhothai;** the new route through **Phitsanulok.** To **Bangkok:** by new route (VIP, 7 and 8pm, 445฿; 1st-class A/C, 8am, 6:30, 6:45, and 7pm, 289฿; 2nd-class A/C, 7 and 10:15pm, 225฿; regular, 9am, 7:30, 8, and 8:30pm, 180฿); by old route (1st-class A/C, 8:30am and 6pm, 319฿; regular, 8:30am, 5:30, and 6:30pm, 177฿).

Rentals: Overseas, 488 Sumonthewarat Rd. (tel. 710 258). Mountain bikes 50฿ per day, motorbikes 150-200฿ per day. Open daily 8am-5:30pm.

Markets: The **produce market** sets up on the *soi* across from the Dheveraj Hotel by the bus terminal. It's open all day, but the main action takes place during the mid-afternoon.

Pharmacies: 345/5 Sumonthewarat Rd. Open daily 8am-10pm.

Medical Services: Nan Provincial Hospital (tel. 710 138), on Sumonthewarat Rd., near the bend 1.5km north of downtown.

Emergency: tel. 191. **Fire:** tel. 199.

Police: (tel. 710 033) on Suriyaphong Rd., opposite City Hall.

Post Offices/Telephones: GPO, 70 Mahawong Rd. (tel. 710 176). Open Mon.-Fri. 8:30am-4:30pm, Sat.-Sun. and holidays 9am-noon. Overseas telephone and fax on 2nd floor. Open daily 7am-10pm. **Postal code:** 55000. **Telephone code:** 054.

ACCOMMODATIONS

Nan Guest House, 57/16 Mahaphrom Rd. (tel. 771 849), a 10-min. walk from the bus station. Turn left onto Ananthaworarittidet Rd. and walk past the municipal market to the 1st major intersection with Pha Kong Rd. Turn right and walk 2 blocks. When you pass Wat Hua Khuang on your right, turn right and follow that road to the Thai Air Office. Go to the end of the *soi* opposite the office. Trying to find it is half the fun. The other half is reveling in your peaceful, cozy room. Trek and local attractions info on the walls. Singles 70฿. Doubles 90฿.

Doi Phuka Guest House, 94/5 Sumonthewarat Rd. (tel. 771 442), outside town. Take a *samlor* from the bus terminal (20฿) or walk north toward the night market (the 1st left after turning left from the northern bus station), then left at the intersection. A sign directs you up a *soi,* past the wat on the left. A splendid teak house with authentic decor. Singles 70฿. Doubles 90฿. Free use of bicycles.

FOOD

Da Dario's, at the north end of town, on the river; go by *songthaew.* Authentic Italian cuisine for lunch and dinner set in a former living room converted for dining. The best place in town for *farang* food. Satisfy that craving for Ceasar Salad (55฿), or share a banana split. Open Mon.-Sat.

Suan Isaan, 2/1 Ananthaworarittidet Rd. (tel. 710 761). From the Dheveraj Hotel, turn left, then left after Bangkok Bank; it's 100m down. Recommended by locals for its spicy Isaan food. Most dishes 25฿. English menu. Open daily 9am-9pm.

Pin Pub Restaurant, 438-440 Sumonthewarat Rd. (tel. 772 640), in the Nan Fah Hotel. One of the town's few nightspots. Live Thai folk music and admirable array of Thai and western dishes 45฿ and up. The specialty is *ho mok ma plaw oun talang* (seafood curry inside a young coconut, 55฿). Open daily 6am-midnight.

SIGHTS

Wat Phumin, on Pha Kong Rd., 200m southwest of the police station and city hall, is the 400-year-old jewel of Nan town. The cruciform *wiharn* with heavy teak doors surrounded by flame carvings, is the undisputed star of the show. The famous murals depicting the culture of the Lanna people are slightly water-damaged, and preservation efforts ban photography. Down the street from Wat Phumin and across from

Wat Phra That Chaeng Kham, is the **Nan National Museum.** (Open Wed.-Sun. 9am-noon and 1-4pm; admission 10฿). Exhibits on the ethnic groups that inhabit the province feature jewelry, royal regalia, weaponry, and large wax figures in traditional clothing. Sneak by the six elephant statues guarding the *chedi* at **Wat Phra That Chang Kham,** across the street from the museum.

Wat Phra That Chae Haeng, the oldest temple in the region, sprawls 2km beyond the Nan River bridge. Nearly 700 years old, the highly revered wat has a bronze-tipped *chedi*, Buddha image, moat, and wall. Water from this canal was used in King Rama IX's (the current king's) wedding ceremony. Equally captivating is the statue of Say Jao Wang Tao Kha Khaong, the first king of old Nan. There's a wooded area perfect for picnics and a small zoo.

Southeast of the town, **Wat Pra That Khao Noi** offers sweeping views of the entire valley cradling the town. Head out onto Hwy. 101 to Phrae. Just after the bridge turn right (marked by a green English sign). The wat is 3km further down the road, past Wat Phayawat on the left. To the left, just before the bridge on the way to the shrine, villagers shape bricks by hand—the blocks are scattered everywhere as they bake in the sun. The **Thai Payap Project** sells Hmong, Yao (Mien), H'tin, and Khmer **handicrafts** from its showrooms on Sumonthewarat Rd. north of the Dhevaraj Hotel. All proceeds help fund community development projects in the surrounding rural areas. (Open daily 8:30am-5pm.)

■ Near Nan

Even accounting for the history of guerilla insurgency, it is astounding that relatively few travelers have glimpsed the mountainous back country of Nan Province. Incredibly wealthy in hill-tribe culture and natural scenery, Nan is waiting in the wings for its moment in the package-tour spotlight. Virtually all of Nan is now safe, but a few mines remain buried in the most remote areas. This should not deter anyone; the risks are negligible, but stick to roads or trails when way off the beaten path. There is a greater danger of getting lost in these parts due to the lack of English signs—it may help to have the Thai names of your destination in writing before departing.

Fhu Travel Service, 453/4 Sumonthewarat Rd. (tel. 710 636), one block south and across the street from the Dhevaraj Hotel, leads excellent expeditions around the province. The Fhus speak English and personally guide customers. Daytrips and treks start at 1500฿ per person, depending on the number of people in the group. A trek with Mr. Fhu is now the only way to visit the **Mrabi people** (also known as Phi Toong Mang, or Spirit of the Yellow Leaves), a small nomadic tribe.

Doi Phukha National Park monopolizes a huge expanse of Nan Province, and is home to the Hmong and Mien who are permitted to live within the park. Dozens of waterfalls and caves remain hidden, waiting to be claimed as a personal haven for those apocalyptic fruitopian moments.

Hop on your Harley and take Hwy. 1080 from the northeast corner of the city of Nan (pass an Esso station on the left as you leave town) for 60 beautiful countryside kilometers to **Pua.** In Pua, turn left just before the police box, then left again 100m up the road at the English sign for the park. From here, follow the main road and the Thai signs of the same yellow/brown color scheme. The road stretches 47km over a mountain peak through the park to **Ban Bor Kleua.** The drive along this road thrusts you into the chilly mountain air and past some of Thailand's highest and most magnificent mountains. Twenty-five km up the road is the park office, which has huts (100฿). Camping in the park is free, but be prepared for freezing temperatures (below 0°C) in the cool season, and penetrating wetness in the rainy season. *Songthaew* also speed to **Pua** from the local bus station in Nan (20฿); one leaves from the market in Pua in the morning for Ban Bor Kleua and can drop you off at the park office (30฿).

A few km past the park office is the prized **Chomphu Phukha tree** *(Bretschneidera sinensis).* Though it is not the only specimen in the world as locals claim, it is extremely rare. A symbol of the province, the tree blossoms once a year in

February, when hordes of Thais come to see it. A few hundred meters past the tree stands a grove of "ancient" palm trees. These distinctive trees, which look more like giant ferns, are relics of Jurassic National Park. From here it is only a few km to the road's highest point and the long, winding descent into Ban Bor Kleua, which features much-lionized salt wells. Turn left off the highway and north from Ban Bor Kleua, however, and a road leads to **Ban Supan,** 6km away. After crossing the bridge just before the village, turn right onto a dirt road to reach the **Supan Waterfall,** off the road to the right and marked by a red Thai sign and a small English one.

You can loop back from Ban Bor Kleua. Head south to Ban Phak Heuak, then west on Hwy. 1081. Swerve south after Ban Huai Lek Lai (the hilly route) or just before Ban Nam Yao (the flat route). Turn right onto Rd. 1225 from either, then left onto 1169, which heads south to Nan.

■ Lampang ลำปาง

Lampang (pop. 50,000) is one of the North's oldest settlements, inhabited as far back as the 7th century, during the Dvaravati period. Only 100km from Chiang Mai, Lampang has always played underdog to its larger, better-known neighbor. Every dog has its day, however, and Lampang is getting the last laugh as its slowly developing tourist facilities have begun to lure overflow and through-traffic from *farang*-saturated Chiang Mai. Although it lacks an abundance of sights and a raging nightlife, Lampang's active market and friendliness are sure to please all but the most cynical.

ORIENTATION

Most major roads radiate from the **clock tower rotary** near the town center. **Boonyawat Road,** pointing directly east, goes past many of the town's hotels, shops, and banks to city hall. In the opposite direction, **Thakhraonoi Road** runs past the Aswin Market. **Suren Road** goes directly to the train station. **Chatchai Road** and **Ban Chiangrai Road** branch out from the station, heading toward the **Wang River** and intersecting **Thipchang Road,** a commercial avenue running parallel to Boonyawat Rd. Across the river, the town turns residential. The bus station, right off **Asia I Highway,** is on **Jantsurin Road** about 2km from the traffic circle. Less expensive accommoddations begin at Kim Hotel, about 1km down Boonyawat Rd.

PRACTICAL INFORMATION

Tourist Offices: (tel. 218 823), on Boonyawat Rd. past all the hotels and banks, behind the main city hall building. Maps available, but little English spoken. Open Mon.-Fri. 8:30am-4:30pm.

Currency Exchange: Banks line Boonyawat Rd. Most open Mon.-Fri. 8:30am-3:30pm. **Bangkok Bank,** 36-44 Thipchang Rd. (tel. 228 135) has an **ATM** that accepts AmEx, Visa, and Plus.

Air Travel: (tel. 218 199), on Sanambin Rd. **Thai Air,** 314 Sanambin Rd. (tel. 217 078). Open daily 8am-5pm. Daily flights to **Bangkok** via **Phitsanulok** (1395฿).

Trains: Lampang Railroad Station (tel. 211 024), on Prasanmaitri Rd. 2km out of town. *Songthaew* run there frequently. To **Bangkok** (6 per day, 8-12hr., depending on service, 3rd-class 106฿) and **Chiang Mai** (2hr., 3rd class 29฿).

Buses: Bus station (tel. 227 410), off Asia 1 Hwy., several km out of town. Go by *songthaew* (10฿) or *samlor* (50฿). Buses running the Nan-Phrae-Denchai-Lampang-Lamphun-Chiang Mai route come through town 9 times per day. Also goes to **Nakhon Ratchasima** (7 per day) and **Bangkok** (10 per day). Private lines and through-buses for Bangkok and points along the way are also available.

Local Transportation: Blue songthaew travel the "Rop Wiang" line (around the circle). Others go anywhere in town for 10฿. **Samlor** costs more than *songthaew*. **Horse-drawn carts** gather near the entrance to city hall, and offer tours (short trip 50฿, circuit of town 80฿).

Markets: Tesaban Market I sets up across the street from city hall along Praisanee Rd. **Aswin Market** (Tesaban Market 2) is on Thakrownoi Rd. off the town's traffic circle. After 7pm, the **night food stalls** move in and stay until midnight, serving dirt-cheap food. Open daily 6am-7pm.

Medical Services: Lampang Hospital (tel. 217 045), on Phahonyothin Rd.

Police: (tel. 217 108) on Boonyawat Rd.

Post Offices/Telephones: GPO (tel. 224 069), on Thipchang Rd. Follow Boonyawat past all the hotels to the city hall; turn left on Praisanee. Open Mon.-Fri. 8:30am-4:30pm, Sat.-Sun. 9am-noon. **Overseas calling** and **fax.** Open daily 8am-8pm. **Postal code:** 52000. **Telephone code:** 054.

ACCOMMODATIONS

Riverside Lampang Guest House, 286 Talat Kao Rd. (tel. 227 005). From Kim Hotel, walk down Suan Dok Rd. past the Pin Hotel until you hit the T-intersection. Turn left; look for the wooden gate on the right. Pure class. Many of the large, gorgeous rooms have balconies and bathtubs; all have hot showers and western toilets (300฿). Breakfast on the veranda with the Wang River.

Srisangar, 213-215 Boonyawat Rd. (tel. 217 070), across the street from Kim Hotel. Inexpensive, yet impersonal. The rooms are clean and the location central. Ease your loneliness with the baht saved by staying here. Rooms 100฿.

FOOD

Riverside Restaurant, 328 Thip Chang Rd. (tel. 221 861). From the Kim Hotel, walk along Suan Dok Rd. toward the Wang River. Take the 1st left. A sign on Boonyawat Rd. points the way. Speedy service with a loving smile. Pizza (60฿) and *tiramisù* (45฿). Open daily 10am-midnight.

Ban Chom Wang, 276 Talat Kao Rd. (tel. 222 845). From Kim Hotel, take Suan Dok Rd. toward the river, past the 1st intersection. Turn left and look for the Thai sign with the Pepsi logo a few meters down. Behold stunning sunsets from the multi-tiered deck overlooking the river. Fried shrimp with garlic and pepper quenches crustacean cravings. No English menu. Open daily 4pm-midnight.

Jeu Jao Kao, 1256-1257 Praisanee Rd., across from the post office. Family-run noodle shop is known for its excellent pork noodles. Fastest bowl of soup this side of the Mekong. Open daily 6am-2pm.

SIGHTS

Wat Phra Kaew Don Tao, in the northeast corner of town, in a residential area by the river, housed the Emerald Buddha during the reign of King Anantayot (1436-68). A typical horse-cart tour stop, the wat has a Burmese-style pagoda in front of its *chedi*. The *wiharn* is open to visitors on certain holidays only. (Wat open daily 6am-6pm; admission 10฿.) **Wat Si Chum,** on Si Chum Rd. past Phahonyothin Rd., south of town, was the victim of a fire due to an electrical mishap a few years ago. During the early evening, tots frolic in the charred remains next to the *chedi*.

■ Near Lampang

Thirty-eight km west of Lampang, the **Thai Elephant Conservation Centre** mounts the highway between Chiang Mai and Lampang, a few km outside Thung Kwian Forest. Elephants begin their training here when they are five years old, and continue with one master until they are 67, when they can legally retire, and are returned to the wild. Exhibitions show them walking in procession, carrying teak logs, and *sawasdee*-ing the crowd (daily at 9:30, 11am, and 2:30pm; admission 50฿). Bundles of sugar cane for the elephants (10฿) are also sold. An extra 100฿ gets a 30-minute elephant-back trip into the surrounding forest; (200฿ for an hour). During peak season, the shows are held 0.5km from the highway. At all other times, the show moves to the school's main grounds. To reach the elephants, take a Chiang Mai bus and ask to be let off at the training center. Catch a bus back along the highway.

The **Kew Lom Dam** is a popular relaxation spot among Lampang youth. The island, which has bungalows and a beach in the middle of the reservoir, can be reached by boat (50฿). North of the dam, another oft-visited spot, the **Jae Sorn**

THAILAND

Waterfalls crash in **Jae Sorn National Park.** The six-tiered cascades are cloaked in dense tropical forest. Camping is permitted. (Open daily 8am-5pm; admission to the falls 20฿.) Food stalls and hot springs make for a steamy combination.

A web of *songthaew* and mini-buses to these sights queue up in several spots in Lampang. To get to Jae Sorn Falls or any stop along the way, look for the dirt parking lot in the *soi* off Thip Chang Rd., one block from Bangkok Ban.

WAT PHRA THAT LAMPANG LUANG

About 18km southwest of Lampang, in the small town of **Khoka**, is **Wat Phra That Lampang Luang,** one of the North's finest displays of religious architecture. The main compound, surrounded by thick plaster walls, dominates a hill and must be entered through one of the four gates. To the left of the front entrance, stalls sell drinks and trinkets, and a small model of the wat bears English labels.

Through the main gate, the central *wiharn* is a large, open-air, Lanna-style structure, supported by 46 laterite columns. Constructed in 1486 by Muen Kum Reg, a vassal of Chiang Mai and ruler of Lampang, the chapel houses two important Buddha images: Phra Jao Lan Tang, cast in 1563, is enclosed in a golden *mondop* near the rear of the temple; and Phra Jao Tan Jai, who sits behind the *mondop.* The 19th-century wall panels give behind-the-scenes glimpses of court life.

To the right of the main temple, **Wiharn Ton Kaew**, built in 1476, and its neighbor **Wiharn Naamtaem**, dating from 1501, display murals. Directly behind the main *wiharn,* the main *chedi* was built in 1449 by Chao Haan Sri Tue Thong, but was reconfigured into its present form in 1496 by Chao Haan Sri. Buddha's hair and ashes from the right side of his forehead and his neck are stashed here.

The 700-year-old Buddha image inside **Phra Phuttha Wiharn** looks spry for his age. Behind that structure, in the small white building named **Haw Phra Phutthabat** (built in 1149), is a replica of Buddha's footprint. The **sacred tree** growing near the bells is believed to have sprouted from a pole a local used to carry offerings to Buddha. Beyond the back wall of the compound, a lackluster shrine actually showcases the temple's most valuable Buddha image, a jade (erroneously called emerald) Buddha from the Chiang Saen period (1057-1757). To the left of the main temple compound, the wat's "museum" contains Buddha images, photos of monks, and paintings from years past. (Open daily 9am-noon and 1-5pm; admission 10฿.)

■ Phitsanulok พิษณุโลก

Phitsanulok was once an important satellite of the Sukhothai kingdom. Ayutthaya kings trained here to become military leaders and coached their armies to fight the Burmese. Both King Naresuan the Great and his brother Prince Ekathotsarot were Phitsanulok natives. Since then the city has maintained a military tradition, but has submerged its history in a morass of modernity. From the late 1960s through the early 1980s, the Third Army of Thailand was stationed in the city to combat the communist rebels in the hills of Nan. The recent Cobra Gold exercises between Thai and American forces have perpetuated the town's military tradition. Friendly, conveniently located, home to one of the world's most fabulous Buddha images, and birthplace of the famed "flying vegetable" dish, Phitsanulok is a popular and worthwhile stopping point on the way north.

ORIENTATION

Roughly shaped like a ladder, the center of Phitsanulok (usually referred to by locals as "Phitlok" or "Philok") is west of the Nan River and densely clustered between two north-south roads: **Ekathotsarot Road,** in front of the train station, and **Phutta Bucha Road,** which streams along the east river bank and contains the night bazaar. A number of important streets flanking the train station, namely **Naresuan Road** (straight out), **Sairuthai Road** (south), and **Phra Ong Dam Road** (north), run perpendicular, forming the rungs. South of the train station, **Borom Trailokanat Road** runs between the two main ladder legs before veering off into Phutta Bucha Rd. Behind the train station, two major roads run parallel (north-south) to the train tracks: **Wisut Kasat Road** and **Sanambin Road.** Both roads can be reached by crossing the tracks south of the station on Ramesuan Rd. The youth hostel and folk museum are on this side of the tracks. A postman's nightmare, the building numbers have little order. Use them for identification but don't depend on them for direction.

PRACTICAL INFORMATION

Tourist Offices: TAT, 209/7-8 Surasi Trade Centre, Borom Trailokanat Rd. (tel. 252 742). Turn left out of the train station and follow Ekathotsarot Rd. for 3 blocks. Take the right at Borom Trailokanat Rd.; it's in the middle of the block on the right. Good, necessary maps. Open daily 8:30am-4:30pm.

Tourist Police: (tel. 251 179), on Borom Trailokanat Rd. near TAT.

Tours and Travel: Phitsanulok Tour Centre, 55/45 Srithammatraipidok Rd. (tel. 242 206), near TAT. Open daily 9am-5pm.

Currency Exchange: Thai Farmers Bank, 144/1 Borom Trailokanat Rd. (tel. 258 599). Open Mon.-Fri. 8:30am-3:30pm. Many more banks on Naresuan Rd.

Air Travel: Phitsanulok Domestic Airport (tel. 258 029), on Sanambin Airport Rd. To **Bangkok** (5 per day, 920฿) and **Chiang Mai** (1 per day, 650฿). **Thai Air,** 209/26-28 Borom Trailokanat Rd. (tel. 258 020), near TAT. Open daily 8am-5pm.

Trains: Phitsanulok Train Station (tel. 258 005), on Ekathotsarot Rd. Most trains on the Bangkok-Chiang Mai route stop in Philok. To **Bangkok** (13 per day, 4-7hr., 3rd-class 69฿) and **Chiang Mai** (6 per day, 7hr., 3rd-class 65฿).

Buses: Phitsanulok Bus Station (tel. 242 430), on Phitsanulok-Lomsak Rd. The city is a popular transfer point for those entering and departing the north, northeast, west, and Bangkok. City bus #1 goes between the train and bus stations. To: **Bangkok** (22 per day, 6:30am-2am, 96฿; A/C 4pm, 163฿); **Chiang Mai** (23 per day, 7:25am-1:30am, 6hr., 86-104฿; A/C 146-155฿); **Chiang Rai** (9 per day, 7hr., 104-115฿; A/C 146-160฿); **Khon Kaen** (11 per day, 5hr., 92฿; A/C 2pm, 129฿, 1:30am, 166฿); **Nakhon Ratchasima** (10 per day, 6hr., 82-110฿; A/C 146฿); **Loei-Udon Thani** (9 per day, 4-7hr., 58-104฿; A/C 91-164฿); **Sukhothai** (every 30min., 5:40am-6pm, 1hr., 16฿; A/C 22฿); **Tak** (every hr., 6:20am-5pm, 3hr., 36฿; A/C 51฿); and **Mae Sot** (6 per day, 5hr.; A/C van 80฿).

Local Transportation: A well-marked **bus system** makes getting around town pretty easy. Bus #1 runs from city bus center along Naresuan Rd. Take a left out of the train station to reach the Philok Bus Station (5฿). Bus #4 runs from city bus center to airport (3฿). Buses stop running around 6pm.

Rentals: Lady Motorcycle Rental, 168/10 Ekathotsarot Rd.

Luggage Storage: at the train station. 5 ฿ per day up to 5 days. Open 24hr.

Markets: In the evening the southern section of Phutta Bucha Rd. along the river is ablaze with the **night bazaar.** Features the mega-publicized *phak bung loi faa* (floating-in-the-sky morning-glory vine), where your meal is launched into the air and caught on a plate by your waiter. The **day market** is located a block from the river adjacent to the night bazaar.

Medical Services: Hospital (tel. 258 812), on Srithammatraipidok Rd.

Post Offices/Telephones: GPO, on Phutta Bucha Rd., 0.5km north of Naresuan Bridge. Open Mon.-Fri. 8:30am-4:30pm, Sat.-Sun. 9am-noon. **Overseas calling** and **fax** next door. Open daily 7am-11pm. **Telephone code:** 055.

ACCOMMODATIONS

Low-priced hotels are scattered around the town center (80-100฿).

Asia Hotel, 176/1 Ekathotsarot Rd. (tel. 258 378). Take a left from the train station and walk 500m; the hotel is on the left. Innocuous rooms, but all the disadvantages of an impersonal hotel. Clean bathrooms with western toilets. Singles 150฿. Doubles 220฿. A/C rooms 350฿-450฿.

Phitsanulok Youth Hostel (HI), 38 Sanambin Rd. (tel. 242 060). Take bus #4, which goes to the airport. After the bus crosses the train tracks and turns right onto Sanambin Rd., look for the hostel on the left. Well-kept rooms are simply furnished and romantic private rooms have a teak four-post bed and mosquito net. Friendly owner speaks fluent English. HI membership is mandatory, but a one-night stamp can be purchased for 50฿. Six stamps and you're a member. All ages. Dorms 50฿. Singles 100฿. Doubles 130฿.

FOOD

The neighborhood around the mosque on **Phra Ong Dam Rd.** is full of Muslim cafés where you can enjoy thick, hot *roti* (10฿). For other eats, try the night bazaar. Flanking **the northern half of the river** is a touristy collection of floating restaurants, where for a few extra baht you can dine while cruising up the muddy Nan River.

Fakara, 52/1 Pra Ong Dam Rd., near the mosque. Muslim café run by an English-speaking Pakistani-Thai woman. Arguably the best food in Phitlok, with delicious 15฿ *lassis,* curries, and even A/C. Open daily 6am-8:30pm.

Sawng Ahung, 26/25 Sanambin Rd. (tel. 251 935), south and across the street from Naresuan University. Look for the pavilion, partially obscured by the bushes. A local favorite for breakfast and lunch. Rice-topped curry soups are popular, as are the excellent desserts. Open daily 6am-2pm.

SIGHTS

A gorgeous Buddha image preens in **Wat Phra Si Ratana Mahathat** (Wat Yai). The spectacular Phra Buddha Chinnarat (Victorious King) was cast in 1557 during the reign of Sukhothai's King Mahatammaracha. Encircled by a golden flame-dragon halo, it is one of the most duplicated of all Buddha images, and can be seen glimmering far outside the mother of pearl trimmed doors of the *wiharn.* (Open daily 7am-5pm.) Part of the temple has been turned into a small museum. (Open Wed.-Sun. 9am-4pm; admission 10฿.) The red #5 city bus which leaves every 10 minutes from the city bus terminal halts at Wat Yai (3฿).

The **Buranathai Buddha Image Factory,** 20/8 Wisut Kasat Rd. (tel. 259 228), handcrafts bronze Buddhas ranging from small figurines to huge wat-sized goliaths. The factory is in the backyard of Dr. Thawee's house. (Open daily 8:30am-5pm; free.) He has opened a fabulous **folk museum** across the street; if you only go to two museums, make this one of them. Dr. Thawee's dedication to the preservation of traditional artifacts has yielded one of the most comprehensive records of daily village life. (Open Tues.-Sun. 8:30am-4:30pm; donations accepted.)

ENTERTAINMENT

Nightlife in Philok is better than in most small tourist towns. Plenty of pubs and cafés have live music and the requisite karaoke bars and discotheques are great places to audition your newest pick-up line. Pubs are clustered on the far north end of Borom Trailokanat Rd. near the Pailyn Hotel. For a muscle relaxant, try **Bualang Thai Traditional Massage,** 57/59-60 Phra Ong Dam Rd. (tel. 259 235). The Wat Poh method (perfectly legit) is practiced here for 100฿ per hour. Open daily 11am-1am.

Studio 54, 38 Borom Trailokanat Rd. (tel. 252 411), in the Pailyn Hotel basement. Classy disco with dark corners and private tables. Open nightly 9pm-2am. Come after 11pm.

Folkway Pub, 20/2 Sanambin Rd. (tel. 21 120), across from Naresuan University, near the youth hostel. Students pack into this tiny restaurant/pub to listen to live performers croon western pop in incomprehensible English. Play "name that tune" all night. Open nightly 7pm-1am.

■ Near Phitsanulok: Phu Hin Rong Khla

The area surrounding Phitsanulok was once the sight of frequent clashes between the Thai army and the military branch of the Communist Party of Thailand, the People's Liberation Army of Thailand (PLAT). From 1967 to 1982, PLAT was able to survive in the hills, thick forests, and strange rock formations of the countryside.

Phu Hin Rong Khla, 123km from town and 30km from the Laotian border, was the Communists' headquarters and training ground, and the town filled with recruits after the bloody crackdown on student demonstrators in Bangkok in 1976. Unable to dislodge the Communists with the combined strength of the army, air force, navy, and national guard, the government finally struck a decisive blow by offering amnesty to all students who joined the movement after 1976. The government over ran the area in 1982 and turned it into a national park. A war monument was erected on **Khao Kur,** a hill 100km from town and the site of the army artillery base. The road to Khao Kur is a knock out; Hwy. 12 whisks past rice paddies, teak forests, and gently rolling hills. TAT provides a map. From Phitsanulok, take a bus to Kakhon Thai (every hr., 6:30am-6pm). From there catch a *songthaew* to the park or rent a scooter for the day to see it all. You can also book **bungalows** rented out by the Forestry Department for a night in Phu Hin Rong Khla. For more information contact the Forestry Department in Bangkok (tel. (02) 579 0529) or Golden House Tour Co. in Phitsanulok (tel. 259 973).

■ Sukhothai สุโขทัย

In 1238, having just sealed an alliance with the Mon people to form the Lannathai ("million Thai rice fields") kingdom, the Thais established a new capital city on fertile land near the Yom River, driving the area's former residents, the Khmers, to the east. Named Sukhothai ("Dawn of Happiness"), this city marked the birth of what came to be considered the first Thai nation. Although the era of Sukhothai rule was brief, its former glory has been preserved in its art and architecture, particularly in its spectacular ruins (now the "classic" Thai style). Today, a muddy river, relaxing atmosphere, and phenomenal guest houses will tempt you to remain.

ORIENTATION

New Sukhothai city is 12km to the east of the old city (*muang gao*), now a historical park. The new city is located in an L-shaped elbow of the Yom River. **Charot Withi Thong Road** runs along the Yom River and then makes a sharp turn to cross it at **Praruang Bridge,** in the corner of the "L." The road continues to the old city. **Nikhon Kasem Road** runs along the other leg of the Yom River "L." **Singhawat Road** runs parallel to Nikhon Kasem Rd., one block away from the river, and intersects Charot Withi Thong Rd. to form the city's largest intersection: the corner of the "L," near Praruang Bridge. **Pravet Nakhon Road** runs parallel to Nikhon Kasem Rd. on the opposite bank of the river. All the guest houses in town provide maps, or you can purchase a comprehensive one at the Chinawat Hotel for 10฿.

PRACTICAL INFORMATION

Currency Exchange: Most banks will change foreign currency and traveler's checks. Open Mon.-Fri. 8:30am-3pm. **Thai Farmers Bank** (tel. 611 932), on Charot Withi Thong Rd., at the base of the bridge. Others are on Singhawat Rd.

Buses: Government buses along with several private companies cluster in town near the cinema on Prasertpong Rd. Government buses to **Bangkok** (106฿) and **Chiang Mai** (91฿). **Win Tour Agency** (tel. 611 039), on Ramkhamphaeng Rd. has A/C buses to: **Bangkok** (10 per day, 5hr., 190฿); **Chiang Mai** (5 per day, 6hr., 91฿); and **Phitsanulok** (every 30min., 6am-6pm, 1hr., 14฿). Guest houses have printed schedules. Otherwise, investigate deals in town.

Local Transportation: The new town can be traversed easily by foot. *Samlor* rides cost 10฿ if you need them. To get to the old city, catch a *songthaew* (last one at 6pm, 5฿) at the terminal across the bridge, about 100m on the right toward the old city. Win Tours has buses to **Si Satchanalai Historical Park** (20฿).

Rentals: Bikes at **Historical Park** (25฿ per day). **Motorbikes** at **Sky Tours** (tel. 611 175), on Prasertpong Rd. near the cinema, or **Traveller Club** (130฿ per day).

Markets: If you cut through the wat at the base of the bridge, Sukhothai's **day market** greets you with durian, funky fish, and big smiles.

Medical Services: (tel. 611 782 or 622 701) is on the road to the old city.

Police: (tel. 611 010), on Nikhon Kasem Rd. Police boxes are at the old Sukhothai bus stop across the bridge and at the 2nd traffic light east of the bridge.

Post Offices/Telephones: GPO, 241 Nikhon Kasem Rd. (tel. 611 752), 1km from the bridge. Open Mon.-Fri. 8:30am-noon, 1-4:30pm, Sat.-Sun. 9am-noon. **Overseas calls** can be made 7am-10pm. **Postal code:** 64000. **Telephone code:** 055.

ACCOMMODATIONS

New Sukhothai is blessed with an abundance of hotels and excellent guest houses, and the competition keeps prices low. All listings are within walking distance of the bus station.

Ban Thai Guest House, 38 Pravet Nakhon Rd. (tel. 610 163), across the Yom River from the main bus stop. Take a left after the bridge at Thai Farmers Bank and walk 300m. Located next to Somprasang Guest House, Ban Thai offers bang for the buck. A patio in the well-kept garden overlooks the river. Bungalows with private bath 150฿. Singles in the refurbished antique house 60฿. Doubles 80฿.

Lotus Village (tel. 621 484), on Rajithanee Rd. From the bus station, head to the wat at the base of the bridge. Exit the wat's compound and go out the back gate. Walk through the market stalls along the river until you see a sign for the guest house. Spacious rooms and quiet teak bungalows nestled among gardens and pools containing catfish. Rooms 80฿ per person.

Somprasong Guest House, 32 Pravet Nakhon Rd. (tel. 611 709), near Ban Thai. Immaculate rooms, quiet atmosphere, and a porch with a view of town. Tidy Thai- and western-style facilities have hot water. Singles 50฿. Doubles with bath 80฿. Triples 120฿. A/C bungalows 300฿. Fabulous food for 20-30฿.

No. 4 Guest House, 97/31 Singhawat Rd. (tel. 610 165). From the traffic circle, take a left at the intersection of Singhawat Rd. and Srintharathid Rd., and then a left onto Soi Ni See. A smaller guest house for those who like homestays. Friendly owners Sud and Lin also offer Thai cooking lessons. Singles 60฿. Doubles 80฿.

FOOD

The best meals you'll find in town are in your guest house—the public eating scene is rather bleak. The **day market,** along the wall of Wat Ratchanee, has a handful of food stalls hawking decent noodles or fried rice (20฿).

Dream Café, 86/1 Singhawat Rd. (tel. 612 081), is across from Bangkok Bank, two blocks from the traffic light. This terribly hip spot is chock-full of antique knick-knacks. The guiding maxim here is "the best coffee is as black as the devil, as hot as hell, pure as a fairy, and fragrant as love." Amen. Cappuccino 45฿. Ten "secret formula" drinks available as well, guaranteed to cure anything from aches and pains to feeble libido (15฿). Open daily 10am-10pm. A smaller version of Dream Café is on Ramkhamhaeng Rd. next to Win Tours. Open daily 7am-10pm.

Traveller Club, 38 Prasertpong Rd. (tel. 611 186). This joint substitutes as the local TAT. Decent food, 2 movies per day, and a talkative owner make this a great place to wait for your bus or just pass the time. Free maps and tourist information. Motorbike rental 130฿. Open daily 8am-11pm.

SIGHTS

The **Old Sukhothai Historical Park** lies within the triple-layered walls of the old city. Outside of it, fragments of wats and *chedi* intermingle with homes, and can be explored along any of the paths branching out from the park's four main gates.

Tourists enter the park through **Kamphaeng Hak (Broken Wall) Gate**. To the left of the gate stands a museum which houses a eclectic collection testifying to the city's rich historical and cultural legacy. Inside the museum, among other artifacts, is a copy of the stone inscribed by King Ramkhamhaeng in Thai script—his own invention—

describing the town of Sukhothai. Also worth checking out are a large white elephant taken from the walls of Wat Chang Rop in Kamphaeng Phet, and a model of a 13-14th century Thai kiln. (Open 9am-4pm; admission 10฿.)

The museum is, however, merely a warm-up bout for the heavyweights inside the old city. (Open 6am-9pm; admission 20฿, good for the whole day.) The grand center-piece of the town is **Wat Mahathat,** one of the first ruins near the museum. The main *chedi* here is known for its lotus-bud shape—you'll see it in the background of many TV commercials advertising Thailand. Nearby **Wat Si Sawai** is an ancient Hindu shrine that was later converted into a Buddhist temple. The three *prang* are not as large as those at Wat Phra Phai Luang, but they are in better condition. You can poke around in the holes at the base of the stupa left by archaeological digs.

Farther north, 500m outside of **Sara Luang Gate,** is **Wat Phra Phai Luang.** Lying on an island encircled by a moat, the ruins have not been renovated to the extent that others in the area have. The magnificent Lopburi-style stupa are the most prominent feature of the site, while the crumbling plaster reliefs of Buddha are just hanging on for dear life. To the west of Wat Phra Phai Luang, you'll come to **Wat Sri Chum,** a square *mondop.* Inside is the massive Buddha sitting serenely as his face seems to drip with mascara streaks. Head 2km back toward New Sukhothai and hang a left at the small green sign leading to **Wat Chang Lom.** The wat has a large Lanka-style *chedi* buttressed by a force of 36 large white elephants. For those who can't navigate the sandy road to Wat Chang Lom, the smaller but structurally similar **Wat Sorasek** is within walking distance of the northern gate.

To get to the historical park, catch a *songthaew* on the west side of the river (5฿). Once you've traveled the 12km to the park, you can rent a bike for 20฿ and tool around. If you want to walk, heck, you can do that too. Bring sunscreen and water.

■ Near Sukhothai: Si Satchanalai

During the 13th century, along with Phitsanulok and Kamphaeng Phet, **Si Satcha-nalai** completed the triangle of power and influence surrounding the capital. The city's fortunes waxed during this period, bringing a wealth and sophistication comparable to that of Sukhothai. As the capital waned in the following century, political power went south to Ayutthaya, and the thriving metropolis of Si Satcha-nalai sunk into anonymity (literally, losing its name).

With the recent and marvelous success of Sukhothai as a tourist attraction, his-tory is repeating itself for the city. The old city continues to rival its former capital in aesthetic appeal; though not yet in popularity. The outlying ruins are diamonds in the rough, yet to be liberated from the jungle soil.

Start at the **Visitors Information Centre,** clearly marked by signs from the roads entering the park. The headquarters contains a scale model of the entire area and a comprehensive museum, detailing the history and architectural significance of the important ruins. They have an English brochure with excellent pictures and an incomprehensible map here as well (5฿).

Backtrack to the main road running along the river and turn left. The old city ruins edge the southwest bank of a turn in the Yom River. The entrance is past Don Laew Gate. Go left at the entrance. Just ahead on the right is **Wat Chang Lom,** the city's central wat. According to the ancient inscriptions, King Ramkhamhaeng ordered the temple's construction in 1287 AD; the style was imported from Sri Lanka concurrent with the introduction of the island's brand of Buddhism.

Five km in the opposite direction, ruins of ancient kilns are found at **Ban Ko Noi.** The unearthing of 200 kilns here destroyed archaeological misconceptions of ancient Thai economic isolation and technological simplicity. The city's kilns produced advanced celadons for export to countries as far away as what is now the Philippines. Kiln #61 has an adjacent museum, displaying ceramics dating back hundreds of years. Open daily 8am-4:30pm; admission 20฿.

Buses deposit you at the highway exit across the river from the park. Bicycles can (and should) be rented here, for 20฿. When waiting for the bus home, be viligent, the bus won't slow unless your in its way. Luckily for those born to be wild, a **motorbike** is the best transport for seeing Si Satchanalai. From new Sukhothai, take Hwy. 1195 (across the river and preferable to Hwy. 101 on the Sukhothai-side of the river), in the direction of Old Sukhothai. Follow this road 31km to its end, turn left and continue for 1km, then right at the sign. Go 15km up to a sign which directs you left to the park. Follow signs to Si Satchanalai Historical Park (not the Si Satchanalai National Park or Si Satchanalai city which is 11km to the north of the ruins). For an interesting detour, stop and check out the wacky **Wat Tawet** 6km out of new Sukhothai on Hwy. 1195. There's a light-green water tower on the left around the 6km mark; go about 200m more and take a right onto the small paved road.

If you cannot return to Sukhothai, shell out big-city bucks to stay at resort-level "bungalows" just outside the park, or take a *songthaew* from the bus stop 12km south to Sawankhalok. **Muang Inn Hotel** is at the intersection of Hwy. 101 and Kasemat Rd. near the Win Tours Agency in town (tel. 642 622). All rooms have fan and private bath. Singles 120฿. Doubles 160฿. **Food** is available from stands at Wat Phra Si Ratana Mahathat or restaurants between there and the park entrance.

■ Mae Sot แม่สอด

People come to Mae Sot expecting border action, mystery, and intrigue. To their surprise, they stumble instead upon fabulous foliage, friendly folk, and phenomenal bargains. Lying 7km from the Burmese border, Mae Sot is one of three trading zones between Thailand and Burma. South of Mae Sot, Um Phang sits barely touched by tourism, offering opportunities for wilderness adventure. The drive from Tak to Mae Sot takes you through splendid mountain scenery and lands you in the middle of paradise.

ORIENTATION

Mae Sot's two major roads run parallel to each other. **Intirakiri Road** has one-way traffic heading east and **Prasatwithi Road** has one-way traffic heading west toward **Moei Market** and the Burmese border 7km away. The large **city market** is off Prasatwithi Rd. near the Siam Hotel. Mae Sot is small enough to explore by foot.

PRACTICAL INFORMATION

Tourist Offices: No such office, but you can stop by **Myawaddy Café** or **West Frontier Guest House** to pick up guides and rap with the owners.

Tourist Police: 738/1 Intirakiri Rd. (tel. 532 960), next to Guest House No.4.

Tours and Travel: Rather than have a company take you down to Um Phang for trekking, consider going down yourself and booking a tour in Um Phang with Mr. T at Trekker Hill. If you want to book in Mae Sot, Mr. Wiboon at B&B House runs **Mae Sot Conservation Tours.** His wife, Boong, is a reporter and is well informed about border events. In 1997, they expect to take trekkers across to Burma. A TAT-approved leader, Mr. Wiboon is friendly and recognizes Um Phang's need to protect its environment. **Mae Sot Travel Centre,** at S&P Guest House (tel. 531 409, in Bangkok 573 7942), has TAT-approved treks to the north or south. **To avoid scams, make sure your guide is TAT approved.**

Currency Exchange: Bangkok Bank, 124/8 Prasatwithi Rd. (tel. 531 639), has a **24-hr. ATM** which takes Visa, AmEx, and PLUS. **Thai Farmers Bank,** 94/9 Prasatwithi Rd. (tel. 531 020). Both open Mon.-Fri. 8:30am-3:30pm.

Air Travel: Airport 3km to the west of town. **Thai Air** office, 110 Prasatwithi Rd. (tel. 531 730). Open daily 9am-5pm. Shuttle is 20฿. Flights leave Tues., Thurs., Sat., and Sun. to: **Chiang Mai** (12:45pm, 590฿) and **Bangkok** (9:50pm, 1405฿).

Buses: There are 4 bus stations in town. The bus station to and from **Bangkok** (10 per day, 6-10hr. depending on class; 125฿, A/C 224฿, VIP 345฿) is on Asia Rd. next to the Michelin Man sign. *Songthaew* to **Mae Sariang** leave from the market area behind the police station (5hr., 150฿). *Songthaew* to **Um Phang** leave from the southern side of town (4hr., 80฿). To find the bus to Um Phang, walk away from

Myawaddy Café on Prasatwithi Rd. Turn right at the Fuji film store. Follow the blue sign just past Haji Yusoof & Sons. Orange and white minivans to **Tak** leave from the station across from Mae Sot Plaza just off Intirakiri Rd. 1 block west (against traffic) of the police station (1½hr., 28฿). Buses to **Chiang Mai** leave from the same station (4 per day, 96฿, A/C 172฿).

Local Transportation: You can walk anywhere in town. To get to **Moei River Market** and the **border,** catch a navy blue **songthaew** across from Myawaddy Café on Prasatwithi Rd. (last one back at 6pm, 7฿).

Medical Services: 1km south of town (tel. 531 224).

Police: (tel. 191) at the intersection of Tang Kim Chiang and Intirakiri Rd.

Post Offices/Telephones: (tel. 531 227), on Intirakiri Rd. Facing the police station, head right. Open Mon.-Fri. 8:30am-4:30pm, Sat.-Sun. 9am-noon. **Overseas calls** can be made 8:30am-4:30pm. **Postal code:** 63110. **Telephone code:** 055.

ACCOMMODATIONS

Neighborhoods on Intirakiri and Prasatwithi Rd. play host to the majority of Mae Sot's crash pads. Guest houses are relatively inexpensive.

West Frontier Guest House and Restaurant, 8/2 Watoon Rd. (tel. 532 038). Facing away from the market area in the Tak bus station, head right; it will be a block away on the left. Spacious rooms and spotless common bathrooms. A great place to feast on delectable Thai dishes. Singles 70฿. Doubles 120฿.

Guest House No. 4, 736 Intirakiri Rd. Facing the police station, head left about 600m. Unwind in the common room with cable TV. Futons in the all-teak dorm room 40฿. Private singles 70฿. Doubles 90฿. Common bathrooms with hot water.

B&B House, 415/17 Tang Kim Chiang Rd. (tel. 532 818). At the police station on Intirakiri Rd., head toward the Pim Hut sign. B&B is a few doors beyond. Orderly and hygienic chambers. Hot water flows lavishly in the exceptionally clean common bathrooms. Dorms 50฿. Private rooms with 2 single beds 100฿. Mr. and Mrs. Wiboon speak perfect English and are ready to help travelers.

FOOD

Mae Sot's ethnic melting pot ladles out a multicultural stew of culinary delights. Family-run restaurants along Prasatwithi and Intirakiri Rd. serve up Muslim, Thai, and Chinese food, but the **night market** makes for mighty slim pickin's.

Myawaddy Café, 100/22 Prasatwithi Rd. (tel./fax 532 549). Head west (with traffic). It is on the right, past all the banks. Doi and Roger sell Burmese lacquerware in one half of the shop and western food in the other. Nightly western meal—salad, garlic bread, the works (100-180฿). Mornings feature all-you-can-drink coffee 15฿. Open Thurs.-Tues. 7am-9pm. The owners also have maps of the area and like to give out information.

SIGHTS

This cross-cultural scene extends to the **Moei River Market** at the Burmese-Thai border 7km west of town, where cheap products are imported from Burma. Go via blue *songthaew* on Prasatwithi Rd. across from the Myawaddy Café (7฿). (Open daily 8am-6pm.) Riding a bike to the market takes you by rice paddies and makes for a pleasant half-day trip.

Between Mae Sot and the town of Tak is **Lan Sang National Park,** where clear water cascades down gneiss rock steps. The first fall may have up to 10,000 visitors a day (in April), but few walk on to the third and most serene fall, Pha Te. The path snakes 8km through dense forests, terminating in Mon, Karen, and Lisu villages. Tourists may ask to see the 20-minute slide show before beginning the trip. Bungalows are available (150฿); the restaurant is open daily 8:30am-5pm. The Tak minibus (28฿) goes to the entrance. From the Tak-Mae Sot highway, you can wait for a *songthaew* (30฿) or walk the 3km to the visitors' center. You'll pass the Park Headquarters and camping area (5฿ per night) on your way up. (Open 8am-4:30pm; admission 5฿, with a vehicle 20฿.)

■ Um Phang อุมผาง

Um Phang is a cultural delight waiting to be discovered. The pint-size polis hosted only 500 trekkers last year, compared with the 6000 visitors stomping around Chiang Mai. Statistically speaking, Um Phang gives off good vibrations: the 3000 Mon and Thai residents are welcoming, and the natural wonders are awe-inspiring. A four-hour *songthaew* ride snakes through rice paddies, corn fields, chili plantations, banana groves, and 1500m-high peaks, finally ending 164km south of Mae Sot, only 30km from Burma. Um Phang can be a heaven for hearty trekkers or a prison for posh city folk. It has a cool climate, night chills, and lots of creepy-crawlies; bring warm clothes and insect repellent.

ORIENTATION AND PRACTICAL INFORMATION

Um Phang is small—very small. Two parallel roads make up the main arteries of this mini-metropolis. **Pravesphywan Road** leads you into town, and there is another street to the west of it. *Songthaew* leave Mae Sot between about 7:30am-4pm to make the four-hour journey (80฿). Most of the *songthaew* back to Mae Sot leave between 6-10am, but a bus will leave around noon. As you enter town, the **post office** is on the left. (Open Mon.-Fri. 8:30am-4:30pm, Sat. 9am-noon.) Taking the first left onto the paved road heading uphill leads to the **morning market** on the left and the **hospital** (24-hr. emergency care) on the right in about 300m. Back on the main road, the **pharmacy** is open daily 7am-9pm. The **police station** (tel. 561 112) is on the road parallel to Pravesphywan Rd. Turn right down the dirt road past Trekker Hill, then left. **There are no banks and no overseas telephone** operators in Um Phang. **Postal code:** 63170. **Telephone code:** 055.

ACCOMMODATIONS AND FOOD

Guest houses in Um Phang are rapidly popping up as locals realize that *farang* are in need of lodging, and that lodgings translate into baht. The **Trekker Hill** (tel./fax 561 090) company, headed by Mr. Jantawong (Mr. T) has a wonderful Thai-style teak shelter decked out with futons, mosquito nets, and toilet paper. The dorm goes for 50฿ per person, or you and your mate can shack up in a private mini-bungalow for 100฿. Mr. T's motley troupe of fun-loving guides will escort you through dense jungles, placid hill-tribe villages, and the breathtaking **Tee Lor Su Waterfalls** by raft, elephant-back, and foot. The food and service are so fabulous you'll almost feel guilty.

To explore Um Phang's other options, go past Mr. T's on the main street, and take a right at the wat. **Um Phang Guest House** (tel. 561 021) is first up on your left, with basic rooms and a woefully common wash area for 50฿. Next up is **Um Phang House** (tel. 561 073). Bungalows range significantly in cleanliness. All go for 350฿ per person. Most guest houses will rustle up chow for 25฿, or head to an open-air restaurant on the main street. Proprietors shut down by 10pm.

SIGHTS

The buzz of crickets, the hum of the river, the green hills, and the smiles of the town-folk will soothe your soul. If the hills, jungle, and river aren't enough, then book a trek and take that body on an adventure. The TAT has made an effort to have trekking companies register with the government. This way, Thailand can keep tabs on trekking companies, ensuring that they adhere to safety and environmental rules, as well as to national hiring practices—Burmese Karens are not allowed to work as guides. As a tourist, you might want to support the TAT, even if it means paying a few more baht. Guides are probably too polite to admonish you for littering, but you should treat Um Phang (and the rest of Thailand) as if it were your own living room—watch where you prop your feet and discard candy wrappers.

Northeast Thailand

NORTHEAST THAILAND

Thais call it "Isaan," denoting prosperity and vastness. This expansive arid plateau encompasses about one-third of Thailand's total land mass, supporting an equal proportion of the nation's population. Among Thais, Isaan has a reputation as an economic and cultural backwater. They have it half right. Isaan *is* one of the country's poorest regions, and the lifestyle remains largely agrarian. The dry season is always excruciatingly hot and dusty, with many water shortages, and the rainy season does not always deliver relief. Many towns and villages appear to be devoid of young adults: males leave home to earn more money as *tuk-tuk* jockeys or construction workers in urban areas, while numerous women are forced into prostitution.

In all other respects, however, this negative attitude is simply a misconception, stemming from differences in history, geography, and culture. In the past, the giant plateau has been isolated geographically from the rest of the kingdom, and the people have had a greater cultural and genealogical kinship with the Laotians and Khmers across the Mekong River. It was due to Isaan's isolation and close ties to the neighboring countries that the U.S. set up air force bases in the region's four largest cities during the Vietnam War. The U.S. military presence helped trigger a period of rapid economic growth in these areas, which remain centers of transportation, commerce, and education.

Unlike other parts of the country, Isaan has yet to trade in its homespun essence for a more commercially appealing countenance. Communication can be an obstacle in Isaan for travelers who don't speak Thai or the local dialect. Perhaps as a result few tourists are willing to brave the region's rudimentary infrastructure and vastness, but those who come are rewarded with a human beauty that is fast disappearing in more developed regions.

THAILAND

■ Khao Yai National Park อุทยานแห่งชาติ เขาใหญ่

For travelers who have a few days left in Thailand and want to rescue their lungs from the clutches of Bangkok fumes, Khao Yai National Park and its gateway city, Pak Chong, can be the salvation. Consecrated as Thailand's first national park in 1961, Khao Yai remains the forerunner of Thailand's extensive and impressive national park network.

PAK CHONG

Stocked with good food and shopping, Pak Chong is the jumping-off point for trips to Khao Yai National Park. The town extends on either side of **Mittaphap (Friendship) Highway.** Streets branching off both sides of the highway have blue signs in Thai and English and are named **Tesaban Road** followed by a number. The entire town is only about 1km long. The **day market,** starting from Tesaban 21, extends one block from the main road from dawn until about 4:30pm, and is stocked with flashlights, dead fish, some camping gear, and more. A **supermarket** on Tesaban 17 sells similar wares daily 9am-10pm. After 4:30, the **night market** (Tesaban 17-19) is the place to be for dinner and people-watching. **Thai Farmers Bank** (tel. 311 501) with its large green English sign, is next to the day market near Tesaban 18. It has a **24-hr. ATM** which takes Visa and MC. Traveler's checks and western currency are exchanged Mon.-Fri. 8:30am-3:30pm. The **post office,** on the corner of Tesaban 25, handles telegrams, money and postal orders, faxes, **international phone calls** (collect for 30฿ and cash), and parcels Mon.-Fri. 8:30am-4:30pm. (**Postal code:** 30130.) There's a privately run **phone center** beside the post office can place HCD calls for a 30฿ service charge. (Open daily 6am-10pm.) **Telephone code:** 044.

The **train station** (tel. 223 37 62) sits at the end of Tesaban 15. Trains go to **Bangkok** via **Ayutthaya** (7 per day, 7:30am-1:50am, 4½hr., 40฿). At the **regular bus station** near Tesaban 18, you can catch daily buses beneath the pedestrian overpass to: **Chiang Mai** (3, 5am, 3pm); **Nakhon Sawan** via **Lopburi** (#121, 6:30, 8:20, 11:20am, 1:20pm); and **Sukhothai** (#572, 7:10, 9:20, 10:20, 12:20pm). The **A/C bus terminal** is beyond the post office next to the Shell station. You can also catch A/C buses at Tesaban 19, kitty-corner to 7-Eleven. Daily buses go to **Bangkok** (6am-2am, 80฿) and **Chiang Mai** via **Phitsanulok** and **Lampang** (8, 9am, 6, 8, 8:30pm).

Light-blue songthaew leave for **Khao Yai National Park** (40km, 20฿) from the highway when they have collected a sizable group of passengers.

Your best bet is Tom and Maew's **Jungle Guest House,** 63 Tesaban 16, Kongvaksin Rd., Soi 3 (tel. 313 836). From the bus terminal, head right to the stoplight at Tesaban 17. Take a left and, when the road forks, veer left. A huge sign announces the guest house about 50m on your right. From the train station, walk down Tesaban 15 until you hit the highway. Hang a left, then a right at the stoplight. Rooms with firm mattress, fan, western toilet, personal shower, and small breakfast go for 70฿. A 1½-day Jungle Adventure tour in Khao Yai National Park is offered here.

THE PARK

Khao Yai National Park, home to one of the last wild elephant herds, has over 40km of gorgeous hiking trails, mostly through rainforest and grasslands. Outlandish reptiles, insects, and vines crawl through it all, with hornbills, gibbons, and rhesus monkeys screeching several meters up in the canopy. The waterfalls alone are worth the trek. Don't mind the leeches—just stay clear of the brownish water.

There are two strategies for exploring the park. The bold should stay in the park and explore with a pal. The other option is to take a day tour. The park is open daily 6am-midnight (admission 10฿). Hitchhiking is common in the park (but *Let's Go* does not recommend this nefarious activity). Trekkers can pick up a road and trail map

(5฿) or hire a guide at the Park Headquarters and Visitors' Centre (at least 200฿ per group per trip).

Nasty relations between Khao Yai and encroaching resorts have left two rustic accommodations. A long wooden house (10฿) where the floor awaits you is near Park Headquarters and has food and shower facilities (10฿). Three km east, a campground has tents (100฿, showers 10฿). For **food**, try the **Khao Yai National Park Club House** located at the mid-point of the road that bisects the park north-south. (Open Mon.-Fri. 6am-11pm, Sat.-Sun. 8am-10pm.)

A simpler method is the **Jungle Adventure,** a 1½-day tour, based at the Jungle Guest House in Pak Chong. Trips leave daily at 3pm and terminate the next day, but you can split the full day and half day. The tour moves at a blistering pace and costs 650฿. Only fruit and soft drinks are included; food runs 40-60฿. Wise trekkers should bring good walking boots, a flashlight, and swim wear.

■ Nakhon Ratchasima (Khorat) นครราชสมา

Nakhon Ratchasima, locally known as Khorat, is the chief point of entry to the rest of Northeast Thailand. Located 256km northeast of Bangkok, Khorat is on the main corridor to all other destinations in Isaan. Most tourists drop in on this large, geographically strategic metropolis (pop. 205,000) for a stopover on their way to other attractions, but some use Khorat as a home base for daytrips to places such as Phimai, Dan Kwian, and Phanom Rung. Khorat is also famed for its silk; bargain-hunters scavenge here for textile deals.

Unfortunately, many travelers view Khorat as they might a trip to the dentist's office—a necessary evil. This reputation is unfair, for *sabaii,* the unique blend of warmth and generosity for which Thailand is justly famous, remains alive in Khorat to a degree not seen often in cities of its size.

ORIENTATION

Khorat is laid out on an east-west grid, divided by **Ratchadamnoen Road;** a rectangular moat surrounds the east side of town. **Chumphon Road** runs parallel to Ratchadamnoen Rd., not to be confused with **Chomphon Road** directly behind the **Thao Suranari Memorial.** The Memorial is an excellent landmark being located smack in the middle of these roads, marking the center of the city. The **train station** is on the west side of town on **Mukkhamontri Road.** The **TAT office** is on the highway-sized **Mittraphap Road,** which runs along the northern edge of the moat and finally curves south along the western edge of town. The office is across the road from the intersection with Mukkhamontri Rd., and a little to the left. The eastern part of Mukkhamontri Rd. forks into three roads before it reaches the moat: **Suranari Road, Phoklang Road,** and **Jomsurangyard Road.** These roads intersect Ratchadamnoen Rd. close to the Memorial. The **Bangkok bus station** is on **Burin Lane,** north of Suranari Rd.

PRACTICAL INFORMATION

Tourist Offices: TAT, 2102-2104 Mittraphap Rd. (tel. 213 666), on the western edge of town, easily reached by bus #1, 2, or 3. Get off just before Mittraphap Rd. and cross it on the footbridge. TAT is immediately on the left before Sima Thani Hotel. Helpful map of Khorat. Check the border situation if you plan to enter Cambodia. English spoken. Open daily 8:30am-4:30pm.

Tourist Police: Directly behind the TAT office (tel. 213 333). Limited English spoken. Open 24hr. **Emergency number:** 1699.

Tours and Travel: Khorat Business Corporation, Ltd., 37-39 Buarong Rd. (tel. 258 631). Offers 2 full-day tours 6am-6pm, covering Phimai, Phanom Rung, and Muang Tham. Car and driver 1500฿, English speaking guide 500฿. Also complete travel agency. Excellent English spoken.

Currency Exchange: Bangkok Bank of Commerce, 30 Phoklang Rd. (tel. 244 288), in the center of town. From the Thao Suranari Memorial, it's about ½ block down Phoklang Rd. on the right. Open Mon.-Fri. 8:30am-3:30pm. **Siam Commer-**

cial Bank, 306 Mukkhamontri Rd. (tel. 251 356). Across the street from the train station and to the right. Open 8:30am-3:30pm.

Air Travel: (tel. 255 425), south of town on Dejudom Rd. A 50-70฿ *tuk-tuk* or 80-100฿ *songthaew* ride. Airport tax 20฿. Daily flights to **Bangkok** (40min., 540฿). Flight times change frequently; contact Thai Air in Bangkok or Khorat. **Thai Airways,** 14 Manaf Rd. (tel. 257 211-13) between Mahatthai and San-Pasit Rd. Open Mon.-Fri. 8am-5pm, Sat. 8am-4pm, Sun. noon-4pm. AmEx, MC, Visa (cash only at the airport). English spoken. Transportation provided from airport to their office.

Trains: Nakhon Ratchasima Railway Station, Mukkhamontri Rd. (tel. 242 044). From the center of town, the station is 0.5km on the left once on the road. To **Bangkok** (9 per day, 8am-midnight, 6hr.) and **Ubon Ratchathani** (9 per day, noon-6am, 5hr.). 2nd class A/C is about 180฿ each way, sleepers are more.

Buses: Terminal 1, (tel. 242 899, for A/C 245 443), on Burin Lane. Service to **Bankok** only. Take bus #2 along Suranari Rd. and get off at the corner with the hospital; walk past it onto Burin Lane. Regular buses are a block up on the right. A/C buses 1 block farther. Buses are number-coded. To **Bangkok** (#21, every 20min., 90฿, A/C 115฿). **Terminal 2,** (tel. 256 007), north of town on Rte. 2 beyond the Takhong River. Take a motorcycle or *tuk-tuk* (30-50฿) there. Handles all traffic to all other destinations. To: **Surin** and **Ubon Ratchathani** (#25, 5 from 11:30am-2:30pm, 17 from 9pm-2:30am); **Khon Kaen, Udon Thani,** and **Nong Khai** (#22 and #211, roughly every hour); **Phimai** (#1305, every 30min., 5am-10pm, 1½hr., 16฿); and **Chiang Mai** (#635, 2 per day). Buses to **Phimai** leave from Mittaphap Rd.

Local Transportation: Samlor and **tuk-tuk** are omnipresent; bargain hard. From the TAT to the Thao Suranari Memorial should not cost more than 40฿. Take the city buses around town (3฿, A/C 5฿)—they're just as convenient (5am-10pm). Buses #1, 2, and 3 start on Mukkhamontri Rd. near the TAT office; they all go into the center of town. They split when Mukkhamontri forks into Suranari Rd. (#2), Phoklang Rd. (#1), and Jomsurangyard Rd. (#3). Exact change necessary. TAT city map has bus routes. *Songthaew* run these routes (3฿) with greater frequency.

Pharmacies: Amarin, 122 Chumphon Rd. (tel. 242 741), behind the memorial a little to the left. The owners speak enough English. "Rx" on the glass doors. Open 7am-9pm.

Medical Services: St. Mary's Hospital, 307 Mittraphap Rd./Rte. 2 (tel. 242 385), 50m south of Bus Terminal #2. Private hospital with excellent English-speaking staff. **Khorat Memorial Hospital,** 348 Suranari Rd. (tel. 230 215), past the Sri Pattana Hotel on the right walking from the Thao Suranari Memorial. Look for a green cross on the roof. English spoken. Visa. Open 24hr.

Emergency: tel. 191. Contact tourist police first (tel. 1699).

Police: (tel. 242 010), on Sapphasit Rd. between Washara Sit and Chainarong Rd.

Post Offices/Telephones: 48 Jomsurangyard Rd. (tel. 259 483). Facing the Thao Suranari Memorial, go right on Ratchadamnoen Rd. until you reach Jomsurangyard Rd. Turn right and pass Klang Plaza; it's on the right. Open Mon.-Fri. 8:30am-4:30pm, Sat. 9am-noon. **Overseas phone,** Mon.-Fri. 8:30am-3pm (tel. 242 046). For better hours, place calls at 371 Assadang Rd. From the moat, follow Assadang Rd. for 2½ blocks into the old city. It's on the left side. International phones open daily 7am-11pm. **Postal code:** 30000. **Telephone code:** 044.

ACCOMMODATIONS

Hotels in Khorat are blighted by the cookie-cutter syndrome. Symptoms include a functional toilet, token furniture, A/C options, and a creaky bed. Hotels of this model are all over town, so at least you can choose by location. Unfortunately, the ever-popular Khorat Doctor's house has closed down.

Potong Hotel, 658 Ratchadamnoen Rd. (tel. 242 084), at the corner of Phoklang Rd. opposite the memorial. Central location and good quality make this one of the better buys in Khorat. Western toilets are a godsend in this blue/green behemoth. Singles with fan 150฿, with TV and A/C 300฿. Doubles with fan 200฿.

Siri Hotel, 688-690 Phoklang Rd. (tel. 242 831), about 350m down Phoklang Rd. after Mukkhamontri Rd. forks. On the left side of the street, next door to the VFW

Thaosura Rd.
Phol Lan Rd.

TO WAT SALA LOI

Suranari Rd.

205

TO WAT THUNG SAWAN

Chok Chai Rd.

224

TO BURIRAM, SURIN AND UBON RATCHATHANI

Assdang Rd.
Wat Phra Narai Maharat
Chomphon Rd.
Mahatthai Rd.
Sapphasit Rd.
Police Station
Kamhaeng Songkhram Rd.
Ratchanikun Rd.

Prajak Rd.

Chang Phuak Rd.

Mittaphap Rd.
Pholsaen Rd.

Yommarat Rd.
Post Office

Night Bazaar

Chum Thang Train Station

Chaiarong Rd.

Juggree Rd.

Thao Suranari Memorial

Telephones

Chumphon Rd.
Ratchadamnoen Rd.

Ratchadamnoen Rd.

TO WAT PAA SALAWAN

Day Market

Clock Tower
Bus Terminal 1

Night Market

Post Office

Wat Suttha Chinda

Mahawirawong Museum

TO PHIMAI AND KHON KAEN

Hospital

Phoklang Rd.

Suranari Rd.

Jomsurangyard Rd.

2

Bus Terminal 2

Lam River

Mittaphap Rd.

Train Station

550

500

yards

meters

0

0

2

Soi Kingsawai Lieng

Soi Lamparoo

Mukkhamontri Rd.

General Post Office

TAT Office

TO BANGKOK

N

Banks $

Nakhon Ratchasima (Khorat)

THAILAND

cafeteria. No Bibles at this hotel, but packs of condoms are complimentary. Singles with bathrooms and fans 130-150฿. Doubles 200฿. A/C costs an additional 100฿. "Special room" with TV, A/C, and fridge, 600฿.

Sri Chompol Hotel, 133 Chompon Rd. (tel. 252 829). A short walk down Chompon Rd. from the statue. The hotel is on the left, opposite a Buddhist paraphernalia shop. Freshly painted walls will brighten your day; bathrooms with flushing squat-style toilet are also a luxury. Singles with fan 150฿, with A/C 220฿. Doubles with fan 220฿, with A/C 330฿.

FOOD

Mouth-watering cuisine is as plentiful as broad smiles and Thao Suranari statuettes in Khorat. The markets are fine places to sample regional specialties. It might be a good idea to try Isaan food in Khorat before moving on to more remote territory. Vegetarians should try **Ran Ahaan Jay Con Im,** 191/2 Suranari Rd. (tel. 252 726). (Open daily 7am-6pm.)

Dok Som, 130 Chumphon Rd. (tel. 252 020), behind the monument and on the left, with a Thai sign. Narrow façade with display case of tortes. The courtyard is in the rear, past the long bar and mirror-lined walls. The menu is bilingual, but the staff isn't. Thai and Chinese dishes with European items, and for the adventuresome, a page of Isaan cuisine. The spicy label is no joke. Entrees 25-100฿, though most are about 50฿. Open daily 10am-midnight.

Cabbages and Condoms (C&C Restaurant), 86/1 Sueb Siri Rd. (tel. 258 100), just a few steps past Soi 4 and before the train tracks. Look for the tiny bridge on the right just below a large neon Pepsi sign. Brainchild of PDA, a non-government group that supports family planning and AIDS education, hence the framed Thai condoms. A clean joint with an English menu. Try the "chicken in herb leaf bikinis" (60฿) or rice cooked in a pineapple (55฿). Open daily 10:30am-10pm.

Suan Pak, 540 Chumphon Rd. (tel. 255 877), behind the shrine and to the left, past Dok Som. Heavily tinted glass windows give the impression of dimly lit interiors with relaxing atmosphere. Wrong! Bright whiteness and waves of Thai pop music, punctuated by the tapping of the waiter's platform shoes, bombard the senses. Thai and Chinese entrees 30-120฿. Open 10am-midnight.

The VFW Cafeteria (tel. 256 522), adjacent to the Siri Hotel on Phoklang Rd. A slice of displaced Americana straight from the silver screen, exemplifying the cinematic "bar-and-grill"/GI hangout in every Vietnam War flick, down to the lazy ceiling fans and Miss February pinups. The expat hangout of Isaan. Cheeseburger 28฿, fries 10฿. Open 8am-9:30pm.

MARKETS

Bathed in the glow of a thousand incandescent bulbs, Khorat's **night bazaar** embraces the free market with abandon. Dozens of vendors fill two blocks of Marat Rd., between Chomphon Rd. and Mahatthai Rd., from 6-10pm daily. Piccadilly Circus meets Yankee Stadium in an orgy of jeans, t-shirts, tapes, and kitsch trinkets. Fiercely competing for sidewalk space, food stalls serve up fruits and Isaan snacks. Needless to say, this is the heartbeat of Khorat. More restrained, if equally raw, **Mae Kim Heng Market** occupies a massive warehouse opening onto both Suranari and Phoklang Rd., about a block beyond the city gate. Filled with lots of fruits and slaughtered livestock, the market opens some time after midnight and runs till the sun is high in the sky.

SIGHTS

Khorat proper is home to several intriguing sights that can be visited in a single, unhurried afternoon. The **Thao Suranari Memorial** in the center of town is the symbol that captures the spirit of Khorat best. Built in 1934 over the city moat between Ratchadamnoen and Chumphon Rd., the bronze statue depicts the heroic Khun Ying Mo, wife of Khorat's deputy governor who, in 1826, rallied the citizens (including 300 women volunteers) in the city's defense against Laotian invaders. Locals reverently refer to her as 'Yah Mo' (Grandmother Mo), wrap the shrine in ribbons, and burn copious amounts of incense. When prayers are answered, they sing their thanks in the local Khorat dialect or hire young women to dance in her honor. An annual **Thao Suranari Fair** (March 23-April 3) draws thousands of pilgrims.

If you're weary of seeing the same old wats all over Thailand, **Wat Sala Loi** offers a chance to set sail for new spiritual horizons. Located on the Takhong River a few hundred meters down a small road off Mittraphap Rd. at the northeast corner of the city moat, the wat has a *bot* shaped like a Chinese junk, symbolizing the passage of the devoted to nirvana.

Every city in Thailand has its sacred city pillar, from which all distances are measured. Khorat's is enshrined at **Wat Phra Narai Maharat** on Prajhak Rd. (between Assadang and Chomphon Rd.) inside the city moat. This wat contains one of Khorat's most sacred objects, a sandstone image of the Hindu god Narayana.

The **Mahawirawong Museum,** (tel. 242 458), Khorat's branch of the National Museum, is on Ratchadamnoen Rd., two blocks south of the shrine on the right. Its small collection contains artifacts from the Angkor and Ayutthaya periods. (Open Wed.-Sun. 9am-noon and 1-4pm; admission 10฿.)

ENTERTAINMENT

The karaoke plague has reached epidemic proportions in Khorat, with little sign of a cure. For temporary relief, the **Simi Thani Sheraton Hotel** (tel. 213 100), directly to the left of TAT, holds outdoor performances of Isaan music and dance (Wed.-Fri. 7-9pm; admission about 200฿). **Thai Boxing** kicks off at Khorat's stadium on Sunday mornings. Inquire at the TAT office. Khorat also has the standard array of movie theaters, nightclubs, and discotheques. **Klang Plaza II,** on the corner of Ratchadamnoen and Jomsurangyard Rd., offers Thai Top 40 and consumptive diversions to teenage mallrats, who swarm to and fro in bell-bottom jeans and primary colors.

Music Bank, on Mahatthai Rd. at the corner with Washire Rd. Coming from the center of town; it's on the right; look for the wooden façade and flashing lights of the restaurant next door. Singha 85฿, and enough whiskey to wet any outlaw's whistle. Munchies also available (40฿). Open daily 6pm-midnight.

Elite 2002 (tel. 260 154), on Jomsurangyard Rd. next to Scanners and across from Klang Plaza. Live Thai music is worth a trip, though the place is a forest of purple bar stools and difficult for dancing; save your Saturday Night Fever routine for the disco next door. 1 drink minimum (80฿). Open daily 9:30pm-1am.

Cocoon Beer House, on Jomsurangyard Rd., opposite Klang Plaza just to the left of the Elite 2002. Water buffalo skulls and old rifles decorate the walls of this small, open-air pub made entirely of packing crates. Remarkably peaceful, considering it faces the dynamic Elite 2002. Single beer 35฿, a pitcher of Carlsberg 150฿. Small snack menu; still can't escape the chicken feet, though. Open daily 7pm-6am.

■ Near Nakhon Ratchasima

DAN KWIAN VILLAGE

Tiny **Dan Kwian village** has long been famous for its distinctive rust-colored pottery, incised with detailed geometric patterns. The crafts are beautiful but also heavy and breakable. Still, vendors sell plenty of beads, necklaces, and belts, which fit nicely into luggage pockets. Take a half-day trip there and visit Mr. Pomsinsab, who produces pottery behind his shop and allows discreet visitors to wander. TAT also sponsors an information center (tel. 375 214). (Open daily 8:30am-4:30pm.)

Follow Chomphon Rd. behind the Thao Suranari Memorial and turn right on Chainarong Rd. At Khorat's south gate, do not exit. Turn left onto Kamhaeng Songkhram Rd. instead and walk past the herds of vendors. Just beyond on the right, you should see a small blue-striped bus (#1307, 30min., 5฿). Indicate to the driver the destination. Disembark when the small road forks into three lanes lined with little shops. To

THAILAND

return, wait on the left side of the road back to Khorat. When the bus comes, gesticulate wildly and make gorilla noises. Hopefully, it will stop for you.

PHANOM RUNG AND MUANG THAM

The ancient Khmer temples of **Phanom Rung** and **Muang Tham** are the tourist magnets of lower Isaan. Phanom Rung is larger, completely restored, and more impressive than Muang Tham. Transportation is not overly difficult, but you should set out early in the morning. From Khorat or Surin, catch bus #274 and get off at **Ban Ta-Ko** (25฿), which is clearly marked as the turn-off for Phanom Rung and Muang Tham. Here you will be accosted by the 'motorcycle mafia,' but if you are just going to Phanom Rung, you can catch a *songthaew* (around 15฿). If you would like to see both Phanom Rung and Muang Tham, motorcycle drivers will take you to the temples and wait while you tour the grounds. A round trip to both temples should cost 150-200฿. Do not pay all at once. This arrangement is especially recommended during the off-season or weekdays, when transport back can be unpredictable. To get back to Surin or Khorat, try to be back at Ban Ta-Ko before 5pm, as the buses plying the highway here run less frequently after that.

Prasat Hin Khao Phanom Rung Historical Park

Phanom Rung lies 383m above sea level, atop an extinct volcano. This superb temple, the closest thing in Isaan to Angkor Wat, was built between the 10th and 13th centuries AD and is among the largest of Khmer monuments, with some of the most detailed architecture and sculpture of its kind in Thailand.

Once inside the complex, climb the three terraced earthen platforms up to the "white elephant hall," a partially reconstructed stone structure on the right directly ahead. In front is the 160-m promenade leading to the main complex and its stairway. This avenue is lined with lotus bud-shaped pillars. You'll encounter the first of three *naga* bridges (a platform flanked by many-headed mythical serpents). The stairs to the main complex are not much of a chore; at the top is the eastern side of the main gallery. Once through the hallway of the gallery, you'll be standing on the third bridge and facing the east portico of the chamber leading to the main sanctuary. The lintel above this entrance is perhaps the most famous door fixture in all of Thailand. It was stolen, then resurfaced in the Art Institute of Chicago, and was eventually returned in 1988. (Open daily 6am-6pm; admission 20฿.)

Muang Tham

Muang Tham does not match the splendor of Phanom Rung, but some aspects of it provide an eerie glimpse of what the temple must have looked like before its restoration. The best sequence is to visit here and then continue to Phanom Rung. The Fine Arts Department has begun renovation of Muang Tham, but it will be a few years before the project is complete. (Open daily 6am-6pm; admission 20฿.)

■ Phimai พิมาย

The lethargic little town of Phimai, northeast of Khorat, boasts only two main streets, but has the good fortune (or savvy town planning) of having grown up around an impressive Angkor-period Khmer temple. The ruins, now largely restored, constitute the Prasat Hin Phimai Historical Park. The recently opened Phimai National Museum, in addition to being an architectural triumph, provides an engaging complement to the temple. A few km east of the town center is Phimai's third don't-miss attraction: Sai Ngam, or "beautiful banyan," a leafy behemoth that dwarfs its arboreal brethren. Two first-rate guest houses and an excellent restaurant make a night in this narcoleptic village worth your while.

ORIENTATION AND PRACTICAL INFORMATION

Buses to Phimai depart from Khorat's Bus Terminal #2 (#1305, every 30min., 5am-10pm, 2hr., 16฿). Stay on the bus until it stops at **Phimai Bus Station,** at the south end of **Chomsudasapet Road.** At the opposite end of the street, the temple is visible. Toward it is **Thai Farmer's Bank** (open Mon.-Fri. 8:30am-3:30pm) on the left. A few doors down is **Baiteiy Restaurant,** an informal tourist information center. Past it, also on the left, is the narrow alley leading to the guest houses. Both offer **bike rentals** (10฿ per hour, 30฿ per day). Chomsudasapet Rd. ends at the gate to the historic park. **Anantajinda Road** runs along the front of the park. To the right, it passes a clock tower, which houses the **police** pavilion and the **night market.** Bus #1305 leaves Phimai for **Khorat** (every 30min., 5am-7pm). For those headed north to **Udon Thani, Khon Kaen,** or **Nong Khai,** get off at Talad Khae, 10km away from Phimai, and ask someone where to wait. To reach the **post and telegraph office,** 123 Srikeaw Rd., go left on Anantajinda Rd. at the gate to the park. **Srikaew Road** is the first right, 100m down, and follows the western edge of the park. The post office is 150m on the left. (Open Mon.-Fri. 8:30am-4:30pm, Sat.-Sun. 9am-noon.)

ACCOMMODATIONS AND FOOD

Old Phimai Guest House, 214 Mu 1 Chomsudasapet Rd. (tel. 471 918). Approaching the park from Chomsudasapet Rd., the alley is on the left just after an Agfa film shop. A wonderfully airy, bright wooden house overseen by a cheerful English-speaking family. Rooms are palatial. Dorms 80฿. Singles 100฿. Doubles 140฿. A/C rooms 300฿. 10฿ discount for HI members. Overseas phone service. Tours of Phanom Rung and Muang Tham available.

S & P New Phimai Guest House, 213 Mu 1 Chomsudasapet Rd. (tel. 471 797), across from the Old Phimai Guest House. Rooms are so big the owner could double his occupancy by dividing them in half. Ideal for those seeking some quiet: no noise except for the family watching Thai TV. Cramped dorm rooms 60฿. Singles 80฿. Doubles 100฿. Triples 150฿. Helpful travel info on the walls downstairs.

Baiteiy Restaurant, 246/1 Chomsudasapet Rd., to the right leaving the alley to Old Phimai and S&P Guest Houses. Unique laterite construction, it's a restaurant as ancient Khmers might have built. No trip to Phimai is complete without a plate of Phimai-style fried noodles (25฿). Extensive English menu boasts a variety of Thai foods (25-150฿). Open daily 7am-midnight.

SIGHTS

Phimai's *raison d'être* are the stately Khmer ruins smack in the middle of town, now the **Prasat Hin Phimai Historical Park.** At its zenith, the Angkor empire (802-1431) covered all of mainland southeast Asia. Testimonies of its power and wealth can be seen in the hundreds of temples which still dot the region. At one time, a laterite highway linked Phimai with the empire's magnificent capital, Angkor Thom, 225km to the south. This red sandstone temple was built in a style similar to that of Angkor Wat in the late 12th century, probably during the reign of Jayavarman VII. Unfortunately the archeologists from the Fine Arts Department went a bit overboard with their "restoration," hence the abundance of cement and the incongruous plaster ceiling in the central sanctuary. On the right as you cross the stone causeway with *naga* balustrades, is a collection of faded sandstone lintels. Although the temple is dedicated to Buddhism, many of the lintels depict Hindu gods and myths or scenes from the epic *Ramayana,* evidence of the Hindu tradition that preceded the spread of Buddhism. (Open daily 7:30am-6pm; admission 20฿.) (For more information, see **Cambodia: History** on page 59.)

North of the park, about 0.5km along the road that runs past the east perimeter of the temple complex, is the **Phimai National Museum** (tel. 471 167), on the right in a large white building with a red tiled roof. The museum is well worth a visit, as it includes an extensive collection of Khmer and Dvaravati art, as well as interesting anthropological exhibits documenting the social, political, and economic history of the Isaan region. (Open Wed.-Sun. 9am-4pm; admission 10฿.)

For a less cerebral diversion, **Sai Ngam**, the largest banyan tree in Thailand, stands on the bales of the Moon River about 2km east of town. It's a 10-minute bike ride tops; facing the park, head to the right on Anantajinda Rd. past the clock tower and follow the signs, sticking to the rust-tinged main dirt road. Descending under Sai Ngam's thick green canopy is like entering some J.R.R. Tolkien-inspired netherworld. Vines brush against your face, and even at high noon much of the brutal tropical sun is filtered out by the leaves. Wizened old men sit at card tables and will read your palm for a few baht. At the center stands a small pagoda, which houses the spirit of this 360-year-old miracle. A long pavilion at the entrance to Sai Ngum houses a number of noodle stalls and souvenir stands. Other attractions in this pleasant pavilion include a traditional Isaan house built on stilts, a flower garden, and a statue of **Sock Prasat Hin,** a famous Thai boxer from Phimai.

■ Surin สุรินทร

Fifty-one weeks out of the year, Surin remains a rare stop on most itineraries, since many travelers prefer to press on to the Mekong River. Their loss is your gain, for those who do venture to this delightful provincial capital find themselves witnesses to a slice of Isaan life the omnipresent tourist industry has yet to devour. One week a year, at the end of November, Surin has its 15 minutes of fame, when hordes of tourists, Thai and *farang* alike, flood the town for the annual Surin Elephant Roundup. In addition, the many small Khmer ruins that dot the province make fine daytrips. Under the stewardship of the Fine Arts Department, these ancient monuments retain an enchanting, if crumbling, grandeur.

ORIENTATION

The provincial capital of Surin is 452km from Bangkok and easily reached by bus or train from Bangkok, Nakhon Ratchasima, and Ubon Ratchathani. The main street, **Thornsarn Road,** runs north-south. At its north end is the train station, just behind the elephant statue. Several blocks away is a prominent traffic circle. To reach it from the bus station, exit to the left, pass the *soi* with the sign for the Petchkason Hotel, and take the next right. Thornsarn Rd. is the first intersection. From the traffic circle, continue south along Thornsan Rd., heading away from the train station. This block contains the post office (immediately on the right past the traffic circle), several banks, and a hotel. The next cross street is **Krung Sri Nai Road.**

PRACTICAL INFORMATION

Currency Exchange: Bangkok Bank, 252 Thonsarn Rd. (tel. 511 443), just past the traffic circle on the right. Open Mon.-Fri. 8:30am-3:30pm.

Trains: Surin Railway Station (tel. 511 295), at the end of Thornsan Rd. To **Ubon Ratchathani** (10 per day, 3hr.) and **Nakhon Ratchasima** (10 per day, 3hr.). Many of these trains continue on to **Bangkok.** Prices vary according to type of train (30-80฿, more to Bangkok).

Buses: Surin Bus Terminal (tel. 511 756), on Chit Bam Rung Rd. From the traffic circle, it's 1 block east, past Mr. Donut and 2 blocks to the left on the right hand side. Bus #274 runs to **Nakhon Ratchasima** (every 25min. until 4pm, 4hr., 41฿). A/C Nakhomchai buses to **Ubon Ratchathani** leave just behind the terminal (every hr., 3-7pm, 3hr., 81฿).

Local Transportation: A samlor around town should cost about 25฿. Pay a little bit more for **tuk-tuk.**

Markets: The **day** and **night markets** are in the same location, along Krung Sri Nai Rd. From the train station, walk one block past the traffic circle and turn right.

Pharmacies: Virat Pharmacy, 6 Chit Bam Rung Rd. Head north on Thonsarn and take a right at the elephant statues. Follow Mitari Rd. until it intersects Chit Bam Rung. The pharmacy is on the left at the corner. Open daily 6am-9pm.

Medical Services: Ruam Paet, Tessabarl 1 Rd. (tel. 513 192). Facing the train station at the traffic circle, turn right. Several blocks down on the right hand side is the hospital. Private and more expensive than **Surin Hospital** on Lakmuang Rd., but there is more of a chance of finding an English-speaking doctor here.
Emergency: tel. 191.
Police: Surin Police Station (tel. 511 007), on Lakmuang Rd.
Post Offices/Telephones: Surin Post Office (tel. 511 009), on the corner of Thornsan and Tessabarl 1 Rd. at the traffic circle. Open Mon.-Fri. 8:30am-4:30pm, Sat.-Sun. 9am-noon. Phone (7am-10pm) and telegram services (8am-6pm) open daily. **Postal code:** 32000. **Telephone code:** 044.

ACCOMMODATIONS

Surin's hotels are mostly empty year-round, except during the elephant round-up festival in November, when rates can go up as much as 50% and finding a room becomes nearly impossible.

Pirom's House, 242 Krung Sri Nai Rd. (tel. 515 140), 2 blocks past the market. Mr. Pirom gives tours (at reasonable prices) that are famed for their spontaneity and the interaction between guests, Mr. Pirom, and the villagers. Their comfortable, Thai-style home has a beautiful pond, which is actually part of the old city moat. Dorms 50฿. Singles 70฿. Doubles 120฿. Gate is locked at 10:30pm.
Santhong Hotel, 279-281 Thornsarn Rd. (tel.512 009). Heading north, it's on the right just before the traffic circle, opposite the Bangkok Bank. Look for the Nid Diew sign. This hotel is clean, airy, and well maintained. Bedsheets so crisp any drill sergeant would be proud. Singles 200฿ or less with shared toilet, with A/C 300฿. Doubles 280฿, with A/C 400฿. Small kiosk and overseas phone too.
New Hotel, 6-8 Thonsarn Rd. (tel. 511 322), immediately outside the train station on the right side of the road. Basic and conveniently located. All rooms come with private bathroom. Singles 150฿. Doubles 240฿. Catch up on any Thai soaps you missed while touring the outback by shelling out 30฿ extra for a TV in your room. Triples available. A/C rooms have warm water.

FOOD

Surin has some of the best Isaan food around, especially at the **market** (at the intersection of Tessabarl 3 and Krung Sri Nai Rd.) which is open almost 24 hours. If Isaan food ain't up your *soi,* pardner, then rustle up the best hamburgers this side of the Rio Grande, cooked just the way you like 'em by a Texas cowpoke.

Pai Ngen (tel. 512 151), on Soi Poi Tanko off Krung Sri Nai Rd. As you leave Pirom's Guest House, head east toward the market and take the first right. It's 100m down on the left. Popular with the locals, and it's no wonder—their Thai and Isaan food is delicious. *Laap* 25-30฿, *nua nam doag* 25-30฿. Mr. and Mrs. Pirom can recommend dishes to those who can't read Thai. Prices are not rock bottom, but the food is worth it. Open daily 9pm-midnight.
Country Roads Café and Guest House, 165/1 Sirirat Rd. (tel./fax 515 721), on the outskirts of town. Facing the train station, turn right and walk parallel to the tracks. Country Roads is 300m down on a corner to the right. Owned and run by a native Texan and his Thai wife, this restaurant/bar sports an English menu with authentic hamburgers, pizza, and fries for the homesick. The bar includes liquors rare in Thailand (Kahlúa, Malibu, etc.). Open 10am-3am.
Wai Wan Restaurant, 44-46 Sanitnikhomrat Rd. (tel. 511 614). From the train station, take the second left onto Sanitnikhomrat Rd. Wai Wan will be halfway down the block on the right. Look for the wood paneling. Wai Wan is three restaurants in one: Western, Thai, and ice-cream parlor. Triple your pleasure with three-colored rice (sausage, olive, and crab) or three-colored cake (vanilla, strawberry and *bai duey*). Steaks (90-250฿) or more traditional Thai rice dishes (30-40฿) available. Open daily 8am-10pm.

SIGHTS

Surin is a pleasant place to relax and enjoy Isaan life, but there's not much in the way of "official" sights, unless you're there for the annual **Elephant Round-Up** at the end of November (check with TAT for exact dates). The stars of this two-day festival are the 200 pachyderms who perform spectacular feats of strength and skill, reaffirming their slot as the national animal. Highlights include a battle re-enactment, fought in the ancient style, and a staged "elephant hunt" exhibiting traditional Suay techniques. The finale features a soccer match played by the surprisingly agile beasts, who would give Pelé a run for his money (or crush him to a bloody pulp anyway). Touristy, but not something to be passed up.

■ Near Surin

Anyone can go to one of the local silk-weaving villages. Communication barriers and wary Thai villagers however, makes learning the entire silk-making process rather difficult for the average traveler. This is where Mr. Pirom's tours (see Pirom's Guest House, above) can come in handy. Pirom knows the people well, and as a go-between for travelers and locals, he makes learning about rural Thailand easier. His tours go to places like **Ban Ta Klang,** a Suay village where elephants are trained and kept as pets, **Ban Khaosinarin,** traditional silk-weaving villages, and numerous Khmer ruins and temples such as **Prasat Srikhoraphum.**

If you are going solo to the villages, walk toward the train station on Thonsarn Rd. After the traffic circle, enter the second alley on the left. Trucks here ferry people the 20-odd km. Get here early to avoid a wait or an overnight in the village.

In the past, travelers have used Surin as a staging ground for trips across the border into Cambodia at Chong Kham. At press time, however, the territory on the Cambodian side has fallen into the hands of the Khmer Rouge and the border remains sealed with no plans to re-open it. Inquire at the TAT for the latest details.

■ Ubon Ratchathani อุบลราชธานี

Ubon Ratchathani (pop. 100,000), the "Lotus City," is known simply as "Ubon" to Thais. One of the larger metropolitan centers in the country, Ubon is the commercial magnet for this corner of Thailand. Despite a small collection of temples, a noteworthy museum, and its renowned silk and cotton cloth, Ubon does not attract many travelers except during the **Candle Festival,** which celebrates the start of Buddhist Lent in late summer. The holiday is a time of great pageantry and rejoicing, and is well worth the trip. Ubon makes an excellent jumping-off point for exploring the archaeological sites, national parks, and charming villages (many of which can only be reached from Ubon) sprinkled along the Mekong River region to the east. Downstream, the river flows into the "emerald triangle" where Thailand, Laos, and Cambodia meet amidst lush jungle.

ORIENTATION

Although the city is readily accessible by air, bus, or train, Ubon is the last stop on the eastern leg of the national railway network. To go farther east or north, travelers must rely on the confusing bus system.

Ubon's main thoroughfare, **Uparat Road,** runs essentially north-south. At its north end, it is called **Chayangkun Road.** To the south, it crosses the **Moon River** into **Warin Chamrap District,** where the train station is located. Buses #2 and #6 go there from Ubon proper. On the north side of the river, Uparat Rd. passes the riverside market, and, two blocks up, intersects **Khuanthani Road.** The hospital and museum are at this intersection and the tourist office several blocks to the right. One block farther on, Uparat Rd. meets **Sinarong Road** on which the tourist police and post office are located. A moat-enclosed park is opposite the police. The airport is in the northeastern corner of the city and bus stations are scattered throughout.

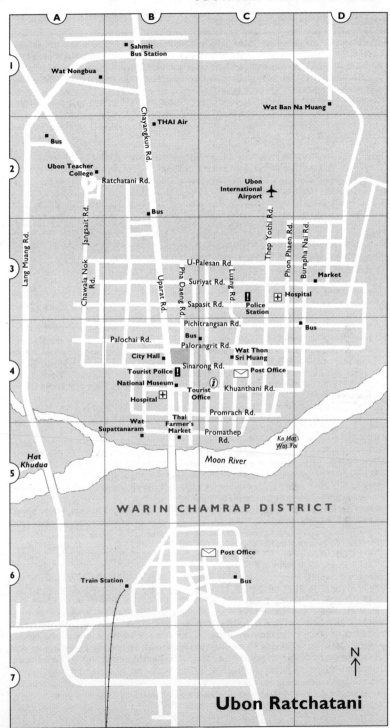

A　B　C　D

1

Sahmit
Bus Station

Wat Nongbua

Chayangkun Rd.

THAI Air

Wat Ban Na Muang

Bus

2

Ubon Teacher
College

Ratchatani Rd.

Ubon
International
Airport

Lang Muang Rd.

Bus

Jangsait Rd.

Thep Yothi Rd.

Phon Phaen Rd.

Burapha Nai Rd.

3

Chawala Nok
Rd.

Uparat Rd.

Pha Daeng Rd.

U-Palesan Rd.

Suriyat Rd.

Luang Rd.

Sapasit Rd.

Market

Hospital

Police
Station

Pichitrangsan Rd.

Palochai Rd.

Bus

Bus

Palorangrit Rd.

Wat Thon
Sri Muang

City Hall

Sinarong Rd.

Post Office

4

Tourist Police

National Museum

Tourist
Office

Khuanthani Rd.

Hospital

Promrach Rd.

Wat
Supattanaram

Thai
Farmer's
Market

Promathep
Rd.

Ko Hat
Wat Tai

Hat
Khudua

Moon River

5

WARIN CHAMRAP DISTRICT

Post Office

6

Train Station

Bus

N

7

Ubon Ratchatani

PRACTICAL INFORMATION

Tourist Offices: Tourism Authority of Thailand (TAT), 264/1 Khuanthani Rd. (tel. 243 770). Going away from the river on Uparat Rd., turn right on Khuanthani Rd. at the National Museum. TAT is on the left two blocks down. Carries city map with bus routes. Friendly staff, some of whom speak decent English. Open daily 8:30am-4:30pm except major holidays.

Tourist Police: (tel. 245 505, emergency 1699), on the corner of Uparat and Sinarong Rd. English spoken, so call here before dialing the police.

Currency Exchange: Krung Thai Bank, 40-46 Uparat Rd. (tel. 242 280). Heading away from the river, it's on the right side just past the Promathep Rd. intersection. Open Mon.-Fri. 8:30am-3:30pm except holidays.

Air Travel: Ubon Ratchathani International Airport (tel. 243 037), on Thepyotee Rd. Thai Air has morning and evening flights to **Bangkok** (1405฿). **Thai Airways,** 364 Chayangkun Rd. (tel. 313 340), 2km north of the river on the right. Open Mon. 10am-4pm, Tues.-Sun. 8am-4pm. MC, Visa.

Trains: Railway Station (tel. 321 878; advance ticketing 321 004), on Sathani Rd., Warin Chamrap District. To **Bangkok** (7 per day, 6:50am-7pm, 13hr., express 175฿) via **Surin** (31฿) and **Nakhon Ratchasima** (88฿).

Buses: There seem to be as many bus stations in Ubon as there are possible destinations. At the far north end of town along Chayangkun Rd. (take bus #2 or #3) is the **Sahmit bus station.** To **Mukdahan** (1 per hour until 1pm, 45฿). Some continue to **Udon Thani** (110฿) or **Nakhon Phanom** (70฿). This station is particularly confusing—always double-check your destination. **Sayan Tour bus station,** 2km beyond the traffic circle, at the northwest end of town along Jangsanit Rd. has daily buses to **Udon Thani** (13 per day, 5:30am-2:30am, 97฿) via **Khon Kaen** (70฿). Buses to **Bangkok** (10 per day, 5am-7pm, 159฿) leave from Uparat Rd., 1 block before Ratchathani Rd. Two blocks east of the Uparat-Palorangit intersection **A/C buses** leave to **Bangkok** (8 per day, 8:15am-9:30pm, 278฿, VIP 325฿) and **Chiang Mai** (6 per day, 12:15-6:30pm, 445฿, VIP 500฿). Buses leave from **Warin Chamrap bus station** south of the Moon River (take bus #1, 3, 6, or 7, 3฿) to **Surin** (every 30min., 7am-5pm, 40฿) and **Phibun** (every 15min., 6:20am-5:30pm, 12฿). From Phibun, *songthaew* run to **Khong Chiam** and **Chong Mek** (see **Near Ubon Ratchathani**).

Local Transportation: City buses cover Ubon and Warin Chamrap. TAT map has bus routes. Buses are 3฿ and run 6am-6pm. **Tuk-tuk** and **samlor** also roam the streets, but they can be expensive. *Samlor* trips shouldn't go beyond the river.

Rentals: Cho Watana, 39/8 Suriyat Rd. (tel. 242 202), 1 block west of the Uparat-Suriyat intersection. Motorbikes cost 250฿ per day, cars 1200฿ and up. A 500฿ deposit for bikes; 5000฿ for cars. International drivers permit required.

Markets: The riverside market is an around-the-clock affair: the "day" market becomes the "night" market at 5pm. Crossing the bridge into Ubon, the market is visible immediately to the right of Uparat Rd.

Pharmacies: Chepwaen, 16-18 Ubonsak Rd. (tel. 242 765). Ubonsak Rd. is opposite TAT and the pharmacy is on the left, just past a small alleyway. Contact lens supplies are available. Open Mon.-Sat. 8am-8:30pm.

Medical Services: Rom Klao, 123 Uparat Rd. (tel. 244 658), 2 blocks down Uparat Rd. From the bridge, it's on the left just before Khuanthani Rd. Private service, English-speaking doctors.

Emergency: tel. 191.

Police: (tel. 254 216), on Sapasit Rd. at the Thebyotee Rd. intersection. Contact the tourist police first (tel. 1699).

Post Offices/Telephones: GPO (tel. 254 000), on Sinarong Rd. Walk past TAT on Khuanthani Rd. and turn left at the 2nd intersection. 1 block north is Sinarong Rd. The post office is on the right hand corner. *Poste Restante* is behind the office. Open Mon.-Fri. 8:30am-4:30pm, Sat.-Sun. 9am-noon. Telephone and telegram service open daily 7am-11pm. AmEx, Visa, MC. **Postal code:** 34000. **Telephone code:** 045.

ACCOMMODATIONS

There are two decent guest houses in **Khong Chiam,** a small town 60km due east of Ubon near the Laotian border, and one in **Warin Chamrap,** only a few km south. The hotel scene in the city is pretty gloomy.

River Moon House, 43-45 Sisaket 2 Rd., Warin Chamrap (tel. 322 592). Exit left on the main road in front of the train station and walk 1½ blocks until the road merges with Sisaket Rd. It's next to the fire station. An abundance of musical instruments provides the tools for an Isaan jam session. Attractive, freshly painted rooms with monster double beds and traditional Isaan furniture (100฿). Free breakfast eaten family-style downstairs.

Ratchathani Hotel, 297 Khuanthani Rd. (tel. 244 388), a small step above the rest. A/C lobby is great for relaxing with Peace Corps volunteers who flock here on their off-days. Color TV and western bath in every room. Uninspiring, high-priced restaurant in the back. Central location. Singles 280฿, with A/C 450฿. Doubles 400฿, with A/C 600฿. VIP rooms 800฿.

Sri Easan Hotel, on Ratchabat Rd., directly across from the riverside market. From the bridge, take the 1st right onto Promathep Rd., and the 1st right from there onto Ratchabat Rd. The Hotel is on the left. Don't let the management or dingy aspect get you down. Singles 150฿. Doubles 200฿. All rooms come with private bath and a powerful fan.

FOOD

For cheap dining use the **market,** off Promathep Rd. east of Uparat Rd. Open virtually 24 hours to serve your stomach. At night, **vendors** also gather off Khuanthani Rd. on Rachabut Rd. near the Ratchathani Hotel. Several Chinese restaurants nearby on Khuanthani Rd. are open well past midnight.

Bua Boo Cha Mangsawirat, 11 Sri Saket Rd., Warin Chamrap (tel. 323 360). From the Warin Chamrap train station, walk straight ahead and turn right onto Uparat Rd. Turn left at the next and Bua Boo is on the immediate right. A large round clay well, framed with gnarled roots, dominates the room. Popular with devout Buddhists, as the Thai and Lao veggie cuisine is first-rate. Each topping is 6฿ and served over special *koklan* rice (whole-grain mixed with wheat grain). Open Mon.-Sat. 6:30am-8pm.

Chiokee Restaurant, 307-317 Khuanthani Rd. (tel. 254 017). With your back to the Ratchathani Hotel, turn left and cross the small intersection. The restaurant is across the street from the National Museum. Very popular, especially in the mornings. Breakfasts 20-50฿ (fresh OJ, 15฿). Voluminous menu has large Thai and western selections. A bit pricey, but worth it. Noodle and rice dishes 30-60฿. Meat dishes 50-100฿. Western standards (25-40฿). Open daily 6am-9pm.

Italian Pizza, 115 Phon Phan Rd. From the post office, walk 3 blocks away from the city center. Turn left on Phon Phan Rd. and walk 2 blocks to the Pichitrangsan Rd. intersection. Look for the red "Italian Pizza" painted on the gables. This is the real thing made by a bona fide Italian from Milan. Seven styles of pasta, eight types of pizza (80-250฿, depending on size), and 6 types of spaghetti (50-70฿), plus other western and Thai favorites. A/C. Open Tues.-Sun. 11:30am-10pm.

SIGHTS

The **Ubon Ratchathani National Museum** (tel. 255 071), considered one of the best in the country, documents the geology, paleontology, archaeology, history, and culture of the region. Most of the exhibits have excellent English translations, and there is even a small replica of the prehistoric paintings at Pha Taem if you can't make it all the way out to see the real thing. The museum is on the left side of Khuanthani Rd. immediately after turning right off Uparat Rd. The building, built in 1873, was formerly the Governor's office. (Open Wed.-Sun. 9am-4pm; admission 10฿.)

Wat Thon Sri Muang is on Luang Rd. opposite the provincial kindergarten school. Built during the Chakri Dynasty, this wat is over 200 years old, and the interior walls have paintings depicting life in ancient Ubon. Two relaxing spots on the Moon River provide idyllic diversions for locals. **Ko Hat Wat Tai** is an island surrounded by a village of huts perched on stilts above the water. Locals order food from the restaurants on the island and picnic in the small thatched huts. Sensational sunsets over the Moon River make for romantic interludes. During the dry season (Dec.-April), the island can be reached by a bamboo footbridge. If you walk east to the end of Promrach Rd. and then turn right and walk down to the river bank, you'll see the island and the bridge. When the bridge is closed, the island is inaccessible and closed to the public. Similar to Ko Hat Wat Tai in terms of what it has to offer, **Hat Khudua** is on the north bank of the river 12km west of town.

ENTERTAINMENT

The Cave, out of town 2 blocks past the Uppalesarn intersection, on the left. This is the place to see and be seen in Ubon. Remarkable "cave art" which proves once and for all that killer whales roamed the streets of prehistoric Ubon. Live music on weekends; the band plays unusually good Thai rock and a smattering of English tunes. Whopping 140฿ weekday and 160฿ weekend cover gets you two drinks. Open daily 9pm-5am.

SHOPPING

Ubon is famous for its silk and cotton cloth. Two stores that sell clothing made from the area's unique handwoven cotton are the **Maybe Cotton Hut,** 142 Sinarong Rd. (tel. 254 932), and **Peaceland,** 189 Thepyotee Rd. (tel. 241 821). Maybe is a block east of the post office. (Open daily 7:30am-9pm.) Peaceland is 2½ blocks north of Maybe; turn left on Thepyotee Rd. and it will be on the left beneath the bougainvillea. (Open daily 10am-8pm.)

Those looking for world-famous Isaan silk should try the **Women's Weaving Cooperative** in the village of **Ban Pa-Ao,** 17km north of Ubon. Begun by CARE international with a staff of three, the cooperative has blossomed into an award-winning operation. Their traditional *mutmee* silk in an array of colors and patterns is beautiful. Prices begin at 650฿ per meter, and run well into the thousands. Weavers will be happy to perform demonstrations upon request. The showroom also sells clothes, mostly women's blouses and skirts, starting at around 450฿. Special tailoring is available. (Open daily 8am-5pm.) Any bus heading north from the Sayan Tour bus station passes Ban Pa Ao. Tell the ticket collector to drop you off there (10฿). From the main road, the cooperative is about 3km east; motorcycle taxis can take you the rest of the way for 10฿. To return to Ubon, simply flag down any bus heading south to the city or catch a *songthaew* directly from the village (6฿).

For a more general selection of local handicrafts, try **Ban Phan Chat,** 158 Ratchabut Rd. (tel. 243 433). Exit right from the TAT office and turn right again at the first intersection. The store is on the immediate right. (Open Thurs.-Tues. 9am-8pm.)

■ Near Ubon Ratchathani

Not far outside Ubon city (about 12km on the way to Si Saket) is **Wat Paa Nanachat Beung Wai,** a forest monastery with predominantly western monks. English is spoken here, so any foreigner studying meditation and the Buddhist religion should visit this wat. Strict rules regulate separation of the sexes. The monastery is behind a peaceful rice field off the highway to Si Saket, near Beung Wai village. Catch a Si Saket-bound bus or *songthaew* from the Warin Chamrap bus terminal and ask to get off at Wat Nanachat (4฿). The best time to visit is before 11am.

Along the southern border of the province with Cambodia is the large, ancient Khmer temple complex of **Khao Phra Wiharn.** It's far away and difficult to access, but can be reached from either Ubon, Si Saket, or Surin. Before making the trip, check at the TAT office to see if it is currently open, since periodic fighting makes things dangerous. To date, it has been closed since June 1994, when Khmer Rouge forces won control of it, and the situation still looks grim. If it is open, however, and the site is deemed safe, you will still have to pass through Thai and Cambodian military checkpoints before entering and pay about 100β at each one. The semi-restored temple is built on a 500m-high escarpment overlooking the Cambodian jungle. To get there, catch a bus to Kantharalak from the Warin Chamrap bus terminal, and from there ride a *songthaew* to the temple. It's a three-hour trip one way.

KHONG CHIAM

Sixty km east of the city, at the confluence of the Moon and Mekong Rivers, lies the tranquil hamlet of Khong Chiam. To local young people it's "Sticksville," but to the traveler, weary of the heat and dust of larger metropolises, it's paradise. Only the two main streets are paved, and children squeal and hide when a sweaty *farang* toting a heavy backpack trudges up the road. The simplest way to get here is to take a bus from the Warin Chamrap bus station to Phibun Mangsahan. From the Phibun market, take a *samlor* to the *songthaew* station near the Moon River (10β). *Songthaew* leave approximately every 30 minutes (12β). Check with the driver to make sure he's headed to Khong Chiam. The Apple Guest House has a list of departure times and destinations of *songthaew* leaving from the market.

The town is shaped like a parrot's beak, jutting out into the two rivers. **Klaewpradit Road** runs from the market and bus stop straight through the center of town, ending at a wat. Walking across the temple grounds leads to a small pavilion that affords an excellent view of the spot where the two rivers meet (called the Two-Color river in reference to the different levels of silt suspension in the water, a phenomenon clearly visible from shore). The **post office** and a small branch of **Krung Thai Bank** are located along Klaewpradit Rd. near the Apple Guest House. **Rimkheng Road** runs along the Mekong River just north of Klaewpradit Rd. Here a stone tablet opposite the police station identifies Khong Chiam as the easternmost point in Thailand. Several good restaurants line Rimkheng Rd. farther down, all affording excellent views of the river, with Laos on the other side.

Khong Chiam supports several fine guest houses of which the **Apple Guest House,** 267 Klaewpradit Rd. (tel. 351 160), is tops. From the market head right on Klaewpradit Rd. It's about 300m down the road, past the bank and opposite the post office on the right. Rooms are large and clean. Singles and doubles are 80β, with A/C 250β. Thai-style bathrooms are communal while A/C rooms have private baths. The small restaurant in front contains a helpful information board. Motorcycles are rented for 150β per day.

The **Khong Chiam Guest House,** 355 Pakumchai Rd. (tel. 351 079), is located off Klaewpradit Rd. From the market take a right onto Klaewpradit, then another right just before the VIP restaurant. Khong Chiam has fairly new, spotless rooms with bath for 100β, with A/C 250β. Motorcycles are rented for 150β, bicycles 50β.

To the north of Khong Chiam is the recently designated **Pha Taem National Park,** where a 200m stretch of prehistoric rock paintings, dating back over 3000 years, has been found. There is no public transport to this park, but you can get there easily with a map and rented wheels from either guest house in Khong Chiam. Road signs along the way make the trip easier. Once at Pha Taem, it's a 500-m walk to the paintings. Trails along the top of the cliff offer gorgeous views of the river and Laos. **Tana Rapids National Park** is about 3km south of Khong Chiam on the Moon River.

BORDER CROSSING: CHONG MEK/VANG TAO

Before the opening of the Friendship Bridge linking Nong Khai with Vientiane, the tiny, remote village of **Chong Mek** was the only location from which travelers could enter Laos on foot. From the even more minuscule village of **Vang Tao** on the Lao side, it is a short ride to **Pakxe,** an excellent springboard for exploring southern Laos. Other than the border crossing itself, there is little of interest to travelers here, unless you come on Saturday or Sunday, when a lively market springs up on both sides of the border. Located in the boonies, 44km southwest of Phibun, Chong Mek can only be reached from Phibun. From Ubon, take a bus from the Warin Chamrap station to

Phibun. At the Phibun market, locals can direct you to *songthaew* heading to Chong Mek (80 min., 13฿).

The Thai market is much larger, although it consists largely of commercial goods, with little in the way of souvenirs or handicrafts. The smaller market on the Lao side consists of a few stalls proffering an array of wicker baskets, lacquer boxes, and rotgut Vietnamese whisky. Only on these two days are foreigners allowed to cross the border freely, but they can proceed no more than 250m onto Lao soil. There are rumors, however, that foreigners can no longer cross to the Lao market now without a visa. Check with the tourist office for more information.

Travelers intending to officially enter Laos here must first obtain a visa stamped with the appropriate entry point (i.e. Vang Tao), from the Lao Embassy in Bangkok. **Visas obtained in Nong Khai are not valid here.** Before crossing the border you must officially register your departure from Thailand at the Thai immigration office on the right, about 30m before the fence. Once in Laos, present your visa to the Lao immigration office, also on the right just beyond the border (entry tax 10฿). From Vang Tao, a *songthaew* can take you to Pakxe for 10฿.

■ Mukdahan มุกดาหาร

Mukdahan was carved out of Ubon Ratchathani and Nakhon Phanom Provinces in 1982. It lies midway along the eastern border of Isaan with the Mekong River to the east, directly opposite the Lao city of Savannakhet. There is a strong Lao flavor to this small, dusty provincial capital, whose population speaks a fifty-fifty mix of Thai and Lao. While admittedly not Ansel Adams territory (good luck finding a postcard in Mukdahan), some beautiful vistas can be had along the river at twilight. Few *farang* make it out this way, and those who do can expect many genuine attempts at conversation. Students on motorbikes cajole you into practicing English with them, and children flee at the approach of a backpack-toting stranger. Even policemen will break from traffic-directing to shower travelers with curious questions.

ORIENTATION

Mukdahan is right on the river, with the Mekong always to the east. The town is laid out on a grid, with streets running roughly parallel (north-south) and perpendicular to (east-west) the river, which is a good point of reference. In the center of town, at the intersection of **Chaiyankan Road** (runs toward the river) and **Phitak Phanomket Road** (parallel to the river), lies a **traffic circle.** Closer to the river, Chaiyankan Rd. crosses **Samut Sakdarak Road.** Along the Mekong's bank is **Samron Chaikhong Road.** This is the site of the daily **Indochina Market.** Facing the river, the immigration pier is at the left end of Samron Chaikhong Rd. From the pier **Song Nang Sathit Road** runs away from the river, parallel to Chaiyankan Rd. Song Nang Suthit Rd. crosses Samus Sakdarak Rd. near Huanum Hotel and crosses Phitak Phanomket Rd. near Hong Kong Hotel, the police station, and the bank. Several blocks farther from the river is the **night market.**

PRACTICAL INFORMATION

Currency Exchange: Thai Farmers Bank, 222 Song Nang Sathit Rd. (tel. 611 056), 2 blocks up the road from the pier and 1 block past Huanum Hotel on the left. Open daily 8:30am-3:30pm except holidays.

Buses: Mukdahan has no central bus station; locations of the stops vary according to the destination and the bus company. There are 2 major companies that operate in Mukdahan. One is **999VIP** (tel. 611 478), whose main stop is located before the night market, opposite the police box. To: **Bangkok** (4:30 and 7:30pm, 164฿; VIP 5:30pm, 445฿); **Nakhon Phanom** (every hr. 6am-5pm, 29฿), via **That Phanom** (15฿); and **Ubon** (every 30min., 6am-2pm). The other company is **927 Tour Co.** (tel. 611 813), across from the City Pillar Shrine on Song Nang Sathit Rd. To **Bangkok** (VIP, 3 per day, 8am-5:30pm, 287฿). More conveniently located, **Sahanit Tour** is along the block of Samut Sakdarak Rd. between Chaiyankan Rd. and

Song Nang Suthit Rd. A/C buses to: **Ubon** (6 per day, 8:30am-5pm, 2½hr., 77฿) and **That Phanom** (5 per day, 9am-4pm, 50฿).

Markets: The **Indochina market** sets up daily at the waterfront. Many merchants come to Savannakhet across the river, bringing bounties of...stuff. The **day market** is off Chaiyankan Rd., 500m west of the traffic circle. Turn right just before the Play Palace Hotel. It is on the right, opposite the post office. The **night market** is on the segment of Song Nang Suthit Rd. in front of city hall, well past Huanum Hotel and the bank.

Pharmacies: Huan Hong Osoth Pharmacy, 38 Samut Sakdarak Rd. (tel. 612 002), opposite Huanum Hotel. English spoken. Open daily 6am-8pm.

Medical Services: The hospital is 2 blocks down on the right. English-speaking doctors can be found at **Mukdahan International Hospital,** 1km south of downtown on Samut Sakdarak (Mukdahan-Domton) Rd., just past Mukdahan Hotel.

Emergency: tel. 191.

Police: Mukdahan Police Station (tel. 611 333), Phitak Phanomket Rd. across the street from Hong Kong Hotel. Some English spoken.

Post Offices: Mukdahan Post and Telegram Office (tel. 611 065)**,** on Chaiyankan Rd. From the traffic circle, head away from the river 500m, passing the hospital to the right. At the motorcycle dealerships and the sign for the Ploy Palace Hotel, take a right. The post office faces the market. Open Mon.-Fri. 8:30am-4:30pm, Sat.-Sun. 9am-noon. **Postal code:** 49000

Telephones: 191/1 Song Nang Sathit Rd. (tel. 611 697). From the pier, walk down Song Nang Sathit Rd., past Huanum Hotel, the bank, and the field in front of the city hall. The overseas phone booth in front of the office will be visible down a small *soi* on the left. Open daily 7am-10pm. **Telephone code:** 042.

ACCOMMODATIONS

The downside to Mukdahan's lack of *farang* visitors is the complete absence of guest houses. Hotels offer simple, clean rooms with a ceiling fan and a communal Thai-style bathroom.

Hong Kong Hotel, 161/1 Phitak Phanomket Rd. (tel. 611 143), across from the police station. From the traffic circle facing the river, go left and it's on the left. Next to the Pith Bakery. Clean rooms, firm beds, and private, western-style toilets for just 140฿ (with fan) or 300฿ (with A/C and TV).

Huanum Hotel, 36 Samut Sakdarak Rd. (tel. 611 197), on the corner of Samut Sakdarak and Song Nang Sathit Rd., 1 block from the pier. Large rooms with enough chairs to host a national *mahjong* tournament. Singles with shared bath 120฿, with private bath 220฿, with A/C 300฿. Doubles with shared bath 200฿, with private bath 300฿, with A/C 400฿. All A/C rooms have hot water and TV.

FOOD

The riverside restaurants are all quite similar. When the sun goes down, tables are set up outside so that diners can enjoy the cool breeze off the Mekong while the lights of Savannakhet begin to wink in the twilight. The **night market** along Song Nong Suthit Rd. is also an excellent place to fill the belly.

Foremost Restaurant, 74/1 Samut Sakdarak Rd. (tel. 612 251). From Huanum Hotel walk past Huan Hong Osoth Pharmacy for 1 block. It's at the next intersection. Elevator music seeps through the A/C air while trendy Thais tap their feet approvingly. The pseudo-translated menu has Thai food and even some western selections. If there's something you want that is unlisted, inquire; chances are they have it. Most dishes 20-80฿. Open daily 7am-11pm.

SIGHTS

If you haven't gotten wats out of your system, you can contemplate the larger-than-life golden buddha as he contemplates the Mekong from **Wat Si Mongkan Tai** on Samron Chaikhong Rd. It is not the sights that make Mukdahan, but instead the people. Take the time to interact with locals who are proud enough of their limited English to approach you.

■ Near Mukdahan

Known for its interesting rock formations and caves, **Phu Pha Theop National Park** also has lots of barely visible prehistoric rock art, varied landscape (unusual rocks, bare plateaus, cliffs, valleys, waterfalls, forests, and streams), protected nature (barking deer, birds, monkeys, wild boar, civets, and late-blooming flowers), and trails throughout. The rangers here know the area well, and one even speaks English. Trail maps in English are available upon request from the park office at the entrance.

The collection of huge, oddly shaped rocks at the main entrance to the park are the chief crowd-pleasers. The undersides of many overhanging rocks are decorated with prehistoric paintings resembling those at Pha Taem. They are 3000 years old and are mostly handprints, enigmatic geometric patterns, shapes of animals, and some indications of calligraphic characters. They're all very faint, so ask one of the park rangers to point some out.

The main 2-km hike to the **Buddha Cave Waterfall** goes straight past the rocks. Most of the other trails are short side hikes offering mountain and cliff scenery as well as more weird rocky areas. The trails aren't always easy to follow; explore carefully. Signs in Thai direct trekkers right, left, and ahead; the arrows pointing straight ahead lead to the waterfall, past a slightly inclined rock plateau. The arrows then pass through to the forested area, down a mountain and up the next one, with beautiful scenery and foliage all along the way. During the rainy or cold season, the cascades of the waterfall can be heard upon approach. During the dry season, the waterfall is likely to have dried up to a pathetic trickle. Rickety wooden stairs lead to the **Buddha Cave,** which is to the left at the top. The large Buddha image here is surrounded by a coterie of thousands of smaller crumbling Buddhas placed on the rock ledges by devout followers.

Phu Pha Theop National Park can only be reached from Mukdahan by blue trucks and *songthaew* leaving town on the Mukdahan-Dontan Rd. (Route 2034) past Mukdahan Hotel on the right (2 per hour; last bus to Mukdahan 6pm; 5฿). Tell the driver to let you off at Phu Pha Theop (poo-PAH-tayp). You'll be dropped off on the main road next to a large 'Mukdahan National Park' sign on the left. The entrance is a 15 minute walk down a small paved road on the right. Go as early as possible; it gets mighty hot while hiking in these parts. (Open 8am-6pm daily.)

■ That Phanom ธาตุพนม

That Phanom overlooks the Mekong River, which flows gently by the southern part of Nakhon Phanom Province. Famous throughout Thailand and Laos, the town boasts the impressive Wat That Phanom. The temple's stunning gold leaf-covered *chedi*, rising nearly 60m above the ground, glints like a 24-carat needle in the noon-day sun, and at night, illuminated by flood lights, it appears like some divine rocket ship bound for nirvana. The region's Laotian and Vietnamese influence is apparent in That Phanom's architecture, its taste in food, and its bi-weekly waterfront market which draws merchants from across the river. Many travelers, enchanted by the slow pace of life, pause their *blitzkreig* itineraries to linger at this sleepy trading post. Accommodations fill up during the February Festival, when room prices inflate faster than a baboon's ass in heat—plan accordingly.

ORIENTATION

That Phanom, mid-way between Nakhon Phanom and Mukdahan is easily reached from either town by bus or *songthaew* (about 15฿). The main drag where buses and *songthaew* stop is **Chayangkun Road.** Wat That Phanom is on this road, but it is visible from almost anywhere in town because of its soaring *chedi*. The road leading directly away from the wat to the river is **Kuson Ratchadamnoen Road,** passing under a Laotian arch of victory and terminating at the **pier.** After the arch there is **Phanom Phanarak Road. Rimkhong Road** runs along the river. Everything is about a 15-minute walk from wherever you get dropped off on Chayangkun Rd., but *tuk-tuk* drivers will take you anywhere for 5฿. The recent widening of Kuson Ratchadamnoen Road to accommodate a grassy common and a fountain opening onto the pier has forced many establishments to seek new locations. Inquire at Niyana Guest House for a local map before striking out on your own.

PRACTICAL INFORMATION

Currency Exchange: Thai Military Bank, 99/13 Chayangkun Rd. (tel. 541 008). Facing Wat That Phanom on Chayangkun Rd., it's to the right about 1½ blocks away. Open Mon.-Fri. 8:30am-3:30pm.

Buses: Leave and arrive from Chayangkun Rd., mostly at the north end. To: **Mukdahan** (every hr., 7am-5pm, 1½hr., 15฿); **Udon Thani** (5 per day, 10am-1:30pm, 5hr., 62฿); and **Bangkok** (8am, 168฿; A/C 5:30pm, 234฿).

Markets: Lan Market is the heartbeat of the border trade, where a flotilla of Laotian vendors set up stalls every Mon. and Thurs. Open dawn to noon.

Medical Services: (tel. 541 255). 2km west of town on the highway.

Emergency: tel. 191.

Police Station: (tel. 541 266), in the north end of town (on the right side of Phanom Phanarak Rd.).

Post Offices/Telephones: GPO (tel. 541 159), sits way outside of town on Chayangkun Rd. After a long walk from Wat That Phanom, past the bank, past the *songthaew*, it's on the left side of the road. Open Mon.-Fri. 8:30am-4:30pm, Sat.-Sun. 9am-noon. **Postal code:** 48110. **International phone service** available during business hours. **Telephone code:** 042.

ACCOMMODATIONS

Niyana Guest House, 65 Soi Wee Tee Saw Ra Chon. From the victory arch facing the river, turn left onto Phanom Phanarak Rd.; 50m down the road, there are signs pointing down a small *soi* on the right to the guest house. Niyana, the free-spirited proprietress, manages the place by herself. On the weekends she teaches local children English; guests are welcome to help (1hr. gets a free curry dinner). If the guest house is full, Niyana will recommend another hotel, or let guests sleep on mats on the floor. Common bathrooms upstairs and downstairs. Dorms 50฿. Singles 70฿. Doubles 90฿. Bike rental available 25฿.

FOOD

Besides Niyana's kitchen, some of the best food comes from the food stalls on Chayangkun Rd (20฿ buys you a savory stick of *gai yang*, a heaping mound of sticky rice, and a bowl of Vietnamese *pho* soup). Several good restaurants on Phanom Phanarak Rd. offer Thai, Lao, and Vietnamese fare. The markets are full of opportunities to sample local cuisine, from eggs boiled on a stick to coconut jello.

SIGHTS

The town's main attraction is **Wat That Phanom,** a symbol of Northeast Thailand and one of the region's most revered temples. This Laotian-style shrine has been restored a total of seven times since its initial construction 1500 years ago, most recently in 1978, after heavy rains in 1975 caused the 57m-high *chedi* to collapse. Every year at the beginning of February is the seven-day **Phra That Phanom Homage Fair,** when thousands of devotees come to pay their respects, accompanied by vendors and entertainers. Pilgrims who journey to Wat That Phanom seven times and "sleep near the Buddha," are believed to have guaranteed passage to heaven.

About 15km northwest of That Phanom is the tiny silk-weaving village of **Renu Nakhon.** Travelers desperate for a culture fix can observe traditional Isaan music and dance (a rare opportunity outside of the major cities) at the **Renu Nakhon** wat every Saturday during the winter. (Niyana's Guesthouse has helpful information on perfor-

THAILAND

Supernatural Stupa?

That Phanom is a holy town, a *Sathanii Saksit*, blessed with a temple which radiates tremendous power. Many townspeople claim that just as the temple can grant everlasting happiness to those who worship there, so too can it bring tragedy to those who defile it. Residents here often point to 1975 as a remarkable year of misfortune for many of their neighbors. That year, the magnificent *chedi* collapsed following torrential rains. Some locals rushed to remove chunks of the fallen stupa as tokens of luck and benediction. Not long afterwards, mysterious accidents and inexplicable illnesses befell the culprits and their families. To this day there remain abandoned houses whose owners have died or run away.

One late June night a couple of years ago, the townspeople again witnessed another show of divine power. A young *songthaew* driver, unable to pay his rent, clambered up the scaffolding around Wat That Phanom, intending to swipe the three large diamonds embedded in the *chedi*. Unable to get back down, he was spotted in the glare of floodlight that illuminates the temple. Word spread through the sleeping town and a crowd soon gathered on the street below, including the police.

One officer, convinced that the thief was an illegal Lao immigrant, drew his pistol, and pulled the trigger. *Click!* The report never came. Again he pulled the trigger, but nothing happened. Exasperated, he grabbed another gun, but had the same result. Perhaps the divine one had taken pity on the would-be burglar and protected him. The hapless bandit was finally dragged down and officers had to forcefully restrain irate townspeople intent on lynching him. Keep in mind that nothing, not even the most innocuous-looking pebble, can be taken beyond the wat's gates. If you inadvertently do so, return it immediately. If not, sleep lightly, and don't say we didn't warn you.

mance times; check here before making the trek as the schedule is by no means set in stone.) To get there, take any Nakhon Phanom-bound *songthaew* and ask to be left off at the Renu Nakhon junction 8km north of That Phanom; from there, hire a *tuk-tuk*.

■ Nong Khai หนองคาย

For a heavy dose of Isaan relaxation and good cheer, ease up to Nong Khai Province, where weary travelers lose themselves in any one of the towns along the Mekong River. Indeed, many *farang* have decided to set up camp and work in some of the guest houses, restaurants, and bookstores around here. Despite the foreign presence and the border-crossing traffic heading toward Laos, the city and the rest of the province refuse to cede any of their original character. Nong Khai Province claims several interesting, sometimes bizarre wats (particularly Phu Thawk and Sala Kaew Ku). With 300km of the provincial border along the Mekong (and hence the Laotian border), a significant Lao-French influence pervades the area, and an abundance of trade (under and above the law) is conducted across the river.

ORIENTATION

In the long and narrow town of Nong Khai, all the main roads run parallel to the river (which flows west-to-east), and are interconnected by a web of *soi*. Because street numbers were assigned haphazardly according to when the buildings were built—not by location—addresses can be confusing. A better way to orient yourself is by using the 19 wats in Nong Khai as landmarks; rest assured there is a temple within 5 minutes of your destination. Good maps are available at all of the guest houses. The **train station** is at the far west end of town on **Kaeworawut Road,** the road closest to the river at that point. As Kaeworawut Rd. runs toward the center of town from the west, it becomes a dirt road which intersects **Haisok Road** (heading to the river). East of Haisok Rd., **Rimkhong Road** is the closest parallel to the river and is where the

Mekhong Guest House, the shopping district, the immigration pier, and several restaurants are located. **Meechai Road, Prajak Road,** and **Highway 212** run parallel to Kaeworawut and Rimkhong Rd. Highway 212 forms the southern border of the town. The **bus terminal** is on the eastern end of Prajak Rd.

PRACTICAL INFORMATION

Currency Exchange: Bangkok Bank Ltd., on Soi Srisaket, which runs from Meechai Rd. opposite Wat Sri Sakes to Rimkhong Rd. near the immigration pier. Open daily 8am-6pm.

Trains: Nong Khai Railway Station (tel. 411 592), Kaeworawut Rd. at the far west end of town. Trains pass through **Khon Kaen,** and **Udon Thani** on their way to **Bangkok** (rapid, 3 per day, 7:40am and 5:40pm, 3rd class 133฿, 2nd class 268฿; express, 7pm, 3rd class 153฿, 2nd class 288฿). Always book in advance. Booking office open 5am-7pm.

Buses: Nong Khai Bus Terminal on Prajak Rd., at the east end of town. To **Udon Thani** (every 30min. until 5:20pm, 1hr. 15฿). Buses to **Bangkok** (every hr., 5:30am-7pm,146฿) pass through **Udon Thani, Khon Kaen,** and **Nakhon Ratchasima.** A/C buses to **Bangkok** leave from the back of the bus terminal (7:30am, 7:30, 8, and 8:30pm, 263฿). Green buses to **Pak Chom** and **Loei** (5 per day, 6am-11am, 7hr., 61฿) pass through **Si Chiang Mai** (2hr., 15฿) and **Sangkhom** (3hr., 25฿). To **Nakhon Phanom** (5 per day, all leave by 9:40am, 7hr., 91฿). To get to **Chiang Khan,** switch buses at **Pak Chom.** To **Beung Kan** and **Ban Ahong** (12:50pm and 6pm, 3hr., 35฿).

Local Transportation: Tuk-tuk, or "skylabs" as they're called in this part of the country, are everywhere and shouldn't cost more than 20฿. Since the town is a tourist enclave, drivers will often demand as much as 50฿. Bargain like a banshee. For short distances, **samlor** can be cheaper.

Rentals: Mut-mee Guest House rents **bicycles** (40฿ per day) as does the **Mekhong Guest House** (30฿ per day). For **motorcycles,** try **Nana Motor,** 1160 Meechai Rd., opposite Chayaporn Market. Motorbikes start at 200฿ per day. Helmets included. Open daily 6am-6pm.

Markets: A market on Rimkhong Rd., east of the immigration pier, hawks everything from chicken statuettes with genuine feathers and beaks (15฿) to electrical goods. **Chayaporn market,** is well past the hospital on Talat Chayaporn Rd., which runs between Kaeworawat Rd. and Meechai Rd.

Pharmacies: Tong Tong Pharmacy, 382/2 Meechai Rd. (tel. 411 690). Exit left from the post office; it's on the corner, a short walk away. Open 7am-9pm.

Medical Services: Nong Khai Hospital (tel. 411 504), on Meechai Rd. close to Mut-mee Guest House and across the street from the police station.

Emergency: tel. 191.

Police: Nong Khai Police Station (tel 411 020), on Meechai Rd.

Post Offices/Telephones: GPO, Meechai Rd. (tel. 411 521). Open Mon.-Fri. 8:30am-4:30pm, Sat.-Sun. 9am-noon. **Telephone** service open daily 7am-10pm; telegram office open daily 8am-6pm. **Postal code:** 43000. **Telephone code:** 042.

ACCOMMODATIONS

These spots (particularly the riverside lodgings) are so enticing that a modern-day Odysseus could easily fall under their siren spells, staying in all day and never venturing out to the real Nong Khai.

Mut-mee Guest House, 1111/4 Kaeworawut Rd., on the river 100m off Kaeworawut Rd. at the end of a *soi.* Arguably the most popular guest house in Northeast Thailand. Cheerful staff has guest house management down to an exact science; service is quick and attentive despite Mut-mee's size (25 rooms for up to 50 guests). Delicious variety of food; portions are generous. Dorms 60฿. Singles 70-100฿ depending on location. Doubles 100-160฿. During the high season teachers-in-residence hold drawing, *tai chi,* and yoga classes. Inquire for details.

Sawasdee Guest House, 402 Meechai Rd. (tel. 412 502), about 5 blocks east of the post office. From the bus station, turn left onto Prajak Rd. and then right at Srikuanmuang, just before the wat. Sawasdee is just across from Meechai. Courtyard garden and remarkable rooms (some have A/C) compensate for lack of river proximity. Ideal for travelers who shun the self-imposed withdrawal from Thai life that occurs at larger, more social guest houses. Singles 80฿. Doubles 120฿, with A/C and hot water 280฿. Twin room 120฿, with A/C and hot water 320฿.

Mekhong Guest House, 519 Rimkhong Rd. (tel. 412 119), a few stores west of the immigration pier. One of several guest house/restaurant combos along the river. Neat, well-kept rooms on two floors with porches that sport expansive views of the river, Laos and the Friendship Bridge. You don't have to pay through the nose to get a glimpse either. Singles start at 50฿. Doubles 70฿.

FOOD

Profit from Nong Khai's epicurean overkill and feast at a riverside eatery. Most have English menus, decent food, and beautiful scenery, but they're none too gentle on the expense account. Prices drop significantly as you move away from the river.

Udomrod, 423 Rimkhong Rd. (tel. 421 014), next to the immigration pier. Standard restaurant with deluxe view. Bony, budget-decimating, but bursting-with-flavor Mekong River fish dishes (the house specialty). Also renowned for its Vietnamese cuisine; try the fried spring rolls. Most dishes 25-50฿; for fresh fish expect to pay 80-160฿. Open daily 2pm-8pm.

Reuan Pae Haisok, (tel. 412 211), behind the dilapidated Wat Haisok near Mut-mee Guest House. Not only is this place genuinely *on* the river, it takes diners on an hour-long spin every evening (5:30pm, 20฿ extra). On a clear day, you'll savor a succulent sunset in addition to a close-up view of the new Friendship Bridge. The food does not meet the exacting standards of penny-pinching gourmets (fried rice and veggies 40฿). Open daily 10am-10pm.

Sala Boat, 527 Rimkhong Rd. (tel. 412 512). Look for the tell-tale "Wall's" ice cream symbol. Enjoy Thai food (20-60฿) and an expansive view of the Mekong. Cheer for real "boats" sailing against the current from the shade of Sala Boat's wooden deck. Open daily 10am-11pm.

The nameless café on Meechai Rd., at the corner of Ho Rd., is literally nameless, but serves some of Nong Khai's best and cheapest food. One block south of the east end of Rimkhong Rd. A short walk toward the post office from Sawasdee Guest House and across the street. English menu with breakfast items. Fried rice and chicken or beef 15฿.

SIGHTS

Seekers of hand-woven *mut-mee* fabrics can visit **Village Weaver Handicrafts**, 786/1 Prachak Rd. (tel. 411 236). The goal of this 13-year-old project is to "promote the professional and social welfare of disadvantaged artisans and families." More specifically, the aim is to promote local industry and prevent young Isaan women from seeking their fortunes in the brothels of Patpong or Pattaya. Traditional cloth is woven on looms in the back of the shop and sold off the bolt or as off-the-rack clothing, hand bags, and other practical items. Seamstresses can make tailor-made outfits in just a few days. Don't worry about trying to fit your lovely purchases into your rucksack—the Village Weaver will ship anywhere in the world at reasonable prices. (Open Mon.-Sat. 8am-5pm, Sun. 9am-3pm.) MC and Visa accepted.

A few km east of Nong Khai on Hwy. 212, **Sala Kaew Ku,** also known as Wat Khaek, is one of the most bizarre temples in all of Thailand. The grounds are populated with towering, concrete statues of Hindu and Buddhist figures narrating scenes from the cycles of life: the good and the evil, the mundane and the fantastic, the innocent and the downright freaky—all the brainchild of an octogenarian Lao mystic. Of these massive images looming high overhead, the newest and most magnificent is a seven-headed, tongue-lashing serpent rearing over a Buddha as he meditates on its coiled lengths. The most bizarre scenario depicts an elephant strolling through a pack of whiskey-drinking, poker-playing, car-driving dogs who snap jealously at its enlightened heels. To get there, bike along Rte. 212, pass "St. Paul Nong Khai School" on the right. Wat Khaek is just two turnoffs later. The turnoff (to the right) has a small English sign that says *"Salakeokoo."* You can also catch any of the buses going east and ask to be let off at the turnoff, or hire a *tuk-tuk* for about 100฿ (or less) round trip. (Open daily 8am-5pm; admission 10฿.)

BORDER CROSSING: NONG KHAI/VIENTIANE

With the opening of the "Friendship Bridge" a few years back and a growing business and tourist interest in Laos, companies offering visas to Laos have multiplied faster than lemmings in Nong Khai. Be wary when choosing an outfit, since a number of them (particularly those along Rimkhong near the immigration pier) are rather shady, fly-by-night affairs and are best avoided. Your best and most legitimate option is to acquire a visa through the Lao Embassy in Bangkok (which will save you piles of baht too). In Nong Khai, count on spending 1500-2500฿ for a 15-day tourist visa. Many travelers recommend the **International Meeting Place** (tel. 421 223) on 1117 Soi Chuen Jitt off Meechai Rd. (heading east, the *soi* is on the right just before Wat Sri-chomchuan). It's a guest house run by an expat Australian and his Thai wife, who can arrange same-day visas for 2500฿. The staff is helpful and the office is chock-full of maps, accommodation suggestions, and travel advice. The International Meeting Place is affiliated with an accredited travel agency in Vientiane. Note that visas purchased in Nong Khai are only valid for crossings from Nong Khai; to enter Laos from anywhere else (i.e. Nakhon Phanom, Mukdahan, or Chong Mek) you must purchase a visa in Bangkok.

■ Near Nong Khai

SANGKHOM

Ninety-five km upriver from Nong Khai, nestled in a range of rolling, jungle-shrouded hills, sits the drowsy hamlet of Sangkhom. The area's mountainous setting not only creates some stunning vistas, but jealously hordes many natural wonders—multi-tiered waterfalls and breathtaking cliffs plummeting straight down to the river below—from the rest of the province and all but the most intrepid *farang*. Rest assured as you gaze across the mighty Mekong toward the rugged, untamed forests of Laos on the opposite bank, that you are about as far from 7-Elevens, karaoke bars, and other signs of industrialization as is possible in Thailand.

Despite its isolation, Sangkhom is home to several fine guest houses. First and fore-most is **Bouy Guest House,** 60 M.4 Sangkhom (tel. 441 065). Romantic bamboo bun-galows in tip-top shape perch on stilts along the banks of a small stream (singles 60฿, doubles 80฿). The remarkable Mr. Toy, owner and chef, prepares scrumptious Thai and Lao specialties. Don't miss the "jungle curry." A wealth of tourist info, and motor-cycles for rent (180฿ per day). Just west of the Bouy Guest House is the brand-new **TXK Guest House,** forced to relocate due to devastating erosion. Mama, the eccen-tric and warm-hearted proprietress, is famous for her Thai and Lao feasts on which guests can gorge themselves for 45฿ per mouth. Single bungalows are 80฿, doubles 100฿. The **post office** is 100m north of the Bouy Guest house on the left (tel. 441 069). Also has **overseas telephone** service. (Open Mon.-Fri. 8:30am-4:30pm, Sat.-Sun. 9am-noon.) **Postal code:** 43160. **Telephone code:** 042.

Sangkhom is an ideal spot to kick off the Tevas and rest road-weary feet. The sur-rounding wilderness is dotted with caves and waterfalls, all of which are marked on a helpful map provided by Bouy Guest House. Particularly impressive are the **Than Thip falls,** about a 30-minute motorbike ride west of town. Signs on the highway will direct you to the dirt turnoff. The cascades' second level contains a swimming hole. East of Sangkhom are the **Than Thong Falls** which, while larger than the Than Thip Falls, are a Thai tourist trap. The designated scenic area just before the falls is a beau-tiful spot to watch a sleepy sun retire for the evening. **Wat Hin Maak Peng,** a monas-tery set among large boulders and bamboo graves, is well worth a visit for the spectacular river views. Remember to dress respectfully. To get to Sangkhom, take the small, green #557 bus which wheezes and chugs its way from Nong Khai to Loei and back again, stopping in Sangkhom (every hr., 25฿).

BAN AHONG

About 185km east of Nong Khai lies Beung Kan. The town itself offers nothing remarkable, but the tiny village of Ban Ahong in the Beung Kan District is worth a visit. Don't expect any frills like banks, post offices, police stations, *tuk-tuk*, or *samlor;* this lonely bus stop on Hwy. 212 consists of a single dirt road and traditional houses on stilts. A sign even reads "Welcome to the middle of nowhere." All told the population consists of 84 roofs in Thai evaluation, about 800 denizens.

The Mekong River narrows here, and often mist-shrouded mountains on the Lao side fall away dramatically to the shore. In the evenings Lao fisherman sing folk songs as they pull in their nets, providing an authentic soundtrack to this spectacular Shangri-La on the Mekong. For travelers with an insatiable urge to take the path less traveled, Ban Ahong is home to the **Hideaway Guest House.** The English- and German-speaking proprietor, Mr. Saksil, opened this romantic bamboo retreat three years ago with the hopes of attracting travelers who want the real scoop on rural village life. Singles go for 70฿, doubles 100฿. The village is quite friendly; the chief's house, just upriver from Hideaway, is the center of social activity, where men go to drink home-brewed moonshine and smoke "Lao cigarettes." The women and children chat nearby in their own circles.

Just downriver from Hideaway across a small brook is **Wat Ba Ahong,** an enchanting place dotted with massive boulders worn smooth by the river in eons past, and shielded by massive leafy trees. Stop in for a mug of traditional Lao medicinal tea brewed from various twigs, herbs, and roots and kept hot all day. Check out the temple's furniture, made from gnarled bamboo roots. Sak, certification from TAT in hand, offers travelers guided treks. The three-day, two-night expeditions pass through a nearby wildlife preserve, stop at a local cave and waterfall, and include bamboo rafting down the mighty Mekong itself. Sak's boyhood friend, Rak, will function as trekking guide, having learned the trade in the famed hills of Chiang Mai. Rak entertains travelers with his quick wit and fascinating autobiographical tales.

Ban Ahong is definitely a worthwhile stop on the long trek between Nakhon Phanom and Nong Khai and is reasonably close to the breathtaking Phu Thawk monastery. To escape the clutches of civilization from Nong Khai take a bus bound for Beung Kan (2hr., 35฿)—make sure the driver knows you're going east to Ban Ahong. From Nakhon Phanom first catch a bus to Beung Kan (57฿). Some will continue on past Ban Ahong (ask the ticket seller) and if not, switch at Beung Kan to a bus going to Nong Khai (7฿); ask to be let off at Ban Ahong.

WAT PHU THAWK

Although it is one of the northeast's most awe-inspiring sights, Wat Phu Thawk is so far removed from any regular tourist destination that is virtually ignored by all foreign pilgrims. In the Isaan dialect, *phu thawk* means single mountain. A mountain range runs behind it, but the shrine stands alone on a massive red sandstone outcropping riddled with caves and ledges.

A wooden staircase twists up, with seven levels representing the stages of enlightenment. Level five contains a sanctuary built into the cliff face and adorned with a regal Buddha image that glows softly at dusk. On the opposite side of the mountain is a unique hermitage built on a rock pinnacle, nestled underneath a huge boulder that threatens to topple any second and smash the entire affair. This island of stone can only be reached by a narrow ridge, with spectacular views falling away to either side Along the walkways are small, wooden platforms and huts for meditation. The top level, mostly forested, is a maze of trails. The monastery's founder, Ajaan Juan, died in a plane crash a few years ago, and a newly built pagoda at the foot of Phu Thawk houses his relics.

Visit Phu Thawk as early in the morning as possible, preferably with your own transportation, a good set of directions, and a healthy tolerance for potholes. By public transportation, go first to Beung Kan; wait at the shelter 50m south of the junction for the *songthaew* heading south to Ban Siwilai (about 10฿)—sit on the left side of the bus and look for the "Ban Siwilai" sign in English. From there, catch another *songthaew* to Phu Thawk (another 10฿). Monday to Friday, morning, noon, and evening, you may be able to share a ride with the local students on their way to and from school. Otherwise, you may have to hire a *tuk-tuk* for about 100฿ to take you the 20km to the mountain and back. (Closed April 12-16.)

■ Chiang Khan เชียงคาน

Of all the riverside towns on the Isaan-Laos border, Chiang Khan comes closest to embodying the term "border town." It's not just the river and surrounding mountains that contribute to the atmosphere of this one-horse village; the town itself is composed of just two parallel roads, lined from end to end with old wooden structures evoking the spirit of American pioneer days. Unfortunately, it's likely that many of these buildings will slowly be replaced. Chiang Khan's halcyon has attracted the attention of investors; land values have increased tenfold in the past few years, with parcels near Kaeng Khut Khu rapids fetching as much as 2 million baht per acre. In the meantime, however, life is still slow and relatively isolated from the clutches of the world.

ORIENTATION

Chiang Khan is on the northern border of Loei Province, 50km from the provincial capital and just across the Mekong River from Laos. East along the river is the small town of Pak Chom, to the west is Tha Li District with several small villages (Ban Nong Phu, Ban Pak Huay, Ban Ahii) on the Heuang River. Chiang Khan can be reached by *songthaew* from either Loei or Pak Chom. Those headed to Chiang Khan from Nong Khai province must take the Nong Khai-Loei bus to Pak Chom and switch there for a *songthaew* to Chiang Khan. The town of Chiang Khan has two main parallel roads, **Chiang Khan Road** (the highway through town) and **Chai Khong Road,** which runs along the river. These two roads are connected by Sois 1-21, from west to east. Buses from Pak Chom drop passengers off around Soi 18.

PRACTICAL INFORMATION

Immigration Offices: next to the post office. Will extend visas (500฿, 2 photos, and photocopies of your passport needed).

Currency Exchange: Thai Farmers Bank, 444 Chiang Khan Rd. (tel. 821 381). Open Mon.-Fri. 8:30am-3:30pm.

Buses: To **Loei** (every 30min., 6am-6:30pm, 1hr., 14฿) from the west end of town. Walk west out of town with the Thai Farmers Bank on your left; turn left onto the highway at the next 3-way intersection. Buses leave across from the gas station a few hundred feet farther down. Last bus 5pm. Buses to **Pak Chom** leave (every 30min., 6am-5pm, 1hr., 15฿) from the east end of Chiang Khan Rd., near Soi 20.

Local Transportation: Tuk-tuk putt around town (5฿).

Rentals: Nong Sam Guest House rents mountain **bikes** (30฿ per 12hr., 50฿ per day). Zen, and Chiang Khan Guest Houses rent regular bicycles (30฿ per day) and **motorbikes** (200฿ per day).

Markets: The **morning/day market** is 1 block south of Chiang Khan Rd. near Sois 9 and 10. The very small **night market** is on Chiang Khan Rd., between Sois 17 and 18. It gets going at sundown and lasts until around 9pm.

Medical Services: Chiang Khan Hospital (tel. 821 101), on Chiang Khan Rd., past Soi 21, on the eastern outskirts of town.

Emergency: tel. 191.

Police: (tel. 821 181), on a *soi* off Chiang Khan Rd. on the outskirts of town, past the hospital on the right, a few hundred feet farther on the left side of the road.

Post Offices/Telephones: Chiang Khan Post and Telegraph Office (tel. 821 011), Chai Khong Rd., at the far east end of town. Open Mon.-Fri. 8:30am-4:30pm, Sat.-Sun. 9am-noon. **Postal code:** 42110. **Telephone code:** 042.

ACCOMMODATIONS

Zen Guest House, 126/1 Soi 12 (tel. 821 119). Owners take Buddhist minimalism and the art of low-pressure maintenance to new levels, spending precious little time on the property. Signs posted throughout this do-it-yourself guest house tell guests what to do in the hosts' absence. Singles 50-60฿. Doubles 100฿.

Nong Sam Guest House, 407 Nam Pon Najan Rd. (tel. 821 457). Follow Chiang Khan Rd. straight out of town past Soi 1 (on the road to Ban Nong Phu) for about 1km until the wooden sign in English appears on the right. Remote location facilitates tranquil riverside contemplation. Singles 120฿. Doubles 150฿. Bike rental and boat trips.

Suksombun Hotel, 243/3 Chai Khong Rd. (tel. 821 064), near Sois 8 and 9. A weathered wooden building right on the river. The preferred choice of many a weary traveler. Some rooms have swell sunset views. Double bed with shared bath 100฿. Rooms with a view (and private bath) 150฿.

FOOD

Ask any local where to eat, and they'll tell you to go to Soi 9. Ask them what's good to eat, and they'll tell you to get the unique local twist on *pad thai.*

Prachamit Restaurant, 263/2 Chiang Khan Rd, in the southwest corner of Chiang Khan Rd. and Soi 9. One of several restaurants on soi 9 serving good *pad thai.* Owner recommends *kow mun gai,* a chicken and rice dish with special sauce (12฿). Cheap and friendly too. Open daily 8am-7pm.

Mekhong Riverside Restaurant, 328/10 Chai Khong Rd. (tel. 821 351), on the river; spot the English sign. Nice porch with tables in back. A bit posh for Chiang Khan; the elegant English menu is more expensive than the restaurants on soi 9 (dishes 30-50฿). Isaan handicrafts for sale in front. Open daily 9am-midnight.

SIGHTS

About 3km east of town, a turn-off leads left to the Kaeng Khut Khu rapids. Follow the sign to Wat Thakhaek and continue another km. A long row of covered picnic areas make for good rapids-watching. The cascades are best in the dry season, but the mountain scenery is always stupendous. Vendors sell Isaan standards like *som tam* and *gai yang.* They've also got two local specialties: *gung thawt* (batter-fried prawns stuck together) and *gung ten* (dancing shrimp, consisting of live wigglies bathed in a spicy sauce). Some guest houses and hotels in town provide transportation by boat to the rapids (see **Accommodations**). Otherwise, you can take a *songthaew* from Chiang Khan Rd. (10฿) or a *tuk-tuk* for about 40฿ roundtrip.

■ Loei เลย

The big billboard on Highway 201 near the hospital greets new arrivals to Loei with, "Welcome to Loei, Land of the Sea of Mountains and Coldest in All Siam." Grammar aside, the billboard has neatly captured the essence of this seldom-visited but pulchritudinous province. Little else is known about this relatively isolated part of Thailand, and life in Loei carries on without much outside intervention—often a shady existence, especially along the northern border with Laos in towns such as Tha Li and Chiang Khan, where smuggled goods sneak into Thailand.

At the end of June is the **Phi Ta Khon Festival,** the region's own version of Halloween. This annual three-day festival takes place in **Dan Sai,** in the west end of the province. The festival originated when Prince Vessandorn, the Buddha's penultimate incarnation, returned to the city and was greeted by a procession so jubilant and fes-

tive that spirits got in on the action. During the festivals, young men don giant colorful masks with long pointy noses and parade around town.

Loei is the perfect base from which to explore the rest of the province. In the evenings, Loei's surprisingly numerous late-night restaurants and pubs are relaxing stops
after a rough day of gallivanting about the mountainous countryside.

ORIENTATION

Loei town is at the center of Loei Province, bordered by Laos to the north and on the
east by the **Loei River. Charoen Rat Road** runs the length of the river. The **post
office** is on the south end of Charoen Rat Rd., and heading north, there is the Savita
Bakery, several banks, the **day** and **night markets,** the Thai Udom Hotel, and the Phu
Luang Hotel. Just past the markets (on the side closer to the river) going north, is the
intersection with **Ruamjai Road,** which has several pharmacies, the Muang Loei
Guest House, and the **main bus terminal** at the west end of the road. **Ararree Road,**
south of Ruamjai Rd., connects Charoen Rat Rd. and **Ruamjit Road** (the road parallel
to Charoen Rat Rd.). One block farther south is **Chuensai Road** (to the east of the traffic circle) and **Nok Kaew Road** (to the west).

PRACTICAL INFORMATION

Currency Exchange: Siam Commercial Bank, 3/8 Ruamjai Rd. (tel. 812 001).
Open Mon.-Fri. 8:30am-3:30pm. **ATM.** Open daily 6am-11pm.

Air Travel: The airport is closed for repair, but should re-open sometime in 1997.
Check with **Thai Air,** 22/15 Chumsai Rd. (tel. 812 344). Open daily 9am-5pm.

Buses: Small green buses to **Nong Khai** via **Pak Chom, Sangkhom,** and **Tha Bo**
(every hr., 5:40-11:40am, 9 and 10:20pm, 60฿) leave from the bus terminal off Ruamjai Rd. If you miss the last bus, go to **Udon Thani** (every 25min., 5am-5:30pm,
68฿), and then catch a Nong Khai bus. Buses to **Chiang Mai** (9hr., 136฿) and
Chiang Rai via **Phitsanulok** and **Lampang** leave *across* from the bus terminal (8
per day, 10am-10:30pm). A private bus company operates from the King Hotel, 11/
9 Chumsai Rd. (tel. 811 225). A/C buses to **Bangkok** (11 per day, 241฿). Buy your
tickets in advance from the hotel. **999 Government Bus Co.** (tel. 811 706), on
Ruamjai Rd., has fan buses to **Bangkok** (every hr., 5-10am; every 30min., 4-11pm).
Exit the Muang Loei Guest House, turn left and walk about 1 block; it's on the left.
Some pass through **Khon Kaen** (138฿, express 188฿). Many long distance buses
start in Nong Khai and may be full upon arrival; make sure your ticket guarantees a
seat.

Local Transportation: The usual **samlor** and **tuk-tuk.** The locals bargain to 5฿,
you may have to settle for 10฿.

Rentals: Bicycles (40฿ per day) and motorbikes (150-200฿ per day) at Muang Loei
Guest House 1.

Markets: The **day** and **night markets** are at the same location at the north end of
Charoen Rat Rd. The night market gets going at around 6pm but closes at 9-10pm.

Pharmacies: Bun Jung Pesat Pharmacy, 83 Charoen Rat Rd. (tel. 812 138), on the
corner of Ruamjai Rd. Open daily 6am-9pm.

Medical Services: Loei Provincial Hospital (tel. 811 679), where Loei-Chiang
Khan Rd. (Hwy. 201) meets Nok Kaew Rd., across from provincial offices. English
spoken.

Emergency: tel. 191.

Police: Loei Police Station (tel. 811 245), at the north end of Charoen Rat Rd.

Post Offices: GPO, (tel. 811 713) on Charoen Rat Rd., south past the footbridge;
cross the river to the fitness park and it's on the left. Open Mon.-Fri. 8:30am-
4:30pm, Sat.-Sun. 9am-noon. **Postal code:** 42000.

Telephones: (tel. 811 253), next to the post office. Open daily 7am-10pm. Does not
accept some calling cards. **Telephone code:** 042.

ACCOMMODATIONS

Friendship House, 257/41 Soi Booncharoen (tel. 832 408). From the post office,
head south, take a left before Wat Sriboonruang, then follow the signs. The only

true guest house in Loei, run by Dom. If his 4-room place is full, he'll help set you up somewhere else. Common baths with hot water. Singles 80฿. Doubles 120฿.

Thai Udom Hotel, 122/1 Charoen Rat Rd. (tel. 811 763), on the corner of Ararree Rd. A friendly hotel close to the markets, the Savita Bakery, and night restaurants. Grand winding staircase hints at more than the run-down rooms offer. But they do have phones, TV, and bottled water. Singles 200฿, with A/C 250฿. Doubles 300฿, with A/C 400฿. VIP room 600฿. Hot water during the cold season.

PR House, 22/16 Chumsai Rd. (tel. 811 416) on the *soi* past the Thai Airways office. New condo-style building offers phone, balconies (perfect for hanging laundry), and hot water. Double 160฿. Twin with A/C, fridge, and TV 350฿.

FOOD

Some of the best (and cheapest) places to break bread are the **open-air restaurants** in front of the movie theater just off Ararree Rd., across from the Thai Farmers Bank, and at the bus terminal. Pyromaniacs can order *pakboong fai daeng* (flaming morning glory vine). Most restaurants are open past midnight.

Savita Bakery, 137-139 Charoen Rat Rd. (tel. 811 526), a bit south of the markets, just past Ararree Rd. Ice cream and pastries, including tiny little banana bread cupcakes (1฿). Staff speaks hesitant English with a smile. A few western dishes (hamburger 20฿). Open daily 6am-10:30pm.

Chinatown, 10/5 Araree Rd. (tel. 812 287). Don't let the name fool you. Thai and (what they call) American dishes, as well as Chinese. Relax with some wonton soup (25฿) or "fried entrails" (demonstrating the problem with dictionary translations, 40฿). Open daily 9am-11pm.

Son Aahaan Thai, 32/106 Nok Kaew Rd. (tel. 813 436), west of the traffic circle, on the right side of the road when walking toward the highway. English sign. A wagon wheel bonanza; the owner managed to use 27 in building the fence and tables of this garden restaurant. The rest are piled in a corner awaiting further inspiration. Extensive English menu, dishes 50฿ and up. Open daily 8am-11pm.

ENTERTAINMENT

For a provincial capital of fewer than 25,000 people, this town has a surprisingly substantial nightlife, representing Isaan's three varieties of nightly entertainment: the country-western-style pub, the karaoke bar, and the swanky, lounge-style nightclub where women take turns crooning off-key. Choose your poison.

Tom's Cabin, 35/10 Ruamjai Rd. Actually off Ruamjai Rd. From Muang Loei Guest House 1, walk to Ruamjai Rd., turn right, take the 1st left and walk halfway down the road; Tom's Cabin is on the left with an English sign. Fabulous pub with live Thai and western folk favorites. The crowd grows as night wears on, hooting and singing along. *The* place to be seen in Loei. Pool table and dart board in back. Open nightly 6pm-6am. You pay for the entertainment in the food (chicken with veggies 60฿) and drinks (Singha 85฿), but it's well worth it.

■ Near Loei

THA LI AND BAN PAK HUAY

Moving westward along the river from Chiang Khan District, the Mekong River splits. The northward branch goes into Laos, meeting the Thai border again up near the Golden Triangle. The Heuang River forms the division between Thailand and Laos where the Mekong leaves off. Around the Heuang River border is the rural **Tha Li** District. *Songthaew* to Tha Li only leave from Loei, and the highway from Chiang Khan to Tha Li District (via Bang Nong Phu), although incredibly scenic, is rarely traveled. Tha Li is best approached from Loei town.

Tha Li's isolation from the rest of the world is its selling point—the region is an area of covert trade across the Lao border. Iron-livered locals knock back *lao khao,* the fierce, rum-like brew that makes Mekong Whiskey seem like root beer. Several nearby villages are on the river.

For those interested in spending some time in this remote area, **Ban Pak Huay** claims the sole accommodation here, the **O.T.S. Guest Home.** Bungalows go for 60-80฿, and there is a commendable menu. Oy, the helpful proprietress, rents out bicycles (20฿ per 12hr., 35฿ per day). Scenic but hilly routes pass through isolated villages such as Ban Ahii and Ban Na Kazeng, and the Lao-style *chedi* called **Wat Phra Tadsadja** can also be visited by bicycle. The Heuang River running past Ban Pak Huay is easily forded—one could easily enter Laos (**not** a good idea). During the cool season, when the water is clear, a section of the river known as Gaeng Thun is a popular place to swim and enjoy a beer.

In Tha Li District, there are frequent Thai-Lao **market** days at the riverside villages, including Ban Pak Huay. These start early—often at 4am—and finish quickly, doing a brisk trade in Laotian contraband, while Lao villagers scoop up Thai goods. Be careful, though: because of Tha Li's reputation, the police make guest appearances, and there are highway checkpoints.

The town of Tha Li is 50km northwest of Loei. Catch a *songthaew* from Loei's main bus terminal (every 30min., 7:20am-5:30pm, 1hr., 15฿). To go to Ban Pak Huay, wait in Tha Li for a *songthaew* continuing down the same road about 8km to Ban Pak Huay. In Ban Pak Huay, the bus stop is at the road leading to O.T.S. Guest Home; turn left. *Songthaew* run back and forth to Tha Li (every hr., 7am-4pm, 5฿).

PHU RUA NATIONAL PARK

A 1375m-high mountain is the majestic centerpiece of this park. Rev up your engines and zip along the road to the peak. At the top, a large Buddha image surveys the scene below and a cliff shaped like the bow of a Chinese junk. For the vehicularly challenged who do not fancy 5km of asphalt, there are alternatives. One route involves a 2km trek to a waterfall, before continuing the 5.5km to the peak. On the way, you must cross a small stream; a sign on the opposite bank directs you 1.6km to the falls. The precipitous cascade is deafening after a good storm, and the spray-laden gusts make a refreshing pit stop. There you'll see a sign in Thai, the bottom of a set of three, directing you to the mountain summit.

Pick up a map and consult park rangers before starting your trip; trail conditions vary throughout the year. It's possible to complete the circuit in one day, but an overnight stay is recommended. Tent rentals for two are 50฿; larger group accommodations for 5-8 people, with bath, are 250-500฿. Food is available on weekends until 6pm, and all week during the busy season. Large parties should make arrangements with the National Parks Division in Bangkok (tel. (02) 579 05 29).

To get to Phu Rua, catch a bus going to Lom Sak (every hr., 5am-5pm, 1hr.); hop off at Phu Rua (15฿). Watch for the large wooden English sign next to the highway on the right side. Disembark across from the market, where you can buy snacks. From here, *songthaew* make the 3.5km trip to park headquarters regularly during the tourist season. Otherwise, pickings are slim. Visitors can hoof it uphill, hire private transport, or catch a ride with one of the guitar-wielding motorcyclists roaming the park. To return to Loei, wait for a bus across from the market (last bus 6pm).

PHU KRADUNG NATIONAL PARK

Its bell-shaped mountain inspired the name of this sanctuary (*kradung* means bell), the second national park established by the Thai government. Today it is one of the most popular reserves in the country. The summit is a 60-sq.km plateau criss-crossed with trails and is a great platform for viewing solar activity. Resident beasties include wild pig, Asian wild dog, black giant squirrel, yellow-throated martin, white-handed gibbon, langur, and macaque. The 9-km hike from the mountain base to park headquarters is facilitated slightly by bamboo stairways; porters can tote you and your gear. Mountain-top board and lodging available.

The park is packed on weekends, holidays, and the peak tourist season. If you plan to visit during these periods, you'll have reservations for a piece of hard ground unless you plan in advance. Contact the National Park Division of the Forestry Department in Bangkok (tel. (02) 579 0529). The park is closed during the rainy season (June-Oct.). To get to Phu Kradung, catch a bus from Loei bound for Khon Kaen, or vice versa (25฿). The bus will drop you off at the Amphoe Phu Kradung administrative office; from there, you can catch a minibus to the National Park Office where the trail begins.

ERAWAN CAVE

Just off the Udon Thani-Loei Hwy. (Hwy. 210), **Erawan Cave** is just slightly closer to Udon Thani. Coming from Loei, the gaping crevice in the distant cliffs which shelters the large Buddha is clearly visible on the left side of the highway as the terrain becomes mountainous. From the highway, it's another 2km to the cave, and if you've just hopped off the Udon-Loei bus, *tuk-tuk* drivers waiting at the turnoff will take you there (10-15฿). For those using their own wheels, no English sign indicates the turnoff for the cave; from Loei, keep an eye out for the *tuk-tuk* clustering on the left side of the road, just after you actually see the cave from the highway. From Udon, they're going to be on the right side, but the cave is not visible before coming upon them. A wat at the cliff base marks the end of the road. To the left, a huge flight of stairs ascends the mountain (marked by a statue of a three-headed elephant). Eventually the steps branch off; take the flight to the left and keep going. It's a long, awkward climb, but the smiling Buddha sitting amidst the echoes of bats will be waiting for you at the top. Once you reach the top, buy a drink, flop down in Buddha's shadow, and revel in his precept of non-action. When your legs recover, say bye-bye to the Buddha and start spelunking.

The cave boasts Dodger Stadium capacity—it could easily host a baseball game, complete with pop flies, though Tommy Lasorda (pre-Slim Fast) would be a tight squeeze. To the right, sunbeams filter through natural skylights. As you creep forward, the darkness deepens and the squeaking of bats becomes an ear-piercing shriek. The winged rodents stay put, mostly. Cryptic signs point out Thai interpretations of the various stalagmites here: "stone tree," "rock *chedi*," etc. The next cavern leads to the "elephant rock" and the "cold room." You are directly under the mountain now, but don't fear—there's light at the end of the tunnel. Through the next cavern and up a wooden staircase, you emerge at the opposite side of the mountain, with a lovely panorama of cultivated fields and the surrounding peaks.

■ Udon Thani อุดรธานี

Sheltering a six-digit population, Udon teems with air-conditioned hotels, restaurants, and coffee shops—a welcome relief after the humble simplicity of small-town, northeast Thailand. Site of a United States Air Force base during the Vietnam War, the American presence is still evident in Udon's western restaurants, its strong expat community, and U.S. consulate. After satiating your appetite for amenities, there are several worthwhile daytrips around the province, notably the UNESCO World Heritage archaeological sites at Ban Chiang, whose discovery practically re-wrote the prehistory of Southeast Asia.

ORIENTATION

Udon Thani is readily accessible by train, bus, or plane. The **train station** is on the eastern fringe of town, and the **TAT office** is on the western fringe, while the hotels are in central Udon Thani. Three **traffic circles** direct vehicles along the length of **Udon-Dusadee Road.** From south to north, at the **Srisuk intersection** is the circle with a statue of the city's founder, Prince Prachak Silpakhom. At the **Phosi Road** intersection, there is a fountain (usually dry), and at **Prachak Road** is the clock tower traffic circle. **Bus stations** are on both the northern and eastern fringes of town, while the **airport** is about 3km outside the city limit, southwest on the **Udon-Loei Highway**. The city bus system is virtually non-existent—bargain viciously with the *tuk-tuk* and *samlor* jockeys for feasible fares.

The northwest part of town has a reservoir surrounded by a peaceful park. Many government offices are in this tranquil section, including the GPO and the U.S. consulate. The rest of town buzzes with shopping districts, department stores, and traffic galore. Maps available at the TAT office and certain hotels will make finding your way around infinitely easier.

PRACTICAL INFORMATION

Tourist Offices: Udon Thani TAT Office (tel. 325 406), located on Mukmontri Rd., turn right off Phasi Rd. A fantastic young staff brimming with helpful information on Udon Thani, Loei, and Nong Khai Provinces. Pick up a free map of the city (you'll need it). Open 8:30am-4:30pm.

Embassies and Consulates: U.S., 35/6 Supphakitchanya Rd. (tel 244 270), along the northern end of Nong Prachak Reservoir, close to Northeastern Wattana Hospital. Open Mon.-Fri. 7:30am-noon and 1-4:30pm. Closed for both Thai and American holidays.

Currency Exchange: Krung Thai Bank, 216 Makkhaeng Rd. (tel. 247 755). **Thai Farmers Bank,** 236 Phosi Rd. (tel. 241 122). Both open Mon.-Fri. 8:30am-3:30pm. **Bangkok Bank,** 154 Prachak Rd. (tel. 221 505). Open Mon.-Fri. 8:30am-3pm. Currency exchange open daily, 8:30am-7pm.

Air Travel: Udon Thani Airport (tel. 246 567), on Udon-Loei Rd. 3km southwest of town. 3 flights per day to **Bangkok. Thai Air,** 60 Makkhaeng Rd. (tel. 243 222). Open Mon.-Fri. 7am-5pm.

Train Station: (tel. 222 061), at the eastern end of Prachak Rd. To: **Bangkok** (8-10hr., 3rd-class 145฿), **Nakhon Ratchasima** and **Khon Kaen** (6hr., 45฿). **Nong Khai** (4 per day, 1hr., 28฿). Book in advance.

Buses: Udon Thani's main bus terminal is on Sayutt Rd. between Prachak Rd. and Phasi Rd. as they approach the train tracks. **407 bus company** manages all A/C buses. To **Bangkok** via **Khon Kaen** and **Nakhon Ratchasima** (every hr., 7:30am-7:30pm, 8hr., 241฿). Behind this building is **bus terminal #1** which sends buses to: **Khon Kaen** (#226, #262, or #211), **Nakhon Ratchasima** (#262 or #211), **Ubon** (#227), and **Ban Chiang/Sakon Nakon** (white bus #230, every 30min.). Northbound buses depart from **bus terminal #2** on the outskirts of town; catch a #6 or #23 *songthaew* from Udon-Dusadee Rd. to Rangsima Market. To: **Nong Khai** (#221, 1hr., 15฿); **Loei** (#220); and **Ban Phu.** Inquire at TAT for the most recent schedule.

Local Transportation: A **city bus** (3฿) runs rings around the city—rather useless if you're in the center of town. The TAT has a list of **songthaew** routes and numbers (3฿). Plenty of **samlor** (10-15฿) and **tuk-tuk** (15-20฿) in town.

Markets: Thai Isaan, between Prachak Rd. and Phosi Rd., just west of the bus station. **Rangsima Market,** on the highway north, just in front of bus terminal #2. Take *songthaew* #6 or #23 from Udon-Dusadee Rd.

Pharmacies: Many pharmacies throughout the city. One to try is at 194 Phosi Rd., beneath the "Consult Your Pharmacist" sign. Open daily 7am-9pm.

Medical Services: Northeastern Wattana Hospital, 70/7-8 Supphakitchanya Rd. (tel. 241 031), at the north end of the Nong Prachak Reservoir.

Emergency: tel. 1699.

Police: Sri Suk Rd. (tel. 222 285).

Post Offices: GPO (tel. 222 304), on Wattana Rd. Open Mon.-Fri. 8:30am-4:30pm, Sat.-Sun. 9am-noon. Telegram office open daily 7am-11pm. **Postal code:** 41000.

Telephones: Telecommunications Ministry of Thailand, 108/2 Udon-Dusadee Rd. (tel. 244 762). North of the clock tower traffic circle before the intersection with Wattana Rd.; look for the antennae and satellite dish. Open daily 7am-11pm.

ACCOMMODATIONS

Prachapakdee Hotel, 156/7-9 Prachak Rd. (tel. 221 804). Heading north on Udon-Dusadee Rd. turn left onto Prachak Rd. The hotel is on the left between the Siam

Commercial and Bangkok Banks. Peaceful location; the owner grows orchids in the rear courtyard. Singles 150฿, with A/C 300฿. Doubles 170฿, with A/C 320฿.

Chai Porn Hotel, 209-211 Makkhaeng Rd. (tel. 222 144). Heading northwest on Phosi Rd., take a right onto Makkhaeng Rd. The hotel is on the right next to the Mandarin Restaurant. Bright, tidy rooms belie this old veteran's age. Doubles boast bathtubs large enough for practicing your synchronized swimming routine. Singles 180฿, with A/C 270฿. Doubles 270฿, with A/C 350฿.

Thailand Hotel, 4/1-6 Surakan Rd. (tel. 221 95). From the bus or train station, head into town on Prachak Rd. and turn left on Surakan. Cross Phosi Rd. and pass "Top World." Thailand Hotel is half a block on the left. Doubles have bathtubs. Clean, with friendly staff. Upper floors sport nice views. Singles 200฿, with A/C 300฿. Doubles with A/C 350฿.

FOOD

Excellent Thai, Isaan, and western restaurants are scattered throughout town. Mediocre coffee shops abound; often, air-conditioning is the best thing on the menu—you'll definitely pay for the privilege.

Yawt Kai Yaang, 7/40-41 Mukmontri Rd. (tel. 241 721), on the corner of Phosi Rd. Popular Isaan restaurant, particularly crowded at lunch time (and for a good reason) despite the mingling of diesel fumes with grill smoke. Rice comes in traditional woven stay-warm baskets; modernity intrudes in the form of mechanized fly dispersers which shoo pests away from the food. A very full meal of *som tam, gai yang, khao niaw,* and water costs 50฿. Open daily 6am-10pm.

Stamp Restaurant, Naresuan Rd. From Phosi Rd., it's on the right. Relax on either A/C-cooled floor. Large portions of Thai or western food. Rice and noodle dishes 30-60฿, steaks 80-100฿, pizzas 120-150฿. Lots of sundaes. Open daily 10am-midnight.

Udon Osha, 170 Prachak Rd. (tel. 243 794), across from Prachapakdee Hotel and 3 stores to the left. This restaurant lists "cooked pig face" among its specialties, but what it really does best is a northern Isaan favorite, *kai dow ga-ta* (2 fried eggs with a minced pork/scallion topping and a few oh-so-delicately arranged slices of the local sweet sausage). Add 2 wee toasted French breadlets with sausage sticks and a cup of hot Ovaltine or coffee all for just 30฿. Open daily 5am-1pm.

SIGHTS

There are several places to visit around the province, but the best you'll do in town is to wander around the edge of **Nong Prachak Reservoir** in the northeast section. The peaceful surrounding area has park benches and open-air pavilions. The landscaping job here is pleasant, albeit imperfect. The work is obvious: the meandering path lacks necessary enclosure and the element of discovery is zippo. A statue of a reclining woman doing leg lifts scandalizes adults and sends teenagers into hysterical laughter. Join mothers with small children and young sweethearts on the footbridge to feed the Jaws-sized catfish, that are truly a spectacle (bag of fish chow 5฿).

ENTERTAINMENT

For a big city, Udon's nightlife options are limited. **The Best Pub,** on a small *soi* off Surakan Rd., across Phosi Rd. from the Thailand Hotel, is one possibility. The cultivated "Wild West" atmosphere is regrettably undermined by the absence of shootouts and duels (a sticker on the door prohibits firearms), and the abundance of lance-bearing knights printed on the walls. At least the Singha (70฿) and snooker would suit the Sundance Kid. American music starts at 9pm, after an hour of Thai warm-up. (Open daily 6pm-1am.)

■ Near Udon Thani

Ban Chiang, 54km east of Udon, is the site of one of the most significant archaeological discoveries in Southeast Asia, which earned it recognition as a UNESCO World

Heritage site in 1992. It is world-renowned for the refined, curvilinear designs of the red buff pottery found here, and its discovery has completely rewritten the prehistory of Southeast Asia, previously dismissed as a cultural black hole.

The story of the site's discovery, scandalous looting, and eventual proper excavation begins in 1966, when Stephen Young, a Harvard student doing archaeological research, tripped over a large root. Just before he kissed *terra firma*, he caught himself, only to find the round rim of a partially unearthed pot staring him in the face. Upon closer scrutiny, he found that the entire 5m x 15m area was littered with half-buried pots. The official excavation by the Fine Arts Department of Thailand and the University of Pennsylvania did not begin in earnest until the mid-70s. In the meantime, valuable artifacts were sold to collectors in shady trading centers around the world. Since then, many objects have been recovered, but without an exact record of their provenance, they have little archaeological significance.

Despite rampant plundering, much has been learned about the people who have lived here continuously for nearly 4000 years. Cord-marked vessels and the burial of infants inside jars represent the period from 3600-1000 BC. The latter practice may indicate unusually high infant mortality rates due to environmental stresses or the widespread practice of infanticide as population control. Carinated vessels with incised patterns and red painting are characteristic of pottery made from 1000-300 BC, while the famous red-on-buff pottery, with its complex red curvilinear designs, is most commonly associated with burial rites of the later periods.

Archaeologists have also found over 100 skeletons which outline the story of the city's original inhabitants. Apparently, the Ban Chiang civilization possessed a knowledge of bronze metallurgy much earlier than previously estimated. (The discovery has changed previously held notions that metallurgy came to Thailand from China; it was probably just the opposite.)

An excellent **village museum** (tel. 223 091) documents the discovery, excavation, and history of the findings unearthed over the past several decades. Second-floor exhibits with comprehensive English captions are most impressive. (Open 9am-4pm; admission 10฿.) At the other end of the village, Wat Phosi Nai's "open-air exhibit" is the first of its kind in Thailand, displaying a burial site excavation as it was initially found, with artifacts intact. Exit left from the museum grounds and walk for about 500m. The excavation will be on the right side, just before the road curves.

Orange and blue *songthaew* from Udon Thani to Ban Chiang (every 30min., 1½hr., 16฿) leave from just beyond the gas station on the left side of Phosi Rd., southeast of the be-statued traffic circle. After crossing the tracks, the road becomes Hwy. 22, the Udon Thani-Sakhon Nakhon Hwy. If the bus drops you off on Hwy. 22 at the road to Ban Chiang, take a *tuk-tuk* the remaining 6km to the museum. The last bus directly from the museum gate back to Udon leaves at noon. Otherwise, hire a *tuk-tuk* (15-20฿) to drive you back to the highway. From there, catch any of the numerous buses heading into Udon.

For those who would prefer to linger at this remarkable site, Ban Chiang's newly-opened **Lakeside Sunrise Guest House** offers basic rooms. Singles cost 90฿, doubles 120฿. It is run by an Aussie and his Thai wife who works at the museum.

Another worthwhile stop is **Erawan Cave**, 90km out of town on Hwy. 210 (Udon-Loei Hwy.). Stalagmites and stalactites stud the interior, and the mouth has a lovely view of the countryside. To get there, leap on a Loei-bound bus at the new terminal on the perimeter road in Udon Thani (30฿). From the highway drop-off, it's a 2-km walk or a 10-20฿ roundtrip *tuk-tuk* ride to the cave. See **Near Loei** for details.

■ Khon Kaen ขอนแก่น

The second-largest city in Isaan, Khon Kaen is the approximate geographic center of the northeast. Tourists often snub this cradle of commerce, but the metropolis deserves credit for its comprehensive museum, exciting night market, decent restaurants, and thriving nightlife. Khon Kaen University, the largest in the Northeast, supplies an energetic young crowd that contributes to the evening *élan*. The educational focus of the city also means that more people speak English. In addition, there's a helpful branch of the TAT worth visiting for information on Khon Kaen city and province, as well as rarely visited northeast regions such as Mahasarakham and Kalasin. In the rest of the province, several sights reward the adventuresome. The pride and joy of Khon Kaen Province are both the discovery of several dinosaur fossils at Phu Wiang National Park, and the silk factories at Chonabot city.

ORIENTATION

The city is an important transportation, communication, and education center for the Isaan region. Because of its size and significance, Khon Kaen is easily reached by plane, bus, or train. The ordinary **bus terminal** is on **Prachasamosorn Road,** as is the tourist office. To reach TAT from the terminal, cross the street and walk three blocks to the left, crossing the main north-south throroughfares **Na Muang Road** and **Klang Muang Road.** Klang Muang Rd. is lined with hotels and restaurants, and the **A/C bus terminal** is several blocks down on the left. Beyond it, Klang Muang Rd. crosses **Srichan Road,** which boasts many of Khon Kaen's best night spots. South of Srichan Rd. are the post office, police station, and the massive day market, which ends at **Ruenrom Road.** At the west end of Ruenrom Rd. (turning right off Klang Muang or Na Muang) is the **train station.**

PRACTICAL INFORMATION

Tourist Offices: TAT, 15/5 Prachasamosorn Rd. (tel. 244 498). A brown and white building on the right, close to the Lang Muang intersection, several blocks east of the ordinary bus terminal. New and very helpful, it's the center for information on Khon Kaen and the surrounding provinces. Some staff members speak excellent English. Free maps as well as intra- and inter-city transportation info. Open 8:30am-4:30pm.

Tourist Police: 15/5 Prachasamosorn Rd. (tel. 236 937), to the left of the TAT office. Also responsible for Nong Khai, Udon Thani, Loei, Sakhon Nakhon, Nakhon Phanom, Nong Bua Lamphu, and Mukdahan Provinces. Before contacting the Thai police in any of these provinces, call the Khon Kaen tourist police.

Currency Exchange: Banks all over the city exchange money. **Bangkok Bank,** 254 Srichan Rd. (tel. 225 142), just before the Parrot Restaurant, offers after-hours exchange. Mon.-Fri. 8:30am-8pm, Sat.-Sun. 9am-5pm.

Air Travel: Khon Kaen Airport (tel. 236 515), on Airport Rd. off Maliwan Rd., which is the name of Prachasamosorn Rd. west of the train tracks. To **Bangkok** (3 per day, 1060฿). For current schedule check with **Thai Airways.** 183/6 Maliwan Rd. (tel. 236 523). Open Mon.-Fri. 8:30am-4:30pm.

Trains: Khon Kaen Railway Station (tel. 221 112), on Ruenrom Rd. To: **Bangkok** (5 per day, 8hr., rapid 107฿, express 127฿) and **Nong Khai** (3 per day, 3hr., 35฿).

Buses: Ordinary bus terminal (tel. 237 300), on Prachasamosorn Rd. To: **Bangkok** (#20, every 30min., 6:30am-10:30pm, 7hr., 107฿); **Udon Thani** (#211 or #262, every 30min., 5:30am-5:30pm, 2hr., 32฿); and **Ubon Ratchathani** (#282, every hr., 5:40am-1:40pm, 70฿). **A/C bus terminal** (tel. 239 910) is on Klang Muang Rd. To: **Bangkok** (#20, every 45min., 7hr., 193฿); **Nong Khai** (#23, 1:30, 3pm, 5hr., 79฿); **Loei** (#217, 6:30, 11:30am, 4:30pm, 3-4 hr., 95฿); **Mukdahan** (#278, 7am, 1:30, 3:30pm, 4hr., 84฿); and **Ubon Ratchathani** (#268, every 2hr., 9am-3pm, 125฿). Check with TAT office for more details.

Local Transportation: Samlor (10-30฿) and **tuk-tuk** (20-30฿). Many **songthaew** (3฿) ply the roads of Khon Kaen, but the routes are confusing. The white *songthaew* goes from the train station to TAT. The navy blue runs from TAT to the National Museum. *Songthaew* #8 and #9 run the length of Klang Muang Rd. Most everything worth seeing in Khon Kaen is within walking distance.

Markets: The **day market,** hidden behind the storefronts along Na Muang Rd. and Klang Muang Rd., stretches south from Srichan Rd. to Ruenrom. Activity lasts 5am-7pm. Vendors also set up each evening on the day market's southern perimeter along Ruenrom Rd. The **night market,** near the A/C bus terminal, is basically an Asian food court beneath corrugated metal.

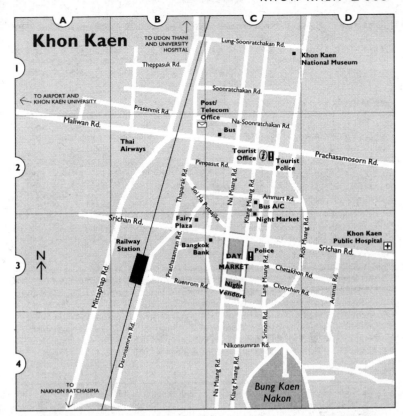

Khon Kaen

Pharmacies: Wattana Pah Sadt, 31/33 Ammart Rd. (tel. 244 468), near Langmuang intersection. Basic first-aid supplies and analgesics. Open daily 7am-10pm.
Medical Services: Khon Kaen Public Hospital (tel. 236 005), on east side of town on Srichan Rd. Thai sign with small green cross. For 24-hr. care, **Mokul Hospital** (tel. 238 934) on Srichan Rd. has English-speaking doctors. From Na Muang or Klang Muang Rd. head toward the train tracks. It is on the right.
Emergency: tel. 1699.
Police: Khon Kaen Police Station (tel. 221 162), on Klang Muang Rd.
Post Offices/Telephones: GPO (tel. 241 560, ext. 4127) on Klang Muang Rd., just past the intersection with Srichan Rd. on the left. Open Mon.-Fri. 8:30am-4:30pm, Sat.-Sun. 9am-noon. **Overseas telephone** and **telegram** open daily 8am-8pm.
Postal code: 40000. **Telephone code:** 043.

ACCOMMODATIONS

Co-Co Guest House, 58/1 Pimpasut Rd. (tel. 241 283), at the corner of Na Muang Rd. and Pimpasut Rd. Check-in at the First Choice Restaurant. The guest house is in the rear, along an alley crowded with karaoke bars. Comfortable, well-maintained wooden complex of rooms. Downstairs baths and A/C rooms sport some unusual architecture (whiskey-bottle windows, woven ceilings, and lacquered brick walls) and noisy non-avian wildlife. Fills up quickly. Noisy on weekend evenings. Singles 100฿. Doubles 150฿, with A/C 300฿.
Sansumran Hotel, 55-59 Klang Muang Rd. (tel. 239 611), a basic hotel with a decent reputation. Look at the pride of wooden lions in the lobby and sympathize with the lone wood antelope. Rooms on the newly renovated 2nd floor are spa-

cious and sparkling, but more expensive. Singles 200฿. Mammoth doubles 250฿. Singles downstairs are cheaper and shabbier but clean (160฿).

Suksawad Hotel, 2/2 Klang Muang Rd. (tel. 236 472). Sign points down a dirt *soi* just off Prachasamosorn Rd. A quiet setting and an English-speaking staff. The miser's choice in Khon Kaen. Small rooms with Asian toilet are just 100฿ for a single. Doubles 140฿. Forgo the bathroom and save 30฿.

FOOD

Typical Thai sidewalk eateries cluster along Pimasut Rd. and Ammart Rd. Inexpensive and authentic Isaan meals can be had at the **night markets** on Lang Muang Rd. and Ruenrom Rd.

The Parrot, 175 Srichan Rd. (tel. 244 692). Heading toward the tracks, it's on the right, on the corner of a *soi* and next to a gas station. Good and inexpensive western meal. Breakfast menu 7:30-11am. Fish and chips (90฿), sandwiches (35฿), pizza (65-160฿), and an entire page of vegetarian selections. Thai food 40-80฿. Fresh-baked white and whole wheat bread 35฿. Wines and other spirits (beer 40) . Staff gives you time to order without hovering. Peruse an English language newspaper while you wait. Open 7:30am-10:30pm, orders taken until 10pm.

SIGHTS

Khon Kaen's only noteworthy sight is the **Khon Kaen National Museum** (tel. 246 170), set back from the intersection of Lung-soomratchakan Rd. and Kasikonthungsang Rd. in a shady park. The navy blue *songthaew* goes past TAT and winds its way to the north end of town, where it will drop you at the side entrance to the museum. This museum documents the history of Thailand's central northeast region. An exhibit on prehistoric artifacts includes pottery from Ban Chiang Archaeological Site in Udon Thani Province. (Open 9am-4pm; admission 10฿.)

ENTERTAINMENT

As the Northeast's premier university city, Khon Kaen majors in hard-core nightlife. For party-hearty dilettantes, the arcade near Co-Co Guest House and First Choice is the premier option for bar-hopping, since the complex is jam-packed with karaoke bars, beer gardens, and other types of pubs.

Hi-tech Music World, on Srichan Rd. across from the well-lit photo of the king where Prachasamran Rd. and Darunsamran Rd. converge. A sea of students bathed in fluorescent lights moves in unison to the beat of Thai rock while screaming orgasmically to the antics of twin playboy bunnies. Enormous plastic insects and suspended sea urchins occupy the cavernous space above, dwarfing both band and audience. Between sets, brightly colored comic-book panels illuminate the floor. 80฿ cover includes 1 drink. Open daily 8pm-1am.

Top West Pub and Restaurant, 6/2 Srichan Rd. (tel. 226 310). Heading toward the tracks along Srichan Rd., it's on the left, after the traffic circle and photo of the King. A country-western bar replete with American flags, animal pelts, and Native American trinkets. A musical showcase of live bands on Saturday night. Soda 50฿. Singha 80฿. Live music daily 10pm-2am.

Funan, 3/1 Srichan Rd. (tel. 239 628). Across the street from Top West and just before the train tracks. MTV holds sway in the early evening until the band takes over, playing exclusively Thai music. The pub fills quickly and the crowd drinks fast. By midnight the band switches to folk/rock standards, as the audience dances at (or on) the tables and sings along. Beer 80฿. Open daily 9:30pm-2am.

Phoebus Music Hall (tel. 332 853), off Pimpasut Rd. From Co-Co Guest House, cross Na Muang Rd.; it's in the arcade on the right. Discophile heaven or teenage hilarity. Don't be surprised if the roving video camera displays your *farang* mug on the screen above the stage. Open daily 8:30pm-2am. Snooker hall upstairs.

■ Near Khon Kaen: Chonabot

Although Khon Kaen Province has plenty of sights, the scant number of tourist facilities (transportation, lodging, etc.) makes exploring the area a healthy challenge. The tiny town of **Chonabot** stocks enough hand-woven silk to outfit Zsa Zsa Gabor and her assorted wedding parties for six lifetimes.

Tour companies often advertise trips to this area, but demand up to a 25% commission from factory owners for every purchase (resulting in higher mark-ups)—it's better to go on your own. Most factories are open Monday-Saturday 8am-5pm; there are no formal showrooms, but they will gladly bring out wares that interest you. Often traditional tie-dyed *mut-mee* silk is sold as a two-*lah* set (one *lah* is 90cm—enough material for one skirt). *Si puen* is plain, solid-color silk, more frequently bought by the meter. Prices vary depending on thickness and weight, of the material. *Mut-mee* silk starts at 250-300฿ per *lah*, and *sipuen* runs 135-200฿ per *lah*.

To get to Chonabot, catch the bus to Nakhon Sawan from Khon Kaen's main bus terminal (every hour, last bus 1:30pm, 1hr., 15฿) and ask to be let off at Chonabot. The bus will deposit you along the highway. After you disembark, turn around to face the wagon-wheel fence and police station. Walk right to the first intersection, then turn left. The first factory is on the right side of the street before the post office.

To return to Khon Kaen, walk back down Phosri Sahat Rd. until it meets the highway. Wait in front of the police station; the last bus back departs at 5pm.

SOUTHERN THAILAND

Southern Thailand is graced with some of the finest shorelines and islands in Southeast Asia. The warm translucent waters of the Gulf of Thailand to the east and the Andaman Sea to the west are at the center of southern life in coastal towns that are financially dependent on the ebb and flow of tourists or the daily shrimp and fish catch. Monstrous luxury hotels have conquered some coastal acreage, but most beaches remain untrammeled and ready for low-impact exploration. Down the bumpier dirt roads, at places yet undiscovered by bulldozer-toting Bangkok developers and tourist guide book writers, Shangri-La is still pristine. You just have to work harder to find it.

Heading down the coast with the Urban Bangkok empire at your back, you pass through a chain of seaside paradise-purgatories and small villages. After squeezing through the narrowest point in Thailand, the road snakes among inland swamps and coastal wetlands, through durian plantations, and along the pale sandstone cliffs that rim glowing white sand beaches. Offshore the resort islands of Ko Samui, Ko Phangan, and Ko Tao gear themselves to please the tens of thousands of foreigners who catalyze the evolution of "paradise on earth."

The ethnic mixture of the deep south slowly appears after Surat Thani, as mosques replace wats and women begin to don veils. Spicy seafoods and local fruits tend to dominate Southern diets. Specialties include *khanom jiin jam yaa* (thin white noodles with fish curry), sweet and sour fish, fish curry paste cooked in banana-leaf cups, and oyster omelettes. Mangosteen, rambutan, *langsads,* and pungent durians are the culinary cooling tools, especially for wimpy *farang* tongues.

In pint-size provinces like those south of Krabi, traveler-oriented services are few, as are the numbers who speak English. Foreigners are something of an anomaly here; don't be surprised if you find yourself under heavy scrutiny. Women may opt to wear long pants in areas with large Muslim populations.

South of Phuket, the west coast's main draw is Ko Tarutao, a group of over 50 islands comprising a national park, thus far protected from the development strangling Ko Phi Phi and Ko Samet. That coast is also home to Trang, the city where the south's feeding frenzy is at a fever pitch. The east coast from Pattani down to Malaysia is lined with blithely beautiful beaches, frequented by locals on the weekends and in the evenings. The deep, deep south from Pattani to Malaysia is rich in lovely countryside as well, plush with vegetation, unlike the area up near Surat Thani, which is stripped and paved for large gas stations and suburban housing projects.

■ Chumphon ชุมพร

All signs point to Chumphon as Thailand's next tourist boom town. It has already usurped Surat Thani as the jumping-off point for that famous tropical trinity: Ko Tao, Ko Phangan, and Ko Samui. The town and its surrounding area are none-too-shabby themselves: 222km of white beaches, fantastic offshore islands, long coral reefs, stunning caves, and waterfalls. Things will only get easier, as an airport is currently under construction and due to be completed by the end of 1996.

Almost 500km from Bangkok, this gateway marks the convergence of the asphalt arteries connecting Phuket, Bangkok, and the tail of Thailand, as well as transition in dialect and food. *Pak tai* refers to the fast, high-toned southern dialect, and to the southern vegetable-laden culinary style which employs some of the country's most merciless spices. *Pak tai* also denotes the region farther south, where Islam is a major influence. Pursuers of trivia will be tickled to know that the town's name was abbreviated from Chumnumphon ("the gathering of blessings"), so named because ancient military troops hosted pep rallies here to raise morale before battles.

ORIENTATION

Chumphon basically follows a simple grid, with a few surprises. **Krom Luang Chumphon Road** runs east from the train station and forms the northern border of the town. **Pobaminthra Manka Road** sprawls east-west as the town's southern limit and is where you'll find the hospital, post office, and buses to Hat Sai Ree. The bus station and several tourist information centers lie on **Tha Thapao Road,** running north-south in the western part of the city. Parallel and one block to the east is hotel-and-eatery-studded **Saladaeng Road.** This is where the city grid begins to break down. Through some quirk of city planning, the last street to the right before the Saladaeng-Krom Luang Chumpon intersection as one walks north has been annexed by Saladaeng Rd. This side-street contains locally famous Ocean Shopping Mall as well as numerous restaurants and the Chumphon Information Centre. **Pracha Uthit Road**, in the shape of a "V," straddles the city center; here you'll find the market and transport to boats to Ko Tao and Hat Thung Wua Laen (Cabana Beach).

PRACTICAL INFORMATION

Tourist Offices: Sornserm Travel, 66/1 Tha Tapao Rd (tel. tel. 502-023), across from the bus station. Organized staff speaks good English and sells packaged deals to the islands. The staff at **Infinity Travel Services,** 68/2 Tha Thapao Rd. (tel. 501 937), greets travelers at the train station in snazzy company jackets. Open daily 7am-11pm. Knowledgeable Mr. O can be found at **Tiw's Restaurant,** 174 Saladaeng Rd. (tel. 502 448), at the 5-way intersection across from the cinema. Look for the English signs advertising tourist information. Open daily 2am-8pm.

Currency Exchange: Bangkok Bank, 111/1-2 Saladaeng Rd. (tel. 511 446). **Thai Farmer's Bank,** 134 Saladaeng Rd. (tel. 511 380). Both open Mon.-Fri. 8:30am-3:30pm, closed holidays.

Trains: Chumphon Railway Station (tel. 511 103), at the intersection of Rot Fai and Krom Luang Chumphon Rd. To: **Bangkok** (9 per day, 7½hr., 3rd-class 102฿; 2nd-class 192฿; sleeper car: top bunk 292฿, bottom bunk 342฿); **Phetchaburi** (5 per day, 5½hr., 3rd class 78฿, 2nd class 142฿, sleeper car: top bunk 242฿, bottom bunk 292฿); **Surat Thani** (11 per day, 3hr., 3rd class, 54฿; 2nd class 91฿); **Padang Besar, Malaysia** (10:54am, 9hr., 2nd class 229฿; sleeper car: top bunk 379฿, bottom bunk 429฿); and **Sungai Kolok** (9:23 and 10:10pm,12hr., 2nd class 250฿; sleeper car: top bunk 400฿, bottom bunk 450฿).

Buses: Regular buses leave from the terminal (tel. 502 725) on Tha Tapao Rd. across from the similarly named hotel. Tickets sold in the station and on the bus. To **Bangkok** (9pm, 7hr., 157฿; A/C tour bus 9:30pm, 202฿; other buses pass ran-

Southern Thailand

Nakhon Pathom

Bangkok

Phetchaburi

Pattaya

Hua Hin

Pran Buri

Khao Sam Roi Yot Nat. Park

Ko Samet

Kui Buri

BURMA

Prachuap Khiri Khan

Thap Sakae

Andaman Sea

Bang Saphan

Pathiu

Gulf of Thailand

Kra Buri

Chumphon

Tham Prakayang

Punya Ban

Sawi

Ko Tao

Ranong

Hat Supin

Lang Sua

Ko Phangan

Laem Son Nat. Park

Ko Ta Luang

Ko Samui

Kapoe

Chaiya

Don Sak

Khura Buri

Tha Chang

Khanom

Tham Waram

Surat Thani

Sichon

Takua Pa

Bang Sak

Khao Sok Nat. Park

Phanom

Na San

Tha Sala

Khao Luk

Phrasaeng

Wiang Sa

Lam Pi

Than Put

Phang Nga

Ao Luk

Khao Phanom Bencha Nat. Park

Thung Yai

Nakhon Si Thammarat

Khok Kloi

Hat Nai Yang Nat. Park

Sasarn Hoi

Ko Yao Noi

Krabi

Thung Sopng

Khlong Thom

Huai Yot

Khuan Khanun

Hua Sai

Ranot

Phuket

Ko Phi Phi

Sikao

Ban Lampam

Thale Luang Thale Sap

Ko Lanta Yai

Trang

Kachong

Sathing Phra

Pak Mong

Ko Li Bong

Yan Ta Khao

Phatthalung

Pak Phayun

Hat Chao Mai Nat. Park

Thung Wa

Thale Ban Nat. Park

Songkhla

Ban Pakbara

Hat Yai

Na Thawi

Pattani

Tarutao Nat. Park

Ko Tarutao

Sadao

Yala

Sai Buri

Ko Rawi

Satun

Kangar

Saba Yoi

Narathiwat

Ban Nang Sata

Pulau Langkawi

Alor Setar

MALAYSIA

Sungai Kolok

Sungai Petani

N

0   50 miles

0   50 kilometers

domly though Chumphon throughout the night but may already be full); **Phuket** (6 per day, 3:30pm-5:30am, 7hr., 102฿); and **Surat Thani** (4 per day, 1:30-5:30pm, 3hr., 57฿). **Suwanathi Tours,** 45/2 Tha Tapao Rd. (tel. 511 422), behind the bus terminal, has A/C buses to **Bangkok** (10:00am, 2:00, and 10:00pm, 202฿). Reserve in advance. Open daily 8am-10pm. **Infinity Tourist Information Service,** 68/2 Tha Tapao Rd. (tel. 501 937) has **mini-van** service to **Surat Thani** (every hr., 7am-5pm, 2½hr., 90฿). Open daily 7am-11pm.

Boats: The daily **slow boat** to **Ko Tao** leaves the pier at midnight (5hr., 200฿). The last *songthaew* (5฿) leaves at 6pm in front of the waterworks offices on Pracha-Uthit Rd. Walk east past the market on Pracha-Uthit Rd. until it curves sharply left. Blue *songthaew* leave just past the covered seating on the left side of the road. The sleek, **high-speed boat** leaves daily from a different pier (8am, 1½hr., 400฿). Red *songthaew* for the speed boat pier also leave from the waterworks office (5฿). Songserm can arrange transportation for both you and your baggage. Infinity (50฿) or Mr. O at Tiw's Restaurant (40฿) can take you to the docks as well. To go to **Ko Maphraw** (Coconut Island), contact the provincial authority at least 15 days in advance for an official tour.

Rentals: Pick-ups and cars can be rented from Tiw's Restaurant (1200฿ per day) or Infinity (900-1200฿ per day). Motorcycles are 200฿; must leave passport. Boats can be hired for daytrips to the islands. Prices range from 1500 to 2500฿ per day, depending on itinerary and boat size. Contact Infinity Tours or Mr. O for details and special events. The **Chumphon Cabana Resort and S.M.C. Travel Centre,** 69/20 Tha Tapao Rd. (tel. 570 395), also offers package tours and sponsors numerous Scuba **PADI** courses (1hr., 300฿; 12 days, 15,000฿). Equipment rentals also available. Costs vary with the season.

Pharmacies: 188/105 Saladaeng Rd. (tel. 501 129), opposite Ocean Shopping Mall. Green sign with orange stripe. Open Mon-Fri 5am-10pm, Sat-Sun. 9:30am-10pm.

Medical Services: Virajsilp Hospital (tel. 503 238), at the south end of Tha Taphao Rd. Open 24hr. English speaking doctors.

Emergency: tel. 191

Police: (tel. 511 300), at the north end of Saladaeng Rd. past the intersection with Krom Luang Chumphon Rd.

Post Offices: GPO (tel. 511 041), on Pobaminthra Manka Rd., past the market and the city shrine in the southeastern corner of town. Open Mon.-Fri. 8:30am-4:30pm, Sat.-Sun. 9am-noon. **Postal code:** 86000.

Telephones: (tel. 511 885), on the 2nd floor of the GPO. Open daily 7am-10pm. Chumphon Cabana Resort and S.M.C. Travel Centre also has overseas telephones. and fax service. Open daily 8am-5pm. **Telephone code:** 077.

ACCOMMODATIONS

There are many Chinese-style hotels along Saladaeng Rd. while new bungalows are constantly appearing on Ao Thung Wua Laen, Hat Sai Ree, and the city fringes.

Mayazes Resthouse, 111/35-36 Soi Bangkok Bank Saladaeng Rd. (tel. 504 452). Take a left from the bus station onto Tha Tapao Rd. and then take the first right. Owner runs a spotless guest house, as well as make outstanding maps of Chumphon and the surrounding site for her guests. All rooms have a writing desk and dresser. Common bathrooms with toilet paper and western-style toilet. Singles 120฿, with A/C 200฿. Doubles 180฿, with A/C 300฿.

Suksamer Guest House, 118/4 Suksamer Rd. (tel. 502 430). From the train station go down Krom Luang Chumphon Rd. until the Suksamer Rd. intersection and turn right. It's at the end of the first *soi* on the left. A thatched-roof house with a big coconut tree, Suksamer has clean, spacious rooms with fans. Shared bathroom with showers. Open-air restaurant serves fresh baked bread (15฿) and pizza (60-130฿). Singles/doubles 150฿.

Suriya Hotel, 125/24-5 Saladaeng Rd. (tel. 511 144), just south of the 5-way intersection on the right side of the road with a red sign over the door. Worn pink fuzzy blankets and once-bright blue walls have seen better days. The nearby street intersection might keep you up at night. Singles with bath 120฿. Doubles 200฿.

Gotta Love Those Swallows

For the lonely budget traveler in Southern Thailand, it's encouraging to know that the nest of the swallow is considered an aphrodisiac by herbalists in Chumphon. Although all nests work just fine, the white nests are the most powerful, and they often sell for up to 70,000฿ per kg. Harvesting nests is difficult, dangerous work, and people have shot each other just over the scraps. Not only is it a risky profession, it is a short-lived one. Harvesting is permitted for only three months during the year. This allows the swallows to make up for the many babies and eggs destroyed in the process (and it keeps the prices up). After harvesting, the nests are torn into strips. The pieces are rinsed in cold water for 24 hr., made into a soup, and sold by the bowl. What bestows such potent powers upon these plain little strips? Perhaps it's because the swallows stay in the air *all day;* these are strong birds. Most believe, however, that it's a combination of the bird's saliva and the "love nest" itself that provides that special something for your special someone.

FOOD

In Chumphon, food-lovers can find meals for chump-change in the markets and shopping mall food courts. The **morning market** actually hustles all day (5am-5pm) in the shade of a city-block-wide mesh of tin roofing—a fresh fruit cornucopia with "fingernail bananas" *(gluay lep meu)* and wonderfully sweet pineapples *(sapah rot),* two first-rate fruits for which Chumphon is renowned. The entrance to the labyrinth is on Pracha-Uthit Rd., by the row of motorcycle taxis along Pobaminthra Manka Rd. The **night market** sprawls along Saladaeng Rd. to the Ocean Shopping Mall and serves delectable dinners like *khao tom aahaan talay* (rice soup with seafood) and *khanom jiin nam ya* (vermicelli with fish curry) at low prices. The **Ocean Shopping Mall,** located on the annexed side-street off Saladaeng Rd., north of the Fuji sign, is an air-conditioned oasis with a food court and typical Thai food—fried rice, noodle soup, ice cream (under 30฿). (Open daily 10am-9:30pm.)

Pai Thong (tel. 501 336), **on** Saladaeng Rd. near the Ocean Shopping Mall. Delicious Isaan dishes 25-30฿: roast pork, roast catfish, and *som tam.* To avoid stomach critters, tell them *"mai sai poo"* (no the raw crabs) and *"mai ped"* (cool off on the chilis). Other dishes 35-50฿. English menu. Open daily 5:30am-11:30pm.

Tiw's Restaurant, 174 Saladaeng Rd. (tel. 502 448), across from the cinema at the 5-way intersection. Decorated with great maps and pictures of the sights around Chumphon. Best place to contact Mr. O. Affordable five-star food. Rice plates 20฿, fried rice 25฿. English menu. Open daily; food served 2am-1pm (yes, 2am), drinks and snacks until 8pm.

■ Near Chumphon

To see anything interesting, a daytrip is in order. The current hot spots for scuba diving and beach bumming, Ko Tao and Ko Nang Yuan, distance themselves from Chumphon's coast. Seldom-visited Ko Ngam Yai and Ko Ngam Noi off nearby Hat Thung Wua Laen, however, are better locations for viewing something besides all the other divers. Renting a boat to visit the islands off Chumphon's shore will set a backpacker's budget back a couple of days; find a group, and share the burden. When your tender skin tires of UV abuse and constant *coup de soleil,* **Rab Ro Caves** and the **Ka Po Waterfalls** offer a soothing change of environment. Hat Thung Wua Laen, Rab Ro Caves, and Ka Po waterfalls can easily be traversed in one daytrip.

For those more adventurous, **Tristar Adventure Tours** (tel. 502 430), in Suksamer Guest House, offers camping and spelunking trips guaranteed to thrill (600฿ for 1 day, 4000฿ for 6 days; includes transportation and food).

THAILAND

HAT THUNG WUA LAEN (CABANA BEACH)

Twelve km north of Chumphon, this is the blockbuster beach in the area (it has no-stick sand). Thankfully, stardom has not spoiled the scene. Laws now prohibit commercial buildings on beachfront property (unfortunately, this gives the already existing Chuan Phan complex a monopoly), ban jet skis and campfires, and maintain tough environmental standards to keep the waters clean. Fishing boats cannot enter the bay, which is naturally protected by hills flanking the gently sloping beach. The influx of bungalows and shops to the outlying area does contribute to a suburbanized sprawl, however. Offshore **Ko Ngam Yai** and **Ko Ngam Noi,** prized for their swallows' nests, underwater coral reefs, and soaring cliffs and caves, are accesible by a boat from Sa Plee Pier. Check tourist information listings for group rates.

In Chumphon, yellow *songthaew* to Cabana Beach lurk behind the marketplace along Pracha-Uthit Rd., which begins across from the cinema at the five-way intersection on Saladaeng Rd. by the Fuji sign. They run the length of the beach (last trip 6pm, ½hr., 20฿). If you've rented your own wheels, head north (across Krom Luang Chumphon Rd.) over the train tracks, following the signs for Chumphon Cabana Resort, which is 16km from town.

Seabeach Bungalow, 4/2 Mu 8, at the very end of Hat Thung Wua Laen, has brick rooms and bright blue curtains. Singles with bath cost 250-300฿, doubles 400฿, with A/C 550฿. The **restaurant** has a fine selection of Thai, seafood, and *pak tai* dishes, but the English menu offers only a limited selection. The only bungalows built directly on the beach are at ~~View Restaurant and Bungalows,~~ 13/2 Mu 8 Hat Thung Wua Laen. The dining area has savory seafood plates (50฿) and the bohemian bungalows have steeply sloped, red-tiled roofs and great views. Bungalows sleeping two go for 300฿, sleeping four 400฿. Best of all, it's close to the main stretch. **Clean Wave Resort,** 54 Mu 8 (tel. 503 621), has a friendly staff and offers single rooms (sleeping three) with fan (250฿), as well as doubles (sleeping four) with fan (400฿) or A/C (550฿). The restaurant has a beautiful view of clean waves, of course.

■ Surat Thani สุราษฎร์ธานี

Many foreign travelers know Surat Thani only as a stopover on the way to Ko Samui or other points south. Granted, there's not much to see in the downtown of this provincial capital, but its outlying areas are home to Thailand's most famous monks (and monkeys). Among the noteworthy sights in this area is Wat Suam Mokkha Phalaram, a respected meditation center that attracts Thais and foreigners seeking a spiritual retreat. Thai gourmands often descend upon Surat Thani to feast on the city's renowned enormous oysters. People boast of the high nutrition of this delicacy, but eat at your own risk.

ORIENTATION

Train service falls about 13km short of Surat Thani, at **Phun Phin.** Public buses (6฿) run from Phun Phin to the Ban Don area. In town, **Talaat Kaset** (Kaset Market), is divided into two sections on either side of **Talaat Mai Road,** which runs straight through town and parallels the **Tapi River. Talaat Kaset 1,** closer to the Tapi River, contains the local **bus station** with most of the connections to towns within the province, such as Phun Phin. **Talaat Kaset 2** contains the bus terminal to other provinces and has connections to **Chaiya.** Numbers on the over-street arches by the entrances indicate which market is which. All of the hotels and many places to eat lie within in a 200m radius of **Phanthip Tour** on Talaat Mai Rd. Toward the river **Na Muang Road** runs parallel to Talaat Mai Rd. and partially along the river. Further toward the river is **Talaat Laang Road** along the riverfront where the night ferry leaves for Ko Samui. **Chonkasem Road** intersects Talaat Mai Rd. at the GPO.

THAILAND

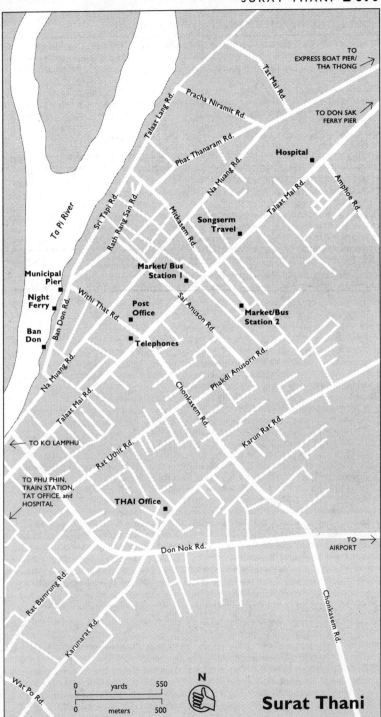

Surat Thani

PRACTICAL INFORMATION

Tourist Offices: Tourism Authority of Thailand (TAT), 5 Talaat Mai Rd. (tel. 288 818), a 20-min. walk south from Talaat Kaset. Useful information and maps for Surat Thani, Ko Samui, Ko Phangan, and Ko Tao. Phone available for emergencies. Open daily 8:30am-4:30pm.

Tourist Police: (24-hr. tel. 281 300), at the TAT.

Tours and Travel: Many places sell transport tickets to *farang* who often can't discern the best or safest deals. Phanthip Tour, Songserm Travel Centre, and Samui Tour are safe, convenient, and reliable. The first 2 own boats to the islands; the last arranges tickets for all modes of transport and charges no "service fee." For road travel, Songserm and Phanthip control almost all the bus/minivan routes. **Phanthip Tour,** 442/24-5 Talaat Mai Rd. (tel. 272 230), between the 2 markets. Open daily 8am-5pm. **Songserm Travel Service,** 30/2 Mu 3 (tel. 285 124), off Talaat Laang Rd., across from the night ferry pier. Open daily 5:30am-6:30pm. **Samui Tour,** 326/12 Talaat Mai Rd. (tel. 282 352), on the way to TAT office on the left. Open daily 5am-6:30pm.

Currency Exchange: Surat Thani has better exchange rates than the islands. Banks line Na Muang Rd. Open Mon.-Fri. 8:30am-3:30pm. **Bangkok Bank,** 195-7 Na Muang Rd. (tel. 273 927), has a booth in front. Open daily 8:30am-5:30pm. **Thai Farmers Bank,** 151 Na Muang Rd. (tel. 282 210).

Air Travel: Thai Air, 3/27-8 Karunarat Rd. (tel. 273 710). To **Bangkok** (12:40 and 8:40pm, 1710฿). Shuttles to and from airport (10:45am and 6:30pm, 20km, 35฿).

Trains: Station (tel. 311 213), 13km away at Phun Phin. Open daily 6am-6pm. Buses (6฿) go to the city center. Arrange tickets through Phanthip Tour, or go directly to the station. Trains tend to be pretty full going through Phun Phin, so buses offer a lot more convenience for a little more money. Plan ahead for train use. Listed fares are for 3rd-, 2nd-, and 1st-class (when available), respectively. To: **Chumphon** (11 per day, 34฿, 71฿, 91฿); **Hat Yai** (5 per day, 6hr., 53฿, 114฿, 228฿); **Trang** (2 per day, 4hr., 59฿, 100฿); **Sungai Kolok** (2 per day, 2nd-class upper 320฿, lower 350฿); **Butterworth** (1:50am, 2nd-class 378฿); and **Bangkok** (9 per day, 13hr.,127฿, 244฿, upper bed, 314฿, lower bed 344฿, 1st-class 470฿, Sprinter 304฿; 10฿ surcharge for express).

Buses: Local bus terminal, Talaat Kaset 1, serves Surat Thani Province. **Regular bus terminal,** Talaat Kaset 2 (tel. 272 341), connects to major cities and provinces around Surat Thani: **Bangkok** (7am and 5pm, 12hr., 158฿; A/C 8pm, 10hr., 285฿); **Chumphon** (7am, 4hr., 58฿); **Hat Yai** (5 per day, 6hr., 85฿; A/C 4 per day, 5hr., 120฿); and **Phuket** (2 per day, 5hr., 85฿; A/C 139฿). **Private buses** also serve Bangkok, and prices vary in quality, service, and hidden commissions (200-300฿). Be wary of any offer under 200฿. Private buses to other cities are generally found at **Phanthip Tour** and **Songserm Travel Service.** Songserm costs a little more, but stops less. Phanthip's 1st-class A/C to: **Phuket** (3 per day, 150-180฿); **Krabi** (3 per day, 150฿); and **Chumphon** (10am, 150฿).

Local Transportation: Motorcycles and **samlor** provide taxi service (10฿). **Tuk-tuk** run regular routes, but have no markings indicating their destination (5฿).

Markets: Talaat Kaset 1 and **2** flood the areas around the bus station with the usual assortment of knick-knacks. The **night market** sprawls between Na Muang Rd. and Talaat Luang Rd. by the Tapi River.

Medical Services: Surat Thani Provincial Hospital (tel. 284 700), 1km past the TAT on Surat-Phih Rd. **Taksin Hospital** (tel. 273 239), on Talaat Mai Rd. 1km north of the intersection with Chonkasem Rd.

Emergency: tel. 191 or tourist police (tel. 281 300). Private and more costly.

Police: 188 Na Muang Rd. (tel. 272 095). Try the tourist police first.

Post Offices: GPO (tel. 272 013), at the corner of Talaat Mai Rd. and Chonkasem Rd. Open Mon.-Fri. 8:30am-4:30pm, Sat.-Sun. 9am-noon. **Branch office** (tel. 273 431), at the intersection of Na Muang Rd. and Chonkasem Rd. Open Mon.-Fri. 8:30am-5:30pm, Sat. 9am-noon. **Postal code:** 84000.

Telephones: Telecom (tel. 281 537), on Don Nok Rd., 2-km from most hotels. Walk down Talaat Mai Rd. toward the TAT from the intersection with Chonkasem Rd. and turn left onto Don Nok Rd. It's on the left about 20min. down the road. **HCD** service to US and UK. Open daily 8am-noon. **Telephone code:** 077.

ACCOMMODATIONS

Those stranded at the train station in Phun Phin can lodge at the **Queen Hotel** (tel. 311 003) down the road (open 24hr.). Rooms cost 150-350฿. The best hotels are in Surat Thani, in a 200m arc around Phanthip Tour and the bus terminals. Some of the less expensive places in town vary in degrees of brotheldom—check out the hotel's scene before signing up for a potentially vile night.

Muang Tai Hotel, 390-2 Talaat Mai Rd. (tel. 286 390), at the intersection with Chonkasem Rd. A recent face-lift has injected youth into the formerly sagging place. Powerful fans actually cool the spacious rooms. An elevator services the 5 floors. Sit-down toilets. Singles/doubles 200฿, with A/C 380฿. Open 24hr.

Thai Thani Hotel, 442/307-9 Talaat Kaset 2 (tel. 272 977), off Talaat Mai Rd. A shy giant hidden by the market. Sanitary rooms have weathered Euro-style baths. The fan struggles to fend off humidity and heat. A/C rooms have pink bathroom sandals and phones. Singles/doubles 240฿, with A/C 320฿. Room with two beds 260฿, with A/C 340฿. 24-hr. reception on the 3rd floor.

Talking Loud, 458/1 Talaat Mai Rd. (tel. 273 577), about 10min. north of the post office. Although the rooms are short of spectacular, they are the cheapest in town and will save the penniless backpacker some cash. Hang out in the jazz club downstairs and pass the time until the boat to Ko Samui comes. Singles without bath 100฿. Doubles 160฿.

FOOD

Talaat Kaset has stalls displaying curries, meats, and vegetables to be ladled over rice. Passengers might want to stock up on provisions from the **food stalls** and the **night market** by the night boat pier before sailing away. The **Sahathai Department Store's food court,** on Na Muang Rd., makes for a nice A/C lunch break. (Open daily 9:30am-9:30pm.) Restaurants along Na Muang Rd. have Thai/English menus.

R. Graphic Restaurant, 522/1 Na Muang Rd. (tel. 283 098), near Sahathai Dept. store. Attentive staff can recommend dishes like fried catfish salad. Or opt for a chicken salad (40฿), fruit shake (20฿), or fried rice (30฿). Open daily 9am-10pm.

Yam Bakery, 460-2 Na Muang Rd. (tel. 281 460), between Sahathai Dept. Store and the post office. Grab the hamburger-sized *khanom pia* (mung bean cake) for 10฿. They also have fresh-baked raisin loaf, breads with stringy sweet pork, and loaves served with butter and sugar (15฿ each). Open daily 4am-8:30pm.

■ Near Surat Thani

Although Ko Samui and company steal the show, the traditional culture and art of the mainland area around Surat Thani make a fine contrast to the islands hedonistic pleasures. The sights around Surat Thani can be planned as daytrips via *songthaew* from Talaat Kaset. It's best to leave early in the morning for Chaiya, since public transportation is less frequent later in the day and disappears after 6pm.

CHAIYA

Chaiya is the site of both an ancient city and one of the most respected meditation centers in the country, **Wat Suan Mokkha Phalarm** (a.k.a. Suan Mok), a 150-acre forest temple along Hwy. 41. Suan Mok is easily recognizable due to the congregation of vehicles parked out front. Inside, devotees invoke the founder, Bhikkhu Phutthathat (or Than Phutthathat), who passed away in July 1993. Masses of people sit under the wat's trees and meditate alongside monks, following the example of Than Phutthathat. His monastic community follows the regimen of Buddha's earliest disciples, and their purist approach is reflected in the temple, which is stark and barren, unlike other wats. The stunning collection of paintings here was described by Than Phutthathat himself as a pictorial interpretation of *dharma.* This "Spiritual Theater" is part of Phutthathat's efforts to make the Buddhist scriptures accessible to all.

Around the wat is the Golden Buddha Shrine, forests, and streams. Anyone can attend **meditation retreats** (both *Vipassana* and *Samatha*—Insight and Tranquil forms) held by resident *farang* monks, usually on the first 10 days of the month. Contact the temple directly, and preferably in person (a minimum contribution of around 50฿ per day covers food and expenses).

Wat Phra Borom That Chaiya (familiarly known as Wat Phra That), the much-revered and elaborately restored 1200-year-old pagoda, contains relics of Lord Buddha and is surrounded by 174 Buddha images. Unlike most of Thailand's temples, this one is consecrated to Mahayana Buddhism, the religion of the then-ruling Srivijaya Empire based in Sumatra. Wat Phra That is also home to a **National Museum** at Chaiya. The well-maintained museum exhibits Thai artifacts from almost 500,000 years ago. (Open Wed.-Sun 9am-4pm; donation 10฿.)

To get to the wats, catch a northbound bus going to Ranong or Chumphon and get off at Wat Suan Mok first. From either Wat Suan Mok or the Chaiya bus/train station, it's a 5฿ motorcycle taxi or *tuk-tuk* ride to Wat Phra That.

MONKEY SCHOOL AND OYSTER FARMS

The Surat Thani area shelters some of the world's least intelligent and brightest creatures. Some of the largest **oysters** (the dumb ones) alive are bred around the Kadaeh and Ta Tong Rivers. If you're interested in how they're raised and harvested, contact the fishing department (tel. 286 922). Far smarter and more animated are the coconut-picking students at the **Monkey Training College.** The show is 300฿, for three people 400฿; check with local travel agents, who can usually give you a better deal with a larger group. To go on your own, catch a *tuk-tuk* or *songthaew* (5฿) on Talaat Mai Rd. on the Phanthip Tour side of the street. Ask to be let off at *rong rian sawn ling.* Then take a motorcycle taxi (20฿) to the school, or face a 2-km hike.

KO SAMUI เกาะสมุย

The third largest island in Thailand sits in calm gulf waters 84km east of Surat Thani and 250km south of Bangkok. Ko Samui is a sun-worshipper's bronzing machine, equipped with enough coconut-ridden sand, cheap bungalows, and fresh seafood to keep seasoned beach aficionados happy. With cleaner water and less large-scale development, Samui beats Phuket in most departments. The air-conditioning coil is slowly conquering Samui, but plenty of rustic accommodations remain.

Tourism has not left Ko Samui untainted, however. With no water-treatment facilities and ballooning quantities of refuse to manage, Ko Samui is hanging in precarious ecological balance. Moreover, many visitors to the island are disturbed by the total absence of indigenous culture. Ko Samui is completely geared toward serving foreign tourists, at any expense.

If you want nightlife and plenty of company, kick up your heels at Chaweng and Lamai. Those seeking a bit more solitude should head to the north beaches of Mae Nam, Bo Phut, and Bangrak, where it's more mellow, but the waves and wind can be as pushy as a lunchtime bully. Although bungalows litter the west and south coasts, the nearby ferry piers, rocky coastline, and occasionally dirty gulf currents washing up from the mainland keep this half of the island tourist-free. Magnificent sunsets are best appreciated from the coves in the southwest, off Rte. 4170.

Peak season seems to be spilling over: last year, tourists stormed the island from August to September and November to March, when accommodations filled to capacity. Prices dip from March to July, but don't expect discounts in the most populated tourist areas. Prices below are for high season unless otherwise noted. In low season, prices may drop 20-50%, automatically or through adroit bargaining.

GETTING THERE

Surat Thani is the main launching point to Ko Samui. Double-check everything as prices and schedules for boats and ferries fluctuate through the tourist season.

There are a few transport options to the island. The best is the **auto ferry,** which departs from Don Sak Pier 60km east of Surat Thani (5 per day, 8am-5pm, 1½hr., 40฿). It arrives at Thong Yang Pier 10km south of Na Thon on Ko Samui, *songthaew* wait to cart newly arrived sun-lovers off to the major beaches. Most tourists opt to go to Na Thon, which is the starting point for trips anywhere on the island. The entire trip is simplified by tour companies that sell combination bus-ferry-bus tickets. Buses depart from the Surat Thani offices of both Phanthip Tour and Samui Tour (5 per day, 6:50am-3:30pm, 3hr., 70฿, A/C 90฿). For more information please see **Surat Thani: Practical Information** on page 674). Samui Tour also picks up folks arriving on overnight trains to Surat, with shuttles departing Phun Phin station at 6:20 and 7:20am, in time to make the first of two trips to Ko Samui.

Songserm Travel Centre runs the **express boat** route, but tickets can be bought almost anywhere. There's a Songserm branch at the pier. The fare to Samui (150฿) includes a bus ride from the Songserm Office to Tha Thong Pier 5km northeast. Buses leave the office at 7:30am and 2pm for Pak Nam boats to Na Thon (8am and 2:30pm, 2½hr.).

The **night/sleeper boat** (11pm, 6hr.) is especially suited for late arrivals in Surat Thani who don't want to spend the night there. Tickets can be purchased at the pier in Surat Thani along Talaat Laang Rd., left of the municipal pier and behind the nightly fruit stalls. There are two fares to Na Thon: the lower deck, no bedding 50฿; and the upper deck, mattresses 70฿.

Samui Airport is between Chaweng and Bangrak beaches. Bangkok Airways makes daily flights to **Bangkok** (2080฿) and **Phuket** (1210฿).

ISLAND ORIENTATION

A new 50-km paved road, **Route 4169** (Tweeratpakdee Rd.), makes a circuit around the island, giving easy access to the major beaches and **Na Thon,** the main pier town. Km markings along the road start at Na Thon (Km0) and run counter-clockwise. Most accommodations sun themselves on the north and east beaches. **Route 4170** loops off the highway to cover the southwest corner of the island and accesses sights like the Butterfly Garden and some of the beaches with more picturesque sunsets. *Songthaew* run along Route 4169 and some beach roads; they will usually drop passengers off at the desired bungalow.

The annually revised maps researched by V. Hongsombud (40฿) are durable, waterproof layouts of Ko Samui, Ko Phangan, and Ko Tao showing every bungalow, sight, and major road along with condensed practical information.

ISLAND SIGHTS

Lounge-about lizards slither to Ko Samui for beaches, not sights. After the sand and countless coconut trees, a couple of graphic rock formations and the generically named "Big Buddha" are the most photographed attractions. The island is made for motorbike exploration (the Big Buddha, and anything along Rte. 4169 can also be reached by *songthaew* until 6pm). The following is a counterclockwise outline, with Km posts.

By the bend in the road by Km18 (Rte. 4169—Southern Lamai), a sign points to **Hin Ta-Hin Yaai** (Grandfather Stone-Grandmother Stone). Supposedly, an old couple died at sea in a shipwreck and their bodies washed ashore, creating mystical rock formations. As you travel down the 400m concrete road, the postcards at the souvenir shops spoil the triple-X surprise. Climb the rocks to see Gramps in erect action (some 3m of solid rock); you may have to hunt to see Granny's stone pudendum. From the tip of the rocky cape, **Hat Lamai** is in full glory below: 2km of undiluted white-sand beach backed by palms shading hundreds of bungalows.

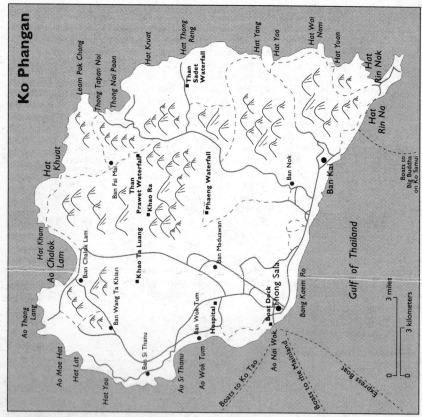

Ko Phangan

Leam Pak Chong
Thong Tapan Noi
Thong Nai Poan
Hat Kruat
Hat Thong Reng
Hat Yang
Hat Tao
Hat Wai Nam
Hat Yuan
Hat Rin Nok
Hat Rin Na

Than Sadet Waterfall

Hat Khuat

Ban Fai Mai

Than Prawet Waterfall

■Khao Ra

Phaeng Waterfall■

Hat Khom

Ao Chalok Lam

Ao Thong Lang

Ban Chalok Lam

Ban Wang Ta Khian

■Khao Ta Luang

Ban Maduawan

Ban Nok

Ban Kai

Ao Mae Hat

Hat Lat

Hat Yao

Ban Si Thanu

Ao Si Thanu

Ao Wok Tum

Ban Wok Tum

Hospital■

Boat Dock
■Thong Sala

Bang Kaem Ro

Gulf of Thailand

Ao Nai Wok

Boats to Big Buddha on Ko Samui

3 miles

3 kilometers

0

0

Boats to Ko Tao

Boats to the Mainland

Express Boat

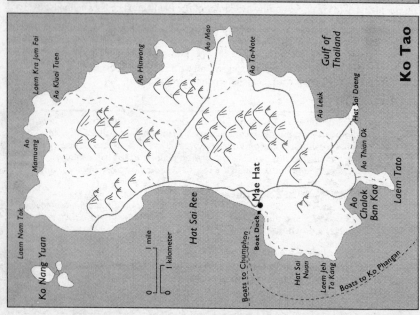

Ko Tao

Laem Nam Tok

Laem Kra Jom Foi

Ao Mamuang

Ao Kluai Tuen

Ao Hinwong

Ao Mao

Ao To-Note

Gulf of Thailand

Ao Leuk

Hat Sai Daeng

Ao Thian Ok

Laem Tato

Hat Sai Ree

Mae Hat

Boat Dock

Ao Chalok Ban Kao

Hat Sai Nuan

Laem Jeh Ta Kang

Ko Nang Yuan

1 mile

1 kilometer

0

0

Boats to Chumphon

Boats to Ko Phangan

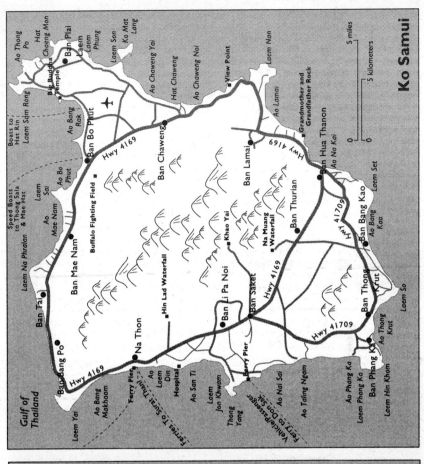

Ko Samui

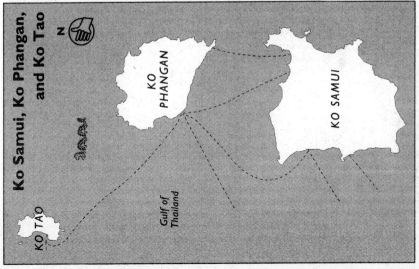

Ko Samui, Ko Phangan, and Ko Tao

Back on Rte. 4169, the road heads for the hills. If you're not careful, you'll plow right through the **Lamai Cultural Hall** at Km20, where the highway takes a sharp right turn. Shift to low gear, and head up the hill. The large rocky cape and **Coral Cove** below form the south end of the longest beach on the island, **Hat Chaweng,** with its coastal reef and **Ko Matlang** in the background.

Continue on down Rte. 4169 until Km27.5 and take a right onto Chaweng Rd. After you pass the 5km of bungalows and bars, it's open road and fresh air. Between Km8 and Km10 on Chaweng Rd., a series of dirt roads lead to the secluded coves and rocky points on the northeast corner of the island. The **Thai Folk Music Instrument Shop** at Km9.5 is open occasionally (every three to four days) depending on the owner's schedule. Farther down the road check out **Big Buddha** himself. Chaweng Rd. becomes Rte. 4171 when the Huge Golden One gleams over the landscape (a good place from which to take in the views). A meditation center also occupies the grounds, and visitors are expected to dress appropriately if they wish to go nearer (but it's just as impressive from afar).

After skirting Big Buddha's beach (also known as **Bangrak**), the road rejoins Rte. 4169 at the town of Bo Phut. Continuing through **Bo Phut Beach,** where houses mingle with bungalows, leads to **Mae Nam Beach,** which has a more urban atmosphere. After this, it's a pretty quiet stretch of 10km to Na Thon along the northwest (the steep road has a superb, high-altitude view of the beach), with the **Laem Yai Lighthouse** (off Km46.5) as the only thing of note after sand, sea, and coconuts.

This points to the active port of **Na Thon** (Km0), which it has the cheapest eats on the island and is a good place to take care of practical matters. There is a major intersection at Km2. Turning left, **Hin Laad Waterfalls** is a little over 1km away past the **Lizard Garden** and an abundance of durian trees. For some impressive cascades, tourists should visit after the rainy season (around November is best) and leapfrog 1km more to **Hunam** and **Hev Khwaay Tok Waterfalls.** For more natural sights, eyeball the white waters of the **Laadwanon River** down the dirt road at Km4.5. The paved road in the other direction goes to the ferry pier at **Thong Yang** and **Laem Chon Kram** (Thief Cave).

A river crosses the road near Km11 (Rte. 4169). About 500m farther, a right turn down a surfaced road leads to **Na Muang Waterfall** (about 1km). It's good for swimming, having received the stamp of approval from His Majesties Rama VI, VII, and IX, who all left their initials on stones nearby. The most impressive waterfall on Ko Samui is probably **Na Muang II,** a solid 1-km hike away. Returning to Rte. 4169 before Km12, **Ban Thurian** grows plenty of Thailand's king of fruits—durian.

Next on this action-packed tour are Ko Samui's religious sights. At Km13, **Wat Khunaram** is the permanent resting place of a mummified clairvoyant monk who predicted his death and planned to die meditating. At Km14.5, the unique **Coral Buddha image** on the left signals a right turn to access **Wat Samret,** about 500m along the dirt road, by the lake. Inside, the **Secret Coral Buddha Image Hall** conceals ancient sculptures.

A right turn onto Rte. 4170 leads to the turn-off for the dirt road to the **Samui Butterfly Garden,** where butterflies foxtrot by the landscaped hill. The **Insect Museum** also provides a bit of diversion for the curious. A bee house and monkey show are included in the admission. (Open 8am-5pm; admission 50฿, children 20฿.) Glass-bottom boat/snorkeling excursions are also available to visit the colorful offshore reefs. A 1-hour stay (plus 30min. transit) costs 150฿ (children 60฿).

Heading back to Rte. 4170, you can turn right, meet up with Rte. 4169, and be back in Lamai in a few minutes, but you'll miss a great sunset. Heading west on Rte. 4170 (km markers go down), the last official sight beckons at Km9.5. The golden **Chedi Laem Sor** and the hill-top **Khao Chedi** are home to the most-respected Buddhist monks on Ko Samui. Off Km6, a 3-km dirt road leads to **Ao Phangka,** a small bay that's perfect for making displays of Harlequin Romance affection as the sun sinks over the blue horizon.

■ Na Thon

Na Thon is the doctor's waiting room of Ko Samui; tourists often end up here for a couple of hours anticipating the next boat. Visitors should instead make use of the lower prices at this communication and shopping center. The daily market on Thaweeratpakdee Rd. offers fruits for the frugal.

ORIENTATION

Walking off the pier, you'll come to **Na Thon Road,** which is lined with travel agents, money changers, restaurants, a TAT branch, and the post/telecom offices. *Songthaew* to the beach arrive and depart in front of the pier. Parallel to Na Thon is **Ang Thong Road** where the police station is located. Beyond this is **Thaweeratpakdee Road,** better known as Km0 of **Route 4169.** Banks, restaurants, and the daily market pepper the road.

PRACTICAL INFORMATION

Tourist Offices: TAT (tel. 420 504), on Na Thon Rd. 200m to the left off the pier in the wooden shack across from the post office. Pamphlets on Ko Samui; some info about Ko Tao and Ko Phangan. Open daily 8:30am-4:30pm.

Tourist Police: (tel. 421 281), in Lipa Yai area by Km2, south of Na Thon, 100m past the road leading to Hin Lad Temple. They usually patrol the streets by Na Thon Chaweng and Lamai. At night, they patrol the Green Mango on Chaweng Beach. Call the TAT and they can radio the nearest patrol.

Tours and Travel: The best places to buy boat/bus/train ticket combinations to Bangkok or other major cities are near the pier in Na Thon: **Phanthip Co., 84/1** Na Thon Rd. (tel. 421 222). Open daily 8am-5pm. **Songserm Travel Centre,** 64/1-2 Na Thon Rd. (tel. 421 316). Open daily 6am-5pm. **Samui Tour** (tel. 421 092), in Bamboo House a few doors from Songserm. Open daily 8am-5pm.

Immigration Offices: 6/9 Thaweeratpakdee Rd. (tel. 421 069), 1km south of the market near the pier. Visa extensions 500฿. Open Mon.-Fri. 8:30am-3:30pm.

Currency Exchange: No problem at Na Thon, Lamai, or Chaweng. Major banks are open daily until 3:30pm and line the major roads; exchange booths open until 5pm. Other beaches' exchangers/travel agents have slightly lower rates.

Air Travel: Plane tickets booked all around Ko Samui, but the main office is **Bangkok Airways,** 72/2 Mu 3 Na Thon Rd. (tel. 420 133). Open daily 8am-5pm.

Trains and Buses: Phanthip and Songserm, both authorized State Railway agents, book bus, train, and boat combinations to the mainland. Songserm quotes: to **Bangkok** (A/C bus 280฿, minivan 450฿, night train with upper bunk 510฿) and **Kuala Lumpur,** Malaysia (minivan and A/C bus 450฿). Phanthip generally offers lower prices but less convenience.

Ferries: By **auto ferry** to **Don Sak** (9 per day, 7am-5pm, 1½hr., 40฿). With a bus-ferry-bus ticket from Na Thon through to Ban Don-Surat Thani, you can catch a bus to Thong Yang in front of either Phanthip Tour or Samui Tour 30min. before the scheduled ferry departure (3hr., 70฿, A/C 90฿). By **express boat** to Tha Thong Pier in **Surat Thani** (7:15am and 2:30pm, 2½hr., 115฿, roundtrip 200฿); includes transport from pier to Surat Thani train station to catch trains to Bangkok, if you buy directly from Songserm. By **sleeper boat** to Surat Municipal Pier (9pm, 6hr., lower deck 50฿, upper deck 70฿). Songserm Travel sells package tickets to **Bangkok** that include the express boat, bus transfer, and the sleeper train. Boat departs at 2:30pm for connection to the train (7pm, 12hr., upper bunk 560฿; lower bunk 610฿). 3rd-class seats are also available at a considerable discount. By **express boat** to **Thong Sala, Ko Phangan** (10:50am and 4:30pm, 50min., 65฿). By **tour boat** from the pier at Big Buddha Beach (Bangrak) to Hat Rin (10:30am and 3:30pm, 45min., 60฿). By **express boat,** the 10:50am departure to Ko Phangan continues to **Mae Hat, Ko Tao** (12:30pm, 2½hr., 250฿). By **speed boat** from Bo Phut pier to Mae Hat (8:30am, 1½hr., 400฿). Check around in Na Thon for new ways to get to Ko Tao.

Boats: The ferry provides a smoother, cheaper, and occasionally faster ride than the express boat. **Ferries leave from Thong Yang, all other boats from Na Thon.** Ferry tickets can be handled at the ferry pier, while general tickets are sold at Na Thon and most travel offices, as well as on board the vessel. The schedules listed change frequently, and the boats occasionally leave late.

Local Transportation: Most *songthaew* (6am-6pm) have set prices posted inside. From Na Thon and Thong Yang piers to: **Ban Mae Nam** (10฿); **Ban Plai Laem** (20฿); **Bo Phut** (15฿); **Hat Chaweng** (20฿); and **Hat Lamai** (20฿). Between **Chaweng** and **Lamai** (10฿). Motorcycle taxis cost about the same.

Rentals: Everywhere. Motorbikes 150฿ per day; jeeps 400฿ per day, with A/C 800฿, with insurance 1000฿.

Medical Services: Samui Hospital, 61 Mui, Tombon Angthong (tel. 421 230), located at Km2 off Rte. 4169 near Na Thon. **Ban Don Hospital** (tel. 425 382), at Km32, between Chaweng and Bo Phut. For first aid and visit clinics in the areas of Na Thon, Chaweng, or Lamai. Serious accidents require emergency transport to the mainland; arrange through the tourist police.

Emergency: tel. 191. **Tourist Police:** tel. 1699.

Police: Call the tourist police first. The police station (tel. 421 095) is on Angthong Rd. From the pier, follow the road into town and take a right.

Post Offices: GPO (tel. 421 013), on Na Thon Rd. 150m left of the pier. Open Mon.-Fri. 8:30am-4:30pm, Sat.-Sun. 9am-noon. Private "officially licensed" branches exist all around the island along Rte. 4169. Many bungalows sell stamps and deliver mail. **Postal code:** 84140.

Telephones: 2nd floor of the GPO. Other overseas call centers transmit through this station, and may add surcharges. Open daily 7am-10pm. Many lodgings have their own services as well. **Telephone code:** 077.

ACCOMMODATIONS

Sea View Guest House, 67/15 Thaweeratpakdee Rd. (tel. 420 052), opposite the Shell gas station. Immaculate establishment with spacious hallway and sitting area. Sinks are outside clean common baths. Private showers are bright, but you still have to share the toilets. Doubles 150฿, with baths 200฿. Slightly bigger room with private flush toilet 200฿, with A/C 300฿. Open 24hr.

Jinta (a.k.a. Can Restaurant), 310 Mu 3, Tombon Angthong (tel. 421 323), off Rte. 4169, south of Sanpetch Mini-Market. Wooden floors and breathing room. Hygienic Thai toilets with sinks. Titanic timbers shade marble benches. Singles 200฿ (low season 150฿). Doubles 250฿ (low season 200฿).

FOOD

While waiting for a boat at the dock, tourists can munch on *khao niaw ping* (grilled sticky rice and bananas wrapped in banana leaves, 3฿ each). On the waterfront, food carts offer fruit, meat-on-a-stick, noodles, and sandwiches.

Ruang Thong Bakery 2, 31-32 Angthong Rd. (tel. 454 241). Head into town along the street left of the pier; it's at the corner of Angthong Rd. Large selection of Thai and western dishes, plus *sukiyaki*. Dishes 35฿ and up. Open daily 7am-7pm.

Vegetarian Restaurant, 196 Angthong Rd., at the south end next to a bird shop behind Thai Farmers Bank. Thai, western, and some Japanese vegetarian dishes. Soya burger or mixed veggie with chili and rice, baked beans with mashed potatoes (50฿), and *miso* soup (25฿). Open daily 10am-7pm.

■ Na Thon to Hat Chaweng

HAT MAE NAM

The first major beach on the Km countdown runs from around Km39 to Km35 along Rte. 4169. Tranquility zealots look no further. The police are around Mu 1 between Km36 and 37, and bungalows are accessible by dirt roads. The rooms are fairly generic—with fan and shower for 200฿ or less (100-150฿ low season). About 1km past the police station, **Friendly Bungalow,** 64/2 Mu 1 Tambon Mae Nam, greets new-comers like old pals. All huts have baths and mosquito nets. Small wooden hut with Thai toilet and sink costs 80-100฿; concrete bungalows with sit toilets are 200฿. (Desk open 8am-10pm.) Off the same dirt road is **Rainbow Bungalow,** 44/4 Mu 1 Tambon Mae Nam (tel. 077 425 484). This charming, family-run pot of gold supplies a magically delicious ambience. Cubbyhole rooms have mosquito nets, barred windows, and Thai toilets. Enticing hammocks can provide hours of relaxation. Small singles go for 80฿, doubles 100฿, with twin beds 150฿. New singles/doubles near the beach have flush toilets (200฿).

HAT BO PHUT

Although it doesn't measure up length-wise to Hat Mae Nam, neighboring Bo Phut proves that good things do come in small packages. Places like **Chai Hat Water Sports** teach windsurfing (400-500฿), and rent sailboards to experienced windsurfers (150฿ per hr.). Speed boats drag people in parasails around the harbor (10min., 400฿). Jet skis are rented for 250฿ per 15min. **Samui Kart Club,** 98 Mu 1 Tambon Bo Phut (tel. 425 097), opposite Ziggy Stardust Bungalow, offers a way to skitter around the island without getting wet. (Open daily 10am-6pm.)

World Bungalow, 175/1 Mu 1 (tel. 425 355), near Km35 on Rte. 4169. It may look expensive, but this is a globe-trotter's bargain-basement bunking spot. Cheap, cozy cottages buried in herbal bushes. The food is anything but mundane (restaurant open 7:30am-11pm). Singles/doubles are concrete-floored, bamboo-walled huts with squat toilet, hot shower, and a small porch 200฿ (low season 150฿). Newer and larger rooms 500฿ (low season 400฿). Doubles with A/C 800฿ (low season 700฿).

Peace Bungalow, 178 Mu 1 Tambon Bo Phut (tel. 425 357), at Km34-35, marked by a wooden signpost. Bungalows, some on stilts, exist harmoniously with breezy, well-kept quarters, double fans, and flush toilet. Singles/doubles 300-350฿ (low season 250-300฿), with A/C 450฿.

Ziggy Stardust, 99 Mu 1 Tambon Bo Phut (tel. 425 410). Clean, upscale inn with enormous tiled baths. Sinks and sit toilets sparkle, though some are missing seats. Beachfront restaurant. A/C rooms have hot showers, fridge, and bathtub. Singles 200฿. Doubles 400฿ (low season 200฿). A/C rooms 1200฿ (low season 800฿).

HAT BANGRAK (BIG BUDDHA BEACH)

Buzzing bungalows swarm between Km2 and 4 of Rte. 4171 which branches off Rte. 4169 at Km33. This path leads to Bangrak and Samui Airport, and eventually becomes the road running near Chaweng. These backpacker-friendly bungalows sit on decent beaches around the windswept emerald bay have small restaurants with a basic Thai-western menu.

Kinnaree Resort, 73/2 Mu 4 Tambon Bo Phut (tel. 245 111), at Km3 of Rte. 4171. Narrow villa among the cooing of flower gardens and turtle doves. Neon jazzes up the basic, white-sheet rooms. Baths with sit toilets, but no sinks. Singles/doubles 100฿ all year, 200฿ for 1-night stays.

Number One Bungalow (tel. 425 446), between Km3 and 4. Typical brown and white-coconut-strewn establishment garners high rankings. Free ride to the airport. Friendly staff. Sit toilets. Singles/doubles 150฿. Doubles/triples 350฿.

LAEM THONGSON, AO THONGSAI, HAT CHOENG MON, AND AO YAI NOI

The northeast cape wraps around some of the island's best views. Beaches are down the dirt roads off the 5km of refreshing mountain highway connecting North Chaweng to Rte. 4171. Laem Thongson can be reached by adventurous motorbikers off Km9 or 10 via 3km of treacherous dirt road. Most of the beach areas belong to Imperial Thongsai. Persistently following the signs for 2km leads to the **Samui Thongson**

THAILAND

Resort on the tip of the promontory, overlooking white caps and a rocky cove with a small stretch of sand. Samui Thongson has singles/doubles with one bed for 150฿, low season 80฿. Doubles/triples with 2 beds cost 300฿, low season 200฿.

Hat Choeng Mon, north of the small Ao Yai Noi, rims the belly of Ao Thongsai and lies just 4km north of Chaweng (between Km8 and 9). It's a world apart from Chaweng, and is worth visiting for the view, serene beaches, good swimming, and the island's grandest hotel: the **Imperial Boat House Hotel** where guests bunk in small arks. Behind the JJ Restaurant, **Choeng Mon Bungalow** (tel. 425 372) has some fancooled stilt houses connected to baths with hot water and sit toilet. Singles/doubles are 200฿, with A/C 350฿.

■ Hat Chaweng

The biggest and brashest of Ko Samui's beaches, Hat Chaweng roars 5km over the eastern coast. It's the nightlife capital of the island, and the beach is the epitome of the sunbathe-eat-party-sleep-sunbathe culture. The shoreline charms some travelers so much that they stay for weeks or months; some open a bar or bungalow and never bother to leave.

ORIENTATION

Hat Chaweng's main thoroughfare is roughly 200m from and parallel to the beach. Anything can be found along or just off this strip: rooms, food, bars, garter belts, TAT, tourist police, post office, golf carts, mini-marts, nightclubs, Jacuzzi tubs, souvenirs, tailors, and on and on. **Chaweng Road** connects to Rte. 4169 via three different branches: Km28 (0.5-km access road), Km29 (1-km road where the afternoon market is located), and Km30 (3-km road). The north and south branches define **Central Chaweng**. Continuing along Chaweng Rd. up the hill at Km4, **North Chaweng** makes up the northernmost km of the beach. **Chaweng Noi** (Lesser Chaweng) makes up the southernmost km and is where all the most expensive resorts have found their niches. The other side of the rock and coral outcropping defines the south end of Chaweng proper, and is accessible from Rte. 4169 off the slope of the mountain that hides Lamai to the south.

ACCOMMODATIONS AND FOOD

Although there are plenty of budget accommodations in Chaweng, rooms go quickly year-round. The most expedient way to hunt on your own is to start with Charlie's Huts; if they're full, keep walking north.

Dining options surround **Chaweng Rd.**, especially near Km3. Most kitchens and restaurants serve similar food and close at 10pm. Explore Rte. 4169 south, where cliffside restaurants above **Thong Takien** offer equivalent prices and quality, as well as a better view.

Charlie's Hut, Viking (Charlie's Hut 2), and **Charlie's Hut 3** (tel. 422 343), Central Chaweng. This angelic trio is legendary among backpackers, and stays packed year round. If everything's full, put your name down on the waiting list. Viking is the best, but all have standard prices: 1-2 person hut 100฿, 140฿ with bath, with 2 beds 300฿. Huts have mosquito nets and electricity only in the evening.

Lotus Bungalow, 60/1 Mu 2 Tambon Bo Put, Central Chaweng, between Suneast and Lucky Mother. In the middle of the action but far enough from the noise to provide a good night's sleep. Singles/doubles 200฿ (150฿ low season). **Chang Diving Centre** (tel. 230 891), with PADI-certified instruction on the grounds.

Suneast Bungalow, 159 Mu 2 Tambon Bo Put, Central Chaweng (tel. 422 115), just past Km3. In the middle of the thickest cluster of huts in Chaweng, with pubs and restaurants nearby. At low tide, the reef appears 200m offshore, but the water's still good for swimming. Fan-cooled bungalows resplendent with fresh sheets 150฿, near beach 200฿. Solid bungalows with double beds 250฿.

Family Bungalow, 119 Mu 2 Tambon Bo Put, North Chaweng, next door to Oasis Restaurant. No feuding in these ultra-clean rooms with shiny tiled floor and very large, clean baths. Restaurant dishes up beauteous beach and boat views. Singles/doubles 200฿ (low season 150฿).

Moon Bungalow (tel. 422 167), North Chaweng. Funky, fanciful owner used to gaze at the moon, but now it's MTV and BBC news off the satellite dish, plus videos every night. Typical, tidy bamboo huts 100฿. Singles/doubles with baths 150฿. Newer and larger rooms 300฿ (low season 200฿). A/C rooms 500-700฿.

Matlang Resort, 154/1 Mu 2 Tambon Bo Put, North Chaweng (tel. 422 172), past the Blue Lagoon. Basic-supplies shop and good ping-pong action. Singles/doubles with fan 300฿ (low season 250฿), with A/C 800฿ (low season 400฿).

ENTERTAINMENT

The **Reggae Pub,** at the footbridge of the leech-livened lake is the most romping night spot on the island. The wildly popular pleasure palace has multiple bars, a huge atrium dance floor, high-tech equipment, and DJs who send almighty, thunderous sonic waves across the inland lake. Don't be fooled by the gigantic, wooden Bob Marley; the Pub plays anything that will induce sweaty bodies to groove. Sunday nights bring the bold to the get-bombed-at-Reggae drinking contest. Those who are up to the challenge may participate for free and perhaps even earn a place on the Wall of Fame.

Action in this partydome picks up late and the raging continues through the night. People whet their nocturnal appetites at the **Green Mango,** 21/5 Mu 3 Tambon Bo Put (tel. 422 165), an equally popular disco, and shuffle over to the Reggae Pub around midnight. (Open daily 8pm-3am.) There's no cover charge at either. Between the two, a strip of pubs tries to pick up the reveling overflow.

■ Hat Lamai

The nightlife at this beach is second only to Chaweng to the north. The best beach glides for 2km between two coral reefs that mark off North Lamai and South Lamai. South Lamai, Ao Bang Nam Cheud, is actually separated from Lamai proper by a small cape that's best known for its R-rated genitalia rock formations. A handful of bungalows are tossed down between Km17 and 21.

ORIENTATION AND PRACTICAL INFORMATION

A small leg of Central Lamai can be reached by dirt roads leading from Km17.5 to 18.5 off Rte. 4169. **Lamai Beach Road** is the access route that branches from Km18.5 to 21 and runs 200m away from the straightest, most beautiful part of Lamai's shore. The highway itself continues inland past the post office and takes a sharp turn at Km20 and the Lamai Cultural Hall. Near the Km21 junction, the shore veers across the stream mouth, and North Lamai actually ends up facing south. A small daily market is off the road, in the Ban Hua Thanon area. Exchange booths, overseas services, and grocery stores dot the street. **Thai House Supermarket,** 126/14 Mu 3 (tel. 424 423), is open 8am to midnight. **Flamingo Bookstore,** opposite Krung Thai exchange booth, deals in books of all languages, reconfirms plane tickets, and has an **overseas call booth.** (Open 8:30am-10pm.) **Night songthaew** at the entrance to Mix Pub run to Na Thon (200฿ per load) and parties at Chaweng (80-100฿ per load) from 6pm to 6am. Lamai Beach Rd. is the center of booze, disco, and video action. For something a wee more sedate, North Lamai hides some of the greatest coves on the island.

ACCOMMODATIONS

North Lamai

People end up at North Lamai when there's no room at the main strip's inns. Bungalows don't jostle for territory as much as those in Central Lamai and the area is generally more subdued. Since restaurants cluster around Central Lamai, you will probably be limited to bungalow food.

Garden Home, 138 Mu 4 (tel. 424 144), along Lamai Beach Rd. near the junction at Km23. Good-natured proprietor built the solid bungalows himself. Fills quickly even in quieter months. Rooms are quite intimate, but in good condition and clean, as are the baths with sit toilets. Singles/doubles 150-200฿, with A/C 500฿. Nearby restaurant serves huge portions of food (30-50฿). Open daily 6am-midnight.

New Hut Bungalows, just off Km21.5 on Rte. 4169 at the north end of the beach. Bare-bones thatched roof quarters with muesli on the menu (30฿), this place draws a loyal backpacker crowd. Double mattress on the floor 60฿, with private bath 150-200฿ (low-season 80-100฿). Food served daily 7am-10pm.

No Name Bungalow (tel. 230 383), 10min. past New Hut from Lamai. Perhaps it was hard for the owners to choose a name, but it is easy for the traveler to appreciate the prices and quiet beach location. Rooms, however, are as spartan as the name. Double mattress 80฿ (low season 60฿). Singles/doubles with bath 150฿ (low season 120฿).

Central Lamai

Between coral to the south and a stream to the north, about 50 places are suitable for backpackers. Pubs and discos tend to run pretty late along Lamai Beach Rd. Expect everything to be occupied during the peak months. The south end of the beach hosts cheap bungalows.

Utopia Bungalow, 124/105 Mu 3 (tel. 233 113), north end of Lamai Beach Rd. High-ceilinged rooms may seem slapped together with white planks, but they're cheap, with lots of windows, and they open up onto perfectly gorgeous beach. Concrete path connects all the bungalows; flowers blooming on the sides would send Thomas More into a tizzy. Singles/doubles 150฿. Larger room with flush toilet 200฿. Doubles/triples with A/C 500฿.

Marina Villa, 124 Mu 3 (tel. 424 259), in the middle of the beach. Big bungalows, tall palms, and a huge, big-screen TV in the restaurant. Room with double bed, fan, and tiled bath 200฿ (low season 150฿). Rooms closer to the beach 200-300฿.

Magic Resort, (tel. 424 229), 2 bungalows south of Utopia. Clean, comfy rooms with fan and sit toilets. Singles/doubles 200฿, with 2 beds 350฿, with A/C 700฿.

FOOD

Lamai's food scene is a copycat version of Chaweng's; all the bungalows serve their versions of Thai-western meals until around 10pm and then let the restaurants and pubs along the main drag pick up the slack. The **daily market** at Ban Hua Thanon has fresh fruits and Thai munchies, but it's over before dinner time.

Shi Bar Restaurant & Cinema, full of Arabian pillows. English movies shown on big-screen TV. The bamboo hut has some low tables and cushions on the floor. No shoes allowed. Upstairs has tables. English and Thai food available, but Israeli food is the star. Mixed plate with kebab, gyros, hummus, falafel, and salad 90฿. Shark steak 70฿, Thai dishes 35-70฿. Four movies every night from 4-11pm.

Nakhon Toe Rung, opposite CIOA Restaurant, look for the sizzling seafood on the grill next to a large wooden boat. Delicious and reasonably priced. Crab fried rice in curry powder 30฿, fried noodles with seafood 30฿, and spaghetti in meat sauce 30฿. Breakfast served as well—muesli 25฿. Open 24hr.

ENTERTAINMENT

During daylight hours, the beach is the setting for it all. Water-skiing costs 250฿ and windsurfing 400฿, but jet-skiing, Hobie-cat, and parasailing require at least 500฿.

At night, some zoom over to the Green Mango and Reggae Pub on their motorbikes, but Lamai has a good share of its own hot spots, even if they don't get rolling until 11pm. The strip of bars and pubs is technically supposed to shut down at 2am, but things usually go later as owners try to stay afloat in the competitive market. **Mix Pub** (tel. 424 200) is the most popular (and loudest) place in town. By 10pm the entrance is posted with staff in their Mix Pub T-shirts, handing out flyers on the special shows. Most drinks fetch 60-80฿, draft beer 30฿. (Open 9pm-4:30am.)

ANG THONG MARINE NATIONAL PARK

For some blow-you-away sea sights, take a daytrip 31km northwest of the "Golden Basin" archipelago. The two-hour boat ride from Na Thon (8:30am, returns at 5pm, 300฿, includes lunch and breakfast) can be booked with most travel agents along the waterfront at Na Thon. Among the 40 islands are small gems like **Ko Wua Talap** (Sleeping Cow Island) where the park office is located, **Ko Saa Sao** (Tripod) with a huge rock arch and fantastic snorkeling waters, and **Ko Mae Ko** (Mother Island) with **Thale Nai** (also known as Lake Crater), the emerald saltwater lake that dazzles visitors who make the exhausting climb. Bashful rhinos and seals shy away from strangers in limestone cliffs and caves. **Ko Lak** and similar limestone formations tower 400m above the water. Dolphins can be seen on the long-tailed boat ride around **Ko Tai Plao. Hat Chan Charat** (Moonlight Beach) does not require any legwork. The waters here are as good as Ko Tao for diving. Visitors who want to snorkel or dive should contact the diving school on the island to arrange diving trips. Advance bed and board arrangements are needed for overnight stays; make reservations through Ang Thong Marine National Park, 145/1 Talaat Lang Rd., Muang District, Surat Thani 84000 (tel. 077 283 025), the **National Parks Division** in Bangkok (tel. 579 05 29), or the park's head office (tel. 286 931). Rooms for four cost 400฿. Camping is allowed for 10฿. Tents are rented for 50฿.

KO PHANGAN เกาะพะงัน

Its big sister a sunshine mecca (Ko Samui) and its little brother a scuba diving Eden (Ko Tao), Ko Phangan suffers a perpetual identity crisis. Although the increasingly famous Full Moon Parties at Hat Rin have placed Ko Phangan on the traveler's circuit, the mish-mash of tourists who wander onto the island don't fund the entire local livelihood. Only 7000 people occupy the 191-sq.km island, pocked with mountainous terrain, and many still depend on fishing and farming for income. Plenty of sun-swept beaches now harvest fast-growing crops of budget bungalows, but the Ko Phangan *sans* full moon extravaganza is often overlooked. When full moon fever hits, however, the party runs all night, bringing with it a path of reckless destruction on Hat Rin, and littering the beach with glass bottles, trash, and cigarette butts. Luckily, the beautiful beaches in the northern part of Ko Phangan have been left intact and serve as a peaceful place to sleep out the hangover.

GETTING THERE

Many boats sailing from Surat Thani make stops at Ko Samui before continuing on to Ko Phangan. Prices and schedules vary greatly through the season; check with the travel agencies for definite figures. The **express boat** drops passengers off on Ko Samui before completing the trip to Phangan (3½hr., 145฿). Transport to Pak Nam, the launching point, is included in the ticket. Buses leave from the Songserm office at 7:30am and 2pm; ferries depart Pak Nam Pier 30min. later. The cheapest route to the island is the **night/sleeper boat** (120฿). Tickets are sold at the pier in Ban Don. Boats depart Ban Don at 11pm and arrive at 6am. For boats from Ko Samui to Thong Sala and Hat Rin see **Na Thon: Practical Information** on page 681 for more details.

ISLAND ORIENTATION

Ko Phangan stakes its claim approximately 100km northeast of Surat Thani and only 12km from Ko Samui at the closest point (between Hat Rin and Bo Phut). The north and west coasts of Ko Phangan have exquisite beaches along several bays created by rocky capes, and provide halcyon getaways for anyone who finds Samui a bit too touristy. The southern coast has a panoramic view of Ko Samui and an ever-increasing onslaught of bargain bungalows at the unusual **Hat Rin,** which can be reached by *songthaew* for 40฿. The interior is slowly being carved away by dirt roads stretching from the main port of **Thong Sala.**

ISLAND SIGHTS

Considering the highly textured terrain, it's no surprise that waterfalls are the major tourist attractions after beaches and full moons. The most famous and probably most stupendous stretches of river on the islands of the Gulf of Thailand belong to **Than Sadet Historical Park.** Kings Rama V, VII, and IX all walked along its many waterfalls and cascades and left their initials as permanent seals of inspection. Than Sadet is best tackled as a daytrip, starting out in the morning on one of the long-tail boats that run from Hat Rin (50฿) and Thong Sala (70฿); they'll drop passengers off at the mouth of the river. It's a refreshing 2-3km trek along the river on its parallel road just to the north.

■ Thong Sala

The southwestern port of Thong Sala is the lifeline for the rest of the island. This is the best place to rent a motorbike, extend your visa, stock up on beach supplies (and batteries, toiletries, and food), as well as change money. The travel agents huddle conveniently by the pier, intercepting the herds to and from the boat. **Thong Sala Road** runs from the pier, past restaurants, travel agencies, and supermarkets. Two major roads branch off Thong Sala Rd., one to Ao Chalak Lam in the north, the other to Ban Kai and Hat Rin along the south coast. The daily market, local restaurants, clinics, and the post office are on this road. Only the **morning market** is at the corner of the road to Ao Chalak Lam.

PRACTICAL INFORMATION

Tourist Offices: Ko Phangan does not have an official TAT office (disregard the sign by the pier). Enterprising travel agencies off the pier can field most questions.

Tours and Travel: Except for the busiest days (after a full moon), you can easily buy tickets on the pier or boat. **Songserm Travel Centre,** 35/1 Thong Sala Rd. (tel. 377 046), to the left of the pier. Open daily 8am-4pm. Express boat to Ko Samui and Surat Thani.

Immigration Offices: Sophie Silver, 2 doors from Siam City Exchange booth handles visa extensions. 1 or 2-week 700฿, 1-month 800฿. Open daily 8am-8pm.

Currency Exchange: Exchange booths straight off the pier. **Siam City Bank,** next to the post office. Open Mon.-Fri. 8:30am-6pm.

Ferries: To the mainland near **Phun Phin** and **Surat Thani** (6:15am, 1, and 10pm, 4hr., 145฿). The afternoon trip is the surer bet. **Express boat** (6:15am and 1pm) to Ko Samui (45min., 65฿) then to Surat Thani (2½hr., 115฿). The afternoon express boat gets to Samui in time for passengers to connect with Songserm's package deal to **Bangkok** (see **Na Thon: Practical Information** on page 681). By **night boat** to the mainland (10pm, 7hr., 120฿). To **Ko Tao** (12:30pm, 2½hr., 150฿). Get tickets at the pier. To **Ko Samui,** take the Hat Rin boat to Big Buddha Beach instead of looping through Thong Sala.

Local Transportation: Go between the pier and the beaches on the labeled taxi-pickup trucks. Fares are based on distance and difficulty of the road. To: **Ban Khai** 30฿, **Ban Tai** 20฿, **Ao Chalok Lam** 30฿, **Thong Nai Paan** 60฿, **Hat Yow** 60฿, and **Hat Rin** 40฿. To get to **Thong Nai Paan,** take the taxi; the road is extremely rough for motorcycles. **Hat Khuat** (Bottle Beach) is accessible by a boat from Ao Chalak Lam (30฿) or Thong Sala (80฿).

Rentals: Around the market area of Thong Sala. 150฿ per day. Larger bikes 200฿, MTX 250฿.

THAILAND

Markets: Bovy Supermarket, 44/25 Mu 1 (tel. 377 231), straight off the pier on the right. Good prices and the largest stock. Open daily 8:30am-8:30pm. For fresh fruits, try the **"morning" market** farther down Thong Sala Rd.

Medical Services: Hospital (tel. 377 036), 3km north of Thong Sala on the way to Chalak Ban Kao. For major procedures go to the mainland. Dr. Charatpong is the only physician who can speak English. He is at Dr. Sanae's **clinic** opposite the GPO Mon.-Fri. from noon-1pm and 4-7pm, Sat.-Sun. 9am-6pm. The nurse can handle first-aid medication. Open Mon.-Fri. 10am-1pm, Sat.-Sun. 9am-6pm.

Emergency: tel. 191

Police: (tel. 377 114), at Ban Don Sai 2km away on the road to Al Chalak Lam. English-speaking staff.

Post Offices: GPO, 12/1 Mu 1 Tambon Ko Phangan (tel. 337 118), next to Siam City Bank. From the pier, take a right at the 1st intersection and head into town; it's on the right side 500m ahead. Open Mon.-Fri. 8:30am-noon and 1-4:30pm, Sat. 9am-noon. **Postal code:** 84280.

Telephones: Overseas calls are expensive. Expect service charges at bungalows and stores. **Café de la Poste,** 25/1 Thong Sala Rd. (tel. 377 043), across from the post office is an authorized agent with a private booth. Collect call 80฿ to Europe and North America, 50฿ to Asia. Open daily 8am-9pm. **Telephone code:** 077.

ACCOMMODATIONS

Staying at Thong Sala means that you missed the boat or intend to catch the morning vessel. Bungalows are off the road to the right of the pier (the one headed for Ban Tai). During the low season, some of these places may be closed. Beware of dogs in this area: they roam in attack-prone packs that have to be "eliminated" occasionally. **Moon Light Bungalow,** 500m from the pier and another 400m off the highway, has rustic bungalows (60฿) that are a little bigger than the mattresses inside. They are clean and have mosquito nets and brooms. Rooms with bamboo walls have spacious cement baths and thatched roof and cost 100฿. Southeast of Thong Sala (right off the pier) within a 1-km walk are a patch of sub-100฿ bungalows like **Petch Cottage** and **Phangan Villa.**

FOOD

Kuai Taew Pak Tai, 145/2 Mu 1, off the southern road along the coast on the way to the market, next to Wantana Book Store. Tables are set up in front of the house. Quick hot dishes to order: rice with pepper, garlic pork or chicken, *raad naa,* rice with basil leaves, chicken, fried rice, and noodle soup—all for 20฿. English menu. Open daily 6am-10pm.

■ Hat Rin

Hat Rin would be just like any other stunning stretch of white Gulf of Thailand sand, if it weren't home to the world-famous Full Moon Party. Every month several thousand travelers converge on Hat Rin to celebrate the rising full moon at a giant beach rave, Thai style. While massive electrical generators plug away to power the pulsating beach-side speakers and spinning disco lights, body-painted revelers dance on the sand and cavort in the warm water until sunrise. The event has attracted a lunar-cycle pilgrimage of bohemian travelers from all over Southeast Asia for several years. It has also attracted increasing numbers of Thai police, who aren't so entertained by Hat Rin's conspicuous hedonism.

ORIENTATION

Two beaches on opposite sides of Ko Phangan's southernmost cape make up Hat Rin. Ground zero during the Full Moon Party is Paradise Bungalow, at the south end of Hat Rin Nok (east). During the high season, the revelry spans most of the rest of sleepless Hat Rin Nok, spilling onto the quieter Hat Rin Na (west) at times. Two dirt roads lined with restaurants and shops cross the cape at its north and south ends.

THAILAND

Another dusty road runs lengthwise between the beaches (along the backdoors of Hat Rin Nok's bungalow resorts) to form an "I" street configuration. The post and telephone office, travel agents, and currency exchangers are clustered around the bottom (south) end of the "I."

PRACTICAL INFORMATION

Tours and Travel: Phanthip Co. (tel. 01 725 0052), at the bottom of the "I." Authorized agent of the State Railway. Joint tickets.

Currency Exchange: Branches of **Siam City** are next to Phangan Bay Resort. Open daily 9:30am-4pm. **Krung Thai,** 100m from the school. Open daily 9am-5pm. Both are along the "I" and have slightly poorer rates than Thong Sala.

Boats: To **Thong Nai Paan** boats leave with favorable winds around noon (50฿), except during the rainy and monsoon season (Oct.-mid-Dec.). Boats to **Big Buddha Beach, Ko Samui** leave from Hat Rin Na June-Oct., and from Hat Rin Nok Nov.-Jan. (9:30am and 2:30pm, 60฿).

Local Transportation: Taxis run to **Ban Khai** (30฿) then to **Thong Sala** (50฿) quite often until 8pm.

Medical Services: Clinics dot the middle of the "I." The one with a gray cross on one side and a blue circle on the other has a regular nurse (tel. 017 050 883). Open daily 9am-9pm.

Emergency: tel. 191

Police: Hat Rin has a police booth next to the school, but it has no phone and is open sporadically. Extra uniformed and undercover police officers patrol the beach during Full Moon Parties. A couple of people get busted each party during high season and have to pay at least a fine of 10,000฿ before leaving the island.

Post Offices/Telephones: A private, licensed branch stands on the bottom of the "I" toward Hat Rin Na. Open Mon.-Fri. 9am-5pm, Sat. 9am-noon. **Overseas calls** are generally 100฿ per minute. Open daily until 9pm. **Postal code:** 84280.

ACCOMMODATIONS

Hat Rin Na (West)

When the moon fills, so do all the rooms. Otherwise, it's a peaceful place to stare at Ko Samui. Beaches are best after the rainy season. For better swimming, head to Hat Rin Nok. The beach gets quieter as it approaches Thong Sala; by the end of the cape, things may get full-mooned during high season.

Sooksom Bungalow, 120 Mu 6 Tambon Ban Tai (tel. 01 958 477), at the top of the "I." Bamboo huts on a small cove. Electricity available from 5-10pm. On the hill 60฿ (low season 50฿). On ground 80฿ (low season 60฿). Restaurant entrees with vegetarian dishes 35฿.

Crystal Palace (tel. 01 725 0511), about 100m before Sooksom Bungalow. Concrete bungalows, tiled patio, and flush toilets. Rooms are dazzling with light and hygiene. Singles/doubles 200฿, but rates fluctuate between 100-300฿.

Hat Rin Nok (East)

The farther you get from the south end of the beach, where the Full Moon Parties rave, the quieter it gets. The drug culture, passing away the time until lunar fever sets in, shuffles up and down the beach. On the actual full moon, forget about sleep. Prices for rooms shoot up during this time and are higher in general than Hat Rin Na. If everything's full during Full Moon, fight for your right to party until dawn and catch a post-revelry boat to somewhere else.

Paradise Bungalow (tel. 01 725 06 61), the southernmost bungalow on Hat Rin Nok and the first to host the Full Moon Party. Quiet beach with some coral reefs. Bamboo bungalows clean, well-built, and picturesque. Bright lights, windows with screens, wholesome baths with Thai toilet, and furnished balcony. Singles/doubles 150฿. Larger room 200฿.

Sun Rise Bungalow, 136 Mu 6 Tambon Ban Tai (tel. 01 725 08 84), in the middle of the beach. Breezy bamboo cottages replete with large beds and mosquito net. Large, tiled floor bath and sit toilet make splendid writing rooms. Not many empty rooms, even in low season. Singles/doubles with bath 150-400฿. A handful of rooms without bath go for 80฿ all year.

Tommy's Resort (tel. 01 725 03 27), at the north end of the beach. Giant beachside speakers feed a steady flow of classic rock and acid jazz to cocktail-toting, volleyball-bouncing residents. Travel agency in back offers tours and overseas phone calls. Open daily 7:30am-11pm. Basic room with double bed and fan 100฿, with the onset of full moon fever 150฿.

FOOD

Barbecued *som tam,* sticky rice, and a few sidewalk restaurants perfume the middle of the "I." Bungalows have large menus of Thai and western food (30-40฿). In the middle of the road connecting the south ends of the beaches, the **Rin Kitchen and Bakery** serves some of the best food in town. Chef Nira's curries and seafoods are well worth their bungalow prices, and her whole-wheat bread (big loaf 25฿) is fresh every morning. (Open daily 8am-10pm.) At the top of the "I," **Mama's Family Restaurant,** whips up economical Indian and Thai meals (curry chicken 20฿, *som yam* 15฿) until the wee hours on party nights.

■ Other Beaches

THONG NAI PAAN AND THONG TAPAN NOI

On the opposite end of the island from Thong Sala, these twin beaches separated by a rocky cliff double the pleasure of those who endure the hour-long jeep ride along the mountains or the boat ride from Hat Rin or the north beaches. The eastern beach, **Thong Nai Paan,** is the longer and more populated of the two. At the end of the road to Thong Nai Paan's eastern point, **Nice Beach Bungalow** offers solid wooden lodgings. All rooms are singles with mosquito nets, high ceilings, and weather screens. Singles/doubles cost 100-500฿. In the middle of Thong Nai Paan beach is the mighty **Pen's Bungalow** which has thatched bungalows with clean tiled baths and sit toilets. Hammocks and benches are plentiful on the beach. Rooms cost 100฿ (low season 80฿), with bath 200฿ (low season 100฿). Tile roof bungalows go for 300฿ (low season 200฿). The owners speak English.

Thong Tapan Noi changes its size quickly with the tides. It is equally beautiful, but more rocky in certain areas near the cliff. Bungalows are off paths that run among coconut trees and high grass. In the middle of the beach, **Honey Bungalow,** 7/2 Mu 5, dribbles bed-sized bungalows on the foothill, with some leaning on enormous rocks. Thatch-roofed, tidy chambers have tiled baths and showers, but no sinks. Plank walls repel the mightiest bloodsuckers. Common baths can be found among banana trees. Bungalows cost 80฿, with shower 150฿; those that are spankin' new and close to the beach go for 200฿. (Reception desk open 8am-10pm.) Circling the owner's home, the concrete bungalows of **Thong Ta Paan Resort** (tel. 377 048), at the north end of Thong Nai Paan Noi on the rocky point, have plain, good-sized rooms. Most have views of the entire beach and the sound of waves on the rocks below. Some peer out toward the secluded cove around the corner known as "Stoned Beach." The resort also has good water pressure and sanitary Thai toilets. Rooms cost 100฿, with bath 150฿, near the beach 250฿.

CHALOK LAM AND HAT KHUAT (BOTTLE BEACH)

About 10km down a surfaced road from Thong Sala, taxis arrive in the belly of Chalok Lam Bay. The quiet beach is partly rocky and blackened by calamari wash from the squid boats that come ashore (April-Oct.). If you decide to stay overnight at Chalok Lam during the squid-free time, **Wantana Resort,** 17 Mu 7 Tambon Ko Phangan, is farther away from the rocky beaches and gives plenty of bang for the baht. Singles/

THAILAND

doubles go for 40฿ all year, with bath 150฿ (low season 80฿). *Songthaew* leave daily at 5, 10am, 3:30, and 7:30pm.

This is the best place to snag a boat to the quaint **Hat Khuat** (Bottle Beach), just to the east and accessible only by water or steep footpaths. The long-tail trip costs 30฿ when a group of six to eight people show up; smaller groups may have to bargain. As Bottle Beach gains popularity, there is talk of inaugurating regular boat service so ask around. The 4-km foot path from Chalok Lam is steep, ill-defined, and a lot of fun, but only worth attempting if you're armed with boots, long pants, water, and a full day of sunlight.

A handful of bungalow resorts occupy Bottle Beach's cookie-cutter sand crescent. The long-tail will probably drop you off in the middle, in front of **Bottle Beach 1.** Ship-shape mattress and mosquito net bungalows cost 80, 100, and 120฿ depending on beach proximity; rates fall to 50, 60, and 80฿ in the low season. White concrete rooms with baths go for 200-250฿. Electricity lights up life from 6:30-11:30pm. Stocking up on food in Thong Sala will help take the sting out of the high food prices (served 7:30am-10pm). If the bungalows are full, **Bottle Beach 2,** next door, offers the same rooms, rates, menu, and cheerful management.

KO TAO เกาะเต่า

Ko Tao (Turtle Island) surfaces 74km southeast of Chumphon and 40km northwest of Ko Phangan. Like Ko Tarutao, Ko Tao was a place of exile for political prisoners; most were taken rapidly with malaria, and all eventually died on the island. Eight years ago, a cold drink couldn't be found because ice hadn't reached the island and electricity was non-existent. Seven years ago, there was a building boom, opening up a steady wave of visitors. Six years ago, electricity started illuminating bungalows in the evening, and today, upstart dive shops seem to take root among the stringy palms almost as frequently as semi-luxurious bungalow resorts. All cater to scuba neophytes who come to take advantage of Ko Tao's inexpensive PADI certification course and veteran divers who want to explore the tepid Gulf waters. Getting here can be an arduous task, but growing numbers of visitors have decided that Ko Tao's pristine underwater world is worth the effort.

Ko Tao is largely underdeveloped, and will probably remain so because of strict regulations by the Thai government. Electricity is only an evening affair, and clean water is the sole thing more valuable than scuba dollars. Beach-side accommodations are inexpensive and backpacker-friendly, and night-time scuba dives still trump the video scene. Sun-crisped coves ring the island where water-logged adventurers can seclude themselves. The local divers and Thai tourism officials, have firmly established most of the island and its surrounding waters as a natural reserve, thus staving off the most onerous trappings of mass tourism for the time being.

GETTING THERE

To get to Ko Tao directly from the mainland, take a bus or train to Chumphon. Catch the **sleeper boat** (midnight, 5-7hr. depending on weather, 200฿) or the **speed boat** (8am, 2hr., 400฿). From Ko Phangan take the daily **express boat** from Thong Sala (12:30pm, 2½hr., 150฿). From Ko Samui, head to Ko Phangan and connect to the Ko Tao boat or take the **speed boat** direct from Bo Phut (8:30am, 1½hr., 450฿). As the number of visitors to Ko Tao rises exponentially every year, so do the transportation alternatives.

ISLAND ORIENTATION

When your boat arrives at the pier at Mae Hat (Mother Beach), you'll have the option of grabbing a taxi, hopping in a long-tail boat, or walking. If you're planning to stay on the west coast near the pier (and scuba-diving schools), you can save 20฿ by following the footpath near the beach which leads to several bungalows in 15-20 minutes.

Otherwise, travelers should find a ride, as most everything else is an arduous hike or only accessible by boat.

Dirt roads connect **Mae Hat, Hat Sai Ree** (2km north on the west coast), **Ao Chalok Ban Kao** (on the south coast), **Ao Thian Ok** (0.5km past Ao Chalok Ban Kao), **Hat Sai Daeng** (the southeast corner), as well as **Ao Hin Wong, Ao Leuk,** and **Ao Ta Node** (on the remote east coast). If you plan to explore the island, the *V. Hongsombud Guide Map of Ko Tao,* sold at most dive shops and some bungalows, is a worthy investment (40฿).

SCUBA DIVING

Ko Tao is touted as the best place in the Gulf of Thailand to learn to scuba dive, although the waters are not as spectacular as the world-famous diving off Phuket and the Similan Islands. The prices are standardized in Ko Tao, so a four-day open-water course costs 6500฿, including equipment, transportation, and snacks. The advanced course costs 5500฿. For those who just want a taste of the scuba experience, the one-day introduction course costs 1400฿ for one dive. Certified divers can go on all-inclusive trips at 700฿ for one dive, 1200฿ for two, 3000฿ for six, and 4500฿ for ten. If you tote your own equipment, a dive trip costs 450฿, or 400฿ for ten or more. Snorkelers can tag along on many trips for about 150฿. For more information, stop in at any one of the dive centers that have proliferated in the pier area.

Scuba Junction and **Planet Scuba** have offices at the pier and Sai Ree beach. **Big Blue** and **Ko Tao Divers**, next to the pier have teamed up to form one of the island's largest schools. Long-time local divers Bryan and Oi run the **Big Fish Dive Centre** near the middle of Hat Sai Ree. At the south point of the island, **Tato Divers** at Tato Lagoon Bungalows offers stunning scenery above and below the emerald waters in a friendly, laid-back atmosphere.

In spite of its small size, Ko Tao has over 20 established dive sights within easy distance. **Chumphon Pinnacle** to the northwest juts up 30m from the sea floor, its peak at a depth of 16m; giant grouper, barracuda, and whale shark are often spotted here. To the southwest, the appropriately named **Shark Island** is known for its clean waters and leopard sharks. Near **Sail Rock,** midway to Ko Phangan, divers can drop into a 22m-high, sub-marine cylindrical rock chimney. Most bays around the island, such as **Ao Hin Wong** and **Ao Mamuang** contain large varieties of coral and fish in shallow waters that are suitable for snorkeling as well as scuba diving.

■ Mae Hat

Mae Hat ("Mother Beach") is the provider for this rocky island, bringing tourists, equipment, food, and fuel. Most of the island's modern facilities, including the post office, the telecommunications office, and the scuba shops, are within walking distance of the pier. Despite its metropolitan status among the island's communities, the beach is as low-key as any other and is an excellent maternal haven for travelers.

PRACTICAL INFORMATION

Tourist Offices: Most dive shop staff dispense plenty of local lore. For transportation info, check with the **Nuan Yang Travel Service Centre,** 10m to the right of the pier. Open daily 8am-9pm.

Currency Exchange: Krung Thai Bank booth, off the pier, has mainland rates. Open daily 11am-3pm. Credit cards accepted at dive shops.

Boats: To **Chumphon** by **night/sleeping boat** leave from Mae Hat Pier (10am, 5hr., 7hr. if the seas are choppy, 200฿) and **speedboat** (7:30am and 3pm, 2½hr., 400฿). To **Surat Thani** via **Ko Phangan ferries** (sporadic days at 9am, 7hr., 200฿). To **Ko Samui** (12pm, 5hr., 250฿). **Speed boat** departs Mae Hat for **Thong Sala** (1pm, 1½hr., 350฿) and **Bo Phut** on Ko Samui (2hr., 450฿). To **Ko Nang Yuan** (10am; returns at 4:30pm, 15min., roundtrip 40฿). During high season, more boats to Ko Nang Yuan leave directly from the beaches.

Local Transportation: Anything beyond a 5-min. walk usually involves traversing unlit dirt roads. If you plan to walk, check the clouds and carry a flashlight; storms hit fast and hard, and some areas fall into complete darkness after dusk.

Taxis: In the form of pick-up trucks and hell-bent motorcycles go almost everywhere on the island. From the pier to **Hat Sai Ree** or **So Chalok Ban Kao** 20฿. To the back of the island 30-50฿. At night, expect 100฿ per person. To get to the morning boat, ask bungalow managers (a day ahead) to arrange a taxi to the pier, but taxis usually make runs to all the bungalows around 8am. During high season, **water taxis** (generally long-tail boats) will also take passengers from the pier to the bays. To: **Ao Chalok Ban Kao** (20฿), **Rocky** or **Kiet Bungalows** (30฿), or the other side of the island (50฿).

Rentals: Some bungalows rent motorcycles for around 150฿ per day; be sure to point out all problems with the bike before you hand over your passport, so you don't get stuck paying for them. Some of the greatest views are only accessible by foot or a "tour boat" ride that loops around the island. This is not a place for inexperienced riders; the roads can be quite rough, sandy, and steep.

Markets: The **Mae Hat pier area** is also called the *talaat* (market). Everything that comes to the island arrives here: fruit, postcards, clothes, swim and snorkel gear, and basic backpacker's supplies. The **mini-mart** at Ko Tao corner to the left off the pier stocks all these goodies and sells boat tickets. Open daily 8:30am-9:30pm.

Medical Services: Public Health Centre, 20m off the road to the right of the pier. Open daily 8:30am-4:30pm. A **private center** (look for the green cross on red circle) is at the entrance to the Public Health Centre. Open daily 7am-5pm; someone is on call 24hr. Call the public phone on the island (tel. 377 196) and people will get in touch with nurses for you.

Police: 600m north of the pier. Shiny new jail but no phone. In case of an emergency, the market area is the best place to find assistance.

Post Offices: GPO, a short right turn off the pier. Open daily 8:30am-5:30pm. **Postal code:** 84280 (for *Poste Restante* 84820-102).

Telephones: At the post office. Overseas calls are generally expensive. Open daily 8:30am-5:30pm. **Nuan Yang Travel Service Centre** has slightly cheaper rates. Open daily 8am-9pm. Some bungalows have overseas calls for similar fees; others rely on radio phones and charge more exorbitant rates.

ACCOMMODATIONS

Coral Beach Bungalow, walk south of the pier until you pass huge boulders on the beach, sky-blue bungalows dot the cape. Guests have free use of their snorkeling gear. Singles/doubles 80-100฿, with shower 100฿, closer to the beach 150฿. Doubles/triples with 2 beds 250฿.

Dam Bungalow, going north, take the first left on the road along the beach. Typical bungalows with mattress, mosquito net, and a balcony. A neon light extravaganza. Electricity 6-11pm. Singles/doubles 80฿ (low season 60฿), closer to the beach 100฿ (low season 80฿). Open 8am-10:30pm.

■ Hat Sai Ree

Sandy beach, peaceful coral reef, sunsets over the sea—sound familiar? They're yours for the taking. Most accommodations can be reached by following the beaten path that winds north from Mae Hat along the beach and over the hill. Take a 10-20 minute walk, or scamper into a cab for 20฿.

Pranee's Bungalow, at the very north end of Hat Sai Ree. Bamboo huts so new and polished you'd think they glow (who needs electricity with these babies?) and surrounded by a garden with fish pools. All rooms have baths with sit toilet, shower, sink, and mirror. 1-2 person huts 250฿ (low season 100-150฿).

Ko Tao Cabana, 137/3 Mu 5 Tambon Ko Tao, a 15-min. walk past the hill. Lola and other showgirls can kick up their heels at these large, family-run bungalows on stilts. Singles/doubles 300฿ (low season 150-200฿). Some of the best food on the island in the restaurant; nightly specials under 50฿.

Sai Ree Cottage, 10/1 Mu 1, in the middle of Hat Sai Ree. Well-ventilated wooden bungalows with high ceilings front the short, narrow beach lined with coconut trees. Friendly manager. Singles/doubles 150฿ (low season 80฿), with fan 200฿ (low season 80-100฿). Larger rooms closer to beach 300฿ (low season 150฿). Simple but clean huts on stilts 50฿. Open 7:30am-11:30pm.

A.C. Resort, at the south end of the beach over the hill. Ah, the irony...no A/C, but all the dark-wood bungalows in a semicircle around the rustic wooden bridge have fans and screens. Singles/doubles 200-350฿ depending on season and management's whims. 10-person rooms 500-1500฿. Full moon parties here are a much tamer version of the Ko Phangan raves. Closed during low season.

North of Hat Sai Ree

Tourists can take a taxi (20฿) to these bungalows 3-4km north of the pier or walk to the end of Hat Sai Ree and then continue around the island on the hillside road. Paths from the road lead to the bungalows.

C.F.T. Bungalow, 31 Mu 1, the northernmost bungalow at the end of the road. Spectacular view of the offshore island trio, and good snorkeling. It is a long walk after the *songthaew* drops you off—most people come by boat. During low season, some rooms are free for those traveling alone. A wooden bridge from the pier leads to simple hillside huts 50฿. Two more rooms higher on the hill are spacious and breezy, with bright, new bathrooms 250฿ (low season 150฿).

Mahana Bay Bungalow, down the path 300m from Hat Sai Ree. Hike up the rocks for a different perspective on Ko Nang Yuan's famous 3-pronged beach. 12 small, basic huts scatter at the foothill 80฿ (low season 50฿).

■ Other Beaches

AO CHALOK BAN KAO

Chalok Ban Kao Bay is carved out of the island's south end, 3km from Mae Hat. Its beach supports the densest pack of bungalows (10 at last count) on the island, but the bay's awesome beauty makes up for the population explosion. The crescent of white-sand beach has clear shallow waters that seem to form a mirror along the rocky, hill-rimmed bay. After the rainy season, the water level rises dramatically (nearly 2m), providing the most picturesque view. Before the rains, low tide turns the beach into white paste; you may think you're hallucinating when hordes of tiny crabs scuttle into holes in the beach in a coordinated disappearing act.

In the middle of the beach, **Carabao Bungalows and Diving Centre** has sturdy cookie-cutter huts lined up among the palms and boasts of being the only place with 24-hour electricity (supposedly through some secret connections). The look for the "coconut diver" strung out over the entrance. Singles/doubles with no bath cost 100฿ (low season 50฿). **View Point Bungalows** (tel. (01) 913 8224) couldn't have a more accurate name. Bungalows line the point out to the right when coming from the beach and boast window screens, sit toilets, showers, and electricity 6pm-noon. One to three person bungalows cost 250฿ (low season 150฿). Farther around the point, the completely secluded **Sunset Bungalow** has also joined the literal-name game. Widely spaced stilt huts show plenty of backpacker traffic, but they're well-maintained and each one affords a commanding view of the fiery evening horizon. After that main event, the friendly, easygoing staff breaks out the guitar and guests feast on some of the best island food. Doubles overlooking Sunset's three tiny beaches go for 80-100฿ (low season 50-80฿).

LAEM TATO

From the mountain viewpoint above Laem Tato, the unique shape of Turtle Island comes into view: you're standing on the south head, with the green hills straight ahead rolling over the turtle's back and the southwest and southeast corners of the island reaching out into the gulf like two front feet. Below, the calm bay waters are translucent; dive boats seem airborne above the dark coral reefs. The **Tato Lagoon Bungalow,** on Tato Beach halfway out the cape, has simple, secluded, dreamy bungalows perched among the massive weather-beaten stones that rim the sand. Many guests are divers-in-training at the bungalow's scuba school, **Tato Divers.** Singles/doubles with bath cost 250฿ (low season 150฿). To make your way to Laem Tato, follow the road up the hill past the bungalows at Ao Chalok Ban Kao and turn right onto the path leading out to the cape. Tato Beach is below you on the right side, 10 minutes ahead. The mountain viewpoint sits 15 sweaty minutes above and beyond the bungalows. A refreshing alternative to trudging along the road out to Laem Tato is to set out from the beach at Chalok Ban Kao and wade through the waist-deep water along the edge of the bay until you come to Tato Beach, where you can strike off onto the paths around the cape.

■ Near Ko Tao: Ko Nang Yuan

This favorite photography subject has some of the best snorkeling in the Gulf of Thailand. The three-pronged trio of beaches makes it possible to walk between its three tiny islands during low tides. Ko Nang Yuan has a viewpoint from the top of the towering rock on the southern isle, where visitors can wave affectionately at sand, snorkelers, and scuba-divers. **Ko Nang Yuan Bungalow,** 10/1 Tambon Ko Tao (tel. (01) 726 00 85) is the only game in town. The office and the restaurant are on the smallest prong, with bungalows fringing the foothill of the south isle. Rooms cost 200-1200฿. A daily boat comes from Mae Hat or Hat Sai Ree (10am, returns at 4:30pm, 40฿ roundtrip), giving just enough time for a beautiful daytrip, and thus avoiding expensive lodgings. It makes more frequent trips during the high season.

PHUKET ISLAND เกาะภูเก็ต

> Phuket is known for treacherous currents during the monsoon season. There are a few casualties almost every year. Exercise caution when swimming and never swim alone. If you are caught in a current float until someone comes to get you.

With its ample natural resources, powdery beaches, and stunning coves and bays, Phuket Island, gleaming 885km south of Bangkok, packs crowds year-round (even during monsoon season). Phuket has always played host to visitors. When colonies, corsets, and Conrad were the fashion, European traders ambled onto this amoeba-shaped island in search of rubber, pearls, and ivory. Their influence, noticeable in the island's older architecture, is just one of the ingredients in Phuket's unique cultural stew. In addition to "sea gypsies," the island's first inhabitants, the population is a mix of Chinese, Malays, Indians, and Thais, most of whom arrived during the tin boom a century ago.

A rhinestone lifestyle is hard to maintain on the "Jewel of the South." Trips to the Similan Islands can be pricey, but offer excellent scuba diving opportunities. Bargaining has withered away in Phuket; merchants scoff at attempts to "cut a deal," knowing that the next fat-cat tourist will happily pay the quoted rates. Nevertheless, there are a few bargains to be snatched up along Kamala Beach and in Phuket Town, connected by *songthaew* (10-30฿) to all the beaches. Great food, a gorgeous coast line, and the alluring Andaman Sea conspire to keep beach bunnies hopping in—just remember that you'll struggle to stay solvent during your sojourn.

GETTING THERE

Phuket International Airport lies 28km outside of Phuket Town on Rte. 4026. International airlines servicing Phuket include Thai Air, Hong Kong Dragon Air, Lauda Air, MAS, Bangkok Airways, and China Airlines. Taxis, and private mini-buses. **Holiday Charter,** 74/56 Phumphon Rd. (tel. 246 088), also runs shuttles from the airport to

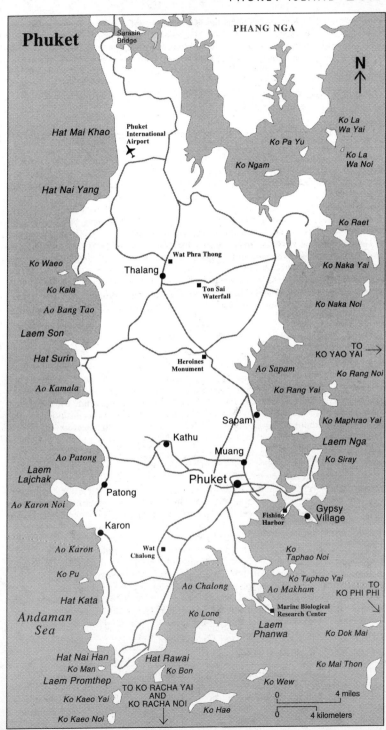

Phuket

PHANG NGA

Sarasin
Bridge

N

Hat Mai Khao

Phuket
International
Airport

Ko La
Wa Yai

Ko Pa Yu

Ko La
Wa Noi

Ko Ngam

Hat Nai Yang

Ko Raet

Wat Phra Thong

Ko Waeo

Thalang

Ko Naka Yai

Ko Kala

Ton Sai
Waterfall

Ao Bang Tao

Ko Naka Noi

Laem Son

Hat Surin

Heroines
Monument

TO
KO YAO YAI →

Ao Sapam

Ko Rang Noi

Ao Kamala

Ko Rang Yai

Sapam

Ko Maphrao Yai

Kathu

Muang

Laem Nga

Ao Patong

Ko Siray

Laem
Lajchak

Phuket

Patong

Ao Karon Noi

Fishing
Harbor

Gypsy
Village

Karon

Wat
Chalong

Ko
Taphao Noi

Ao Karon

Ko Pu

Ko Taphao Yai

Hat Kata

Ao Chalong

Ao Makham

TO
KO PHI PHI

Andaman
Sea

Ko Lone

Marine Biological
Research Center

Laem
Phanwa

Ko Dok Mai

Hat Nai Han

Hat Rawai

Ko Man

Ko Bon

Ko Mai Thon

Laem Promthep

Ko Wew

TO KO RACHA YAI
AND
KO RACHA NOI

Ko Kaeo Yai

0   4 miles

Ko Kaeo Noi

Ko Hae

0   4 kilometers

THAILAND

Phuket Town (70฿) and to the beaches (100฿). In town, the **Thai Air International Office** is at 78 Ranong Rd. (tel. 211 195). (Open daily 8am-5pm.) There is no train service. The most common means of transportation to Phuket is by bus. Most towns around and south of Bangkok have at least one daily bus line.

ISLAND ORIENTATION

No longer a meek island escape, Phuket is now an oversized resort. Pioneers in search of that "off the beaten track" spot should forge a path elsewhere. Mangroves and prawn farms span Phuket's east coast, making it unsuitable for swimming. The west coast's bleached beaches are undergoing exponential development, and the crashing surf is drowned out by the relentless pounding of jackhammers. For the penny-wise, Phuket Town is a realistic base from which to explore the various beaches. *Songthaew* run from town to all the beaches (30-45min., 10-30฿) and the town still contains budget-minded bed and board. Renting a motorbike (150฿ per day) allows the flexibility of dallying through several beaches in one day. Be aware that motorcycles have no insurance, often no helmet, and that accidents are very common. The police are tired of careless tourists: as a "rich" *farang,* you may end up paying through the nose, even if an accident is not your fault.

Moving clockwise from Phuket Town are the less developed and more serene southern beaches of **Rawai** and **Nai Harn,** where travelers can find peace and sun without the traffic and noise of Phuket Town. The western beaches of **Kata, Karon,** and **Patong** have mini-cities built up around them with extensive entertainment options (e.g., jet skiing, bars, clubs, and scuba diving). Farther up the northwest coast the beaches are increasingly beautiful and untouched by development. Head to **Kamala, Bang Jao,** and **Nai Yang** for complete solitude.

■ Phuket Town

Phuket is famed in Thailand for its culinary delights. This, however, may not be an obvious distinction for the budget traveler unwilling to shell out big baht. Rather than cheap eats, the city holds overpriced antique and gold shops, 10-minute waits to cross traffic-ravaged streets, and the blank stares of tourists searching for the "Jewel of the South" promised by travel guides. Colonial architecture, old-fashioned cafés, and antique eateries with marble table tops allow a retreat with a fruit-shake.

ORIENTATION

Although Phuket has undergone tremendous development, it is not an overwhelming metropolis. Nevertheless, the **central area** of Phuket Town is a jumbled grid. The traveler's first move should be to pick up the free TAT map. Four main streets, two north-bound and two south-bound, radiate from the clock tower in the middle of town (the smaller one in the center of the rotary, not the broken Seiko tower on the corner of Phang Nga and Thep Kasattri roads). **Thep Kasattri Road** (north) jets to the airport, intersecting **Ratsada Road,** where the morning market buzzes. The market is farther down the street past the rotary, where the street becomes **Ranong Road.** The *songthaew* station is on Ranong Rd. in front of the market; vehicles serve most destinations around the island (10-30฿). The GPO sits on **Montri Road** (north), which also originates from the clock tower, and crosses Phang Nga Rd., site of the bus station and many hotels. **Phuket Road** (south) passes the Ocean Shopping Mall and also creeps a few blocks north to claim the TAT office. **Thilok Uthit I Road** (south) runs parallel to Phuket Rd. and ends in a T-intersection with **Ong Sim Phai Road.** The night market sets up near here.

PRACTICAL INFORMATION

Tourist Offices: Tourism Authority of Thailand (TAT), 73-75 Phuket Rd. (tel. 212 213). With the Seiko Tower at your back, go south on the right side of Phuket Rd. Cross one bridge and it's across the street from the Honda dealership. Maps, bus schedules, hotel lists, and pamphlets on entertainment, food, and shopping. Listings of official budget travel offices and agencies with bikes/jeeps for rent. Staff speaks English. Open daily 8:30am-4:30pm.

Tourist Police: 5/39-40 Sakdidet Rd. (tel. 219 878; emergency 1699), off the road in the St. Plaza Hotel.

Tours and Travel: Sea Tours Co. Ltd., 95-4 Phuket Rd. (tel. 218 417), 1 block down from TAT on the left. Authorized representative of both **Thai Air** and **AmEx.** Competitive prices for tours and flights. Books bus tickets. Open Mon.-Fri. 8:30am-5pm, Sat. 8:30am-noon. **K. International Tour,** 41/33 Montri Rd. (tel. 222 853-4), next to Downtown Tourist Shop. Affordable tours of **Similan Islands.** Reserves bus tickets. Open Mon.-Fri. 8am-6:30pm, Sat.-Sun. 8am-5pm.

Currency Exchange: Banks gather on Phang Nga Rd. in front of the On On Hotel. **Bangkok Bank,** 22 Phang Nga Rd. (tel. 211 292-5). Outside exchange booth is open daily 8:30am-5pm. Accepts Visa, AmEx at booth and **ATM. Thai Farmer's Bank,** 14 Phang Nga Rd. (tel. 217 125). Exchange booth accepts MC, Visa. ATM machine accepts Visa. Booth open daily 8:30am-6pm.

Buses: The **inter-city bus station** (tel. 211 480) is just off Phang Nga Rd. in the eastern section of the city, set back from the road behind a newly built shopping plaza. To: **Bangkok** (6 per day, 6am-6:30pm, 15hr., 210฿; A/C 7 per day, 8:25am-5:30pm, 14hr., 1st class 368-570฿, 2nd class 294฿); **Hat Yai** (4 per day, 6:20-10:20am, 8hr., 112฿; A/C 7 per day, 7:30am-9:30pm, 7hr., 192-202฿); **Surat Thani** (8 per day, 4:45am-1:50pm, 6hr., 77฿; A/C 7:30am and 9am, 5hr., 139฿); **Trang** (9 per day, 4:15am-12:20pm, 6hr., 78฿; A/C 12 per day, 7am-6:30pm, 5hr., 140฿); **Krabi** (3 per day, 10:50am-2:30pm, 4hr., 47฿; A/C 17 per day, 7am-6:30pm, 3hr., 84฿); and **Phang Nga** (5 per day, 10:10am-4:30pm, 2½hr., 26฿).

Local Transportation: The **songthaew** station is on Ranong Rd. in front of the town market; vehicles leave for destinations around the island (every 30min., 6am-6pm): **Kata Karon** (15฿); **Surin** (15฿); **Patong** (10฿); **Phromtep** (30฿); **Rawai** (10฿); and **Kamala** (15฿). To get around town use local **mini-vans.** Bargain hard for a 10฿ fare.

Rentals: Phuket Travel, 188 Phuket Rd. (tel. 226 175), opposite TAT. Rents motorbikes (150-200฿ per day), jeeps (700฿), trucks (800-1000฿), and cars (1200-1800฿). IDP (except motorbikes) and passport deposit required.

Pharmacies: Pleon Pharmacy, 41/8 Montri Rd. (tel. 215 129), opposite the Pearl Hotel, north of rotary. Open daily 10am-midnight. Fulfills minor medicinal needs.

Medical Services: Mission Hospital, 4/1 Thepkasatri Rd. (tel. 211 173). 24-hr emergency service. **The Medical Centre,** 69 Krabi Rd. (tel. 212 853), is closer to budget area. Open daily 8am-5pm. Both have English-speaking doctors.

Emergency: tel. 1699.

Police: (tel. 212 115). Contact TAT first.

Post Offices: 183/57-59 Phang Nga Rd. Temporarily in the newly finished shopping plaza next to the bus terminal until the new office is finished. Open Mon.-Fri. 8:30am-4:30pm. *Poste Restante.* **Branch:** 158 Montri Rd (tel. 211 020), on the corner with Thalang Rd.; open Mon.-Fri. 8:30am-4:30pm, Sat.-Sun. 9am-noon.

Telephones: 112/2 Phang Nga Rd. (tel. 216 861), the tall building with satellite dish east of the Phang Nga-Montri intersection toward the bus station. Overseas calling and fax (95-110฿ per page). Sells domestic phone cards. Open daily 8am-midnight. MC, Visa, AmEx. **Telephone code:** 076.

ACCOMMODATIONS

Budget lodgings in Phuket are rare, and they cluster in the middle of town. Hours tend to undergo unpredictable changes, while low-end rates remain fixed all year; middle and upscale prices fluctuate more.

Suk Sabai Hotel, 82/9 Thep Kasattri Rd. (tel. 212 287). From the Phang Nga-Phuket Rd. intersection, go down Phuket toward the bridge. The street becomes Thep Kasattri Rd. and Suk Sabai is visible in a bright yellow structure down the next right (Suthat Rd. Soi 2). Nice, quiet, new, and clean. Singles/doubles with double bed and fan 140฿. Security box at the reception desk. Open daily 6am-midnight.

On On Hotel, 17 Phang Nga Rd. (tel. 211 154), on opposite end of Phang Nga Rd. from the bus station, across from Thai Farmer's Bank. The façade sports blue-green arches. Tidy rooms along winding wooden halls. Common shower/toilet areas sport peeling paint and interesting views. Rooms without baths have a sink. Singles (with 1 double bed) 100฿, with bath 150฿, with A/C 250฿. Doubles with bath 220฿, with A/C 360฿. Reception desk open daily 8am-9:30pm. Security box.

Thara Hotel, 184/24 Thep Kasattri Rd. (tel. 216 208), north of Suk Sabai. Dim, down-trodden doubles with fan and refurbished private bath 160฿, with A/C 300฿. Open at 8am; knock on the door when office is closed.

FOOD

The array of culinary specialties available in Phuket masks some of its aesthetic short-comings. The Ranong Rd. daily **market** has aisles upon aisles of produce, tropical fruit, and friends of the sea. Eateries are mainly of the point-and-eat variety. The **night market,** at the junction of Tilok Uthit 1 and Ong Sim Phai Rd., stretches for several square blocks. With the giant broken Seiko at your back, follow Phuket Rd. south past the rotary to Metropolis Hotel; the market is on the left.

Ka Jok See, 26 Takuapa Rd. (tel. 217 903), several shops south of the Takuapa-Ratsada intersection, half-hidden by a tangle of potted plants. Gracious dining in turn-of-the-century style. Colored windows and well-worn wooden tables amidst shelves of old china and pottery. Even the food comes dressed; fried shrimp in noodle sarongs 60฿. Most dishes 50-60฿. English menu. Open Tues.-Sun. 6-11pm.

Muslim Restaurant, 1/1 Thep Kasattri Rd. (tel. 223 930), at the Thalang Rd. intersection. In the morning, there's *roti,* chicken curry, and of course *kow mook gai* (saffron rice with chicken, 25฿). Hot tea with sweet condensed milk balances this vicious breakfast. Insure your tongue before trying a flammable curry dinner. Open daily 7am-9pm (hours may vary).

SIGHTS

A good excuse to bask in temperate A/C is the **Phuket Aquarium and Marine Biological Research Centre** (tel. 391 126). *Songthaew* to the aquarium (Makahm Bay, until 5pm, 10฿) leave from Ranong Rd. The aquarium at Laem Phanwa is the last stop. It is home to exotic undersea critters: electric eels, spiny lobsters, clown fish with rouged lips, and other aquatic wonders which glide and slither, and peck at the divers cleaning the tanks. Whet your appetite here before going out for seafood. (Admission 20฿, children 5฿.)

■ Hat Kata

Hat Kata, a 2km banana-shaped sandy streak, is split into two sections, Kata Yai and Kata Noi, and garnished with humanely priced sleeping quarters and a splash of budget traveler flavor. At the junction between the two beach halves, Kata Centre is a small town of night-owl bars, restaurants, hotels, and shops. During low season, especially May-July, the area clears out, and prices plummet.

PRACTICAL INFORMATION

Tourist Police: tel. 212 468.

Tours and Travel: Kata Centre Service, 114/24 Mu 4, Kata Centre (tel. 330 582), on Patak Rd. next to Dan Kwian Restaurant, has competitive prices for trips to **Phang Nga** (450฿, low season 300฿), **Coral Island** (400฿ per day, high season only), and **Phi Phi Island** (550฿, low season 500฿). Open daily 9am-9pm.

Currency Exchange: Thai Farmers Bank, 114/6 Kata Beach (tel. 330 592), down the street from Kata Centre Service. Open daily 9:30am-8pm.

Local Transportation: Songthaew from Phuket Town leave from the market on Ranong Rd. until 5 pm (30min., 15฿). *Songthaew* stop near Kata Noi; or flag them on the main highway. **Tuk-tuk** charge upwards of 150฿. Many shops have motor-bike rentals (150฿ per day).

Medical Services: AR Clinic, 112/7 Patak Rd. (tel. 330 666), across from Thai Farmers Bank. Open Mon.-Sat. 10am-7pm. For **emergencies,** try Dr. Arin's beeper; dial 162 for an operator and then 078 679.
Police Station: Chalong Police Station (tel. 381 247).
Post Offices/Telephones: (tel. 330 937), lies on the main highway linking Phuket, Kata, and Patong. From Patak Rd. walk from the sea and turn right onto the highway. The office is 1 block up. *Poste Restante*, overseas phone, and telegram. Open Mon.-Fri. 8:30am-noon and 1-4:30pm, Sat. 9am-noon. **Postal code:** 83100. **Telephone code:** 076.

ACCOMMODATIONS AND FOOD

Most guest houses have eateries and there are plenty of pricey seafood joints selling lobster, tiger prawns, and fish by the kilo.

Lucky Guest House, 110/44 Mu 4 Patak Rd. (tel. 330 572), halfway between the sea and main highway. From Pitak Rd. take the right fork at the Kata Centre, go past Kata On Sea and look for the sign. Beautiful and extraordinarily clean. Singles have double beds, all rooms have private baths, and some have balconies. Singles/doubles 250฿, with bath 400-450฿ (low season 250฿). Rooms with A/C 500-600฿ (low season 400฿). Reception open daily 9am-10pm. Safe deposit box available daily 8am-8pm.
Rose Inn, 110/24 Pitak Rd. Mu 4 (tel. 330 572), behind Kata Centre Office. Quiet walkway lined with potted plants. Tidy rooms with private bath. Singles/doubles 250-300฿ (low season 200฿).
Dive Café, 111/25-26 Patak Rd. (tel. 330 683, about 1 block away from the water on the left from Rose Inn. D House specialty is *gai manao* (lemon chicken) 60฿, coffee shakes 15-20฿. Open daily 9am-10pm.

ENTERTAINMENT

If you have the cash, this area has world-class **snorkeling** and **diving** around the Similan or Racha Islands (off the eastern and southern coasts, respectively). Otherwise, make a splash at the bar scene in Kata Centre. Wince at all types of music and video.

Siam Diving Centre, 121/9 Patak Rd. (tel. 330 936), at the midpoint between Kata and Karon. A PADI five-star center with divemasters. Explore some of the world's best **diving** and **underwater coral reef formations.** 4-day diver certification courses cost 5900฿ (1 dive) or 8200฿ (2 dives), including transport, equipment, and food. Rentals available for 600฿ per day. Open daily 9am-6pm.

■ Other Beaches

HAT RAWAI

Hat Rawai, on the southern tip of the island, can't brag about its ocean views, but it does scare up some meager budget options. During low tide, the beach becomes a swamp; its neighbor, Hat Nai Han, is more attractive and worth an overnight stay (despite the deluxe resort rooted there). Both are deserted in the low season when monsoons menace the water. On Rawai, **Pornmae Bungalows,** 58/1 Wisa Rd. (tel. 381 300), offers tidy bamboo bungalows with a double bed and bath for 800฿ per month, but these fill up fast year-round. For something sturdier, hole up in a concrete bunker with a double bed, bath, and western toilets for 300฿ (low season 200฿) available all year. Additions to this package include refrigerator (350฿, low season 300฿) and A/C (450฿, low season 400฿). Reception is open daily 8am-10pm.
Friendship Beach, 27/1 Soi Mittrapap (tel. 381 281), has two-for-one beers during happy hour (6am-7pm), excellent Thai and Euro food (ribs 100฿, lasagna 75฿), cable TV, a pool table, and occasional jazz. It is the watering hole of many an expat and visiting *farang*. Beach-side bungalows come in large (sleeps 2-3 people, 350฿, low season 300฿), and *really* large (sleeps 4 people, 700฿, low season 500฿). To the left of

the restaurant is the **Friendship Beach Second Hand Shop** (tel. 381 424). The owner, Steve Brickley, stocks a modest selection of novels in English, French, and German, but the bulk of the shop is marine equipment. Sometimes Steve also has information on yachts seeking crews for their jaunts across Southeast Asia. Yacht owners frequently ask for money from sea-faring backpackers during high season, but will often pay for help during low season. The catch is, of course, fewer yachts pass through during the monsoons. Prior experience not necessarily a prerequisite.

Save your appetite for Phuket Town. Otherwise, **Lair Lae Thong** (tel. 381 300), next to the bungalows, has a breezy sitting area and pricey service with a smile. Basic noodle/rice dishes start at 40฿. (Open daily 8:00am-11pm.)

PATPONG BEACH

For those who crave more entertainment options, Patpong, on the west coast, is where it's at. Budget accommodations here are almost nonexistent, and travelers should expect to pay much higher rates than in Phuket Town. **B&B Guest House,** 116/11 Soi Kepsup (tel. 292 147), off Thaweewong Rd., offers clean white rooms with hot water and flush toilet. Singles go for 250-300฿ (low season 200฿), doubles 400฿ (low season 300฿), with A/C 600฿ (low season 450฿). Near B&B Guest House is **Restaurant Pizzeria Garden,** 116/13-14 Soi Kepsup (tel. 293 045), which offers spacious rooms complete with sofa, mirror, dresser, and cabinets. Singles/doubles 350-400฿ (low season 250-300฿).

HAT KAMALA

Escapees from the rat race can scurry to the quiet-as-a-mouse **Hat Kamala,** on the way to Surin from Phuket for a 20฿ bus ride (last bus to Phuket Town, 3pm). There are no big hotels (yet), and the aquamarine water and snowy sand are the same as anywhere else on the island. If you want to hibernate up here, guest houses are popping up all over. Stays should be in the range of 325-375฿ (about 75฿ less in low season). **Kamala Group House,** located past the police station on the left at 93/4 Mu 3 (tel. 324 426), offers miraculously spotless second floor rooms (doubles with bath 300฿ year round). Downstairs, multi-lingual testaments to **Kamala Seafood's** culinary exploits graffiti the walls. Dishes average 50฿ and up. Complete the Kamala Group experience with a novel (20฿ per day) from the **Kamala Group Service Library** or rent one of their motorcycles (150-200฿ per day with passport deposit) or jeeps (700-800฿ with insurance).

HAT SURIN, BANG TAO, AND HAT NAI YANG

The deep blue waters at nearby **Surin Beach** have been spared the voracious jaws of beachfront development, however, the beast is beginning to surface. The only lodgings here are large resorts up the road, but guest houses are in the works. Small, costly seafood joints dot the beach. **Bang Tao** is a long attractive beach dominated by two resort complexes that have monopolized access to the water, denying penniless pilgrims. Restaurants on the beach charge 60-100฿ for basic seafood meals. With your own food, a towel, and some Faulkner, Bang Tao makes a nice daytrip, especially between May and July, when the heavy rains haven't hit but crowds have skedaddled. **Hat Nai Yang,** a 13km Eden of coconut and rubber trees, is part of a national park. The government recognition has kept private developers at bay, although the condo vultures anxiously circle the park boundaries. Currently, the only **accommodation** is a set of government-run bungalows. The **visitors office** (tel. 327 407) is near the entrance (open daily 8am-4:30pm). Two-person concrete bungalows with bath cost 250฿, 4-person set-up 400฿. Rooms away from the water (shared bath) are 200฿. **Camp** on the beach (bring your own equipment) for 10฿ per night. The office has a safe and serves food from 8am to 9pm (fried rice 25฿).

ON THE MAINLAND

■ Phang Nga พังงา

Splashing about halfway between Phuket and Krabi, Phang Nga Bay has become a popular spot for boat tours that weave between the craggy islets jutting abruptly from the water. The beautiful bay forms a spectacularly chaotic labyrinth of caves, islets, and rock formations. Long tail boats bring visitors into the bat-infested caves during low tide, and if they're lucky, tourists can catch a glimpse of the wild monkeys frolicking on the island's shores. The steep, unique rock formations are worth a climb early in the morning or late in the afternoon, when the Phuket crowds have dwindled. The nearby fishing village of Ko Panyi offers good access to the bay. It houses over 1000 Muslims in a town built entirely on stilts over the ocean water—infinitely more satisfying lodgings than sightless Phang Nga town. The bay is not as developed as Phuket or Krabi, meaning fewer hotels and English-menu restaurants.

ORIENTATION

The **bus station** is outside the town center on **Phetkasem Road.** Hotels, banks, and eating spots are several blocks off to the right of the station. The police station, post office, and hospital are to the left. Phang Nga town runs along this road about 3-4km, thinning out in both directions. Most facilities are within walking distance, except for the post office and hospital, which are a few km outside of town.

PRACTICAL INFORMATION

Tourist Offices: Sayan Tour (tel. 430 348), next to the bus terminal. Offers tours of Phang Nga Bay and Ko Panyi, maps, and bus schedules. Run by English-speaking Sayan Tamtopol. TAT-approved and helpful. Open daily 7am-6pm.

Currency Exchange: Bangkok Bank, 120 Phetkasem Rd. (tel. 411 362), 2 blocks from the bus station. **Krung Thai Bank,** 109 Phetkasem Rd. (tel. 412 010). Both open Mon.-Fri. 8:30am-3:30pm.

Buses: Station is on Phetkasem Rd., marked by a sign. To: **Bangkok** (5pm, 14hr., 205฿; A/C, 13hr., 346฿; VIP, 13hr., 510฿); **Hat Yai** (4 per day, 8:45am-12:30pm, 6hr., 94฿; A/C 6 per day, 8:30am-1:10pm, 6hr., 163฿); **Krabi** (13 per day, 7:30am-6:30pm, 2hr., 25฿; A/C 5 per day, 8:30am-1:10pm, 43฿); **Phuket** (18 per day, 6:30am-5:45pm, 2hr., 25฿; A/C 9 per day, 11:40am-7pm, 2hr., 47฿); **Surat Thani** (4 per day, 6:30am-1:30pm, 3hr., 50฿; A/C 3 per day, 9:30am-1:30pm, 3hr., 120฿); **Ko Samui** (9:30, 11:30am, 6½hr., 180฿ including ferry); and **Trang** (6 per day, 7:30am-6:30pm, 4hr., 57฿; A/C 4 per day, 9:30am-3pm, 4hr., 102฿). **A/C minivans** for **Malaysia** stop at Sayan Tour (ask for times). To: **Surat Thani** (2½hr., 650฿); **Hat Yai** (5hr. 200฿); **Penang** (9hr., 520฿); **Kuala Lumpur** (20hr., 720฿); and **Singapore** (24hr., 820฿).

Local Transportation: Songthaew (5฿) run up and down Phetkasem Rd.

Pharmacies: 91 Phetkasem Rd., near the market. Open Mon.-Fri. 7-8:30am and 4:30-9pm, Sat.-Sun. 7am-9pm.

Medical Services: Phang Nga Hospital, 436 Phetkasem Rd. (tel. 412 032), about 2km on the left from the bus station.

Police Station: 193 Phetkasem Rd. (tel. 412 073), 0.5km left of the bus station.

Post Offices/Telephones: (tel. 412 171), On Phetkasem Rd. about 2km to the left of the bus station. *Poste Restante.* Open Mon.-Fri. 8:30am-4:30pm, Sat.-Sun. 9am-noon. **Overseas calls** and telegram located upstairs. Open daily 8:30am-4:30pm. **Postal code:** 82000. **Telephone code:** 076.

ACCOMMODATIONS

Luk Muang Hotel, 1/1 Phetkasem Rd. (tel. 411 512), about 500m past Muang Thong Hotel, next to a wat. Rooms bask in the radiance of the sunlight filtered in through orange curtains. Blue sofas and red floors decorate spotless rooms with flush toilets. Singles 150฿. Doubles 200฿. 4-person room 250฿.

Thaweesuk Hotel, 79 Phetkasem Rd. (tel. 412 100), on the bus station side of the street, several blocks to the right as you exit the station. Rooms are basic, but the best part is the easily accessible roof-top, which commands a view of the Phang Nga mountain range. Singles/doubles 100฿, with 2 beds (2-3 people) 150฿. The reception desk, in the front of the grocery store next door, is open daily 6am-11pm. Safe deposit box and tours available.

Muang Thong Hotel, 128 Phetkasem Rd. (tel. 412 132), across from the bus station about 1 block down to the left. The manager speaks little English, but an English sign lists prices for a decent room, bath, and fan. Singles 120฿, with A/C 250฿. Doubles 180฿, with A/C 320฿. Desk open daily 7am-midnight.

FOOD

Phang Nga won't be over-run by galloping gourmets anytime soon. A few places have English menus, but often have higher prices too. The **morning market,** off Phetkasem Rd. near the Fuji shop, offers handfuls of fruit. Late afternoon **vendors** set up along Phetkasem Rd. near the hospital and post office and along Riverside Rim Kong Rd. Open daily about 4:30pm-midnight.

Duang Seafood, 122 Phetkasem Rd. (tel. 412 216), near Muang Thong Hotel, next to Thai Farmer's Bank. One of the few seafood restaurants in town, it outclasses rivals with snazzy English menu and requisite mark-up. Dishes above 40฿. Shrimp with corn 50฿. Open daily 9am-10:30pm.

■ Near Phang Nga

The top-heavy calcite formations that spring from the sea have made Phang Nga Bay an increasingly popular tourist attraction. Travel offices in Phuket and Krabi book tours (at least 350฿ for a daytrip), sending squadrons of high-powered boats racing about the Bay's mangrove-lined waterway between 10am and 2pm. Expensive sights are **Khao Ping Kan** and **Ko Tapu,** the twin nail-shaped rock-islands that preen in the bay of Khao Ping Kan island and appear in the James Bond film *Man With the Golden Gun.* The rock's base is gradually dissolving, threatening the total collapse of the precarious formation.

Songthaew from Phang Nga town go to the pier (10฿), where long-tailed boats can be chartered for a spin around the islands (over 550฿ for a few hours). Sayan (tel. 430 348), whose office is located in the same lot as the Phang Nga bus terminal, offers a reputable tour service (see **Practical Information** above). Sayan's excursions include lesser-explored caves such as the **Naga cave,** a prehistoric site where paintings and burial sites can be found. Furthermore, his tour gets going before most of the tourists from Phuket and Krabi arrive. Four-hour (7:30am and 2pm, 150฿) and full-day tours (7:30am, 350฿) are available daily. During the low season prices and schedule may vary based on the number of people. During the high season Sayan sometimes offers a tour of Phang Nga's wats and waterfalls as well.

KO PANYI

Most tours dock at **Ko Panyi,** a Muslim fishing village constructed on stilts over the water. Over 250 years ago, an enterprising Indonesian fisherman agreed with two fellow seamen to search for fertile islands. Each fisherman had to raise a flag over a newly discovered island as a sign that the land was ready for habitation. Ko Panyi was settled in this way, with seafaring colonists spotting the tell-tale *panyi* (flag) and moving in. The present population is about 1500; there is a post office, health clinic, primary school, cemetery, and a mosque where almost everyone in the village prays five times a day. An overnight stay at Ko Panyi is definitely worthwhile, since the village is completely different after the daytrippers have packed up and gone back to the mainland. At the end of the day, people emerge from their homes to carry on the tasks of everyday living: cooking, cleaning, and gossiping with neighbors.

For an additional 150฿, Sayan will gladly arrange **accommodation** in his own home, a yummy Thai breakfast, and a sunrise boat trip back to Phang Nga pier the next morning. He has a notebook overflowing with multi-lingual superlatives from former house guests. Beware of imposters; many people have used Sayan's name and plagiarized his brochure to entice tourists and rip them off.

■ Krabi กระบี่

A paradigm of southern cities, Krabi is not a destination in and of itself, but rather a transit point for travelers who have made the *pak Thai* pilgrimage to shack up on a sassy beach nearby or set sail for a spectacular isle off the coast. From November to March, the blue waters of the Andaman Sea are calm and clear, making for smooth passage to Ko Phi Phi and Ko Lanta. Few families remain in town during the low season, when the monsoons move in and turn the water a turbulent opaque, but young backpackers still slouch about, relishing the silence, solitude, and reduced hotel rates. Prices in town vacillate greatly with the seasons, as do the community's tourist services. Boats to beaches and islands halt on monsoon days, ferries to Ao Nang quiet their engines from April to September, and low-budget bungalows in Krabi as well as on Phi Phi and Lanta often shut down for the low season while remaining establishments ransom rooms for paltry sums. Ko Phi Phi and Ko Lanta, along with Ko Poda and Ko Hua Khwaan (Chicken Island), offer opportunities to observe a plethora of aquatic critters. Of the nearby beaches, Rai Lay and Phra Nang beaches are the most secluded (reached only by boat) and the most beautiful. Get the goods before everyone else does.

ORIENTATION

Buses entering Krabi usually go only as far as the station, 5km out of the town. Red *songthaew* go from the station to **Maharat Road** in town (5฿). Running parallel, between Maharat Rd. and the **Krabi River**, is **Utarakit Road**, home to banks, the post office, and tour offices. Krabi's small **TAT office** is also located on Utarakit Rd. From Maharat Rd., Utarakit Rd. is accessible via **Prachachoen Road** or any other cross street. The daily **morning market** is at the intersection of **Pruk-sa-uthit** and **Srisawat Road**. Boats to Phra Nang Beach, Ko Phi Phi, and Ko Lanta leave from **Chao Fah Pier**, down **Chao Fah Road** directly ahead on the water. A small **night market** is on **Kong Ka Road**, which intersects Utarakit Rd. and runs along Chao Fah Pier. **P.S. Tours and Guest House** sells good maps of the area for 40฿, useful not only for navigating Krabi town, but also for locating the area's beaches and islands.

PRACTICAL INFORMATION

Tourist Offices: TAT office (tel. 612 740), on Utarakit Rd., along the river near the Floating Restaurant. Get better info at P.S. Tours. Open daily 8:30am-4:30pm.

Tours and Travel: P.S. Tours and Guest House, 71/1 Utarakit Rd. (tel. 611 308). Info on Krabi's beaches, as well as those on the Ko Phi Phi and Ko Lanta. Boat tours of **Ko Poda, Ko Taloo,** and **Phra Nang Cave.** Day tour 280฿ (lunch, snorkeling equipment). To **Ko Phi Phi** and **Ao Nang** 670฿. Arranges bus service to other cities and boats to beaches. Open daily 8am-10pm. **Grand Tours,** 73/1 Utarakit Rd. (tel. 621 456), 1 block back toward the TAT, from the intersection of Utarakit and Chao Fah Rd. Similar services as P.S. Open daily 6:30am-9pm. **Jungle Book Tour,** 141 Utarakit Rd. (tel. 611 148). Pamphlets of guest houses in Krabi, plus the standard services. Open daily 7am-9pm.

Currency Exchange: Bangkok Bank, 147 Utarakit Rd. (tel. 811 186), on the left, about 1 block from the TAT office. Open Mon.-Fri. 8:30am-3:30pm. 24-hr. **ATM** accepts Visa. **Siam City Bank,** 93 Utarakit Rd. (tel. 611 320), 1 block from Bangkok Bank toward P.S. Tours. Exchange booth. Open daily 8:30am-4pm.

Buses: The **bus station** (tel. 611 804) is 5km outside town. Red *songthaew* run between town and the bus station (every 15min., 5฿). Hail them anywhere or from Maharat Rd., where they often stop. To: **Bangkok** (4 per day, 3:30-5:20pm, 14hr., 204฿; A/C 2 per day, 4:30pm and 5pm, 12hr., 368-377฿; VIP 4pm, 4:30pm, 5pm, 12 hr., 540฿); **Hat Yai** (4 per day, 10:30am-2:10pm, 5hr., 78฿; A/C 10 per day, 7am-5:20pm, 127฿); **Phang Nga** (every hr., 7am-4pm, 2hr., 25฿; A/C 5 per day, 9:30am-4pm, 2hr., 45฿); **Phuket** (16 per day, 6:20am-3:10pm, 5hr., 46฿; A/C 13 per day, 9:30am-5:20pm, 4hr., 84฿); and **Trang** (14 per day, 6:20am-4pm, 3hr., 36฿; A/C 15 per day, 9:30am-8:30pm, 2½hr., 66฿). A private A/C bus to **Surat Thani** leaves from Chao Fah Pier (7, 11am, and 3:30pm, 3hr., 150฿).

Boats: Long-tailed boats leave from Chao Fah Pier at the end of Chao Fah Rd. to **Phra Nang Beach** and **Rai Lay Beach** (45min., 40฿) and to **Ao Nang Beach** (1hr., 65฿), 9am-6pm (to 4pm low season). To **Ko Lanta** (Oct.-April, 10am and 1:30pm, 2½hr., 150฿). These leave when there's 6-8 people. Boat service is irregular in the low season (May-Sept.). Convince the boatman to leave with 4 people during this time, since it's usually less crowded, or charter the boat for 200฿. **Ferries** to **Ko Phi Phi** leave regularly during the high season (10-11am, 2hr., 125฿) and return 8-9pm. During the low season, ferry service may be irregular. Tour companies, including P.S. and Grand, arrange boat trips (150฿).

Local Transportation: Krabi is small enough to permit getting anywhere (except the bus station and beaches) by foot. *Songthaew* to Ao Nang Beach, Hat Noppharat Thara, and Shell Cemetery leave Utarakit Rd. near the Floating Restaurant, or from Pattana Rd., across from the New Hotel (15฿).

Rentals: Grand Tour, 73/1 Utarakit Rd. (tel. 612 948). Motorbikes 200฿ per day. Jeep with insurance 800฿ per day, with A/C 1200฿.

Markets: Krabi's **day-turn-night market** sprawls between Maharat Soi 10 and Soi 8. A smaller **night market** also sets up along the Krabi River on Kong Ka Rd.

Pharmacies: 2/4 Pattana Rd. (tel. 620 545), facing Rimnam Restaurant, with the large sign advertising birth control pills. Open daily 6:30am-9pm.

Medical Service: (tel. 611 210), 5km out of town on Utarakit Rd. **24-hr. number:** 611 227. Some doctors speak English.

Emergency: tel. 191 or call the TAT (tel. 612 740).

Police: (tel. 611 222), on Utarakit Rd. on the same side of the street as the post office, about 0.5km down, heading out of town. Little English spoken.

Post Offices/Telephones: 190 Utarakit Rd. (tel. 611 050), across from P.S. Tours about ½ block up. *Poste Restante.* Open Mon.-Fri. 8:30am-4:30pm, Sat. 9am-noon. **Overseas calls,** telegram, and fax service upstairs open daily 7am-midnight. MC, Visa, AmEx. **Postal code:** 81000. **Telephone code:** 075.

ACCOMMODATIONS

Grand Tower Guest House, 73/1 Utarakit Rd. (tel. 611 741), on the corner of Chao Fah Rd. Lowest rates for 7th-floor rooms, which contain a double mattress and flaking paint chips. No elevator. Other chambers are bright and brand new. Ceiling fan and a big window dissipate heat. Open daily 7am-10pm. Singles/doubles 120฿, with bath 230฿, with double beds 280฿. Safe-deposit in high season.

Jungle Book Guest House, 141 Utarakit Rd. (tel. 611 148), behind the tour office and restaurant. Just the bare necessities here. Box-like rooms with fans. Bright lights make up for small windows. Common showers and bathrooms. 50฿ all year. Newly assembled boxes 80฿.

KR Mansions and Guest House, 52/1 Chao Fah Rd. (tel. 612 761). From Grand Tower Guest House walk 0.5km up Chao Fah Rd., away from the river. Away from downtown din, with rooftop and deck chairs for enjoying breezy days. Common baths have sinks outside. Singles/doubles 120฿, with bath 220฿. Rooms with twin bed 150฿, with bath 250฿. Prices may fluctuate with lunar cycles. Open daily 7am-10pm.

FOOD

Ruenmai Thai, 319 Utarakit Rd. (tel. 611 365), on the outskirts of town, 2km toward the hospital (take a *tuk-tuk*). Savory examples of Krabi's local cuisine. Forget *pad thai*—foreigners rave over coconut prawn soup with *pak mieng* (40฿) and spicy manila pea salad (45฿). The soft-spoken owner is a local activist for sustainable development in Krabi's tourist industry. Open daily 10:30am-10pm.

Jungle Book Restaurant, 141 Utarakit Rd. (tel. 611 148), in the tour office. Your tummy will roar like Simba for their breakfasts. Muesli with fruit and yogurt 25฿, cereal 20฿, American breakfast 55฿, ham 'n cheese omelette 25฿. Excellent English menu. Open daily 7am-8pm.

■ Near Krabi

Krabi's nearby world-renowned beaches are some of the most popular tourist magnets in Thailand. The fact certainly is not lost on the local population, which heartily embraces the arrival of sun-and-sand lovers and their wallets. Hotels, guest houses, and bungalows spring to life in the high season from their monsoon-drenched dormancy and fill to capacity. Recently, the local industry has shifted its target from the low-budget market to more upscale, middle-budget vacationers. There is still plenty of surf for the cash-clogged, but prices are rapidly rising, and several expensive resorts stud nearby beaches. During the low season, many beaches are inaccessible.

AO NANG

The cove is the only beach, besides Hat Noppharat Thara, that is a national park area reached by land. The sand on the long beach is not as plush as the silky silica on Phra Nang Beach or Ko Phi Phi, and rivers of traffic lend a somewhat urban atmosphere, which dries up past the Phra Nang Inn. From here, walk down a dirt road into forested areas and more secluded hideaways. Prices on Ao Nang have skyrocketed within the past year. Most bungalows fold up during the low season.

During the high season, in the center of the road that runs past the beach, there's a small branch of **Bangkok Bank,** a **supermarket,** a restaurant, and two **tour offices,** but these are often closed during the low season. For **police,** the number is the same as Krabi's (tel. 611 222; **emergency** tel. 191). *Songthaew* from Krabi to Ao Nang (and Hat Noppharat Thara) leave from Pattana Rd. across from the New Hotel, a half-block in from the river (every 15min. or when full, 15฿). Last *songthaew* back to Krabi leaves at 6pm (low season 4:30pm).

Gift Bungalows (tel. 637193), at the center of Ao Nang Beach, screened from the road by masses of exuberant tropical vegetation, presents a decent restaurant (open during the high season) and small but well-kept bungalows. Baths are roofless—no need to turn on the faucet come rainy season. Singles cost 250฿ (low season 150฿), doubles 300฿ (low season 200฿). All rooms have bath. (Open daily 7:30am-midnight; low season 7:30am-5pm.) **Gift's Restaurant** is endowed with a solid selection of western and Thai food: brown bread with jam, beans, or Nutella, Thai omelettes, and fruit pancakes (open daily in high season 7:30am-9:30pm).

At the terminus of Ao Nang Beach, where the road becomes a dusty dirt trail, there's **Last Café,** which is only open in the high season (drinks available in low season). Homemade brown bread rises to the occasion, and customers keep rolling in for Muesli with fruit and yogurt (30฿), Thai omelettes (40฿), or Thai noodle soup (30฿). Without electricity, the restaurant must rely on lanterns for nocturnal luminescence—the final word in romantic dining (open daily 6:30am-midnight). The ideally situated **Phra Nang Inn** (tel. 612 173) is a nice alternative to bungalow basics with surprisingly proletarian prices (45-70฿) for a *bourgeois* linen-napkined resort. Green curry soup with shrimp and rice is exceptional and rich enough to satisfy an ocean-sized appetite (70฿). Shrimp in tamarind sauce is another savory item (70฿). (Open daily 7-10am for breakfast buffet, 10am-2pm, and 5-10pm.)

Sea Canoe was founded in 1983 with the goals of developing "sustainable business opportunities with local people that promote environmental conservation by providing high-quality recreational adventures specializing in natural history and cross-cultural education." Sea Canoe Krabi (tel. (01) 464 44 03) is located opposite Phra Nang

THAILAND

Inn and offers half-day (700฿) and full-day (1200฿) self-paddled trips along the coast, as well as rental equipment. MC, Visa, and AmEx are accepted.

HAT PHRA NANG AND HAT RAI LAY

Road-less **Hat Phra Nang** has whiter sand and more aqua-colored water than Ao Nang. Unfortunately, the only beach-front lodging is a resort whose rooms command 8000-60,000฿ per night (low season 6000฿). Bungalows clump among the coconut palms on a narrow spit of land that spans east and west Hat Rai Lay. On the **East Rai Lay Beach** side, the scene is generally quieter and cheaper. **West Rai Lay Beach,** however, has a wider, whiter stretch of sand with clear water that practically washes up to you and begs for a belly-flop. Boats stop on East Rai Lay Beach. Along the walkway between East and West Rai Lay Beach lounges an **English bookstore** with paperbacks for rent (10฿).

Wherever you stay, you'll never be farther than a few minutes walk to either beach. The first bungalow on the north end is **Viewpoint Bungalows** (tel. (01) 722 01 15), which has concrete bungalows with small balconies, fans, sit-down toilets, and a great view. Singles or doubles cost 300฿ (low season 150฿). Rooms nearer to the beach are 400฿ (low season 200฿). Next to Viewpoint is **Tex Rock Climber's Bar,** featuring reggae and rock music and hosting occasional parties.

An exotic new species has begun to haunt the cliffs that crowd Rai Lay's beaches. Rock climbers have found the mild climate, nightlife, and the vertical rise of Rai Lay perfect for a winter retreat. **Tex Rock Climbing School** (next to Viewpoint Bungalows) of East Rai Lay offers beginner courses to the beach-bored: half-day (400฿), full-day (700฿), and three-day (2000฿) courses with a signed waiver of liability. Equipment rental (800฿ per day) and guides are available for the experienced. One-day treks (700฿) and pinnacle-top camping trips (1200฿) are also offered.

West Rai Lay Beach can be reached by the walkway between Sun Rise Bungalow and **Rai Lay Bay Bungalow I** (tel. (01) 722 0112). Passports are required to check in. Singles or doubles go for 350-600฿ (low season 150-300฿). All rooms have concrete floors, bamboo walls, tin-walled bath with passably clean flushing toilets. (Reception open daily 7:30am-10pm.) Restaurant is pricey, but popular for its outdoor seating and gorgeous beach views (open daily 7:30am-9:30pm). *Pad thai* costs 40฿ or fried rice 40฿. Two English movies shown nightly during the high season, one during the low. Also has bus schedules and an **overseas call booth.**

Next door, **Sand Sea** (tel. (01) 228 4426) has bamboo huts with mosquito nets, clean rooms, and bathrooms with tiled floors and squat toilet. Singles or doubles are 350-750฿ (low season 150-350฿), with A/C 900฿ (low season 500฿). Deluxe room with hot water and mini bar are 1200฿ (low season 500฿). Restaurant offers fried rice with seafood 35-40฿, as well as spaghetti 40฿. (Open daily 7am-9:30pm. Reception open daily 8am-9:30pm; **currency exchange** daily 9am-9pm.)

Next to Sand Sea is **Rai Lay Village Bungalows** (tel. (01) 228 4366). Ramble along the coconut palm alley to quiet singles or doubles for 600฿ (low season 200฿). Doubles or triples with two beds cost 700฿ (low season 300฿). Fabulous A/C rooms are 1500฿ (low season 700฿). The surfside **restaurant** serves ginger beef (40฿) and other Thai and American favorites. (Reception open daily 7am-10pm.)

KO PHI PHI AND KO LANTA

Cheap deals and quiet, safe bungalows are rapidly becoming endangered species on **Ko Phi Phi,** as the island becomes an exploited paradise for increasing numbers of visitors. Phi Phi has the white sandy beaches, the coconuts, the lush vegetation, and blue water of paradise, but is also one of the worst examples of overdevelopment in a national park. Some hold-out bungalows still go for prices within the backpacker's range during the high season (no fan or bath) at **Phi Phi Andaman** (tel. (01) 723 1073) for 200-400฿, **Maphrao Resort** (180-400฿), and **Gipsy Village** (100-250฿). Most other bungalows charge a minimum of 200-300฿ during high season.

> ### Equation for Exploitation
> $\dfrac{\text{Natural Beauty}}{\text{distance from mainland}}$ x H_2O clarity (% coral remaining) = tourism coefficient

Daytrips to Phi Phi can be arranged at P.S. Tours in Krabi; they include snorkeling around **Phi Phi Don, Ao Maya** (with prehistoric cave paintings), **Ko Yung (**Mosquito Island**), Mai Phai** (Bamboo Island)**, Ko Poda,** and **Ko Hua Khwaan** (Chicken Island). The snorkeling is particularly good around Ko Hua Kwaan and Ko Poda. Reportedly, a lonely set of **bungalows** with an electrical generator mopes on Ko Poda (around 550฿ with fans and baths). It costs 300฿ to hire a long-tailed boat to go there. Camping is 100฿ per night (bring your own tent and food). Call 612 160 for more information or contact the TAT (available only during high season). Long-tailed boats for five people run between Phi Phi Don and Phi Phi Lay and around the islands for 300฿.

Ko Lanta, a 20km-long giant among Lilliputian islands, is fast climbing the charts among tourists fleeing overcrowded Ko Phi Phi. The island retires in the low season, but has bungalows in the 40-50฿ range. During the high season, bungalows with bath can be found for 80฿. Budget traveler options are generally concentrated on Hat Klong Down. Bamboo bungalow singles at **Lanta Golden Bay Cottages** (tel. (01) 723 0879) have mosquito nets and a price tag of 100฿ (low season 70฿). Newer, concrete rooms with fans and potted shrubs are 120-150฿ (low season 80฿). Both have clean baths with Thai toilet. For the tenderfoot, **Lanta Sea House** (tel. (01) 722 0160) has brand-new concrete bungalows with balconies, tiled floors, and flush toilets, but no sink for 500฿ (low season 250฿). Their wooden-floored bamboo bungalows are older. Singles cost 200฿ (low season 150฿), doubles 400฿.

Two hours by boat from Krabi, Ko Lanta is actually closer to Trang. Krabi, however, dominates the industry in these parts, and holds the cards on transport and tours there for now. Boats from Krabi go to Ko Lanta's **Ban Saa Laadaan Pier** daily during the high season (Oct.-May, 1pm, 2hr., 150฿) and return at 8am. During the high season, boats also leave from Ko Phi Phi for Ko Lanta (1pm, 1½hr., 150฿). Otherwise, mini-vans depart year-round from Krabi to Baw Muang (10:30 and 11am, 2hr.) to catch a boat to Ko Lanta, and a minibus to the bungalows (total trip 150฿).

INLAND

The **Khao Nawe Choochee Lowland Forest** is one of the last remaining forests of its kind in Thailand. Among the 290-plus species of birds that nest in the forest is the endangered *Pitta gurneyi*, a brightly colored ground-dwelling bird of which there are only about 150 living. The **Thung Tieo nature trail,** a 2.7-km path, eases you through some of Thailand's most lush and currently undisturbed slices of nature. Motorbike there from Krabi or take a *songthaew* out to **Khlong Thom,** the capital of that district. Contact Mr. Koyou at the **Krabi Bird Club,** 24 Phetkasem Rd. (tel. 699 089). TAT officials can also find him for you. Mr. Koyou can haul tourists around the area in his pick-up truck (300฿). A motorcycle taxi can be hired from Khlong Thom (100฿), but be sure to arrange return transport.

■ Trang ตรัง

When it comes to economic opportunity, Trang has lived a charmed existence. In the 7th and 12th centuries, it was a major trading outpost for the Srivijaya Empire. At the turn of this century, rubber trees (the first in Thailand) were introduced to the area, and countless plantations sprouted. Finally, about 30 years ago, Highway Rte. 4 hit town and, since then, Trang has been riding another wave of prosperity. The provincial capital stockpiles 119km worth of national park beaches and a formidable collection of small islands nearby, both of which remain miraculously undisturbed by the brazen bandits of large-scale development. Located off the well-trodden tourist circuit, Trang is perfect for travelers seeking relief from *farang*-heavy traffic. The area is a local vacation spot, however, which keeps prices up and vacancies down. Day tours of the islands can be arranged from Trang, but they all close down in the low season.

ORIENTATION

Buses arrive at the **bus terminal** on **Ploenpitak Road;** the **train station** forms a central axis and gathering place at the city's northern tip. **Phra Ram VI Road,** a large avenue lined with hotels, originates at the train station and runs through most of Trang. **Ratchadamnoen Road** winds alongside it, and the daily **market** is between these two roads, a few blocks from the railroad. **Visetkul Road** intersects Phra Ram VI Rd. at the clock tower. **Ratsada Road** runs parallel to it. The rest of Trang's layout is an arbitrary maze of streets winding around themselves. Trang Travel has very helpful **maps** of the city with a decent province map on the back (50฿). Most of the city is within walking distance.

PRACTICAL INFORMATION

Tourist Offices: Trang Travel, on Phra Ram VI Rd. (tel. 219 598), on the right side, 1 block down from the train station, facing Thumrin Hotel. Some English spoken. Decent maps (50฿). Open daily 8am-8pm. **Trang Tour Service,** 22 Sathani Rd. (tel. 214 564). Excellent information on region and beyond.

Currency Exchange: Bangkok Bank, 2 Phra Ram VI Rd. (tel. 218 203), 1 block from the train station on the right. Open Mon.-Fri. 8:30am-3:30pm.

Air Travel: Trang Airport (tel. 210 804), on Trang-Palian Rd, 7km south of the city. Airport fee 30฿. Trang Travel runs airport vans (30฿), or take a *tuk-tuk* (30฿). Thai Air to: **Bangkok** (Tues., Fri., and Sun., 10:40am, 2005฿); **Phuket** (Mon., Wed., Thurs., and Sat., 10:40am, Fri., Sun., 6pm, 435฿). **Thai Air,** 199/2 Visetkul Rd. (tel. 218 066). From the train station, turn left at the clock tower and it's on the left about 5 blocks down, across from a school. Open daily 8am-5pm.

Trains: (tel. 213 082), at the end of Phra Ram VI Rd. To: **Bangkok** (1:35pm, 14½hr., 3rd class 165฿; 2nd class 312฿; sleeper upper 412฿, lower 462฿; A/C upper 562฿, lower 682฿); **Surat Thani** (1:35pm, 4hr., 3rd class 69฿; 2nd class 110฿; 6pm, 3rd class 89฿, 2nd class 130฿); and **Chumphon** (1:35pm, 8hr., 3rd class 94฿; 2nd class 164฿; 6pm, 3rd class 114฿; 2nd class 184฿).

Buses: Station (tel. 210 455) is on Ploenpitak Rd., but some vans and buses leave from random points around the city. To: **Phuket** (A/C 6 per day, 7am-7pm, 5hr., 140฿); **Krabi** (6 per day, 6am-11pm, 2-3hr., 35฿; A/C 5 per day, 8am-7:30pm, 2hr., 66฿); **Phang Nga** (A/C 6 per day, 7:30am-7:30pm, 3½hr., 102฿), **Hat Yai** (A/C vans every hr. or when full, 6am-4pm, 2hr., 35฿; regular local orange bus every 30min., 5:30am-4:30pm, 3hr., 30฿); **Surat Thani** (vans every hr., 8am-5pm, 3hr., 100฿; on Tha Klang Rd. near railroad crossing); and **Satun** (buses every hr. or when full from Ratsada Rd. on the way out of town, 6am-5pm, 38฿; take a *tuk-tuk* to the stop). To **Bangkok** (7am and 4:30pm, 12-13hr., 203฿; A/C 4pm, 13hr., 375฿; 2 VIP at 5pm, 13hr., 565฿).

Local Transportation: Tuk-tuk (5฿) within the city. No main stop. **Minivans** go to points around Trang. **Taxis** (15฿) and minivans (10฿) leave when full (5am-7pm, 20min.). For vans to **Kantang Pier,** go from the station, turn right on Kantang Rd.; they're on the right down the road. Vans to **Pakmeng Beach** leave from Tha Klang Rd. (6am-6pm, 20฿; schedule is erratic in low season).

Medical Services: Ratchadamnoen Hospital, 25 Soi 1, Sai Ngam Rd. 2 (tel. 211 200), off Ratchadamnoen Rd. near market. Some English spoken. Open 24hr.

Pharmacies: 117/1 Phra Ram VI Rd., near Koh Teng Hotel.

Emergency: tel. 191.

Police: 6 Phattalung Rd. (tel. 218 019). From the clock tower, walk down Phra Ram VI Rd. to the next major intersection. Take a left; Phattalung Rd. is the next intersection. Some officers speak English.

Post Offices/Telephones: GPO (tel. 218 521), on the corner of Phra Ram VI and Jermpanya Rd. From the train station, pass the clock tower, and travel about 0.5km until the road makes a sharp turn. You might want to take a motorcycle. *Poste Restante*. Open Mon.-Fri. 8:30am-4:30pm, Sat. 9am-noon. Upstairs has **overseas phone,** fax, and telegram. Open daily 7am-10pm. More convenient **branch** (tel.

218 021) is near the train station on the corner of Kantang Rd. and Phra Ram VI Rd. Overseas telephone service during regular hours. Open Mon.-Fri. 8:30am-4:30pm. **Postal code: 92000. Telephone code: 075.**

ACCOMMODATIONS

Akachai Apartments, 3-11 Khao Rd. (tel. 218 751), off Kantang Rd. near the busy 4-way intersection; look for the red English sign. Quiet, pleasant neighborhood (except for the nearby 6am temple bell). Light snoozers should ask for back rooms. All rooms have high-powered ceiling fans, double bed, and clean bath (130฿). Monthly rates available. Open daily 6am-4am.

Koh Teng Hotel, 77-79 Phra Ram VI Rd. (tel. 218 148), 5 blocks down from the train station. Notebook of *farang* travel experiences. Large, tidy rooms, with phones, ceiling fans, antique mirrors, an enormous private bath, and so much toilet paper. Singles 160฿. Doubles 250฿. Reception open daily 7:30am-9pm.

FOOD

Unlike many of southern Thailand's largely Muslim cities, Trang embraces a distinct Chinese presence. Crispy roasted honey-dipped pork with *paa tong ko* (Chinese doughnuts) and *dim sum* make a distinctly Trang breakfast. Dredge up mouth-watering meals from the **night market** mother lode. One belly-filling bazaar is next to Diamond Department Store by the train station; another extends down Phra Ram VI Rd. near the Trang and Wattana Hotels.

Ko Lun Restaurant, 201/2 Huai Yod Rd. (tel. 219 403). Exit the bus station and cross the street. Turn left and it's on the corner of the second alley you cross. A famous coffee shop among bottomless-stomached locals who enjoy the Trang breakfast feast. Huge selection of *dim sum* dishes (3-8฿). Don't worry about not consuming all they put in front of you—they only charge for what you actually eat. Noodle soup (12฿), *goa bii* (5฿), and roast pork for 2-3 people (30฿). Open daily 5am-4pm. *Dim sum* served 5-10am.

Koh Teng Restaurant, 77-79 Phra Ram VI Rd. (tel. 218 148), at the Koh Teng Hotel. Park your knees under their round, antique marble tables. Thin rice noodles in Chinese sauce with pork or chicken (25฿), excellent iced coffee and tea (8฿), and French toast (15฿). Most dishes run about 50-60฿.

Wee Rot Muslim Restaurant (tel. 219 579), on Kantang Rd. From the train station take a left at the 1st light; the restaurant is 1 block down on the left, next to Siam Commercial Bank. Sweet *roti* (3฿, with egg 6฿), topped with either sweet condensed milk or curry base silences morning stomach snarls. Hot tea can wash it down (6฿). Good selection of curries 15-20฿. Open daily 6am-8pm.

SIGHTS AND ENTERTAINMENT

Violence is rampant in the mean streets of Trang. Walking along Pra Ram VI in the morning, visitors can see bags of colorful **fighting-fish** for sale. Below many stilt houses are makeshift **cock-fighting** arenas. The biggest and goriest of all are the **bullfights.** No longer as popular as they once were, they still take place one weekend a month, drawing people from neighboring provinces. Day tickets cost as much as 750฿, a trifle compared to the bets made on the blood-soaked bovines, which can exceed a million baht. The fight itself is unpleasant, but for locals it's an art form, an exciting sport, and a legacy that spans many generations. To get to the bull-fight field, direct *tuk-tuk* drivers to go to Sanam Wuah Chon (5฿). Ask people in town for the schedule. Tickets for one round average 200฿. The fights starts around 10:45am.

Trang's infamous **Vegetarian Festival** is held in September or October (the exact date depends on the Chinese calendar). Endless ceremonies are performed, but hands-down the singular most freakish is the ritualized self-mutilation of locals, who pierce their cheeks and tongues with long metal spikes, and handfuls of pencils. The squeamish may wish to avoid Trang during this grisly time of year. Otherwise bring your camera for some unprecedented photo moments.

THAILAND

■ Near Trang

Most visitors to Trang don't dwell on the city itself. The high season (November-May) brings locals on the run from city life to the national park beaches or to the islands off the west coast in the Andaman Sea. Low season monsoons use the islands for target practice, and at that time there is no transport to them; re-route during these months. Though not quite idyllic, the shores are sedate, and Hat Yong Ling has wonderful rock formations. Pakmeng Beach is the busiest, leaving Yong Ling and Jao Mai relatively isolated.

HAT PAKMENG

Hat Pakmeng is the only mainland beach with any significant commercial presence. Several food stands and restaurants line the road set back from the water and can serve customers in their beach chair if they wish (pork with garlic and basil, 50฿). **Pakmeng Resort,** 60/1 Mu 4 (tel. 210 321), is at the south end of the beach, 2km from the *songthaew* drop-off, toward Hat Yong Ling and Hat Jao Mai. The resort has a pleasant restaurant and bungalows in the back. Well-kept single cottages with clean bath and fan for 1-2 people cost 200-400฿. Pakmeng Resort arranges high season day tours on long-tailed boats for groups of 10, going to Ko Mook, Ko Hai, and Ko Kradan (800-1000฿ per boat). Motorbikes are rented at 200฿ per day. (Open daily 7am-10pm.) Minivans to Pakmeng cost 10฿. Returning from Pakmeng may take awhile in the low season. Vans rendezvous at the north end of the beach near the road leading away from the water.

HAT JAO MAI AND HAT YONG LING

The national park head office (tel. 210 664; open daily 8am-4pm) is located 6km from Hat Pakmeng on **Hat Jao Mai.** There are government-run concrete bungalows here—two large bedrooms with simple beds and two floor mattresses, but no showers (100฿ for 2, 200฿ for 3, and 200-300฿ for 4 or 5). Tents are also rented for 100฿. There is no restaurant, but the staff can whip up something on request. Travelers should still bring extra food. Call ahead for reservations.

   Hat Yong Ling, 16km from Hat Jao Mai, also has a national park head office (open 8am-4pm). Plain rooms (no mattress) in stilt houses with baths in the opposite shack are available for free, or camp out in your own tent. The beach has two coves sheltered by rocky mountains covered in wild orchids. To get to an isolated patch of sand, simply trek across a lush patch of tropical forest and through a bat cave to reach one of the best sand and sea combos in the country. Spelunkers may want to bring a flashlight. At points along the mountain base, the salty waves have carved out small coves where locals often set up camp and grill seafood. If you're lucky they might ask you to join them. Vans run to Hat Pakmeng (10฿); *songthaew* to Hat Jao Mai or Hat Yong Ling will have to be arranged, but at a steep cost (100฿), since there is no regular service. Some travelers go there by motorbike from Pakmeng.

ISLANDS NEAR TRANG

Trang's tourists are irresistibly drawn to the endless possibilities of island snorkeling. In addition to the cheaper Pakmeng Resort, **Trang Travel** (tel. 219 598) in Trang arranges day tours (590฿, including lunch). Equipment is an additional 30฿. Ko Hai, Mook, Kradan, Libong, and Sukorn all have a few accommodations. Boats to islands near Pakmeng, such as Ko Hai and Ko Mook, leave from Pakmeng Pier (around 100฿, depending on island). Everything is closed during the low season.

   Ko Mook is the most popular island with the bottom-dollar backpacker, as its lodgings start as low as 75฿. The **Ko Mook Resort** has its head office at 45 Phra Ram III (tel. 212 613), and offers rooms in a longhouse without baths at 125฿ per person (each room sleeps 2). A twin-bed bungalow with bath is 200฿, with fan 250฿. (Open daily 8am-6pm.) From Trang, take a minibus to Pakmeng Pier, and then board a long-tail boat for Ko Mook before noon (1hr., 70฿). Ko Mook Resort also offers car/boat service via Pakmeng Beach for 80฿ per person.

Ko Hai has the **Ko Hai Resort** (tel. 210 317 or 211 104). Bungalows (minus bath) start at 250฿. Boats to Ko Hai from Pakmeng's northern pier are about 100฿, leaving Pakmeng at 9-10am, and coming back from Ko Hai at 8-9pm (45min). **Ko Hai Villa,** office at 112 Phra Ram VI (tel. 210 496) has bungalows without fans for 300฿, concrete rooms for one-two people with fan 600฿ (two-three people 800฿). Their boats for Ko Chenk (Emerald Cave), Ko Kradan, and Ko Wan leave at 9am, returning at 4pm (240฿). **Ko Kradan's** bungalow options are limited to expensive resorts with villas (800-950฿). To get to **Ko Sukorn, Ko Lao Lieng,** or **Ko Petra** (the latter two have no accommodations), board a boat from the ferry pier or at Hat Jao Mai.

■ Hat Yai หาตใหญ่

Squatting 26km away from the provincial capital, Hat Yai maintains its considerable commercial girth, fueled by a protein-packed flow of Malaysian and Singaporean tourists. Shopping is the main event in this metropolitan arena, since commodities and food are about 35% cheaper here than they are in Singapore and Malaysia. Streets are paved with closet-like shops merchandising watches, electric razors, clothes, and gourmet cookies. Muslim women on the sidewalks sell apples, plums, and juicy grapes imported from Australia; street hawkers pace back and forth trying to convince you that you cannot function completely without a purple, fluffy ostrich on a string. Large department stores blast radio chatter into the street as *tuk-tuk* threaten to run over visitors bargaining for "Rolexes."

ORIENTATION

The heart of Hat Yai pumps in a relatively small area close to the train station and plaza market, where most out-of-town buses deposit passengers on **Phetkasem Road** near the **clock tower.** The daily **municipal market** and the **night market** extend from Phetkasem Rd. down **Montri 2 Road** to **Ratakan Road,** which runs parallel to Phetkasem Rd. The front of the train station faces **Thamnoonvithi Road,** a large cross street that runs through vendor packed **Niphat Uthit 1, 2,** and **3 Roads,** Hat Yai's busiest streets. Running perpendicular to these streets, **Suphasan Rangsan Road** is the northernmost cross street; several other busy streets run parallel to it (including **Pratchathipat Road,** Thamnoonvithi Rd., and **Manasruedee Road**). Phetkasem Rd., which comes into the city running by Wat Hat, crosses the train tracks and then curves to the left going by the Plaza Cinema and market area up to the intersection with **Niphat Songkraw 1 Road** (where the GPO is located), at which point Phetkasem Rd. continues off to the right of the rotary.

PRACTICAL INFORMATION

Tourist Offices: TAT Office, 1/1 Soi 2 Niphat Uthit 3 Rd. (tel. 245 986), 3 blocks south of Hat Yai Central Hotel on the left. English-speaking staff responsible for Songkhla and Satun Provinces. Decent maps of Hat Yai and information on Ko Tarutao. Open daily 8:30am-4:30pm.

Tourist Police: (tel. 212 213), on Sripoovanart Rd. From TAT, walk down Niphat Uthit 3 Rd. (toward the Florida Hotel) 1 block and take a right 1 block down. It's on the right, just before the next intersection. English spoken.

Tours and Travel: Pakdee, 93/1 Niphat Uthit 2 Rd. (tel. 234 535), below the Cathay Guest House. Lodging available upstairs. English-speaking staff organizes trips to major Thai cities. Open daily 7am-8pm (low season 7am-6pm). Accepts MC (3% service charge), Visa and AmEx (5% service charge).

Immigration Offices: (tel. 243 019), on Phetkasem Rd., near the bridge and the police station. Visa extensions. Open Mon.-Fri. 8:30am-3:30pm.

Currency Exchange: Bangkok Bank, 39 Niphat Uthit 2 Rd. (tel. 235 330), near the intersection of Suphasan Rangsan Rd. Accepts MC, Visa, and AmEx. **ATM** accepts only Visa. Open daily 8:30am-5pm. **Thai Farmers Bank,** 188/1 Suphasan Rangsan

Rd. (tel. 243 027), on the corner of Phetkasem Rd., near the bridge. Open Mon.-Fri. 8:30am-4:30pm.

Air Travel: (tel. 251 008), 13km west of Hat Yai. To: **Bangkok** (3-5 per day, 2280฿); **Kuala Lumpur** (Tue. 4:40pm, Fri., Sun. 2:50pm, 2275฿); and **Singapore** (4:40pm, 4260฿). Surcharge with credit card. 300฿ airport tax for international flights. **Thai Air** has 2 offices in Hat Yai: 190-6 Niphat Uthit 2 Rd. (tel. 232 352). Open Mon.-Fri. 8am-5pm. Also 166/4 Niphat Uthit 2 Rd. Open Mon.-Sat. 8am-5pm, Sun. 9am-4pm. Runs minivans to and from the airport 1½-2hr. before take-off (40฿) with hotel pick-up. **Flight Information:** tel. 311 175.

Trains: Hat Yai Railway Station (tel. 243 705), at the end of Thamnoonvithi Rd. To: **Bangkok** (rapid 3:55pm and 5:05pm; express 6:10pm and 6:40pm, 15-17hr., 2nd class 313฿); **Surat Thani** (6:05am, 11:37am; rapid 3:55pm and 5:05pm; express 6:10pm and 6:40pm, 5-6hr., 2nd class 144฿); **Sungai Kolok** (4 per day, 7:05am-12:34pm; rapid 6:30am; express 6:56am, 4-5hr., 2nd class 87฿); **Butterworth** (express 12:40pm, 4hr., 2nd class 75฿); and **Kuala Lumpur** (express 5:45am, 13hr). Extra charges to train tickets: rapid 20฿; express 50฿; 2nd-class top sleeper 100฿, lower sleeper 150฿; 2nd-class A/C upper sleeper 200฿, lower 250฿. For a full schedule, contact the train station or TAT office.

Buses: City bus terminal (tel. 232 789), at the south end of town on Ranchanawanit Rd. Buses stop in front of the plaza market on Phetkasem Rd., arriving 10-15min. after scheduled departure time from bus terminal. *Tuk-tuk* to the terminal 10฿. For buses to Bangkok, go to the terminal. To: **Bangkok** (3 per day, 7:30am-4pm, 16hr., 238฿; A/C 6 per day, 7am-6pm, 14hr., 425฿; VIP 4pm and 5pm, 14hr., 625฿); **Phuket** (4 per day, 5:30-9:45am, 8½hr., 115฿; A/C 7 per day, 8am-9:30pm, 7hr., 192฿); **Krabi** (4 per day, 5:30-9:45am, 5hr., 91฿; A/C 7 per day, 8-11:45am and 9:30pm, 4hr., 127฿); **Surat Thani** (5 per day, 5:20-11:20am, 6½hr., 86฿; A/C 4 per day, 7:10am-3pm, 5½hr., 120฿); **Trang** (every 15-45min., 5:10am-4:55pm, 3hr., 40฿); **Sungai Kolok** (A/C 4 per day, 6am-3pm, 4hr., 96฿) via **Narathiwat** (3hr., 75฿); and **Padang Besar** (every 30min., 5am-6pm, 2hr., 50฿). For a complete schedule, contact TAT. Most travel agents in Hat Yai organize **minibuses** to Phuket (200฿), Krabi (150฿), and Surat Thani (150฿). Government buses do not cross the Malaysian border. **Pakdee Tour** has daily buses to Malaysia and Singapore. The buses are Malaysian but Thai travel agents are authorized to book tickets. No visa is required for Malaysia unless you are from Bangladesh, Pakistan, India, South Africa, China, Sri Lanka, or Burma. Thai travel agents do not arrange or process visas. To: **Penang** (9:30am, 12:30, and 3:30pm, 4½hr., 200฿); **Sungai Kolok** (every hr., 8am-5pm, 4hr., 150฿); **Kuala Lumpur** (9am and noon, 9hr., 350฿); and **Singapore** (VIP 12:30pm, 15hr., 500฿).

Taxis: Operate more as inter-city transport and leave from the bus terminal. Taxis to **Satun** (50฿) leave from Ratakan Rd. across from the post office. To **Sungai Kolok** (130฿) leave from Suphasan Rangsan Rd.

Local Transportation: Tuk-tuk (10฿). Motorcycle rides cost 10-20฿ in town.

Markets: Both the **day** and **night markets** bustle around the clock near the plaza cinema between Montri 1 and 2 Rd. During the day, get clothing, watches, or handicrafts. In the evenings, feast on noodle soups, curries, and gelatinous desserts. A **morning market** also sets up on Niphat Uthit 3.

Pharmacies: Thong Cun Ting, 129/11 Niphat Uthit 3 Rd. (tel. 243 411). Open daily 8am-10pm.

Medical Services: Prince of Songkhla University Hospital (24-hr. tel. 212 070), to the east of the city off Rajyindee Rd.

Emergency: tel. 1699.

Police: Contact the tourist police first. The main Songkhla police station (tel. 243 021) is on Phetkasem Rd. near the bridge.

Post Offices/Telephones: GPO (tel. 243 013), at the corner of Niphat Songkraw 1 and Soi 4. The post office is on the right a few blocks down. Open Mon.-Fri. 8:30am-4:30pm, Sat. 9am-noon. Telegram and **overseas calling** upstairs (tel. 245 293). Open daily 8am-6pm. **Communications Authority of Thailand (CAT),** 490/1 Phetkasem Rd. (tel. 2310804). Northeast part of city; take a *tuk-tuk* there. Overseas phone calls: collect calls 30฿ flat charge. Open daily 8am-midnight. **Postal code:** 90110. **Telephone code:** 074.

ACCOMMODATIONS

Many of the cheapest hotels in Hat Yai offer sleazy services, often under the name of "ancient Thai massage." To avoid such establishments, opt for a slightly more expensive but reputable guest house suggested by the TAT hotel list.

Sorasilp Guest House, 251/7-8 Phetkasem Rd. (tel. 232 635), near the market area just off Phetkasem Rd., with a small English sign. Breakfast service and proximity to the bus. Clean chambers and spotless private baths with sit toilets, towels, sheets, and soap. Open daily 5am-2am. Singles 150฿. Singles/doubles 180฿, with A/C 250฿. Doubles with 2 beds 250฿, with A/C 350฿. Reservations recommended during Thai and Malaysian holidays.

Cathay Guest House, 93/1 Niphat Uthit 2 Rd. (tel. 243 815). A mecca for travelers coming from or going to Malaysia. Westerners congregate over beers in the lounge. Geriatric but large and fairly dust-free rooms in a somewhat noisy area. Years of backpacker bathing have worn down the baths to a smooth, clean surface. Open daily 6am-2am. Dorms 70฿. Singles/doubles 140฿. Doubles with 2 beds 160฿. Triples 200฿. Breakfast daily 6:30am-noon.

Hok-Jin Heng Hotel, 87 Niphat Uthit 1 Rd. (tel. 243 258), across from Bank of Ayutthaya. 6 floors of fresh rooms are amazingly pristine. Baths with flush toilets; facilities shine like a new penny. Knock if you get there past midnight. Singles 150฿, with A/C 240฿. Doubles 240฿. Fine 1st-floor Chinese restaurant.

FOOD

Food vendors set up day and night in the Niphat Uthit Rd. area and near the plaza market and cinema on Phetkasem Rd. For local flavor, try crepes with shredded coconut (*khanom bueng*). In the evening, the Suphasan Rangsan Rd. stalls offer a variety of freshly cooked dinner items like *pad thai* (15฿).

Best Kitchen, 13-15 Juti Uthit 2 Rd. (tel. 234 479), along Kong Toey canal, next to J.B. Hotel. Look for the pop-arty, neon duck and lobster sign. Affordable alternative to sidewalk noodle shops. Special roast duck with special sauce leaves customers quacking with glee (50฿). Fried beef or chicken with basil leaves 65฿, fried pork ribs with garlic and pepper 65-85฿. Fried rice dishes 35฿. English menu. Open daily 10:30am-10pm.

ENTERTAINMENT

All good credit cards come to die in Hat Yai. Retire your trusty Visa before it collapses from consumer overload. Phetkasem Rd. stocks birds, fish, shoes, ethnic garb, belts, and, of course, watches. For more structured entertainment, slather yourself with western pop culture at **Post Laser Disk,** 82-3 Thamnoonvithi Rd. (tel. 232 30 27), about two blocks past Niphat Uthit Rd., on the right. There's no charge for watching the English-language movies on the second floor, but you do have to order from the pricey menu (coffee 35฿). Movies are shown noon-midnight daily; the sign outside lists what's playing.

Promote peace and harmony at the **Thai Boxing stadium** which has fighting bouts on Saturday afternoons, one or two times a month. Admission price varies according to the boxer, but averages around 50-100฿. The boxing schedule can be erratic, so contact TAT for details. *Tuk-tuk* go to the stadium for 20-30฿ per person. Another equally stomach-churning Hat Yai spectator sport is **bullfighting;** bovines lock horns on the first Saturday of each month (except Buddha's Day), 10am-3pm, in the stadium up Niphat Songkraw 1 Rd. toward the Klong Wa intersection. One round has about three bullfights and admission costs 100-200฿ per round, depending on the bull. *Tuk-tuk* go to Nernkhomthong Stadium for 50-100฿ per person.

Wat Hat Yai Nai is known for its 35m-long and 15m-high reclining Buddha, the third-largest in the world. The wat is located on the way into Hat Yai (coming in on the eastern side) near Klong U. Thapao Bridge. Foreigners should wear long pants and shirts that cover the shoulders. No shoes are allowed inside, and visitors may not enter the shrine after 6pm. *Tuk-tuk* go to the wat for 20฿ per person.

■ Satun สตูล

Despite the gangs of motorcycles that roar through the streets at all hours, the rural province of Satun, situated on the Straits of Melaka, turns a deaf ear to the din. Tourists pass through Satun headed for Ko Tarutao, the national park island off the coast, or to cross the border by boat to Pulau Langkawi. Ko Tarutao is only open from November through May, so from June to October, Satun plays solitaire.

ORIENTATION

Satun is one of Thailand's southernmost provinces, located only 20km from the Malaysian border. Buses deliver people to north-south-running **Sulakanukul Road,** which changes to **Buriwanit Road** after crossing **Samanta Pradit Road.** The main stretch of Satun is **Satun Thani Road,** beginning at the junction with Samanta Pradit Rd. and running parallel to Buriwanit. The gold-domed **Bambang Mosque** is in the town center. The large daily **market** is along the river, to the left of the Rain Tong Hotel, as are **long-tail boats** that go to **Tamalang Pier** (when the water is high enough), the point where boats leave to Kuala Perlis in Malaysia.

PRACTICAL INFORMATION

Tours and Travel: Satun Travel and Ferry Service, 45/16 Satun Thani Rd. (tel. 711 453), off Satun Thani Rd., on a small road next to the large Wang Mai Hotel. Representative of Kuala Perlis-Langkawi Ferry Service. To **Phuket** (350฿) and **Krabi** (250฿); both leave 10am. Tours of other islands in the Andaman Sea are also available. **Thanapat Tour,** 45/18 Satun Thani Rd. (tel. 711 426), 2 shops down from Satun Travel, sells boat tickets to **Ko Tarutao** (200฿) and **Langkawi** (360฿). Reserves bus tickets as well. Open daily 6:30am-10pm.

Currency Exchange: Thai Farmers Bank, 31 Sulakanukul Rd. (tel. 721 354), down from Samanta Pradit Rd. on the left. Open Mon.-Fri. 8:30am-3:30pm.

Immigration Offices: (tel. 711 080), on Buriwanit Rd. next to the library. Open daily 8:30am-4:30pm.

Buses: Leave from Buriwanit Rd. in front of the library. To **Trang** (every 30min., 6am-4pm, 3hr., 38฿) and **Hat Yai** (orange bus, every hr., 6am-4pm, 2hr., 28฿). **Minivans** to Hat Yai leave from the temple on Satun Thani Rd. (every 30min., 6am-5pm). **Taxis** headed that way depart when full from Buriwanit Rd., in front of the market, and P. Ying store (40฿). Buses to **Bangkok** (1:30pm, 16½hr., 234฿; A/C 2:30 and 3pm, 660฿) leave from the corner of Sarit Phuminat and Hatthakam Senksa Rd. Buses to **Phuket** (A/C 10:50am, 7hr., 350฿) stop in **Trang** (1½hr., 150฿), **Krabi** (5hr., 250฿), and **Phang Nga** (6hr., 300฿). They leave from Satun Travel off Satun Thani Rd. across from the Wang Mai Hotel. Satun also has buses to **Surat Thani** and **Ko Samui** (both, 5hr., 350฿). For other bus services, take a bus to Trang and transfer.

Boats: Catch boat rides to **Tamalang Pier** near Rain Tong Hotel and the market (5am-noon 30฿) when the water is high in the river. Go by *songthaew* when the water is low; departs from in front of Chana Temple (every hr., 6am-5pm, 20฿). From Tamalang, 10km south of Satun, long-tail boats travel to **Kuala Perlis,** Malaysia as they fill up (6am-1pm, 40-50฿) and **Langkawi Island,** Malaysia (9:30am, 1pm, and 4pm, 1½hr., 180฿, children 130฿). Satun Travel can arrange passage and has an A/C minivan to the pier (9am, 12:30, 3:30pm, 20฿).

Pharmacies: Pon Phaesaj, 62 Buriwanit Rd. (tel. 711 329), near the police box. Open daily 7am-9pm.

Medical Services: Satun Hospital, 55/1 Hatthakam Senksa Rd. (24-hr. tel. 711 028), sits in the center of town. English-speaking doctors.

Emergency: tel. 191.

Police: (tel. 711 025), on corner of Yarttrasawaddee Rd. and Satun Thani Rd. about 0.5km up from Samanta Pradit Rd. They lock and close their huge gate at night.

Post Offices/Telephones: (tel. 711 013), on the corner of Samanta Pradit Rd. and
Satun Thani Rd. *Poste Restante.* Open Mon.-Fri. 8:30am-4:30pm, Sat.-Sun. 9am-
noon. **Overseas calling** and telegram upstairs. Open daily 8am-6pm. No credit or
calling card calls accepted. **Postal code:** 91000. **Telephone code:** 074.

ACCOMMODATIONS AND FOOD

Rain Tong Hotel, 4 Samanta Pradit Rd. (tel. 711 036), is on the Bambang River,
around the bend from the municipal market. The extremely kind, elderly staff will be
ecstatic to assist guests. Tidy but weathered bedrooms have baths and sinks. Singles
cost 120฿, doubles 160฿. (Open daily 6am-midnight.) Satun's Muslim majority sets
the tone of local cuisine. Several breakfast *roti* places also serve patrons throughout
the day (one stays open all night). In addition to an extensive daily **municipal market,**
there is a **night market** on Tammango Uthit Rd. (open daily 3pm-midnight). Duck
noodle soup costs 20฿, Thai chicken noodle soup 15฿. **Sri Trang,** 127 Satun Thani
Rd., opposite the cinema, doesn't have an English sign, but locals can point you in the
right direction. Lots of curry styles available, as well as rice dishes: with one item 10฿,
with two items 12฿. (Open daily 4-9pm.)

■ Near Satun: Ko Tarutao National Marine Park

This park is an archipelago in the Indian Ocean along the Straits of Melaka, consisting
of 51 islands off the west coast of the Thai peninsula in the Andaman Sea, near the
Malaysian border. **Ko Tarutao** proper is only 6km from Langkawi Island, a major
point of entry into Malaysia. Covering 151sq.km, it is the largest of the park's islands
and in the 1940s was a concentration camp for political prisoners. During WWII, the
government ran out of food supplies for the detainees, who turned to piracy on the
high seas to support themselves. After the prisoners were pardoned, locals from the
mainland moved to the island but were forced off when it became a protected area.
Tarutao's best beaches sprawl on its west coast, which has a **coral reef.** The inland
area seethes with waterfalls, mountains, caves, and wildlife. A two-hour **hiking trail**
from Ao Phante Melaka to Ao Talo Wao, east of the island, also extends south for
another three hours to Ao Talo U-Dang. From November to January, **sea-turtles** paddle ashore to deposit their ovoid offspring on **Ko Khai** (Egg Island), 15km southwest
of Ko Tarutao.

The **park office** (tel. 711 383) is at Ao Phante Melaka at the north tip of Tarutao
near the pier. Row housing is the cheapest government accommodation. Each room
sleeps four (280฿ per room). Bungalows have two bedrooms and two baths (400฿
per room). Larger cottages are also available with two bedrooms and one bath (600฿
per room). **Camping** is allowed (10฿ per night, bring your own tent). Make reservations in advance with the National Park Division of the Royal Forest Department in
Bangkok (tel. (02) 579 0529), or the Pak Bara office (tel. (074) 781 285). The park is
only open from November to May.

To get to Ko Tarutao from **Satun** take a local **bus** headed for Trang and get off in La
Ngu about 60km from Satun (every 45min., 20฿) in front of the library on Buriwanit
Rd. In La Ngu, there's a stop for *songthaew* to Pak Bara Pier, about 11km away (15฿).
From Pak Bara Pier, **boats** leave daily for Ko Tarutao (Nov.-May 10:30am and 2:30pm,
200฿ roundtrip). Boats from Tarutao to Pak Bara leave daily at 9am and 2pm. **Long-
tail boats** can also be chartered at the pier (500฿ and up).

From Hat Yai **share-taxis** go to La Ngu (60฿) or Pak Bara (60฿) in front of the post
office on Ratakan Rd. near the U Thaphao Bridge, or pay 360฿ for the whole car,
which holds six. Local **buses** leave from Hat Yai for Pak Bara (7:05, 11:05am, and
2:55pm, 40฿) at the plaza market on Phetkasem Rd. near the clock tower. The regular bus from Satun to Hat Yai goes by Chalung T-intersection, from which *songthaew*
go to Pak Bara. **A/C vans** also deposit you in the midst of Pak Bara for 50฿. Vans leave
from Duang Chan Rd, just off of Niphat Uthit 1 Rd., near Krung Thai Bank (every hr.,
6am-4pm, 2hr.). From **Trang,** take a local **bus** to Satun which stops in La Ngu (45฿).

For **taxis** from Trang to La Ngu, contact Trang Travel on Phra Ram VI Rd. across from the Thumrin Hotel near the train station (around 60฿).

■ Narathiwat นราธิวาส

Proving that the east coast becomes increasingly photogenic farther south, the beaches around Narathiwat are long, white stretches of sand, unspoiled by tourist-oriented hotels and beer bars. Narathiwat itself is relatively quiet and extremely lovely, a good place to escape the grime of urban areas and the fervent crowds of other beaches. A predominantly Muslim town with a beachside space-age mosque, Narathiwat echoes with early morning calls to prayer, a soothing prelude to the small barrage of fishing boat motors. While Narathiwat may seem far removed from the country's commercial economy, the closed doors hide black market trading and thriving prostitution. All traffic, idyllic and illicit, comes to a standstill at 6pm, however, as the national anthem is broadcasted in the streets. This slightly contrived display of patriotism reminds everyone that they haven't left Thailand, yet.

ORIENTATION

Narathiwat rests on the east coast, just before the Malaysian border. From here to Pattani, the coast is lush with relatively deserted beaches. **Puphapugdee Road** runs along the river in the east and **Pichit Bamrung Road** runs parallel, one block inland, crossing the bridge at the north end of town, near the mosque, and to Hat Narathat. Other roads intersect these two, forming a ladder. The most easily identified landmark is the **clock tower** on Pichit Bamrung Rd. At this intersection, take a right up **Wichit Chaibun Road** to get to Puphapugdee Rd. close to the Narathiwat Hotel, which stands on the left, a bit across the street. Most inter-city buses stop on Pichit Bamrung Rd. a couple km south where *songthaew* to Ban Thom congregate.

PRACTICAL INFORMATION

Tourist Offices: The TAT for the province is in Sungai Kolok.
Currency Exchange: Thai Farmers Bank, 319 Puphapugdee Rd. (tel. 511 360). About 2 blocks up from the Narathiwat Hotel going up toward Hat Narathat. Open Mon.-Fri. 8:30am-3:30pm. **Siam Commercial Bank,** 133/4 Pichit Bamrung Rd. (tel. 512 737), near the corner of Chamroonnara Rd. Open Mon.-Fri. 8:30am-3:30pm. If you plan on crossing the border, you must change money in Sungai Kolok; no banks here sell Malaysian ringgit.
Air Travel: Airport (tel. 511 595), 13km northwest of town. Thai Air flies to **Bangkok** via **Hat Yai** (Wed., Fri., and Sun. 3:05pm). From Hat Yai you can go to **Phuket.** Shuttles go to and from the airport (40฿). Check for van departure time (usually around 1:30pm). **Thai Air,** 322-4 Puphapugdee Rd. (tel. 511 161), across from Narathiwat Hotel, near Thai Farmers Bank. Manager speaks English well and can give info on Narathiwat Province. Open daily 8:30am-5pm.
Trains: The closest train station is **Tanyongmat** (tel. 611 162), 20km outside town. Take a taxi or *songthaew* from in front of the market on Pichit Bamrung Rd. (20฿ per person). To **Bangkok** (12:48 and 3:47pm) via **Surat Thani.**
Buses: Transportation is quite casual. Buses to **Bangkok** (A/C, 1:30pm, 506฿) leave from across from the police station on Suriyapradit Rd. Buses to **Sungai Kolok** stop at the end of Pichit Bamrung Rd., away from Hat Narathat.
Minivans: (tel. 511 148). Depart in front of the Yaowaraj Hotel to: **Sungai Kolok** (every hr., 7am-6pm, 1hr., 40฿); **Tak Bai** (every hr., 6am-5pm, 45min., 30฿); and **Hat Yai** (every hr., 6am-5pm, 3hr., 100฿). There are also companies on the right of Pichit Bamrung Rd., past the clock tower as you walk away from the beach.
Local Transportation: Songthaew head south to **Tak Bai** (10฿) down Puphapugdee Rd. via **Wat Khao Keng** (5฿), and from near the hospital on Rangamanka Rd. (also for **Tanyongmat**). They circulate through town all day (4-5฿ per person within 10km), but **motorcycle taxis** are more common (5฿).
Medical Services: (tel. 513 480), on the right side of Rangamanka Rd., about 2km south of town if you're heading out to Tanyongmat.

Emergency: tel. 191.
Police: (tel. 511 236), on Suriyapradit Rd. From the clock tower, walk down Pichit Bamrung Rd. At the end of the road turn right. The station is 2km down on the left. Some English spoken. Probably your best bet in an **emergency**.
Post Offices/Telephones: (tel. 511 093), on Pichit Bamrung Rd. about 2 blocks from the clock tower. Open Mon.-Fri. 8:30am-4:30pm, Sat. 9am-noon. Telegram and **overseas calls** are upstairs. Telegram open daily 8am-6pm. Overseas calls (tel. 511 002) open daily 7am-10pm. **Postal code:** 96000. **Telephone code:** 073.

ACCOMMODATIONS

Cathay Hotel, 275 Puphapugdee Rd. (tel. 511 014). If you are not one of the lucky few with a river view, ask the manager to let you onto the roof. He speaks excellent English and will enthusiastically point out landmarks across the stunning panorama. Large rooms with clean sheets, spotless private bath, and plenty of light. Singles 120฿. Double 170฿. Open daily 6:30am-9:30pm.
Yaowaraj Hotel, 131 Pichit Bamrung Rd. (tel. 511 148), on the corner of Chamroonnara Rd. Peppy staff maintains fairly large and sterile rooms with well-kept bathrooms in this concrete Thai-style hotel. Singles/doubles 140฿, with A/C 230฿. Doubles/triples with 2 beds 200฿, with A/C 280฿. Open daily 7am-10pm.

FOOD

There is a **market,** although small and bland, between Puphapugdee Rd. and Pichit Bamrung Rd. A few portable **food stands** spring up at night in the market area. Several **roti stands** also open up in the evening along Puphapugdee Rd. and Pichit Bamrung Rd. The **open-sided restaurant** on the corner of Puphapugdee Rd. and Chamroonnara Rd. has a lot of prepared meat dishes (open all day through dinner).

Ruste, on Pichit Bamrung Rd. Walk up Chamroonnara Rd. from Puphapugdee and take a left, it's right after the Siam Commercial Bank. A fine Muslim restaurant. Noodle soups with greens and fish balls 20฿. One man speaks decent English and can order you a big plate of fried vegetables for 20฿, a good way to get the riboflavin lacking in many Thai treats. Open daily noon-midnight.
Restaurant No. 5, at Hat Narathat gets pretty loud, but serves good food. Most restaurants tend to offer more than food for the typically male clientele, but No. 5 is more respectable. Superb beef salad and spicy hot shellfish on top of rice. Dishes around 40-50฿. Open for lunch and dinner daily until 10pm.

SIGHTS

On the way to Hat Narathat on Pichit Bamrung Rd., visitors pass by fishermen casting their nets where the Bang Nara River gushes into the sea. Intricately painted fishing boats bob around as naked children splash in the low tide, looking half-heartedly for shellfish. Over the small bridge, is **Hat Narathat,** a large, shaded area back from the water, lined with coconut trees and several small restaurants which are great for having a beer and watching the sunset. The sand stretches for km around, undisturbed by tourists, bungalows, or trinket peddlers. It is basically deserted until evening, when locals come for picnics to bid farewell to the departing sun. Walk to Hat Narathat or take a motorcycle taxi for 5฿.

About 10km south of town, **Wat Khao Keng** is known for the mammoth Buddha that stands its ground about 100m back from the road. The 25m-high Buddha, set in the midst of peaceful, tropical forest, is daunting even to seasoned Buddha-watchers. Young entrepreneurs sell flowers and incense. *Songthaew* go from Puphapugdee Rd. to the Buddha (5฿ per person).

■ Sungai Kolok สไหงโก-ลก

Sungai Kolok is a vociferous concrete border town at the southeast tip of Thailand. Most travelers usually go straight from the border to the train station or vice-versa without staying in the primarily "short-time trade" hotels that plague the city. If you do spend the night, almost any hotel features this disturbing sideline. Ban Taba, a small town 5km south of Tak Bai (on the Gulf of Thailand), is increasingly becoming the preferred border crossing point. Ferries from Ban Taba to Malaysia cost 5-10฿, and the border there is open the same hours as in Sungai Kolok.

ORIENTATION

Most of Sungai Kolok is laid out in a grid. The **border crossing** is on **Asia 18 Road,** the main thoroughfare through the city, parallel to the train tracks, 1km to the right of the train station if you're facing it. Coming from Malaysia, the TAT and tourist police are on the right, next door to the border police. The **train station** is about 1km down from the border on the right, an easy walk. Those entering Sungai Kolok from another point in Thailand via bus, might want to take a rickshaw or a motorcycle taxi to get to the border. **Charoen Khat Road** runs perpendicular to Asia 18 Rd. and the train tracks, beginning at Asia 18 Rd., directly across from the station. The daily **market** runs along Asia 18 Rd., set back on smaller streets and alleys between the train station and the border.

PRACTICAL INFORMATION

Tourist Offices: TAT, Asia 18 Rd. (tel. 615 230), next to the border on the left, from the town center. You have to walk through motor vehicle customs, so don't be put off by road blocks on Asia 18 Rd. Maps of Sungai Kolok, info about the city and Narathiwat Province, and transportation schedules. Open daily 8:30am-5pm.

Tourist Police: (tel. 612 008), in the building with the TAT. Open daily 8am-6pm.

Immigration Offices: Narathiwat Immigration Office, 70 Charoen Khat Rd. (tel. 611 231), across from the police station, after Shern Marcar Rd., coming from the train station. Open Mon.-Fri. 8:30am-4:30pm.

Currency Exchange: Thai Farmers Bank, 1/6 Vorakamin Rd. (tel. 611 578), on the corner of Charoen Khat and Vorakamin Rd. Open Mon.-Fri. 8:30am-3:30pm. Change currency here, since banks in other provinces probably won't do it.

Air Travel: Thai Air, 31 Thespathom Rd. (tel. 612 132), across from Plaza Hotel.

Trains: Train Station, Asia 18 Rd. (tel. 611 162). Opposite Charoen Khat Rd. To: **Bangkok** (rapid noon, 20½hr., 200฿, sleeper top 468฿, bottom 498฿, plus 100฿ for A/C; express 3pm, 19½hr., 230฿, sleeper top 528฿, bottom 578฿, plus 100฿ for A/C); **Surat Thani** (6:30am, 12hr., 86฿ and 180฿; rapid noon, 9hr., 106฿ and 200฿; express 3pm, 9hr., 126฿ and 230฿); **Hat Yai** (4 per day, 6:30am-1:25pm, 4½hr., 42฿ and 87฿; rapid noon, 4hr., 62฿ and 107฿; express 3pm, 4hr., 92฿ and 137฿); **Chumpon** (rapid noon, 12hr., 130฿ and 250฿; express 3pm, 12hr., 160฿ and 280฿); and **Trang** (3:15pm, 15½hr. with layover, 79฿ and 165฿). **Advance booking ticket office** window open daily 7am-4pm. Advance booking can only be made for Phattalung and farther destinations.

Buses: 45/2 Worakamin Rd. (tel. 612 045), at the intersection of Wongvitee Rd. To: **Bangkok** (A/C 8am, 18hr., 414฿, with bathroom, 12:30pm, 18hr., 533฿); stops in **Narathiwat** (19฿, 26฿, and 33฿) and **Surat Thani** (9am, 10hr., 143฿; A/C 8am and 12:30pm, 10hr., 200-256฿). Buses to **Hat Yai** leave in front of the Valentine Hotel on the corner of Waman Amoey Rd. and Thespathom Rd., across from the post office (A/C, 4 per day, 7am-3pm, 4hr., 98฿). To **Narathiwat,** from in front of the train station (every 30min., 6:30am-4:30pm, 1hr., 16฿).

Minivans: A/C vans leave from Charoen Khat Rd. across from the train station, next to Asia hotel to **Narathiwat** (every hr., 7am-6pm, 1hr., 40฿) and **Hat Yai** (every hr., 6am-5pm, 4hr., 110฿).

Local Transportation: Motorcycle taxis are the best way around, 10฿ to the border. **Bicycle rickshaws** are 20฿ per person to the border and may cost less within the busier streets. Both run regular fares from 5am-dark. After hours costs more.

Medical Services: (tel. 611 109), Saitong 2 Rd., behind the train tracks. Some doctors speak enough English to get by.

Emergency: tel. 1699 for tourist police.

Police Station: (tel. 611 070), on Charoen Khat Rd., near the intersection of Shern Marcar Rd., on the left if you're coming from the train station, across from the immigration office and Thai Farmers Bank. Call the tourist police first.

Post Offices/Telephones: (tel. 611 141), on Thespathom Rd. about 3 blocks from Thailiang Hotel and across the street, near Plaza Hotel. *Poste Restante.* Open Mon.-Fri. 8:30am-4:30pm, Sat. 9am-noon. The telegram and **overseas calling** office (tel. 612 124) is around the back. Open Mon.-Fri. 8:30am-4:30pm. **Postal code:** 96120. **Telephone code:** 073.

ACCOMMODATIONS

Savoy Hotel, 34 Charoen Khat Rd. (tel. 611 093), on the right from the train station, 1 or 2 blocks down. A concrete immensity. Well-lit, decent-sized rooms have clean sheets, hard mattresses and pillows, fans, and bearable bathrooms. Get a room off the street to avoid traffic noise. Singles with bath 120฿. Doubles with bath 150฿. Open daily 4am-midnight. Chinese restaurant open daily 7am-4pm.

Paradise Hotel, 34 Wamanumnoi Rd. (tel. 611 313), near the intersection with Thespathom Rd. Large rooms with windows, double beds, and bath in a quiet neighborhood. Newly painted an exotic gray—not bad for a concrete slab. Rooms with bath 140฿, with TV 180฿, and A/C 260฿. Open daily 6am-midnight.

FOOD

Sungai Kolok's daily **market** spreads out before the sun gets out of bed behind Asia 18 Rd. The agony of choosing from a wide selection of tasty foods can leave visitors writhing in ecstasy. At night there is a string of **food vendors** along Shern Marcar Rd. selling local specialties. Those who want to sit down while they eat can try the vendors along Vorakamin Rd., starting at the Thai Farmer's Bank. A plate of fried vegetables with garlic and spicy sauce on rice runs 20-25฿. **Siam Restaurant,** 2-4 Shern Marcar Rd. (tel. 611 360), cooks up several extravagantly garnished seafood dishes at steep prices. There is a small section on the menu (English and Thai) with 20-25฿ dishes. They have good prawn fried rice for 25฿, or fried vegetables with baby corn, giant mushrooms, and greens on rice for 25฿. (Open daily 10:30am-9pm.)

BORDER CROSSINGS

The Thailand/Malaysia border, on Asia 18 Rd. near the Sungai Kolok River, is open daily 5am-9pm Thai time (1hr. ahead of Malay time). There may be improvised Malaysian-run tour offices in Sungai Kolok, but most companies that organize buses or book flights between Thailand and Malaysia are located in Hat Yai. Thai buses do not cross through to Malaysia, nor do trains on the eastern coast. On the Thai side a small blue English sign guides you to two booths—one for arrivals and one for departures; check out and walk across the bridge to the small town of **Rantau Panjang** in Malaysia. A short distance farther (30m or so) are the taxis. Both buses and taxis run every hour from the border to Kota Bharu. Buses cost RM2.4 , taxis RM3.5 per person. The same schedules and fares apply from Kota Bharu to the border.

Whichever way you cross, travel early. Transportation options on both sides of the border are most abundant in the morning. Arriving during banking hours saves you from getting stuck with no appropriate currency, and possibly being forced to recross the border. If you are arriving from Malaysia and plan to cash traveler's checks for Thai baht, be sure to arrive between Mon. and Fri., 8:30am-3:30pm. If you are crossing in the other direction, you can go to Thai Farmer's Bank to exchange any left-over baht for Malaysian ringgit, good for taxis to Kota Bharu. Most banks in Kota Bharu are closed on Fridays.

> If you are exiting Thailand, make sure to get an exit stamp on your passport. If not, you will have exited the country *illegally,* and the next time you come to Thailand, you will face deportation..

VIETNAM

Prepared to be the next Asian powerhouse, Vietnam wants to prove a point to the world: this country, whose guerilla soldiers outwitted and humiliated two big-shot western powers, can once again triumph over odds. The "free world" tried to punish this nation for choosing communism over democracy. After twenty years of struggle, neglect, and rejection, however, Vietnam has resuscitated itself, and the world waits avidly at its doorstep. Signs of the brutal war which was burned into the memory of a generation around the globe still linger here, and thousands of Vietnamese remain unaccounted for, but these people are ready to make peace with the past. Vietnam is no longer a war zone; it's a thriving country.

The passage of time has finally quelled the bitterness of defeat, as the U.S. finally extended a hand to its former enemy in July 1995, ready to put that war comfortably behind it. To the international community, the establishment of diplomatic ties is a stamp of approval, ushering in a stampede of venture capitalists ready to bless the Vietnamese with free enterprise. Massive development slated for the next few years means that all doors will soon be open and visitors will be able to travel more easily across the land. The time to see Vietnam is now. From the spectacular mists and rocky limestone crags of Halong Bay to the tangled rivers and emerald rice paddies of the Mekong Delta, Vietnam's charm and beauty still entice foreigners to its shores as it did during a former era.

ESSENTIALS

◼ Geography

Vietnam extends 1600km from China to the Gulf of Thailand, encompassing rugged mountains, flat lowlands, fertile valleys, and white sand beaches. The Hoang Lien Son Mountains circle the Red River Delta in the north and, to the south, the 1200km-long Truong Son Mountains stretch from Thanh Hoa Province to just north of Ho Chi Minh City. At either end of the country are two alluvial plains, the Red River Delta in the north and the Mekong Delta in the south. Monsoon rains often overflow the tributaries of the Red River, causing devastating floods. The central coastal strip runs along the eastern seaboard of central Vietnam, forming a narrow, low plain sometimes cut through with towering mountains that fall into the sea.

◼ When to Go

Vietnam's extension over several latitudes makes for some variable climates between the three historically divided regions of the country. The weather in North Vietnam (Bac Bo) is much cooler than in the south, with mild temperatures and little rainfall during the winter (November-April) and heavy rains which can culminate in violent typhoons during the summer (May-October). In the South (Nam Bo), temperatures remain constant and humid, averaging 30°C (86°F). Here, the dry season starts in November and ends in April with two months of unbearable heat just before the rain breaks, bringing in the wet season (May-October). Central Vietnam (Trung Bo) has transitional weather. Hue, sitting in the middle of Vietnam's coastal curve, tends to be overcast throughout most of the year with constant rainfall, even in the dry season between February and April. In the interior highlands of the country, temperatures at night are pleasant and cool and can be downright freezing during the winter (October-March). The "infernal" months of March and April average a cool, pleasant 26°C (79°F).

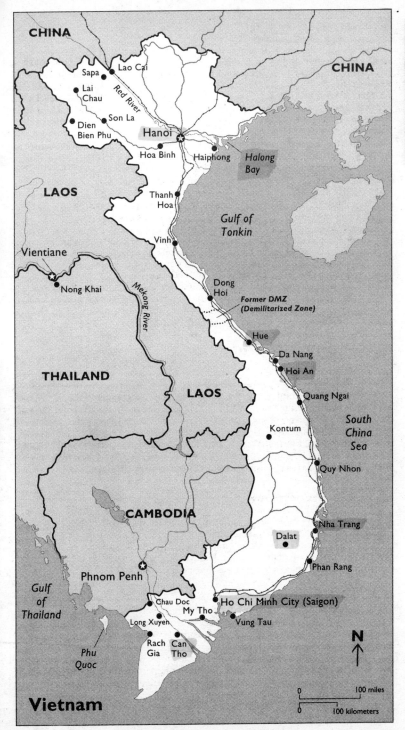

Vietnam

100,000 Đ = £6.

VIETNAM

■ Money

US$1=11,018.50Đ (dong)
CDN$=8030.98Đ
UK£1=17,186.70Đ
IR£1=17,425.74Đ
AUS$1=8165.440Đ
NZ$1=6680.213Đ
SARand=3090.549Đ

1000Đ=US$0.091
1000Đ=CDN$0.125
1000Đ=UK£0.59
1000Đ=IR£0.057
1000Đ=AUS$0.122
1000Đ=NZ$0.149
1000Đ=SARand0.324

The monetary system in Vietnam is based on the **dong.** Denominations come in 200Đ, 500Đ, 1000Đ, 2000Đ, 5000Đ, 10,000Đ, 20,000Đ, and 50,000Đ. Many establishments, however, quote prices only in US$; as a result, *Let's Go* lists prices in US$ and dong accordingly. **Try to pay for everything in dong.** Fluctuating exchange rates make things cheaper in dong and, moreover, as of October 1994 it's illegal to use US$ in transactions. *Let's Go* advises non-Americans to exchange their currencies into US$ before going to Vietnam, as this will facilitate transactions once there.

US$ can also be exchanged unofficially at hotels and in jewelry shops at slightly better rates than at banks. It's best to carry **traveler's checks** in US$ which can be exchanged for dong at certain banks—Vietcombank, Cosevina, and ANZ—for a 2% commission. Most hotels and airline offices do not accept traveler's checks. **Lost or stolen traveler's checks cannot be replaced in Vietnam.**

Tipping is not necessary, although it's customary to leave some small change. At more expensive restaurants and hotels, 10% is added to the bill. **Bargaining** should always be done in dong and with a smile. When prices are not fixed, you should expect to receive a "discount" anywhere from 10-50%.

■ Getting Around

BY PLANE

Travel by plane is the best way to get from one end of the country to the other. The two hubs are Hanoi in the north and Ho Chi Minh City in the south. From each of these major cities, trains, buses, motorcycles, or cars can transport travelers to their destination. Haiphong, Hue, Da Nang, Nha Trang, Dalat, and Dien Bien Phu have airports of their own, but flights there are relatively infrequent. There is a 15,000Đ departure tax for all domestic flights. **Do not lose your baggage claim tickets; you won't be allowed to take your luggage out of the airport without them.**

BY TRAIN

Trains in Vietnam do exist, but solely for the pleasure of existing. Because the gauge of Vietnamese trains are smaller than those in the west, they move at a sluggish pace (maximum speed of 50km per hour), and require a lifetime's worth of patience. Furthermore, train tracks that once extended throughout the country are now in disrepair having been destroyed during the Vietnam War. Passengers should retain their tickets or will be charged a fee upon disembarking.

BY BUS

The national bus transportation system is a dirt-cheap way to travel through Vietnam. It is not, however, for the impatient, faint of heart, or those sensitive about their personal space. Buses are actually large flat-bed trucks with seats bolted in and a roof overhead. The rides are loud, dusty, and tiring. Furthermore, these "buses" are tailor-made for those of small stature. For long distance trips, purchase tickets at least one day in advance, and arrive one hour before the departure time to ensure a seat. Expect to be packed in with bikes, fruits, vegetables, and lots of sweating commuters. Hang on to your life as the driver ignores all safety precautions and hang on to your valuables, too; pickpockets can have a field day amidst the confusion.

BY BIKE AND MOTORCYCLE

Traveling by motorbike is a good alternative mode of getting from city to city without relying on the nightmarish public transportation system. The laws in Vietnam allow foreigners to operate motorbikes which are 100cc and under without a motorcycle license; consequently, you can rent one anywhere. Tourists with an operator's license, however, can choose from more powerful machines.

For those who have recently won the Tour de France and would like to train while vacationing in Vietnam, bikes are readily available. Used bicycles cost 200-500,000Đ and will take some cunning deal-making to get a fair price. Many complain about the poor quality of Chinese bicycles (e.g. the Phoenix), but for tourist purposes, they are perfectly adequate and the logical budget choice. Practically all guest houses rent out bikes and motorbikes.

BY THUMB

Let's Go urges you to use common sense and consider all the risks involved before hitchhiking. We do not recommend hitchhiking to anyone.

Hitchhiking is a commonplace practice all along the major highways. If you flag down a bus or minibus, expect to negotiate and pay a fare. This is how many Vietnamese catch an inter-city bus when the bus station is already too far afield. Private vehicles and trucks that stop to offer you a ride might or might not ask for money.

■ Keeping in Touch

The **postal service** in Vietnam could use a little competition to speed it up; your friends might as well hold on to their mail and give it to you upon your return. Mail can take as long as three weeks to and from Vietnam. **Poste Restante** service is available in major cities, but cross your fingers and make a wish upon every star, fountain, and tooth you can find. Packages to Vietnam will be opened and inspected. **Telephones** were scarce not too long ago, but today almost all businesses have phone and fax. **Long-distance calls** placed from Vietnam can cost you a paycheck or two. It's impossible to make **collect calls** from private phones; collect calls can be placed for a 11,000Đ charge. Also try asking your hotel operator for this service. Dial 10 for long-distance calls, if you must. Vietnam is seven hours ahead of Greenwich Mean Time (GMT).

■ Staying Safe

Travelers in Vietnam should keep in mind some of the general rules about safety and follow your instincts. Hold on tight to all your belongings, as many pickpockets rove the streets for unsuspecting tourists, and keep your eyes out for con artists, especially prevalent in Ho Chi Minh City. In addition, keep in mind that the police in Vietnam are generally unfriendly and should, in most cases, be avoided. A new law prohibits the police from collecting fines directly—they can only hand out tickets—so don't be fooled into paying fines to them directly. **Be sure not to photograph any bridges or other military structures.**

■ Hours and Holidays

Most offices and museums open around 7 or 8am and close by 4 or 5pm with a break at midday, 11:30am-2pm. Most offices close on Sundays except museums, which close on Mondays instead. All offices close public holidays (noted below).

Good News For Grandma!

Although most visitors are aware that Tet, the Lunar New Year, is the most celebrated holiday in Vietnam, few people are aware of Ram Thang Bay, Vietnam's other significant celebration. Also called Tet Trung Nguyen, it falls on the 15th day of the seventh lunar month (around the second week of August). The festival is a time for forgiveness and centers around absolving the sins of the dead. According to legend, there once was an impoverished woman who committed one petty crime after another; her son, on the other hand, was a paradigm of virtue who equaled his mother's bad deeds with a succession of good ones. When the mother passed away she was sent to hell to suffer for her crimes. But when her son died, he instead went to heaven, where he could see all the deeds of man, on earth as well as in hell. Seeing his mother's unspeakable torments, the son approached the King of the Underworld to appeal for his mother's soul. The King weighed the deeds of the son against the sins of the mother and decided to vindicate her. He was so moved by the son's piety, in fact, that he declared a day of forgiveness in hell—a respite for those serving their penance. During the Ly (1009-1225) and Tran (1225-1400) dynasties, even prisoners were allowed to return home to visit their families during their holiday.

January 1: New Year's Day (official).
February: Tet, Traditional New Year, 1st to 7th day of new lunar month (official).
February 3: Anniversary of the Communist Party of Vietnam (official).
March: Hai Ba Trung Day (6th day of the 2nd lunar month).
April: Thanh Minh, New Year of the Dead (5th day of the 3rd lunar month).
April 30: Liberation of South Vietnam and Saigon (official).
May 1: International Labor Day (official).
May 19: Ho Chi Minh's Birthday (official).
May 28: Celebration of the Buddha (official).
August: Trung Nguyen (15th day of the 7th lunar month). See gray box below.
September 2: National Day (official).
September 3: President Ho's Anniversary (official).
September: Mid-Autumn Festival, (15th day of the 9th lunar month).
November: Confucius' Birthday (28th day of the 9th lunar month).

LIFE AND TIMES

■ The People of Vietnam

The Vietnam War dramatically shifted the demographics of Vietnam. Today, two-thirds of Vietnam's 78 million people are under the age of 25.

VIETNAMESE

Constituting 85% of the population, the **Vietnamese** are descended from the Kinh people who migrated into the Red River Delta about 2000 years ago. Most ethnic Vietnamese are Buddhist, but many also practice a mix of Taoism and Confucianism.

CHINESE

Today there are about one million ethnic **Chinese** (Hoa) in Vietnam, most of whom live in the south. Nearly all of them have adopted Vietnamese citizenship, but most continue to follow Chinese customs and traditions. The Vietnamese government has recognized the importance of the once-persecuted Chinese in the development of Vietnam. As merchants and tradespeople, the Chinese play a leading role in the economy of the country.

CHAM

The central and southern provinces of Vietnam are home to about 100,000 **Chams.** Following the complete and final destruction of their kingdom in 1720 by the expanding Vietnamese, the Cham king and many of his people fled to Cambodia, where their descendants still live to this day. Those who remained in Vietnam were dispossessed and pushed off their land, while their artistic traditions died out due to hardship and extreme poverty. Although once culturally similar, differences can be discerned among the Chams of today. Chams living in the central region still follow old Brahminic traditions while those in the south have converted to Islam.

MONTAGNARD

Montagnard is a common term used to describe the numerous hill tribes that live in the mountains of North and Central Vietnam. These ethnic minority groups vary in size, but altogether there are 6-8 million Montagnards. The way of life of these hill tribes is changing fast. Montagnards have found their traditions and customs undermined by alien cultural influences in their villages, and assaulted under the pressure of constant fighting with the French, Vietnamese, and even each other. Most of the hill tribes migrate every few years and cultivate upland crops using shifting cultivation. Relatively isolated from Vietnam's mainstream society, Montagnards are often autonomous and have their own systems of government within their respective groups. Larger Montagnard tribes include the **Tay,** who live in the northwest; the **Thai** (ethnically distinct from those in Thailand), who can be found in the river valleys of the north, as well as on the slopes of the northwest mountains; the **Moung,** who make their homes in Thanh Hoa and Yen Bai Provinces in the north central part of the country; the **Nung,** who inhabit northeast Vietnam near the border; the **Hmong,** who dwell in the highest altitudes, near the Chinese border; the **Gia Rai** (or Zria), which is the largest group in Central Vietnam; and the **Dao,** who occupy the northern frontier in Lao Cai and Ha Giang Provinces.

■ History

PRE-HISTORY

Little remains of the ancient civilizations of Vietnam, but the earliest inhabitants known to historians were the **Negritos,** who vanished from the region with the arrival of peoples from the Indonesian archipelago. Not long afterward came the **Kinh,** who were forced southward from the lower Yangtze River Valley into the **Red River Delta** by the encroaching Chinese.

Located on a strategic land mass on the crossroads of trade, Vietnam was later inundated by migrating **Mon-Khmer** and **Tai-Kadai** ethnic groups, some of whom intermarried with their predecessors. These are the ancestors of the **Viet** people of today. The language of the Mon-Khmers formed the basis of the Vietnamese language, while tonality was borrowed from the Thais. However, it was the later arrival of the ethnic **Chinese** who left an indelible cultural stamp on Vietnam.

In the Red River Delta, the Viet people (descendents of the **Kinh**) established the kingdom of **Au Lac** which prospered peacefully until 207BC when the Chinese began filtering into the region. A Chinese general from Guangdong subjugated the Red River Delta, which then became the southern province of the kingdom Nan Yueh, or **Nam Viet,** referring to the peoples of the south.

THE CHINESE MILLENNIUM

The **Han Dynasty** incorporated Nam Viet into its empire in 111 BC. Thus began a millennium of brutal Chinese rule during which Chinese immigrants flooded the Red River Delta and intensified the Sinicization of the region, making Vietnam culturally distinct from the other Indianized countries of mainland Southeast Asia. The Han emperors divided Nam Viet into three administrative districts of **Annam, Tonkin,** and **Thanh Hoa.** Despite the cruelty of their oppressors, the Vietnamese people, most notably the elite, accepted Chinese cultural influences—the classics, Confucian principles, Mahayana Buddhism, and Chinese characters—while thoroughly resisting Chinese rule. All revolts were harshly suppressed, intensifying the hatred.

The decline of the **Tang Dynasty** (618-907) marked the rise of Nam Viet. In 939, the Vietnamese, under the leadership of **Ngo Quyen,** successfully overthrew Chinese rule. Ngo declared himself king of the kingdom of **Dai Viet.**

While controlling northern Vietnam, the Chinese tried to assert itself over the **Chams** living in the south. According to early Chinese records, the Chams overthrew Chinese authority in the 1st century AD and established a kingdom near Hue. **Champa** came to be a powerful state that challenged Chinese rule outside of China proper, occasionally invading Nam Viet. A contemporary of **Funan**, Champa absorbed its neighbor's Indianized culture when it annexed the Funanese province of Panduranga (Phan Rang). Champa outlasted Funan, but it was finally destroyed in 1471 by the expanding Vietnamese.

INDEPENDENT VIETNAM (939-1860)

After the downfall of the Chinese, Vietnam enjoyed nearly a thousand years of autonomy under several strong dynasties that ruled from Hanoi and Hue. Yet, the first few years of self-rule were plagued by internal disputes and incursions from the Thai kingdom of **Nanchao** and Champa. As a result, Dai Viet eventually sought protection from China, entering an overlord-vassal relationship with its former enemy.

The rise of the **Ly Dynasty** (1009-1225) brought stability to the region over the next two hundred years. During their reign, the Lys displaced war lords and moved the capital to modern-day **Hanoi** where they created a strong centralized government based on a nine-level hierarchical bureaucracy adapted from China. The new government was thoroughly Confucian in principle, and the mandarins, the intellectual leaders, promoted Confucian values throughout the kingdom.

In 1225, the **Tran Dynasty** (1225-1400) arose to overthrow the Lys. A series of strong, capable rulers pursued public works projects including the building of irrigation and water control systems and embankments along the Red River. In the waning years of the Tran Dynasty the Chinese once again overpowered Dai Viet. This time, their rule was even more cruel. Led by **Le Loi,** the Vietnamese rebelled against these harsh actions, and drove out the hated Chinese in 1428. Le Loi then established the **Le Dynasty** (1428-1776) and the language, writing, religion, art, and government system of China became firmly established in Vietnamese life.

In addition to the constant threat from their northern neighbors, internal disputes broke out within the royal family. In this vulnerable state, the Le family succumbed to a despotic general named **Trinh.** Meanwhile, in Hue, the prominent **Nguyen** family, once aligned with the Le, established their own sphere of influence, posing a threat to the Trinhs in the north. A struggle ensued between the two families, and a wall near the 17th parallel divided the kingdom into two territories. The Nguyen power in Annam (Central Vietnam) soon spread to the south and, by 1720, they had pushed out the Chams, most of whom fled to present-day Cambodia. With Champa out of the way, the Nguyens were able to extend their jurisdiction into the Mekong Delta, then a part of the Khmer kingdom of Angkor, and incorporated **Saigon** into their growing kingdom.

As the Nguyens grew in strength, the Trinhs waned in authority. The **Nguyen brothers** (not to be confused with the Nguyens of Hue) from the northern district of **Tayson** rebelled against the tyranny of the Trinh family and eventually united both kingdoms. The people of Tonkin hailed these three brothers as heroes who freed the land from the despotic and corrupt Trinhs, while those of Annam viewed them as usurpers who had taken advantage of the Nguyen king's recent death. The teenage **Prince Nguyen Anh** fled into exile, as a victorious Nguyen Hue of Tayson declared himself **Emperor Quang Trung.**

By 1802, Nguyen Anh had installed himself at Hue as **Emperor Gia Long** of Annam, the first king of the **Nguyen Dynasty** (1802-1883), Vietnam's last royal family. Gia Long proved to be a remarkable and strong ruler who reinstituted a Chinese-based administration, Confucian principles, and a code of law. With the help of the French, the king created a navy and fortified the kingdom by constructing forts and casting weapons. The crumbling irrigation system was restored and new roads connecting the three main cities of Saigon, Hue, and Hanoi were built. Today Gia Long is regarded as the father of Vietnam and his dynasty marks the country's golden age, even though it hailed the arrival of the French.

COLONIAL RULE AND NATIONALISM (1860-1954)

In 1535, a Portuguese captain had sailed into Da Nang Bay and claimed most-favored-nation trading status for Portugal, but the Portuguese could not fully subjugate the Vietnamese. A century later came the Dutch, just in time for the territorial dispute between the Trinh and Nguyen families.

A truce ended the war and a trade slump drove out the Portuguese and Dutch merchants by 1700, leaving behind them a handful of Catholic missionaries intent on "civilizing" the Vietnamese. Officials kept missionary activity to a minimum, fearing that ideas promulgated by the Europeans would lead to a conquest of their kingdom and a breakdown of the traditional Vietnamese order. Missionary activities continued doggedly, however, until they were banned and made punishable by death. **France,** outraged at the persecution of European missionaries (not to mention the Catholicism-bashing), invaded Vietnam and attacked Da Nang in 1858 and Saigon in 1861, forcing **Emperor Tu Duc** to cede three southern provinces and pay an indemnity.

The delta was annexed and became **Cochin China.** In 1883, Vietnam was formally divided into the French territories of Tonkin (north), Annam (central), and Cochin China (south). The emperor continued to rule over Tonkin and Annam, although the French had the final say in all major decisions, while Cochin China was strictly governed by the colonialists. Over the next few years, France also expanded its influence in the region and annexed Laos and Cambodia to form **French Indochina.**

The early 20th century saw the rise of **nationalism** in Indochina, most notably in Vietnam. Having been introduced to western ideas by elite Vietnamese who had studied in France, numerous anti-French societies spread rapidly, although most were clandestine and lacked well-defined political goals. Eventually, these organizations were united under the leadership of the **Indochinese Communist Party (ICP)** which was founded in 1930 by **Ho Chi Minh.** Ignored by western representatives at Versailles when he urged France to improve the administration of Vietnam, Ho turned to communist doctrine, and ultimately headed to Moscow in 1924. After 30 years of self-exile, Ho returned to Vietnam in 1942 to lead a revolution.

The Japanese invasion of Indochina in 1941 was a welcome respite from the French, but Ho Chi Minh's forces resisted the occupation. The French remained in nominal control, but were virtual slaves to their Axis enemy. The communists, in an effort to broaden and strengthen their political and social base, willingly collaborated with non-communist groups. This united-front organization became the Vietnam Independence League, better known as the **Viet Minh.** When World War II ended, Ho Chi Minh acted quickly, expecting the French to return to reclaim Vietnam. **Emperor Bao Dai** also feared French domination, and practically handed his power over to Ho by abdicating. Already in control of much of the country, the Viet Minh declared independence for their country. France was not willing to recognize Vietnam's independence and, consequently, a long, bitter war ensued. In May 1954, France's surrender to the ragtag Viet Minh at **Dien Bien Phu,** signaling an end to its colonial might (see **Dien Bien Phu: Sights** on page 751).

THE VIETNAM CONFLICT

Dien Bien Phu marked the end of the **First Indochina War.** The **Geneva Accords** that same year divided Vietnam temporarily along the 17th parallel into two countries. Ho Chi Minh took control of North Vietnam while U.S.-backed **Ngo Dinh Diem** proclaimed himself president of South Vietnam. An all-Vietnamese election scheduled for 1956 to unify the country was never approved by either the U.S. or South Vietnam; they feared the vote would have gone to the communists. After that failed attempt at democracy, the 17th parallel became the border between the **Democratic Republic of Vietnam** (north) and the **Republic of Vietnam** (south).

With the withdrawal of the French came the arrival of the Americans, who assumed responsibility for the survival of democracy by providing financial aid and military advice to South Vietnam. Diem, however, was extremely unpopular in South Vietnam. The U.S. supported Diem because of his anti-French, anti-Communist, and Christian sentiments, but unlike "Uncle Ho," he was out of touch with the Vietnamese people. Under the pressure of a continual guerilla war waged by the **Viet Cong** (a derogatory term for the Viet Minh), Diem was so oppressive a leader that he was overthrown and assassinated in 1963 by his own troops.

The civil war in Vietnam escalated with the intervention of the U.S. in August of 1964, when North Vietnamese naval crafts supposedly attacked the **USS Maddox** while it was engaged in espionage activities in the Gulf of Tonkin. President Lyndon Johnson, long afraid of losing the next presidential election, saw in the situation a way to salvage his image. The U.S. retaliated to the outrageous "attack" by bombing North Vietnam and sending troops to the South.

Meanwhile, South Vietnam had been in a state of anarchy since Diem's assassination. In 1965, **Nguyen Van Thieu** seized power. In an effort to control the South's dictatorial government and to escalate the war against the north, the U.S. sent 3500 Marines to Da Nang on March 7, 1965. Three years later, in the spring of 1967, over 500,000 American soldiers were stationed in South Vietnam.

The Vietnam War reached a climax with the **Tet Offensive** of February 1968 when the Viet Cong attacked more than 100 cities and military bases in the south during new year celebrations. Although a devastating military defeat for the communists, the offensive was a crucial psychological victory. Both sides suffered heavy losses and, for the first time, it was evident that the North Vietnamese were willing to make extensive sacrifices in order to win the war. Thus, the U.S. resolved to withdraw from the conflict before further embarrassing itself. Johnson decided not to seek office again and Richard Nixon was elected on the promise that he would withdraw American troops from Southeast Asia.

Although the U.S. began to withdraw its troops, it continued and increased saturation bombing of Vietnam, Laos, and Cambodia, culminating in an overt invasion of the latter country. The **Paris Agreements of 1973** called for a cease-fire, the total withdrawal of U.S. combat forces from all three countries, and the release of American prisoners of war. Without further hesitation, the 200,000 North Vietnamese troops left in South Vietnam launched a massive offensive and were joined by comrades from across the 17th parallel. The South, suffering from severe losses, was unable to protect itself, and Saigon fell on April 30, 1975.

The new government moved to crush all opposition. They rounded up hundreds of thousands of people and imprisoned them without trial in forced labor camps, or "re-education camps." Rather than face the terror that came with the communist victory, thousands of South Vietnamese fled their homeland.

With the loss of much of the country's educated elite and the physical destruction wrought by the U.S., the task of rebuilding Vietnam was phenomenal. Furthermore, herbicides used by Americans to destroy foliage in South Vietnam proved to have long-term detrimental effects on rainfall, soil erosion, and consequently the productivity of the land. It is estimated that in an attempt to defoliate the rainforests which camouflaged communist guerilllas, the U.S. wiped out a 30-year supply of timber that will take at least another century to replace.

Without enough outside aid, Vietnam's ambitious plans to rebuild the economic, social, and political infrastructure of the country were fruitless. The Soviet Union, Eastern European countries, and China contributed to the reconstruction effort, but the U.S. refused to give the aid that had been promised in the Paris Agreements.

Instead, America led a worldwide trade embargo against Vietnam and pressured the International Monetary Fund to deny it credit. To make matters worse, a campaign of repression against Vietnam's ethnic Chinese incurred the wrath of China. In addition, Vietnam's invasion of Cambodia in 1978 to stop the Khmer Rouge drew condemnation from western nations. (See **The Vietnamese Intervention,** page 63.)

■ Vietnam Today

The end of the Cold War and the collapse of the USSR in 1991 has forced Vietnam to seek rapprochement with the west and its capitalist Southeast Asian neighbors. In 1996, Vietnam became a member of the Association of Southeast Asian Nations (ASEAN) and has since increased its efforts to promote cross border trade. The establishment of diplomatic relations with the U.S. marks the beginning of Vietnam's quest for economic success in the footsteps of Thailand, Malaysia, and Singapore, so that by the year 2020, Vietnam hopes to be an industrialized nation.

The Eighth Party Congress, the landmark meeting of the Vietnam Communist Party (VCP), took place in June 1996 and established the government's current stand on political, economic, and religious issues. Among other things, the VCP produced a 57-page political report, a set of goals and commands for the next five years. According to this report, the Vietnamese government intends to thwart all attempts to abuse issues of democracy, encourage private capitalist economy, and make radical reforms of administrative procedures. With the memories of failed hard-lined communism in mind, it would appear as though this party is committed to an open market economy.

While willing to liberalize the market economy to a prosperous end, the not-so-hard-lined-but-still-communist leaders will not relinquish their unchallenged political authority and privilege. Having a dim view of organized religion, the Communist Party continues to claim control over people's belief and religious activities.

HUMAN RIGHTS

The death penalty in Vietnam is applicable for a wide variety of offenses ranging from actions violating national security to treason. In 1995 alone, 100 Vietnamese were sentenced to death. Fair trials occur rarely and defendants are usually not allowed defenders until a few days before their trial, preventing adequate preparation. In addition to this, the Vietnamese government still does not tolerate the practice of certain religions, and has been known to take action against those who do not adhere to Buddhism. In yet a further demonstration of intolerance, the government discriminates against hill tribes, the vast majority of which seek autonomy.

■ The Arts

Unlike its Southeast Asian neighbors, Vietnam developed a rich literary tradition rather than an artistic one. Although magnificent artistry and architecture can be found throughout the country (most notably the imperial palace at Hue), the art of Vietnam is a reflection of Chinese styles. Vietnamese art and architecture progressed through several periods coinciding with the various dynasties, but since they were Chinese prototypes, they never gained their own characteristics.

ART AND ARCHITECTURE

The earliest art found in Vietnam dates from 500BC and belonged to the **Dong Son** civilization near modern-day Thanh Hoa. Little is known about this culture, but the magnificent bronzes left behind were clearly of Chinese influence.

Early architecture can be found in Central Vietnam, where the Hindu kingdom of **Champa** once prospered. Between the 6th and 11th centuries, Champa produced some splendid temples and fine carvings, although most traces of them have disappeared with time and war. At the beginning of the 8th century, Cham art was strikingly similar in style and form to that of the Gupta period in India. Even this early in its development, Cham art already showed native influences; by the end of the 9th century, it had become distinctively Cham. The complete defeat of Chams in the 15th century by the Vietnamese marked the end of Cham architecture.

DANCE AND DRAMA

Many Vietnamese enjoy a popular theater form known as **cai luong** (old music). Similar to American musicals, *cai luong* uses dialogue and singing to communicate with the audience. *Cai luong* is universally appealing in its simplicity, understandable to even non-Vietnamese people. Today, *cai luong* is written by writers who have modernized classic plots. Actors perform in traditional Vietnamese as well as western dress. **Hat boi,** once a popular dance form, originated from classical Chinese opera, in which gestures are of primary importance and singing replaces dialogue. Performances incorporate old Chinese music and traditional Chinese dress. Unfortunately, there has been no attempt to revive *hat boi,* since it nearly vanished after the division of Vietnam in 1954. In addition to these foreign-inspired theatrical forms, Vietnam has cultivated its own dramatic art form called *mua roi nuoc* or **water puppet theater.** *Mua roi nuoc* originated in North Vietnam perhaps as early as the 1st century AD. In water puppet theater, all the water's a stage and the puppets in it are legendary heroes from historical and religious epics. Puppets are carved from a water resistant wood and then painted. Hanoi boasts the most famous water puppet theater tradition, but the art form has spread to most major cities in Vietnam.

LITERATURE

Before the Vietnamese adopted a written script similar to Chinese, folk tales, legends, songs, and proverbs were passed on orally from generation to generation. In the 13th century, a new script called **nom** was developed and used thereafter to immortalize literary works, even though this literature remained largely Chinese in style. From the 15th century on, *nom* literature took on a form of its own. Considered to be truly Vietnamese in nature, these works were simple and addressed the problems and injustices of the age. The many pieces composed during the *nom* literary movement continue to be favorites among the Vietnamese today.

The 17th and 18th centuries saw the birth of **truyen** (verse novel) which was much like Homer's epic poems. Although traveling storytellers mesmerized audiences with *truyen* tales, it was not until the 19th century—a period fraught with social and political unrest—that Vietnamese literature attained its height. Prolific poets and writers churned out Vietnam's greatest masterpieces during this epoch, including the highly celebrated **Truyen Kieu** (Tale of Kieu).

The arrival of the French proved to be another important marker in the development of Vietnamese literature. The **quoc ngu** script created by Father Alexandre de Rhodes in the 17th century came into more widespread use and, Vietnam's dependence on Chinese traditions ceased. The new script was adopted in the 1920s and a decade later, Vietnamese literature had taken on a decidedly western tone.

NORTH VIETNAM

■ Hànôi

Stern and austere, Hanoi has been the intellectual, artistic, and political center of Vietnam throughout its long history. It has weathered French colonialism, revolutionary communism, and today, the opening of its economy to the world market. Each of these historic influences is visible throughout Hanoi, from the tree-lined avenues which vaunt yellow French villas, to the massive no-nonsense state buildings, to the presence of small companies which have the words "joint-venture" or "foreign

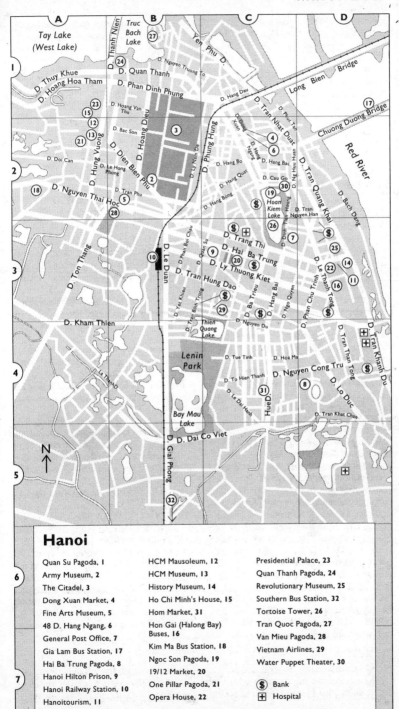

VIETNAM

Hanoi

Quan Su Pagoda, 1
Army Museum, 2
The Citadel, 3
Dong Xuan Market, 4
Fine Arts Museum, 5
48 D. Hang Ngang, 6
General Post Office, 7
Gia Lam Bus Station, 17
Hai Ba Trung Pagoda, 8
Hanoi Hilton Prison, 9
Hanoi Railway Station, 10
Hanoitourism, 11

HCM Mausoleum, 12
HCM Museum, 13
History Museum, 14
Ho Chi Minh's House, 15
Hom Market, 31
Hon Gai (Halong Bay) Buses, 16
Kim Ma Bus Station, 18
Ngoc Son Pagoda, 19
19/12 Market, 20
One Pillar Pagoda, 21
Opera House, 22

Presidential Palace, 23
Quan Thanh Pagoda, 24
Revolutionary Museum, 25
Southern Bus Station, 32
Tortoise Tower, 26
Tran Quoc Pagoda, 27
Van Mieu Pagoda, 28
Vietnam Airlines, 29
Water Puppet Theater, 30

$ Bank
✚ Hospital

investment" in their names. The city that spawned a communist revolution is now going through a revolution itself. In 1988, the government took a cue from Gorbachev's *perestroika* policies, and adopted a new course of economic policy dubbed *Doi Moi* (Renovation). Hanoians have since put down their Russian textbooks for English and have forsaken Marx for Smith. Towering construction cranes stand like sentinels across the city-scape, harbingers of more change to come. The stream of bikes and motorcycles can be dizzying, but the narrow streets of the Old Quarter and peaceful shores of numerous lakes keep Hanoi on a human scale.

Even in the process of development, Hanoi retains a distinctly communist flavor. While neither as warm nor as prosperous as their southern counterparts, Hanoians proudly display their multi-faceted heritage as cyclo drivers wearing imitation Viet Minh helmets and fatigues pedal past outdoor Chinese chess games. While Saigon may remain the pocket book, Hanoi will always be the heart and mind of Vietnam.

GETTING THERE AND AWAY

By Plane

Flights into Hanoi land at **Noi Bai International Airport,** 35km north of the city. If you have filled out your customs and entry/exit cards, the wait should be no more than one hour. Keep your baggage claim tickets secure—you will not be allowed to exit with your bags without them. **Note:** Keep your stamped, white immigration card with your passport. Accommodations are required to register guests with the local police and will need your card for that purpose.

A metered taxi goes into town for 220-275,000Đ. Vietnam Airlines **minibuses** run between the airport and the city every hour until 4:30pm; if going to the airport, purchase your ticket a day in advance (44,000Đ). The shuttle picks up and drops off passengers at the **Vietnam Airlines office,** 1 Quang Trung (reconfirmation tel. 821 66 66), just south of Hoan Kiem Lake. Flights out of Hanoi are subject to a departure tax of 15,000Đ for domestic flights and 77,000Đ for international flights. Domestic flights go to **Ho Chi Minh City (HCMC)** (1,900,000Đ), **Hue** and **Da Nang** (1,000,000Đ), and **Nha Trang** (1,450,000Đ). Buy tickets at the office at least a day ahead. Regular connections with major cities in Southeast Asia are available.

By Train

Travelers arriving in Hanoi from Haiphong, Lao Cai, and all southern points disembark at **Hanoi Railway Station** (Ga Hanoi), 126 Trang Tien, at the west terminus of Tran Hung Dao, about 1km southwest of Hoan Kiem Lake. A 10-minute cyclo ride (5000-8000Đ) from the station will quickly bring visitors to the heart of the city. Foreigners must purchase tickets at window #7, on the left when entering, where they pay higher prices than native Vietnamese. Buy train tickets two to three days in advance, as seats disappear quickly.

Three classes of trains depart from Hanoi for **HCMC:** slow (S1, Mon., Thurs., and Sat., 7pm, 36hr.), slower (S3, daily, 7:30pm, 40hr.), and slowest (S5, daily, 10am, 44hr.). Soft seats on trains to: **Da Nang** (268-335,000Đ); **HCMC** (572-719,000Đ): **Hue** (235-293,000Đ); and **Nha Trang** (470-596,000Đ). For trips overnight, take hard sleepers to: **Da Nang** (379-553,000Đ); **HCMC** (814-1,193,000Đ); **Hue** (331,000-482,000Đ); and **Nha Trang** (675-1,039,000Đ). Daily trains go to: **Lao Cai** (5:10am and 9pm, 10hr., seats 94-111,500Đ, berths 155-173,000Đ); **Lang Son** (5am and 10pm, 7hr., 70,000Đ hard); and **Haiphong** (5:45am, 2½hr., 40,000Đ hard). **Note:** Save your ticket or you will be forced to pay again upon arriving at your destination. Watch valuables carefully; trains are favorite haunts for thieves, and North Vietnam is notorious for pickpockets.

By Bus

Kim Ma Bus Station (to west and northwest destinations), on the left of Nguyen Thai Hoc just after the intersection with Giang Vo (8-10,000Đ cyclo ride), has buses to: **Dien Bien Phu** (5am, 18-30hr., 50,000Đ) via **Son La** (1hr., 35,000Đ). Buses to

Haiphong and **Halong Bay** depart from **Gia Lam Bus Station** across the Red River. A motorcycle taxi to the station is 10,000Đ. Inter-city bus to all points south leave from the **Southern Bus Station** on Giai Phong, the extension of Le Duan, 5km south of the train station. **Tourist minibuses,** which can be booked through your hotel or a tourist café, go to: **Hue** (14hr., 242,000Đ) and **HCMC** (48 hr., 385,000Đ).

GETTING AROUND

By Bicycle (Xe Dap) and Motorbike (Xe May)

Most hotels and guest houses rent motorbikes for 55-110,000Đ per day. A motorbike can be a great way to explore beyond the Hoan Kiem and Ba Dinh Districts and get you to the pockets of Hanoi seldom visited by backpackers. Be prepared to fork over 500-1000Đ each time you park your bike, however. Insist on a helmet when you rent. Although Hanoi may be too large to navigate by bike, the fit and hearty may find it a great alternative to the motorbike. The best way to obtain a bicycle is through your hotel or guest house (6-10,000Đ per day).

By Cyclo and Motorcycle Taxi

Perhaps one of the most delightful and comfortable ways to get from place to place is on the three wheels of a **cyclo.** These ubiquitous vehicles can be found on almost every corner or in the streets. Always agree on a price before you get on (5-8000Đ should get you anywhere within 3-4km). You can also hire cyclos by the hour (11,000Đ per hour). Motorcycle taxis are more useful for distant rides and have slightly higher rates of 2-3000Đ per km. They can also be found loitering on street corners with cyclo drivers or found at signs that say *"Xe Om."*

By Car

Cars are still not commonplace in the city, but this doesn't mean you can't rent one. **Especen** (see **Tours and Travel** below) charges 330,000Đ per day in town, 3300Đ per km for travel outside of Hanoi.

By Taxi

Taxis line up across the street from the Vietnam Airlines office on Bai Trieu. **Hanoi Taxi** (tel. 853 52 52) can pick you up and deliver you to your destination for a heavy toll (11,000Đ, plus 6600Đ per km). Metered taxis also cruise the streets and at the train station. It would be wise to insist on the meter.

ORIENTATION

Throughout Hanoi, lakes serve as hubs of business and centers of leisure. At the heart of the city is **Hoan Kiem Lake,** Hanoi's most useful and picturesque landmark. Just to the north of Hoan Kiem Lake is the **Old Quarter** of the city, a backpacker's haven of narrow, winding streets crowded with shops, cafés, and hotels. To the south of the lake are five parallel, east-west boulevards. From north to south: **Duong Trang Thi/Hang Khay/Trang Tien, Duong Hai Ba Trung, Duong Ly Thuong Kiet, Duong Tran Hung Dao,** and **Duong Nguyen Du** border an area full of banks, embassies, businesses, shops, restaurants, and street merchants. These three sections form the downtown area, **Hoan Kiem District.** To the south of Hoan Kiem is **Hai Ba Trung District,** where **Lenin Park** and small specialty shops can be found. **Dong Da District,** one of the poorest sections of Hanoi, sprawls out west of Hai Ba Trung. **Ba Dinh,** Hanoi's fourth district, lies to the west of Hoan Kiem Lake and is bounded on the east by the **citadel** and on the south by **Duong Nguyen Thai Hoc.** This district has attracted a lot of foreign investment and is now under heavy development. In the center of this section of the city sits the **Ho Chi Minh Mausoleum,** a mecca of the communist world. **Tay Lake** swallows up almost the entire area north of the mausoleum, and its north shore is heavily settled by expatriates. Bordering the southeast corner of Tay Lake is **Truc Bach Lake;** the strait separating the two lakes is a popular night hangout for the young and hip of Hanoi.

VIETNAM

PRACTICAL INFORMATION

Tourist Offices: Vietnamtourism, 30A Ly Thuong Kiet (tel. 826 40 89), and **Hanoitourism,** 18 Ly Thuong Kiet (tel. 825 60 36), offer a wide array of pricey tours, as well as a variety of visa services. Both are open Mon.-Sat. 8am-noon and 1-4:30pm. Vietnamtourism's 4-week visa extension (US$25) is the cheapest in town. **Especen,** 79 Hang Trong (tel. 825 16 59), is the choice of the backpacker community. Offers the same services as the other two, in addition to money exchanges and bike, car, and motorbike rentals. Open Mon.-Sat. 7:30-11:30am and 1:30-5pm. MC, Visa, AmEx. Many **tourist cafés** double as package tour operators. One-day and multi-day excursions to Hoa Lu, Halong Bay, Sapa, and Dien Bien Phu are popular. The cost (US$11-17 per day) includes transportation, accommodations, and food, placing them within the budget of most backpackers. **Queen, Darling, Red River, Green Bamboo,** and other operators familiar to those coming from the south, can all be found near Hoan Kiem Lake. **Note:** Be forewarned that tour quality is notoriously unreliable and promised accommodations and meals don't always come as advertised.

Embassies and Consulates: Australia, 66 Ly Thuong Kiet (tel. 825 27 63; fax 825 92 68). **Cambodia,** 71A Tran Hung Dao (tel. 825 37 89). **Canada** (embassy closed; call 823 55 00 to contact Canadian consulate). **China,** 46 Hoang Dieu (tel. 845 37 36). **Indonesia,** 64 Ngo Quyen (tel. 825 17 85). **Laos,** 22 Tran Binh Trong (tel. 825 45 76; fax 822 84 14). **Malaysia,** A3 Van Phuc (tel. 825 33 71; fax 823 21 66). **Singapore,** 41-43 Tran Phu (tel. 823 39 66). **Thailand,** 63-65 Hoang Dieu (tel. 823 50 42). **UK,** 16 Ly Thuong Kiet (tel. 825 25 10; fax 826 75 62). **US,** 7 Lang Ha (tel. 843 15 00; fax 835 04 84).

Immigration Offices: Don't bother going to the Ministry of Foreign Affairs for visa services; they will send you to one of the tourist companies above.

Currency Exchange: Vietcombank, 47-49 Ly Thai To (tel. 826 55 01). Exchanges major currencies and traveler's checks at no commission. Open Mon.-Sat. 8-11:30am and 1:30-3pm. **Citibank,** 17 Ngo Quyen (tel. 825 19 50) offers full **ATM** services for Citibank cardholders and also exchanges cash and traveler's checks. Open Mon.-Fri. 8:30am-12:30pm and 1:30-3:30pm, Sat. 8:30-11:30am.

American Express: 51 Ly Thai To. Don't know much about traveler's checks or what to do if you lose them. Good luck getting help at all.

Pharmacies: Nha Thuoc Nguyen Van Luan, 3 Trang Thi (tel. 826 86 44), just south of Hoan Kiem Lake. Open daily 8am-noon and 2-6pm. Many western prescription drugs are available over the counter in Vietnam.

Medical Services: Swedish Clinic (tel. 845 24 64), in the Van Phuc area opposite the Swedish embassy, 3.5km west of the center of town. Western hospital with western prices. **Dr. Raphael Kot,** Van Phuc A2, Room 101 and 102 (tel. 843 07 48), is a western-trained doctor whose clinic offers vaccinations at cost and charges 550,000Đ per consultation. **Medevac** services through **AEA International,** 4 Tran Hung Dao, 4th Fl. (tel. 821 35 55).

Police: Central station, 2 Le Thi To (tel. 825 41 08), on the southwest corner of Hoan Kiem Lake, at the intersection with Trang Thi.

Emergency: tel. 815. **Police:** tel. 813.

Post Offices: GPO, 75 Dinh Tien Hoang, southeast of Hoan Kiem Lake. Pick up *Poste Restante* and packages at 77 Dinh Tien Hoang. Telegram and telex services available. **DHL** has a booth on the corner of Dinh Tien Hoang and Le Thach. The entire postal complex is open daily 7:30am-7:30pm.

Telephones: Telephone office, 75B Dinh Tien Hoang (tel. 825 52 36), next to the GPO. Most reliable place for **overseas calls.** Exorbitant rates; give your party the above telephone number and have him or her call back. It costs 4400Đ to receive an overseas call. **Fax** service. Open daily 6-9:30pm. **Branch office,** 66 Luong Van Can (tel. 826 29 99). Domestic and overseas calls at the same rates. Open daily 6am-9pm. **Information:** tel. 116. **Telephone code:** 4.

ACCOMMODATIONS

Hotels are plentiful in Hanoi, but finding budget digs with good value isn't as easy as in the south. Negotiate yourself a better deal than the first offer, particularly for multiple-day stays. Rooms are usually two-bed doubles; negotiate for singles. The **Old Quarter,** just north of Hoan Kiem Lake, is the heart of Hanoi's massive mini-hotel industry and the ideal haunt for backpackers. Hunt around and drive a hard bargain. Students can ask about discounts for *sinh vien*. Most hotels will hold luggage for almost nothing. Many also place overseas phone calls at later hours—but at higher rates—than the post office.

Especen Hotels, with 10 locations in Hanoi, furnish clean, reasonably priced rooms. If one is full, they will help reserve a room at another. **Especen No. 9,** 10B Dinh Liet (tel. 825 30 69), is on the left heading north from the lake. Massive, A/C doubles with TV, fridge, and phone for as little as 165,000Đ. **No. 8,** 23 Hang Quat (tel. 825 13 01), at the corner of Luong Van Can, is cheaper but more basic. **No. 10,** 2B Hang Vai (tel. 828 11 60). Heading north on Luong Van Can, turn left onto Hang Vai and walk several blocks; it's on the left past the posh Continental Hotel. Small, A/C doubles 132,000Đ.

Bao Long Hotel, 39 Hang Be (tel. 824 04 34). From the east side of Hoan Kiem Lake, walk straight up Dinh Tien Hoang to Hang Dau past the Water Puppet Theatre. Hang Dau becomes Hang Be; Bao Long is 50m down on the right. Long on budget, short on privacy, but it's cheap. Dorm-style rooms have 4 beds with net, fans, and attached bath. Beds 33,000Đ. English and French spoken.

Binh Minh Hotel, 50 Hang Be (tel. 826 73 56), across the street from Bao Long. At the center of all the action with the sounds of traditional Vietnamese music outside on occasional evenings. The 18 rooms have soothing blue walls with mosquito-hungry geckoes patrolling for prey. Helpful staff, down to the playful parrot. Basic, fan-cooled singles 55,000Đ. Doubles with bath 88,000Đ.

Guesthouse, 55 Luong Ngoc Quyen (tel. 826 85 39). From the northern tip of the lake, walk up Dinh Liet/Ta Hien 3 blocks and take a left on Luong Ngoc Quyen. Guesthouse is several paces down on the left. Rooms are a bit sterile, but you can't get a bathroom and A/C for less. Singles 77,000Đ. Doubles 110,000Đ.

A Dong Hotel, 46 Luong Ngoc Quyen (tel. 825 69 48), just across the street from Guesthouse. Small, 10-room hotel offers outstanding rooms at bargain basement rates. An open courtyard offers visitors an island of peace and quiet in the middle of it all. Friendly staff is ready to serve up some of the local cuisine. Doubles with A/C and TV 110,000Đ, with shower 132,000Đ, with balcony 165,000Đ.

Pham Guest House, 22 Nguyen Thai Hoc (tel. 823 25 45). From the lake walk 1.5km west on Trang Thi; after a large intersection the road becomes Nguyen Thai Hoc; Pham's on the right at the end of a short alley. To experience life with a Vietnamese family, this is the place. They look after the 2 rooms and will take you in as if you were a long-lost relative and offer you meals. Doubles with A/C and bath 165,000Đ. Extra person 33,000Đ. Call ahead to reserve.

Lotus Guest House, 42V Ly Thuong Kiet (tel. 826 86 42), 2 blocks from the intersection with Ba Trieu. Lotus is what every guest house should be—warm, friendly, and cozy. Hang out in the small living room, order from a small menu of drinks and snacks, and swap stories. Most importantly this is the place to stay if you are sick—two doctors are at your disposal. Dorms 44,000Đ. Singles 66-88,000Đ. Doubles 88-132,000Đ. Additional guests 22,000Đ.

FOOD

Hanoi, the hub of the north, offers up many of the great specialities of this region. The best place to get your hands on traditional Vietnamese dishes like *pho* or *bun* is out in the markets, from the vendors on the street, or from small stalls and one-room operations where ordering is looking and pointing. To dine this way, arrive early (7-8am for breakfast, 11:30am-noon for lunch, and 5:30-6pm for dinner) for fresh, hot food. Gorge on exotic fruits from street vendors at the **19/12 Market.** Cool off with refreshing drinks like *mia da* (pressed sugarcane with ice) or *che* (sweet bean drink). And don't forget to try Hanoi's two local brews, Halida (brewed in conjunction with Carlsberg) and Bia Hanoi, which comes in bottles and draft (*bia hoi*).

Bia Hoi, 36 Bat Dan, on the corner with Hang Dieu. From the lake, head north up Luong Van Can 2 blocks and turn left on Hang Bo. Walk 200m and look to the right. Not a restaurant *per se,* but the best damn *bia hoi* stand and food stall this side of the 17th parallel. A consensus pick by locals, expats, and visitors alike, this is a place not to be missed. Tam, the proprietor of this humble establishment, is a sweet lady who'll stuff you full of food and beer. A meal and beers will not exceed 22,000Đ. Open daily 6:30am until everyone is passed out drunk.

Quan Hue, 6 Ly Thuong Kiet (tel. 826 40 62). Coming from the lake, turn left on Ly Thuong Kiet and it's on the left. Menu graced with an extensive selection of seafood, including *banh beo* and other classic shrimp dishes from Hue. Most entrees 20-50,000Đ. Open daily 7am-2pm and 5-9:30pm.

Quang An Restaurant (Restaurant 22), 22 Hang Can (tel. 826 71 60). Go up Luong Van Can until it turns into Hang Can. The restaurant is on the left up a small alleyway. Frog, pigeon, crab, fish, pork, beef, and chicken each cooked in a variety of ways. If it moves, they'll throw it in the pot. Try the *duck l'orange* or a rabbit dish. Many dishes go heavy on garlic, so bring mints lest your breath kill your companions. Entrees 20-50,000Đ. Open daily 11am-10:15pm.

Piano Restaurant & Bar, 50 Hang Vai (tel. 828 44 23), around the corner from Quang An Restaurant. Take a left on Lan Ong, which becomes Hang Vai. No piano and no bar, but plenty of restaurant. Specializing in Vietnamese and Chinese cuisine and everything from eel to *escargot.* Do you have the intestinal fortitude to stomach the tortoise soup? Entrees 20-50,000Đ. Open daily 9am-10pm.

Banh Tom Ho Tay, 1 Thanh Vien (tel. 257 839), on the north tip of Truc Bach Lake. Park your motorbike and find a table outside on the water. Don't bother looking at the menu. Just order a double serving of the shrimp cakes (*banh tom*) and 2 bottles of Hanoi beer. Then sit back and enjoy the flashing neon signs on the other side of the lake. Open daily 11am-10pm.

Hanoi Café, 252 Hang Bong (tel. 825 02 16), near the amazingly chaotic intersection with Dien Bien Phu and Nguyen Thai Hoc. One of the few good things that the French left in Vietnam was delicious pastry, and you'll find a lot of that here. The café is quick to brag that it was visited by Catherine Deneuve during the filming of *Indochine,* this café offers sandwiches and fluffy sweets. Beats the pants off the other cafés for food quality and ambiance. Open daily 7am-10:30pm.

Tram Phan Tram! (Bottoms up!)

The Vietnamese take beer-drinking seriously—so seriously that you might think you're in Germany when it comes to quaffing *lager* with the locals. Although most *bia hoi* (draft beer) stands on the sidewalks and side roads fall short of a Munich *biergarten,* the enthusiasm and passion with which the Vietnamese drink their beer rivals malt-drinkers anywhere in the world, and for good reason: the beer in Vietnam is fresh and delicious. Every morning, beer is delivered fresh in mini-kegs (known affectionately as "beer bombs"), which means that there are no preservatives and less of a chance of getting a hangover should you imbibe too liberally. But be warned: while Vietnamese beer may not have as much body as many international beers, it certainly has a kick.

Almost every city or region has its own local brews: in Hanoi, try Bia Hanoi and Halida; in Hue, drink Huda; in Saigon, don't miss 333 and Bia Saigon. Regardless of where you go, locals will insist that their city's beer is the best in Vietnam—and we all know that the only way to know for sure is to do careful, empirical research. To locate a good beer stall, look for peanut shells on the floor or a crowd of people. You'll find that a good *bia hoi* is the great social equalizer: doctors and lawyers share the camaraderie of good beer elbow-to-elbow with cyclo drivers and shoe-shine boys. Get to your favorite stall early, since kegs are often kicked by mid-afternoon, and grab a handful of peanuts in the shell (*lac*) or dried squid (*muc*) to help it go down right. Sorry, no beer nuts Norm.

SIGHTS

Concentrated in the districts of Hoan Kiem and Ba Dinh, most of Hanoi's attractive and interesting sights can be reached on foot. Those preferring not to leg it can be a part of Hanoi's most hypnotic sight—the traffic—by renting a bike or motorbike.

Hoan Kiem District

Hoan Kiem Lake (Lake of the Restored Sword) takes its name from a 15th-century legend. The **Emperor Le Thai To** (1428-33), having returned victorious from a confrontation with an army of invading Ming Chinese, was cruising the lake in search of quiet and relaxation. His day cruise was rudely interrupted, however, when an overly rambunctious giant turtle rose from the waters and snatched away his sword. Having no other explanation for his butterfingers, the emperor declared it was divine intervention—a sign from the heavens that the struggle had ceased and that the sword had been returned to its divine source. The **Tortoise Tower** on a tiny island in the center of the lake commemorates this event, and is one of the enduring symbols of Hanoi. Today the park serves as a meeting place, napping quarters, and exercise grounds for the city's residents.

In the northeast quadrant of the lake is a tree-laden island on which **Ngoc Son Temple** (Jade Mountain) is situated. Dating back to the Tran dynasty (1225-1400), the small shrine was successively embellished over generations. It was last renovated in 1865 and is dedicated primarily to **Van Xuong,** the god of literature. **Tran Hung Dao,** the 13th-century hero, and the physician **La To** are also honored and worshipped here. The entrance to the temple is through **Tam Quan** (Three Passage) gate on the northeast shore. From there, a striking red bridge arches from the shore to the island. Named **The Huc** (Morning Sunbeam), the bridge is lit up with lights during Tet. Once over the bridge, the temple stands beyond a pavilion and embankment. The sanctuary to Van Xuong is behind the **Hall of the Cult** as you enter. (Open daily 7:30am-6pm; admission 12,000Đ.)

North of Hoan Kiem Lake is the **Old Quarter.** Bordered on the west by the Hanoi Citadel, the labyrinthine part of town stretches up to Long Bien Bridge, which was continually bombed and repaired during the war. The Viet people built villages of stilt houses here 2000 years ago, then, in the 11th century, **Ly Thai To,** the first emperor of independent Vietnam, built his palace. Not long after, the Old Quarter gained a reputation for lovely crafts. Over time, guilds began to form as the Old Quarter became a patchwork of craft communities. Because street-front real estate was valuable and merchants were taxed by the length of their storefronts, the houses were long, thin structures which extended their way deep into the middle of the block. Typical dimensions of such homes can be 3m by 50-60m long and such structures earned the fitting name **tube houses.** These traditional homes still exist today, but are under growing threat from developers. Also in the Old Quarter is **48 Hang Ngang,** where Ho Chi Minh drew up his Declaration of Independence for Vietnam in 1945. (Open daily 8-11am and 1-4pm; free.)

Southwest of the lake stands the former **Hanoi Hilton,** the nickname given to the prison which held American POWs during the war. Bounded by Hai Ba Trung, Tho Nhuom, and Hoa Lo, you won't find much here today except a massive construction project. The former **Hao Lo Prison** was torn down for the construction of a massive five-star hotel and shopping center. One can only hope guests there will receive better treatment.

A block south from the famous prison is **Quan Su (Ambassador's) Pagoda,** 73 Quan Su, between Ly Thuong Kiet and Tran Hung Dao. The official center of Buddhism in Hanoi, this site was a guest house for visiting Buddhist ambassadors. The structure as it stands today was completed in 1942. Inside are many interesting depictions of Buddha, including the Buddha as school teacher. (Open Tues.-Sun. 8:30-11am and 1-4pm; free, but donations asked for at the altar.)

Moving back east down Ly Thuong Kiet from Quan Su is the **19/12 Market** on the left. Five blocks farther down Ly Thuong Kiet, take a left on Phan Chu Trinh. Go two blocks north and look to your right. In the large open square stands the majestic, French-built **Opera House.** Looking like a little piece of Versailles, the off-yellow structure, built in 1911, is less used as a performance center than as an advertising space out front. Inside is a grand theater with box and balcony seats and a two-story stage. Ask the guard at the side entrance to let you in to take a look around. Bring a flashlight if you can (sometimes the guard will provide one) because the theater is unlit inside.

To the north of the Opera House is the **Revolutionary Museum,** 25 Ton Dan. Re-opened in August 1995 after renovations, the museum presents Vietnam's continual struggle for independence, elucidating how 1000 years of conflict with the Chinese, an additional 200 years with the French, and a decade of American-fueled civil war led fatefully and inevitably to the victory of the communist proletariat. Exhibits include artifacts like a guillotine, anti-war banners in several languages, and pictures of protests from around the world saved by the North's wartime propaganda machine. (Open Tues.-Sun. 8-11:30am and 1-4pm; admission 10,000Đ.)

Behind the Opera House and a short distance from the Revolutionary Museum is the **History Museum,** 1 Trang Tien (tel. 825 35 18). Beyond the statue of Ho Chi Minh that greets visitors is the museum's collection of Vietnamese artifacts, labeled only in Vietnamese. Although there are no official tours, it's possible to find a curator to guide you through for a small fee (around 5-10,000Đ). Even if you do it on your own, there are interesting things such as the Dong Son bronze drums and ceramics on the second floor, in addition to objects from the Khmer and Champa civilizations. (Open Tues.-Sun. 8-11:45am and 1:15-4pm; admission 10,000Đ.)

Ba Dinh District

Ba Dinh Square, the site of Ho Chi Minh's delivery of Vietnam's Declaration of Independence from Japanese and French authority on September 1, 1945, and the **Ho Chi Minh Mausoleum** overlooking the square are the principle sights west of Hoan Kiem Lake. The most convenient and interesting way to head out to this area is via Dien Bien Phu. Along the way is a small park with a **statue of Lenin,** one of the few left standing in the country.

Across the street from Lenin's statue is the large **Hanoi Citadel,** comprising a 12 city-block area to the north. Inside its gates is the **Army Museum,** 28A Dien Bien Phu. Built in 1859, the museum presents the checkered history of Vietnamese military might. Out front is a symbolic image of communist superiority over the west: a propped up MiG-21 jet "flies" over the wreckage of a U.S. plane. Inside are relics from the battle at Dien Bien Phu and the tank that crashed through the gates of the Presidential Palace in Saigon. On the grounds of the museum the **Hanoi Flag Staff,** built in 1872, stands 31m tall. (Open Tues.-Sun. 8-11:30am and 1:30-4:30pm; admission 10,000Đ, an extra 2000Đ for a camera.)

From the gates of the Army Museum, turn right and head northwest up Dien Bien Phu toward the **Ho Chi Minh Mausoleum.** After 200m, turn left on the Le Hong Phong and right onto Ong Ich Khiem toward the grassy Ba Dinh Square. No one comes to Hanoi without paying their respects to Bac Ho (Uncle Ho) at his primely situated residence across from the square. With the communist propensity to preserve their great leaders, Ho Chi Minh could not escape his present fate despite his wishes to be cremated. Completed in 1975, the raised, granite structure strikes an imposing figure. Used as a receiving stand for high officials and party leaders during parades and state ceremonies, the complex keeps the well-preserved Ho Chi Minh in the middle of all the action *sans* pulse.

When visiting Uncle Ho, be certain to wear respectable attire: no shorts, short skirts, or tank tops. Be polite and refrain from talking or putting your hands in your pockets. In a room at the top of the flight of stairs lies Ho Chi Minh in a glass case covered up to his stomach with a wool blanket (probably because of the A/C), and his hands folded together on his chest. (Open Tues.-Thurs. and Sat., 8-11am (April-Oct.) and 8-11am (Nov.-March), Sun. 7:30-11am or 8-11:30am, depending on season.) It's closed for one month (usually September) when Ho Chi Minh takes a vacation to Russia to visit Lenin and join him in a relaxing formaldehyde bath.

The exit of the mausoleum leads to the garden behind it. Head north to the **Presidential Palace.** The former residence of the Governor's General of French Indochina, the palace has served as a state guest house since 1954, when the Viet Minh unceremoniously expelled the French. Ho Chi Minh shunned the palace as a residence, believing the building belonged to the people. Instead, he chose an electrician's house on the palace grounds. On the shore of his favorite carp pond, **Ho Chi Minh's residence** is an austere structure which has a meeting room on the ground floor. His personal area upstairs has been attentively preserved, right down to his slippers and book collection. (Open daily 8am-5pm.)

South of the palace and park, past the mausoleum, stands **One Pillar Pagoda,** one of the few structures remaining from the original city. Although one of the most-revered monuments in Hanoi, it's a little disappointing at first sight. Built in 1049, the pagoda is dedicated to Quan An, the goddess of mercy. The heirless Emperor Ly Thang Tong built the pagoda after he dreamed that he saw the goddess, sitting on a lotus flower, hand a boy to him; soon afterwards he was gifted with the birth of a son. (Open daily 8am-5pm.)

Behind One Pillar Pagoda, the huge granite mass of the **Ho Chi Minh Museum** soars out of the landscape. The three stories of the museum chronicle Ho Chi Minh's life and times. Among the highlights is a 1958 Edsel crashing through a wall, a symbol of American commercial and capitalist failure. Many captions are translated into English. Nevertheless, the major themes of the museum are fun to decipher and no big mystery. (Open Tues.-Sun. 8-11am and 1:30-4pm; free.)

Three blocks south of the mausoleum and Ba Dinh Square is the **Vietnam Museum of Fine Arts,** 66 Nguyen Thai Hoc. Despite its diverse collection of silk paintings and ancient sculptures from dynastic Vietnam, the museum is an undiscovered treasure. (Open Tues.-Sun. 8am-noon and 1-4pm; admission 10,000Đ.)

To the north of the art museum, across the street is the **Temple of Literature.** To gain access to the walled complex, head to the south side of the temple to the bonsai-tree laden entrance of the **Four Pillars.** Built in 1070, during the reign of Emperor Ly Thang Tong, the Temple of Literature and National University are two of the oldest vestiges of the history of ancient Hanoi. Once an important Confucian center for the imperial court and the children of mandarins, the complex today takes up the area of two city blocks. The succession of open courts is established by a series of gates, in analogy to the academic experience, passing through each gate as one attains more experience, wisdom, and education. The first set of gates are the **Gates of Talent and Virtue.** The next set heading north are those of letters, which lead to one of the most interesting artifacts in the temple, the **82 Tortoise Stelae** on which the names of the 1306 doctoral laureates from the years 1484 to 1780 are inscribed. Proceed farther into the temple means passing through the **Gate of Synthesis** and into the sanctuary, which houses a colorful statue of Confucius and his four greatest disciples. The Temple of Literature often hosts small rituals and performances of traditional Vietnamese music and dance, and sometimes even water puppet performances. (Open Tues.-Sun. 8-11:30am and 1:30-5pm; admission 12,000Đ.)

To the north of the Ho Chi Minh Mausoleum and Ba Dinh Square lies **Tay Lake,** or West Lake. The location of choice for foreign investors and developers, this area is the front-runner for the site of New Hanoi. The largest lake in the city, Tay Lake covers 5sq.km. The shore of the lake bordering Truc Bach Lake is a popular hangout spot for Hanoi's young lovers.

Trekking out from the city center lets you see the face of Hanoi without the mask of tourism. Spend a relaxing day at **Lenin Park,** the largest in Hanoi, lying 1km south of the train station. Another 1km south down Hwy. 1 (Le Duan) from Lenin Park, right on Trung Chinh, and another 1km on the left is the **Air Force Museum.** Hardly anyone visits this museum, but it has an interesting collection of planes. (Open Tues.-Sun. 8-11am and 1-4pm; free.)

MARKETS AND SHOPPING

Virtually all of Hanoi could be characterized as a public market—street vendors and shops abound. **Dong Xuan Market,** Vietnam's oldest and largest market, is in the north part of the Old Quarter. The French used the market to facilitate tax collection and enlarged it in 1885 with five gates; each one for specific goods. The market was recently gutted by fire. As of August 1996, repairs were nearing completion. **Hom Market,** on Hue, burgeons six blocks south of Hoan Kiem Lake (open daily 6:30am-7pm). **19/12 Market** comprises a city block between Hai Ba Trung and Ly Thuong Kiet just to the west of Quang Trung. It is a frenetic produce market; live chickens and ducks look on as buyers and merchants perform the haggling tango. The produce right at the entrance tends to be more expensive (and of poorer quality) than at the stands deeper within (open daily 6am-6pm).

In addition to these markets, Hanoi's Old Quarter, also known as the **36 Street Area,** is a gold mine of shops with specialized services and products. The names of the streets are believed to have been derived from the original number of guilds in ancient times, when the streets were named after their product, service, or location. A majority of the streets start off with the word *hang* (merchandise). Although most of the streets have been transformed from their original name and function, merchants offering similar products and services still cluster together. **Hang Gai** sells ready-made and tailored silk clothing, embroidery, and silver products; **Hang Quat** originally sold feather fans and silk, and now peddles brightly colored funeral flags and religious objects; **Hang Ma** sells paper products, including votives burned for ancestors; **Lang Ong** emanates the sweet scent of herbal and medicinal products; **Hang Bac** specializes in silver (formerly in metal currency exchange) and has several jewelry smiths; **Hang Dao,** formerly the central silk-dying and silk products street, now sells ready-made clothing; and **Hang Thiec** was and is the street of tinsmiths—you can still hear and watch the smiths pounding out the sheet metal.

ENTERTAINMENT

Travelers to Hanoi will find a dearth of entertainment options in this quaint capital city. There are, however, the **water puppets**—a definite must-see—at Kim Dong Theatre, 57B Dinh Tien Hoang (tel. 255 450), up the street two blocks north of the GPO. Named after the king who was a great patron of the art, the Thang Long Water Puppet Troupe has performed its art in festivals all over the world. Dating back as far as the 1st century AD, this form of puppetry originated in the rice paddies among the peasants. More delightful than the physical movements of the puppets themselves are the individual skits and stories presented. Each has some sort of aquatic theme and funky special effects. (Shows nightly at 8pm; 1½-2hr.; tickets 20-40,000Đ depending on location.)

For simple, mindless entertainment, catch the latest (in Vietnam, that is) movie at **Fansland Theatre,** 84 Ly Thuong Kiet (tel. 825 74 84), next to Saigon Hotel. Operated by a man who loves American films, the small screen here is adequate for viewing movies, but you'll have to bring your own popcorn. (Shows usually 5:30 and 8pm, sometimes with a matinee at 3pm; tickets 5-8000Đ.) Call for a schedule.

NIGHTLIFE

Full-blown communism has left a nightlife scene that is still nascent. When the *bia hoi* runs out, most travelers and expats take shelter in the bars. The more lively head to one of the few clubs.

Centropell Club and Café, 46 Hang Cot (tel. 825 77 73), in the north half of the Old Quarter. Although plagued by karaoke, this is a terrific venue to hear live music. It becomes a romping discotheque as the evening wanes. The ethic here is the appreciation of music and the arts, and the occasional art movies cater to the sensitive and sophisticated. Cover varies. Drinks 44,000Đ. Open daily 11am-2am.

Gold Cock, 5 Bao Khanh (tel. 825 04 99). From Le Thai To on the west side of Hoan Kiem Lake, turn onto Bao Khanh. Walk 20m up and turn right on the small street heading north. The bar will be on the right. The preeminent gay bar in Hanoi, this place is popular among expats and tourists alike. Clientele munches on burgers, hot dogs, pizzas, and salads while slurping their beers (12-35,000Đ). Open daily 4pm-midnight.

The Emerald, 53 Hang Luoc (tel. 825 92 85), up Luong Van Can until it becomes Hang Luoc. It's on your right. A bit o' Dublin in Hanoi. The ale house's luscious wood bar and a couple of pints of Bass will make you forget you're in Vietnam. Pool, darts, and other pub games will keep you busy. Pints 44-66,000Đ (no one said bringing Ireland to Vietnam was cheap). Open daily 11am-midnight.

Tin Tin Pub, 14 Hang Non (tel. 828 71 75). Heading north on Luong Van Can, turn left on Hang Quat and bear right onto Hang Non. Tin Tin is a tiny place on your right. Fans of Tin Tin will be happy to find their pal happy and healthy in Hanoi. In addition to the bottled and canned beers, patrons come for the Vietnamese versions of hamburgers, pizzas, and crepes. Patrons prefer the tofu burger to the bloody one. Open daily 7am-midnight.

Techno Night Club, 2 Nguyen Thai Hoc (tel. 823 15 12), just before the train tracks. A restaurant by day, this dive metamorphoses each night: the orange and black decor gives the impression of being inside a jack-o-lantern. Dance your worries away or drink yourself into oblivion; the colorful psychedelic mural proclaiming "No money, no future, no problem," begins to look pretty convincing after a few bottles of Bass (25,000Đ). Disco open nightly 8pm-midnight.

■ Hảiphóng

Haiphong tourist literature never fails to boast that Haiphong is Vietnam's third largest city and largest port. There's not much else to brag about. Short on tourist attractions, Haiphong receives little attention from travelers on their way to Halong Bay. Back during the war, however, it received somewhat more from American bombers as the gateway to the Red River, lifeline of the north. The Vietnamese merchant marine helped rebuild the port and revitalize the city with an influx of foreign trade, and today Haiphong is a thriving market town with renewed economic optimism.

ORIENTATION

Located 103km east of Hanoi in the Red River Delta, Haiphong has a compact population center with its heavy industry and ports radiating out from there. The city center is a triangle bordered by three thoroughfares, **Dien Bien Phu** (east-west), **Hoang Van Thu** (north-south), and **Tran Hung Dao** (diagonally between the two, to the southeast of their intersection). Dien Bien Phu is flanked with hotels while Hoang Van Thu is lined with eateries. The **GPO** is on Hoang Van Thu one block north of Dien Bien Phu. From the Municipal Theatre, at the intersection of Tran Hung Dao and Hoang Van Thu, **Quang Trang** runs 1km west along the canal-like Tan Bac Lake before ending at the **bus station** and Steel Market. The **train station** is on **Luong Khanh Thien,** parallel to Tran Hung Dao. From the station, head northwest up Pham Ngu Lao, across **Tran Phu** and a grassy common, to Tran Hung Dao. From here, **Minh Khai** runs north to the Dien Bien Phu area.

PRACTICAL INFORMATION

Tourist Offices: Vietnamtourism, 15 Le Dai Hanh (tel. 842 989). Friendly staff offers useful info about the city, trips to Do Sen Beach and Halong Bay, and provides detailed city maps. **Branch office,** 57 Dien Bien Phu. Open Mon.-Sat. 7:30-11:30am and 1:30-5pm.

Currency Exchange: Vietcombank, 11 Hoang Dieu (tel. 842 658). Exchanges currencies and traveler's checks, no fee. MC, Visa, AmEx advances at 4% commission. Open Mon.-Sat. 7:30-11am and 1:30-4:30pm.

Air Travel: Cat Bi Airport, 7km southwest of the center of town. To: **HCMC** (11:30am); **Da Nang** (Mon., Wed., and Sat., 2:20pm); and **Nha Trang** (Thurs. and

Sun., 11:30am). **Vietnam Airlines Office,** 30 Tran Phu (tel. 842 414). Open Mon.-Sat. 8-11:30am and 1:30-4:20pm. Get to the airport by taxi (40-50,000Đ), motorcycle taxi, or cyclo (15-20,000Đ).

Trains: Haiphong Railway Station, 75 Luong Khanh Thien (tel. 846 433), at the end of Pham Ngu Lao. To **Hanoi** (5:55pm, 2½hr., hard seat 40,000Đ).

Buses: Ben Oto Tam Bac, across the street from Cho Sat, the market. Buses run to **Hanoi** (3-4hr., 15-20,000Đ). Buses to Hanoi and other destinations leave from **Ben oto Niem Nghia,** 3km south of Cho Sat on the left.

Ferries: Pier on the Cua Cam River. From the west end of Dien Bien Phu, head north toward the port. Service to **Bai Chay,** Halong Bay (9am, 3hr., 44,000Đ) and **Cat Ba** (6am, noon, and 2 pm, 3hr., 55,000Đ). Purchase tickets at the dock.

Local Transportation: Cyclos (5-10,000Đ) should get you anywhere in the city.

Taxis: Haiphong Taxi (tel. 841 999).

Pharmacies: Hong Bang Haiphong Pharmacy, 63 Dien Bien Phu (tel. 842 926). Well-stocked with necessities. Open Mon.-Sat. 8am-7pm, Sun. 8am-2pm.

Medical Services: Vietnam-Czechoslovakia Friendship Hospital, 1 Nha Thuong (tel. 846 236).

Emergency: Police: tel. 813. **Ambulance:** tel. 815.

Post Offices: GPO, 5 Nguyen Tri Phuong (tel. 842 563), at the intersection with Hoang Van Thu. DHL International overnight service. *Poste Restante.* Telegram. Telex. Open daily 8am-8pm.

Telephones: (tel. 842 005), inside the GPO. Standard overseas rates. Can receive calls and faxes. Open daily 6:30am-9pm. **Telephone code:** 31.

ACCOMMODATIONS

Bach Dang Hotel, 42 Dien Bien Phu (tel. 842 444). Rooms with bath, A/C, and telephone for surprisingly reasonable rates are the reward for tolerating tacky furniture. Cheapest singles 110,000Đ. Doubles 132,000Đ. Twins 165,000Đ.

Ben Binh Hotel, 6 Ben Binh (tel. 842 260), 100m east of the ferry dock. Stumble out of bed to the pier. This pumped-up B&B makes you feel like a VIP. Gated complex—quiet, comfortable nights. Doubles with bath and A/C 115-440,000Đ.

Mini Hotel, 20B Minh Khai (tel. 842 443). Heading east, on Dien Bien Phu, turn right on Minh Khai and go 100m. Split into two complexes, rooms at 20B are better. If these are gone, you're exiled across the street. Modest rooms with mosquito net and fan. Doubles and triples 44,000Đ, with bath and A/C 110,000Đ.

FOOD AND ENTERTAINMENT

The **food stalls** on the corner of Dien Bien Phu and Minh Khai have a good selection of local cuisine. There are also a number of great stalls on Tran Hung Dao. For a restaurant atmosphere, check out some of the eateries that line the segment of Hoang Van Thu between Dien Bien Phu and Tran Hung Dao.

You would think a port city like Haiphong, overrun with sailors and ship captains, would have a plethora of entertainment options. Well, think again. Although there is no lack of sidewalk cafés and small bars, you'll be hard-pressed to find a rollicking time. If dancing is your thing, head to **Trivoli,** 107 Dien Bien Phu (tel. 841 748), which pumps out disco music most nights and occasionally has live music (open daily 7:30pm-midnight; cover 33,000Đ).

MARKETS AND SIGHTS

An enduring symbol of Haiphong, the **Municipal Theatre,** often called the Great Theatre, dominates the center of the city, at the intersection of Quang Trung/Tran Hung Dao and Hoang Van Thu. It was built in 1904 in the style of the Hanoi Opera House, using materials imported from France. The square in front of the theater was the site of a bloody four-day stand-off between French colonial forces and Viet Minh revolutionaries on November 20, 1946. Now a popular hangout for city residents, the square hosts state and municipal ceremonies.

Nearby on Quang Trung, the fine, pagoda-like, four-post **Flower Stalls,** built in 1944, dot the city landscape with vibrant colors. Farther west on the same street is one of the busiest trading and merchant areas in the city. Here, hawker shops flank Quang Trung and its side streets, overflowing with cloth, blankets, clothes, durable goods, shoes, hats, and crafts. At the far east end of Quang Trung on the site of one of the city's most ancient rice markets, the modern behemoth known as **Cho Sat** (Steel Market) rises six stories above the rest of Haiphong. Built in 1992 as a joint venture with China, Cho Sat is a bustling conglomeration of restaurants, clubs, and offices on the upper floors, and a center of trade on the lower levels.

Heading back east on Nguyen Canh, **Tam Bac Lake** is on the left with numerous *sampan* and rafts scattered across on the placid surface. Walk farther about 1km, then turn right onto Linh and take an immediate left on Le Chan. Keep walking to reach **Nghe Temple.** The colorful temple commemorates Le Chan who led the Two Tung Sisters' insurrection against the Chinese and then founded An Bien Village, Haiphong's predecessor. Inside the sanctuary, a statue of the petite yet proudly defiant Le Chan guards the temple. (Open daily 8am-4:30pm.) Le Chan's birth and death are celebrated on the eighth day of the second lunar month and the 25th day of the 12th lunar month respectively. On the eve of the Lunar New Year, throngs pay homage to Le Chan by laying little red sacks of salt on her altar.

Move on south down Me Linh and turn left on To Hieu. Walk 500m down and then make a right onto Hang Kenh. Another km south leads to the **Hang Kenh Communal House.** Wood carvings, statuettes, and icons of worship clutter the rooms of the house. Dragons, gongs, drums, bronze flamingos, elephants, and horses festoon all objects and surfaces imaginable within the walled compound. At its center stands a statue of Ngo Quyen, the legendary liberator and king of Dai Viet (for more details, see **The Chinese Millennium** on page 727).

From Hang Kenh head back up to To Hieu, go east for 1.5km, and then turn left on Chua Hang. On the left, 500m down stands **Du Hang Pagoda** with a well-kept garden and a large bell tower. Built between 980 and 1308 during the Tran dynasty, the pagoda was restored earlier this century. The pagoda houses various mainly bronze artifacts, including bells, gongs, cauldrons, and an ornate altar.

■ Near Haiphong

With Vietnam's mist-shrouded and phenomenal Halong Bay a hop, skip, and a jump away, many people forget that other natural wonders exist nearby. **Cat Ba Island National Park,** a popular destination among backpackers, lies some 50km east of Haiphong, covering over 200 sq.km. This pristine island and its elements, including artifacts dating back 6000 years, remain well-preserved. The park covers most of the island, but a small town and beautiful fine sand beaches grace the south side, the most popular spot being **Cat Co Beach.** The slopes of Cat Ba teem with grottoes, stalagmites, and other attractive geological formations, while the clear waters offer fantastic views of coral and sea floor life. Cat Ba's mountains rise over 300m and primeval forest blankets the rugged terrain. To get to Cat Ba, take the ferry from Haiphong (6am, noon, and 2pm, 55,000Đ). From the drop-off on Cat Ba, a bus will transport you into Cat Ba town (2000Đ).

▨ Halong Bay

Apart from Hanoi, Halong Bay is the chief tourist magnet in north Vietnam. Located northeast of Haiphong, the bay contains over 1500 limestone islands rising steeply from the sea. Halong (Descending Dragon) has long been an area of legend and mystery. One tale recounts the story of a dragon who helped the Vietnamese defeat an invading Chinese fleet. The dragon descended from heaven and spat out divine pearls which linked themselves into a defensive barrier against the invaders. Once the enemy had been turned back, the dragon settled in the bay, converting its scales into a multitude of rocky islets. Both natives and tourists have taken to naming the formations for things they resemble; the French even took to calling one the Mitterrand Rock, and are now looking for a large-nosed Chirac Rock. Despite their unreliability and somewhat packaged feel, group tours are probably the best way to see Halong Bay; independent travelers report paying exorbitant fees for boat rental.

ORIENTATION

Halong Bay is 165km east of Hanoi and can be reached by road from Hanoi or Haiphong or by ferry from Haiphong. Overnight boat tours of the bay's limestone spires include a night at anchor in their midst. Landlubbers can stay in Bai Chay or Hon Gai, which comprise Halong City. These ports are in the northeast corner of the bay and are separated by the strait that connects Halong Bay to **Cua Loc Bay** in the north. In both Bai Chay and Hon Gai, the main road runs parallel to the shore. In Bai Chay, it's a reverse L and has no name. In Hon Gai, the larger of the two cities, the main drag is **Duong Le Thanh Tong.**

PRACTICAL INFORMATION

Tourist Offices: Halong Tourist Company (tel. 846 405), in Bai Chay, just south of the ferry to Hon Gai. **Vietnam Tourism,** 2 Le Thanh Tong (tel. 827 250). Both can arrange tours, and are open Mon.-Sat. 7:30-11am and 1:30-5pm.

Currency Exchange: Commercial Bank of Quang Vinh (tel. 825 297), 1.5km south of the ferry to Hon Gai. All major currencies and traveler's checks exchanged. Open Mon.-Sat. 8-11am and 1-4pm.

Buses: Bai Chay Bus Station, 1km south of the ferry. Daily routes to **Hanoi** (every hr., 5am-2pm, 20,000Đ); **Hue-Da Nang** (Wed.-Mon., 6:30am, 65,000Đ); and **HCMC** (Sun.-Mon., 7am, 110,000Đ).

Ferries: From Bai Chay to Hon Gai (6am-midnight, 1000Đ per person).

Medical Services: Quang Minh Provincial Hospital, 651 Le Thanh Tong, 1km east of Hon Gai GPO (tel. 825 490).

Emergency: tel. 825 486.

Post Offices: Hong Gai GPO, at the end of Le Thanh Tong, in the center of town, 2km from Bai Chay ferry. Open daily 6:30am-8pm. **Halong City Post Office** (tel. 846 417), near the ferry to Hon Gai. Open daily 7am-7pm.

Telephones: (tel. 825 539), international office in the GPO. Receives calls and faxes. **Telephone code:** 33.

ACCOMMODATIONS

Bai Chay houses the more expensive choices and the bargain-basement steals. Good mid-range rooms are in Hon Gai, closer to downtown, but a ferry ride away from the modest Bai Chay beach and the docks.

Bai Chay

Nha Nghi Xuan Huong (tel. 846 418), 1km south of the ferry. Centrally located and close to the water. It ain't the Ritz-Carlton, but you'll spend more time in it asleep than not. Doubles with fans 77-110,000Đ, with A/C 132-165,000Đ.

Nha Nghi Binh Dan, just under 2km south of the ferry. Welcome to summer camp, Vietnamese-style. The hard beds and cold shower outside your room might have you writing home about homesickness, but at least it's cheap. Doubles with fan 55-66,000Đ. Dorms 22,000Đ.

Hon Gai

Nha Nghi Son Ha, 63 Le Thanh Tong (tel. 826 553). Down the street from the ferry, easy to reach from anywhere in Halong City. This small, family-run guesthouse is charming and cheap. Doubles, a few with A/C 88-132,000Đ.

Nha Nghi Huong Giang, 39 Le Thanh Tong (tel. 827 497). Extremely well-kept and friendly, this 3-room guesthouse actually makes you feel like a guest in somebody's house. All rooms have bath. Doubles with fan 110,000Đ, with A/C and TV 132,000Đ. Double suites 165,000Đ.

FOOD AND ENTERTAINMENT

Although Halong City lies on the rich waters of the bay, its food is relatively disappointing. Just south of the ferry dock are several **food** and **bia hoi stalls** where a good bowl of *pho* and a glass of beer comes to less than 5000Đ. Farther south on Le Thanh Tong as it veers east sprawls the **market,** with a variety of seafood to sample. At night, most visitors sit out on the beach snacking on dried squid and beer. Others shake their booty down at the **Top Disco Club,** near Bai Chay Beach.

SIGHTS

Among the principal sites that most tours hit is the cavernous **Dango Grotto.** Carved by thousands of years of sea erosion, the grotto includes three caverns whose entrance is close to 200m above sea level. The monstrous outer cavern can easily hold several thousand people while the central cavern houses stalagmites standing up from the ground like miniature Cham towers. The last cavern is narrow but replete with fresh water year-round. Legend has it that the Vietnamese hid wood here for shipbuilding during their conflicts with the Chinese around the turn of the millennium, hence the name *dango* (hiding wood). Another site is the **Virgin Grotto,** named for a stalagmite figure that resembles a young maiden. This amazing hole winds more than 2km into the island with a showcase of natural limestone sculptures along the way.

If you are not seeing the bay via a tour from Hanoi, check out boat options at the Travel Wharf (1km south of the ferry on the Bai Chai side). To join a tour, purchase a ticket from the small travel booth at the wharf. A four-hour tour runs 55,000Đ per person, leaving when full. Groups can charter their own boat: a wooden ship with a 25-person capacity is around 220,000Đ; steel ships 50% more. The ideal way to cruise the bay is to set sail on a **junk,** although they are hard to find. Tourist cafés in Hanoi offer excursions to the bay.

Halong Bay may be the prime tourist destination in the north outside of Hanoi, but other small diversions await to amuse the landlocked. Those with an itch for sun and sand should head out to **Bai Chay Beach,** but don't expect any killer waves. The limestone islands that so majestically rise out of the water also serve to neutralize it.

NORTHWEST VIETNAM

Although the remote Hoang Lien Son Mountains are rarely a common image evoked of Vietnam, they offer some of the most arresting scenery in Southeast Asia. Rice-covered valleys wind between basalt hills, while mountainous roads traverse majestic passes and shallow fords. The area's waterfalls, cloud-piercing peaks, and impossibly steep cornfields provide a spectacular backdrop to the region's numerous hill tribes. These people, famed for their colorful garments and beautiful jewelry, carry on subsistence agriculture as in ancient times.

Despite the offerings of Northwest Vietnam, few travelers brave the difficulties inherent in visiting this enchanting region. Consequently, it remains relatively uncorrupted by tourism, except for the market settlement of Sapa, where hotels and tourist cafés exist in greater density than in Hanoi. The rewards are difficult to fathom due to the lack of tourist services and the abysmal road conditions. The northwest has long been ignored by Hanoi, and the lack of international phones and banking services are no small hurdle. Neither are the roads, which date back to the days of French colonialism. Saint-like patience in transit, however, pays large dividends in dramatic vistas and warm, colorful people.

Those who wish to travel the entire circuit can strike out west from Hanoi, passing through Son La, Dien Bien Phu, and Lai Chau (a small town where buses going in either direction stop for the night) on the way to Sapa. Alternatively, Sapa can be reached via Lao Cai on some combination of train tracks and pavement.

■ Sapa

The crown-jewel of the northwest, Sapa is a town of stunning landscapes and many cultures. During the week, this market hamlet features extraordinary views of the Hoang Lien Son Mountains, as well as bevies of Hmong women selling clothing. Each Friday, Montagnards from surrounding districts trek to trade at the weekend market. Their arrival coincides with a flood of package tourists, and the town overflows with a multitude of ethnic groups, exotic foods, and brands of cameras. Room rates sky-rocket, and cloth hawkers harass their quarry with unwelcome persistence. On Sunday morning, the pastel-checked Giay join the indigo-garbed Hmong and red-capped Dao to round out the diverse cast. An even greater number of Indo-European ethnicities are represented, but the bulk of these tourists depart by mid-day, leaving the field to the indigenous people and independent travelers.

From Monday to Thursday, when the tide of tourists ebbs to a moderate level, the town doffs its hectic weekend garb and dons some more accessible to the budget traveler. This mid-week lull welcomes those seeking asylum from the muggy, fume-fouled streets of Hanoi. The hill tribes are less active in town, their villages are accessible by hiking down any of several valleys of breathtaking scenery. Today, the impact of tourism is tremendous and the rapid pace of construction currently underway is quickly obliterating all signs of war-caused ruin.

ORIENTATION

Over 350km northwest of Hanoi, Sapa is a town of unnamed streets just off **Highway 4,** 34km west of Lao Cai. From the highway, a road leads to the center of town, passing a strip of hotels, the **GPO** on the left, and the **new market,** near the Catholic church. Shop-lined streets branch off in every direction; the one to the right of the church leads to a **stone staircase** down to the main street. Hotels and cafés line this avenue as well, and 100m to the left is another **post office** where **tourist buses** servicing **Lao Cai** stop. Another set of steps goes from the street down to the plaza where the old market once existed. A new building will be completed in late 1997 and the market will reoccupy this site, abandoning the temporary location uphill.

PRACTICAL INFORMATION

Tours and Travel: Pick up the informative guide *Sapa* at the Auberge Restaurant and Guest House (34,000Đ). This rare gem details all aspects of the town and surrounding area, including the minority hill tribes.

Currency Exchange: Almost all guest houses exchange US$, but at rates about 10% lower than in Hanoi. Traveler's checks can be exchanged at Auberge.

Buses: Tourist minibuses to **Lao Cai** leave in front of the post office branch (6:20am and 2pm, 2hr., 20,000Đ). Buy tickets at the post office 1 day in advance. **Public buses** must be flagged down on Hwy. 4 as they rumble past town. To: **Lai Chau** (7am, 8hr., 30-35,000Đ); **Lao Cai** (6 and 10am and 2pm, 2hr., 10-15,000Đ).

Pharmacies: Two, both next to the GPO. Both open daily 6am-9pm.

Post Offices: GPO, east of the church on the road leading back to Lao Cai, on the right. *Poste Restante.* Open daily 7am-9pm (summer), 7:30am-8pm (winter). A smaller post office, on the street above the old market, is open daily 7am-11pm.

Telephones: Both post offices have overseas service; the GPO (tel. 871 300) is less expensive but has shorter hours. **Telephone code:** 20.

ACCOMMODATIONS

Finding a room in Sapa during the weekend can be traumatic. Guest houses are plentiful, but high demand creates little pressure to provide quality service, and some are dodgy, flea-ridden affairs. Always ask to inspect the room before negotiating a rate; check that lights work, that the shower has water pressure, and settle on a check-out time. Blankets are standard and A/C unnecessary. Rates fluctuate wildly based on demand, but generally rise 20-100% for Fri.-Sun. nights. Those willing to shell out a bit more money generally have better luck at mid-range hotels. **Ham Rong Hotel** (tel. 871 251), past the church from the new market, is one such option. Doubles and triples are available for US$20-25. Budget hotels with the best value are just downhill of the old market plaza. **Phuong Nam Hotel** (tel. 871 286) commands a ledge over the valley. The terrace out back has an unbeatable view and the rooms are clean and reasonably priced at US$6-12. **Son Ha Guest House** (tel. 871 273), around the corner behind the half-constructed market complex, has cheap rooms and is run by a friendly, English-speaking family. The slew of minihotels on the main street vary widely in quality.

FOOD

Local cuisine is hardly spectacular. Fruits such as plums and apricots, however, grow in abundance due to Sapa's temperate climate. **Stalls** in the market serve *pho* and rice dishes, including such delicacies as snake and dog. It's also worth trying the grilled corn-on-the-cob sold by street vendors. Sapa Wine, though neither wine nor a product of Sapa, is the choice spirit for travelers on chilly winter evenings.

> **Observatory Restaurant and Hotel,** on the road to Hwy. 4, just before the GPO. Excellent vegetarian food at rock-bottom prices. Tomato, cabbage, garlic and tofu with rice 7000Đ. Vietnam's best vegetable *pho* for just 4000Đ. Sit outside and keep warm with a bottle of Sapa Wine (12,000Đ). Open daily 7am-11pm.
>
> **Auberge Dang Trung Restaurant and Guest House** (tel. 871 243). Facing downhill on the main street, it's to the left, just around the corner at the end of the street. Tourists come in droves to the 2nd-floor restaurant for the huge vegetarian plate (15,000Đ) and the irresistible banana shakes (3000Đ). Excellent view and a good source of tourist info. Open daily 6:30am-10pm.
>
> **Nha Khach Ham Rong** (tel. 871 254), on the ground floor of the Ham Rong Hotel. The hotel is up the steps near the Auberge Restaurant, from the market past the church. Snake is the specialty (90,000Đ). Killed before your eyes and cooked to order with veggies and rice, one animal serves two. Open daily 1-9pm.

MARKETS AND SIGHTS

The French dubbed the mountains surrounding Sapa the Tonkinese Alps. This 3000-m range certainly has beauty worthy of the name, although it lacks an alpine ecosystem. Phan Si Pan Mountain (3163m), directly across the valley, is the highest peak in Vietnam. It's possible for experienced mountaineers to climb to the summit via a hard three-to-five day expedition, but slopes in this area are deceptively steep and treacherous. You shouldn't set off without a competent guide.

Sapa's main attraction is the **weekend market.** Sapa's market is open daily, but Montagnards are present in their highest density on Saturday afternoons and Sunday mornings. Fruit, grains, and meat are bought and sold and tourist dollars are a commodity as well. The Hmong in particular recognize that tourists can be a source of income, and many arrive in town carrying baskets filled with silver bangles and patterned caps rather than rice. Bargaining is done with the fingers, as most Montagnards' knowledge of western language is limited to the exclamation *"jolie!"*

The **Love Market,** which takes place on Saturday nights, is the equivalent of Sapa's dating scene. The Dao tradition is designed to enable friends from distant villages to meet with some degree of regularity. Both sexes perform traditional songs and dances to impress and entertain their peers. Unfortunately, with tourists filming their every move at the market, it's no wonder that many Dao have stopped coming.

■ Near Sapa

TREKKING AROUND SAPA

Upon arrival in Sapa, some travelers are discouraged by the quality of interaction with the hill tribes, as encounters are generally limited to bartering with cloth hawkers.

Day hikes (ranging from all-day treks to short excursions) into the surrounding villages offer less commercial contact with the hill tribes. Remember to treat these people with respect. Don't go into any home or snap a picture of someone without permission. Going with a guide will facilitate interaction with the Montagnards and reduce their anxiety about dealing with westerners.

The roundtrip to all three villages takes anywhere from four to eight hours, and can be appended at any point by backtracking to Sapa. From Sapa, head out of town past the Auberge Restaurant. Along this road many of the hill-tribe people enter and leave town sporting backpacks or straw baskets. Stalls along the road keep your fuel gauge near full with tea, fruit, and snacks. About 1½hr. into the hike (about 7km), a bridge over the river appears far below the road. After a series of waterfalls and just behind a Hmong homestead, a steep trail leads downhill toward the river and across a foot bridge to the Hmong village of **Lao Chai.** From here, the river downstream leads to the Giay village of **Ta Van,** just past a second bridge. Backtrack and cross this bridge to get back to the main road. From here, it's about two hours back to town or 1½ hours on to the Dao village of **Chai Man.** Prehistoric etchings adorn rocks along the road. The village is across the river and to the left at the fork. The path crosses a waterfall to the village.

To get to villages in other directions, go downhill from the market and follow the path that leads northwest along the valley. On it is one of the old, destroyed French villas built in the 30s. About 10 minutes later, a small path splits off of the main track to the left. After 5km, the main path leads to the Hmong village of **Sin Chai.** If you decide to turn left, you will reach **Cat Cat,** another Hmong village, less than 1km away. Past the village, deeper into the valley, is an old **hydroelectric power station** and **San Sa Ho waterfall.**

LAI CHAU

Lai Chau might be described as a truck stop, expect that most trucks don't bother to shift gears here. Buses do stop, so many travelers get stuck here for the night. To some, this spells welcome relief from the rough strip of mud stretching away in both directions. If you get stuck here, don't despair, as buses will leave the next day to more desirable locales: **Hanoi** (6 per month, 5am, 18-30hr.); **Dien Bien Phu** (11:30am, 4½hr., 15,000Đ); and **Lao Cai** (6am, 10hr.), via **Sapa** (9h., 35,000Đ). For stranded travelers, **Lan Anh Hotel** offers clean triples with bath and simpler doubles with shared bath upstairs. Rates start at US$15 and US$10 respectively, as they exploit their monopoly (50,000Đ per bed). **Hawker stalls** at the back of the station offer light meals, snacks, and beverages.

■ Diện Biên Phu

Having recently been named the new capital of Lai Chau Province, Dien Bien Phu is in the midst of a boom, as state buildings are built to accommodate the relocation. As the site of the disastrous French defeat in 1954 at the hands of Ho Chi Minh's Viet Minh forces, Dien Bien Phu is a popular street name around the country. Despite all this advance billing and storied history, most find there's really not much to the budding city. It just so happens that here French military strategy suffered humiliating defeat, but maybe that's reason enough to visit.

ORIENTATION AND PRACTICAL INFORMATION

Over 450km northwest of Hanoi and just 34km from the Laotian border, Dien Bien Phu is situated in the Muong Thanh Valley. **Duong Be Van Dan,** the main street, runs north-south along the east bank of the **Nam Yum River.** To the west of the Nam Yum is the **battlefield. Highway 12** connects Dien Bien Phu to Lai Chau, and runs north on the west side of the river. The **bus station,** on Highway 12, is adjacent to the main bridge over the river. Buses run to **Hanoi** (5am, 18-30hr., 60,000Đ) via **Son La** (7hr., 25,000Đ) and **Lai Chau** (11am, 4-5hr., 15,000Đ). Passenger vans also depart for Lai

Chau (3-5 per day, leave when full, 16,000Đ). The **airstrip** runs parallel to Hwy. 12 and the terminal is on the left, 1km north of the bus station on the road to Lai Chau. It services flights to **Hanoi** (Sat. and Sun., noon). On the east side of the bridge is a large rotary where meat and produce vendors set up each morning. A **hospital** is located off Be Van Dan. Head south from the GPO about 500m, turn left on the street before the War Memorial, then walk 200m and take the right fork; it's on the right. A **pharmacy** is on the east side of Be Van Dan at the intersection with the bridge. (Open daily 7am-7pm.) The **GPO** is on Be Van Dan, 500m south of the bridge on the west side of the street. It has *Poste Restante* and an **international telephone office** (tel. 825 837). **Telephone code:** 23.

ACCOMMODATIONS AND FOOD

For comfort at a moderate price, try **Dien Bien Phu Beer Plant Guesthouse** (Nha May Bia Dien Bien Phu), 62 Pho Tran Can (tel. 825 576), 400m east of Be Van Dan. Turn at the massive sign next to the War Memorial and Cemetery. Spacious, A/C doubles with hot showers and pastel trim open onto a lovely balcony (120,000Đ). Sample the local brew at the street-side pub. More centrally located, **Cong Ty Xay Dung So 2** is on the right just across the bridge from the bus station. Fairly clean triples with bath, fan and thin mattresses start at 120,000Đ but can be bought for less.

Rice and *pho* can be had along the length of Be Van Dan, and some of the bamboo huts near the GPO offer a wider selection of meals. Protocol is point-and-eat. Both the **market** next to the bridge and the one south of the GPO feature produce hawkers. Fresh crab makes a tasty snack (sold live at 1500Đ for three dozen).

SIGHTS

The main draw of Dien Bien Phu, for Vietnamese and foreign tourists alike, is its military history. To the Vietnamese, the battle was the triumph of self-determination over colonialism. It was the decisive moment that they sent the French packing, and so the Viet Minh thought, won autonomy for a united Vietnam. In the early morning of May 6, 1954, the day before the Geneva Conference on Indochina was to convene, the Vietnamese detonated a charge behind French lines in a tunnel. The explosion signaled the beginning of the Viet Minh's final assault in the two-month siege that forced the French to pull out their second national flag, the white one. In the resulting negotiations in Switzerland, the Geneva Accords of 1954 were hammered out, granting Vietnam independence but dividing the country at the 17th parallel, thus setting the stage for the two decades of civil war that were to follow

To view what remains of the battle, start at the **Dien Bien Phu Museum,** 100m south of the War Memorial and Cemetery on the right. Its grounds are littered with scraps of vintage artillery. The displays inside show tactical positions and photos of the aftermath, but captions are only in Vietnamese. Across the street, just north of the cemetery, is **Al Hill**, the scene of some of the fiercest fighting. In front of the hill, a map shows the locations of a hollowed-out tank, an old bunker, and a war memorial. Around back, on the east side of the hill, is the entrance to the tunnel the Viet Minh dug to get behind enemy lines.

From the hill, cut across the street and through the market to a small bridge across the river to the battlefield. On the battlefield is a mishmash of artillery pieces. In the middle of the field lies **Colonel Christian de Castries' command bunker,** recently restored by the Vietnamese government. The hollow structure offers the imagination an eerie window on the experience of the besieged French soldiers. 100m up the path stands a monument dedicated to the French dead. The French government has done nothing to support this privately-funded project (paid for by a French veteran) and it lies as barren as French colonialist aspirations. (All four open daily 8-11am and 1:30-5pm; admission 5000Đ each, including guide.)

■ Sơn La

Originally a hill-tribe village, this rarely visited town is where the French colonial government once sent Vietnamese dissidents to ponder their misguided convictions. While Son La, for many, is nothing more than a stopover on the grueling but beautiful journey between Dien Bien Phu and Hanoi, this former prison-colony has a subtle charm not unlike Australia's. The infrequent traveler who lingers here will discover hospitable residents, great beer, and an horrific penal history.

ORIENTATION AND PRACTICAL INFORMATION

Son La rests between two high hills, 320km west of Hanoi and two-thirds of the way from the capital to Dien Bien Phu on **Route 6. Duong Cau Trang,** which runs west toward Dien Bien Phu, and **Duong Truong Chinh,** which runs south to Hanoi, meet to form the center of Son La. Running parallel to Truong Chinh to the west, just across the **Nam La River,** is **Duong To Hieu.** Between these two main boulevards is a giant rice paddy. The **bus station** is on the left of Truong Chinh, 100m north of the intersection with Cau Trang and sends buses to **Hanoi** (4am, 12hr., 35,000Đ) and **Dien Bien Phu** (every other day, 5am, 7hr., 25,000Đ). An alternate way to get to Dien Bien Phu is to take a bus to **Tuan Giao** and find connecting service there. A **pharmacy** sits at the intersection of Truong Chinh and Cau Trang. (Open daily 7:30am-7pm.) The **GPO,** on To Hieu, 500m from the intersection with Cau Trang on the right, contains an **international telephone office** (tel. 852 421). (Open daily 6:30am-8pm.) **Telephone code:** 22.

ACCOMMODATIONS AND FOOD

True budget hotels are a rarity in Son La, but numerous mid-range options are available. **Khach San Cong Duan** (tel. 857 244), run by the Son La Trade Union, is off To Hieu. From the GPO, go 500m north and take a left at the small market. The hotel is 200m up on the right. Clean rooms with a pair of large beds, hot bath, and TV are 165,000Đ. Those unimpressed by the view of the mountainous landscape may find solace in the wall paintings of tropical beaches. **Son La Hotel** (tel. 852 702), on Can Trang, 100m east of the intersection with Truong Chinh, is centrally located near the bus station. The balconies sport beautiful views. Basic rooms with two hard pallets and a bath start at 132,000Đ. Quads with bath, TV, and fan are 165,000Đ.

Com/pho shops abound in Son La. The popular one with a blue sign across the street from the Son La Hotel offers hot food with a warm smile. **Thit De,** at the corner of To Hien and Can Trang, serves regional specialties such as goat kebab and roast duck. Don't miss the local brew, Bia Son Duong, which is on tap (1500Đ) at **Khach Hang La Thuong De,** north of the GPO and across the street.

SIGHTS

In Son La, the legacy of colonialism takes the form of an old **French prison,** built in 1908 to hold fomenters of anti-colonial sentiment. Inmates were subjected various unpleasant punishments, including group incarceration in the underground dungeons of the prison. The prison was liberated in 1954 with the departure of French colonial forces. To get to the old prison, head toward Dien Bien Phu from the center of town for about 1km. Along the way, **To Hieu Monument** is on the left, dedicated to the favorite son of Son La. Just 100m beyond the monument, take a right at Khau Ca and head another 200m to the top of the hill. The entrance to the prison itself is down a path to the right of the museum. Best preserved is the dismal dungeon. Upstairs is a small **cultural museum** containing clothing and artifacts of the Black Thai hill-tribe, the earliest settlers of Son La, as well as a photographic history of the prison. A peach blossom tree, whose roots are beginning to displace the stones in the walls around it, serves as the prison's only memorial to those prisoners who died during incarceration. (Both open daily 7-11:30am and 1:30-4pm.)

The hills around Son La are still home to Montagnard settlements which predate the arrival of both ethnic Vietnamese and French. Colorfully dressed hill-tribe women frequent the **day market** 1km north of the bus station on Truong Chinh, as well as the **morning produce bazaar** next to the station.

■ Lào Cai

At the northern terminus of Highway 1, Lao Cai is one of two border crossings into China. A portal for trade between China and Vietnam, the town is experiencing a flurry of construction. The imposing administrative buildings ensure that bureaucracy and red tape keep pace with commerce. Apart from hard-hat jobs, however, Lao Cai has little to offer visitors; most hardly pause before speeding away. Perhaps this explains Lao Cai's unofficial motto, "We're more fun than a root canal."

ORIENTATION AND PRACTICAL INFORMATION

Over 300km northwest of Hanoi, Lao Cai is situated on the Red River on the border of south China. It is where both **Highway 1** and the rail line from Hanoi terminates. The bulk of the city runs along two parallel north-south streets on opposite sides of the Red River connected by a large bridge. On the east side is **Duong Pho Moi Lao Cai** on which the **border checkpoint** is located in the north end. The **train station** is over 2km south of it. Most hotels are on this street near the border station. On the west side of the river is **Duong Hoang Lien** which runs south into Hwy. 1. Travelers should note that if Lao Cai is not entered on their visa as an entry point, 440,000Đ must be paid to change it.

Currency exchange (US$ only) is available at **Nhan Hang Nong Nghiep Lao Cai** (tel. 830 013), on Pho Moi Lao Cai, on the right if heading north, just around the bend from the border. (Open daily 7-11:30am and 1-5pm.) Ground transportation to and from Lao Cai stops at the **bus station** (Ben Xe Khach Lao Cai) just over the bridge on the west side of the river. Buses service **Sapa** (6, 6:20am, and 3pm, 2hr., 20,000Đ) and **Haiphong** via **Hanoi** (2 or 4am, 10-14hr., 50,000Đ). If heading to Sapa, other options include renting a **taxi** (220,000Đ) or hiring a **motorcycle taxi** (55,000Đ per person). Most taxis wait in and around the bus station. The easiest way to get to **Sapa** is to catch a **tourist minibus** (22,000Đ). These leave from the train station each morning and evening shortly after the train arrives from Hanoi. The **train station** is on Pho Moi Lao Cai, about 2km south of the bridge. The **LC2** (6:30pm) and **LC4** (9:40am) depart to **Hanoi** (10hr., 93,500Đ hard seat; scalpers sell upgrades to sleepers). Motorcycle taxis between the station and the border/hotel strip or the market/bus station cost 10,000Đ.

A **pharmacy, Quay Ban Thuoc** (tel. 301 87), lies on the west side of the bridge near the rotary circle. (Open daily 7am-9pm.) The large provincial **hospital** is on the edge of town off Hoang Lien. When coming into town from Hwy. 1, turn right at the first turn after the city road divides. It is a three-story white building on the right. The **GPO**, 200 Hoang Lien, has an **international telephone office** and **fax** service. There is a **branch office,** 13 Pho Moi Lao Cai (tel. 822 003). (Open daily 7am-8pm.) **Telephone code:** 20.

ACCOMMODATIONS AND FOOD

The **Post Office Guest House,** 13 Pho Moi Lao Cai (tel. 830 006), has a variety of options to suit the budget of most travelers. Dorms with fans are 30,000Đ. Doubles with A/C, TV, and bath go for 100,000Đ. Across the street is **Khach San Hong Ha** (tel. 830 007). Food stalls near the hotels serve *pho* or simple plates of chicken or pork with rice. The **market** just beyond the bus station is the place to pick up fruit, snacks, and sweeter delights. A smaller market across from the train station offers fruit, biscuits, and other provisions for the haul back to Hanoi.

CENTRAL VIETNAM

■ Huế

Hue hesitates to surrender to the bustle of the modern world, maintaining the heart of a small city at the core of a large one. Excessively gracious and accommodating citizens welcome visitors to the ancient imperial capital with open arms and a friendly curiosity not found in many other parts of Vietnam. As the spiritual, artistic, and cultural center of the nation, Hue has a rich, storied past and an incredible concentration of impressive sights and ruins.

In the 19th century, under the capable rule of the Nguyen Dynasty (1802-1945), Hue reached preeminence and, for the first time, Vietnam was united under a single court. In Hue, the dynasty established an admirable city. It was not long, however, before the death knell sounded for this brilliant golden age. French ships blockaded and prepared to attack the city in 1833. The Emperor, recognizing the technological might of the French, sued for peace, and Vietnam became a French protectorate. The colonial administration did much to protect the treasures of Hue and preserve its historic integrity, but it was to no avail. Hue became a combat zone during the Vietnam War, particularly during the 1968 Tet Offensive, during which the citadel was constantly taken and retaken by both sides as fighting raged even on the sacred grounds of the Imperial City.

The city dwells not on the memory of this traumatic recent past, but rather on the glory of a more distant heyday. The real Hue, the royal Hue, remains in the quiet, tree-lined boulevards of the old Citadel and the majestic ruins of the Imperial City. The aroma of some of Vietnam's finest food and the melodies of traditional folk music engage the senses and restore to life Hue's ancient grandeur.

ORIENTATION

A little over 100km south of the 17th parallel and 16km inland from the South China Sea, Hue is bisected by the **Perfume River** (Song Huong). On the northwest side of the river is the ancient, square-shaped **Citadel,** within which is the protected **Royal Palace** and **Imperial City** of the Nguyen Dynasty. On the southeast side is new Hue, where the lion's share of hotels, restaurants, and tourist services flourish.

On the Citadel side, **Duong Le Duan/Tran Hung Dao** runs between the river and the Citadel wall. At the center of this side of the wall, just inside the Citadel, is the **Flagstaff of Hue,** which marks the front gate of the Royal Palace and the Imperial City. **Duong Nguyen Trai** and **Duong Dinh Tien Hoang** intersect with Le Duan/Tran Hung Dao and run northwest through the gates of the Citadel flanking the Imperial City on either side. On the southeast bank of the Perfume River, **Duong Le Loi,** the main tourist strip on this side, runs parallel to the water. **Duong Hung Vuong,** the other major tourist drag, starts at the **Trang Tien Bridge,** crosses Le Loi and heads southeast to **Highway 1.** A little farther upstream, **Phu Xuan Bridge** spans the river between Le Loi and Le Duan.

PRACTICAL INFORMATION

Tourist Offices: Tour agencies abound, all offering the same trips for the same rates (1-day tours 165,000Đ, ½-day on the Perfume River 33,000Đ). Shop around for pleasant staff or go on the recommendation of other travelers. **DMZ Tours,** 26 Le Loi (tel. 825 242). The definitive place for tours of the DMZ. Book the tour from your hotel or directly from the office. Open daily 5am-10pm. **Art Tourist Services Centre (ATC),** 44 Le Loi (tel. 824 500), will book plane and train tickets and arrange for car rentals. Open daily 7am-8pm.

Currency Exchange: Vietcombank, 5 Hoang Hoa Tham (tel. 824 629), next door to the GPO. Exchanges all major currencies and traveler's checks. Cash advance on

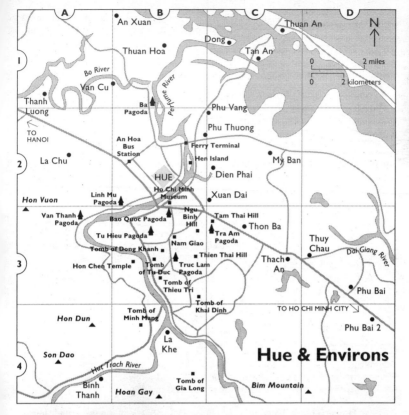

Hue & Environs

MC, Visa. AmEx moneygram. Open Mon.-Sat. 7-11:30am and 1:30-4:30pm (summer) or 1-4pm (winter).

Air Travel: Phu Bai Airport, 10km south of the city off Hwy. 1. Expect to pay 88-110,000Đ for a taxi to the airport (no meters). **Vietnam Airlines,** 7 Nguyen Tri Phuong St. (tel. 824 709), in the lobby of Thuan An Hotel. Open daily 7-11am and 2-5pm. To: **Dalat** (Tues. and Sat. 11:50am, Wed. and Fri. 2:25pm); **Hanoi** (daily, 8:50am and 12:30pm, plus Wed. 9:20am, 99,000Đ); **HCMC** (8:30am and 4:30pm, plus additional times on Tues., Wed., Fri., and Sun.; 99,000Đ); **Bangkok** (Mon.-Wed. and Fri., 8:30am); **Hong Kong** (Mon., Thurs., Sat., and Sun, 8:30am); **Kuala Lumpur** (Mon., Wed., and Fri. 8:30am); and **Phnom Penh** (8:30am).

Trains: Hue Railway Station, on Đ. Le Loi, at the southwest end over the bridge. To: **HCMC** (4am, 26hr., berth, 494-608,000Đ, 9am, 22hr., soft seats 437,000Đ, berths 608-722,000Đ, 11:30am, 24hr., seats 379,000Đ, berths 551-722,000Đ), and **Hanoi** (12:48pm, 17hr., seats 235,000Đ, berths 331-420,000Đ, 4:55pm, 14hr., seats 293,000Đ, berths 407-482,000Đ, 7:46pm, 17hr., seats 255,000Đ, berths 369-482,000Đ). Purchase tickets 3 days in advance.

Buses: An Hoa Bus Station, outside the walls of the Citadel at its northwest corner off of Hwy. 1, runs north to: **Khe Sanh** (5am, 6hr., 30,000Đ); **Dong Hoi** (6am, 7hr., 25,000Đ); and **Hanoi** (5am, 24-28hr., 100,000Đ). **An Cuu Bus Station,** 1km south of the Perfume River on Hung Vuong, primarily serves points south. To: **Da Nang** (every hr., 5am-4pm, 3-4hr., 25,000Đ); **Dalat** (6am, 20-24hr., 150,000Đ); **HCMC** (6am, 36hr., 190,000Đ); and **Hanoi** (5:30am, 24-28hr., 120,000Đ). Purchase tickets for long trips 1 day in advance. The **local bus station** (Ben Xe Dong Ba) is on Tran Hung Dao, on the Citadel side of the Perfume River. Transport to **Thuan An Beach** all day (5000Đ). **Tourist minivans** leave for Hanoi (5am, 15hr.,

$22) and **HCMC** (5am, 20hr., $35). They can be booked (1 day in advance) through hotels or any travel agency. The politely persistent may be rewarded with a discount of several dollars.

Taxis: ATC Taxi (tel. 833 333). Unmetered rides to anywhere within reason. Call 1 hr. in advance to ensure a ride.

Boats: Tourist Boat Pier, 5 Le Loi, next to the Floating Restaurant. Hire a boat for a 1-day tour up the Perfume River to **Thien Mu Pagoda** and the **Royal Tombs** or to **Thuan An Beach** ($10 for a 10 person boat to Thuan An for the day). The **Folk Songs of Hue** boat tour and performance, given rave reviews, leaves every night at 7pm and returns 2-3 hr. later (352,000Đ for 8-person boat).

Rentals: Rent through your hotel or any of a multitude of street corner operations. **Bikes** run 7-8000Đ per day, motorcycles 77-110,000Đ. Compare rates and equipment before going to rent.

Markets: Dong Ba Market, Hue's largest, sprawls along the north bank of the Perfume River, just past the bus station. Activity is feverish daily 7am-7pm. **An Cuu Market** is on Hung Vuong, a block past the bus station. Perched above a small stream, the narrow labyrinth of produce-filled alleys has perhaps the world's highest density of conical hats. Open every morning.

Pharmacies: Pharmacy Hung Vuong, 5 Hung Vuong (tel. 821 225). Carries antimalarial drugs. Staff speaks English. Open daily 7:30am-10pm.

Medical Services: Hue City Hospital, 16 Le Loi (tel. 822 325). Some western-trained physicians. A little bit of English spoken by some staff.

Post Offices: GPO, 8 Hoang Hoa Tham, south of Le Loi. *Poste Restante.* US dollar currency exchange. Open daily 6:30am-9pm. **Train station post office** (tel. 823 109). Open daily 7am-9pm.

Telephones: International Phone Office (tel. 822 000), in the GPO lobby. Receives and sends faxes. Open daily 6:30am-9pm. After hours phone calls possible; inquire. **Telephone code:** 54.

ACCOMMODATIONS

Due to the high density of tourists, there is a hotel, guest house, or mini-hotel every 50m on the southeast side of the Perfume River—and more are on the way. Bargain until you are satisfied with what you are getting and the price.

Guest House Thanh Thuy, 46/4 Le Loi (tel. 824 585), down a small alley across from the Century Riverside Hotel, one of 3 small guest houses. A total family operation. They work hard to make sure their fledgling hotel offers all the creature comforts. Balconies off the front rooms are great for hanging out and soaking in the night air. Clean bathrooms. Ask for a discount for long stays. Rooms have A/C, bath, and some have balconies $8-12. Rooms fill quickly—call ahead.

Truong Tien Hotel, 8 Hung Vuong (tel. 823 127), on the right coming from the river. A backpacker's motel, the bus from Hanoi actually stops next door. Clean 3-bed dorms $3 per person. Singles start at $6. 10pm lockout.

Thanh Loi Hotel, 7 Dinh Tien Hoang (tel. 824 803), just outside Thuong Tu Gate to the Citadel. Across-the-river location grants a little relief from the hordes of touts and cyclo that patrol Le Loi and Hung Vuong. Small, clean rooms start at $6 for a double bed with private bath. A/C rooms $10-15 depending on view.

Binh Minh Hotel, 12 Nguyen Tri Phuong (tel. 825 526). Head down Hung Vuong away from the river and turn right on Nguyen Tri Phuong. A run-of-the-mill hotel/restaurant combo, with fan rooms $5, with private bath $8, with A/C $10.

FOOD

The food in Hue is some of the best in Vietnam. Scores of restaurants filled with tourists and greasy, sterile, fried rice dishes line Hung Vuong and Le Loi. Venture a little farther for more authentic vittles.

Quan Ba Do, 9 Nguyen Binh Khiem. From the Citadel side of the river, head northeast on Tran Hung Dao and across a small bridge. Go straight through the rotary onto Chi Lang and proceed about 1km to Nguyen Binh Khiem. It is 50m up from

Hue-Cool Cuisine

Warning: this copy of *Let's Go: Southeast Asia* will self-destruct if you visit Hue without sampling the excellent regional dishes. Great local favorites include *banh khoai* (a crispy, fried flour-batter folded in half, stuffed with pork, shrimp, bean sprouts, onions, and other fresh, minty greens) and *banh xeo*, which resembles an omelette. Two simple ingredients—rice flour and fresh shrimp—comprise the basis of three other tasty delights: *banh beo, banh loc,* and *banh nam*. Cooking *banh beo* involves pouring water and rice flour into circular molds, steaming until the consistency becomes gelatinous, and then sprinkling dried shrimp and fried onions or rinds on top. In *banh nam*, long rectangular pieces of gelatinized rice flour are sprinkled with dried shrimp and wrapped inside a banana leaf. *Banh loc* uses a whole shrimp, encased in the gelatinized rice flour and wrapped inside a banana leaf. Fish sauce accompanies all of the above dishes. A popular breakfast in Hue—definitely *not* for the squeamish—is *com hen*. This spicy rice chowder, mixed with miniature clams, will ignite if left unattended. Put out the fire and wash down all of Hue's food with Huda, the local brew touted on its bottle as "brewed by Danish technology."

the intersection on the left. Local fishermen bring in baskets of fresh shrimp before sunrise. Throngs pour in all day long craving *banh beo, banh loc,* and *banh nam*. 4000Đ per serving. Open daily 10am-7pm.

Quan Chay, 44 Hung Vuong (tel. 824 081), a block past the elongated rotary on the right. Regarded as the best vegetarian restaurant in Hue. A large selection of dishes available, from rice to soups to small appetizers. Most entrees around 10,000Đ. Open daily 7am-10pm.

Restaurant Vuon Hong, 4 Chu Van An (tel. 821 111). Heading northeast on Le Loi, turn right onto Chu Van An. Open dining patio on the right. Vietnamese dishes with a touch of French influence makes for delicious dining. Most entrees 15-20,000Đ. Open daily 7am-midnight.

Restaurant Huong Sen, 42 Nguyen Trai (tel. 823 201), inside the Citadel. Cross Phu Xuan Bridge and turn left on Le Duan; enter the last gate on the southeast side by turning right on Nguyen Trai. Delicious food, prompt service, inviting atmosphere. What more could you ask for? Give the blood curd with crab a try; you won't regret it. Entrees 22-55,000Đ. Open daily 7am-11pm.

Sinh Coffee, 20 Le Loi (tel. 25 726), in the Hue public library complex. Stop for a delicious fruit shake. Hook up with other travelers and swap stories over flan or ice cream. Mr. Trung Toan, the amiable proprietor, is a knowledgeable soccer fanatic and has good deals for motorscooter or boat rental. Open daily 7am-11pm.

SIGHTS

The ancient Citadel, Imperial City, and Royal Tombs dominate the tourist landscape of Hue. The grandeur of the ancient palaces and tombs captures the undivided attention of nearly all. Trying to see all that Hue has to offer can be overwhelming at first, but renting a bike and splitting up the sights over at least two days will allow you to attack the city's great monuments and find some hidden gems along the way.

The Citadel and Imperial City

Emperor Gia Long, founder of the Nguyen Dynasty, began constructing the Citadel in 1805 with rampart walls made of piled-up dirt from excavations of the surrounding moat. Emperor Minh Mang completed the fortification by bricking the 6m-high, 20m-wide wall and expanding the moat to its current size (4m deep, 23m wide). Today, the massive square-shaped citadel is 10km in circumference, with four gates on its front side along the Perfume River and two on each of the other three sides.

Just inside the Citadel, between the central front gates, the 47-m high **Flag Pole of Hue** is one of the city's landmarks. The tallest in Vietnam, it has been rebuilt several times since its construction in 1807. Opposite the flag pole and outside the citadel, just off Hwy. 1, lies the **Pavilion of Edicts.** Built in 1810, the large square was used by

Gia Long to announce successful candidates of the national exam and declare important edicts. The Emperor Minh Mang is said to have enjoyed watching duels between tigers and elephants staged here.

Across from the flagpole inside the citadel is the **Noon Gate** (Ngo Mon). This is the grand entrance to the Imperial City, a square within the square of the Citadel. Built in 1833, the gate served both as an entrance and a ceremonial enclave called the **Five-Phoenix Pavilion,** which sits atop the gate where the emperor and his court would watch the ceremonial proceedings below. The middle of the three arched entrances to the Imperial City was reserved exclusively for the emperor and even today remains closed to the public, who enter through flanking entrances (foreigners to the left). (Open daily 7am-6pm; admission 55,000Đ.) Behind this, the **Palace of Supreme Harmony**—the spiritual center of the imperial grounds—once housed the emperor's throne. Emperor Gia Long built it in the center of the Imperial City in 1803, but Minh Mang moved the ornate red and gold structure to its present location. The different levels of the courts in front of the throne correlated to the standing of the mandarins (the court's intellectual elite); they were further differentiated with military leaders on the right and the civil leaders on the left.

North of the throne, the Imperial City has suffered both the trials of time and nature and the ravishes of the Viet Minh, who used it as a base during the war. These open fields once housed the grand residences of the emperor and empress. Called the **Forbidden Purple City,** the formerly walled residence area lies on the same vertical axis as the Imperial City and Citadel. The **Royal Library,** on the right when facing north, is one of the few structures still intact inside the Purple City. West of the Purple City are the residences of the Queen Mother and Great Queen Mother. These structures are undergoing extensive renovations with funds from UNESCO, which has declared Hue a World Heritage Site. In the west corner of the Imperial City is **Thien Mieu Temple,** dedicated to Gia Long and his successors. Offerings were made to the small thrones on the altars. In front of the temple squat the **Nine Dynastic Urns,** representing members of the dynasty. Ornate reliefs concerning nature and man are cast into the potbelly sides of each giant bronze vessel.

About 3km west of the Citadel is **Thien Mu Pagoda.** Head west on Le Duan and continue across the train tracks to Kim Long. Situated on a high hill overlooking the Perfume River, the pagoda is dedicated to a legendary 16th-century woman who declared that a time of great prosperity would come if a Buddhist pagoda were built on the site. Lord Nguyen Hoang heard her decree and built the pagoda in 1601. The seven-level tower at the top of the stairs is one of the many representative icons of Hue. The first monk to publicly immolate himself in Saigon during Ngo Dinh Diem's presidency came from this pagoda, and his car is on display as a memorial.

Royal Tombs

In addition to the magnificent Citadel and Imperial City, Hue is home to the tombs of seven emperors of the Nguyen Dynasty. Located a few km outside the city center, predominantly to the southwest, the tombs are accessible by motorscooter or bike. These tombs provided not just noble burials, but also comfortable afterlives. Many of the tombs were the crowning life pursuits of the emperors; each designed his individually. In this way, each tomb represents the expressive spirit of an emperor as well as the architecture of the time, Vietnamese with French influences.

Although the tombs are visually and structurally different, they share certain formal elements. Each encloses a large open court guarded by statues of mandarins, a stele inscribed with the eulogy, and a temple dedicated to the worship of the emperor. (All open daily 6am-sunset; admission 22-55,000Đ.)

Starting from Le Loi, head west toward the train station. After crossing the small bridge, turn right on Bui Thi Xuan. Follow this street along the river for just under 3km and turn left. About 100m on the right is the **Royal Arena,** built in 1830. Similar in size and function to a Roman arena, Hue's version primarily hosted duels between elephants and tigers. Head south from the arena another 2km, and turn left to the **tomb of Tu Duc** (take care not to turn at the first left after 1.5km). Ruling from 1848 to 1883, Tu Duc had the longest—and perhaps most challenging—reign of any Nguyen emperor. The scholarly and literary leader had to face the challenges that European influences, particularly the French, posed to Vietnam's future. Although he had many children, Tu Duc never sired an heir; he often found solace from this misfortune in the fairy-tale construction of his tomb, particularly the island in the middle of the lake. (Admission 55,000Đ.)

Down the street, 500m from the tomb of Tu Duc, is the **tomb of Danh Khanh.** In contrast to his uncle Tu Duc, Danh Khanh ruled only three years, 1886-89. The absence of an outer wall to tie together the tombs of his mother, wife, and himself reflects the incompleteness of his reign. Relatively few visitors to Tu Duc's tomb walk over to this one. (Admission 25,000Đ.) From here, backtrack out to the street that led into the two tombs. Then head south down the road for 1km and turn onto the gravel access road to the entrance of **the tomb of Thieu Tri.** Taking the left fork just before the tomb leads to the tomb of Khai Dinh. Basically abandoned, this tomb has a design similar to that of Dong Khanh's tomb. The caretaker may lavish you with a personal tour. (Admission 22,000Đ.)

Back on the road, head south 2km until you see the boats that ferry passengers over to the **tomb of Minh Mang;** built from 1841 to 1843, it is considered by many to have the greatest architectural balance and poise, in comparison to the other tombs. From the three porticoes of the Hong Mon Gate in front, you'll enter the largest greeting court of all the tombs, filled with stone elephants and mandarins guarding and paying homage to the emperor. Next, three sets of stairs lead to the stele pavilion that bears Minh Mang's eulogy, composed by Thieu Tri. Descending from the pavilion, you'll reach three large courtyards dedicated to Minh Mang and his wife. Opposite these stands the **Minh Lau Temple,** which houses an altar to the king's eternal prosperity and longevity. Over a stone bridge is the tomb proper; look for the large mound of dirt. The bronze circular door represents the sun.

The **tomb of Gia Long** (ruled 1802-20) lies several km from Minh Mang's, so it is best bike there. Follow the road southeast, passing through Minh Mang Village until you reach a tributary of the Perfume River. Cross over on a ferry (1000Đ) and take the dirt path there, which will lead to the tomb. Due to its distance from the other tombs, Gia Long receives few visitors. This mausoleum, built 1814-1820, boasts a courtyard surrounded by a lotus pond and guarded with horses, elephants, and mandarins. A set of steps will take you to the burial chamber where Gia Long and his wife lay in eternal slumber.

Head back on the road from the tomb to the ferry dock and go back across the Perfume River. From there, turn left up the road and, after 200m, turn right toward the **tomb of Khai Dinh.** Constructed on the side of a hill over a span of 11 years, completed in 1931, six years after Khai Dinh's nine-year reign. The last of the tombs to be built, this one has a style strikingly different from the others—it shows great deference to European styles, and many visitors comment on the similarity of its ornamentation to that of France's Palace of Versailles. Here you have to climb a long flight of stairs to reach each successive pavilion and court. At the top of the tomb, a large altar houses a guilded statue of Khai Dinh; this is the only tomb containing a visual representation of the emperor.

From Khai Dinh's tomb, head north up the road until it terminates near the **Nam Giao Altar,** a giant open-air monument reminiscent of a wedding cake. It was here that the emperor made sacrifices to God in supplication and thanksgiving. The three levels represent the concepts of Heaven, Earth, and Man. To get back to the city center, just head north up Phan Boi Chau. Before returning to the city, however, stop at the **Bao Quoc Pagoda;** take a left down Dien Bien Phu and then a right just after the train tracks. Built in 1670, this pagoda sits at the top of the stairs in a quiet sanctuary among the trees. The altar is flanked by classrooms, where monks have been teaching their students for over 50 years.

■ Near Hue

THUAN AN BEACH

The perfect place to kick back between long days of sight-seeing is the beach in nearby Thuan An. Head northeast on Le Loi/Thuan An until it leaves the Perfume River, about 3km north of the post office. The road follows a stream 10km to the beach, past the **Huda beer factory.** The trip takes one hour by bicycle, but can also be made by boat from the pier or bus from the intra-city bus station in **Dong Ha,** near the large market by the east corner of the citadel. The beach is pretty empty on weekdays, but receives a flood of visitors from the city on weekends.

THE DEMILITARIZED ZONE (DMZ)

According to the guidelines of the Geneva Accord following the First Indochina War with France in 1954, Vietnam was divided at the 17th parallel. It was stipulated that a buffer area above and below the dividing line would be established as a zone where no military presence or buildup would be permitted. Ironically, the area known as the **Demilitarized Zone (DMZ)** became home to some of Vietnam's bloodiest fighting. It was also the location of the extensive networks of the Ho Chi Minh Trail, which the U.S. military tried with great effort to detect and destroy in order to cut off the supply and intelligence lines of the Viet Minh. Nonetheless, the McNamara Wall, the military line against the communists, did little to stem the tide.

Touring the area is next to impossible without a guide and proper vehicle, as most of the prominent military sites are spread far apart and there are still **live mines and undetonated shells. Use extreme caution.** Although you can find a guide in Dong Hoi and even in Dong Ha (halfway between Dong Hoi and Hue), the easiest and most reliable way to tour is from Hue, where tour services come a dime a dozen. For the war history enthusiast, hiring a guide is a more edifying and interesting experience, yet not too much more expensive than the packaged tours. Renting a motorscooter is adequate transportation to cover this ground.

The **Ben Hai River** delineates the 17th parallel political division. The **Hien Luong Bridge,** 59km north of Hue, crosses the river and was one of the first transfluminal targets destroyed by American fighter jets. On the north side of the rebuilt bridge is a large concrete spire with the requisite communist star and commemorative date, dedicated to the struggle of war and the reunification. North of the river, a set of winding roads leads to perhaps the most interesting sight in the DMZ, the **Vinh Moc Tunnels.** "Tunnels" is somewhat of a misnomer; Vinh Moc was more of an underground city which, unlike the Cu Chi Tunnels in the south, had less of a direct military purpose. Started in 1966 and finished less than two years later, Vinh Moc was built as the U.S. bombings became increasingly threatening to the area around the village. The 2.8km of tunnels burrow for 25m underground and were dug by hand using a clever system of pulleys to carry the earth out of the excavation. The underground city has walkways high enough for people up to 1.5m tall and 1.2m wide, a maternity ward (where tours are quick to mention that 17 babies were born), and a deep freshwater spring. Small arched chambers line the sides of the passageways that served as family residences and utility areas. During the war, Vinh Moc was a vital supply link to Con Co Island, a strategic Viet Minh stronghold.

Twenty km south of the 17th parallel is **Dong Ha.** On Hwy. 1, here called Duong Le Duan, **Khach Trung Tau Bus Station** runs buses to Hue and Da Nang (every 30min., 6am-2pm, to Hue 20,000Đ, to Da Nang 30,000Đ). 100m south, **Dong Ha Hotel,** 15 Le Duan (tel. 522 92), has an adjoining tour office that works with tour services in Hue (guide 132,000Đ). Guides are also available (110,000Đ per day) at the **Quang Tri Tourism Company,** 135 Le Duan (tel. 529 27).

From Dong Ha, Rte. 9 runs 60km west to Laos. This road was one of the principal highways the Americans used for artillery and troop transport in holding the line against further Viet Minh ingressions south. About 15km west on the highway is **Cam Lo,** where a road heads north to both **Con Thien Firebase,** the site of a fierce battle in 1968 that served as a diversion for the general offensive and uprising of Tet and **Ruong Son National Cemetery,** a memorial to the tens of thousands of soldiers who died in the Annamite Mountains along the Ho Chi Minh Trail. Five km west of Cam Lo, an unpaved road turns left off Rte. 9 to **Camp Carroll.** Now overseen by a state agricultural enterprise, the overgrown camp was once a strategic headquarters for the U.S. military. Another 7km west on Rte. 9 from Camp Carroll stands the **Rockpile.** This large rock outcropping rises from the landscape and was an unassailable (or so the Marines thought, until it was stormed by Viet Minh commandos) helicopter landing pad where essential military supplies like Budweiser were dropped. Another 20km west toward Khe Sanh is **Dakrong Bridge,** built from 1975 to 1976 with the assistance of the Cubans. Finally, 10km from the bridge on the climb toward Khe Sanh is the **Khe Sanh Combat Base** of Bruce Springsteen fame. Site of perhaps the bloodiest battle of the war, this is the base where Marines were airlifted to safety when the U.S. abandoned the outpost; now it is just a barren field of mud.

PHONG NHA CAVES

Queued up behind Halong Bay, **Phong Nha Caves** are perhaps Vietnam's second greatest natural landmark. Vietnam is trying hard to attract more people to this wondrous monument forged by the lithe hands of time and water. The caves are accessible through Dong Hoi, charters (with some negotiation) can be arranged at the tourist office there. Dong Hoi is on Highway 1 and can be reached by bus from Hue (daily, 5-7hr., 18,000Đ) or by train from Hanoi. Transportation to the caves from Dong Hoi can arranged by Tour and Guide Service for 66-110,000Đ per person roundtrip. Admission and a 2-hr. boat trip through the caves is 66,000Đ per person. Be prepared to wait; the boat will not push off until it reaches critical mass. An even better option for touring is offered through the Hue tourist office (275,000Đ one day, 385,000Đ two day).

■ Đà Nẵng

In Da Nang, tourists are not the same point-stare-and-wave-at-the-*tay ba lo* spectacle that they are in other Vietnamese cities. The town overall seems indifferent to their presence and proceeds at its own pace. Perhaps this is because the city has played host to foreigners for so long. In ancient times, Da Nang saw the presence of the Chinese, Chams, and Khmers. Then the French came and renamed the city Tourane. Recognizing Da Nang as an important port, the colonial administration urged its settlement in the early 1900s. A decade after the expulsion of the French, an amphibious operation by the U.S. military washed up on Da Nang's shores to secure the nearby airfield. For the next 10 years, the city was a principal base of American military operation, and nearby China Beach became the celebrated R&R spot for men fighting near the 17th parallel. Today, an assortment of foreigners are back in Da Nang doing business or just visiting. But, as usual, it doesn't matter to the locals.

ORIENTATION

Almost at the dead center of Vietnam, some 750km south of Hanoi and 990km north of Ho Chi Minh City, Da Nang lies on the **Han River,** protected from the South China Sea by **Da Nang Bay.** The main thoroughfares of the city generally run north-south along the river. **Duong Bach Dang** runs one way north along the east bank of the river while one block inland, **Duong Tran Phu** runs south. Another three blocks east is **Duong Phan Chu Trinh,** a two-way street parallel to Bach Dang and Tran Phu. These three main streets are intersected by **Duong Dien Bien Phu/Ly Thai To/Hung Vuong,** the east-west boulevard which spurs off from Hwy. 1 and dissects the city into northern and southern halves. Although these streets effectively provide a grid in which to easily navigate the city, pick up a tourist map from newsstands along the river; the irregular networks of tributary streets can be confusing.

PRACTICAL INFORMATION

Tourist Offices: Da Nang Tourist, 92A Phan Chu Trinh (tel. 823 660). Helpful office with good info on local attractions like Marble Mountain, China Beach, and Hai Van Pass/Lang Co Beach. Open Mon.-Sat. 7-11:30am and 1-4:30pm.

Embassies and Consulates: Laos, 7 Tran Quy Cap (tel. 821 208). Tourist visas to cross the border at **Lao Bao** take 1hr. to process; fees vary by nationality. Open Mon.-Sat. 8-11:30am and 2-4:30pm.

Currency Exchange: Vietcombank, 104 Le Loi (tel. 822 110), exchanges major foreign currency and traveler's checks. MC, Visa, and AmEx Moneygram. Open Mon.-Sat. 7:30-11am and 1-4pm.

Air Travel: Da Nang International Airport (tel. 826 394), 3km from the city center. **Vietnam Airlines,** 35 Tran Phu (tel. 827 286), has flights to major cities in Vietnam. Open daily 7:30-11am and 1:30-4:30pm. To **Hanoi** (988,000Đ); **HCMC** (988,000Đ) and **Nha Trang** (549,000Đ). Schedules subject to change. Also to: **Bangkok, Hong Kong, Kuala Lumpur, Phnom Penh,** and **Singapore**.

Trains: Da Nang Railway Station, at 4 Hai Phong (tel. 823 810). To **HCMC** (daily #S1 noon, S3 3pm, and S5 7:50am) and **Hanoi** (#S2 2pm, S4 4:30pm, and S6 9am). Local trains run to **Hue** (6am, 2:30pm, 54,000Đ). Ticket office open daily 6am-5pm. Cyclos to the train station cost 5000-10,000Đ.

Buses: Lien Tinh Station, 33 Dien Bien Phu (tel. 821 265), 2km west of the city toward Hwy. 1, 500m past 29/3 Park. To: **Dalat** (5am, 18-20hr., 167,000Đ); **Dong Hoi** (7am, 8-10hr., 15,000Đ); **Haiphong** (5am, 28hr., 173,000Đ); **Hanoi** (5am, 24hr., 170,000Đ); **HCMC** (4, 4:30, 5, 5:30, 6, and 7am, 36hr., 212,000Đ); **Hue** (every 90min., 6am-2pm, 4hr., 30,500Đ); **Nha Trang** (5am, 14hr., 117,500Đ); **Quy Nhon** (6am, 10hr., 11,000Đ); and **Thanh Hoa** (5am, 20hr., 146,000Đ). Buy tickets to Hanoi and HCMC 1 day in advance. **Minibus** travel in Toyota minivans is more comfortable but more expensive. A **private minibus chartering service,** 111 Le Loi (tel. 828 205), can accommodate your needs. Vehicles run to all destinations listed above. All leave at 5am from in front of the ticket office. Purchase tickets (176-352,000Đ) as far in advance as possible. There is also another private minibus company on 93 Le Loi (tel. 825 136) with daily service to: **Hue** (46,000Đ); **Nha Trang** (122,000Đ); **HCMC** (255,000Đ); **Quy Nhon** (110,000Đ); and **Savannakhet,** Laos (255,000Đ).

Ferries: Ben Pha Da Nang, 9C Bach Dang (tel. 821 528), just south of the Hung Vuong intersection. Regular ferries go across the Han River (500Đ) to the shanties and fishing villages of Da Nang. Open daily 4:30am-10pm.

Local Transportation: Cyclos offer rides all over town, and some motorcycle taxis compete for fares. Getting anywhere around town should never exceed 10,000Đ. **Taxis** are easiest to obtain by booking through hotels. Bike and motorbike rentals available at most accommodations.

Rentals: Tram Du Lich, 69 Le Loi (tel. 824 451), rents 4-seat (242,000Đ per day) and 12-seat (297,000Đ per day) vehicles with driver to nearby places: China Beach, Marble Mountains, Hoi An, and My Son. Also sells tickets to Hue for 66,000Đ (daily departure). **Motorscooters** can be rented at the Danang Hotel.

Markets: Cho Han, at the intersection of Hung Vuong and Tran Phu. Open 6:30am-7pm. A large outdoor **produce market** is just south of Cho Han on Bach Dang. Massive **Cho Con,** at the corner of Hung Vuong and Ong Ich Kiem, lies in one of the busiest parts of town. Open daily 7am-7pm.

Pharmacies: Pharmacy Nghia An, 16 Phan Chu Trinh (tel. 825 660). Open daily 7am-9pm.

Medical Services: Da Nang Hospital, 74-76 Haiphong (tel. 822 118).

Emergency: tel. 14.

Post Offices/Telephones: GPO, 60 Bach Dang (tel. 238 81), just north of the intersection with Hung Vuong. Open daily 6am-10pm. **International phone office** inside. Closes 30min. before the post office. Pick up *Poste Restante* at the **international post office** at 62 Bach Dang. **Telephone code:** 51.

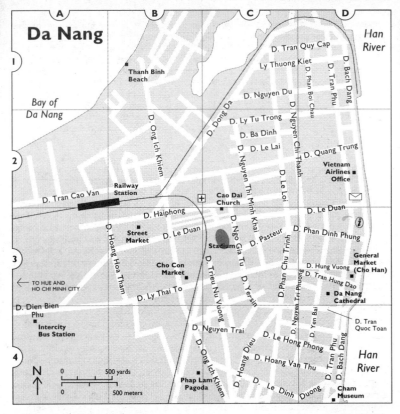

Da Nang

Bay of Da Nang

Han River

Thanh Binh Beach

D. Ong Ich Khiem

D. Dong Da

D. Tran Quy Cap

Ly Thuong Kiet

D. Nguyen Du

D. Ly Tu Trong

D. Ba Dinh

D. Le Lai

D. Bach Dang

D. Tran Phu

D. Phan Boi Chau

D. Nguyen Chi Thanh

D. Quang Trung

Vietnam Airlines Office

D. Tran Cao Van

Railway Station

Cao Dai Church

D. Haiphong

D. Le Duan

Street Market

D. Le Duan

D. Hoang Hoa Tham

D. Nguyen Thi Minh Khai

D. Ngo Gia Tu

Stadium

D. Pasteur

D. Le Loi

D. Phan Dinh Phung

D. Le Duan

General Market (Cho Han)

Cho Con Market

D. Trieu Nu Vuong

D. Yersin

D. Phan Chu Trinh

D. Hung Vuong

D. Tran Hung Dao

Da Nang Cathedral

← TO HUE AND HO CHI MINH CITY

D. Ly Thai To

D. Dien Bien Phu

Intercity Bus Station

D. Nguyen Trai

D. Hoang Dieu

D. Le Hong Phong

D. Nguyen Tri Phuong

D. Yen Bai

D. Tran Phu

D. Bach Dang

D. Tran Quoc Toan

Han River

D. Ong Ich Khiem

D. Hoang Van Thu

D. Le Dinh Duong

Phap Lam Pagoda

Cham Museum

N

0   500 yards

0   500 meters

ACCOMMODATIONS

Mini Hotel Thuan An, 14 Bach Dang (tel. 820 527), is a small, family-run operation. Near the northern terminus of Bach Dang, this hotel retains its quiet charm, but remains close enough so that the city is accessible by foot. Watch the fishing boats and *sampan* glide on the Han River from your room. Doubles with bath and fan 88,000Đ, with A/C 155,000Đ.

Thanh Thanh Hotel, 50 Phan Chu Trinh (tel. 821 230), near the Danang Cultural Theatre. 53 rooms of wondrous joy play host to numerous tourists and businessmen alike. Doubles with bath and fan 110-122,000Đ, with A/C 155-339,000Đ.

Thuy San Hotel, 12 Bach Dang (tel. 835 005), just past the Thuan An Hotel. "Thuy San" means seafood—an odd name for a hotel, even in a port city. In truth, the hotel is owned by a state-run seafood export company (don't worry, they fish somewhere else). Very good value for the money. Doubles with A/C, hot water, and TV 155,000Đ. Large rooms with attached living room 220,000Đ.

Danang Hotel, 3-5 Dong Da (tel. 823 258), at the far northern end of town. This relic from the war years is today a haven for Vietnamese tourists. Rooms cluster together with four individual rooms radiating off a shared common room. All rooms with A/C and bath. Singles 66,000Đ. Doubles 88,000Đ. Triples 110,000Đ. Larger rooms 132-165,000Đ. Rooms in the adjacent but much ritzier **Da Nang I** start at 255,000Đ.

FOOD

Nha Hang Vietnam, 25-27 Ly Tu Trong (tel. 823 845). Throngs of people, tourists and locals alike come here to enjoy a meal. Offers a wide selection of basic Vietnamese dishes. If you're in the mood for steamed rice and traditional side orders, this is one of the best economical bets in the city. Large crowds at night. Valet parking for your motorscooter. Entrees 11-33,000Đ. Open daily 7am-11pm.

Nha Hang Thoi Dai, 5 Bach Dang (tel. 826 404). Also called the "Modern Restaurant," it spreads the sweet scents of Vietnamese cuisine along the banks of the Han. Particularly crowded at breakfast and lunch. Wide selection of local seafood specialities. Most dishes 20,000Đ for a generous portion. Open daily 7am-11pm.

Song Xanh, 179 Tran Phu (tel. 820 051). This ice cream shop/café serves Vietnamese versions of universal delights. Its special selection of yogurts (or, as the Vietnamese say, *yaourt*) is a great sampler of local flavor. Will also dish up luscious plates of fresh fruit and other local sweets. If that's not enough, tell them to crank up the karaoke. Open daily 6:30am-10pm.

SIGHTS

There is little in the way of sights in Da Nang, but it does boast Vietnam's premier museum of Cham artifacts collected from the 7th to 15th centuries. Built in the style of Cham architecture, the **Cham Museum,** 1 Tieu La (walk southward down Tran Phu or Bach Dang) is, for good reason, the most visited tourist attraction in Da Nang. Founded in 1915 by the French School of the Orient, the small museum houses a collection of Cham sandstone carvings. Cham art, throughout its evolution, reflects elements from all over Southeast Asia; Indonesian art figured prominently in its early phases while Khmer art influenced its latter phase. Guides are available. An informative guidebook, *Museum of Cham Sculpture—Danang,* can also be purchased (15,000Đ). (Open daily 6am-6pm; admission 20,000Đ.)

A block west of the museum stands an elegant yellow-orange pagoda known as **Tam Bao Pagoda,** 253 Phan Chu Trinh. Built in 1953, this towering combination of French, Chinese, and Cham architectural styles has five tiers, which represent the steps in the ascension to heaven. North from here, six blocks over on Tran Phu, is the **Danang Cathedral,** built in 1923 to serve the French Catholic community. More commonly referred to as the "rooster cathedral" by locals due to the weathercock atop the cross on the steeple, this massive, unbuttressed white church is well-preserved and cuts an imposing figure against the sky. Masses are held daily at 5am and 5pm, Sunday Mass at 6am and 4:30pm.

Cut back over to Phan Chu Trinh and head north to get to the **Danang Cultural Theatre,** where large concerts and special performances are often held. Three blocks farther north up this street (Phan Chu Trinh changes its name to Le Loi along the way), turn left at Haiphong. On the right after two blocks and across the street from Da Nang Hospital is the **Cao Dai Temple.** Built in 1955, this is the largest Cao Dai structure outside of its site of origin. The two gates for entering the complex are reserved for either sex—the left one for women, the right for men. The entrance to the temple is organized similarly, with a center door reserved for priests of the church. Inside the temple, prayer services are conducted daily at 6am, noon, 6pm, and midnight. A simple sentence epitomizes this seemingly odd combination of deities: "All religions have the same source."

ENTERTAINMENT

Christie's Harbourside, 9 Bach Dang (tel. 826 645), on the river south of the Hung Vuong intersection. This place moves like a butterfly and stings like a bee. Bob Christie, the New Zealand proprietor, just wants his visitors to be comfortable, well-fed, and laden with beer. Along with beers (33,000Đ) and cocktails (55,000Đ), this bar and grill also serves up burgers, pasta, and steak imported from Australia. If that isn't enough, there's a satellite TV. Open daily 11am-11pm.

VIP Club, 11C Quang Trung (tel. 823 295). Home of the rich, famous, and cool of Da Nang. Ever hip, ever bad, and always stylish. If you've got clubbing gear, live it up. Otherwise suffer the stares, you poorly dressed backpacker. Cover 33,000Đ. Mixed drinks 50,000Đ and up. Open daily 8pm-2am.

■ Near Da Nang

CHINA BEACH

China Beach is famous for two reasons: U.S. troops landed here during the Vietnam War, and the TV series of the same name was a post-M.A.S.H. hit. Today the beach makes a great daytrip from either Da Nang or Hoi An, but don't expect to run into any Dana Delaney look-alikes. You'll find few foreigners here and even fewer Vietnamese, though the new **Non Nuoc Resort Hotel** complex (tel. 836 216) has been constructed in the hopes of luring another wave of invaders to the area. The hotel offers everything a good resort should: taxi service, lockers on the beach, tennis courts, dance hall, and souvenir shops, to name a few. Rooms start around 330,000Đ, and services are priced for a foreign clientele (read: high). There should be no need to stay here overnight, however, since the beach is so close to the larger cities. Rent a motorbike and drive yourself. The clean, wide, quiet beach is perfect for an afternoon's repose and a dip in the ocean; stone benches and tables shaded by small thatched roofs can shield you from the sun. You will be required to pay an access fee for the beach as well as some nominal charges for your vehicle (should be less than 11,000Đ total).

MARBLE MOUNTAIN (NGU HANH SON)

Marble Mountain, 17km north of Hoi An and 12km south of Da Nang, has a setting straight out of an adventure flick. The mountain gets its name from—you guessed it—the marble and limestone quarries that cluster at the base. The huge, naturally hollowed caves, winding paths punctuated with carved icons and breathtaking views combine to form a worthwhile daytrip from either of the two bigger cities. Originally Cham people lived here; in the 19th century, Emperor Minh Mang made this place one of his retreats. Even more recently, the mountain served as a base for the Viet Cong; when U.S. troops found out, they bombed the site heavily.

Climbing 123 steps leads to the **Linh Ung Pagoda,** which is decorated with mosaics of bottle and ceramic pieces. The Buddha inside brings luck and talent, but people also come here to pray for children of a certain sex. On this level of the path there is also a square stone platform on which, according to legend, fairies and gods used to play checkers. The path continues up through natural rock arches, and niches along the way reveal Buddha statues—sometimes carved directly out of the living rock and still a part of the mountain. Sixty steps up from the Linh Ung Pagoda is the **Vong Hai Dai** (Simply Stunning Sea View). Squeeze past the photo-happy Vietnamese tourists on a clear day to catch a glimpse of the ocean.

A mere 58 steps later is the **main cave.** The four rather cartoonish warrior statues guarding the entrance of the cave date from Emperor Minh Mang's time, and are intended to protect the cave from evil spirits. The ceiling in this cathedral-like cavern is 15m high. Two bridges flank the entrance of the cave. **Cau Duyen** (Happiness Bridge), the one on the right of the entrance, is thought to bring happiness to married couples. Behind the bridge is a small cave where childless couples go to pray for fertility. Similarly, people come to pray at the altar next to **Cau Lok** (Luck Bridge) for luck and prosperity. Just before Cau Lok, there is a small hole in the stone; reach in to where you can hit a drum, and then see if you can figure out what makes the noise. Behind both of the bridges are the Marble Mountain Rorschach Tests: locals claim that you can see an ostrich and an elephant carved into the cave's wall by running water. If you fail that test, you can't miss the five-meter Buddha carved high into the wall at the far end of the cave. One of the chambers here has stairs leading to a lookout perch known as Dong Van Thong (The Way to the Clouds), but *Let's Go* does not recommend trying to ascend to heaven from here. (Marble Mountain open 6am-6pm; admission 10,000Đ.)

▌Hôi An

In a country which has seen so much of its cultural heritage laid waste by numerous wars, the superb state of preservation of this "ancient town" is not just unique, it's extraordinary. Strolling along the town quay at dawn, visitors will encounter Chinese merchants opening their doors for business as they have for two centuries, as well as ships gliding through the morning mist.

Hoi An's beauty and laid-back pace of life have made it one of the most popular tourist destinations in Central Vietnam, so much so that, according to the locals, during the high season foreigners outnumber Vietnamese on the streets by a hefty margin. From the 16th to the 19th centuries, Hoi An (known to Europeans as Faifo) was a bustling port frequented by Chinese, Japanese, and European traders and it was in Hoi An that Jesuit missionaries first began proselytizing among the Vietnamese. But it was the Chinese who, more than any other group, have left a lasting impression on the town. Hailing from places like Quang Dong (Canton), Hai Nam, and Phuc Kien (Fukien), they constituted a large percentage of the population until the late 1970s, when many of them fled the country. Today only about 1000 remain, but the ornate pagodas and meeting halls built by their ancestors are surely some of the most impressive architectural relics in Vietnam.

ORIENTATION AND PRACTICAL INFORMATION

This small, ancient town unfurls on the north banks of the **Thu Bon River,** which then divides into smaller tributaries just west of Hoi An. One main street curves along the river; it starts out from the west as **Duong Nguyen Thi Minh Khai,** then morphs into **Duong Bach Dang** between two bridges, and finally a third time into **Duong Phan Boi Chau. Duong Tran Phu,** the next major street over, is lined with pagodas and ancient Chinese houses. Two main thoroughfares cut through these streets: **Duong Le Loi/Nguyen Truong To** and **Duong Hoang Dieu,** the latter of which extends into a bridge over Thu Bon.

The Hoi An **tourist office** is in the Hoi An Hotel complex, 6 Tran Hung Dao (tel. 861 362). The staff offers other typical tourist services. **Exchange currency** at any hotel, the post office, or the **bank,** 4 Hoang Dieu (tel. 861 340). (Open daily 7-11:30am and 1:30-4:30pm.) Trains do not stop here but there is a **bus station** (tel. 861 284) on the west edge of town on Phan Chu Trinh runs between the two towns. (Open daily 5am-6pm.) Frequent buses to **Da Nang** (1hr., 15,000Đ) are slow and uncomfortable but much cheaper than private minibuses. Check with the Vinh Hung Hotel for information on **minibuses.** Slightly cheaper **motorbike** and **car rentals** are across the street from the Hoi An Hotel with Six Brothers Transportations Service, 15 Tran Hung Dao (tel. 615 18). Proprietor Hieu also leads tours in English. Bikes cost 5000Đ per day, motorbikes 55,000Đ per day. The **market** is at the intersection of Nguyen Hue and Bach Dang. The **post office** (tel. 861 167) is on Tran Hung Dao just past the right of the Hoi An Hotel. (Open daily 6:30am-9:30pm.) **International calls** can be placed here. **Telephone code:** 51.

ACCOMMODATIONS

Hoi An's newly acquired status as a prime-time tourist destination has led to a five-fold increase in the number of hotels over the last year. Unfortunately for backpackers, however, even a basic double with fan can run 110-155,000Đ.

Hoi An Hotel, 6 Tran Hung Dao (tel. 861 362). Several renovated buildings make up this gigantic complex. Owned by the Hoi An Tourist Service Company, its monopoly is now being challenged by smaller hotels. Features immaculate, modern rooms, attentive service, and all the amenities of a 4-star hotel. Singles with fan 80-120,000Đ. Doubles 110-200,000Đ, with A/C 250-330,000Đ.

Cong Doan Hotel, 50 Phan Dinh Phung (tel. 861 899), west of the intersection with Nhi Trung. Operated by the local labor union, the rooms are about as proletarian as pricey Hoi An gets. Very clean, freshly painted doubles with hot water and fan 133-155,000Đ (110,000Đ low season); with A/C 188-210,000Đ (133-155,000Đ low season).

Thuy Duong Hotel 2, 68 Huynh Thuc Khang (tel. 861 394), between a Cao Dai temple and the bus station. A pleasant budget-traveler oriented hotel; the only drawback is the 1-km hike into town. Rooms with fan 110-188,000Đ, with A/C 210-255,000Đ. Also a location at 11 Le Loi (tel. 861 574).

Thanh Binh Hotel, 1 Le Loi (tel. 861 297). You can't miss the hot-pink stucco. Freshly painted interior with tile floors can get a bit noisy, but the price leaves little room for complaint. Immaculate doubles with fan and hot water 122-155,000Đ, with A/C 220-255,000Đ.

Thien Trung Hotel, 63 Phan Dinh Phung (tel. 861 720), at the western edge of town, just past the Cong Doan Hotel on the left. Gorgeous new whitewashed villa has 2 stories of clean rooms. Open interior courtyard with fountain can be noisy. Travelers often gather at the small restaurant/café to socialize and exchange travel tips. Doubles and triples with fan 155-210,000Đ, with A/C 255-310,000Đ.

FOOD

The specialty of Hoi An is *cao lau,* a soup containing rice noodles made with special water found only in a local well. Prices tend to be low and portions generous. Bach Dang is lined with several eateries. Most establishments are open daily 6am-10pm.

Han Huyen Floating Restaurant (tel. 861 462), on Bach Dang just before the covered Japanese Bridge. Sit inside or outside this wooden hut while enjoying a view of the river and daily Vietnamese life. Tourists rave about the food and you'll see why: excellent service, rock-bottom prices, a huge selection, and meals all run less than 20,000Đ. Savory stewed duck 18,000Đ.

Restaurant Cao Lau, 42 Tran Phu. Guess what their main dish is? Packed to the gills every morning with locals setting their daily *cao lau* fix, but don't worry, the cheery proprietor will squeeze you in. *Cao lau* and a pot of coffee run 7000Đ.

Café Can, 74 Bach Dang (tel. 861 525). The riverside location has potential for a much more romantic ambiance, but the café is not as charming as one might hope. The menu is obviously geared toward foreigners, and offers western-style drinks and vegetarian dishes. Try the set seafood menu for 35,000Đ.

Huong Xuan Restaurant, 8 Le Loi (tel. 861 498). Their location opposite Hoi An Pagoda and two hotels assures a foreign clientele. Clean and spacious interior. One page of the menu is devoted to local specialities with a detailed English description. Good food, cheap prices (10-20,000Đ).

SIGHTS

The state recently instituted a new admission policy for touring Hoi An's many historic sights. Every visitor now must purchase a 50,000Đ ticket (available at whatever sight you happen to visit first) which gives access to one old home, one assembly, and the museum. All additional sights are 10,000Đ. One of the first things seen in town is the **Japanese Covered Bridge,** at the west end of Tran Phu. The bridge is believed to have been built by the Japanese in the 16th century, although no documentation exists to support this.

The **Phung Hung Home,** 4 Nguyen Thi Minh Khai, was built over 200 years ago and has housed eight generations of the Vietnamese Phung Hung family. Inside visitors will find a mixture of Chinese, Vietnamese, and Japanese architectural styles, along with 80 ironwood columns, yin-yang tiles on the ceiling, and a stunning assortment of Vietnamese furniture. The square opening in the ceiling was originally for storing trade goods in case of floods. (Open daily 7:30am-6pm.)

The most well-known historical home in Hoi An is unquestionably **Tan Ky Old House,** 101 Nguyen Thai Hoc (tel. 861 474). It also holds the distinction of being the first private house to be recognized by the Ministry of Culture for its historical and cultural value. Tan Ky was built nearly 200 years ago and has seen seven generations of happy Chinese. Wooden columns with marble bases support the interior, while the exterior bricks and tiles keep the house cool in the summer and warm in the winter. The house is also famous for its curved "crabshell" ceiling design (they claim the wood ceiling beams look like a crabshell; you make the call). Family members can show you heirlooms from great-grandfather's time. (Open daily 8am-noon and 2-5pm; admission 2000Đ.)

Phuoc Kien Pagoda, 46 Tran Phu, is a 300-year-old temple built by the Fukien *kongsi,* one of Hoi An's four prominent clans. It's the biggest pagoda in Hoi An. An ornate pink and green gate in the courtyard opens to the pagoda. In a glass box on the altar sits fat lady Thien Hau Thanh Mau, goddess of the sea and protector of sailors. She's very popular in Hoi An; a mural to the right of the entrance depicts Her Largeness rescuing a sinking vessel. (Open daily 6:30am-6pm; admission 10,000Đ.)

Continuing down this lane of pagodas leads to **Guangdong Assembly Hall/Pagoda,** 176 Tran Phu, (tel. 861 736), which can effectively satisfy any urges you have for the color red. This spate of ruddiness is typical of pagodas in Guangdong, China, even up to the happy, red-faced Buddha inside. The pagoda was built in the early 18th century, and has undergone four name changes since. Like the Phuoc Kien Pagoda, it is dedicated to the worship of our large lady Thien Hau, and once specialized in helping sick and unfortunate sailors. (Open daily 7:30am-5pm; admission 10,000Đ.) **Hai Nam Pagoda,** 110 Tran Phu, commemorates the 108 merchant-sailors from Hai Nam Island who were mistakenly executed by the king in 1851; he thought they were traitors. (Open 6am-noon and 1-8pm; free.)

Quan Cong Mieu or **Ong Pagoda,** 24 Tran Phu, is actually two pagodas built back-to-back. The Quan Cong and Quan Am pagodas, both constructed in 1653, are dedicated to the heroes Cong and Am. Standing right on the street, it fits in like a house; look for the red doors with dragons on them. The **museum** in back displays millennia-old relics; the three periods represented are pre-Champa, Champa, and Greater Viet. (Open daily 7am-7pm; admission 5000Đ to the museum and pagoda.)

■ Near Hoi An

When the Chinese architecture in Hoi An finally loses its picture-perfect pulchritude, rent a motorcycle and putter to **Cau Dai Beach.** This somewhat crowded and small beach lies 5km east on Tran Hung Dao from Hoi An. Boat rentals to reach the following places on the banks of the river run about 80,000Đ roundtrip to both and last roughly two hours. Hire a boat (usually marked Tourist) at the Hoi An dock on Bach Dang next to the market. Tours leave from 6:30am to 5pm. Hoi An Tourist Service Company also runs boat trips to these sites, but they're more expensive. The **Ceramics Village (Lang Gom)** is the first stop from Hoi An. Brick kilns fire the products that hard-laboring locals create by hand. (Admission 2000Đ.) Don't be misled by the name of the **Carpenter's Village (Lang Moc):** only one family here does any carpentry. Many people come here to custom-order their dream piece of furniture, which can be shipped anywhere in the world. The village itself is beautiful, and the 10-minute walk to the carpenter's house is a good chance to enjoy the serene setting.

MY SON

The **My Son Cham ruins,** the largest group of Cham ruins in Vietnam, are 37km from Hoi An. Be aware that if you don't hook up with a tour group leaving from Da Nang or Hoi An, you are guaranteed to lose about 110,000Đ per person in the numerous "admission" fees charged by the provincial police.

From Hoi An, Hwy. 1 leads south for 7km to Tam Ky town. At the town, drivers turn right (east) and continue down a rough road for 20km until a wooden bridge comes into view. Cross the bridge and continue on. A few km later, but still some distance from the site, you must pay for a tour guide and motorcycle, if you don't have one already (they make you leave your vehicle at this point; this is where the random charges begin). Admission is 10,000Đ; each photo you take will cost 5000Đ, while a permit to make video recordings runs 20,000Đ.

The ruins are an impressive collection of five groups of temples, even if the statues that once adorned the temples now reside in museums around the world. The first two groups of temples should satisfy the most Cham-starved tourist, but you can also take the whole day and visit all five.

The complex was built as a pilgrimage site for the Chams in the 3rd century, and 70 towers sprung up at the site when it became the center of the Cham kingdom. The Vietnamese pushed the Cham out in the 13th century, but are currently trying to atone for their insensitivity by restoring the towers. As one of the head locations of the Viet Cong during the Vietnam War, many of the ruins in the area were bombed by U.S. forces. In 1990, a generous German woman donated money toward the restoration of the towers' interiors.

SON MY (MY LAI)

The stopover point to see the village of Son My (the site of the My Lai Massacre) is **Quang Ngai,** a small town 98km south of Hoi An. Do your best to arrive early and catch a bus or minibus to somewhere else as soon as possible. **Buses** (tel. 822 895) to other cities leave from 26 Le Thanh Ton, off Hwy. 1 about 2km south of the Hung Vuong intersection (take a cyclo 3000Đ). Foreigners may have trouble purchasing a ticket here, and they may jack up fares considerably. A better option may be to flag down a mini-bus outside the Song Tra Hotel at the north end of Quang Trang just before the bridge. Money can be exchanged at **Vietcombank,** 89 Hung Vuong (tel. 822 626). Traveler's checks are not accepted. (Open Mon.-Sat. 7-11:30am and 1:30-5pm.) Calls can be made from the **post office** (tel. 849 231) at the end of Hung Vuong. (Open daily 6am-9pm.) **Telephone code:** 55. For travelers who are forced to stay here, the best option is the **Kim Thanh Hotel,** 19 Hung Vuong (tel. 823 471), where singles with fan cost 66,000Đ, doubles 88,000Đ, with A/C 110,000Đ, quads 165,000Đ. After this, it's a sharp step down in quality to the **Vietnam Hotel,** 41 Hung Vuong (tel. 823 610). Singles here are 66,000Đ, doubles 110,000Đ, with A/C 155,000Đ. For food, mosey on over to **Restaurant 26,** 27 Phan Dinh Phung. Cheap plastic tables and chairs contrast with the pricey food (44,000Đ per person for a meal). **Note:** minibuses may drop passengers off at the state run Song Tra Hotel at the north end of town; avoid staying here. Rooms (110,000Đ) are theoretically available, but for a fan and unclean bathroom it's an astonishing 220,000Đ.

Motorcycles (60,000Đ per day) or cars can be rented in Quang Ngai to get to one of Vietnam's most tragic villages. On March 16, 1968, **Son My** (also referred to as Tinh Khe) went from being a collection of quiet farming villages to a somber testimony of war-time atrocities. U.S. soldiers came in and opened fire on four of the hamlets that make up Son My. Almost all of the inhabitants of **Son My** were killed: 504 died, mostly women, children, and elderly people. The officers responsible went on trial the following year. The museum that now rests at the former site of My Lai enshrines the memory of this tragedy.

From Quang Ngai, the ride begins 1km north on Hwy. 1 (Quang Trung) over the grayish cement bridge near the Song Tra Hotel; a huge memorial sign directs drivers down the dirt road to the right. Bamboo thickets, thatch houses, rice paddies, corn fields, and water buffalo line the serene 13-km road, at the end of which stands a huge cement gate reading. Visitors should leave their vehicle here and proceed through the red iron gates up the stone path. Visitors must stop first at the museum office, the first building on the left after the gate, to secure a photo permit. Truong Thiem Huong, who heads the office, lives in the village and leads tours in English. The well-manicured gardens to the right are dotted with statues commemorating the people killed in the massacre. The blooming flowers, trimmed hedges, and chirping birds are a strange contrast to the bloody history of this site.

The center of the former town is the **Memorial Museum.** Its facade reads: *Mai Mai Khac Sau Long Cam Thu Giac My Xam Luoc* (We Will Never Forgive the Evil Acts of the American Imperialist Forces). To the right of the entrance is an altar with the world-famous picture of crying My Lai residents before their deaths; above the altar is a black stone engraved with the names of all the My Lai victims. Pictures on the walls of the museum feature those considered responsible for the tragedy: President Diem, President Eisenhower, Colonel Henderson (the leader of the 11th brigade), and Captain Medina (the leader of the platoon that razed the village) in front of the U.S. Court Marshall. (Open daily 7am-5pm; admission 11,000Đ.)

SOUTH VIETNAM

▩ Nha Trang

Travelers journeying south from Hoi An will most likely receive their first introduction to the wonders of South Vietnam in Nha Trang. After the barren, rocky terrain of the central provinces, Nha Trang's green hills falling away to azure waters and bone-white sand couldn't be more welcoming. Indeed, Nha Trang has been compared favorably to the French Riviera or the Caribbean. Thankfully, though, the "City of the Blue Sea" has yet to become Kuta North despite the alarming rate at which hotels are sprouting up. Fishing, however, remains Nha Trang's principle economic enterprise, and at night the horizon is ablaze with lights from off-shore shrimp boats. Nha Trang does not offer much in the way of culturally enlightening sights, but the snorkeling, diving, and other water-borne activities is unparalleled, and still fairly cheap…for now.

ORIENTATION

The 6-km **Duong Tran Phu** runs along the beach from north to south. Everything else (meaning the rest of town) spreads off to the west of Tran Phu. Just outside of the train station on **Duong Thai Nguyen** lurks the town's only six-street intersection; take **Duong Ly Tu Trong** from here to get to the beach. Farther west Thai Nguyen becomes 23 Thang 10. The long distance **bus terminal** is along 23 Dong 10 at the outskirts of town. If you're on the beach, walk north (with the beach on the right) along Tran Phu until the post office; turn left onto **Duong Le Loi** to get to the market and restaurants in town.

PRACTICAL INFORMATION

Tourist Offices: Khanh Hoa Tourism, 1 Tran Hung Dao (tel. 823 704). Open daily 7-11:30am and 1:30-5pm. **Lang's Tour and Travel Service** (tel. 828 514) on Tran Phu across from the Grand Hotel. Open daily 7-11am and 1:30-9pm. They do everything: book train and air tickets, extend visas, book tours and hotels, rent boats and cars, and sell maps (5000Đ).

Currency Exchange: Vietcombank, 17 Quang Trung (tel. 821 054), open Mon.-Sat. 7:30-11am and 1:30-4pm. Most hotels will also change currency

Air Travel: Nha Trang Airport (tel. 823 797), south of town off Tran Phu. The yellow Vietnam Airlines Airport Bus (tel. 823 589) drops tourists at any hotel (22,000 per person). Motorcycles drivers and cars may try to take you into town for much more. The **Vietnam Airlines Booking Office,** 12B Hoang Hoa Tham (tel. 823 797). To: **Da Nang** (549,000Đ); **Hanoi** (1,426,100Đ); and **HCMC** (659,000Đ). Schedules subject to change. Flights to **Bangkok, Hong Kong, Kuala Lumpur, Phnom Penh,** and **Singapore** fly through HCMC first.

Trains: The **train station** is on Thai Nguyen past the 6-street intersection and before the inter-city bus station. Book **tickets** at 17 Thai Nguyen (tel. 822 113) 7:30-11am and 2-4:30pm, or at any hotel. Trains run to all major cities. Prices depend on which train you take. Average prices for hard seats to: **HCMC** (132,000Đ); **Hanoi** (407,000Đ); **Da Nang** (154,000Đ); and **Hue** (187,000Đ).

Buses: Noi Tinh Station, on 2/4 the west of the market, is the local bus station. **Lien Tinh Station,** 58 23/10 (tel. 822 397), next to Long Son Pagoda, is the long-distance station. Open daily 5am-4pm. Regular connections with major cities. To: **Hanoi** (3days, 309,000Đ); **HCMC** (10hr., 107,000Đ); **Hue** (24hr., 160,000Đ); **Dalat** (14hr., 63,000Đ); and **Da Nang** (13hr., 127,000Đ). Private **minibuses** organized by travel agencies are cheaper and more comfortable than regular buses or trains. Book one at any hotel or travel agency; they'll pick you up at your hotel.

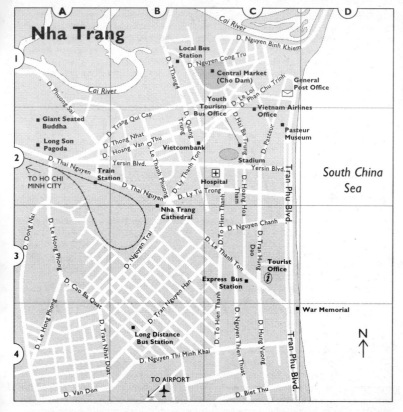

Nha Trang

Minibuses usually leave in the early mornings and late afternoons. To: **HCMC** (122,000); **Dalat** (88,000Đ); **Hoi An** and **Da Nang** (both 155,000Đ).

Rentals: Car rentals available at any hotel or travel agency, like **Hung Dao Garage**, 22B Tran Hung Dao (tel. 823 008), and **Hung Vu Travel Service**, 64 Thong Nhat (tel. 823 106). Prices average 220,000Đ per day in the city and 440,000Đ per day outside of the city for a 4-seat sedan. **Bike rentals** also at any hotel for 10,000Đ per day. **Motorbike rentals** across from Grand Hotel: 11,000Đ per hour or 66,000Đ per day.

Markets: Dam Market is to the north of the city west of the post office near Phan Boi Chau. A typical market with an emphasis on electronic equipment.

Police: tel. 821 079.

Medical Services: Hospital, 19 Yersin (tel. 822 175).

Emergency: tel. 822 175 (hospital number).

Post Offices: 4 Le Loi (tel. 821 250), at the northern end of Tran Phu, on the first block of Le Loi. Take a left from Tran Phu on to Le Loi. Fax, mail and telephone services. Open daily 6:30am-8pm.

Telephones: 50 Le Thanh Ton (tel. 823 866), across the street from the Vien Dong Hotel. Open daily 6:30am-10pm. **Directory Information:** tel. 108. **Telephone code:** 58.

ACCOMMODATIONS

Most budget accommodations in Nha Trang congregate around the beachfront on Tran Phu. During the low season (April-July) prices are negotiable.

78 Guest House, 78 Tran Phu (tel. 826 342), near the southern end of the beach. The 78 is the best budget option on Tran Phu, which makes it popular and nearly always full by late afternoons. Doubles with fan 66,000Đ, with bath 88,000Đ, with hot water 122,000Đ, with A/C 144,000Đ. Triples 122,000Đ. Excellent info on travel in Vietnam, as well as tourist activities in Nha Trang.

Huu Nghi Hotel, 3 Tran Hung Dao (tel. 826 703), just up Tran Hung Dao from the Khanh Hoa Tourist Office on Le Thanh Ton. Formerly the Hung Dao. A 5-min. walk from the beach but a very attractive option, since the rooms here are nicer than in many beach-front hotels. Singles with fan and IDD phone 80,000Đ; with A/C 150,000Đ. Doubles 100,000Đ, with A/C 170,000Đ. Triples 130,000Đ. Add 20,000Đ for hot water.

Hotel 62, 62 Tran Phu (tel. 825 095), about 200m south of the war memorial at the intersection with Biet Du. Another rather uninspiring example of Vietnamese architects' penchant for concrete, it nonetheless has cheap rooms and sports a prime location on the main beach. Singles with fan 70,000Đ. Doubles 88,000Đ, with A/C 122,000Đ, also with hot water 155,000Đ.

Nha Trang Hotel, 129 Thong Nhat (tel. 826 645), about 200m west of the intersection with the war memorial. On a busy street, a cyclo ride from the beach, but it's cheap and clean, making it a decent last resort. Doubles with fan 100,000Đ, with A/C 122,000Đ. The Nha Trang II is just around the corner at 21 Le Thanh Phuong (tel. 822 956). It's smaller and in a more peaceful location. Singles with fan 100,000Đ. Doubles 122,000Đ. The Nha Trang III, 22 Tran Hung Dao (tel. 823 933), near Huu Nghi Hotel, has more of a guest house feel but is more expensive. Doubles with A/C and hot water 122,000Đ.

Ha Phuong Hotel, 30 Hoang Hoa Tham (tel. 829 015), not far from the intersection with Tran Phu. A lovely new mini-hotel, run by a local traveler's café. Singles with fan and bathroom 10,000Đ, with A/C 122,000Đ. Information office in the lobby offers many services such as visa extensions and boat trips.

FOOD

Don't leave Nha Trang without trying *nem nuong,* the regional specialty of grilled pork and vegetables rolled into rice paper and dipped in a special fish sauce mix. Restaurants specializing only in *nem nuong* abound in the Dam Market area, around the west end of Le Loi. Cheap restaurants with Vietnamese food also congregate in this area. The few restaurants on the beach front may provide better ambiance, but also serve less tasty food at higher prices.

Nem Ninh Hoa, 16 Lan Ong (tel. 826 737). Large servings of delicious *nem nuong* for 7000Đ per person. In the evenings, they pack 'em in with a shoe horn. The service is indifferent, but the food is great. Open daily 7am-10pm.

Nem #9, 9 Le Loi (tel. 829 063), on the corner near the GPO. One of the *nem* specialty shops the locals recommend. Often crowded. The menu (for what it's worth) is painted on the wall, but everyone comes for one thing: *nem.* Large serving of *nem* and a Coke 9000Đ. Open daily 8am-10pm.

Phuc Thinh Quan, 17 Le Loi (tel. 828 428). Serves *nem* and other Vietnamese dishes. *Nem* 6000Đ. Grilled shrimp 22,000Đ. Open daily 7:30am-10:30pm.

Vietnam Restaurant 2, 7 Hoang Van Thu (tel. 826 588). Aggressive owners wave you down from blocks away, guaranteeing "good food, or no pay." Highly-acclaimed by locals, but pricier than most joints. Dishes average 15-20,000Đ, more for larger servings. Steamed fish 20-30,000Đ. The **Vietnam Restaurant I** (though it is, in fact, newer than #2), is just up the street. Open daily 7am-11pm.

SIGHTS

The **Ponagar Cham Temples** or **Thap Ba (Temple of the Lady)** are just north of the city on Duong 2/4, immediately past Xom Bong Bridge. Walk or bike the 2km from town, or take a cyclo (10,000Đ). Once there, a flight of stone steps leads past vendors to the temples at the top of the hill. The main tower, measuring 22.5m, was dedicated to the Goddess Ponagar (Mother of the Land). This matriarch-creator was, like most big mamma goddesses, responsible for birth, agriculture, and household tasks. The local importance of agriculture is evident in the worshipping of a stone fruit in one of the towers.

The main tower was constructed in the year 817 AD, and part of it was still under renovation in 1996. The hexagonal monument of 10 columns on the side of the hill offers a photo-worthy view of the fishing dock and estuary below. Contributions to help the preservation effort are appreciated. (Open daily 6am-6pm; admission 6000Đ.)

The **Long Son Pagoda,** Nha Trang's postcard temple, stands at the western end of Yersin. The pagoda was built in 1963 and is dedicated to the memory of the Buddhists who gave their lives protesting the American-supported Diem regime. Long Son is most renowned for its 9m-high white hilltop statue of Buddha sitting in the lotus position. (Open daily 6am-6pm.)

Cau Da Villa is another former vacation residence of King Bao Dai, Vietnam's last monarch. The yellow colonial villa perches on a hilltop at the south end of Tran Phu, between the Linh Son Pagoda and Cau Da Pier. The villa has been converted to a luxury hotel, so budget travelers should content themselves with joining the photo-taking tourist crowds outside. Contact Khanh Hoa Tourism for information and reservations if you want a night's stay (roughly 440,000Đ per night).

Boat tours go to the islands off the coast of Nha Trang. Travelers will pass Han Mun (Ebony Island) on the way out; **Hon Mieu** contains the Tri Nguyen "Aquarium," which is actually two rather large ponds with fish and some turtles. **Hon Yen** (Salangane Island) features the bird's nests (complete with eggs) that Nha Trang inhabitants harvest and send as delicacies to wealthy Asian gourmands. Another island featured on the boat tours is **Hon Tre** (Bamboo Island), uninteresting except for the snorkeling opportunities offshore. Look out for the blobs of oil in the water and the sharp coral underfoot. Book tours at any hotel or travel agency, or directly with Mama Linh (tel. 826 693) in front of the Hai Yen Hotel (8am, return 5pm, 77,000Đ per person). Price includes transportation from the hotel to Cau Da Pier, snorkeling equipment, and lunch. Serious scuba divers can book dives at the **Blue Diving Club** (tel. 825 340) at the Coconut Cave Resort, opposite the Hai Yen Hotel on Tran Phu. The club's three licensed instructors lead daily dive excursions for certified divers for $60 (includes 2 dives, all equipment, and meals). PADI certifications cost $340 per person (4 days, 4 dives).

The **Poklong Garai Towers** (Cham Towers) stand on Trau Hill, 7km northwest of Phan Rang town, on the highway to Nha Trang. These towers were built at the end of the 13th century to honor the generous King Poklong Garai (1151-1205), who was known for his good deeds toward the Cham people and for constructing the local irrigation system. It's an easy climb up an untended path to the three red-brick towers. Carved gods and dragons and the ornate, cursive Cham script adorn the exteriors of the towers. Inside the main tower is the statue of a kneeling calf that doubles as an altar. A bust of the thin, bearded King Poklong Garai reposes underneath the redwood lattice ceiling. The hill itself features a great view of the rather dry and cactus-friendly surrounding area. (Open daily 7am-5pm; admission 5000Đ.)

▓ Dàlat

Dalat certainly ranks among the most unique tourist destinations in Indochina, if not all of Southeast Asia. For some places it is intriguing architecture, natural beauty, or a colorful local population which draws crowds. Dalat, fortunately, boasts an abundance of all three, but what really sets it apart is something quite different: the weather. The contrast between the steamy lowland deltas and the decidedly non-tropical climate of this mountain retreat couldn't be more dramatic. Whereas in the Delta women weave straw *non* hats to shield themselves from the sun, here they knit wool caps to ward off the often chilling breeze.

Traditionally, this region, dominated by the Langbian Mountains, was the exclusive domain of hill-tribe minorities. The French founded Dalat in the late nineteenth century as a retreat from the travails of the lowlands (after all, forcing others to labor like slaves all day in the heat was draining work). The legacy of this period is a large number of European-style villas which somehow seem less out of place amidst Dalat's towering pine trees and rolling hills then they do elsewhere in Indochina.

Today Dalat is one of the country's premier tourist spots, for Vietnamese and foreigners alike. For Vietnamese visitors, sights like the Lake of Sighs and the Valley of Love (whose names are far more romantic than the places themselves) are don't-miss highlights. More popular with foreigners are excursions into the highlands to visit hill-tribe communities. As you make your way from the sultry streets of Ho Chi Minh City to the hot hands of Nha Trang, be sure to chill out for a few days in Dalat.

ORIENTATION

Dalat is the capital of Lam Dong Province, 300km north of HCMC on National Highway 20. Flights from HCMC and other cities land at **Lien Khuong Airport,** 30km south of town. Dalat's narrow, maze-like streets follow the contours of the hills upon which the city was built. At the center of town is **Cho Dalat.** Just up the side of concrete steps to the left of the market is **Hoa Binh Square,** dominated by the mammoth 3/4 Cinema. Most of Dalat's budget hotels can be found along **Truon Cong Dinh** and **Phan Dinh Phung.** The former, which runs into the latter, is to the left when facing the cinema. Dalat Tourist publishes a helpful map, available for 10,000Đ at any of their hotels.

PRACTICAL INFORMATION

Tourist Offices: Lamdong Tourist Company, 4 Tran Quoc Toan (tel. 822 125). The prime tourist info stop. The English-speaking staff is helpful and does everything: rents bikes and cars, and runs tours to the Lat villages and hikes into the Langbian Mountains. Open daily 7:30-11:30am and 1:30-4:30pm. **Dalat Tourist,** 9 Le Dai Hanh (tel. 822 479). A smaller, less patronized office.

Currency Exchange: Exchange at major hotels or **Industrial and Commercial Bank,** 46 Hoa Binh (tel. 822 495). Open Mon.-Sat. 7-11:30am and 1-4:30pm.

Air Travel: Lien Khuong Airport (tel. 843 373), 30km south of the city. Airport to city transport 33,000Đ. **Vietnam Airlines Office,** 5 Truong Cong Dinh (tel. 822 895). To **HCMC** ($40) and **Hue** ($75).

Trains: 1 Nguyen Trai (tel. 822 170). Offers service only to the village of **Trai Ma,** 7km away (8am and 2pm, returning at 10am and 3:30pm respectively, 55,000Đ roundtrip). There's a 4,000Đ charge just to enter the station.

Buses: Two private bus stations: on Nguyen Thi Minh Khai south of Cho Dalat and behind the 3/4 Cinema directly north of the market. Similar services with express buses to major cities. Leaves early mornings and late afternoons, as soon as they fill up. To: **Nha Trang** (5hr., 60,000Đ); **Da Nang** (13hr., 105,000Đ); **Hanoi** (3 days, 160,000Đ); and **Hue** (24hr., 140,000Đ). Tickets sold at small stands near the stairs leading from the market to Hoa Binh Square. Dalat Tourist operates a "tourist bus" to **Nha Trang,** stopping briefly at **Thap Cham** in Phan Rang. The minibus picks passengers up at their hotels (8am, 6hr., 88,000Đ). Book at any hotel. The public bus station is several km south of town on 3 Thang 4; they apparently don't like to sell tickets to foreigners.

Rentals: Expect to pay 165-220,000Đ per day for **car rental** within the city, and 330-550,000Đ per day for inter-city trips for a 4-seat car with driver. Foreigners cannot rent a car without a driver. 12-seat vans cost slightly more. Ask at any hotel reception desk or try **Lien Hiep Tourist Service,** 147 Phan Dinh Phung (tel. 822 556), or **Tourist Transportation Enterprise,** 9 Le Dai Hanh (tel. 822 479). For **motorcycle rentals,** ask at any hotel, at the bus stations in town, or around the market area. 110,000Đ per day, with driver 9900Đ per hour. **Bicycles** are 15,000Đ, although the hills are grueling.

Markets: Cho Dalat, in the center of town. Crowded and colorful with floors for clothing and crafts, ready-to-eat food, groceries, and souvenirs. In a country of market cultures, Dalat's really stands out.

Medical Services: Lamdong Hospital, 4 Pham Ngoc Thach (tel. 821 369).

Police: 19 Tran Phu (tel. 822 468).
Post Offices/Telephones: 14-16 Tran Phu (tel. 822 347). Place **international calls** here. Open daily 7:30am-10pm. **Telephone code:** 63.

ACCOMMODATIONS

Although Dalat appears to have more hotels than busts of Uncle Ho, foreigners are for the most part required to stay in more expensive accommodations operated by Dalat Tourist (read: the state). Most hotels do not offer A/C (at this altitude, who needs it?), though hot water is a must.

Hoa Binh Hotel, 64 Truon Cong Dinh (tel. 822 787). Clean, friendly, and recently given a facelift. All rooms have hot water. The bathrooms are outside but don't fret, they have hot water too. Closet-sized singles in the attic $3. Larger singles $5. Doubles $7. Triples $12. If Hoa Binh is full, try **Hoa Binh 2** up the hill at 67 Truon Cong Dinh (tel. 822 982). Smaller, with charming singles and doubles for $5 and $8, respectively.

Mimosa II Hotel, 118 Phan Dinh Phung (tel. 822 180). One of the best combinations of quality and value in Dalat. First-class rooms with desk, 2 beds, hot water, and bath tub $9, 2 people $15. Slightly smaller rooms $7-12. Even cheaper rooms with shared bath can be had for $5-6 ($8-10 for 2 people). **The Mimosa I** is up the street at 170 Phan Dinh Phung (tel. 822 656) with identical prices.

Lao Nguyen Hotel, 90 Phan Dinh Phung (tel. 823 738), between Hoa Binh and Mimosa II. Same management as the two Mimosas. Offers very clean, bright, if spartan, rooms at prices as cheap as you'll find in Dalat. Outside bathrooms. Singles $6. Doubles $8. Rooms on the 3rd floor $5-6.

Lam Son Hotel, 5 Hai Thuong (tel. 822 362). From Hoa Binh Square head down Duong 312 and take a right after the intersection with Hai Ba Trung; this converted French villa is on a hill to the left. Slightly inconvenient location but worth the walk. All the rooms have attractive wooden furniture and high ceilings, with hot water. Doubles $15. Smaller, but equally nice rooms $10.

Thanh Binh Hotel, 41 Nguyen Thi Minh Khai (tel. 822 909), just to the right of the market, though the convenient location also means it can be quite noisy from 5am-10pm no matter what side of the hotel you're staying in. Friendly, helpful staff. Basic singles with hot water and seatless toilet $7. Doubles $12. Nicer rooms with desk and furniture $10, doubles $16.

Hang Nga Tree House, 3 Huynh Thuc Khang (tel. 822 070), near the intersection with Le Hong Phong. Undoubtedly one of the most unique (or bizarre) guest houses you'll encounter in Southeast Asia. Hang Nga's 8 rooms are built in two fanciful concrete tree trunks, surrounded by vines and massive concrete giraffes. The rooms are cut from gnarled logs. The owner/architect is the daughter of the late Truon Chinh, former president of Vietnam and Ho Chi Minh's right-hand man. Worth a peek even if you don't want to pay 220-600,000Đ for a night.

FOOD

Dalat's natural setting supplies cartloads of fruits and vegetables, as well as an array of wild meats like boar and rabbit. Try to shop in the inexpensive markets or your wallet could suffer. There is a large food cart on the second floor of Cho Dalat, where a bowl of *hu tieu* soup and all-you-can-drink hot tea cost 5000Đ. Many popular restaurants are on Phan Dinh Phung, near the main budget hotels.

Dong A Restaurant, 82 Phan Dinh Phung (tel. 821 033), between the Hoa Binh and Lao Nguyen Hotels. Combines a pleasant atmosphere and reasonable prices (7-25,000Đ). Basic rice dishes are cheap and filling (7-10,000). The more adventurous can choose from the wild beasts section of the menu (20-30,000Đ). A few vegetarian dishes as well. Open daily 8:30am-9pm.

Lien Hiep Restaurant, 147 Phan Phung (tel. 823 024), diagonally across the street from the Dong A on the first floor of the mini-hotel of the same name. It's a bit short on ambiance, but the cheap, delicious food more than compensates. Menu includes rice dishes, duck, beef, chicken, crab, eel, and shrimp. Most dishes 12,000Đ or less. Open daily 9am-11pm.

Thanh Thuy Restaurant, 2 Nguyen Thai Hoc (tel. 822 262). One of two lakeside cafés owned by Dalat Tourist, the more upscale Thuy Ta across the lake is ridiculously expensive. A nice spot for an evening cup of coffee; watch Vietnamese teeny-boppers paddle around the lake in swan boats. Hot tea 4000Đ, hot cocoa 5000Đ, coffee 6-7000Đ. Open daily 6:30am-11pm.

Kim Linh Restaurant, 58 Phan Phung (tel. 825 406), across from the Cam Do Hotel south of the intersection with D. Truon Cong Dinh. Serves rather expensive (20-30,000Đ) Chinese and Vietnamese dishes, though the portions are generous. A great place to go with a group, where a few dishes can feed a crowd. Beef with curry powder 20,000Đ, sauteed squid 20,000Đ. Open daily 8am-11pm.

SIGHTS

Lake Xuan Huong ripples gently at the center of town. While somewhat less impressive than its national reputation for beauty would indicate, it is still appealing for its tranquil setting and the beautiful houses that line its banks.

The creative Buddha, Thich Ca, sits in **Linh Son Pagoda,** a short walk from the market. Head north up Nguyen Van Troi, passing the town cathedral to the red brick staircase with two cement dragons along the bannisters and columns topped by pink lotuses. Inside to the left reposes the God of Talent, with eyes on his stomach (a sign of his all-seeing powers—talent and skill are thought to reside in the stomach). In case you're wondering, the square design on the straw mats all over the pagoda say "Happy Family." (Pagoda open 6am-8pm. Knock if the door is closed; monks will allow visitors in upon request.)

The former **Governor General's Residence** or Palace II stands southeast of the lake at 12 Tran Hung Dao. Unfortunately, the lovely yellow building is closed to tourists, but the parking lot in front offer an unparalleled view. Two km southwest of Lake Xuan Huong is the slightly more impressive **Palace of King Bao Dai** or Palace III (tel. 822 093), on Trieu Viet Vuong, at the end of Le Hong Phong. King Bao Dai was the last king of the Nguyen Dynasty and of Vietnam. He reigned as King from 1926 to 1945, but kept his hold on power when he became Chief of State under the Republic in 1949 and chose Dalat as the capital city. Bao Dai left the country in 1954 to live in France. King Bao Dai, Queen Nam Phuong, and their five children lived here during vacations and holidays. The Palace, based on the design of a French-Vietnamese architect team, was begun in 1933 and completed five years later. (Open daily 7-8am and 1-5pm; admission 10,000Đ.)

■ Near Dalat

Dalat's train only goes to **Trai Mat Village.** There's not much to see in the village, but the beautiful **Linh Phuoc Pagoda,** 120 Tu Phuoc (tel. 825 410), features a colorful cement dragon around the fountain in the courtyard. One wall of the pagoda lists the names of the temples benefactors, who come from around the world. The pagoda is still being built, but visitors can go inside. (Open daily 6am-7pm.)

Camly Falls is a touristy nightmare 2km from Dalat's city center. Hardly a waterfall despite its name, Camly's brown water flows into a pond with cement shores. A colorful gazebo awaits the photo-addicted, and the staff there provides visitors with plastic "ethnic" costumes for 2000Đ. (Open 7am-6pm; admission 5000Đ.)

Vendors await the unwary 10km south of Dalat at **Prenn Falls** (Prenn Pass). After your driver drops you off, walk over a little wooden bridge, turn right down a steep, winding, and rocky path, pass a statue of horse and rider to the left, and you'll arrive at Dalat's premiere waterfall. A huge bamboo bridge allows you to walk under the waterfall; cool off in the waters, but be careful—it can be very slippery. Some of the most interesting sights here are the women dressed in long, tight, traditional evening dresses and high heels. (Open 7am-5pm; admission 10,000Đ.)

The **Langbian Mountains** are a rural retreat 12km north of Dalat, with peaks as high as 2163m. Here you can go mountain climbing, para-gliding and trekking. At the foot of the mountains lies **Lat Village,** home to the Lat and Chill ethnic groups. The climb up features some scenic views, but all tourists must secure a **visitor's license** before heading up (55,000Đ from the tourist office), or take the easy way up and go with a tour. Lamdong Tourist Company organizes three-hour treks into the Langbian Mountains for about 165,000Đ per person. Book a day in advance or before the morning you want to go.

VALLEY OF LOVE

Honeymooners and hikers may want to hire a motorcycle and driver (10,000Đ per hour) and putter over to the **Valley of Love** (Thung Lung Tinh Yeu), which lies 6km north of Dalat's city center, and features forests, trails, rolling hills, lakes, views of the Langbian Mountains, and swarms of tourists (tel. 821 448 for information). On the other side of the crowds and souvenir stands, horses and guides chomp at the bit to take you through the valley for 66,000Đ per hour. Boats can also be rented near the lakes. The romantic nature of this valley is rooted in history: the **Lake of Sighs** (Ho Than Tho) gets it name from the story of the Vietnamese Romeo and Juliet. Two star-crossed lovers came here to bemoan their separated fates, and eventually committed suicide rather than remain apart. (Of course, no one seems to know how they did it—but that's not the important part.) Their graves are next to the lake. The name conjures up romantic images of some remote, mist-surrounded lake; in fact, the lake is a rather disappointing limpid pond. Employees dressed in bear costumes cavort in the woods, but they may ask for money if you want to take their picture. The lake is about 4km east of town off Ho Xuan Huong. (Open daily 7am-5pm; admission 10,000Đ.)

■ Hồ Chí Minh City (Saigon)

From as far back as any Vietnamese can remember, this former "Pearl of the Orient" has been the center of wealth for Vietnam. Saigon is the place where Vietnamese can dress *comme* the westerners, own more motorbikes than bicycles, and go dancing without attracting neighborhood rumors. At the same time, this metropolis is home to more beggars, thieves, and prostitutes than any other city in the country.

In 1975 when the North Vietnamese seized Saigon, ending 30 years of nearly continuous warfare, it was renamed after their greatest revolutionary hero, Ho Chi Minh. Today, both names are used interchangeably, though more often than not it is referred to simply as *thanh pho,* "the city." This third moniker best fits Saigon's position as the unofficial capital of the new Vietnam. Hanoi may be the cathedral and political hub, but for the thousands of young Vietnamese who flock here from all over the country to make it big, Saigon is where it's at.

Most foreign visitors delight in the astounding array of bars and nightclubs while frowning at such side-affects of modernity as pollution, overcrowding, and fast living. Love or hate it, Saigon is the new image of Vietnam—no longer a colonial jewel or the fallen city, it is developing at an astounding rate, embracing capitalism wholeheartedly. Indeed, trade has always been the city's *raison d'etre.* After suffering impatiently through 10 years of high socialism, the city didn't just re-enter the capitalist maelstrom in 1986—it jumped in with both feet. Economic changes are slow, but are already affecting the daily lives of Saigon's inhabitants. School girls in flowing white *ao dai*'s peddle down broad boulevards, oblivious to the din around them, while delivery boys, their faces hidden behind sunglasses, zip through mid-day traffic on Japanese motorbikes. Meanwhile construction sites seem to have sprung up overnight, casting eerie orange spotlights against the city's skyline.

GETTING THERE AND AWAY

By Plane

Foreigners arrive at **Tan Son Nhat International Airport** (tel. 844 65 13). The airport shuttle transports visitors from the plane to the terminal. The least insane and most

In Vietnam, prices at many hotels, guest houses, and restaurants are quoted in U.S. dollars; in fact, some places will only take U.S. dollars, even though this practice is now illegal. *Let's Go* lists prices in both dollars and dong. It would be wise to keep small U.S. dollar bills handy.

secure way to leave the airport is to hop into a metered taxi. (55-77,000Đ). Big groups can rent a van for about 165,000Đ (tel. 844 17 04).

The **Vietnam Airlines** office is at 116 Nguyen Hue (tel. 829 21 28). **Royal Air Cambodge,** 343 Le Van Sy (tel. 829 93 63), has daily flights to **Phnom Penh** ($70). **Thai Airways,** 65 Nguyen Du (tel. 829 28 09), offers daily service to **Bangkok** ($173). **Singapore Airlines,** 6 Le Loi (tel. 823 18 95), flies daily to **Singapore** ($279). **Lao Aviation,** 95A Pasteur (tel. 822 69 90), has one flight per week to **Vientiane** (Friday, $170). **Malaysian Airlines,** 116 Nguyen Hue (tel. 829 25 29), flies daily to **Kuala Lumpur** ($150).

By Bus

Ho Chi Minh City (HCMC) has five major bus stations, all located outside the city center, which serve domestic destinations. Buses to **Cambodia** leave from the bus stop at 145 Nguyen Du Mon.-Sat. at 4:30am. Tickets must be purchased at least one day in advance from the garage at 155 Nguyen Hue (tel. 823 07 54), directly across from the Vietnam Airlines office (open Mon.-Sat. 8-11:30am and 1:30-4:30). Tickets for the Mon.-Wed. buses are $12; tickets for the Thurs.-Sat. buses are $5. **Note:** Cambodian visas specifying entry at **Moc Bai** must be obtained in HCMC first.

GETTING AROUND

Because regulations are strictly enforced by the watchful police, traffic flows surprisingly smoothly in HCMC. However, it's best to avoid the streets during rush hours (7-10am and 4-6pm). Four **taxi** companies service HCMC, the two cheapest being: **Vina-taxis** (tel. 842 28 88), with rates of 7500Đ for the first km, 1500Đ per 200m thereafter; and the **purple Saigon Taxis** (tel. 424 242). **Cyclos** run anywhere in the city for 10,000Đ, but are banned from certain streets. In general, if you're looking to see the city overall, rent a **bike** or a **motorcycle;** if you're staying on the tourist path, just walk. Many hotels and guest houses rent bikes (55-88,000Đ per day). HCMC also has a small but convenient and comfortable **inner-city bus system. Ben Thanh Station** (tel. 865 11 11), the main terminal, is across the street from Ben Thanh Market. From here A/C buses move down Tran Hung Dao into Cho Lon stopping at the market and the bus station (2000Đ). Other buses run from the terminal to the inter-city bus stations for 3000Đ (see **Practical Information** below).

ORIENTATION

The **Saigon River** curves to the east, forming that border of HCMC, while a series of canals and channels runs through the southern part of the city. **Districts 1** and **5** are major centers of tourism and commercial activity; they form a quarter-moon sickle along the bend of the river, traversing almost the entire length of the metropolis, from northeast to southwest. The **Ben Nghe Canal** flows southwest from the river. **Duong Tran Hung Dao** runs parallel to the canal and connects District 1 to **Cho Lon,** the Chinatown of Saigon. Tourist traffic radiates from **Ben Thanh Market,** sprawled out near the traffic circle closest to the river and canal. Here, Tran Hung Dao divides the circle and continues on the other side, changing into **Duong Le Loi.** The area west of this traffic circle comprises the **Pham Ngu Lao area,** where most budget accommodations cluster. **Duong Pham Ngu Lao** cuts through the area at an angle from the traffic circle. **Duong Dien Bien Phu** forms the border of Saigon proper to the northwest. Running southeast and crossing Dien Bien Phu, **Duong Phan Dinh Phung** intersects **Duong Nguyen Thai Minh Khai** and **Duong Le Duan** almost at the geographical center of the city, ending at **Duong Ton Duc Thang,** which parallels the Saigon River.

VIETNAM

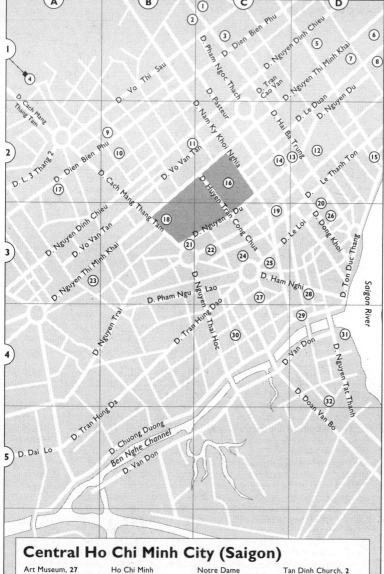

Central Ho Chi Minh City (Saigon)

Art Museum, 27
Bac Ton Museum, 15
Ben Thanh Market, 24
Binh Dan Hospital, 17
Central Saigon
Mosque, 26
Culture Park, 18
Dien Bien Phu
Hospital, 9
Foreign Exchange
Bank, 29
Historical Museum, 6

Ho Chi Minh
Museum, 31
Immigration Police
Office, 21
Le Van Tham Park, 3
Main Post Office, 13
Mariamman Hindu
Temple, 22
Mililtary Museum, 7
Nhi Dong II
Hospital, 12

Notre Dame
Cathedral, 14
Opera Theatre, 20
Phung Son Tu
Pagoda, 30
Reunification Hall, 16
Revolutionary
Museum, 19
Saigon Hospital, 25
Saigon Station, 4
Stadium, 5

Tan Dinh Church, 2
Tan Dinh Market, 1
Vietnam Bank, 28
War Crimes
Museum, 11
Women's Hospital, 23
Xa Loi Pagoda, 10
Xom Chieu Market, 32
Zoo/
Botanical Garden, 8

PRACTICAL INFORMATION

Tourist Offices: Saigon Tourist, 49-55 Le Thanh Ton (tel. 829 89 14), at the intersection with Dong Khoi. Operates more than 50 hotels and 40 restaurants. Helpful staff can answer questions and may try to recruit visitors for their pricey tours (1-day city tour, 144,000Đ). Open daily 7:30-11:30am and 1-6:30pm.

Tours and Travel: Sinh Office, 179 Pham Ngu Lao (tel. 835 56 01). Office of the renowned Sinh Café across the street. Tours to **Vung Tao, Cu Chi,** and the **Mekong Delta.** Also operates a popular "open tour" of 4 cities. Bus leaves from the office every morning at 7:30am, stopping at **Dalat,** then **Nha Trang,** then **Hoi An,** and finally **Hue** (open ended ticket $35). Open daily 7:30am-10pm.

Embassies and Consulates: Australia, 5B Ton Duc Thong (tel. 829 60 35; fax 829 60 31), on the 5th floor of the Landmark Building. Open Mon.-Thurs. 9am-noon and 1-4pm, Fri. 9am-noon. **Canada,** 203 Dong Khoi (tel. 824 20 00, ext. 1209; fax 829 45 28). Open Mon.-Fri. 8:30am-noon and 1-4:30pm. **UK,** 261 Dien Bien Phu (tel. 829 84 33; fax 822 57 40). Open Mon.-Fri. 8-11am. **Laos,** 181 Hai Ba Trung (tel. 829 76 64; fax 829 76 64). Tourist visas take 1 week to process, $25 extra for a rush job. Fees vary by country $25-42. $25 processing fee. Open Mon.-Fri 8:30-11:30am and 2-4pm. **Indonesia,** 18 Phung Khac Khoan (tel. 825 18 88). Open Mon.-Fri. 8-11am and 2-5pm. **Singapore,** 5 Phung Khac Khoan (tel. 822 51 74; fax 825 16 00). Open Mon.-Fri. 8:30am-12:30pm and 1:30-5pm. **Cambodia,** 4 Phung Khac Khoan (tel. 829 27 51). Open Mon.-Fri. 7:30-11:30am and 2-5pm, Sat. 7:30-11:30am. **Thailand,** 77 Tran Quoc Thao (tel. 822 26 37), District 3. Open Mon.-Fri. 8:30am-noon and 1:30-5pm. Visa applications 8:30-11:30am and 2-4pm. **New Zealand,** 41 Nguyen Thi Minh Khai (tel. 822 69 07), on the 5th floor of the Yoko Building. Open Mon.-Fri. 8:30am-5pm.

Currency Exchange: At most hotels, gold shops, and the GPO. **Vietcombank,** 17-29 Ben Chuong Duong (tel. 825 13 21). MC and Visa cash advances. Open Mon.-Sat. 8-11:30am and 1-4pm. **Sacombank,** 211 Nguyen Thai Hoc (tel. 835 56 07), at the intersection with Pham Ngu Lao. Visa and MC cash advance. Open Mon.-Sat. 7:30am-4:30pm. In addition, there are several currency exchange booths on Le Loi near the city theater and major hotels.

Air Travel: Daily flights to **Hanoi** ($170); **Haiphong** ($170); **Hue** ($90); and **Da Nang** ($90). Open Mon.-Sat. 7:30am-6pm, Sun. 8:30am-12:30pm. For airline offices, see **Getting There and Away,** above.

Trains: Railway Station, 1 Nguyen Thong (tel. 844 39 52), in District 3 off Cach Mang Thang Tam. Foreigners and overseas Vietnamese must buy tickets at counter 1. The **Reunification Express** links HCMC with all the major cities of the central and northern regions, ending in Hanoi. There are several classes of trains. The fastest go to: **Hanoi** on Mon., Thurs., and Sat. (365,000Đ) and pass through **Nha Trang** (95,000Đ), **Da Nang** (203,000Đ), and **Hue** (224,000Đ). Slower, cheaper trains leave daily to: **Nha Trang** (10hr.); **Da Nang** (16hr.); **Hue** (19hr.); and **Hanoi** (40hr.). The most convenient place to buy tickets is from the booking office in the headquarters of the Vietnam Railway Union, 136 Ham Nghi (tel. 823 01 05), opposite Ben Thanh Market. Open Mon.-Sat. 7:30-11am and 1-3pm.

Buses: Mien Dong Station (tel. 899 40 56), north of the city center on Hwy. 13 in Binh Thanh District, sends buses to points north. To: **Hanoi** (9:30am and 3:30pm, 48hr., 123,000Đ); **Hoi An** (20hr., 68,500Đ); **Da Nang** (22hr., 80,000Đ); **Quy Nhon** (15hr., 69,000Đ); **Pleiku** (10am, 20hr., 70,000Đ); and **Kontum** (8am, 21hr., 76,000Đ). **Mien Tay Station** (tel. 875 29 53), on Hung Vuong in Binh Chanh District west of the city center, sends buses to the **Mekong Delta.** Regular and express bus service to: **Can Tho** (4hr., 15,000Đ); **Ha Tien** (31,000Đ); **Rach Gia** (8hr., 24,000Đ); **Chau Doc** (8hr., 23,500Đ); **Long Xuyen** (6hr., 19,800Đ); **Ca Mau** (12hr., 33,000Đ); and **Bac Lieu** (10hr., 27,400Đ). **Tan Binh Station,** 15 Lach Mong Thang Tam (tel. 864 55 35), in Tan Binh District runs buses to **Tay Ninh** (3hr., 8400Đ). **Cho Lon Station,** 86 Trang Tu (tel. 855 55 29), off Tran Hung Dao, 2 blocks north of Binh Tay Market. Buses go to **My Tho** in the Mekong Delta. **Van Thanh Station,** 152 Dien Bien Phu (tel. 899 48 39, northeast of the city center in Binh Thanh District. Express minibuses leave when full to **Dalat** (5hr., 28,000Đ) and **Vung Tau** (2hr., 16,000Đ).

Ferries: Leave from Vina Express Pier (tel. 829 78 92) on Ton Duc Thang near the intersection with Nguyen Hue. To **Vung Tau** (8am and 2pm, 1hr., $10). Ticket office open Mon.-Sat. 7-11am and 1-5pm, Sun. 7-11am and 1-3pm.

Rentals: Sinh Office, 179 Pham Ngu Lao (tel. 835 56 01). $5 per day for a 90cc motorbike, $6 for a 100cc. Passport deposit required. Open daily 6am-10pm. **Travel agency** at 114A Nguyen Hue (tel. 829 54 17), near city hall and the Vietnam Airlines office. Small bikes $5, larger bikes $8. Open Mon.-Sat. 8am-5pm.

English Language Bookstore: Bookstore Quoc Su, 20 Ho Huan Nghiep (tel. 824 43 88), 50m from the statue of Tran Hung Dao. Mostly used English and French books. Attached outdoor café. Open daily 8am-10pm.

Pharmacies: 678 Nguyen Dinh Chien (tel. 839 59 57), in District 3. The owner speaks English and French. Open daily 7:30am-12:30pm and 2-9pm.

Medical Services: Saigon Hospital, 125 Le Loi (tel. 829 77 09), the emergency center of the city. Also try **Cho Ray Hospital,** 201 Nguyen Chi Thanh (tel. 855 41 37) or the **Australian AEA International Emergency Service and 24-hr. Clinic,** 65 Nguyen Du (tel. 829 85 20), which are popular with foreigners.

Post Offices: GPO, 2 Cong Xa Paris (tel. 829 96 15), to the left of the Notre Dame Cathedral. Considered one of HCMC's architectural treasures. Info desk to the left of the entrance. *Poste Restante.* EMS, DHL, FedEx as well as photocopying, fax, and telex service. Sells domestic calling cards. Open daily 6:30am-10pm.

Telephones: Domestic and **international calls** can be made at hotels (with a surcharge), post offices (the cheapest option), and telephones-for-hire (look for a square blue sign with a red telephone). **HCD** calls at the post office 19,000Đ. Public telephones only place domestic calls. Purchase a calling card from any post office or major book store. **Directory Assistance:** 108. **Telephone code:** 8.

ACCOMMODATIONS

HCMC's largest selection of budget accommodations and services concentrate in District 1 on Pham Ngu Lao. The best and cheapest abodes, however, lie elsewhere. Bui Vien, one block south of Pham Ngu Lao, has nice guest houses, as does Lo Giang, two blocks south of Tran Hung Dao. There are some decent budget spots in Cho Lon, but that area is better known for its prostitutes and pickpockets.

Miss Loi's Guest House, 178/20 Lo Giang (tel. 835 29 73). Hidden away down a narrow alley near the end of Lo Giang past an Isuzu warehouse. If you get lost, ask the locals. Undoubtedly one of the friendliest operations in town. Dorms $3. Clean, simple singles $5. Larger rooms with fan and private bath $8-10. Rooms with balcony, bath and A/C $15. Free coffee, tea, and drinking water.

Phuong Lan Guest House, 70 Bui Vien (tel. 833 05 69), near the intersection with De Tham. Close enough to the restaurants and bars along Pham Ngu Lao to be convenient. Congenial husband and wife management team keeps the rooms clean. Rooms with fan and shared toilet $7, with A/C $22. Doubles with A/C and hot water shower $20. Fruit and tea are on the house.

Ngoc Hue, 171/22 Lo Bac (tel. 836 00 89), just down the alley and on the left from Miss Loi's. Popular with Japanese and French travelers. Quiet and peaceful, with roof top terrace where guests can enjoy an evening beer and take in the HCMC skyline. Excellent value; new rooms with ceiling fan, writing table, and private bath $6, with A/C $10-15. Breakfast included.

Dung, 185/6 H. Pham Ngu Lao (tel. 835 70 49), down a narrow alley, about 30m from the intersection with Nguyen Thai Hoc. One of several nearly identical guest houses on the alleyway, friendly family-run Dung (pronounced "zoom") is a recent addition to the Pham Ngu Lao scene. Nearly sterile rooms with fan and western bath $7, with A/C and hot water $12.

Van Canh Hotel, 184 Calmette (tel. 829 49 63), near the intersection with Tran Hung Dao, across from the Ben Thanh Market. The Soviet-style design won't win any awards, but the location is unbeatable. Rooms are large and clean, although the brown-on-brown color scheme won't brighten anyone's day. Rooms with fan and shared bath 40,000Đ, with A/C and shared bath 70,000Đ. Deluxe rooms with fridge, TV, phone, and hot water 170,000Đ.

Hotel 269, 269 Pham Ngu Lao (tel. 832 23 45), past the intersection with De Tham on the left; look for the vertical sign. Ideal for travelers willing to shell out a few extra dong for more comfortable lodgings. 269 is clean, affordable, and friendly—a combination not always found on Pham Ngu Lao. Bright rooms with ceiling fan, telephone, and flush toilet/shower $10. Larger rooms with A/C, fridge, and hot water $15. Deluxe triples with bathtub $20. All prices negotiable.

Phuong Hoang Hotel, 41 Tran Hung Dao B (tel. 855 18 88), at the intersection with Chau Van Liem, 1 block from the Cho Lon post office. Don't let the drab lobby put you off; upstairs halls and rooms are spotless and freshly painted. Spacious rooms with fan, fridge, writing desk, and private bath go for 135,000Đ, with A/C 270,000Đ. The street below can be rather noisy, but who comes to Cho Lon for tranquility anyway?

Truong Thanh Hotel, 111-117 Chau Van Liem (tel. 855 60 44), 2 blocks north of the intersection with Tran Hung Dao, opposite a theater. Saigon Tourist runs this establishment. A bit dark and worn around the edges, but the friendly staff keeps the rooms in good shape. The higher the hike, the cheaper the bed. Rooms with fan and two beds 55,000Đ, on the middle floors 60,000Đ. A/C rooms with a writing desk and flush toilet 140,000Đ.

Mid-range Accommodations

Hotel 69, 69 Hai Ba Trung (tel. 829 15 13), 50m from the Tran Hung Dao statue, in a central location. Ideal for those who want to see HCMC in style. All rooms have A/C, telephone, hot water, and complimentary toothbrushes. Rates begin at $24 for a small room. Larger rooms with bathtub $29 and $34. Free breakfast.

Thien Thien, 177 Tran Binh Trong (tel. 839 41 89), near the intersection with Nguyen Trai. May be the classiest mid-range digs in Cho Lon, and the location is as quiet as you'll find in this chaotic district. The friendly family who runs this place keeps the rooms clean and serene. Decked-out doubles with A/C, telephone, fridge, writing desk, and hot water $20. Larger rooms with two beds $25.

FOOD

Market food stalls, sidewalk stands, and steamy, hole-in-the-wall greasy spoons may not care much for ambiance, but their food is unbeatable. **Com binh dan** (family restaurants), universally equipped with plastic and metal furniture, feature rice with any number of toppings. Along Pham Ngu Lao and De Tham, tourist cafés can be found, which serve good and cheap food, but cater exclusively to foreigners. The best restaurants in this area are along Nguyen Thai Hoc between the intersections with Pham Ngu Lao and Tran Hung Dao; many of these eateries specialize in seafood. Look to the droves of locals for the best restaurants.

Tin Nghia, 9 Tran Hung Dao (tel. 821 25 38), at the intersection with Pham Ngu Lao, about 300m from Ben Thanh Market. This tiny vegetarian-only haunt predates the liberation of Saigon in 1975. The skillful cook reproduces all the signature Vietnamese dishes using only vegetarian-friendly ingredients. All dishes are under 10,000Đ. Noodles with curry 5000Đ. Fresh spring rolls 1000Đ each. Open daily 7am-2pm and 4-9pm.

Restaurant 13, 13 Ngo Duc Ke (tel. 829 14 17), 2 blocks from the intersection with Nguyen Hue, near the Tran Hung Dao monument. The string of tables set up along the sidewalk outside affirms its popularity with locals and expats alike. The flawless Vietnamese cuisine, generous portions, and efficient service make it well worth the extra dong. Most dishes run 36-45,000Đ. Spring rolls (10,000Đ for 10) are a must. A plethora of seafood options. Open daily 7am-midnight.

Pho Hoa, 260C Pasteur (tel. 829 79 43), in District 3, opposite the Pasteur Institute. Widely regarded as having the best *pho* in the city—ask any Saigonese for confirmation. Combines tasty food with personal service and eclectic decor. 12,000Đ gets a large, mouth-watering bowl of soup, best if eaten with bean sprouts, mint, lime, and chili sauce. Open daily 6am-midnight.

Giural Restaurant, 2A Le Loi (tel. 824 27 50), at the corner with Dong Khoi across from the Continental Hotel. Satiate your sweet-tooth in this A/C bakery-restaurant.

Its central location makes it an ideal place for a mid-afternoon snack while sightseeing. Mouth-watering pastries and Japanese-style *kotobuki* treats 4500-10,000Đ. The restaurant serves expensive western and Asian cuisine (30,000Đ), but most people come for the pastries. Open daily 6am-10:30pm.

Kim Cafeteria, 270 De Tham (tel. 839 81 77). A favorite backpacker hangout. Don't expect to be rubbing shoulders with any locals here, but if it's western company (and food) you crave, Kim's is a fine option. The only thing foreign here is ambiance. Lengthy menu makes up for the lack of decor. Tasty food, friendly prices. Most dishes 6-15,000Đ. Open daily 7am-10pm. Tour office next door.

MARKET

Ho Chi Minh City is, to a large degree, one giant market. **Cho Ben Thanh,** on Le Loi not far from Pham Ngu Lao, is the largest market in District 1 (open daily 6am-6pm). The art deco structure houses textiles, clothing, jewelry, and dried foodstuffs. A better place to shop for clothing is **Cho Tan Dinh** on Hai Ba Trung, at the north end of District 1 opposite the Tan Dinh Catholic Church (open daily 6am-6pm). Tan Dinh Market also has a large fruit and flower section.

The colossal **Cho Lon,** which literally means "big market," dominates District 5. Here motorbikes and delivery trucks careen down the narrow streets, while shops literally ooze out onto the sidewalks. Foreigners are wise to keep an eye out at all times to avoid getting run down by a cartload of diced shrimp or pirated stereos. **Cho An Dong,** also in District 5 between An Duon Vuong and Hung Vuong, is another good place to shop for clothes. The quickest and cheapest way to get to this district from District 1 is to take one of the small blue and yellow buses that run along Tran Hung Dao, and get off at the Cho Lon bus terminal (12,000Đ).

Individual streets are frequently known for a particular product; Huyhn Thuc Khang in District 1 and Tran Hung Dao in Cho Lon are known for electronics and bootlegged CDs imported from China. Nguyen Dinh Chien has quality foreign goods while Pham Hong Thai displays a dizzying assortment of bicycles.

SIGHTS

Most of HCMC's sights are within District 1, except for the famous markets and pagodas of Cho Lon. The most efficient way to cover all the sights downtown is to follow a horseshoe path starting with the Historical Museum and City Zoo in the northeast and ending with the Ho Chi Minh Museum in the southeast. Travelers should get an early start as the heat becomes unbearable by mid-morning. All of these sights can be easily covered in a day or two.

The **Historical Museum,** 2 Nguyen Binh Khiem (tel. 829 81 46), inside the Botanical Garden/Zoo complex, offers a comprehensive history of Vietnam to visitors. Entrance to the museum is only through the main gates of the zoo on Nguyen Binh Khiem. The Historical Museum is the orange structure to the left of the zoo entrance. Inside, the first floor highlights clothing, tools, handicrafts, and artwork from many of Vietnam's minority ethnic cultures. The room with the big, black bust of Uncle Ho contains a 3000-year-old Dong Son bronze drum discovered in 1902. An array of bronze Chinese incense burners points to the heavy influence of the Chinese on Vietnam. (Open Mon.-Sat. 8-11:30am and 1:30-4:30pm, Sun. 8:30am-4:30pm; admission 10,000Đ, visitors must also pay the zoo admission.)

Although it's Vietnam's largest, the **zoo and botanical garden** has only a modest collection of animals, but the landscape is quite attractive with lily ponds and flowering vegetation (open 6am-6pm; admission 11,000Đ). From the exit of the Historical Museum, there is a pagoda on the opposite side of the zoo entrance. Visitors come here to worship at the **altar of Emperor Hung**. The revered first (and, historians will tell you, mythical) emperor is highly regarded as the father of ancient Vietnam. The pagoda carries displays of some of the emperor's tools and armor (open Tues.-Sun. 8-11:30am and 1:30-4:30pm).

Just next door at 2 Le Duan is a **military museum** devoted to documenting the history of the "Ho Chi Minh Campaign," Hanoi's first successful drive to overrun the south in the spring of 1975. The collection includes a few captured American and South Vietnamese knick-knacks with exhibits commemorating the "liberation" of each major South Vietnamese city, culminating with the seizure of Saigon itself on April 30,1975. (Open Tues.-Sun. 8-11:30am and 1:30-4pm.)

Near the intersection of Le Duan and Dong Khoi stands the **Notre Dame Cathedral.** The red structure, built around 1880, is a miniature of its more grand and more famous sibling in Paris, twin spires and all. Three stained-glass windows barely shed enough light on the interior. A mix of Romanesque and pagoda-esque altar styles adorn prayer cubicles along the sides of the cathedral. In front, a white statue of Mother Mary blesses passersby from atop her pedestal. (Open daily 5-11am and 2:30-5:30pm. Wed. masses at 5:30am and 5pm. Sun. masses at 5:30, 6:30, 7:30, 9:30am, 4:30, and 6:30pm.)

Steps away from the Army Museum on Nam Ky Khoi Nghia, is the **Reunification (Thong Nhat) Palace** (open 7:30-10:30am and 1-4pm; admission 40,000Đ, includes brochure and guide). This 60s-style building is actually the second of two palaces built on this site. The original Norodom Palace was constructed in 1868 by the French to house their Governor General. After the French left the country in 1954, South Vietnam's President Ngo Dinh Diem took over the colonial mansion and changed its name to Independence Palace. On February 27, 1962, two Saigon Air Force pilots attempted to assassinate Diem by bombing the palace. The president survived, but his humble abode had to be razed to the ground and replaced by the present structure. Not long after, on April 30, 1975, a communist tank plowed through the gates of the palace to set up the current regime. Independence Palace then became Reunification Palace, undergoing a new political era and another name change. Visitors see the palace as it was in 1975. Among the highlights of the tour are the President's International Reception Room, which resembles a hunter's den with the giant tusks of some poor ancient mammoth; the Credentials Presentation Room with an impressive 40-piece, wall-size lacquer painting; the private living space of the president and his family, the most serene and least ostentatious part of the palace; and the helicopter on the rooftop terrace. For 11,000Đ, tourists can pose for a picture in the helicopter with panoramic HCMC in the background.

The **War Remnants Museum,** 28 Vo Van Tan, formerly known as the War Crimes Museum, lies one block north of the palace (open 7:30-11:45am and 1:30-4:45pm; admission 7000Đ). The museum is about as cheery as you'd expect, filled with an assemblage of war mementos and extensive coverage of the My Lai (Son My) massacre. Weapons, defused bombs, an F-5A plane, fetuses damaged by side-effects of Agent Orange, and the requisite tank in the courtyard are supplemented by brochures in Chinese, French, and English. One of the simplest and most eloquent exhibits in the museum is a statue of a mother, made from bomb fragments.

Past the municipal library is the **Revolutionary Museum,** 65 Ly Tu Trong (tel. 829 97 41). Traditionally dressed Vietnamese women lead tours in broken English through this white, colonial building. Exhibits of inspiring socialist statues of heroes, mothers, and soldiers await tourists around every corner. Chocolate-brown chairs from a more vinyl era are available for resting tour-tired feet. (Open Tues.-Sun. 8-11:30am and 1:30-4:30pm.)

Near the museum at 45 Trung Dinh stands the **Mariamman Hindu Temple** (open daily 7am-7pm). This aqua and pink house of worship is distinguished from the more common red ones by lions, multi-headed icons, and other figurines gracing the facade. The interior features the standard raised prayer platform. Although consecrated to Hinduism, Buddhists also come here to worship.

From the temple, head to the intersection containing the Rex Hotel, City Hall, and the Municipal Theatre. The **Rex Hotel** is a holdover from French glory days; it was once the place for late-night carousing among the French elite. You can now enjoy a panoramic view of the city and a cup of coffee on the rooftop terrace for a relatively exorbitant 20,000Đ. Christmas lights and manicured trees add that certain *je ne sais quoi*. The **Municipal Theatre** is on the way to City Hall coming from the Rex. This slightly dilapidated white colonial building occasionally houses propaganda rallies

On the Trail with Ho Chi Minh:
30 Years of Budget Travel

The Vietnamese have a saying that goes, "A day on the road is a day of wisdom gained." Although most are not aware of it, Ho Chi Minh spent thirty years traveling across the globe in search of adventure, wisdom, and a path to deliver his country from French colonialism, before returning to Vietnam at age 55. Behind the mask of this charismatic revolutionary leader lies a mysterious figure with a penchant for pseudonyms, who remains to this day a conundrum to historians. As is often the case, it is difficult to separate the man and his personal history from the image and the idealism.

In 1912 at age 22, Ho Chi Minh left his homeland after being turned down for admissions at a prestigious colonial school in Vietnam. Assuming the name of Nguyen Va Ba (already his fourth alias), he spent some time tracing the shores of North Africa and the Iberian Peninsula. Eventually, he found his way to the "melting pots" of New York and Boston. Two years later, he skipped across the pond to London where he spent a few years doing odd jobs and even had a stint as an apprentice to a renowned pastry chef. He hung out with Irish nationalists, Fabian socialists, and migrant workers from China and India, then British subjects. Following World War I, Ho, now known as Nguyen Ai Quoc, the "patriot," hopped the Channel to the Paris of Picasso and Hemingway, and engaged himself in politics, joining the anti-colonial crowd of Vietnamese expatriates. During these years, he wrote voluminous political tracts, numerous letters of petition, pamphlets, and newspaper articles.

Despite his absorption with French sophism, he grew weary of the French (as many do) and headed for Moscow in 1924 under the new name of Ly Thuy. There he was recruited by the Comintern and founded the Revolutionary Youth League to train Vietnamese activists. While in Moscow, the Chinese national struggle was under way, and Ho hoped Southeast Asia would soon follow. The next year, he made his way to China, changing his name to Wang, but the splintered Vietnamese struggle and the adverse political climate slowed his plans. From China he went to Hong Kong where he was able to consolidate the various leaders of other independence movements under the aegis of the newly formed Indochinese Communist Party (ICP) in 1930. But an informer tipped off the French, and Ho was thrown in jail for two years before he was diagnosed with tuberculosis. A series of medical transfers found him back in Moscow, but he returned to China after the Japanese invasion of Manchuria. In the spring of 1941, he and his tattered group of revolutionaries made their way along a jungle trail into Vietnam where he made his last name change to Ho Chi Minh, "He who enlightens." He bided his time until the expulsion of the Japanese when he delivered his historic Vietnamese Declaration of Independence in Ba Dinh Square, Hanoi on September 2, 1945. And he did it all without an internal frame pack!

and traditional concerts. Those still craving pictures with Uncle Ho have a perfect opportunity in front of **City Hall** (also referred to as Independence Hall). The beautiful, massive, and well-preserved pastel yellow colonial building features a statue in the mini-park of Uncle Ho consoling a child.

One block south of the quadrangle at 66 Dong Du is the blue **Saigon Central Mosque** (open daily 7am-8pm). Built in 1935 by Indian Muslims living in Saigon, the building still conducts services for a practicing Muslim community of roughly 200 Cham, Vietnamese, and Indian faithfuls. Those accustomed to densely decorated temple interiors will be surprised by the relatively austere interior (no iconography allowed). A shallow, tranquil pool surrounded by cool, clean tiles waits peacefully to the right of the entrance. Unlike traditional mosques, visitors are allowed into the main prayer room. The large niche in the wall marks the main altar; in front of it is a prayer rug pointing toward Mecca.

Head away from the mosque to the east, and turn right down Hai Ba Trung toward the water. In the square at the water's edge sits a **statue of Tran Hung Dao,** the well-loved Vietnamese hero who successfully defended the kingdom from a Chinese incursion in 1228. **Floating restaurants** lurk in large numbers along the river; these are restaurants on boats that tour the river starting around 8pm. Many feature dancing on board. Organize a dinner *à la mer* yourself or inquire with Saigon Tourist (dinner runs around 220,000Đ).

Those who want to know more about Ho Chi Minh, Vietnam's premiere hero and revolutionary leader, should cross the river and turn left to the **Ho Chi Minh Museum,** Nguyen Tat Thanh (tel. 825 10 94). While many Vietnamese might not agree with everything he did, most everyone admires him. One of the most interesting exhibits is a map documenting the many countries Ho visited as a young man. Student groups come here for the requisite history field trips, and your Vietnam tour would never be complete without one more picture with Uncle Ho. (Open Mon.-Fri. 7:30-11:30am and 1:30-4:30pm.)

NIGHTLIFE AND ENTERTAINMENT

Nightlife is the biggest form of entertainment in HCMC and, not surprisingly, the most developed sector of the economy. Every night is fun night in HCMC, but save your best threads for Fridays and Saturdays, when rich locals jam the streets heading for the hippest discos, karaoke parlors, or cafés. The action never stops on Nguyen Hue and Dong Khoi near the Rex Hotel; they're packed around the clock with the hip, the hep, and the slap-happy.

Bars and Cafés

Buffalo Blues, 72A Nguyen Du (tel. 822 28 74). Watch Tuyet Loan pump out "New York, New York" and other jazz favorites with a Harlem accent and a no-nonsense attitude. She's been singing the blues for over 20 years. The Brothers Jazz Band also play here. Barbecue food and plenty of boozin' blues. Beer $3-5.50 per pint. Mixed drinks $3-5.30. Open daily 10am-midnight.

Apocalypse Now, 2C Thi Sach (tel. 824 14 63). New location. Casual hangout for budget travelers and expats alike. Black walls, helicopters on ceilings, blaring rock music, and pool table—a little perverse given HCMC's recent history. Free popcorn with the beer. Witty menu has a wisecrack for every drink. Open daily from 6pm until the last stragglers head home.

Nightclubs and Discos

Nightclubs and discos in HCMC are like any in the west: loud rock and techno, flashing lights, video screens, and the occasional live band. Most clubs here, however, cater to foreigners and house "hostesses" (often prostitutes), who get paid to provide conversation and company to the lone male. The joints listed below are cleaner (or at least less obtrusive) than most. Shorts and sandals are not allowed.

My Man, 27 Ngo Duc Ke (tel. 822 57 53). Claustrophobes shouldn't go past the entrance of this popular disco. Dance skin to skin with wealthy young Saigonese doing the MC Hammer in hardly a square foot of space. No roving hostesses. Cover 30,000Đ. Open daily 8:30pm-midnight.

Queen Bee, 104-106 Nguyen Hue (tel. 829 36 81). Very chic: video screens awe as professional dancers groove on stage. Get down on the packed dance floor or relax on the second floor lounge. Popular with expats and locals alike. 65,000Đ cover includes 1 drink. After that, drinks 17,000Đ. Open daily 8am-1am.

■ Near Ho Chi Minh City: Cu Chi

Perhaps even more than the countless war museums and memorials, few sights capture the remarkable tenacity of the Vietnamese revolutionaries during the war better than the tunnel complex at Cu Chi, 40km away from HCMC. The first tunnels were constructed during the 1940s by the Viet Minh. During the early 1960s, the newly-

The best places to travel may be the best places to get hepatitis A.

You can pick up hepatitis A when traveling to high-risk areas outside of the United States. From raw shellfish or water you don't think is contaminated. Or from uncooked foods — like salad — prepared by people who don't know they're infected. At even the best places.

Symptoms of hepatitis A include jaundice, abdominal pain, fever, vomiting and diarrhea. And can cause discomfort, time away from work and memories you'd like to forget.

The U.S. Centers for Disease Control and Prevention (CDC) recommends immunization for travelers to high-risk areas. *Havrix*, available in over 45 countries, can protect you from hepatitis A. *Havrix* may cause some soreness in your arm or a slight headache.

Ask your physician about vaccination with *Havrix* at your next visit or at least 2 weeks before you travel. And have a great trip.

Please see important patient information adjacent to this ad.

Havrix®
Hepatitis A Vaccine, Inactivated

The world's first hepatitis A vaccine

For more information on how to protect yourself against hepatitis A, call

1-800-HEP-A-VAX (1-800-437-2829)

Manufactured by
SmithKline Beecham Biologicals
Rixensart, Belgium

Distributed by
SmithKline Beecham Pharmaceuticals
Philadelphia, PA 19101

Havrix is a registered trademark of SmithKline Beecham.
HA8606   © SmithKline Beecham, 1996

Hepatitis A Vaccine, Inactivated
Havrix®

See complete prescribing information in SmithKline Beecham Pharmaceuticals literature. The following is a brief summary.

INDICATIONS AND USAGE: *Havrix* is indicated for active immunization of persons ≥ 2 years of age against disease caused by hepatitis A virus (HAV).

CONTRAINDICATIONS: *Havrix* is contraindicated in people with known hypersensitivity to any component of the vaccine.

WARNINGS: Do not give additional injections to patients experiencing hypersensitivity reactions after a *Havrix* injection. (See CONTRAINDICATIONS.)

Hepatitis A has a relatively long incubation period. Hepatitis A vaccine may not prevent hepatitis A infection in those who have an unrecognized hepatitis A infection at the time of vaccination. Additionally, it may not prevent infection in those who do not achieve protective antibody titers (although the lowest titer needed to confer protection has not been determined).

PRECAUTIONS: As with any parenteral vaccine (1) keep epinephrine available for use in case of anaphylaxis or anaphylactoid reaction; (2) delay administration, if possible, in people with any febrile illness or active infection, except when the physican believes withholding vaccine entails the greater risk; (3) take all known precautions to prevent adverse reactions, including reviewing patients' history for hypersensitivity to this or similar vaccines.

Administer with caution to people with thrombocytopenia or a bleeding disorder, or people taking anticoagulants. Do not inject into a blood vessel. Use a separate, sterile needle or prefilled syringe for every patient. When giving concomitantly with other vaccines or IG, use separate needles and different injection sites.

As with any vaccine, if administered to immunosuppressed persons or persons receiving immunosuppressive therapy, the expected immune response may not be obtained.

Carcinogenesis, Mutagenesis, Impairment of Fertility: *Havrix* has not been evaluated for its carcinogenic potential, mutagenic potential or potential for impairment of fertility.

Pregnancy Category C: Animal reproduction studies have not been conducted with *Havrix*. It is also not known whether *Havrix* can cause fetal harm when administered to a pregnant woman or can affect reproduction capacity. Give *Havrix* to a pregnant woman only if clearly needed. It is not known whether *Havrix* is excreted in human milk. Because many drugs are excreted in human milk, use caution when administering *Havrix* to a nursing woman.

Havrix is well tolerated and highly immunogenic and effective in children.

Fully inform patients, parents or guardians of the benefits and risks of immunization with *Havrix*. For persons traveling to endemic or epidemic areas, consult current CDC advisories regarding specific locales. Travelers should take all necessary precautions to avoid contact with, or ingestion of, contaminated food or water. Duration of immunity following a complete vaccination schedule has not been established.

ADVERSE REACTIONS: *Havrix* has been generally well tolerated. As with all pharmaceuticals, however, it is possible that expanded commercial use of the vaccine could reveal rare adverse events.

The most frequently reported by volunteers in clinical trials was injection-site soreness (56% of adults; 21% of children); headache (14% of adults; less than 9% of children). Other solicited and unsolicited events are listed below:

Incidence 1% to 10% of Injections: Induration, redness, swelling; fatigue, fever (>37.5°C), malaise; anorexia, nausea.

Incidence <1% of Injections: Hematoma; pruritus, rash, urticaria; pharyngitis, other upper respiratory tract infections; abdominal pain, diarrhea, dysgeusia, vomiting; arthralgia, elevation of creatine phosphokinase, myalgia; lymphadenopathy; hypertonic episode, insomnia, photophobia, vertigo.

Additional safety data

Safety data were obtained from two additional sources in which large populations were vaccinated. In an outbreak setting in which 4,930 individuals were immunized with a single dose of either 720 EL.U. or 1440 EL.U. of *Havrix*, the vaccine was well-tolerated and no serious adverse events due to vaccination were reported. Overall, less than 10% of vaccinees reported solicited general adverse events following the vaccine. The most common solicited local adverse event was pain at the injection site, reported in 22.3% of subjects at 24 hours and decreasing to 2.4% by 72 hours.

In a field efficacy trial, 19,037 children received the 360 EL.U. dose of *Havrix*. The most commonly reported adverse events were injection-site pain (9.5%) and tenderness (8.1%), reported following first doses of *Havrix*. Other adverse events were infrequent and comparable to the control vaccine Engerix-B® (Hepatitis B Vaccine, Recombinant).

Postmarketing Reports: Rare voluntary reports of adverse events in people receiving *Havrix* since market introduction include the following: localized edema; anaphylaxis/anaphylactoid reactions, somnolence; syncope; jaundice, hepatitis; erythema multiforme, hyperhidrosis, angioedema; dyspnea; lymphadenopathy; convulsions, encephalopathy, dizziness, neuropathy, myelitis, paresthesia, Guillain-Barré syndrome, multiple sclerosis; congenital abnormality.

The U.S. Department of Health and Human Services has established the Vaccine Adverse Events Reporting System (VAERS) to accept reports of suspected adverse events after the administration of any vaccine, including, but not limited to, the reporting of events required by the National Childhood Vaccine Injury Act of 1986. The toll-free number for VAERS forms and information is 1-800-822-7967.

HOW SUPPLIED: 360 EL.U./0.5 mL: NDC 58160-836-01 Package of 1 single-dose vial.

720 EL.U./0.5 mL: NDC 58160-837-01 Package of 1 single-dose vial; NDC 58160-837-02 Package of 1 prefilled syringe.

1440 EL.U./mL: NDC 58160-835-01 Package of 1 single-dose vial; NDC 58160-835-02 Package of 1 prefilled syringe.

Manufactured by **SmithKline Beecham Biologicals**
Rixensart, Belgium
Distributed by **SmithKline Beecham Pharmaceuticals**
Philadelphia, PA 19101
BRS–HA:L5A

Havrix is a registered trademark of SmithKline Beecham.

formed National Liberation Front (Viet Cong) greatly expanded the tunnel complex; at one point the network of underground passageways stretched from Cu Chi, clear to the Cambodian border. The tunnels were used to extend NLF control over the area and as a base for commando raids and infiltrations of Saigon. Not surprisingly, the Americans in turn used every means at their disposal to eliminate the underground sanctuaries. The area around Cu Chi, known as the "Iron Triangle," became one the most bombed pieces of real estate on earth.

Today you can visit the **tunnel complex** and, although it's quite touristy—the tunnels have been widened to accommodate broad-shouldered foreign guerrillas and are reinforced with concrete—it remains interesting (open daily 8am-5pm; admission 55,000Đ includes a tour in English). At times the Vietnamese efforts to make Cu Chi a tourist destination seem chilling; it is likely few visitors will opt to don the black pajamas and "Ho Chi Minh sandals" that were de rigeur for a Viet Cong guerrilla. To get there via public transportation take a bus heading for Tay Ninh from Tan Dinh Bus Station (1½hr., 5000Đ). Ask to be let out at Cu Chi. From Cu Chi tourists will have to take a motorcycle taxi the final 20km to the tunnels (10-15,000Đ). Beware that gleaning transportation back to Ho Chi Minh City may be tough. An easier, if less adventurous, option is to book a one-day tour with one of the tourist cafés on Pham Ngu Lao. Sinh Café (see **Budget Travel** above) runs a tour to Cu Chi and the Cao Dai temple at Tay Ninh for $4 per person.

▓ Vũng Tàu

For over a century now, Vung Tau has been to the Saigonese what the Hamptons are to New Yorkers: a place to escape the grind of their urban existence for a little R&R, but still close enough (100km) to scuttle back on Sunday afternoon. The French colonialists, who called the place Cap St. Jacques, began the trend, erecting a number of luxurious villas which played host to generations of Vietnamese elites. It is a safe bet that Vung Tau was far more attractive in the 1890s than the 1990s; today its ugly gray sand beaches are lined with even uglier concrete pillbox-style hotels and cheap cafés catering to the weekend crowd.

If it's sandy white beaches and crystal-clear water you're after, head north to Nha Trang, but Vung Tau does offer a very respectable series of sights as well as the opportunity to mix with Vietnamese tourists to a degree not possible in other, more segregated destinations.

ORIENTATION

Four beaches run the length of Vung Tau's peninsula: **Bai Dau** lies in a small alcove northwest of town; **Bai Truoc** (Front Beach) guards the shore in front of the town but is too rocky for swimming; **Bai Dua** lies on the coast south of Nui Nho; and **Bai Sau** (Back Beach) runs up the east coast. **Duong Tran Phu** traverses the coast from Bai Dau to the town, where it becomes **Duong Quang Trung**. Once past Bai Truoc, Quang Trung becomes **Duong Ha Long,** which extends to the point of the cape, curves northeast along Bai Sau, and mutates once again into **Duong Thuy Van. Duong Hoang Hoa Tham** connects Bai Truoc to Bai Sau.

PRACTICAL INFORMATION

Currency Exchange: Vietcombank, 27-29 Tran Hung Dao (tel. 852 309), near the center of town. Open Mon.-Fri. 7-11:30am and 1:30-4:30pm (no transactions on Thurs. afternoon), Sat. 7-11:30am and 1-4pm.

Buses: Vung Tau Station, 50 Nam Ky Khoi Nghia (tel. 859 727). Frequent buses to **HCMC** (5am-2am, 2hr., 14,000Đ).

Ferries: Vina Express (tel. 859 515) hydrofoils leave from the pier on Bai Truoc opposite Hai Au Hotel. To **HCMC** (11am and 4:15pm, 1hr., 110,000Đ).

Rentals: Bikes are the optimum means of transportation in Vung Tau, available at most hotels and guest houses for about 5000Đ per day.

Markets: The **old market,** at the intersection of Ly Thuong Kiet and Do Chien in the center of town. Tiny, with a few clothing stalls. **Cho Mo,** on Nam Ky Khoi Nghia past the bus station, is larger and more vibrant. A number of **food stalls** sell mammoth bowls of *pho* and other dishes. Open daily 6am-6pm. Numerous souvenir stalls line Quang Trung along Bai Truoc.

Pharmacies: 8 Nam Ky Khoi Nghia. Open daily 7am-noon and 3-9pm.

Medical Services: Le Loi Hospital, 22 Le Loi (tel. 832 432), operates a small clinic for foreigners. English and French spoken. **Friendship Hospital,** 99 Le Loi (tel. 838 348), just up the street. Financed and built in 1989 by a group of American Vietnam War veterans and their Vietnamese counterparts.

Post Offices/Telephones: GPO, 4 Le Hong Pheng. Has **international telephones,** fax, telegram, FedEx, and DHL. Open daily 6am-9pm.

ACCOMMODATIONS AND CAMPING

Accommodations in Vung Tau are expensive, while the ones that fit the budget traveler's pocket are often former Russian compounds. Most of these cluster around the more popular beach areas of Bai Truoc and Bai Sau. Bai Truoc's conveniently located accommodations in town are more costly, but it's a long hike to the more pleasant beach at Bai Sau. Bai Dau and Bai Dua are tucked away from the hustle and bustle but lack decent accommodations and favorable swimming conditions.

Bai Truoc

Most of Vung Tau's nicest (and most expensive) hotels are in this area. The accommodations are all former Russian compounds. Far and away the most pleasant of the compound-style hotels is the **Thang Long,** 45 Thong Nhat (tel. 852 175), east of the intersection with Tran Hung Dao opposite a Catholic church. Recently renovated, it's still reasonably priced. Small rooms with fan go for $7, while bright, airy rooms with A/C cost $15. Larger rooms with writing desk and hot water are still more at $20. **Nha Nghi 14,** 14 Le Loi (tel. 854 648), is at the southern end of Le Loi. Leave your pro-democracy propaganda at home; this guest house is run by the Ministry of the Interior. Actually it is quite clean, cheap, and friendly. Rooms with two beds, fan, and hot water cost $7, with A/C and TV $15. **Hai Son,** 27 Le Loi (tel. 832 955), resembles the best Stalingrad has to offer, but the price is right. Rather unkempt doubles with fan go for 80,000Đ, much cleaner and more pleasant rooms with A/C are 100-250,000Đ depending on the size and accoutrements. For more frills, the **Song Hong Hotel,** 12 Hoang Dien (tel. 852 137), offers cheap rooms starting at $25, which gets you wall-to-wall carpeting, telephone, stocked fridge, and hot water.

Bai Dua

Not much here for anything approaching a backpacker's budget. For comfy rooms and great views, try the **Bai Dua Villas,** 22 Ha Long, directly across from the Bai Dua restaurant. Rooms farthest from the ocean are cheapest, with A/C, bathtub, and fridge for $20, closer to the water $30.

Bai Sau

29 Thuy Van (tel. 853 481) is located where you would imagine it to be. The extremely polite and convivial family speaks great English. Popular with backpackers, 29 has a refreshing side yard and inexpensive rooms which share a toilet. Doubles cost 44-88,000Đ. **Bimexco** (tel. 859 916), on Thuy Van, lies on the northern end of the beach, in a tree-filled, quiet camp environment. The bathrooms are tiny and toilets sometimes leak, but it's still nicer than the other compounds. Rooms with fan cost 120-200,000Đ, with A/C 150-300,000Đ. For a cheaper bed, the traveler might try **Thang Muo Hotel,** 46 Thuy Van (tel. 852 665), which has huge rooms with A/C and fridge for 160,000Đ (includes breakfast). Nicer rooms with TV, phone, and bathtub go for 270,000Đ. There is also a swimming pool and volleyball to keep the backpacker amused and fit.

FOOD

Vung Tau is packed with pricey seafood joints where you can plan on spending at least 50,000Đ for a simple meal. For cheaper eats, make tracks for Do Chien in the center of town, where *quan com binh dan* (food shops) abound and a meal of *pho* or fried rice can be had for 10,000Đ tops.

Bai Dua Restaurant, 22 Ha Long (tel. 856 281), at the tip of the peninsula. Doric columns, cloth napkins, and a terrace overlooking the water. As chic as Vung Tau gets. If it swims, you can eat it here. Sea cucumbers with pig's feet like Mom used to make 40,000Đ. Open daily 7am-9pm.

Hue Anh, 446 Truong Cong Dinh (tel. 856 663), about 50m from the intersection with Ha Long. Expensive Chinese food and a hyper-kinetic monkey in the courtyard. Most dishes 30-80,000Đ. Open daily 9:30am-9:30pm.

SIGHTS

There isn't much to do in Vung Tau aside from rolling in the sand and macerating in the water. With that in mind, those who'd like a break from the beaches should head to **Lang Ca Ong Pagoda** on Dinh Thang Tam. This three-building complex sits amidst verdant plants and surrounds a simple courtyard. The pagoda was built in 1911 to honor the whale (not Moby Dick but his older, more friendly, Vietnamese cousin Ca Ong, Vung Tau's patron god) for protecting and rescuing men at sea (open daily 7am-4pm).

The **Thich Ca Phat Dai Pagoda** and sculpture park is popular with Vietnamese tourists. Built in 1961, this huge complex is dedicated to the Thich Ca Buddha, the god of creativity. The Buddha worship seems to have created a miraculous number of souvenir shops in the area around the pagoda. Follow the winding, untended path through the complex and you'll see locals making their way up the steep path to their homes. The first pagoda, with the overwhelming tangy smell of incense, houses the typical gold-clad Buddha and bell, but remains humble in its other furnishings. The top of the hill features a stunning view of the ocean. To get here head all the way down Le Loi. When you can't go any farther, turn left. The pagoda is 500m down Toan Phu (open 6am-6pm; admission 15,000Đ).

The **Bach Dinh Museum** is on Quang Trung, just north of Bai Truoc. The museum is housed in a small mansion originally built by the French as a retreat for the governor-general and his mistresses. Later on it was occupied by Bao Dai, Vietnam's last emperor, and his mistresses. During the 1960s, South Vietnamese President Nguyen Van Thien occasionally frolicked here as well. The collection is small but interesting, and remarkably apolitical. Highlights include an extensive collection of Vietnamese and Chinese porcelain. After taking in the museum, some Chinese travelers quaff glasses of snake blood, a veritable potion of youth and virility, at the shop next to the mansion. (Open daily 7am-5pm; admission 20,000Đ.)

Vung Tau has its share of large statues. The **Thich Ca Phat Dai,** a giant white statue of Buddha in the lotus position, meditates atop the hill at Bai Dau north of the U.S. Airforce Base. Christianity, not to be outdone, provides the graying **Statue of Jesus** atop Nui Nho at the top of the cape.

MEKONG DELTA

What the rest of the world calls the Mekong Delta, the Vietnamese call *dong bang song cuu lang* (river of the nine-headed dragon), a reference to its nine principle tributaries. Rural life in the Delta is very different from rural society in Central or North Vietnam. Villages here are less insular, and their social structures less restrictive. This is due both to history and geography—there is far more land here than in the densely populated North, making for a more mobile population. The Vietnamese are in fact relatively new to the region, as large scale migrations only began in the early 19th century, roughly contemporaneous with the settlement of the American west. The Vietnamese displaced large numbers of ethnic Khmers living in the Delta (this territory once belonged to the Angkor Empire), a move which explains the ethnic tension between the two nations today. These Vietnamese immigrants, many of whom were from among the lowest social class in the North, did not duplicate the hierarchical, patriarchal social systems which characterized northern villages. When the French arrived in the 1860s, they realized the region's agricultural potential and began massive land reclamation projects turning thousands of hectares of swamp into some of the most fertile paddie land in the world.

Today the Delta feeds much of the country and produces enough surplus to make Vietnam the world's third leading rice exporter. Life here is hard, but the always friendly locals invariably greet the odd foreign traveler with warm smiles and big waves. Traveling in this region can be taxing, as the public buses are far from luxurious. The rewards, however, are great, for it affords a chance to view a way of life as yet largely unchanged by economic development.

■ Mỹ Tho

My Tho might well be dubbed the gateway to the Mekong Delta region because of its proximity to HCMC, yet many travelers choose to skip it entirely and begin their Delta explorations instead in more popular Can Tho. The strong-arm tactics of the local tourism authority have also kept budget travelers at bay. Despite the criticism that it is neither as large nor as interesting as Can Tho, this quiet, riverine town has much to recommend itself, including river excursions, gregarious locals, and a delicious style of *hu tieu* noodle soup. Particularly if you are traveling by local transport and wish to avoid overly taxing bus rides, My Tho makes a pleasant, gentle introduction to the Delta before pushing on to other choice locales.

ORIENTATION

My Tho, just 70km south of HCMC, is the capital of Tien Giang Province. Although a provincial seat, this sleepy town should pose no significant navigational challenge. **Duong Ap Bac** runs from the northern outskirts of town, past the bus station, intersecting **Duong Hung Vuong,** My Tho's principle north-south thoroughfare, 3km later. **Duong 30 Thong 4,** running along the banks of the Tien Giang River, marks the town's southern border. At the large statue of Thu Khoa Huan, 30 Thong 4 turns north, becoming **Duong Trung Trac.** My Tho's central market sprawls along Trung Trac north of the intersection with **Duong Dinh Bo Linh.**

PRACTICAL INFORMATION

Tourist Offices: Tien Giang Tourist, 8 D. 30 Thang 4 (tel. 873 477), just west of the public landing. Run by the People's Committee of Tien Giang Province, it operates most of the hotels and several restaurants in My Tho. Organizes pricey tours of the province's principal attractions including river excursions. Glossy brochures with maps in Vietnamese and French. Open Mon.-Sat. 7am-4pm.

Currency Exchange: from the bank at 15B Nam Ky Khoi Nghia (tel. 873 420), at the corner with Thu Khoa Huan. Open Mon.-Sat. 7:30-11am and 1:30-4pm.

Buses: Bus station, 4km northwest of town at 42 Ap Bac (tel. 875 274) on the way to HCMC. Daily buses to: **Tay Ninh** (13,400Đ); **Vung Tau** (15,400Đ); **Can Tho** (10,800Đ); **Chau Doc** (18,500Đ); and **HCMC** (6200Đ). Most long distance buses leave early in the morning (5-8am).

Rentals: Bikes are available from most hotels, or a second Tien Giang Tourist office at 63 Trung Trac. Standard price 10,000Đ per day.

Markets: My Tho has two large markets. The closest one lies along the west bank of the Bao Dinh River, north of Dinh Bo Linh. Chock full of producer sellers, fish mongers, and food stalls. Open sunrise to sunset. The new **indoor market** is at the corner of Le Loi and Le Dai Hanh, one block west of the Bao Dinh River. The place for sandals and clothes. Open daily 6am-8pm.

VIETNAM

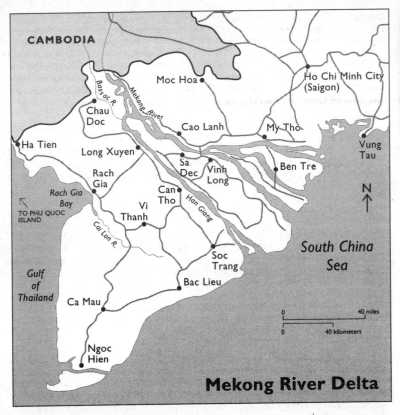

Mekong River Delta

Medical Services: My Tho General Hospital, 2 Hung Vuong (tel. 872 354).
Post Offices/Telephones: GPO, 59 30 Thong 4 (tel. 873 245), across the street
from the public landing. Fax, **international telephones,** and telegrams. Open
Mon.-Sat. 6am-9pm. **Telephone code:** 073.

ACCOMMODATIONS

Due in part to the overbearing approach of the Tien Giang Tourist Company, tourism
in My Tho has long lagged behind that in other popular Delta destinations. The dearth
of decent hotels here is a testament to this. Note: As of summer 1996, several hotels,
including the **Khach San 43,** 43 Ngo Quyen, were not accepting foreigners. This situation could change at any time so it may be worth checking.

Cong Doan Hotel, 61 30 Thong 4 (tel. 874 324), next door to the post office. Run
by the provincial labor union, the Cong Doan offers pleasant rooms at proletarian
prices (for My Tho, that is). Nice views of the Tien Giang River from the 2nd floor
balcony. Bright, airy rooms with fan and shared bath for 1-3 people 70,000Đ, for 4
people 80,000Đ. Rooms with fan and private bath 80-100,000Đ. Doubles with TV,
fridge, A/C, and hot water 200,000Đ.
Song Tien Hotel, 101 Trung Trac (tel. 872 009), just before the intersection with
Dinh Bao Linh, about 2 blocks north of the Huong Duong Hotel. Alternatively
known as the Ap Bac Hotel. A very friendly place, and the views of My Tho and the
surrounding countryside from the higher floors are exceptional. A/C rooms are
good value at $10 for a double, with fridge $15, with hot water $20.

FOOD

Aside from a few touristy establishments operated by Tien Giang Tourist, there is little in the way of fine dining to be had in My Tho. Your best option is to head for one of the many cheap eateries along Trung Trac between the Thu Khoa Hoan statue and the bridge. **Chi Thanh Restaurant,** 56 Trung Trac (tel. 873 756) is packed at night and most dishes cost less than 10,000Đ. This is a good spot to try *hu tieu* My Tho, a local variation on the noodle soup sold throughout southern Vietnam.

SIGHTS

One day is more than enough time to take in My Tho's fairly meager amount of attractions. Across the Nguyen Trai Bridge off Nguyen Trung Trac is the **Vinh Trang Pagoda,** a large, slightly faded temple surrounded by water fountains (open daily 7:30am-noon and 2-5pm). The inside of the temple is quite beautiful, constructed of hardwood and decorated with ornately carved dragons covered in gold leaf.

Twelve km outside My Tho to the west is the **Dong Tam Snake Farm** (open daily 7am-5pm), where a variety of pythons and cobras are raised for their skin, meat, and venom (to make snake-bite antidotes). Motorcycles can be hired for about 30,000Đ roundtrip to run there.

Boat trips on the Tien Giang River are another popular activity in My Tho (although they are cheaper in Can Tho). Potential destinations include the **Coconut Monk Island,** a small island 30 minutes from My Tho that was once home to a bizarre religious community overseen by the "coconut monk," a French-educated mystic who preached a doctrine that blended Buddhism and Christianity. The remains of his fanciful retreat still stand. **Tan Long Island,** a 15-minute boat trip from My Tho, is famous for its fruit orchards. Small boats can be hired from the public landing opposite the Cong Doan at the intersection of 30 Thong 4 and Le Loi. Getting to Tan Long Island costs 30,000Đ, to Coconut Monk Island 50,000Đ.

■ Cần Tho'

Can Tho (population 400,000) is the official capital of Can Tho Province and the unofficial capital of the entire nine-province Mekong Delta. From here roadways and waterways link the city with more far-flung destinations. The city has always been the focus of most of the foreign investment in the Delta; at night illuminated billboards hawking Japanese electronics glow on the opposite bank of the river.

But don't think for a moment that this development has spoiled Can Tho's tourist appeal. This picturesque town, with its broad boulevards and welcoming locals, is arguably the most popular destination in the Delta, and with good reason. Can Tho is probably the best place to experience the Delta as it was meant to be seen—by boat. For a dollar or two per hour, *sampan* can be hired to visit vibrant floating markets and paddle up tiny canals to explore quiet villages and fruit orchards.

Can Tho's wide range of accommodations and cheap, tasty food also offers a degree of variety not found elsewhere. For all these reasons Can Tho makes the ideal springboard to the Delta detour.

ORIENTATION

Can Tho is 170km southwest of Ho Chi Minh City, at the confluence of the Hau Giang and Can Tho Rivers. **Duong Hoa Binh** is the principle thoroughfare, and several museums, the bank, and post office lie along the northern end. **Duong Hai Ba Trung** runs along the bank of the Can Tho River. Several budget hotels can be found here, north of the statue of Ho Chi Minh; south of the statue is the vast **market district.** **Duong Nguyen An Ninh** and **Duong Chau Van Liem** link Hai Ba Trung with Hoa Binh; a number of budget hotels line Chau Van Liem between **Duong Phan Dinh Phung** and **Duong Dong Khoi.** Maps, should one be necessary, are available at the GPO for 1500Đ.

PRACTICAL INFORMATION

Tourist Offices: Can Tho Tourism, 20 Hai Ba Trung (tel. 821 852), organizes expensive tours to destinations in the Delta. Open daily 7:10-11am and 1-5pm.
Currency Exchange: Vietcombank, 7 Hoa Binh (tel. 820 445). Open Mon.-Sat. 7:30-11:30am and 1-3pm. **Exchange Bureau,** 27 Phan Dinh Phung (tel. 820 192). Open Mon.-Fri. 7:30-11am and 1:30-4pm, Sat. 7:30-11am. Hotels often have exchange services as well.
Air Travel: Vietnam Airlines Office, 20 Hai Ba Trung (tel. 821 853), run by Can Tho Tourism (see above).
Buses: Bus station (tel. 821 475 for info), northwest of town on Nguyen Trai, near the intersection with Hung Vuong and Rte. 4. Daily buses to: **Long Xuyen** (5500Đ); **Chau Doc** (9600Đ); **Rach Gia** (10,000Đ); **HCMC** (15,600Đ); and **Dalat** (38,600Đ).
Ferries: Dock is on the corner of Hai Ba Trung and Ngo Quyen near the market. A blackboard in the terminal lists destinations and prices, but most are obscure. At present there are no regular ferries to HCMC. To **Ca Mau** (10,400Đ).
Rentals: Bikes and **motorbikes** are available at most accommodations. Try Huy Hoang Hotel (see **Accommodations** below).
Markets: On Hai Ba Trung, between Ngo Quyen and Chau Van Liem.
Medical Services: Can Tho General Hospital, 4 Chau Van Liem (tel. 821 288), at the corner with Hoa Binh.
Post Offices/Telephones: 2 Hoa Binh (tel. 822 105). Telegrams, **international phones,** and fax. EMS and DHL service in the EMS building to the left of the post office (tel. 820 584). Both open daily 6:30am-8pm. **Telephone code:** 071.

ACCOMMODATIONS

Hotels cluster along Hai Ba Trung north of the Ho Chi Minh statue, along Chau Van Liem, and along smaller Ngo Duc Ke one block south of Chau Van Liem.

Huy Hoang Hotel, 35 Ngo Duc Ke (tel. 825 833), 1 block south of the Chau Van Liem-Phan Dinh Phung intersection. As close as Can Tho gets to a decent guest house; it's clean, cheap, and friendly. Freshly painted doubles with writing desk, private bath, and ceiling fan 77,000Đ. Rooms with A/C 130,000Đ.
Khach San 31, 31 Ngo Duc Ke (tel. 825 287), next door to the Huy Hoang. A copy-cat operation if there ever was one; the friendly owners are obviously trying to capitalize on the Huy Hoang's success. The 31's rooms are newer and slightly cheaper than next door. Singles with private bath 66,000Đ. Doubles 75,000Đ. Larger rooms with A/C 100,000Đ.
Hau Giang B Hotel, 27 Chau Van Liem (tel. 821 950). Not to be confused with the more upscale Hau Giang Hotel on Nam Ky Khoi Nghia, this is a Can Tho Tourist-run operation. Rooms are good value. Spacious, sweet-smelling abodes with writing desk and ceiling fan for 88,000Đ, with A/C 122,000Đ. Deluxe rooms with A/C and hot water go for 155,000Đ.
Phong Nha, 75 Chau Van Liem (tel. 821 615). The myriad English signs in the lobby instruct guests how to behave at this popular backpacker hangout. Decent English spoken. Simple, clean singles with fan, bath, and writing desk $5. Doubles $6. Triples $10. Larger rooms with A/C $15.
Viet Huong, 33-35 Chau Van Liem (tel. 824 832), 2 blocks closer to the river from Phong Nha Hotel. Don't let the dank, vaguely cave-like lobby scare you; the rooms are recently renovate A/C rooms may be the best in town; doubles with desk and gorgeous bathroom $10. Equally attractive singles with fan $7. Non-renovated rooms are, er, liveable. Singles with fan and bathroom $4. Doubles $6.

FOOD

The few restaurants in Can Tho tend toward the functional rather than the froofy, but the food is definitely filling. All the restaurants offer the same kind of food. Seafood is generally fresh and good. Specialties of the area include *lau* (seafood vegetable soup), and *canh chua* (sour fish soup). A number of cheap restaurants line Nam Ky Khoi Nghia east of the intersection with Dien Bien Phu.

Vinh Loi Restaurant, 42 Hai Ba Trung (tel. 821 124). If you wake up in the middle of the night with your tummy rumblin' for attention, stumble over to Vinh Loi. This greasy spoon features good food, average prices, friendly staff, and chirping locusts to make it go down just right. Rice with chicken or spareribs, or breakfast 6000Đ. Open all day, every day.

Thien Hoa Restaurant, 26 Hai Ba Trung (tel. 821 942). Friendly servers offer a comprehensive and mouth-watering menu of seafood dishes. Chinese stewed shrimp is the specialty. All entrees under 15,000Đ. Open daily 9:30am-midnight.

California Ice Cream, 18 Hoa Binh. Not quite Ben and Jerry's, but enough to remind you of home. They claim the ice cream is imported from America, but the only thing that might have arrived from those foreign shores is the machine. Teeny tiny dish 3000Đ. Open daily 8am-10pm.

SIGHTS

The principle attraction in Can Tho is to hire a small boat and explore the provincial waterways. A typical trip includes a visit to the **floating market** at Phung Hiep, where vendors sell fruits or vegetables from boats. Even more interesting is an excursion up one of the many canals that criss-cross the area. Don't worry about finding a boat; simply head down Hai Ba Trung at the beginning of the market and plenty of offers will be made. (Trips average 20,000Đ per hour.)

For those who want to wander through Can Tho, there are two temples that can be viewed briefly. The **Munirangsyaram Pagoda,** 36 Hoa Binh, is a Theravada Buddhist temple built by the Khmers; it has distinctive detail carvings and a slender design (open daily 6am-5pm). Inside rests a Thich Ca Buddha. The **Vang Pagoda,** also on Hoa Binh, is an unexceptional town pagoda.

Ho Chi Minh Museum, on Hoa Binh to the left of post office, awaits anyone still not saturated with socialist sights, but may not satisfy the seeker; the museum remains in a state of disrepair, with random construction materials scattered among the displays. (Supposedly open 7am-4pm, but the sleeping guard may ignore your knocks if you come during his 4-hr. mid-day nap; free.) The brand new **Weapons Museum** behind the Ho Chi Minh Museum features canons, surface-to-air missile launchers, and a hollowed-out Huey helicopter.

Can Tho Park, at the intersection of Chau Van Liem and Hoa Binh, has a friendly ferris wheel and an appealing patch of greenery. It's a welcome break from the concrete of the city; tourists can come here to watch the submarine races.

■ Long Xuyên

Long Xuyen, the capital of An Giang Province, is no one's favorite destination in the Mekong Delta, but buses to Chau Doc or Rach Gia invariably stop here. Cheerful Long Xuyen plays its role as transit point admirably, providing decent accommodations and food to road-weary travelers. A paddle on the Hau Giang River and a wander through Long Xuyen's gargantuan market are about all this city of 100,000 denizens can offer to the traveler.

While perhaps not Vietnam's next tourist hot spot, Long Xuyen is nevertheless crucial to the country's economic future. It is largely due to An Giang's fertile rice fields that Vietnam has established herself as the world's third leading rice exporter (behind the U.S. and Thailand). Indicators of the province's relative prosperity can be seen in the TV antennae perched above many bamboo huts while shiny new motorbikes wait out front.

In 1939 the Hoa Hao religious sect was founded here by Huynh Phi So, a mystic who believed himself to be a reincarnation of the Maitreya Buddha (Buddha of the Future). Along with the Cao Dai sect, the Hoa Hao remains a powerful regional force, with its own military until the late 1950s.

PRACTICAL INFORMATION

Tourist Offices: An Giang Tourist, 83-85 Nguyen Hue (tel. 852 036). Big smiles, glossy brochures, and pricey package tours. Get all info for Chau Doc here since there's no branch office there. Open Mon.-Sat. 8am-4pm.

Currency Exchange: Vietcombank, 20-22 Ngo Gia Tu (tel. 844 210). Open Mon.-Sat. 7-11am and 1-5pm.

Buses: Bus station, 414 Tran Hung Dao (tel. 841 125), about 1km south of the traffic circle on the outskirts of town. To: **Chau Doc** (2hr., 5500Đ); **Can Tho** (2hr., 5500Đ); **HCMC** (6hr., 19,800Đ); **Rach Gia** (2hr., 6500Đ); **Ha Tien** (4hr., 14,000Đ); and **Ca Mau** (5hr., 18,200Đ).

Ferries: For what it's worth, the Long Xuyen ferry terminal (tel. 854 846) is on Tran Quoc Toan, the small dirt road that is the first right after crossing Duy Tan Bridge. Ferries go to more isolated Delta towns and sometimes HCMC.

Local Transporation: 3-wheeled **pedicabs** and motorized **trishaws** provide local transport, although Long Xuyen is small enough to walk around. From the bus station into town is 2000Đ, but they'll ask for 5 times that at first.

Markets: The **Long Xuyen Market** occupies a vast swath of territory along the river north and south of Nguyen Hue (see **Sights** below).

Medical Services: Chau Van Liem (tel. 852 862), to the right off Ly Trieu Kiet, 1km beyond Duy Tan Bridge. It should only be for the desperate.

Post Offices/Telephones: GPO, 11-13 Ngo Gia Tu (tel. 841 467), diagonally across from the Vietcombank. **International phone calls,** faxes, and telegrams here. Open daily 6am-9pm. **Telephone code:** 076.

ACCOMMODATIONS

There is no shortage of hotels in Long Xuyen although decent budget options are in rather short supply.

Khach San Phat Thanh, 2 Ly Tu Trong (tel. 841 708), near the corner of Ly Tu Trong and Doan Van Phoi. Long Xuyen's best budget offering. The color scheme indicates the decorators' rather intense fondness for Pepto-bismol pink. Pleasant singles with 1 double bed, ceiling fan, and cramped but clean bath 60,000Đ. Doubles with 2 beds and writing desk 70,000Đ, with A/C 100,000Đ.

Khach San Thai Binh 2, 4 Nguyen Hue A (tel. 841 859), on the left just before the intersection with Doan Van Phoi; look for the vertical sign. Much nicer than the original Thai Binh just up the street, it lacks the latter's subterranean feel. Maybe the cleanest bathrooms in An Giang Province. Fresh shiny singles with ceiling fan, phone, and even a packet of smokes 70,000Đ. Doubles with A/C 120,000Đ, with fridge and TV 150,000Đ.

An Giang Hotel, 40 Hai Ban Trung (tel. 841 297), just before the provincial library on the right; look for the sign. The rules strictly forbid gambling and "violent or depraved films" in the rooms. A good choice for those willing to spend a little more; slightly overpriced but clean singles with fan $9, with A/C $12. Doubles $13, with hot water $14. Deluxe rooms with TV and fridge $15.

Binh Dan Hotel, 12 Ly Tu Trong (tel. 844 557), 2 blocks north of Nguyen Trai. Enter through the motorcycle shop. In Vietnamese *binh dan* refers to the common people; the cramped rooms are certainly common, but recent renovation has made them bright and clean, and at 50,000Đ for a single (1 double bed) the price can't be beat. Foreigners are welcome and the elderly managers will make every effort to make their stay pleasurable.

FOOD

A number of cheap, street-side restaurants line Nguyen Trai between the traffic circle and the intersection with Hai Ba Trung. For a more formal dining experience, try **Com Viet Nam** at 43 Le Minh Nguon (tel. 842 353). The street is one block from the river in the market district, and the restaurant is one block north of the large textile barns; look for the large red Tiem Com sign painted on the side of the building. It's an air-conditioned refuge from the crush of the streets. The menu is in Vietnamese but the friendly staff can recommend dishes (10-20,000Đ), such as their delicious *canh* (soups) for 7000Đ. "Soviet-style beef" should raise a few eyebrows. (Open daily 10am-10pm.)

SIGHTS

There is little to see in Long Xuyen itself; most travelers use it as a springboard to trip to Chau Doc or Rach Gia, both of which are about 70km away. Nevertheless, if you find yourself in town with an afternoon to kill there's enough to keep you occupied. One of the town's most interesting "sights" is Long Xuyen's vast and colorful **market** which lies along the river bank for several blocks north and south of Nguyen Hue. The market includes several large barns devoted solely to clothing and textiles, much of which is imported from Thailand.

For those of a more spiritual bent, Long Xuyen's **Catholic Church** is one of the largest in the Delta; its bell tower is far and away the tallest structure in town. The large structure was built in the late 1960s. Mass is held daily and the church is open to the public until 8pm. On Sundays children gather for catechism and English classes—native speakers are always welcome.

Small boats can be hired for a tour of Long Xuyen's large **river-home community** from the landing at the end of Nguyen Hue for about 10,000Đ. The best time to go is in the early morning or late afternoon when the sun is less brutal.

Directly across the river is **Cho Mer District,** famed for its fruit orchards. Ferries run continuously between Long Xuyen and An Hoa on the other side (1000Đ), leaving from the ferry terminal about 1km south of town off Thoai Ngoc Hau. There is little to see, however, since most of the fruit is sold in Long Xuyen's market.

■ Châu Dốc

The slumbering town of Chau Doc snoozes along the banks of the Hau Giang River 60km west of Long Xuyen. Chau Doc is fast becoming one of the most popular destinations in the Mekong Delta, although at first glance it is a little difficult to ascertain why. A visit to the nearby shrine of Lady Xu or Nui Sam Mountain is a must-see for every visitor, but the real source of Chau Doc's charm is the syrupy pace of life here.

Maybe it's the water, or the air, but even the saleswomen in Chau Doc's fabulous market lack the pushiness of their counterparts in other Delta towns. Indeed, although Chau Doc's narrow pot-holed streets are positively teeming with humanity (the town claims a population of about 50,000), somehow everyone manages to live in harmony, if not quietude. The town is ideal for wandering, particularly in the evening, although flat-footed foreigners would be wise to keep an eye out for errant soccer balls, decidedly free-range chickens, and careening youngsters on bicycles.

Chau Doc's proximity to the Cambodian border, in addition to raising questions about smuggling operations, gives it a strong Cambodian flavor. During the late 1970s Pol Pot's Khmer Rouge frequently invaded the area, eventually providing the pretense for Vietnam's invasion of Cambodia in 1979.

ORIENTATION

Chau Doc requires no map to get around. The town, lying on the northern bank of the Hau Giang River, is laid out in a simple grid, and distances are easily navigable on foot. **Duong Le Loi/Gia Long/Tran Hung Dao** runs the length of the town along the shore; during the day the middle section of the road encompasses part of Chau Doc's vibrant market. The rest of the market, and many cheap restaurants, are sandwiched between **Duong Chi Lang** and **Duong Bach Dang,** which parallel each other and run smack through the middle of town. **Duong Thu Khoa Nghia** crosses Chi Lang and Bach Dang like a "T" two blocks north of the market.

PRACTICAL INFORMATION

Currency Exchange: 68 Nguyen Huu Canh (tel. 866 259), at the corner with Phan Van Vang. Does not take traveler's checks. Open Mon.-Sat. 7-11am and 1-5pm.

Buses: Station (tel. 868 570), 2km southwest of town at the intersection of Hwy. 91 and Le Loi. Buses to: **Long Xuyen** (4400Đ); **Can Tho** (9600Đ); **HCMC** (23,600Đ); **My Tho** (18,500Đ); and **Vung Tau** (31,600Đ). **Express minibuses** to **HCMC** leave daily from Chau Doc Hotel (3pm, 6hr., 50,000Đ).

Ferries: Ferries to **Ha Tien** in Kien Giang Province leave from the ferry station, 86 Tran Hung Dao, 1km east of the center of town and 100m past the army barracks on the right. Boats leave at 4am and arrive at Ha Tien at 3pm (25,000Đ). Ferries make the short hop across the river to **Con Tien Island** (500Đ) and leave continuously from the pier (tel. 867 151) just past Tran Hung Dao.

Local Transportation: 3-wheeled **pedicabs** and **motorcycle taxis.** From the bus station to town is 2000Đ. To **Nui Sam** (3000Đ).

Medical Services: 5 Le Loi (tel. 867 184), across from the children's garden.

Post Offices/Telephones: GPO, 73 Le Loi (tel. 866 191). Place **international calls** here. Open daily 6am-10pm. **Telephone code:** 076.

ACCOMMODATIONS

Thanh Tra Hotel, 77 Thu Khoa Nghia (tel. 866 788). From the town gardens turn right onto Thu Khoa Nghia; the hotel is 400m down on the left. Quiet, with a peaceful enclosed courtyard and mammoth lobby; popular with the Sinh Café tour crowd from HCMC. Rooms are small but very clean with gorgeous bathrooms. A bit overpriced at 80,000Đ for doubles with fan, with A/C 120,000Đ.

Chau Doc Hotel, 17 Doc Phu Thu (tel. 866 484). A recent facelift has left corridors and rooms bright and freshly painted. Singles with overhead fan and shared toilet 65,000Đ. Doubles with writing desk and A/C 75,000Đ. Triples with A/C 125,000Đ. Sells express bus tickets to HCMC; minibus leaves at 3pm.

Tai Thanh Hotel, 86 Bach Dang (tel. 966 147). May look a little dilapidated and has somewhat cramped rooms (just enough room for the bed), but the spotless bathrooms make up for it all. Doubles with fan 70,000Đ. Quads 100,000Đ.

Nha Khoch 44, 44 Doc Phu Thu (tel. 866 540), diagonally across from the Chau Doc Hotel. Basic, no frills budget hotel, but the rooms are big. The tiled floor and walls resemble a locker room. Singles with fan 50,000Đ. Doubles with fan and writing desk 80-90,000Đ.

FOOD

Most of the good joints concentrate on Chi Lang. All are open about 9am-9pm. Even cheaper eats can be had at the food stalls at the northern end of the market where Quang Trung intersects Chi Lang.

Lam Hung Ky, 71 Chi Lang (tel. 866 745). The cleanest and best-looking restaurant on the block. Delicious food and generous portions (average 10-20,000Đ). Chicken and ginger 20,000Đ. Open daily 8am-9pm.

Restaurant 88, 88 Doc Phu Thu (tel. 866 843). Great location in Chau Doc Square opposite the public gardens. Polite service, good-size portions, excellent food, and rare delicacies like snake, turtle, and bird (order 1hr. ahead) make this a great place to eat. Most dishes 10-15,000Đ. Open daily 7am-10pm.

Hong Phat, 77 Chi Lang (tel. 866 950). Lam Hung Ky's main competition comes from this friendly Chinese and Vietnamese joint. Service can be a bit slow but is worth the wait. Most dishes 15-20,000Đ. Open daily 8am-8pm.

SIGHTS

Most people come to Chau Doc to enjoy its easy-going lifestyle and friendly population. There is little of historical or cultural significance in this frontier town. Nevertheless, the **Chau Phu Temple,** at the corner of Le Loi and Bao 16 Thoai at the beginning of the market section, is worth a visit. In fact, it's not a temple at all but a *dinh* (town meeting house). The inside of the Chinese-inspired structure contains several altars (the central one boasting a portrait of Ho Chi Minh, of course) and beautiful wooden columns decorated with ornate gold dragons. Visitors are welcome. (Open daily about 7am-6pm.) Just across the street from the *dinh* small boats can be hired for about 20,000Đ per hour to explore the Hau Giang River and check out Chau Doc's many **floating village** communities.

The "Famed Beauty Spot" and primo pilgrimage point of **Nui Sam Mountain** lies 5km from town. The **Lady Xu Temple** was built here in the early 19th century when Lady Xu's holy statue was found atop the mountain. (The truly dedicated can look for Lady Xu's original pedestal; it's still there.) The people of nearby Vinh Te Village moved her to her current abode, but had to rebuild it in 1972 because of structural problems. Curved roofs covered with glazed tiles currently shelter the red statue and her monstrously large headdress from the elements. The Lady even gets bathed by the faithful in the Tam Ba (Bathing the Lady) Ceremony. The 23-25th days of the fourth lunar month are the Lady's official pilgrimage days.

■ Rach Giá

Rach Gia, like Long Xuyen 54km to the north, is usually one of those towns everyone passes through en route to someplace else. Here in Kien Giang Province, "someplace else" usually means Phu Quoc Island or the border town of Ha Tien. But don't overlook this bustling port city; its friendly locals, massive market, and delicious seafood make it well worth a visit in its own right.

Rach Gia has earned a few footnotes in Vietnamese history. As early as the first century AD, the nearby ancient city of Oc Eo, not far from Rach Gia, was believed to be the major port of the Indic kingdom of Funan. The few findings here—including Roman coins—provide archaeologists with some of their only clues about the nature of this mysterious civilization. More recently, it was here in 1868 that the resistance leader Nguyen Trung Truc was beheaded by the newly arrived French colonialists.

ORIENTATION

Rach Gia is the capital of Kien Giang Province, with a population of over 100,000 Vietnamese, Khmers, and Chinese. Rach Gia is a deceptively confusing city to navigate, although the key destinations (hotels, post office, bank, ferry terminal) are all clustered near each other in the center of town. **Duong Nguyen Trung Truc** runs from the distant inter-province **bus terminal** in Rach Soi beneath the large yellow city gates and over the **Cai Lon River,** where it becomes **Duong Le Loi** ending at the statue of Nguyen Trung Truc in front of the market near several hotels. On the other end of the market is a small bridge leading to the post office and the bank. Turning left here leads to the **ferry terminal** at the end of Nguyen Trung Truc where the traveler can go to Phu Quoc Island. **Duong Tran Phu,** Rach Gia's main drag, is three blocks east of the Nguyen Trung Truc statue.

PRACTICAL INFORMATION

Tourist Offices: Kien Giang Tourist, 12 Ly Tu Trong (tel. 862 081). With your back to the Nguyen Trung Truc statue turn left onto Le Hong Pheng, then take the first right onto Ly Tu Trong. It's opposite Thanh Binh Hotel. Helpful staff can help plan a trip to Phu Quoc Island and won't try to force an expensive package tour. Open Mon.-Sat. 7-11am and 1-5pm.

Currency Exchange: Vietcombank, 1 Huynh Mon Dat (tel. 863 427), just across the bridge, next to the post office. Open Mon.-Sat. 7-11am and 1:30-5pm. **Note:** Those heading out to Ha Tien should change money here; Ha Tien has no currency exchange.

Buses: Rach Soi Station (tel. 864 086), 7km south of town on Nguyen Trung Truc, sends buses to other provinces. To: **HCMC** (24,000Đ); **Can Tho** (9600Đ); **Long Xuyen** (6500Đ); **Chau Doc** (10,000Đ); and **Vung Tau** (132,000Đ). To get into town take a *xe lam* (2000Đ). A **small station** (tel. 862 274), at the far end of 30 Thang 4, across the bridge at the northern end of Tran Phu, has buses to other towns in the province. To **Ha Tien** (4hr., 8000Đ). **Express minibuses** to **HCMC** leave from a parking lot (tel. 862 718) opposite house #51 on Tran Quoc Tuan, 0.5km past the post office. Buses leave at 10pm (7hr., 78,000Đ).

Ferries: Ferries to **Phu Quoc Island** leave from the terminal at the far end of the pier (tel. 863 242) on Nguyen Cong Tru. At the time of press, the boat left once per day at 9am (arrive 1hr. early to ensure a seat), but this could easily change; ask at the pier or at the tourist office. Tickets to **Duong Dong Town**, Phu Quoc (52,000Đ). Ferries to nearby **Lai Son Island** leave from the same pier (tel. 863 242), opposite the shiny new customs house (15,000Đ).

Rentals: Inquire at hotels. Khach San Thanh Binh rents **bikes** for 15,000Đ per day.

Medical Services: 15 Le Loi (tel. 866 015), at the corner with Tran Hung Dao.

Post Offices/Telephones: GPO, 2 Tu Duc (tel. 862 551). Place **international calls** here. Open daily 6:30am-9pm. **Telephone code:** 077.

ACCOMMODATIONS

Khach San Thanh Binh, 11 Ly Tu Trong (tel. 863 053), opposite the tourist office. This is the cheapest option in Rach Gia, and the quality is actually much better than many hotels in the same price range. The friendly staff may ask you to give an impromptu English lesson or two. Singles with high ceilings, writing desk, and shower (bathroom outside) 35,000Đ. Doubles 60,000Đ.

Binh Minh Hotel, 48 Pham Hong Thai (tel. 862 154), on the corner about 20 steps from the statue. Their business card describes the rooms as "elegant." Well, it ain't the Ritz, but doubles with fan and clean bathroom for 50,000Đ are certainly livable for a night or two. Slightly more kempt doubles with A/C 70,000Đ. Great views of town, the market, and the ocean from the upper floors.

To Chau Hotel, 4F Le Loi (tel. 863 718), near the Nguyen Trung Truc statue. Run by the Kien Giang Tourist, it's clean, friendly, and professional. Nice singles (1 double bed) with ceiling fan, writing desk, and shower 80,000Đ. Doubles with A/C and hot water 110,000Đ, with fridge 120,000Đ. Huge rooms with all this plus a TV 140,000.

FOOD

Rach Gia is famous for its seafood, particularly cuttlefish, served with *nuoc mam* (fish sauce), another local specialty. The *nuoc mam* produced on Phu Quoc Island is universally regarded as the best in Vietnam. Several small restaurants line Tran Phu between the bridges, and two pleasant café/noodle shops overlook the river along Tran Hung Dao near the Le Loi intersection. Don't leave Rach Gia without trying the seafood at **Tay Ho Restaurant,** 112 Tran Phu (tel. 863 031), opposite the Lao Dong Cultural Centre near the southern end of Tran Phu. Choose from eel, cuttlefish, shrimp, crab, fish, or snake. Most dishes average 15,000Đ. (Open daily 8am-10pm.)

SIGHTS

For most travelers Rach Gia is merely a transit point on the way to Phu Quoc Island or Ha Tien. There is, however, still enough to see in this amiable little city to keep travelers occupied for a few hours until the next ferry or bus leaves. There is no excuse for not paying homage to home-town martyr Nguyen Trang Truc at the **Nguyen Trang Truc Pagoda** on Nguyen Cong Tru on the way to the Phu Quoc ferry. Nguyen Trung Truc led the Vietnamese people in their futile attempts to resist the French during the 1860s. He led a daring raid against the French warship *Esperance*, successfully sinking the ship but losing his own head shortly thereafter in Rach Gia's market in 1868. The interior of the temple is decorated with prayer flags and contains a large portrait of the rebel leader. It's open daily to the public.

About 2km north of the post office on Quang Trung is **Phat Lon Temple**, a Theravada Buddhist temple serving Rach Gia's large Cambodian population. A large gold Buddha is enshrined in the main sanctuary, and many tall stupas stand in the yard in front. The temple provides an interesting comparison with the many Mahayana temples in Vietnam, although travelers familiar with Theravada temples in Thailand or Cambodia will find it rather unimpressive.

■ Near Rach Giá: Phú Quốc Island

After a week or two of hard travel through the Delta, braving the dust and discomfort of the public bus system, what could be a greater reward than a few lazy days on a paradisical, yet-to-be-discovered tropical isle? **Phu Quoc Island** offers just this. The Thais and Cambodians might dispute the Vietnamese claim to this 48km-long island, but to Hanoi it's a district of Kien Giang Province. While the diplomats haggle over its sovereignty, Phu Quoc is still just a gleam in the eye of rapacious real estate moguls and your only dilemma is where on its miles of sandy white beach to lay down your towel. To the more active beach bum, the crystal clean waters of the Gulf of Thailand offer fantastic **snorkeling** and **fishing** opportunities. Although actually much closer to Ha Tien (45km from Ha Tien and 15km from Kamet Province, Cambodia), at present foreigners can only access Phu Quoc via Rach Gia. Ferries depart daily from the Rach Gia Pier (see **Practical Information** above). Make sure yours is bound for Dong Duong Town, the only village on the island prepared for tourists. At last count there was one pricey hotel and two guest houses here, including the **Huong Bien Guest House** (tel. 846 050). Check with the helpful staff at the Rach Gia Tourist office for the latest information. There is also a guest house on the much closer island of **Lai Son;** check at the tourist office for details.

■ Hà Tiên

Anyone who says every Delta town looks the same obviously hasn't been to Ha Tien, a three-hour ride west of Rach Gia. Jagged limestone karsts rise dramatically above the rice paddies, providing a break from the pancake-flat terrain that makes up most of the region.

Historically Ha Tien was a part of Cambodian territory (the mountains of Kampot Province are easily visible to the west). Then, in 1708, the town's Chinese governor decided to seek the protection of the Nguyen lords at Hue. Like most of the towns in this region, it is home to a large *mien* (Cambodian) population. Khmer women are easily recognized by the checked scarves they wear instead of the traditional Vietnamese conical straw hat. Hopefully one day in the not-too-distant future it will be possible to reach Phu Quoc Island from Ha Tien; fears of Khmer Rouge piracy currently prevent this. Nonetheless, Ha Tien's obliging locals, engaging sights, and a bonafide beach are sure to make it a highlight of any Delta excursion.

ORIENTATION AND PRACTICAL INFORMATION

Ha Tien is a small fishing town 90km from Rach Gia and just 7km from the Cambodian border. The **bus station** (tel. 852 560) is just across To Chau River from town. Regular buses go to: **Rach Gia** (4400Đ); **Chau Doc** (14,500Đ); **Long Xuyen** (14,000Đ); and **HCMC** (31,000Đ). **Express buses** to **HCMC** leave at 8pm and 9pm (31,000Đ). Crossing the pontoon bridge (toll 500Đ) brings travelers to **Duong Ben Tran Hau,** which parallels the river. Most of Ha Tien's accommodations, the **market,** and a number of small cafés and restaurants line this street. Turning left onto Ben Tran Hau and walking four blocks goes to the intersection with **Duong Phuong Thanh,** which leads to several temples and 5.5km later, **Thach Dong cave,** and the Vietnamese/Cambodian **border.** Money should be changed in Rach Gia, as there is **no exchange bank** in Ha Tien; some travelers, however, are able to exchange cash at the market. A new **post office** is being constructed on **Duong To Chau,** which intersects Ben Tran Hau between the To Chau and Dong Ho hotels. **International phone calls** can be made from here. The Ha Tien branch of the **Kien Giang Tourist Company** is on the ground floor of the Dong Ho Hotel. **Bicycles** can be rented from the To Chau Hotel for 20,000Đ per day.

ACCOMMODATIONS

Dong Ho Hotel (tel. 852 141), on Ben Tran Hau, right by the bridge. Operated by Kien Giang Tourist Company. Unbeatable location and large, airy rooms (many with balconies) make this the place to stay in Ha Tien. Doubles with fan and shared toilet 45,000Đ. Large rooms with private bath 65,000Đ.

Khai Hoan Hotel, 239 Phuong Thanh (tel. 852 254), near the Phuong Thanh Hotel. Far and away the newest and cheeriest hotel in Ha Tien. Bright, freshly painted singles with writing desk and fan 60,000Đ (the shared bathrooms are equally spotless). Doubles with inside bathroom 80,000Đ, with A/C 120-150,000Đ depending on the size.

Phuong Thanh Hotel (tel. 852 626), on Phuong Thanh, at the intersection of Phuong Thanh and Ben Tran Hau, 4 blocks west of the pontoon bridge. The office doubles as a tailoring shop. They are very proud of the karaoke café downstairs. Large, simple rooms with 3 beds and a fan are very clean, but a bit barren with only a stool for furniture. Bathrooms are outside. 1 person 60,000Đ, each additional person (up to 3) 10,000Đ.

FOOD

A number of cheap streetside cafés selling *hu tieu* soup, *pho,* and basic rice dishes line Ben Tran Hau to the left of the pontoon bridge. Several of the cafés boast mammoth stereos and blast Asian remixes of American pop music all day. The food here is ultra-cheap, a meal of *hu tieu* and *sinh to* (fruit shake) costs about 8000Đ.

Nha Hang Huong Bien (tel. 852 072), 30m down from the Dong Ho on the right, serves tasty seafood in a slightly more formal environment. The specialty is *ca chien sot ca,* scrumptious fried fish in a sweet and sour sauce (15,000Đ). Other delicacies include snake, eel, squid, crabs, and shrimp (most dishes 15,000Đ). The Vietnamese menu has more options than the English. Open daily 7am-8pm.

SIGHTS

Ha Tien has more to see than Rach Gia, although one of the most pleasant activities is to simply rent a bike and explore the countryside. Well worth a visit is the **tomb of Mac Cuu,** Ha Tien's Chinese governor who was appointed by the Cambodian court, but defected to the Vietnamese Nguyen lords. Mac Cuu's tomb, a fine example of Chinese architecture, adorned with fierce dragons, was erected in 1809 by Emperor Gia Long. A number of Mac Cuu's descendants are also buried in tombs along the hillside, giving the area its name, Nui Lang (Hill of tombs). To get there, head down Phuong Thanh; turn left just before the large yet-to-be finished church and go straight. The tombs are beneath the gate on the right. Continuing straight along Phuong Thanh leads to the **Sac Tu Tan Bao Tu Pagoda,** first built by Mac Cuu in 1730. A large statue of Quan Am, the Goddess of Mercy, stands in the yard.

Three km out of town down this same road is **Thach Dong Cave,** a limestone grotto within sight of the Cambodian border. The subterranean temple is rather unimpressive (it's flanked by a subterranean souvenir stand), but the view of Cambodia is quite beautiful, as is the bike ride out to the grotto (admission 500Đ).

Bai Mui Nai (Deer's Head Beach) is not far from Thach Dong. Ha Tien's main beach, this narrow strip of gray sand is certainly not Vietnam's most tropical but is quite popular with local tourists. Phu Quoc Island and the mountains of Kamet Province in Cambodia can be clearly seen in the distance. To get there, continue down the dirt road past Thach Dong, turn left at the first opportunity (a border checkpoint forbids you to go straight any farther anyway), and continue down the dirt road for about 2km. The entrance to the beach is on the right.

Appendix

▨ Climate & Temperatures

Temp in °C	January		April		July		October	
Rain in cm/mo.	Temp	Rain	Temp	Rain	Temp	Rain	Temp	Rain
CAMBODIA								
Phnom Penh	21/31	0.7	24/35	7.7	24/32	17.1	24/30	25.7
HONG KONG	13/18	3.3	19/24	13.7	26/31	38.1	23/27	11.4
INDONESIA								
Jakarta	23/29	30.0	23/30	14.7	23/31	6.4	23/31	11.2
Ujung Pandang	23/29	68.6	23/30	15.0	21/30	3.6	22/31	4.3
Medan	22/29	13.7	22/32	13.5	23/32	13.2	22/30	25.9
LAOS								
Luang Prabang	13/28	1.5	21/36	10.9	23/32	23.1	21/32	7.9
Vientiane	14/28	0.5	23/34	9.9	24/31	26.7	21/31	10.9
MALAYSIA								
Cameron HL	13/22	16.8	14/23	29.7	13/23	12.2	14/22	34.0
Georgetown	23/32	9.4	24/33	18.8	23/32	19.1	23/32	42.9
Kuala Lumpur	22/32	15.8	23/33	29.2	22/32	9.9	23/32	24.9
Kuching	22/29	61.0	23/32	27.9	22/32	19.6	23/32	26.7
SINGAPORE	23/30	25.2	24/31	18.8	24/31	17.0	23/31	20.8
THAILAND								
Bangkok	20/32	0.8	25/35	5.8	24.32	16.0	24/31	20.6
Chiang Mai	13/29	0.0	22/36	3.6	23/31	21.3	21/31	9.4
VIETNAM								
Da Nang	19/24	10.2	23/30	1.8	25/34	9.9	23/28	53.0
Hanoi	13/20	1.8	20/28	8.1	26/33	32.3	22/29	9.9
Ho Chi Minh City	21/32	1.5	24/35	4.3	24/31	31.5	23/31	26.9

▨ Weights & Measures

1 millimeter (mm) = 0.04 inches (in.)
1 meter (m) = 1.09 yards (yd.)
1 kilometer (km) = 0.621 miles (mi.)
1 gram (g) = 0.04 ounces (oz.)
1 kilogram (kg) = 2.2 pounds (lbs.)
1 "stone" (weight) = 14 pounds
1 liter = 1.057 U.S quarts (qt.)
1 liter = 0.88 Imperial quarts
1 Imperial gallon = 1.19 U.S. gallons (ga.)
1 British pint = 1.19 U.S. pints (pt.)

1 inch = 25mm
1 yard = 0.92m
1 mile = 1.61km
1 ounce = 25g
1 pound = .45kg
1 pound = .71 stone
1 U.S quart = 0.94 liters
1 Imperial quart = 1.14 liters
1 U.S. gallon = .84 Imperial gallons
1 U.S. pint = .84 British pints

To convert from °C to °F, multiply by 1.8 and add 32.
To convert from °F to °C, subtract 32 and multiply by 5/9.

°C	30	26	22	18	14	10	6	2	-1	-5
°F	86	79	72	64	57	50	43	36	34	23

■ Country Codes

Australia	61	**Laos**	856	**Thailand**	66
Cambodia	855	**Malaysia**	60	**U.K.**	44
Canada	1	**N. Zealand**	64	**U.S.**	1
Hong Kong	852	**Singapore**	65	**Vietnam**	84
Indonesia	62	**South Africa**	27		

■ Languages

NUMBERS

No.	Indonesian	Malaysian	Lao	Thai	Khmer	Vietnam
1	satu	satu	neung	neung	mouy	mot
2	dua	dua	sawng	sorng	pee	hai
3	tiga	tiga	saam	sahm	bei	ba
4	empat	empat	sii	see	boun	bon
5	lima	lima	haa	hah	bram	nam
6	eman	eman	hok	hok	bram-mouy	sau
7	tujuh	tujuh	jet	jet	bram-pee	bay
8	delapan	delapan	paet	bpairt	bram-bei	tam
9	sembilan	sembilan	kao	gao	bram-boun	chin
10	sepuluh	sepuluh	sip	sip	duop	muoi
11	sebelas	sebelas	sip-et	sip-et	duop-mouy	muoi mot
12	duabelas	duabelas	sip-sawng	sip-sahm	duop-pee	muoi hai
20	duapuluh	duapuluh	sao	yee-sip	maphei	hai muoi
30	tigapuluh	tigapuluh	saam-sip	sahm-sip	samseb	ba muoi
40	empatpuluh	empatpuluh	sii-sip	see-sip	sairseb	bon muoi
50	limapuluh	limapuluh	haa-sip	hah-sip	hahseb	nam muoi
100	seratus	seratus	neung hawy	neung roy	mouy-rouy	mot tram
1000	seribu	seribu	neung phan	neung pun	mouy-paun	mot nghin

WORDS AND PHRASES

English	Khmer	Vietnamese
Hello	joom reab suor	xin chao
Yes/No	baht (male), jas (female)/te	vang/khong
Thank you	ar kun	cam on rat nhieu
Excuse me	suom tous	xin loi
Good-bye	lear heouy	chuc ngu ngon
How are you?	tau neak sok sapbaiy jea te	co khoe khong
Train	rout phleoung	xe lua
Bus	lan thom deouk monous	xe buyt
Bus stop	ben lan	ben xe
Market	psar	cho
Station	ben lan	ga xe lua
Doctor	krou peit	bac si
Police	police	cong an
How much does this cost?	t'lai bpon-mahn?	cai nay gia bao nhieu?
Now	eilov nees	bay gio
Tomorrow	sa-ek	ngay mai

English	Indonesian	Malaysian
Hello	Selamat Siang	Selamat Siang
Yes/No	ya/tidak	ya/tidak
Please: To ask for something	minta	minta
Please: To ask for help	tolong	tolong
Thank you	terima kasih	terima kasih
Excuse me	ma'af	ma'af
Good-bye: To one staying	Selamat Tinggal	Selamat tinggal
Good-bye: To one going	Selamat Jalan	Selamat jalan
Good Morning	Selamat Pagi	Selamat pagi
Good Night	Selamat Malam	Selamat malam
How are you?	Apa kabar?	Apa kabar?
Fine, thank you	Baik, terima kasih	Baik, terima kasih
Where is…?	Mana?	Mana?
How much does this cost?	Berapa yang ini?	Berapa yang ini?
Do you speak English?	Bisa bicara Bahasa Ingles?	Bisa bicara Bahasa Ingles?
I don't speak…(language)	Saya tidak bisa bicara Bahasa Indonesia	Saya tidak bisa bicara Bahasa Malaysia
Bus	bis	bis
Train	kerata api	kerata api
Car	mobil	kerata
Taxi	taksi	taksi
Bathroom	kamar kecil	tandas
Restaurant	rumah makan	rumah makan
Guest House	wisma	wisma
Market	pasar	pasar
Bank	bank	bank
Hospital	rumah sakit	rumah sakit
Yesterday	kamarin	kamarin
Today	hari ini	hari ini
Tomorrow	besok	besok
Sunday	Hari Minggu	Hari Minggu
Monday	Hari Senen	Hari Senen
Tuesday	Hari Selasu	Hari Selasu
Wednesday	Hari Rabu	Hari Rabu
Thursday	Hari Kamis	Hari Kamis
Friday	Hari Jum'at	Hari Jum'at
Saturday	Hari Sabtu	Hari Sabtu

English	Lao	Thai
Hello	Sa-bai-dii	Sa-wut-dee
Yes/No	ya/baw	chai/mai chai
Thank you	khawp jai	korp-koon
Excuse me	tat si	kor-toht
Good-bye	pai jao	lah gorn na
How are you?	Sa-bai-dii baw?	Bpen yung-ngai bahng?

English	Lao	Thai
Bus	lot meh	rot may
Bus stop	bawn jawt	bpai rot ma
Market	talaat	dta-laht
Shower	aap nam	fuk boo-a
Station	sa-thaa-nii	sa-tahn-nee rot fai (rot may)
When?	Mëfalni?	meu-arai
Where is…?	Yuu sai?	…yuu thii nai?
How much does this cost?	Thao dai?	nee tao-rai?
Do you have…?	Mii…baw?	mii…mai?
I don't understand	Baw khao jai	mai khao jai
Do you speak English?	Jao paak pha-saa	Poot pah-sah ung-grit bpen mai?
I don't speak… (language)	Khawy paak phaa-saa lao baw dai	poot pah-sah tai mai bpen
I need…	Tawng kaan…	yaak dai
Tomorrow	meu eun	proong nee
Yesterday	meu waan nii	wun nee

Index

INDEX